D0204337

Consumer Behavior

Building Marketing Strategy

The Irwin/McGraw-Hill Series in Marketing

Alreck & Settle
The Survey Research Handbook
Second Edition

Anderson Hair & Bush
Professional Sales Management
Second Edition

Arens
Contemporary Advertising
Seventh Edition

Bearden, Ingram & Laforge
Marketing: Principles & Perspectives
Second Edition

Belch & Belch
Introduction to Advertising & Promotion: An Integrated Marketing Communications Approach
Fifth Edition

Bernhardt & Kinnear
Cases in Marketing Management
Seventh Edition

Berkowitz, Kerin, Hartley and Rudelius
Marketing
Sixth Edition

Bowersox and Closs
Logistical Management
First Edition

Bowersox and Cooper
Strategic Marketing Channel Management
First Edition

Boyd, Walker & Larreche
Marketing Management: A Strategic Approach with a Global Orientation
Third Edition

Cateora & Graham
International Marketing
Tenth Edition

Churchill, Ford, Walker, Johnston, & Tanner
Sales Force Management
Sixth Edition

Churchill & Peter
Marketing
Second Edition

Cole & Mishler
Consumer and Business Credit Management
Eleventh Edition

Cravens
Strategic Marketing
Sixth Edition

Cravens, Lamb & Crittenden
Strategic Marketing Management Cases
Sixth Edition

Crawford & Di Benedetto
New Products Management
Sixth Edition

Dwyer & Tanner
Business Marketing
First Edition

Etzel, Walker & Stanton
Marketing
Twelfth Edition

Futrell
ABC's of Relationship Selling
Sixth Edition

Futrell
Fundamentals of Selling
Sixth Edition

Hair, Bush & Ortinau
Marketing Research
First Edition

Hasty and Rearden
Retail Management
First Edition

Hawkins, Best & Coney
Consumer Behavior
Eighth Edition

Hayes, Jenster & Aaby
Business To Business Marketing
First Edition

Johansson
Global Marketing
Second Edition

Lambert & Stock
Strategic Logistics Management
Third Edition

Lambert, Stock & Ellram
Fundamentals of Logistic Management
First Edition

Lehmann & Winer
Analysis for Marketing Planning
Fourth Edition

Lehmann & Winer
Product Management
Second Edition

Levy & Weitz
Retailing Management
Fourth Edition

Mason & Perreault
The Marketing Game
Second Edition

McDonald
Direct Marketing: An Integrated Approach
First Edition

Meloan & Graham
International and Global Marketing Concepts and Cases
Second Edition

Monroe
Pricing
Second Edition

Oliver
Satisfaction: A Behavioral Perspective on the Consumer
First Edition

Patton
Sales Force: A Sales Management Simulation Game
First Edition

Pelton, Strutton, Lumpkin
Marketing Channels: A Relationship Management Approach
First Edition

Perreault & McCarthy
Basic Marketing:
A Global Managerial Approach
Thirteenth Edition

Perreault & McCarthy
Essentials of Marketing:
A Global Managerial Approach
Eighth Edition

Peter & Donnelly
A Preface to Marketing Management
Eighth Edition

Peter & Donnelly
Marketing Management:
Knowledge and Skills
Sixth Edition

Peter & Olson
Consumer Behavior and Marketing Strategy
Fifth Edition

Rangan
Business Marketing Strategy:
Cases, Concepts & Applications
First Edition

Rangan, Shapiro & Moriarty
Business Marketing Strategy:
Concepts and Applications
First Edition

Rossiter & Percy
Advertising Communications and Promotion Management
Second Edition

Stanton, Spiro & Buskirk
Management of a Sales Force
Tenth Edition

Sudman & Blair
Marketing Research:
A Problem Solving Approach
First Edition

Ulrich & Eppinger
Product Design and Development
Second Edition

Walker, Boyd and Larreche
Marketing Strategy:
Planning and Implementation
Third Edition

Weitz, Castleberry and Tanner
Selling: Building Partnerships
Fourth Edition

Zeithaml & Bitner
Services Marketing
Second Edition

Consumer Behavior

Building Marketing Strategy 8/e

Del I. Hawkins
University of Oregon

Roger J. Best
University of Oregon

Kenneth A. Coney
Late of Arizona State University

Boston Burr Ridge, IL Dubuque, IA Madison, WI New York San Francisco St. Louis
Bangkok Bogotá Caracas Lisbon London Madrid
Mexico City Milan New Delhi Seoul Singapore Sydney Taipei Toronto

McGraw-Hill Higher Education
A Division of The ***McGraw-Hill*** *Companies*

CONSUMER BEHAVIOR: BUILDING MARKETING STRATEGY

Published by Irwin/McGraw-Hill, an imprint of The McGraw-Hill Companies, Inc., 1221 Avenue of the Americas, New York, NY 10020.

This book is printed on acid-free paper.

domestic 2 3 4 5 6 7 8 9 0 VNH/VNH 0 9 8 7 6 5 4 3 2 1
international 2 3 4 5 6 7 8 9 0 VNH/VNH 0 9 8 7 6 5 4 3 2 1

ISBN 0-07-231602-0

Publisher: *David Kendric Brake*
Sponsoring editor: *Jill Braaten*
Senior developmental editor: *Nancy Barbour*
Editorial assistant: *Mary Shannon*
Marketing manager: *Colleen J. Suljic*
Project manager: *Rebecca Nordbrock*
Production supervisor: *Debra Sylvester*
Cover and interior design: *Keith J. McPherson*
Supplement coordinator: *Carol A. Bielski*
New media: *Ann Rogula*
Cover illustrator: *Michael Steirnagle*
Compositor: *Interactive Composition Corporation*
Typeface: *10/12 Times Roman*
Printer: *Von Hoffmann Press, Inc.*

Library of Congress Cataloging-in-Publication Data

Hawkins, Del I.
Consumer behavior : building marketing strategy / Del I. Hawkins, Roger J. Best
Kenneth A. Coney. — 8th ed.
p. cm.
ISBN 0072316020
Includes bibliographical references and indexes.
1. Consumer behavior—United States. 2. Market surveys—United States.
3. Consumer behavior—United States—Case studies. I. Best, Roger J.
II. Coney, Kenneth A. III. Title
HF5415.33.U6H38 2000
658.8'342'0973 dc—21 00-027293

INTERNATIONAL EDITION ISBN 0-07-118039-7

www.mhhe.com

Preface

Marketing attempts to influence the way consumers behave. These attempts have implications for the organizations making the attempt, the consumers they are trying to influence, and the society in which these attempts occur. We are all consumers and we are all members of society, so consumer behavior, and attempts to influence it, are critical to all of us. This text is designed to provide an understanding of consumer behavior. This understanding can make us better consumers, better marketers, and better citizens.

MARKETING CAREERS AND CONSUMER BEHAVIOR

A primary purpose of this text is to provide the student with a usable, managerial understanding of consumer behavior. Most students in consumer behavior courses aspire to careers in marketing management, sales, or advertising. They hope to acquire knowledge and skills that will be useful to them in these careers. Unfortunately, some may be seeking the type of knowledge gained in introductory accounting classes; that is, a set of relatively invariant rules that can be applied across a variety of situations to achieve a fixed solution that is known to be correct. For these students, the uncertainty and lack of closure involved in dealing with living, breathing, changing, stubborn consumers can be very frustrating. However, if they can accept dealing with endless uncertainty, utilizing an understanding of consumer behavior in developing marketing strategy will become tremendously exciting.

It is our view that the utilization of knowledge of consumer behavior in the development of marketing strategy is an art. This is not to suggest that scientific principles and procedures are not applicable. Rather, it means that the successful application of these principles to particular situations requires human judgment that we are not able to reduce to a fixed set of rules.

Let us consider the analogy with art in some detail. Suppose you want to become an expert artist. You would study known principles of the visual effects of blending various colors, of perspective, and so forth. Then you would practice applying these principles until you developed the ability to produce acceptable paintings. If you had certain "natural" talents, the right teacher, and the right topic, you might even produce a "masterpiece." The same approach should be taken by one wishing to become a marketing manager, a salesperson, or an advertising director. The various factors or principles that influence consumer behavior should be thoroughly studied. Then, one should practice applying these principles until acceptable marketing strategies result. However, while knowledge and practice can in general produce acceptable strategies, "great" marketing strategies, like masterpieces, require special talents, effort, timing, and some degree of luck (what if Mona Lisa had not wanted her portrait painted?).

The art analogy is useful for another reason. All of us, professors and students alike, tend to ask: "How can I use the concept of, say, social class to develop a successful marketing strategy?" This makes as much sense as an artist asking: "How can I use blue to create a great picture?" Obviously, blue alone will seldom be sufficient for a great work of art. Instead, to be successful, the artist must understand when and how to use blue in conjunction with other elements in the picture. Likewise, the marketing manager must understand when and how to use a knowledge of social class in conjunction with a knowledge of other factors in designing a successful marketing strategy.

This book is based on the belief that knowledge of the factors that influence consumer behavior can, with practice, be used to develop sound marketing strategy. With this in mind, we have attempted to do three things. First, we present a reasonably comprehensive description of the various behavioral concepts and theories that have been found useful for understanding consumer behavior. This is generally done at the beginning of each chapter or at the beginning of major subsections in each chapter. We believe that a person must have a thorough understanding of a concept in order to successfully apply that concept across different situations.

Second, we present examples of how these concepts have been utilized in the development of marketing strategy. We have tried to make clear that these examples are *not* "how you use this concept." Rather, they are presented as "how one organization facing a particular marketing situation used this concept."

Third, at the end of each chapter and each major section, we present a number of questions, activities, or cases that require the student to apply the concepts.

CONSUMING AND CONSUMER BEHAVIOR

The authors of this book are consumers, as is everyone reading this text. Most of us spend more time buying and consuming than we do working or sleeping. We consume products such as cars and fuel, services such as haircuts and home repairs, and entertainment such as television and concerts. Given the time and energy we devote to consuming, we should strive to be good at it. A knowledge of consumer behavior can be used to enhance our ability to consume wisely.

Marketers spend billions of dollars attempting to influence what, when, and how you and I consume. Marketers not only spend billions attempting to influence our behavior, they also spend hundreds of millions of dollars studying our behavior. With a knowledge of consumer behavior and an understanding of how marketers use this knowledge, *we can study marketers.* A television commercial can be an annoying interruption of a favorite program. However, it can also be a fascinating opportunity to speculate on the commercial's objective, target audience, and the underlying behavior assumptions. Indeed, given the ubiquitous nature of commercials, an understanding of how they are attempting to influence us or others is essential to understand our environment.

Throughout the text, we present examples that illustrate the objectives of specific marketing activities. By studying these examples and the principles on which they are based, one can develop the ability to discern the underlying logic of the marketing activities encountered daily.

SOCIAL RESPONSIBILITY AND CONSUMER BEHAVIOR

Should commercial sites on the World Wide Web (Internet) that focus on children be strictly regulated, banned completely, or left alone? This issue is currently the source of a major debate. As educated citizens, we have a responsibility to take part in this debate and to influence its outcome. Developing a sound position on this issue requires an understanding of children's information processing as it relates to advertising—an important part of our understanding of consumer behavior.

The debate described above is only one of many that require an understanding of consumer behavior. We present a number of these topics throughout the text. The objective is to develop the ability to apply consumer behavior knowledge to social and regulatory issues as well as to business and personal issues.

NEW TO THE EIGHTH EDITION

Marketing and consumer behavior, like the rest of the world, is changing at a rapid pace. Both the way consumers behave and the practices of studying that behavior continue to evolve. In order to keep up with this dynamic environment, several changes have been made for the eighth edition.

Internet Applications

The Internet is rapidly changing many aspects of consumer behavior. We have integrated the latest research and practices concerning the Internet throughout the text and the cases.

Consumer Insights

These boxed discussions are now in every chapter. They provide an in-depth look at a particularly interesting consumer study or marketing practice. Each has several questions with it that are designed to encourage critical thinking by the students.

More Global Examples

While previous editions have included a wealth of global material, this edition further integrates this important area. Most chapters contain multiple global examples woven into the text. In addition, Chapter 2 and several of the cases are devoted to global issues.

CHAPTER FEATURES

Each chapter contains a variety of features designed to enhance students' understanding of the material as well as to make the material more fun.

Opening Vignettes

Each chapter begins with a practical example that introduces the material in the chapter. These involve situations in which businesses, government units, or nonprofit organizations have used or misused consumer behavior principles.

Integrated Coverage of Ethical/Social Issues

Marketers face numerous ethical issues as they apply their understanding of consumer behavior in the marketplace. We describe and discuss many of these issues. These discussions are highlighted in the text via Y. In addition, Chapter 20 is devoted to the consumerism movement and the regulation of marketing practice. Several of the cases are also focused on ethical or regulatory issues, including all of the cases following Part Six.

Internet Exercises

The Internet is rapidly becoming both a major source of data on consumer behavior and a medium in which marketers use their knowledge of consumer behavior to influence consumers. A section at the end of each chapter has Internet assignments. These serve two purposes. One is to teach students how to use the Internet as a research tool to learn about consumers and consumer behavior. The second purpose is to enhance students' understanding of how marketers are approaching consumers using this medium.

DDB Needham Lifestyle Data Analyses

Each relevant chapter poses a series of questions that require students to analyze data from the annual DDB Needham Lifestyle survey. These data are available in spreadsheet format on the disk that accompanies this text. These exercises increase students' data analysis skills as well as their understanding of consumer behavior.

Four-Color Illustrations

Print ads, storyboards, and photos of point-of-purchase displays appear throughout the text. Each is directly linked to the text material both by text references to each illustration and by the descriptive comments that accompany each illustration.

Review Questions

The review questions at the end of each chapter allow students or the instructor to test the acquisition of the facts contained in the chapter. The questions require memorization, which we believe is an important, though insufficient, part of learning.

Discussion Questions

These questions can be used to help develop or test the students' understanding of the material in the chapter. Answering these questions requires the student to utilize the material in the chapter to reach a recommendation or solution. However, they can be answered without external activities such as customer interviews (therefore, they can be assigned as in-class activities).

Application Activities

The final learning aid at the end of each chapter is a set of application exercises. These require the students to utilize the material in the chapter in conjunction with external activities such as visiting stores to observe point-of-purchase displays, interviewing customers or managers, or evaluating television ads. They range in complexity from short evening assignments to term projects.

OTHER LEARNING AIDS IN THE TEXT

Three useful sets of learning material are presented outside the chapter format—cases, an overview of consumer research methods, and a format for a consumer behavior audit.

Cases

There are cases at the end of each major section of the text except the first. The cases can be read in class and used to generate discussion of a particular topic. Students like this approach, and many instructors find it a useful way to motivate class discussion.

Other cases are more complex and data intense. They require several hours of effort to analyze. Still others can serve as the basis for a term project. We have used several cases in this manner with success (the assignment is to develop a marketing plan clearly identifying the consumer behavior constructs that underlie the plan).

Each case can be approached from a variety of angles. A number of discussion questions are provided with each case. However, many other questions can be used. In fact, while the cases are placed at the end of the major sections, most lend themselves to discussion at other points in the text as well.

Consumer Research Methods Overview

Appendix A provides a brief overview of the more commonly used research methods in consumer behavior. While not a substitute for a course or text in marketing research, it is a useful review for students who have completed a research course. It can also serve to provide students who have not had such a course with relevant terminology and a very basic understanding of the process and major techniques involved in consumer research.

Consumer Behavior Audit

Appendix B provides a format for doing a consumer behavior audit for a proposed marketing strategy. This audit is basically a list of key consumer behavior questions that should be answered for every proposed marketing strategy. Many students have found it particularly useful if a term project relating consumer behavior to a firm's actual or proposed strategy is required.

SUPPLEMENTAL LEARNING MATERIALS

We have developed a variety of learning materials to enhance the student's learning experience and to facilitate the instructor's teaching activities. Please contact your local Irwin/McGraw-Hill sales representative for assistance in obtaining ancillaries. Or, contact us directly at our Web site, www.mhhe.com.

DDB Needham Lifestyle Data Analyses Disk

A disk accompanying the text contains data in spreadsheet format from the annual DDB Needham Lifestyle survey. It enables students to access consumer market data and draw marketing strategy recommendations based on these data.

Instructor's Manual

The Instructor's Manual contains suggestions for teaching the course, learning objectives for each chapter, additional material for presentation, lecture tips and aids, answers to the end-of-chapter questions, suggested case teaching approaches, and discussion guides for each case.

Test Bank and Computerized Test Bank

A test bank of over 1,500 multiple-choice questions accompanies the text. These questions cover all the chapters, including the material in the opening vignettes and in the Consumer Insights. The questions are coded according to degree of difficulty. A computerized version is available in MAC, DOS, and Windows platforms.

Four-Color Acetates

A packet of 70 four-color acetates of ads, picture boards, point-of-purchase displays, and so forth is available to adopters. These acetates are keyed to specific chapters in the text. The Instructor's Manual relates the acetates to the relevant concepts in the text.

Video Cases

A set of video cases is available to adopters. These videos describe firm strategies or activities that relate to material in the text. A guide for teaching from the videos is contained in the Instructor's Manual.

Electronic Slides

180 PowerPoint slides accompany the eighth edition. The slides contain key figures from the text as well as additional images.

CD-ROM Presentation Manager

This instructor CD-ROM contains PowerPoint electronic slides, video clips, advertisements from the text, plus many nontext ads, the Instructor's Manual, and the test bank. This supplement is available to adopters of the text.

ACKNOWLEDGMENTS

We enjoy studying, teaching, consulting, and writing about consumer behavior. Most of the faculty we know feel the same. As with every edition, we have tried to make this a book that students would enjoy reading and that would get them excited about a fascinating topic.

Numerous individuals and organizations helped us in the task of writing this edition. We are grateful for their assistance. A special thanks is due to Nancy Barbour for her patience and skill. We would also like to thank the many other members of the McGraw-Hill Higher Education team, including Colleen Suljic, Rebecca Nordbrock, Keith J. McPherson, Keri Johnson, and Debra Sylvester. Particular thanks are also due to the many people who helped us in the development of this text. We believe that the eighth edition is improved because of your efforts: John Drea, Western Illinois University; Paul Herr, University of Colorado—Boulder; Michelle Kunz, Morehead State University; James Leigh, Texas A&M University; Lois Mohr, Georgia State University; James Munch University of Texas—Arlington; Sue L. O'Curry, DePaul University; Phil Titus, Bowling Green State University; and Janice Williams, University of Central Oklahoma.

Our colleagues at Oregon—David Boush, Marian Friestad, Dennis Howard, Lynn Kahle, Bob Madrigal, Yigang Pan, and Peter Wright—generously responded to our requests for assistance. All should be held blameless for our inability to fully incorporate their ideas.

The text would have had higher quality, been more fun to read, and been much more fun to write had Ken Coney been able to write it with us. Once again, this edition is dedicated to his memory. By his life he said to us:

Cherish your dreams
Guard your ideals
Enjoy life
Seek the best
Climb your mountains

Del I. Hawkins
Roger J. Best

DDB Needham Lifestyle Data Analyses

DDB Needham Worldwide is one of the leading advertising agencies in the world. One of the many services it provides for its clients as well as to support its own creative and strategy efforts is a major, annual lifestyle survey. This survey is conducted using a panel maintained by Consumer Mail Panel. In a panel such as this, consumers are recruited such that the panel has demographic characteristics similar to the U.S. population. Members of the panel agree to complete questions on a periodic basis.

THE DATA

The 1996 Lifestyle study involved over 3,500 completed questionnaires. These lengthy questionnaires included approximately 200 interest and opinion items (I like to pay cash for everything I buy, I am an avid sports fan); 160 frequency of activity questions (worked in the garden, gambled in a casino), questions on preferred marital style (traditional, modern, or other), over 200 questions on product purchase and use, approximately 75 questions on product ownership and purchase intentions, over 100 questions on one's self-concept and ideal self-concept, and numerous questions collecting demographic and media preference data.

DDB Needham has allowed us to provide a portion of these data in spreadsheet format in the disk that accompanies this text. The data are presented in the form of cross-tabulations at an aggregate level with the cell values being percents. For example:

	Household Size			
	1	*2*	*3–5*	*>5*
Number in sample	550	1,377	1,626	162
Rented a video	7.0%	10.7%	18.8%	20.0%
Used the Internet	6.1	5.6	5.7	1.9
Made pancakes	2.0	5.9	9.5	19.3

The above example indicates that 7.0 percent of the 550 respondents from one-person households were heavy renters of videos, compared to 10.7 percent of the 1,377 from two-person households, 18.8 percent of those from households with three, four, or five members, and 20.0 percent of those from households with more than five members.

It is possible to combine columns within variables. That is, we can determine the percent of one- and two-person households combined that made pancakes. Because the number of respondents on which the percents are based differs across columns, we can't simply average the cell percent figures. Instead, we need to convert the cell percent to numbers by multiplying each cell percent times the number in the sample for that column. Add the numbers for the cells to be combined together and divide the result by the sum of the number in the sample for the combined cells' columns. The result is the percent of the combined column categories that engaged in the behavior of interest.

The data available on the disk are described below.

Column Variables for the Data Tables

Tables

- 1 & 1A Household size, marital status, number of children at home, age of youngest child at home, and age of oldest child at home.
- 2 & 2A Male's report of female level of employment and motivation for working, female's report of female work level and motivation for working.
- 3 & 3A Household income, education level of respondent.
- 4 & 4A Occupation.
- 5 & 5A Ethnic subculture, age.
- 6 & 6A Gender, geographic region.
- 7 & 7A Personality/self-concept traits (humorous, friendly, affectionate, dynamic, shy, assertive, sensitive, independent, traditional, romantic, intellectual, competitive).

Row Variables for Tables 1, 2, 3, 4, 5, 6, and 7

Activity

Heavy User (25+ times in last year)

Food delivered to home
Made pancakes
Purchased from mail catalog
Used a price-off coupon at grocery store
Attended a lecture
Went to movies
Took photographs
Used the Internet
Cooked outdoors
Jogged
Visited health club
Rented a video
Car trip over 100 miles
Attended church

Heavy User (personal use several times a week or more)

Pain relievers
Shower gel
Dandruff shampoo
Lipstick (females)
Presweetened cereal
Cigarettes

Ownership

Personal computer
Camcorder
Microwave oven
Common stock
A handgun
Cellular phone
35mm camera

Favorite Television Shows (personal preference, not family)

"E.R."
"Melrose Place"
"X-Files"
"Seinfeld"
"Frasier"
"Murphy Brown"
"Saturday Night Live"
"David Letterman"

Row Variables for Tables 1A, 2A, 3A, 4A, 5A, 6A, and 7A

Attitudes/Interests/Opinions

I am uncomfortable when the house is not completely clean.

I love to eat different food with interesting flavors.

I usually check ingredient labels when buying food.

I am confused by all the nutrition information that is available today.

I like to cook.

I have trouble getting to sleep.

I work very hard most of the time.

I have a lot of spare time.

When I have a favorite brand I buy it—no matter what else is on sale.

I always check prices even on small items.

I'm willing to pay more to shop at stores where I get better service.

I am usually among the first to try new products.

I make a special effort to buy from companies that support charitable causes.

Our family is too heavily in debt.

Most big companies are just out for themselves.

A drink or two at the end of the day is a perfect way to unwind.

Americans should always buy American products.

I make a strong effort to recycle everything I can.

Everything is changing too fast today.

My greatest achievements are still ahead of me.

Dressing well is an important part of my life.

The car I drive is a reflection of who I am.

I seek out new experiences that are a little frightening or unconventional.

I like the feeling of speed.

Children are the most important thing in a marriage.

A woman's place is in the home.

I think the women's liberation movement is a good thing.

Television is my primary form of entertainment.

I refuse to buy a brand whose advertising I dislike.

TV commercials place too much emphasis on sex.

I like to be among the first to see a new movie.

Personality (terms that would describe me)

Interesting

Winner

Self-confident

Sexy

Life-of-the-party

Tense

Patient

ACCESSING THE DATA

The data can be used on either a Macintosh or Windows-based machine. Once accessed, you should immediately create a backup copy of all the files either on your hard drive or on another disk.

If you have a Macintosh system 7 or later, you should be able to get an immediate translation of the disk into Macintosh format. If you have an earlier Macintosh system, you may need to run a utility program such as Apple File Exchange to translate the program. Simply follow the instructions that come with this program. Be sure to make a backup copy of the translated files before you begin to work with them.

Contents in Brief

Contents

Consumer Behavior

Building Marketing Strategy

part one

Introduction

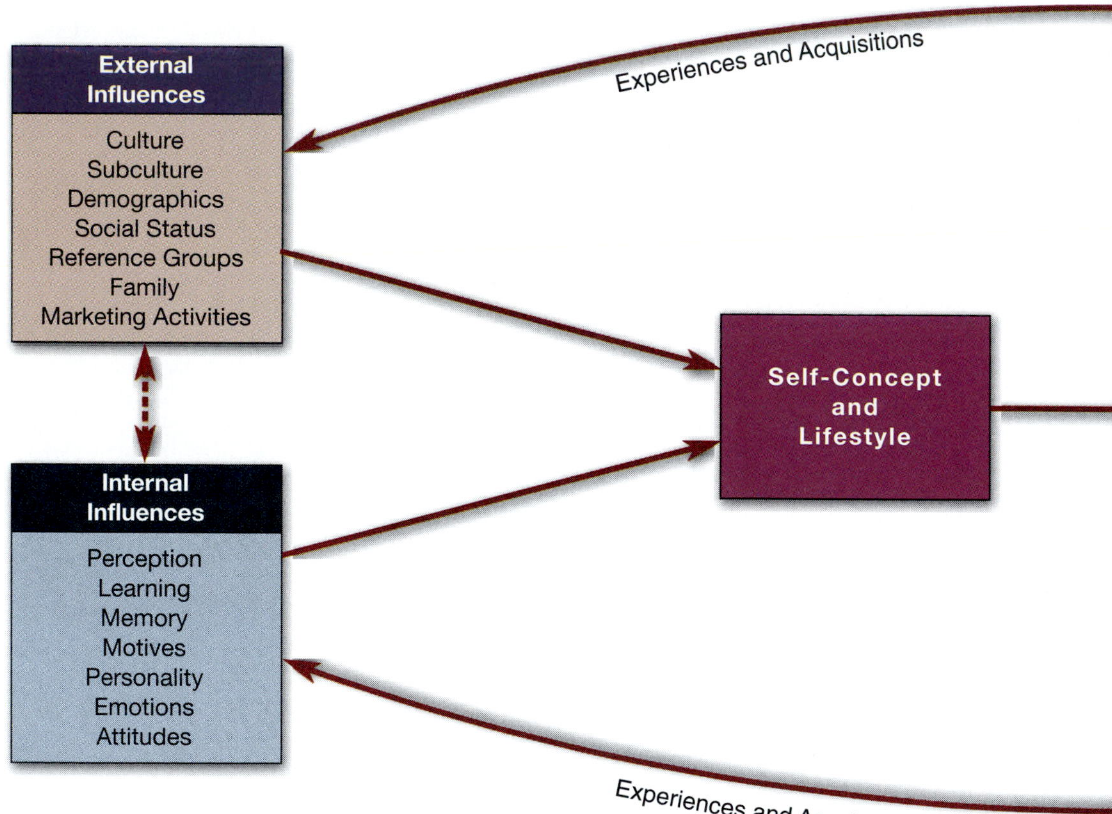

■ What is consumer behavior? Why should we study it? Do marketing managers, regulators, and consumer advocates actually use knowledge about consumer behavior to develop marketing strategy? Will a sound knowledge of consumer behavior help me in my career? Will it enable me to be a better citizen? How does consumer behavior impact the quality of our lives and environment? How can we organize our knowledge of consumer behavior in order to understand and use it more effectively?

■ These and a number of other interesting questions are addressed in the first chapter of the text. This chapter describes the importance and usefulness of the material to be covered in the remainder of the text and provides an overview of this material. In addition, the logic of the model of consumer behavior shown on these pages is developed.

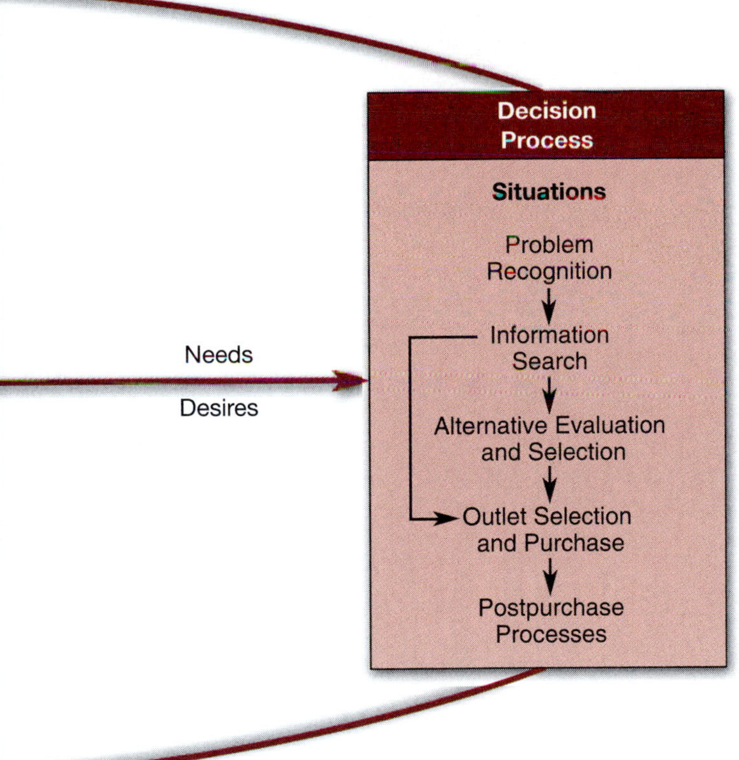

Courtesy PETA.

chapter one

Consumer Behavior and Marketing Strategy

■ The mission of People for the Ethical Treatment of Animals (PETA) is to end all abuse and exploitation of animals. While it is best known for its anti-fur campaign (see Case 6–2, page 739), it works in all areas where animals and humans interact. It faces the monumental task of convincing people to change long-held attitudes and beliefs with respect to animals.

PETA promotes a vegan lifestyle based on its belief that animals raised for food are typically raised in cruel conditions and that animals should not be killed to meet human needs unnecessarily. It also encourages the use of products ranging from stitches to shoes that do not contain animal products. Likewise, it urges the use of products such as "cruelty-free" hair dyes from Revlon that have not been tested on animals.

PETA issues educational materials, maintains several Web sites, sponsors rallies and boycotts, issues press releases, sponsors local organizations, and sells merchandise designed to educate consumers, change attitudes, and alter behaviors toward animals. Its most renowned activities are its anti-fur billboards, such as the one on the facing page featuring Pamela Lee that appeared in New York, London, Paris, and Berlin.

■ In March 1996, the Center for Media Education released a report entitled *Web of Deception: Threats to Children from Online Marketing.* This report unleashed a barrage of calls for regulation of marketing practices on the World Wide Web. A press release from the National PTA stated in part: "The National PTA joins the Center for Media Education and others this morning in sounding the alarm—Madison Avenue is once again 'giving kids the business,' and this time it's on the Internet and the World Wide Web. Parents and families beware!!! The wires of the next generation of telecommunications are barely warm, but the advertising targeted at children is heating up." A similar release from the Consumer Federation of America proposed that: "This emerging issue will require increased protection by the government and increased vigilance by parents. (While) our children are fearless when sitting in front of a computer, (they) are very vulnerable. They are not sophisticated consumers . . . They have little experience or knowledge about how marketers operate."

The American Academy of Child and Adolescent Psychiatry's statement concluded that: "We know that children are gullible and that advertising targeted at children can be very powerful. In the isolated world of cyberspace, where a child is interacting with a computer, a child becomes much more vulnerable to manipulation from promotional programs that promise rewards for compliance with requests for information . . . vulnerable children are unable to understand the consequences of choices made in response to computerized prompts that entice them to advance through the program, much like the computer games with which they are familiar. Children isolated on-line are highly vulnerable to the clever manipulations of the very compelling advertising practices in cyberspace." (See Case 6–1 for details.)

One result of this report (and other studies) was the passage of the Children's Online Privacy Protection Act (COPPA).

■ Procter & Gamble created the disposable diaper market in Japan when it introduced Pampers. The product was an unmodified version of the American product and was marketed using the same rational approach used in the United States. However, Japanese competitors soon reduced P&G's share to less than 10 percent. "We really didn't understand the consumer," explained P&G's CEO.

Based on consumer research, P&G redesigned the diapers to be much thinner. It also introduced pink diapers for girls and blue for boys. Advertising was changed from a rational approach (a diaper is shown absorbing a cup of water) to a more indirect, emotional approach (a talking diaper promises toddlers that it won't leak or cause diaper rash). Finally, the Procter & Gamble corporate name was made prominent in both packaging and design. Unlike Americans, Japanese consider corporate identity and reputation to be critical. P&G is now in second place in Japan, with more than a 20 percent share.

■ Linda Smith, vice president, Marketing, for L'eggs Products, describes the philosophy of L'eggs' award-winning Web site as follows: "We want it to be more than 'Everything you always wanted to know about pantyhose.'" The site (www.leggs.com) offers a complete on-line women's magazine. Its introduction says:

> We're about lifestyles, having fun and dealing with issues that we all face; and then of course we've got great *products*. Each week we're adding new articles and features to keep the content fresh.

It currently contains sections on health and fitness, L'eggs products, career/personal finance, legal/politics, entertainment/style, home and family, shopping spree (L'eggs on-line store), and women's resources. The entertainment/style section recently featured movie reviews, a game, and a celebrity profile. The career/personal finance section had articles titled "Getting Your Financial Life in Order," "What Career Is for You," and "The Biggest Financial Mistake Women Make." For its Web site to succeed and enhance the sales and image of its products, L'eggs must understand much more about its customers than their hosiery requirements![1]

The field of **consumer behavior** is *the study of individuals, groups, or organizations and the processes they use to select, secure, use, and dispose of products, services, experiences, or ideas to satisfy needs and the impacts that these processes have on the consumer and society.* This is a broader view of consumer behavior than the traditional one, which focused much more on the buyer and the immediate antecedents and consequences of the purchasing process. This view will lead us to examine indirect influences on consumption decisions as well as consequences that involve more than the purchaser and seller.

The opening examples summarize several attempts to apply an understanding of consumer behavior in order to develop an effective marketing strategy, to regulate a marketing practice, or to cause socially desirable behavior. The examples cited reveal four main facts about the nature of our knowledge of consumer behavior. First, successful marketing decisions by commercial firms, nonprofit organizations, and regulatory agencies require extensive information on consumer behavior. It should be obvious from these examples that *organizations are applying theories and information about consumer behavior on a daily basis.* A knowledge of consumer behavior is critical for influencing not only product purchase decisions but decisions about which college to attend, which charities to support, how much recycling to do, or whether to seek help for an addiction or behavioral problem.

The examples also indicate the need to collect information about the specific consumers involved in the marketing decision at hand. At its current state of development, *consumer behavior theory provides the manager with the proper questions to ask.* However, given the importance of the specific situation and product category in consumer behavior, it will often be necessary to conduct research to answer these questions. One executive explains the importance of consumer behavior research this way:

> Understanding and properly interpreting consumer wants is a whole lot easier said than done. Every week our marketing researchers talk to more than 4,000 consumers to find out:
>
> - What they think of our products and those of our competitors.
> - What they think of possible improvements in our products.
> - How they use our products.
> - What attitudes they have about our products and our advertising.
> - What they feel about their "roles" in the family and society.
> - What their hopes and dreams are for themselves and their families.
>
> Today, as never before, we cannot take our business for granted. That's why understanding—and therefore learning to anticipate—consumer behavior is our key to planning and managing in this ever-changing environment.[2]

The examples also indicate that *consumer behavior is a complex, multidimensional process.* The Center for Media Education, PETA, L'eggs, and P&G have invested millions of dollars researching consumer behavior and much more trying to influence it, yet none of them are completely successful.

Finally, the examples indicate that *marketing practice designed to influence consumer behavior influences the firm, the individual, and society.* Pampers, while providing substantial benefits to individual consumers and profits for Procter & Gamble, raises resource use and disposition issues that impact all of society. More obvious concerns arise around products such as cigarettes and alcohol. Likewise, specific marketing practices such as targeting children on the Web have implications for the family and society. We will explore these types of issues throughout the text.

Courtesy Weider Nutrition Group—Tiger's Milk/Tiger Sport.

Courtesy PowerBar Inc.

ILLUSTRATION 1-1

These ads are targeting the same consumers with very similar products, yet they use two very different approaches. Why? They are based on different assumptions about consumer behavior and how to influence it.

Sufficient knowledge of consumer behavior currently exists to provide a usable guide to marketing practice for commercial firms, nonprofit organizations, and regulators, but the state of the art is not sufficient for us to write a cookbook with surefire recipes for success. We will illustrate how some organizations were able to combine certain ingredients for success under specific conditions. However, as conditions change, the quantities and even the ingredients required for success may change. It is up to you as a student and future marketing manager to develop the ability to apply this knowledge to specific situations. To assist you, we have included example situations and questions at the end of each chapter and a series of short cases at the end of each section that can be used to develop your application skills. Also, Appendix B at the end of the text provides a list of key questions for a consumer behavior audit for developing marketing strategy.

It is important to note that *all marketing decisions and regulations are based on assumptions about consumer behavior.* It is impossible to think of a marketing decision for which this is not the case. For example, regulations designed to protect children from various marketing practices on the Web must be based on assumptions about children's ability to process information and make decisions in this environment. Likewise, a decision to match a competitor's price reduction must be based on some assumption about how consumers evaluate prices and how they would respond to a price differential between the two brands. Examine Illustration 1-1. Both these ads appeared in the same issue of *Outside* magazine and are targeted at the same consumers. What assumptions about consumer behavior underlie each ad? Which approach is best? Why?

APPLICATIONS OF CONSUMER BEHAVIOR

Marketing Strategy

As stated above, all marketing strategies and tactics are based on explicit or implicit beliefs about consumer behavior. Decisions based on explicit assumptions and sound theory and research are more likely to be successful than are decisions based solely on implicit intuition. Thus, knowledge of consumer behavior can be an important competitive advantage. It can greatly reduce the odds of bad decisions such as the following:

> BIC Corp. introduced a small $5 bottle of perfume to be sold in supermarkets and drugstore chains where it had tremendous distribution strength. The perfume was to be easy and convenient to buy and use. However, as one expert said in examining the $11 million loss project: "Fragrance is an emotional sell, not convenience or utility. The BIC package wasn't feminine. It looked like a cigarette lighter."[3]
>
> Nestea launched a yellowish carbonated beverage named Tea Whiz. As you might suspect, it failed, as did Miller Clear Beer and Gerber adult foods.

Our primary goal is to help you obtain a usable managerial understanding of consumer behavior. The key aspect of this objective is found in the phrase *usable managerial understanding*. We want to increase your understanding of consumer behavior in order to help you become a more effective marketing manager. We will take a more in-depth look at marketing strategy and consumer behavior shortly.

Regulatory Policy

The Food and Drug Administration (FDA) recently ordered three manufacturers of vegetable oil to remove claims on their labels that state that the products contain no cholesterol. The FDA believes that the claims of *No Cholesterol* are misleading *even though they are true.*[4]

The FDA staff that issued these regulations did so based on their beliefs and knowledge about how consumers process information. If they are correct, the rules will result in better (healthier or more economical) choices by consumers. However, if they are incorrect, both consumers and firms delivering a superior product are harmed. Clearly, effective regulation of many marketing practices requires an extensive knowledge of consumer behavior. We will discuss this issue throughout the text and provide a detailed treatment in Chapter 20.

Social Marketing

Recently, some states began investing cigarette tax revenues in high-quality, prime-time antismoking television commercials (see Case 3–9). Researchers at the University of Vermont spent $2 million on a four-year television campaign that showed popular kids disdaining cigarettes or smokers being unable to get dates. Smoking rates among teenagers were 35 percent lower in communities where the campaign was shown than in similar communities without the campaign. The effect was still strong two years after the campaign quit airing.[5]

How did these researchers decide to stress negative social consequences of smoking rather than negative health consequences? The decision was based on their knowledge and assumptions about the consumer behavior of teenagers.

ILLUSTRATION 1-2

Nonprofits as well as commercial firms attempt to influence consumption patterns. Both types of organizations must base their efforts on knowledge of consumer behavior to maximize their chances of success.

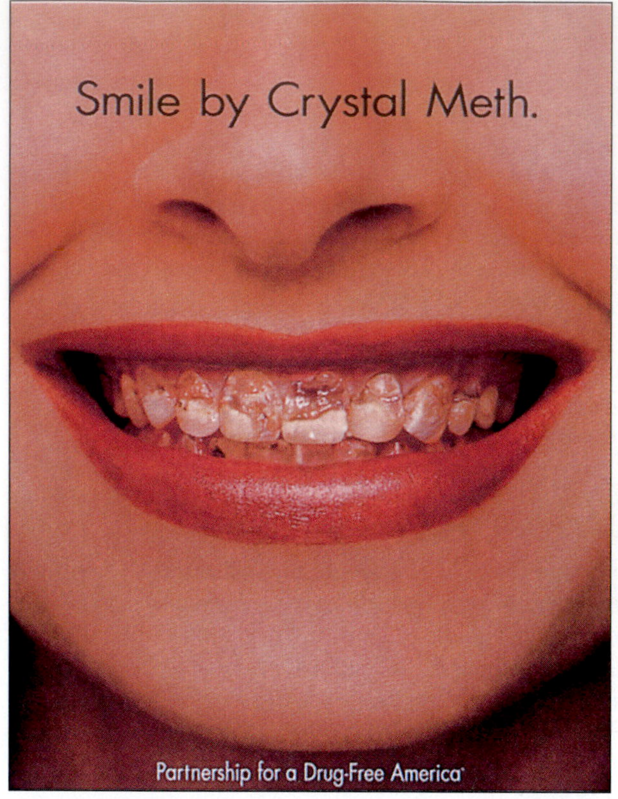

Courtesy Partnership for a Drug-Free America.

Social marketing is *the application of marketing strategies and tactics to alter or create behaviors that have a positive effect on the targeted individuals and/or society as a whole.*[6] Social marketing has been used in attempts to reduce smoking, as noted above, to increase the percentage of children receiving their vaccinations in a timely manner,[7] to encourage environmentally sound behaviors such as recycling,[8] to reduce behaviors potentially leading to AIDS,[9] to enhance support of charities,[10] to reduce drug use,[11] and many other important causes.

Just as for commercial marketing strategy, successful social marketing strategy requires a sound understanding of consumer behavior. For example, the Partnership for a Drug-Free America uses a fear-based campaign in its efforts to discourage the use of crystal meth. Illustration 1-2 contains one of its milder ads. In Chapter 11, we will analyze the conditions under which such campaigns are likely to succeed.

Informed Individuals

Most economically developed societies are legitimately referred to as consumption societies. Most individuals in these societies spend more time engaged in consumption than in any other activity, including work or sleep (both of which also involve consumption). Therefore, knowledge of consumer behavior can enhance our understanding of our environment and ourselves. Such an understanding is essential for sound citizenship, effective purchasing behavior, and reasoned business ethics.

Literally thousands of firms are spending millions of dollars to influence you, your family, and your friends. These influence attempts occur in ads, packages, product features, sales pitches, and store environments. However, they also occur in the content of many television shows, in the products that are used in movies, and in the materials presented to children in the schools.[12] Given the magnitude of these direct and indirect influence attempts, it is important that consumers accurately understand the strategies and tactics that are being used.[13] It is equally important that all of us, as citizens, understand the consumer behavior basis of these strategies so that we can set appropriate limits on them when required.

MARKETING STRATEGY AND CONSUMER BEHAVIOR

Since all four of the applications of consumer behavior described above focus on the development, regulation, or effects of marketing strategy, we will now examine marketing strategy in more depth.

To survive in a competitive environment, an organization must provide target customers more value than is provided by its competitors. **Customer value** is *the difference between all the benefits derived from a total product and all the costs of acquiring those benefits.* For example, owning a car can provide a number of benefits (depending on the person and the type of car), including flexible transportation, image, status, pleasure, comfort, and even companionship. However, securing these benefits requires paying for the car, gasoline, insurance, maintenance, and parking fees, as well as risking injury from an accident, adding to environmental pollution, and dealing with traffic jams and other frustrations. It is the difference between the total benefits and the total costs that constitutes customer value.

The importance of understanding value *from the customer's perspective* can be seen in a product introduction by La Choy (a Hunt-Wesson Inc. brand). La Choy was a well-known brand. Frozen food sales had been growing rapidly, as had ethnic food sales. La Choy management decided to launch a line of large, meaty, frozen egg rolls to be used as a main course rather than as appetizers, as the smaller egg rolls then available were used. The logic seemed sound. Unfortunately, the large egg rolls could not be microwaved (the shells became soggy) and they took 30 minutes to heat in a regular oven. Consumers considered value in frozen foods of this type to include quick preparation. The egg rolls were a market failure and were withdrawn within two years.[14]

Providing superior customer value requires the organization to do a better job of anticipating and reacting to customer needs than the competition does. As Figure 1-1 indicates, an understanding of consumer behavior is the basis for marketing strategy formulation. Consumers' reactions to this marketing strategy determine the organization's success or failure. However, these reactions also determine the success of the consumers in meeting their needs, and they have significant impacts on the larger society in which they occur.

Marketing strategy, as described in Figure 1-1, is conceptually very simple. It begins with an analysis of the market the organization is considering. This requires a detailed analysis of the organization's capabilities, the strengths and weaknesses of competitors, the economic and technological forces affecting the market, and the current and potential customers in the market. Based on the consumer analysis portion of this step, the organization identifies groups of individuals, households, or firms with similar needs. These market segments are described in terms of demographics, media preferences, geographic location, and so forth. One or more of these segments are then selected as target markets based on the firm's capabilities relative to those of the competition (given current and forecast economic and technological conditions).

Next, marketing strategy is formulated. Marketing strategy seeks to provide the customer with more value than the competition while still producing a profit for the firm.

FIGURE 1-1 Marketing Strategy and Consumer Behavior

Marketing strategy is formulated in terms of the marketing mix. That is, it involves determining the product features, price, communications, distribution, and services that will provide customers with superior value. This entire set of characteristics is often referred to as the **total product.** The total product is presented to the target market, which is consistently engaged in processing information and making decisions designed to maintain or enhance its lifestyle (individuals and households) or performance (businesses and other organizations).

Look at Illustration 1-3. What is the Rainforest Cafe's total product? Clearly, it is much more than food. The Rainforest Cafe, the Hard Rock Cafe, and similar restaurants are selling experiences as much as or perhaps more than food! As Consumer Insight 1-1 indicates, this is an increasingly important aspect of marketing.

For the firm, the reaction of the target market to the total product produces an image of the product/brand/organization, sales (or lack thereof), and some level of customer satisfaction among those who did purchase. Sophisticated marketers seek to produce satisfied customers rather than mere sales—because satisfied customers are more profitable in the

Courtesy Rainforest Cafe, Inc.

ILLUSTRATION 1-3

What do you buy when you go to a theme restaurant? The experience is the product as much or more than the actual food.

long run. For the individual, the process results in some level of need satisfaction, financial expenditure, attitude development/change, and/or behavioral changes. For society, the cumulative effect of the marketing process affects economic growth, pollution, social problems (illnesses caused by smoking and alcohol), and social benefits (improved nutrition, increased education). These individual and societal impacts are not always in the best interests of the individual or society, so the development and application of consumer behavior knowledge has many ethical implications.

Note again that an *analysis of consumers* is a key part of the foundation of marketing strategy, and *consumer reaction* to the total product determines the success or failure of the strategy. Before providing an overview of consumer behavior, we will examine marketing strategy formulation in more detail.

MARKET ANALYSIS COMPONENTS

Market analysis requires a thorough understanding of the organization's own capabilities, the capabilities of current and future competitors, the consumption process of potential customers, and the economic, physical, and technological environment in which these elements will interact.

The Consumers

It is not possible to anticipate and react to customers' needs and desires without a complete understanding of consumer behavior. Discovering customers' current needs is a complex

Consumer Insight 1-1

The Experience Economy

Not too many years ago, a child's birthday cake was made at home from scratch. Then, cake mixes became the most common means of preparing a cake. Increasingly, this has been replaced by cakes made (standard or customized) at bakeries or grocery stores. Now, many birthday cakes are provided as part of the birthday package arranged by Chuck E. Cheese's, the Discovery Zone, or a similar company. These companies are not selling products or services; they are selling experiences. The primary evaluation of a birthday party "conducted" by such a firm is not the taste of the cake and ice cream, the promptness of the service, or the nature of the party favors. Rather, it is the quality of the experience: Did the kids have fun? Did it have a "Wow factor"? Were the adults comfortable?

An experience occurs when a company intentionally creates a memorable event for customers. While products and services are, to a large extent, external to the customer, an experience is largely internal to each customer. The experience exists in the mind of an individual who has been engaged on an emotional, physical, intellectual, or even spiritual level. Experiences can be categorized along two dimensions. *Participation* refers to how active or passive the individual is in the experience. *Connection* relates to whether the individual is absorbing the event (such as reading a book) or is immersed in the event (such as acting in a play).

Theme parks, theme restaurants, adventure travel, and similar activities are experiences that are marketed as such. Customers patronize them in order to acquire the experience. Today, many firms are wrapping experiences around their traditional products and services in order to sell them better. Niketown, the Sharper Image, Cabella's, and REI all draw customers to their outlets in part because of the experiences that are available at those outlets. The Mall of America and the Forum Shops in Las Vegas have developed shopping areas that are visited for the experiences as much as for the merchandise.

Critical Thinking Questions

1. What services could become experience-provoking events? How would they do this?
2. How can retailers, including Internet outlets, provide their customers with experiences?
3. What would a store like Niketown (or a local shopping mall in your area) have to do to charge admission for customers to enter?

process, but it can generally be accomplished by direct marketing research, as the following example illustrates.

Black & Decker (B&D) had a moderately successful line of relatively inexpensive power tools with the Black & Decker brand and a successful expensive line called *DeWalt* for the professional market. Initial research with consumers revealed that the serious Do-It-Yourselfer (DIYer) wanted higher quality tools than the inexpensive line but few were willing to pay for the level of quality in the DeWalt line. Therefore, B&D identified 50 serious DIYers. B&D managers questioned these DIYers about the tools they used and why they had picked particular brands. They went with them on shopping trips and watched as they purchased tools and other items for projects. They observed them in their shops and questioned them as they used the tools. B&D tried to determine what these DIYers liked and disliked about particular brands and tools, how the tools felt when they used them, what problems they had while doing projects or cleaning up afterward, and so forth. They also tried to understand the emotional side of DIY projects by asking questions such as: *What was your project? How did you feel when you completed it?*

The color of the tools was carefully researched as well. Consumer research found that the deep green used on B&D's garden products was associated with quality and reliability. The name Quantum was also based on consumer research. It beat out such names as Excell, Caliber, and Excaliber. Consumers said it implied a product that was a step ahead of others and they could pronounce it easily. The Black & Decker name does not appear on the DeWalt products or packages because the professional contractors did not think B&D could make sophisticated tools. However, the serious DIYers had high regard for B&D, and its name appears prominently on Quantum products and packages.

The Quantum line has been very successful. As one analyst says: "Black & Decker has become very good at taking market share away from rival companies. They just know their customer."[15]

However, anticipating evolving consumer needs requires *understanding* the consumer, which in turn requires understanding the behavioral principles that guide consumption behaviors. These principles are covered in depth in the balance of this text.

The Company

A firm must fully understand its own ability to meet customer needs. This involves evaluating all aspects of the firm, including its financial condition, general managerial skills, production capabilities, research and development capabilities, technological sophistication, reputation, and marketing skills. Marketing skills would include new product development capabilities, channel strength, advertising abilities, service capabilities, marketing research abilities, market and consumer knowledge, and so forth.

Failure to adequately understand one's own strengths can cause serious problems. IBM's first attempt to enter the home computer market with the PC Jr. was a failure in part for this reason. While IBM had an excellent reputation with large business customers and a very strong direct sales force for serving them, these strengths were not relevant to the household consumer market.

The Competitors

It is not possible to consistently do a better job of meeting customer needs than the competition without a thorough understanding of the competition's capabilities and strategies. This requires the same level of knowledge of a firm's key competitors that is required of one's own firm. In addition, for any significant marketing action, the following questions must be answered:

1. If we are successful, which firms will be hurt (lose sales or sales opportunities)?
2. Of those firms that are injured, which have the capability (financial resources, marketing strengths) to respond?
3. How are they likely to respond (reduce prices, increase advertising, introduce a new product)?
4. Is our strategy (planned action) robust enough to withstand the likely actions of our competitors, or do we need additional contingency plans?

The Conditions

The state of the economy, the physical environment, government regulations, and technological developments affect consumer needs and expectations as well as company and competitor capabilities. The deterioration of the physical environment has produced not only consumer demand for environmentally sound products but also government regulations affecting product design and manufacturing.

International agreements such as NAFTA (North American Free Trade Agreement) have greatly reduced international trade barriers and increased the level of both competition and consumer expectations for many products. The development of computers has changed the way many people work and has created new industries.

Clearly, a firm cannot develop a sound marketing strategy without anticipating the conditions under which that strategy will be implemented.

MARKET SEGMENTATION

Perhaps the most important marketing decision a firm makes is the selection of one or more market segments on which to focus. A **market segment** is *a portion of a larger market whose needs differ somewhat from the larger market.* Since a market segment has unique needs, a firm that develops a total product focused solely on the needs of that segment will be able to meet the segment's desires better than a firm whose product or service attempts to meet the needs of multiple segments.

To be viable, a segment must be large enough to be served profitably. To some extent, each individual or household has unique needs for most products (a preferred color combination, for example). The smaller the segment, the closer the total product can be to that segment's desires. Historically, the smaller the segment, the more it costs to serve the segment. Thus, a tailor-made suit costs more than a mass-produced suit. However, flexible manufacturing and customized media are making it increasingly cost effective to develop products and communications for small segments or even individual consumers, as the following example shows:

Fingerhut, a catalog retailer with $2 billion in sales, has a database that stores over 500 pieces of information on each of more than 50 million potential customers. The data include not only past purchases and credit information but demographics such as age, marital status, and number of children and personal data such as hobbies and birthdays. This database enables Fingerhut to send consumers individualized catalogs at times when they are most likely to buy.[16]

Market segmentation involves four steps:

1. Identifying product-related need sets.
2. Grouping customers with similar need sets.
3. Describing each group.
4. Selecting an attractive segment(s) to serve.

Product-Related Need Sets

Organizations approach market segmentation with a set of current and potential capabilities. These capabilities may be a reputation, an existing product, a technology, or some other skill set. The first task of the firm is to identify need sets that the organization is capable (or could become capable) of meeting. The term **need set** is used to reflect the fact that most products in developed economies satisfy more than one need. Thus, an automobile can meet more needs than just basic transportation. Some customers purchase cars to meet transportation and status needs. Others purchase them to meet transportation and fun needs. Still others purchase automobiles to meet status, fun, and transportation needs. Illustration 1-4 shows two ads for automobiles. What needs does the Acura ad appeal to? The Isuzu ad? These ads differ because the firms are pursuing different market segments with distinct need sets.

Customer needs are not restricted to product features. Their needs also include types and sources of information about the product, outlets where the product is available, the price of the product, services associated with the product, the image of the product or firm, and even where and how the product is produced. For example, Nike recently lost sales due to publicity about child labor and abusive working conditions at some of the factories in

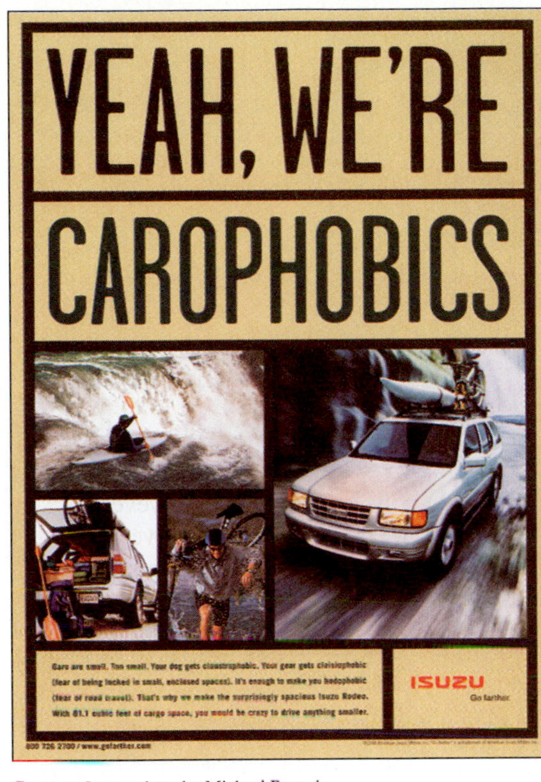

Courtesy Isuzu; photo by Michael Rausch.

Courtesy Acura Division, American HondaMotor Co., Inc.

ILLUSTRATION 1-4

Acura and Isuzu are both cars. Both provide flexible, individual transportation. Yet, as these ads show, they are designed to meet a different set of needs in addition to basic transportation.

developing countries where many of its products are made. In response, it has changed some practices and engaged in a variety of public relations activities, but the criticism continues.[17]

Identifying the various need sets that the firm's current or potential product might satisfy typically involves consumer research (particularly focus groups and depth interviews) as well as logic and intuition. These need sets are often associated with other variables such as age, stage in the household life cycle, gender, social class, ethnic group, or lifestyle, and many firms start the segmentation process focusing first on one or more of the groups defined by one of these variables. Thus, a firm might start with various ethnic groups and attempt to discover similarities and differences in consumption-related needs across these groups. While better-defined segments will generally be discovered by focusing first on needs, then on consumer characteristics associated with those needs, both approaches are used in practice and both provide a useful basis for segmentation.

Customers with Similar Need Sets

The next step is to group consumers with similar need sets. For example, the need for moderately priced, fun, sporty automobiles appears to exist in many young single individuals, young couples with no children, and middle-aged couples whose children have left home. These consumers can be grouped into one segment as far as product features and perhaps even product image are concerned despite sharply different demographics.

This step generally involves consumer research—including focus group interviews, surveys, and product concept tests (see Appendix A). It could also involve an analysis of

TABLE 1-1

Market Segment Attractiveness Worksheet

Criterion	Score*
Segment size	________
Segment growth rate	________
Competitor strength	________
Customer satisfaction with existing products	________
Fit with company image	________
Fit with company objectives	________
Fit with company resources	________
Distribution available	________
Investment required	________
Stability/predictability	________
Cost to serve	________
Sustainable advantage available	________
Communications channels available	________
Risk	________
Other (__________)	________

*Score on a 1 to 10 scale, with 10 being most favorable.

current consumption patterns and deductions based on an understanding of consumer behavior.

Description of Each Group

Once consumers with similar need sets are identified, they should be described in terms of their demographics, lifestyles, and media usage. In order to design an effective marketing program, it is necessary to have a complete understanding of the potential customers. It is only with such a complete understanding that we can be sure we have correctly identified the need set. In addition, we cannot communicate effectively with our customers if we do not understand the context in which our product is purchased and consumed, how it is thought about by our customers, and the language they use to describe it. Thus, while many young single individuals, young couples with no children, and middle-aged couples whose children have left home may want the same features in an automobile, the media required to reach each group and the appropriate language and themes to use with each group would undoubtedly differ.

Attractive Segment(s) to Serve

Once we are sure we have a thorough understanding of each segment, we must select our **target market**—*that segment(s) of the larger market on which we will focus our marketing effort.* This decision is based on our ability to provide the selected segment(s) with superior customer value at a profit. Thus, the size and growth of the segment, the intensity of the current and anticipated competition, the cost of providing the superior value, and so forth are important considerations. Table 1-1 provides a simple worksheet for use in evaluating and comparing the attractiveness of various market segments.

It is important to remember that each market segment requires its own marketing strategy. Each element of the marketing mix should be examined to determine if changes are required from one segment to another. Sometimes each segment will require a completely different marketing mix, including the product. At other times, only the advertising message or retail outlets may need to differ.

MARKETING STRATEGY

It is not possible to select target markets without simultaneously formulating a general marketing strategy for each segment. A decisive criterion in selecting target markets is the ability to provide superior value to those market segments. Since customer value is delivered by the marketing strategy, the firm must develop its general marketing strategy as it evaluates potential target markets.

Marketing strategy is basically the answer to the question: *How will we provide superior customer value to our target market?* The answer to this question requires the formulation of a consistent marketing mix. The **marketing mix** is *the product, price, communications, distribution, and services provided to the target market.* It is the combination of these elements that meets customer needs and provides customer value. For example, in Illustration 1-1, the Tiger Sport Energy Bar promised superior value through better taste and a lower price than its competitors.

The Product

A **product** is *anything a consumer acquires or might acquire to meet a perceived need.* Consumers are generally buying need satisfaction, not physical product attributes.[18] As the former head of Revlon said, "in the factory we make cosmetics, in the store we sell hope." Thus, consumers don't purchase quarter-inch drill bits but the ability to create quarter-inch holes. Federal Express lost much of its overnight letter delivery business not to UPS or Airborne but to fax machines and the Internet because they could meet the same consumer needs faster, cheaper, or more conveniently. Consider one analyst's description of McDonald's product:

> The source of McDonald's pre-eminence is neither hamburgers nor fast-food service. It's giving a wide range of people the experience of a reliable break from fatigue, stress, grown-up responsibility. More variety, fewer calories, even enhanced freshness are not the principal criteria for success if what those people seek is "a break today."[19]

We use the term *product* to refer to physical products and primary or core services. Thus, an automobile is a product, as is a transmission overhaul or a ride in a taxi. Over 15,000 new products and new versions of existing products are introduced to supermarkets alone each year. Obviously, many of these will not succeed. To be successful, products must meet the needs of the target market better than the competition does.

Consider the Chinese computer market. A few years ago, a state-owned company—Legend—appeared headed for oblivion as China opened its market to Western firms. Today it dominates all competitors. How? According to its general manager, "We have much more insight into the needs of Chinese customers." These insights have been translated into bundling software products for first-time buyers (most of the market) into its computers. These include tutorials on such topics as using the computer, using the Internet, and organizing home finances.[20]

Communications

Marketing communications include *advertising, the sales force, public relations, packaging, and any other signal that the firm provides about itself and its products.* An effective communications strategy requires answers to the following questions:

1. *With whom, exactly, do we want to communicate?* While most messages are aimed at the target-market members, others are focused on channel members or those who

ILLUSTRATION 1-5

All aspects of the marketing mix should be designed around the needs and characteristics of the target market. Many segments would not understand the language in this ad, but it works with the targeted segment.

Courtesy Mervin Manufacturing, Inc.

influence the target-market members. For example, pediatric nurses are often asked for advice concerning diapers and other nonmedical infant care items. A firm marketing such items would be wise to communicate directly with these individuals.

Often it is necessary to determine who within the target market should receive the marketing message. For a children's breakfast cereal, should the communications be aimed at the children or the parents or both? (The answer depends on the target market and varies by country.)

2. *What effect do we want our communication to have on the target audience?* Often a manager will state that the purpose of advertising and other marketing communications is to increase sales. While this may be the ultimate objective, the behavioral objective for most marketing communications is often much more immediate. That is, it may seek to have the audience learn something about the product, seek more information about the product, like the product, recommend the product to others, feel good about having bought the product, or a host of other communications effects.
3. *What message will achieve the desired effect on our audience?* What words, pictures, and symbols should we use to capture attention and produce the desired effect? Marketing messages can range from purely factual statements to pure symbolism. The best approach depends on the situation at hand. Developing an effective message requires a thorough understanding of the meanings the target audience attaches to words and symbols, as well as knowledge of the perception process. Consider Illustration 1-5. Many older consumers would not relate to the phrase "full time enjoyer of all that is sick." However, it communicates clearly to this target market for snowboards.

4. *What means and media should we use to reach the target audience?* Should we use personal sales to provide information? Can we rely on the package to provide needed information? Should we advertise in mass media, use direct mail, or rely on consumers to find us on the Internet? If we advertise in mass media, which media (television, radio, magazines, newspapers) and which specific vehicles (television programs, specific magazines, and so forth) should we use? Answering these questions requires an understanding both of the media that the target audiences use and of the effect that advertising in those media would have on the product's image.
5. *When should we communicate with the target audience?* Should we concentrate our communications near the time that purchases tend to be made or evenly throughout the week, month, or year? Do consumers seek information shortly before purchasing our product? If so, where? Answering these questions requires knowledge of the decision process used by the target market for this product.

Price

Price is *the amount of money one must pay to obtain the right to use the product.* One can buy ownership of a product or, for many products, limited usage rights (i.e., one can rent or lease a product such as a video). Economists often assume that lower prices for the same product will result in more sales than higher prices. However, price sometimes serves as a signal of quality. A product priced "too low" might be perceived as having low quality. Owning expensive items also provides information about the owner. If nothing else, it indicates that the owner can afford the expensive item. This is a desirable feature to some consumers. Therefore, setting a price requires a thorough understanding of the symbolic role that price plays for the product and target market in question.

It is important to note that the price of a product is not the same as the cost of the product to the customer. The **consumer cost** is *everything the consumer must surrender in order to receive the benefits of owning/using the product.* As described earlier, the cost of owning/using an automobile includes insurance, gasoline, maintenance, finance charges, license fees, parking fees, time and discomfort while shopping for the car, and perhaps even discomfort about increasing pollution, in addition to the purchase price. One of the ways that firms seek to provide customer value is to reduce the nonprice costs of owning or operating a product. If successful, the total cost to the customer decreases while the revenue to the marketer stays the same or even increases.

Distribution

Distribution, *having the product available where target customers can buy it,* is essential to success. Only in rare cases will customers go to much trouble to secure a particular brand. Obviously, good channel decisions require a sound knowledge of where target customers shop for the product in question, as the following example shows:

> Huffy Corp., a $700 million bicycle manufacturer, did careful research before launching a new bicycle called Cross Sport. The new bike was a cross between a mountain bike and the traditional thin-framed 10-speed bicycle. Focus groups and product concept tests revealed strong consumer acceptance. Huffy quickly launched the $159 Cross Sport through its strong mass distribution channels such as Kmart and Toys "R" Us. Unfortunately, the fairly serious adult rider that these bikes targeted demands individual sales attention by knowledgeable salespeople. Such salespeople are found at specialty bike shops, not at mass retailers. As Huffy's president said: "It was a $5 million mistake."[21]

Service

Earlier, we defined *product* to include primary or core services such as haircuts, car repairs, and medical treatments. Here, **service** refers to *auxiliary or peripheral activities that are performed to enhance the primary product or service.* Thus, we would consider car repair to be a product (primary service) while free pickup and delivery of the car would be an auxiliary service. While many texts do not treat service as a separate component of the marketing mix, we do because of the critical role it plays in determining market share and relative price in competitive markets. A firm that does not explicitly manage its auxiliary services is at a competitive disadvantage.

Auxiliary services cost money to provide. Therefore, it is essential that the firm furnish only those services that provide value to the target customers. Providing services that customers do not value can result in high costs and high prices without a corresponding increase in customer value.

CONSUMER DECISIONS

As Figure 1-1 illustrated, the consumer decision process intervenes between the market strategy (as implemented in the marketing mix) and the outcomes. That is, the outcomes of the firm's marketing strategy are determined by its interaction with the consumer decision process. The firm can succeed only if consumers see a need that its product can solve, become aware of the product and its capabilities, decide that it is the best available solution, proceed to buy it, and become satisfied with the results of the purchase. A significant part of this entire text is devoted to developing an understanding of the consumer decision process (Chapters 13–18).

OUTCOMES

Firm Outcomes

Product Position The most basic outcome for a firm of a marketing strategy is its **product position**—*an image of the product or brand in the consumer's mind relative to competing products and brands.* This image consists of a set of beliefs, pictorial representations, and feelings about the product or brand. It does not require purchase or use for it to develop. It is determined by communications about the brand from the firm and other sources, as well as by direct experience with it. Most marketing firms specify the product position they want their brands to have and measure these positions on an ongoing basis. This is because a brand whose position matches the desired position of a target market is likely to be purchased when a need for that product arises.

Sauza Conmemorativo tequila attempts to build a product position as a smooth, lighthearted tequila by running a series of humorous ads all with the tag line: *LIFE IS HARSH. Your Tequila shouldn't be* (see Illustration 1-6). This positioning has helped the brand's sales grow at more than twice the industry average.[22]

Sales Sales are a critical outcome, as they produce the revenue necessary for the firm to continue in business. Therefore, virtually all firms evaluate the success of their marketing programs in terms of sales. As we have seen, sales are likely to occur only if the initial consumer analysis was correct and if the marketing mix matches the consumer decision process.

Courtesy Domecq Importers, Inc.

ILLUSTRATION 1-6

Sauza Conmemorativo has built a strong product position—a smooth, somewhat irreverent tequila—by using a long running humorous campaign with the tag line: "Life is harsh. Your tequila shouldn't be."

Customer Satisfaction Marketers have discovered that it is generally more profitable to maintain existing customers than to replace them with new customers. Retaining current customers requires that they be satisfied with their purchase and use of the product. Thus, **customer satisfaction** is a major concern of marketers.

As Figure 1-2 indicates, convincing consumers that your brand offers superior value (relative to the competition) is necessary in order to make the initial sale. Obviously, one must have a thorough understanding of the potential consumers' needs and of their information acquisition processes to succeed at this task. However, *creating satisfied customers,* and thus future sales, requires that customers continue to believe that your brand meets their needs and offers superior value *after they have used it.* That is, you must deliver as much or more value than your customers initially expected, and it must be enough to satisfy their needs. This requires an even greater understanding of consumer behavior.

Creating Satisfied Customers **FIGURE 1-2**

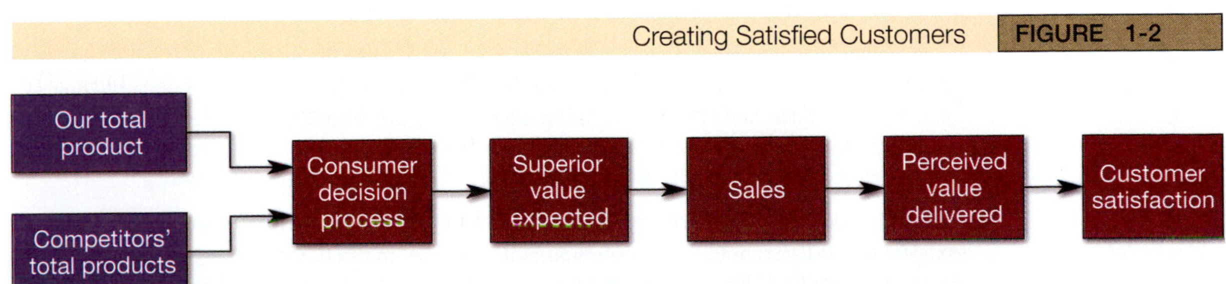

Honda's recent efforts in this area are described below:

> Honda had the factory workers who actually assemble the cars as well as marketing managers conduct telephone interviews with over 47,000 Accord owners. The interviews sought to determine customer satisfaction levels with all aspects of the Accord as well as ideas for improvements. The interviews were conducted by those who would have to make any necessary changes. The results of the three months of interviews were incorporated into the redesigned Accord.[23]

Individual Outcomes

Need Satisfaction The most obvious outcome of the consumption process for an individual, whether or not a purchase is made, is some level of satisfaction of the need that initiated the consumption process. This can range from none (or even negative if a purchase increases the need rather than reduces it) to complete. Two key processes are involved—the actual need fulfillment and the perceived need fulfillment. These two processes are closely related and are often identical. However, at times they differ. For example, people might take a food supplement because they believe it is enhancing their health while in reality it could have no direct health effects or even negative effects. One objective of regulation and a frequent goal of consumer groups is to ensure that consumers can adequately judge the extent to which products are meeting their needs.

Injurious Consumption While we tend to focus on the benefits of consumption, we must remain aware that consumer behavior has a dark side. **Injurious consumption** occurs *when individuals or groups make consumption decisions that have negative consequences for their long-run well-being.*

For most consumers, fulfilling one need impacts their ability to fulfill others due to either financial or time constraints. For example, some estimates indicate that most Americans are not saving at a level that will allow them to maintain a lifestyle near their current one when they retire.[24] The cumulative impact of many small decisions to spend financial resources to meet needs now will limit their ability to meet what may be critically important needs after retirement. For other consumers, readily available credit, unrelenting advertising, and widespread, aggressive merchandising results in a level of expenditures that cannot be sustained by their income.[25] The result is often financial distress, delayed or bypassed medical or dental care, family stress, inadequate resources for proper child care, bankruptcy, or even homelessness.

Cigarette consumption is encouraged by hundreds of millions of dollars in expenditures, as is the consumption of alcoholic beverages, snacks with high sugar and/or fat content, and other potentially harmful products. These expenditures cause some people to consume these products or to consume more of them. Some of these people (and their families) in turn are then harmed by this consumption.[26]

Companies are not the only entities that promote potentially harmful products. Most states in the United States now promote state-sponsored gambling, which has caused devastating financial consequences for some. The following quote indicates the magnitude of the problem:

> Every year over 10 million American consumers suffer financial losses from their addiction to gambling . . . There are currently 10 million alcoholics and 80 million cigarette smokers in the United States . . . Every year 25,000 people die as a result of alcohol related traffic accidents . . . All of these disturbing and disturbed behaviors result from consumption gone wrong.[27]

While these are issues we should be concerned with and we will address throughout this text, we should also note that alcohol consumption seems to have arisen simultaneous with civilization and evidence of gambling is nearly as old. Consumers smoked and chewed tobacco long before mass media or advertising as we know it existed, and illegal drug consumption continues to grow worldwide despite the absence of large-scale marketing (or at least advertising). Thus, though marketing activities based on knowledge of consumer behavior undoubtedly exacerbate some forms of injurious consumption, they are not the sole cause and, as we will see shortly, may also be part of the cure.

Society Outcomes

Economic Outcomes The cumulative impact of consumers' purchase decisions (including the decision to forgo consumption) is a major determinant of the state of a given country's economy. Consumers' decisions on whether to buy or save impact economic growth, the availability and cost of capital, employment levels, and so forth. The types of products and brands purchased influence the balance of payments, industry growth rates, and wage levels. Decisions made in one society, particularly large wealthy societies like the United States, Western Europe, and Japan, have a major impact on the economic health of many other countries. A recession in the United States or a strong shift toward purchasing only American-made products would have profound negative consequences on the economies of many other countries both developed and developing.

Physical Environment Outcomes Consumers make decisions that have a major impact on the physical environments of both their own and other societies. The cumulative impact of American consumers' decisions to rely on relatively large private cars rather than mass transit results in significant air pollution in American cities as well as the consumption of significant nonrenewable resources from other countries. The decisions of consumers in most developed and in many developing economies to consume meat as a primary source of protein results in the clearing of rain forests for grazing land, the pollution of many watersheds due to large-scale feedlots, and an inefficient use of grain, water, and energy to produce protein. It also appears to produce health problems for many consumers. The destruction of the rain forests and other critical habitat areas receives substantial negative publicity. However, these resources are being used because of consumer demand, and consumer demand consists of the decisions you and I and our families and our friends make!

As we will see in Chapter 3, many consumers now recognize the indirect effects of consumption on the environment and are altering their behavior to minimize environmental harm.

Social Welfare Consumer decisions affect the general social welfare of a society. Decisions concerning how much to spend for private goods (personal purchases) rather than public goods (support for public education, parks, health care, and so forth) are generally made indirectly by consumers' elected representatives. These decisions have a major impact on the overall quality of life in a society.

Injurious consumption, as described above, impacts society as well as the individuals involved. The social costs of smoking-induced illnesses, alcoholism, and drug abuse are staggering. To the extent that marketing activities increase or decrease injurious consumption, they have a major impact on the social welfare of a society. Consider the following:

> According to the U.S. Public Health Service, of the 10 leading causes of death in the United States, at least seven could be reduced substantially if people at risk would change just five behaviors: compliance (e.g., use of antihypertensive medication), diet, smoking, lack of exercise, and alcohol and drug abuse. Each of these behaviors is inextricably linked with marketing efforts and the reactions of consumers to marketing campaigns. The link between consumer choices and social problems is clear.[28]

However, the same authors conclude: "Although these problems appear daunting, they are all problems that are solvable through altruistic (social) marketing." Thus, marketing and consumer behavior can both aggravate and reduce serious social problems.

THE NATURE OF CONSUMER BEHAVIOR

Figure 1-3 is the model of consumer behavior that we use to capture the general structure and process of consumer behavior and to organize this text. This model is a **conceptual model.** It does not contain sufficient detail to predict particular behaviors. However, it does reflect our beliefs about the general nature of consumer behavior. Individuals develop self-concepts and subsequent lifestyles based on a variety of internal (mainly psychological and physical) and external (mainly sociological and demographic) influences. These self-concepts and lifestyles produce needs and desires, many of which require consumption decisions to satisfy. As individuals encounter relevant situations, the consumer decision process is activated. This process and the experiences and acquisitions it produces in turn influence the consumers' self-concept and lifestyle by affecting their internal and external characteristics.

This model, while simple, is both conceptually sound and intuitively appealing. Each of us has a view of ourselves (self-concept), and we try to live in a particular manner given our resources (lifestyle). Our view of ourselves and the way we try to live are determined

FIGURE 1-3 Overall Model of Consumer Behavior

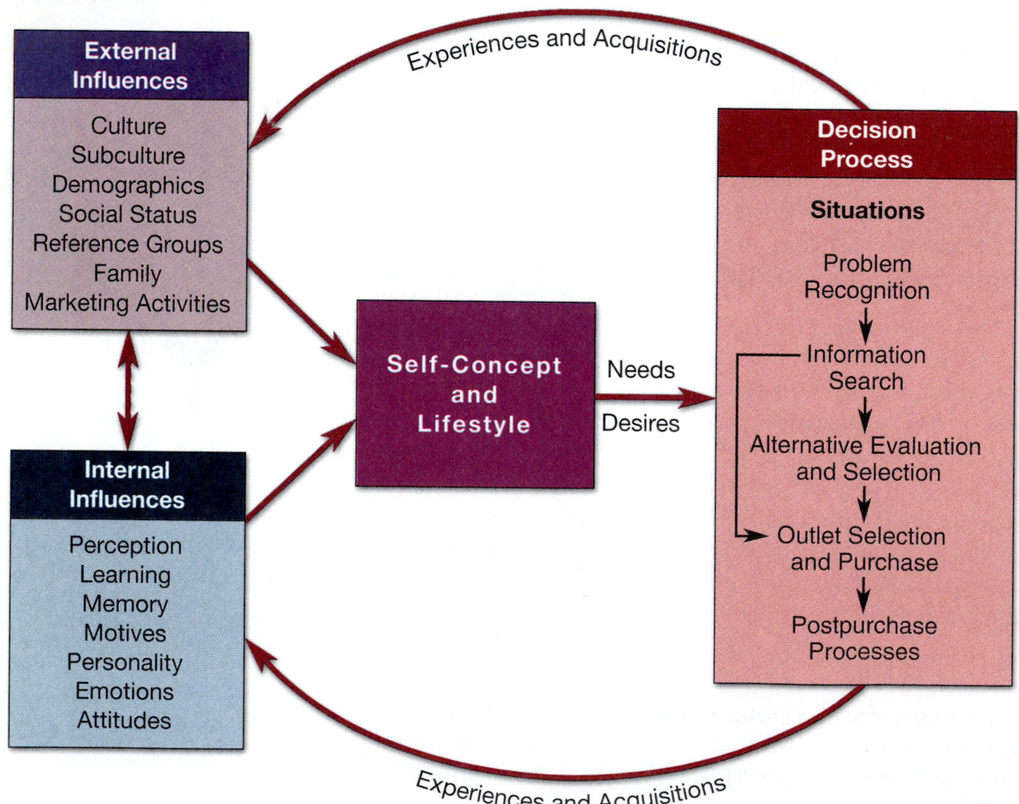

by internal factors (such as our personality, values, emotions, and memory) and external factors (such as our culture, age, friends, family, and subculture). Our view of ourselves and the way we try to live results in desires and needs that we bring to the multitude of situations we encounter daily. Many of these situations will cause us to consider a purchase. Our decision (and even the process of making it) will cause learning and may affect many other internal and external factors that will change or reinforce our current self-concept and lifestyle.

Figure 1-3 and our initial discussion of it make consumer behavior seem simple, structured, conscious, mechanical, and linear. A quick analysis of your own behavior and that of your friends will reveal the fallacy of this perception. Consumer behavior is frequently complex, disorganized, nonconscious, organic, and circular. Unfortunately, we must present it in a relatively simple, linear manner due to the limitations of written communications. As you look at the model and read the following chapters based on this model, continually relate the descriptions in the text to the rich world of consumer behavior that is all around you.

Each of the factors shown in Figure 1-3 is given a detailed treatment in the chapters that follow. In the next sections, we will provide a brief overview so that you can see how they fit together. Our discussion and the text move through the model from left to right.

External Influences

Dividing the factors that influence consumers into categories is somewhat arbitrary. For example, we treat learning as an internal influence despite the fact that much human learning involves interaction with, or imitation of, other individuals. Thus, learning could also be considered a group process. In Figure 1-3, the two-directional arrow connecting internal and external influences is used to indicate that each set interacts with the other.

We organize our discussion of external influences from large-scale macrogroups to smaller, more microgroup influences. Culture is perhaps the most pervasive influence on consumer behavior. We begin our consideration of culture in Chapter 2 by examining differences in consumption patterns across cultures. In Chapter 3, we focus on the American culture, specifically cultural values. As we will see, while Americans share many values and consumption behaviors, there is also rich diversity and ongoing change in this society that creates both marketing opportunities and unique social energy. Illustration 1-7 reflects the changing role of women in our society, as well as our ethnic diversity.

Chapter 4 continues our examination of the American society by analyzing its demographics (the number, education, age, income, occupation, and location of individuals in a society) and social stratification. Chapter 5 considers ethnic, religious, regional, and age-based subcultures. While our main focus in Chapters 3, 4, and 5 is on the American culture, we continuously compare and contrast this culture with others throughout the world.

Chapter 6 analyzes families and households, including discussions of how they evolve over time, the role of families in teaching children how to consume, and household decision making. In Chapter 7, we look at the processes by which groups influence consumer behavior and group communication, including the role of groups in the acceptance of new products and technologies.

Internal Influences

Internal influences begin with perception, the process by which individuals receive and assign meaning to stimuli (Chapter 8). This is followed by learning—changes in the content or structure of long-term memory (Chapter 9). Chapter 10 covers three closely related topics: motivation—the reason for a behavior; personality—an individual's

ILLUSTRATION 1-7

America's gender roles and demographics are changing rapidly. Ads such as this one reflect these changes.

Courtesy Avalon Beverage Company.

characteristic response tendencies across similar situations; and emotion—strong, relatively uncontrolled feelings that affect our behavior. We conclude our coverage of internal influences by examining attitudes in Chapter 11. An attitude is an enduring organization of motivational, emotional, perceptual, and cognitive processes with respect to some aspect of our environment. As such, our attitudes are heavily influenced by the external and internal factors that we have discussed in the preceding chapters.

Self-Concept and Lifestyle

Chapter 12 is a detailed discussion of the key concepts around which our model revolves. As a result of the interaction of all the variables described earlier, individuals develop a self-concept that is reflected in a lifestyle. The **self-concept** is the *totality of an individual's thoughts and feelings about him- or herself.* It is the total image one has of one's self as a result of the culture one lives in and the individual situations and experiences that comprise one's daily existence. It is the sum of past decisions and future plans. **Lifestyle** is, quite simply, *how one lives.* It includes the products one buys, how one uses them, and what one thinks and feels about them. It is the manifestation of one's self-concept.

Both individuals and families exhibit distinct lifestyles. We often hear of "career-oriented individuals," "outdoor families," or "devoted parents." One's lifestyle is determined by both conscious and unconscious decisions. Often we make choices with full awareness of their impact on our lifestyle, but generally we are unaware of the extent to which our decisions are influenced by our current or desired lifestyle. Our model shows that consumers' self-concepts and lifestyles produce needs and desires that interact with the situations in which consumers find themselves to trigger the consumer decision process.

We do not mean to imply that consumers think in terms of lifestyle. None of us consciously thinks *I'll have an Evian bottled water in order to enhance my lifestyle.* Rather, we make decisions consistent with our lifestyles without deliberately considering lifestyle. Most consumer decisions involve very little effort or thought on the part of the consumer. They are what we call *low-involvement* decisions. Feelings and emotions are as important in many consumer decisions as logical analysis or physical product attributes. Nonetheless, most consumer purchases involve at least a modest amount of decision making, and most are influenced by the purchaser's current and desired lifestyle.

Situations and Consumer Decisions

Consumer decisions result from perceived problems (*I'm thirsty*) and opportunities (*That looks like it would be fun to try*). We will use the term *problem* to refer both to problems and to opportunities. Consumer problems arise in specific situations, and the nature of the situation influences the resulting consumer behavior. Therefore, we provide a detailed discussion of situational influences on the consumer decision process in Chapter 13.

As Figure 1-3 indicates, a consumer's needs/desires may trigger one or more levels of the consumer decision process. It is important to note that for most purchases, consumers devote very little effort to this process, and emotions and feelings often have as much or more influence on the outcome as do facts and product features. Despite the limited effort that consumers often devote to this process, the results have important effects on the individual consumer, the firm, and the larger society. Therefore, we provide a detailed coverage of each stage of the process: problem recognition (Chapter 14), information search (Chapter 15), alternative evaluation and selection (Chapter 16), outlet selection and purchase (Chapter 17), and use, disposition, and purchase evaluation (Chapter 18). The increasing role of technology, particularly of the Internet, in consumer decision making is highlighted throughout these chapters.

In Chapter 19, we show how our model of individual and household consumer behavior can be modified to help understand organizational consumer behavior. Chapter 20 focuses our attention on consumerism and the regulations that have resulted from this and other forces. We pay particular attention to the role that knowledge of consumer behavior has or could play in these areas.

THE MEANING OF CONSUMPTION

As we go through this text, we will present the results of studies of consumer behavior, theories about consumer behavior, and examples of marketing programs designed to influence consumer behavior. In reading this material, it is easy to lose sight of the fact that consumer behavior is not just a topic of study or a basis for developing marketing or regulatory strategy. Consumption frequently has deep meaning for the consumer.[29]

Consider Consumer Insight 1-2. Andre, just escaping homelessness, is clearly proud of the fact that he was able to save and buy a pair of Nikes. He could undoubtedly have purchased a different brand that would have met his physical needs as well for much less money. While he does not say why he bought the more expensive Nikes, a reasonable interpretation is that they serve as a visible symbol that Andre is back as a successful member of society. In fact, Nike is currently being criticized for creating, through its marketing activities, symbols of success or status that are unduly expensive. What do you think? Does Nike manipulate people like Andre into spending more than necessary for a product because of its symbolism? If ads were banned or restricted to showing only product features, would products and brands still acquire symbolic meaning?

Consumer Insight 1-2

The Meaning of Consumption

"I (Andre Hank) worked eight-hour shifts at one restaurant, then drove to the other one for another eight-hour shift. One day I came home and my girlfriend and our 6-year-olds were gone. When she left, I fell apart. I stopped going to work, stopped sleeping. I wasn't doing anything, just going crazy . . . they took me to the hospital where I got a shot to help me sleep. I woke up in a psyche ward. After three or four months, they released me.

"When I came out of the hospital I didn't have anything. I wanted to get my old job back, but they wouldn't give me a second chance. I tried to get another job but it's hard when you don't have a phone, or an answering machine, or a pager. And I was sleeping in abandoned buildings, then on the El for a long time.

"One day more than three years ago I was hungry and didn't have any money and I saw a guy selling newspapers. I asked him what he was selling and he told me about *StreetWise* (a nonprofit, independent newspaper sold by the homeless, formerly homeless, and economically disadvantaged men and women of Chicago). So I [began to sell *StreetWise*] . . . I don't make a lot of money but I'm good at saving it. Right now I'm saving for a coat for next winter.

"I'm no longer homeless. I've got a nice little room in a hotel . . . I can buy food . . . I even saved for [and bought] Nikes."

Andre is not unique among low-income consumers in wanting and buying items such as Nike shoes. As one expert says: "These people (low-income consumers) want the same products and services other consumers want." He suggests that marketing efforts reflect those desires. Another expert states that: "There's this stereotype that they don't have enough money for toothpaste, and that's just not true. There has to be some significance to them being called lower-income, but they do buy things."

The working poor are forced to spend a disproportionate percent of their income on housing, utilities, and medical care (due to a lack of insurance). They generally rely on public transportation. They spend a smaller portion of their relatively small incomes on meals away from home and on all forms of entertainment such as admissions, pets, and toys. They spend very little on their own financial security. However, as Andre illustrated, they spent the same percent of their income (though a smaller dollar amount) on apparel and accessories.

Critical Thinking Questions

1. What does the consumption of a product like Nikes mean to Andre?
2. What does this story say about our society and the impact and role of marketing?

Source: C. Miller, "The Have-Nots," *Marketing News,* August 1, 1994, pp. 1–2; P. Mergenhagen, "What Can Minimum Wage Buy?" *American Demographics,* January 1996, pp. 32–36; and A. Hank, "Hank Finds Two Families," *StreetWise,* May 16–31, 1996, p. 7.

Perhaps some insight into these questions can be found in the following description of the attitudes of several goat-herders in a narrow mountain valley in northeastern Mexico in 1964. Modern advertising was not part of their environment.

> I asked Juan what were his major economic concerns. He answered very quickly, "food and clothes," he said. "How about housing?" I asked. "That is never a problem," he said, "for I can always make a house." For Juan and the others, a house is not a prestige symbol but simply a place to sleep, a place to keep dry in, a place for family privacy, and a place in which to store things. It is not a place to live, as the word is so meaningfully used in the United States.
>
> It seems difficult to overestimate the importance of clothing. A clean set of clothes is for a pass into town, or a fiesta. Clothes are the mark of a man's self-respect, and the ability of a man to clothe his family is in many ways the measure of a man. I once asked Mariano in the presence of Isidro and Juan why he wanted the new pair of trousers he had just purchased, when the pair he was wearing in the field seemed perfectly acceptable. He told me that while they were acceptable for the field, they could not be worn into town, for they were much too shabby. "They would call me a hick," he said, "if they saw me go into town this way." "Who?" I asked. "Why, everyone," he answered, adding some delightful obscenities to punctuate his feelings. Isidro thought my questions hysterically funny, for everyone knows what it is like to go into town without a good set

of clothes. "Oh they would laugh; they would call him many funny things; they would call him______________________________. They would call anyone these things if they came into town badly dressed."[30]

Understanding the meaning of consumption is not a simple task.[31] Most research on consumer behavior has been based on a set of beliefs and assumptions called **positivism** or **modernism.**[32] These terms refer to the philosophical and sociocultural ideas and conditions that have characterized Western societies for the past 400 years or so. With respect to research and knowledge, modernism assumes the rule of reason and a rational order; autonomous, self-determining investigators and subjects; the validity and value of science and the scientific process; and the presence of a single, objective reality. The research methods described in Appendix A are generally based on these assumptions.

Postmodernism is a varied set of views and philosophies that have in common the rejection of all or most of the assumptions that underlie modernism.[33] Postmodernist researchers believe that all reality is constructed by the individual or group and is determined by that individual or group as much as or more than it is by an external, "objective" reality. Thus, there are multiple realities. Postmodernists tend to view knowledge as being time, culture, and context dependent. They generally view consumption as a symbolic system as much as or more than an economic system. These and many other differences with modernism have led postmodern researchers to attempt to understand consumer behavior using ethnography and participant/observer studies,[34] content analysis of popular media,[35] and introspection.[36] As postmodernism evolves, it will continue to enrich our understanding of consumer behavior (and it will continue to stress that this understanding is neither universal nor permanent).

SUMMARY

This should be a fascinating course for you. The fact that you are enrolled in this class suggests that you are considering marketing or advertising as a possible career. If that is the case, you should be immensely curious about why people behave as they do. Such a curiosity is essential for success in a marketing-related career. That is what marketing is all about—understanding and anticipating consumer needs and developing solutions for those needs.

Even if you do not pursue a career in marketing, analyzing the purpose behind advertisements, package designs, prices, and other marketing activities is an enjoyable activity. In addition, it will make you a better consumer and a more informed citizen.

Finally, much of the material is simply interesting. For example, it is fun to read about China's attempt to market Pansy brand men's underwear in America, or Ford having to change the name of its Pinto automobile in Brazil after it learned that pinto was slang for a small male sex organ. So have fun, study hard, and expand your managerial skills as well as your understanding of the environment in which you live.

KEY TERMS

Conceptual model 26
Consumer behavior 7
Consumer cost 21
Customer satisfaction 23
Customer value 11
Distribution 21
Injurious consumption 24
Lifestyle 28
Market segment 16
Marketing communications 19
Marketing mix 12
Marketing strategy 19
Modernism 31
Need set 16
Positivism 31
Postmodernism 31
Price 21
Product 19
Product position 22
Self-concept 28
Service 22
Social marketing 10
Target market 18
Total product 12

INTERNET EXERCISES

1. Market segmentation is one of the most important parts of developing a marketing strategy. Many commercial firms provide information and services to help define and/or describe market segments. Visit USAData's Web site (http://www.usadata.com). Select one of the "Data Reports" (found under the "Data to Go" section), for a topic, company, consumer profile, geography or media that interests you. Prepare a report on the characteristics of your selection. How valuable do you think this service would be to a marketer?
2. Visit the WorldOpinion Web site (http://www.worldopinion.com). What information can you find that is relevant to understanding consumer behavior?
3. Marketers of many products target young (under 29) single adults who live alone. How will the number of such adults change between now and 2010. (Hint: Visit http://www.census.gov).
4. Examine magazine ads for a product category that interests you. Visit two Web sites identified in the ads. Which is most effective? Why? What beliefs about consumer behavior are reflected in the ads?
5. What ethical and legal issues involving the interaction of consumers and marketing are currently the concern of the:
   a. Federal Trade Commission (http://www.ftc.gov).
   b. Better Business Bureau (http://www.bbb.org).
6. Evaluate several People for the Ethical Treatment of Animals Web sites (http://www. peta-online.org, http://www.circuses.com, http://www.nofishing.net, http://www.taxmeat.com, and http://www. furisdead.com).
7. Evaluate L'Eggs' Web site (http://www.leggs.com). What assumptions about consumer behavior are reflected in this Web site?

DDB NEEDHAM LIFESTYLE DATA ANALYSES

1. Examine the DDB Needham data in Tables 1 through 7 for differences among heavy consumers of the following. Why do you think these differences exist? How would you use these insights to develop marketing strategy?
   a. The Internet
   b. Church attendance
   c. Cellular phones
   d. Lipstick
2. Cigarettes are frequently injurious to those who consume them. Examine the DDB Needham data. What variables are most associated with smoking cigarettes? To what extent do these variables explain why people smoke?

REVIEW QUESTIONS

1. How is the field of consumer behavior defined?
2. What conclusions can be drawn from the examples at the beginning of this chapter?
3. What are the four major uses or applications of an understanding of consumer behavior?
4. What is *social marketing?*
5. What is *customer value* and why is it important to marketers?
6. What is required to provide superior customer value?
7. What is a *total product?*
8. What is involved in the *consumer* analysis phase of market analysis in Figure 1-1?
9. What is involved in the *company* analysis phase of market analysis in Figure 1-1?
10. What is involved in the *competitor* analysis phase of market analysis in Figure 1-1?
11. What is involved in the *conditions* analysis phase of market analysis in Figure 1-1?
12. Describe the process of *market segmentation.*

13. What is *marketing strategy?*
14. What is a *marketing mix?*
15. What is a *product?*
16. What does an effective communications strategy require?
17. What is a *price?* How does the *price* of a product differ from the *cost of the product to the consumer?*
18. How is *service* defined in the text?
19. What is involved in creating satisfied customers?
20. What are the major outcomes for the firm of the marketing process and consumers' responses to it?
21. What are the major outcomes for the individual of the marketing process and consumers' responses to it?
22. What are the major outcomes for society of the marketing process and consumers' responses to it?
23. What is a *product position?*
24. What is meant by *injurious consumption?*
25. What is meant by *consumer lifestyle?*
26. Describe the consumer decision process.
27. What is meant by *positivism* or *modernism?*
28. What is meant by *postmodernism?*

DISCUSSION QUESTIONS

29. Why would someone shop on the Internet? Buy a mountain bike? Eat at McDonald's frequently?
    a. Why would someone else not make those purchases?
    b. How would you choose one outlet, brand, and/or model over the others? Would others make the same choice in the same way?
30. Of what use, if any, are models such as the one in Figure 1-3 to managers?
31. What changes would you suggest in the model in Figure 1-3? Why?
32. Describe your lifestyle. How does it differ from your parents' lifestyle?
33. Do you anticipate any changes in your lifestyle in the next five years? What will cause these changes? What new products or brands will you consume because of these changes?
34. Describe a recent purchase you made. To what extent did you follow the consumer decision-making process described in this chapter? How would you explain any differences?
35. Describe several "total products" that are more than their direct physical features.
36. Describe the needs that the following items might satisfy and the total cost to the consumer of obtaining the benefits of the total product.
    a. Casual shoes
    b. Car insurance
    c. Cat
    d. Notebook computer
37. As described in the chapter, the FDA recently ordered three manufacturers of vegetable oil to remove claims on their labels stating that the products contain no cholesterol. The FDA believes that the claims of no cholesterol are misleading *even though they are true.* How would you explain this?
38. How would you define the product that the Hard Rock Cafe provides? What needs does it meet?
39. To what extent, if any, are marketers responsible for injurious consumption involving their products?
40. How could social marketing help alleviate some of society's problems?
41. Is the criticism of Nike for creating a shoe that is symbolic of success to some groups (see Consumer Insight 1-2) valid? Why or why not?
42. Robert's American gourmet snack foods produces herbal-based snacks such as Spirulina Spirals and St. John's Wort Tortilla Chips. According to the company president, "We're selling like crazy. We don't do research. We react as sort of a karma thing."[37] How would you explain the firm's success? What are the advantages and risks of this approach?

APPLICATION ACTIVITIES

43. Interview the manager or marketing manager of a firm that sells to households or individuals. Determine how this individual develops the marketing strategy. Compare this person's process with the approach described in the text.
44. Interview the managers of a local charity. Determine what their assumptions about the consumer behavior of their supporters are. To what extent do they use marketing strategy to increase support for the organization and/or compliance with its objectives?
45. Interview five students. Have them describe the last three restaurant meals they consumed and the situations in which they were consumed. What can you conclude about the impact of the situation on consumer behavior? What can you conclude about the impact of the individual on consumer behavior?
46. Visit one or more stores that sell the following items. Report on the sales techniques used (point-of-purchase displays, store design, salesperson comments, and so forth). What beliefs concerning consumer behavior appear to underlie these strategies? It is often worthwhile for a male and a female student to visit the same store and talk to the same salesperson at different times. The variation in salesperson behavior is sometimes quite revealing.
    a. Expensive furniture
    b. Inexpensive furniture
    c. Expensive jewelry
    d. Camping equipment
    e. Power tools
    f. Personal computers
47. Interview individuals who sell the following items. Try to discover their personal "models" of consumer behavior for their products.
    a. Bicycles
    b. Luxury cars
    c. Inexpensive cars
    d. Skis
    e. Pets
    f. Personal computers
48. Interview three individuals who recently made a major purchase and three others who made a minor purchase. In what ways were their decision processes similar? How were they different?

REFERENCES

1. C. Kaydo, "Faces of Change," *Sales & Marketing Management*, December 1997, pp. 41–48.
2. "Marketing-Oriented Lever Uses Research," *Marketing News*, February 10, 1978, p. 9.
3. C. Power, "Flops,"pp. 79–80. Reprinted from the August 16, 1993 issue of *Business Week* by special permission. © 1993 McGraw-Hill and Companies, Inc.
4. "FDA Orders Vegetable Oil Makers to Drop No-Cholesterol Claim," *Marketing News,* June 10, 1991, p. 8.
5. "Slick TV Ads Divert Child Smoking," *Marketing News,* August 29, 1994, p. 30. See also C. Pechmann and S. Ratneshwar, "The Effects of Antismoking and Cigarette Advertising on Young Adolescents' Perceptions of Peers Who Smoke," *Journal of Consumer Research,* September 1994, pp. 236–51.
6. See A. R. Andreasen, "Social Marketing," *Journal of Public Policy & Marketing*, Spring 1994, pp. 108–14; A. R. Andreasen, *Marketing Social Change* (San Francisco: Jossey-Bass, 1995); P. Braus, "Selling Good Behavior," *American Demographics*, November 1995, pp. 60–64; and R. E. Petty and J. T. Cacioppo, "Addressing Disturbing and Disturbed Consumer Behavior," *Journal of Marketing Research*, February 1996, pp. 1–8.
7. R. W. Jones, C. Marshall, and T. P. Bergman, "Can a Marketing Campaign Be Used to Achieve Public Policy Goals?" *Journal of Public Policy & Marketing,* Spring 1996, pp. 98–107.
8. J. A. McCarty and L. J. Shrum, "The Recycling of Solid Wastes," *Journal of Business Research,* May 1994, pp. 53–62; K. R. Lord, "Motivating Recycling Behavior," *Psychology & Marketing*, July 1994, pp. 341–58; and G. R. Foxall "Environment-Impacting Consumer Behavior," in *Advances in Consumer Research XXII*, ed. F. R. Kardes and M. Sujan (Provo, UT: Association for Consumer Research, 1995), pp. 262–68.
9. K. D. Frankenberger and A. S. Sukhdial, "Segmenting Teens for AIDS Preventive Behaviors," *Journal of Public Policy & Marketing,* Spring 1994, pp. 133–50; and P. Raghuber and G. Menon, "AIDS and Me, Never the Twain Shall Meet," *Journal of Consumer Research,* June 1998, pp. 52–63.
10. See footnote 6.

11. K. J. Kelly, R. C. Swaim, and J. C. Wayman, "The Impact of a Localized Antidrug Media Campaign," *Journal of Public Policy & Marketing*, Fall 1996, pp. 238–51.
12. "The New Hucksterism," *Business Week,* July 1, 1996, pp. 76–84.
13. See M. Friestad and P. Wright, "The Persuasion Knowledge Model," *Journal of Consumer Research*, June 1994, pp. 1–31; and M. Friestad and P. Wright, "Persuasion Knowledge," *Journal of Consumer Research,* June 1995, pp. 62–74.
14. See footnote 3.
15. S. Caminiti, "A Star Is Born," *Fortune*, Autumn 1993, pp. 44–47.
16. S. Chandler, "Data Is Power," *Business Week*, June 3, 1996, p. 69.
17. See W. McCall, "Nike Battles Backlash from Overseas Sweatshops," *Marketing News*, November 9, 1998, p. 14.
18. T. F. McMahon, "What Buyers Buy and Sellers Sell," *Journal of Professional Services Marketing*," No. 2 (1996), pp. 3–16.
19. P. Murtaugh, "Finding a Brand's Real Essence," *Advertising Age,* August 10, 1998, p. 12.
20. D. Roberts, "How Legend Lives Up to Its Name," *Business Week,* February 15, 1999, pp. 75–76.
21. See footnote 3.
22. T. Pruzan, "Sauza Tequila Ads," *Advertising Age,* July 8, 1996, p. 29.
23. See footnote 15.
24. B. Morris, "The Future of Retirement," *Fortune,* August 19, 1996, pp. 86–94.
25. See D. N. Hassey and M. C. Smith, "Compulsive Buying," *Psychology & Marketing,* December 1996, pp. 741–52; and N. A. Mendoza and J. W. Pracejus, "Buy Now, Pay Later," in *Advances in Consumer Research XXIV,* ed. M. Bruck and D. J. MacInnis (Provo, UT: Association for Consumer Research, 1997), pp. 499–503.
26. See P. Mergenhagen, "People Behaving Badly," *American Demographics,* August 1997, pp. 37–43.
27. E. C. Hirschman, "Secular Mortality and the Dark Side of Consumer Behavior," in *Advances in Consumer Research XVIII*, ed. R. Holman and M. R. Solomon (Provo, UT: Association for Consumer Research, 1991), pp. 1–4. See also R. J. Faber, "Two Forms of Compulsive Consumption," *Journal of Consumer Research,* December 1995, pp. 296–304.
28. See Petty and Cacioppo, footnote 6, p. 1.
29. See M. L. Richins, "Special Possessions and the Expression of Material Values," *Journal of Consumer Research,* December 1994, pp. 522–33.
30. J. F. Epstein, "A Shirt for Juan Navarro," in *Foundations for a Theory of Consumer Behavior*, ed. W. T. Tucker (New York: Holt, Rinehart & Winston, 1967), p. 75.
31. See C. J. Thompson, H. R. Pollio, and W. B. Locander, "The Spoken and the Unspoken," *Journal of Consumer Research,* December 1994, pp. 432–52.
32. See A. F. Firat and A. Venkatesh, "Liberatory Postmodernism and the Reenchantment of Consumption," *Journal of Consumer Research,* December 1995, pp. 239–67; and S. Brown, "No Representation without Taxation," in *Enhancing Knowledge Development in Marketing,* ed. B. B. Stern and G. M. Zinkhan (Chicago: American Marketing Association, 1995), pp. 256–62.
33. Ibid.
34. See E. J. Arnould and M. Wallendorf, "Market-Oriented Ethnography," *Journal of Consumer Research*, November 1994, pp. 484–504.
35. R. W. Belk and W. Bryce, "Christmas Shopping Scenes," *International Journal of Research in Marketing*, August 1993, pp. 277–96.
36. See M. Wallendorf and M. Brucks, "Introspection in Consumer Research," *Journal of Consumer Research,* December 1993, pp. 339–59; and S. J. Gould, "Researcher Introspection as Method in Consumer Research," *Journal of Consumer Research*, March 1995, pp. 719–22.
37. M. W. Fellman, "New Age Dawns for Product Niche, " *Marketing News,* April 27, 1998, p. 1.

part two

External Influences

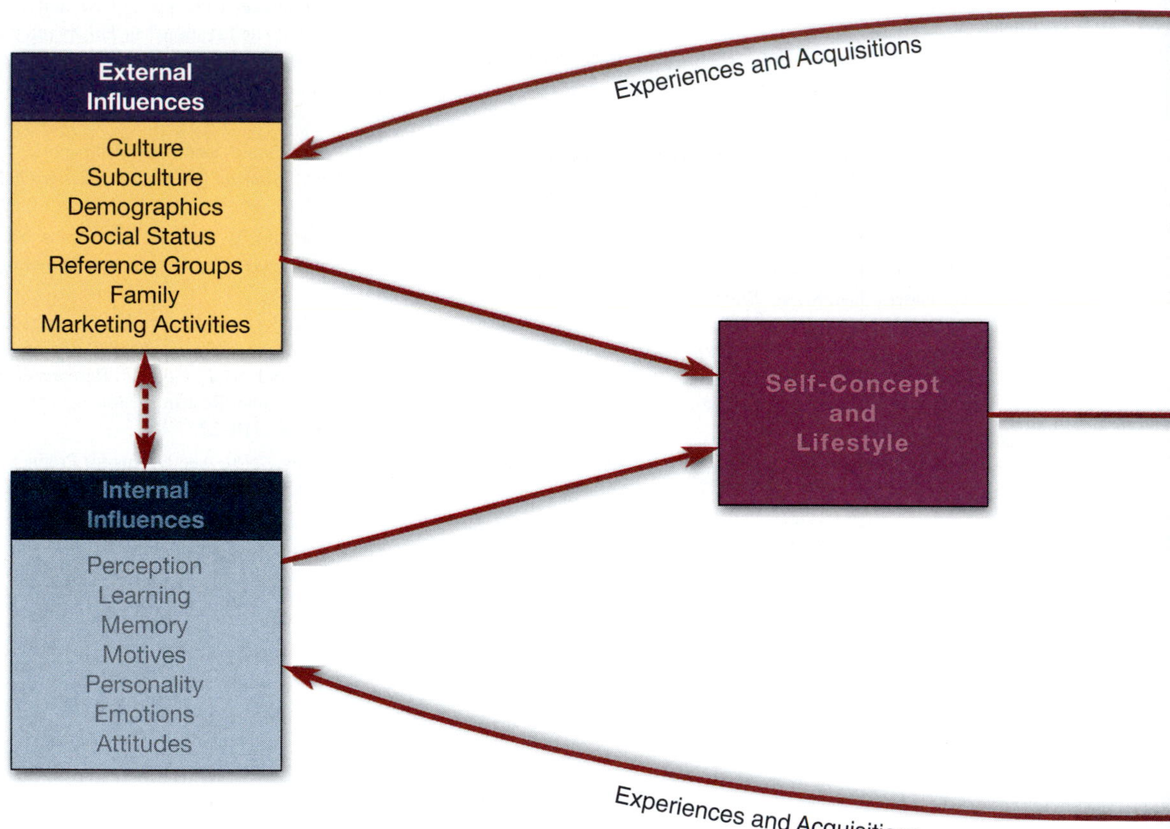

■ The external influence area of our model shown at the left is the focal point of this part of the text. Any division of the factors that influence consumer behavior into separate and distinct categories is somewhat arbitrary. For example, we consider learning in the next part of the text, which focuses on internal influences. However, a substantial amount of learning involves interaction with, or imitation of, other individuals. Thus, learning clearly involves external influences such as family and peers. In this part, we will consider groups and other external influences in terms of their functioning and direct impact on consumer behavior. Our focus in this part is on the functioning of the various groups, not the process by which the individual reacts to these groups.

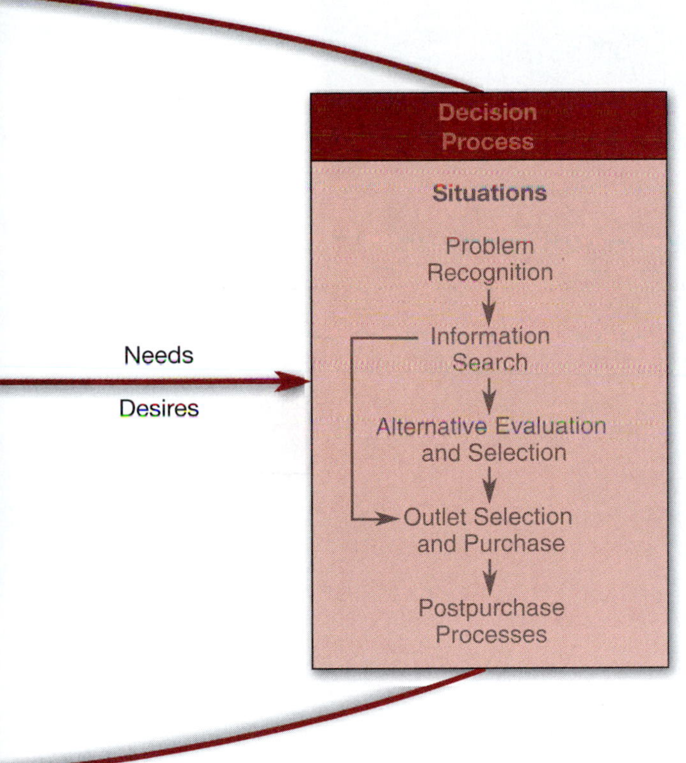

In this part, we begin with large-scale, macrogroup influences and move to smaller, more microgroup influences. As we progress, the nature of the influence exerted changes from general guidelines to explicit expectations for specific behaviors. In Chapter 2, we examine how cultures cause differing behaviors across countries or other cultural units. Chapters 3, 4, and 5 focus primarily on the American society by examining its values, demographics, social stratification, subcultures, and family structure. Chapter 7 examines the mechanisms by which groups influence our behaviors. Contrasting examples from other cultures are presented throughout these chapters.

Jonathan Drake/Sygma.

chapter two

Cross-Cultural Variations in Consumer Behavior

China evokes many images. One aspect of China's image is the growth and consumption of tea. The ubiquitous nature of tea in China is captured in the common expression: "I wouldn't do that for all the tea in China." To visit a store or home in China is to be offered hot tea, and it comes automatically with food throughout the country.

Given the dominant position of tea in the Chinese culture, would you consider China to be a good country in which to launch a chain of coffee shops? Starbucks does! In January 1999, Starbucks, in conjunction with its Chinese partner, opened its first retail outlet in China in Beijing. While the opening ceremony was traditionally Chinese with dragons and flower wreaths, the outlet and most of its products are strictly Western.

David Sun, CEO of Starbucks' Chinese partner, states: "At Starbucks, we offer the very best of class in everything we do, from brewing the perfect cup of coffee to inspiring magical moments in the lives of our customers. This is the heart and soul of the Starbucks experience."

However, does a perfect cup of coffee provide value to a consumer who normally drinks tea? Will a Western-style coffee shop provide "inspiring magical moments" to Chinese consumers?

Not long ago, similar questions were being asked about the Starbucks concept in America. For its first 10 years, Starbucks operated a single retail outlet in Seattle. In 1983, Howard Schultz, Starbucks' director of marketing, was vacationing in Italy where he noticed the immense popularity of espresso bars. Upon his return, the firm launched a coffee bar in downtown Seattle. This experiment was successful, and the firm began its rapid expansion across the United States.

The coffee bar concept coupled with high-quality, strong flavored coffee obviously transferred successfully from the Italian to the American culture. However, America has traditionally embraced coffee. Will Starbucks work in countries where tea is the dominant drink? Will the social and status aspects of Starbucks find acceptance in Asian cultures?

The answers to the above questions are not yet clear. Starbucks now has over 30 outlets in Pacific Rim countries, including Japan, Thailand, Taiwan, the Philippines, Malaysia, and Singapore, as well as the new outlet in China. Plans call for 200 outlets in the region within a year or two despite the region's current economic doldrums. Outlets will soon open in South Korea, with Hong Kong on the horizon. The firm has also recently opened outlets in England and New Zealand.[1]

Marketing across cultural boundaries is a difficult and challenging task. As Figure 2-1 indicates, cultures may differ in demographics, languages, nonverbal communications, and values.[2] Starbucks' success in Asia and elsewhere depends on how well it understands and adapts to these differences. One step Starbucks has taken to ensure its success is to work with local partners in each foreign culture.

In this chapter, we focus on cultural variations in *values* and *nonverbal communications.* In addition, we briefly describe how demographic variations across countries and cultures influence consumption patterns.

Before we begin our discussion, we need to point out that while marketing strategy is heavily influenced by such variables as values, demographics, and languages, it also influences these variables. For example, television advertising in China is extensive and reflects many Western values. Over time, such advertising will influence not only how many Chinese choose to live (lifestyle) but also what they value and how they think and feel.

FIGURE 2-1 Cultural Factors Affect Consumer Behavior and Marketing Strategy

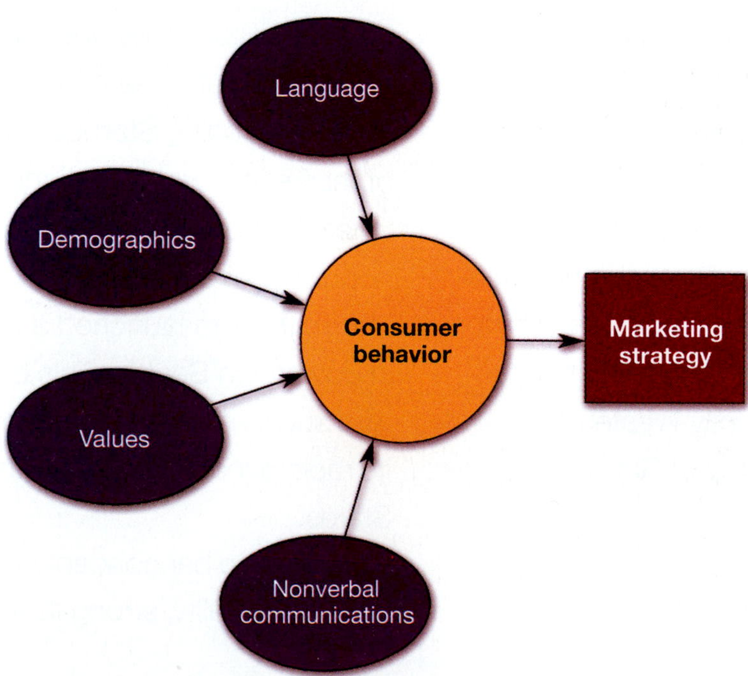

Munshi Ahmed.

ILLUSTRATION 2-1

American tobacco companies have aggressive marketing campaigns in most developing countries. Many challenge the ethics of this practice.

Even countries such as Vietnam are eager for Western products and the lifestyle associated with them:

> Young people want to adopt the lifestyle of America. Everyone wants to smoke *Marlboros. Apocalypse Now* is Vietnam's version of *TGIFriday.* Started in Ho Chi Minh City, it has become a chain and is spreading North.[3]

Thus, the massive export and multinational advertising of consumer goods, particularly heavily symbolic goods such as cigarettes, soft drinks, clothing, and athletic gear, as well as experiential goods such as music, movies, and television programming, impacts the culture and desired lifestyles of the importing countries.[4] Often these products are adapted to the local culture and assume meanings and uses that greatly enrich the culture and the lives of its members. However, many countries, both developed and developing, are concerned about the *Westernization,* and particularly the *Americanization,* of their cultures. This has led to attempts to ban or limit the importation of various American products. Europe has attempted to limit the importation of American movies, while Canada has restricted the Nashville-based Country Music Television channel. Both the French and Chinese governments have tried to restrict the use of English in brand names or advertising.

Despite concerns such as those described above, most categories of American products are generally prized throughout the world, as are those of Japan and Europe.[5] One American industry that has taken advantage of this fact is the tobacco industry. American tobacco companies are aggressively marketing their products internationally where government restrictions and public attitudes are more favorable than they are in the United States. For example, the required label on the side of the cigarette package in Japan indicates that smoking is considered as much a problem of politeness toward nonsmokers as it is a health hazard:

> Smoking too much can damage your health, so please be careful. Please observe good manners when smoking.

As Illustration 2-1 shows, tobacco firms have been particularly aggressive in the developing countries of Asia, Latin America, Africa, and Eastern Europe. Their advertising and promotions, frequently using Western models (including well-known movie stars who do not promote cigarettes in the United States) and alluring settings, along with the marketing activities of local tobacco firms, have been quite successful. Worldwide cigarette consumption rose by 18 percent over the past two decades despite sharp drops in consumption in the United States, Canada, and much of Western Europe. Smoking-related deaths are now Asia's number one killer.[6] In China, one out of three men are projected to die of smoking-related causes.[7] Clearly, there are both subtle (exported ads and products impacting other cultures' values) and direct (exporting harmful products) ethical issues involved in international marketing.

THE CONCEPT OF CULTURE

Culture is *the complex whole that includes knowledge, belief, art, law, morals, customs, and any other capabilities and habits acquired by humans as members of society.*[8]

Several aspects of culture require elaboration. First, culture is a *comprehensive* concept. It includes almost everything that influences an individual's thought processes and behaviors. While culture does not determine the nature or frequency of biological drives such as hunger or sex, it does influence if, when, and how these drives will be gratified. It not only influences our preferences but how we make decisions[9] and even how we perceive the world around us. Second, culture is *acquired.* It does not include inherited responses and predispositions. However, since much of human behavior is learned rather than innate, culture does affect a wide array of behaviors.

Third, the complexity of modern societies is such that culture seldom provides detailed prescriptions for appropriate behavior. Instead, in most industrial societies, culture supplies *boundaries* within which most individuals think and act. Finally, the nature of cultural influences is such that we are *seldom aware* of them. One behaves, thinks, and feels in a manner consistent with other members of the same culture because it seems "natural" or "right" to do so. The influence of culture is similar to the air we breathe; it is everywhere and is generally taken for granted unless there is a fairly rapid change in its nature.

Imagine a pizza that you and some friends are sharing. If you are an American, odds are you envisioned pepperoni on your pizza. However, in Japan, squid is the most popular topping; in England, it's tuna and corn; in Guatemala, black bean sauce; in Chile, mussels and clams; in the Bahamas, barbecued chicken; in Australia, eggs; and in India, pickled ginger.[10] Some of these toppings probably seem strange or even disgusting to you and yet are perfectly natural to members of other cultures. This is the nature of culture. We don't think about the fact that our preference for pizza topping, as well as most of our other preferences, is strongly influenced by our culture.

Culture operates primarily by setting rather loose boundaries for individual behavior and by influencing the functioning of such institutions as the family and mass media. Thus, *culture provides the framework within which individual and household lifestyles evolve.*

The boundaries that culture sets on behavior are called norms. **Norms** are simply *rules that specify or prohibit certain behaviors in specific situations.* Norms are derived from cultural values. **Cultural values** are *widely held beliefs that affirm what is desirable.*

Violation of cultural norms results in **sanctions** or penalties ranging from mild social disapproval to banishment from the group. Conformity to norms is usually given explicit and obvious rewards only when a child is learning the culture (socialization) or an individual is learning a new culture (acculturation). In other situations, conformity is expected without reward. For example, in America we expect people to arrive on time for business and social appointments. We do not compliment them when they do arrive on time, but we tend to become angry when they arrive late. Thus, as Figure 2-2 indicates, cultural values give rise to norms and associated sanctions, which in turn influence consumption patterns.

Values, Norms, Sanctions, and Consumption Patterns **FIGURE 2-2**

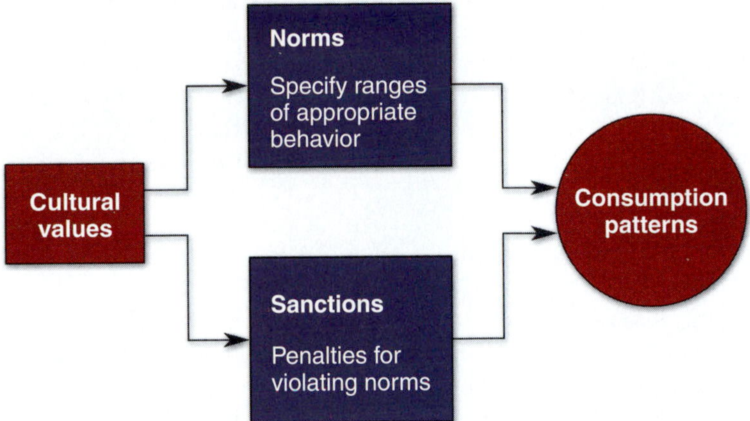

The preceding discussion may leave the impression that people are aware of cultural values and norms and that violating any given norm carries a precise and known sanction. This usually is not the case. We tend to "obey" cultural norms without thinking because to do otherwise would seem unnatural. For example, we are seldom aware of how close we stand to other individuals while conducting business. Yet, this distance is well defined and adhered to, even though it varies from culture to culture.

Cultures are not static. They typically evolve and change slowly over time.[11] Marketing managers must understand both the existing cultural values and the emerging cultural values of the societies they serve. The examples in Table 2-1 illustrate the negative consequences of a failure to understand cultural differences.

Cross-Cultural Marketing Mistakes **TABLE 2-1**

- A U.S. electronics firm landed a major contract with a Japanese buyer. The U.S. firm's president flew to Tokyo for the contract-signing ceremony. Then the head of the Japanese firm began reading the contract intently. The scrutiny continued for an extraordinary length of time. At last, the U.S. executive offered an additional price discount. The Japanese executive, though surprised, did not object. The U.S. executive's mistake was assuming that the Japanese executive was attempting to reopen negotiations. Instead, he was demonstrating his personal concern and authority in the situation by closely and slowly examining the document.
- Another electronics company sent a conservative American couple from the Midwest to represent the firm in Sweden. They were invited for a weekend in the country where, at an isolated beach, their Swedish hosts disrobed. The Americans misinterpreted this not uncommon Swedish behavior, and their response to it destroyed a promising business relationship.*
- Crest initially failed in Mexico when it used its U.S. approach of providing scientific proof of its decay-prevention capabilities. Most Mexicans assign little value to the decay-prevention benefit of toothpaste.
- Coca-Cola had to withdraw its 2-liter bottle from the Spanish market after discovering that it did not fit local refrigerators.†
- Procter & Gamble's commercials for Camay, in which men directly complimented women on their appearance, were successful in many countries. However, they were a failure in Japan, where men and women don't interact in that manner.‡

*S. P. Galante, "U.S. Companies Seek Advice on Avoiding Cultural Gaffes Abroad," *The Wall Street Journal,* European ed., July 20, 1984, sec. 1, p. 7.

†P. Kotler, "Global Standardization: Courting Danger," *Journal of Consumer Marketing,* Spring 1986, p. 13.

‡J. S. Hill and J. M. Winski, "Goodbye Global Ads," *Advertising Age,* November 16, 1987, p. 22.

ILLUSTRATION 2-2

Malaysian shoppers buy American products at Makro, a Dutch-owned retail chain. The combination of low price, wide selection, and world brands are changing traditional shopping patterns around the world.

Munshi Ahmed.

Numerous American companies have awakened to the need for general cultural sensitivity. General Motors, Procter & Gamble, and Exxon committed $500,000 each for cross-cultural training for their employees. Red Wing Shoe Company put 21 executives through a three-day training program on the Middle East. As Red Wing's president explained: "We always give the customer what he wants. If we're playing in his ballpark, we'd better know his rules."[12] As Illustration 2-2 indicates, sophisticated retailers and manufacturers are able to succeed throughout the world.

VARIATIONS IN CULTURAL VALUES

Cultural values are widely held beliefs that affirm what is desirable. These values affect behavior through norms, which specify an acceptable range of responses to specific situations. A useful approach to understanding cultural variations in behavior is to understand the values embraced by different cultures.

There are numerous values that vary across cultures and affect consumption. We will present a classification scheme consisting of three broad forms of cultural values—*other oriented, environment oriented,* and *self oriented.*[13] The cultural values that have the most impact on consumer behavior can be classified in one of these three general categories. Individual values can affect more than one area, but their primary impact is generally in one of the three categories.

Other-oriented values reflect a society's view of the appropriate relationships *between individuals and groups* within that society. These relationships have a major impact on marketing practice. For example, if the society values collective activity, consumers will look toward others for guidance in purchase decisions and will not respond favorably to "be an individual" promotion appeals.

Environment-oriented values prescribe a society's relationship *to its economic and technical as well as its physical environment.* As a manager, you would develop a very different marketing program for a society that stressed a problem-solving, risk-taking, performance-oriented approach to its environment than you would for a fatalistic, security- and status-oriented society.

Self-oriented values reflect the objectives and approaches to life *that the individual members of society find desirable.* Again, these values have strong implications for marketing management. For instance, the acceptance and use of credit is very much determined by a society's position on the value of postponed versus immediate gratification.

Table 2-2 provides a list of 18 values that are important in most cultures. The list is not meant to be exhaustive but does include the major values that are relevant to consumer behavior in industrialized societies. Most of the values are shown as dichotomies (e.g., materialistic versus nonmaterialistic). However, this is not meant to represent an either/or situation. Instead, a continuum exists between the two extremes. For example, two societies can each value tradition, but one may value it more than the other and, therefore, be closer

TABLE 2-2 Cultural Values of Relevance to Consumer Behavior

Other-Oriented Values	• *Individual/Collective.* Are individual activity and initiative valued more highly than collective activity and conformity? • *Youth/Age.* Is family life organized to meet the needs of the children or the adults? Are younger or older people viewed as leaders and role models? • *Extended/Limited family.* To what extent does one have a life-long obligation to numerous family members? • *Masculine/Feminine.* To what extent does social power automatically go to males? • *Competitive/Cooperative.* Does one obtain success by excelling over others or by cooperating with them? • *Diversity/Uniformity.* Does the culture embrace variation in religious beliefs, ethnic background, political views, and other important behaviors and attitudes?
Environment-Oriented Values	• *Cleanliness.* To what extent is cleanliness pursued beyond the minimum needed for health? • *Performance/Status.* Is the culture's reward system based on performance or on inherited factors such as family or class? • *Tradition/Change.* Are existing patterns of behavior considered to be inherently superior to new patterns of behavior? • *Risk taking/Security.* Are those who risk their established positions to overcome obstacles or achieve high goals admired more than those who do not? • *Problem solving/Fatalistic.* Are people encouraged to overcome all problems, or do they take a "what will be, will be" attitude? • *Nature.* Is nature regarded as something to be admired or overcome?
Self-Oriented Values	• *Active/Passive.* Is a physically active approach to life valued more highly than a less active orientation? • *Sensual gratification/Abstinence.* To what extent is it acceptable to enjoy sensual pleasures such as food, drink, and sex? • *Material/Nonmaterial.* How much importance is attached to the acquisition of material wealth? • *Hard work/Leisure.* Is a person who works harder than economically necessary admired more than one who does not? • *Postponed gratification/Immediate gratification.* Are people encouraged to "save for a rainy day" or to "live for today"? • *Religious/Secular.* To what extent are behaviors and attitudes based on the rules specified by a religious doctrine?

to the tradition end of the scale. For several of the values, a natural dichotomy does not seem to exist. For a society to place a low value on cleanliness does not necessarily imply that it places a high value on "dirtiness." These 18 values are described in the following paragraphs.

Other-Oriented Values

Individual/Collective Does the culture emphasize and reward individual initiative, or are cooperation with and conformity to a group more highly valued? Are individual differences appreciated or condemned? Are rewards and status given to individuals or to groups? Answers to these questions reveal the individual or collective orientation of a culture. Based on a major study by Hofstede, the United States, Australia, United Kingdom, Canada, the Netherlands, and New Zealand are high in individualism. Taiwan, Korea, Hong Kong, Mexico, Japan, and India are more collective in their orientation.[14]

This value is one of the core factors differentiating cultures.[15] It is so fundamental that it affects the self-concept and self-consciousness of individuals.[16] Not surprisingly, consumers from cultures that differ on this value differ in their reactions to many marketing activities such as reactions to fast-food restaurants,[17] luxury goods,[18] advertising,[19] and preferred sources of information.[20]

Thus, motivating and compensating Japanese, Indian, or Korean sales personnel using individual-based incentive systems and promotions may not be effective. Likewise, such themes as "be yourself," "stand out," and "don't be one of the crowd" are often effective in the United States but generally are not in Japan, Korea, or China. One expert describes the role that brands play in many Asian societies:

> Brands take on roles as symbols that extend well beyond the intrinsic features of the category. One is not buying a watch, or even a status brand, one is buying club membership, or an "I am just like you" (symbol). If brands are such powerful symbols it is again not surprising to find very entrenched levels of brand loyalty.[21]

However, these generalizations are less accurate today than in the recent past, at least as far as Japan is concerned. Evidence indicates that the Japanese, particularly the younger generation, are becoming more individualistic:

> Mizuho Arai knows what she likes. A 20-year-old uniformed office worker by day, at night she wears loafers, a sweater, Levi's 501s, and a black parka. Shopping with an L. L. Bean bag over her shoulder, she prefers bargain outlets to traditional department stores and designer boutiques. "I don't like to be told what's trendy. I can make up my own mind."[22]

Arai is typical of the younger generation of Japanese consumers. "They don't listen to us," complains Kenichi Mizorogi, the cosmetics manager for Shiseido Co. In the late 1980s, Shiseido launched its very successful *Perky Jean* makeup line with the theme: "Everyone is buying it." "That would never work now," says Mizorogi. Indeed, recent research has found that the 18–21 age group (a $33 billion market) places major emphasis on individuality.

The different values held by younger and older Japanese illustrate the fact that few cultures are completely homogeneous. Marketers must be aware of differences both *between* cultures and *within* cultures.[23] Marketers must also avoid making simplistic assumptions about what will be most effective in each type culture. For example, one study found that ego-focused emotional ads worked better in a collectivist culture while other-focused emotional ads were superior in an individualistic culture. The apparent reason for these

Kellogg in Brazil

Consumer Insight 2-1

Brazil should be a great market for cold cereal. It has a large population and nearly half are under 20. It has a reasonable per capita income. Kellogg Company noticed this and the absence of any established competitors and decided to enter the Brazilian market. The difficulty was that Brazilians do not eat an American-style breakfast. Thus, Kellogg was faced with the daunting task of changing long-established eating patterns.

Novelas—soap operas—are very popular in Brazil. Therefore, Kellogg began advertising on the novelas. The first campaign showed a boy eating the cereal out of the package. While highlighting the good taste of the product, it also positioned it as a snack rather than as part of the breakfast meal. The campaign was soon withdrawn.

An analysis of the Brazilian culture revealed a very high value placed on the family, with the adult male the dominant authority. Therefore, the next campaign focused on breakfast themes with the father pouring the cereal into bowls and adding milk. This second campaign was much more successful than the first one.

Critical Thinking Question

1. What ethical issues should Kellogg consider before launching its cereals in Brazil?

counterintuitive results was the generation of and elaboration of novel thoughts triggered by the ads that did not conform to the cultural value.[24]

Youth/Age To what extent do the primary family activities focus on the needs of the children instead of on those of the adults? What role, if any, do children play in family decisions? What role do they play in decisions that primarily affect the child? Are prestige, rank, and important social roles assigned to younger or older members of society? Are the behavior, dress, and mannerisms of the younger or older members of a society imitated by the rest of the society? While American society is clearly youth oriented, Confucian beliefs practiced in Korea emphasize age. Thus, mature spokespersons would tend to be more successful in Korean advertisements than would younger ones.

Variation in attitudes toward children can be seen in the percent of the respondents from various countries that agree with the statement: "Marriage without children is not complete." This percent ranges from around 70 in France, Greece, and Portugal to 30 or less in the Netherlands, Norway, Sweden, Great Britain, and Denmark.[25]

China's policy of limiting families to one child has produced a strong focus on the child. In fact, many of these children receive so much attention that they are known in Asia as "little emperors." H. J. Heinz is successfully marketing a rice cereal for Chinese babies. Its premium price (75 cents a box, where average workers earn only $40 a month) and American origin give it a quality image. The convenience of the instant cereal is also an advantage in a country where 70 percent of the women work outside the home.[26]

Consumer Insight 2-1 indicates the importance of understanding this value in marketing to families.

Extended/Limited Family The family unit is the basis for virtually all known societies. Nonetheless, the definition of the family and the rights and obligations of family members vary widely across cultures.[27] As we will see in Chapter 8, our families have a lifelong impact on all of us both genetically and through our early socialization, no matter what culture we come from. However, cultures differ widely in the obligations one owes to other family members at various stages of one's life, as well as who is considered to be a member of one's family.

In the United States, the family is defined fairly narrowly and is less important than in many other cultures. In general, strong obligations are felt only to immediate family members (siblings, parents, and children), and these diminish as family members establish new families. That is, one's sense of obligation toward one's brother, sister, or even parent tends to decrease when one marries.

In many other cultures, the role of families is much stronger. Families, and obligations, often extend to cousins, nieces, nephews, and beyond. One has responsibilities to one's parents, grandparents, and even ancestors that must be fulfilled. Families are of critical importance in Korea and China. In Korea, there are only about 273 family names, and over half of all Koreans have a family name of *Kim, Lee, Pak,* or *Choi.* In China, the per capita income has historically been too low to allow the purchase of such consumer durables as television sets. This led many firms to avoid this market. However, the extended families that are the basis of Chinese society pooled funds and television ownership in China's urban areas matches that of many industrialized nations.

Clearly, marketers need to understand the role of families in the cultures they serve. For example, in Mexico, compared to the United States, adolescents are much more likely to seek parental advice or to respond positively to ads with parental figures in the purchase of items ranging from candy to movies to fashion clothing.[28] These differences call for related changes in the advertising of products to teenagers in these two cultures.

Masculine/Feminine Are rank, prestige, and important social roles assigned primarily to men? Can a female's life pattern be predicted at birth with a high degree of accuracy? Does the husband, wife, or both, make important family decisions? Basically, we live in a masculine-oriented world, yet the degree of masculine orientation varies widely, even across the relatively homogeneous countries of Western Europe.

This dimension influences both obvious and subtle aspects of marketing (see Chapter 3). Obviously, you would not portray women executives in advertisements in Muslim countries. However, suppose you were going to portray a furniture or household appliance purchase decision for a Dutch market. Would you show that the decision would be made by the husband, by the wife, or jointly? A joint decision process would probably be used. Or suppose you had an office in a Muslim country. Would you follow the common American practice of hiring a female secretary? To do so would be an affront to many of your Muslim clients.

The role of women is changing and expanding throughout much of the world. This is creating new opportunities as well as problems for marketers.[29] In China, this change is taking place fairly rapidly, while in Japan it is coming at a slower pace. The increasing percentage of Japanese women who continue to work after marriage has led to increased demand for time-saving products as well as other products targeted at the working woman:

- Many Japanese women "feel guilty" preparing frozen vegetables in a microwave rather than preparing fresh vegetables. Pillsbury Japan's Green Giant decided to promote its frozen vegetables stressing convenience and nutrition and to position them as part of "modern up-to-date cooking." Sales increased 50 percent. They have followed up with Dough Boy frozen bite-sized meat pies for busy mothers to pack in their children's school lunches.
- Lotte had dominated the caffeinated chewing gum market (used for a pick-me-up on the way to work or during working hours) by targeting men with a very masculine positioning strategy. Warner-Lambert K.K. decided that working women were under the same stresses as men and developed a brand called *Sting,* targeted at working women.

©Shiseido Cosmetics (America) Ltd.

ILLUSTRATION 2-3

The changing role of women creates new needs and products even in relatively traditional cultures such as Japan. This lipstick is targeted at Japan's new working women.

Using fashionable advertising and sleek gold and silver packaging, Sting has been a solid success.

- Long-lasting, no-smear lipstick didn't exist in Japan a few years ago but now has sales of $45 million a month (see Illustration 2-3). Targeted at working women, Shiseido's brand, Reciente Perfect Rouge, features a popular model racing through her busy day wearing the no-smear lipstick.
- Virginia Slims has grown sales by 25 percent annually with ads showing a woman wearing jeans and repairing a motorcycle or a woman with her face smeared with grease holding a wrench.[30]

Competitive/Cooperative Is the path to success found by outdoing other individuals or groups, or is success achieved by forming alliances with other individuals and groups? Does everyone admire a winner? Variation on this value can be seen in the way different cultures react to comparative advertisements. For example, Germany and Spain ban such ads, while the United States encourages them.

As one would expect in a cooperative culture, the Japanese have historically found comparative ads to be distasteful. However, focus group research for Pepsi-Cola Japan found that younger consumers would appreciate advertising that mocked a rival in a frank and funny way. Based on this research, PepsiCo launched a TV spot in which rap singer Hammer depicted market leader Coke as the beverage that turns you into a nerd. Pepsi's sales jumped 19 percent.[31] However, in other cooperatively oriented countries, comparative ads have not fared as well.[32]

Diversity/Uniformity Do members of the culture embrace variety in terms of religions, ethnic backgrounds, political beliefs, and other important behaviors and attitudes? A culture that values diversity will not only accept a wide array of personal behaviors and attitudes but is also likely to welcome variety in terms of food, dress, and other products and services. In contrast, a society valuing uniformity is unlikely to accept a wide array of tastes and product preferences (though such a society may be subject to fads, fashions, and other changes over time).

Environment-Oriented Values

Cleanliness Is cleanliness "next to godliness," or is it a rather minor matter? Are homes, offices, and public spaces expected to be clean beyond reasonable health requirements? In the United States, a high value is placed on cleanliness. In fact, many Europeans consider Americans to be paranoid on the subject of personal hygiene. For example, over 90 percent of all adult Americans use deodorant. In contrast, the percentage of adult males and females using deodorants from various European countries are:[33]

	Male	*Female*		*Male*	*Female*
Austria	30%	53%	Italy	52%	60%
Belgium	46	61	Luxembourg	44	65
Denmark	80	89	Netherlands	60	76
Finland	75	81	Norway	83	85
France	47	66	Portugal	63	52
Germany	60	70	Spain	53	66
Great Britain	69	81	Sweden	80	86
Greece	28	35	Switzerland	71	74
Ireland	56	72			

While there are differences in the value placed on cleanliness among the economically developed cultures, the largest differences are between these cultures and many of the underdeveloped nations. In many poorer countries cleanliness is not valued at a level sufficient to produce a healthy environment. This is true even in large parts of a rapidly developing country such as China where a lack of basic hygiene still causes significant health problems.

Performance/Status Are opportunities, rewards, and prestige based on an individual's performance or on the status associated with the person's family, position, or class? Do all people have an equal opportunity economically, socially, and politically at the start of life, or are certain groups given special privileges? Are products and brands valued for their ability to accomplish a task or for the reputation or status of the brand?

Performance/status is closely related to the concept of **power distance**, which refers to *the degree to which people accept inequality in power, authority, status, and wealth as natural or inherent in society.* India, Brazil, France, Hong Kong, and Japan are relatively high in their acceptance of power. Austria, Denmark, New Zealand, Sweden, and the United States are relatively low.[34]

A status-oriented society is more likely to prefer "quality" or established brand names and high-priced items to functionally equivalent items with unknown brand names or lower prices. This is the case in Japan, Hong Kong, Singapore, the Philippines, Malaysia,

Indonesia, Thailand, and most Arabic countries, where consumers are attracted by prestigious, known brands.

A recent study found that almost 80 percent of the respondents in the United Kingdom agreed that a well-known brand name would have a moderate or strong influence on their purchase decisions. In contrast, less than 30 percent of the German respondents assigned that level of importance to the brand name.[35] The marketing implications in terms of advertising strategies, branding, and new-product development are significant. How would your strategy change if you were exporting an established American product to Germany versus to the United Kingdom? What if it were a new product from Mexico?

Tradition/Change Is tradition valued simply for the sake of tradition? Is change or "progress" an acceptable reason for altering established patterns? Compared to Americans, Koreans and Chinese consumers are much less comfortable dealing with new situations or ways of thinking.[36] While Koreans and Chinese may feel uncomfortable with change, overall both cultures are enthusiastically embracing change. In China, "modernness" (often symbolized by a Western name) is an important product attribute.

Another study found that female Irish consumers, compared to American females, had a lesser need to engage in variety-seeking behavior, and they achieved their optimum level of consumption variety at a lower level.[37] The marketing impact of England's tradition-oriented culture can be seen in the fact that three-fourths of its population claim to be generally brand loyal (compared to half in France and Germany).[38] Further, British ads, compared to those in America, are much more likely to stress tradition and history.[39]

Risk Taking/Security Do the "heroes" of the culture meet and overcome obstacles? Is the person who risks established position or wealth on a new venture admired or considered foolhardy? This value has a strong influence on entrepreneurship and economic development as well as new-product acceptance. The society that does not admire risk taking is unlikely to develop enough entrepreneurs to achieve economic change and growth. New-product introductions, new channels of distribution, and advertising themes are affected by this value.

Problem Solving/Fatalistic Do people react to obstacles and disasters as challenges to be overcome, or do they take a "what will be, will be" attitude? Is there an optimistic, "we can do it" orientation? In the Caribbean, difficult or unmanageable problems are often dismissed with the expression "no problem." This actually means: "There is a problem, but we don't know what to do about it—so don't worry!" Mexico also falls toward the fatalistic end of this continuum. As a result, Mexican customers are less likely to express formal complaints when confronted with an unsatisfactory purchase.

Nature Is nature assigned a positive value, or is it viewed as something to be overcome, conquered, or tamed?[40] Americans historically considered nature as something to be overcome or improved. In line with this, animals were either destroyed or romanticized and made into heroes and pets.[41] Dogs, for example, are pets in the United States, and few Americans would feel comfortable consuming them as food. However, they are a common food source in countries such as China.

Most Northern European countries place a very high value on the environment. Packaging and other environmental regulations are stronger in these countries than in America. In turn, Americans and Canadians appear to place a higher value on the environment than the southern European countries and most developing countries (though this may reflect variations in the financial ability to act on this value rather than in the value itself).[42]

These differences in attitudes are reflected in consumers' purchase decisions, consumption practices, and recycling efforts.[43] The average number of categories of items regularly recycled per household across a number of European countries illustrates this point:[44]

Austria	5.1	Luxembourg	3.9
Belgium	3.0	Netherlands	4.1
Denmark	3.8	Norway	2.8
France	2.0	Portugal	0.7
Germany	4.8	Spain	0.7
Greece	0.3	Sweden	4.1
Ireland	0.7	Switzerland	5.0
Italy	3.0	United Kingdom	2.2

The power of environmental concern in countries such as Germany can be seen by the success of the family-owned Greuner Frosch (Green Frog) household cleaners. Despite its small size and limited advertising, the firm has captured market share from such multinationals as Unilever, P&G, Henkel, and Colgate-Palmolive by offering products less harmful to the environment.

Self-Oriented Values

Active/Passive Are people expected to take a physically active approach to work and play? Are physical skills and feats valued more highly than less physical performances? Is emphasis placed on doing? Americans are much more prone to engage in physical activities and to take an action-oriented approach to problems. "Don't just stand there, *do something,*" is a common response to problems in America. Active exercise is rare among women in most countries other than the United States. This is true even in European countries.[45] While this obviously limits the market for exercise equipment in these countries, it also affects advertising themes and formats. For example, the ad shown in Illustration 1-7 (page 28) would not be appropriate in many countries.

Sensual Gratification/Abstinence Is it acceptable to pamper oneself, to satisfy one's desires for food, drink, or sex beyond the minimum requirement? Is one who forgoes such gratification considered virtuous or strange? Muslim cultures are very, very conservative on this value. Advertisements, packages, and products must carefully conform to Muslim standards. Polaroid's instant cameras gained rapid acceptance because they allowed Arab men to photograph their wives and daughters without fear that a stranger in a film laboratory would see the women unveiled.

In contrast, Brazilian advertisements contain nudity and blatant (by U.S. standards) appeals to sensual gratification. Consider the following prime-time television ad for women's underwear:

> A maitre d' hands menus to a couple seated at a restaurant table. When the man opens his menu to the "chef's suggestion," he has a "vision" of a woman's bare torso and arms. She then pulls on a pair of panties. "What a dish!" he exclaims, only to have another "vision," this time of a woman unclasping her front-closing bra to fully expose her breasts. The man slumps under the table, to the consternation of both his wife and the waiter.[46]

Illustration 2-4 is an Australian ad for milk. Its strong sensual appeal works well in Australia but would not be as successful in more conservative cultures.[47]

1. ***Video:*** A young man returns from his morning jog to the apartment he shares with others. His flatmate is on his way out.
Audio: The Tex-Mex 60s hit "Wooly Bully" throughout.

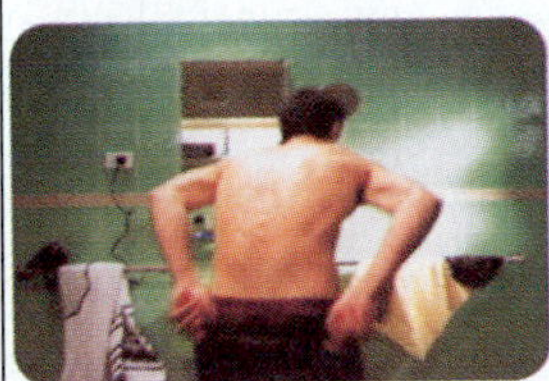

2. ***Video*** (cut): In the bathroom he is stripping off his sweaty jogging gear when he spots something black and lacy hanging from the towel rack.

3. (Cut) In the shaving mirror he sees the legs of the lingerie's owner.

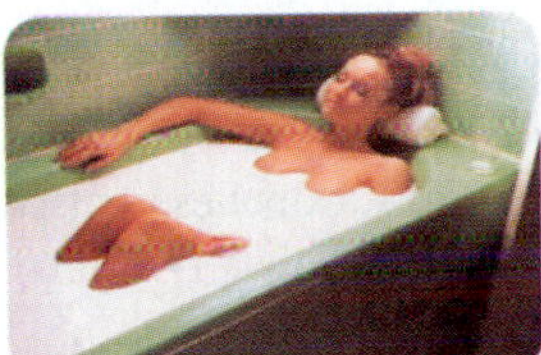

4. (Cut) She is dozing in a bathtub full of milk.

5. (Cut) The young man is fascinated and embarrassed at the same time.

6. (Cut) The beauty is sound asleep. He decides to steal away.

7. (Cut) But not before chancing a final look. Suddenly, he discovers ...

8. (Cut) ... a glass and a straw at the edge of the tub. This gives him an idea.

9. (Cut) He starts sucking the milk from the straw to lower the milk level and to get an even better look at the natural wonders in front of him.

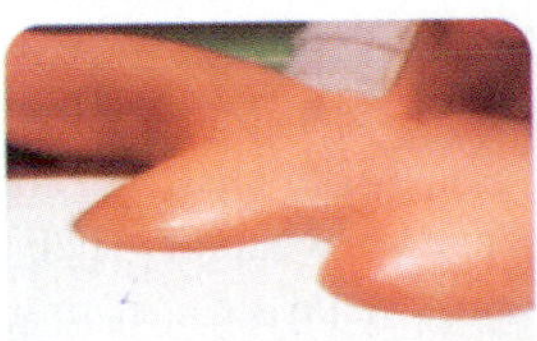

10. Cut.

11. (Cut) He notices that the milk tastes quite delicious.

12. Hence he concentrates more on the tasty liquid than on the bathing beauty.

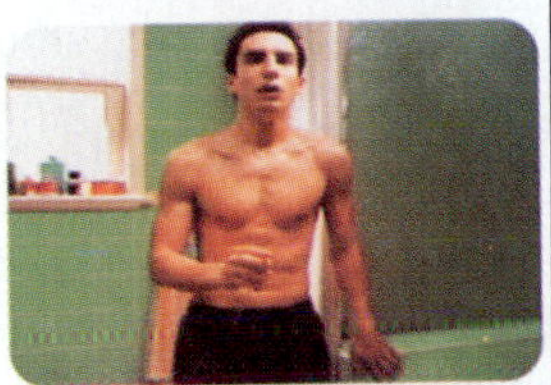

13. His enjoyment is rudely interrupted.
Audio (MVO): "Honey, I'm back."

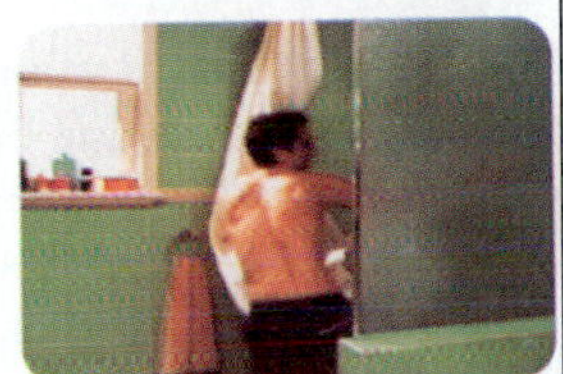

14. ***Video:*** Quickly, he jumps into in the shower stall to hide.

15. Cut.
Audio (MVO): "Rev. It's the taste you can't resist."

Courtesy Australian Milk Marketing; agency: Clemenger Melbourne

ILLUSTRATION 2-4

Cultures differ in their acceptance of sensual gratification. This ad works well in Australia, but it would not be appropriate in cultures that place a high value on abstinence.

Material/Nonmaterial Is the accumulation of material wealth a positive good in its own right? Does material wealth bring more status than family ties, knowledge, or other activities? Consider the following conclusion from a study of Chinese television ownership.

> The television one owns is very much a representation of one's own self-worth. For most, the television had become almost as much a part of getting married as saying their vows. One engaged

man (age 24), who was saving for his TV so he could get married, noted that he wanted a 25-inch or 29-inch Japanese model. He was willing to save for up to two years (a commonly quoted time frame) before revising his sights downward. Price was not nearly as important as projecting "a good image" to others. He was concerned about getting off to a good start. Several respondents noted that the purchase of the appropriate television set was more important than having furniture when considering marriage.[48]

There are two types of materialism. **Instrumental materialism** is *the acquisition of things to enable one to do something.* Skis can be acquired to allow one to ski. **Terminal materialism** is *the acquisition of items for the sake of owning the item itself.* Art is generally acquired for the pleasure of owning it rather than as a means to another goal. Cultures differ markedly in their relative emphasis on these two types of materialism. For example, a substantial percentage of advertisements in both the United States and Japan have a materialistic theme. However, instrumental materialism is most common in U.S. advertising, while terminal materialism is predominant in Japanese ads.[49]

A further description of cultural variation in the meaning of material items is presented in the section on nonverbal communications later in this chapter.

Hard Work/Leisure Is work valued for itself, independent of external rewards, or is work merely a "means to an end"? Will individuals continue to work hard even when their minimum economic needs are satisfied, or will they opt for more leisure time? In parts of Latin America, work is viewed as a necessary evil. However, in much of Europe, work is considered essential for a full life. Consequently, labor-saving products and instant food often meet with failure in countries such as Switzerland.

Postponed Gratification/Immediate Gratification Is one encouraged to "save for a rainy day," or should one "live for today"? Is it better to secure immediate benefits and pleasures, or is it better to suffer in the short run for benefits in the future (or in the hereafter or for future generations)?

This value has implications for distribution strategies, efforts to encourage savings, and the use of credit.[50] For example, in Germany and the Netherlands, buying on credit is widely viewed as living beyond one's means. In fact, the word for debt in German (*schuld*) is the same word used for "guilt."

Religious/Secular To what extent are daily activities determined by religious doctrine? The United States is relatively secular. Many Islamic cultures as well as some Catholic countries are much more religiously oriented.[51] In contrast, religion plays a very small role in Chinese culture. However, even in a country such as China, where very few are actively involved with a formal religion, many of the culture's values were formed in part by historical religious influences. The same is true for the secular nations of the West. Understanding the extent and type of religious influences operating in a culture is essential for effectively designing all elements of the marketing mix.[52]

Clearly, the preceding discussion has not covered all of the values operating in the various cultures. However, it should suffice to provide a feel for the importance of cultural values and how cultures differ along value dimensions.

CULTURAL VARIATIONS IN NONVERBAL COMMUNICATIONS

Differences in **verbal communication systems** (languages) are immediately obvious to anyone entering a foreign culture. An American traveling in Britain or Australia will be able to communicate, but differences in pronunciation, timing, and meaning will be readily apparent. For example, Griptight Ltd. had a successful line of infant products with the brand name *kiddiwinks* in the United Kingdom. When it decided to import these items to the United States, research revealed that, while the product generally could remain the same, the name *BinkyKids* would work better, the term *soother* had to be changed to *pacifier,* and the white, medicinal-style packaging needed to be brightened and enlivened. An examination of the German market revealed additional differences. Germans preferred glass baby bottles in modern shapes. These bottles are more environmentally friendly, are scratch resistant and so are more hygienic, and they keep the milk warm longer. However, U.S. and U.K. parents stated that they would not buy the glass bottles due to the risk of breakage.[53]

Variations in verbal language are easy to notice and accept because we realize that language is an arbitrary invention. The meaning assigned to a particular group of letters or sounds is not inherent in the letters or sounds—a word means what a group of people agree that it will mean.

Attempts to translate marketing communications from one language to another can result in ineffective communications, as Ford Motor Company is painfully aware:

> Fiera (a low-cost truck designed for developing countries) faced sales problems since *fiera* means "terrible, cruel, or ugly" in Spanish. The popular Ford car *Comet* had limited sales in Mexico, where it was named Caliente. The reason—*caliente* is slang for a streetwalker. The Pinto was briefly introduced in Brazil without a name change. Then it was discovered that *pinto* is slang for a "small male sex organ." The name was changed to Corcel, which means horse.[54]

Coca-Cola Company avoided the problems Ford encountered by realizing that *enjoy,* which is part of its famous logo Enjoy Coca-Cola, has sensual connotations in Russian and several other languages. Coca-Cola solved this problem by changing the logo to Drink Coca-Cola where appropriate. It also altered the successful "The real thing" theme to "I feel Coke" in Japan and several other countries with great success.

Table 2-3 indicates that Ford is not the only company to encounter translation problems. The problems of literal translations and slang expressions are compounded by symbolic meanings associated with words, the absence of some words from various languages, and the difficulty of pronouncing certain words:

TABLE 2-3

Translation Problems in International Marketing

- An American airline operating in Brazil advertised the plush "rendezvous lounges" on its jets only to discover that *rendezvous* in Portuguese means a room hired for lovemaking.
- General Motors' "Body by Fisher" was translated as "corpse by Fisher" in Flemish.
- Colgate's Cue toothpaste had problems in France, as *cue* is a crude term for "butt" in French.
- In Germany, Pepsi's advertisement, "Come alive with Pepsi," was presented as "Come alive out of the grave with Pepsi."
- Sunbeam attempted to enter the German market with a mist-producing curling iron named the Mist-Stick. Unfortunately, *mist* translates as "dung" or "manure" in German.
- Pet milk encounters difficulties in French-speaking countries where *pet* means, among other things, "to break wind."
- Fresca is a slang word for "lesbian" in Mexico.
- Esso found that its name pronounced phonetically meant "stalled car" in Japanese.
- Kellogg's Bran Buds translates to "burned farmer" in Swedish.
- United Airline's in-flight magazine cover for its Pacific Rim routes showed Australian actor Paul Hogan in the outback. The caption stated, "Paul Hogan Camps It Up." Unfortunately, "camps it up" is Australian slang for "flaunts his homosexuality."
- A car wash was translated into German as "car enema."
- China attempted to export Pansy brand men's underwear to America.

- Mars addressed the problem of making the M&M's name pronounceable in France, where neither ampersands nor the apostrophe "s" plural form exists, by advertising extensively that M&M's should be pronounced "aimainaimze." Whirlpool is facing a similar problem in Spain, as its name is virtually unpronounceable in Spanish.
- In the Middle East, consumers often refer to a product category by the name of the leading brand. Thus, all brands of vacuum cleaners are referred to as Hoovers and all laundry detergents are Tide.
- To market its Ziploc food storage bags in Brazil, Dow Chemical had to use extensive advertising to create the word *zipar*, meaning to zip, since there was no such term in Portuguese.

In addition, such communication factors as humor and preferred style and pace vary across cultures, even among those speaking the same basic language. Nonetheless, verbal language translations generally do not present major problems as long as we are careful. What many of us fail to recognize, however, is that each culture also has nonverbal communication systems or languages that, like verbal languages, are specific to each culture. **Nonverbal communication systems** are *the arbitrary meanings a culture assigns to actions, events, and things other than words.*

Unlike verbal languages, most of us think of our nonverbal languages as being innate or natural rather than learned. Therefore, when we encounter a foreign culture, we tend to assign our own culture's meanings to the nonverbal signs being utilized by the other culture. The problem is compounded by the fact that the "foreigner" is interpreting our nonverbal cues by the "dictionary" used in his or her own culture. The frequent result is misunderstanding, unsuccessful sales calls and advertising campaigns, and, on occasion, long-lasting bitterness.

The following discussion examines the seven variables shown in Figure 2-3 that we consider to be nonverbal languages: time, space, symbols, friendship, agreements, things, and etiquette.[55]

FIGURE 2-3 Factors Influencing Nonverbal Communications

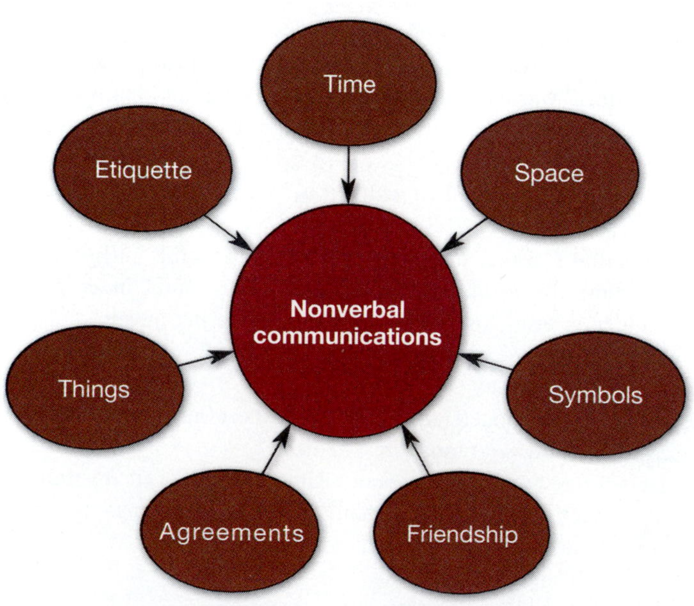

Time

The meaning of time varies between cultures in two major ways. First is what we call time perspective: this is a culture's overall orientation toward time. The second is the interpretations assigned to specific uses of time.

Time Perspective Most Americans, Canadians, Western Europeans, and Australians tend to view time as inescapable, linear, and fixed in nature. It is a road reaching into the future with distinct, separate sections (hours, days, weeks, and so on). Time is seen almost as a physical object: we can schedule it, waste it, lose it, and so forth. We believe a person does one thing at a time. We have a strong orientation toward the present and the short-term future. This is known as a **monochronic time perspective.**

Other cultures have different time perspectives. Most Latin Americans, Asians, and Indians tend to view time as being less discrete and less subject to scheduling. They view simultaneous involvement in many activities as natural. People and relationships take priority over schedules, and activities occur at their own pace rather than according to a predetermined timetable. They have an orientation toward the present and the past. This is known as a **polychronic time perspective.**

Some of the important differences between individuals with a monochronic perspective and those with a polychronic perspective are listed below.[56]

Monochronic Culture	*Polychronic Culture*
Do one thing at a time	Do many things at once
Concentrate on the job	Highly distractible and subject to interruptions
Take deadlines and schedules seriously	Consider deadlines and schedules secondary
Committed to the job or task	Committed to people and relationships
Adhere religiously to plans	Change plans often and easily
Emphasize promptness	Base promptness on the relationship
Accustomed to short-term relationships	Prefer long-term relationships

How would marketing activities vary between monochronic and polychronic cultures? Personal selling and negotiation styles and strategies would need to differ, as would many advertising themes. Contests and sales with deadlines would generally be more effective in monochronic than in polychronic cultures. Convenience foods frequently fail when positioned in terms of timesavings and convenience in polychronic cultures where "saving time" is not part of cultural thought processes. The following quote illustrates the impact of time perspective on the positioning strategy of fast-food outlets in polychronic cultures:

> In Argentina, McDonald's has an image of an expensive, modern restaurant where the majority of the customers are teenagers and young adults who patronize McDonald's to express their modern and liberated value systems. This is equally true in Turkey. In fact, a major reason for the popularity of fast-food restaurants in many developing countries is neither convenience nor reasonable prices. Time savings does not have the same priority in these countries as it does in the United States. What makes these restaurants popular in developing countries such as Argentina, Turkey, and many others is their "Americanness." Patronization of these restaurants enables consumers to express their "aspirational" links with developed nations.[57]

Meanings in the Use of Time Specific uses of time have varying meanings in different cultures. In much of the world, the time required for a decision is proportional to the importance of the decision. Americans, by being well prepared with "ready answers," may adversely downplay the importance of the business being discussed. Likewise, both

Japanese and Middle Eastern executives are put off by Americans' insistence on coming to the point directly and quickly in business transactions. Greek managers find the American habit of setting time limits for business meetings to be insulting. Consider the following advice from a business consultant:

> In many countries we are seen to be in a rush; in other words, unfriendly, arrogant, and untrustworthy. Almost everywhere, we must learn to wait patiently and never to push for deadlines. Count on things taking a long time, the definition of "a long time" being at least twice as long as you would imagine.[58]

Promptness is considered very important in America and Japan. Furthermore, promptness is defined as being on time for appointments, whether you are the person making the call or the person receiving the caller. The variation in waiting time between cultures is illustrated in this story:

> Arriving a little before the hour (the American respect pattern), he waited. The hour came and passed; 5 minutes—10 minutes—15 minutes. At this point he suggested to the secretary that perhaps the minister did not know he was waiting in the outer office—20 minutes—25 minutes—30 minutes—45 minutes (the insult period)! He jumped up and told the secretary that he had been "cooling his heels" in an outer office for 45 minutes and he was "damned sick and tired" of this type of treatment.

The principal source of misunderstanding lay in the fact that in the country in question, the five-minute delay interval was not significant. Forty-five minutes, instead of being at the tail end of the waiting scale, was just barely at the beginning. To suggest to American secretaries that perhaps their boss didn't know you were there after waiting 60 seconds would seem absurd, as would raising a storm about "cooling your heels" for five minutes. Yet this is precisely the way the minister registered the protestations of the American in his outer office.[59]

Space

The use people make of space and the meanings they assign to their use of space constitute a second form of nonverbal communication.[60] In America, "bigger is better." Thus, office space in corporations generally is allocated according to rank or prestige rather than need. The president will have the largest office, followed by the executive vice president, and so on.

Americans tend to personalize their work space and consider it their own. Few Americans would be comfortable in the following environment:

> In Tokyo, . . . IBM Japan provides only 4,300 desks for its 5,000 sales representatives since at least 700 are generally out on a sales call at any point in time. When sales representatives arrive at the office, they check a computer to see which desk is empty, take their personal filing cabinet from storage and roll it to the available desk where they work until they need to visit a customer. Each time they leave, they clear the desk and return their file cabinet to storage.[61]

A second major use of space is **personal space.** It is the nearest that others can come to you in various situations without your feeling uncomfortable. In the United States normal business conversations occur at distances of 3 to 5 feet and highly personal business from 18 inches to 3 feet. In parts of Northern Europe, the distances are slightly longer, while in most of Latin America they are substantially shorter.

An American businessperson in Latin America will tend to back away from a Latin American counterpart in order to maintain his or her preferred personal distance. In turn, the host will tend to advance toward the American in order to maintain his or her personal space. The resulting "chase" would be comical if it were not for the results. Both parties generally are unaware of their actions or the reasons for them. Furthermore, each assigns a meaning to the other's actions based on what the action means in his or her own culture. Thus, the North American considers the Latin American to be pushy and aggressive. The Latin American, in turn, considers the North American to be cold, aloof, and snobbish.

Symbols

If you were to see a baby wearing a pink outfit, you would most likely assume the child is female. If the outfit were blue, you would probably assume the child is male. These assumptions would be accurate most of the time in the United States but would not be accurate in many other parts of the world such as Holland. Colors, animals, shapes, numbers, and music have varying meanings across cultures.[62] Failure to recognize the meaning assigned to a symbol can cause serious problems:

- A manufacturer of water-recreation products lost heavily in Malaysia because the company's predominant color, green, was associated with the jungle and illness.
- A leading U.S. golf ball manufacturer was initially disappointed in its attempts to penetrate the Japanese market. Its mistake was packaging its golf balls in sets of four. Four is a symbol of death in Japanese.
- Pepsi-Cola lost its dominant market share in Southeast Asia to Coke when it changed the color of its coolers and vending equipment from deep "regal" blue to light "ice" blue. Light blue is associated with death and mourning in Southeast Asia.
- Most Chinese business travelers were shocked during the inauguration of United's concierge services for first-class passengers on its Pacific Rim routes. To mark the occasion, each concierge was proudly wearing a white carnation—an Asian symbol of death.
- AT&T had to change its "thumbs-up" ads in Russia and Poland where showing the palm of the hand in this manner has an offensive meaning. The change was simple. The thumbs-up sign was given showing the back of the hand.

Table 2-4 presents additional illustrations of varying meanings assigned to symbols across cultures.[63] Despite frequent cultural differences in symbols, many symbols work well across a wide range of cultures. Kellogg's *Tony the Tiger* works in the United States, Japan (see Illustration 2-5), and many other cultures (see Case 2–4).

Friendship

"Our intention is to drive down the cost of manufacturing to provide lower costs to the customer," McConville (CEO of Diebold China, a manufacturer of ATM machines) tells three government officials through his translator, JiLin Shi, a Diebold deputy general manager.

McConville is seated at a long table in a conference room in Diebold's manufacturing plant. He is flanked by four of his employees, all Chinese. The officials sit across the table, where cans of Coca-Cola and bottles of mineral water are offered. "The duty is paid by the customer in the end," McConville says.

To get the duty lowered from 25 to 12 percent, Diebold has to prove that 60 percent of the parts it uses in manufacturing are Chinese-made. One of the officials starts speaking in Mandarin. Shi translates, "The localization looks good. We'll produce a letter for customs. We wish you prosperity."

McConville shakes hands with the officials and gives each one a gift—a shopping bag full of Tupperware. "As with most things in today's environment, team effort makes things successful, and we consider you part of our team," he says to the officials. The officials smile and the group goes to celebrate over lunch in a private, second-floor room in a nearby restaurant.

The lazy Susan in the middle of the round table groans under plates piled high with fried snake and Peking ducks and other delicacies. A waitress lifts the shell off a cooked turtle and scoops the

TABLE 2-4

The Meaning of Numbers, Colors, and Other Symbols

Symbol	Meaning
White	Symbol for mourning or death in the Far East; happiness, purity in the United States.
Purple	Associated with death in many Latin American countries.
Blue	Connotation of femininity in Holland; masculinity in Sweden, United States.
Red	Unlucky or negative in Chad, Nigeria, Germany; positive in Denmark, Rumania, Argentina. Brides wear red in China, but it is a masculine color in the United Kingdom and France.
Yellow flowers	Sign of death in Mexico; infidelity in France.
White lilies	Suggestion of death in England.
7	Unlucky number in Ghana, Kenya, Singapore; lucky in Morocco, India, Czechoslovakia, Nicaragua, United States.
Triangle	Negative in Hong Kong, Korea, Taiwan; positive in Colombia.
Owl	Wisdom in United States; bad luck in India.
Deer	Speed, grace in United States; homosexuality in Brazil.

meat into bowls of steaming broth. As the employees and government officials chat in mandarin and smoke Marlboros, McConville sips a Tsingtao beer and whispers to a visitor, "That meeting was only the beginning. Now we have to meet with customs to see if they even know what the process for lowering customs is." He dips his duck in plum sauce. "That'll mean dinner, some wine. In China, it doesn't matter who it is. You have to get to know them."[64]

The rights and obligations imposed by friendship are another nonverbal cultural variable. Americans, more so than most other cultures, make friends quickly and easily and drop them easily also. In large part, this may be due to the fact that America has always had a great deal of both social and geographic mobility. People who move every few years must be able to form friendships in a short time period and depart from them with a minimum of pain. In many other parts of the world, friendships are formed slowly and carefully because they imply deep and lasting obligations. As the following quote indicates, friendship and business are deeply intertwined in most of the world:

> To most Asians and Latin Americans, good personal relationships and feelings are all that really matter in a long-term agreement. After all, the written word is less important than personal ties. Once personal trust has been established, cooperation increases. The social contacts developed between the parties are often far more significant than the technical specifications and the price. In many countries the heart of the matter, the major point of the negotiations, is getting to know the people involved.
>
> Brazilians and many Latin Americans cannot depend on their own legal system to iron out conflicts, so they must depend on personal relationships. Americans negotiate a contract; the Japanese negotiate a relationship. In many cultures, the written word is used simply to satisfy legalities. In their eyes, emotion and personal relations are more important than cold facts. The key issue is, "Can I get along with these people and their company and do I want to sell (or buy) their products?" rather than "Can I make money on this deal?" They are particularly interested in the sincerity of those with whom they are negotiating. The Japanese are especially unwilling to do business with someone they think may be arrogant or unpleasant: "I do not do business with someone who does not like us!" The Japanese do not separate personal feelings from business relationships.

KELLOGG'S FROSTED FLAKES® is a registered trademark of Kellogg Company. All rights reserved. Used with permission.

ILLUSTRATION 2-5

Kellogg's tiger is an effective symbol in many cultures. Here the tiger and a contest work as well in Japan as they do in America.

Personal affinity is also immensely important to Mexicans and other Latin Americans. The goal is to nurture a mutual confidence, engage in informal discussions, and seek solutions to problems. Therefore, personal rapport, preliminary meetings, telephone conversations, and social activities are necessary.[65]

Agreements

Americans rely on an extensive and, generally, highly efficient legal system for ensuring that business obligations are honored and for resolving disagreements. Many other cultures have not evolved such a system and rely instead on friendship and kinship, local moral principles, or informal customs to guide business conduct. For example, in China the business relationship is subordinate to the moralistic notion of a friendship. Under the American system, we would examine a proposed contract closely. Under the Chinese system, we would examine the character of a potential trading partner closely. In the words of an American CEO based in China:

> Relationships are everything in China, more so than in the U.S., which is more focused on business. The Chinese want to know and understand you before they buy from you.[66]

When is an agreement concluded? Americans consider the signing of a contract to be the end of negotiations. However, to many Greeks and Russians such a signing is merely the signal to begin serious negotiations that will continue until the project is completed. At the other extreme, presenting a contract for a signature can be insulting to an Arab, who considered the verbal agreement to be completely binding.

We also assume that, in almost all instances, prices are uniform for all buyers, related to the service rendered, and reasonably close to the going rate. We order many products such as taxi rides without inquiring in advance about the cost. In many Latin American and Arab countries, the procedure is different. Virtually all prices are negotiated prior to the sale. If a product such as a taxi ride is consumed without first establishing the price, the customer must pay whatever fee the seller demands.

Things

The cultural meaning of things leads to purchase patterns that one would not otherwise predict. One observer noted a strong demand for expensive, status brands whose absolute cost was not too high among those Russians beginning to gain economically under capitalism. He concluded that:

> They may stick to their locally produced toothpaste, but they want the Levi's, the Mont Blanc pens, the Moet Chandon champagne to establish their self-esteem and their class position.[67]

The differing meanings that cultures attach to things, including products, make gift-giving a particularly difficult task.[68] For example, giving a Chinese business customer or distributor a nice desk clock (a common gift in many countries) would be inappropriate. Why? In China, the word for *clock* is similar to the word for *funeral,* making clocks inappropriate gifts.

The business and social situations that call for a gift, and the items that are appropriate gifts, vary widely. For example, a gift of cutlery is generally inappropriate in Russia, Japan, Taiwan, and Germany. In Japan, small gifts are required in many business situations, yet in China they are less appropriate. In China, gifts should be presented privately, but in Arab countries they should be given in front of others.

Etiquette

Etiquette represents generally accepted ways of behaving in social situations. Assume that an American is preparing a commercial that shows people eating an evening meal, with one person about to take a bite of food from a fork. The person will have the fork in the right hand, and the left hand will be out of sight under the table. To an American audience this will seem natural. However, in many European cultures, a well-mannered individual would have the fork in the left hand and the right hand on the table. Likewise, portraying the American custom of patting a child on the head would be inappropriate in much of Asia, where the head is considered sacred.

Behaviors considered rude or obnoxious in one culture may be quite acceptable in another. The common and acceptable American habit (for males) of crossing one's legs while sitting, such that the sole of a shoe shows, is extremely insulting in many Eastern cultures. In these cultures, the sole of the foot or shoe should never be exposed to view.

Normal voice tone, pitch, and speed of speech differ between cultures and languages, as do the use of gestures. Westerners often mistake the seemingly loud, volatile speech of some Asian cultures as signifying anger or emotional distress (which it would if it were being used by a Westerner) when it is normal speech for the occasion.

As American trade with Japan increases, we continue to learn more of the subtle aspects of Japanese business etiquette. For example, a Japanese executive will seldom say *no* directly during negotiations, as this would be considered impolite. Instead, he might say,

"That will be very difficult," which would mean *no*. A Japanese responding *yes* to a request often means, "Yes, I understand the request," not "Yes, I agree to the request." Many Japanese find the American tendency to look straight into another's eyes when talking to be aggressive and rude.

Consider the following example of Japanese business etiquette:

"Your *meishi* is your face."

"*Meishi* is most necessary here. It is absolutely essential."

"A man without a *meishi* has no identity in Japan."

The exchange of *meishi* is the most basic of social rituals in a nation where social ritual matters very much. It solidifies a personal contact in a nation where personal contacts are the indispensable ingredient for success in any field. The act of exchanging *meishi* is weighted with meaning. Once the social minuet is completed, two people know where they stand in relation to each other and their respective statures within the hierarchy of corporate or government bureaucracy.

What is this mysterious "exchange of *meishi*"? It is the exchange of business cards when two people meet! A fairly common, simple activity in America, it is an essential, complex social exchange in Japan.

The importance of proper, culture-specific etiquette for sales personnel and advertising messages is obvious. Although people are apt to recognize that etiquette varies from culture to culture, there is still a strong emotional feeling that "our way is natural and right."

Conclusions on Nonverbal Communications

Can you imagine yourself becoming upset or surprised because people in a different culture spoke to you in their native language—say, Spanish, French, or German—instead of English? Of course not. We all recognize that verbal languages vary around the world. Yet we generally feel that our nonverbal languages are natural or innate. Therefore, we misinterpret what is being "said" to us because we think we are hearing English when in reality it is Japanese, Italian, or Russian. It is this error that marketers can and must avoid.

A GLOBAL TEENAGE CULTURE?

> After classes, ____________________________, 17, a high school junior in ______________ ______________, peels off his school clothes, puts three gold and silver hoop rings in his left ear, and slips into jeans and Nikes. Then he goes to the moving company where he works after school. His job pays not only for his wardrobe but also for his record collection, which includes recordings by his favorite rappers, Doctor Dre and Ice Cube.[69]

Can you fill in the blanks in the above story with any degree of confidence? The young man is Nasoshi Sato and he lives in Tokyo. However, his behavior differs little from that of millions of other teenagers in Europe, North and South America, and Asia. One study videotaped the bedrooms of teens from 25 countries. The conclusion:

> From the gear and posters on display, it's hard to tell whether the rooms are in Los Angeles, Mexico City, or Tokyo. Basketballs sit alongside soccer balls. Closets overflow with staples from an international, unisex uniform: baggy Levi's or Diesel jeans, NBA jackets, and rugged shoes from Timberland or Doc Martens.[70]

"Teenagers—who make up a huge and growing part of the population around the world—represent the first truly international market in history," according to Larry McIntosh,

Pepsi-Cola's vice president for international advertising.[71] Consider the following data on teenage clothing ownership around the world (the data for Asia exclude China).[72]

	United States	*Europe*	*Asia*	*Latin America*
Jeans	93%	94%	93%	86%
T-shirt	93	94	96	59
Running shoes	80	89	69	65
Blazer	42	43	27	30
Denim jacket	39	57	23	41

Teenagers around the world not only tend to dress alike, they are very similar in the things they find enjoyable. A large-scale global survey found remarkable consistency in the things teenagers enjoy doing.[73]

Activity	*Percent Doing Activity for Enjoyment*
Be with friends	93%
Watch TV	93
Watch movies at home	83
Go to movies	80
Go to parties	78
Be with family	76
Play sports	76
Talk on phone	76
Travel	75

What is causing this movement toward uniformity? The largest single influence is worldwide mass media. Teens throughout the world can tune in *MTV* or *Baywatch*. Teenagers around the world watch many of the same shows, see the same movies and videos, and listen to the same music. They not only idolize the same musicians but they copy these musicians' dress styles, mannerisms, and attitudes, which provides them with many shared characteristics. This interconnectedness is rapidly increasing with the growth of the World Wide Web.

Sports and sports figures are another unifying force. Soccer, basketball, and baseball are increasingly every country's home sports. Track, American-style football, and winter sports, particularly snowboarding, are also popular with teenagers. The Olympics have become a worldwide media event. In a school in China's rural Shaanzi province, students were asked to name the "world's greatest man," living or dead. Michael Jordan tied with the late Zhou En-lai for the title.[74] Products used or endorsed by such stars often find quick acceptance among teenagers around the world.

Marketers are using the similarities among teenagers across cultures to launch global brands or to reposition current brands to appeal to this large market. For example, Pepsi Max was introduced around the world with a single set of commercials aimed at teenagers. The ads showed a quartet of teens vying to perform the most outrageous feats such as skydiving from Big Ben, rollerblading off the Sphinx, or surfing down the dunes of the Sahara. Likewise, 7 UP recently launched similar ads targeting teenagers in Spain, Russia,

Ireland, and the Netherlands. The theme is "Air conditioning for a passionate world." Companies such as Kodak and Apple are also advertising to teens globally because they often influence or determine the purchase of cameras, computers, and other consumer electronics.

It is important to note that teenagers also have a great many culturally unique behaviors, attitudes, and values. Also, the similarities described above are most noticeable among middle-class teens living in urban areas. Poorer, rural teens often conform more closely to their society's traditional culture.

GLOBAL DEMOGRAPHICS

China's economy grew rapidly throughout the 1990s, as did personal disposable income.[75] In the more prosperous regions, this has produced an explosion in the use of motorbikes as replacements for bicycles (private automobile ownership is limited). This sudden, large increase in motorbike usage triggered demand for gasoline in cities with no gasoline stations and few available sites. Illustration 2-6 shows how one firm dealt with this challenge by developing and deploying "mobile" service stations in the form of fuel trucks with attached gasoline pumps.

Disposable income is one aspect of demographics. **Demographics** *describe a population in terms of its size, structure, and distribution. Size* refers to the number of individuals in the society, while *structure* describes the society in terms of age, income, education, and occupation. *Distribution* refers to the physical location of individuals in terms of geographic region and rural, suburban, and urban location.

Demographics are both a result and a cause of cultural values. That is, densely populated societies are likely to have more of a collective orientation than an individualistic one because a collective orientation helps such societies function smoothly. Cultures that value

© Del Hawkins.

ILLUSTRATION 2-6

The rapid growth in personal income in parts of China has led to an explosion in motorbike ownership. The Chinese have responded with innovative distribution and service outlets.

hard work and the acquisition of material wealth are likely to advance economically, which alters their demographics both directly (income) and indirectly (families in economically advanced countries tend to be smaller).

A critical aspect of demographics for marketers is income. However, the average income in a country is not as important as the distribution of income. One country with a relatively low average income can have a sizable middle-income segment, while another country with the same average income may have most of the wealth in the hands of a few individuals. For example, Kenya and Indonesia have similar average per capita incomes. However, as can be seen in Figure 2-4, the distribution of that income differs sharply, with almost half of Indonesia's income going to the middle 60% of the population compared to only a third of Kenya's. How will these differences affect consumption? The percent of households in Indonesia that can afford discretionary consumer items is much larger than in Kenya, enhancing Indonesia as a market for consumer goods firms.

Marketers increasingly use **purchasing power parity (PPP)** rather than average or median income to evaluate markets. PPP is based on a standard market basket of products bought in each country based on U.S. dollars. Suppose a product in the United States is purchased primarily by families with $20,000 annual income. A PPP analysis would show that

FIGURE 2-4 Income Distribution across Countries

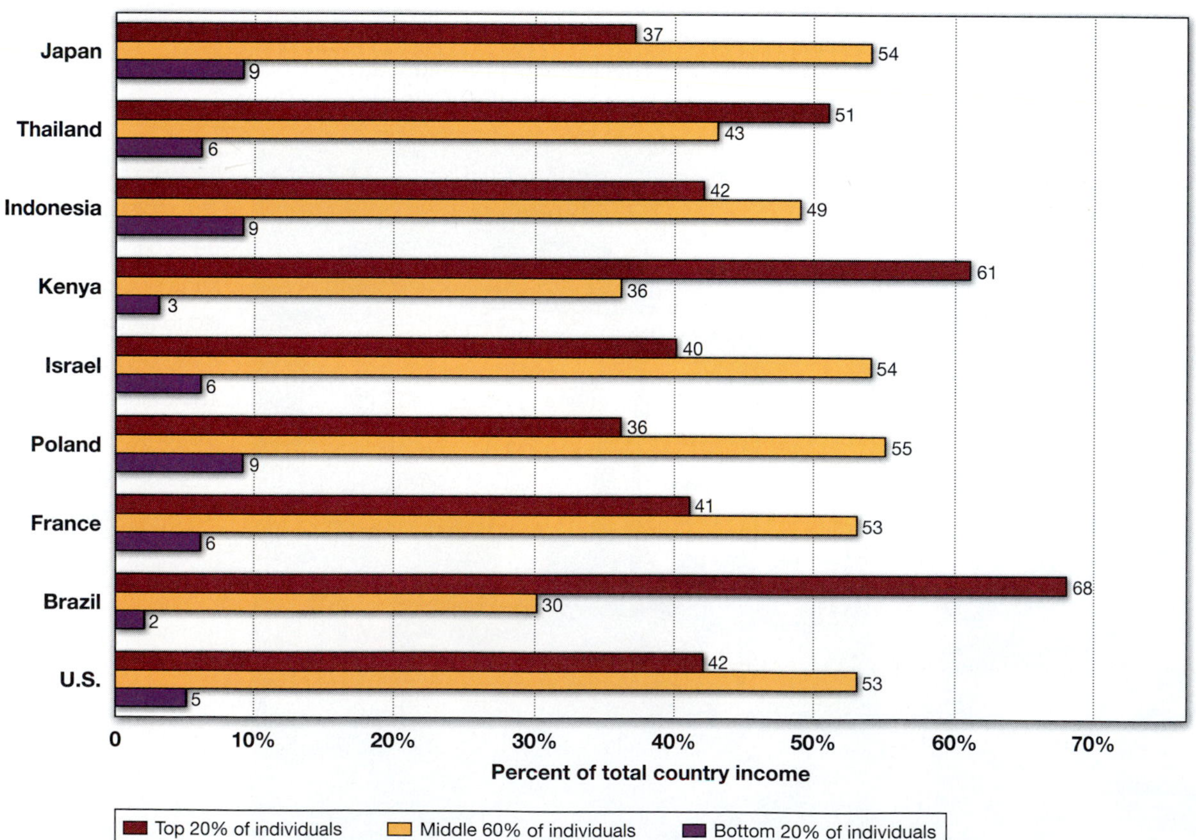

Source: R. Sookdeo, "The New Global Consumer," *Fortune,* Autumn–Winter 1993, pp. 68–76. © 1993 Time Inc. Reprinted by permission.

Venezuela has 2.5 million households with incomes that allow them to consume as much as a typical U.S. household with $20,000 income. The Venezuelan household may have a lower income in U.S. dollars but it may be able to buy more because of a lower local cost structure, government-provided health care, and so forth.[76] The World Bank now describes all countries in terms of PPP in its annual *World Bank Atlas*. The importance of considering purchasing power rather than just income can be seen in the following table (in U.S. dollars):[77]

	Per Capita Income	*Per Capita PPP*
Brazil	$ 3,020	$ 5,470
China	490	2,120
Denmark	26,510	18,940
Germany	23,560	20,980
Indonesia	730	3,140
Korea	7,670	9,810
Malaysia	3,160	8,630
Mexico	3,510	7,100
Switzerland	36,410	23,620

The economic, climatic, and social structures of a country influence how consumers allocate their income. Table 2-5 shows large differences across countries in the manner in which households allocate their resources. For example, Mexican households spend twice as much of their income on appliances and other nonessential consumer goods as do Indian households. What do this and the other differences in this table suggest for marketers?[78]

The estimated age distribution of the United States, the Philippines, and Japan for the year 2000 is shown on page 68.[79] Note that almost half the population of the Philippines is less than 20 years of age compared to less than a third for the United States and about one-fifth for Japan. What product opportunities do this and the other age differences among

How Households Allocate Their Income **TABLE 2-5**

	Country						
Category	*United States*	*Mexico*	*Iran*	*Kenya*	*Singapore*	*Thailand*	*India*
Food	10%	35%	37%	38%	19%	30%	52%
Clothing	6	10	9	7	8	16	11
Housing, utilities	18	8	23	12	11	7	10
Medical care	14	5	6	3	7	5	3
Education	8	5	5	10	12	5	4
Transportation	14	12	6	8	13	13	7
Other*	30	25	14	22	30	24	13
Per capita income (000)†	22.5	3.2	1.5	.4	13.9	1.6	.4

*Includes appliances and other consumer durables.

†In 1992 U.S. dollars. Source: *World Fact Book 1992* (Washington, D.C., Central Intelligence Agency, 1992).

Source: R. Sookdeo, "The New Global Consumer," *Fortune,* Autumn–Winter 1993, pp. 68–76. © 1993 Time Inc. Reprinted by permission.

these countries suggest? Even if all other aspects of the countries were identical, the demographic variable *age* would dictate different product and communications mixes.

Age	*United States*	*Philippines*	*Japan*
<10	14.7%	25.0%	10.1%
10–19	13.9	22.0	11.1
20–29	13.3	17.6	14.7
30–39	15.3	13.5	13.3
40–49	15.3	10.0	13.3
50–59	11.2	6.1	15.1
60–69	7.2	3.7	11.6
>69	8.9	2.1	10.9

CROSS-CULTURAL MARKETING STRATEGY

There is continuing controversy over the extent to which cross-cultural marketing strategies, particularly advertising, should be standardized.[80] Standardized strategies can result in substantial cost savings. Maybelline's new Manhattan line of cosmetics designed for the Asian market uses one ad campaign in China, Taiwan, Hong Kong, Thailand, and Singapore. The ads feature an attractive Asian model in a low-cut, short dress against the Manhattan skyline at night. This combination of appeals to youth, beauty, and sophistication could be used in many other countries, though this ad would be inappropriate (and probably banned) in most Islamic countries. Illustration 2-7 is another appeal to beauty and sensuality that would require little alteration (other than language) across most Western cultures.

Campbell's Soup is succeeding worldwide, but the particular soups range from the traditional chicken noodle in the United States to cream of chili in Mexico, split pea with ham in Argentina, peppery tripe in Poland, and watercress and duck gizzard in China. McDonald's used to strive for uniformity around the globe. Now it adopts its products as appropriate, adding fried eggs to burgers in Japan and offering Samurai Pork Burgers with a sweet barbecue sauce in Thailand. However, its most dramatic changes are being made as it enters India for the first time:

> Eighty percent of Indians are Hindu who don't eat beef so there will be no *Big Macs* in India. Instead, the menu will feature the Maharaja Mac—"two all mutton patties, special sauce, lettuce, cheese, pickles, onions on a sesame-seed bun." For the strictest Hindus who eat no meat, McDonald's will offer deep fried rice patties flavored with peas, carrots, red pepper, beans, onions, coriander, and other spices. Pork is also banned from the menu, as India's 110 million Muslims believe it is unclean.[81]

The critical decision is whether utilizing a standardized marketing strategy in any given market will result in a greater return on investment than would an individualized campaign. Thus, the consumer response to the standardized campaign and to potential individualized campaigns must be considered in addition to the cost of each approach.

Considerations in Approaching a Foreign Market

There are seven key considerations for each geographic market that a firm is contemplating. An analysis of these seven variables provides the background necessary for deciding whether or not to enter the market and to what extent, if any, an individualized marketing strategy is required. A small sample of experts, preferably native to the market under consideration, often will be able to furnish sufficient information on each variable.

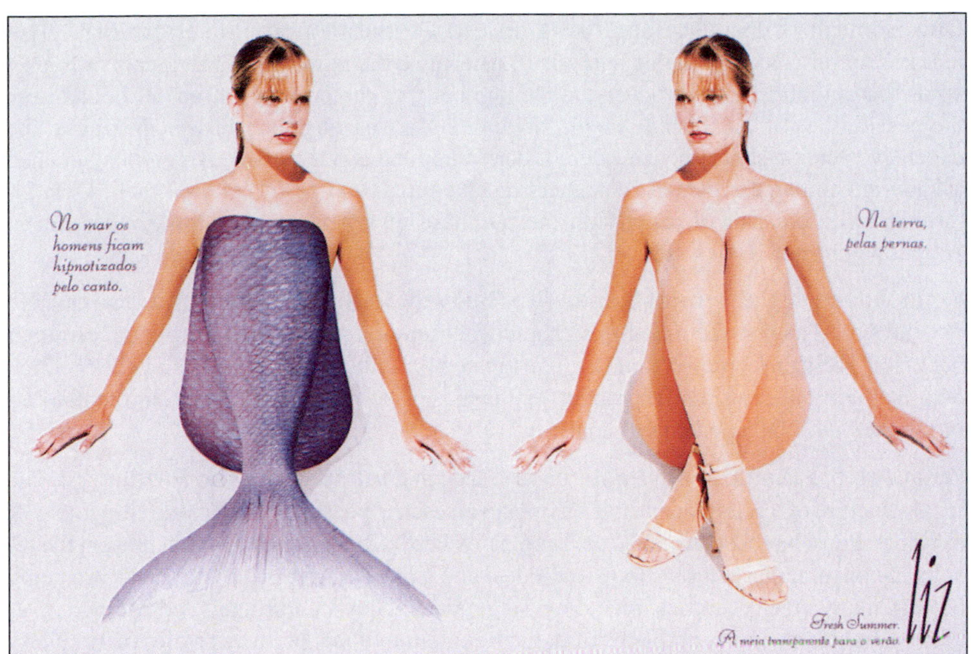

DM9DDB, São Paulo.

ILLUSTRATION 2-7

Ads appealing to beauty can be used with little or no alteration across many cultures. This ad would work well in most Western cultures, but it would not be appropriate for some others such as traditional Muslim societies.

Is the Geographic Area Homogeneous or Heterogeneous with Respect to Culture? Marketing efforts are generally directed at defined geographic areas, primarily political and economic entities. Legal requirements and existing distribution channels often encourage this approach. However, it is also supported by the implicit assumption that geographical or political boundaries coincide with cultural boundaries. This assumption is incorrect more often than not. For example, a recent Gallup study suggested that strategies in Latin America need to be designed at the metropolitan level because of major within-country differences.[82]

Canada provides an even clearer example. Many American firms treat the Canadian market as though it were a single cultural unit despite the fact that they must make adjustments for language differences. However, studies have found that French Canadians differ from English Canadians in attitudes toward instant foods and spending money; in spending patterns toward expensive liquors, clothing, personal care items, tobacco, soft drinks, candy, and instant coffee; in television and radio usage patterns; and in eating patterns.[83] Thus, marketing campaigns must be developed for cultural groups, not just countries.

What Needs Can This Product or a Version of It Fill in This Culture? Most firms examine a new market with their existing product or product technology in mind. The question they must answer is what needs their existing or modified product can fill in the culture involved. For example, bicycles and motorcycles serve primarily recreational needs in the United States, but they provide basic transportation in many other countries.

General Foods has successfully positioned Tang as a substitute for orange juice at breakfast in the United States. However, in analyzing the French market, it found that the French drink little orange juice and almost none at breakfast. Therefore, a totally different positioning strategy was used; Tang was promoted as a new type of refreshing drink for any time of the day. In contrast, the Maybelline's Manhattan cosmetic line described earlier was developed specifically for Asian women but is positioned similarly to its cosmetics targeting young women in the United States.

Can Enough of the Group(s) Needing the Product Afford the Product? This requires an initial demographic analysis to determine the number of individuals or households that might need the product and the number that can probably afford it. In addition, the possibilities of establishing credit, obtaining a government subsidy, or making a less expensive version should be considered. For example, Levi-Strauss de Argentina launched a trade-in campaign in which consumers received a 50,000 peso "reward" (about $7) for turning in an old pair of jeans with the purchase of a new pair. A strong recession in Argentina prompted the action.

What Values or Patterns of Values Are Relevant to the Purchase and Use of This Product? The first section of this chapter focused on values and their role in consumer behavior. The value system should be investigated for influences on purchasing the product, owning the product, using the product, and disposing of the product. Much of the marketing strategy will be based on this analysis.

What Are the Distribution, Political, and Legal Structures for the Product? The legal structure of a country can have an impact on each aspect of a firm's marketing mix. For example, Pepsi has been banned from running its Pepsi Challenge ads (which present the results of consumer taste tests comparing Pepsi and Coke) in Argentina. These ads are being used in many other countries, including Singapore, Malaysia, Portugal, and Mexico. Colgate encountered similar problems in India. Regulation of marketing activities, particularly advertising, is increasing throughout the world. China recently banned "superlative claims" and comparative ads. Duracell had to withdraw its famous bunny ads because of the ruling, and Budweiser was not able to launch its beer into China with its familiar tag-line, "The King of Beers."[84]

Regulations also affect distribution channels. Until recently, Japan prohibited yen-based transactions on the Internet, which slowed the development of this distribution channel.[85] China recently announced a ban on direct sales to consumers, which has major consequences for Amway, Avon, Mary Kay, and other direct marketers in China.[86]

Traditional distribution patterns also differ across countries. In China, vanilla is considered a chemical and is sold in paint stores. Nutmeg, cinnamon, and some other spices are often distributed through Chinese medicine stores. Similar variations in what Americans consider "normal" distribution channels exist in most countries.

In What Ways Can We Communicate about the Product? This question requires an investigation into (1) available media and who attends to each type, (2) the needs the product fills, (3) values associated with the product and its use, and (4) the verbal and nonverbal communications systems in the culture(s).[87] All aspects of the firm's promotional mix (including packaging, nonfunctional product design features, personal selling techniques, and advertising) should be based on these four factors. In Illustration 2-8, note the bright colors Whirlpool uses for the refrigerators it markets in Thailand and other Asian countries. This is based on the fact that many consumers in these countries keep their refrigerators in their living rooms (the kitchens are too small) and want them to serve as attractive pieces of furniture, not just as appliances.

Money-back guarantees are one of the most credible advertising claims to U.S. citizens, but most Latin Americans simply do not believe them. Instead, they are influenced by claims that the brand is the "official" product of a sports group or an event, a claim that has little credibility in the United States.[88]

What Are the Ethical Implications of Marketing This Product in This Country? All marketing programs should be evaluated on ethical as well as financial dimensions. As discussed at the beginning of the chapter, international marketing activities raise many ethical issues. The ethical dimension is particularly important and complex in marketing to

Krapit Phanrut/Sipa.

ILLUSTRATION 2-8

Whirlpool uses bright colors for its refrigerators sold in Malaysia. Refrigerators are often placed in the living room and serve as furniture as well as appliances in much of Asia.

Third World and developing countries.[89] Consider Kellogg's attempt to introduce cold cereal as a breakfast food in Brazil. The following questions represent the type of ethical analysis that should go into the decision:

- If we succeed, will the average nutrition level be increased or decreased?
- If we succeed, will the funds spent on cereal be diverted from other uses with more beneficial long-term impacts for the individuals or society?
- If we succeed, what impact will this have on the local producers of currently consumed breakfast products?

Understanding and acting on ethical considerations in international marketing is a difficult task. However, it is also a necessary one.

SUMMARY

Culture is defined as the complex whole that includes knowledge, beliefs, art, law, morals, customs, and any other capabilities acquired by humans as members of society. Culture includes almost everything that influences an individual's thought processes and behaviors.

Culture operates primarily by setting boundaries for individual behavior and by influencing the functioning of such institutions as the family and mass media. The boundaries or *norms* are derived from *cultural values.* Values are widely held beliefs that affirm what is desirable. Cultures change when values change, the environment changes, or when dramatic events occur.

Cultural values are classified into three categories: other, environment, and self. *Other-oriented values* reflect a society's view of the appropriate relationships between individuals and groups within that society. Relevant values of this nature include *individual/collective, youth/age, extended/limited family, masculine/feminine, competitive/cooperative,* and *diversity/ uniformity.*

Environment-oriented values prescribe a society's relationships with its economic, technical, and physical environments. Examples of environment values are *cleanliness, performance/status, tradition/change, risk taking/security, problem solving/fatalistic,* and *nature.*

Self-oriented values reflect the objectives and approaches to life that individual members of society find desirable. These include *active/passive, sensual gratification/abstinence, material/nonmaterial, hard work/leisure, postponed gratification/immediate gratification,* and *religious/secular.*

Differences in *verbal communication systems* are immediately obvious across cultures and must be taken into account by marketers wishing to do business in those cultures. Probably more important, however, and certainly more difficult to recognize are *nonverbal communication systems.* Major examples of nonverbal communication variables that affect marketers are *time, space, friendship, agreement, things, symbols,* and *etiquette.*

There is evidence that teenagers around the world share at least some aspects of a common culture. This is driven by worldwide mass media and common music and sports stars.

Demographics describe a population in terms of its size, structure, and distribution. These differ widely across cultures and influence cultural values (and are influenced by them) as well as consumption patterns.

Seven questions are relevant for developing a cross-cultural marketing strategy: (1) Is the geographic area homogeneous with respect to culture? (2) What needs can this product fill in this culture? (3) Can enough people afford the product? (4) What values are relevant to the purchase and use of the product? (5) What are the distribution, political, and legal structures concerning this product? (6) How can we communicate about the product? and (7) What are the ethical implications of marketing this product in this country?

KEY TERMS

Cultural values 42
Culture 42
Demographics 65
Environment-oriented values 44
Instrumental materialism 54
Monochronic time perspective 57
Nonverbal communications systems 56
Norms 42
Other-oriented values 44
Personal space 58
Polychronic time perspective 57
Power distance 50
Purchasing power parity (PPP) 66
Sanctions 42
Self-oriented values 45
Terminal materialism 54
Verbal communications systems 54

INTERNET EXERCISES

1. Contact the Michigan State University (MSU) "International Business Resources on the WWW" site (http://ciber.bus.msu.edu/busres.htm). Which of the resources listed is most useful for:
   a. Worldwide consumer data.
   b. Data on consumer markets in China.
   c. Data on consumer markets in Europe.
   d. Data on industrial markets in Brazil.
2. Using the Michigan State University site described in Exercise 1, select and describe one of the sources such as STAT-USA. Evaluate its usefulness for understanding international markets and other cultures.
3. Using the WWW, prepare a brief report on the following as a market for soft drinks. Provide addresses for all Web sites used.
   a. Taiwan
   b. France
   c. European Union
   d. Mexico
4. Prepare a report that describes how useful, if at all, the information available at the World Bank Web site (http://www.worldbank.org) is in terms of helping you understand the following as a market for microwave ovens:
   a. Korea
   b. China
   c. Germany
   d. Canada
5. Use the Internet to find an attractive country in which to introduce a small, economical, easy to repair automobile that would cost about $5,000 U.S.
6. Visit the CIA site (http://www.cia.gov). Select the "Publications and Reports" link from the home page. Evaluate the usefulness of the *World Fact Book* site for international marketers.

REVIEW QUESTIONS

1. What are some of the ethical issues involved in cross-cultural marketing?
2. What is meant by the term *culture?*
3. What does the statement "Culture sets boundaries on behaviors" mean?
4. What is a *norm*? From what are norms derived?
5. What is a *cultural* value?
6. What is a *sanction?*
7. Cultural values can be classified as affecting one of three types of relationships—other, environment, or self. Describe each of these, and differentiate each one from the others.
8. How does the first of the following paired orientations differ from the second?
   a. Individual/Collective
   b. Performance/Status
   c. Tradition/Change
   d. Limited/Extended family
   e. Active/Passive
   f. Material/Nonmaterial
   g. Hard work/Leisure
   h. Risk taking/Security
   i. Masculine/Feminine
   j. Competitive/Cooperative
   k. Youth/Age
   l. Problem solving/Fatalistic
   m. Diversity/Uniformity
   n. Postponed gratification/Immediate gratification
   o. Sensual gratification/Abstinence
   p. Religious/Secular
9. What is meant by nonverbal communications? Why is this such a difficult area to adjust to?
10. What is meant by each of the following as a form of nonverbal communication?
    a. Time
    b. Space
    c. Friendship
    d. Agreements
    e. Things
    f. Symbols
    g. Etiquette
11. What is the difference between *instrumental* and *terminal* materialism?
12. What are the differences between a *monochronic* time perspective and a *polychronic* time perspective?
13. What forces seem to be creating a global teenage culture?
14. What are demographics? Why are they important to international marketers?
15. What is *purchasing power parity?*
16. Are standardized or individualized strategies best for marketing to multiple cultures?
17. What are the seven key considerations in deciding whether or not to enter a given international market?
18. What does determining if a geographic area or political unit is "homogeneous or heterogeneous with respect to culture" mean? Why is this important?

DISCUSSION QUESTIONS

19. Why should we study foreign cultures if we do not plan to engage in international or export marketing?
20. Is a country's culture more likely to be reflected in its art museums or its television commercials? Why?
21. Are the cultures of the world becoming more similar or more distinct?
22. Why do values differ across cultures?
23. The text lists 18 cultural values of relevance to marketing practice. Describe and place into one of the three categories two additional cultural values that have some relevance to marketing practice.
24. Select two cultural values from each of the three categories. Describe the boundaries (norms) relevant to that value in your society and the sanctions for violating those norms.
25. What are the most relevant cultural values affecting the consumption of each of the following? Describe how and why these values are particularly important.
    a. Television

b. Bicycles
c. Pet food
d. Clothes washers
e. Cosmetics
f. Beer

26. What variations between the United States and other societies, *other than cultural variations,* may affect the relative level of usage of the following?
    a. Television
    b. Bicycles
    c. Pet food
    d. Clothes washers
    e. Cosmetics
    f. Beer
27. Is the European Union (EU) likely to become a relatively homogeneous culture by 2010?
28. What are the marketing implications of the differences in the percent of adults using deodorants between countries such as Greece and Austria compared to countries such as Denmark, Norway, and Sweden?
29. How should marketing practices differ between a culture with a limited family focus and one with an extended family focus?
30. What are the marketing implications of the differences in recycling across the 16 European countries shown in the text (page 52)?
31. Why do nonverbal communication systems vary across cultures?
32. What, if any, nonverbal communication factors might be relevant in the marketing of the following?
    a. Soft drinks
    b. Cosmetics
    c. Automobiles
    d. Hand soap
    e. Computers
    f. Mountain bikes
33. To what extent do you think teenagers are truly becoming a single, global culture?
34. Will today's teenagers still be a "global culture" when they are 35? Why or why not?
35. How do demographics affect a culture's values? How do a culture's values affect its demographics?
36. What insights can you gain from examining Figure 2-4 and Table 2-5 simultaneously?
37. What causes the differences between purchasing power parity and income as shown in the text (page 67)?
38. What are the marketing implications of the differing age distributions across the United States, the Philippines, and Japan?
39. The text provides a seven-step procedure for analyzing a foreign market. Using this procedure, analyze your country as a market for:
    a. Automobiles from Indonesia
    b. Men's shoes from Korea
    c. Expensive watches from Poland
    d. Wine from Canada
40. What are the major ethical issues in introducing prepared foods such as breakfast cereals to Third World countries?
41. Should U.S. tobacco firms be allowed to market cigarettes in developing countries? Why or why not?

42. How can developing countries keep their cultures from being overly Westernized or Americanized?

APPLICATION ACTIVITIES

43. Interview two students from two different cultures. Determine the extent to which the following are used in those cultures and the variations in the values of those cultures that relate to the use of these products.
    a. Bicycles
    b. Perfume
    c. Beer
    d. Health food
    e. Cigarettes
    f. Television viewing
44. Interview two students from two different foreign cultures. Report any differences in nonverbal communications they are aware of between their culture and your culture.

45. Interview two students from two different foreign cultures. Report their perceptions of the major differences in cultural values between their culture and your culture.
46. Interview a student from Korea. Report on the advice that the student would give an American firm marketing consumer products in Korea.
47. Interview two students from EU countries. Report on the extent to which they feel the EU will be a homogeneous culture by 2010.
48. Imagine you are a consultant working with your state or province's tourism agency. You have been asked to advise the agency on the best promotional themes to use to attract foreign tourists. What would you recommend if Japan and Germany were the two target markets?
49. Analyze a foreign culture of your choice, and recommend a marketing program for a brand of one of the following made in your country:
    a. Bicycle
    b. Perfume
    c. Beer
    d. Bottled water
    e. Dried fruit
    f. Personal computer

REFERENCES

1. N. Madden, "Starbucks Ships its Coffee Craze to Pacific Rim," *Advertising Age,* April 27, 1998, p. 28, and various company press releases.
2. For another approach, see A. C. Samli, "Toward a Model of International Consumer Behavior," *Journal of International Consumer Marketing* 7, no. 1 (1994), pp. 63–84.
3. C. Miller, "Not Quite Global," *Marketing News,* July 3, 1995, p. 9.
4. See R. W. Pollay, D. K. Tse, and Z. Y. Wang, "Advertising Propaganda and Value Change in Economic Development," *Journal of Business Research* 20 (1990), pp. 83–95.
5. See W. Bailey, "Country of Origin Attitudes in Mexico," *Journal of International Consumer Marketing,* no. 3 (1997), pp. 25–41; and J. Marcoux, P. Filiatrault, and E. Cheron, "The Attitudes Underlying Preferences of Polish Consumers towards Products Made in Western Countries," *Journal of International Consumer Marketing,* no. 4 (1997), pp. 5–29.
6. S. Efron, "Smokers Light Up All Over the World," *The Register-Guard,* September 9, 1996, p. 1.
7. "Smoking-Related Deaths Almost Epidemic in China," *The Register-Guard,* November 20, 1998, p. 13A.
8. For a thorough discussion of the meaning of culture, see D. J. McCort and N. K. Malhotra, "Culture and Consumer Behavior," *Journal of International Consumer Marketing,* no. 2 (1993), pp. 91–127.
9. See W. J. McDonald, "Developing International Direct Marketing Strategies," *Journal of Direct Marketing,* Autumn 1994, pp. 18–27; W. J. McDonald, "American versus Japanese Consumer Decision Making," *Journal of International Consumer Marketing* 7, no. 3 (1995), pp. 81–93; and J. B. Ford, L. E. Pelton, and J. R. Lumpkin, "Perception of Marital Roles in Purchase Decision Processes," *Journal of the Academy of Marketing Science,* Spring 1995, pp. 120–31.
10. "And Then There's Global Pizza," *The Register-Guard,* August 25, 1996, p. C-1.
11. See D. K. Tse, R. W. Belk, and N. Zhou, "Becoming a Consumer Society," *Journal of Consumer Research,* March 1989, pp. 457–72.
12. S. P. Galante, "Clash Courses," *The Wall Street Journal,* European ed., July 20, 1984, p. 1.
13. For different value sets, see G. Hofstede, *Cultures and Organizations* (London: McGraw-Hill, 1991); S. E. Beatty, L. R. Kahle, and P. Homer, "Personal Values and Gift-Giving Behaviors," *Journal of Business Research,* March 1991, pp. 149–57; and F. Hansen, "From Lifestyle to Value Systems to Simplicity," in *Advances in Consumer Research XXV,* ed. J. W. Alba and J. W. Hutchinson (Provo, UT: Association for Consumer Research, 1998), pp. 181–95.
14. G. Hofstede, *Culture's Consequences* (Newbury Park, CA: Sage Publications, 1980); and F. Zandpour et al., "Global Reach and Local Touch," *Journal of Advertising Research,* September 1994, pp. 35–63.
15. F. Hansen, "From Life Style to Value Systems to Simplicity," in *Advances in Consumer Research XXV,* ed. J. W. Alba and J. W. Hutchinson (Provo, UT: Association for Consumer Research, 1998), pp. 181–95.
16. S. Abe, R. Bagozzi, and P. Sadarangani, "An Investigation of Construct Validity and Generalizability of the Self-Concept," *Journal of International Consumer Marketing,* no. 3–4 (1996), pp. 97–123.
17. M. Lee and F. M. Ulgado, "Consumer Evaluations of Fast-Food Services," *Journal of Services Marketing,* no. 1 (1997), pp. 39–52.
18. N. Y. Wong and A. C. Ahuvia, "Personal Taste and Family Face," *Psychology & Marketing,* August 1998, pp. 423–41.
19. Z. Caillat and B. Mueller, "The Influence of Culture on American and British Advertising," *Journal of Advertising Research,* May–June 1996, pp. 79–88; Y. Zhang and B. D. Gelb, "Matching Advertising Appeals to Culture," *Journal of Advertising,* Fall 1996, pp. 29–46; N. D. Albers-Miller and B. D. Gelb, "Business Advertising as a Mirror of Cultural Dimensions," *Journal of Advertising,* Winter 1996, pp. 57–70; B. D. Culter, S. A. Erdem, and R. G. Javalgi, "Advertising's Relative Reliance on Collectivism-Individualism Appeals," *Journal of International Consumer Marketing,* no. 3 (1997), pp. 43–55; M. P. Leach and A. H. Liu, "The Use of Culturally Relevant Stimuli in International Advertising," *Psychology & Marketing,* September 1998, pp. 523–46; and L. Ha, "Advertising Appeals Used by Services

Marketers," *Journal of Services Marketing,* no. 2 (1998), pp. 98–112.

20. G. D. Gregory and J. M. Munch, "Cultural Values in International Advertising," *Psychology & Marketing,* March 1997, pp. 99–119; and R. B. Money, M. C. Gilly, and J. L. Graham, "Explorations of National Culture and Word-Of-Mouth Referral Behavior," *Journal of Marketing,* October 1998, pp. 76–87.
21. C. Robinson, "Asian Culture," *Journal of the Market Research Society,* January 1996, pp. 55–62.
22. K. L. Miller, "You Just Can't Talk to These Kids," *Business Week,* April 19, 1993, pp. 104–6.
23. See "Changing Lifestyle," *Japan Marketing/Advertising Yearbook 1994* (Tokyo: Dentsu, 1994), p. 93; and M. S. Roth, "The Effects of Culture and Socioeconomics on the Performance of Global Brand Image Strategies," *Journal of Marketing Research,* May 1995, pp. 163–75.
24. J. L. Aaker and P. Williams, "Empathy versus Pride," *Journal of Consumer Research,* December 1998, pp. 241–53.
25. *Reader's Digest Eurodata—A Consumer Survey of 17 European Countries* (Pleasantville, NY: The Reader's Digest Association, Inc., 1991), p. 26. The German data are for the former West Germany.
26. P. Duggan, "Feeding China's 'Little Emperors,'" *Forbes,* August 6, 1990, pp. 84–85.
27. S. H. C. Tai and J. L. M. Tam, "A Comparative Study of Chinese Consumers in Asian Markets," *Journal of International Consumer Marketing,* no. 1 (1996), pp. 25–42; and S. H. C. Tai and J. L. M. Tam, "A Lifestyle Analysis of Female Consumers in Greater China," *Psychology & Marketing,* May 1997, pp. 287–307.
28. B. D. Keillor, R. S. Parker, and A. Schaffer, "Influences on Adolescent Brand Preferences in the United States and Mexico," *Journal of Advertising Research*, May–June 1996, pp. 47–56.
29. N. Razzouk and J. Al-Khatib, "The Nature of Television Advertising in Saudi Arabia"; J. Huang, "National Character and Sex Roles in Advertising"; and B. D. Cutler, R. G. Javalgi, and D. Lee, "The Portrayal of People in Magazine Advertisements"; all in *Journal of International Consumer Marketing* 6, no. 2 (1993), pp. 65–90; 7, no. 4 (1995), pp. 81–96; and 8, no. 2 (1995), pp. 45–58; B. A. Browne, "Gender Stereotypes in Advertising on Children's Television in the 1990's"; and J. B. Ford et al., "Gender Role Portrayal in Japanese Advertising"; both in *Journal of Advertising,* Spring 1998, pp. 83–96 and 113–24.
30. J. Russell, "Working Women Give Japan Culture Shock," *Advertising Age,* January 16, 1995, p. I-24.
31. See footnote 22, p. 106; and P. Sellers, "Pepsi Opens a Second Front," *Fortune,* August 8, 1994, pp. 70–76.
32. See N. Donthu, "A Cross-Country Investigation of Recall of and Attitude toward Comparative Advertising," *Journal of Advertising,* Summer 1998, pp. 111–22.
33. See footnote 25, p. 19.
34. See footnote 14.
35. N. Giges, "Europeans Buy Outside Goods," *Advertising Age,* April 27, 1992, p. I-26.
36. D. Kim, Y. Pan, and H. S. Park, "High- versus Low-Context Culture," *Psychology & Marketing,* September 1998, pp. 507–21.
37. N. M. Murray and L. A. Manrai, "Exploratory Consumption Behavior," *Journal of International Consumer Marketing,* no. 1 (1993), pp. 101–19.
38. Ibid.
39. Caillat and Mueller, footnote 19.
40. An interesting approach to environmental protection and culture is R. P. McIntyre, M. S. Meloche, and S. L. Lewis, "National Culture as a Macro Tool for Environmental Sensitivity Segmentation," in *Enhancing Knowledge Development in Marketing,* ed. D. W. Cravens and P. R. Dickson (Chicago: American Marketing Association, 1993), pp. 153–59.
41. See B. J. Phillips, "Advertising and the Cultural Meaning of Animals," in *Advances in Consumer Research XXIII,* ed. K. P. Corfman and J. G. Lynch (Provo, UT: Association for Consumer Research, 1996), pp. 354–60.
42. See G. Levin, "Too Green for Their Own Good," *Advertising Age*, April 12, 1993, p. 29.
43. T. S. Chan, "Concerns for Environmental Issues," *Journal of International Consumer Marketing,* no. 1 (1996), pp. 43–55.
44. *Trends in Europe: Consumer Attitudes & the Supermarket* (Washington, D.C.: Food Marketing Institute, 1992), p. 56.
45. C. Miller, "No Exercise, and They Like to Smoke," *Marketing News*, August 17, 1992, p. 13.
46. J. Michaels, "Nudes Dress Up Brazil Undies Ads," *Advertising Age,* August 3, 1987, p. 42.
47. See also F. Piron and M. Young, *Journal of International Consumer Marketing,* no. 3–4 (1996), pp. 211–28.
48. K. B. Doran, "Symbolic Consumption in China," in *Advances in Consumer Research XXIV,* ed. M. Bruck and D. J. MacInnis (Provo, UT: Association for Consumer Research, 1997), pp. 128–31.
49. R. W. Belk and R. W. Pollay, "Materialism and Status Appeals in Japanese and U.S. Print Advertising," in *Comparative Consumer Psychology*, ed. A. Woodside and C. Keown (Washington, D.C.: American Psychological Association, 1985). See also E. C. Hirschman and P. A. LaBarbera, "Dimensions of Possession Importance," *Psychology & Marketing*, Fall 1990, pp. 215–33; and C. Webster and R. C. Beatty, "Nationality, Materialism, and Possession Importance," in *Advances in Consumer Research XXIV,* ed. M. Bruck and D. J. MacInnis (Provo, UT: Association for Consumer Research, 1997), pp. 204–10.
50. See L. R. Kahle and P. Kennedy, "Using the List of Values (LOV) to Understand Consumers," *The Journal of Consumer Marketing,* Summer 1989, pp. 5–12.
51. See S. S. Al-Makaty, "Attitudes toward Advertising in Islam," *Journal of Advertising Research,* May–June 1996, pp. 16–25.
52. See L. C. Huff and D. L. Alden, "An Investigation of Consumer Response to Sales Promotions in Developing Markets," *Journal of Advertising Research,* May–June 1998, pp. 47–56.
53. C. Miller, "Kiddi Just Fine in the U.K," *Marketing News*, August 28, 1995, p. 8.
54. D. A. Ricks, *Big Business Blunders* (Burr Ridge, IL: Richard D. Irwin, 1983), p. 39.
55. See E. T. Hall, *The Silent Language* (New York: Fawcett World Library, 1959), p. 39; E. T. Hall, "The Silent Language in Overseas Business," *Harvard Business Review,* May–June 1960,

pp. 87–96; and E. T. Hall and M. R. Hall, *Hidden Differences* (Garden City, NY: Doubleday, 1987).

56. C. J. Kaufman, P. M. Lane, and J. D. Lindquist, "Exploring More than 24 Hours a Day," *Journal of Consumer Research,* December 1991, pp. 392–401; and L. A. Manrai and A. K. Manrai, "Effect of Cultural-Context, Gender, and Acculturation on Perceptions of Work versus Social/Leisure Time Usage," *Journal of Business Research,* February 1995, pp. 115–28.
57. Manrai and Manrai, footnote 56. See also footnote 17.
58. L. Copeland, "Foreign Markets: Not for the Amateur," *Business Marketing,* July 1984, p. 116.
59. Adapted from E. T. Hall, *The Hidden Dimension* (Garden City, NY: Doubleday, 1966).
60. See M. Chapman and A. Jamal, "Acculturation," in *Advances in Consumer Research XXIV,* ed. M. Bruck and D. J. MacInnis (Provo, UT: Association for Consumer Research, 1997), pp. 138–44.
61. S. Smith, "The Sales Force Plays Musical Chairs at IBM Japan," *Fortune,* July 3, 1989, p. 14.
62. N. M. Murray and S. B. Murray, "Music and Lyrics in Commercials," *Journal of Advertising,* Summer 1996, pp. 52–63.
63. J. Cohen, "The Search for Universal Symbols," *Journal of International Consumer Marketing,* no. 3–4 (1996), pp. 187–210.
64. Adapted from G. Brewer, "An American in Shanghai," *Sales & Marketing Management,* November 1997, pp. 39–44.
65. Reprinted from *Industrial Marketing Management,* Vol. 4, P. A. Herbig and H. E. Kramer, "Do's and Don'ts of Cross-Cultural Negotiations," p. 293, Copyright 1992, with permission from Elsevier Science.
66. Footnote 64, p. 42.
67. Footnote 3.
68. S. E. Beatty et al., "Gift-Giving in the United States and Japan," *Journal of International Consumer Marketing,* no. 3 (1993), pp. 49–66; and S. Y. Park, "A Comparison of Korean and American Gift-Giving Behaviors," *Psychology & Marketing,* September 1998, pp. 577–93.
69. S. Tully, "Teens," *Fortune,* May 1994, pp. 90–97.
70. Ibid.
71. B. G. Yovovich, "Youth Market Going Truly Global," *Advertising Age,* March 27, 1995, p. 10.
72. *The World's Teenagers* (New York: D'Arcy Masius Benton & Bowles, 1994).
73. Ibid.
74. Footnote 69, p. 96.
75. See L. Tong, "Consumerism Sweeps the Mainland," *Marketing Management,* Winter 1998, pp. 32–35.
76. C. Walker, "The Global Middle Class," *American Demographics*, September 1995, pp. 40–46.
77. Per Capita Income and PPP. Source: *The World Bank Atlas*, 1995, pp. 18–19. Reprinted by permission of The World Bank.
78. See P. Oyewole, "Country Segmentation of the International Market Using ICP-Based Consumption Patterns," *Journal of Global Marketing,* no. 4 (1998), pp. 75–94.
79. *The Sex and Age Distribution of the World Populations* (New York: United Nations, 1994).
80. T. Duncan and J. Ramaprasad, "Standardized Multinational Advertising," *Journal of Advertising,* Fall 1995, pp. 55–68; M. S. Roth, "Effects of Global Market Conditions on Brand Image Customization and Brand Performance," *Journal of Advertising,* Winter 1995, pp. 55–72; S. J. Chhabra, "Marketing Adaptations by American Corporations in South America," *Journal of Global Marketing,* no. 4 (1996), pp. 57–74; C. L. Wang, "The Degree of Standardization," *Journal of Global Marketing*, no. 1 (1996), pp. 89–107; J. Whitelock and C. Pimblett, "The Standardization Debate," *Journal of Global Marketing,* no. 3 (1997), pp. 45–66; B. Rosenbloom, Trina Larson, and R. Mehta, "Global Marketing Channels and the Standardization Debate," *Journal of Global Marketing,* no. 1 (1997), pp. 49–64; and S. Byfield and L. Caller, "Horses for Courses," *Journal of the Market Research Society,* October 1997, pp. 589–601.
81. D. Bryson, "Hindus Eat Mutton in their Macs," *The Register-Guard,* October 12, 1996, p. 1.
82. C. Rubel, "Survey," *Marketing News,* July 15, 1996, p. 5.
83. See C. M. Schaninger, J. C. Bourgeois, and W. C. Buss, "French-English Canadian Subcultural Consumption Differences," *Journal of Marketing,* Spring 1985, pp. 82–92.
84. D. Roberts, "Winding Up for the Big Pitch," *Business Week,* October 23, 1995, p. 52; and M. M. A. Khan, "Indian Court Tells Lever to Clean Up Ad Claims," *Advertising Age International,* January 1998, p. 32.
85. M. Haffenberg, "Report from Tokyo," *Marketing News,* May 25, 1998, p. 2.
86. N. Madden, "China's Direct Sales Ban," *Advertising Age,* May 18, 1998, p. 56.
87. See F. Zandpour, C. Chang, and J. Catalano, "Stories, Symbols, and Straight Talk"; C. A. diBenedetto, M. Tamate, and R. Chandran, "Developing Creative Advertising Strategy for the Japanese Marketplace"; J. Ramaprasad and K. Hasegawa, "Creative Strategies in American and Japanese TV Commercials"; and B. D. Cutler, and R. G. Javalgi, "A Cross-Cultural Analysis of the Visual Components of Print Advertising"; all in *Journal of Advertising Research,* January–February 1992, pp. 25–38, 39–48, 59–67, and 71–80; and T. Nevett, "Differences between American and British Television Advertising"; and A. Biswas, J. E. Olsen, and V. Carlet, "A Comparison of Print Advertisements from the United States and France," both in *Journal of Advertising* December 1992, pp. 61–71 and 73–81.
88. I. Galceran and J. Berry, "A New World," *American Demographics,* March 1995, p. 26.
89. R. W. Belk and N. Zhou, "Learning to Want Things," in *Advances in Consumer Research XIV,* ed. M. Wallendorf and P. Anderson (Provo, UT: Association for Consumer Research, 1987), pp. 478–81; N. Dholakia and J. F. Sherry, Jr., "Marketing and Development," in *Research in Marketing IX,* ed. J. N. Sheth (Greenwich, CT: JAI Press, 1987), pp. 119–43; and R. W. Pollay, D. K. Tse, and Z. Y. Wang, "Advertising Propaganda and Value Change in Economic Development," *Journal of Business Research* 20 (1990), pp. 83–95.

WNBA
98
WNBA
1
WNBA
60
WNBA
57

The Changing American Society: Values

What do Nike, American Express, Coca-Cola Co., Kellogg Co., Sears, General Motors, and Lee Jeans have in common? They have all committed to three-year television sponsorships of the Women's National Basketball Association (WNBA). WNBA stars are becoming spokespersons for a wide array of firms. Sheryl Swoopes has appeared for Discover Card and Nike, Rebecca Lobo has been in ads for Reebok, and Cynthia Cooper has done a commercial for Bud Light.

Two new magazines are based on the rapid increase of women as sports participants and spectators: *Conde Nast Sports for Women* and *Sports Illustrated's Women/Sport*. Even more impressive evidence of the acceptance of women's sports is the fact that Mattel recently launched a line of WNBA Barbie dolls.

Women's participation in professional sports is just one sign of perhaps the most significant change in American society in the past 50 years—the changing role of women. For example, a few years ago, a new Barbie doll generated a substantial amount of publicity. Introduced with the theme "We girls can do anything, right, Barbie?" the *Day-to-Night Barbie* represented the career woman. This Barbie had a calculator, business card, credit card, newspaper, and business magazines. *Home & Office,* a dollhouse-like accessory, provided an office desk with a personal computer terminal. However, her business suit was a feminine pink with white accents. Today, Army Barbie (in combat fatigues), Navy Barbie, and Policewoman Barbie look completely natural on the shelf next to Beach Barbie.

In Chapter 2, we discussed how variations in values influence consumption patterns *across* cultures. In this chapter, we will describe how changes in values over time influence consumption patterns *within* cultures. The changing role of women in American society reflects changes in the "masculine/feminine" value described in Chapter 2. Cultural values are not constant. Rather, they evolve over time. Twenty years ago, Barbie dolls were limited to very "traditional" female portrayals. However, America's values and beliefs concerning gender-based behaviors have changed radically, as have gender-related products and marketing activities. Other values are also evolving. In the first section of this chapter, we will examine the evolution of American values in general. Next, we examine three marketing trends that have evolved in response to changing values: green marketing, cause-related marketing, and gender-based marketing.

CHANGES IN AMERICAN CULTURAL VALUES

Observable shifts in behavior, including consumption behavior, often reflect underlying shifts in **cultural values,** *widely held beliefs that affirm what is desirable.* Therefore, it is necessary to understand the underlying *value shifts* in order to understand current and future behavior.[1]

While we discuss American values as though every American has the same values, in fact there is substantial variance in values across individuals and groups. In addition, changes in values tend to occur slowly and unevenly across individuals and groups. Thus, while the popular press often trumpets "the new values of Americans," sound studies of these new or changing values generally indicate less change than is implied by the popular press. For example, a "return to traditional values" is often described as a major value change. However, the percent who regard religion as important or who attend church at least once a month has not increased, while the percent in favor of living together before marriage and in favor of legalized abortions has remained constant or increased.[2]

Likewise, we should not confuse the many changes in how we do things with changes in the values that lead us to do them. The explosion in communications and entertainment technology does not necessarily mean that we suddenly value change, contacts with others, or entertainment more than in the past. It may only signify the availability of more exciting ways to act on existing values. Thus, marketers must carefully analyze value shifts of relevance to their products and markets before developing strategy based on assumed changes.

Figure 3-1 presents our estimate of how American values are changing. These are the same values used to describe different cultures in Chapter 2 (see page 45 for definitions). It must be emphasized that Figure 3-1 is based on the authors' subjective interpretation of the American society. You should feel free to challenge these judgments.

Self-Oriented Values

Traditionally, Americans were active, materialistic, hardworking, religious people who were inclined toward abstinence and postponed gratification. Beginning after the end of World War II and accelerating rapidly during the 1970s and early 1980s, Americans placed increased emphasis on leisure, immediate gratification, and sensual gratification. An examination of American advertising, product features, and personal debt levels indicates that these changes have significantly affected consumers' behaviors and marketing practice. It appears that several of these trends are now reversing direction and moving back toward their traditional positions.

Traditional, Current, and Emerging American Values **FIGURE 3-1**

	Self-Oriented	
Active	ECT*	Passive
Material	T C E	Nonmaterial
Hard work	T C E	Leisure
Postponed gratification	T EC	Immediate gratification
Sensual gratification	C E T	Abstinence
Religious	T E C	Secular
	Environment-Oriented	
Maximum cleanliness	TCE	Minimum cleanliness
Performance	T E C	Status
Tradition	EC T	Change
Risk taking	T E C	Security
Problem solving	T CE	Fatalistic
Admire nature	E C T	Overcome nature
	Other-Oriented	
Individual	T EC	Collective
Limited family	TEC	Extended family
Diversity	EC T	Uniformity
Competition	T C E	Cooperation
Youth	T C E	Age
Masculine	T C E	Feminine

*T = Traditional, E = Emerging, and C = Current.

Religious/Secular America is basically a secular society. That is, a religious group does not control the educational system, government, and political process and most people's daily behaviors are not guided by strict religious guidelines. Nonetheless, 90 percent of all Americans claim a religious affiliation and over 75 percent of women and over 60 percent of the men in a recent survey claimed that religion was an important part of their life. However, less than 40 percent say they attend church with any regularity (a percent that hasn't changed much since 1940). Further, there is evidence that only about half of those who claim to attend church actually do so.[3]

While many Americans may profess to be more religious than their behavior would suggest they are, religious-based beliefs do influence many decisions. For example, the Pax TV network was recently launched as a "family-oriented" network that would not show programs with excessive sex or violence. While one does not have to be religious to prefer less sex and violence on television, many of the programs on the new network, such as "Touched By an Angel," carry religious themes.

In addition, religion is very important to a significant number of Americans.[4] Many of those for whom religion is especially important are conservative in their beliefs. They are quite active politically and as consumers. Their political activism involves attempts to regulate various marketing activities, including products (particularly "sin" products such a liquor, gambling, and pornography) and advertising. Their consumption patterns include both positive consumption (purchasing religious objects and books) and negative consumption (avoiding or boycotting products and companies).

ILLUSTRATION 3-1

American culture values sensual gratification. Products and ads based on this are generally well received.

Courtesy Norwegian Cruise Line.

While conservative religious groups generate substantial publicity and there is some evidence that more Americans are embracing religion, the culture remains relatively secular. We treat religion and its impact on our society in considerable depth in Chapter 5 when we discuss subcultures.

Sensual Gratification/Abstinence Closely tied to America's traditional religious orientation was a belief in the virtue of abstinence. As American society became more secular, sensual gratification became more acceptable. By the 1960s, sensual gratification was an important objective for many consumers. Now, sensual gratification is less acceptable than in the recent past. While it is still perfectly acceptable to consume products for the sensual pleasures they provide, the range of products and occasions for which this is acceptable has narrowed.[5] This has produced some interesting marketing opportunities and challenges. For example, consumption of both frozen nonfat yogurt *and* superpremium, high-fat ice cream has increased, while consumption of regular ice cream has declined. It appears that many consumers are indulging themselves less frequently but more lavishly. Illustration 3-1 contains an ad that appeals to sensual gratification.

Postponed/Immediate Gratification As with abstinence, Americans are no longer as willing to forgo pleasures. While concern about personal debt is high[6] and more consumers are shopping for value and waiting for sales, personal debt, personal bankruptcies, and credit sales continue to climb.

Material/Nonmaterial Americans also retain their material orientation. An outcome of America's focus on materialism is a consumption-driven society. As we will explore later in the text, more Americans work and they work more hours now than in the past.[7] While

Courtesy Rio Suite Hotel & Casino.

ILLUSTRATION 3-2

This resort and its ad are consistent with American values for leisure, activeness, sensual gratification, and risk taking.

the causes of this are complex, in part Americans are trading time and energy for things and services such as cars and travel. Consider the fact that the size of the average American family has dropped sharply over the past 30 years while the size of the average American home has dramatically increased. While there is some evidence that this strong value on material possessions (including the consumption of nonessential services) is moderating, it remains a central part of America's culture.

Hard Work/Leisure As stated above, more Americans are working more now than at any time in recent history. Over 85 percent of all adults agree with the statement "I work very hard most of the time." Partly in response to this increase in work hours, the value placed on work relative to leisure has dropped sharply since 1985. A recent survey found that 30 percent felt that work was of primary importance (down from 48 percent in 1975), 36 percent felt that leisure was of primary importance, and 24 percent rated them equally important.[8] Thus, we have a situation where hard work and leisure are both valued, often by the same people. In response, ads promoting leisure[9] *and* ads stressing hard work are common.[10]

Active/Passive Americans continue to value an active approach to life. While less than a third of all American adults exercise regularly, Americans take an active approach to both leisure and problem-solving activities. Television viewing as a primary form of entertainment has dropped sharply from its peak in the mid-1980s. Instead, using the Internet, cooking, gardening, and a host of other activities are popular. The strength of this orientation is reflected in the tremendous acceptance given Nike's "Just Do It" theme. Illustration 3-2 describes a resort designed for active leisure.

Environment-Oriented Values

Environment-oriented values prescribe a society's relationship with its economic, technical, and physical environments. Americans have traditionally admired cleanliness, change, performance, risk taking, problem solving, and the conquest of nature. While this cluster of values remains basically intact, there are some significant shifts occurring.

Cleanliness Americans have long valued cleanliness, particularly personal hygiene. This strong focus seems to be declining somewhat.[11] Messier homes are more acceptable,[12] though personal hygiene remains very important to most Americans. However, these shifts are minor and do not suggest major changes.

Tradition/Change Americans have always been very receptive to change. *New* has traditionally been taken to mean *improved.* While still very appreciative of change, Americans are now less receptive to change for its own sake. New-product recalls, the expense and the failure of various government programs, and the energy required to keep pace with rapid technological changes are some of the reasons for this shift. Another reason is the aging of the American population. As we will see in the next chapter, the average age of the population is increasing and people are generally somewhat less change-prone as they age. However, as Internet shopping, welfare reforms, and a host of other new products, services, and programs illustrate, Americans are still very accepting of change.

Risk Taking/Security Our risk-taking orientation seems to have changed somewhat over time. There was an increased emphasis on security during the period from 1930 through the mid-1980s. This attitude was a response to the tremendous upheavals and uncertainties caused by the Depression, World War II, and the Cold War. However, risk taking remains highly valued and is gaining appreciation as we look to entrepreneurs for economic growth and to smaller firms and self-employment to obtain desired lifestyles.

Problem Solving/Fatalistic Americans take great pride in being problem solvers. By and large, Americans believe that virtually anything can be fixed given sufficient time and effort. Marketers introduce thousands of new products each year with the theme that they will solve a problem better than existing products will. We will examine the results of this value later in this chapter in the sections on green marketing and cause marketing.

Admire/Overcome Nature Traditionally, nature was viewed as an obstacle. We attempted to bend nature to fit our desires without realizing the negative consequences this could have for both nature and humanity. This attitude has shifted dramatically over the past 30 years.

Recent surveys report that nearly 80 percent of the public is concerned about the condition of the environment. One survey found that 64 percent would pay more for environmentally sound grocery products, 76 percent would boycott manufacturers of polluting products, and 81 percent would sacrifice some convenience to save natural resources.[13] Another poll found over 90 percent stating they would (1) make a special effort to buy products from companies that protect the environment, (2) give up some convenience for environmentally safer products or packaging, and (3) pay more for such products.[14] These values are being translated into actions, with over half of all Americans now classified as environmentally active.[15] Firms that convince these consumers that their products are environmentally sound can reap huge rewards. Tom's of Maine markets environmentally sound personal care products (see Illustration 3-3). Its products command a 20 to 50 percent price premium and its sales grew 25 percent from 1995 to 1997! According to an

Courtesy Tom's of Maine, Inc.

ILLUSTRATION 3-3

Americans are increasingly concerned about the environment. Firms that convince Americans that their practices are as environmentally sound as possible tend to enjoy success.

executive, the firm gains additional advantages as well:

> The environmental and social responsibility policies are a barrier to competitive advances. Even a competitor with much greater resources cannot just replicate our formula and expect to take our market share. Our corporate practices add a richness and depth to our product appeal that creates an unusually strong brand loyalty.[16]

Concerns in Canada are similar if somewhat less intense than in America.[17] We describe the marketing response to this value in the section of this chapter on green marketing.

Performance/Status Americans are shifting back to a focus on performance rather than status. While consumers are still willing to purchase "status" brands, these brands must provide style and functionality in addition to the prestige of the name. This has led to substantial increases in sales at various types of discount stores and for retailer and other private-label brands.[18] For example, Gap Inc. found that many of its Gap stores featuring higher priced, status items were struggling. In 1993, 48 of them were converted into *Old Navy* stores, which feature lower-cost, quality clothing. Old Navy presents "shopping as theatre, with big stores, low prices, loud music, concrete floors, exposed pipes, and whimsical displays."[19] Old Navy stores are now a major, national chain.

Procter & Gamble has responded to the consumer's desire for quality performance at a modest price by completely altering its pricing and promotion strategy away from periodic discounts and coupons toward "everyday low prices." It is also eliminating unpopular sizes, flavors, and other variants of its products to make it easier for consumers to find what they want as well as to reduce its costs. For example, P&G has reduced the number of items in its hair care line by almost half in recent years, and yet its market share increased by over 15 percent.[20] Other marketers are following suit.

Other-Oriented Values

Other-oriented values reflect a society's view of the appropriate relationships between individuals and groups within that society. Historically, America was an individualistic, competitive, masculine, youth, limited family, and uniformity-oriented society. Several aspects of this orientation are undergoing change.

Individual/Collective A strong emphasis on individualism is one of the defining characteristics of American society. Watch any American hit movie. The leading character will virtually always behave as an individual, often despite pressures to compromise to the "group." Americans believe in "doing your own thing." Even the "uniform" that each generation of teenagers invents for itself allows ample room for individual expression. This value affects incentive systems for salespeople, advertising themes, and product design.[21]

Diversity/Uniformity While American culture has always valued individualism, it has also valued a degree of uniformity, particularly with respect to groups. America was founded in part by people seeking religious freedom or fleeing from various forms of persecution. The Constitution and many laws seek to protect diverse religions, political beliefs, and so forth. Nonetheless, Americans historically insisted that immigrants quickly adopt the language, dress, values, and many other aspects of the majority. Those who did not were often subject to various forms of discrimination.

Beginning after World War II and accelerating since the 1960s, Americans have increasingly valued diversity. The cultural backgrounds of immigrant groups are celebrated by both the immigrants and the larger community. While far from free from racial, religious, ethnic, or class prejudice, American culture is evolving toward valuing diversity more than uniformity. The Toyota ad shown in Illustration 3-4 reflects the positive view of diversity held by most Americans.

We examine one aspect of America's increasing acceptance of diversity—marketing to gay consumers—in the marketing strategy section of this chapter.

Limited/Extended Family Beginning in the 1500s, America became a nation of immigrants as settlers from Europe and elsewhere replaced the Native American population. These immigrants left their extended families behind. As America grew, the westward movement produced a similar phenomenon. Even today, frequent geographic moves and continued immigration as well as differential rates of social mobility mean that few children grow up in close interaction with aunts, uncles, cousins, nieces, or nephews. It is also common for children to leave their hometowns and parents once they begin their own careers. The physical separation of traditional family members often reduces the sense of family among those members. This, in turn, reduces the impact that the family has on the individual.

This is not to say that Americans do not love their family members or that how an American is raised does not influence the person for life. Rather, it means that a 35-year-old American is unlikely to have a cousin who would feel obligated to respond positively to a loan request (this is not the case in many other cultures). Likewise, this 35-year-old would be unlikely to have one or more cousins, aunts, or nephews live with him or her for an extended time period.

Youth/Age Traditionally, age has been highly valued in almost all cultures. Older people were considered wiser than young people and were, therefore, looked to as models and leaders. This has never been true in American culture, probably because transforming a wilderness into a new type of producing nation required characteristics such as physical strength, stamina, youthful vigor, and imagination. This value on youth continued as we

Courtesy Toyota Motor Sales, U.S.A., Inc.; agency Saatchi & Saatchi/L.A.

ILLUSTRATION 3-4

Americans increasingly value diversity. As a result, firms develop programs that recognize and honor the diverse nature of American society.

became an industrial nation. Since World War II, it has increased to such an extent that products such as cars, clothing, cosmetics, and hairstyles seem designed for and sold only to the young! For example, while only about 20 percent of the population is between 16 to 30 years of age, a study found that almost 40 percent of American print ads featured models that appeared to be in this age range.[22]

However, there is a slow reversal of this value on youth. Because of their increasing numbers and disposable income, older citizens have developed political and economic clout and are beginning to use it. There are cosmetics, medicines, and hair care products being marketed specifically to older consumers. Middle-aged consumers now constitute the largest single market segment. As we will see in the next chapter, this segment has lifestyles distinct from the youth markets.

Competition/Cooperation America has long been a competitive society, and this value remains firmly entrenched. It is reflected in our social, political, and economic systems. We reward particularly successful competitors in business, entertainment, and sports with staggering levels of financial compensation. While there is increased focus on cooperation and teamwork in schools and businesses, this is generally done so that the team or group can outperform some other team or group. It is no wonder that America was one of the first countries to allow comparative advertising.

Masculine/Feminine American society, like most others, has reflected a very masculine orientation for a long time. This chapter's opening story indicates how this orientation is changing. The marketing implications resulting from changes in this value are discussed in detail in the marketing strategy section of this chapter.

MARKETING STRATEGY AND VALUES

We have examined a number of marketing implications associated with values and changes in values. It is critical that all aspects of the firm's marketing mix be consistent with the value system of its target market. Different groups will have different value systems and marketers must adjust their activities to the values of their target group. Marketers must also change their marketing mix as the value systems of their target groups evolve. Fortunately, values generally change slowly. Firms will have time to allow their practices to evolve if they monitor customer values. Firms can conduct their own monitoring surveys or subscribe to one of the many commercial surveys that measure values. However, caution should be used in responding to popular press declarations of major value shifts.

We will now examine four marketing responses to evolving American values: green marketing, cause-related marketing, marketing to gay consumers, and gender-based marketing.

Green Marketing

Marketers have responded to Americans' increasing concern for the environment with an approach called **green marketing.** Green marketing generally involves: (1) producing products whose production, use, or disposal is less harmful to the environment than the traditional versions of the product, (2) developing products that have a positive impact on the environment, or (3) tying the purchase of a product to an environmental organization or event. Examples include the following:

- With the cooperation of software producers, GreenDisk collects diskettes from obsolete boxes of software, reformats them, packages them in funky, low-tech packaging, and sells them. In 1997, they sold 60 million disks that would have otherwise gone into landfills and saved the materials and energy it would have required to produce 60 million new disks.
- Wal-Mart has launched an "eco-store." The store carries Wal-Mart's usual merchandise mix but highlights environmentally superior products. Recycling is the theme. The store recycles much of its own waste and provides recycling services for its customers. The store itself is designed to be energy efficient and uses recycled materials both in its construction and in the shopping bags it provides for consumers.
- Organic fertilizers, such as those produced by Ringer Corp., can have a positive effect on the environment. Organic fertilizers now have a 10 percent market share despite costing about twice as much as chemical fertilizers. The Church & Dwight Company, Inc., developed sodium bicarbonate products to help purify wastewater and to restore lakes damaged by acid rain.
- Americans also spend hundreds of millions of dollars on the environment through their support of environmental groups such as the Nature Conservancy, the National Audubon Society, the National Park Foundation, and Greenpeace.
- Chevrolet's *Geo* plants and cares for a tree in the buyer's name when a Geo is purchased. Since a major attribute of the Geo is its fuel efficiency, the environmental tie-in makes sense to consumers and works effectively. Over 500,000 trees have been planted in this campaign.
- Heinz changed the formula of its squeezable plastic ketchup containers to make them more readily recyclable. Church & Dwight eliminated the plastic overwrap and converted to 100 percent recycled paperboard boxes for its Arm & Hammer *Carpet Deodorizer.*

Courtesy Dixon Ticonderoga Company.

ILLUSTRATION 3-5

Almost 10 percent of new products introduced in America are "green" products. These new crayons are made from soybeans rather than petroleum.

- Estée Lauder launched, under the *Origins* label, a complete line of cosmetics that are made of natural ingredients, are not tested on animals, and are packaged in recyclable containers.
- Canon USA gives the Nature Conservancy 50 cents for each laser-printer toner container that is returned for recycling. This is producing over $750,000 for the Conservancy annually.
- Prang Crayons are made from soybeans rather than petroleum-based wax (see Illustration 3-5).

Concern with the environment is not a unidimensional issue. Individual and environmental organizations often focus on a subset of five concerns: (1) solid waste disposal, (2) air/water pollution, (3) resource depletion, (4) chemical additives, or (5) harm to nature.[23]

Marketers need to be cautious when making environmental claims. Those most concerned with the environment are opinion leaders who are active shoppers. These people carefully evaluate advertising claims and are skeptical about them.[24] While specific environmental claims enhance consumers' attitudes toward the product and advertiser, vague environmental claims have a negative impact.[25] Consumers consider a specific environmental claim to be one that (1) provides detailed, useful information, (2) indicates that the product has environmental benefits superior to competing products, and (3) shows a clear improvement to the environment.[26]

As concern for the environment grew throughout the 1980s and into the 1990s, many firms began to improve their products and processes relative to the environment and to advertise those improvements. Unfortunately, different marketers used the same claims, such as *environmentally friendly* or *environmentally safe,* to refer to vastly differing performance levels. Further, some firms made green claims that were misleading if not completely false. For example, some firms made claims such as "Now completely phosphorus free!" when they had contained only a trace amount of phosphorus before. While the claim is true, the elimination of trace amounts of phosphorus from the product in question had no beneficial environmental impact.

Such contradictory and misleading claims produced cynicism among many consumers for all green claims and a variety of conflicting state and federal government regulations concerning green claims. This, in turn, caused reputable firms to drop environment claims and may well have reduced the impetus to produce environmentally sound products. The primary problem from the marketers' standpoint was the impossibility (or high cost) of complying with a multitude of complex and conflicting state and federal regulations.

To enable consumers to receive the information they need to make environmentally sound choices and to allow marketers to benefit from their efforts to develop environmentally sound products, the Federal Trade Commission (FTC) recently issued a set of voluntary guidelines for green claims. While neither the states nor the firms have to follow the guidelines, it appears that state and federal agencies will not prosecute firms within the guidelines and will prosecute those who fall outside them. The general guidelines include dozens of examples of acceptable and unacceptable practices to guide marketers, including the following:

- A "recycled" label on a soft-drink bottle made from recycled material wouldn't be considered misleading even if the cap isn't made from recycled material.
- An ad touting a package as having "50 percent more recycled content than before" could be misleading if the recycled content had increased from 2 to 3 percent.
- An ad calling a trash bag "recyclable" without qualification would be deemed misleading because bags aren't ordinarily separated from other trash at landfills or incinerators.
- An ad touting a shampoo bottle as containing "20 percent more recycled content" would be considered misleading if it didn't say whether the product is being compared with a rival or the product's previous container.
- Labels promoting products as "environmentally safe" or "environmentally friendly" must specify what portion of the product is being referred to; otherwise, they would be deceptive.
- A shampoo advertised as "biodegradable" without qualification wouldn't be deceptive if the marketer has competent and reliable scientific support showing it will decompose in a short time.[27]

Green marketing is complex. Environmental concerns are only one criteria consumers use in making purchase decisions.[28] For example, over half those interviewed in a recent survey expressed concern about the level of pesticide residue found in food products but less than one in five looked for food grown in a pesticide-free manner.[29] Thus, firms must balance concern for the environment with other consumer expectations and financial constraints.

Although using recycled materials generally elicits a positive response from consumers,[30] other environmentally sound actions may not work as well. For example, McDonald's and other chains were widely criticized for using polystyrene hamburger containers. However, they had originally shifted to this product in part in response to environmental concerns. The polystyrene container actually uses 30 percent less energy to produce than does coated paper or paperboard, and their manufacture results in 40 percent less air pollution and 42 percent less water pollution.[31] However, the solid waste problem they create is much more visible to consumers than the air pollution and energy depletion areas in which they create great savings. *Should a firm like McDonald's spend millions to educate a skeptical public about polystyrene or should it use coated paper?* In fact, McDonald's is currently testing a compostable "Earth Shell" to replace both paper and polystyrene.

There is a conflict between conservation and most business strategies. The basic thrust of environmentalism is the "three Rs"—*reduce, reuse, recycle.* Two of the three core thrusts of the environmental movement conflict with the objective of most businesses, which is growth in sales and profits. This conflict between producing and conserving

The Ford Excursion versus the Environment

Ford's incoming chairman, William Ford, Jr., has pledged that going green will be Ford's priority in the future—"The environment will become like quality. It's a prism through which we will look when we make product decisions."

Despite Ford's environment concerns, sport-utility vehicles (SUVs), which consume significantly more gas and other resources than standard cars, are critical to the company's success. In 1997, SUVs were nearly 20 percent of its sales and contributed $5 billion in pretax earnings (almost 60 percent of the total). Now, Ford is launching a super SUV, the Ford Excursion. This vehicle will be 230 inches long (10 inches longer than the longest passenger vehicle now on the road) and will weigh nearly three tons. The Sierra Club has labeled it the "Ford Valdez" and suggested "Have you driven a tanker lately" for an advertising slogan. The Excursion is so large that the government does not classify it as a "light vehicle," which excludes it from federal fuel economy standards. At a price of around $50,000 Ford may make as much as $20,000 on each Excursion and sales could easily exceed 50,000 per year!

Ford didn't just decide to build a giant SUV and hope it would sell. Consumer demand has pushed sales of its other SUVs to the point where Ford has trouble supplying them and demand has been particularly strong for the larger models. As one dealer says, "There is a ready market of bigger-is-better SUV buyers." William Ford, Jr., explains his dilemma:

> It's a delicate balance between what the customer wants and being completely environmentally driven. You can make a completely clean vehicle, but if it sits unsold on the dealer's lot it's not helping the environment, either. We just have to make these vehicles cleaner and cleaner every year.

Critical Thinking Questions

1. Why is there so much demand for SUVs, which are not environmentally friendly, when American values strongly support environmental protection?
2. How should a company such as Ford balance the ethics of providing environmentally sound products with the need to provide consumers with the products they desire in order to remain profitable?

Source: K. Naughton, "Ford's Green Dilemma," *Business Week*, December 21, 1998, pp. 96–97.

Consumer Insight 3-1

mirrors the conflict between the value Americans place on the environment and their materialistic orientation. This same conflict exists in most developed and many developing nations. How it is resolved will have major consequences for the economic and environmental health of the next generation.[32] Consumer Insight 3-1 describes how this conflict is playing out at Ford Motor Co.

Cause-Related Marketing

The term *cause marketing* is sometimes used interchangeably with *social marketing* to refer to the application of marketing principles and tactics to advance a cause such as a charity (United Way), an ideology (environmental protection), or an activity (breast cancer exams). Social marketing differs from traditional marketing in the intangible and abstract nature of the "product" and in the absence of a profit motive. At one extreme, such as a health-related campaign, there are potential direct benefits to the individual. However, in general, the benefits to the individual are very indirect (a better society in which to live). Often, the benefit is purely or primarily emotional.[33] Individuals are requested to change beliefs or behaviors or provide funds because it is "the right thing to do" and you will "feel good" or "be a better person" because of it.

Examine the two ads in Illustration 3-6. What are the benefits being promised to those who respond? Why would an individual "buy" one of these "products"? Why do most individuals fail to "purchase" the "products" advertised in these ads?

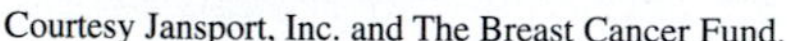
Courtesy Jansport, Inc. and The Breast Cancer Fund.

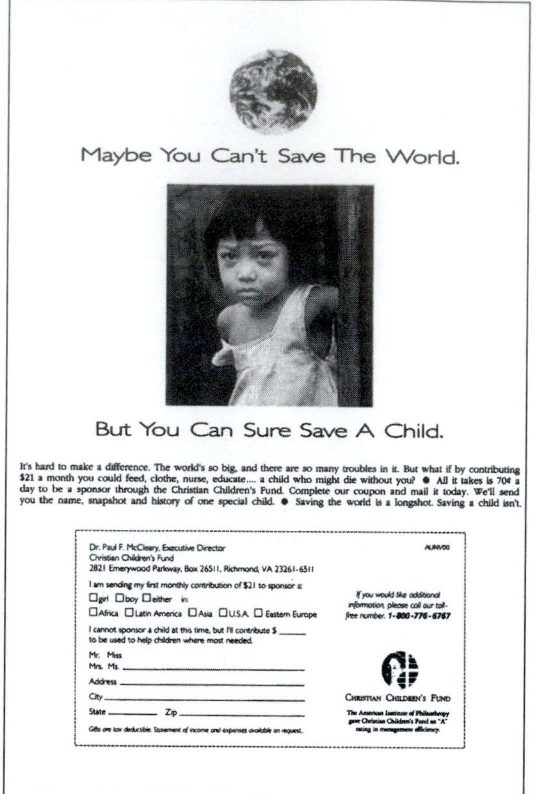

Courtesy Christian Children's Fund.

ILLUSTRATION 3-6

The Christian Children's ad promotes a benefit to the world community without advancing the profits or image of a commercial firm. It is an example of social marketing. The Jansport ad represents cause-related marketing as it benefits a cause and enhances the image and sales of a commercial firm.

As noted in Chapter 1, social marketing is marketing done to enhance the welfare of individuals or society without direct benefit to a firm. In contrast, cause marketing or **cause-related marketing (CRM)** is *marketing that ties a company and its products to an issue or cause with the goal of improving sales and/or corporate image while providing benefits to the cause.*[34] Companies associate with causes to create long-term relationships with their customers, building corporate and brand equity that should eventually lead to increased sales.[35] The Christian Children's Fund in Illustration 3-6 is an example of social marketing, as it promotes a benefit to the world community without advancing the profits or image of a commercial firm. The Jansport ad in Illustration 3-6 is an example of cause-related marketing. It attempts to benefit a cause *and* to enhance the image and sales of a commercial firm.

The foundation of cause-related marketing is marketing to consumers' values, and it is effective. Consider the following results, conclusions, and recommendations from a national survey of Americans:

- 61 percent believe that CRM is a good way to solve social problems.
- 64 percent believe it should be a standard business practice.
- 85 percent believe it improves a product or firm's image.
- 62 percent believe that corporate commitment to a cause should be for more than a year.
- 66 percent are likely to switch brands based on CRM when price and quality are equal.
- 62 percent are likely to switch stores based on CRM when price and quality are equal.

Cause-Related Marketing at Avon

Consumer Insight 3-2

Joanne Mazurki was put in charge of linking the Avon name to a woman's issue or a family issue. "We know that consumers will choose to buy from a company that stands for something and that serves their needs, and our customer's needs are more than just lipstick. [This is] . . . a sound business judgment because it enhances our image with current and potential customers and differentiates us from our competitors in the cosmetics industry."

Mazurki selected breast cancer awareness as Avon's issue in America. The logic was simple. Most of Avon's customers and its 415,000 U.S. sales representatives are female. Research showed that breast cancer had reached epidemic proportions and was women's number one health concern. Fifty-nine percent of women were not following the guidelines for early detection, and education and access to testing were underfunded by both the government and private sector.

Avon made a five-year commitment to the cause. It created pink enameled breast cancer awareness ribbons to be distributed by its 2,000-member in-store sales force as well as its outside sales representatives. Avon projected selling 6 million of the ribbons at $2 each, with all proceeds going to breast cancer education and early detection programs.

According to Mazurki, "Passion branding [CRM] goes beyond a marketing program. It becomes an umbrella for the kind of company you are and the kind of relationship you have with your customers and your sales reps. You can't overestimate the value of a program like this in motivating your sales force."

Avon supports breast cancer education and testing in the United States and Britain, where breast cancer is a major problem. In Malaysia, it focuses on violence against women, in China, child nourishment, and in Thailand, AIDS. In each country, it matches its cause with the concerns of its customers and sales representatives.

Critical Thinking Questions

1. What ethical issues do cause-related marketing efforts such as this raise?
2. Evaluate Avon's cause-related marketing program from both Avon's and the supported cause's perspective.

Source: N. Arnott, "Marketing with a Passion," *Sales & Marketing Management,* January 1994, pp. 64–71; and G. Smith, "Are Good Causes Good Marketing?" *Business Week,* March 21, 1994, p. 64.

- Influentials (the 10 percent of the population who are socially active opinion and group leaders) are much more favorable toward and influenced by CRM than the general population. Upscale individuals (income, education, and/or occupation) are more favorable than are other groups.[36]

While CRM is clearly effective, particularly with upscale customers and opinion leaders, it also faces considerable skepticism. A majority of consumers doubt firms' interest in the causes and attribute their entire motivation to increased sales or image. The best defense against this type of skepticism is long-term, concrete actions focused on providing significant benefits to a broadly defined cause rather than a specific group or charity.[37] Consumer Insight 3-2 provides a glimpse of the logic and process Avon used as it moved to a successful cause-related marketing campaign.

Other examples of CRM include the following:

- Lee Apparel is sponsoring a National Denim Day in which companies allow employees to wear denim to work that day in exchange for a $5 contribution to the Susan G. Komen Breast Cancer Foundation.
- During the last quarter of the year, American Express donated 2 cents per transaction to the antihunger organization Share Our Strength. The heavily advertised campaign produced $5 million for the organization and helped increase the firm's charge volume by over 9 percent.
- Midas launched a project called Project Baby Safe. Drivers who purchase a $42 *Century 1000 STE* baby car seat get a certificate worth that amount in Midas services.

- Members Only spends its entire promotion budget on social issues, primarily drug abuse. In most of its television commercials, the company's name appears only as a tagline at the end of the social message.

Cause-related marketing is often effective because it is consistent with several strongly held American values. A common theme in most CRM programs is the presentation of a problem such as breast cancer, AIDS, or pollution and an action that individuals can take to help solve the problem. This theme ties directly into America's strong problem-solving orientation. It is also consistent with a focus on individualism—CRM programs tend to encourage individuals to take individual actions that can contribute directly to the solution of the problem. The specific cause being promoted often taps other cultural or individually held values or concerns.

Marketing to Gay Consumers

As Americans have increasingly embraced ethnic, religious, and racial diversity, marketers have responded by developing marketing programs targeting a wide array of diverse groups. One of the last groups to gain public acceptance is the gay and lesbian community (and this acceptance is still far from complete).[38] In this section, we will follow the convention of the business press and refer to gay and lesbian consumers as the gay market.

Size estimates of the number of people in the gay market are suspect due to methodological and response bias concerns in surveys on this topic. It is generally assumed that the actual population size will be understated in surveys. Many gays do not want to be categorized based solely on this dimension of their identity, and there are concerns about social taboos, religious censure, legal statutes, and the real or perceived risk of jeopardizing jobs, reputations, and family situations. Several relatively large-scale surveys produced the following population estimates (percent of the adult population):[39]

	Gay Male	*Lesbian*	*Gay/ Homosexual/ Lesbian*
1993 Janus Report	9%	5%	
1993 Yankelovich Monitor			5.7%
1994 *Parade* Magazine Survey	3	1	
1994 Sex in America	2.8	1.4	

The gay market is generally considered to be wealthier and in higher status occupations than the general population. Again, measurement issues are a major concern. Most surveys that collect data on the demographic characteristics of the gay market are actually surveys of subscribers to gay publications who may not represent the overall gay population. For example, a 1997 study of readers of the National Gay Newspaper Guild's publications found them to be 12 times more likely to be in a professional job and twice as likely to own a second home or individual stocks as the average American. The $47,000 average income of the 750,000 readers represents a $35 billion market.[40] However, two 1998 studies found average gay *household* income to be only slightly above the U.S. average.[41]

While the exact dimensions of the gay market remain unclear, many firms have concluded that it represents a significantly attractive market to pursue aggressively. For example, American Express recently spent $250,000 on a study of this market before committing to additional marketing effort. Likewise, Subaru conducted a major study before deciding the market warranted a special effort.[42]

Any firm that desires to capture the loyalty of members of the gay community must have internal policies that do not discriminate against gay employees. Without such policies and practices, companies are unlikely to receive a positive response to advertising appeals. In addition to having appropriate internal policies, firms face a number of decisions in approaching this market.

- Does the product need to be modified in any way to meet the needs of this market?
- Should we advertise in gay-oriented media using our standard ads?
- Should we advertise in gay media using ads with gay themes?
- To what extent should we be involved in gay community activities?
- Should our major media ads include ads with gay themes?

Product Issues With the exception of a few areas, the lifestyles of gay consumers do not differ sufficiently from other consumers to require product modifications. United Airlines, Coors, Barnes & Noble, and Procter & Gamble have programs that target the gay market using their standard products. However, IBM recently introduced a special WorkPad palm computer loaded with gay travel information software.

One area in which standard products do frequently require alteration is financial services. As the director of segment marketing for American Express explains:

> Often, gay couples are very concerned about issues like Social Security benefits and estate planning, since same-sex marriages often are not recognized under the law.[43]

The following ad content reflects one of American Express's product offerings targeting the gay market.

> When you're ready to plan a future together, who can you trust to understand the financial challenges that gay men and lesbians face?
>
> At American Express Financial Advisors we offer Domestic Partner Planning services that can help you address issues like protecting assets from unnecessary taxation and getting around restrictions placed on unmarried couples. We offer you the expertise and insight you need to make smart decisions.

Hartford Financial Services developed Diverse Household Auto Insurance, which offers discounts to both heterosexual and gay couples. In a humorous ad, two blue cars are shown side-by-side with the caption: *The Hartford offers auto insurance discounts to gay couples.* Beneath these cars are two side-by-side pink cars with the caption: *We also offer discounts to lesbian couples.* At the bottom of the ad, a blue and a pink car are side-by-side and have the caption: *Heck, we even offer discounts to heterosexual couples. (Not that there's anything wrong with that.)*

Communication Issues There are a large number of gay-oriented media in the United States and Canada. Rivendell Marketing Co. is a national advertising representative for 185 such publications, with a combined circulation of 3.5 million. The National Gay Newspaper Guild has 12 publications with a readership of over 750,000. There are a number of gay-oriented magazines, with *Out* (circulation 140,000) the largest. Advertising expenditures in gay-oriented print media more than doubled from 1994 to 1998.

Compared to the general population, gays are heavy Web subscribers (52 percent), and a number of gay Web sites are capitalizing on this fact.[44] PlanetOut is one of the more successful. It has more than 500,000 unique monthly visitors. American Airlines, Citibank, Pfizer, and Starbucks are among the firms that advertise on the site.

Since most products don't require alteration for the gay market, most firms initially approach the market by placing one of their standard ads in gay-oriented media. Anheuser-Busch, Miller Brewing, Bailey's Original Irish Cream, and American Express are among the firms that first approached this market with standard ads and then developed gay-themed ads.

According to one expert in this area:

> Gay people want to support companies that reach out to them in a way that is tasteful and shows that they're included in the company's message.[45]

In order to be inclusive and clearly reach out to the gay community, firms are increasingly creating ads specifically for this market. The ads may merely portray a gay couple instead of a heterosexual couple in a standard ad. Or, the entire ad may contain a gay theme. Baileys developed a gay-focused ad for its limited-edition coffee cups (used to promote Baileys and coffee). The cups, which are sold in sets of two, are designed like a face with one eye winking. The ad the firm ran in *Out* showed a picture of the two cups side-by-side with the caption: *Our limited-edition coffee cups are available nationwide, though only recognized as a set in Hawaii* (a play on the fact that, at that time, Hawaii was the only state in the United States to recognize same-sex marriages).

In addition to advertising in gay media, support of gay community events such as Gay Pride week is another avenue firms use in approaching this market. Tanqueray gin has sponsored a number of events to raise funds for AIDS programs, which is an area of great concern of the gay community.

It has been estimated that slightly more than a fourth of the gay community does not use gay-oriented media. Those who do also spend considerable time using standard media, particularly television. However, very few firms have used ads with gay themes in standard mass media. The Hartford ad described earlier is being used on billboards and some local newspapers. This was unusual enough to generate an article in *Advertising Age* entitled "Insurer places gay-themed ads in mainstream media." Concern about "backlash" from that portion of the market that does not accept the gay community as well as a desire to have ads that directly appeal to the largest number of viewers are the primary reasons for the lack of gay-themed ads in mainstream media.

Gender-Based Marketing

Until recently, the prevailing stereotype of an automobile purchase involved a male making the purchase alone. If accompanied by his wife or girlfriend, she only offered suggestions concerning color and interior features.

Today, research indicates that women influence 80 percent of all automobile purchases, buy 26 percent of all new trucks and over half of all new cars, and are the predominant buyers of many models, including Nissan *Pulsars,* Cadillac *Cimarrons,* Toyota *SR5s*, Pontiac *Fieros,* Ford *Escort EXPs*, and all Saturn models.[46] Marketers who have clung to the outdated stereotype by either ignoring women purchasers or by focusing on excessively "feminine" themes have lost substantial sales opportunities. For example, one of Chevrolet's first ads aimed at women backfired because it contained limited product feature information but showed lots of pinks and lavenders. Likewise, Chrysler failed with a model named "La Femme" that was designed for the stereotyped woman of yesterday.

Although surveys of American consumers consistently indicate that women want the same basic features in a car as males do, there are subtle differences. For example, many automobiles have radios, heaters, and other accessories that are difficult to operate with long fingernails. Likewise, women find unrealistic role portrayals in automobile advertising offensive and are frequently frustrated in their attempts to deal with auto sales personnel who don't treat them seriously. They are also more attentive to the showroom environment. Examples of the response of automobile manufacturers and others to the changing role of

Courtesy Pontiac GMC.

ILLUSTRATION 3-7

Women are now the dominant buyers of many types of automobiles. GMC is expending considerable effort to position its new sport-utility vehicle as being appropriate for women.

women include the following:

- An ad for the Pontiac *Grand Am* shows a young woman who brings her brother with her when she buys a car. His role is to help her pick the color.
- Four of the five introductory ads for GMC's sport-utility vehicle featured women. One illustrates the ease with which a woman executive in a suit can enter the vehicle due to its lower entry step. Illustration 3-7 shows one of these ads.
- Sixty percent of the buyers of the new Mercury Mountaineer sport-utility vehicle are expected to be women. It is being promoted on the Women's Open golf tournament and in magazines such as *Mirabella* and *Vanity Fair.*
- *Good Housekeeping* is now offering a "Women's Automobile Satisfaction Award" to brands that score 5 percent or more above the average satisfaction rating among female owners.
- *Elle* recently launched an "Auto Buyers Guide for Women" service on its Web site (www.elle.com).

The terms *sex* and **gender** are used interchangeably to refer to *whether a person is biologically a male or female.* ***Gender identity*** refers to the traits of *femininity* (expressive traits such as tenderness and compassion) and *masculinity* (instrumental traits such as aggressiveness and dominance). These traits represent the ends of a continuum, and individuals have varying levels of each trait, with biological males tending to be toward the masculine end of the continuum and biological females toward the feminine end.[47]

Gender roles are *the behaviors considered appropriate for males and females in a given society.* As the previous discussion of automobile purchasing indicates, gender roles in America have undergone massive changes over the past 25 years. The general nature of this shift has been for behaviors previously considered appropriate primarily for men to be acceptable for women, too.[48]

Gender roles are ascribed roles. An **ascribed role** is based on *an attribute over which the individual has little or no control.* This can be contrasted with **achievement roles,** which are based on *performance criteria over which the individual has some degree of control.* Individuals can, within limits, select their occupation (achievement role), but they cannot generally determine their gender (ascribed role).

Researchers find it useful to categorize women into **traditional** or **modern gender orientations** based on their preference for one or the other of two contrasting lifestyles:

- *Traditional.* A marriage with the husband assuming the responsibility for providing for the family and the wife running the house and taking care of the children.
- *Modern.* A marriage where husband and wife share responsibilities. Both work, and they share homemaking and child care responsibilities.

In a 1977 survey, 65 percent of the adult respondents expressed a preference for a traditional lifestyle. By 1994, this figure had dropped to less than 40 percent. While 69 percent of Americans over 60 and 44 percent of those between 45 and 60 prefer the traditional lifestyle, only 30 percent of those under 45 prefer it. In addition to varying by age, preference for a traditional lifestyle varies with geographic region (it is lowest on the West Coast) and education (it decreases as education level increases).[49]

While males and females both express strong preferences for the modern lifestyle as a general concept, attitudes and behaviors toward specific aspects of that lifestyle remain very conservative. For example, a majority of both sexes believes that "a woman with young children should not work outside the home". Studies consistently find that many men resent and resist housework even if their spouses are employed. The following quote illustrates the struggle that this can produce:

> I told him (husband), "I don't like the example. I don't want the boys to see mommy does the housework and daddy doesn't do it." I even told him I wanted him to cook supper at least one night a week. Not only would it give me a break from cooking supper but the kids would see daddy doing it. But he cooked spaghetti every single Saturday night for months. I mean there wasn't even a salad with it, it was just a blob. (Laughs.) I think he didn't like cooking and I think he didn't like me asking him to do it, and this was his way of doing it but not doing it.[50]

Thus, we find a pattern typical of a changing value: growing acceptance of the change, but not for all aspects of it, and substantial resistance to the new behaviors from the more traditional groups or those who stand to lose as the new value is accepted.

This pattern of conflict exists not only between groups within the society but within individuals who are torn between the two orientations. Consider the following quote from a 41-year-old woman with four children who is a social worker:

> Sometimes I go through guilt trips because I work. I think women are getting out of this cycle, but I am still of the school that feels women's responsibilities are to be mothers and to be homemakers. Unfortunately, it's not changing for me. I hope it's changing for my children . . . but I'm of the generation where a lot of us still carry those guilt feelings around if your family can't come home to homemade bread and a hot meal every night. I know that's unrealistic, but, I still sort of feel like that's my responsibility.[51]

Social change is often painful for the individuals and groups involved.

As we have seen, women have a variety of role options and a range of attitudes concerning their gender. The ads in Illustration 3-8 reflect two sharply contrasting views of the

Courtesy Giant Bicycle, Inc.

Courtesy IVEX Personal Care Products Group.

ILLUSTRATION 3-8

Women fulfill a multitude of roles today and have a wide range of attitudes about their role in society. These two ads take radically different approaches to their portrayal of women and women's attitudes.

female role. In the following sections, we examine some of the marketing implications of the changing role of women in American society.

Market Segmentation Neither the women's nor the men's market is as homogeneous as it once was. At least four significant female market segments exist.[52]

1. *Traditional housewife.* Generally married. Prefers to stay at home. Very home- and family-centered. Desires to please husband and/or children. Seeks satisfaction and meaning from household and family maintenance as well as volunteer activities. Experiences strong pressure to work outside the home and is well aware of forgone income opportunity. Feels supported by family and is generally content with role.
2. *Trapped housewife.* Generally married. Would prefer to work, but stays at home due to young children, lack of outside opportunities, or family pressure. Seeks satisfaction and meaning outside the home. Does not enjoy most household chores. Has mixed feelings about current status and is concerned about lost opportunities.
3. *Trapped working woman.* Married or single. Would prefer to stay at home, but works for economic necessity or social/family pressure. Does not derive satisfaction or meaning from employment. Enjoys most household activities, but is frustrated by lack of time. Feels conflict about her role, particularly if younger children are home. Resents missed opportunities for family, volunteer, and social activities. Is proud of financial contribution to family.
4. *Career working woman.* Married or single. Prefers to work. Derives satisfaction and meaning from employment rather than, or in addition to, home and family. Experiences some conflict over her role if younger children are at home, but is generally content. Views home maintenance as a necessary evil. Feels pressed for time.

While the above descriptions are oversimplified, they indicate the diverse nature of the adult female population. However, it should be noted that this diversity is declining. With two-thirds of American women preferring to work and 75 percent of this group employed, the career working woman category now contains half of all adult women (compared to 30 percent in 1977).[53] Nonetheless, the other segments are still sizable and each has somewhat different needs and communications requirements.

Product Strategy

The Gillette Company had traditionally focused on the men's market. Razors were designed by and for men. While all major razor manufacturers had long marketed "women's razors," most were merely slight variations on razors designed primarily for men. According to a Gillette executive, "the general approach was to take a man's razor, change the handle a bit, color it pink, and say, 'Here, honey, this is for you.'" Most women shunned this approach and simply used the razor their husbands used.

Several years ago, Gillette gave one of the industrial designers in its shaving division, Jill Shurtleff, the task of looking at women's razors. Shurtleff first tried all the women's razors on the market and concluded that none worked well: "They were ergonomically terrible."

The next step was to conduct research to answer the question, "How do women shave?" The answer was—"differently from men." The average woman shaves 9 times more surface area than a man, shaves 2.5 times a week, and changes the blade 10 times a year. While men generally shave in front of a well-lit mirror, most women shave in a slippery, often poorly lit, shower or tub. Women also shave parts of the body that they cannot see well, such as underarms and backs of thighs. Not surprisingly, many women complained of nicks and cuts and considered shaving an unpleasant task.

Shurtleff concluded that razor features such as the T-shape were excellent for shaving men's faces but were inappropriate for women's needs. Therefore, she developed the radically new *Sensor for Women.* A distinct break with the pink women's razors of the past was achieved with a white and aqua design, to evoke a clean, watery feeling. A traditional naming strategy would have produced *Lady Sensor;* however, *Sensor for Women* was chosen—as a more direct statement. When men, including the Gillette managers, saw the new product, they were skeptical, at best. Women, however, quickly saw its advantages. The *Sensor for Women* produced $40 million in sales in its first six months on the market for a 60 percent market share![54]

Many products are losing their traditional gender typing. Guns, cars, motorcycles, computer games and equipment, golf equipment, financial services, and many other once-masculine products are now designed with women in mind.[55]

While new products are being developed or altered to satisfy positive needs created by the changing role of women, others are emerging to deal with more negative consequences of the evolving roles of women. More women work more hours outside the home today than at any time in our history.[56] This has created great time pressures on most households, as the following quotes from two working wives illustrate:

I have no time. I have absolutely no disposable time at all. I shopped at that Kroger's for probably seven or eight years, and I know where everything is and I don't have to spend any time searching for things. In fact it's real frustrating to me when Kroger's rearranges even small areas in their store, because I don't want to have to go hunt for things.

The poor kids have to make do with you know, canned ravioli, or fish sticks or whatever I can round up. I run into the guilt type thing I guess. Like I should be performing what my mother did, cooking the good wholesome meal with the potatoes and the green vegetables and the meat. But if I can manage to defrost the meat and get it into the crock pot where it's doing its thing while I'm at work, then, you know, we might have a decent dinner.[57]

This time pressure has produced a wealth of time-saving products and services that these consumers use (though often with some guilt feelings).[58]

Courtesy Kraft Food, Inc.

ILLUSTRATION 3-9

As time pressure has mounted for women, firms have responded with new products and positioning strategies. Minute rice's campaign features an 800 number to call for quick recipes and the tagline—"The perfect last-minute idea."

Minute rice has responded to these time pressures with advertising positioning Minute rice as perfect for fast but good meals (see Illustration 3-9). Sara Lee recently began losing market share in its dessert line. Research found that "Sara Lee was one of those golden brand names but consumers didn't find it relevant in terms of how they live today. No one eats dessert as a family anymore. Consumers are more often grabbing a dessert to eat in front of the TV at 9 P.M. rather than sitting down to a cake after dinner." As a result, Sara Lee is revamping both its advertising and its product mix.[59]

As women's roles have expanded, the consumption of potentially harmful products has become socially acceptable for women. This raises the ethical issue of targeting groups that have not historically been heavy users of products such as alcohol or tobacco. Examples include the following:

- Hiram Walker attempted to reach women while introducing its *Royale Cream Liqueur* by sponsoring "Melrose Place" parties at bars throughout the country. The show is very popular with women.
- Consolidated Cigar Corporation is introducing two new cigars designed for female smokers. The new cigars will be near regular size but "will be tapered at both ends to make them easier to light and more comfortable for the smaller female hand."
- A controversial but expanding product category for women is personal protection devices, particularly handguns. Smith & Wesson recently launched *LadySmith*, a line of guns designed specifically for women. Other manufacturers had attempted to reach the female market by "feminizing" men's guns with colored handles and engraved roses on the side plates. Smith & Wesson found through research that "if a woman is going to pull out a gun for personal protection, she doesn't want a cute gun." Smith & Wesson redesigned its guns to fit women's hands and has a very successful new line.

One female gun owner gives her reasoning for gun ownership as follows:

> It's me or them. I have no other choice. Today right on freeways women have been killed, raped, and assaulted . . . I feel like we are victimized. The odds of getting from birth to death without being in a life-jeopardizing situation as females is pretty dad-blamed nonexistent.[60]

While assaults against women are a major social problem, controversy surrounds the danger associated with expanding handgun ownership (independent of gender). Some evidence indicates that the odds of an accidental shooting of a family member or friend are as great or greater than the effective use of a gun for self-defense.

Marketing Communications As gender roles evolve, it is increasingly necessary to communicate how an existing product or brand is appropriate for the gender that traditionally did not use it. Beer ads, once targeted exclusively at males, are now targeted at females as well. Miller, Budweiser, Michelob, and Coors have all launched advertising campaigns aimed at female consumers, and females now consume over 20 percent of domestic beer volume. As with developing guns for women, promoting alcoholic beverages to women raises ethical questions, given the harmful effects alcohol can have, particularly on pregnant women.

State Farm Insurance targets working mothers who have children or who are expecting a child as prospects for their life insurance products. It runs ads in magazines such as *Working Mother, Working Woman,* and *American Baby.* The ads feature a picture of a woman life insurance agent with her own child. The copy from one ad is:

> A mother's love knows no bounds. And there's no better way to show how much you love them than with State Farm life insurance. Nobody knows better than Gail Coleman—a State Farm agent and mom. When she sits down with you to talk about life insurance, she knows you need a plan designed for working moms. One that will grow as your needs grow. And she's always there to answer your questions. So when it comes to life there are two things you can always count on. A mother's love and your State Farm agent. Like a good neighbor, State Farm is there.

Advertisements portraying women must not offend any of the various segments.[61] For example, an ad that implied that housework was unimportant or that women who work outside the home are somehow superior to those who do not could insult traditional housewives. The type of role portrayal most acceptable to a wide range of women appears to be an egalitarian image in which a working woman and her husband share the household chores (a traditional and a superwoman image were less effective across the various segments).[62]

Ads that show women primarily as decoration or as clearly inferior to males tend to produce negative responses across all female segments.[63] Despite these negative reactions, many ads still use these tactics. An analysis of cigarette and alcoholic beverage ads reached this conclusion:

> The world of smoke and drink is more the domain of men than women. While men balance work with smoking and drinking, women tend to occupy that world as sexual objects, interested in socializing, not working.[64]

There are relatively few ads showing men using products traditionally designed for women or performing tasks traditionally performed by women. Illustration 3-10 shows an exception. One advertising agency offers the following advice for portraying men performing household tasks:

> It is important to keep in mind that most men, while they do some housework, resent having to do it. Therefore, the houseworking husband should be shown as a no-nonsense person knocking off a job because it has to be done. The pleasure is in the completion of the task, not in the act of doing it.
>
> The husband should not be shown as doing the wife a favor by helping her out. While this might appeal to the husband, it may well alienate the wife. As more and more women pursue careers, they will expect the sharing of household tasks as a right and obligation, not as a favor on the part of their mates.[65]

Courtesy Fisher-Price.

ILLUSTRATION 3-10

This ad is still quite unusual in that it portrays a male involved in a traditional female task. Although gender roles are changing, it is much more common to portray women performing traditional male tasks than the reverse.

Retail Strategy Men are increasingly shopping for household products, and females are shopping for "masculine" products such as lawn mowers and hammers. When men shop for household items for the family, they generally select the brand for items such as soups and soft drinks but serve primarily as purchasing agents for other items such as cleaning and baby products.[66] In response to these changes, retailers such as Kmart are showing very masculine men shopping for household products at their stores. Campbell Soup has begun advertising its Chunky Soup in *Sports Illustrated* and *Field & Stream.*

SUMMARY

American values have evolved and will continue to evolve. In terms of those values that influence an individual's relationship with *others,* Americans remain individualistic. We have substantially less of a masculine orientation now than in the past. We also place a greater value on older persons and diversity.

Values that affect our relationship to our *environment* have become somewhat more performance oriented and slightly less oriented toward change. There is a strong and growing value placed on protecting the natural environment, and we increasingly value risk taking.

Self-oriented values have also undergone change. We place somewhat less emphasis on hard work as an end in itself and on sensual gratification. We are more content to delay our rewards than in the recent past.

While religion is important and is perhaps becoming more so, America remains a relatively secular culture.

Americans assign a high value to the environment. Marketers have responded to this concern with *green marketing:* (1) Producing products whose production, use, or disposition is less harmful to the environment than the traditional versions of the product; (2) developing products that have a positive impact on the environment; or (3) tying the purchase of a product to an environmental organization or event.

Cause-related marketing is marketing that ties a company and its products to an issue or cause with the goal of improving sales and corporate image while providing benefits to the cause. Companies associate with causes to create long-term relationships with their customers, building corporate and brand equity that should eventually lead to increased sales.

Roles are prescribed patterns of behavior expected of a person in a situation. *Gender roles* are *ascribed roles* based on the sex of the individual rather than on characteristics the individual can control. In contrast, an *achievement role* is acquired based on performance over which an individual does have some degree of control.

Gender roles, particularly female roles, have undergone radical changes in the past 25 years. The fundamental shift has been for the female role to become more like the traditional male role. Virtually all aspects of our society, including marketing activities, have been affected by this shift.

KEY TERMS

Achievement role 98
Ascribed role 98
Cause-related marketing (CRM) 92
Cultural values 80
Gender 97
Gender identity 97
Gender role 98
Green marketing 88
Modern gender orientation 98
Traditional gender orientation 98

INTERNET EXERCISES

1. Visit a site such as Yahoo's daily news page (http://dailynews.yahoo.com). What value does it have in helping track American values? What other sites are useful for this?
2. Search for a newsgroup that is relevant for understanding the following. Report on the insights that it can provide.
   a. American values in general
   b. Cause-related marketing
   c. Green marketing
   d. Gender roles
3. Use the Internet to discover what, if any, cause-related marketing activities the following firms are involved with.
   a. Nike
   b. Wendy's
   c. Mary Kay Cosmetics
   d. A firm you would like to work for
4. Evaluate an on-line green shopping mall (such as http://www.ecoexpo.com, or www.greenmarketplace.com). What value do these malls provide consumers? Advertisers? What types of firms advertise here? How would you characterize their ads?
5. Evaluate Ben & Jerry's Web site (http://www.benjerry.com).
6. Determine the size and average income of the gay market using the Web (you should start with the James C. Hormel Gay and Lesbian Center at the San Francisco Public Library Web site—http://206.14.7.53/glcenter).
7. Use the Internet to determine the role of women in purchasing the following.
   a. Cigars
   b. Mountain bikes
   c. Stocks

DDB NEEDHAM LIFESTYLE DATA ANALYSES

1. What characterizes individuals with a very traditional view of the female role? How do these individuals differ from those with a much more modern view? (Use the DDB Needham data in Tables 1a, 2a, 3a, 4a, 5a, 6a, and 7a.)
2. Based on the data in DDB Needham Tables 1a, 2a, 3a, 4a, 5a, 6a, and 7a, what characterizes individuals who subscribe strongly to the cleanliness value?
3. What characterizes consumers who are particularly responsive to cause-related marketing? What are the marketing strategy implications of this? (See DDB Needham data in Tables 1a, 2a, 3a, 4a, 5a, 6a, and 7a.)
4. Examine the DDB Needham data in Tables 1a, 2a, 3a, 4a, 5a, 6a, and 7a. What characterizes individuals who are active recyclers? What are the marketing strategy implications of this?

REVIEW QUESTIONS

1. What is a cultural value? Do all members of a culture share cultural values?
2. Describe the current American culture in terms of each of the 18 values discussed in this chapter.
3. What is *green marketing?*
4. What are the dimensions of concern with the environment?
5. What problems did the questionable use of environment claims by some firms cause for consumers? For other firms? How did the Federal Trade Commission respond?
6. Describe the basic conflict between the environmental movement and many businesses.
7. What is *cause-related marketing?* Why is it often successful?
8. What are the major decisions a firm faces with respect to the gay market?
9. What is meant by *gender?*
10. What is *gender identity?*
11. What is a *gender role?*
12. How does an *ascribed role* differ from an *achievement role?*
13. What is happening to male and female gender roles?
14. What are the differences between a traditional and a modern gender role orientation?
15. Describe a segmentation system for the female market based on employment status and gender role orientation.
16. What are some of the major marketing implications of the changing role of women?

DISCUSSION QUESTIONS

17. Describe additional values you feel could (or should) be added to Figure 3-1. Describe the marketing implications of each.
18. Pick the three values you feel the authors were most inaccurate about in describing the *current* American values. Justify your answers.
19. Pick the three values you feel the authors were most inaccurate about in describing the *emerging* American values. Justify your answers.
20. Which values are most relevant to the purchase or use of the following? Are they currently favorable or unfavorable for ownership/use? Are they shifting at all? If so, is the shift in a favorable or unfavorable direction?
    a. Dog
    b. Habitat for Humanity contribution
    c. Mutual funds
    d. Large sport-utility vehicles

e. Mountain bikes
f. American Express card

21. Do you believe Americans' concern for the environment is a stronger value than their materialism?
22. What are the primary ethical issues involved in green marketing?
23. Cause-related marketing is done to enhance the firm's sales or image. This has caused some to consider it to be unethical. What is your position?
24. Suppose AT&T showed a gay couple using its long-distance service or P&G showed a gay couple using one of its laundry products in ads on network television. Is a "backlash" by those who do not accept the gay community a likely response? If not, how are such consumers likely to respond? Why?
25. Do you think housewives may be defensive or sensitive about not having employment outside of the home? If so, what implications will this have for marketing practice?
26. What is your position on targeting women as a market for the following?

    a. Handguns
    b. Alcoholic beverages
    c. Cigarettes
27. Develop an advertisement for the following for each of the four female market segments described in the chapter.
    a. Casual restaurant
    b. Electric mop
    c. Dish detergent
    d. Fruit drink
    e. American Express card
    f. Perfume

APPLICATION ACTIVITIES

28. Find and copy or describe an advertisement for an item that reflects Americans' position on the following values.
    a. Active/Passive
    b. Material/Nonmaterial
    c. Hard work/Leisure
    d. Postponed/Immediate gratification
    e. Sensual gratification/Abstinence
    f. Religious/Secular
    g. Cleanliness
    h. Performance/Status
    i. Tradition/Change
    j. Risk taking/Security
    k. Problem solving/Fatalistic
    l. Admire/Overcome nature
    m. Individual/Collective
    n. Limited/Extended family
    o. Diversity/Uniformity
    p. Competition/Cooperation
    q. Youth/Age
    r. Masculine/Feminine
29. Interview a salesperson who has been selling the following for at least 10 years. See if this individual has noticed a change in the purchasing roles of women over time.
    a. Automobiles
    b. Camping equipment
    c. Do-it-yourself equipment
    d. Guns
    e. Life insurance
30. Interview a career-oriented working wife and a traditional housewife of a similar age. Report on differences in attitudes toward shopping, products, and so forth.
31. Find one advertisement you think is particularly appropriate for each of the female market segments (traditional housewife, trapped housewife, trapped working woman, and career working woman). Copy or describe each ad and justify its selection.
32. Interview a salesperson for each of the following. Ascertain the interest shown in the item by males and females. Determine if males and

females are concerned with different characteristics of the item and if they have different purchase motivations.

a. Stereo equipment
b. Computer
c. Automobile
d. Golf equipment
e. Refrigerator
f. Flowers

33. Interview 10 male and 10 female students. Ask each to describe the typical owner or consumer of the following. If they do not specify, ask for the gender of the typical owner. Then probe to find out why they think the typical owner is of the gender they indicated. Also determine the perceived marital and occupational status of the typical owner and the reasons for these beliefs.

a. Large dog
b. In-line skates
c. Sports car
d. Mountain bike
e. United Way contributor
f. Waterbed

REFERENCES

1. See A. Jolibert and G. Baumgartner, "Values, Motivations, and Personal Goals," *Psychology & Marketing,* October 1997, pp. 675–88.
2. J. W. Winski, "Who We Are," *Advertising Age,* January 20, 1992, pp. 16, 18; A. W. Fawcett, "The Consumer Mindset in the 90's," *Advertising Age,* April 18, 1994, pp. 13–14; and M. Spiegler, "Scouting for Souls," *American Demographics,* March 1996, p. 47.
3. K. L. Woodward, "The Rites of Americans," *Newsweek,* November 29, 1993, p. 80.
4. See P. S. La Barbera, and Z. Gurhan, "The Role of Materialism, Religiosity, and Demographics in Subjective Well-Being," *Psychology & Marketing,* January 1997, pp. 71–97.
5. F. Rose, "If It Feels Good, It Must Be Bad," *Fortune,* October 21, 1991, pp. 91–108.
6. See footnote 2.
7. J. B. Schor, *The Overworked American,* (New York: Basic Books, 1991).
8. W. B. Fay, "The Great Time Famine," *Marketing Research,* September 1992, pp. 50–51.
9. C. R. Wiles, J. A. Wiles, and A. Tjernlund, "The Ideology of Advertising," *Journal of Advertising Research,* May–June 1996, pp. 57–66.
10. R. Tansey et al., "An Advertising Test of the Work Ethic in the U.K. and the U.S.," *Journal of International Consumer Marketing,* no. 3 (1997), pp. 57–77.
11. Fawcett, footnote 2.
12. See J. P. Robinson and M. Milke, "Dances with Dust Bunnies," *American Demographics,* January 1997, pp. 37–40.
13. S. Hayward, "The Environmental Opportunity," *Marketing Research,* December 1989, pp. 66–67.
14. S. Hume and P. Strand, "Consumers Go 'Green,'" *Advertising Age,* September 25, 1989, p. 3; and J. Ottman, "Innovative Marketers Give New Products the Green Light," *Marketing News,* March 1998, p. 10.
15. P. Stisser, "A Deeper Shade of Green," *American Demographics,* March 1994, pp. 24–29. See also T. L. Speere, "Growing the Green Market," *American Demographics,* August 1997, pp. 45–49.
16. J. Ottman, "Environmental Branding Blocks Competitors," *Marketing News,* August 17, 1998, p. 8.
17. G. H. G. McDougall, "The Green Movement in Canada," *Journal of International Consumer Marketing* 5, no. 3 (1993), pp. 69–87.
18. S. Sherman, "How to Prosper in the Value Decade," *Fortune,* November 30, 1992, pp. 90–103; F. Rice, "What Intelligent Consumers Want," *Fortune,* December 28, 1992, pp. 56–60; and "Economy Puts Focus on Value," *Advertising Age,* July 26, 1993, pp. 11.
19. S. Caminiti, "Will Old Navy Fill the Gap?" *Fortune,* March 18, 1996, p. 59.
20. Z. Schiller, "Make It Simple," *Business Week,* September 9, 1996, pp. 96–104.
21. See G. D. Gregory and J. M. Munch, "Reconceptualizing Individualism-Collectivism in Consumer Behavior," in *Advances in Consumer Research XXIII,* ed. K. P. Corfman and J. G. Lynch (Provo, UT: Association for Consumer Research, 1996), pp. 104–10.
22. See footnote 9.
23. L. C. Troy, "Consumer Environmental Consciousness," in *Enhancing Knowledge Development in Marketing,* ed. D. W. Cravens and P. R. Dickson (Chicago: American Marketing Association, 1993), pp. 106–13.
24. L. J. Shrum, J. A. McCarty, and T. M. Lowrey, "Buyer Characteristics of the Green Consumer," *Journal of Advertising,* Summer 1995, pp. 71–82.

25. A different conclusion is reached in E. Thorson, T. Page, and J. Moore, "Consumer Response to Four Categories of 'Green' Television Commercials," in *Advances in Consumer Research XXII,* ed. F. R. Kardes and M. Sujan (Provo, UT: Association for Consumer Research, 1995), pp. 243–50.

26. J. L. Davis, "Strategies for Environmental Advertising," *Journal of Consumer Marketing,* no. 2 (1993), pp. 19–36. See also J. K. Ross III, L. T. Patterson, and M. A. Stutts, "Consumer Perceptions of Organizations that Use Cause-Related Marketing," *Journal of the Academy of Marketing Science,* Winter 1992, pp. 93–97; S. Banerjee, C. S. Gulas, and E. Iyer, "Shades of Green," *Journal of Advertising,* Summer 1995, pp. 21–32: and M. R. Stafford, T. F. Stafford, and J. Chowdhury, "Predispositions toward Green Issues," *Journal of Current Issues and Research in Advertising,* Spring 1996, pp. 68–79.

27. S. W. Colford, "FTC Green Guidelines May Spark Ad Efforts," *Advertising Age,* August 3, 1992, p. 11. See also D. L. Scammon and R. N. Mayer, "Agency Review of Environmental Marketing Claims," *Journal of Advertising,* Summer 1995, pp. 33–54.

28. See L. R. Stanley and K. M. Lasonde, "The Relationship between Environmental Issue Involvement and Environmentally Conscious Behavior," in *Advances in Consumer Research XXIII,* ed. K. P. Corfman and J. G. Lynch (Provo, UT: Association for Consumer Research, 1996), pp. 183–88; and T. S. Chan, "Concerns for Environmental Issues and Consumer Purchase Preferences," *Journal of International Consumer Marketing,* no. 1, 1996, pp. 43–55.

29. Speere, footnote 15, p. 49.

30. A. S. Mobley et al., "Consumer Evaluation of Recycled Products," *Psychology & Marketing,* May 1995, pp. 165–76.

31. Ibid., p. 113.

32. See G. M. Zinkhan and L. Carlson, "Green Advertising and the Reluctant Consumer"; and W. E. Kilbourne, "Green Advertising"; both in *Journal of Advertising,* Summer 1995, pp. 1–6 and 7–19.

33. See R. P. Bagozzi and D. J. Moore, "Public Service Advertisements," *Journal of Marketing,* January 1994, pp. 56–70.

34. For a thorough discussion of CRM, see M. E. Drumwright, "Company Advertising with a Social Dimension," *Journal of Marketing,* October 1996, pp. 71–87.

35. *The Cone/Roper Study: A Benchmark Survey of Consumer Awareness and Attitudes towards Cause-Related Marketing* (New York: Roper/Starch Worldwide, Inc., 1994), p. 1.

36. Ibid.

37. N. Arnott, "Marketing with a Passion," *Sales & Marketing Management,* January 1994, pp. 64–71. See also A. R. Andreasen, "Profits for Nonprofits," *Harvard Business Review,* November 1996, pp. 47–52.

38. See M. Wilke, "Conservative Groups Ready 'Ex-Gay' TV Ads," *Advertising Age,* October 26, 1998, p. 3.

39. "How Many Lesbians and Gay Men Are There," James C. Hormel Gay and Lesbian Center, San Francisco Public Library Web site (http://206.14.7.53/glcenter), February 1999.

40. L. Koss-Feder, "Out and About," *Marketing News,* May 25, 1998, p. 1.

41. M. Wilke, "Fewer Gays Wealthy, Data Say," *Advertising Age,* October 19, 1998, p. 58.

42. M. Wilke, "Ads Targeting Gays Rely on Real Results," *Advertising Age,* June 22, 1998, p. 3.

43. Footnote 40, p. 20.

44. M. Wilke, "Burgeoning Gay Web Sites Spark Advertiser Interest," *Advertising Age,* June 22, 1998.

45. Footnote 40, p. 1.

46. See T. Triplett, "Automakers Recognizing Value of Women's Market," *Marketing News,* April 11, 1994, pp. 1–2; and J. Halliday, "GM Looking to Woo Developing Clout of Females," *Advertising Age,* June 17, 1996, p. 39.

47. E. Fischer and S. J. Arnold, "Sex, Gender Identity, Gender Role Attitudes, and Consumer Behavior," *Psychology & Marketing,* March 1994, pp. 163–82; L. J. Jaffe, "The Unique Predictive Ability of Sex-Role Identity in Explaining Women's Response to Advertising," *Psychology & Marketing,* September 1994, pp. 467–82; and S. J. Gould, "Gender Identity and Gender Salience," in *Advances in Consumer Research XXIII,* ed. K. P. Corfman and J. G. Lynch (Provo, UT: Association for Consumer Research, 1996), pp. 478–83.

48. See P. Ireland, *What Women Want* (New York: E. P. Dutton, 1996); D. J. Swiss, *Women Breaking Through* (Peterson's/Pacesetter Books, 1996); and P. McCorduck and N. Ramsey, *The Futures of Women* (Reading, MA; Addison-Wesley Publishing, 1996).

49. J. S. Grigsby, "Women Change Places," *American Demographics,* November 1992, p. 48, and Fawcett, footnote 2.

50. C. J. Thompson, "Caring Consumers," *Journal of Consumer Research,* March 1996, p. 397.

51. Ibid., p. 388.

52. These segments are similar to the four categories popularized by Bartos. See C. M. Schaninger, M. C. Nelson, and W. D. Danko, "An Empirical Evaluation of the Bartos Model," *Journal of Advertising Research,* May 1993, pp. 49–63; and R. Bartos, "Bartos Responds to 'The Bartos Model,'" *Journal of Advertising Research,* January 1994, pp. 54–56.

53. R. E. Wilkes, K. M. Palan, and J. J. Burnett, "Is a Modern Feminine Orientation Synonymous with Working Status?" C. Droge and R. Calantone, *Enhancing Knowledge Development in Marketing* (Chicago: American Marketing Association, 1996), pp. 244–51.

54. M. Maremont, "A New Equal Right: The Close Shave," pp. 58–59. Reprinted from the March 29, 1993 issue of *Business Week* by special permission. © 1993 McGraw-Hill and Companies, Inc.

55. See J. A. Bellizzi and L. Milner, "Gender Positioning of a Traditionally Male-Dominant Product," *Journal of Advertising Research,* June–July 1991, pp. 64–72; and G. Myers, "Selling a Man's World to Women," *American Demographics,* April 1996, pp. 36–42.

56. See J. Larson, "The New Homemakers," *American Demographics,* September 1997, pp. 45–50.

57. Footnote 50, pp. 395–96.

58. Footnote 8, p. 50. See also G. M. Rose, L. R. Kahle, and A. Shoham, "The Influence of Employment-Status and Personal Values on Time Related Food Consumption Behavior and Opinion Leadership"; and J. J. Madill-Marshall, L. Heslop, and L. Duxbury, "Coping with Household Stress in the 1990s"; both in

Advances in Consumer Research XXII, ed. F. R. Kardes and M. Sujan (Provo, UT: Association for Consumer Research, 1995), pp. 367–72 and 729–34; and J. K. Maher, L. J. Marks, and P. E. Grimm, "Overload, Pressure, and Convenience," in *Advances in Consumer Research XXIV,* ed. M. Bruck and D. J. MacInnis (Provo, UT: Association for Consumer Research, 1997), pp. 490–98.

59. J. Pollack, "Sara Lee Urges Daily Indulgence in $15 Mil Effort," *Advertising Age,* October 19, 1998, p. 6.

60. M. E. Blair and E. M. Hyatt, "The Marketing of Guns to Women," *Journal of Public Policy & Marketing,* Spring 1995, pp. 117–27. See also E. Blair and E. M. Hyatt, "Using Promises of Protection and Empowerment to Market Guns to Women," in *Advances in Consumer Research XXV,* ed. M. Bruck and D. J. MacInnis (Provo, UT: Association for Consumer Research, 1997), pp. 355–59.

61. See L. J. Jaffe, "The Unique Predictive Ability of Sex-Role Identity in Explaining Women's Response to Advertising," *Psychology & Marketing,* September 1994, pp. 467–82; J. B. Ford and M. S. LaTour, "Contemporary Female Perspectives of Female Role Portrayals in Advertising," *Journal of Current Issues and Research in Advertising,* Spring 1996, pp. 81–95; and R. Widgery, M. G. Angur, and R. Nataraajan, "The Impact of Employment Status on Married Women's Perceptions of Advertising Message Appeals," *Journal of Advertising Research,* January 1997, pp. 54–62.

62. L. J. Jaffe and P. D. Berger, "The Effect of Modern Female Sex Role Portrayals on Advertising Effectiveness," *Journal of Advertising Research,* July 1994, pp. 32–42.

63. R. W. Pollay and S. Lysonski, "In the Eye of the Beholder," *Journal of International Consumer Marketing* 6, no. 2 (1993), pp. 25–43; D. Walsh, "Safe Sex in Advertising," *American Demographics,* April 1994, pp. 24–30; M. S. LaTour, T. L. Henthorne, and A. J. Williams, "Is Industrial Advertising Still Sexist?" *Industrial Marketing Management,* 1998, pp. 247–55; and M. Y. Jones, A. J. S. Stanaland, and B. D. Gelb, "Beefcake and Cheesecake," *Journal of Advertising,* Summer 1998, pp. 33–51.

64. L. N. Reid, K. W. King, and H. L. Wyant, "Gender Portrayals in Cigarette and Alcohol Ads," in *Enhancing Knowledge Development in Marketing,* ed. R. Achrol and A. Mitchell (Chicago: American Marketing Association, 1994), pp. 48–56.

65. "Males Don't Like New Women: DDB," *Advertising Age,* October 20, 1980, p. 60. See also A. W. Fawcett, "Ads Awaken to Fathers' New Role in Family Life," *Advertising Age,* January 10, 1994, p. S-8; and R. Elliott, S. Eccles, and M. Hodgson, "Re-Coding Gender Representations," *International Journal of Research in Marketing,* August 1993, pp. 311–24.

66. *Men in the Marketplace* (Emmaus, PA: Rodale Press, 1989).

Lisa Quinones/Black Star.

chapter four

The Changing American Society: Demographics and Social Stratification

■ Studies have shown that between 78 and 98 percent of inner-city urban homes and apartments have cockroach infestations. Evidence also indicates that roaches are the leading cause of asthma and allergies in many urban areas. Residents were not getting the information needed to deal with the problem and were not using appropriate health-enhancing behaviors.

In response, S. C. Johnson & Son worked with BR&R Communications to host *Raid Max* "roach evictions" at inner-city housing developments. The evictions involve using Raid Max and Raid Max Roach Bait Plus Egg Stoppers to kill roaches and prevent their return. They also have medical specialists test those residents who are interested for cockroach allergies. Two entomologists are on hand to answer questions about cockroach allergies and give advice on controlling the bugs.

According to the company, the program "really makes a difference with the consumer." When they go into the store, they remember that the company "cared enough to come into their neighborhoods and provided them with something they can use to make a difference."[1]

■ "There's a lot of neat stuff. It reminds me of a living J. Peterman catalog," says one customer. She is speaking of Restoration Hardware (see facing photo). Restoration Hardware does not stock paints and power tools. It does carry nickel-plated hammers, Swedish Formula hardwood Floor Cleaner, Atomic Robot Man toys, and chenille throws. All are sold at significant mark-ups. The nickel-plated martini shaker modeled on a 1936 original sells for $48. The stores have elegant displays, soft jazz, unique items, and an index card essay on most items in the stores.

Ninety-five percent of Restoration's customers are college educated with relatively high incomes. The chain is growing rapidly toward a target of 200 stores.[2]

The concerns and lives of the various social classes in America are clearly different. Although Americans like to think of America as an egalitarian society, there are sharp differences among Americans on every dimension related to social status.

In this chapter, we are going to discuss the closely related concepts of demographics and social status. As we will see, several demographic variables—income, education, and occupation—serve as dimensions of social status. We will first take a broad look at the demographics of the American society. Then we will consider social status and the role that demographics play in social status.

DEMOGRAPHICS

Just as our value structure is changing, so are our demographics. As defined in Chapter 2, **demographics** *describe a population in terms of its size, distribution, and structure. Size* means the number of individuals in a population, while *structure* describes the population in terms of age, income, education, and occupation. *Distribution* of the population describes the location of individuals in terms of geographic region and rural, urban, or suburban location. Each of these factors influences the behavior of consumers and contributes to the overall demand for various products and services.

Population Size and Distribution

The population of the United States is approximately 270 million today and is expected to reach 285 million by 2010. The population has grown steadily since 1960 despite a declining birthrate. This increase has been caused by longer life expectancies, the large baby boom generation moving through their child-bearing years, and significant immigration. Population growth was a critical factor in the profitability and even survival of many industries. For example, per capita coffee consumption has declined steadily from 3.5 cups per day in the 1960s to an average of less than 1.5 cups today. However, the addition of 80 million people to the U.S. population during this period enabled the industry to maintain its total sales.

In addition to the growth rate of a population, it is important for marketers to know where this growth is likely to take place. For example, from 2000 to 2010, Arizona, Florida, Georgia, and Hawaii are predicted to grow by about 15 percent. In contrast, Illinois, Indiana, Michigan, Iowa, Ohio, and Pennsylvania are predicted to decrease slightly.[3] As we will discuss in detail in the next chapter, regions of the country serve as subcultures whose members (residents) have tastes, attitudes, and preferences that are unique to that region. Several examples of these differences are shown in Figure 4-1. Unique regional lifestyles create tremendous marketing opportunities for those who understand the needs of people in rapidly growing regions.[4]

Age

In describing the response of consumers to the first Tiger Woods line of golf products, the manager of a major sporting store stated:

A Tale of Three Cities FIGURE 4-1

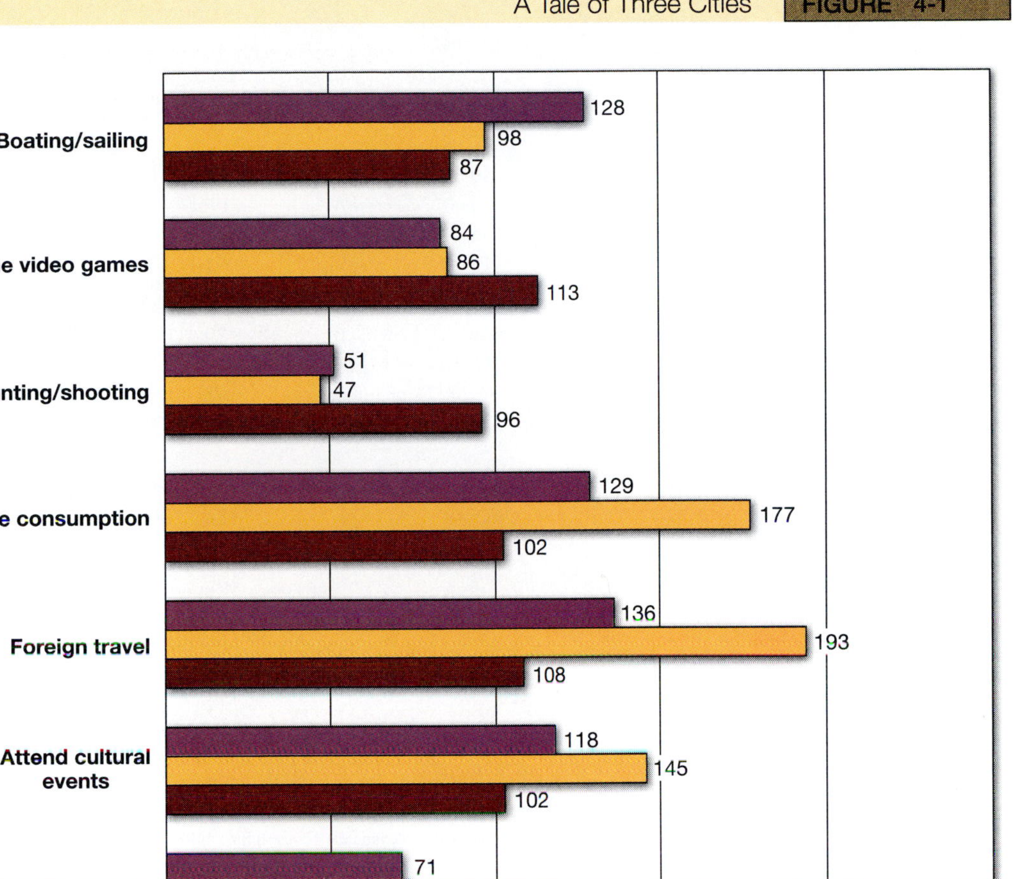

*An Index of 100 represents the average for the entire United States.

Reprinted from the 1998 edition of *The Lifestyle Analyst,* published by SRDSwith data supplied by Polk.

To tell you the truth, we did not have people busting down our doors for it. The product is not grunge enough for the kids, and it's too flashy for older people. Nike is trying to market something that there is not a market for.

Proper age positioning is critical for many products. Age has been found to affect the consumption of products ranging from beer to toilet paper to vacations. Our age shapes the media we use, where we shop, how we use products, and how we think and feel about marketing activities.[5] Table 4-1 illustrates some consumption behaviors that vary with age. Illustration 4-1 shows an ad with the type of humor appreciated by many young adults.

TABLE 4-1

Age Influences on Consumption*

	Age					
	18–24	*25–34*	*35–44*	*45–54*	*55–64*	*65+*
Products						
Tequila	156	174	115	57	64	5
Scotch	44	66	98	143	119	137
Laptop/notebook	94	115	124	139	98	15
Doctor visits	74	88	91	107	110	135
Activities						
Barbecuing	69	116	139	130	82	32
Aerobics	171	140	118	99	28	18
Cruise ship	60	80	95	114	144	121
Volunteer work	75	96	117	121	97	82
Shopping						
Montgomery Ward	91	87	106	94	117	110
The Gap	217	140	85	82	52	26
Domino's Pizza	161	132	124	80	52	30
Marie Callender's	77	80	105	135	110	96
Media						
Reader's Digest	64	75	96	109	119	144
Rolling Stone	290	158	93	46	14	2
MTV	286	153	81	42	22	16
CNN	73	93	99	114	117	107

*100 = Average level of use, purchase, or consumption.

Source: *Mediamark Spring 1997* (New York: Mediamark Research Inc., 1997).

Cadillac's research revealed that older and younger potential customers had differing needs with respect to a luxury car. Therefore, they began using a service called selective binding for their ads in such magazines as *Fortune, Sports Illustrated, Time,* and *Money.* Selective binding allows different ads to be placed in copies of a magazine going to subscribers with different demographics. Thus, younger potential buyers subscribing to one of these magazines will see ads for the Seville or Eldorado, while older subscribers to the same magazine will see ads for the Fleetwood Brougham.

The estimated age distributions (millions in each age category) of the U.S. population for 2000 and 2010 are:[6]

Age Category	*2000*	*2010*	*Percent Change*
<5	17	17	0%
5–17	49	46	−6.3
18–24	25	27	+7.6
25–34	37	38	1.1
35–44	44	37	−15.3
45–54	37	43	+16.1
55–64	24	35	+46.7
65–74	18	21	+15.3
>74	16	18	+10.1

Courtesy K2 Skis.

ILLUSTRATION 4-1

Age affects how individuals think, feel, and behave. The humor in this ad would be appreciated more by younger consumers than older consumers.

Even a quick look at these age distributions indicates that momentous changes are occurring. Some of the profound marketing implications of these changes are:

- Demand for children's products such as toys, diapers, and clothes will remain constant, as the population less than 5 years of age will be stable over this period.
- Products consumed by older children and younger teenagers will decrease in demand. The entertainment industry, personal electronics, grade and middle schools, and clothing firms will all be affected.
- Products consumed by adults aged 35 to 44 will decline as this population group grows smaller. This will have significant implications for the overall economy as well as for specific products, as this is the age when many families acquire their first home or buy a larger one, upgrade their automobiles, and begin significant savings programs. Housing construction, financial services, automobiles, and similar products will be impacted.
- The largest impact will be caused by the huge increase (almost 20 million) in the number of individuals between 45 and 64. This is the age of highest earning, so luxury items should do well. As children leave home, vacations, restaurants, and financial services aimed at the mature market should flourish. Television programs will change to meet the interests of this mature market. With over half of the population 45 or older, the general "tone" of the American society will undoubtedly change significantly.
- The large growth in the number of individuals over 65 will also create many opportunities for marketers ranging from beauty aids and travel and leisure to retirement homes and health care.

Age groups as defined by the census and as presented above can be very useful as a means of understanding and segmenting a market. For example, P&G recently launched the *Oil of Olay ProVital* line targeting women over 50 years old. According to P&G, this is the fastest growing consumer segment in North America. Today, there are about 70 million women in that group in America and this is expected to grow by 50 percent over the next 15 years. The prime spokeswoman for the product will be 51-year-old actress Anne Roberts. However, the product line will not be positioned as just an antiwrinkle solution:

> Age is just a number. Many women 50 and over have told us that as they age, they feel more confident, wiser, and freer than ever before. These women are redefining beauty. Our research shows that when it comes to skin, dryness and vitality are their key concerns, not just a few wrinkles.[7]

While age groups as defined by the census or in five-year increments are often a useful way to understand and segment a market, analyzing age cohort groups or generations will often provide more meaningful segments and marketing strategies. This approach is covered in depth in the next chapter.

Occupation

The number of professional workers such as engineers, scientists, and lawyers has grown rapidly over the past 15 years. Likewise, managerial, marketing, sales, health care, and social services jobs have also seen rapid growth. Service occupations have added more jobs over the past 15 years than any other category. In contrast, traditional blue-collar occupations have grown slowly if at all.[8] Because our occupation influences the clothes we wear, cars we drive, and foods we eat, products and services that serve the professional, managerial, or service worker have experienced greater growth in demand than those targeted at the traditional blue-collar worker.

Differences in consumption between occupational classes have been found for products such as beer, detergents, dog food, shampoo, and paper towels. Media preferences, hobbies, and shopping patterns are also influenced by occupational class (see Table 4-2).

Education

The level of education in the United States continues to rise. The percentage of the population age 25 and over completing high school and college is going up, while the percentage with only some high school or elementary education is decreasing. Unfortunately, the high school dropout rate is still high, particularly in disadvantaged populations.

Education is becoming increasingly critical for a "family wage" job. Traditional, high-paying manufacturing jobs that required relatively little education are rapidly disappearing. High-paying jobs in the manufacturing and service sectors today require technical skills, abstract reasoning, and the ability to read and learn new skills rapidly. These capabilities are acquired through meaningful education. Individuals without these skills are generally forced into minimum wage and often part-time jobs. Such jobs will not keep a family above the poverty level.[9] Education clearly drives income in today's economy:[10]

Median Income: Individuals 25 and Older

Education Level	*Males*	*Females*
High school degree	$22,765	$13,266
Some college	26,873	16,611
Associate's degree	30,052	19,642
Bachelor's degree	40,590	26,417

TABLE 4-2

Occupational Influences on Consumption*

	Administration/ Managerial	*Technical/ Clerical/ Sales*	*Precision/ Craft*
Products			
Domestic beer	98	72	185
Luggage	136	106	84
Cigarettes	87	83	165
Diet colas	128	111	89
Laptop/notebook	234	143	56
Activities			
Sailing	299	67	105
Archery	91	82	239
Dining out	147	118	98
Lottery	105	101	131
Shopping			
Wal-Mart	94	102	1,009
Ann Taylor	245	131	33
Olive Garden	123	122	77
Bonanza	53	100	109
Media			
Playboy	85	96	230
Outside	193	94	58
Jazz radio	189	126	66
Country radio	96	109	126

*100 = Average level of use, purchase, or consumption.

Source: *Mediamark Spring 1997* (New York: Mediamark Research Inc., 1997).

Since individuals tend to have spouses with similar education levels, these income differences are magnified when spousal income is considered.[11]

These data clarify the deep concern that America is splitting into a nation of haves and have-nots. Unfortunately, as the cost of advanced education continues to increase, America's traditional path to upward social mobility is not as open as it once was. If today's parents did not attend college, it is increasingly difficult for them to send their children to college.

Education influences what one can purchase by partially determining one's income and occupation. It also influences how one thinks, makes decisions, and relates to others.[12] Those with a limited education are generally at a disadvantage not only in earning money but also in spending it wisely.[13] Not surprisingly, education has a strong influence on one's tastes and preferences, as shown in Table 4-3.

Income

A household's income level combined with its accumulated wealth determines its purchasing power. While many purchases are made on credit, one's ability to buy on credit is ultimately determined by one's current income and past income (wealth).

With the exception of the Depression in the 1930s, modern American history has been characterized by consistently increasing real per capita income. For most middle- and lower-income Americans, this increasing trend stopped in the 1980s, and household incomes were

TABLE 4-3

Education Level Influences on Consumption*

	Graduated College	Attended College	Graduated High School	Did Not Graduate High School
Product				
Champagne	143	117	86	53
Chewing tobacco	56	98	114	134
Laptop/notebook	227	118	52	16
Heavy video rental	73	125	112	74
Activities				
Tennis	188	129	54	41
Lottery	78	100	120	91
Hunting (with rifle)	88	102	118	77
Cook for fun	131	119	83	69
Shopping				
Venture	87	98	104	110
Banana Republic	174	131	62	39
Churchs Fried Chicken	59	90	107	48
TGI Friday's	152	125	78	46
Media				
National Enquirer	46	107	127	112
National Geographic	148	113	77	61
The Nashville Network	62	97	123	106
BRAVO	146	130	82	40

*100 = Average level of use, purchase, or consumption.

Source: *Mediamark Spring 1997* (New York: Mediamark Research Inc., 1997).

stagnant or declining until they increased again in 1995.[14] For example, from 1984 to 1994, incomes of the top 5 percent of Americans grew by 37 percent, while those on the bottom experienced only a 1 percent increase. Younger households and those without specialized skills suffered the most during this period.

Half a decade of economic uncertainty as well as limited or no increase in purchasing power for many caused consumers at virtually all income levels to demand products that deliver value—significant performance for the price. Lower-income consumers sought value in lower-priced products such as the Geo, while Buick advertised that it provides the same performance as several luxury imports for "thousands less."

The economic boom of the past five years has enhanced the purchasing power of most Americans. At the lower (but not lowest) and middle-income levels this increased purchasing power is reflected in rapidly growing sales for premium products and "small luxuries" such as Gillette's Mach3 razor (35 percent more expensive than its SensorExcel) and Huggies Supreme diapers. As income rises, luxury purchases increase. Luxury cars are now 12 percent of the market (up from 7 percent a decade ago) and yacht makers can't keep up with demand.[15]

Income *enables* purchases but *does not generally cause or explain them.* For example, individuals making over $60,000 a year are almost five times more likely to read the *New Yorker* magazine than individuals making less than $10,000 per year. However, relatively few low-income individuals who won a lottery paying over $60,000 per year would suddenly subscribe to the *New Yorker*. Occupation and education directly influence preferences for products, media, and activities; income provides the means to acquire them.[16] Thus, income is generally more effective as a segmentation variable when used in conjunction with other demographic variables.

An example of using income with other demographic variables is Vons, a West Coast grocery chain. Vons analyzed the demographics and purchase patterns of consumers in the shopping area of each of its outlets. It found that the income and age distribution, along with ethnicity, of each area had a major influence on the types and amounts of items purchased at each store. As a result, it moved from a single store format to five based on the shopping area demographics, particularly income and ethnicity.[17]

Marketing Strategy and Demographics

Frito-Lay developed a Light product line, including Cheetos Light, Doritos Light, and Ruffles Light. Marketing research identified the primary target market as age 35 to 54, college-educated, white-collar workers with annual incomes above $35,000. While Frito-Lay used its knowledge of the values, attitudes, and media habits of this group to structure its communication campaign, its most creative use of demographics was in distribution.

Frito-Lay used Market Metrics—a firm with a database on 30,000 supermarkets. Market Metrics defines trading areas around each supermarket, considering distance and the presence of travel barriers such as freeways or rivers. It then uses Census Bureau data to profile the demographics of the shoppers in each store's trade area. Market Metrics took Frito-Lay's target demographics and ranked the 30,000 supermarkets in terms of how well they matched the target market. This approach has allowed Frito-Lay to focus maximum sales, point-of-purchase, and promotional efforts on those specific stores with the greatest market potential based on demographics. It plans to increase its use of this approach in the future: "If we wanted to target Hispanics or Italians or married couples with children under the age of five, we could do it with this program."[18]

Demographics clearly influence consumption behaviors both directly and by impacting other attributes of individuals such as their personal values and decision styles, which also influence consumption.[19] Frito-Lay combined all of the demographic variables that we have discussed separately to define a primary target market. It then developed a marketing strategy to reach this segment. The benefits of such a thorough approach are obvious, and many firms use demographic data in this manner.

SOCIAL STRATIFICATION

We are all familiar with the concept of social class, but most of us would have difficulty explaining our class system to a foreigner. The following quotes illustrate the vague nature of social class in America and Canada:

> Like it or not, all of us are largely defined, at least in the eyes of others, according to a complex set of criteria—how much we earn, what we do for a living, who our parents are, where and how long we attended school, how we speak, what we wear, where we live, and how we react to the issues of the day. It all adds up to our socioeconomic status, our ranking in U.S. society.[20]
>
> I would suppose social class means where you went to school and how far. Your intelligence. Where you live. The sort of house you live in. Your general background, as far as clubs you belong to, your friends. To some degree the type of profession you're in—in fact, definitely that. Where you send your children to school. The hobbies you have. Skiing, for example, is higher than the snowmobile. The clothes you wear . . . all of that. These are the externals. It can't be (just) money, because nobody ever knows that about you for sure.[21]

FIGURE 4-2 Social Standing Is Derived and Influences Behavior

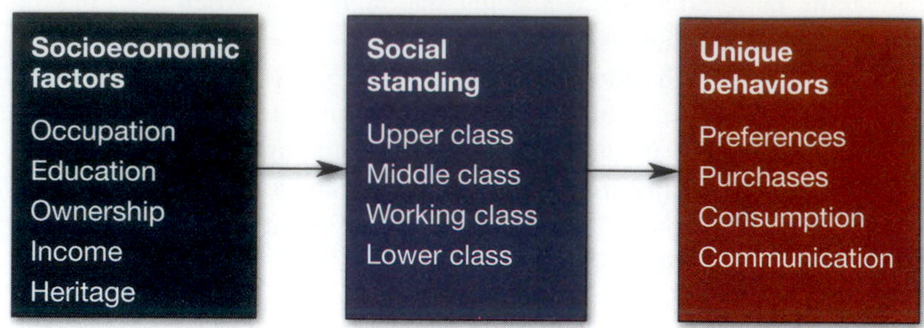

The words *social class* and *social standing* are used interchangeably to mean **societal rank**—*one's position relative to others on one or more dimensions valued by society.* How do we obtain a social standing? Your social standing is a result of characteristics you possess that others in society desire and hold in high esteem. Your education, occupation, ownership of property, income level, and heritage (racial/ethnic background, parents' status) influence your social standing, as shown in Figure 4-2. Social standing ranges from the lower class, those with few or none of the socioeconomic factors desired by society, to the upper class, who possess many of the socioeconomic characteristics considered by society as desirable. Individuals with different social standings tend to have different needs and consumption patterns. Thus, a **social class system** can be defined as:

> a hierarchical division of a society into relatively distinct and homogeneous groups with respect to attitudes, values, and lifestyles.

The fact that members of each social class have a set of unique behaviors makes the concept relevant to marketers. It is important for marketers to understand when social class is an influencing factor and when it is not. Not all behaviors differ between social strata. In fact, most are shared. Therefore, we should recognize that the applicability of social class in the formulation of marketing strategy is product-specific and often situation-specific.

For a social-class system to exist in a society, the individual classes must meet five criteria: they must be (1) bounded, (2) ordered, (3) mutually exclusive, (4) exhaustive, and (5) influential. *Bounded* means that there are clear breaks between each social class. In other words, it is necessary that a rule be devised for each class that will include or exclude any particular individual. *Ordered* means that the classes can be arrayed or spread out in terms of some measure of prestige or status from highest to lowest. *Mutually exclusive* means that an individual can only belong to one social class (though movement from one class to another over time is possible). Requiring social classes to be *exhaustive* means that every member of a social system must fit into some class. Finally, the social classes must be *influential*. That is, there must be behavioral variations between the classes.

Based on these five criteria, it is clear that a strict and tightly defined social class system does not exist in most industrialized nations. The first criteria, that the classes be distinctly bounded, obviously is not so in the United States. The two classic studies of social class in America developed differing numbers of classes (and other researchers have reported yet other breakdowns).[22] If there were indeed firm boundaries, reasonably careful researchers would identify the same number of classes. Likewise, various criteria of social class will place individuals into differing categories. That is, a person may be considered upper-middle class if education is the placement criterion but upper-lower if income is used. This casts doubt on the ability to construct mutually exclusive social classes.

Status Crystallization

"Pure" social classes do not exist in the United States or most other industrialized societies. However, it is apparent that these same societies do have hierarchical groups of individuals and that individuals in those groups do exhibit unique behavior patterns that are different from behaviors in other groups.

What exist are *not a set of social classes,* but a *series of status continua.*[23] These status continua reflect various dimensions or factors that the overall society values. In an achievement-oriented society such as the United States, *achievement-related factors* constitute the primary status dimensions. Thus, education, occupation, income, and, to a lesser extent, quality of residence and place of residence are important status dimensions in the United States. Race and gender are *ascribed* dimensions of social status that are not related to achievement. Likewise, the status of a person's parents is an ascribed status dimension that also exists in the United States. However, heritage is a more important factor in a more traditional society such as England.[24]

The various status dimensions are related to each other both functionally and statistically. In a functional sense, the status of one's parents influences one's education, which in turn influences occupation that generates income, which sets limits on one's lifestyle. Does this mean that an individual with high status based on one dimension will have high status based on the other dimensions? This is a question of **status crystallization.** The more consistent an individual is on all status dimensions, the greater the degree of status crystallization for the individual. Status crystallization is moderate in the United States. For example, many blue-collar workers (such as plumbers and electricians) earn higher incomes than many professionals (such as public school teachers).

SOCIAL STRUCTURE IN THE UNITED STATES

The moderate level of status crystallization in the United States supports the contention that a social class system is not a perfect categorization of social position. However, this does not mean that the population cannot be subdivided into status groups that share similar lifestyles, at least with respect to particular product categories or activities. Furthermore, there are many people with high levels of status crystallization who exhibit many of the behaviors associated with a class system. It is useful for the marketing manager to know the characteristics of these relatively pure class types, even though the descriptions represent a simplified abstraction from reality.

A number of different sets of social classes have been proposed to describe the United States. We will use the one developed by R. P. Coleman and L. Rainwater. Coleman and Rainwater base their social class structure on "reputation," relying heavily on the "man in the street" imagery. A **reputationalist approach:**

> is designed to reflect popular imagery and observation of how people interact with one another—as equals, superiors, or inferiors. Personal and group prestige is at its heart.[25]

In their system, shown in Table 4-4, the *upper class* (14 percent) is divided into three groups primarily on differences in occupation and social affiliations. The *middle class* (70 percent) is divided into a middle class (32 percent) of average-income white- and blue-collar workers living in better neighborhoods and a working class (38 percent) of average-income blue-collar workers who lead a "working-class lifestyle." The *lower class* (16 percent) is divided into two groups, one living just above the poverty level and the other visibly poverty-stricken. Note that the average income associated with each class, particularly the upper classes, will have increased dramatically since Table 4-4 was developed.

TABLE 4-4

The Coleman-Rainwater Social-Class Hierarchy

Upper Americans	• Upper-upper (0.3%). The "capital S society" world of inherited wealth, aristocratic names. • Lower-upper (1.2%). The newer social elite, drawn from current professional, corporate leadership. • Upper-middle class (12.5%). The rest of college graduate managers and professionals; lifestyle centers on careers, private clubs, causes, and the arts.
Middle Americans	• Middle class (32%). Average pay white-collar workers and their blue-collar friends; live on "the better side of town," try to "do the proper things." • Working class (38%). Average pay blue-collar workers; lead "working-class lifestyle" whatever the income, school background, and job.
Lower Americans	• Upper-lower (9%). "A lower group of people but not the lowest"; working, not on welfare; living standard is just above poverty. • Lower-lower (7%). On welfare, visibly poverty-stricken, usually out of work (or have "the dirtiest jobs").

	Typical Profile			
Social Class	*Percent*	*Income*	*Education*	*Occupation*
Upper Americans				
Upper-upper	.3%	$600,000	Master's degree	Board chairman
Lower-upper	1.2	450,000	Master's degree	Corporate president
Upper-middle	12.5	150,000	Medical degree	Physician
Middle Americans				
Middle class	32.0	28,000	College degree	High school teacher
Working class	38.0	15,000	High school	Assembly worker
Lower Americans				
Upper-lower	9.0	9,000	Some high school	Janitor
Lower-lower	7.0	5,000	Grade school	Unemployed

Source: R. P. Coleman, "The Continuing Significance of Social Class in Marketing," *Journal of Consumer Research,* December 1983, p. 267.

The percent of the American population assigned each class in the Coleman-Rainwater system closely parallels the way Americans classify themselves. In one study, Americans were asked to classify themselves into one of five classes.[26] The results were:

Poor	8%
Working	37
Middle	43
Upper-middle	8
Upper	1

The largest difference is the tendency of more Americans to see themselves in the working or middle class than the Coleman-Rainwater does. The Coleman-Rainwater groups are described in more detail in the following sections. An alternative view of social class in America is presented in Consumer Insight 4-1.

Consumer Insight 4-1

Cultural Capital: An Alternate View of Social Status

The traditional view of social class structure is based on the presumption that societies segregate into differential reputational groupings based on economic position and on noneconomic criteria such as morals, culture, and lifestyle that are sustained because people tend to interact with their social peers. The basis for this research was "a Rockwellian image of small town life that represents a minuscule and declining fraction of the contemporary United States . . . Status construction now must deal with the tremendous geographic mobility of American professionals and managers, the privatization of social life, the proliferation of media and travel, and the anonymity of urban environments."

An alternative view of social class and consumption was developed by Bourdieu and modified by Holt. This theory proposes three types of capital that individuals use to produce status. *Social capital* consists of relationships, organizational affiliations, and networks. *Economic capital* represents financial resources that are expressed through consuming goods and activities of material scarcity and imputed luxury. *Cultural capital* consists of a set of socially rare and distinctive tastes, skills, knowledge, and practices.

A high level of cultural capital is acquired in upbringing in families with well-educated parents whose occupations require cultural skills, interaction with peers from similar families, high levels of formal education at institutions that attract other cultural elites studying areas that emphasize critical abstract thinking and communication over the acquisition of particularized skills and knowledge. These reinforcing experiences become embodied as ways of feeling, thinking, and acting.

Cultural capital secures the respect of others through the consumption of objects that are ideationally difficult and so can only be consumed by those few who have acquired the ability to do so. For example, a dinner discussion of the directorial powers reflected in a current movie serves as a claim to particular resources such as knowledge of directorial styles in movies and the ability to analyze these styles. These resources provide reputational currency. Such actions are perceived not as explicit class signals but as bases for whom one is attracted to and admires, or not. Thus, status boundaries are expressed simply through expressing one's tastes.

In addition to tastes expressed in actions, tastes and preferences expressed in product or service ownership or use also signal status. However, cultural tastes are signaled not in terms of the economic value of the items but from the inferred cultural aptitude on the consumer of the item. Thus, owning abstract art implies that the owner has the background and skills necessary to understand and appreciate the art.

The tastes of individuals low in cultural capital are organized to appreciate that which is practical; goods, services, and skills are valued for their functional benefits. Corporeal pleasures are preferred. As an example, these individuals want their houses and furnishings to be comfortable, functional, durable, and easy to care for. In contrast, the tastes of individuals high in cultural capital center on abstract benefits and self-expression. They view their homes as canvasses upon which they express their aesthetic sensibilities.

Critical Thinking Questions

1. Is this view of status in America accurate?
2. If this view of status is accurate, how will individuals high in cultural capital differ from those low in cultural capital in what, how, and why they (a) eat, (b) dress, (c) decorate, (d) read, (e) exercise, and (f) socialize?

Source: D. B. Holt, "Does Cultural Capital Structure American Consumption," *Journal of Consumer Research,* June 1998, pp. 1–24.

Upper Americans (14 Percent)

The Upper-Upper Class Members of the upper-upper social class are aristocratic families who make up the social elite. Members with this level of social status generally are the nucleus of the best country clubs and sponsors of major charitable events. They provide leadership and funds for community and civic activities and often serve as trustees for hospitals, colleges, and civic organizations.

The Kennedy family is a national example of the upper-upper class. Most communities in America have one or more families with significant "old money." These individuals live in excellent homes, drive luxury automobiles, own original art, and travel extensively. They generally stay out of the public spotlight unless it is to enter politics or support a charity or community event.

The Lower-Upper Class The lower-upper class is often referred to as "new rich—the current generation's new successful elite." These families are relatively new in terms of upper-class social status and have not yet been accepted by the upper crust of the community. In some cases, their incomes are greater than those of families in the upper-upper social strata. Bill Gates (founder of Microsoft) and Ted Turner are national examples of the lower-upper class. Most communities have one or more families who have acquired great wealth during one generation.

Many members of this group continue to live lifestyles similar to those of the upper-middle class. This is particularly true of those who acquired their wealth relatively slowly through professional accomplishments. These individuals do not try to emulate or out-do the upper-upper classes. Their income generally exceeds the amount needed to support their lifestyle. They are a prime market for investment services of all types.

Other members of the lower-upper class strive to emulate the established upper-upper class. Entrepreneurs, sports stars, and entertainers who suddenly acquire substantial wealth often engage in this type behavior. However, they are frequently unable to join the same exclusive clubs or command the social respect accorded the true "blue bloods." Many respond by aggressively engaging in **conspicuous consumption.** That is, they purchase and use automobiles, homes, yachts, clothes, and so forth primarily to demonstrate their great wealth. Thus, it is not unusual to read about a star professional athlete who owns 5 or 10 luxury cars, multiple homes, and so forth. These individuals are referred as the **nouveaux riches.** Doing the "in thing" on a grand scale is important to this group. High-status brands and activities are actively sought out by the nouveaux riche.

Together, the upper-upper and lower-upper constitute less than 2 percent of the population. However, shows such as "The Lifestyles of the Rich and Famous" as well as numerous magazines and newspaper articles make the consumption patterns of these two groups quite visible to the general population. Many members of lower social classes would like to emulate at least some aspects of the lifestyles of these groups. Therefore, these groups serve as important market segments for some products and as a symbol of "the good life" to the upper-middle class. Illustration 4-2 shows a product and ad that would appeal to the upper classes.

The Upper-Middle Class The upper-middle class consists of families who possess neither family status derived from heritage nor unusual wealth. Their social position is achieved primarily by their occupation and career orientation. Occupation and education are key aspects of this social stratum, as it consists of successful professionals, independent businesspeople, and corporate managers. As shown in Table 4-4, members of this social class are typically college graduates, many with professional or graduate degrees.

The more successful members of this group prospered during the 1990s. In fact, many accumulated substantial wealth as the stock market rose to record highs. The more marginal members of the upper-middle class have not fared as well. Many were negatively affected by corporate downsizing, reduced government budgets, and the stagnation of earnings during the first half of the decade.

Upper-middle-class individuals tend to be confident and forward looking. They worry about the ability of their children to have the same lifestyle they enjoy. They realize that their success depends on their careers, which in turn depend on education. As a result, they are very concerned about their children's education. Having their children get a sound education from the right schools is very important to them.

Courtesy Sabre Corporation.

ILLUSTRATION 4-2

This product and ad stress elegance and craftsmanship as well as performance. These features appeal to the upper classes.

This group is highly involved in the arts and charities of their local communities. They belong to private clubs where they tend to be quite active. They are a prime market for financial services that focus on retirement planning, estate planning, and college funding issues. They consume fine homes, expensive automobiles, quality furniture, good wines, and nice resorts. Illustration 4-3 contains an advertisement aimed at this group.

While this segment of the U.S. population is small (approximately 12.5 percent), it is highly visible and many Americans would like to belong to it. Because it is aspired to by many, it is an important positioning variable for some products. Figure 4-3 describes this "upward pull" strategy. The ad for Kahlua shown in Illustration 4-4 contains an example of this approach. Kahlua, a relatively inexpensive liqueur, is shown being consumed in very elegant surroundings. Thus, a product readily affordable by the middle and working class is positioned as one that will allow its users to experience some elements of the upper-middle-class lifestyle. However, as we discuss later, this "upward pull" strategy will not work for all products or groups.

Middle Americans (70 Percent)

The Middle Class The middle class is relatively large (approximately 32 percent of the population) and is composed of white-collar workers (office workers, school teachers, lower-level managers) and high-paid blue-collar workers (plumbers, factory supervisors).

ILLUSTRATION 4-3

An ad such as this would appeal to the upper-middle class. It emphasizes celebrating a special event in an elegant and yet private way.

Courtesy Four Seasons Hotels, Inc.

FIGURE 4-3 "Upward Pull" Strategy Targeted at Middle Class

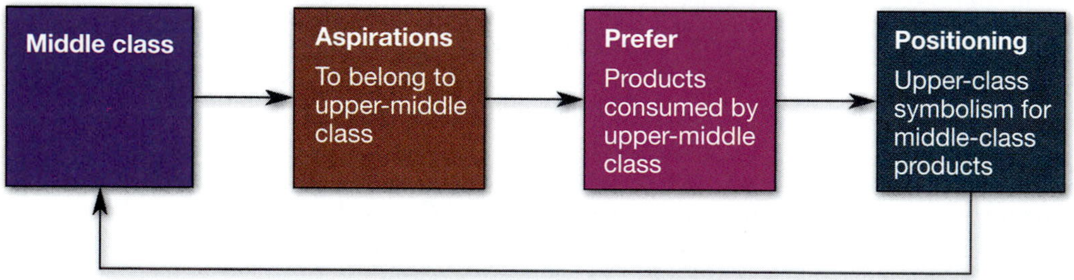

Middle class	→	Aspirations	→	Prefer	→	Positioning
		To belong to upper-middle class		Products consumed by upper-middle class		Upper-class symbolism for middle-class products

(Positioning → back to Middle class)

Thus, the middle class represents the majority of the white-collar group and the top of the blue-collar group. The middle-class core typically has some college (though many do not have a degree), a white-collar or a factory supervisor position, and an average income.

The middle class is concerned about respectability. They care what the neighbors think. They generally live in modest suburban homes. They are deeply concerned about the quality of public schools, crime, drugs, the weakening of "traditional family values," and their family's financial security. Retirement is an increasing concern as firms reduce pension plans and doubts about the Social Security system grow.

Courtesy Hiram Walker, Inc.

ILLUSTRATION 4-4

By positioning a moderately priced product as one that will allow its users to experience some elements of the upper-middle-class lifestyle, Kahlua is using an upward-pull strategy.

Members of the middle class generally avoid elegant furniture and are likely to get involved in do-it-yourself projects. They represent the primary target market for the goods and services of home improvement centers, garden shops, automotive parts houses, as well as mouthwashes and deodorants. With limited incomes, they must balance their desire for current consumption with aspirations for future security. Illustration 4-5 shows a product targeted at this group.

The Working Class The working class (38 percent) is the largest social class segment in the U.S. population, although it is declining in relative size. It consists of skilled and semiskilled factory, service, and sales workers. Though some households in this social stratum seek advancement, members of this stratum are more likely to seek security for and protection of what they already have. This segment suffered seriously during the first half of the 1990s as their average real earnings declined. Automation and the movement of manufacturing activities to developing countries also led to economic insecurity among the working class.

Working-class families live in modest homes or apartments that are often located in marginal urban neighborhoods, decaying suburbs, or rural areas. They are greatly concerned about crime, gangs, drugs, and neighborhood deterioration. They generally cannot afford to move to a different area should their current neighborhood or school become unsafe or otherwise undesirable. Immigration rates concern them as a threat to their jobs. With modest education and skill levels, the more marginal members of this class are in danger of falling into one of the lower classes. Unfortunately, they also often lack the skills and resources to avoid the danger.

The ad shown in Illustration 4-6 would appeal to those members of this class seeking advancement as well as those concerned about downward mobility due to work force reductions.

Many **working-class aristocrats** dislike the upper-middle class and prefer products and stores positioned at their social class level.[27] These individuals are proud of their ability to do "real work" and see themselves as the (often unappreciated) backbone of America. They

ILLUSTRATION 4-5

This ad will appeal to the middle class's focus on home and family, as well as their desire for value and performance.

Advertisement reprinted by permission of Whirlpool Corporation.

are heavy consumers of pickups and campers, hunting equipment, power boats, and beer. Miller Brewing Company gave up attempts to attract a broad audience for its Miller High Life beer. Instead, it is targeting working-class aristocrats with ads that feature bowling alleys, diners, and country music. The ad shown in Illustration 4-7 would appeal to this group.

Lower Americans (16 Percent)

The Upper-Lower Class Approximately 9 percent of the U.S. population can be categorized as members of the upper-lower class. The upper-lower class consists of individuals who are poorly educated, have very low incomes, and work as unskilled laborers (janitor, dishwasher). Most of these jobs are minimum wage. A full-time, 50-week-a-year minimum wage job is not enough to keep a one-earner family of three above the poverty level. In fact, it keeps the family almost 30 percent below the poverty line (this is a major change from the late 1960s, when the minimum wage would support a family of three). Compounding the problem is the fact that many of these jobs are part-time and few provide meaningful benefits such as health insurance or a retirement plan. Consider John Gibson, a 50-year-old part-time janitor in Nashville who makes somewhat more than minimum wage:

"I'd like to work more," John says. However, he is not qualified for many jobs. "I have to make sacrifices but I get by. When I get my check, the first thing I do is pay my rent." John lives alone

Courtesy Olsten Corporation.

ILLUSTRATION 4-6

This ad would appeal to members of the working class seeking advancement as well as to those concerned about downward social mobility due to the changing economy. It would also appeal to some members of the upper-lower classes as well as marginal members of the middle class.

in a small efficiency apartment. One of the things John sacrifices in order to get by is eating at fast-food restaurants. Although he likes the food and the convenience, a co-worker convinced him that it was much cheaper to prepare food at home.

Until recently, John drove a 1978 Pontiac Bonneville: "it started costing me a lot of money. Little things were going wrong, and it was giving me fits." His co-workers helped him buy a 1987 Ford Escort. He minimizes his expenses on clothing by shopping at thrift stores such as the one operated by the Salvation Army.

As a part-time employee, he has no company health insurance but he is now eligible for some coverage from the state of Tennessee. A few years before he had this coverage he was hospitalized. Afterward, his wages were garnished to cover his bills and he was forced to rely on social service agencies. Today he spends a great deal of his spare time volunteering at these same agencies. He would enjoy golf, but is seldom able to play. He has no pension plan or personal insurance and wonders what his retirement years will be like.[28]

Members of the upper-lower class live in marginal housing that is often located in depressed and decayed neighborhoods. Crime, drugs, and gangs are often close at hand and represent very real threats. They are concerned about the safety of their families and their and their children's future. Painfully aware of the lifestyle of the class below them, they strive to avoid slipping into the ranks of the society-dependent, lower-lower class.

Unfortunately, due to their limited education, members in this social stratum have a difficult time moving up in occupation and hence, social status. The lack of education, role models, and opportunities often produces despair that can result in harmful consumption (cigarettes and alcohol). It may also produce inefficient purchasing and a short-term time focus.

ILLUSTRATION 4-7

This product and ad would appeal to the working class, particularly the working-class aristocrats.

Courtesy Wolverine World Wide, Inc.

The Lower-Lower Class The lower-lower social stratum (7 percent), the poverty class, or the "bottom layer" as Coleman and Rainwater have categorized them, has the lowest social standing in society. They have very low incomes and minimal education. This segment of society is often unemployed for long periods of time and is the major recipient of government support and services provided by nonprofit organizations. Andre Hank, as described in Consumer Insight 1-2, is an example of an individual who was in the upper-lower class and then wound up in the lower-lower class when he lost his job.

Many members of this group lack the personal resources in terms of educational background, work habits, health, and attitude to escape unemployment and poverty without external assistance. The major debate of the 104th Congress was over the best means to assist (or some would say force) people to escape a cycle of poverty and hopelessness. It is still too early to tell if the approach taken (sharply limiting the length of time adults can receive welfare) was the correct one.

Marketing to the lower classes is frequently controversial. The rent-to-own business flourishes by renting durable goods such as televisions and refrigerators to lower-class households who frequently cannot afford to acquire them for cash and lack the credit rating to charge the purchases at regular outlets. While this service appears to meet a real need, the industry is frequently criticized for charging exorbitant interest rates on the purchases.[29]

The marketing of "sin" products is even more controversial. Malt liquors and fortified wines sell heavily in lower-class neighborhoods. However, firms that actively promote such products to this market risk significant negative publicity. When R. J. Reynolds tried to market its *Uptown* cigarettes to lower-class urban blacks, public protests became so strong that the product was withdrawn. While one might applaud this outcome, the unstated assumption of the protest is that these individuals lack the ability to make sound consumption decisions and thus require protections that other social classes do not require. This assumption is certainly controversial.

Nike has been criticized for marketing expensive shoes to this market. The argument is that Nike is creating demand for a product that members of the lower class cannot readily afford and that is not a necessity. The assumption is that if Nike did not develop products that appealed to these segments, or if it developed less expensive products, the funds thus saved would be put to better use. *What do you think?* It should be noted that inner-city teenagers are currently trendsetters for several types of fashion and music. Thus, despite limited income, they are an influential market for some products.

Other firms are criticized for not marketing to the lower classes. Major retail chains, particularly food chains, and financial firms seldom provide services in lower-class neighborhoods. Critics argue that such businesses have a social responsibility to locate in these areas. The businesses thus criticized respond that this is a problem for all of society and the solution should not be forced on a few firms. However, as the opening vignette to this chapter described, S. C. Johnson & Son has effectively served this market. Sophisticated chain retailers such as Dollar General Corporation have also begun to meet the unique needs of this segment. As one specialist in this area said:

> people with lower household incomes are still consumers. They still have to buy food. They still wear clothing. They still have to take care of their kids.[30]

The challenge for business is to develop marketing strategies that will meet the needs of these consumers efficiently and at a reasonable profit to the firm.

Conclusions on Social Structure in the United States

The descriptions provided above are brief. In part, this reflects our belief that it is relatively unproductive to attempt to provide very specific descriptions for social classes. The complexity and variety of behaviors and values involved precludes doing a thorough job. Rather, marketing managers must investigate the various status dimensions to determine which, if any, affect the consumption process for their products. In the next section, we discuss how this can be done.

THE MEASUREMENT OF SOCIAL CLASS

As described earlier, education, occupation, income, and, to a lesser extent, place of residence are the primary achievement-based status dimensions used to determine social standing. How do we measure these dimensions in the most useful manner? There are two basic approaches:

1. A single dimension: a single-item index.
2. A combination of several dimensions: a multi-item index.

Single-Item Indexes

Single-item indexes *estimate social status based on a single dimension.* Since an individual's overall status is influenced by several dimensions, single-item indexes are generally less accurate at predicting an individual's social standing or position in a community than are well-developed multi-item indexes. However, single-item indexes allow one to estimate the impact of specific status dimensions on the consumption process. The three most common single-item indexes are (1) education, (2) occupation, and (3) income.

Education Education has traditionally been highly valued in our culture. It has served as the primary path for upward social mobility. Thus, education is a direct measure of status. The higher one's educational level, the more status one has in this and most other societies. Education is a commonly used measure and is a component in two of the three common multiple-item indexes.

Education not only provides status; it influences an individual's tastes, values, and information-processing style. As Table 4-3 indicates, educational level influences all aspects of one's lifestyle and consumption patterns. However, education seldom provides a complete explanation for consumption patterns. For example, a lawyer earning $30,000 per year as a public defender will have a different lifestyle from a lawyer earning $250,000 per year in private practice, despite similar educational backgrounds.

Occupation Occupation is the most widely used single-item index in marketing studies. In fact, occupation is probably the most widely used single cue that allows us to evaluate and define individuals we meet. That this is true should be obvious when you stop to think of the most common bit of information we seek from a new acquaintance: "What do you do?" Almost invariably we need to know someone's occupation to make inferences about his or her probable lifestyle. Occupation is strongly associated with education (which to some extent causes occupation) and income (which to some extent is caused by occupation).

One's occupation provides status. However, the type of work one does and the types of individuals one works with over time also directly influence one's values, lifestyle, and all aspects of the consumption process (see Table 4-2).

A number of approaches are used to assign scores or rankings to the hundreds of occupational categories that exist in an industrial society. The most widely used is the **socioeconomic index (SEI).** This scale is based on the education level and income of individuals in various occupations. The weight given each component was derived so that the score given each occupation was similar to the "standing" assigned that occupation by a large sample of the public. Once the appropriate weights were derived, any occupation could be ranked.

This scale has been revised several times and is the most up-to-date scale available. Table 4-5 provides the SEI scores for a number of job titles.

TABLE 4-5

SEI Scores for Selected Occupations

Occupation	*SEI Score*	*Occupation*	*SEI Score*
Accountant	65	Marketing manager	58
Aerospace engineer	84	Marketing professor	83
Athlete	49	Mail carrier	28
Auto mechanic	21	Plumber	27
Bartender	24	Police	38
Chemist	78	Registered nurse	46
Dentist	89	Sales, Apparel	25
Elementary school teacher	70	Sales, Engineer	78
Housekeeper	15	Stevedore	22

Source: G. Stevens and J. H. Cho, "Socioeconomic Indices," *Social Science Research* 14 (1985), pp. 142–68.

Income Income has traditionally been used as a measure of both purchasing power and status. Wealth clearly provides status. It also enables consumption. However, income *per se* generally *does not cause or direct consumption* to nearly the extent that education and occupation do. For example, over 70 percent of those with annual incomes above $50,000 use the Internet while less than 25 percent of those with incomes less than $25,000 do so.[31] Does income cause one to use the Internet? No. Income allows one to use it by providing funds to purchase the required equipment and pay the service charges. Income is also highly correlated with education and occupation, both of which tend to influence lifestyle, which in turn creates needs that the Internet can meet.

Using income poses a number of measurement problems. Basically, the researcher must decide which income to measure. This involves such decisions as:

- Individual or family income.
- Before or after taxes.
- Salary or total income.

Many individuals may not have accurate knowledge of their incomes as defined by the researcher (i.e., total family pretax income). In addition, individuals are often reluctant to reveal their income, and if they do respond, they may not provide an accurate answer.

Income is clearly necessary to maintain a lifestyle. Likewise, there is a higher status attached to higher incomes than to lower incomes. Still, income does not explain lifestyles very effectively. A college professor or lawyer may have the same income as a truck driver or plumber. Nonetheless, it is likely that their consumption processes for a variety of products will differ. As we will see shortly, income relative to other variables such as occupation may be quite useful, and a number of studies have found it useful when used alone.

Relative Occupational Class Income Thus far, we have been discussing the relative merits of one status dimension over another. However, in some cases, it may be more productive to consider using one status dimension *in conjunction with another.* This is what the concept of **relative occupational class income (ROCI)** involves. ROCI is the "relationship of a family's total income to the median income of other families in the same occupational class."[32] Thus, occupational class is viewed as setting the basic lifestyle, while relative income provides (1) excess funds, (2) neither excess nor deficient funds, or (3) deficient funds for the desired lifestyle. The three categories are referred to as *overprivileged, average,* and *underprivileged,* respectively.

Consider two working-class families with two children each. One has a household income of $22,000 while the second has an income of $60,000. Both desire standard working-class lifestyles, as they have similar education levels and somewhat similar occupations. They are likely to live in similar neighborhoods. However, the first family is underprivileged relative to the average income of the class and will have to sacrifice in order to live in a working-class neighborhood. It may drive an older or smaller car, save less, and take fewer, less expensive vacations. The second family is overprivileged and is a likely market for sport-utility vehicles, power boats, snowmobiles, good camping equipment, and so forth. Studies have found ROCI to influence the consumption of such products as coffee and automobiles. Relative class income (used with Coleman's multi-item index) influences the types of stores shopped.[33]

A closely related concept is **subjective discretionary income (SDI).** SDI is an estimate by the consumer of how much money he or she has available to spend on nonessentials. It is measured by using the responses on a 1-to-6, agree-to-disagree scale to the following statements:

1. No matter how fast our income goes up, we never seem to get ahead.
2. We have more to spend on extras than most of our neighbors do.
3. Our family income is high enough to satisfy nearly all our important desires.

In one large-scale study, SDI was found to add considerable predictive power to total family income (TFI) measures and, for some product categories, to predict purchases when family income did not. Some of the findings include the following:

- Investments such as mutual funds, IRAs, stocks, and luxury cars require relatively high levels of both TFI and SDI.
- Loans and second mortgages are associated with relatively high TFI (necessary to qualify) but low levels of SDI (a felt need for extra cash).
- Fast-food restaurant patronage is predicted by relatively high TFI but relatively low SDI.
- Consumption of low-cost foods such as bologna and packaged spaghetti is not predicted by TFI but is associated with a low SDI.[34]

A study in Australia reached similar conclusions on the value of SDI and TFI for predicting use of various financial services.[35]

Multi-Item Indexes

The use of social class as an explanatory consumer behavior variable has been heavily influenced by two studies, each of which developed a **multi-item index** to measure social class.[36] The basic approach in each of these studies was to determine, through a detailed analysis of a relatively small community, the classes into which the community members appeared to fit. Then, more objective and measurable indicators or factors related to status were selected and weighted in a manner that would reproduce the original class assignments.

Hollingshead Index of Social Position The **Hollingshead Index of Social Position (ISP)** is a two-item index that is well developed and widely used. The item scales, weights, formulas, and social class scores are shown in Table 4-6.

It is important to note that this scale, like most multi-item indexes, was designed to measure or reflect *an individual or family's overall social position within a community.* Because of this, it is possible for a high score on one variable to offset a low score on another. Thus, the following three individuals would all be classified as middle class: (1) someone with an eighth-grade education who is a successful owner of a medium-sized firm; (2) a four-year college graduate working as a salesperson; and (3) a graduate of a junior college working in an administrative position in the civil service. All of these individuals may well have similar standing in the community. However, it seems likely that their consumption processes for at least some products will differ, pointing up the fact that overall status may mask potentially useful associations between individual status dimensions and the consumption process for particular products.

Warner's Index of Status Characteristics Another widely used multi-item scale of social status is Warner's **Index of Status Characteristics (ISC).** Warner's system of mea-

Hollingshead Index of Social Position (ISP) **TABLE 4-6**

	Description	*Score*
Occupation Scale (Weight of 7)	Higher executives of large concerns, proprietors, and major professionals	1
	Business managers, proprietors of medium-sized businesses, and lesser professionals	2
	Administrative personnel, owners of small businesses, and minor professionals	3
	Clerical and sales workers, technicians, and owners of little businesses	4
	Skilled manual employees	5
	Machine operators and semiskilled employees	6
	Unskilled employees	7

	Description	*Score*
Education Scale (Weight of 4)	Professional (MA, MS, ME, MD, Ph.D., LLD, and the like)	1
	Four-year college graduate (BA, BS, BM)	2
	One to three years college (also business schools)	3
	High school graduate	4
	Ten to 11 years of school (part high school)	5
	Seven to nine years of school	6
	Less than seven years of school	7

ISP score = (Occupation score × 7) + (Education score × 4)

	Social Strata	*Range of Scores*
Classification System	Upper	11–17
	Upper-middle	18–31
	Middle	32–47
	Lower-middle	48–63
	Lower	64–77

Source: Adapted from A. B. Hollingshead and F. C. Redlich, *Social Class and Mental Illness* (New York: John Wiley & Sons, 1958).

surement is based on four socioeconomic factors: occupation, source of income, house type, and dwelling area. Each of these dimensions of status is defined over a range of seven categories, and each carries a different weight. This system classifies individuals into one of six social status groups:

Category	*Percent of Population*
Upper-upper	1.4%
Lower-upper	1.6
Upper-middle	10.2
Lower-middle	28.8
Upper-lower	33.0
Lower-lower	25.5

Census Bureau's Index of Socioeconomic Status The U.S. Bureau of the Census uses a three-factor social status index based on occupation, income, and education. This scale, referred to as the **Socioeconomic Status Scale (SES),** produces four social status categories:

Category	*Percent of Population*
Upper	15.1%
Upper-middle	34.5
Middle	34.1
Lower-middle	16.3

Which Scale Should Be Used?

The selection of a measure of social status or prestige requires one first to select the most appropriate prestige or status dimension for the problem at hand. When an individual's total personal or family status is the dimension of concern, perhaps in a study of opinion leadership, a multi-item index such as the Warner or Hollingshead index would be most appropriate. Studies of taste and intellectually oriented activities such as magazine readership or television viewing should consider education as the most relevant dimension. Occupation might be most relevant for studies focusing on leisure-time pursuits.

Issues and Assumptions in Using Social Class

A number of issues and assumptions are involved in using social class. First, there is a tendency for marketers to assume that all individuals desire upward social mobility and/or want to emulate the behaviors and consumption patterns of those above them. However, as we have seen, this is frequently not the case. Many individuals are quite content with their social standing and lifestyle. This is true not only for older individuals but also for younger people. Many teenagers and young adults today are aspiring to the lifestyle and social status enjoyed by their parents. Appeals to upward social mobility are not effective with these individuals.

Class consciousness is generally quite low in American society. Americans don't generally think in terms of social classes, and most describe themselves as "middle class" when asked. Thus, direct or obvious class-based appeals would not work with many individuals.

Most social-class measures and theories were developed before *the rapid expansion of the role of women.* Traditionally, women acquired the status of their husbands. They had few opportunities outside the home and had limited access to education or careers. This has changed radically in recent years. Now women bring educational, financial, and occupational prestige to the household just as males do. Other than using total household income rather than the male's income, no scale has been developed that fully accounts for the new reality of dual sources of status for a household. The fact that marriages are generally among individuals with similar educational and occupational backgrounds minimizes the problems this would otherwise cause.

Finally, as we will see in Chapter 12, *lifestyle segments* that have much in common with social class but with less emphasis on status and permanence are frequently a superior way to understand society.

SOCIAL STRATIFICATION AND MARKETING STRATEGY

While social stratification does not explain all consumption behaviors, it is certainly relevant for some product categories. For clear evidence of this, visit a furniture store in a working-class neighborhood and then an upper-class store such as Ethan Allen Galleries.

The first task managers must perform is to determine, for their product categories, which aspects of the consumption process are affected by social status. This will generally require research in which relevant measures of social class are taken and associated with product/brand usage, purchase motivation, outlet selection, media usage, and so forth.

Product/brand utilization often varies widely across social strata. Income clearly restricts the purchase of some products such as expensive sports cars and boats. Education often influences consumption of fine art as well as mass media. Occupation appears to be related closely to leisure activities.

The consumption of imported wine, liqueurs, and original art varies with social class. Beer is consumed across all social classes, but Michelob is more popular at the upper end and Pabst is more popular at the lower end. A product/brand may have different meanings to members of different social strata. Blue jeans may serve as economical, functional clothing items to working-class members and as stylish, self-expressive items to upper-class individuals. Likewise, different purchase motivations for the same product may exist between social strata. Individuals in higher social classes use credit cards for convenience (they pay off the entire balance each month), while individuals in lower social classes use them for installment purchases (they do not pay off the entire bill at the end of each month).

For products such as those described above, social class represents a useful segmentation variable. Having selected a segment based on usage rate, purchase motivation, or product/brand meaning, the marketer must position the brand in a manner consistent with the desired target market.

Figure 4-4 illustrates how Anheuser-Busch covers more than 80 percent of the U.S. population by carefully positioning three different brands. Table 4-7 indicates that consumers perceive these brands very clearly in social class terms.

TABLE 4-7 Perceived Social-Class Appeal of Various Beer Brands

	Social Class*				
	Upper/ Upper Middle	*Middle*	*Lower Middle*	*Upper Lower/ Lower*	*All Classes*
Brand					
Coors	22	54	16	2	3
Budweiser	4	46	37	7	4
Miller	14	50	22	6	6
Michelob	67	23	4	1	2
Old Style†	3	33	36	22	1
Bud Light	22	53	14	3	5
Heineken	88	9	1	—	1

*Percent classifying the brand as most appropriate for a particular social class.

†Local beer on tap.

Source: K. Grønhaug and P. S. Trapp, "Perceived Social Class Appeals of Various Branded Goods," *Journal of Consumer Marketing,* Winter 1989, p. 27.

FIGURE 4-4 Anheuser-Busch Positioning to Social Class Segments

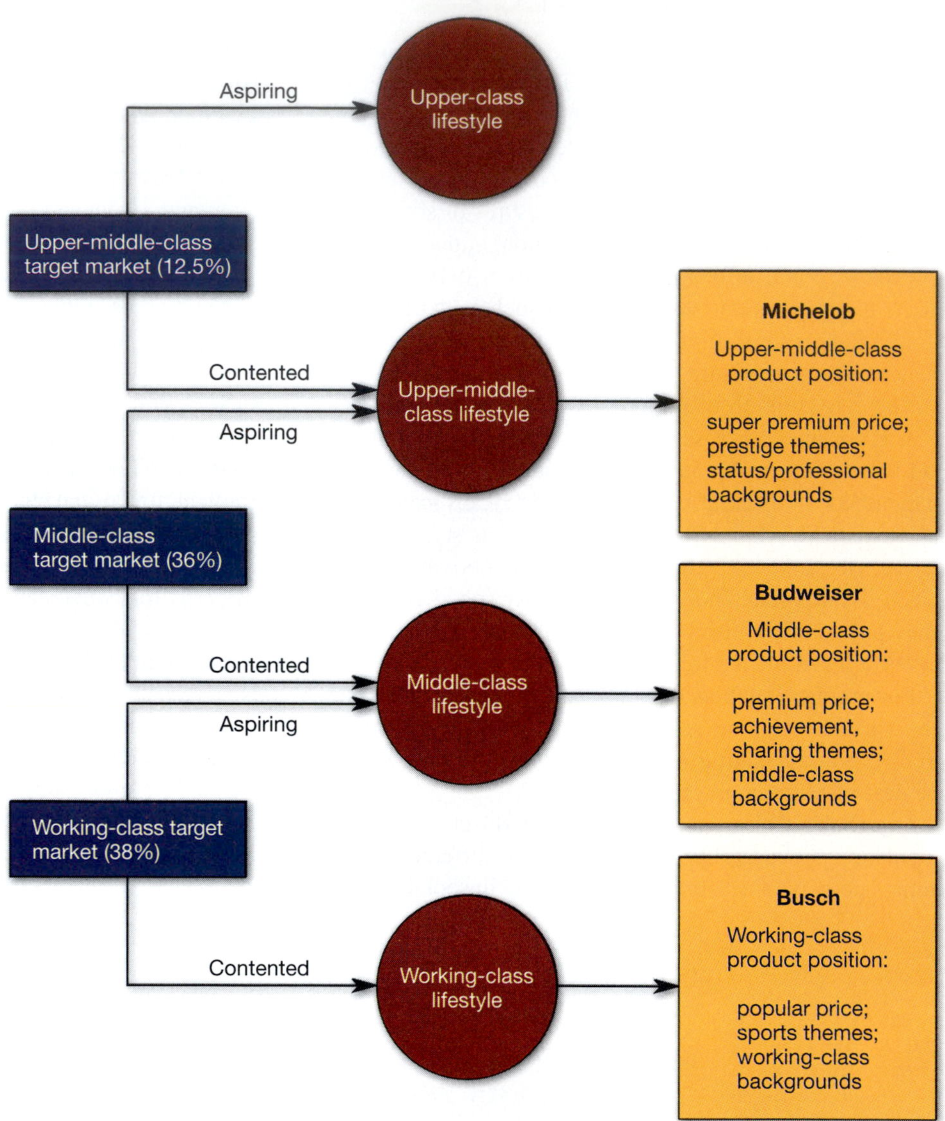

SUMMARY

American society is described in part by its *demographics,* which include a population's size, distribution, and structure. The structure of a population refers to its age, income, education, and occupation makeup. Demographics are not static. At present, the rate of population growth is moderate, average age is increasing, southern and western regions are growing, the workforce contains more women and white-collar workers than ever before, and per capita income grew in 1995 after six years of stagnation or decline. Since demographics affect all aspects of the consumption process, marketers must anticipate these shifts and adjust their marketing mixes accordingly.

A *social class system* is defined as the hierarchical division of a society into relatively permanent and homogeneous groups with respect to attitudes, values, and lifestyles.

For a social class system to exist in a society, the individual classes must meet five criteria. They must be (1) *bounded,* (2) *ordered,* (3) *mutually exclusive,*

(4) *exhaustive,* and (5) *influential.* Using these criteria, it is obvious that a strict and tightly defined social-class system does not exist in the United States. What does seem to exist is a series of status continua that reflect various dimensions or factors that the overall society values. Education, occupation, income, and, to a lesser extent, type of residence are important status dimensions in this country. *Status crystallization* refers to the consistency of individuals and families on all relevant status dimensions (e.g., high income and high educational level).

While pure social classes do not exist in the United States, it is useful for marketing managers to know and understand the general characteristics of major social classes. Using Coleman and Rainwater's system, we described American society in terms of seven major categories (*upper-upper, lower-upper, upper-middle, middle, working class, upper-lower,* and *lower-lower*).

There are two basic approaches to the measurement of social classes: (1) use a combination of several dimensions, a *multi-item index,* or (2) use a single dimension, a *single-item index.* Multi-item indexes are designed to measure an individual's overall rank or social position within the community. Problems occur in doing this because of inconsistencies between status items. Single-item indexes estimate status based on a single-status dimension. Income, education, and occupation are the most frequently used measures of social status.

Since there is no one, unidimensional status or class continuum, it is impossible to state which is the best measure. Rather, the choice of the measure to be used should depend on its appropriateness or relevance to the problem at hand. Increasingly, the use of one status dimension in conjunction with another seems appropriate. *Relative occupational class income* (ROCI) is a good example of such an approach. *Subjective discretionary income* (SDI), which measures how much money consumers feel they have available for nonessentials, is also useful to marketers.

KEY TERMS

Conspicuous consumption 124
Demographics 112
Hollingshead Index of Social Position (ISP) 134
Index of Status Characteristics (ISC) 134
Multi-item indexes 134
Nouveaux riches 124
Relative occupational class income (ROCI) 133
Reputationalist approach 121
Single-item indexes 131
Social class system 120
Societal rank 120
Socioeconomic index (SEI) 132
Socioeconomic Status Scale (SES) 136
Status crystallization 121
Subjective discretionary income (SDI) 133
Working-class aristocrats 127

INTERNET EXERCISES

1. Use the Internet to describe the following characteristics of the U.S. population in 2010. (Hint: http://www.census.gov is a good place to start, as is http://www.easidemographics.com.) How will this differ from the way it is today? What are the marketing strategy implications of these shifts?
   a. Total size and size by major census region
   b. Age distribution
   c. Education level
   d. Occupation structure
   e. Income level
2. Use the Internet to provide a demographic description of your community now and as forecast for 2010.
3. Using the Internet, prepare a report on the social status structure of the United States. Provide the name and URL of all Web sites that you used in this report.
4. What is available on the Internet relevant to the role that education, occupation, and income play in the purchase of the following? What do you conclude about the usefulness of the Internet for gathering this type data at this point in time?
   a. Mountain bikes
   b. Internet shopping
   c. Television viewing
   d. Cigarette smoking
5. Evaluate the services provided at http://www.easidemographics.com.

DDB NEEDHAM LIFESTYLE DATA ANALYSES

1. Which demographic variables are most closely associated with heavy consumption of the following? What would explain this association? Which contributes most to causing the consumption? (See Tables 1 through 7.)
   a. Pancakes
   b. Movie attendance
   c. Video rental
   d. Cigarettes
2. Which demographic variables are most closely associated with ownership of the following? What would explain this association? Which contributes most to causing the ownership? (See Tables 1 through 7.)
   a. 35mm camera
   b. Personal computer
   c. Handgun
   d. Common stock
3. Examine the DDB Needham data in Tables 1 through 7. Which demographic variables are most closely associated with enjoying the following? What would explain this association? Which contributes most to causing this enjoyment?
   a. "E.R."
   b. "Melrose Place"
   c. "Seinfeld"
   d. "Saturday Night Live"
4. Which demographic variables are most closely associated with the following? What would explain this association? Which contributes most to causing the attitude or belief? (See Tables 1a, 2a, 3a, 4a, 5a, 6a, and 7a.)
   a. Liking to cook.
   b. Having a lot of spare time.
   c. Believing in buying American products.
   d. Feeling that commercials place too much emphasis on sex.
   e. Feeling like a winner.
   f. Feeling sexy.

REVIEW QUESTIONS

1. What are demographics?
2. Why is population growth an important concept for marketers?
3. What trend(s) characterizes the occupational structure of the United States?
4. What trend(s) characterizes the level of education in the United States?
5. What trend(s) characterizes the level of income in the United States?
6. What trend(s) characterizes the age distribution of the American population?
7. What is a social class system?
8. Describe the five criteria necessary for a social class system to exist.
9. What is meant by the statement, "What exists is not a set of social classes but a series of status continua"?
10. What underlying cultural value determines most of the status dimensions in the United States?
11. What is meant by status crystallization? Is the degree of status crystallization relatively high or low in the United States? Explain.
12. Briefly describe the primary characteristics of each of the classes described in the text (assume a high level of status crystallization).
13. What ethical issues arise in marketing to the lower social classes? 
14. What are the two basic approaches used by marketers to measure social class?
15. Why is education sometimes used as an index of status?
16. What are the advantages of using occupation as an indication of status?
17. What are the problems associated with using income as an index of status?
18. What is meant by relative occupational class income? Why is the general idea behind this concept particularly appealing?
19. What is meant by subjective discretionary income? How does it affect purchases?
20. What are the advantages of multi-item indexes? The disadvantages?
21. Describe the Hollingshead Index of Social Position.
22. How should a marketing manager select the most appropriate measure of status?

DISCUSSION QUESTIONS

23. Which demographic shifts, if any, do you feel will have a noticeable impact on the market for the following in the next 10 years? Justify your answer.
    a. Snowboards
    b. Vacations
    c. Casual restaurants
    d. Soft drinks
    e. "Green" products
    f. Magazines
24. Given the changes in America's demographics, name five products that will face increasing demand and five that will face declining demand.
25. Why do the regional differences shown in Figure 4-1 exist? What are the implications of such differences for marketers of products such as soft drinks?
26. Will the increasing median age of our population affect the general "tone" of our society? In what ways?
27. Which status variable, if any, is most related to:
    a. Watching professional football on TV
    b. Snowboarding
    c. Foreign travel
    d. Luxury car ownership
    e. Type of pet owned
    f. Charity contributions
28. How could a knowledge of social stratification be used in the development of a marketing strategy for:
    a. A men's clothing store
    b. A magazine
    c. A health club
    d. Clothes detergent
    e. Foreign vacations
    f. The United Way
29. Do you think the United States is becoming more or less stratified over time?
30. Do your parents have a high or low level of status crystallization? Explain.
31. Based on the Hollingshead two-factor index, what social class would your father be in? Your mother? What class will you be in at their age?
32. Name four products for which each of the three following single-factor indexes would be most appropriate as measurements of status. Justify your answer.
    a. Income
    b. Education
    c. Occupation
33. Name four products in addition to automobiles for which the relative occupational class income concept would be particularly useful. Justify your selection.
34. Evaluate the subjective discretionary income concept. How does it differ from ROCI? Which is more useful? Why?
35. How do you feel about each of the ethical issues or controversies the text described with respect to marketing to the lower classes? What other ethical issues do you see in this area?

36. Is it ethical for marketers to use the mass media to promote products that most members of the lower classes and working class cannot afford?

37. Would your answer to Question 36 change if the products were limited to children's toys?

38. Name five products for which the "upward pull strategy" shown in Figure 4-3 would be appropriate. Name five for which it would be inappropriate. Justify your answers.
39. What causes the results shown in Table 4-7?
40. Social classes evolved under the communist system in China despite government opposition. Why?

APPLICATION ACTIVITIES

41. Interview a salesperson at the following locations and obtain a description of the "average" purchaser in demographic terms. Are the demographic shifts predicted in the text going to increase or decrease the size of this average-purchaser segment?
    a. Mercedes dealership
    b. Mountain bike outlet
    c. Travel agent (vacation travel)
    d. Pharmacy
    e. Golf equipment outlet
    f. Florist
42. Using Standard Rate and Data or Simmons Research Bureau studies, pick three magazines that are oriented toward different social classes. Comment on the differences in content and advertising.

43. Interview a salesperson from an expensive, moderate, and inexpensive outlet for the following. Ascertain their perceptions of the social classes or status of their customers. Determine if their sales approach differs with differing classes.
    a. Men's clothing
    b. Women's clothing
    c. Furniture
    d. Jewelry
44. Examine a variety of magazines/newspapers and clip or describe an advertisement that positions a product as appropriate for each of the seven social classes described in the text (one ad per class).
45. Interview an unskilled worker, schoolteacher, retail clerk, and successful businessperson all in their 30s or 40s. Measure their social status using one of the multi-item measurement devices. Evaluate their status crystallization and their unique and similar consumer behaviors.
46. Visit a bowling alley and a tennis club parking lot. Analyze the differences in the types of cars, dress, and behaviors of those patronizing these two sports.
47. Volunteer to work two days or evenings at a homeless shelter, soup kitchen, or other program aimed at very-low-income families. Write a brief report on your experiences and reactions.

REFERENCES

1. C. Miller, "The Have-Nots," *Marketing News,* August 1, 1994, pp. 1–2.
2. E. Neuborne, "Welcome to Yuppie Hardware," *Business Week,* December 21, 1998, pp. 94–95.
3. *U.S. Census Bureau, Population Division, Population Projections Branch,* March 29, 1999.
4. See S. Mitchell, "Birds of a Feather," *American Demographics,* February 1995, pp. 40–48.
5. For example, see M. Goode and L. Moutinho, "The Effects of Consumers' Age on Overall Satisfaction," *Journal of Professional Services Marketing,* no. 2 (1996), pp. 93–112.
6. "Resident Population of the United States: Middle Series Projections, 2001–2005, by Age and Sex," (Washington, D.C.: U.S. Bureau of the Census, March 1996).
7. P. Sloan and J. Neff, "With Aging Boomers in Mind, P&G, Den-Mat Plan Launches," *Advertising Age, April 13, 1998,* p. 3.
8. "Changes in the Occupational Structure," in *Statistical Forecasts of the United States,* ed. J. E. Person, Jr., (Washington, D.C.: Gale Research Inc., 1993), pp. 444–45.
9. P. Mergenhagen, "What Can Minimum Wage Buy?" *American Demographics,* January 1996, pp. 32–36; and W. O'Hare and J. Schwartz, "One Step Forward, Two Steps Back," *American Demographics,* September 1997, pp. 53–56.
10. "Median Income in the United States: 1997," *Current Population Reports* (Washington, D.C.: U.S. Bureau of the Census, 1997), p. 26.
11. D. Crispell, "Dual-Earner Diversity," *American Demographics,* July 1995, p. 35.
12. Ibid.; and G. E. Smith, "Framing in Advertising and the Moderating Impact of Consumer Education," *Journal of Advertising Research,* September 1996, pp. 49–64.
13. See A. D. Mathios, "Socioeconomic Factors, Nutrition, and Food Choice," *Journal of Public Policy & Marketing,* Spring 1996, pp. 45–54.
14. S. Fulwood III, "Americans Draw Fatter Paychecks," *Eugene Register-Guard,* September 27, 1996, p. 1; and E. Kacapyr, "Are You Middle Class?" *American Demographics,* October 1996, pp. 31–35.
15. See F. H. Frank, *Luxury Fever* (New York: Free Press, 1999).
16. For an example, see F. J. Mulhern, J. D. Williams, and R. P. Leone, "Variability of Brand Price Elasticities across Retail Stores," *Journal of Retailing* no. 3 (1998), pp. 427–45.
17. M. Johnson, "The Application of Geodemographics to Retailing," *Journal of the Market Research Society,* January 1997, p. 212.
18. J. Lawrence, "Frito's Micro Move," *Advertising Age,* February 12, 1990, p. 44.
19. J. A. McCarty and L. J. Shrum, "The Role of Personal Values and Demographics in Predicting Television Viewing Behavior," *Journal of Advertising,* December 1993, pp. 77–101; W. J. McDonald, "The Role of Demographics, Purchase Histories, and Shopper Decision-Making Styles in Predicting Consumer Catalog Loyalty," *Journal of Direct Marketing,* Summer 1993, pp. 55–65; and M. R. Stafford, "Demographic Discriminators of Service Quality in the Banking Industry," *Journal of Services Marketing,* no. 4 (1996), pp. 6–22.
20. K. Labich, "Class in America," *Fortune,* February 7, 1994, p. 114.
21. R. P. Coleman and L. Rainwater, *Social Standing in America: New Dimensions of Class* (New York: Basic Books, 1978), p. 18.
22. See A. B. Hollingshead, *Elmstown's Youth* (New York: John Wiley & Sons, 1949); and W. L. Warner, M. Meeker, and K. Eels, *Social Class in America: A Manual of Procedure for the Measurement of Social Status* (Chicago: Science Research Associates, 1949).
23. J. E. Fisher, "Social Class and Consumer Behavior," in *Advances in Consumer Research XIV,* ed. M. Wallendorf and P. Anderson (Provo, UT: Association for Consumer Research, 1987), pp. 492–96.

24. See R. P. Heath, "The New Working Class," *American Demographics*, January 1998, pp. 51–55.
25. R. Coleman, "The Continuing Significance of Social Class in Marketing," *Journal of Consumer Research*, December 1983, p. 265.
26. See footnote 24.
27. See J. P. Dickson and D. L. MacLachlan, "Social Distance and Shopping Behavior," *Journal of the Academy of Marketing Science,* Spring 1990, pp. 153–62.
28. Footnote 9.
29. R. H. Hill, D. L. Ramp, and L. Silver, "The Rent-to-Own Industry and Pricing Disclosure Tactics," *Journal of Public Policy & Marketing,* Spring 1998, pp. 1–10.
30. Footnote 1, p. 2.
31. *1998 Interactive Media Survey* (Chicago: Advertising Age, 1998), p. 1.
32. W. H. Peters, "Relative Occupational Class Income: A Significant Variable in the Marketing of Automobiles," *Journal of Marketing,* April 1970, p. 74.
33. S. Dawson, B. Stern, and T. Gillpatrick, "An Empirical Update and Extension of Patronage Behaviors across the Social Class Hierarchy," in *Advances in Consumer Research XVII,* ed. M. E. Goldberg, G. Gorn, and R. W. Pollay (Provo, UT: Association for Consumer Research, 1990), pp. 833–38.
34. T. C. O'Guinn and W. D. Wells, "Subjective Discretionary Income," *Marketing Research*, March 1989, pp. 32–41; see also P. L. Wachtel and S. J. Blatt, "Perceptions of Economic Needs and of Anticipated Future Income," *Journal of Economic Psychology,* September 1990, pp. 403–15.
35. J. R. Rossiter, "'Spending Power' and the Subjective Discretionary Income (SDI) Scale," in *Advances in Consumer Research XXII,* ed. F. R. Kardes and M. Sujan (Provo, UT: Association for Consumer Research, 1995), pp. 236–40.
36. See footnote 1.

144

Chris Usher.

chapter five

The Changing American Society: Subcultures

Laura Schaefer (facing page), a salesperson at the Wavedancer surf-and-skateboard shop, is handling Christmas returns. The returns consist of clothes that fit snugly and shoes unsuitable for skateboarding. "My mom and dad got me these," usually accompanies each return. These teens prefer brands like Mudd, Paris Blues, In Vitro, Cement. Brands most of their parents have never heard of. Nike and Levi's are no longer "cool." "They just went out of style," says a 13-year-old shopper. A Levi's market research director says: "We all got older, and as a consequence, we lost touch with teenagers."

"Mom and dad" are not the only ones struggling to understand this emerging generation. Manufacturing and retailing are awaking to the fact that the largest generation since the baby boom is coming of age and is very different from the older generations. Firms such as Universal Studios, Coca-Cola, and McDonald's use "street teams" of young people to research this market. These teams hang out in clubs, parks, and malls talking to teens about everything from fashion to finance in an attempt to discover trends as they emerge. General Motors brings teens and younger children into car clinics to measure their attitudes about current and prototype future cars. These and many other established firms echo Levi's feeling: "This is a generation that must be reckoned with. They are going to take over the country."

Researchers and other experts have noted a number of characteristics of what some call Generation Y.

- One in three is not Caucasian. One in four lives in a single-parent household. Three in four have working mothers. Most have grown up with a computer.
- The old-style advertising that works very well with boomers, ads that push a slogan and an

image and a feeling, the younger consumer is not going to go for. Instead, they respond to humor, irony, and the (apparently) unvarnished truth. Sprite has done well with its ads that parody celebrity endorsers and carry the tagline: "Image is nothing. Obey your thirst."

- The Internet is their medium. No Doubt, a band with a teen following, was recently booked into a small Manhattan venue. On opening night the house was packed with teenage girls dressed just like the lead singer. Says the promoter: "How do they know this? How do they keep up with what she's wearing? It's not from network television. It's online."
- This is a very pragmatic group. At 18 years old, they already have five-year plans. They are already looking at how they will be balancing their work/family commitments.

While many firms have consistently targeted the teenage market, most assumed a relatively stable continuum over preferences and values over time. However, this generation is distinct in a number of ways from the one that preceded it. Generation Y will carry its unique characteristics into the future as it enters early adulthood during the next decade. As one marketer states:

> Most marketers perceive them as kids. When you do that, you fail to take in what they are telling you about the consumers they're becoming. This is not about teenage marketing. It's about the coming of age of a generation.[1]

In the previous chapter, we described how changes in American values were creating challenges and opportunities for marketers. Another extremely important aspect of the American society is its numerous subcultures such as the teenage subculture described above. Although American society has always contained numerous subcultures, until recently many marketers treated it as a homogeneous culture based primarily on Western European values. Though this view of America was never accurate, it is even less so today as non-European immigration, differential birthrates, and increased ethnic identification accentuate the heterogeneous nature of our society.

An array of racial, ethnic, nationality, religious, age, and regional groups or subcultures characterize American society. These subcultures are growing at different rates and are themselves undergoing change.

In this chapter, we describe the more important subcultures in America. We also highlight the marketing strategy implications of a heterogeneous rather than a homogeneous society.

THE NATURE OF SUBCULTURES

A **subculture** is *a segment of a larger culture whose members share distinguishing patterns of behavior.* The unique patterns of behavior shared by subculture group members are based on the social history of the group as well as on its current situation. Subculture members are also part of the larger culture in which they exist. Subculture members generally share many behaviors and beliefs with the core culture. As Figure 5-1 indicates, the degree to which an individual behaves in a manner unique to a subculture depends on the extent to which the individual identifies with that subculture.

America has traditionally been viewed as a melting pot or a soup bowl. Immigrants from various countries would come to America and quickly (at least by the second generation) surrender their old languages, values, behaviors, and even religions. In their place, they

Identification with a Subculture Produces Unique Market Behaviors **FIGURE 5-1**

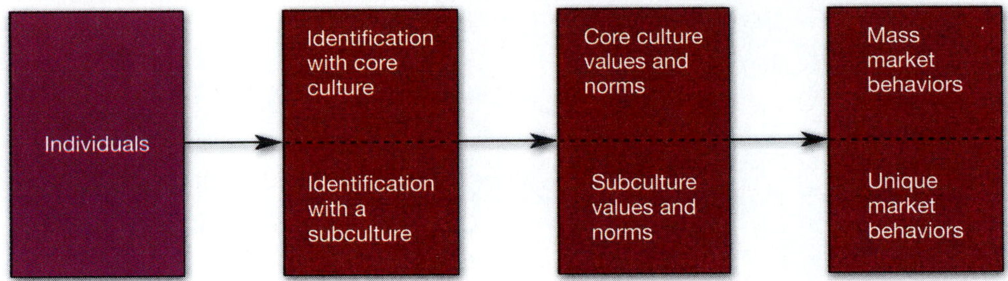

would acquire American characteristics that were largely a slight adaptation of Western European, particularly British, features. The base American culture was vast enough that new immigrants did not change the flavor of the mixture to any noticeable extent. While this view was a reasonable approximation for most Western European immigrants, it was never very accurate for African, Hispanic, Asian, or Arabic immigrants. Nor did it accurately describe the experience of the Native American.

Today, America is often described as a salad rather than a melting pot or a soup bowl. When a small amount of a new ingredient is added to soup, it generally loses its identity completely and blends into the overall flavor of the soup. In a salad, each ingredient retains its own unique identity while adding to the color and flavor of the overall salad. The soup analogy is probably most accurate for European immigrants and nationality groups,[2] while the salad analogy most closely describes the experience of non-European immigrants and nationality groups. However, even in the salad bowl analogy, we should add a large serving of salad dressing that represents the core American culture and that blends the diverse groups into a cohesive society.

Astute marketers are aggressively pursuing opportunities created by increased diversity. AT&T runs broadcast and print ads in 20 different languages in the United States! EABC, a cable and satellite network, broadcasts programming in Arabic, Asian, Indian, Chinese, Filipino, Greek, Italian, Korean, Polish, and Russian. Chrysler advertises its New Yorker model by stressing safety features to the general market, styling to African-Americans, and aspiration and achievement to Hispanics. However, marketing to ethnic groups requires a thorough understanding of the attitudes and values of each group. For example, a New York Life Insurance ad designed to appeal to Koreans was a disaster because it used a Chinese model.[3]

Ethnic groups are the most commonly described subcultures, but generations, religions, and geographic regions are also the bases for strong subcultures in the United States. Thus, *we are all members of several subcultures.* Each subculture may influence different aspects of our lifestyle. Our attitudes toward new products or imported products may be strongly influenced by our regional subculture, our taste in music by our generation subculture, our food preferences by our ethnic subculture, and our alcohol consumption by our religious subculture. The communications manager at Miller Brewing describes his firm's view of the influence of ethnicity and age on consumption:

> We used to have an ethnic marketing department up until several years ago . . . (But now we believe) the things that young Hispanic or young African-American or young white people have in common are much stronger and more important than any ethnic difference.[4]

ILLUSTRATION 5-1

The degree to which a message needs to be customized for an ethnic audience varies by product and strategy. This billboard continues Mountain Dew's successful approach but uses the Spanish language.

Michael Hruby.

This manager believes that age is more important than ethnicity in influencing the behaviors of the members of his target market for his product. The Mountain Dew billboard shown in Illustration 5-1 reflects a modified version of this view. This ad, targeting young Hispanics, uses the same theme and style as other Mountain Dew ads but it uses Spanish in the copy.

Determining which subculture, if any, is an important determinant of behavior for a specific product is an important task for marketing managers. In the sections that follow, we describe the major ethnic, religious, regional, and age subcultures in America. While we will describe the mode or general nature of these subcultures, it must be emphasized that *there are very large variations within each subculture.* Our focus in this chapter is on America, but all countries have a variety of subcultures that marketers must consider.

ETHNIC SUBCULTURES

Until the 2000 Census, the Bureau of the Census used the terms *black, white, Asian/Pacific Islander,* and *American Indian/Alaskan Native/Aleut* and *Other* to describe America's major racial groups. *Hispanic* was used as an ethnic term to describe individuals from Spanish-speaking cultures regardless of race. Under this system, people of Arab background were considered white and people from China, India, and Samoa were grouped together. There are obvious problems with such a system, and over 10 million Americans

Ethnic Subcultures in the United States: 1990–2010 **FIGURE 5-2**

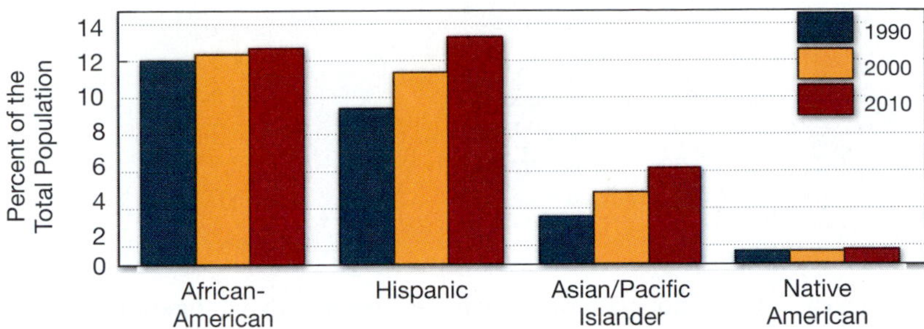

refused to place themselves into one of the racial categories used in the 1990 Census. In addition, many younger Hispanics do not consider themselves to be white or black, but to be Hispanics or Latinos. Other individuals have parents from two different races and are proud of their mixed heritage.[5] Romona Douglas, of white, black, and American Indian descent, describes her feelings as follows:

> The assumption is that black people are a certain way, and white people are a particular way, and Asians are a certain way. Well, what about multi-racial families? I don't appreciate a McDonald's commercial with a street-wise black person. That is not me, that is not my upbringing. A lot of marketing campaigns are based on stereotypes of mono-racial communities.[6]

In the 2000 Census, the Hispanic question will appear before the race question. Respondents will be asked if they are *Spanish/Hispanic/Latino.* To answer yes, respondents select a nationality group as well (*Mexican/Mexican Am./Chicano, Puerto Rican, Cuban, Other—please print*). In the race question that follows, respondents will be able to make multiple selections from 15 categories (*White, Black, African American/Negro; American Indian/Alaskan Native; Asian Indian; Chinese; Filipino; Japanese; Korean; Vietnamese; Native Hawaiian; Guamanian/Chamorro; Samoan; Other Asian; Other Race*). With this system, Douglas could accurately identify herself. However, Americans of Arab or Middle-Eastern descent are disappointed that there is not a category for them. Despite such shortcomings, marketers are excited about the additional insights the new data will provide. Unfortunately, data from the 2000 Census will not be readily available until 2002.[7]

We will define **ethnic subcultures** broadly as *those whose members' unique shared behaviors are based on a common racial, language, or nationality background.* Figure 5-2 provides the current and projected sizes of the major ethnic groups in America. As this figure makes clear, non-European ethnic groups constitute a significant and growing part of our population (from 24 percent in 1990 to 32 percent by 2010). The percentages shown in the figure understate the importance of these ethnic groups to specific geographic regions. Ethnic groups tend to concentrate in relatively few areas of the country.[8] Thus, Hispanics are the largest population group in parts of Arizona, Florida, New Mexico, and Texas, while Asian-Americans are the largest group in Honolulu, and African-Americans are a majority in parts of the South.

The relatively faster growth rate of non-European groups is due to a higher birthrate among some of these groups and to greater immigration. Immigration has accounted for over a third of the U.S. population growth over the past several decades. About 800,000 legal immigrants arrive each year. In 1997, the sources of these immigrants were (these percents have been relatively stable over the past decade):

Asia	33.3%
Mexico	18.4
Europe	15.0
Caribbean	13.2
Central/South America	12.1
Africa	6.0[9]

Clearly, immigration patterns have fueled the growth of ethnic subcultures. The influx of ethnic immigrants not only increases the size of the ethnic subcultures, it also reinforces the unique behaviors and attitudes derived from the group's home culture. In the following sections, we describe the major ethnic subcultures. It is critical to remember that *all subcultures are very diverse, and general descriptions do not apply to all of the members.*[10]

AFRICAN-AMERICANS

Debra Sandler, director of Flavor Brands (*Slice, Mountain Dew, Mug Root Beer,* etc.) for PepsiCo, recently discussed the differences in marketing to the overall market and marketing to African-Americans.

> The strategy does not differ, the tactics differ. For example, if we say we want to be the beverage of choice to all teens, one of the things we have to do if we want to get to where teens are, to where they live and breathe, is to be wherever they are. We want to be available; we also want to be seen as part of their lifestyle. The difference is we may go about that differently for an 18-year-old Anglo male who lives in the suburbs than for an 18-year-old African-American male who happens to live in an urban environment.
>
> For example, we did a promotion where we gave away prizes—jet skis and convertibles. One thing we heard loud and clear from the urban teens was that they didn't participate in the promotion because they didn't think the prizes were relevant. So sometimes the tactics must change . . . While we, African-American consumers, are our own segment, we are also very much a part of the mainstream. In fact, in many cases we are driving the mainstream . . . Again, in reaching teens, if I can produce television creative that appeals to an urban 18-year-old male, chances are that creative will appeal to all teens. It doesn't always work the other way around.
>
> One of the challenges I think is how to get this done on a regional level where we have local application and local relevance, while taking advantage of national efficiencies . . . How do we combine national and regional focus to make it one effort. Your overall strategy should be national, but your execution should be regional.
>
> For example, when it comes to promotional activities like Black History month, is it better for us to develop one promotion that we execute throughout the country, or do we give the top 5 or 10 markets the budget and allow them to spend against local needs.
>
> It's funny because I was an international business major in my undergraduate studies, and I often feel like I am doing international marketing in the domestic environment. Yes, you must take into account the cultural differences. That, in my mind is how you bring your strategy to life for that consumer.[11]

African-Americans, or blacks (surveys do not indicate a clear preference for either term among African-Americans[12]), constitute 12 percent of the American population. Concentrated in the South and the major metropolitan areas outside the South, African-Americans represent a $320 billion market. Thus, it is not surprising that marketers are very interested in this group.

Demographics

African-Americans are somewhat younger than the general population. They also tend to have lower household income levels ($25,050 versus $40,577 for non-Hispanic whites) and to be single-parent households.[13] However, stereotyping African-Americans as poverty-ridden would not be accurate, as the data below (for 1997) indicate:

African-American Household Income	*Percent*
>$75,000	7.9%
$50,000–$74,999	13.1
$25,000–$49,999	29.1
$15,000–$24,999	17.9
<$15,000	32.0

In addition, for historical reasons many African-American families often purchase or rent less expensive homes than would be expected for their income level. This provides "extra" funds to spend on clothing, personal care items and services, and shopping trips to upscale malls and retailers.[14]

Cadillac is one company that is targeting the affluent black consumer. In Houston and Washington, D.C., Cadillac is testing a direct marketing campaign to affluent black consumers in which it promises to donate $50 to minority-oriented charities in the name of each person who takes a test drive.

Many of the consumption differences noted between African-Americans and other groups relate as much to age, education, and economic circumstances as to race.[15] However, other differences are caused by differing values and lifestyles associated with the group's unique African-American identity.[16]

Consumer Groups

Market Segment Research conducted a major study of the African-American, Hispanic, and Asian-American markets in America.[17] This study identified four distinct consumer groups among African-Americans.

Contented (37 percent) This is the largest group and it is the oldest (mean age = 44). Forty percent of the group are married; 32 percent are widowed or divorced. The average household size is 2.3. Fifty-six percent are female. Half are not employed. Three-fourths finished high school and 13 percent completed college.

This is a mature segment that is basically content with life. They are not concerned with social appearances or status. They are not impulsive. They prefer to stay at home and they are moderately health conscious. They tend to save and are followers rather than leaders. They are the least optimistic about their financial future.

Upwardly Mobile (24 percent) This group has an average age of 37. Slightly more than half are male. Sixty-two percent are married; less than 10 percent are widowed or divorced. The average household size is 3.1. Over 80 percent are employed and 50 percent attended college.

This segment is composed of active, status-oriented professionals. They have materialistic aspirations and are quality oriented. They are impulsive shoppers but are also smart shoppers. They are financially secure, health conscious, and optimistic about the future.

Living for the Moment (21 percent) This is the youngest group; two-thirds are less than 34. Fifty-eight percent are male; 61 percent are single. The average household size is 2.4. Almost 80 percent are employed and 90 percent completed high school.

This segment is self-oriented and lives for the moment. They are not concerned with social issues or responsibility. They are socially active, carefree, and image conscious.

Living Day-to-Day (18 percent) This group has the lowest income and the largest average household size (5.4), although only a third are married. Its average age is 36, and 56 percent are female. Only half are employed, and over a fourth have less than a high school education.

This is basically an unskilled, poverty group. They are not status conscious nor are they socially active. They are most concerned with price and least concerned with quality. They are not health conscious and they are not optimistic about their financial future.

The four-segment scheme described above is only one of many ways the African-American subculture could be segmented. Other approaches include segmenting the black subculture by the social class structure described in Chapter 4 or the generation subcultures described later in this chapter. However, the scheme described above has been useful to marketers and it also indicates the diversity that exists within this population. Clearly, marketing strategies that target "the African-American market" as a single market are likely to fail. It and the other ethnic groups we examine are as diverse as the "white market."

Media Usage

African-Americans make greater use of mass media than do whites and they have different preferences. In 1998, there was no overlap between the 5 most popular shows among black and white audiences. The top five shows of each group and their ranking with the other group were:[18]

Blacks' Top Five	*Rank with Whites*	*Whites' Top Five*	*Rank with Blacks*
1. Steve Harvey Show	118	1. E.R.	15
2. Jamie Foxx Show	124	2. Friends	91
3. Monday Night Football	7	3. Frasier	93
4. For Your Love	118	4. Jesse	106
5. CBS Sunday Movie	10	5. Veronica's Closet	84

Clearly, African-Americans prefer shows with African-American themes or performers. Likewise, radio stations that play music popular with African-Americans and magazines like *Essence* and *Ebony* focused on African-American concerns receive most of the attention from this segment.

African-Americans have not been heavy users of the Internet, but that is now changing, with an estimated 23 percent of black households having Internet access.[19] Black-focused sites such as *NetNoir* (www.netnoir.com) and *Black Voices* (www.blackvoices.com) are attracting advertisers such as IBM, Hewlett-Packard, Wells Fargo, and Walt Disney. The availability of a wide array of black-focused media makes the delivery of messages targeting various segments of the African-American market feasible.

As stressed earlier, subcultures are not homogenous. The data above indicate limited overlap between the television shows watched by adult blacks and whites. However, 11 programs appeared on both black and white teenagers' top 20 lists.[20] Thus, the television preferences of black and white teenagers are more similar than are those of their parents.

Courtesy Alberto Culver USA, Inc.

ILLUSTRATION 5-2

African-American consumers have distinct needs from other ethnic groups for product categories such as skin and hair care and cosmetics.

Marketing to African-Americans

Marketing to African-Americans should be based on the same principles as marketing to any other group. That is, the market should be carefully analyzed, relevant needs should be identified among one or more segments of the market, and the entire marketing mix should be designed to meet the needs of the target segments. At times, the relevant segment of the African-American market will require a unique product. At other times, it will require a unique package, advertising medium, or message. Or, no change may be required from the marketing mix used to reach a broader market. However, it is critical that the decision on how to appeal to this market be based on a sound understanding of the needs of the selected segments.

Products African-Americans have different skin tones and hair from white Americans. Cosmetics and similar products developed for white consumers are often inappropriate for black consumers. Recognition of this fact by major firms has created aggressive competition for the $750 million that African-American women spend each year on cosmetics, hair care, and skin care.

Estée Lauder's subsidiary, Prescriptives, recently launched a product line called *All Skins* with 115 different shades designed to reach this market. Maybelline introduced *Shades of You* to meet the unique needs of this market. Illustration 5-2 shows a print advertisement for a product designed specifically for this market.

Other manufacturers have found it worthwhile to alter their products to meet unique social needs of African-Americans. Hallmark has a *Mahogany* line of greeting cards that features black characters and sayings. Mattel had considerable success with a black version of *Barbie* and *Shani,* a Barbie-type doll with broader facial features and dark skin. Tyco Toys and others now offer a variety of African-American dolls. Bank of America offers *Kente* checks with *Kente* cloth borders and the option of several symbols of relevance to the black community in the center of the check.

Blacks often use the same product as whites but use it in a different way. Carnation's *Instant Breakfast Drink* is popular with black consumers. However, while whites use it as

ILLUSTRATION 5-3

This product is widely used by African-Americans and white Americans. However, ads targeting African-Americans are designed to reflect the fact that they generally refer to this product category as *dressing* while whites term it *stuffing*.

Used with permission of Kraft Foods, Inc.

a low-calorie substitute for breakfast, African-Americans often consume it with breakfast because they enjoy the taste. Likewise, African-Americans tend to prefer their coffee sweeter and with more cream or nondairy creamer than the general population. Coffee-Mate used this fact to develop a marketing campaign with ads in *Ebony* and *Essence,* black-oriented radio stations, billboards in black neighborhoods, and a sweepstakes promotion that was featured in black-oriented local newspapers. It was rewarded with significant sales and market share gains.

Communications A common mistake when communicating with any ethnic group is to assume that its members are the same as the larger culture except for superficial differences. However, as one expert says: "Black people are not dark-skinned white people."[21] Failure to recognize this fact often produces commercials "targeted" at African-Americans that simply place the firm's standard ad in black media or that replace white actors with black actors, without changing the script, language, or setting. For example, Greyhound Bus targeted blacks by placing its standard commercials on black radio stations. Unfortunately, the soundtrack for the commercials was country-western, which is not popular with most black audiences.

Not all messages targeted at African-Americans need to differ significantly from those targeted at other groups. The appeal in Illustration 5-2 is to the desire to feel beautiful, which is the same for whites and blacks, though the product and model in this ad are targeted at African-American consumers. In other instances, advertisers can simply change the race of the models in the ads and perhaps the consumption setting to help indicate that the product is appropriate for the needs of the African-American consumer. This works when the product, the appeal, and the appropriate language are the same for the black target market and the other groups being targeted. This is common in ads for automobiles. Such ads can be effectively run in both black and general media.

In contrast, the ad for *Stove Top Stuffing* shown in Illustration 5-3 is used specifically to target African-Americans. Research revealed that many African-Americans refer to foods of this type as dressing rather than stuffing. Thus, in ads targeting this segment the word *dressing* is used. Note also the use of the term *Mama* and the outdoor basketball court setting.

Another means of communicating with the African-American and other ethnic communities is **event marketing.** Event marketing involves creating or sponsoring an existing event that has a particular appeal to a market segment. For example, Coors Light sponsored the "Roots of Rhythm" concert tour along with a nationwide sweepstakes in conjunction with Black Music Month. The brand also helped sponsor such events as the Indianapolis Black Expo and Harlem Day in New York.

Retailing JCPenney Co. has had great success with its *Authentic African* boutiques in stores located near significant African-American populations. These small shops, located inside JCPenney stores, feature clothing, handbags, hats, and other accessories imported from Africa.

KFC has launched a "neighborhood program" to tie its neighborhood outlets to the character of the neighborhood in which they operate. In African-American neighborhoods, this involves having the employees wear traditional African-style uniforms, piping in up-tempo rhythm and blues music, and offering additional menu items that reflect local tastes such as soul sides—red beans and rice, sweet potato pie, Honey BBQ Wings, and Mean Greens.

Surveys reveal that a major difference between white and black shoppers' store selection criteria is respect. More than 60 percent of African-American shoppers say that one of their most important reasons for choosing a store is that it treats its customers with respect.[22] This focus on respect is caused by the sad fact that many black shoppers still encounter disrespectful acts such as being closely watched while shopping. The need for cultural sensitivity training for retail employees is clear.

African-Americans also use shopping as a form of recreation more than whites (it ranks 4th among blacks and 13th among whites). This suggests that stores with black customers should pay particular attention to providing a pleasant and fun shopping environment. Blacks also respond to sales differently than whites and have differing desires with respect to credit card, cash, and check payments.[23] Thus, all aspects of the shopping experience need to be carefully aligned to the needs of the target shoppers.

HISPANICS

The Bureau of the Census defines **Hispanic** as *a person of any race whose primary language, or the primary language of an ancestor, is Spanish.*[24] The use of the Spanish language among Hispanic-Americans is increasing rather than decreasing. Extensive immigration is one reason for the increased use of Spanish. It is estimated that over 70 percent of Hispanic-Americans were born outside the United States.[25] Another reason is the growth of self-contained Spanish-speaking communities, coupled with the impact of national Spanish-language media. However, while Hispanic communities are growing, many affluent Hispanics are leaving these communities for the suburbs.[26]

Like the other ethnic groups in America, Hispanics are diverse. Many marketers feel that the Hispanic subculture is not a single ethnic subculture but instead is three main and several minor nationality subcultures: Mexican-Americans (60 percent), Puerto Ricans (12 percent), Cubans (5 percent), and other Latinos, mainly from Central America (23 percent). Each group speaks a slightly different version of Spanish and has somewhat distinct values and lifestyles. Further, each group tends to live in distinct regions of the country: Mexican-Americans in the Southwest and California, Puerto Ricans in New York and New Jersey, Cubans in Florida, and other Latinos in California, New York, and Florida.[27] Income levels also vary widely across the groups, with Cuban-Americans having incomes slightly below those of non-Hispanics, while Puerto Ricans average incomes are only half that level. Anheuser-Busch is beginning to target nationality groups within the Hispanic market.

Others argue that while one must be sensitive to nationality-based differences, the common language, common religion (Roman Catholic for most Hispanics), and the emergence of national Spanish-language media and entertainment figures create sufficient cultural homogeneity for many products and advertising campaigns. Thus, the decision to treat Hispanics as a single ethnic subculture or several nationality subcultures depends on the product and the nature of the intended communication.

Whether one treats the Hispanic market as a single market or as several nationality markets, it may still be necessary to segment the market further using social class, generation, stage in the family life cycle, or other appropriate variables. A Hispanic heritage is only one of the factors influencing this group's consumption behaviors.

Identification with Traditional Hispanic Culture

Acculturation is *the degree to which an immigrant has adapted to his or her new culture.*[28] The Market Segment Research study used level of identification with the traditional Hispanic culture as a measure of acculturation. It found three Hispanic groups based on this measure:

- *Strong Hispanic identification.* Members of this group are almost entirely Spanish speaking. They tend to live in areas populated exclusively by Hispanics. They are recent arrivals and retain close ties to family and friends "at home." They are generally low on all measures of social status. Their media usage is heavily Spanish language. About 60 percent of all Hispanic nationality groups except Puerto Ricans (38 percent) are in this group.
- *Moderate Hispanic identification.* This group speaks both Spanish and English but is most comfortable with Spanish. Members live in areas of moderate Hispanic density. Most have been in the United States for 12 years or more. They have average levels of income and social status. Their ties to the "old country" are moderate. They use both Spanish-language and English media. About 25 percent of all Hispanic nationality groups except Puerto Ricans (35 percent) are in this group.
- *Limited Hispanic identification.* This group speaks both Spanish and English. It is very comfortable with English. Members live in areas dominated by non-Hispanics. They have lived in the United States for a long time and many are second- or third-generation Americans. Their ties to their country of origin are limited. They tend to use English-language media. Their income and social status are relatively high. About 18 percent of all Hispanic nationality groups except Puerto Ricans (27 percent) are in this group.[29]

As the above discussion indicates, most Hispanics identify more or less strongly with a Hispanic culture. This culture is heavily influenced by the Roman Catholic religion. It is very family oriented, with the extended family playing an important role. It is also a very masculine culture and sports are very important to Hispanics, particularly boxing, baseball, and soccer. This masculine orientation manifests itself in many ways, including "macho" rules for interaction between males and male-dominant relationships between males and females. While it varies with the product category, a strong Hispanic identification is associated with husband-dominant household decision making.[30]

The Hispanic culture generally has a fairly traditional view of the appropriate role of women. For example, the wife is expected to prepare the food for the family. This produces challenges and opportunities for marketers.

- Churchs Chicken encounters resistance to its eat out and takeout foods among Hispanic consumers. Churchs' vice president of marketing states: "In the Latino community, there are a number of cultural barriers to not cooking." A result of these barriers is a social stigma against women who do not prepare meals for their families. To counter this, Churchs has launched an advertising campaign to make eating out more acceptable. The new campaign will try to position the chain as a place that provides a value-price dinner that frees up consumers to engage in more pressing activities.[31]

- The California Milk Processor Board targets Mexican-Americans in California with ads that position milk as a vehicle through which families come together. Their research found that in this culture, cooking is not only the wife's responsibility, it is central to her role. However, cooking is not only a responsibility, it is a way of expressing love for her family and a source of great pleasure. Commercials focus on women preparing food for the family with milk as a key ingredient. One of the most successful ones shows a grandmother teaching her six-year-old granddaughter how to cook using milk.[32]

While most Hispanics identify with their Hispanic roots, most also view themselves first and foremost as Americans. Many are quite conservative on issues such as increased immigration and bilingual education.[33]

Marketing to Hispanics

Although average Hispanic household income is relatively low ($26,628 versus $40,577 for non-Hispanic whites), the Hispanic market is estimated to be worth over $225 billion and it is the most rapidly growing segment of our population.[34] Thus, many marketers are targeting it with a variety of approaches:

- "It's tough to get Hispanics to switch brands. And while the general buyer looks at price first, Hispanics are willing to pay extra to purchase quality products for their family. So handing out coupons or reducing price is not an effective way to get them to try our products. A far better approach is to do in-store promotions to get Hispanics to sample our product." [Martin Serna, president of the firm that does Borden's promotions in the Hispanic community.]
- Anheuser-Busch, Campbell Soup, and Coca-Cola sponsor the nine-day Carnival Miami, one of the largest Hispanic festivals in America. Adolph Coors sponsors a variety of events, including community cook-offs and Cinco de Mayo celebrations. American Honda Motor Company helped fund the U.S. tour of Mexico City's Ballet Folklorico. Ford has helped fund soccer teams in Hispanic communities.
- See's Candies shows ads on Spanish television that feature a tour of their manufacturing plant. The fact that 70 percent of their workforce is Hispanic is apparent and shows their support of the Hispanic community.
- Pepsi developed an advertisement that appealed to all the Hispanic nationality groups. It produced a Spanish version of its Pepsi-generation campaign that focuses on a "sweet 15" party, the *quinceañera,* which celebrates the coming of age for Hispanic girls. In contrast, Nestlé had to depart from its normal one-ad approach for *Butterfinger* candy. It found that peanut butter was *mantequilla de maní* for Hispanics from the Caribbean and *crema de cacahuete* for those from Mexico. Therefore, they created two different sets of copy for their Spanish-language ads.[35]

Communications As we saw earlier, most Hispanics speak Spanish most of the time and prefer Spanish-language media. Therefore, although it is possible to reach part of this market using mass media, any serious attempt to target Hispanics must use Spanish-language media as well. As shown below, among Hispanics who speak Spanish, advertising copy recall is much higher for Spanish language ads, even among those whose dominant language is English:[36]

Respondent's Dominant Language	Ad Language: *Spanish*	Ad Language: *English*
Spanish	59%	32%
Equal/English	61	46
Total	60	38

Reaching the majority of Hispanics in Spanish is a straightforward task. There are two Spanish-language television networks in the United States—Telemundo and Univision. Coca-Cola spent $8 million advertising to Hispanics on Univision in 1998 and Pepsi spent over $5 million in 1999.[37] Spanish-language radio is widespread with both local and network stations. Heavy radio advertisers include American Airlines, Sears, AT&T, McDonald's, and other major consumer goods marketers.

There are numerous Spanish-language magazines, including Spanish versions of *Cosmopolitan, National Geographic, Men's Health, People,* and *Reader's Digest.* One company represents 18 such magazines with a paid circulation of over 750,000 and an estimated 4.9 million readers. *Latina* targets younger, affluent Hispanic women. Its readers have an average household income of almost $50,000. There are also many Spanish-language newspapers.

Hispanics are not heavy users of the Internet, with less than 10 percent estimated to have access. However, LatinoLink (www.latinolink.com) averages over 200,000 users per month. The U.S. Navy, IBM, AT&T, and Charles Schwab are advertisers. Hispanics receive relatively little direct mail but have a positive response to it. Gillette is one firm that has been successful using direct mail, though it has had difficulty getting good mailing lists.[38]

Successfully communicating to Hispanic consumers involves more than directly translating ad copy from English to Spanish. Tang introduced itself in its Spanish ads as *jugo de chino,* which worked well with Puerto Ricans who knew it meant orange juice. However, the phrase had no meaning to most other Hispanics. Other examples of translation difficulties include the following:

- Frank Perdue's chicken slogan, "It Takes a Tough Man to Make a Tender Chicken," was translated to: "It Takes a Sexually Excited Man to Make a Chick Affectionate."
- Budweiser's slogan ended up being, "The Queen of Beers," while another brand was "Filling; Less Delicious."
- A candy marketer wanted to print a statement on its package bragging about its 50 years in the business. When a tilde (˜) did not appear over the appropriate *n,* the package claimed it contained 50 anuses.
- One food company's burrito became *burrada,* a colloquialism for "big mistake."
- Coors' beer slogan, "Get loose with Coors" came out as "Get the runs with Coors."[39]

Successful marketing to Hispanics moves beyond accurate translations into unique appeals and symbols.

- Sears recognized the importance of the extended family in a successful ad for baby furniture. In the English ad, a husband and wife are shown selecting the furniture. In the Spanish ad, a teenage daughter and the grandparents join the expectant couple.
- Prego spaghetti sauce recognized the traditional Hispanic family role structure in its advertising. In its English ad, a father and son are shown alone in the kitchen preparing

dinner. In the Spanish-language ad, the entire family—mother, father, and child—are shown in the kitchen. Showing men cooking would not appeal to many traditional Hispanics.

- A car ad for Honda showed a young man enthusiastically washing a new car and admiring its features. The commercial ends with the man handing the keys to his brother who is the owner of the car. This humorous approach reflected the importance of the family in the Hispanic culture. When someone in the family buys a car, it belongs to the entire family.[40]
- Hispanic teens are particularly difficult to target with effective communications. Frito-Lay's successful campaign for Doritos was themed "Sabor a todo volumen" (roughly "The loudest taste on earth"). TV ads featured loud Hispanic music and Hispanic teens with an emphasis on Doritos' bold and spicy taste. Research revealed that the music was key to the success of the campaign. According to a spokesperson: "Music is one of the major attributes of Hispanic teens that bind them together. The styles differ from salsa to Latin pop, but all are based on Latin roots."[41]

Examine Illustration 5-4 (the voice-over was only in Spanish). Note the family focus and the strong presence of the male.

Products Other than specialty food products, few marketers have developed unique products or services for the Hispanic market. However, an emerging trend is for marketers with food and household products developed for the Central and South American markets to distribute them in areas of the United States with large Hispanic populations. Examples include:

- Colgate-Palmolive distributes its Mexican household cleaner *Fabuloso* in Los Angeles and Miami.
- Nestlé sells *Nido,* its Mexican powdered milk brand, and *Nestum,* one of its cereals from Venezuela, in the United States.
- PepsiCo is marketing its *Gamesa* brand cookies from Mexico in Hispanic areas in the United States.

MCI Communications targets U.S. Hispanics with family and friends in Mexico *Servicio Llámame* (Call Me Service). The service costs $5 per month. The U.S. customer is provided a residential toll-free number plus a four-digit security code that may be given to friends and family in Mexico. This allows the Mexican residents to dial the U.S. resident directly. The call is billed to the U.S. resident (who generally has more disposable income) at a significant discount from the normal collect-call rate. The new service was launched with Spanish-language television ads featuring boxer Oscar De La Hoya receiving calls from friends in Mexico critiquing his last fight.[42]

Retailing The primary retailing responses to this market have been increasing the number of bilingual salespeople, the use of Spanish language signs, directions, and point-of-purchase displays, and merchandise assortments that reflect the needs of the local Hispanic community. The following examples describe more focused responses:

- Tiangus, a grocery chain aimed at the Mexican-American market in Southern California, was launched with a fiesta atmosphere. Stands served a wide variety of Mexican foods, the walls were splashed with bright colors, and shoppers were serenaded with mariachi bands. The shelves were stocked with empanadas, handmade tortillas, and other items typically found only in specialty stores.

  The stores are not just standard stores with a Latin flair and a few specialty items. The chain is based on extensive research. For example, it was found that the Hispanic shopper "is fussier about freshness, so she shops more frequently and uses less refrigeration. She may have less disposable income but she'll spend a higher share of it on

Courtesy of Bank of America.

ILLUSTRATION 5-4

The family is very important to the Hispanic subculture, and the male plays a major role. This television ad is in Spanish and has a strong family theme. It also emphasizes the dominant American cultural values of achievement and financial success.

food." Based on these findings, Tiangus stores emphasize fresh food. Half the selling space is devoted to fresh food, with reduced space for packaged items and freezer foods.[43]

- Warehouse Entertainment recently launched a chain of Tu Música (Your Music) stores catering to Hispanic consumers. The stores carry music ranging from Hispanic rock to pop crossover to Mexican favorites. The logic of starting the stores was simple according the firm's president: "The market in which we operated was changing and we needed to change with it." Tu Música targets first- to third-generation Hispanics who speak Spanish and seek Latino music. It advertises on Spanish-language TV, radio, and newspapers. It uses Spanish language–speaking sales personnel. About one-third of its titles (more than 10,000) are in Spanish compared to 2 percent in a typical outlet.[44]
- Bank of America converted its 5,000 ATM machines into a bilingual format. In regions of the country with large Hispanic populations, its branches have a Spanish-language service line, first-time home buyer education programs in Spanish, and a Spanish-language

loan-by-phone program. Its brochures are available in a bilingual format. These and other activities are tied together in an image campaign called "Cerca de ti" or "Close to you."

ASIAN-AMERICANS

Although substantially smaller than the African-American and Hispanic subcultures, Asian-Americans are a rapidly growing subculture, due primarily to immigration. Asian-Americans have the highest average household income of any ethnic group ($45,249 compared to $40,577 for non-Hispanic whites). This is also the most diverse group, with numerous nationalities, languages, and religions. Figure 5-3 shows that Chinese and Filipinos are the two largest nationality groups. However, Koreans, Vietnamese, and others (primarily Laotian, Cambodian, and Thai) are the most rapidly growing due to high immigration rates.

Asian-Americans are concentrated in the West and in New York. More than half live in California, New York, and Hawaii.[45] As shown below, the percent of each nationality group that primarily uses its native language is high (except for Filipinos).

Country	*Percent Using Native Language Primarily*
Vietnam	85%
Hong Kong	82
China	64
Korea	64
Taiwan	64
Japan	46
Philippines	27

Consumer Groups

The Market Segment Research study identified three groups of Asian-Americans based on their demographics and attitudes: traditionalist, established, and live for the moment.

National Background of Asian-Americans **FIGURE 5-3**

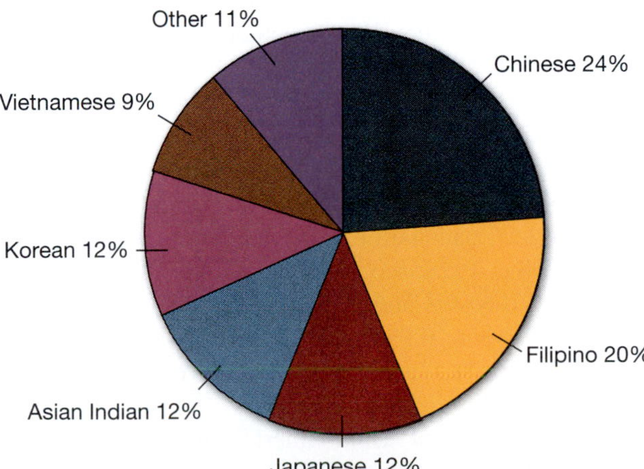

Traditionalist (49 percent) This group has an average age of 41, but almost 40 percent are over 50. Seventy percent are married. Almost half are unemployed but a large number of these are retired. They have relatively limited educations, with 50 percent having a high school diploma or less. Their average household size is small (3.1).

Traditionalists have a strong identification with their original culture. Almost half speak their native language exclusively and three-fourths speak only their native language at home. They are not status conscious. They are not highly concerned with price or quality when shopping. While not concerned with financial security, they are also not optimistic about their financial future.

Established (27 percent) This group's average age of 40 is almost the same as the traditionalists', but only 22 percent are over 50. Eighty percent are married and 60 percent are employed full-time. Seventy-three percent have at least some college and over half have a college degree. Their average household has 4.1 members.

Individuals in this group have relatively weak identification with their native cultures. Only a fourth speak their native language exclusively and less than half prefer native-language television programming.

This is a conservative, professional group. They are financially secure and optimistic about their financial futures. They are quality oriented and are willing to pay a premium for high quality.

Live for the Moment (24 percent) This is the youngest of the three segments (average age = 35). Most (70 percent) are married and half are employed full-time. Almost half have at least some college. Their average household size is 4.0.

This group has a moderate level of identification with their traditional cultures. About 30 percent speak their native language exclusively, though two-thirds do so at home. This is a spontaneous, materialistic group. They are impulsive shoppers and are concerned about status and quality. They are spenders rather than savers.

Marketing to Asian-Americans

As the preceding discussion indicates, there is not a single Asian-American market. Rather, there are several Asian-American markets, based primarily on nationality and language. Each of these in turn can be further segmented based on degree of acculturation,[46] social class, generation, lifestyle, and other variables. Thus, while the number and average income of Asian-Americans makes them attractive to marketers, the diversity of languages and cultures has precluded major marketing efforts focused on them as a group.[47]

There are, however, opportunities to market effectively to the nationality subgroups. As mentioned earlier, these groups tend to be clustered in limited geographic regions (half live in just three states). Where there is a concentration of any of the nationality groups, there are native-language television and radio stations, as well as newspapers. Thus, targeted nationalities can be efficiently reached with native-language ads. For example, in San Francisco, KTSF presents a live one-hour newscast in Cantonese every weeknight. It covers both mainstream news and news of particular interest to the Chinese community. Many KTSF advertisers, such as McDonald's, dub their existing ads in Cantonese. Others, such as Colgate-Palmolive, run the ads they are using for the same products in Asia.

Over 40 percent of Asian-American households are estimated to have personal computers in their homes. Web-based marketing to the Asian community is growing rapidly.

Courtesy of Bank of America.

ILLUSTRATION 5-5

Marketing to Asian-Americans involves more than translating ads into the appropriate languages. This promotion is based on the Lunar New Year, which is special to many Asian cultures.

Firms can reach Chinese consumers in their native language on Chinese.Yahoo.com, Sinanet.com, and Chinese Cyber City (ccchome.com). Similar sites are gaining popularity among other Asian-American nationality groups, and firms such as Charles Schwab are using them as communications channels.

Examine Illustration 5-5. It is bilingual and can communicate with Vietnamese with differing language preferences. More importantly, it is a special promotion based on the Lunar New Year that is meaningful to this group. It shows that Bank of America is doing more than just translating an ad used for the broader market but is focusing special attention on the Vietnamese market.[48]

Other examples of successful marketing to Asian-Americans include the following:

- A Los Angeles chain selected four outlets with large numbers of Chinese and Vietnamese customers. At the time of the Moon Festival (a very important holiday in many Asian cultures), the store ran ads and distributed coupons for free moon cakes and lanterns. Sales increased by 30 percent in these stores during the promotion.
- The Filipino Channel mainly broadcasts time-shifted programs from Manila. Geffin Records recently tested the channel by advertising a single by Kia on "Flames," a program that appeals to young American Filipinos. The result was an immediate and sharp sales increase.
- During a recent Chinese Lunar New Year celebration, Bank of America in California sponsored special events and offered premiums for opening accounts, including a

chance to win a family reunion at Disneyland. Together with AT&T and Disneyland, the bank paid for airfare from Tokyo for family members, a free visit to Disneyland, and AT&T calling cards.

NATIVE AMERICANS

Native Americans are just under 1 percent of the U.S. population (approximately 2.5 million). Nearly half live in the West, and 30 percent reside in the South. While many Native Americans live on or near reservations, others are dispersed throughout the country.

There are numerous Native American tribes, each with its own language and traditions. Many of the tribes have reservations and quasi-independent political status. In general, Native Americans have limited incomes (about two-thirds of the national average), but this varies widely by tribe:[49]

Tribes	*Size in 1990*	*1990 Household Income*
Cherokee	369,000	$21,992
Navajo	225,000	12,817
Sioux	107,000	15,611
Chippewa	106,000	18,801
Choctaw	86,000	21,640
Pueblo	55,000	19,097
Apache	53,000	18,484
Iroquois	53,000	23,640
Lumbee	51,000	21,708
Creek	46,000	21,913

The diversity in the income figures across tribes is increasing, as some tribes have gained significant revenue and employment by opening casinos on their reservations in states that otherwise prohibit gambling.

In recent years, Native Americans have taken increased pride in their heritage and are less tolerant of inaccurate stereotypes of either their history or their current status. Thus, marketers using Native American names or portrayals must ensure accurate and appropriate use. Although each tribe is small relative to the total population, the geographic concentration of each tribe provides easy access for marketers. Sponsorship of tribal events and support for tribal colleges, training centers, and community centers can produce good results for firms that do so over time.

ASIAN-INDIAN AMERICANS

There are approximately 1 million Americans of Indian heritage (from India). This segment of the population is growing rapidly due to immigration. Asian-Indian Americans are concentrated in New York and California, with significant numbers in New Jersey, Illinois, and Texas as well. As a group, they are well educated, affluent, and fluent in English; yet most retain cultural ties to their Indian background. Thus, they form an attractive market segment for many products.

Those unfamiliar with India often assume that it is a homogeneous country. However, in some ways it is more like Europe than America. It has 25 states, 7 union territories, 15 official languages, and dozens of other languages and dialects. Thus, while those who immigrate to America have much in common, they also have many differences based on their background in India.

The first large wave of Asian-Indian Americans immigrated shortly after the Immigration and Nationality Act was amended in 1965. Due in large part to the nature of U.S. immigration policy, this group was almost exclusively professionals. More recent immigrants have tended to have less education and training, due again to U.S. immigration policy, which is now heavily based on family reunification.

A specialist on Asian-Indian Americans, Dr. Arun Jain, divides the group into three market segments. The First Wave (our name, not Dr. Jain's) is composed of the highly educated men who arrived in the 1960s and their wives. These men are virtually all highly paid professionals. Their wives tend to have a limited education, they do not work outside the home, and their English language skills may be limited. Most of the children of this group attended college and are now beginning to start their own families. The parents tend to focus on their children's marriage and their own approaching retirement.

The Second Wave arrived in the 1970s. Like the First Wave, the men are highly educated professionals. However, the women in this group are also highly educated and most work outside the home. Their children are college-bound teenagers and the parents are actively involved in the process of selecting a college and major.

The Third Wave arrived after 1980. While some are similar to those in the Second Wave, most are relatives of those who arrived earlier. They are generally less educated and are younger than the other two groups. Many are working in service jobs such as driving a taxi. However, most of these are saving aggressively to enable them to move into business or other opportunities. Many others are running motels, small grocery stores, or gas stations. While the three groups differ significantly in a number of ways, most share a number of important cultural traits:

- They place great value on education, particularly their children's education.
- They are concerned with financial security, and save at a rate much higher than the average American.
- They do not have a "throw-away" mentality. They shop for value and look for quality and durability.
- Husbands tend to have a dominant role in family decisions.

In addition to these cultural traits, children who were born in the United States or who immigrated at an early age are often more knowledgeable about many American products than their parents. They may exert significant influence on food, clothing, and even electronics purchases.

Asian-Indian Americans attend to the general mass media. They can also be targeted via specialty magazines such as *Masal, Onwars, Hum,* and *India Abroad;* and cable TV, radio stations, and newspapers in regions with significant populations. For example, Western Union advertises to this segment on Eye on Asia, a cable channel focused on this group. Long-term involvement in the Indian community is an effective way to gain support from this segment:

> Metropolitan Life was a major sponsor of a Navaratri, a religious festival that attracted 100,000 participants from around New York and New Jersey. As one participant said: "One of the chief executives of the company attended the festival, and the company took out a series of ads in the souvenir program. Now we feel we should reward the company for taking an interest in us."[50]

ARAB-AMERICANS

There are about 1 million Arab-Americans in the United States. Perhaps no group in America has a more inaccurate stereotype. For example: What is the most common religion of Arab-Americans? About half identify themselves as Christians, about half are Muslim, and a few are Jewish.

Arab-Americans come from a variety of countries, including Morocco, Algeria, Egypt, Lebanon, Jordan, Saudi Arabia, and Kuwait. They share a common Arabic heritage and the Arabic language. Since World War II, many Arab immigrants have been business proprietors, landowners, or influential families fleeing political turmoil in their home countries. Many of these individuals attended Western or Westernized schools and were fluent in English before arriving.

Eighty-two percent of Arab-Americans are U.S. citizens and 63 percent were born in the United States. They are somewhat younger than the general population, better educated, and have a higher than average income. They are also much more likely to be entrepreneurs. A third of all Arab-Americans live in California, New York, and Michigan.

Most Arab-Americans are tired of negative stereotyping and misrepresentations about their culture. Even the film *Aladdin* contained insults and mistakes. Aladdin sings about the "barbaric" country from which he came. A guard threatened to cut off a young girl's hand for stealing food for a hungry child. Such an action would be contrary to Islamic law. The storefront signs in the mythical Arabic land had symbols that made no sense in Arabic or any other language.

Thus, the first rule in reaching this market is to treat its members with respect and accuracy. There are specialized newspapers, magazines, and radio and television stations focused on this market. Attention to the unique traditions of this community can pay large dividends.[51]

RELIGIOUS SUBCULTURES

America is basically a **secular society.** That is, the educational system, government, and political process are not controlled by a religious group and most people's daily behaviors are not guided by strict religious guidelines. Nonetheless, 90 percent of all Americans claim a religious affiliation, and over 95 percent of those are Christian.[52] Over 75 percent of women and over 60 percent of the men in a recent survey claimed that religion was an important part of their life. However, less than 40 percent say they attend church with any regularity (a percent that hasn't changed much since 1940). Further, there is evidence that only about half of those who claim to attend church regularly actually do so.[53]

The fact that the American culture is largely secular is not viewed as optimal by all of society. Many conservative Christians would prefer a society and legal system more in line with their faith. The intense debates over abortion, prayer in schools, the teaching of evolution versus creationism, homosexual rights, and a host of other issues is evidence of this division in American society.

Religion is important to, and influences the behaviors of, many Americans. The different religions in America prescribe differing values and behaviors. Thus, a number of **religious subcultures** exist in America.

Christian Subcultures

Much of the American value system and the resultant political and social institutions are derived from the Christian, and largely Protestant, beliefs of the early European settlers.

Demographic Differences across the Major Religious Subcultures in America **TABLE 5-1**

Religion	Percent of U.S.	Employed Full-Time	College Graduates	Median Income (000$)	Own Home
Christian					
Roman Catholic	26.2%	54.3%	20.0%	$27.7	69.3%
Baptist	19.4	52.3	10.4	20.6	66.6
Methodist	8.0	49.6	21.1	25.1	75.2
Lutheran	5.2	50.0	18.0	25.9	76.5
"Christian"	4.5	51.8	16.0	20.7	63.7
Presbyterian	2.8	48.8	33.8	29.0	76.9
Pentecostal	1.8	52.8	06.9	19.4	60.8
Episcopalian	1.7	52.6	39.2	33.0	70.6
Mormon	1.4	49.9	19.2	25.7	74.0
Non-Christian					
Jewish	1.8	50.1	46.7	36.7	61.7
Muslim	0.5	62.5	30.4	24.7	43.3
Buddhist	0.4	59.4	33.4	28.5	50.6
Agnostic	0.7	63.5	36.3	33.3	59.7
No religion	7.5	60.5	23.6	27.3	60.6

Although our culture is basically secular, many of our traditions and values are derived from the Judeo–Christian heritage of the majority of Americans. Most of the major American holidays, including Christmas, Easter, and Thanksgiving, have a religious base. However, except for Easter, the pure religious base of these holidays is no longer the central theme that it once was.

While the United States is 90 percent Christian, Christianity takes many forms in this country, each with some unique beliefs and behaviors.

Table 5-1 lists the major Christian faiths as well as the other major religions in America. As the table shows, there are significant demographic differences across the various religions.

Roman Catholic Subculture The Catholic church is highly structured and hierarchical. The Pope is the central religious authority, and individual interpretation of scripture and events is minimal. A controversial tenet of the Catholic church is that the sole purpose of sex is for procreation. Therefore, the use of birth control devices is prohibited (though many Catholics deviate from this tenet). A result of this is a larger average family size for Catholics than for Protestants or Jews. The larger family size makes economic gains and upward social mobility more difficult. It also has a major influence on the types of products consumed by Catholics relative to many other religions.

Over 20 percent of Catholics are ethnic minorities—15 percent are Hispanic, 5 percent are African-American, and 2 percent are Asian. Catholics are concentrated in the Northeast and in areas with large Hispanic populations.

Like Protestants, Catholics vary in their commitment and conservatism. The more conservative members share many values and behaviors with Protestant religious conservatives.

Catholics have few consumption restrictions or requirements associated with their religion. Marketers targeting this group can reach the more committed members through specialized magazines and radio programs. It is important for marketers to recognize that since one in four Americans is a Roman Catholic, they are part of almost all market segments. Marketing activities, particularly advertising, should be reviewed to avoid being disrespectful to Catholic ideas and practices. This is particularly true for ads that use Catholic symbols such as priests or nuns.

Protestant Subcultures Approximately 60 percent of all Americans identify themselves as Protestant. While there are many types of Protestant faiths with significant differences between them, most stress direct individual experience with God as a core tenet. In general, Protestant faiths emphasize individual responsibility and control. This focus has been credited with creating a strong work ethic, desire for scientific knowledge, a willingness to sacrifice for the future, and relatively small families. These characteristics in turn have created upward social mobility and produced the majority of the ruling elite in America.

Since almost two-thirds of Americans are Protestants, they are not generally considered a subculture. Rather, Protestant values and attitudes tend to define the core American culture. This is particularly true for white Protestants of western European heritage—WASPs (white Anglo-Saxon Protestants). This group has historically dominated America in terms of numbers, wealth, and power (with power historically belonging to the male members of this group). Its leaders established the rules for appropriate behaviors, styles, manners, and products to own. This group also established barriers that made it difficult for other groups to gain power or wealth. These ranged from rigid segregation and legal restrictions against African-Americans to subtler barriers against Catholics and Jews.

Marketers were active participants in erecting and maintaining many of these barriers. Obvious discrimination took place when firms, generally retailers and service firms, refused to serve African-Americans, Jews, or other ethnic or religious groups. More subtle participation by marketers involved ads and television programs that only showed WASPs living the good life. Today, the legal barriers have been removed, the subtler attitudinal barriers are much lower than in the past, and marketers are using a more diverse cast in their commercials. Nonetheless, subtle biases remain.

While Protestants constitute the basic core culture of America, the diversity across and within denominations creates numerous subcultures within the larger group. Many of these religious groups have unique beliefs of direct relevance to marketers. These generally involve the consumption of products containing stimulates such as caffeine (prohibited by the Mormon Church) or alcohol (prohibited by the Southern Baptist church, among others). However, the basic distinction among Protestants, like the Catholics, is degree of conservatism in their religious beliefs. The majority of Protestants are "middle of the road" in terms of conservatism. This is consistent with America's dominant cultural values. However, a sizable minority are very conservative and, along with conservative Catholics, represent a significant subculture.

The Born-Again Christian Subculture Born-again Christians have been referred to as the Christian Right, Religious Right, Conservative Christians, Evangelical Christians, and Fundamentalist Christians. **Born-again Christians** are *characterized by a strong belief in the literal truth of the Bible, a very strong commitment to their religious beliefs, having had a "born-again" experience, and encouraging others to believe in Jesus Christ.* Depending on the definition used, somewhere between 20 and 33 percent of adult Americans are born-again Christians.[54]

Born-again Christians tend to have somewhat lower education and income levels than the general population. They tend to have a more traditional gender role orientation. Born-again Christians are best known for their political stands on issues such as abortion, homosexual rights, and prayer in the schools. They have substantial political influence, particularly within the Republican Party and in certain geographic regions such as Texas.

Their beliefs also influence their consumption patterns. They generally oppose the use of alcohol and drugs. They do not consume movies or television programs that are "overly" focused on sex or other "immoral" activities. In fact, various groups of born-again Christians have organized boycotts against advertisers that sponsor shows they find inappropriate.

In contrast, they are very receptive to programs, books, and movies that depict traditional (i.e., Protestant) family (husband, wife, children) values. Firms with a reputation for supporting similar values would be well received by this segment. In contrast, Disney products have faced boycotts because of Disney's personnel policies, which extend some benefits to same-sex couples.

Non-Christian Subcultures

Jewish Subculture Judaism is unique in that historically it has been an inseparable combination of ethnic and religious identity. Until recently, Jews in America tended to marry other Jews. Today, about 30 percent of all married Jews in America are married to a member of another faith.[55] Jews are heavily concentrated in the Northeast (44 percent, down from 63 percent in 1971), but are increasingly dispersing throughout the United States, particularly into the Sunbelt.[56] American Jews tend to have higher than average incomes and education levels. In most ways, Jewish consumption patterns are similar to those of other Americans with similar education and income levels.

As with other religious groups, committed, conservative Jews represent a distinct subculture from mainstream Jews. Orthodox Jews have strict dietary rules that prohibit some foods such as pork and specify strict preparation requirements for other foods (see Illustration 5-6). They also strictly observe Jewish holidays and many do not participate in even secular aspects of the major Christian holiday, Christmas. Reformed Jews and Jews less committed to the strict interpretations of Judaism are less influenced by these practices. They tend to celebrate Chanukah, which coincides with Christmas, and Passover, which coincides with Easter, more so than Sukkot and Shavuot, which do not coincide with American holidays.[57]

Muslim Subculture It is important to recall from our earlier discussion that Muslim and Arab are not synonymous in America. While the core of the 3 to 4 million Muslims in America are of Arabic heritage, many others are African-Americans (about 25 percent) or are from Asian, Hispanic, or European backgrounds. Like the Protestants, there are a variety of Muslim sects with varying belief patterns, though all are based on the Koran. Like Protestants, Catholics, and Jews, the most obvious division among Muslims is the degree of conservatism and the importance attached to the literal teachings of the religion. As with the other religious groups in America, most Muslims' lives are centered on work, family, school, and the pursuit of success and happiness.

In general, Muslims tend to be conservative with respect to drug and alcohol use and sexual permissiveness. In fact, many oppose dating. They also place considerable emphasis

ILLUSTRATION 5-6

Many religions prescribe dietary practices for their members. This product is designed to meet the food preparation guidelines of the Jewish religion.

Courtesy of Empire Kosher.

on the family (with the eldest male as the head of the family) and on respect for elders. The more devout Muslims not only avoid pork products but also any foods that have not been prepared in accordance with the strict rules of Islam. The following quote from a devout Pakistani Muslim on why he does not eat in Western restaurants illustrates the stress this can cause:

> Well, how can I be sure that the cook who has cooked pork or bacon in a pan did not cook my vegetables in the same pan? How can I be sure that even if he used different pans he washed his hands in between cooking bacon and a vegetable? I do not think there is any way I can get a pure food out there.[58]

These beliefs conflict with the practices in the larger society and the images portrayed on television and in the movies. They are also a source of conflict between older Muslims who immigrated to America and their children who were raised here.[59] Muslims in America have their own magazines, schools, social clubs, marriage services, and bookstores. There are over 1,100 Moslem mosques and sanctuaries in America. In general, this subculture has not attracted the attention of marketers except as it overlaps with the Arab-American subculture.

Buddhist Subculture There are nearly as many Buddhists in America as there are Muslims. They are primarily Asian-American or white. It is important to note that only about 5 percent of Asian-Americans are Buddhists. Buddhists tend to be slightly above average in income and education and they are concentrated in the West.

There are a variety of Buddhist sects in America. All stress the basic idea that all beings are caught in *samsara,* a cycle of suffering and rebirth that is basically caused by desire and actions that produce unfavorable *karma.* Samsara can be escaped and a state of *nirvana* reached by following the noble *Eightfold Path.* This combines ethical and disciplinary practices, training in concentration and meditation, and the development of enlightened wisdom.

Thus far, marketers have largely ignored this market. Its small size and diverse ethnic composition make it difficult to target. However, as specialized media evolve to serve Buddhists, opportunities will exist for astute marketers.

REGIONAL SUBCULTURES

Distinct **regional subcultures** arise due to climatic conditions, the natural environment and resources, the characteristics of the various immigrant groups that have settled in each region, and significant social and political events. These distinct subcultures present numerous opportunities and challenges for marketers. Examples include:

- Anheuser-Busch divided Texas into several regions and developed unique marketing programs for *Budweiser* in each. In the northern part of the state, it used a cowboy image, while in the southern region, a Hispanic identity was stressed. Market share rose from 23 percent to 37 percent.
- Campbell Soup's original pork and beans did not sell well in the Southwest. In response, Campbell's removed the pork and added chili pepper and ranchero beans. Sales increased dramatically. A Campbell's subsidiary developed Zesty Pickles for the Northeast because consumers there prefer sourer pickles than do other Americans.
- Mercedes Benz has half of its total advertising budget controlled by its four regional divisions. Chevrolet allocates 20 percent of its advertising budget to regional ads, some of which are targeted at the state level (Suburbans are advertised in Texas as the "national car of Texas"). Coca-Cola has developed specific ad campaigns for Texas and Minnesota. In addition, Coca-Cola bottlers conduct extensive local advertising campaigns.
- Frito-Lay potato chips are darker and oilier in the Northeast, lighter tasting and heavier textured in the Southeast. Its Pizza Hut unit allocates half its ad budget for local advertising.
- McDonald's Egg McMuffin was an instant success in most of the country but was a disaster in the Southeast, where most people had never heard of eggs Benedict and English muffins were not commonly consumed. Only after the Southeastern McDonald's franchisees developed a customized regional marketing strategy to explain the new product in a humorous way did Eggs McMuffin become a nationwide success.[60]

While the most effective regional marketing strategies are often based on small geographic areas, we can observe significant consumption differences across much larger regions. Table 5-2 illustrates some of the consumption differences across the four U.S. census regions. Given such clear differences in consumption patterns, marketers are beginning to realize that, for at least some product categories, the United States is no more a single market than is the European Union (see Chapter 2). Since specialized (regional) marketing programs generally cost more than standardized (national) programs, marketers must balance potential sales increases against increased costs.[61] This decision process is exactly the same as described in the section on multinational marketing decisions in Chapter 2.

TABLE 5-2

Regional Consumption Differences*

	Northeast	*North Central*	*South*	*West*
Media				
Cosmopolitan	96	84	106	111
Outdoor Life	97	131	89	88
Vibe	179	100	67	81
Premiere	83	105	83	138
Religious radio	54	109	143	63
"Nick at Nite"	122	110	90	85
Hobbies/Activities				
Hunting (with rifle)	96	132	92	81
Tennis	100	78	84	151
Movie attendance	107	82	81	145
Attend high school sports	82	148	93	75
Product Use				
Imported wine	136	95	90	87
Domestic wine	118	68	68	171
Diet cola drinks	94	129	95	82
Regular cola drinks	75	87	134	81
Mouthwash	111	100	99	92
Laptop/notebook	111	72	75	161
Restaurants/Shopping				
Fast-food restaurants	74	110	113	92
Kmart	93	123	91	95
The Gap	162	93	74	93
Eddie Bauer	103	123	59	139
Banana Republic	134	82	75	128

*100 = Average consumption or usage.

Source: *Mediamark Spring 1997* (New York: Mediamark Research Inc., 1997).

AGE-BASED SUBCULTURES

A **generation** or **age cohort** is *a group of persons who have experienced a common social, political, historical, and economic environment.* Age cohorts, because their shared histories produce unique shared values and behaviors, function as subcultures.

Cohort analysis is *the process of describing and explaining the attitudes, values, and behaviors of an age group as well as predicting its future attitudes, values, and behaviors.*[62] A critical fact uncovered by cohort analysis is that each generation behaves differently from other generations as it passes through various age categories. For example, in 2010, the baby boom generation will be entering retirement. However, it would be a mistake to assume that retiring baby boomers will behave like the pre-Depression generation does today. The forces that shaped the lives of these generations were different and their behaviors will differ throughout their life cycles. Stated another way, you won't become your parents.[63]

In the following sections, we will examine the five generations that compose the primary American market.[64] It is important to emphasize that generation is only one factor influencing behavior, and the differences within generations are often larger than the differences across generations. In addition, generations do not have sharp boundaries. Those near the age breaks between generations often do not clearly belong to either generation.

Pre-Depression Generation

The Pre-Depression generation was referred to as the "Greatest Generation" in Tom Brokaw's best-selling book (which provides an outstanding discussion of this group).[65] Also termed the *mature market* or *seniors,* it refers to those individuals born before 1930. Over 30 million Americans are in this generation. These individuals grew up in traumatic times. Most were children during the Depression and entered young adulthood during World War II. They have witnessed radical social, economic, and technological change. As a group, they are conservative and concerned with financial and personal security.

As with all generations, the Pre-Depression generation is composed of many distinct segments, and marketing to it requires a segmented strategy.[66] In addition to the variations in consumption related to differences in such variables as social class, geographic region, gender, and ethnicity, physical and mental health are major causes of consumption differences within this generation. As you would expect, health and age are closely related, with health declining over time. For example, 70 percent of the younger members of this market are married and 37 percent have activity limitations, while only 24 percent of the oldest members are married and 57 percent have activity limitations. **Gerontographics** is *a segmentation approach to the mature market that is based on the physical health and mental outlook of older consumers* (see Consumer Insight 5-1).

Communications strategies need to consider media selection, message content, and message structure. For example, some aspects of information processing, memory, and cognitive performance decline with age.[67] The rapid, brief presentation of information that younger consumers respond to is generally not appropriate for older consumers.[68]

Most adult consumers report feeling 70 to 85 percent of their chronological age. This suggests using spokespersons somewhat younger than the target segment.[69] Illustration 5-7 contains an ad from *Modern Maturity* magazine that uses a mature spokesperson. The copy stresses health benefits but for an active lifestyle rather than just for staying well. The stated message, as well as the message implied by using Big John in the ad, position this product for the Healthy Indulger segment described in Consumer Insight 5-1.

In general, age should not be the point of the message.[70] As one experienced marketer stated: "It's important to appeal to the things they are interested in, rather than appealing to the age they've reached—because they aren't thinking about age."

Products related to the unique needs of mature consumer segments range from vacations to health services to single-serving sizes of prepared foods. As this generation continues to age, assisted living services are growing rapidly. Assisted living arrangements vary from housing (generally apartment or condominium) with meals, cleaning, and assistance with personal care such as bathing to limited services provided on a scheduled basis at the consumer's home.[71]

Depression Generation

This is the cohort born between 1930 and 1946. It is also referred to as the "bridge" generation, the "Ike" or "Eisenhower" generation, and the "silent" generation. These people were small children during the Depression or World War II. They matured during the prosperous years of the 1950s and early 60s. They discovered both Sinatra and Presley. They

Consumer Insight 5-1

Gerontographics

Gerontographics is based on the theory that people change their outlook on life when they experience major life events such as becoming a grandparent, retiring, losing a spouse, or developing chronic health conditions. Individuals who have confronted similar events are likely to have a similar outlook on life and, given similar economic resources, similar lifestyles. This approach has identified four segments in the elderly market.

Healthy Indulgers This group is physically and mentally healthy. Both spouses are generally still alive. They have prepared for retirement both financially and psychologically. They are basically content and set to enjoy life. They often sell their fairly large homes and move into apartments, townhouses, or condos. They like activities, convenience, personal service, and high-tech home appliances. They are a strong part of the market for cruises and group travel.

Ailing Outgoers These people have experienced health problems, which limits their physical abilities and frequently their financial capability. However, they maintain positive self-esteem. They accept their "old-age" status, acknowledge their limitations, and still seek to get the most out of life. They like the feeling of independence as well as the socializing that eating out provides, but they frequently have limited funds as well as dietary restrictions. International Kings Table, a restaurant chain, has responded to this by offering a moderately priced, cafeteria-style meal consisting of eight entrees, several hot vegetables, a salad bar, a variety of desserts, and a drink. It also provides senior discounts, coupons, and other promotions. Other restaurants in areas with many seniors offer "early bird specials" where the evening meal is priced at a significant discount if taken before the normal meal hour. Many seniors prefer relatively early meals and respond favorably to a discount that is not directly tied to age.

Ailing outgoers are a key market for retirement communities and assisted living housing. They need clothing that enables them to dress without assistance even with limited mobility or arthritis. However, they also want their clothes to be stylish. In response, JCPenney's Easy Dressing catalog features fashionable clothing for older women. The clothes have Velcro fasteners rather than buttons, roomier armholes for easier access, and other features that make it easier to dress.

Healthy Hermits Members of this group retain their physical health but life events, often the death of a spouse, have reduced their self-concept and self-worth. They have reacted by becoming psychologically and socially withdrawn. Many then resent the isolation and the feeling that they are expected to act like old people. This group does not want to stand out. They prefer clothing styles that are popular with other seniors. They will pay a premium for well-known brands. They tend to stay in the homes in which they raised their families, and they are an important part of the do-it-yourself market.

Frail Recluses Frail recluses have accepted their old-age status and have adjusted their lifestyles to reflect reduced physical capabilities and social roles. They focus on becoming spiritually stronger. Frail recluses may have been in any one of the other categories at an earlier age. They tend to stay at home and many require home and lawn care services. They are a major market for health care products, home exercise and health-testing equipment, and emergency response systems. They like high levels of personal service, particularly in the area of financial services.

Critical Thinking Questions

1. The percent of the American population that is elderly is going to increase dramatically over the next 20 years. How is this going to change the nature of American society?
2. What ethical and social responsibilities do marketers have when marketing to the elderly?

Source: G. P. Moschis, "Life Stages of the Mature Market," *American Demographics,* September 1996, pp. 44–51.

Courtesy of Campbell Soup Company.

ILLUSTRATION 5-7

The mature market is composed of many distinct segments. This ad would appeal to the "healthy indulger" segment, which is healthy, content, and out to enjoy life.

"invented" rock and roll and grew up with music and television as important parts of their lives.

There are about 35 million individuals in this group. They are at the height of their earning power or are recently retired, and they have substantial accumulated wealth in the form of home equity and savings. They dominate the top positions in both business and government. Here are some of the ways they and others describe their lives and dreams:[72]

- This is a group of people who believe they should take advantage of their life situation; they should enjoy themselves; and their purchasing habits are a reflection of that attitude.
- We have some of those Depression-type abilities our parents had—thrift, saving money for the rainy day, don't put all your eggs in one basket . . . [but] we also have that freewheeling spirit of the younger generation.
- It's hard to find clothing that's geared to us. Somebody could make a fortune by making more clothes for our age group—something so we don't look like teenagers, but are still with it.
- I can't wait for the weekends. It's just nice to get away from your job and go to the beach. We fly kites, ride bikes—very relaxing, definitely.

- When the kids leave home and the dog dies, then you have the time and money to do something.

Recognizing both the economic power and the attitudes of this group, Lincoln recently redesigned its Town Car to appeal to 54- to 63-year-old upper-income individuals. It made the car shorter and improved its handling. Its advertising now focuses on this group as well as on the older consumers that are its current core market.

While still in excellent health, they are beginning to notice the physical effects of aging. Comfort as well as style is important. Levi's Action Slacks have been a major success with this generation. These slacks, which have an elastic waistband, are cut for the less lean, maturer body. This generation has given rise to many of the products low in fat, sugar, salt, and/or cholesterol on the market today.

Retirement planning is important to this group, and firms such as Merrill Lynch have developed products and services to meet these needs. This generation is a major consumer of recreational vehicles, second homes, new cars, travel services, and "recreational" adult education.

Members of this generation are also grandparents with sufficient incomes to indulge their grandchildren. This makes them a major market for upscale children's furniture, toys, strollers, car seats, and clothing.

Baby Boom Generation

The baby boom generation refers to those individuals born during the dramatic increase of births between the end of World War II and 1964. There are about 80 million baby boomers, which is substantially more than the two preceding generations combined. Most of this group grew up during the prosperous 1950s and 1960s. They were heavily influenced by the Kennedy assassination, the Vietnam War, recreational drugs, the sexual revolution, the energy crisis, the rapid growth of divorce, and the Cold War, as well as rock and roll and the Beatles. Although there are significant differences between the boomers born early in this generation and those born later, boomers are considered to be more self-centered, individualistic, economically optimistic, skeptical, suspicious of authority, and focused on the present than other generations.[73]

One reason for the focus on youth in advertising and product development has been the size of this segment and the fact that, until recently, it was young. It *is* the mass market, and as it ages, marketers will have to deal with a much more mature market.[74]

Baby boomers are characterized by high education levels, high incomes, and dual-career households. Most baby boomers are parents, and the early boomers are beginning to become grandparents. Parenthood provides a consistency of lifestyle between the older and younger members of this generation. Parenthood is also causing many boomers to return to the organized religion that they abandoned in their younger years.

Baby boomers are also characterized by time poverty as they try to manage two careers and family responsibilities. Many have recently faced economic hardships and uncertainties as companies reduced the size of their workforces, including middle management. However, the economic boom of the past several years has mitigated these effects.

In 2000, the age range of this generation is 36 to 54. This is an age range characterized by a family and home orientation. It also involves the need to save for, or to pay for, children's college and weddings. In addition, it is the time that individuals begin seriously to plan for retirement. This is a particular concern of baby boomers, as many doubt the ability of the Social Security system to handle the large influx of demand that this generation will produce.

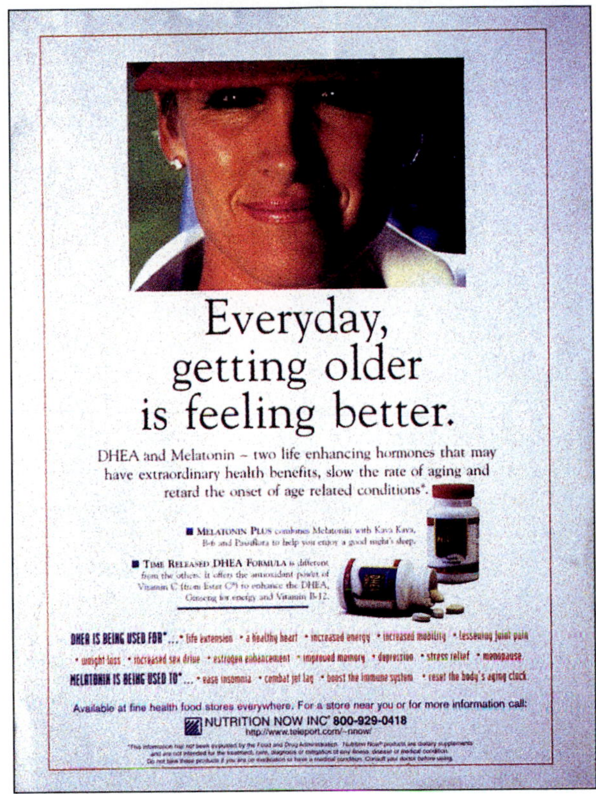

Courtesy of Nutrition Now.

ILLUSTRATION 5-8

The baby boom generation is entering its 50s. As it matures, it is creating demand for weight control products, hair dyes, and other "antiaging" devices.

As this generation enters its 50s, it will profoundly change marketing practice.[75] As boomers age, their physical needs will change. The number of women going through menopause will increase radically, as will demands for products and services related to this transition. Weight gain will become an increasing concern, and demand for plastic surgery, baldness treatments, health clubs, cosmetics for both men and women, hair coloring, health foods, and related products is likely to explode.[76] Illustration 5-8 shows an ad focused on the needs of this group. Other examples of firms focusing on the maturing needs of this generation include the following:

- Den_Mat Corp. launched Rembrandt Age Defying mouthwash and toothpaste line. The theme line will be "Do your teeth make you look 10 years older?" The product will have "revolutionary antiaging products that help restore teeth and gums to a healthier, whiter and younger look." Jaclyn Smith is the spokesperson for the line.
- Kellogg Co. is dropping its Special K ads featuring young, slim, attractive women putting on tight fitting jeans or short skirts. Research revealed that boomers were alienated by these ads: "They told us they couldn't relate to advertising techniques that used unrealistic body images." One of Kellogg's new ads has men talking in a bar. "I have my mother's thighs. I have to accept that," says one. "Do these make my butt look big?" asks another. The ad uses humor to say, "Men don't obsess about these things. Why should women?"[77]
- Nestlé Drumstick has grown sales rapidly by introducing new flavors (Strawberry Swirl, Cappuccino coffee, and Coffee with Chocolate Layers) targeted at baby boomers.

They are advertised in a TV commercial showing an adult couple consuming them in a horse-drawn carriage with Frank Sinatra's "The Best Is Yet to Come" playing.
- Motorcycles, snowmobiles, and personal watercraft sales are expanding rapidly in this market as manufacturers launch products that are larger, safer, more comfortable, and loaded with extras.

Generation X

The Generation X, often referred to as the baby bust generation, was born between 1965 and 1978. It is a smaller generation than its predecessor. This generation reached adulthood during difficult economic times. It is the first generation to be raised mainly in dual-career households, and 40 percent spent at least some time in a single-parent household before the age of 16. The divorce of one's parents is often a cause of stress and later emotional problems for the children involved.[78] However, these changes have also caused many members of Generation X to have a very broad view of a family, which may include parents, siblings, stepparents, half-siblings, close friends, live-in lovers, and others.

This is the first American generation to seriously confront the issue of "reduced expectations." These reduced expectations are based on reality for many "busters" as wages and job opportunities for young workers were limited until recently.[79] Not only has the path to success been less certain for this generation, but many Generation Xers do not believe in sacrificing time, energy, and relations to the extent the boomers did for the sake of career or economic advancement.

This generation faces a world racked by regional conflicts, an environment that continues to deteriorate, and an AIDS epidemic that threatens their lives. Members of this group tend to blame the "me generation" and the materialism associated with the baby boom generation for the difficult future they see for themselves.

A higher percent of Generation X attended college than any other generation, but a higher percent also failed to obtain a degree. This generation is a more visual generation than previous generations. While its members read less, they visit art museums and galleries more often and they watch television programming about art more than the general population. They watch about the same amount of television as the baby boomers (about three hours per day), and they watch the same popular shows as the mass audience. They attend movies regularly but no more so than the previous generation did at the same age. They are more avid users of the Internet than are the older generations. Likewise, they are generally very comfortable with computers and related technologies.

A noticeable change in this generation has been the decline in physical activity. Participation in virtually every form of sports or exercise from skiing to hiking to weight lifting is down from the previous generation. Surprisingly, the decline seems to be the greatest among females.

A final characteristic of this generation is that they tend to leave home later and the males tend to return to live with their parents more than was common in most previous generations. A tendency to marry later as well as the difficulty of obtaining a job that will support independent living are the major reasons. However, with one in five 25-year-olds living with their parents, a market segment with a low total income but high disposable income has been created.[80]

Finally, it should be stressed that this is a very diverse generation. Marriage and the presence of children are two factors that segment this generation. Likewise, while many members of this generation have struggled with careers and financial matters, others have fast-track careers and high incomes.

The baby bust generation is a $125 billion market, and it is vital for products such as beer, fast food, cosmetics, and electronics. As it enters the household formation age over the next 10 years, it will be critical for cars, appliances, and children's products. However, it is not an easy generation to reach. It is both cynical and sophisticated about products, ads, and shopping. It is materialistic and impatient. In many aspects, its tastes are "not baby boom." Thus, it created the grunge look and snowboarding. New magazines such as *Spin, Details,* and *YSP* were created for this generation, as was the *X Games.* It responds to irreverence in advertising but not to many traditional approaches. For example, almost half of those aged 18 to 24 preferred Coca-Cola's *Polar Bear* ads to its previous campaign, while less than a fifth of those aged 45 to 54 did.[81]

Busters need value because many have low-paying jobs, and they want products and messages designed uniquely for their tastes and lifestyles.[82] Marketers are increasingly targeting this group. Apple's decision to advertise computers on MTV and MCI's 1-800-COLLECT service are both targeted at baby busters. Other successful approaches to this generation include the following:

- Budweiser's talking frogs commercial represents the humorous, irreverent advertising that this group likes. Its Web site also uses the frogs and is designed to appeal to this generation.
- Volkswagen's TV ad showing two young guys tooling around in a VW, picking up a discarded couch, discarding it (apparently because it smells bad), and continuing to drive around with the musical lyrics "da da da" playing has been very successful. Volkswagen also has a Web site focused on Generation X that it promotes in media read by the more successful members of this generation.
- Kia Motors America recently launched its Sportage convertible targeting Generation X. It is advertised on cable TV with an ad showing "Ed," the owner chauffeuring a couple in the convertible.
- Philips Electronics is targeting the younger members of this generation with its new $599 CD-Recording home audio deck, which allows customers to make custom CDs. According to a company spokesperson: "It's targeted toward a younger audience because of their appetite for music and the role it plays in their life." It will be advertised on MTV and other targeted programs.

Generation Y

Today's 22-year-olds are the leading edge of the next generation. It is a significant one for our society because it is the next baby boom, with 72 million members. These children of the original baby boomers were born between 1978 and 1994 and are sometimes referred to as the "echo boom."

It is the first generation to grow up with virtually full-employment opportunities for women, with dual-income households the standard, with a wide array of family types seen as normal, with significant respect for ethnic and cultural diversity, with computers in the home and schools, and with the Internet. It has also grown up with divorce as the norm,[83] AIDS, terrorism, visible homelessness (including many teenagers), drug abuse, gang violence, parents losing employment due to downsizing, and, until a few years ago, stagnant or declining purchasing power for many families.

The traditional mass marketing approaches that were so successful with older generations don't work well with Generation X and are even less effective with Generation Y.

ILLUSTRATION 5-9

Attracting Generation Y requires new approaches to marketing. Traditional media and mass techniques are not as effective with this group as they were with their parents.

Courtesy of The Pepsi Cola Company.

Pepsi is successfully appealing to the older members of Generation Y as well as the younger members of Generation X by inventing Pepsi Ball (a combination basketball, Frisbee, hockey, and team handball played on a triangle field with three goals) and promoting it on college campuses (see Illustration 5-9). Many marketers are particularly interested in the teenage portion of this generation.

Most teenagers have positive self-images and view themselves as kind, trustworthy, likable, funny, intelligent, happy, affectionate, creative, active, and tolerant. Over a third of all teenagers work for wages, and over half of those over 15 have jobs. The average number of hours per week spent on various activities includes:[84]

Household chores/shopping	10.5
Watching TV	8.7
Listening to the radio	7.1
Talking on the phone	5.5
Listening to CDs, tapes	5.2
Hanging out with friends	5.1
Sports, athletic activities	5.1
Watching videos	4.9
Dating	4.4
Homework	4.1
Job	3.7

The vast majority of teenagers were raised and currently reside in dual-income or single-parent households. Therefore, they have grown up assisting in household management, including shopping. This fact, coupled with the ubiquitous presence of advertising throughout their lives, has made them cynical, smart shoppers:

Courtesy Delia's

ILLUSTRATION 5-10

Teenagers are shunning the brands and channels their parents used. Many prefer Mudd and Delia's to Levi's and The Gap.

> They're even more pragmatic than the baby boomers ever were, and they have a B.S. alarm that goes off quick and fast. They walk in and usually make up their minds very quickly about whether its phat or not phat, and whether they want it or don't want it. They know a lot of advertising is based on lies and hype.[85]

Like all recent generations, this group of teenagers has its own language and way of speaking. "In" words, expressions, and tones change quickly. Clothing styles likewise change quickly. However, musical and other aesthetic tastes acquired during teenage and early adult years tend to last a lifetime.[86] Brand and store preferences can also be enduring.

The teenage market is attractive to marketers for two reasons. As stated above, preferences and tastes formed during the teenage years can influence purchases throughout life. Second, it currently spends over $140 billion annually for personal consumption (two-thirds from its own money and one-third from parents). It spends billions more while doing the household shopping and influences the purchase of additional items:

> Kerri, age 16, hated the family's "clunky" Jeep Cherokee. She insisted on going along when her father, an attorney, went car shopping. She persuaded him to buy a Toyota *Camry* with a CD player and sunroof. According to Kerri: "It looks more like a hip-hoppier car."[87]

Marketers targeting teens need to use appropriate language, music, images and media. The portrayal of multiple racial and ethnic groups in ads aimed at this generation is common. This is a multiethnic generation, and single-race ads would seem unnatural to them. In addition, urban African-American teenagers and the hip-hop culture they often embody are frequently the style leaders of this generation.[88]

Successful approaches to this market include the following:

- Sassaby has a line of cosmetics for teenagers called Jane. It is positioned as "totally new, tell-it-like-it-is cosmetics for a new generation." In addition to teen-oriented ads in teen-oriented media, it is planning a 24-hour bulletin board on Prodigy for teenage girls. Called Jane's Brain, it is being billed as "the thinking girl's guide to the highway of life . . . where young women talk, to each other and to Jane . . . [about] boys, school, parents, politics, music, the future, and of course, makeup." As part of its promotion strategy, Sassaby will use the bulletin board to identify social issues of importance to the participants. It will then launch special promotional cosmetics shades tied to one of those issues, with a portion of the sales donated to that cause.

- "Everyone loves Delia's. It's the big excitement," says 15-year-old Emily. The catalog did well over $100 million in sales in 1998 offering downtown fashion to the 4 million teenage girls on its mailing list. The clothes are designed and promoted strictly for this Generation. Emily's mother doesn't like them: "I think they are too revealing. I tell her I'll buy her anything at The Gap." But Emily thinks The Gap is "too preppy." Delia's catalogs don't just offer clothes for sale (see Illustration 5-10). They dispense fashion advice including how to order pants so that they will drop well below the hips and drag the hems. In addition, the models look like regular teenagers. It drops its catalogs at schools and has a hot Web site. It also bought gurl.com, a popular fashion, chat, and game site for girls. It plans to target male teenagers next with a catalog titled *Droog.*[89]

SUMMARY

The United States is becoming increasingly diverse. Much of this diversity is fueled by immigration and an increase in ethnic pride and by identification with non-European heritages among numerous Americans. Most members of a culture share most of the core values, beliefs, and behaviors of that culture. However, most individuals also belong to several subcultures. A *subculture* is a segment of a larger culture whose members share distinguishing patterns of behavior. An array of ethnic, nationality, religious, regional, and age subcultures characterize American society. The existence of these subcultures provides marketers with the opportunity to develop unique marketing programs to match the unique needs of each.

Ethnic subcultures are defined broadly as those whose members' unique shared behaviors are based on a common racial, language, or nationality background. Non-European ethnic groups constitute a significant and growing part of the U.S. population (from 24 percent in 1990 to 32 percent by 2010).

African-Americans are the largest non-European ethnic group, with 12 percent of the U.S. population. While African-Americans are, on average, younger and poorer than the general population, they are a large, diverse group with many segments.

Hispanics are the second largest non-European ethnic group, and they are predicted to surpass African-Americans in numbers by 2010. While Hispanics have a variety of national backgrounds (Mexico = 60 percent, Puerto Rico = 12 percent, Cuba = 5 percent), the Spanish language, a common religion (Roman Catholic), and national Spanish-language media and entertainment figures have created a somewhat homogeneous Hispanic subculture.

Asian-Americans are the most diverse of the major ethnic subcultures. They are characterized by a variety of nationalities, languages, and religions. From a marketing perspective, it is not appropriate to consider Asian-Americans as a single group. Instead, Asian-Americans are best approached as a number of nationality subcultures.

Native Americans, Asian-Indian Americans, and *Arab-Americans* are smaller but important subcultures. Each is diverse yet shares enough common values and behaviors to be approached as a single segment for at least some products. Geographic concentration and specialized media allow targeted marketing campaigns.

While the United States is a relatively secular society, 90 percent of all Americans claim a religious affiliation, and 40 percent claim to attend church regularly. Although 95 percent of those with a religious affiliation are Christian, a variety of *religious subcultures* exist both within the Christian faiths and within the Jewish, Muslim, and Buddhist faiths that several million other Americans embrace. Within each faith, the largest difference is the degree of conservatism between the members. Conservatism in this case refers to the extent to which the initial teachings of the faith are taken in their literal context as the only truth. The born-again Christian movement is the most visible example of a subculture based on religion.

Regional subcultures arise due to climatic conditions, the natural environment and resources, the characteristics of the various immigrant groups that have settled in each region, and significant social and political events. Regional subcultures affect all aspects of consumption behavior, and sophisticated marketers recognize that the United States is composed of numerous regional markets.

An *age cohort* is a group of persons who have experienced a common social, political, historical, and economic environment. Age cohorts or generations, because their unique shared histories produce unique shared values and behaviors, function as subcultures. *Cohort analysis* is the process of describing and explaining the attitudes, values, and behaviors of an age group as well as predicting its future attitudes, values, and behaviors. There are five major generations functioning in America today—Pre-Depression, Depression, Baby Boom, Generation X, and Generation Y.

KEY TERMS

Acculturation 156
Age cohort 172
Born-again Christian 168
Cohort analysis 172
Ethnic subculture 149
Event marketing 155
Generation 172
Gerontographics 173
Hispanic 155
Regional subcultures 171
Religious subcultures 166
Secular society 166
Subculture 146

INTERNET EXERCISES

1. Visit the U.S. Census Web site (http://www.census.gov). What data are available there on the following? Which of this is most useful to marketers? Why?
   a. Native Americans
   b. African-Americans
   c. Hispanics
2. Use the Internet to determine the cities in the United States that have the largest population of the following. Why is this useful to marketers?
   a. Native Americans
   b. African-Americans
   c. Hispanics
   d. Asian-Indian Americans
   e. Arab-Americans
   f. Individuals over 65
3. Visit American Demographics' Web site (http://www.marketingpower.com).
   a. What information is available there on generations? Which is most useful to marketers? Why?
   b. What information is available there on African-Americans? Which is most useful to marketers?
4. Identify and describe two Web sites that provide useful information on the following.
   a. Roman Catholic subculture
   b. Protestant subcultures
   c. Jewish subculture
   d. Muslim subculture
   e. Buddhist subculture
5. Evaluate Delia's Web site and its on-line magazine (http://www.delias.com and http://www.gurl.com).
6. Find and evaluate Web sites targeting the members of:
   a. Each of the generations
   b. Different religions
   c. Different ethnic groups
7. Find one or more Web sites that focus on the hip-hop culture (Yahoo has a list, or try http://www.vibe.com).

DDB NEEDHAM LIFESTYLE DATA ANALYSES

1. Which heavy user consumption categories have the greatest differences across the ethnic subcultures? Why is this the case?
2. For which products does ownership differ the most across ethnic groups? Why is this the case?
3. For which television shows do preferences differ the most across the ethnic subcultures? Why is this the case?
4. Based on the DDB Needham data in Table 5a, which attitudes/interests/activities vary the most across the ethnic subcultures ? Why is this the case?
5. Using the DDB Needham data in Table 5a, create age groups that approximate the generations described in the text. For which attitudes/interests/activities are there the greatest differences across the generations? Why is this the case?
6. Using the DDB Needham data in Table 5, create age groups that approximate the generations described in the text. For which products and activities are there the greatest differences in heavy consumption across the generations? Why is this the case?

REVIEW QUESTIONS

1. What is a *subculture?*
2. What determines the degree to which a subculture will influence an individual's behavior?
3. Is the American culture more like a soup or a salad?
4. What is an *ethnic subculture?*
5. How large are the major ethnic subcultures in America? Which are growing most rapidly?
6. What countries/regions are the major sources of America's immigrants?
7. Are the various ethnic subcultures homogeneous or heterogeneous?
8. Describe the income distribution of African-Americans. What are the marketing implications of this distribution?
9. Describe the four African-American consumer groups found by the Market Segment Research study.
10. What are the basic principles that should be followed in marketing to an African-American market segment?
11. To what extent is the Spanish language used by American Hispanics?
12. Can Hispanics be treated as a single market?
13. How homogeneous are Asian-Americans?
14. To what extent do Asian-Americans use their native language?
15. Describe the three Asian-American consumer groups identified by the Market Segment Research study.
16. Why is the United States considered to be a *secular society?*
17. Describe the *Roman Catholic subculture.*
18. Describe the *born-again Christian subculture.*
19. Describe the *Jewish subculture.*
20. Describe the *Muslim subculture.*
21. Describe the *Buddhist subculture.*
22. What is a regional subculture?
23. What is an *age cohort? Cohort analysis?*
24. Describe each of the major generations in America.

DISCUSSION QUESTIONS

25. Do you agree that America is becoming more "like a salad than a soup" in terms of the integration of ethnic groups? Is this good or bad?
26. Do you agree with Miller Brewing that "the things that young Hispanic or young African-American or young white people have in

common are much stronger and more important than any ethnic difference"? For what types of products is this view most correct? Least correct?

27. Most new immigrants to America are non-European and have limited English-language skills. What opportunities does this present to marketers? Does this raise any ethical issues for marketers?

28. A significant number of African-Americans live in inner cities or rural areas and have household incomes below the poverty level. What are the marketing implications of this fact? Does a firm's social responsibility play a role here? If so, what?

29. While many of the following have very limited incomes, others are quite prosperous. Does marketing to prosperous members of these groups require a marketing mix different from the one used to reach other prosperous consumers?
   a. African-American
   b. Hispanic
   c. Asian-American

30. Describe how each of the following firms' product managers should approach the (*i*) African-American market, (*ii*) the Hispanic market, (*iii*) the Asian-American market, (*iv*) the Asian-Indian American market, (*v*) the Arab-American market, or (*vi*) the Native American market.
   a. Coca Cola
   b. Chili's
   c. NBC television
   d. *Time* magazine
   e. United Way
   f. Sony televisions
   g. Amazon.com
   h. Crest toothpaste

31. Describe how each of the following firms' product managers should approach each of the (*i*) African-American, or (*ii*) Asian-American consumer groups identified by the Market Segment Research study.
   a. Coca Cola
   b. Chili's
   c. NBC television
   d. *Time* magazine
   e. United Way
   f. Sony televisions
   g. Amazon.com
   h. Crest toothpaste

32. What, if any, unique ethical responsibilities exist when marketing to ethnic subcultures?

33. Do you agree that the United States is a secular society? Why or why not?

34. Describe how each of the following firms' product managers should approach the (*i*) Catholic, (*ii*) Christian, (*iii*) born-again Christian, (*iv*) Jewish, (*v*) Muslim, and (*vi*) Buddhist subcultures.
   a. Coca Cola
   b. Chili's
   c. NBC television
   d. *Time* magazine
   e. United Way
   f. Sony televisions
   g. Amazon.com
   h. Crest toothpaste

35. Will regional subcultures become more or less distinct over the next 20 years? Why?

36. Select one product, service, or activity from each category in Table 5-2 and explain the differences in consumption for the item across the regions shown.

37. Why does the consumption of laptop/notebook computers differ across regions? Are regions a better explanation for laptop/notebook use than the demographic factors identified in Chapter 4 (see Tables 4-1, 4-2, and 4-3)?

38. Describe how each of the following firms' product managers should approach the (*i*) Pre-Depression generation (*ii*) Depression generation, (*iii*) Baby Boom generation, (*iv*) Generation X, and (*v*) Generation Y.
   a. Coca Cola
   b. Chili's
   c. NBC television
   d. *Time* magazine
   e. United Way
   f. Sony televisions
   g. Amazon.com
   h. Crest toothpaste

39. How will your lifestyle differ from your parents' when you are your parents' age?

APPLICATION ACTIVITIES

40. Watch two hours of prime-time major network (ABC, CBS, FOX, or NBC) television. What subculture groups are portrayed in the programs? Describe how they are portrayed. Do these portrayals match the descriptions in this text? How would you explain the differences? Repeat these tasks for the ads shown during the programs.
41. Pick a product of interest and examine the Simmons Market Research Bureau or MediaMark studies in your library (these are often in the journalism library) on the product. Determine the extent to which its consumption varies by ethnic group and region. Does consumption also vary by age, income, or other variables? Are the differences in ethnic and regional consumption due primarily to ethnicity and region or to the fact that the ethnic group or region is older, richer, or otherwise different from the larger culture?
42. Examine several magazines and/or newspapers aimed at a non-European ethnic or nationality group. What types of products are advertised? Why?
43. Interview three members of the following subcultures and ascertain their opinions of how their ethnic and/or nationality group is portrayed on network television shows and in national ads.
    a. African-Americans
    b. Asian-Americans
    c. Hispanics
    d. Arab-Americans
    e. Asian-Indian Americans
    f. Native Americans
44. Interview three members of the following subcultures and ascertain the extent to which they identify with the core American culture, their ethnic subculture within America, or their nationality subculture. Also determine the extent to which they feel others of their ethnic/race group feel as they do and the reasons for any differences.
    a. African-Americans
    b. Asian-Americans
    c. Hispanics
    d. Arab-Americans
    e. Asian-Indian Americans
    f. Native Americans
45. Interview three members of the following subcultures and determine the extent to which their consumption patterns are influenced by their religion.
    a. Catholics
    b. "Mainstream" or "moderate" Christians
    c. Born-again Christians
    d. Jews
    e. Muslims
    f. Buddhists
46. Interview two students from other regions of the United States and determine the behavior and attitudinal differences they have noticed between their home and your present location. Try to determine the causes of these differences.
47. Interview two members of the following generations. Determine the extent to which they feel the text description of their generation is accurate and how they think their generation differs from the larger society. Also determine what they think about how they are portrayed in the mass media and how well they are served by business today.
    a. Pre-Depression
    b. Depression
    c. Baby Boom
    d. Generation X
    e. Generation Y

REFERENCES

1. E. Neuborne, "Generation Y," pp. 80–88. Reprinted from the February 15, 1999 issue of *Business Week* by special permission. © 1999 McGraw-Hill and Companies, Inc.
2. For conflicting data, see S. Reese, "When Whites Aren't a Mass Market," *American Demographics,* March 1997, pp. 51–54.
3. T. McCarroll, "It's a Mass Market No More," *Time,* Fall 1993, p. 80.
4. M. G. Briones, "Coors Turns Up the Heat," *Marketing News,* June 22, 1998, p. 15.
5. See G. Sandor, "The Other Americans," *American Demographics,* June 1994, pp. 36–42; N. McNamee, "Should the Census Be Less Black and White," *Business Week,* July 4, 1994, p. 40; and S. Evinger, "How to Record Race," *American Demographics,* May 1996, pp. 36–41.

6. C. Fisher, "It's All in the Details," *American Demographics,* April 1998, p. 45.
7. W. O'Hare, "Managing Multiple-Race Data," *American Demographics,* April 1998, pp. 42–44
8. W. H. Frey, "Immigrant and Native Migrant Magnets," *American Demographics,* November 1996, pp. 37–40; and W. H. Frey, "The Diversity Myth," *American Demographics,* June 1998, pp. 39–43.
9. *Legal Immigration, Fiscal 1997* (Washington D.C.: U.S. Department of Justice, January 1999), p. 9.
10. See L. R. Oswald, "Culture Swapping," *Journal of Consumer Research,* March 1999, pp. 303–18.
11. M. L. Rossman, *Multicultural Marketing* (New York: American Management Association, 1994), pp. 153–57.
12. E. Morris, "The Difference in Black and White," *American Demographics,* January 1993, p. 46.
13. L. McAllister, "Ethnic Customs Influence How Ethnic Americans Gift," *Gifts & Decorative Accessories,* July 1993, p. 53; and "Table A: Comparison of Summary Measures of Income by Selected Characteristics" (Washington, D.C.: U.S. Bureau of the Census, March Current Population Survey), September 8, 1998, p. vii.
14. C. Fisher, "Black, Hip, and Primed to Shop," *American Demographics,* September 1996, pp. 52–59.
15. For example, see B. E. Bryant and J. Cha, "Crossing the Threshold," *Marketing Research,* Winter 1996, pp. 21–28.
16. E. Morris, "The Difference in Black and White," *American Demographics,* January 1993, pp. 44–49.
17. *The 1993 Minority Market Report* (Coral Gables, FL: Market Segment Research, Inc., 1993).
18. J. Sterngold, "A Racial Divide Widens in Black and White," *The New York Times,* December 29, 1998, p. A12. Copyright © 2000 by the New York Times Co. Reprinted by permission.
19. K. Cleland, "Narrow-Marketing Efforts Winning the Internet Savy," *Advertising Age,* November 16, 1998, p. s26.
20. J. Hodges, "Black, White Teens Show Similarity in TV Tastes," *Advertising Age,* May 13, 1996, p. 24.
21. H. Schlossberg, "Many Marketers Still Consider Blacks 'Dark-skinned' Whites," *Marketing News,* January 19, 1993, p. 1.
22. Footnote 14, p. 56.
23. N. Delener, "Consumer Payment System Attribute Perceptions and Preferences," *Journal of Professional Services Marketing,* no. 1 (1995), pp. 53–71; and F. J. Mulhern, J. D. Williams, and R. P. Leone, "Variability of Brand Price Elasticities across Retail Stores," *Journal of Retailing,* no. 3 (1998), pp. 427–45.
24. For a thorough discussion of this issue, see G. R. Soruco and T. P. Meyer, "The Mobile Hispanic Market," *Marketing Research,* Winter 1993, p. 8.
25. P. Braus, "What Does Hispanic Mean?" *American Demographics,* June 1993, pp. 46–50.
26. G. R. Soruco and T. P. Meyer, "The Mobile Hispanic Market," *Marketing Research,* Winter 1993, pp. 6–11.
27. M. Winsberg, "Specific Hispanics," *American Demographics,* February 1994, pp. 44–53.
28. An excellent description of this process for Mexican immigrants is L. Penaloza, "*Atravesando Fronteras*/Border Crossings," *Journal of Consumer Research,* June 1994, pp. 32–54.
29. See footnote 17, pp. 41–43. For data on how identification with the Hispanic culture influences information search, see C. Webster, "The Effects of Hispanic Subcultural Identification on Information Search Behavior," *Journal of Advertising Research,* September 1992, pp. 54–62.
30. C. Webster, "The Effects of Hispanic Identification on Marital Roles in the Purchase Decision Process," *Journal of Consumer Research,* September 1994, pp. 319–31.
31. L. Kramer, "Churchs Chicken Chain Courts Latino Audience," *Advertising Age,* October 19, 1998, p. 12.
32. R. Maso-Fleischman, "Archetype Research for Advertising," *Journal of Advertising Research,* October 1997, pp. 81–84.
33. See footnote 26.
34. See C. Fisher, "Telcos Lead Hispanic Ad Stampede," *Advertising Age,* January 23, 1995, p. 30; and J. D. Zbar, "Marketing to Hispanics," *Advertising Age,* March 18, 1996, p. 27.
35. S. Livingston, "Marketing to the Hispanic-American Community," *Journal of Business Strategy,* March 1992, pp. 54–57.
36. J. A. F. Nicholls and P. Roslow, "Main Message Retention," *Marketing Research,* Spring 1996, pp. 39–45.
37. See M. Mogelonsky, "Watching in Tongues," *American Demographics,* April 1998, pp. 48–52.
38. C. Krol, "Few Direct Efforts Target Hispanics," *Advertising Age,* August 24, 1998, p. s6.
39. "Marketing to Hispanics," *Advertising Age,* February 8, 1987, p. S–23; and M. Westerman, "Death of the Frito Bandito," March 1989, pp. 28–32.
40. K. Morral, "Connecting with the Hispanic Market," *Bank Marketing,* June 1996, pp. 43–48.
41. L. Giegoldt, "Brand Loyalty Opportunities Abound," *Advertising Age,* August 24, 1998, p. s10. See also S. Shim and K. C. Gehrt, "Hispanic and Native American Adolescents," *Journal of Retailing,* no. 3 (1996), pp. 307–24.
42. S. Hume, "MCI Seeks Mexican Friends and Family," *Advertising Age,* March 8, 1993, p. 7.
43. M. Johnson, "The Application of Geodemographics to Retailing," *Journal of the Market Research Society,* January 1997, p. 213.
44. J. D. Zbar, "'Latinization' Catches Retailers' Ears," *Advertising Age,* November 16, 1998, p. S22.
45. See B. Edmundson, "Asian Americans in 2001," *American Demographics,* February 1997, pp. 16–17.
46. S. F. Ownby and P. E. Horridge, "Acculturation Level and Shopping Orientations of Asian-American Consumers," *Psychology & Marketing,* January 1997, pp. 1–18.
47. See W. P. O'Hare, W. H. Frey, and D. Fost, "Asians in the Suburbs," *American Demographics,* May 1994, pp. 32–38; and C. Fisher "Marketers Straddle the Asia-America Curtain," *Advertising Age,* November 7, 1994, p. S–21.
48. See also D. Fost, "Asian Homebuyers Seek Wind and Water," *American Demographics,* June 1993, pp. 23–24.

49. "Targeting American Indians," *Marketing Power,* May 1995, p. 4; and C. Russell, "Native Americans," *Marketing Power,* September 1996, p. 4.
50. This section was based on M. Mogelonsky, "Asian-Indian Americans," *American Demographics,* August 1995, pp. 32–39.
51. This section was based on S. El-Badry, "The Arab-American Market," *American Demographics,* January 1994, pp. 22–30.
52. B. A. Kosmin and S. P. Lachman, *One Nation Under God* (New York: Harmony Books, 1993), pp. 88–93.
53. K. L. Woodward, "The Rites of Americans," *Newsweek,* November 29, 1993, p. 80. See also A. W. Fawcett, "The Consumer Mindset in the '90s," *American Demographics,* April 18, 1994, p. 12; and M. Spiegler, "Scouting for Souls," *American Demographics,* March 1996, pp. 42–49.
54. S. W. McDaniel and J. J. Burnett, "Targeting the Evangelical Market," *Journal of Advertising Research,* August 1991, p. 27.
55. Footnote 52, p. 245.
56. R. Thau, "The New Jewish Exodus," *American Demographics,* June 1994, p. 11.
57. Footnote 52, p. 12.
58. M. Chapman and A. Jamal, "The Floodgates Open," *Enhancing Knowledge Development in Marketing* (Chicago: American Marketing Association, 1996), p. 198.
59. See S. El-Badry, "Understanding Islam in America," *American Demographics,* January 1994, p. 10.
60. S. L. Hapoienu, "The Rise of Micromarketing," *The Journal of Business Strategy,* November–December 1990, p. 3.
61. R. E. Linneman and J. L. Stanton, Jr., "A Game Plan for Regional Marketing," *Journal of Business Strategy,* November–December 1992, pp. 19–25.
62. A. Rindfleisch, "Cohort Generational Influences on Consumer Socialization," in *Advances in Consumer Research XXI,* ed. C. T. Allen and D. R. John (Provo, UT: Association for Consumer Research, 1994), pp. 470–76; and R. T. Rust and K. W. Y. Yeung, "Tracking the Age Wave," in *Advances in Consumer Research XXII,* ed. F. R. Kardes and M. Sujan (Provo, UT: Association for Consumer Research, 1995), pp. 680–85.
63. S. Mitchell, "Are Boomers Their Parents?" *American Demographics,* August 1996, pp. 40–45.
64. For a detailed treatment, see J. W. Smith and A. Clurman, *Rocking the Ages* (New York: HarperBusiness, 1997).
65. T. Brokaw, *The Greatest Generation* (New York: Random House, 1998).
66. See N. Long, "Broken Down by Age and Sex," *Journal of the Market Research Society,* April 1998, pp. 73–91; G. P. Moschis, "Life Stages of the Mature Market," *American Demographics,* September 1996, pp. 44–51; G. P. Moschis, "Consumer Behavior in Later Life," *Journal of the Academy of Marketing Science,* Summer 1994, pp. 195–204; D. Crispell and W. H. Frey, "American Maturity," *American Demographics,* March 1993, pp. 31–42.
67. See C. Yoon, "Age Differences in Consumers' Processing Strategies," *Journal of Consumer Research,* December 1997, pp. 329–40; and S. Law, S. A. Hawkins, and F. I. M. Craik, "Repetition-Induced Belief in the Elderly," *Journal of Consumer Research,* September 1998, pp. 91–107.
68. R. L. Johnson and C. J. Cobb-Walgren, "Aging and the Problem of Television Clutter," *Journal of Advertising Research,* July 1994, pp. 54–62; and P. Sorce, "Cognitive Competence of Older Consumers," *Psychology & Marketing,* September 1995, pp. 467–80. See also J. Perrien et al., "Exploring the Persuasive Effects of a Commercial for a Pharmaceutical Product," in *Advances in Consumer Research XXV,* ed. J. W. Alba and J. W. Hutchinson (Provo, UT: Association for Consumer Research, 1998), pp. 513–16.
69. T. Bristol, "Persuading Senior Adults," *Journal of Current Issues and Research in Advertising,* Fall 1996, pp. 59–67.
70. See G. P. Moschis, A. Mathur, and R. K. Smith, "Older Consumers' Orientations toward Age-Based Marketing Stimuli," *Journal of the Academy of Marketing Science,* Summer 1993, pp. 195–205; K. Tepper, "The Role of Labeling Processes in Elderly Consumers' Responses to Age Segmentation Clues," *Journal of Consumer Research,* March 1994, pp. 503–19; and R. T. Peterson, "The Portrayal of Senior Citizens," *Journal of Professional Services Marketing* 12, no. 2, pp. 95–106.
71. L. J. Barton, "Assisted Living in the U.S," *American Demographics,* July 1997, pp. 45–51
72. L. Freeman, "Completing the Span of 'Bridge' to Boomers," *Advertising Age,* November 7, 1994, p. S–8; and W. Dunn, "The Eisenhower Generation," *American Demographics,* July 1994, pp. 34–40.
73. C. Gibson, "The Four Baby Booms," *American Demographics,* November 1993, pp. 36–41; and P. Braus, "The Baby Boom at Mid-Decade," *American Demographics,* April 1995, pp. 40–45.
74. R. A. Lee, "The Youth Bias in Advertising," *American Demographics,* January 1997, pp. 47–50
75. C. Russell, "The Baby Boom Turns 50"; and J. Langer, "Eight Boomers' Views"; both in *American Demographics,* December 1995, pp. 22–33 and 34–41.
76. See P. Braus, "Boomers against Gravity," *American Demographics,* February 1995, pp. 50–57.
77. D. Goodman, "Special K Drops Thin Models for Health Theme," *Marketing News,* March 02, 1998, p. 8.
78. N. Zill and J. Robinson, "The Generation X Difference," *American Demographics,* April 1995, pp. 24–33.
79. Ibid.
80. M. Mogelonsky, "The Rocky Road to Adulthood," *American Demographics,* May 1996, pp. 26–35.
81. A. W. Fawcett, "CAA Ads Make Big Splash with Youth, Women," *Advertising Age,* April 12, 1993, p. 1.
82. P. Herbig, W. Koehler, and K. Day, "Marketing to the Baby Bust Generation," *Journal of Consumer Marketing,* no. 1 (1993), pp. 4–9; K. Ritchie, "Marketing to Generation X," *American Demographics,* April 1995, pp. 34–39; and K. Ritchie, *Marketing to Generation X* (New York: Lexington Books, 1995).
83. For a discussion of the consequences of this, see A. Rindfleisch, J. E. Burroughs, and F. Denton, "Family Structure, Materialism,

and Compulsive Consumption," *Journal of Consumer Research,* March 1997, pp. 312–25.

84. *Targeting Today's Teens* (New York: Simmons Market Research Bureau, 1994). See also S. Mitchell, "The Next Baby Boom," *American Demographics,* October 1995, pp. 22–31.

85. C. Miller, "Phat is Where It's At for Today's Teen Market," *Marketing News,* August 15, 1994, p. 6. See also D. M. Boush, M. Friestad, and G. M. Rose, "Adolescent Skepticism toward TV Advertising and Knowledge of Advertising Tactics," *Journal of Consumer Research,* June 1994, pp. 165–75. See also S. Shim, "Adolescent Consumer Decision-Making Styles," *Journal of Consumer Research,* September 1996, pp. 547–69.

86. See M. B. Holbrook, "Nostalgia and Consumption Preferences," *Journal of Consumer Research,* September 1993, pp. 245–56; and M. B. Holbrook and R. M. Schindler, "Age, Sex, and Attitude toward the Past as Predictors of Consumer's Aesthetic Tastes for Cultural Products," *Journal of Marketing Research,* August 1994, pp. 412–22.

87. L. Zinn, "Teens," *Business Week,* April 11, 1994, p. 79.

88. M. Spiegler, "Marketing Street Culture," *American Demographics,* November 1996, pp. 29–34

89. Footnote 1.

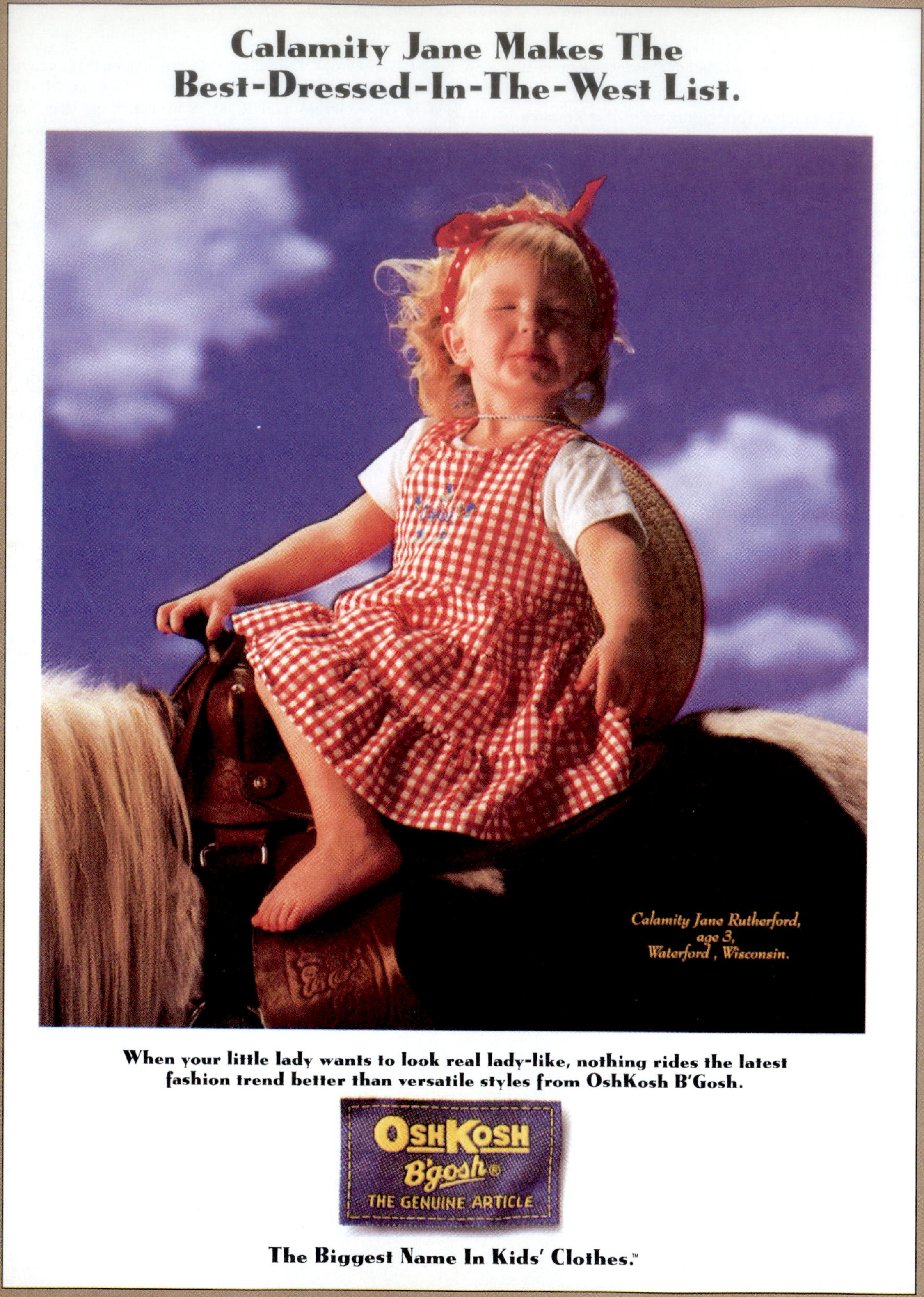
Calamity Jane Makes The
Best-Dressed-In-The-West List.
Calamity Jane Rutherford,
age 3,
Waterford, Wisconsin.
When your little lady wants to look real lady-like, nothing rides the latest fashion trend better than versatile styles from OshKosh B'Gosh.
OshKosh
B'gosh®
THE GENUINE ARTICLE
The Biggest Name In Kids' Clothes.™

© Oshkosh B'Gosh, Inc.

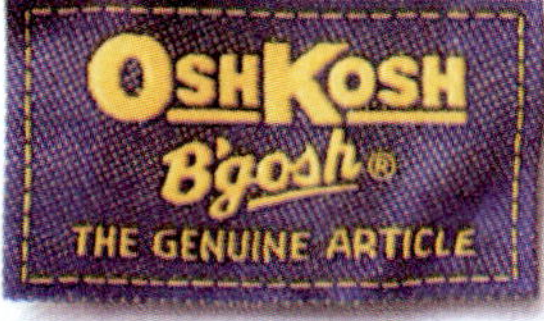

The American Society: Families and Households

OshKosh B'Gosh is a 100-year-old firm that was noted primarily for its work clothes until the 1970s. At that time, children's wear represented only 5 percent of OshKosh's sales. Then the "echo boom" (a sharp increase in births as the baby boom generation entered the prime child-bearing years) of the late 1970s and early 1980s began. The sudden growth in the number of young children, coupled with the status focus of their parents, resulted in rapid growth for the high-quality but expensive OshKosh kids bib overalls and other branded items. Sales grew from $40 to $340 million in a decade. OshKosh became identified with expensive children's clothes. Its clothes were considered almost a uniform for yuppie toddlers.

However, this great success brought serious problems. First, OshKosh was so identified with clothes for young children that it could not sell to other age groups. While parents choose toddlers' clothes, children begin to influence and then make these decisions as young as four or five. OshKosh learned this the hard way. They introduced a line of clothes aimed at older kids, which failed. A major reason was that eight-year-olds did not want to wear "baby" clothes. Attempts to market women's casual clothes and maternity wear also failed, as did a line of men's casual clothes.

By 1990, the number of births had declined as the baby boom generation matured. Generation X found Gap Kids, Lands' End, and other brands better suited to their tastes and desires. Values also began to change and status lost some of its appeal. Value and thrift became the focus of many new parents facing an uncertain economic environment. Value-oriented shoppers stopped buying kids' clothing in department stores (OshKosh's primary distribution channel) and started buying imitations at Kmart and other discount stores.

OshKosh's net income fell from $29.5 million in 1990 to $4.5 million in 1993. However, it has begun to grow again primarily by focusing on the children's market.

It has added two new product lines to the *OshKosh B'Gosh* line (sizes 2T through 6x/7): *Genuine Kids* (12 months through size 16) and *Baby B'Gosh* (newborn through 24 months). The Genuine Kids line is targeted at affluent consumers (with median household incomes of $75,000), and most of the sales are in youth sizes. OshKosh B'Gosh is focused on the preschool market. It also launched a Hispanic advertising campaign for this line.

Baby B'Gosh was created to allow a clear focus on the needs of this segment. A similar name was used to encourage parents to move from *Baby B'Gosh* to *OshKosh B'Gosh* as the baby matures. Research revealed a number of unique features about the purchase process for infant clothing:

- Gifts are a significant part of the market.
- Traditional department stores are a preferred channel.
- New mothers look to other mothers in deciding what to buy.
- Mothers want a special look for their baby that is different from other kids.
- Collections and coordination are not critical.
- Comfort is important, durability less so.
- Practical features such as ease of dressing are very important.
- Price/value is important, as the baby quickly outgrows the clothing.

Based on this and additional research on how families make purchase decisions for clothing for children of differing ages, OshKosh has successfully reversed its sales and profit decline.[1]

The household is the basic consumption unit for most consumer goods.[2] Major items such as housing, automobiles, and appliances are consumed more by household units than by individuals. Furthermore, the consumption patterns of individual household members seldom are independent from those of other household members. For example, deciding to grant a child's request for a bicycle may mean spending discretionary funds that could have been used to purchase an evening out for the parents, new clothing for a sister or brother, or otherwise used by another member of the household. Therefore, it is essential that marketers understand the household as a consumption unit, as shown in Figure 6-1.

Households are important not only for their direct role in the consumption process but also for the critical role they perform in socializing children. The family household is the primary mechanism whereby cultural and social-class values and behavior patterns are passed on to the next generation. Purchasing and consumption patterns are among those attitudes and skills strongly influenced by the family household unit.

This chapter examines (1) the nature and importance of families and households in contemporary American society; (2) the household life cycle; (3) the nature of the family decision process; and (4) consumer socialization.

The Household Influences Most Consumption Decisions FIGURE 6-1

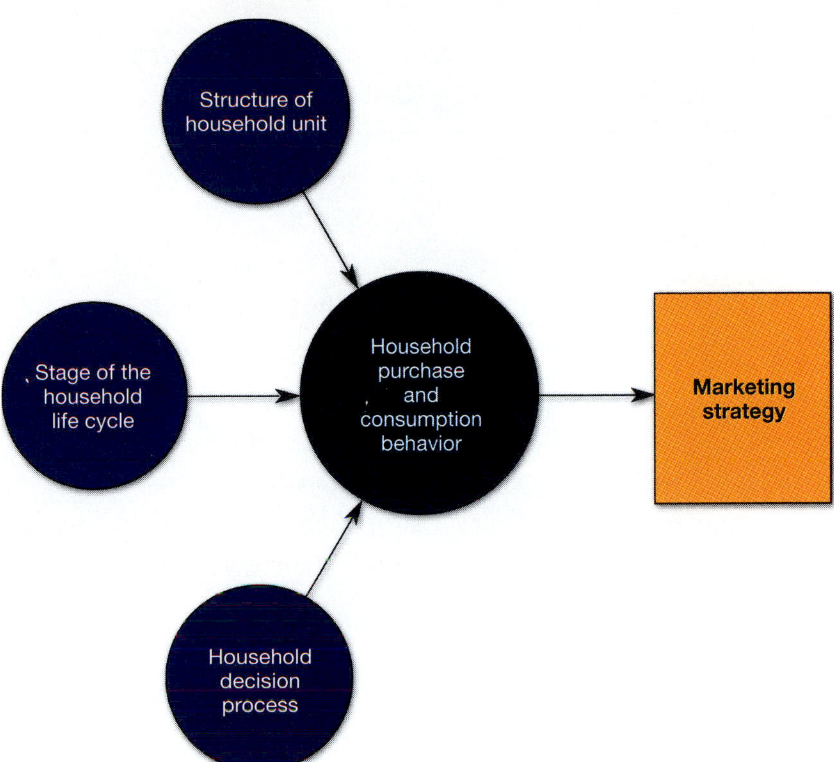

THE NATURE OF AMERICAN HOUSEHOLDS

Types of Households

The term *household* designates a variety of distinct social groups. The Census Bureau defines a **family household** as a household unit that consists of two or more related persons, one of whom (i.e., the householder) owns or rents the living quarters. The **nuclear family** consists of two adults of opposite sexes, living in a socially approved sex relationship with their own or adopted children. The nuclear family is important in virtually every culture.

The nuclear family described above represents the prescriptive (culturally desirable) and descriptive (most common) version of the nuclear family (see Table 6-1). However, there are several variations of the nuclear family. The most common variation in the United States is the single-parent family household created by the death of one spouse or, more commonly, divorce. In either case, the children and the mother are likely to remain together as a nuclear family.

The **extended family household** is a household that includes the nuclear family plus additional relatives. The most common form of the extended family involves the inclusion of one or both sets of grandparents. In addition, aunts, uncles, cousins, in-laws, and other

TABLE 6-1 Family and Nonfamily Households: 2000–2010

Type of Household	2000 *Number (000)*	2000 *Percent*	2010 *Number (000)*	2010 *Percent*	*Percent Change 2000–2010*
All Households	110,140	100.0%	117,696	100.0%	6.9%
Families	77,705	70.6	80,193	68.1	3.2
Married couples	60,969	55.4	61,266	52.1	0.5
Children under 18 at home	24,286	22.1	23,433	19.9	(3.5)
Children over 18 at home	5,318	4.8	6,884	5.8	29.4
No children under 18 at home	31,365	28.5	30,950	26.3	(1.3)
Single fathers	1,523	1.4	1,660	1.4	9.0
Single mothers	7,473	6.8	7,779	6.6	4.1
Other families	7,741	7.0	9,488	8.1	22.6
Nonfamilies	32,434	29.4	37,503	31.9	18.0
Men living alone	10,898	9.9	12,577	10.7	15.4
Women living alone	16,278	14.8	18,578	15.8	14.1
Other nonfamilies	5,258	4.8	6,347	5.4	20.7

relatives may be included. This is not as common in America as it is in other countries such as China and India.

Household units that are not families also have several variations. The Census Bureau defines a **nonfamily household** as households made up of householders who either live alone or with others to whom they are not related. It is estimated that almost 30 percent of all households were nonfamily households in 2000, and this percentage is growing.

These definitions are important because the Census Bureau, which provides most of the available data on households, uses them. Unfortunately, these terms do not cover the richness of the American family structure. The **blended family**—a family consisting of a couple, one or both of whom were previously married, their children, and the children from the previous marriage of one or both parents—is one missing form.[3] While half or more of all first marriages end in divorce, most of these divorced individuals remarry (and many others engage in long-term cohabitation).[4] Thus, a significant percentage of American children grow up with stepparents and siblings. Many of these children spend significant time in two such families, one formed by their mother and the other by their father.

Kraft recognizes the diversity and importance of families in its new campaign featuring brief, unscripted videos of actual families interacting around food. One spot features an apparently single mother shopping with her teenage sons, another features a nuclear family of seven, while the third portrays an extended family get-together. At the end of the family get-together commercial, the grandmother says: "Everyone needs to connect as a family. Just a simple thing such as making dinner. Everybody gets a little bit of attention—which I don't mind giving. I like that." Illustration 6-1 contains a television ad that shows how Merita bread can be used to create the favorite sandwiches of various family members.

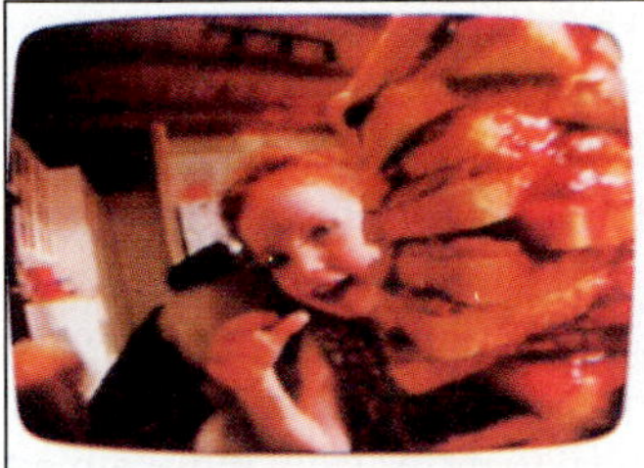

VOICE OVER: Merita Bread knows beauty is in the eye of the beholder. Especially when it comes to sandwiches.

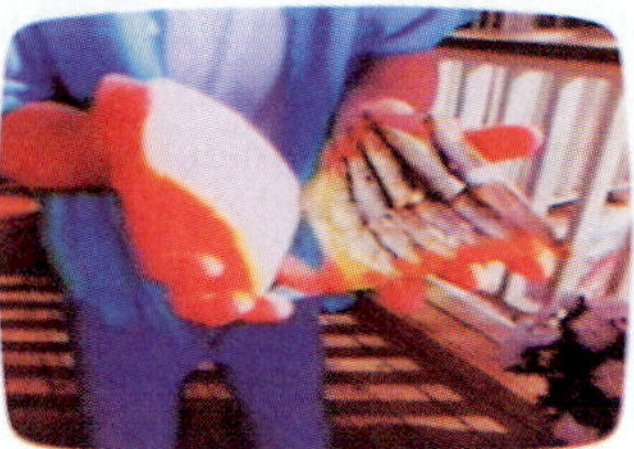

Of course, no matter what unique ingredients are inside,

Moms know... the perfect bread is Merita Old Fashioned. So soft, so delicious, and healthy too...

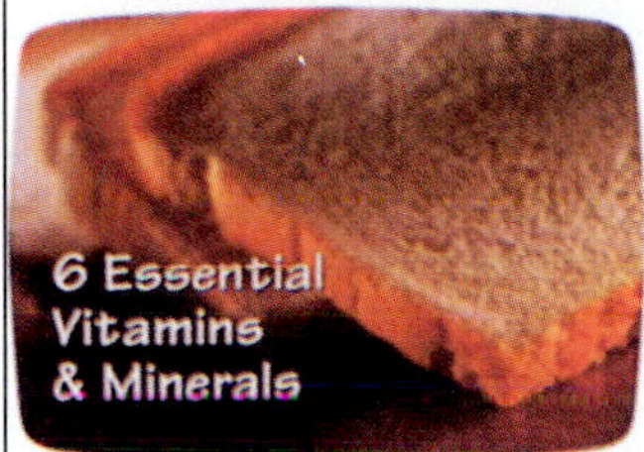

with six essential vitamins and minerals. Merita Old Fashioned makes any sandwich better.

(Co-worker reacts negatively to Dad's favorite sandwich.)

Merita Old Fashioned. Your family. Merita Bread. Perfect together.

Courtesy Interstate Bakeries Corporation.

ILLUSTRATION 6-1

Members of the same family often have differing desires. Marketers who can appeal to all members of the family unit have an advantage.

Changes in Household Structure

Households, family and nonfamily, are important to marketing managers because they constitute consumption units and therefore represent the proper unit of analysis for many aspects of marketing strategy. The fact that the number of household units is growing and is projected to continue to grow is more important than population growth for marketers of refrigerators, televisions, telephones, and other items purchased primarily by household units. Equally important to homebuilders, appliance manufacturers, and automobile manufacturers are the *structure* and *size* of households. Between 2000 and 2010, changes such as those cited below will have a major impact on a wide variety of marketing practices:

- Family households will grow by 7.5 million, but married couples with children under 18 living at home will shrink by almost a million.
- Family households with children over 18 living at home will increase by over 1.5 million.
- Nonfamily households will grow by 5 million and will constitute almost a third of all households.

These changes in household structure are reflected in the reduced average size of households, which has declined from 3.33 in 1960 to 2.42 in 2000. This decline has been caused by an increase in single-parent and single-person households, as well as by a decline in the birthrate.

The age of the householder also plays a role in purchase and consumption behavior. As we saw in Chapter 4, the greatest household growth during the early 2000s will occur in those with householders in the 45 to 54 age category. The kinds of household products this age group consumes are different from products consumed by younger and older householders.

This growth implies a strong demand for upgraded household furnishings, vacations, luxury items, and sports and entertainment items targeted at a more mature market. The fact that much of this growth is coming from single-person households suggests that apartments, appliances, and food containers should be produced in sizes appropriate for the single individual.

The growth in single-parent families also implies a need for convenience items, day care centers, and appliances that relatively young children can operate. The timing and content of advertising aimed at singles and single-parent families may need to differ from those aimed at the traditional nuclear families. As with most variables affecting consumer behavior, the marketing manager must examine the shifts in the American family structure for specific product category implications.

Household structure is of importance to marketers not only because it influences both the needs and resources of the primary consumer purchasing unit, it also influences the well-being and consumer socialization of children.[5]

THE HOUSEHOLD LIFE CYCLE

The traditional view of the American household life cycle was quite simple. People married by their early 20s (in 1960, the median age was 20.3 for women and 22.8 for men), had several children, these children grew up and started their own families, the original couple retired, and the male would eventually die followed after a few years by the female. This was known as the *family life cycle,* and it was a useful tool for segmenting markets and developing marketing strategy. The basic assumption underlying the family life cycle approach is that most families pass through an orderly progression of stages, each with its own characteristics, financial situation, and purchasing patterns.

However, as suggested earlier, the American household follows a much more complex and varied cycle today. In fact, there is no longer a single dominant household life cycle through which most families progress. Instead, there are a variety of cycles through which different families progress. Researchers have developed several models of the **household life cycle (HLC).**[6] All are based on the age and marital status of the adult members of the household and the presence and age of children. The version used in this text and shown in Figure 6-2 is a condensed version of one developed by Gilly and Enis.[7]

The HLC assumes that households move into a variety of relatively distinct and well-defined categories over time. There are a variety of routes into most of the categories shown in Figure 6-2, and movement from one category into another frequently occurs. For example, it is common for singles to marry and divorce within a few years without having children (move from single to young couple back to young single). Or one can become a single parent through divorce or through birth or adoption without a cohabiting partner.

While the route taken into a category influences some aspects of the family's life, it is generally of secondary importance. Thus, the fact that a family is a young, single-parent family with a child under six influences much of its consumption expenditures. Whether the family was created by divorce or was initially formed as a single-parent family is less critical to our understanding of its needs and purchases.[8]

Each category in the household life cycle poses a set of problems that household decision makers must solve. The solution to these problems is bound intimately to the selection and maintenance of a lifestyle and, thus, to product consumption. For example, all young couples with no children face a need for relaxation or recreation. Solutions to this common problem differ. Some couples opt for an outdoors-oriented lifestyle and consume camping equipment and related products. Others choose a sophisticated urban lifestyle and consume

Stages of the Household Life Cycle **FIGURE 6-2**

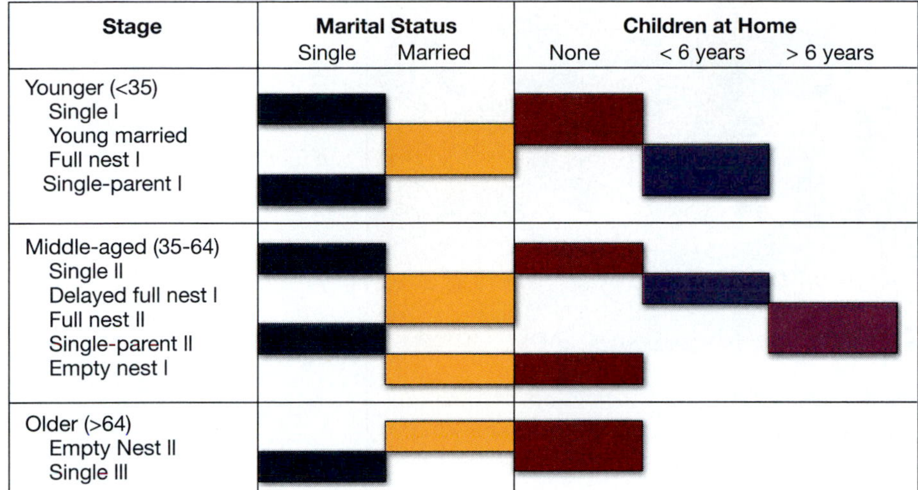

tickets to the theater and opera, restaurant meals, and so forth. As these families move into another stage in the HLC such as the "full nest I" stage, the problems they face also change. The amount of time and resources available for recreation usually diminishes. New problems related to raising a child become more urgent.

Each stage presents unique needs and wants as well as financial conditions and experiences. Thus, the HLC provides marketers with relatively homogeneous household segments that share similar needs with respect to household-related problems and purchases.

While Figure 6-2 categorizes households into married and unmarried, it is "coupleness" rather than the legal status of the relationship that drives the behavior of the household. Committed couples, same sex or opposite sex, tend to exhibit most of the category specific behaviors described below whether or not they are married.

Single I This group consists of young (under 35), unmarried individuals. It is basically the unmarried members of Generation X, as described in Chapter 5. Individuals generally leave home and establish their own distinct identities. It is a time of growth and change, both exciting and positive and frightening and painful. As one 30-something said:

> I wouldn't go through my 20's again for all the money in the world. You are out of undergraduate school and it's like, "What's expected of me?" You still haven't come to know yourself, and it's like that there is this gigantic world out there and you must somehow get all the experiences you can under your belt before you can get to know yourself. So you try on a lot of labels and I guess that somehow you think that that assemblage is you, when it isn't.[9]

This group can be subdivided into those younger than 25 and those 25 and over. Individuals younger than 25 have limited incomes and many of these individuals live with their families or are supported in part by their families. A significant number are in school or have recently graduated from high school or college and are beginning their working careers. Some have returned home after a divorce. Though this group has a low income, they also have few fixed expenses. They lead an active social life. They go to bars, movies, and concerts, and purchase sports equipment, clothes, and personal care items.

Singles between 25 and 35 have higher incomes and are more likely to be independent. While many live in multi-individual households, they have more financial obligations and

ILLUSTRATION 6-2

Young singles are active and often have significant discretionary income. They are an excellent market for a wide array of recreational and leisure items.

Courtesy Ford Motor Company.

must invest more time in household management than at-home singles. Many have experienced the pain of divorce and are trying to rebuild their lives.

These older singles are a good market for the same types of products as the younger singles as well as for convenience-oriented household products. They are also a prime market for nice apartments, sports cars, Club Med vacations, and similar activities. They are also beginning to develop financial portfolios such as life insurance, savings, and stocks or mutual funds. The ad shown in Illustration 6-2 would appeal to both groups.

Although the average age at marriage has increased by four years since the mid-1950s (to 24.4 for women and 26.5 for men) and is forecast to continue increasing,[10] the small size of this age cohort means that there will be fewer young single households in 10 years than there are now.[11]

	2000 (000s)	*2010 (000s)*	*Percent Change*
Females 25	495	488	−7.7%
Females 25–34	1,351	1,224	−9.4
Males 25	466	378	−19.0
Males 25–34	1,836	1,602	−12.7

Young Couples: No Children The decision to marry (or to live together) brings about a new stage in the household life cycle. The lifestyles of two young singles are greatly altered as they develop a shared lifestyle. Joint decisions and shared roles in household responsibilities are in many instances new experiences. Savings, household furnishings, major appliances, and more comprehensive insurance coverage are among the new areas of problem recognition and decision making to which a young married couple must give serious consideration.

Like the young single stage, the time spent by a young couple in this stage of the HLC has grown as couples either delay having children or choose to remain childless. However, the relatively small size of Generation X means that the total number of households in this category will decline over the next 10 years:[12]

Age	*2000 (000s)*	*2010 (000s)*	*Percent Change*
<25	526	505	−3.9%
25–34	2,268	2,231	−1.6

Despite the declining size of this segment, it is very attractive to marketers. Eighty-five percent of all households in this group have dual incomes and thus are relatively affluent. Compared to full nest I families, this group spends heavily on theater tickets, expensive clothes, luxury vacations, restaurant meals (more than half their food expenditures are for restaurant and take-out meals), and alcoholic beverages. They can afford nice cars (they spend 72 percent more than the average household on new cars), stylish apartments, and high-quality home appliances.[13]

Illustration 6-3 contains an ad that would appeal to this group as well as to some members of the single I and full nest I segments. Note that romance plays a major role in the ad. It also plays on the desire to escape worries and everyday responsibilities.

Full Nest I: Married with Young Children The addition of the first child to a family creates many changes in lifestyle and consumption. Naturally, new purchases in the areas of baby clothes, furniture, food, and health care products occur in this stage. Lifestyles are also greatly altered. The couple may have to move to another place of residence since their current apartment may not be appropriate for children. Likewise, choices of vacations, restaurants, and automobiles must be changed to accommodate young children. McDonald's, for example, attempts to occupy children in a restaurant environment by providing recreational equipment at their outlets that cater heavily to families with young children. Some of the changes in annual expenditures that occur as a household moves from childless to a new child stage include the following:

Expenditure	*Percent Change*
Food	2.4%
Alcoholic beverages	−33.8
Housing	9.5
Apparel	10.8
Health care	49.3
Entertainment	−5.6
Education	−28.9
Contributions	−32.1
Investments	−8.3

ILLUSTRATION 6-3

This ad positions Westin Hotels and Resorts as an ideal place for couples to escape the pressures of a hectic work schedule for relaxation and romance.

Courtesy Starwood Hotels & Resorts.

As these data indicate, discretionary expenditures are reduced by the need to spend on child-related necessities such as housing, health care, and clothing. Income tends to decline as one spouse often stays home with young children (only 61 percent have dual incomes). However, the increasing average age of parents before the birth of the first child and the smaller families common today have reduced this impact.

Obtaining competent child care first becomes an issue at this or the single-parent I stage. It remains a major concern of parents at all stages of the household life cycle. Households with a stay at home spouse confront this issue mainly for evenings out or weekends away. Single-parent and dual-earner households generally require daily child care. This often requires stressful trade-offs:

> Sure, like everyone I wanted a place that was reasonable, convenient, stimulating, full of warmth and caring, and also safe. I wanted care provided by trained, competent, and loving care givers, just like I would, but finding such care is impossible. So what do I do, I get realistic, have fewer expectations and become extra vigilant. I know I can't have it all.[14]

Illustration 6-4 contains an ad aimed at this market segment. It shows how the choice of recreational activities such as vacations changes with the addition of young children. Another example of marketing to this group is Cox Direct, which mails packets of discount coupons to parents of new babies (a program called "Just Delivered") and to parents of toddlers (a program called "See Them Grow"). The latter program sends coupons to 750,000 families quarterly.

Courtesy Smuggler's Notch Resort.

ILLUSTRATION 6-4

Parenthood brings both great pleasures and great responsibilities. This ad emphasizes the pleasures of family activities such as vacations.

Single-Parent I: Young Single Parents Birth or adoption by singles is increasingly common. Although the rate has declined over the past several years, around 25 percent of children are born to unmarried mothers.[15] Divorce also continues to be a significant part of American society. One in every three marriages will end in divorce, and this occurs most frequently early in a marriage. While most divorced individuals remarry and most women who bear children out of wedlock eventually get married, over 8 percent of American households are single-parent households, and 30 percent of U.S. children live in single-parent households. As shown below, the number of young single-parent families is predicted to grow sharply over the next 10 years:[16]

		2000 (000s)	*2010 (000s)*	*Percent Change*
Females	<25	931	1,234	32.5%
Females	25–34	2,605	2,834	8.8
Males	<25	102	120	17.3
Males	25–34	482	571	18.5

The younger members of this group, particularly those who have never been married, tend to have a limited education and a very low income. These individuals are often members of one of the lower social classes, as described in Chapter 4. The older members of this segment and the divorced members receiving support from their ex-spouses are better off financially, but most are still under significant stress as they raise their young children without the support of a partner who is physically present.

This type of family situation creates many unique needs in the areas of child care, easy-to-prepare foods, and recreation. The need to work and raise younger children creates enormous time pressures and places tremendous demands on the energy of these parents. Most are renters and so are not a major market for home appliances and improvements. Their purchases focus on getting by and time- and energy-saving products and services that are not overly expensive.

Single II: Middle-Aged Single The middle-aged single category is made up of those who have never married and individuals who are divorced and have no child-rearing responsibilities. These individuals are in the 35 to 64 age category. This group represents about 11 percent of U.S. households but a much smaller percent of the adult population, since most of these are single-person households. This segment is expected to grow by almost 25 percent over the next 10 years.

Middle-aged singles generally live alone. They have higher incomes than young singles. However, all live-alone singles suffer from a lack of scale economies. That is, a couple or family needs only one dishwasher, clothes dryer, and so forth for everyone in the household. The single-person household needs the same basic household infrastructure even though only one person uses it.

The needs of middle-aged singles in many ways reflect those of young singles. But middle-aged singles are likely to have more money to spend on their lifestyles. Thus, they may live in nice condominiums, frequent expensive restaurants, own a luxury automobile, and travel often. They are a major market for gifts, and the males buy significant amounts of jewelry as gifts.

Empty Nest I: Middle-Aged Married with No Children The lifestyle changes in the 1970s and 1980s influenced many young couples to not have children. In other cases, these households represent second marriages in which children from a first marriage are not living with the parent. This group also includes married couples whose children have left home. These three forces have produced almost 19 million households consisting of middle-aged couples without children at home. The size of this segment is expected to remain fairly constant for the next 10 years.

Both adults typically will have jobs, so they will be very busy. However, the absence of responsibilities for children creates more free time than they have enjoyed since their youth. They also have money to spend on dining out, expensive vacations, second homes, luxury cars, and time-saving services such as house-cleaning, laundry, and shopping. They are also a prime market for financial services.

Delayed Full Nest I: Older Married with Young Children Many members of the baby boom generation delayed having their first child until they were in their mid-30s. This produced the new phenomenon of a large number of middle-aged, established families entering into parenthood for the first time.

A major difference between this group and the younger new parents is income. Older new parents' incomes average $15,000 more than those of younger new parents. They have had this income flow longer and so have acquired more capital and possessions. They outspend all groups on child care, mortgage payments, home maintenance, lawn care, and household furnishings. They can also spend more on nonchild expenditures such as food, alcohol, entertainment, savings, and contributions.

Full Nest II: Middle-Aged Married with Children at Home The children of this group are generally over six years old and are less dependent than the children of the younger couples. However, the fact that the children are older creates another set of unique consumption needs. Families with children six and older are the primary consumers of lessons of all types (piano, dance, gymnastics, and so on), dental care, soft drinks, presweetened cereals, and a wide variety of snack foods. Greater demands for space create a need for larger homes and cars. Transporting children to multiple events places time demands on the parents and causes this group to spend a third more for gas and oil than the typical household.[17] These factors, coupled with heavy demand for clothing and an increased need to save for college, places a considerable financial burden on households in this stage of the household life cycle. This is offset somewhat by the tendency of the wife to return to work as the children enter school.

As we saw in Chapter 5, the teenage members of this segment, as well as those in the single-parent II segment (described next) are important consumers in their own right as well as important influencers on household consumption decisions.

Single-Parent II: Middle-Aged Single with Children at Home Single individuals in the 35 to 64 age group who have children are often faced with serious financial pressures. As shown below, women head most of these households, and the size of segment will not change much over the next 10 years.

	2000 (000s)	*2010 (000s)*	*Percent Change*
Females	3,910	3,681	−5.6%
Males	918	943	2.7

The same demands that are placed on the middle-aged married couple with children are present in the life of a middle-aged single with children. However, the single parent often lacks some or all of the financial, emotional, and time support that the presence of a spouse generally provides. Many individuals in this position are thus inclined to use time-saving alternatives such as ready-to-eat food, and they are likely to eat at fast-food restaurants. The children of this segment are given extensive household responsibilities.[18]

Empty Nest II: Older Married Couples There are about 10 million households in the segment, and it is expected to grow modestly over the next 10 years. For the most part, couples in the over-64 age group are either fully or partially retired. Because of age, social orientation, and weakening financial status (due to retirement), the older married couple has unique needs in the areas of health care, housing, food, and recreation. For example, this group has a great deal of time but not a great deal of money. This has made the sale of travel trailers and group vacations very attractive to many older married couples. Illustration 6-5 shows an ad for a product designed to meet one of this segment's needs.

Single III: Older Single The older single represents more than 2 percent of our adult population. Older singles typically are female and this segment is growing rapidly. Again, the conditions of being older, single, and generally retired create many unique needs for housing, socialization, travel, and recreation. Many financial firms have set up special programs to work with these individuals. They often have experienced a spouse's death and now are taking on many of the financial responsibilities once handled by the other person.

ILLUSTRATION 6-5

As consumers mature, their financial situation, free time, and physical and social needs change. Roadtrek appeals to many members of the empty nest II segment.

Courtesy Home & Park Motorhomes; agency: Martron IDG.

MARKETING STRATEGY BASED ON THE HOUSEHOLD LIFE CYCLE

The preceding sections have illustrated the power of the HLC as a segmentation variable. The purchase and consumption of many products is driven by the HLC. The reason for this is that each stage in the HLC poses unique problems and/or opportunities to the household members. The resolution of these problems often requires the consumption of products. Our earlier discussion and illustrations indicated how marketers are responding to the unique needs of each stage in the HLC.

While a stage in the HLC causes many of the problems and/or opportunities individuals confront as they mature, it does not provide solutions. Thus, while all full nest I families face similar needs and restrictions with respect to recreation, their social class heavily influences how they will meet those needs. As we saw in Chapter 4, *social class provides consumption-related attitudes and values as well as the financial resources required to enact a desired lifestyle.* Social class provides solutions to many of the problems posed as one moves through the various stages of the HLC.

For example, think of how the need for vacations differs as you move across the stages of the household life cycle. Young singles often desire vacations focused on activities, adventure, and the chance for romance. Full nest I families need vacations that allow both parents and young children to enjoy themselves. The manner in which these needs will be met will vary sharply with social class due to both income and taste differences across the various classes. Upper-class singles may vacation in Paris or at an exclusive resort in the tropics. Middle-class singles may visit a ski resort or join a package vacation tour that targets young singles. Lower-class individuals may visit friends or family.

TABLE 6-2

Household Life Cycle/Social Stratification Matrix

Stage of Household Life Cycle	Social Class					
	Lower-Lower	*Upper-Lower*	*Working*	*Middle*	*Lower-Upper*	*Upper-Upper*
Single I						
Young married						
Full nest I						
Single-parent I						
Single II						
Delayed full nest I						
Full nest II						
Single-parent II						
Empty nest I						
Empty nest II						
Single III						

Table 6-2 presents the **HLC/Social Stratification Matrix.** One axis is the stages in the HLC (which determines the problems the household will likely encounter) and the other is a set of social strata (which provide a range of acceptable solutions).

This matrix can be used to segment the market for many products and to develop appropriate marketing strategies for the targeted segments. An effective use of the matrix is to isolate an activity or problem of interest to the firm such as preparing the evening meal, snacks, weekend recreation, and so forth. Research, often in the form of focus group interviews, is used to determine the following information for each relevant cell in the matrix:

1. What products or services are now being used to meet the need or perform the activity?
2. What, if any, symbolic or social meaning is associated with meeting the need or using the current products?
3. Exactly how are the current products or services being used?
4. How satisfied are the segment members with the current solutions, and what improvements are desired?

Attractive segments are those that are large enough to meet the firm's objectives and that have needs that current products are not fully satisfying. This approach has been used successfully for movies, regional bakeries, and financial services.[19]

Abercrombie & Fitch has achieved great success by focusing on the younger members of the young single I category who are in the middle and upper social classes. Its 162 stores blast contemporary music at corporate specified decibel levels designed to discourage conversation. Service is provided by "brand representatives" selected to embody the brand's Greek fraternity/sorority lifestyle and attitude positioning. It advertises in only three magazines—*Out, Rolling Stone,* and *Vanity Fair.* The stores feature oversized posters of black and white photos of frolicking college students with sexual undertones, designed to appeal to both heterosexuals and homosexuals. Its "magolog" generated significant controversy recently when it provided instructions for a variety of drinking games. (After a complaint from Mothers Against Drunk Driving, the company agreed to send postcards to students urging responsible drinking.)

FAMILY DECISION MAKING

Family decision making is *the process by which decisions that directly or indirectly involve two or more family members are made.* Decision making by a group such as a family differs in many ways from decisions made by an individual. Consider the purchase of a breakfast cereal that children, and perhaps the adults, will consume. Who recognizes the need for the product? How is a type and brand selected? Does everyone consider the same attributes? A parent typically makes the actual *purchase;* does that mean that the parent also makes the *choice?* Or, is the choice made by the children, the other parent, or some combination? Which parents are involved, and how does this change across products and over time? How does it differ by stage in the household life cycle?

Family purchases are often compared to organizational buying decisions. While this can produce useful insights, it fails to capture the essence of family decision making. Organizations have relatively objective criteria such as profit maximization that guide purchases. Families lack such explicit, overarching goals. Most industrial purchases are made by strangers or have little impact on those not involved in the purchase. Most family purchases directly impact the other members of the family.

Most importantly, *many family purchases are inherently emotional and affect the relationships between the family members.*[20] The decision to buy a child a requested toy or new school clothes is more than simply an acquisition. It is a symbol of love and commitment to the child. The decision to take the family to a restaurant for a meal or to purchase a new television has emotional meaning to the other family members. Disagreements about how to spend money are a major cause of marital discord. The processes families use to make purchase decisions and the outcomes of those processes have important impacts on the well-being of the individual family members and the family itself. Thus, while family decision making has some things in common with organizational decision making, it is not the same.

The Nature of Family Purchase Roles

Figure 6-3 illustrates the six roles that frequently occur in family decision making, using a cereal purchase as an example.[21] It is important to note that individuals will play various roles for different decisions:

- *Initiator(s).* The family member who first recognizes a need or starts the purchase process.
- *Information gatherer(s).* The individual who has expertise and interest in a particular purchase. Different individuals may seek information at different times or on different aspects of the purchase.
- *Influencer(s).* The person who influences the alternatives evaluated, the criteria considered, and the final choice.
- *Decision maker(s).* The individual who makes the final decision. Of course, joint decisions also are likely to occur.
- *Purchaser(s).* The family member who actually purchases the product. This is typically an adult or teenager.
- *User(s).* The user of the product. For many products there are multiple users.

The Household Decision-Making Process for Children's Products **FIGURE 6-3**

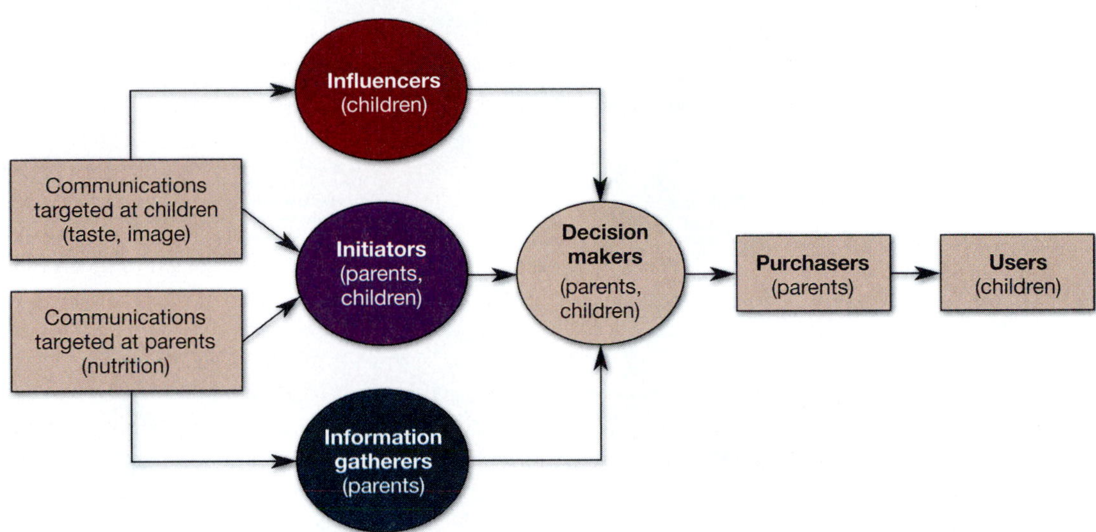

In many family purchase decisions, the primary product users are neither the decision maker nor the purchaser. For example, women (wives and girlfriends) purchase most of the fragrances used by men. Thus, marketers must decide who in the family plays which role before they can affect the family decision process. After thorough study, Crayola shifted its advertising budget from children's television to women's magazines. Its research revealed that mothers rather than children were more likely to recognize the problem, evaluate alternatives, and make the purchase. Illustration 6-6 shows a product designed for use by children that is selected by both the children and the parents and purchased by parents.

Family decision making has been categorized as *husband-dominant, wife-dominant, joint,* or *individualized.* Husband-dominant decisions traditionally occurred with the purchase of such products as automobiles, liquor, and life insurance. Wife-dominant decisions were more common in the purchase of household maintenance items, food, and kitchen appliances. Joint decisions were most likely when buying a house, living room furniture, and vacations. These patterns are much less pronounced today. As women's occupational roles have expanded, so has the range of family decisions in which they participate or dominate.[22]

A moment's reflection will reveal that the above four categories of decisions omit critical participants in many family decisions. Until recently, most studies have ignored the influence of children.[23] Yet, children, particularly teenagers, often exert a substantial influence on the consumption process.[24] Thus, we need to recognize that *child-dominant,* and various combinations of *husband-, wife-, child joint decisions* are also common in both single-parent and two-parent households.

Studies of family decisions have focused on direct influence, ignoring indirect influence. For example, a wife might report that she purchased an automobile without discussing it with any member of her family. Yet she might purchase a van to meet her perceptions of the desires of the family rather than the sports car that she personally would prefer. Most research studies would classify the above decision as strictly wife-dominated. Clearly, however, other family members influenced the decision.

ILLUSTRATION 6-6

Children often determine the products and brands they use. At other times they influence these choices, but the parents play the dominant role. In such cases, the marketer must meet the needs of both the child and the parents.

Different family members often become involved at different stages of the decision process. Figure 6-4 shows the influence of wives and husbands, at each stage of the decision process, for a variety of services. As can be seen, roles vary across services and across stages in the decision process.

Family decisions also allow different members to make specific subdecisions of the overall decision. When an individual makes a decision, he or she evaluates all the relevant attributes of each alternative and combines these evaluations into a single decision. In a family decision, different members often focus on specific attributes. For example, a child may evaluate the color and style of a bicycle while one or both parents evaluate price, warranty, and safety features.

Determinants of Family Purchase Roles

How family members interact in a purchase decision is largely dependent on the *role specialization* of different family members, the degree of *involvement* each has in the product area of concern, the *personal characteristics* of the family members, and the *culture and subculture* in which the family exists.[25]

Culture and Subculture Determinants In Chapter 2, we listed a masculine versus feminine orientation as one of the values that differentiates societies. In Chapter 3, we indicated that America was relatively less masculine oriented than many other cultures. As masculine orientation increases, the role of females in decisions tends to decrease. Thus, we find that wives are more involved in a wider range of decisions in the United States than they are in a more traditional culture.[26]

As we saw in Chapter 5, subcultures in the United States have some values that differ from those of the dominant culture. The Hispanic subculture was described in that chapter as having more of a masculine orientation than the broader culture. Research indicates that

Husband/Wife Decision Roles for Services **FIGURE 6-4**

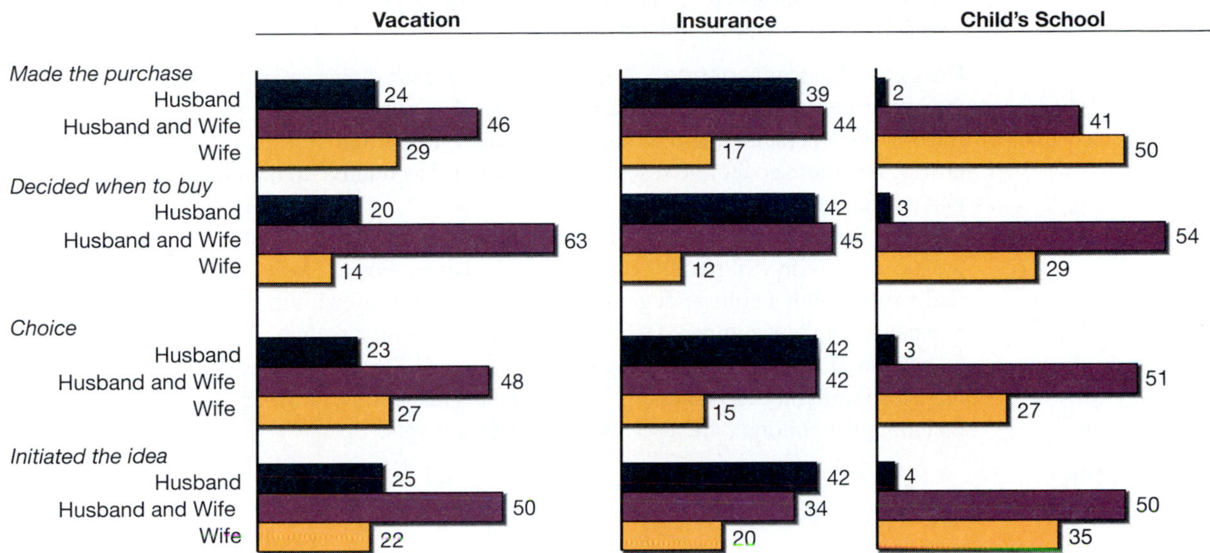

Note: Totals do not add to 100 because other individuals were involved in some decisions.

Source: M. R. Stafford, G. K. Ganesh, and B. C. Garland, "Marital Influence in the Decision-Making Process for Services," *Journal of Services Marketing* 10, no. 1 (1996), p. 15.

Hispanics who identify strongly with the Hispanic culture tend to make more husband-dominant decisions than do others.

Role Specialization Over time, each spouse develops more specialized roles as a part of the family lifestyle and family responsibilities. Husbands traditionally specialized in mechanical and technical areas and therefore established criteria and evaluated alternatives in areas such as automobiles, lawn care, and insurance (as we saw in Chapter 3, this has changed sharply). Wives often have a more specialized role in certain aspects of child rearing and, as a result, have a more specialized role in buying children's clothing and food. While particular roles are no longer automatically assigned to one gender in the marriage, they still tend to evolve over time. It is simply much more efficient for one person to specialize in some decisions than it is to have to reach a joint decision for every purchase.

Because role specialization within any family takes time to develop, younger couples engage in greater degrees of joint decision making than more established families. As children age and acquire capabilities and responsibilities, their purchase roles within the family also evolve.

Involvement/Expertise *Involvement* or expertise in a product area is another major factor that has an impact on how a family purchase decision will be made. Naturally, the more involved a spouse is with a product area, the more likely he or she will be to exert influence over other family members during a purchase in that product area. For example, teenagers who are involved with computers might dominate the decision for a family computer or the choice of an Internet access service. The following quote reveals how even a fairly young adolescent can influence adult purchases:

> Occasionally I will ask her to go along with me when I need to select a new cologne or a new tie or a new shirt and get some feedback from her as to her opinion of how it looks and how it would fit into today's goings-on . . . Whether we agree on it or not is two different things; you know, I value her opinion. (Father with daughter, age 12.)[27]

Personal Characteristics A wide array of personal characteristics have an effect on the influence individuals will have on purchase decisions.[28] Relative power within the marriage is one characteristic that has been studied. It is often defined in terms of economic power. The more economic resources one partner has relative to the other, the more power that partner has.

Education is another important personal characteristic. The higher a wife's education, the more the wife will participate in major decisions. For example, 70 percent of the married women with a college degree claim to have equal say with their husband in the brand of a new car to buy compared to 35 percent of those with less than a high school degree and 56 percent of those with only a high school degree.[29] Though rarely studied, personality influences family decision making. The age and capabilities of the various family members, including the children, are also important determinants.

Conflict Resolution

Given the number of decisions families make daily, disagreements are inevitable. How they are resolved is important to marketers as well as to the health of the family unit. A recent study revealed six basic approaches that individuals use to resolve purchase conflicts after they have arisen (most couples generally seek to avoid open conflicts):[30]

- *Bargaining.* Trying to reach a compromise.
- *Impression management.* Misrepresenting the facts in order to win.
- *Use of authority.* Claiming superior expertise or role appropriateness (the husband/wife should make such decisions).
- *Reasoning.* Using logical argument to win.
- *Playing on emotion.* Using the silent treatment or withdrawing from the discussion.
- *Additional information.* Getting additional data or a third-party opinion.

While this study did not include children, a study focused on how children and parents attempt to influence each other found a similar though more complex set of influence strategies.[31]

Conclusions on Family Decision Making

Much remains to be learned about family decision making. But we can offer five general conclusions:

1. Different family members are often involved at different stages of the decision process.
2. Different family members often evaluate different attributes of a product or brand.
3. The direct involvement of family members in each stage of the decision process represents only a small part of the picture. Taking into account the desires of other family members is also important, though seldom studied.
4. Who participates at each stage of the decision process and the method by which conflicts are resolved are primarily a function of the product category and secondarily a function of the characteristics of the individual family members and the characteristics

of the family. The product category is important because it is closely related to who uses the product.

5. Overt conflicts in decision making are less common than agreement.

MARKETING STRATEGY AND FAMILY DECISION MAKING

Formulating an effective marketing strategy for most consumer products requires a thorough understanding of the family decision-making process in the selected target markets with respect to that product. Table 6-3 provides a framework for such an analysis.

The family decision-making process often varies across market segments such as stages in the family life cycle or social class. Therefore, it is essential that we analyze family decision making *within* each of our defined target markets. Within each target market, we need to:

- Discover which family members are involved at each stage of the decision process.
- Determine what their motivations and interests are.
- Develop a marketing strategy that will meet the needs of each participant.

For example, younger children are often involved in the problem recognition stage related to breakfast. They may note a new cartoon character–based cereal or discover that their friends are eating a new cereal. They are interested in identifying with the cartoon character or being like their friends. When they request the new cereal, the parents, generally the mother, may become interested. However, she is more likely to focus on nutrition and price. Thus, a marketer needs to communicate fun, taste, and excitement to children and nutrition, value, and taste to the parents. The children can be reached on Saturday cartoons, appropriate Internet sites, and similar media while the mother may be more effectively communicated with through magazine ads and package information.

Consider Illustration 6-7. This product is being positioned as one that will be used by the father and the children. The ad is targeted at the father and stresses the pleasure he will bring to the children if he buys the *Polaris*. It also implies that it will increase the popularity of his children. Note that the last line says "mother approved." This suggests the potential for some conflict over such a purchase.

TABLE 6-3

Marketing Strategy Based on the Family Decision-Making Process

Segment: ____________

Stage in the Decision Process	*Family Members Involved*	*Family Members' Motivation and Interests*	*Marketing Strategy and Tactics*
Problem recognition			
Information search			
Alternative evaluation			
Purchase			
Use/Consumption			
Disposition			
Evaluation			

ILLUSTRATION 6-7

This product is positioned as one that the kids and father will use. It indicates that most of the pleasure will go to the kids. However, the ad is targeted at the father who is likely to be the primary participant in the decision process for this type of product.

Courtesy of Polaris Industries.

CONSUMER SOCIALIZATION

The family provides the basic framework in which consumer socialization occurs. **Consumer socialization** is *the process by which young people acquire skills, knowledge, and attitudes relevant to their functioning as consumers in the marketplace.* Learning, including acquiring consumption-related knowledge, is a lifelong process. However, the quantity and nature of learning that take place before early adulthood (around 18), as well as their impact on subsequent learning, are sufficiently unique to justify focusing on this time period.

We are concerned with understanding both what behaviors children learn and how those behaviors are associated with the purchase and use of goods and services. The *what* of consumer learning refers to the content of learning, and the *how* refers to the methods by which that content is acquired. Before we address these two issues, we need to consider the ability of children of various ages to learn consumption-related skills.

The Ability of Children to Learn

Younger children have limited abilities to process certain types of information.[32] **Piaget's stages of cognitive development** present a widely accepted set of stages of cognitive development:

Stage 1 *The period of sensorimotor intelligence (0 to 2 years).* During this period, behavior is primarily motor. The child does not yet "think" conceptually, though "cognitive" development is seen.

Stage 2 *The period of preoperational thoughts (3 to 7 years).* This period is characterized by the development of language and rapid conceptual development.

Stage 3 *The period of concrete operations (8 to 11 years).* During these years, the child develops the ability to apply logical thought to concrete problems.

Stage 4 *The period of formal operations (12 to 15 years).* During this period the child's cognitive structures reach their greatest level of development and the child becomes able to apply logic to all classes of problems.

Other researchers have proposed other stages, with learning rather than maturation as the underlying cause of observed differences. However, the general pattern of less ability to deal with abstract, generalized, unfamiliar, and/or large amounts of information by younger children is common to all approaches.[33]

The changing capabilities of children to learn as they age presents challenges to parents who are attempting to teach their children appropriate consumption behaviors. As we will discuss shortly, it also poses ethical and practical issues for marketers.[34] This limited learning capacity is the basis for substantial regulation of advertising to children. We describe existing and proposed regulations of marketing to children in depth in Chapter 20.

The Content of Consumer Socialization

The content of consumer learning can be broken down into two categories: *directly relevant* and *indirectly relevant.* Directly relevant aspects of consumer learning are those necessary for purchase and use to actually take place. In other words, a child has to learn particular skills, such as how to shop, how to compare similar brands, how to budget available income, and so forth. Knowledge and attitudes about stores, products, brands, salespeople, clearance sales, advertising media, and coupons are examples of directly relevant consumer learning content. The following quotes are examples of attempts to teach adolescents appropriate (from the parent's perspective) shopping rules:

> Son, look at this. This is just going to wash nicer, it will come through the laundry nicer, and you do a lot of the laundry yourself, and I just would rather that it's something that would wash easy, that doesn't have to be ironed, that isn't 100 percent cotton. (Mother with son, age 13.)
>
> Well, I usually try to get her to shop a little bit more and see if she can't find the same item for a little less, so I always suggest, "Look around, just because you found this one, maybe you can find another one that's a better buy." Or I get her to try to think about sales, maybe it's not exactly what she wanted, but I try to get her to go that route. (Mother with daughter, age 14.)[35]

Indirectly relevant consumer learning content refers to everything that has been learned that motivates purchase and use behavior. In other words, it is the knowledge, attitudes, and values that cause people to want certain goods or services and that allow them to attach differential evaluations to products and brands. For example, some consumers know (have learned) that Calvin Klein is a prestigious brand name, and they may respond positively to various products carrying this name. This information about Calvin Klein's prestige is not necessary to carry out the actual purchase (directly relevant), but it is extremely important in deciding *to* purchase and *what* to purchase (indirectly relevant).

The Process of Consumer Socialization

While advertising and other marketing activities also have a strong influence, the family is the primary source of consumer socialization. Parents teach their children both directly and indirectly relevant consumption knowledge. They do so both deliberately and casually through instrumental training, modeling, and mediation.[36]

Consumer Insight 6-1

Consumer Socialization and Birthday Parties

A study of birthday parties for children aged three to five revealed that the mothers used the situation to (1) teach children how to plan a party, (2) indicate approval or disapproval of certain themes (Barbie, Ninja Turtles), (3) teach sharing and other positive values, and (4) instill social skills. The following quotes indicate the instrumental nature of the process.

Planning Skills

- She was involved in choosing some of the little prizes and the cake. We took her with us when we went to the store . . . that has a bakery and they make these birthday cakes on various themes . . . she was allowed to choose which one.
- He was pretty involved . . . he knew what he wanted on his cake . . . I knew that if I just went and got something and he knew how he wanted it, it just did not work. So we did a lot together.

Theme Approval

- [Explaining why she would not let her son have a commercial theme at his party.] It is not so much the money but the values I have about it . . . but I have to explain to Carl that we decided to do it this way because we think birthdays are very special, but we celebrate them differently than other people . . . that's what we think is important that is the lesson we try to show.
- We don't encourage [Jake] to be into Ninja Turtles . . . in fact we discourage him. [When he requested a Ninja Turtle theme for his party.] I was fighting it all the way . . . I think I gave him some other options. I think they are too aggressive.

Positive Values

- [I use] outdoor games . . . something where everybody wins. [In a treasure hunt] they all got in like one big cohort, and they all helped each other . . . It was really nice, they really liked it, and everyone got a prize in the end.
- [My daughter] has a class with 9 or 10 girls and I made it very clear that if it was a big group, we'd invite all of the girls even if we had to sacrifice. Rather than exclude three or four. It has been very hurtful to her in the last year where, you know, the majority is invited and a few are excluded.

Social Skills

- I am petrified they are going to say something like, "Hey, I already have this." My eight-year-old would never do this because he knows I'll take all his toys and give them to the Salvation Army if I find out . . . With the four-year-old, I worry.
- I think (birthday parties) should teach them to be good . . . I've always emphasized the importance of thank-you notes.

Critical Thinking Questions

1. Parents need to teach their children appropriate consumption skills. However, parents are not taught how to do this. How should parents learn what and how to teach their children about consumption?
2. Should consumption skills be taught in school? If so what should be taught and in which grades?

Source: C. Otnes, M. Nelson, and M. A. McGrath, "The Children's Birthday Party," in *Advances in Consumer Research XXII,* ed. F. R. Kardes and M. Sujan (Provo, UT: Association for Consumer Research, 1995), pp. 622–27.

Instrumental training *occurs when a parent or sibling specifically and directly attempts to bring about certain responses through reasoning or reinforcement.* In other words, a parent may try directly to teach a child which snack foods should be consumed by explicitly discussing nutrition. Or, rules may be established that limit the consumption of some snack foods and encourage the consumption of others.[37]

Parents use many venues to teach consumption skills and related values. Consumer Insight 6-1 describes how some mothers of three- to five-year-olds use birthday parties for instrumental training. The quotes below show an approach used with older children:

> I'm always trying to get her to learn the relative value of things and particularly the impact of advertising and its effect on driving purchases and desires. So we try to talk about that. I point out

Courtesy of International Home Foods.

ILLUSTRATION 6-8

Rewarding children for desirable behavior is a basic part of consumer socialization. However, as this ad indicates, some types of rewards may prove harmful to the long-run interests of the child. Providing food as a reward or incentive may result in the child learning to eat when not hungry, which can produce unnecessary weight gains.

> manipulative or deceptive advertising, and give her a sense of being a critical consumer. (Father with daughter, age 13.)
>
> One thing that we always talk about when we're looking at something is the price of it. "For what you're buying, is the price worth the quality of what you're buying?" (Mother with son, age 13.)[38]

Illustration 6-8 shows how easy it is to inadvertently teach children dysfunctional behavior. The Chef Boyardee ad (one of a series of such ads) provides a valuable service by alerting parents to the danger of using food as a reward for positive behavior.

Modeling *occurs when a child learns appropriate (or inappropriate) consumption behaviors by observing others.* Modeling generally, though not always, occurs without direct instruction from the role model and frequently without conscious thought or effort on the part of the child. Modeling is an extremely important way for children to learn relevant skills, knowledge, and attitudes. Children learn both positive and negative consumption patterns through modeling. For example, children whose parents smoke are more likely to start smoking than are children whose parents do not smoke.

Mediation *occurs when a parent alters a child's initial interpretation of, or response to, a marketing or other stimulus.* This can easily be seen in the following example:

CHILD: Can I have one of those? See, it can walk!

PARENT: No. That's just an advertisement. It won't really walk. They just make it look like it will so kids will buy them.

The advertisement illustrated a product attribute and triggered a desire, but the parent altered the belief in the attribute and in the believability of advertising in general. This is not to suggest that family members mediate all commercials. However, children often learn about the purchase and use of products during interactions with other family members. Thus, the firm wishing to influence children must do so in a manner consistent with the values of the rest of the family.

The Supermarket as a Classroom

Professor James McNeal has a five-stage model of how children learn to shop by visiting supermarkets and other retail outlets with a parent.[39]

Stage I: Observing Parents begin taking children to the store with them at a median age of 2 months (ranging from 1 to 33 months). During this stage, children make sensory contact with the marketplace and begin forming mental images of marketplace objects and symbols. In the early months, only sights and sounds are being processed. However, by 12 to 15 months, most children can begin to recall some of these items. This stage ends when children understand that a visit to the market may produce rewards beyond the stimulation caused by the environment.

Stage II: Making Requests At this stage, children begin requesting items in the store from their parents. They use pointing and gesturing as well as statements to indicate that they want an item. Throughout most of this stage, children make requests only when the item is physically present, as they do not yet carry mental images of the products in their minds. In the latter months of stage II, they begin to make requests for items at home, particularly when they are seen on television.

Some children enter this stage as early as 6 months, but the median age is 2 years. By three years, two-thirds are making requests in the store and at home.

Stage III: Making Selections Actually getting an item off the shelf without assistance is the first act of an independent consumer. At its simplest level, a child's desire is triggered by an item in his or her immediate presence and this item is selected. Soon, however, children begin to remember the store location of desirable items, and they are allowed to go to those areas independently or to lead the parent there.

Children begin to do this almost as soon as they can walk. Some are in this stage as one-year-olds, but the median age is three and a half years.

Stage IV: Making Assisted Purchases Most children learn by observing (modeling) that money needs to be given in order to get things from a store. They learn to value money given to them by their parents and others as a means to acquire things. Soon they are allowed to select and pay for items with their own money. They are now primary consumers. Some enter this stage as early as two, though the median age is five and a half years.

Stage V: Making Independent Purchases Making a purchase without a parent to oversee it requires a fairly sophisticated understanding of value as well as the ability to visit a store (or a section of a store) safely without a parent. Most children remain in stage IV a long time before their parents allow them to move into stage V. Thus, the median age for entering stage V is eight years.

McNeal's research indicates that children learn to shop, at least in part, by going shopping. Retailers are developing programs based on these learning patterns. A&P has installed child-sized shopping carts in 100 of its outlets. The objectives are to occupy the children and make their visit to the store fun (which will also increase the parents' pleasure) and to get the children involved in the shopping process. Piggly Wiggly is starting Piggly Wiggly Pals Clubs in many of its outlets. Children can get their membership cards stamped at the store and receive such items as the Earth Pals kit, which includes tree seedlings.

MARKETING TO CHILDREN

Children are a very large market. Spending by children aged 4 to 12 was estimated to be over $24 billion in 1997, an increase of almost 300 percent from 1991! On average, 10-year-old children receive over $6 per week as an allowance and a slightly larger amount from earning money for doing chores and from gifts.[40]

Marketing to children is fraught with ethical concerns. The major source of these concerns is the limited ability of younger children to process information and to make informed purchase decisions. There are also concerns that marketing activities, particularly advertising, produce undesirable values in children, result in inappropriate diets, and cause unhealthy levels of family conflict. The opening vignette for Chapter 1 and Case 6-1 describe concerns that using the Internet to market to younger consumers has raised. We examine questionable marketing practices focused on children and the regulations designed to control them in detail in Chapter 20.

Although marketers need to be very sensitive to the limited information processing skills of younger consumers, ethical and effective marketing campaigns can be designed to meet the needs of children and their parents. All aspects of the marketing mix must consider the capabilities of the child. The most obvious is product safety. Young children put things in their mouths and can choke on a wide array of materials. Packaging should be safe when the product is removed. Advertisements should promote positive values such as sharing and good nutrition, as well as the product.

Reaching children used to mean advertising on Saturday morning cartoons. Now there are many more options, even for the very young. *Barbie, Outside Kids,* and *Sports Illustrated for Kids* have wide circulation among children who can read. CD-ROMs with interactive capabilities and titles such as "The Magic School Bus" are becoming big sellers. They provide the opportunity to offer entertainment, education, and commercial messages to children and their parents. On-line firms provide services for children as young as three. For example, Prodigy has "Sesame Street" on-line. It uses a graphic interface that attracts kids between the ages of three and six.

Direct mail can be an effective means to reach even very young children. Many firms target children or families with young children by forming "kid's clubs." Unfortunately, many of these clubs engage in sales techniques that are controversial if not clearly unethical (see Chapter 20). However, if done properly, they can be fun and educational for the children while delivering responsible commercial messages. Consider the *Burger King Kids Club:*

> Kids (or their parents) can pick up a membership form at any Burger King for free. After it is sent in, they receive a kit containing a membership certificate, stickers, a membership card and iron-on transfers for T-shirts. On their birthdays, they receive a card good for a free meal at their local Burger King. Bimonthly Kids Club newsletters are distributed through the restaurants. A quarterly

32-page, full-color magazine is sent to the members' homes. There are three different versions of the magazine geared to the age of the member. Each issue has six pages of outside advertising. Burger King does not sell its membership list.[41]

If the content is sound and the ads are constructed in a manner appropriate for the age groups, this program appears to be one that children would benefit from and enjoy.

SUMMARY

The household is the basic purchasing and consuming unit and is, therefore, of great importance to marketing managers of most products. Family households also are the primary mechanism whereby cultural and social-class values and behavior patterns are passed on to the next generation.

The *family household* consists of two or more related persons living together in a dwelling unit. *Nonfamily households* are dwelling units occupied by one or more unrelated individuals.

The *household life cycle (HLC)* is the classification of the household into stages through which it passes over time based on the age and marital status of the adults and the presence and age of children. The household life cycle is a valuable marketing tool because members within each stage or category face similar consumption problems. Thus, they represent potential market segments.

The *household life cycle/social stratification matrix* is a useful way to use the HLC to develop marketing strategy. One axis is the stages in the HLC (which determines the problems the household will likely encounter) and the other is a set of social strata (which provide a range of acceptable solutions). Each cell represents a market segment.

Family decision making involves consideration of questions such as who buys, who decides, and who uses. Family decision making is complex and involves emotion and interpersonal relations as well as product evaluation and acquisition.

Marketing managers must analyze the household decision process separately for each product category within each target market. Household member participation in the decision process varies by *involvement with the specific product, role specialization, personal characteristics,* and one's *culture and subculture.* Participation also varies by stage in the decision process. Most decisions are reached by consensus. If not, a variety of conflict resolution strategies may be employed.

Consumer socialization deals with the processes by which young people (from birth until 18 years of age) learn how to become consumers. Children's learning abilities are limited at birth, then slowly evolve with experience over time. Consumer socialization deals with the learning of both *directly relevant purchasing skills* (budgeting, shopping) and *indirectly relevant skills* (symbols of quality and prestige, for example). Families influence consumer socialization through direct *instrumental training, modeling,* and *mediation.* Consumers appear to go through five stages of learning how to shop. This learning takes place primarily in the retail outlet in interaction with the parent.

Marketing to children is fraught with ethical issues. The main source of ethical concern is the limited ability of children to process information and make sound purchase decisions or requests. There are also concerns about the role of advertising in forming children's values, influencing their diets, and causing family conflict. However, ethical and effective marketing programs can be developed for children.

KEY TERMS

INTERNET EXERCISES

1. Prepare a report on the information available on the Internet concerning the percent of the U.S. population that is in each stage of the household life cycle (provide the addresses for all sites used).
2. What information is available on the Internet concerning the magnitude of purchases by children?
3. Visit the Federal Trade Commission (http://www.ftc.gov) and Better Business Bureau (http://www.bbb.org) sites. What ethical and legal issues involving marketing to children appear?
4. Visit two of the sites listed below. Evaluate the effectiveness of the site in terms of marketing to children and the degree to which it represents an ethically sound approach to marketing to children.
   a. http://www.kelloggs.com
   b. http://www.fritolay.com
   c. http://www.warnerbros.com
   d. http://www.crayola.com
   e. http://www.nabisco.com
5. Find and describe two sites targeting children under six. What is your evaluation of these sites?

DDB NEEDHAM LIFESTYLE DATA ANALYSES

1. For which products, activities, or programs does consumption, participation, or viewing vary the most by household size (see Table 1)? Why is this the case?
2. Based on Table 1, consumption, participation, or viewing of which products, activities, or programs varies the most by marital status? Why is this the case?
3. Examine the data in Table 1. For which products, activities, or programs does consumption, participation, or viewing vary the most by number of children at home? Why is this the case?
4. For which attitudes/interests/activities in Table 1a are there the greatest differences across various size households? Why is this the case?

REVIEW QUESTIONS

1. The household is described as "the basic consumption unit for consumer goods." Why?
2. What is a *nuclear family?* Can a single-parent family be a nuclear family?
3. How does a *nonfamily household* differ from a *family household?*
4. What is an *extended family household?*
5. How has the distribution of household types in the United States been changing? What are the implications of these shifts?
6. What is meant by the *household life cycle?*
7. What is meant by the statement: "Each stage in the household life cycle poses a series of problems that household decision makers must solve"?
8. Describe the general characteristics of each of the stages in the household life cycle.
9. Describe the HLC/social stratification matrix. What is the logic for this matrix?
10. What is meant by *family decision making?* How can different members of the household be involved with different stages of the decision process?
11. How does family decision making differ from most organizational decision making?
12. The text states that the marketing manager must analyze the family decision-making process separately within each target market and for each product. Why?

13. What factors influence involvement of a household member in a purchase decision?
14. How do family members attempt to resolve conflict over purchase decisions?
15. What is *consumer socialization?* How is knowledge of it useful to marketing managers?
16. What are Piaget's stages of cognitive development?
17. What do we mean when we say that children learn *directly relevant* and *indirectly relevant* consumer skills and attitudes?
18. What processes do parents use to teach children to be consumers?
19. According to the text, what types of consumer socialization occur at young children's birthday parties?
20. Describe each of the five stages children go through as they learn to shop at stores.
21. What ethical issues arise in marketing to children? 

DISCUSSION QUESTIONS

22. Rate the stages of the household life cycle in terms of their probable purchase of the following. Justify your answers.
    a. Sport-utility vehicle
    b. Snowboard
    c. Internet service
    d. Expensive wine
    e. Life insurance
    f. Recreation vehicle
23. Pick two stages in the household life cycle (HLC). Describe how your marketing strategy for the following would differ depending on which group was your primary target market.
    a. Sport-utility vehicle
    b. Toothpaste
    c. Vacation
    d. Bank
24. Do you think the trend toward nonfamily households will continue? Justify your response.
25. What are the primary marketing implications of Table 6-1?
26. How would the marketing strategies for the following differ by stage of the HLC (assume each stage is the target market)?
    a. Tennis club
    b. Health insurance
    c. Sports drink
    d. Toothpaste
    e. Vacuum cleaner
    f. Mountain bike
27. What are the marketing implications of Figure 6-4?
28. Complete Table 6-2 for the following if the target market is full nest I and (1) working class, (2) middle class, or (3) lower-upper class.
    a. Soft drink
    b. Vacation
    c. Toothpaste
    d. Insurance
29. Complete Table 6-2 for the items in Question 28 if the target market is:
    a. Single I
    b. Young married
    c. Single-parent I
    d. Single II
    e. Delayed full nest I
    f. Full nest II
    g. Single-parent II
    h. Empty nest I
    i. Single III
    j. Empty nest II
30. How can a marketer use knowledge of how family members seek to resolve conflicts?
31. Describe a recent family purchase in which you were involved. Use this as a basis for completing Table 6-3 for a marketer attempting to influence that decision.
32. Describe four types of activities or situations in which *direct instrumental training* is likely to occur.
33. Describe four types of activities or situations in which *modeling* is likely to occur.
34. Describe four types of activities or situations in which *mediation* is likely to occur.
35. Are Piaget's stages of cognitive development consistent with the five stages of learning to shop that McNeal identified?

APPLICATION ACTIVITIES

36. Interview a junior high student and determine and describe the household decision process involved in the purchase of his or her (*a*) clothes, (*b*) breakfast foods, (*c*) bedroom furniture, and (*d*) expensive hobby items such as a snowboard or computer.
37. Interview two automobile salespersons from different dealerships. Try to ascertain which stages in the household life cycle constitute their primary markets and why this is so.
38. Interview one individual from each stage in the household life cycle. Determine and report the extent to which these individuals conform to the descriptions provided in the text.
39. Interview a family with at least one child under 13 at home. Interview both the parents and the child, but interview the child separately. Try to determine the influence of each family member on the following products *for the child's use.* In addition, ascertain what method(s) of conflict resolution are used.
    a. Toothpaste
    b. Shoes
    c. Snacks
    d. Major "toys," such as a bicycle
    e. Television viewing
    f. Restaurant meals
40. Interview a couple that has been married for the following periods. Ascertain and report the degree and nature of role specialization that has developed with respect to their purchase decisions. Also determine how conflicts are resolved.
    a. Less than 1 year
    b. 1–5 years
    c. 6–10 years
    d. Over 10 years
41. Pick a product and market segment of interest and interview five households. Collect sufficient data to complete Table 6-3.
42. Pick a product of interest and with several fellow students complete enough interviews to fill the relevant cells in Table 6-2. Develop an appropriate marketing strategy based on this information.
43. Interview several parents of preschool children. Determine the extent to which they agree with Piaget's four stages and McNeal's five stages.
44. Watch several hours of Saturday morning cartoons. What ethical concerns, if any, did they cause?

REFERENCES

1. Based on material provided by OshKosh and S. Chandler, "Kids' Wear Is Not Child's Play," *Business Week,* June 19, 1995, p. 118.
2. See F. L. Williams, "The Family as an Economic System," *Psychology & Marketing,* March–April 1993, pp. 111–20.
3. See P. Kiecker and N. R. McClure, "Redefining the Extended Family in Recognition of Blended Family Structures," *Enhancing Knowledge Development in Marketing* (Chicago: American Marketing Association, 1996), pp. 242–43.
4. See C. Otnes, K. Zolner, and T. M. Lowery, "In-Laws and Out-Laws"; and M. J. Bates and J. W. Gentry, "Keeping the Family Together"; both in *Advances in Consumer Research XXI,* ed. C. T. Allen and D. R. John (Provo, UT: Association for Consumer Research, 1994), pp. 25–33 and 30–34; and F. F. Furstenberg, Jr., "The Future of Families," *American Demographics,* June 1996, pp. 34–40.
5. A. Rindfleisch, J. E. Burroughs, and F. Dento, "Family Structure, Materialism, and Compulsive Consumption," *Journal of Consumer Research,* March 1997, pp. 312–25. See also J. E. Burroughs and A. Rindfleisch, "Materialism as a Coping Mechanism," in *Advances in Consumer Research XXIV,* ed. M. Bruck and D. J. MacInnis (Provo, UT: Association for Consumer Research, 1997), pp. 89–97.
6. See C. M. Schaninger and W. D. Danko, "A Conceptual and Empirical Comparison of Alternative Household Life Cycle Models," *Journal of Consumer Research,* March 1993, pp. 580–94; and R. E. Wilkes, "Household Life-Cycle Stages, Transitions, and Product Expenditures," *Journal of Consumer Research,* June 1995, pp. 27–42.
7. M. C. Gilly and B. M. Enis, "Recycling the Family Life Cycle," in *Advances in Consumer Research IX,* ed. A. A. Mitchell (Provo, UT: Association for Consumer Research, 1982), pp. 271–76.
8. See footnote 6.
9. G. J. Thompson, "Interpreting Consumers," *Journal Marketing Research,* November 1997, p. 448.
10. D. Crispell, "Marital Bust," *American Demographics,* June 1994, p. 59.
11. "The Future of Households," *American Demographics,* December 1993, p. 39.
12. Footnote 11, p. 35.

13. M. K. Ambry, "Receipts from a Marriage," *American Demographics,* February 1993, pp. 30–39.

14. J. Mukherui, "Consumption of Child Care," in *Advances in Consumer Research XXIV,* ed. M. Bruck and D. J. MacInnis (Provo, UT: Association for Consumer Research, 1997), p. 77.

15. Furstenberg, footnote 4, p. 36.

16. Footnote 11, p. 37.

17. Footnote 13, p. 33.

18. See *Targeting Today's Teens* (New York: Simmons Market Research Bureau, 1994); C. Miller, "Phat Is Where It's At for Today's Teen Market," *Marketing News,* August 15, 1994, p. 6; L. Zinn, "Teens," *Business Week,* April 11, 1994, p. 79; and S. Mitchell, "The Next Baby Boom," *American Demographics,* October 1995, pp. 22–31.

19. For a different approach, see L. G. Pol and S. Pak, "Consumer Unit Types and Expenditures on Food Away from Home," *Journal of Consumer Affairs,* Winter 1995, pp. 403–28.

20. See J. Park, P. Tansuhaj, and E. R. Spangenberg, "An Emotion-Based Perspective of Family Purchase Decisions," in *Advances in Consumer Research XXII,* ed. F. R. Kardes and M. Sujan (Provo, UT: Association for Consumer Research, 1995), pp. 723–28.

21. C. Lackman and J. M. Lanasa, "Family Decision-Making Theory," *Psychology & Marketing,* March–April 1993, pp. 81–113.

22. For an expanded view of this in an international context, see J. Ruth and S. R. Commuri, "Shifting Roles in Family Decision Making," in *Advances in Consumer Research XXV,* ed. J. W. Alba and J. W. Hutchinson (Provo, UT: Association for Consumer Research, 1998), pp. 400–406. See also W. Na, Y. Son, and R. Marshall, "An Empirical Study of the Purchase Role Structure in Korean Families," *Psychology & Marketing,* September 1998, pp. 563–76.

23. Notable exceptions are E. R. Foxman, P. S. Tansuhaj, and K. M. Ekstrom, "Family Members' Perceptions of Adolescents' Influence in Family Decision Making," *Journal of Consumer Research,* March 1989, pp. 482–91; and S. E. Beatty and S. Talpade, "Adolescent Influence in Family Decision Making," *Journal of Consumer Research,* September 1994, pp. 332–41.

24. See F. Holbert and G. Antonides, "Family Type Effects on Household Members' Decision Making," in *Advances in Consumer Research XXIV,* ed. M. Bruck and D. J. MacInnis (Provo, UT: Association for Consumer Research, 1997), pp. 48–54; C. Kim and H. Lee, "Development of Family Triadic Measures for Children's Purchase Influence," *Journal Marketing Research,* August 1997, pp. 307–21; B. Dellaert, M. Prodigalidad, and J. Louviere, "Family Members' Projections of Each Other's Preference and Influence," *Marketing Letters,* no. 2 (1998), pp. 135–45; and K. M. Palan, "Relationships between Family Communication and Consumer Activities of Adolescents," *Journal of the Academy of Marketing Science,* Fall 1998, 338–49.

25. See D. J. Burns, "Husband-Wife Innovative Consumer Decision Making," *Psychology & Marketing,* May–June 1992, pp. 175–89; C. Webster, "Determinants of Marital Power in Decision Making," in *Advances in Consumer Research XXII,* ed. F. R. Kardes and M. Sujan (Provo, UT: Association for Consumer Research, 1995), pp. 717–22; and R. Madrigal and C. M. Miller, "Construct Validity of Spouses' Relative Influence Measures," *Journal of the Academy of Marketing Science,* Spring 1996, pp. 157–70.

26. J. B. Ford, L. E. Pelton, and J. R. Lumpkin, "Perception of Marital Roles in Purchase Decision Processes," *Journal of the Academy of Marketing Science,* Spring 1995, pp. 120–31.

27. K. M. Palan and R. E. Wilkes, "Adolescent-Parent Interaction in Family Decision Making," *Journal of Consumer Research,* September 1997, pp. 159–69.

28. See C. Webster and S. Rice, "Equity Theory and the Power Structure in a Marital Relationship," in *Advances in Consumer Research XXIII,* ed. K. P. Corfman and J. G. Lynch (Provo, UT: Association for Consumer Research, 1996), pp. 491–97; M. C. Reiss and C. Webster, "Relative Influence in Purchase Decision Making," in *Advances in Consumer Research XXIV,* ed. M. Bruck and D. J. MacInnis (Provo, UT: Association for Consumer Research, 1997), pp. 42–47; and C. Webster, "The Meaning and Measurement of Marital Power," in *Advances in Consumer Research XXV,* ed. J. W. Alba and J. W. Hutchinson (Provo, UT: Association for Consumer Research, 1998), pp. 395–99.

29. D. Crispell, "Dual-Earner Diversity," *American Demographics,* July 1995, pp. 32–37.

30. C. Kim and H. Lee, "A Taxonomy of Couples Based on Influence Strategies," *Journal of Business Research,* June 1996, pp. 157–68. See also L. Mallalieu and C. Faure, "Toward an Understanding of the Choice of Influence Tactics," in *Advances in Consumer Research XXV,* ed. J. W. Alba and J. W. Hutchinson (Provo, UT: Association for Consumer Research, 1998), pp. 407–14.

31. Footnote 27.

32. See L. A. Peracchio, "How Do Young Children Learn to Be Consumers?" *Journal of Consumer Research,* March 1992, pp. 425–40; M. C. Macklin, "The Effects of Advertising Retrieval Cue on Young Children's Memory and Brand Evaluations," *Psychology & Marketing,* May 1994, pp. 291–311; and M. C. Macklin, "The Impact of Audiovisual Information on Children's Product-Related Recall," *Journal of Consumer Research,* June 1994, pp. 154–64.

33. See J. Gregan-Paxton and D. R. John, "The Emergence of Adaptive Decision Making in Children," *Journal of Consumer Research,* June 1997, pp. 43–56.

34. For example, see M. C. Macklin, "Preschoolers' Learning of Brand Names from Visual Cues," *Journal of Consumer Research,* December 1996, pp. 251–61; and D. R. Pawlowski, D. M. Badzinski, and N. Mitchell, "Effects of Metaphors on Children's Comprehension and Perception of Print Advertisements," *Journal of Advertising,* Summer 1998, pp. 83–98.

35. Footnote 27.

36. See S. Grossbart, L. Carlson, and A. Walsh, "Consumer Socialization and Frequency of Shopping with Children," *Journal of the Academy of Marketing Science,* Summer 1991, pp. 155–64; O. A. J. Mascarenhas and M. A. Higby, "Peer, Parent, and Media Influences in Teen Apparel Shopping," *Journal of the Academy of Marketing Science,* Winter 1993, pp. 53–58; and S. Shim, L. Synder, and K. C. Gehrt, "Parent's Perception Regarding

Children's Use of Clothing Evaluative Criteria," in *Advances in Consumer Research XXII,* ed. F. R. Kardes and M. Sujan (Provo, UT: Association for Consumer Research, 1995), pp. 628–32.

37. See J. L. Haynes, D. C. Burts, A. Dukes, and R. Cloud, "Consumer Socialization of Pre-schoolers and Kindergartners," *Psychology & Marketing,* March–April 1993, pp. 151–66.

38. Footnote 27.

39. J. U. McNeal, *Kids as Consumers* (New York: Lexington Books, 1992); and J. U. McNeal and C. Yeh, "Born to Shop," *American Demographics,* June 1993, pp. 34–39.

40. J. U. McNeal, "Tapping the Three Kids' Markets," *American Demographics,* April 1998, p. 38.

41. C. Miller, "Marketers Hoping Kids Will Join Club," *Marketing News,* January 31, 1994, pp. 1–2.

© David Strick/Outline.

chapter seven

Group Influences on Consumer Behavior

For most products and brands, a consumer or family makes a purchase decision, acquires the item, and consumes it. While friends and acquaintances frequently influence whether or not a product will be purchased, which brand will be selected, and how it will be used, the basic purchase motivation relates to the ability of the product or service itself to meet a need of the consumer.

Other purchases are fundamentally different. The consumer buys more than the product or brand. Membership in a group is also being purchased. A prime example of this is the purchase of a Harley-Davidson motorcycle. Most purchasers of a Harley-Davidson acquire not only the bike and some aspect of the image that comes with it, they also join a group or subculture. While there are a number of distinct Harley-Davidson groups, most share a core ethos or value system.

Although various subgroups exist, the "status" of the groups varies depending of how authentic it is (how close the group is to the outlaw biker). Clearly, simply buying a Harley does not automatically make one a member of the group, as this quote from a "real" biker indicates:

> To get down to task, there are several new classes of riders fouling the wind with the misapprehension that merely owning a Harley will transform them into a biker. This is the same type of dangerous ignorance that suggests that giving a dog an artichoke turns him into a gourmet. (We) . . . have identified several classes of these offenders:
>
> | | |
> |---|---|
> | Rubies: | Rich Urban Bikers |
> | Sewers: | Suburban Weekend Riders |
> | Riots: | Retired Idiots on Tour |
> | Mugwumps: | My Ugly Goldwing Was Upsetting My Peers |
> | Ahabs: | Aspiring Hardass Bikers |
> | Bastards: | Bought a Sportster, Therefore a Radical Dude |
> | Igloos: | I Got the Look, Own One Soon |

Hoots: Have One Ordered, True Story
Assholes: Assholes

New bikers appear to go through three stages as they become fully part of the particular Harley group to which they aspire: (1) experimentation with the biker identity, (2) identification and conformity, and (3) mastery and internalization.

An important part of the biker identity involves product consumption. Obviously, one must own a Harley. However, just owning a Harley isn't enough. People, both other bikers and the general public, have expectations about the dress and behaviors of Harley bikers. As one study found: "the newcomer becomes acutely aware of another aspect of Harley ownership, performance before an audience. Much of what guides the newcomer's purchases of protective clothing, footwear, helmets, and accessories can be explained as tasks of impression management driven by perceptions of audience expectation."[1]

Purchasing a Harley and "becoming a biker" is clearly a group-based process. Even in an individualistic society like America, group memberships and identity are very important to most of us. And, while we don't like to think of ourselves as conformists, most of us conform to group expectations most of the time.

When you decided what to wear to the last party you attended, you probably based your decision in part on the anticipated responses of the other individuals at the party. Likewise, your behavior at an anniversary celebration for your grandparents probably would differ from your behavior at a graduation party for a close friend. These behaviors are responses to group influences and expectations.

Almost all consumer behavior takes place within a group setting. In addition, groups serve as one of the primary agents of consumer socialization and learning. Therefore, understanding how groups function is essential to understanding consumer behavior.

TYPES OF GROUPS

The terms *group* and *reference group* need to be distinguished. A **group** is defined as *two or more individuals who share a set of norms, values, or beliefs and have certain implicitly or explicitly defined relationships to one another such that their behaviors are interdependent.* A **reference group** is *a group whose presumed perspectives or values are being used by an individual as the basis for his or her current behavior.* Thus, a reference group is simply a group that an individual uses as a guide for behavior in a specific situation.

Most of us belong to a number of different groups and perhaps would like to belong to several others. When we are actively involved with a particular group, it generally functions as a reference group. As the situation changes, we may base our behavior on an entirely different group, which then becomes our reference group. We may belong to many groups simultaneously, but we generally use only one group as our primary point of reference in any given situation. This is illustrated in Figure 7-1.

Groups may be classified according to a number of variables. Marketers have found three classification criteria to be particularly useful: (1) membership, (2) type of contact, and (3) attraction.

The *membership* criterion is dichotomous: either one is a member of a particular group or one is not a member of that group. Of course, some members are more secure in their membership than others are. That is, some members feel they really "belong" to a group while others lack this confidence.

Reference Groups Change as the Situation Changes **FIGURE 7-1**

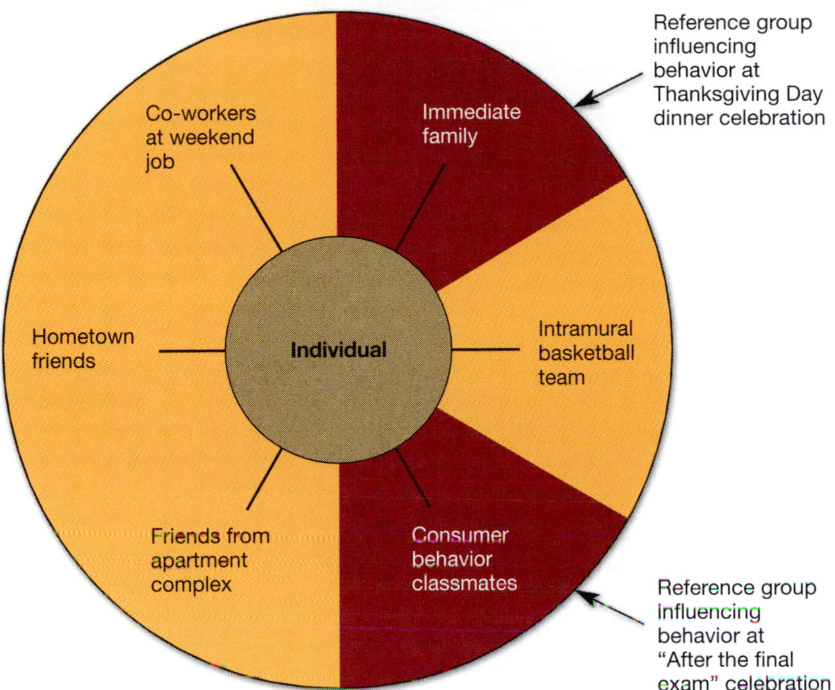

Type of contact refers to how much interpersonal contact the group members have with each other. As group size increases, interpersonal contact tends to decrease. Type of contact is generally treated as having two categories. Groups characterized by frequent interpersonal contact are called **primary groups.** Groups characterized by limited interpersonal contact are referred to as **secondary groups.** Consumer Insight 7-1 discusses the unique nature of groups formed when contact is based on the Internet.

Attraction refers to the desirability that membership in a given group has for the individual. This can range from negative to positive. Groups with negative desirability—**dissociative reference groups**—can influence behavior just as do those with positive desirability. For example, teenagers tend to avoid clothing styles associated with older consumers.

Nonmembership groups with a positive attraction, **aspiration reference groups,** also exert a strong influence. Individuals frequently purchase products thought to be used by a desired group in order to achieve actual or symbolic membership in the group. For example, many who aspire to the Harley biker group cannot currently acquire membership due to the expense of the bike or opposition from family members. These aspiring group members often purchase and wear Harley apparel and related products.

A recent study identified an aspiration and a dissociative reference group for junior- and senior-level undergraduate business majors.[2] The students were asked to rate the lifestyle groups listed in the PRIZM lifestyle clusters (a set of 62 types of American lifestyles—see Chapter 13) in terms of: "These people are very similar to how I would like to be" (aspiration group) and "These people are very similar to how I would not like to be" (dissociative group). The students were provided with descriptions of some of the consumption patterns of each of the groups on which to base their ratings. These college students aspired to be like the "Money & Brains" PRIZM group and to avoid the "Smalltown Downtown" group. The consumption descriptions of these two groups are:

Money & Brains	*Smalltown Downtown*
Heavy Users of:	
Travel/entertainment cards	Saltwater fishing gear
Aperitif/specialty wines	Pro wrestling
Classical music	Gospel music
Valid passports	Cafeterias
Natural cold cereal	Canned meat spreads
Whole wheat bread	Instant mashed potatoes
TV Movies	"The Today Show"
Light Users of:	
Hunting	Money market funds
Pickup trucks	Racquetball
CB radios	Travel/entertainment cards
Roller derby	Chewing tobacco
Presweetened cereal	Natural cold cereal
Canned stews	Mexican foods
"As the World Turns"	"David Letterman"

There were 38 other groups that were evaluated, but these were the groups most and least aspired to. To which group would you like to belong? Would you want to avoid belonging to the other group? Based on these consumption patterns, what kinds of jobs, attitudes, and hobbies do you think each group has? What other products do they use?

The business students in this study thought (with a good degree of accuracy) that the Money & Brains group would drive BMWs and Mercedes, read travel magazines, *Vogue,* and *Business Week,* drink Heineken, expensive wine, and Scotch, and use Polo and Obsession. In contrast, the students described the Smalltown Downtown group as driving Fords and Chevrolets, reading *People, Sports Illustrated,* and *TV Guide,* drinking Budweiser and Miller, and using Brut and Old Spice. Since people tend to consume products associated with aspiration groups and avoid products associated with dissociative groups, this study suggests that Ford and Chevrolet are not well positioned to capture the next generation of upper-middle-class consumers. What other marketing implications do you see? What should the various brands mentioned above do?

Consumption-Based Groups

A consumption-based group, often termed a **consumption subculture,** is *a distinctive subgroup of society that self-selects on the basis of a shared commitment to a particular product class, brand, or consumption activity.* These groups have (1) an identifiable, hierarchical social structure; (2) a set of shared beliefs or values; and (3) unique jargon, rituals, and modes of symbolic expression.[3] Thus, they are reference groups for their members as well as those who aspire to join or avoid them.

In the opening vignette, we described some aspects of a consumption subculture built around a product—Harley-Davidson motorcycles. Other subcultures that have been studied

Virtual Communities?

The terms *virtual community* and *cybercommunity* are increasingly used to describe groups of people who interact over time around a topic of interest on the Internet. These interactions generally take place in the Usenet portion of the Internet or on sites maintained by firms, media, or professional and nonprofit groups. Examples would include Jeep owners, scuba divers, *Star Wars* fans, and Planned Parenthood.

While it is easy to imagine that true communities are evolving on the Internet, the evidence is less clear. Such groups lack the wide range of functions and interactions that characterize "real" communities. Many participants in virtual communities lack any ongoing commitment to the group. The lack of face-to-face or even voice-to-voice interaction removes much of the symbolic and emotional meaning conveyed in "real" communities. The anonymity of participants removes responsibility for the consequences of their communications. Finally, there is seldom the explicit or implicit *quid pro quo* that characterizes most ongoing social relations.

Despite these distinctions from "real" communities or traditional groups, research indicates that for many participants in these Usenet and similar groups they are indeed virtual communities. Studies have found ongoing communications among subsets of these interest groups. In addition, the patterns of communication indicate a group structure with the more experienced members serving as experts and leaders and the newer members seeking advice and information.

Not everyone involved with an interest group on the Internet is part of a community or group. Many "participants" are "lurkers" who peruse the group discussions without participating. Others participate at a very limited level. Still others are "drop-ins." For example, one of the authors of this text visits a scuba diving interest group once a year or so. He inquires about dive sites and other recreational opportunities in the area of his planned vacation.

Critical Thinking Questions

1. Can meaningful communities exist on the Internet?
2. What are the implications for society of the emergence of Internet-based communities?
3. What are the ethical implications of marketers monitoring Internet interest groups for product and advertising insights? 
4. What are the ethical implications of marketers participating in Internet interest groups without identifying themselves? 

Source: N. A. Granitz and J. C. Ward, "Virtual Community," in *Advances in Consumer Research XXIII*, ed. K. P. Corfman and J. G. Lynch (Provo, UT: Association for Consumer Research, 1996), pp. 161–66; C. Okleshen and S. Grossbart, "Usenet Groups, Virtual Community and Consumer Behaviors"; and S. Dann and S. Dann, "Cybercommuning"; both in *Advances in Consumer Research XXV*, ed. J. W. Alba and J. W. Hutchinson (Provo, UT: Association for Consumer Research, 1998). pp. 276–82 and 379–85.

Consumer Insight 7-1

in some detail have focused on a style/attitude (the "punk" culture),[4] an organization (an art museum),[5] and an activity (bodybuilding).[6] Harley-Davidson is somewhat unique, as it is unusual to have a strongly formed consumption subculture built around a product. Saturn, through the image it portrays of its customers in its advertising, the barbecues, workshops, and other events local dealers sponsor for owners, and the annual "vacation get-together at the factory" program (attended by over 40,000 people), is trying to create such a group.

Activity-based subcultures are much more common. Snowboarding, golfing, home brewing beer, and gardening all have consumption subcultures built around them. Each has a set of self-selecting members. They have hierarchies at the local and national levels. For example, home brewing status is determined by whether or not one is a "serious" brewer, one's skill, length of time as a brewer, awards won, amount and type of equipment, role in the local club, and so forth. Each also has shared beliefs and unique jargon and rituals (relax, have a home brew). Most hobbies and participation sports have consumption-based subcultures built around them.

Another focus for consumption-based groups is the consumption of entertainment (art, movies, and sports). Consumption need not be shared physically to be a shared ritual that

ILLUSTRATION 7-1

Clothing styles originating in consumption subcultures for functional or symbolic reasons are often adopted by other groups as well. Surfers have initiated several styles that gained widespread popularity.

Illustrations in ad by Rick Rietveld; advertising design and layout by Rick Rietveld; © Rietveld, USA.

creates and sustains a group.[7] Serious fans of professional football, "Dawson's Creek," or "Star Trek" form consumption subcultures. For example, following a team gives a fan something in common with other fans of the same team, and enthusiasm for the sport itself provides a common ground for all members of the group.[8] The same is true for all forms of entertainment that attract devout followers.

Marketing and Consumption Subcultures Consumption subcultures are important to marketers for a variety of reasons. For product-based groups, the firm must market the subculture itself as well as, or even instead of, the product. This is certainly the case for Harley-Davidson. It markets a slightly sanitized version of the original outlaw biker culture that initially formed around the bikes.[9]

Groups based on activities obviously are markets for the requirements of the activity itself, such as golf clubs for golfers. However, these groups develop rituals and modes of symbolic communication that often involve products or services. Golf is renowned for the "uniform" that many of its adherents wear. Clothes, hats, and other items designed for golfers are based as much on providing symbolic meaning as they are for functional benefits. Snowboarders and downhill skiers both require protection from the cold, yet their outfits have little in common in terms of appearance.

While these subcultures adopt consumption patterns in large part to affirm their unique identity, the larger market often appropriates all or parts of their symbols, at least for a time.[10] Thus, clothing initially worn by a consumption subculture such as snowboarders or surfers for functional or symbolic reasons may emerge as a style for a much larger group (see Illustration 7-1). Marketers such as Nike observe such groups closely for clues to new trends.

Courtesy *Runner's World.*

ILLUSTRATION 7-2

Marketers increasingly encourage the formation of consumption-based groups and/or tie group-related activities and benefits to their products.

Participating in a shared consumption experience is a means of developing and maintaining social relationships among individuals. When two or more individuals share a consumption event such as attending a performance, the consumption experience is not just the direct effect of seeing the performance. It includes the social interactions with the other individual(s), the fact of sharing, and the meanings attached to these interactions. Thus, organizations marketing the arts, as well as sports marketers and others, should focus on providing and promoting the social, group aspects of the experience as well as the artistic and entertaining features. College and professional football teams that encourage tailgate parties before the games are an example of one approach to this. Illustration 7-2 shows how *Runner's World* promotes the formation of consumption groups and social experiences around the often solitary act of running.

REFERENCE GROUP INFLUENCES ON THE CONSUMPTION PROCESS

We all conform in a variety of ways to numerous groups. Look around your classroom. The odds are that, except for gender differences, most of you will be dressed in a similar manner. In fact, a student who comes to class dressed in a suit will generally be asked about the job interview that others will assume is the cause of the more formal clothing. Note that we, as individuals, do not generally consider these behaviors to constitute conformity. Normally, we conform without even being aware of doing so, though we also frequently face conscious decisions on whether or not to go along with the group.

Drs. Junkins, Kwiatkowski, Cuervo, and Huang haven't been doctors long enough to know they're supposed to drive one of those overpriced luxury imports.

When Ed, Janet, Beth, and Jim emerged, successfully, from medical school, they felt the gratification of having achieved a lifelong goal, while also confronting a hard reality common to most young doctors—a ton of student loan debt. (You could buy five Saturns with what a new M.D. typically owes.)

In Ed's case, that hard reality also included his 10-year-old car—nobody could tell him how much time it had left. Since a pediatric resident's life is ruled by a beeper (and because you can't tell a sick kid that the tow truck was late), Ed bit the bullet and went looking for a new car.

While he was making the rounds of the car dealerships in town, Ed discovered Saturn. Where, along with the simple, painless way one shops at our showrooms, he liked the rather healthy range of standard features offered and (especially) the fact that the price of a Saturn did not put him into a state of shock.

Since then, mostly on his referral, many of Ed's colleagues have been filling the hospital parking lot with new Saturns. (Apparently, the people who pay most attention to a doctor's advice are other doctors.)

The Saturn SL1

SATURN.

A Different Kind *of* Company. A Different Kind *of* Car.

Courtesy Saturn Corporation.

ILLUSTRATION 7-3

Group members often use other members as a source of information for their purchase decisions. This is known as *informational influence.* It can be based on the similarity of the members (he is like me and he uses it) or their perceived expertise (she knows a lot about this and she uses this brand). This example describes similarity-based informational influence.

Norms are *general expectations about behaviors that are deemed appropriate for all persons in a social context, regardless of the position they hold.* Norms arise quickly, often without verbal communication or direct thought, any time a group exists. Norms tend to cover all aspects of behavior relevant to the group's functioning and violation of the norms can result in sanctions.

Reference groups have been found to influence a wide range of consumption behaviors. Before examining the marketing implications of these findings, we need to examine the nature of reference group influence more closely.

The Nature of Reference Group Influence

Conformity can take three forms: *informational, normative,* and *identification.*[11] It is important to distinguish among these types, since the marketing strategy required depends on the type of influence involved.

Informational influence occurs when an individual uses the behaviors and opinions of reference group members as potentially useful bits of information. This influence is based on either the similarity of the group's members to the individual or the expertise of the influencing group member. Thus, a person may notice several members of a given group using a particular brand of coffee. He or she may then decide to try that brand simply because there is evidence (its use by friends) that it may be a good brand. Or, one may decide to purchase a particular brand and model of computer because a friend who is very knowledgeable about computers owns or recommends it. In these cases, conformity is the result of information shared by the group members. Illustration 7-3 shows the nature of informational influence. Notice that the text of the ad indicates that one of the new doctors engaged in a fairly extensive search process before purchasing the *Saturn.* Then, many of his colleagues purchased a Saturn based on his recommendation.

The ad agency for Hennessy cognac hired attractive models and actors to visit trendy bars. In the bars, they would invent an excuse to order "Hennessy martinis" for everyone or selected groups. The hope was that by having "in" looking individuals ordering this new drink, others would consider it acceptable or stylish.[12] Is this an ethical application of group influence?

Normative influence, sometimes referred to as *utilitarian* influence, occurs when an individual fulfills group expectations to gain a direct reward or to avoid a sanction.[13] You may purchase a particular brand of clothing to win approval from your colleagues. Or you may refrain from wearing the latest fashion for fear of teasing by friends. The essence of normative influence is the presence of a direct reward or sanction. Ads that promise social acceptance or approval if a product is used are relying on normative influence. Likewise, ads that suggest group disapproval if a product is not used (such as a mouthwash or deodorant) are based on normative influence.

Identification influence, also called value-expressive influence, occurs when individuals have internalized the group's values and norms. These then guide the individuals' behaviors without any thought of reference group sanctions or rewards. The individual has accepted the group's values as his or her own. The individual behaves in a manner consistent with the group's values because the individual's values and the group's values are the same.

Figure 7-2 illustrates a series of consumption situations and the type of reference group influence that is operating in each case. While this figure indicates the wide range of situations in which groups influence the consumption process, there are other situations in which groups have at most a limited, indirect effect.[14] For example, purchasing a particular brand of aspirin or noticing a billboard advertisement generally are not subject to group influence.

Degree of Reference Group Influence

Reference groups may have no influence in a given situation or they may influence usage of the product category, the type of product used, and/or the brand used. Brand influence is most likely to be a category influence rather than a specific brand. That is, a group is likely to approve (or disapprove) a range of brands such as private-label soft drinks or luxury automobiles.

Table 7-1 shows how two consumption situation characteristics—necessity/nonnecessity and visible/private consumption—combine to influence the degree of reference group influence likely to operate in a specific situation.[15] In the following paragraphs, we will discuss these two, and three additional determinants of reference group influences.

1. Group influence is strongest *when the use of product or brand is visible to the group.* For a product such as aerobic shoes, the product category (shoes), product type (aerobic), and brand (Reebok) are all visible. A dress is visible in terms of product category and product type (style), but the brand is less obvious. The consumption of other products such as vitamins is generally private. Reference group influence typically affects only those aspects of the product (category, type, or brand) that are visible to the group.[16]
2. Reference group influence is higher *the less of a necessity an item is.* Thus, reference groups have strong influence on the ownership of products such as snowboards and designer clothes, but much less influence on necessities such as refrigerators.

FIGURE 7-2 Consumption Situations and Reference Group Influence

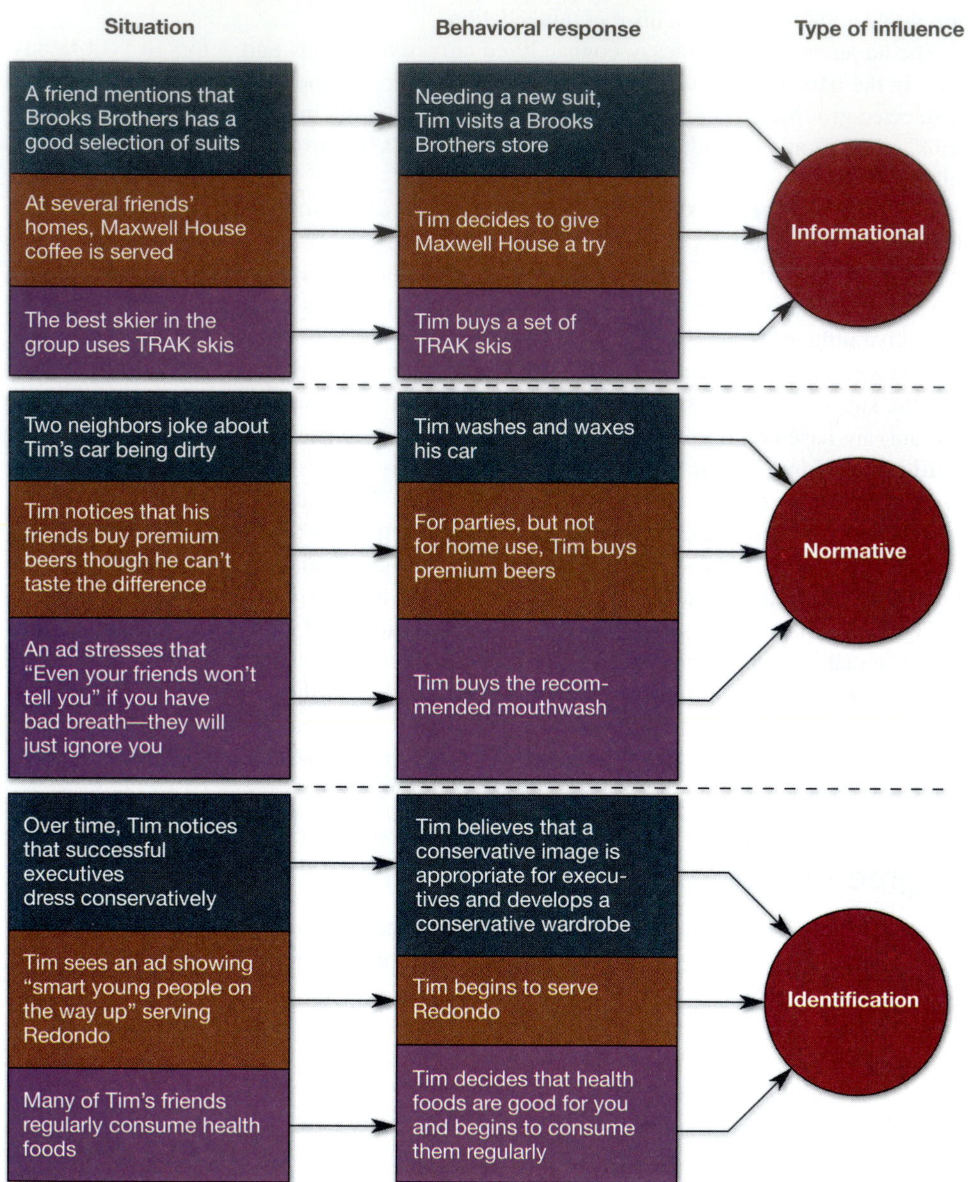

3. In general, *the more commitment an individual feels to a group, the more the individual will conform to the group norms*. We are much more likely to consider group expectations when dressing for a dinner with a group we would like to join (stay with) than for dinner with a group that is unimportant to us. This was demonstrated in a recent study that found that Hispanic consumers who strongly identified with the Hispanic ethnic community were more subject to normative and identification influence from the Hispanic community than were those with weak identification to this group.[17]

TABLE 7-1

Two Consumption Situation Characteristics and Product/Brand Choice

	Degree Needed	
	Necessity	Nonnecessity
Consumption	Weak reference group influence on product	Strong reference group influence on product
Visible Strong reference group influence on brand	*Public Necessities* Influence: Weak product and strong brand Examples: Wristwatch Automobile	*Public Luxuries* Influence: Strong product and brand Examples: Snow skis Health club
Private Weak reference group influence on brand	*Private Necessities* Influence: Weak product and brand Examples: Mattress Refrigerator	*Private Luxuries* Influence: Strong product and weak brand Examples: Hot tub Home entertainment center

Source: "Reference Group Influence on Product and Brand Purchase Decision," *Journal of Consumer Research,* September 1982, p. 185.

4. The *more relevant a particular activity is to the group's functioning, the stronger the pressure to conform to the group norms concerning that activity*. Thus, style of dress may be important to a social group that frequently eats dinner together at nice restaurants and unimportant to a reference group that meets for basketball on Thursday nights.
5. The final factor that affects the degree of reference group influence is *the individual's confidence in the purchase situation*. One study found the purchase of color televisions, automobiles, home air conditioners, insurance, refrigerators, medical services, magazines or books, clothing, and furniture to be particularly susceptible to reference group influence. Several of these products such as insurance and medical services are neither visible nor important to group functioning. Yet they are important to the individual and are products about which most individuals have limited information. Thus, group influence is strong because of the individual's lack of confidence in purchasing these products. In addition to confidence in the purchase situation, there is evidence that individuals differ in their tendency to be influenced by reference groups.[18]

   Confidence is not necessarily the same as product knowledge. One study found that knowledgeable car buyers were more prone to informational reference group influence than were novice buyers. The explanation is that knowledgeable buyers are quite interested in automobiles and enjoy exchanging information and opinions with knowledgeable peers. Novices tend to be uninterested in automobiles, do not enjoy seeking information on the product, and are more influenced by ads and salespeople.[19]

Figure 7-3 summarizes the manner in which reference groups influence product and brand usage. Marketing managers can use this structure to determine the likely degree of group influence on the consumption of their brand.

FIGURE 7-3 Consumption Situation Determinants of Reference Group Influence

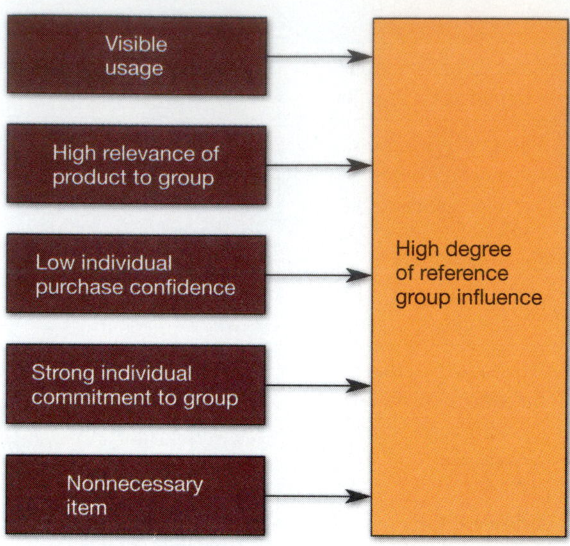

MARKETING STRATEGIES BASED ON REFERENCE GROUP INFLUENCES

The first task the manager faces in using reference group influence is to determine the degree and nature of reference group influence that exists—*or can be created*—for the product in question. Figure 7-3 provides the starting point for this analysis.

Personal Sales Strategies

The power of group norms was initially demonstrated in a classic series of studies now generally referred to as the Asch experiments or the **Asch phenomenon.** Eight subjects are shown four straight lines on a board—three close together and one some distance from them. They are asked to determine which one of the three unequal lines that are grouped together is closest to the length of the fourth line shown some distance away. The subjects are to announce their judgments publicly. Seven of the subjects are working for the experimenter, and they announce incorrect matches. The order of announcement is arranged so that the naive subject responds last. The naive subject almost always agrees with the incorrect judgment of the others.

Note that the conformity being obtained was among strangers with respect to a discrete, physical task that had an objective, correct answer. This study has been repeated in a variety of formats and has generally achieved the same results. For example, students' evaluations of the nutritional value of a new diet food were strongly affected by the stated opinions of other students even when they did not know the other students.[20] Imagine how much stronger the pressures to conform are among friends or when the task is less well defined, such as preferring one brand or style to another.

Consider this direct application of the Asch phenomenon in personal selling. A group of potential customers are brought together for a sales presentation. As each design is

Courtesy of Food and Wines from France, Inc.

ILLUSTRATION 7-4

French champagne is viewed by many as being appropriate only for very special occasions. This ad indicates that French champagne is appropriate for fun, casual group activities.

presented, the salesperson scans the expressions of the people in the group, looking for the one who shows approval (e.g., head nodding) of the design. The salesperson then asks that person for an opinion, since the opinion is certain to be favorable. The person is asked to elaborate. Meanwhile, the salesperson scans the faces of the other people, looking for more support, and then asks for an opinion of the next person now showing most approval. The salesperson continues until the person who initially showed the most disapproval is reached. In this way, by using the first person as a model, and by social group pressure on the last person, the salesperson gets all or most of the people in the group to make a positive public statement about the design.

Tupperware and other firms using the "party" sales approach rely on situations in which reference group behavior encourages sales. Tupperware products are ones for which we would not normally predict a strong level of reference group influence—private usage, limited relevance to the group, fairly high individual purchase skills, and a necessary item. However, by making the purchase itself part of a party at a friend's home, the situation is dramatically changed. Now the purchase act is the focus of attention, and it is visible and highly relevant to the party group to which the individual usually has a fair degree of commitment.[21] Do you see any ethical issues in using group influences in this way?

Advertising Strategies

Marketers often position products as appropriate for group activities. French wines gained an image of being somewhat expensive and snobbish. Many consumers viewed them as appropriate only for very special occasions. A trade group, Food and Wines from France, launched a campaign to broaden their appeal. Illustration 7-4 shows an ad that positions French champagne as appropriate for casual, fun group parties.

ILLUSTRATION 7-5

This 30-second television commercial is aimed at preteens. It indicates that smoking pot is a strong violation of group norms and that those who do smoke pot will be confronted with sanctions such as personal rejection.

(Music underneath throughout)
TOMMY: Whoa, look at . . .
GIRLS: Tommy. He's so stoned.
TOMMY: This is totally . . . happening;
GIRLS: Look what's happened to him.
TOMMY: You know I look like . . .
GIRLS: . . . such a mess. What a loser .
TOMMY: Yeah, this weed is definitely . . .
GIRLS: Gross. Ever since he started smoking pot, he's gross.
TOMMY: Like everybody's doing it.
GIRLS: and it's so uncool.
TOMMY: They're really into me. They think I'm so . . .
GIRLS: Out of it.
GIRLS: He's really out of it.

Courtesy of a Partnership for a Drug-Free America.

Marketers use all three types of reference group influence when developing advertisements. Informational influence in advertising was shown earlier in Illustration 7-3. Ads using informational influence typically show members of a group using a product, with the message that if you are or want to be in a group such as this one, you should use this product. However, the reason is not because you will be accepted or rewarded by the group members for using it or punished for not using it. Rather, the message is that "these types of people find this brand to be the best; if you are like them, you will too."

Normative group influence is not portrayed in ads as much as it once was. It involves the explicit or implicit suggestion that using (or not using) the brand will result in members of a group you belong to or wish to join rewarding (punishing) you. One reason for the reduced use of this technique is the ethical questions raised by implying that a person's friends would base their reactions to the individual on his or her purchases. Ads showing a person's friends saying negative things about them behind their back because their coffee was not great (yes, there was such an ad campaign) were criticized for playing on peoples' insecurities and fears.

Identification influence is based on the fact that the individual has internalized the group's values. The advertising task is to demonstrate that the advertised product is consistent with the group's and therefore the individual's values.

Group influence and conformity are normal and powerful influences on behavior. This is generally neither good nor bad, it is just a component of human existence. However, it can be harmful to individuals. Teenagers and preteenagers are strongly influenced by "peer pressure" or normative and identification group influence. To an unfortunate extent, these influences can lead to injurious consumption involving cigarettes, alcohol, drugs, sexual activities, and so forth.[22] Organizations working to combat these behaviors are up against a powerful foe. It is difficult to "just say no to drugs" if your friends are doing them and you face teasing and being ostracized if you don't join them.

One way to succeed in such a situation is to alter the group norms. That is, engaging in the injurious behavior needs to become a violation of the group norms. The 30-second Partnership for a Drug-Free America commercial shown in Illustration 7-5 is targeted at preteens. It clearly defines smoking pot as inappropriate group behavior subject to group sanctions (girls won't like you). Similar antismoking ads (one said, "Your friends won't come near you") targeting teenagers have been very effective.[23]

COMMUNICATIONS WITHIN GROUPS

Delores Sotto, a long-time resident of a large apartment building on Manhattan's West End Avenue, is explaining the problem with dry cleaning in her neighborhood. "If you ask me," she says, "none of the dry cleaners in this area is any good. They all should have gone out of business long ago." Over the course of the next 10 minutes, Delores relays horror stories about ruined Armani ("Collezin, for God's sake!"), shrunken custom-made shirts now suitable for only a preteen nephew, and stains mysteriously appearing on garments days after they have been cleaned.

It turns out that Delores's information comes not from direct experience but from the collective wisdom of her apartment building. In the laundry room, hallways, and elevators of her building, Delores's neighbors pass on the negative experiences they have with neighborhood vendors.[24]

As Delores illustrates, consumers are particularly likely to tell others about negative experiences in the marketplace. Do they also share positive experiences? An analyst with Morgan Stanley & Company characterizes Wal-Mart as "a company built on word-of-mouth reputation." What does this mean? By providing "everyday low prices" before they were popular, along with a broad selection of merchandise, fully stocked shelves, and superior customer services, Wal-Mart was able to generate excitement among its customers who, in turn, told their friends about the store. Based on this, Wal-Mart has become America's largest retailer. However, it spends just 0.5 percent of its sales on advertising (compared to 2.5 percent for Kmart and 3.8 percent for Sears). This translates into a *billion dollars more profit* per year compared to Sears' performance.[25] Clearly, positive word-of-mouth communications are worth a great deal to a firm.

Word-of-mouth (WOM) communications, *individuals sharing information with other individuals,* are a critical influence on consumer decisions and business success.[26] We learn about new products, restaurants, and retail outlets from our friends and other reference groups (1) by observing or participating with them as they use product and services, or (2) by seeking or receiving advice and information from them. About half of Americans agree that they "often seek the advice of others before making a decision to buy products or services," and 40 percent feel that people often come to them for purchase advice.[27] Below are the percent of men and women who rely on the advice of others before purchasing various products and services:

Product	*Men*	*Women*
New doctor	45%	47%
Legal advice	41	42
Car mechanic	40	49
Restaurant	39	38
Movie	26	28
Personal loan	17	20
Automobile purchase	15	22
Hair cut	10	24

As the above discussion indicates, (1) using WOM in making purchase decisions is common, (2) it varies by product category, and (3) it varies somewhat with demographics.

OPINION LEADERSHIP

Information is the primary tool that marketers use to influence consumer behavior. While an individual ultimately processes information, in a substantial number of cases one or more group members filter, interpret, or provide the information for the individual. The person who performs this task or role is known as an **opinion leader.** The process of one person receiving information from the mass media or other marketing sources and passing that information on to others is known as the **two-step flow of communications.** The two-step flow explains some aspects of communication within groups, but it is too simplistic to account for most communication flows. What usually happens is a multistep flow of communication.[28] Figure 7-4 contrasts the direct flow with a multistep flow of mass communications.

The **multistep flow of communication** involves opinion leaders for a particular product area who actively seek relevant information from the mass media as well as other sources. These opinion leaders process this information and transmit their interpretations of it to some members of their groups. These group members also receive information from the mass media as well as from group members who are not opinion leaders. The figure also indicates that these nonopinion leaders often initiate requests for information and supply feedback to the opinion leaders.[29]

Situations in Which Opinion Leadership Occurs

The exchange of advice and information between group members can occur when (1) one individual seeks information from another, (2) one individual volunteers information, and (3) as a by-product of normal group interaction.

Imagine that you are about to make a purchase in a product category with which you are not very familiar. Further imagine that the purchase is important to you—perhaps a new sound system, skis, or a bicycle. How would you go about deciding what type and brand to buy? Chances are you would, among other things, consult someone you know who you believe to be knowledgeable about the product category. This person would be an opinion leader for you. Notice that we have described a *high-involvement* purchase situation in which the purchaser had limited product knowledge about an important

FIGURE 7-4 Mass Communication Information Flows

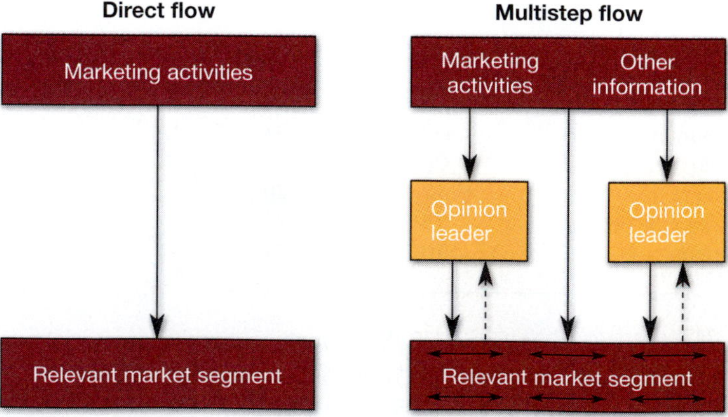

decision. Figure 7-5 illustrates how these factors lead to varying levels of opinion leadership.[30]

In a low-involvement purchase, one is less likely to seek an opinion leader. (Imagine seeking out a friend and asking which brand of wood pencil is best!) However, opinion leaders may well volunteer information on low-involvement products. Of course, such products and purchases would not be low involvement for the opinion leader. For example, many people consider the choice of a plastic or paper grocery bag to be an unimportant (low-involvement) decision. However, a person very interested in the environment might be highly involved with such decisions. Such a person might well seek out information of the environmental consequences of such decisions and provide unsolicited opinions about them.

In addition to *explicitly* seeking or volunteering information, group members provide information to each other through observable behaviors. For example, suppose you visit a friend's house, a digital camera is used to take pictures, and these are then shown on the television screen. You have learned that your friend likes this product and you have gained personal experience with it.

Opinion Leader Characteristics

What characterizes opinion leaders? The most salient characteristic is greater long-term involvement with the product category than the nonopinion leaders in the group. This is referred to as **enduring involvement,** and it leads to enhanced knowledge about and experience with the product category or activity.[31] This knowledge and experience makes opinion leadership possible.[32] Thus, an individual tends to be an opinion leader only for specific product or activity clusters.

Opinion leadership functions primarily through interpersonal communications and observation. These activities occur most frequently among individuals with similar demographic characteristics. Thus, it is not surprising that opinion leaders are found within all demographic segments of the population and seldom differ significantly on demographic

Likelihood of Seeking an Opinion Leader **FIGURE 7-5**

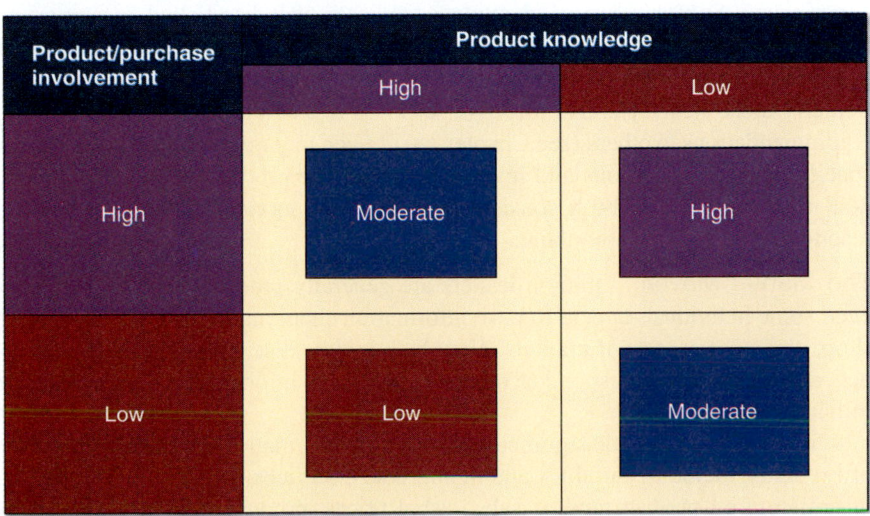

variables from the people they influence. The data below support the idea that people generally seek purchase advice from people like themselves.[33]

Product	Most Trusted Source	
	Men (percent using)	*Women (percent using)*
New doctor	Female relative (26%)	Female relative (29%)
Legal advice	Male relative (26%)	Male relative (31%)
Car mechanic	Male friend (40%)	Male relative (50%)
Restaurant	Female friend (26%)	Female friend (42%)
Movie	Male friend (27%)	Female friend (40%)
Personal loan	No one (29%)	Male relative (33%)
Automobile purchase	No one (31%)	Male relative (46%)
Hair cut	No one (38%)	Female friend (45%)

It is important to note the important role family members play in opinion leadership. Another study has found that family members and close friends are particularly important information sources for difficult decisions for which the consumer has limited prior knowledge.[34]

Opinion leaders tend to be more gregarious than others are. A personality trait, public individuation, also seems to characterize opinion leaders. **Public individuation** is *a willingness to act differently from one's peers even if it attracts attention.*[35] Opinion leaders also have higher levels of exposure to relevant media than do nonopinion leaders.

The findings described above are based primarily on studies conducted in the United States. A study of opinion leadership for personal computers among undergraduate business students in eight countries (Australia, Germany, Hong Kong, India, Indonesia, Korea, New Zealand, and the United States) reached similar conclusions while noting some differences across countries. Expertise (a function of involvement) and sociability were important in all eight countries. In three of the Asian countries (Korea, Indonesia, and India), the opinion leaders tended to be older than those they influenced (in all three countries, a greater value is place on maturity than in most Western countries). In Indonesia, opinion leaders tended to be wealthier than the nonopinion leaders.[36]

In addition to the above individual characteristics associated with opinion leadership, a very important situational characteristic has been identified: the product, service, or store experience.[37] Substantial research evidence indicates that dissatisfied consumers are highly motivated to tell others about the reasons for their dissatisfaction, and these negative messages influence the recipients' attitudes and behaviors. Likewise, satisfied customers, particularly those with a positive affective response to a service, frequently provide positive recommendations to others (see Chapter 18).[38] Such recommendations may influence both specific purchase decisions and involvement with the product category.[39] This phenomenon makes imperative both consistent product and service quality and quick, positive responses to consumer complaints.

The Market Maven Opinion leaders are generally product or activity specific. However, some individuals appear to have information about many kinds of products, places to shop, and other aspects of markets. They both initiate discussions with others about products and shopping and respond to requests for market information. They are referred to as **market mavens.**

Market mavens provide significant amounts of information to others across a wide array of products, including durables and nondurables, services, and store types. They provide information on product quality, sales, usual prices, product availability, store personnel characteristics, and other features of relevance to consumers. Like opinion leaders, market mavens do not differ demographically from those they provide information to except they are more likely to be female.

Although market mavens are demographically similar to others, they have unique media habits. They are extensive users of media, particularly direct mail and homemaking magazines. They also watch television more and listen to the radio more than others. These media patterns provide an avenue for marketers to communicate with this important group.[40] Market mavens also appear to differ on several personality dimensions, including extraversion and conscientiousness.[41]

Market mavens have also been found to exist in industrial markets.[42]

Market Helping Behavior and Purchase Pals Consumers do more than respond to requests for information or volunteer advice. Many consumers engage in **market helping behavior**—*actively helping others acquire goods and services.* We have discussed the provision of various types of information in the previous sections. However, individuals clip coupons, collect information from a variety of sources, visit stores, and buy and return products for others. They teach others how to shop and connect them with helpful salespeople.

Not surprisingly, those who are most active in market helping behaviors have much in common with market mavens and many are market mavens. Others are more narrowly focused on one product category. Marketplace involvement and altruism are the key defining characteristics of those actively engaged in market helping behaviors. This suggests a marketing strategy that appeals to the altruism of those highly involved in the marketplace. This would be similar to the "Friends don't let friends drive drunk" approach. A promotion such as "Bring a senior citizen shopping to the Bon Marche and receive a 10 percent discount on your purchases" would be one approach.[43]

A **purchase pal** is *a person who accompanies another on a shopping trip primarily to aid in the purchase process.* Two types of aid are generally sought and/or provided: symbolic/social and functional/technical. Buyers seeking symbolic or social support (Does this look good on me? Should I really buy this?) tend to request help from close personal sources such as family members or very close friends. The purchase pal must know and understand the buyer's personal needs and use situations. Buyers seeking functional or technical support (Is this a good price? Is this superior quality?) tend to seek help from experts who are often colleagues or acquaintances.

Purchase pals spend the time and effort to help for both personal benefits (ego enhancement and status) and altruism (affection or concern for the shopper). Of course, both motives are frequently involved.[44]

Retailers need to recognize the role of purchase pals and train their sales personnel to effectively consider the role of both the purchaser and the pal. It is particularly important that the salesperson recognize the motive (ego enhancement versus altruism) that is driving the behavior of the pal. For example, ego enhancement motives may cause the pal to recommend more sophisticated or expensive items than the purchaser needs. While this might help make the immediate sale, it could also produce a product return or a dissatisfied customer (who is more likely to blame the store than the pal).

Marketing Strategy and Opinion Leadership

The importance of opinion leadership varies radically from product to product and from target market to target market. Therefore, the initial step in using opinion leaders is to determine—through research, experience, or logic—the role opinion leadership has in the situation at hand. Once this is done, marketing strategies can be devised to make use of opinion leadership.

ILLUSTRATION 7-6

Consumers use personal sources as their primary opinion leaders. However, experts whom they don't know personally can also fill this role. Survey results indicating that the brand is recommended by experts or typical users are also effective.

Courtesy CNS, Inc.

Advertising Advertising attempts to both *stimulate* and *simulate* opinion leadership. Stimulation involves themes designed to encourage current owners to talk about the product/brand or prospective owners to ask current owners for their impressions. Before such a campaign is used, the firm needs to be certain that there is a high degree of satisfaction among existing owners.

Simulating opinion leadership involves having an acknowledged opinion leader—such as Shaquille O'Neill or Sheryl Swoopes for basketball equipment—endorse a brand. Illustration 7-6 is an example of this approach. Or, it can involve having an apparent opinion leader recommend the product in a "slice of life" commercial. These commercials involve an "overheard" conversation between two individuals in which one person provides brand advice to the other. Finally, advertising can present the results of surveys showing that a high percentage of either knowledgeable individuals (9 out of 10 dentists surveyed recommend . . .) or typical users (see Illustration 7-6) recommend the brand.

Product Quality and Customer Complaints An obvious fact that has been confirmed by research is that consumers talk to other consumers about their experiences with products, stores, and services. Therefore, it is absolutely essential that marketers meet or exceed customer expectations concerning their products. When customer expectations are not met, the firm must respond quickly and fairly to customer complaints. Unhappy customers tell an average of nine others about their dissatisfaction.[45] This issue is discussed in detail in Chapter 18.

Marketing Research Since opinion leaders receive, interpret, and relay marketing messages to others, marketing research should focus on opinion leaders rather than "representative" samples in those product categories and groups in which opinion leaders play a critical role. Thus, product-use tests, pretests of advertising copy, and media preference studies should be conducted on samples of individuals likely to be opinion leaders. It is essential that these individuals be exposed to, and respond favorably to, the firm's marketing mix. Of course, for those product categories or groups in which opinion leadership is not important, such a strategy would be unwise.

Product Sampling Sampling—sending a sample of a product to a group of potential consumers—is an effective means of generating interpersonal communications concerning

SAGE ADVANCE CORPORATION
"JUST REWARDS" PROGRAM

We at Sage Advance Corporation have discovered that our satisfied customers have been giving very positive testimonials for our product and referring new customers to us. Our "Just Rewards" Program acknowledges the value of your word-of-mouth referrals. The program also offers you another means to recoup the cost of your Copper Cricket solar water heating system.

WHAT IS THE "JUST REWARDS" PROGRAM?

Sage Advance Corporation will pay a $100 reward to any owner of a Copper Cricket system who introduces the Copper Cricket to another person IF that introduction results in the sale of a new system to that person.

HOW DOES THE PROGRAM WORK?

1. You must be a Copper Cricket Owner.
2. The new purchaser of a Copper Cricket system must identify you as the person who introduced them to the system. The only way to do this is to have the new purchaser fill out the "Just Rewards" card which they then present to the Sage Advance representative at time of purchase. If there is no Sage Advance representative in their area, call Sage Advance direct (503) 485-1947, and we will record your claim in the customer file.
3. You are eligible for the "Just Rewards" Program for two (2) years from the date of your purchase of the Copper Cricket System.
4. The new purchaser can reside in any state of the U.S.A.
5. This $100 reward per system sale is not a rebate or otherwise a part of the sales price of the system.

Sage Advance Corporation is committed to establishing a sustainable energy future. We welcome your assistance in reaching this goal. The rewards for us and you are many. Not only can you help reduce our national dependency on fossil fuels and nuclear energy, you can also reduce your living expenses and make a personal statement about your concern for the future. Pure, safe, renewable solar energy has been, and will continue to be, the public's choice. So, call a friend and share the rewards.

Courtesy Sage Advance Corporation.

ILLUSTRATION 7-7

Positive WOM can be a critical component of the success of a firm. Here Sage Advance tries to encourage its current customers to recommend its system to others.

the product. However, instead of using a random sample, marketers should attempt to send the samples to individuals likely to be opinion leaders.

Chrysler introduced its LH cars by offering the use of a new car to 6,000 presumed opinion leaders for a weekend. These included executives and community leaders. However, it also included less obvious people who often offer advice—for example, barbers. Follow-up research found that over 32,000 people drove or rode in the car, and the positive WOM reached many more.[46]

Retailing/Personal Selling Numerous opportunities exist for retailers and sales personnel to use opinion leadership. Clothing stores can create "fashion advisory boards" composed of likely style leaders from their target market. An example would be cheerleaders and class officers for a store catering to teenagers. Restaurant managers can send special invitations, 2-for-1 meal coupons, and menus to likely leaders in their target markets, such as officers in Junior League, League of Women Voters, and Rotary.

Retailers and sales personnel can encourage their current customers to pass along information to potential new customers. For example, an automobile salesperson, or the dealership, might provide a free car wash or oil change to current customers who send friends in to look at a new car. Real estate agents might send a coupon good for a meal for two at a nice restaurant to customers or other contacts who send them new clients. Illustration 7-7 illustrates one firm's efforts in this area.

TABLE 7-2

Opinion Leadership and Opinion Seeking Scales*

Instructions: This short questionnaire is about _______________ (product category). Please read each statement carefully. For each statement, please circle the number that most closely matches your view of the opinions stated. The items are scaled from 1 to 7, with a higher number meaning stronger agreement.

1. My opinion on _______________ seems not to count with other people.
2. When I consider buying a _______________, I ask other people for advice.
3. When they choose a _______________, other people do not turn to me for advice.
4. I don't need to talk to others before I buy _______________.
5. Other people come to me for advice about choosing _______________.
6. I rarely ask other people what _______________ to buy.
7. People that I know pick _______________ based on what I have told them.
8. I like to get others' opinions before I buy a _______________.
9. I often persuade other people to buy the _______________ that I like.
10. I feel more comfortable buying a _______________ when I have gotten other people's opinions on it.

*Even-numbered items measure opinion seeking and odd-numbered items measure opinion leadership. Scoring needs to be reversed on some items for consistency.

Source: L. A. Flynn, R. E. Goldsmith, and J. K. Eastman, "Opinion Leaders and Opinion Seekers," *Journal of the Academy of Marketing Science,* Academy of Marketing Science, Spring 1996, p. 146.

Identifying Opinion Leaders Opinion leaders can be identified by using sociometric techniques, key informants, and self-designating questionnaires such as the one shown in Table 7-2. While the instrument in Table 7-2 allows you to identify opinion leaders through direct research, what if you want to know who the opinion leaders are for a product on a national scale? Opinion leaders are hard to identify *a priori* because they tend to be demographically similar to those they influence.

The fact that opinion leaders are heavily involved with the mass media, particularly media that focus on their area of leadership, provides a partial solution to the identification problem. For example, Nike could assume that many subscribers to *Runner's World* serve as opinion leaders for jogging and running shoes. Likewise, the fact that opinion leaders tend to be gregarious and tend to belong to clubs and associations suggests that Nike could also consider members, and particularly leaders, of local running clubs to be opinion leaders.

Some product categories have professional opinion leaders. For products related to livestock, county extension agents are generally very influential. Barbers and hair stylists serve as opinion leaders for hair care products. Pharmacists are important opinion leaders for a wide range of health care products. Computer science majors may be natural opinion leaders for other students considering purchasing a personal computer.

Levi Strauss has taken a unique and productive approach to identifying and influencing opinion leaders. In an attempt to increase Dockers preferences among the key 24- to 35-year-old urban market, it has created the position of "urban networker" for such key cities as San Francisco, Chicago, Los Angeles, New York, and Boston. The job of the urban networker is to identify emerging trendsetters in their cities and tie them to Dockers. This could involve noticing a new band that is beginning to catch on and providing the members with Dockers. Or, the networker might sponsor the band or a performance at which the band will perform. Emerging artists, entertainment promoters, athletes, and other potential opinion leaders are contacted and encouraged to wear Dockers and are provided with various types of assistance, not the least of which is connections to other emerging individuals in their field. Emerging events, activities, and charities are also targeted. The objective is not to cause events or stars (which Nike tends to do), but to be associated with emerging urban "happenings" and young influentials as they evolve.[47]

DIFFUSION OF INNOVATIONS

An **innovation** is *an idea, practice, or product perceived to be new by the relevant individual or group.* Whether or not a given product *is* an innovation is determined by the perceptions of the potential market, not by an objective measure of technological change. The manner by which a new product is accepted or spreads through a market is basically a group phenomenon. In this section, we will examine this process in some detail.[48]

Categories of Innovations

Try to recall new products that you have encountered in the past two or three years. As you reflect on these, it may occur to you that there are degrees of innovation. For example, the Internet is more of an innovation than a new fat-free snack. For consumers, changes required in one's behavior (including attitudes and beliefs) or lifestyle if the new product or service is adopted determine the degree of innovation, not the technical or functional changes in the product. Thus, acquiring and using a Philips Audio CD-Recorder to record songs from existing CDs onto blank CDs would not require a significant behavior change for most CD users. However, purchasing and using a computer for the first time requires significant behavior changes.

We can place any new product somewhere on a continuum ranging from no change to radical change, depending on the target market's perception of the item. This continuum is often divided into three categories or types of innovations.

Continuous Innovation Adoption requires relatively minor changes in behavior or changes in behaviors that are unimportant to the consumer. Examples include Pepsi One, and Prang Fun Pro crayons made from soybeans. Illustration 7-8 is another example of a continuous innovation.

Dynamically Continuous Innovation Adoption requires a moderate change in an important behavior or a major change in an area of behavior that is of low or moderate importance to the individual. Examples would include digital cameras, personal navigators, and Internet shopping. Illustration 7-9 shows a product that is a radical technological change but is probably a dynamically continuous innovation for most consumer groups.

Discontinuous Innovation Adoption requires major changes in behavior in an area of significant importance to the individual or group. Examples would include Norplant contraceptive, laser eye surgery, and electric cars.

Keep in mind that both degree of innovation and importance are determined by the consumer. Thus, for consumers deeply involved with photography, the digital camcorder shown in Illustration 7-9 would be a discontinuous innovation.

Most of the more than 20,000 new products or alterations introduced each year tend toward the no-change end of the continuum. Much of the theoretical and empirical research, however, has been based on discontinuous innovations. For example, individual consumers presumably go through a series of very distinct steps or stages known as the **adoption process** when purchasing an innovation. These stages are shown in Figure 7-6.

Figure 7-6 also shows the steps in extended decision making described in Chapter 1. As can be seen, the *adoption process* is basically a term used to describe extended decision

ILLUSTRATION 7-8

The degree to which a product is considered to be an innovation is determined by the market's perception, not the underlying technology. Will consumers consider this to be a radical innovation?

Courtesy Gillette Co.

FIGURE 7-6 Adoption Process and Extended Decision Making

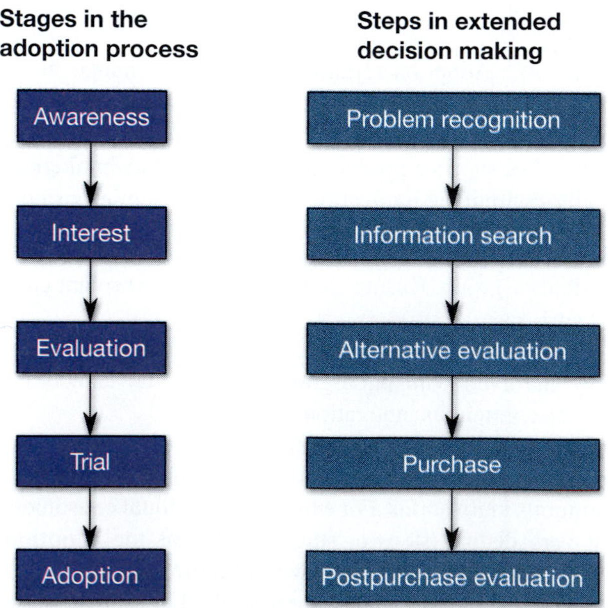

Courtesy of JVC Company of America.

ILLUSTRATION 7-9

This product has significant technological changes that provide it with radically increased capabilities. For some consumers, it will be considered a dynamically continuous innovation, while others will react to it as a discontinuous innovation.

making when a new product is involved. As we will discuss in detail in Chapter 14, extended decision making occurs when the consumer is *highly involved* in the purchase. High purchase involvement is likely for discontinuous innovations such as the decision to purchase an electric car or have laser eye surgery, and most studies of innovations of this nature have found that consumers use extended decision making.

However, it would be a mistake to assume that all innovations are evaluated using extended decision making (the adoption process). In fact, most continuous innovations probably trigger limited decision making. That is, as consumers, we generally don't put a great deal of effort into deciding to purchase such innovations as Hershey Food's new *Marabou Milk* chocolate rolls or the new *Scotch-Brite Never Rust* soap pad.

Diffusion Process

The **diffusion process** is *the manner in which innovations spread throughout a market.* The term *spread* refers to purchase behavior in which the product is purchased with some degree of regularity.[49] The market can range from virtually the entire society (for a new soft drink, perhaps) to the students at a particular junior high (for an automated fast-food and snack outlet).

No matter which innovation is being studied or which social group is involved, the diffusion process appears to follow a similar pattern over time: a period of relatively slow

FIGURE 7-7 Diffusion Rate of an Innovation over Time

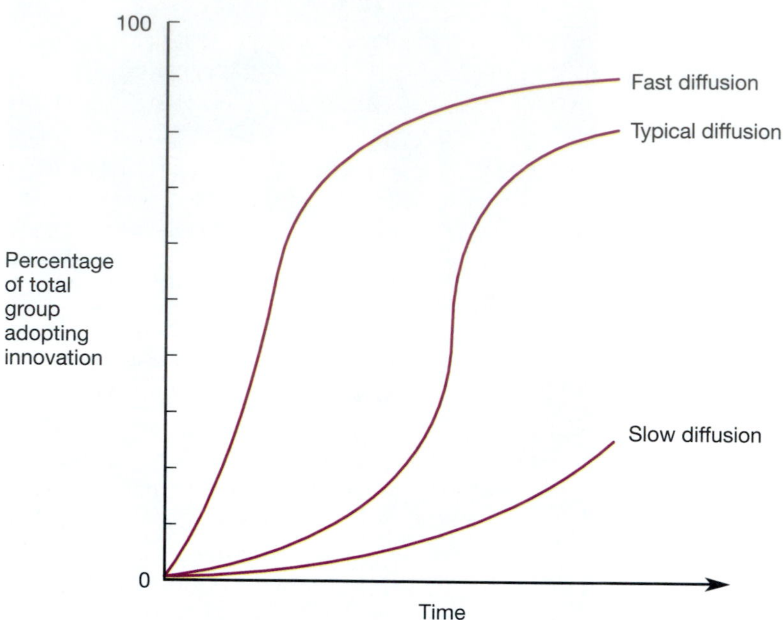

growth, followed by a period of rapid growth, followed by a final period of slower growth. This pattern is shown in Figure 7-7. However, there are exceptions to this pattern. In particular, it appears that for continuous innovations such as new ready-to-eat cereals, the initial slow-growth stage may be skipped.

An overview of innovation studies reveals that the time involved from introduction until a given market segment is saturated (i.e., sales growth has slowed or stopped) varies from a few days or weeks to years. This leads to two interesting questions: (1) What determines how rapidly a particular innovation will spread through a given market segment? and (2) In what ways do those who purchase innovations relatively early differ from those who purchase them later?

Factors Affecting the Spread of Innovations The rate at which an innovation is diffused is a function of 10 factors. We describe each below.

1. *Type of group*. Some groups are more accepting of change than others. In general, young, affluent, and highly educated groups accept change, including new products, readily. Thus, the target market for the innovation is an important determinant of the rate of diffusion.
2. *Type of decision*. The type of decision refers to an individual versus a group decision. The fewer individuals involved in the purchase decision, the more rapidly an innovation will spread. Therefore, innovations likely to involve two or more household members will generally spread slower than innovations that affect primarily one individual.
3. *Marketing effort*. The rate of diffusion is heavily influenced by the extent of marketing effort involved. Thus, the rate of diffusion is not completely beyond the control of the firm.

4. *Fulfillment of felt need.* The more manifest or obvious the need that the innovation satisfies, the faster the diffusion. Rogaine, a cure for some types of hair loss, gained rapid trial among those who are uncomfortable with thin hair or baldness.
5. *Compatibility.* The more the purchase and use of the innovation is consistent with the individual's and group's values or beliefs, the more rapid the diffusion.
6. *Relative advantage.* The better the innovation is perceived to meet the relevant need compared to existing methods, the more rapid the diffusion.[50] Both the performance and the cost of the product are included in relative advantage. Thus, some innovations offering noticeable performance advantages such as CD players for automobiles are accepted slowly or not at all because of a high price. *To succeed, an innovation must have either a performance advantage or a cost advantage.* It is the combination of these two that we call relative advantage.
7. *Complexity.* The more difficult the innovation is to understand and use, the slower the diffusion. The key to this dimension is ease of use, *not* complexity of product. For example, Panasonic's portable videodisk player, while a very complex product, is very simple for most consumers to use.

   Complexity involves both attribute complexity and trade-off complexity. **Attribute complexity** deals with the difficulty encountered in understanding or using the attributes of a product. Many new or novice users may perceive the JVC digital camera as having a high level of attribute complexity. Such consumers may be afraid that they could not understand or properly use such features as "100x digital zoom, and sophisticated effects which offer 18 scene transitions and 12 special effects," or the "docking station, which . . . allows it to perform digital zoom and five other digital effects, all during post production."

   Trade-off complexity refers to the degree and number of conflicting benefits. An electric car has a high degree of trade-off complexity for many consumers because it contains such conflicting attributes as environmental benefits versus range and cost of purchase versus economy of operation.[51]
8. *Observability.* The more easily consumers can observe the positive effects of adopting an innovation, the more rapid its diffusion will be. Cellular telephones are relatively visible. Laser eye surgery, while less visible, may be a frequent topic of conversation. On the other hand, new headache remedies, such as naproxen sodium (*Aleve*), are less obvious and generally less likely to be discussed.
9. *Trialability.* The easier it is to have a low-cost or low-risk trial of the innovation, the more rapid its diffusion. The diffusion of products like laser eye surgery has been hampered by the difficulty of trying out the product in a realistic manner. This is much less of a problem with low-cost items such as headache remedies, or such items as videodisk players that can be rented, borrowed, or tried at a retail outlet.
10. *Perceived risk.* The more risk associated with trying an innovation, the slower the diffusion. Risk can be financial, physical, or social. **Perceived risk** is a function of three dimensions: (1) *the probability that the innovation will not perform as desired;* (2) *the consequences of its not performing as desired;* and (3) *the ability to reverse, and the cost of reversing, any negative consequences.*[52] Thus, many consumers feel a need for the benefits offered by laser eye surgery and view the probability of its working successfully as being quite high. However, they perceive the consequences of failure as being extreme and irreversible and therefore do not adopt this innovation.

An additional type of risk exists for durable technological innovations such as palm computers and videodisk players. Consumers have observed that such products are typically characterized by rapid performance improvements and price declines. Thus, they see

FIGURE 7-8 Diffusion Rates for Popular Consumer Electronics

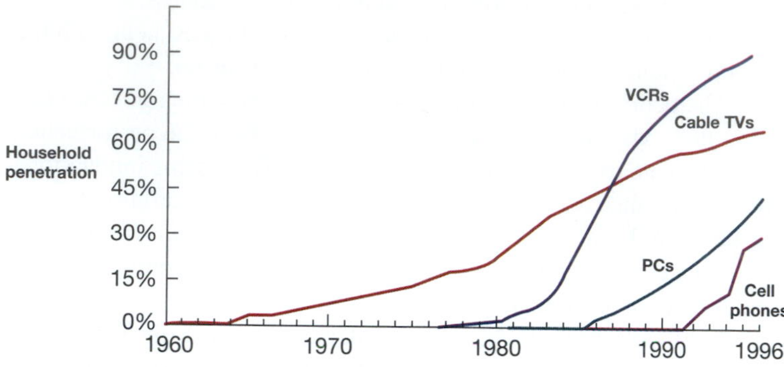

Source: "New Technologies Take Time," p. 8. Reprinted from the April 19, 1999 issue of *Business Week* by special permission. © 1999 McGraw-Hill and Companies, Inc.

FIGURE 7-9 Adoptions of an Innovation over Time

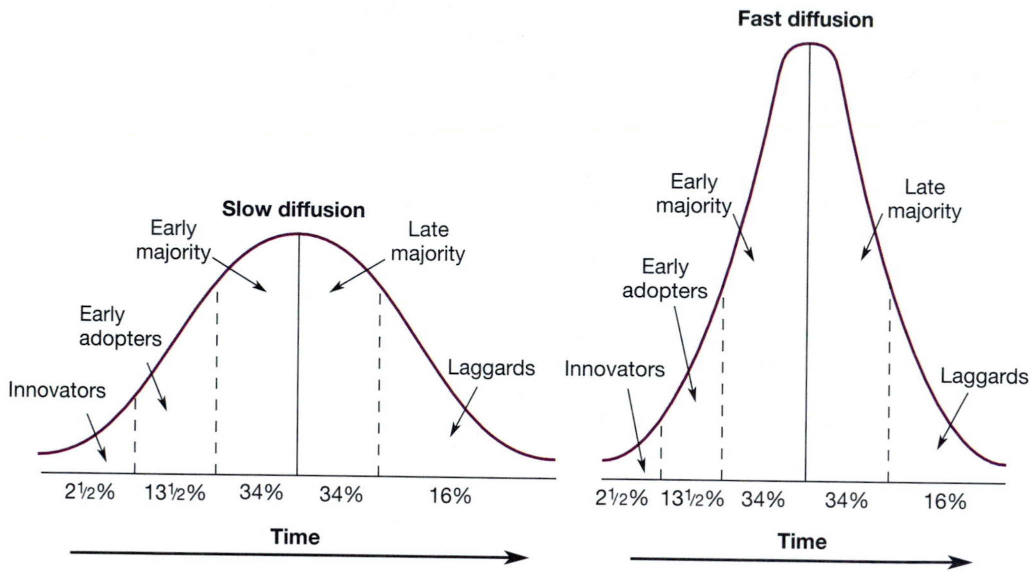

a risk in adopting such products too early and paying "too much" and/or having a product that is soon out-of-date.

Figure 7-8 shows the diffusion curves for four popular consumer electronic products. How would you explain the differences in the rate and level of penetration of U.S. households?

Characteristics of Individuals Who Adopt an Innovation at Varying Points in Time The curves shown in Figures 7-7 and 7-8 are cumulative curves that illustrate the increase in the percentage of adopters over time. If we change those curves from a cumulative format to one that shows the percentage of a market that adopts the innovation at any given point in time, we will have the familiar bell-shaped curves shown in Figure 7-9.

Figure 7-9 reemphasizes the fact that a few individuals adopt an innovation very quickly, another limited group is very reluctant to adopt the innovation, and the majority of the group adopts at some time in between the two extremes.

Researchers have found it useful to divide the adopters of any given innovation into five groups based on the relative time at which they adopt. These groups, called **adopter categories,**[53] are shown in Figure 7-9 and are defined below:

Innovators	The first 2.5 percent to adopt an innovation
Early adopters	The next 13.5 percent to adopt
Early majority	The next 34 percent to adopt
Late majority	The next 34 percent to adopt
Laggards	The final 16 percent to adopt

How do these five groups differ? The first answer is: *It depends on the product category being considered.* Table 7-3 illustrates the rather dramatic differences between early

TABLE 7-3

Early Purchasers of Home Computers and VCRs

	Home Computer	*VCR*
Age*		
18–24	103	163
25–34	113	91
35+	94	84
Education*		
College graduate	179	152
Attended college	125	86
High school	77	92
Marital status*		
Married	209	92
Single	107	136
Products owned†		
Tennis clothing	0	+
Squash racquet	0	–
Water skis	–	+
Target gun	–	+
Bowling ball	–	+
Ski boots	–	0
Luxury car	–	0
Men's diamond ring	–	+
Classical folk records/tapes	0	–
Contemporary jazz records/tapes	–	0
Book club	0	–
Solar heating	+	–
Food dehydrator	+	–
Electric ice-cream maker	–	+

*Results are index numbers, where 100 equals average consumption.

† + = Heavy consumption; 0 = Moderate consumption; and – = Light consumption

Source: A. J. Kover, "Somebody Buys New Products Early—But Who?" Unpublished paper prepared for Cunningham & Walsh, Inc.

purchasers of home computers and VCRs.[54] Thus, while we propose some broad generalizations, they may not hold true for a particular product category.

Innovators are venturesome risk takers. They are capable of absorbing the financial and social costs of adopting an unsuccessful product. They are cosmopolitan in outlook and use other innovators rather than local peers as a reference group. They tend to be younger, better educated, and more socially mobile than their peers. Innovators make extensive use of commercial media, sales personnel, and professional sources in learning of new products.

Early adopters tend to be opinion leaders in local reference groups. They are successful, well educated, and somewhat younger than their peers. They are willing to take a calculated risk on an innovation but are concerned with failure. Early adopters also use commercial, professional, and interpersonal information sources, and they provide information to others.

Early majority consumers tend to be cautious with respect to innovations. They adopt sooner than most of their social group but also after the innovation has proven successful with others. They are socially active but seldom leaders. They tend to be somewhat older, less well educated, and less socially mobile than the early adopters. The early majority relies heavily on interpersonal sources of information.

Late majority members are skeptical about innovations. They often adopt more in response to social pressures or a decreased availability of the previous product than because of a positive evaluation of the innovation. They tend to be older and have less social status and mobility than those who adopt earlier.

Laggards are locally oriented and engage in limited social interaction. They tend to be relatively dogmatic and oriented toward the past. Innovations are adopted only with reluctance.

TABLE 7-4

Innovation Analysis and Diffusion Enhancement Strategies

Diffusion Determinant	*Diffusion Inhibitor*	*Diffusion Enhancement Strategies*
1. Nature of group	Conservative	Search for other markets Target innovators within group
2. Type of decision	Group	Choose media to reach all deciders Provide conflict reduction themes
3. Marketing effort	Limited	Target innovators within group Use regional rollout
4. Felt need	Weak	Extensive advertising showing importance of benefits
5. Compatibility	Conflict	Stress attributes consistent with values norms
6. Relative advantage	Low	Lower price Redesign product
7. Complexity	High	Distribute through high-service outlets Use skilled sales force Use product demonstrations Extensive marketing efforts
8. Observability	Low	Use extensive advertising
9. Trialability	Difficult	Use free samples to early adopter types Special prices to rental agencies Use high-service outlets
10. Perceived risk	High	Success documentation Endorsement by credible sources Guarantees

Marketing Strategies and the Diffusion Process

Market Segmentation The fact that earlier purchasers of an innovation differ from later purchasers suggests a "moving target market" approach. That is, after a general target market is selected, the firm should initially focus on those individuals within the target market most likely to be innovators and early adopters.[55]

Messages to this group can often stress the newness and innovative characteristics of the product as well as its functional features. Since this group is frequently very involved with, and knowledgeable about, the product category,[56] marketing communications may be able to focus on the new technical features of the product and rely on the audience to understand the benefits these features will provide.

As the innovation gains acceptance, the focus of attention should shift to the early and late majority. This will frequently require different media. In addition, message themes should generally move away from a focus on radical newness. Instead, they should stress the acceptance the product has gained and its proven performance record.

Diffusion Enhancement Strategies Table 7-4 provides a framework for developing strategies to enhance the market acceptance of an innovation. The critical aspect of this process is to analyze the innovation *from the target market's perspective*. This analysis will indicate potential obstacles—*diffusion inhibitors*—to rapid market acceptance. The

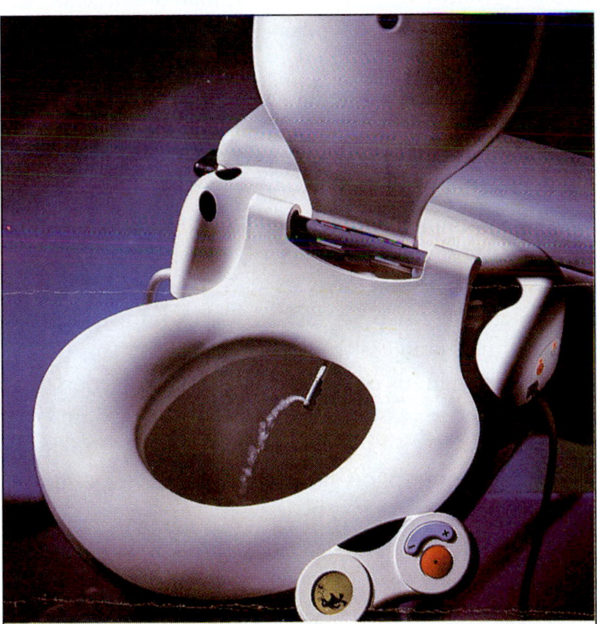

Toto U.S.A.

ILLUSTRATION 7-10

Ten factors determine the success of innovations. How do you think this innovation will fare based on these factors?

manager's task is then to overcome these inhibitors with *diffusion enhancement strategies*.[57] Table 7-4 lists a number of potential enhancement strategies. Many others are possible.

Of course, one would want as much research as practical to determine the way the target market is likely to perceive an innovation as well as its reactions to the various potential diffusion enhancement strategies. However, even in the absence of research, this approach can uncover weaknesses in an innovation as well as suggest strategies to overcome them. Consider the innovation shown in Illustration 7-10. Which factors will inhibit its diffusion and what strategies can be used to overcome them?

SUMMARY

A group in its broadest sense includes two or more individuals who share a set of norms, values, or beliefs and have certain implicit or explicit relationships such that their behaviors are interdependent. Some groups require membership; others (e.g., aspiration groups) do not. The nature of contact is based on the degree of interpersonal contact. Groups that have frequent personal contact are called primary groups, while those with limited interpersonal contact are called secondary groups. Attraction refers to the degree of positive or negative desirability the group has to the individual.

Norms are general expectations about behaviors that are deemed appropriate for all persons in a social context, regardless of the position they hold. Norms arise quickly and naturally in any group situation. The degree of conformity to group norms is a function of (1) the visibility of the usage situation, (2) the level of commitment the individual feels to the group, (3) the relevance of the behavior to the functioning of the group, (4) the individual's confidence in his or her own judgment in the area, and (5) the necessity/nonnecessity nature of the product.

A consumption-based group or consumption subculture is a distinctive subgroup of society that self-selects on the basis of a shared commitment to a particular product, brand, or consumption activity. These subcultures also have (1) an identifiable, hierarchical social structure, (2) a set of shared beliefs or values, and (3) unique jargon, rituals, and modes of symbolic expression.

Consumption subcultures are important to marketers because (1) sometimes a brand (for example, Harley-Davidson) is the basis for the subculture, (2) the subcultures require products to perform the activities on which they are based and to signal membership and status, (3) these products sometimes become appropriated by the mass market, and (4) the consumption of some products are or can become part of the consumption ritual for other products or for specific situations.

Group influence varies across situations. Informational influence occurs when individuals simply acquire information shared by group members. Normative influence happens when an individual conforms to group expectations to gain approval or avoid disapproval. Identification influence exists when an individual identifies with the group norms as a part of his or her self-concept and identity.

Communication within groups is a major source of information about certain products. It is a particularly important source when an individual has a high level of *purchase involvement* and a low level of *product knowledge*. In such cases, the consumer is likely to seek information from a more knowledgeable group member. This person is known as an *opinion leader*. Opinion leaders are sought out for information, and they also volunteer information. Of course, substantial product information is exchanged during normal group interactions.

Opinion leaders are product-category or activity-group specific. They tend to have greater product knowledge, more exposure to relevant media, and more gregarious personalities than their followers. They tend to have demographics similar to their followers. A situational variable, *product dissatisfaction,* motivates many individuals to become temporary opinion leaders. The term *market maven* is used to describe individuals who are opinion leaders about the shopping process in general.

Many consumers engage in *market helping behavior*—actively helping others acquire goods or services. Others serve as *purchase pals*—a person who accompanies another on a shopping trip primarily to aid in the purchase process.

Marketers attempt to identify opinion leaders primarily through their media habits and social activities. Identified opinion leaders then can be used in marketing research, product sampling, retailing/personal selling, and advertising.

Groups greatly affect the diffusion of innovations. *Innovations* vary in degree of behavioral change required and the rate at which they are diffused. The first purchasers of an innovative product or service are termed *innovators;* those who follow over time are known as *early adopters, early majority, late majority,* and *laggards*. Each of these groups differs in terms of personality, age, education, and reference group membership. These characteristics help marketers identify and appeal to different classes of adopters at different stages of an innovation's diffusion.

The time it takes for an innovation to spread from innovators to laggards is affected by several factors: (1) nature of the group involved; (2) type of innovation decision required; (3) extent of marketing effort; (4) strength of felt need; (5) compatibility of the innovation with existing values; (6) relative advantage; (7) complexity of the innovation; (8) ease in observing usage of the innovation; (9) ease in trying the innovation; and (10) perceived risk in trying the innovation.

KEY TERMS

Adopter categories 253
Adoption process 247
Asch phenomenon 236
Aspiration reference group 227
Attribute complexity 251
Consumption subculture 228
Diffusion process 249
Dissociative reference group 227
Early adopters 254
Early majority 254
Enduring involvement 241
Group 226
Identification influence 233
Information influence 232
Innovation 247
Innovators 254
Laggards 254
Late majority 254
Market helping behavior 243
Market maven 242
Multistep flow of communication 240
Norm 232
Normative influence 233
Opinion leader 240
Perceived risk 251
Primary group 227
Public individuation 242
Purchase pal 243
Reference group 226
Secondary group 227
Trade-off complexity 251
Two-step flow of communication 240
Word-of-mouth (WOM) communication 239

INTERNET EXERCISES

1. Monitor a chat group or bulletin board on a topic that interests you for a week. Are the participants in this activity a group? A reference group? A virtual community?
2. Find a consumption-based group or subculture that uses the Internet as one means of communication. What can you learn about this group by monitoring the Internet?
3. Find and describe an example of a marketer using the Internet to encourage the formation or communications of a group or consumption subculture around its product.
4. Find and describe evidence of market maven and/or everyday market helping behavior on the Internet.
5. Find and describe two examples of opinion leadership and two examples of seeking an opinion leader on the Internet.
6. Pick a very recent innovation of interest. Prepare a report on the information available about this innovation on the Internet.

DDB NEEDHAM LIFESTYLE DATA ANALYSES

1. Use the DDB Needham data to determine the characteristics of likely innovators for the following. Why is this the case? What are the marketing implications?
   a. Foods
   b. New products in general
2. Based on the DDB Needham data, what characterizes one who is likely to be an opinion leader for new movies? Why is this the case? What are the marketing implications?
3. What characterizes one who is likely to be a late adopter or laggard for many items (see Tables 1a, 2a, 3a, 4a, 5a, 6a, and 7a)? Why is this the case? What are the marketing implications?

REVIEW QUESTIONS

1. How does a *group* differ from a *reference group?*
2. What criteria are used by marketers to classify groups?
3. What is a *dissociative reference group?* In what way can dissociative reference groups influence consumer behavior?
4. What is an *aspiration reference group?* How can an aspiration reference group influence behavior?
5. What factors determine the degree of influence a reference group will have on a given consumer decision?
6. What is a *consumption-based group* or a *consumption subculture*? What are the characteristics of such a group?
7. How can marketers develop strategy based on consumption subcultures?
8. What types of group influence exist? Why must a marketing manager be aware of these separate types of group influence?
9. What five factors determine the strength of reference group influence in a situation?
10. What is the *Asch phenomenon* and how do marketers utilize it?
11. How can a marketer use knowledge of reference group influences to develop advertising strategies?
12. What is an *opinion leader?* How does an opinion leader relate to the *multistep flow of communication?*
13. What characterizes an opinion leader?
14. What determines the likelihood that a consumer will seek information from an opinion leader?
15. How does a *market maven* differ from an *opinion leader?*
16. What is a *purchase pal?* What are the marketing implications of purchase pals?
17. What is *market helping behavior?* Why is it important to marketers?
18. How can marketing managers identify opinion leaders?
19. How can marketers utilize opinion leaders?
20. What is an *innovation?* Who determines whether a given product is an innovation?
21. What are the various categories of innovations? How do they differ?
22. What is the *diffusion process*? What pattern does the diffusion process appear to follow over time?
23. Describe the factors that affect the diffusion rate for an innovation. How can these factors be utilized in developing marketing strategy?
24. What are *adopter* categories? Describe each of the adopter categories.
25. How can a marketer use knowledge of adopter categories to develop marketing strategy?

DISCUSSION QUESTIONS

26. Using college students as the market segment, describe the most relevant reference group(s) and indicate the probable degree of influence for each of the following decisions:
    a. Brand of toothpaste
    b. Purchase of life insurance

REFERENCES

1. J. W. Schouten and J. H. McAlexander, "Subcultures of Consumption," *Journal of Consumer Research,* June 1995, pp. 43–61.
2. B. G. Englis and M. R. Solomon, "To Be *and* Not to Be," *Journal of Advertising,* Spring 1995, pp. 13–28.
3. Footnote 1, p. 43.
4. K. J. Fox, "Real Punks and Pretenders," *Journal of Contemporary Ethnology,* October 1987, pp. 344–70.
5. C. B. Bhattacharya, H. Rao, and M. A. Glynn, "Understanding the Bond of Identification," *Journal of Marketing Research,* October 1995, pp. 46–57.
6. A. M. Klein, "Pumping Iron," *Sociology of Sport Journal,* June 1986, pp. 68–75.
7. B. Gainer, "Ritual and Relationships," *Journal of Business Research,* March 1995, pp. 253–60. See also E. J. Arnould and P. L. Price, "River Magic," *Journal of Consumer Research,* June 1993, pp. 24–45.
8. See R. J. Fisher, "Group-Derived Consumption," in *Advances in Consumer Research XXV,* ed. J. W. Alba and J. W. Hutchinson (Provo, UT: Association for Consumer Research, 1998), pp. 283–88; and R. J. Fisher and K. Wakefield, "Factors Leading to Group Identification," *Psychology & Marketing,* January 1998, pp. 23–40.
9. Footnote 1, p. 58.
10. G. McCracken, "Culture and Consumption," *Journal of Consumer Research,* June 1985, pp. 71–84; and E. M. Blair and M. N. Hatala, "The Use of Rap Music in Children's Advertising," in *Advances in Consumer Research XIX*, ed. J. F. Sherry, Jr., and B. Sternthal (Provo, UT: Association for Consumer Research, 1992), pp. 719–24.
11. See W. O. Bearden, R. G. Netemeyer, and J. E. Teel, "Further Validations of the Consumer Susceptibility to Influence Scale," in *Advances in Consumer Research XVII,* ed. M. E. Goldberg, G. Gorn, and R. W. Pollay (Provo, UT: Association for Consumer Research, 1990), pp. 770–76; and O. A. J. Mascarenhas and M. A. Higby, "Peer, Parent, and Media Influences in Teen Apparel Shopping," *Journal of the Academy of Marketing Science,* Winter 1993, pp. 53–58.
12. M. Kuntz, "The New Hucksterism," *Business Week,* July 1, 1996, p. 79; and C. Walker, "Word of Mouth," *American Demographics,* July 1995, p. 44.
13. See R. J. Fisher and D. Ackerman, "The Effects of Recognition and Group Need on Volunteerism," *Journal of Consumer Research,* December 1998, pp. 262–77.
14. P. W. Miniard and J. P. Cohen, "Modeling Personal and Normative Influences on Behavior," *Journal of Consumer Research,* September 1983, pp. 169–80. See also D. F. Midgley, G. R. Dowling, and P. D. Morrison, "Consumer Types, Social Influence, Information Search and Choice," in *Advances in Consumer Research XVI,* ed. T. K. Srull (Provo, UT: Association for Consumer Research, 1989), pp. 137–43.
15. See also T. L. Childers and A. R. Rao, "The Influence of Familial and Peer-Based Reference Groups on Consumer Decisions," *Journal of Consumer Research,* September 1992, pp. 198–211.
16. See E. Day and M. R. Stafford, "Age-Related Cues in Retail Services Advertising," *Journal of Retailing,* no. 2 (1997), pp. 211–33.
17. C. Webster and J. B. Faircloth III, "The Role of Hispanic Ethnic Identification on Reference Group Influence," in *Advances in Consumer Research XXI,* ed. C. T. Allen and D. R. John (Provo UT: Association for Consumer Research, 1994), pp. 458–63.
18. See D. N. Lascu, W. O. Bearden, and R. L. Rose, "Norm Extreme and Interpersonal Influences on Consumer Conformity," *Journal of Business Research,* March 1995, pp. 201–13; L. R. Kahle, "Role-Relaxed Consumers," *Journal of Advertising Research,* May 1995, pp. 59–62; and B. D. Keillor, R. S. Parker, and A. Schaefer, "Influences on Adolescent Brand Preferences," *Journal of Advertising Research,* May 1996, pp. 47–56.
19. P. Choong and K. R. Lord, "Experts and Novices and Their Use of Reference Groups," *Enhancing Knowledge Development in Marketing* (Chicago: American Marketing Association, 1996), pp. 203–8.
20. Lascu, Bearden, and Rose, footnote 18. See also P. F. Bone, "Word-of-Mouth Effects on Short-Term and Long-Term Product Judgments," *Journal of Business Research,* March 1995, pp. 213–23.
21. J. K. Frenzen and H. L. Davis, "Purchasing Behavior in Embedded Markets," *Journal of Consumer Research,* June 1990, pp. 1–12.
22. See R. L. Rose, W. O. Bearden, and J. E. Teel, "An Attributional Analysis of Resistance to Pressure Regarding Illicit Drug and Alcohol Consumption," *Journal of Consumer Research,* June 1992, pp. 1–13.
23. C. Pechmann, "The Effects of Antismoking and Cigarette Advertising on Young Adolescents' Perceptions of Peers Who Smoke," *Journal of Consumer Research,* September 1994, pp. 236–51. See also D. D. Schoenbachler and T. E. Whittler, "Adolescent Processing of Social and Physical Threat Communications," *Journal of Advertising,* Winter 1996, pp. 37–54.
24. C. Walker, "Word of Mouth," *American Demographics,* July 1995, p. 38.
25. C. Fisher, "Wal-Mart's Way," *Advertising Age,* February 18, 1991, p. 3.
26. See P. M. Herr, F. R. Kardes, and J. Kim, "Effects of Word-of-Mouth and Product-Attribute Information on Persuasion," *Journal of Consumer Research,* March 1991, pp. 454–62.
27. Footnote 24, p. 40.
28. P. H. Reingen and J. B. Kernan, "Analysis of Referral Networks in Marketing," *Journal of Marketing Research,* November 1986, pp. 370–78.
29. See L. J. Yale and M. C. Gilly, "Dyadic Perceptions in Personal Source Information Search," *Journal of Business Research,* March 1995, pp. 225–37.
30. For a thorough discussion, see D. F. Duhan, S. D. Johnson, J. B. Wilcox, and G. D. Harrell, "Influences on Consumer Use of

Word-of-Mouth Recommendation Sources," *Journal of the Academy of Marketing Science,* Fall 1997, pp. 283–95.

31. G. M. Rose, L. R. Kahle, and A. Shoham, "The Influence of Employment-Status and Personal Values on Time Related Food Consumption Behavior and Opinion Leadership," in *Advances in Consumer Research XXII,* ed. F. R. Kardes and M. Sujan (Provo, UT: Association for Consumer Research, 1995), pp. 367–72; and U. M. Dholakia, "Involvement-Response Models of Joint Effects," in *Advances in Consumer Research XXV,* ed. J. W. Alba and J. W. Hutchinson (Provo, UT: Association for Consumer Research, 1998), pp. 499–506.
32. See M. C. Gilly, J. L. Graham, M. F. Wolfinbarger, and L. J. Yale, "A Dyadic Study of Interpersonal Information Search," *Journal of the Academy of Marketing Science,* Spring 1998, pp. 83–100.
33. Footnote 24, p. 44.
34. D. F. Duhan, S. D. Johnson, J. B. Wilcox, and G. D. Harrell, "Influences on Consumer Use of Word-of-Mouth Recommendation Sources," *Journal of the Academy of Marketing Science,* Fall 1997, pp. 283–95.
35. K. K. Chan and S. Misra, "Characteristics of the Opinion Leader," *Journal of Advertising,* no. 3 (1990), pp. 53–60.
36. R. Marshall and I. Gitosudarmo, "Variation in the Characteristics of Opinion Leaders across Borders," *Journal of International Consumer Marketing* 8, no. 1 (1995), pp. 5–22.
37. See D. S. Sundaram, K. Mitra, and C. Webster, "Word-of-Mouth Communications," in *Advances in Consumer Research XXV,* ed. J. W. Alba and J. W. Hutchinson (Provo, UT: Association for Consumer Research, 1998), pp. 527–31.
38. M. Johnson, G. M. Zinkhan, and G. S. Ayala, "The Impact of Outcome, Competency, and Affect on Service Referral," *Journal of Services Marketing,* no. 5 (1998), pp. 397–415.
39. J. L. Giese, E. R. Spangenberg, and A. E. Crowley, "Effects of Product-Specific Word-of-Mouth Communication on Product Category Involvement," *Marketing Letters,* no. 2 (1996), pp. 187–99.
40. L. F. Feick and L. L. Price, "The Market Maven," *Journal of Marketing,* January 1987, pp. 83–97. See also R. A. Higie, L. F. Feick, and L. L. Price, "Types and Amount of Word-of-Mouth Communications about Retailers," *Journal of Retailing,* Fall 1987, pp. 260–78; M. E. Slama and T. G. Williams, "Generalization of the Market Maven's Information Tendency across Product Categories," in *Advances in Consumer Research XVII,* ed. M. E. Goldberg, G. Gorn, and R. W. Pollay (Provo, UT: Association for Consumer Research, 1990), pp. 48–52; K. C. Schneider and W. C. Rodgers, "Generalized Marketplace Influencers' Attitudes toward Direct Mail as a Source of Information," *Journal of Direct Marketing,* Autumn 1993, pp. 20–28; and J. E. Urbany, P. R. Dickson, and R. Kalapurakal, "Price Search in the Retail Grocery Market," *Journal of Marketing,* April 1996, pp. 91–104.
41. T. A. Mooradian, "The Five Factor Model and Market Mavenism," in *Advances in Consumer Research XXIII,* ed. K. P. Corfman and J. G. Lynch (Provo, UT: Association for Consumer Research, 1996), pp. 260–63.
42. R. Nataraajan and M. G. Angur, "A Quest for the 'Industrial Maven,'" *Industrial Marketing Management,* July 1997, pp. 353–62.
43. L. L. Price, L. F. Feick, and A. Guskey, "Everyday Market Helping Behavior," *Journal of Public Policy & Marketing,* Fall 1995, pp. 255–66.
44. C. L. Hartman and P. Kiecker, "Buyers and Their Purchase Pals," in *Enhancing Knowledge Development in Marketing,* ed. R. Achrol and A. Mitchell (Chicago: American Marketing Association, 1994), pp. 138–44; and P. Kiecker and C. L. Hartman, "Predicting Buyers' Selection of Interpersonal Sources," in *Advances in Consumer Research XXI,* ed. C. T. Allen and D. R. John (Provo, UT: Association for Consumer Research, 1994), pp. 464–69.
45. Footnote 24, p. 40.
46. Footnote 24, p. 44.
47. A. Z. Cuneo, "Dockers Strives for Urban Credibility," *Advertising Age,* May 25, 1998, p. 6.
48. See also E. M. Rogers, *Diffusion of Innovations* (New York: Free Press, 1983); H. Gatignon and T. S. Robertson, "A Propositional Inventory for New Diffusion Research," *Journal of Consumer Research,* March 1985, pp. 849–67; and V. Mahajan, E. Muller, and F. M. Bass, "New Product Diffusion Models in Marketing," *Journal of Marketing,* January 1990, pp. 1–26.
49. See M. I. Nabith, S. G. Bloem, and T. B. C. Poiesz, "Conceptual Issues in the Study of Innovation Adoption Behavior," in *Advances in Consumer Research XXIV,* ed. M. Bruck and D. J. MacInnis (Provo, UT: Association for Consumer Research, 1997), pp. 190–96.
50. See M. A. Eastlick, "Predictors of Videotex Adoption," *Journal of Direct Marketing,* Summer 1993, pp. 66–74.
51. For another type of complexity, see D. G. Mick and S. Fournier, "Paradoxes of Technology," *Journal of Consumer Research,* September 1998, pp. 123–43.
52. For a more complete analysis, see U. M. Dholakia, "An Investigation of the Relationship between Perceived Risk and Product Involvement," in *Advances in Consumer Research XXIV,* ed. M. Bruck and D. J. MacInnis (Provo, UT: Association for Consumer Research, 1997), pp. 159–67.
53. For different schemes, see V. Mahajan, E. Muller, and R. K. Srivastava, "Determination of Adopter Categories by Using Innovation Diffusion Models," *Journal of Marketing Research,* February 1990, pp. 37–50; and D. M. Midgley and G. R. Dowling, "A Longitudinal Study of Product Form Innovation," *Journal of Consumer Research,* March 1993, pp. 1–25.
54. See also M. P. Venkatraman, "The Impact of Innovativeness and Innovation Type on Adoption," *Journal of Retailing,* Spring 1991, pp. 51–67.
55. For a discussion of when this is not appropriate, see V. Mahajan and E. Muller, "When Is It Worthwhile Targeting the Majority Instead of the Innovators in a New Product Launch," *Journal Marketing Research,* November 1998, pp. 488–95.
56. See S. Ram and H. Jung, "Innovativeness in Product Usage," *Psychology & Marketing,* January 1994, pp. 57–67.
57. For a similar but distinct approach, see J. N. Sheth, "Consumer Resistance to Innovations," *Journal of Consumer Marketing,* Spring 1989, pp. 5–14.

Cases

2-1 The Copper Cricket

Bob Block, president of Sage Advance, which manufactures and markets the Copper Cricket (a patented geyser-pumping solar water heater for home use), describes the history of the firm as follows:

> By November 1986, after working for three years, Eldon Haines and I were looking over the edge of frustration. Eldon, a nuclear chemist from the Jet Propulsion Lab, had invented geyser pumping with a friend in 1979. He dabbled with it for a few years, and in 1983 we built the first working prototype. By the end of 1984, we had a patent and were searching for licensees for the technology.
>
> In 1985, the worst fears of the solar industry were realized; the tax credits were canceled, and within the next year 85 percent of the solar manufacturers disappeared. We were ready with our new product and no one was around to manufacture it. We built about 30 systems and sold them to individuals who had written to us after reading about the technology in *New Shelter* magazine. All of those systems are still out there and working perfectly.
>
> While walking one rainy autumn night, around midnight I realized that we had to do something. We were at the lowest point in the solar market in 20 years and yet we had a great new technology. Our altruistic investors were morally supportive but didn't have any more discretionary capital to invest in our rapidly decaying personal energy. Our board of directors had effectively disbanded, and we were two scientists with no desire to become businessmen.
>
> The next day I offered a plan to Eldon: We should start a new company to manufacture the geyser pump, join up with some businesspeople who know marketing and manufacturing, build a production prototype and write a business plan. We found two people who were perfect; one had just lost his own solar manufacturing company to the tax credits and the other had a still-successful solar engineering and sales firm. We put together $10,000 that we borrowed from family and friends and wrote our plan.

The new firm was named Sage Advance, and the geyser-pump-driven solar hot water system was named the Copper Cricket. Despite Bob and Eldon's enthusiasm and the experience of their new partners, the firm was not at the break-even sales level as of January 1, 1994.

The Product

The geyser pump is protected by a strong patent. The absence of moving parts, zero maintenance requirements, and the fact that it is freezeproof are significant advantages over all other systems on the market.

The Copper Cricket, at about $2,100, costs somewhat more than competitive systems. It can provide over half the hot water used by a family of four (47 percent in Boston to 95 percent in Phoenix). It saves $100 per year in electricity bills in Portland, Oregon (those figures vary, depending on the climate and utility rates).

The Copper Cricket can be installed in an existing home. In fact, many are installed by do-it-yourselfers. Of course, they can also be installed in new construction.

The virtues of the Copper Cricket have been widely recognized. *Popular Science* named it one of 1989s "Greatest Achievements in Science and Technology." Christopher Flavin of the World Watch Institute describes it as "the most cost-effective solar hot water system to be developed in the last decade." Amory Lovins, director of the Rocky Mountain Institute, says: "It's what solar always should have been. Personally, I'd recommend it as the best system on the market." A recent survey of Copper Cricket owners found that 98 percent would recommend the product to a friend.

The Environment

The energy crises of the late 1970s and early 1980s coupled with the federal government's and many states' tax credit programs created a huge market for solar energy systems, particularly solar water heating systems. Hundreds of firms began to produce such systems. Unfortunately, many of them produced systems that were inefficient, flawed, subject to freezing, or that required extensive maintenance. The easing of the energy crisis and the removal of the federal tax credit program in 1985 devastated the industry. Within a year, approximately 90 percent of the solar water heater producers dropped out of the business. Unfortunately, tens of thousands of poorly performing systems had been sold. Both consumers and distributors were left holding the bag.

In December 1993, the market picture was uncertain. The environment was a major concern, and both nuclear- and coal-based energy generation were under attack. However, in recent elections, most "green" initiatives nationwide had failed (many by votes of two to one). The Persian Gulf crisis had increased fuel prices, but they were again quite low. The lingering recession had consumers nervous about capital outlays.

Marketing Efforts

The firm's marketing efforts have been extremely limited due to its severe cash flow problems. A significant percent of the firm's sales occur in Oregon, where the firm is headquartered. Oregon also has an energy tax credit program. In Oregon, the Copper Cricket has been advertised in newspapers, on radio, and via direct mail. The product is also shown at home shows, which appears to be particularly effective.

Sage Advance has developed a high-quality four-page brochure and a one-page ad slick for mass mailings and to hand out at trade and home shows. It has also developed a direct-mail program and newspaper ads for its dealers to use.

Unfortunately, Sage's attempts to attract dealers have not been very successful. It is attempting to secure distributors (individuals) who will both sell the system to homeowners and set up a group of retail dealers within a defined geographic area. Despite a training program and generous commissions, few effective distributors have signed on. (Two large manufacturers who survived the 1985 shakeout have substantial distribution and sales despite having a less advanced product.)

At the national and regional levels, the product and company have received substantial publicity. Two articles on the Copper Cricket appeared in *Popular Science* in 1989 (July and December). These produced over 1,000 inquiries. The product has also appeared in the *Environmental Products Resource Guide, Brown's Business Reports, Pacific Northwest Magazine,* and numerous newspapers and trade periodicals.

To encourage word-of-mouth communications, Sage will pay Copper Cricket owners $100 for a referral that results in a sale (see Illustration 7-7, p. 245). So far, this has produced relatively few sales.

Sage is also working with a number of large electrical utilities. Many utilities now sponsor programs to conserve energy, and several are evaluating the Copper Cricket as a means to this end. A standard program would involve the utility's underwriting part of the cost of the system and/or providing financing at a very low rate. However, utilities generally make such decisions only after observing a new system in use under controlled conditions for several years.

The January 1994 Board Meeting

The board of directors left the January 1994 board meeting with mixed emotions. They were thrilled that Sage had shown its first quarterly profit in the last quarter of 1993. Sales projections were also strong for 1994. However, cash was perilously low and the management team had not been paid their full salaries for several years. This resulted in a large "deferred salaries" liability on the balance sheet that was hampering new fund-raising efforts. Management remained convinced that all that stood between the firm and significant success was enough cash to launch a major marketing program.

There was some concern among the board members about launching a sizable program. Current sales were strong only in Oregon, though they were projected to expand significantly into other states in the Northwest. Pacific Power recently certified the Copper Cricket as the first solar water heater eligible for an $800 rebate under its Super Good Cents program. While this was good news, the board was concerned about the permanence of Pacific Power's program and Sage's inability to successfully market the Copper Cricket in the absence of government or utility rebates. The need for a profitable 1994 appeared essential for the future of Sage Advance.

Discussion Questions

1. Conduct an innovation analysis of the Copper Cricket using Table 7-4 as the basis. What insights does the innovation analysis provide into its slow sales growth?
2. What strategies does the innovation analysis suggest to increase the diffusion of the Copper Cricket?

3. Evaluate Sage's attempt to increase word-of-mouth communications (see Illustration 7-7). How would you improve its effectiveness?
4. Who do you think the innovators are for this product? How will they differ from the early adopters? The early majority?
5. Would an environmental theme or an economic theme be most effective for the Copper Cricket in 1994? (Fewer than 1,800 units have been sold.)
6. Evaluate the effectiveness of an appeal claiming that, for a particular region of the country, a $2,000 purchase of a Copper Cricket is better than a certificate of deposit (or savings account) paying 9 percent tax free because the Copper Cricket will save $200 per year in electricity (a 10 percent tax-free return).

2-2 Norelco's Advantage Razor Introduction

While electric razors represent a $400 million market, less than a third of U.S. males use electric shavers and only one in seven females use them. Norelco dominates the men's segment, followed by Remington, Braun, and Panasonic. Remington, Norelco, and Panasonic had major shares of the women's market until 1998.

In the early 1990s, electric razor marketers sharply increased their marketing efforts, but this had little impact on electric razors' share of shavers. In fact, the percent of both men and women using electric razors declined slightly between 1991 and 1993. By 1996, Norelco (a division of Philips Electronics) had well over 50 percent of the $400 million plus market. In late 1996, Pat Dinley, Norelco's president, described the firm's new approach:

> Over the years, we've fought the market share battle with other electric shavers. Long term, the big opportunity is in converting people who use blades to electric.

Norelco will use a two-pronged approach to gain share in the overall shaving market, focusing on younger shavers and directly targeting blade users. According to Dinley:

> Traditionally, our target market has been 35-plus. We believe we've got a real opportunity to bring some new people into the category, so we're going after 18- to 54-year-olds.

Targeting younger consumers has involved using different media and themes. Some of the media used include ESPN sports, "Monday Night Football," and "Friends," as well as select men's magazines.

The creative theme is focused heavily on the irritation that can be associated with blade shaving. One television ad features sneering blade razors that turn into dragons and snakes. The comfort of a Norelco shave is stressed with the tagline "Anything closer would be too close for comfort."

In 1998, Philips Electronics, Norelco's parent company made two major moves. First, it focused Norelco strictly on men's products (except for pet grooming products). Women's electric razors and other products targeting women were redesigned and introduced under the Philips Personal Care name.

Norelco then launched a new flagship razor, the Advantage. The advantage razor has a Nivea for Men shaving lotion cartridge built inside the razor chamber. This unique system dispenses the lotion while shaving to offer a wet shave experience without the hassle associated with water and lather. While the razor comes with five lotion cartridges, it can be used wet or dry and it can be rinsed clear with tap water.

The product was launched with an estimated $35 million campaign. The ads take a humorous approach that challenges consumers to put the razor "to the test." One ad makes this offer: "If you don't make it part of your routine after 21 days, we'll give you your money back, guaranteed." According to VP-marketing Rich Sorota, "The advertising is part of our holistic approach to get consumers to put it to the test. [The objective] is to get really dissatisfied blade users to trade up to electrics. [Marketing research has found] over 10 million dissatisfied blade users out there."

A spokesperson for the ad agency says the ads also try to eliminate the perception that electric razors are "some old razor your grandmother gave you in high school" and instead position them as the "high-tech way to shave." Advantage commercials will run on network, cable, and syndicated TV and in such magazines as *Rolling Stone, Details, Spin,* and *Sports Illustrated.*

Table A provides demographic data on the users of electric razors, disposable razors, and replaceable-blade razors and on the users of Remington and Norelco electric shavers.

TABLE A

Demographics and Razor Use*

Variable	Type: Electric	Type: Disposable	Type: Blades	Brand: Norelco	Brand: Remington
Percent Adults Using	30.1%	54.3%	40.7%	16.6%	6.8%
Age					
18–24 years	86	99	114	74	104
25–34	87	105	108	83	77
35–44	90	106	102	84	90
45–54	92	108	96	97	85
55–64	112	97	90	122	99
>64	150	77	83	164	166
Education					
College graduate	113	93	108	107	103
Some college	106	97	104	102	109
High school graduate	92	105	100	97	95
No degree	90	104	84	94	93
Occupation					
Professional	114	91	107	97	117
Managerial/Administrative	102	99	106	104	92
Technical/Clerical/Sales	102	97	109	98	100
Precision/Craft	80	104	99	87	72
Other employed	81	112	105	75	86
Race/Ethnic Group					
White	104	99	101	107	104
Black	61	111	91	44	70
Spanish speaking	80	106	107	77	92
Region					
Northeast	111	98	108	112	89
North central	114	93	102	132	100
South	76	109	92	69	96
West	112	96	103	103	116
Household Income					
<$10,000	87	108	73	104	86
$10,000–19,999	96	106	92	94	99
$20,000–29,999	102	98	93	114	103
$30,000–39,999	89	105	95	91	89
$40,000–49,999	97	90	111	101	97
$50,000–59,999	98	105	106	88	82
$60,000–74,999	101	101	106	96	111
$75,000+	115	95	109	106	115
Household Structure					
1 person	105				
2 people	110	94	97	110	114
3 or more	93	105	103	92	92
Any child in HH	87	107	102	84	84

*100 = Average use or consumption unless a percent is indicated. Base = Adult males.
Source: *Mediamark Spring 1997* (New York: Mediamark Research Inc., 1997).

Discussion Questions

1. Prepare a two-page summary (accompanied by no more than four graphs) that conveys the key information in Table A to a manager.
2. Describe the typical user of an electric razor, a disposable razor, and a blade razor, in one paragraph each.
3. Conduct an innovation analysis of the Advantage using Table 7-4 as the basis. What insights does the innovation analysis provide into its probable sales growth?
4. Which of the demographic factors are most relevant for developing marketing strategy for the Advantage? Why?
5. Based on demographics, describe the best target market for the Advantage.
6. What additional demographic data would you like to have in order to develop marketing strategy for the Advantage? Justify your answer.
7. Why would "10 million dissatisfied blade users" continue to use blades?
8. Evaluate Norelco's objective to, and strategy for, switching dissatisfied blade users to electric razors.
9. Based on the available data, develop a marketing strategy for the Advantage.

Source: R. A. Davis, "Electric Razors Plan Aggressive Fourth-Quarter," *Advertising Age,* October 12, 1992, p. 20; L. Petrecca, "Norelco Courts Younger Crowd," *Advertising Age,* September 1996, p. 64; L. Petrecca, "Norelco Puts New Shaver to the Test," *Advertising Age,* August 31, 1998, p. 10; and "Electric Razors Retain Strong Category Position," *MMR,* January 1999, p. 30.

2-3 Frito-Lay's Wow! Chips

One of Frito-Lay's first entries into the "better-for-you" snack area was the Sunchip. Sunchips are made from whole wheat, corn, other grains, and canola or sunflower oil.

Dwight Riskey, vice president of marketing at Frito-Lay, explains the strategy behind Sunchips:

> The aging baby boomers were a very significant factor. We were looking for new products that would allow them to snack. But we were looking for "better-for-you" aspects in products and pushing against that demographic shift.

The success of Sunchips has been followed by a variety of additional new better-for-you product successes. In fact, it is estimated that 70 percent of Frito-Lay's growth is coming from better-for-you products.

Baked Lay's were launched in late 1995 with a $50 million ad campaign that featured supermodels such as Naomi Campbell and Vendela eating the chips. The campaign became such a huge success that the firm could not keep up with demand.

Frito-Lay launched a line of Reduced Fat Doritos in July 1996 to go along with its Reduced Fat Ruffles, Baked Tostitos, and Baked Lay's.

In 1998, Frito-Lay's Wow! chips became "the most successful new product in a decade" according to the company. Sales for 1998 are estimated at $346 million. However, a number of industry observers are warning that the company is celebrating too soon. While the following sales data (52 weeks ending March 1999) appear to support the firm's claim, observers note that the most recent sales periods have shown sales declines.

Tortilla/tostada chips		Potato chips	
Brand	*Sales ($ millions)*	*Brand*	*Sales ($ millions)*
1. Doritos	709.5	Lay's	783.5
2. Tostitos	543.5	Ruffles	391.5
3. Baked Tostitos	107.8	Private labels	161.3
4. Doritos Wow!	76.0	Lay's Wow!	142.0
5. Santitas	55.0	Ruffles Wow!	117.6
6. Mission	38.2	Wavy Lay's	113.6
7. Tostitos Wow!	30.9	Utz	54.7

Wow! are made with Olestra fat substitute. To date, Pringles is the only other chip maker using Olestra, though a number of regional firms are expected to launch Olestra-based products soon. The advantage of Olestra is that the body cannot absorb it and so it provides no calories. One reason producers have been slow to utilize Olestra is persistent rumors that it causes gastric distress. According to one industry expert, "There is real concern about the reports of

TABLE A

Demographics and Chip Consumption*

Variable	Sun Chip	Ruffles	Ruffles Light	Lay's Potato Chips	Doritos	Doritos Light
Age						
18–24 years	119	117	94	102	95	127
25–34	120	115	78	113	118	101
35–44	134	125	125	117	124	101
45–54	100	87	129	103	119	138
55–64	59	88	84	90	80	68
>64	54	64	82	68	50	72
Education						
College graduate	127	92	135	98	145	97
Some college	115	106	121	109	99	130
High school graduate	82	100	86	102	90	104
No degree	85	100	61	85	73	53
Occupation						
Professional	124	96	114	106	133	106
Managerial/Administrative	127	110	124	96	156	158
Technical/Clerical/Sales	119	109	87	109	112	136
Precision/Craft	116	85	22	85	165	127
Other employed	98	104	100	112	88	78
Race/Ethnic Group						
White	98	101	105	100	106	104
Black	99	91	49	95	64	54
Spanish speaking	109	106	105	96	153	112
Region						
Northeast	85	84	70	89	107	81
North central	112	117	129	88	107	120
South	80	96	92	106	95	91
West	138	104	111	113	93	113
Household Income						
<$10,000	71	88	70	87	58	54
$10,000–19,999	66	79	65	90	97	72
$20,000–29,999	79	95	92	97	64	51
$30,000–39,999	114	114	97	100	100	108
$40,000–49,999	119	113	125	121	114	149
$50,000–59,999	110	121	105	110	115	95
$60,000–74,999	141	116	88	102	105	105
$75,000+	123	95	161	103	152	152
Household Structure						
1 person	55	58	68	64	38	40
2 people	87	79	86	92	82	101
3 or more	122	126	119	116	130	118
Any child in HH	130	127	114	119	139	117

*100 = Average use or consumption unless a percent is indicated. Base = Female homemakers.

Source: *Mediamark Spring 1997* (New York: Mediamark Research Inc., 1997).

some people getting sick. The regional chip makers want to wait and see what happens with that." The president of a regional chip firm states:

> The jury is still out as far as the popularity of Wow! and the new Pringles that use Olestra. Consumers don't want to eat things that can cause diarrhea.

Indeed, Wow! chips carry a warning that they "may cause abdominal cramping and loose stools."

Sales first softened for Wow! chips in the summer of 1998. At that time, Frito-Lay changed its introductory campaign that featured a woman in a tree house with a child and a man floating on a lake eating Wow! chips. The tag line was "Life tastes good again." The new campaign was a harder sell featuring "Saturday Night Live" cheerleader Cheri Oteri and the theme "Bet you can't taste the difference! Or it's free!" Less than a year later, sales appear to be dropping again.

Table A contains demographic data relevant to the consumption of chips.

Discussion Questions

1. What type of innovation was Sunchips? Baked Lay's? Reduced Fat Doritos? Wow! chips?
2. Analyze Wow! chips, using the innovation analysis methodology of Table 7-4.
3. What values might explain Baked Lay's success? Will these also explain Wow! chips?
4. Based on the demographic material available, what target market(s) would you select for Wow! chips? What additional demographic data would you like to have? How would you use it?
5. How should Frito-Lay deal with the rumors and concerns about gastric problems caused by consuming Olestra?
6. Why are Wow! chip sales declining or flat? What should Frito-Lay do about this?
7. How should Frito-Lay proceed in introducing Wow! chips to the following?
   a. The European Union
   b. Taiwan
   c. Japan
   d. Brazil
   e. Mexico
8. What role, if any, do you feel reference group influences played in the success and current problems with Wow! chips?
9. Which stage in the family life cycle is the best market for Wow! chips? Why?
10. What would you do to continue the growth of Wow! chips?

Source: J. Pollack, "Frito-Lay Revamps Strategy for Struggling Wow!" *Advertising Age,* September 14, 1998, p.1; "Hot Potatoes," *Snack and Wholesale Bakery,* August 1999, p. 14, "Americans Remain Dedicated Snackers," *MMR,* August 9, 1999, p. 10; K. Yung, "Fat-Free Chips Not a Sure Bet," *The Houston Chronicle,* January 31, 1999, p. 3; and K. Yung, "Concerns about Sales," *The Dallas Morning News,* January 25, 1999.

2-4 Tony the Tiger Goes Global

Kellogg Company has distribution in over 150 countries and yet is still "unknown to half the world's population," according to Arnold Langbo, Kellogg's CEO. Langbo plans to change that.

Kellogg recently built a company-owned cereal plant in Latvia and currently has sales in Poland, Hungary, and Czechoslovakia. It has also started construction on a plant in India and is entering China. These efforts will greatly expand non-U.S. sales, which in 1995 contributed 38 percent of total operating earnings. However, international expansion and the development of global brands will not be easy.

To become more international, the firm recently reorganized into four divisions: North America, Latin America, Europe, and Australasia. According to Langbo:

> The way we used to be organized, we were a U.S.-based multinational—a company with a big domestic business and, by the way, some international business. That was the way we were thinking; that's the way the organization was structured.
>
> Today, if you talk to customers in the U.K., Canada, or Australia, they think of Kellogg as being based in the U.K. or Canada or Australia. We're global in organizational structure and business but also multidomestic.
>
> We now have a number of truly global brands (Frosted Flakes and Corn Flakes, with Froot Loops and Rice Krispies close, and Frosted Mini-Wheats and Honey Nut Loops moving rapidly). There used to be slight variations in our food around the world, but now you'll recognize the product wherever you go.

Expanding into many markets will involve more than trying to gain share from other cereal marketers.

It will require altering long-held traditions:

> In Eastern Europe it's going to be pretty slow because we're going to have to go in there and literally create the habit—much as we did in Germany 25 years ago or France 20 years ago. Cereal is a whole new breakfast concept for these people. However, they do eat breakfast in those countries and they eat fairly substantial breakfasts.
>
> In Asia, consumers are used to eating something warm, soft, and savory for breakfast—and we're going to sell them something that's cold, crisp, and sweet or bran tasting. That's quite a difference.

The challenge is made greater by the presence of aggressive competition in many developed or developing markets. Competition is particularly intense in Europe, where Nestlé and General Mills formed a joint venture called Cereal Partners Worldwide. Langbo characterizes the new competitor this way:

> They are a very formidable competitor with Nestlé's distribution strength and knowledge of the European market and General Mills' technology and cereal marketing expertise.

The result of the entry of the new competitor, which spent an estimated $35 to $50 million in advertising in the top six European markets, and the response of existing firms such as Kellogg, was an increase in the growth rate of total cereal sales as well as share erosion among the weaker brands.

Competition is strong even in some countries where consumption is low. For example, in Japan, with consumption at four bowls per year per person compared to 10 pounds in the United States, there are more than 100 products fighting for shelf space.

According to Langbo, a global brand requires a core position strategy or product benefit that will work in multiple countries and local execution of that idea to reflect local attitudes. The key ideas for three of Kellogg's global or near global brands are described by Langbo in the following paragraphs.

Frosted Flakes

Frosted Flakes is based on the concept of vitality. This idea originated in the United States but is a universal idea that translates and travels well. Because the product has a special appeal to children, the cultural differences are not so pronounced. Tony the Tiger illustrates the vitality theme in a universally understandable manner. Tony is loved throughout the world, symbolizing appeals that are truly global. We use Tony and the vitality message everywhere from the United States to Taiwan to Argentina.

Corn Flakes

The basic positioning concept for Corn Flakes is simple, unadulterated food that tastes surprisingly good. This concept also has universal appeal. It is typically the first product we introduce in a new market. It is the foundation of our line, and it is the world's most popular cereal.

All-Bran

The value proposition for All Bran is the health benefits of fiber in the diet. This proposition does not have universal appeal without development. The concept of the value of fiber in the diet is new to many countries and is often resisted.

In 1984, we began a massive campaign to countries where the benefits of fiber were not widely accepted. The campaign varied across countries due to differences in the attitudes of local medical and nutritional professionals, specific diseases that were most on the minds of the local population, and local restrictions on health claims. However, the basic approach was to educate and support the medical and nutritional community in each country. We would sponsor symposia on dietary fiber. As a country's experts became convinced of the value of fiber, they told their story in their academic press, the general press, and in public service announcements. Today, despite competition from many other high-fiber cereals, All Bran is one of the top 15 cereals worldwide.

Discussion Questions

1. What type of innovation would cold cereal be to a country not accustomed to this type of food?
2. Conduct an innovation analysis based on Table 7-4 for cold cereal in China.
3. What values are involved in the consumption of a product such as breakfast cereal?
4. What values would support and what values would harm the chances of Kellogg succeeding with cold cereal in the following countries? What other factors would be important?
   a. China
   b. Mexico
   c. Japan
   d. France
5. What nonverbal communications factors would be important in developing an advertising campaign for a cold cereal?

6. Develop a marketing program to market one of Kellogg's cold cereals in the following countries:
   a. China
   b. Mexico
   c. Japan
   d. France
7. Why does Tony the Tiger "travel" so well?
8. Evaluate the communications process Kellogg used to gain acceptance for All Bran. Could a version of this work for gaining acceptance of cold cereals in China?

Source: J. Liesse, "Kellogg Chief to Push Harder for Int'l Growth," *Advertising Age,* August 24, 1992, p. 4; A. G. Langbo, "Building a Global Company," in *Marketing's New Strategic Direction* (New York: The Conference Board, 1995), pp. 14–16; A. G. Langbo, "Touring the World with Tony the Tiger," *Across the Board,* July 1995, p. 56; and P. Galarza, "Snap, Crackle, Flop?" *Financial World,* March 25, 1996, p. 26.

2-5 Wal-Mart Enters China

Retailing is rapidly becoming a global business. Among other international locations, Kmart has 13 stores in Eastern Europe, 7 in Mexico, and 1 in Singapore. Office Depot, Saks Fifth Avenue, and J. C. Penney have recently launched major expansions in Mexico. The Gap, Pier 1, and the Foot Locker have been part of the wave of U.S. retailers expanding into Europe, where the number of such firms grew from 14 in 1992 to 50 in 1995. In 1991, Wal-Mart opened its first store outside the United States in Mexico City. In 1997, Wal-Mart had 2,744 stores in the United States, 145 in Mexico, 136 in Canada, 11 in Puerto Rico, 6 in Argentina, 5 in Brazil and 2 in Indonesia. By 1999, it had over 600 outlets outside the United States. Its international sales were $7.5 billion in 1998, with rapid growth forecast.

U.S. firms are not the only ones expanding across the globe. Makro, a Dutch wholesale club, is Southeast Asia's leading store group, with sales of over $2 billion. Carrefour of France is the leading retailer in Brazil and Argentina and recently opened an outlet in Shanghai. Yaohan, a Japanese retail chain with headquarters in Hong Kong, has plans to open 1,000 stores in South China. The chain is also expanding into Europe and the United States. In fact, four non-U.S. retailers operate in more countries and have significantly more foreign sales than Wal-Mart, America's largest retailer.

Some analysts feel that internationalization is essential for retailers to prosper in the future. One expert predicts the rise of four or five dominant global retailers that will enjoy substantial advantages in pricing, sourcing, and logistics. Another states: "We're really moving to boundaryless retailing."

Retail firms that succeed internationally find a way to bring value to local markets that local competitors cannot match. This value may be in the form of low price, selection, service, image, unique products, or other features desired in multiple cultures. Toys "R" Us has found unmatched selection a feature that offers it a strong brand image and a competitive advantage in Europe and Japan despite prices higher than in the United States. Michael Goldstein, the CEO, notes:

> I remember talking to customers who were leaving one of our stores in Wales. When I asked what they liked about the store, every one of them said selection. No one paid attention to pricing, which was one of our big concerns.

In Hong Kong, as elsewhere, it is Disney's products and image that draw customers. There was a near riot when a Disney store opened in Hong Kong in 1994. The outlet can hold only 150 people at a time, and 5,000 people routinely show up each day. The store has giant screens continually showing clips from Disney films and clerks dressed in 1950s collegiate gear.

The Hong Kong Market

Hong Kong shoppers are very price sensitive. Many appear to treat shopping almost as a competitive sport in which the person who gains the lowest price wins. However, despite the desire for low price, convenience often plays a dominant role in store choice. Few Hong Kong Chinese have access to a private car. Instead, they rely on buses and taxis. Carrying large items or bulk purchases home by bus is difficult or impossible. Using a taxi is expensive. Thus, most Hong Kong residents shop within a few kilometers of their residence.

Even if transportation were not an issue, house size would be. Most residents live in very small apartments. Many of these apartments are only 300 square feet. Given small refrigerators and very limited storage space, Hong Kong consumers shop for food and other items virtually daily. They cannot easily buy in large quantities or sizes and store the product no matter what savings they might obtain by doing so. Frequent shopping is made easier by the fact that most of the large apartment buildings contain a number of retail outlets such as a small grocery store, pharmacy, laundry, and restaurant.

Hong Kong has thousands of small businesses. However, most face the same purchasing constraints that households do. They do not have access to private transportation and lack storage space. The small business often doubles as the family residence, and potential storage space is required for family activities.

Wal-Mart's Approach

Wal-Mart is entering the market with a small chain of Value Clubs that are similar to small Sam's Clubs. That is, they will be small-scale retail/wholesale, cash and carry, membership warehouse operations. Wal-Mart's traditional approach is to give customers the goods and services they desire at a price well below the competition. However, it also relies on relatively large, bulk purchases for much of its sales.

One opportunity for Wal-Mart is to open outlets near the many new apartment houses being constructed in the New Territories. The enormous building boom in this region will house many less sophisticated new residents from China who may be particularly appreciative of the low price and selection Value Clubs will offer.

Wal-Mart has learned how to make its U.S. customers feel like they are shopping at their own personal store. It will continue this approach in Hong Kong. For example, it will accept returned goods with a smile. This policy basically does not exist in Hong Kong, even if the items are defective. However, it remains to be seen if low price and unique service will be enough. As one shopper commented while visiting the store and looking at a four-pound jar of Skippy peanut butter: "The price is right, but where would I put it?"

Discussion Questions

1. Will Wal-Mart succeed? What would you recommend to help it succeed?
2. What values are relevant to the success of retail stores such as Wal-Mart? How should Wal-Mart adjust its strategies to be consistent with the prevailing value system in Hong Kong?
3. How will Wal-Mart need to alter its approach as it opens stores in the following countries?
   a. Japan
   b. Egypt
   c. Germany
   d. Great Britain
4. How can Wal-Mart use reference group influences to its advantage in Hong Kong?

Source: N. Herndon, "Wal-Mart goes to Hong Kong," *Marketing News,* November 21, 1994, p. 2; C. Rapoport, "Retailers Go Global," *Fortune,* February 20, 1995, pp. 102–8; and W. Zellner, "Wal-Mart Spoken Here," *Business Week,* June 23, 1997, pp. 138–43.

2-6 Tom's of Maine

Tom's of Maine has a unique view of the firm and its role in society. This unique view is reflected in its mission, purpose, and belief statements.

The Tom's of Maine Mission

To serve our customers by providing safe, effective, innovative, natural products of high quality.

To build relationships with our customers that extend beyond product usage to include full and honest dialogue, responsiveness to feedback, and the exchange of information about products and issues.

To respect, value, and serve not only our customers, but also our co-workers, owners, agents, suppliers, and our community; to be concerned about and contribute to their well-being, and to operate with integrity so as to be deserving of their trust.

To provide meaningful work, fair compensation, and a safe, healthy work environment that encourages openness, creativity, self-discipline, and growth.

To contribute to and affirm a high level of commitment, skill, and effectiveness in the work community.

To recognize, encourage, and seek a diversity of gifts and perspectives in our worklife.

To acknowledge the value of each person's contribution to our goals and to foster teamwork in our tasks.

To be distinctive in products and policies which honor and sustain our natural world.

To address community concerns in Maine and around the globe, by devoting a portion of our time, talents, and resources to the environment, human needs, the arts, and education.

To work together to contribute to the long-term value and sustainability of our company.

To be a profitable and successful company while acting in a socially and environmentally responsible manner.

The Purpose of Tom's of Maine Is:

To serve our customer' health needs with imaginative science from plants and minerals;

To inspire all those we serve with a mission of responsibility and goodness;

To empower others by sharing our knowledge, time, talents, and profits; and

To help create a better world by exchanging our faith, experience, and hope.

Statement of Beliefs

We believe that both human beings and nature have inherent worth and deserve our respect.

We believe in products that are safe, effective and made of natural ingredients.

We believe that our company and our products are unique and worthwhile, and that we can sustain these genuine qualities with an ongoing commitment to innovation and creativity.

We believe that we have a responsibility to cultivate the best relationships possible with our co-workers, customers, owners, agents, suppliers, and our community.

We believe that different people bring different gifts and perspectives to the team and that a strong team is founded on a variety of gifts.

Company Actions

The firm engages in a wide array of actions consistent with its mission, purpose, and beliefs. It gives 10 percent of its pretax profits to nonprofit organizations benefiting the environment, human needs, arts, and education. All employees are encouraged to use up to 5 percent of their paid work time to do volunteer work in nonprofit organizations of their choosing. Its sponsorship program is a separate program that "promotes important causes and work while contributing to the strategic goals of Tom's. Sponsorships integrate our dual interests: to profit while contributing to the Common Good. Our major national sponsorship is E-Town, the environmental radio show."

However, being a socially responsible business means that Tom's is still a business.

Succeeding at what we do is what enables all of our other contributions. Our financial success helps to demonstrate that it isn't necessary for business to discard its social conscience in order to profit in today's economy.

Tom's product line includes natural toothpaste (Natural Toothpaste for Children, Natural Fluoride Toothpaste, Natural Fluoride-Free Toothpaste), deodorant (Aloe, Lichen & Coriander Deodorant, Gentle Deodorant), soap (Children's Soap, Deodorant Bar Soap, Moisturizing Bar Soap), mouthwash, shampoo, flossing ribbon, shaving cream. All its products are based on natural ingredients, and the packaging makes extensive use of recycled materials. Here is their description of their soap line:

Our premium natural bar soaps are gentle, 100% vegetable-based soaps containing no animal fat, artificial detergents, fragrances, or dyes. To avoid the use of synthetic preservatives such as EDTA and BHT, we combined rosemary extract and Vitamin C to create an innovative natural stabilizer. Our three distinctive bar soap lines meet the needs of the entire family.

Illustration 3-3 in the text is an ad for Tom's toothpaste. The following is a promotional message for Tom's children's toothpaste:

Dear Parent, The Story Of Our Children's Natural Toothpaste

We think the time is right to make a natural toothpaste just for children. For over 20 years we have committed ourselves to natural oral and body care products. Many adults have come to trust our natural toothpastes made without saccharin or synthetic flavors, preservatives, dyes or animal ingredients.

We now offer a delicious and effective natural toothpaste with sensible ingredients and natural fruit flavors created with your child's taste in mind. It contains none of the stripes and "sparkles": neon colors and sweet bubble gum flavors you see in other brands. Our gentle formulation is low in abrasivity and contains fluoride to help prevent dental decay.

Try it and let us know what you and your child think.

Your friends, Kate & Tom Chappell

TABLE A

Demographics and Toothpaste Use*

Variable	Heavy User	Arm & Hammer	Close-Up	Colgate Baking Soda	Tom's of Maine
Gender					
Male	78	107	88	89	88
Female	120	94	111	110	111
Age					
18–24 years	109	112	149	128	139
25–34	108	94	109	122	91
35–44	116	100	114	103	119
45–54	98	91	95	90	118
55–64	63	111	88	85	114
>64	73	100	45	65	29
Education					
College graduate	104	103	72	103	202
Some college	107	115	98	103	101
High school graduate	100	91	101	91	73
No degree	85	92	132	108	32
Occupation					
Professional	104	89	86	98	149
Managerial/Administrative	100	100	90	91	195
Technical/Clerical/Sales	113	115	95	105	128
Precision/Craft	73	96	109	96	33
Other employed	106	92	118	108	73
Race/Ethnic Group					
White	101	94	88	94	105
Black	94	143	190	132	7
Spanish speaking	111	85	114	138	70
Region					
Northeast	97	119	81	144	174
North central	88	82	76	91	19
South	105	97	132	86	30
West	108	107	92	91	234
Household Income					
<$10,000	83	128	115	96	53
$10,000–19,999	93	74	114	101	55
$20,000–29,999	100	99	108	83	35
$30,000–39,999	103	75	124	98	70
$40,000–49,999	92	100	103	103	141
$50,000–59,999	105	116	74	113	73
$60,000–74,999	99	129	77	109	139
$75,000+	115	102	81	103	201
Household Structure					
1 person	95	89	85	73	73
2 people	99	97	89	84	84
3 or more	102	104	110	116	116
Any child in HH	103	98	122	122	122

*100 = Average use or consumption unless a percent is indicated. Base = All adults.

Source: *Mediamark Spring 1997* (New York: Mediamark Research Inc., 1997).

Part of the package message for this product (similar to information on many of its products) is:

> **WHAT MAKES THIS NATURAL?** All major brands of toothpaste for children contain saccharin, artificial color, and taste super sweet. We take a simple approach—use natural ingredients to make it taste good and work well. Compare our natural ingredients with any other brand and make your choice.

Active Ingredient	**Purpose**	**Source**
Sodium monofluorophosphate	Decay prevention	Fluorspar (calcium fluoride), an ore
Ingredient		
Glycerin	Moistener	By-product of vegetable soap (Kosher)
Water	Consistency	Branch Brook
Calcium carbonate	Mild abrasive	Purified calcium from the earth
Hydrated silica	Mild abrasive	Purified silica from the earth
Fruit extracts	Flavor	Orange, Banana, Pineapple, & other natural flavors
Carrageenan	Thickener	Seaweed
Sodium lauryl sulfate	Disperse the calcium	Derived from coconut oil

NO SACCHARIN OR ARTIFICIAL SWEETENERS, NO PRESERVATIVES, NO ARTIFICIAL COLOR OR FLAVOR & NO ANIMAL INGREDIENTS

Table A contains demographic data relevant to toothpaste usage.

Discussion Questions

1. How is Tom's of Maine able to survive competing against some of the largest and most sophisticated firms in the world?
2. Who should Tom's market be in terms of demographics?
3. What values support the success of Tom's?
4. How would you market Tom's products in these countries?
   a. France
   b. Mexico
   c. Japan
   d. Germany
   e. Australia
   f. Singapore
5. Which cells in the HLC/Social Stratification Matrix (Table 6-2) represent the best target markets for Tom's products? Why?
6. What role do reference groups and group communications play in the success of firms such as Tom's?
7. Should Tom's advertising focus solely on product features and benefits or should it also cover the positive social actions of the firm?

2-7 Understanding Teens

American teens spend well over $100 billion a year. Many are the primary grocery shoppers for their family. Most influence a wide array of family purchases from pets to cars and computers. Marketers have historically had a difficult time understanding this market in part because it changes so quickly. Firms today are engaging in a variety of activities to keep up with today's teens.

Teen Link™

Bates USA, a major advertising agency, recently started a survey called Teen Link™. In this survey, a demographically representative cross section of teens is paid to file a "report" to the firm every other month for a year. A company vice president states:

> Because we will be following the same group of teens for one year and developing relationships with them, we will not only have a very close-up perspective on the trends, issues, hopes and dreams that are important to teens today, but will also gain an understanding of the values and attitudes they will carry into adulthood.

The bi-monthly "reports" involve innovative and involving research approaches. For the first, the teens were given a disposable camera and told to photograph the most important people, places, and things in their lives and to write about why they took each photo. One described his reason for submitting a photo of a kitchen sink as "This is a picture of my kitchen sink, which I have to clean every weekend, along with all the other sinks and the bathtub."

Another assignment provided the teens with magazines and the requirement to use pictures from the magazines to create collages depicting where they see themselves 15 years into the future. To measure clothing trends, it asks them to describe how they would dress the characters on "Dawson's Creek." The image of fast-food restaurants was measured by asking them to match a list of restaurants to celebrities likely to eat there. One 17-year-old said the Spice Girls, Ally McBeal, and Puff Daddy would eat at McDonald's while Martha Stewart and the cast of "Golden Girls" would go to Wendy's.

Based on this and other research, Bates believes that today's teens are:

- Independent minded.
- Altruistic and concerned with issues of world peace, making a positive impact and being a leader.
- More concerned with "How do I feel about myself?" rather than "How do I fit in?"

Teenage Research Unlimited's Focus Groups

Teenage Research Unlimited is a research firm that specializes in the teenage market. It conducts roughly 1,000 focus group discussions per year. Most of these are with "influencers,"—teens who respond "I do" to questions such as "Who decides what you and your friends do on a Saturday night?"

Focus groups, loosely structured discussions with small groups led by a trained moderator, are difficult to do with teens. They tend to "clam up, cut up, or gang up on the moderator." Teenage Research uses moderators experienced with teens, does not mix genders in the groups, and has only one teen from a school in each group (so they won't have to worry about what they say being repeated at school).

In addition to general discussion on topics such as retail stores, the focus groups involve other techniques as well. In one session, each girl filled out a page showing a stick figure, a radio and a blank magazine cover. One 16-year-old portrayed herself wearing wide-cuff jeans and a Tori Amos T-shirt, listening to Soul Coughing and reading *Rolling Stone* and *Sports Illustrated.*

Discussion Questions

1. Evaluate the Teen Link™ approach. What are its strengths and weaknesses?
2. Evaluate the use of focus groups to understand teenagers.
3. How would you study teenagers?
4. Assume that the three conclusions that Bates has reached about teens are correct. What are their implications for the following organizations?
   a. JCPenney
   b. Mudd
   c. Calvin Klein
   d. Taco Bell
   e. Kodak
   f. United Way
5. Assume the 17-year-old quoted above about the types of celebrities that would eat at McDonald's and Wendy's is typical of teens in general. What are the implications for Wendy's? For McDonald's?

Source: Bates USA News Release, S. Elliot; "Advertising," *The New York Times,* October 23, 1998; and M. J. McCarthy, "Stalking the Elusive Teenage Trendsetter," *The Wall Street Journal,* November 11, 1998, p. B1.

2-8 Dixon Ticonderoga's Prang Soybean Crayon

At the Purdue University's 1994 contest to develop new uses for soybeans, one entrant was to use them to make crayons. Dixon Ticonderoga entered into an agreement to develop and market the new crayon. After years of research, the product was launched as the "first new crayon in 100 years."

The new crayon was named the Prang Fun Pro Soybean Crayon. It promises a number of advantages over traditional crayons.

- It is made from soybeans, a renewable resource. Most crayons are made from paraffin, a petroleum product.
- It doesn't flake like petroleum-based crayons.
- It doesn't create a waxy build-up.
- It allows users to blend or layer colors, which is not possible with traditional crayons.

While Prang crayons have a number of desirable features, they also face a serious obstacle. Crayola is virtually synonymous with crayons. It dominates the market in terms of sales, distribution, and advertising. In addition to traditional crayons, some of the products Crayola is featuring for the 1999 school year include Crayola Construction Paper crayons that provide consistent, true color across all types of paper, including black construction paper, brown paper bags, and colored poster board.

Crayola Washable highlighters and Crayola Erasable highlighters are improved this year, as are Crayola Poster markers. Crayola School glue, Crayola Student scissors, Crayola Metallic colored pencils, Crayola Computer & Craft Paper, Crayola Color WipeOffs Whiteboard Combo sets, and Crayola Color WipeOffs (washable dry erase markers) are other school-related products.

Crayola Kids' Katchalls designed for organizing kids' crayons, markers, and supplies are durable plastic boxes with a snap-close top and handle that makes them easy for kids to grip and carry. Crayola backpacks come in a variety of colors and sizes, and some styles include a matching lunch bag. Crayola shoes are available in infant size 1 through children's size 12.

Discussion Questions

1. What type innovation is the new Prang crayon? Evaluate it as an innovation using Table 7-4 as a structure.
2. How can the firm use opinion leaders to help the Prang Crayon succeed?
3. How can the firm use reference group influence to help the Prang Crayon succeed?
4. What values will help this product succeed?
5. Would you target children or adults? How would your approach differ between the two groups?
6. What demographic groups would you target?
7. How would you compete against Crayola?
8. How would you market the Prang Crayon in these countries or regions?
   a. Japan
   b. European Union
   c. Mexico
   d. Egypt

Source: Prang Home Page (www.prang.com); D. Gardner, "Soy-Based Crayons Color the Countryside," *Agri Marketing,* February 1998, pp. 18–19; and "Soybean Crayons Add Color," *PR Newswire,*" August 31, 1999.

2-9 Marketing Bottled Sauces to Ethnic Groups

As Table A indicates, African-Americans are relatively heavy users of bottled barbecue and seasoning sauces. Spanish-speaking consumers are also relatively heavy consumers of these products compared to non-Spanish-speaking whites. Because of these relatively high consumption levels and the fact that both these groups are growing faster than the overall population, marketers of bottled sauces are very interested in both segments.

TABLE A

Ethnic Group Bottled Sauce Consumption*

	White	*Black*	*Spanish Speaking*
Heavy sauce users	96	139	101
A-1 Original	104	77	111
A-1 Bold	95	140	100
Heinz 57	102	112	126
Lawry's	95	146	89
Lea & Perrins Steak Sauce	99	112	69
Bull's Eye Barbecue Sauce	102	80	83
Heinz Barbecue Sauce	95	133	107
Hunts BBQ Sauce	96	133	115
Kraft BBQ Sauce	97	133	83
Kraft Thick 'N Spicy	101	102	82
Tabasco Sauce	103	83	118
Durkee Red Hot Sauce	92	166	33
Louisiana Hot Sauce	881	244	86

*100 = Average use or consumption. Base = Female homemakers.

Source: *Mediamark Spring 1997* (New York: Mediamark Research Inc., 1997).

TABLE B

African-American Shopping Patterns Relevant to Sauces

1. Frequency of shopping for groceries:
   At least once a week = 35%
   Once every two weeks = 30%
   Less frequently = 31%
   Mean number of times per month = 2.4
2. Most important factor in selecting a store:
   Quality = 76%
   Price = 24%
3. Repeat purchasing behavior:
   Generally purchase the same brand = 57%
   Purchase whatever brand is on sale = 43%
4. When in a store, I often buy an item on the spur of the moment.
   Strongly agree/Agree = 47%
   Strongly disagree/Disagree = 33%
5. When I go to the supermarket, I shop based on a budget.
   Strongly agree/Agree = 64%
   Strongly disagree/Disagree = 21%
6. I definitely/probably would make a purchase based on
   Buy 1—Get 1 free = 58%
   Cents-off coupon = 54%
   In-store samples = 48%
   Rebates = 34%
   Sweepstakes = 29%
7. Used cents-off coupon in past 30 days = 43%
   Source of coupons:
      Newspaper = 79%
      Mail = 42%
      In-store = 17%
8. I prefer lighter foods to heavy meals.
   Strongly agree/Agree = 53%
   Strongly disagree/Disagree = 27%
9. Major leisure activities:
   Watching TV = 66%
   Going shopping = 50%
   Reading = 48%
   Going to parties = 39%
   Cooking for pleasure = 37%
   Hanging out with friends = 36%
   Eating out at restaurants = 31%

Source: *The 1993 MSR Minority Market Report* (Coral Gables, FL: Market Segment Research, Inc., 1993).

Table A also indicates that there is considerable variation in the success that various firms have with each segment. Table B provides data relevant to African-American sauce shopping patterns, and Table C provides similar data for Hispanics.

Discussion Questions

1. Why do African-Americans consume relatively more bottled sauces than whites or Hispanics?
2. How would you explain the variation in the relative consumption of various brands of hot sauce across the three groups?
3. How would you explain the variation in consumption across the various brands of steak sauce among Hispanic consumers?
4. Which of the African-American segments described in Chapter 5 would be the best target market(s) for Heinz 57 Sauce? Why?

TABLE C

Hispanic Shopping Patterns Relevant to Sauces

1. Frequency of shopping for groceries:
   At least once a week = 57%
   Once every two weeks = 27%
   Less frequently = 13%
   Mean number of times per month = 3.1
2. Most important factor in selecting a store:
   Quality = 72%
   Price = 28%
3. Repeat purchasing behavior:
   Generally purchase the same brand = 64%
   Purchase whatever brand is on sale = 36%
4. When in a store, I often buy an item on the spur of the moment.
   Strongly agree/Agree = 40%
   Strongly disagree/Disagree = 35%
5. When I go to the supermarket, I shop based on a budget.
   Strongly agree/Agree = 69%
   Strongly disagree/Disagree = 16%
6. I definitely/probably would make a purchase based on:
   Buy 1—Get 1 Free = 57%
   Cents-off coupon = 46%
   In-store samples = 42%
   Rebates = 37%
   Sweepstakes = 25%
7. Used cents-off coupon in past 30 days = 36%
   Language of coupons used:
      Spanish = 52%
      English = 15%
      Both = 33%
   Source of coupons:
      Newspaper = 67%
      Mail = 62%
      In-store = 12%

Source: *The 1993 MSR Minority Market Report* (Coral Gables, FL: Market Segment Research, Inc., 1993).

5. Does it make sense to treat African-Americans as a separate segment for these products? Why?
6. Develop a complete marketing strategy for the following to use to gain sales among African-American consumers. What additional data would you like to have to develop your strategy?
   a. Bull's Eye Barbecue Sauce
   b. Tabasco Sauce
7. Which of the Hispanic market segments described in Chapter 5 would be the best target market(s) for Kraft BBQ Sauce? Why?
8. Would it make more sense to treat Hispanics as several nationality groups or as a single Hispanic group (perhaps with demographic submarkets) with respect to bottled sauces? Why?
9. Develop a complete marketing strategy for the following to use to gain sales among Hispanic consumers.
   a. Lawry's
   b. Louisiana Hot Sauce
   c. Kraft BBQ Sauce

part three

Internal Influences

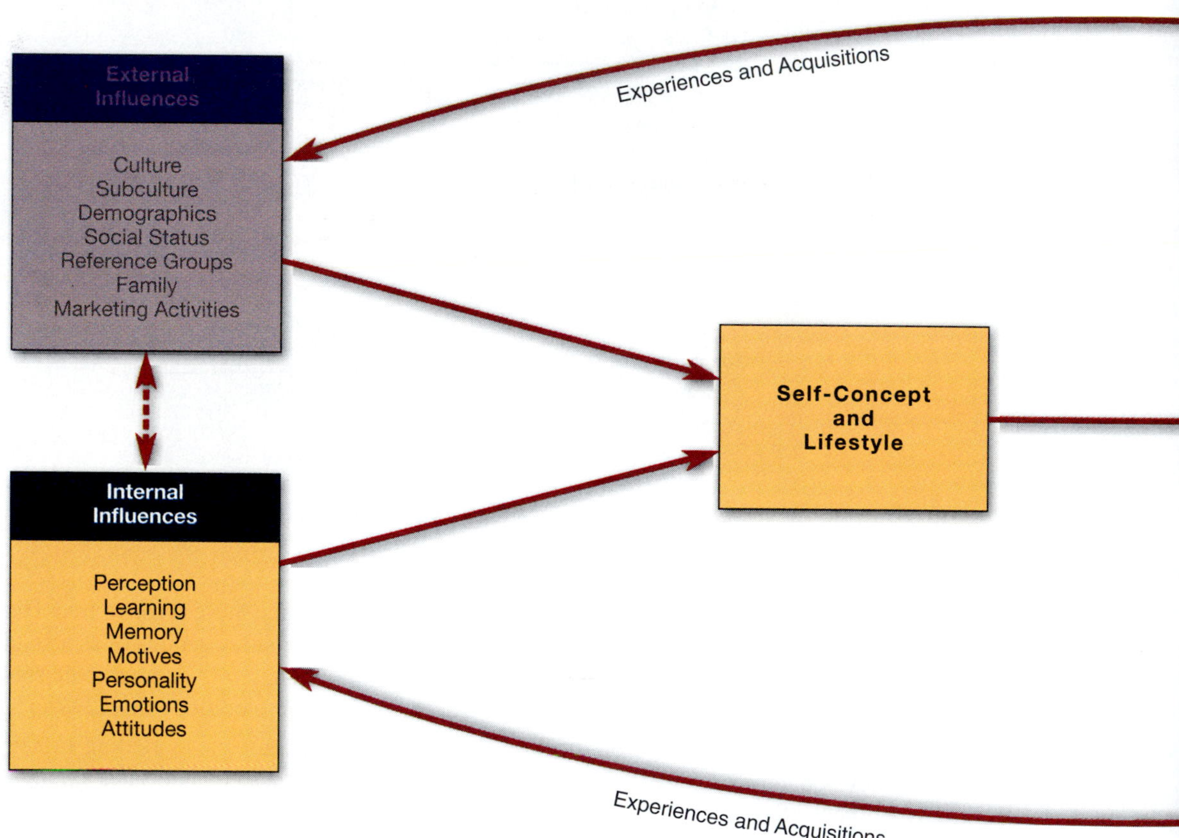

■ The highlighted areas of our model, internal influences and self-concept and lifestyle, are the focal point of this part of the text. Our attention shifts from forces that are basically outside the individual to processes that occur primarily within the individual.

This part begins with a discussion of perception, the process by which individuals assign meaning to environmental stimuli. In Chapter 9, we consider learning and memory. Chapter 10 covers motivation, personality, and emotions. Chapter 11 focuses on the critical concept of attitudes and the various ways attitudes are formed and changed.

As a result of the interaction of the external influences described in the previous part of the text and the internal processes examined in this part, individuals form self-concepts and desired lifestyles. These are the hub of our model of consumer behavior. Self-concept refers to the way individuals think and feel about themselves as well as how they would like to think and feel about themselves. Their actual and desired lifestyles are the way they translate their self-concepts into daily behaviors, including purchases.

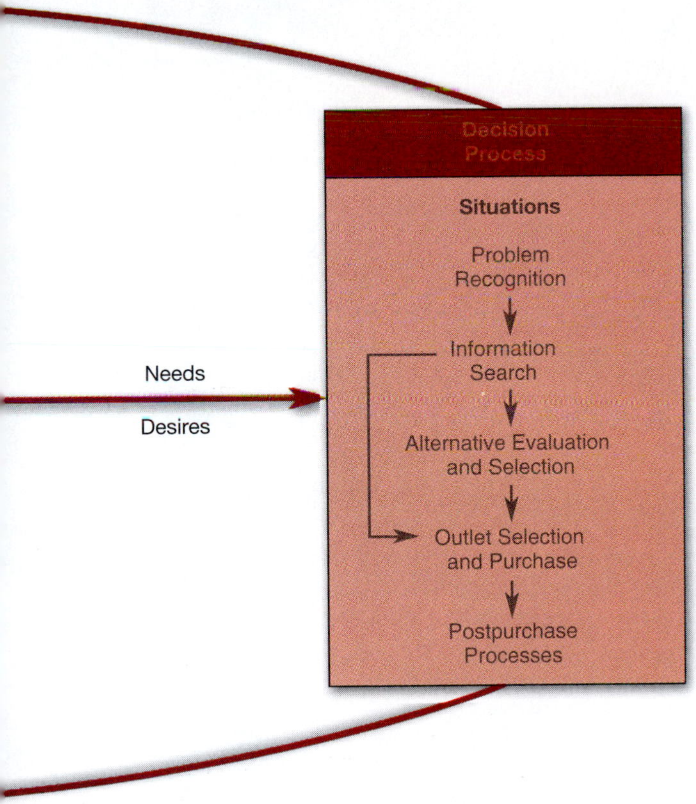

Courtesy Imperial Schrade Corporation.

chapter eight

Perception

Marketers often use attractive models to attract attention to their advertisements. This is particularly true when the advertisement is directed toward males. How effective is this tactic?

An eye-tracking device is a combination of computer and video technology that allows one to record eye movements in relation to a stimulus such as a package or a commercial. The respondent sits in a chair at a table and reads a magazine, watches television commercials, or observes slides of print advertisements, billboards, shelf facings, point-of-purchase displays, and so forth. Respondents control how long they view each scene. The eye-tracking device sends an unnoticeable beam of filtered light, which is reflected off the respondent's eyes. This reflected beam represents the focal point and can be superimposed on whatever is being viewed. This allows the researcher to determine how long an ad or other marketing stimulus is viewed, the sequence in which it was examined, which elements were examined, and how much time was devoted to looking at each element.

RCA used an attractive model in a television ad for its Colortrack television sets. The model wore a conservative dress. Eye tracking revealed that the audience focused substantial attention on the product. Seventy-two hours later, brand name recall was 36 percent. In contrast, a similar commercial used an attractive female in a revealing dress. Eye tracking showed that the ad attracted considerable attention but most of it was focused on the attractive model. Seventy-two hours later, brand name recall was only 9 percent![1]

Marketers do not want their target audience to look only at the models in their ads. They want to communicate something about their product as well. However, since there are many more commercials than consumers can possibly look at, marketers often use attractive models, humor, or other factors to attract the target market's interest. The opening example illustrates that if not well done, these factors may attract attention only to themselves, not to the advertising message. Will the Schrade ad on the facing page effectively communicate its message to its target audience?

A sound knowledge of perception is essential to avoid this and other problems encountered when communicating with various target audiences. Perception is the critical activity that links the individual consumer to group, situation, and marketer influences.

THE NATURE OF PERCEPTION

Information processing is *a series of activities by which stimuli are perceived, transformed into information, and stored.* Figure 8-1 illustrates a useful information-processing model having four major steps or stages: exposure, attention, interpretation, and memory. The first three of these constitute **perception.**

FIGURE 8-1 Information Processing for Consumer Decision Making

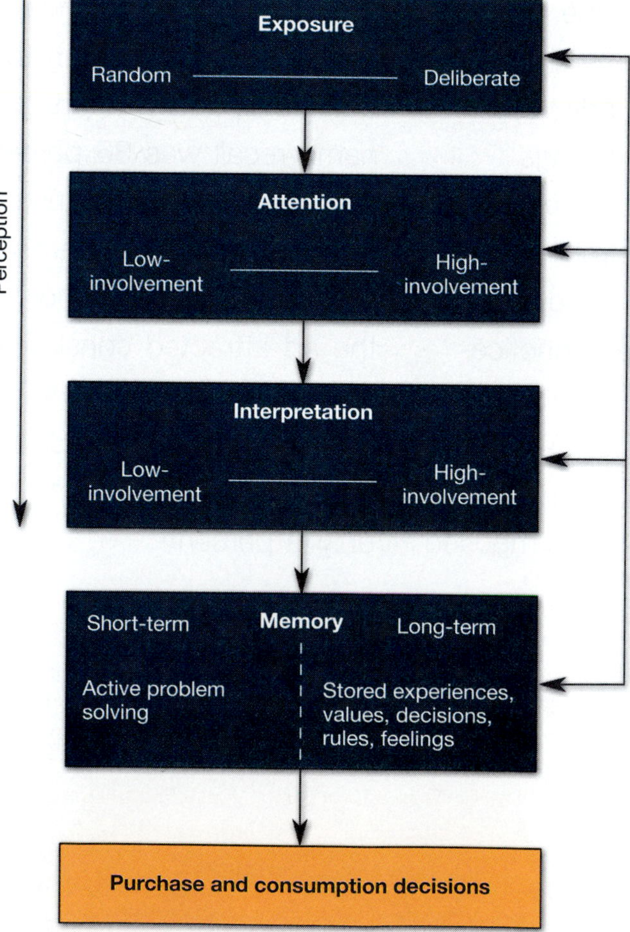

Exposure occurs when a stimulus such as a billboard comes within range of a person's sensory receptor nerves—vision, for example. *Attention* occurs when the receptor nerves pass the sensations on to the brain for processing. *Interpretation* is the assignment of meaning to the received sensations. *Memory* is the short-term use of the meaning for immediate decision making or the longer-term retention of the meaning.

Figure 8-1 and the above discussion suggest a linear flow from exposure to memory. However, *these processes occur virtually simultaneously and are clearly interactive*. That is, our memory influences the information we are exposed to, attend to, and the interpretations we assign. At the same time, memory itself is being shaped by the information it is receiving.

Both perception and memory are extremely selective. Of the massive amount of information available, an individual can be exposed to only a limited amount. Of the information to which the individual is exposed, only a relatively small percentage is attended to and passed on to the central processing part of the brain for interpretation. The meaning assigned to a stimulus is as much or more a function of the individual as it is the stimulus itself. Much of the interpreted information will not be available to active memory when the individual needs to make a purchase decision.

This selectivity, sometimes referred to as **perceptual defenses,** means that *individuals are not passive recipients of marketing messages*. Rather, consumers largely determine the messages they will encounter and notice as well as the meaning they will assign them. Clearly, the marketing manager faces a challenging task when communicating with consumers.

EXPOSURE

Exposure occurs *when a stimulus comes within range of our sensory receptor nerves*. For an individual to be exposed to a stimulus requires only that the stimulus be placed within the person's relevant environment. The individual need not receive the stimulus for exposure to have occurred. That is, you have been exposed to a television commercial if it aired while you were in the room, even if you were talking to a friend and did not notice the commercial.

An individual is generally exposed to no more than a small fraction of the available stimuli. There are now hundreds of television channels, thousands of radio stations, and an exponentially increasing number of sites on the Internet. Yet, one normally watches only one television station at a time, reads one magazine, newspaper, or book at a time, and so forth. What determines which stimuli an individual will be exposed to? Is it a random process or purposeful?

Why are you reading this text? Clearly, you are doing so for a reason. Most of the stimuli to which individuals are exposed are "self-selected." That is, we deliberately seek out exposure to certain stimuli and avoid others.

Generally, we seek *information that we think will help us achieve our goals*. These goals may be immediate or long range. Immediate goals could involve seeking stimuli such as a television program for amusement, an advertisement to assist in a purchase decision, or a compliment to enhance our self-concept. Long-range goals might involve studying this text in hopes of passing the next exam, obtaining a degree, becoming a better marketing manager, or all three. An individual's goals and the types of information needed to achieve those goals are a function of the individual's existing and desired lifestyle and such short-term motives as hunger or curiosity.

Of course, we are also exposed to a large number of stimuli on a more or less random basis during our daily activities. While driving, we may hear commercials, see billboards and display ads, and so on, that we did not purposefully seek out.

The impact of the active, self-selecting nature of exposure can be seen in the zipping, zapping, and muting of television commercials. **Zipping** occurs when one fast-forwards through a commercial on a prerecorded program. **Zapping** involves switching channels when a commercial appears. **Muting** is turning the sound off during commercial breaks. The nearly universal presence of remote controls makes zipping, zapping, and muting very simple.

One study of zipping found that most commercials were zipped and most of these were zipped without any viewing at all. This is important, as it means that the advertiser has only limited ability to reduce zipping by creative advertising.[2] However, there is evidence that moderately unique ads and ads that arouse positive feelings are less subject to zipping than are other ads.[3]

Zapping has been found to be influenced by the same ad characteristics as zipping. In addition, the situation itself (presence of a remote control, a VCR time shifter, cable TV), the amount of clutter (number of ads during a time period), placement of the ad (at the end of a program rather than in the middle), and the type of household (multiple-person, higher income, with males present, with children under 18) increase zapping.[4] As with zipping, most commercials were zapped as soon as they appeared. Many consumers habitually zap all commercials, though about 40 percent of consumers rarely zap commercials.[5] Those who zip or zap commercials appear to do so for enjoyment (it is fun), to alleviate boredom, to avoid commercials (dislike of commercials), for relaxation (it helps me unwind), and curiosity (zapping to see what is on other channels).[6]

These findings are valid only for the American market, with its immense array of television channel choices, a long history of advertising during programs (in some countries, ads are limited to the times between programs), and the widespread diffusion of remote controls. A recent study of commercial viewing in New Zealand (with basically only three channels) found very little viewing drop-off during commercials and no consistent demographic characteristics associated with those who did switch channels.[7] However, a large-scale study in the Netherlands (with five main channels) found significant zapping during commercial breaks.[8]

Avoidance of commercials is not limited to television. Automobile drivers avoid about half of the radio commercials broadcast by switching stations.[9] Newspaper readers now read only about half the daily paper compared to reading almost two-thirds 10 years ago.[10] Ads in magazines are also frequently avoided, and many individuals remove all advertising inserts before reading a magazine.[11] Forty percent of Internet users claim they never look at banner ads while using the Internet.[12]

Of course, consumers not only avoid commercials, they also actively seek them out. Many viewers look forward to the commercials developed for the Super Bowl. More impressive is the positive response consumers have to **infomercials**—program-length commercials (often 30 minutes), generally with an 800 number to order the product or request additional written information. One study found that over half the population had watched an infomercial in the past year, with viewership heaviest among younger, more affluent consumers.[13] Another study found that early adopters, opinion leaders, and active shoppers are more likely to view infomercials than are other consumers.[14] This suggests that they may have significant indirect effects through their impact on word-of-mouth communications.

Consumers also actively seek out commercial information on the Internet. In one survey, 45 percent of the respondents reported using the Internet in the past six months. Of these, three-fourths have visited a company's home page, primarily to obtain product information. Eighty-five percent of these have sought out a Web site because they saw or heard it in a mass media ad. The study also found that half of those using the Internet sometimes click on banner ads for additional information.[15] Thus, while there are very few studies in this area and the use and nature of the Internet is changing rapidly, it is clear that many consumers are using it as a means of gaining exposure to marketing messages.

ATTENTION

Attention occurs *when the stimulus activates one or more sensory receptor nerves and the resulting sensations go to the brain for processing*. We are constantly exposed to thousands of times more stimuli than we can process. The average supermarket has 30,000 individual items. It would take hours to attend to each of them. Each television network shows 6,000 commercials per week and radio stations air many more. Therefore, we have to be selective in attending to marketing as well as to other messages.

This selectivity has major implications for marketing managers and others concerned with communicating with consumers. For example, a Federal Trade Commission staff report indicates that fewer than 3 percent of those reading cigarette ads ever notice the health warning.[16] Less than half of the direct-mail ads received are read.[17] As the following story illustrates, anyone wishing to communicate effectively with consumers must understand how to obtain attention after obtaining exposure.

> The Federal Crop Insurance Corporation (FCIC) spent $13.5 million over a four-year period on an advertising campaign to increase awareness and knowledge among farmers of the federal crop insurance program. The campaign included "direct mailings to millions of producers of crops covered by the farmers' disaster program and to FCIC policyholders; national and local news releases; feature stories in national magazines, a radio campaign; publication of several brochures . . ."
>
> However, "farmers ended up knowing no more about this program after the ad campaign than they did before." A spokesperson described the problem with the program: "It was very good and very effective advertising. The trouble is that we had a hard time getting people to read it."[18]

What determines or influences attention? At this moment, you are attending to these words. If you shift your concentration to your feet, you will most likely become aware of the pressure being exerted by your shoes. A second shift in concentration to sounds will probably produce awareness of a number of background noises. These stimuli are available all the time but are not processed until a deliberate effort is made to do so. However, no matter how hard you are concentrating on this text, a loud scream or a sudden hand on your shoulder would probably get your attention. Of course, attention always occurs within the context of a situation. The *same individual* may devote different levels of attention to the *same stimulus* in *different situations*. Attention is determined by three factors—the *stimulus,* the *individual,* and the *situation.*

Stimulus Factors

Stimulus factors are physical characteristics of the stimulus itself. A number of stimulus characteristics tend to attract our attention independently of our individual characteristics.

Size and Intensity The *size* of the stimulus influences the probability of paying attention. Larger stimuli are more likely to be noticed than smaller ones. Thus, a full-page advertisement is more likely to be noticed than a half-page advertisement. In one study, consumers seeking a business from the Yellow Pages attended to over 90 percent of the quarter page ads but only a quarter of the plain listings.[19] Figure 8-2 indicates the relative

FIGURE 8-2 The Impact of Size on Advertising Readership*

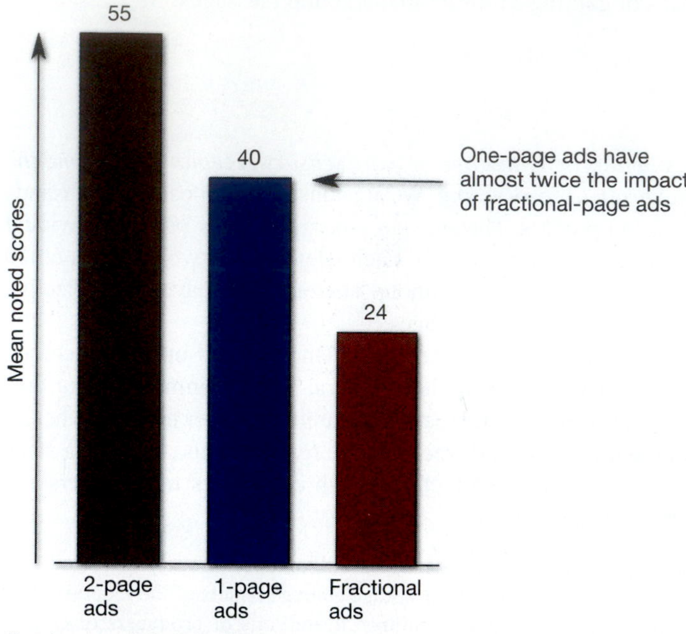

*Based on an analysis of 85,000 ads.

Source: *Cahners Advertising Research Report 110.1B* (Boston: Cahners Publishing, undated).

attention-attracting ability of various sizes of magazine ads. Another analysis of 86,000 ads found the following average number of inquiries for additional information in relation to ad size:[20]

Size	*Number of Responses*
Spread	107
1 page	76
2/3 page	68
1/2 page	56
1/3 page	47

Insertion frequency, the number of times the same ad appears in the same issue of a magazine, has an impact similar to ad size. Multiple insertions were found to increase recall by 20 percent in one study and by 200 percent in another.[21] The *intensity* (e.g., loudness, brightness) of a stimulus operates in much the same manner.

Color and Movement Both *color* and *movement* serve to attract attention, with brightly colored and moving items being more noticeable. A brightly colored package is more apt to receive attention than a dull package. In an eye-tracking study of Yellow Page usage, it was found that color ads were attended to before noncolor ads, more frequently than noncolor ads, and for longer time periods than noncolor ads.[22] Figure 8-3 shows the relative attention-attracting ability of black and white and of four-color magazine ads of different sizes.

Color and Size Impact on Attention **FIGURE 8-3**

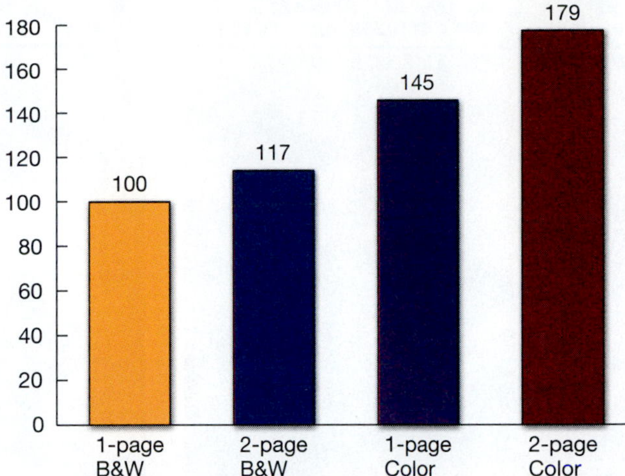

Readership of a 2-page black and white ad was set at 100.

Source: "How Important Is Color to an Ad?" *Starch Tested Copy,* February 1989, p. 1, Roper Starch Worldwide, Inc.

Illustration 8-1 shows two ads that are identical except for the use of color. The ad with the color was noticed by 40 percent more readers than the black and white ad. However, while color can increase attention and readership, if not used properly, it can also distract from the message and the ability of the audience to effectively process the message.[23]

Position *Position* refers to the placement of an object in a person's visual field. Objects placed near the center of the visual field are more likely to be noticed than those near the edge of the field. This is a primary reason why consumer goods manufacturers compete fiercely for eye-level space in grocery stores. Likewise, advertisements on the right-hand page receive more attention than those on the left. The probability of a television commercial being viewed drops sharply as it moves from being the first to air during a break to the last to air.[24]

Isolation *Isolation* is separating a stimulus object from other objects. The use of "white space" (placing a brief message in the center of an otherwise blank or white advertisement) is based on this principle, as is surrounding a key part of a radio commercial with a brief moment of silence.[25] Illustration 8-2 shows an effective television ad that uses isolation and contrast (discussed shortly). This ad for the Green Burrito fast-food chain contains only the green smiley face set on a black background. The mouth moves as the face speaks or sings the ad message in a "calming but off-key" male voice.

Format Catalog merchants wishing to display multiple items per page often create an environment in which the competition for attention across items reduces attention to all of the items. However, with proper arrangement and formatting this competition for attention can be reduced and sales improved.[26] *Format* refers to the manner in which the message is presented. In general, simple, straightforward presentations receive more attention than complex presentations. Elements in the message that increase the effort required to process the message tend to decrease attention. Advertisements that lack a clear visual point of reference or have inappropriate movement (too fast, slow, or "jumpy") increase the processing effort and decrease attention. Likewise, audio messages that are difficult to understand due to foreign accents, inadequate volume, deliberate distortions (computer voices), loud background noises, and so forth also reduce attention.[27]

ILLUSTRATION 8-1

Color can attract attention to an ad. In this case, the color ad had a noted score of 62 percent compared to 44 percent for the identical black and white ad.

Courtesy of Konica Business Machines, U.S.A.

Contrast *Contrast* refers to our tendency to attend more closely to stimuli that contrast with their background than to stimuli that blend with it. Ads that differ from the type of ad consumers expect for a product category often motivate more attention than ads that are more typical for the product category.[28] The headline, colors, and design of the ad in Illustration 8-3 contrast with expectations and will cause many to attend to the ad.

Over time, we adjust to the level and type of stimuli to which we are accustomed. Thus, an advertisement that stands out when new will eventually lose its contrast effect and its ability to capture or hold attention.[29] The body of knowledge called **adaptation level theory** deals with this phenomenon.

Information Quantity A final stimulus factor, information quantity, relates more to the total stimulus field than to any particular item in that field. Although there is substantial variation among individuals, all consumers have limited capacities to process information. **Information overload** occurs when consumers are confronted with so much information that they cannot or will not attend to all of it. Instead, they become frustrated and either postpone or give up the decision, make a random choice, or utilize a suboptimal portion of the total information available.

One study found that consumers purchased more items as the number of catalogs they received increased, and then at a certain point the number of items purchased decreased as additional catalogs were received. The explanation was that information overload had been reached and consumers had stopped reading any of the catalogs.[30]

There are no general rules or guidelines concerning how much information consumers can or will use. Marketers, the federal government, and various consumer groups want product labels, packages, and advertisements to provide *sufficient* information to allow for an informed decision. Marketers must determine the information needs of their target markets and provide the information those consumers desire. In general, the most important information should be presented first, and it should be highlighted or otherwise made to stand out from the main part of the text. More detailed and less important data can be provided in

Courtesy Mendelsohn/Zien.

ILLUSTRATION 8-2

This television commercial for the Green Burrito food chain makes effective use of isolation and contrast to capture and hold attention to its message.

brochures, videotapes, Web sites, and infomercials that interested consumers can seek out. The regulatory implications of information overload are discussed in Chapter 20.

Individual Factors

Individual factors are characteristics of the individual. *Interest* and *need* seem to be the primary individual characteristics that influence attention. Interest is a reflection of overall lifestyle as well as a result of long-term goals and plans (e.g., becoming a sales manager) and short-term needs (e.g., hunger). Short-term goals and plans are, of course, heavily influenced by the situation. In addition, individuals differ in their *ability* to attend to information.[31]

ILLUSTRATION 8-3

Consumers are exposed to many more ads than they can read or even notice. Marketers often use bright colors and surprising headlines to capture the audience's attention.

Courtesy Robert Stock.

Individuals seek out (exposure) and examine (attend to) information relevant to their current needs. For example, an individual contemplating a vacation is likely to attend to vacation-related advertisements. Individuals attending to a specialized medium such as *Runner's World* or *Business Week* are particularly receptive to advertisements for related products. Not surprisingly, products are generally advertised in magazines with editorial copy related to the product or product usage.

Interest or involvement with a brand or product category implies that an individual is likely to attend to messages about the brand or product, and research supports this.[32] Thus, advertisers targeting consumers that are involved with their product or brand will not have much trouble attracting attention while those trying to reach uninterested consumers face a significant challenge.

Situational Factors

Situational factors include stimuli in the environment other than the focal stimulus (i.e., the ad or package) and temporary characteristics of the individual that are induced by the environment, such as time pressures or a very crowded store. For example, consumers pay less attention to a commercial in a large cluster of commercials than they do to one in a smaller set. This negative impact on attention is diminished if the commercial is first in the time cluster.[33]

Obviously, individuals in a hurry are less likely to attend to available stimuli than are those with extra time (if you have ever been on a long flight without a book, you may recall

Involvement with a Magazine and Advertising Effectiveness **FIGURE 8-4**

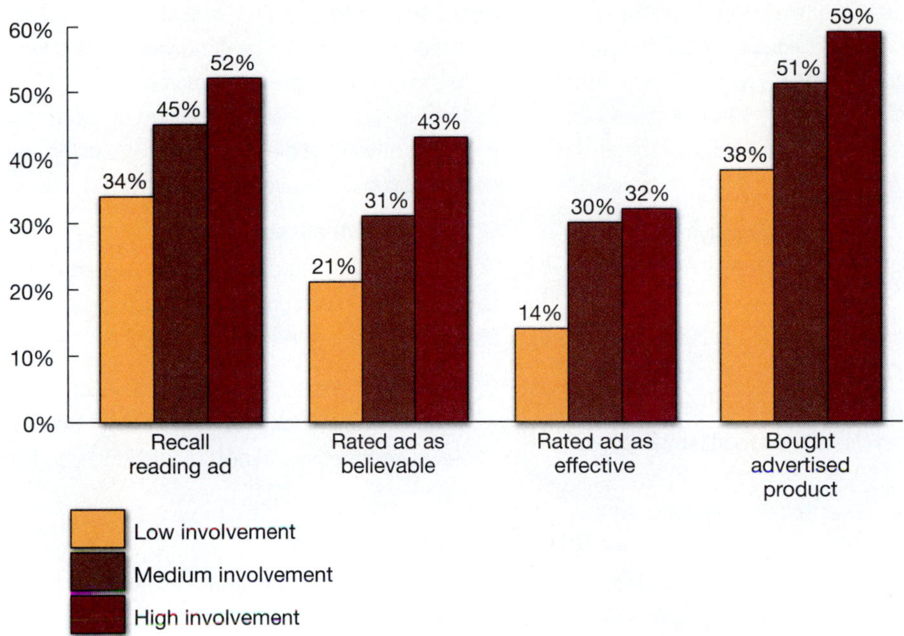

Source: *Cahners Advertising Research Report 120.1* and *120.12* (Boston: Cahners Publishing, undated).

reading even the ads in the airline magazine). Individuals in an unpleasant environment—such as an overcrowded store or a store that is too noisy, too warm, or too cold—will not attend to many of the available stimuli as they attempt to minimize their time in such an environment.

Program Involvement Print, radio, television, and Internet ads occur in the context of a newspaper, magazine, program, or site. In general, the audience is attending to the medium because of the program or editorial content, not the advertisement. In fact, as we saw earlier, many individuals actively avoid commercials by zapping them. Does the nature of the program or editorial content in which an ad appears influence the attention that the ad will receive? The answer to this question is clearly *yes*.[34] Figure 8-4 demonstrates the positive impact that involvement with a magazine has on attention to print ads. Below, we see that a high level of television program involvement greatly increases the percent of viewers who (1) recall the ads aired during the commercial, (2) find them to be credible, and (3) form positive purchase intentions:[35]

	Program Involvement		
	Low	*Medium*	*High*
Unaided recall	18%	21%	22%
Aided recall	34	48	54
Copy credibility	24	37	41
Purchase interest	13	16	18

Consumer Insight 8-1

Why People Watch TV

Research has consistently shown that people generally engage in other activities while watching TV or leave the room while the television is on. Yet at other times, these same individuals will be deeply engrossed in the program being shown. A recent study identified four levels of television "viewing" based on physical proximity to the set and degree of focus on the program:

- *Level I.* Television is the sole activity and concentration is high; the viewer is in front of the set.
- *Level II.* Television is one of two activities and concentration is divided; the viewer is in front of the set but visual focus is divided between viewing and another task such as reading the newspaper.
- *Level III.* Television is a peripheral activity, an accompaniment to a primary activity; the viewer is not in front of the set but is in contact with it.
- *Level IV.* Television is a background noise; the viewer may or may not be in the same room.

Most viewing at levels I and II appear to be fairly routinized. That is, consumers have shows they like and they tend to watch those shows regularly. There is very little "channel surfing" just to select a program to watch. Television viewing is also a social activity. About two-thirds of prime-time viewing is done in the presence of others. Prime-time viewing is a family or household affair, not a solo activity.

People not only watch television at differing levels, they also have multiple motives for watching. Six predominant motives have been discovered:

Committed/Ritualized

This involves viewing one's favorite programs on a regular basis. The programs have become like friends. The following quote exemplifies this motive:

> When you watch . . . the same newscasters, they become like friends. You watch the 11 o'clock news and he says "Good night," and you feel like saying, "Good night, Charles."

Mood Improvement

Many people view TV to elevate their moods or to escape from cares and worries:

> You work, you come home . . . the same old dull routine every day. (TV) sort of takes you away from your everyday working life and lets you forget about your own problems for a while.

It should be noted that most of the gain in attention occurs when program involvement moves from low to moderate levels. There is some evidence that high levels of program involvement may detract from the attention paid to some types of commercials.[36] Program involvement not only increases the attention paid to the ad; it also affects the viewer's attitude toward the ad and the product being advertised.[37]

There are multiple reasons or motives underlying program involvement.[38] Several of these are described in Consumer Insight 8-1.[39]

Nonfocused Attention

Thus far, we have been discussing a fairly high-involvement attention process in which the consumer focuses attention on some aspect of the environment due to stimulus, individual, or situational factors.[40] However, stimuli may be attended to without deliberate or conscious focusing of attention. For example, products contained in ads to which subjects were exposed but to which they paid little or no attention nonetheless had an enhanced probability of being considered for purchase.[41]

Hemispheric Lateralization **Hemispheric lateralization** is a term applied to activities that take place on each side of the brain. The left side of the brain is primarily responsible for verbal information, symbolic representation, sequential analysis, and the

It's a security blanket . . . a decompression chamber, immersion in a fantasy world for a few moments, a few hours.

Information/Cognitive Benefit

Television is used to keep viewers up-to-date on current events, to provide new and interesting information, to acquaint viewers with people and places they would not otherwise encounter, and to provide "food for thought."

Social Learning

Viewers use situations shown on television to examine their own behaviors and as a source of guidance:

> You have done something to somebody and you didn't even think it was wrong—it never even crossed your mind. You can look at a program and you think, "How could he say that to somebody?" And you think, "Gee, I said something like that to this person just the other day."

Social Grease

Many programs are watched because one's family or friends are watching them. They are the source of conversation while they are on (or during the commercials) or in the days following the show:

> We discuss (stories) and talk about what we didn't like, about what happened with the different characters we don't like or we do like . . . sometimes people think you are talking about some people you know, real people.

Engrossing Different World

This a type of escapism in which the television induces a kind of substitute consciousness. Rather than relaxation, it produces suspense, excitement, and emotional arousal:

> Out of touch . . . I don't think about anything. I don't think about my kids, my wife or anything . . . I'm not there . . . I'm not at school and I'm not at home. I'm in the TV screen . . . I'm there with them.

Critical Thinking Questions

1. How should commercials differ depending on the motive a target market has for viewing a particular program?
2. What programs are likely to be watched for each of these six reasons?

Source: B. Lee and R. S. Lee, "How and Why People Watch TV," *Journal of Advertising Research,* November 1995, pp. 9–18.

ability to be conscious and report what is happening. It controls those activities we typically call rational thought. The right side of the brain deals with pictorial, geometric, timeless, and nonverbal information without the individual being able to verbally report it. It works with images and impressions.

The left brain needs fairly frequent rest. However, the right brain can easily scan large amounts of information over an extended time period. This had led Krugman to suggest that "it is the right brain's picture-taking ability that permits the rapid screening of the environment—to select what it is the left brain should focus on."[42] Evidence indicates that there is some validity to this theory. This indicates that advertising, particularly advertising repeated over time, will have substantial effects that traditional measures of advertising effectiveness cannot detect. The nature of these effects is discussed in more detail in the next chapter. At this point, we need to stress that applied research on this topic is just beginning, and much remains to be learned.[43]

Subliminal Stimuli A message presented so fast or so softly or so masked by other messages that one is not aware of "seeing" or "hearing" it is called a **subliminal stimulus.** Subliminal stimuli have been the focus of intense study as well as public concern.

Two books triggered public interest in masked subliminal stimuli.[44] The author "documents" numerous advertisements that, once you are told where to look and what to look for, appear to contain the word *sex* in ice cubes, phalli in mixed drinks, and nude bodies in the shadows. Most, if not all, of these symbols are the chance result of preparing thousands of print ads each year (a diligent search could no doubt produce large numbers of religious symbols, animals, or whatever). Such masked symbols (deliberate or accidental) do not appear to affect standard measures of advertising effectiveness or influence consumption behavior.[45] Research on messages presented too rapidly to elicit awareness indicates that such messages have little or no effect.

Thus, though the general public is concerned about subliminal messages,[46] such messages do not present a threat to the general public nor do they offer a potentially effective communications device.[47] In addition, there is no evidence marketers are using subliminal messages.[48]

INTERPRETATION

Interpretation *is the assignment of meaning to sensations*. It is a function of the *gestalt* or pattern formed by the characteristics of the stimulus, the individual, and the situation. Thus, the entire message, including the context in which it occurs, influences our interpretation, as does the situation in which we find ourselves. For example, our beliefs about a new product are influenced by our beliefs about the capabilities and social responsibility of the company that produces it.[49] Likewise, consumers may interpret a high level of advertising for some products as meaning that the products are of low quality.[50]

We assign meaning to the tone and "feel" of the message as well as the actual words and symbols. For example, in a television ad, one actor can say "Thanks a lot" to another. Is this an expression of gratitude? It depends. Sometimes it is, and sometimes it means just the opposite. Members of the same culture or subculture easily and accurately assign the correct meaning based on voice tone or context.[51]

Cognitive interpretation is a process whereby stimuli are placed into existing categories of meaning. This is an interactive process. The addition of new information to existing categories also alters those categories and their relationships with other categories. When the compact disc player was first introduced to consumers, they most probably grouped it in the general category of record players in order to be able to evaluate it. With further experience and information, many consumers have gained detailed knowledge about the product and have formed several subcategories for classifying the various brands and types.

It is the individual's interpretation, not objective reality, that will influence behavior. For example, a firm may introduce a high-quality new brand at a lower price than existing brands because the firm has a more efficient production or marketing process. If consumers interpret this lower price to mean lower quality, the new brand will not be successful regardless of the objective reality.[52]

The above example indicates the critical importance of distinguishing between *semantic meaning,* the conventional meaning assigned to a word such as found in the dictionary, and *psychological meaning,* the specific meaning assigned a word by a given individual or group of individuals based on their experiences and the context or situation in which the term is used.[53]

Marketers must be concerned with psychological meaning. For example, the semantic meaning of the expression *on sale* is "a price reduction from the normal level." However, when applied to fashion clothes, the psychological meaning that some consumers would derive is "these clothes are, or soon will be, out of style."

Affective interpretation is the emotional or feeling response triggered by a stimulus such as an ad. Like cognitive interpretation, there are "normal" (within-culture) emotional responses to many stimuli (e.g., most Americans experience a feeling of warmth when seeing pictures of young children with kittens). Likewise, there are also individual variations to this response (a person allergic to cats might have a very negative emotional response to such a picture).[54]

Individual Characteristics

Marketing stimuli have meaning *only* as individuals interpret them.[55] A number of *individual characteristics* influence interpretation. For example, gender and social class affect the meaning assigned to owning various products. Likewise, gender affects the nature of the emotional response to nudity in ads.[56] There is evidence that our language may influence how we interpret and recall written and verbal information.[57] Two particularly important personal variables affecting interpretation are *learning* and *expectations.*

Learning We saw in Chapter 2 that the meanings attached to such "natural" things as time, space, friendship, and colors are learned and vary widely across cultures. Even within the same culture, different subcultures assign different meanings to similar stimuli. For example, dinner refers to the noon meal for some social classes in some geographic regions of the United States and to the evening meal for other social classes and geographic regions.

Likewise, many consumers have a very warm emotional response when presented with pictures of fried chicken or people frying chicken. They learned this response because of fried chicken's role in picnics and family gatherings when they were young. Thus, we are referring to learning in this context not as formal learning such as one encounters in an academic setting but as the accumulation of life experiences. Consider how Kim, a young woman who values control, responded to several beer ads:

INTERVIEWER: (referring to beer party ad): What evidence did the advertiser provide for conveying the theme that beer makes the party?

KIM: They wanted you to see the party. Everyone looks like they're having fun. When you go to a party, someone is out of control or doing something stupid. Everything here is under control. That was trying to portray a positive image of a party.

KIM: (responding to a question about a bar scene beer ad): Beer makes you smile, laugh, get along. Everyone's attractive, younger, having a good time. They don't look like they'd been drinking. No one looked like they've been drinking numerous beers.

INTERVIEWER: You've said that several times. Do you expect to see the downside of drinking?

KIM: Yeah, I guess I'm used to it. I wouldn't expect them to show that to a customer. I compare it to what I see. In college and high school, people don't really have control over it. They go too far. It's difficult for me to see leisurely drinking.[58]

Clearly, consumers base their interpretation of marketing messages and activities on their own experiences and needs.

Expectations Individuals' interpretations of stimuli tend to be consistent with their *expectations.* For example, we expect dark brown pudding to taste like chocolate, not vanilla, because dark pudding is generally chocolate flavored and vanilla pudding is generally cream colored. In a recent taste test, 100 percent of a sample of college students accepted dark brown *vanilla* pudding as chocolate. Further, in comparing three versions of the vanilla pudding that differed only in degree of darkness, the students rated the darkest as having the best chocolate flavor.[59] Thus, their expectations, cued by color, led to an interpretation that was inconsistent with "objective" reality. The ad in Illustration 8-4 uses color to reinforce an interpretation that Godiva truffles are "rich" and "luscious." This works because we have learned, through our culture, to assign this type of meaning to the color gold.

ILLUSTRATION 8-4

Colors do more than just attract attention to an ad. They provide an important part of the meaning of the ad. The use of gold in this ad conveys a meaning of richness that is consistent with the intent of the advertiser.

Courtesy Godiva Chocolatier, Inc.

Consumers will frequently evaluate the performance of a well-known brand or a more expensive brand as higher than that of an identical product with an unknown brand name or a lower price. Consumers also frequently attribute advertisements for new or unknown brands to well-known brands. Even an "objective" product feature such as price is sometimes interpreted to be closer to an expected price. Likewise, brands with promotional signs on them in retail stores are interpreted as having reduced prices even when the sign does not indicate that prices have been reduced and when, in fact, prices have *not* been reduced.[60]

Situational Characteristics

Consider the following situation:

> Three stores sell coffeemakers. The first store offers two brands of comparable quality, Braun and Krups. The second store carries only one brand, Braun, and the third carries only Krups. Will customers who visit the first store and evaluate the two brands of coffee makers jointly value those brands differently than consumers who go to the second or third store and evaluate only one of the two brands? If so, in which store will these brands be valued most?

The answer is, it depends. It depends on how attractive the consumer perceives each brand to be relative to his or her requirements or expectations. If both brands are initially relatively attractive, evaluating them jointly reduces their perceived value. If they are initially relatively unattractive, evaluating them jointly tends to increase their perceived attractiveness.[61] Thus, the situation (joint or separate evaluations) interacts with individual and product characteristics to determine interpretation.

A variety of situational characteristics influence interpretation. Temporary characteristics of the individual, such as hunger or loneliness, influence the interpretation of a given stimulus, as do moods. The amount of time available also affects the meaning assigned to marketing messages. Likewise, physical characteristics of the situation such as temperature, the number and characteristics of other individuals present, the nature of the material surrounding the message in question, external distractions, and the reason the message is being processed affect how the message is interpreted.

Will consumers interpret a price or sale ad or display that asks them to "compare at" another store or an ad that asks them to compare to the store's regular price as offering the most value (given identical savings)? The answer depends in large part on *where* the consumer is when attending to the ad. If at home, the "compare to another store" tends to be evaluated as offering the best value while the opposite is true if the ad is read in the store.[62]

Both Coca-Cola and General Foods have refused to advertise some products during news broadcasts because they believe that "bad" news might affect the interpretation of their products. According to a Coca-Cola spokesperson:

> It's a Coca-Cola corporate policy not to advertise on TV news because there's going to be some bad news in there, and Coke is an upbeat, fun product.[63]

The above quote expresses a concern about context effects, or what researchers refer to as **contextual priming effects.** This refers to the impact that the content of the material surrounding an ad will have on the interpretation of the ad. The immediate contexts in which ads appear are generally the television/radio program in which they are embedded or the magazine/newspaper/Web site in which they appear. As Coca-Cola suspects, it appears that ads are evaluated in a more positive light when surrounded with positive programming.[64]

Stimulus Characteristics

The stimulus sets the basic structure to which an individual responds. The structure and nature of the product, package, advertisement, or sales presentation have a major impact on the nature of the mental processes that are activated and on the final meaning assigned to the message.[65]

In recognition of the critical importance of the meaning associated with stimuli, marketers are beginning to use semiotics. **Semiotics** is *the science of how meaning is created, maintained, and altered.* It focuses on **signs,** which are *anything that conveys meaning, including words, pictures, music, colors, forms, smells, gestures, products, prices, and so forth.*[66] Thus, while signs are part of the stimulus, the audience assigns meanings to them. As a recent study concludes:

> [T]he consumption of any product is richly embroidered by the symbolism of the practices, rituals, and texts surrounding it and, further, the meanings associated with products are crucial to understanding their exchange value in the marketplace.[67]

The following example shows how the same ad can elicit different meanings based on the audience's viewpoint. The stimulus was a clothing ad for Jordache:

> The consultant saw the virtues of wisdom, justice and temperance, faith and envy in this ad, while the pastor saw lust and temperance. The consultant derived wisdom and justice from the perceived conservative nature of the product. The product was not faddish and was thus correct for many social occasions. Both interpreted the calm look on the model's face as temperance. The color of the outfit (white) also suggested temperance to the pastor. While the consultant did not take notice of how the blouse was buttoned . . . the minister focused on this slight dishabille as a sign of lust. This was a subtle sign, but still a strong referent for lust.
>
> The consultant also stated that the setting and especially the boat could "elicit" envy in the viewer. The sailboat, or in her words "yacht," would signify wealth and status and thus elicit envy.[68]

Colors can be used to further illustrate the importance of semiotics. In Chapter 2, the different meanings that various societies assign different colors were described. For example, red is considered to be unlucky or negative in Chad, Nigeria, and Germany, but it has positive connotations in Denmark, Rumania, and Argentina. Brides wear red in China, but it is a masculine color in the United Kingdom and France.

Earlier in this chapter, we saw how color influenced taste perceptions of pudding. When *Barrelhead Sugar-Free Root Beer* changed the background color on its cans from blue to beige, consumers rated it as *tasting* more like old-fashioned root beer. Canada Dry's sugar-free ginger ale sales increased dramatically when the can was changed to green and white from red. Red is interpreted as a cola color and thus conflicted with the taste of ginger ale.[69]

The U.S. Supreme court recently ruled that color can serve as a trademark. In a case involving Qualitex Co., a marketer of dry cleaning pads, the court ruled that the distinctive green-gold color that it had been using (1) *acts as a symbol,* (2) *having developed secondary meaning it serves as a mark and identifies the source of the product,* and (3) *the color does not serve any other product-related function.*[70] The first two standards listed above are based on the meanings that consumers learn to associate with particular colors in specific situations.

Consumers across many cultures use brand name, price, warranty, physical product appearance, and retailer reputation as signals of product quality.[71] In addition, factors indirectly related to the product, such as its country of origin, can have a major influence on the meaning assigned the product (see Chapter 16). For example, would you rather have a sweater designed and made in Japan or Italy, a watch from Switzerland or Brazil? Many consumers would answer Italy and Switzerland. Further, many would evaluate the actual products in a manner consistent with their predispositions. This poses significant challenges for marketers competing with brands made in countries with superior reputations for that product category.[72]

All aspects of the message itself influence our interpretation. This can include our reaction to the overall style, visual and auditory background, and other nonverbal and verbal aspects of the message, as well as its explicit content. For example, the type of background music played during an ad has been found to influence the interpretation of and response to the ad.[73] Likewise, the set of brands available affects the interpretation assigned individual brands. Thus, the entry of a brand into a market results in a revaluation of existing brands as well as an initial evaluation of the new brand.[74] Likewise, promoting a new product in conjunction with an existing product influences the perceived quality of the new product.[75]

In Illustration 8-5 the attention-attracting device, the mannequin being pulled into the billboard by the vacuum cleaner, reinforces the verbal content of the message ("The incredible suction power of the AEG Vampyr Rosso"). This billboard is likely to attract attention and communicate the key message that the AEG vacuum cleaner is powerful.

Sensory Discrimination The ability of an individual to distinguish between similar stimuli is called **sensory discrimination.** This involves such variables as the sound of stereo systems, the taste of food products, or the clarity of display screens. Marketers obviously must know how much they need to change a brand in order for consumers to notice the change.

The minimum amount that one brand can differ from another with the difference still being noticed is referred to as the **just noticeable difference (j.n.d.).** Marketers seeking to find a promotable difference between their brand and a competitor's must surpass the j.n.d. in order for the improvement or change to be noticed by consumers. On the other hand, a marketer sometimes may want to change a product feature but not have the consumer perceive any change and hence not surpass the j.n.d.

Courtesy HVR/FCB Advertising/The Netherlands.

ILLUSTRATION 8-5

This billboard uses a unique attention-attracting device, ample white space, and a brief message. All the elements of the ad are consistent. It is likely to both capture attention and be interpreted as intended.

The higher the initial level of the attribute, the greater the amount that attribute must be changed before the change will be noticed. Thus, a small addition of salt to a pretzel would not distinguish the product from a competitor's unless the competitor's pretzel contained only a very limited amount of salt. This relationship is expressed formally as:

$$\text{j.n.d.} = \Delta I/I = K$$

where

j.n.d. = Just noticeable difference
I = Initial level of the attribute
ΔI = Change in the attribute
K = Constant that varies with each sense mode

Example: Lifting weights

$I = 100$ lbs

$K = .02$ for weight

$\text{j.n.d.} = \Delta I/100 = .02$

$\Delta I = 100 \text{ lbs.} \times .02$

$\Delta I = 2$ lbs. for j.n.d.

For one to detect a weight change, more than 2 pounds would have to be added or taken away from the original 100 pounds. This formula is known as **Weber's law.** Values for *K* have been established for several senses and can be utilized in the development of functional aspects of products.[76] More useful than the formula itself is the general principle behind it—*individuals typically do not notice relatively small differences between brands or changes in brand attributes*. Makers of candy bars have utilized this principle for years. Since the price of cocoa fluctuates widely, they simply make small adjustments in the size of the candy bar rather than altering price. Marketers want some product changes, such as reductions in the size of the candy bars, to go unnoticed. These changes must be below the j.n.d. Positive changes, such as going from a quart to a liter, must be above the j.n.d. or it may not be worthwhile to make them, unless advertising can convince people that meaningful differences exist.

Interpreting Images

Clinique ran an ad that pictured a tall, clear glass of mineral water and ice cubes. A large slice of lime was positioned on the lip of the glass. In the glass with the ice cubes and mineral water were a tube of Clinique lipstick and a container of cheek base. Nothing else appeared in the ad. What does this mean?

Until recently, actual pictures in marketing messages were thought to convey "reality." Since they duplicated a part of the visual world, it was assumed that they carried no cultural or individual meaning beyond the meaning attached to the objects they portrayed. If this is indeed the case, the Clinique ad is irrelevant or nonsensical: "the (ad) would be utterly unintelligible for a theory in which advertising pictures illustrate tangible product attributes or represent the consumption experience in a relevant way. No one stores open lipsticks in glasses of soda water and the ability of makeup to withstand such icy submersion would be an improbable benefit at best. It is not a common consumption practice to garnish mineral water with lipstick, cheek base, and a slice of lime."[77]

Is Clinique guilty of ineffective or even foolish advertising in this case? No. All of us intuitively recognize that pictures do more than represent reality, they supply meaning. Thus, one interpretation of the Clinique ad is "Clinique's new summer line of makeup is as refreshing as a tall glass of soda with a twist." The verbal translation of the meaning conveyed by images is generally incomplete and inadequate. Words and pictures have differing communications capabilities. Marketers constantly use images to communicate with consumers, yet we have only a very limited knowledge of how consumers interpret and respond to such messages.

A useful approach to designing ads using pictures and other nonverbal images is rhetorical theory. **Rhetoric** *approaches messages by framing them as an attempt by the sender of the message to influence the recipient of the message*. The intent to influence is a critical part of the analysis of the message and its interpretation. Thus, the receiver evaluates the message in light of assumptions about the sender's persuasive intentions. The sender crafts a message with the intention of influencing the audience. The sender selects the symbols—words, pictures, colors, and so forth—to use based on the anticipated response of the audience. The sender makes assumptions about the audience's response based on knowledge of the learned meanings the various elements of the message will have for the audience. The audience uses its vocabulary of meanings to read the message, infer the sender's intention, evaluate the argument, and formulate a response.[78]

In this view, images have learned meaning beyond their direct representation of reality. "A picture is worth a thousand words" not just because it may convey reality more efficiently than words but because it may convey meanings that words cannot adequately

Courtesy Guerlain, Inc.

ILLUSTRATION 8-6

Pictures do more than represent the visual part of "reality." By their elements and construction they can communicate rich meanings to which audiences will respond.

express. This approach requires us to construct ads whose total meaning, the interpretation formed by the words and the images in the ad, is internally consistent (the words and images convey consistent or complementary meanings) and will produce the desired response in the audience.

Any images used in an ad will convey meaning to an audience both as individual symbols and through their interaction with other symbols in the ad. Thus, a picture of a pumpkin and a haystack in an ad will produce the meaning of a ritual—Thanksgiving—in many consumers. The same pumpkin paired with a black cat will conjure up images and feelings associated with a different ritual—Halloween. As marketers, we must understand the meanings our audiences assign various images and use them to construct messages with the same care and precision we use with the verbal part of the messages.

One well-established principle for organizing ad elements is proximity. The *proximity principle* refers to a tendency to perceive objects or events that are close to one another as being related or as sharing attributes. Thus, Hershey's introduced its new *Kisses With Almonds* by placing them next to its well-known *Kisses* in an ad with the expression "Kissin' cousins."

Illustration 8-6 is an example of an ad based primarily on imagery. What does this ad mean to you? Would it mean the same to older consumers? Consumers of the opposite gender? Consumers from other cultures?

Consumer Inferences

When it comes to advertising, "what you see is not what you get." That is, consumers use available data and their own ideas to make inferences about information not contained in the ad. A **consumer inference** is the process by which consumers assign a value to an attribute or item not contained in an ad based on other data in the ad. When data about an attribute are missing, consumers may assign it a value based on a presumed relationship between that attribute and one for which data are available, they may assign it the average of their assessments of the available attributes, they may assume it to be weaker than the attributes for which data are supplied, or any of a large number of other strategies may be used.[79]

While we are just beginning to study consumer inferences, it is clear that certain types of information portrayal may lead to incorrect inferences and suboptimal consumer decisions. For example, a price comparison advertisement showing UPS to have a lower charge for overnight delivery than FedEx will cause many consumers to assume that (1) it has the lowest price in the market, and/or (2) that its total cost, including other services that may be required, is lower than that of FedEx. Neither case need be true. Airborne might have lower prices than either UPS or FedEx. Likewise, UPS may charge enough more than FedEx for pickup so that it would not be a better buy for those needing pickup.[80] Likewise, an ad stating that a product contains no cholesterol may induce consumers to infer that the product is also low in fat.[81]

Both marketers and regulators need to be aware of message structures that may produce incorrect inferences by consumers. This is particularly likely to occur when comparative ads are used.

Misinterpretation of Marketing Messages

Marketing managers and public policy officials both want consumers to interpret messages accurately—that is, in a manner consistent with what others or experts would consider to be the "true" or "objective" meaning of the messages. Having read the previous material on interpretation, you probably suspect that widespread agreement on, or accurate interpretation of, mass media messages is difficult to obtain. Several studies indicate that this is indeed the case. A study of both commercial and noncommercial television communications reached the following conclusions:[82]

- A large proportion of the audience miscomprehends communications broadcast over commercial television.
- No communication (program content or advertisement) is immune from miscomprehension.
- An average of 30 percent of the total information was miscomprehended.
- Nonadvertising communications had higher levels of miscomprehension than did advertising messages.
- Some demographic variables appear to be slightly associated with miscomprehension.

A second study, which focused on editorial and advertising content in general-circulation magazines, reached essentially the same conclusions.[83] Evidence also indicates that package information, including FTC-mandated disclosures, is subject to miscomprehension. Neither the consumer nor the marketer benefits from such miscomprehension.

We are just beginning to learn about methods to minimize miscomprehension. This is a complex task. For example, repetition does not appear to reduce miscomprehension. And while very simple television messages are less subject to miscomprehension, the same is not true for print messages. Unfortunately, we do not yet have a workable set of guidelines for eliminating this problem. Thus, marketers, public officials, and others wishing to communicate with the public should carefully pretest their messages to ensure that they are being interpreted correctly.

PERCEPTION AND MARKETING STRATEGY

Information is the primary raw material the marketer works with in influencing consumers. Therefore, an understanding of the perception of information is an essential guide to marketing strategy. In the following sections, we briefly discuss a number of areas where such an understanding is particularly useful. The role of theories of perception in the regulation of advertising is discussed in Chapter 20.

Retail Strategy

In recent years, many retailers have felt a need to reduce the number of SKUs (stock-keeping units—individual items such as brands, sizes, and versions) within product categories in order to reduce operating costs. However, they have been reluctant to do so for fear that consumers would perceive this as a reduction in choice and shop elsewhere. What should they do? Research shows that eliminating low preference items while holding total product category shelf space constant does not have a negative impact on consumer perceptions.[84]

Retailers often use exposure very effectively. Store interiors are designed with frequently purchased items (canned goods, fresh fruits/vegetables, meats) separated so that the average consumer will travel through more of the store. This increases total exposure. High-margin items are often placed in high-traffic areas to capitalize on increased exposure.

Shelf position and amount of shelf space influence which items and brands are allocated attention. Point-of-purchase displays also attract attention to sale and high-margin items. Stores are designed with highly visible shelves and overhead signs to make locating items (an information-processing task) as easy as possible. Stores provide reference prices to increase consumers' abilities to accurately interpret price information. Unit price information by brand may be displayed on a separate sign in ascending or descending order to facilitate price comparisons. Nutrition information provided in a similar manner enhances consumers' abilities to choose nutritious brands.

Brand Name and Logo Development

Shakespeare notwithstanding, marketers do not believe that "a rose by any other name would smell as sweet." Would you rather have a soft drink sweetened with NutraSweet or with aspartame? Brand names can influence how food products taste to consumers.[85]

Companies such as NameLab use linguists and computers to create names that convey the appropriate meaning for products. For example, NameLab created "Compaq" for a portable computer that was originally to be called "Gateway." The focus of NameLab is the total meaning conveyed by the interaction of the meanings of the name's parts. For Compaq, *com* means computer and communications while *paq* means small. The unique spelling attracts attention and gives a "scientific" impression. In general, concrete terms with relevant, established visual images such as Mustang, Apple, or Cup-a-Soup are easier to recognize and recall than are more abstract terms. However, alphanumeric names (word and letter combinations such as Z210) are very effective for some product categories (generally technical or chemical) and target markets.[86]

The impact of the image conveyed by a name was vividly demonstrated in a study in which three groups of consumers evaluated the same sporting goods product.[87] The *only* difference among the three groups was the name associated with the product. The perceptual

TABLE 8-1

Meanings Conveyed by Type Style

	Highest Quality	*Best for Recording Music*	*Poorest Value*	*Preference*
A. MEMOREX	**1st**	2nd	5th	2nd
B. Memorex	5th	5th	3rd	5th
C. **MEMOREX**	3rd	3rd	**1st**	3rd
D. ***Memorex***	4th	4th	2nd	4th
E. **memorex**	2nd	**1st**	4th	**1st**

Reprinted with permission from the *Marketing News,* published by the American Marketing Association. Source: D. L. Masten, "Logo's Power Depends on How Well It Communicates with Target Market," December 5, 1988, p. 20.

differences caused by the name are shown in the following table:

	Percent Attributing Feature to Product		
Feature	*Name A*	*Name B*	*Name C*
For all surfaces	11%	26%	17%
Easy to see	8	34	19
For professionals	42	53	30
Large	38	53	18

Clearly, brand name influences how consumers interpret product features.

Marketers are increasingly **co-branding** (also referred to a co-marketing, brand alliances, and joint marketing) in which two brand names are given to a single product. Examples include "Intel Inside" Compaq computers, Breyer's ice cream containing Reese's Pieces candies, and the vast array of Visa cards affiliated with airlines and other organizations. Co-branding has been shown to modify attitudes toward the participating brands. However, the effects can be positive or negative and can differ for the two brands involved. Thus, a firm considering co-branding should be sure that its target market views the potential partner positively and that the two brands "fit" together in a way that ads value to the product.[88]

How a product or service's name is presented (its *logo*) is also important.[89] Table 8-1 illustrates the power of type style in influencing consumers' perceptions of the attributes of Memorex audiotapes. Memorex was using style C at the time of the study and a key competitor, Maxell, was using E. What advice would you give Memorex?

Other studies have found equally impressive impacts.[90] Figure 8-5 shows the additional positive or negative impact the graphic part of a logo can have on the image associated with a name. The scores shown in the table are the percent of the respondents who rated the company very high on such attributes as "trustworthy," "high quality," "relevant for today's lifestyles," and "I would use." One rating was obtained from consumers who saw only the company name; the second was in response to the full logo including the name.[91] What advice would you offer these firms?

Media Strategy

The fact that the exposure process is selective rather than random is the underlying basis for effective media strategies. Since exposure is not random, the proper approach is to

Logos Influence the Image Consumers Have of Firms **FIGURE 8-5**

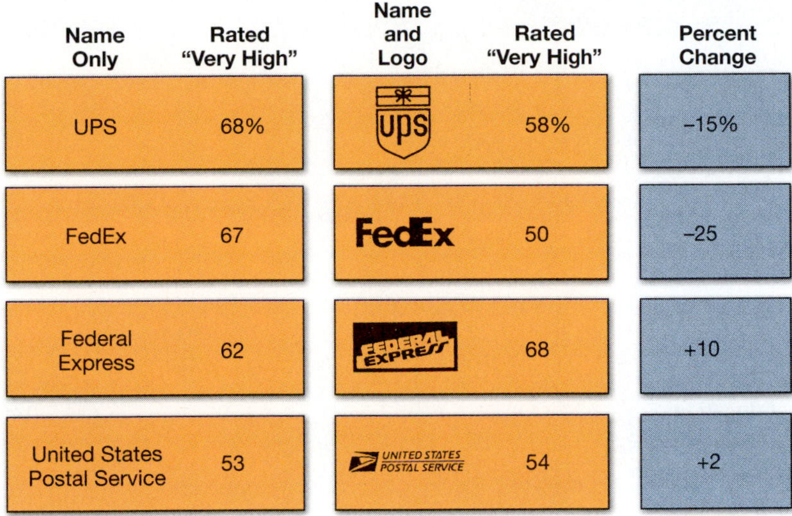

Name Only	Rated "Very High"	Name and Logo	Rated "Very High"	Percent Change
UPS	68%	UPS	58%	−15%
FedEx	67	FedEx	50	−25
Federal Express	62	FEDERAL EXPRESS	68	+10
United States Postal Service	53	UNITED STATES POSTAL SERVICE	54	+2

Note: The percentage shown on the Name and Logo columns is average top-box ratings ("agree strongly") within a 5-point rating scale on the image contribution attributes, based only on respondents who are aware of the company or brand.

determine to which media the consumers in the target market are most frequently exposed and then place the advertising messages in those media. As one executive stated:

> We must look increasingly for matching media that will enable us best to reach carefully targeted, emerging markets. The rifle approach rather than the old shotgun.[92]

For some products and target markets, consumers are highly involved with the product category itself and will go to considerable trouble to secure product-relevant information. This occurs most frequently among heavy users of hobby items such as skis and stereo equipment or for fashion items.

For other products and target markets, consumers have limited involvement with the product category. Products such as salt or detergents are examples. In a situation such as this, the marketer must find media that the target market is interested in and place the advertising message in those media. As we learned earlier, potential target markets as defined by age, ethnic group, social class, or stage in the family life cycle have differing media preferences. Table 8-2 illustrates selective exposure to several magazines based on demographic characteristics.

Advertisements and Package Design

Advertisements and packages must perform two critical tasks—capture attention and convey meaning. Unfortunately, the techniques appropriate for accomplishing one task are often counterproductive for the remaining task.

What should a manager do to attract attention to a package or advertisement? As with most aspects of the marketing process, it depends on the target market, the product, and the situation. If the target market is interested in the product category, or in the firm or brand, attention will not constitute much of a problem. Once consumers are exposed to the

TABLE 8-2

Selective Exposure to Magazines Based on Demographic Characteristics*

Demographic Characteristics	*Better Homes & Gardens*	*Playboy*	*National Geographic*	*Family Circle*	*Forbes*
Gender					
Male	47	173	112	58	137
Female	148	33	89	139	66
Age					
18–24	47	186	83	41	61
25–34	93	149	79	91	109
35–44	115	107	111	103	130
45–54	112	91	118	106	118
55–64	122	32	110	132	75
65+	103	16	101	126	76
Education					
Graduated college	107	81	153	75	244
Graduated high school	105	102	76	122	41
Household Income					
$75,000+	111	88	137	91	240
$40,000–$49,999	107	118	103	97	73
$20,000–$29,999	95	112	85	96	49

*100 represents an average level of usage.

Source: Adapted from *MRI Magazine Total Audience Report: Fall 1997* (New York: Mediamark Research, Inc., 1997).

message, they will most likely attend to it. Unfortunately, most of the time consumers are not actively interested in a particular product. Interest in a product tends to arise only when the need for the product arises. Since it is difficult to reach consumers at exactly this point, marketers have the difficult task of trying to communicate with them at times when their interest is low or nonexistent.

Assume that you are responsible for developing a campaign designed to increase the number of users for your firm's toilet bowl freshener. Research indicates that the group you wish to reach has very little interest in the product. What do you do? Two strategies seem reasonable. One is to *utilize stimulus characteristics* such as full-page ads, bright colors, animated cartoons, or surrealism to attract attention to the advertisement. The second is to *tie the message to a topic the target market is interested in*. Celebrities are often used in advertisements in part for this reason, as is humor. Sex, in the form of attractive models, is also frequently used. The opening vignette for this chapter shows an ad that uses both sex and humor to capture attention.

Using either stimulus characteristics or consumer interests unrelated to the product category to attract attention presents two dangers. The first danger is that the strategy will be so successful in attracting attention to the stimulus object that it will reduce the attention devoted to the sales message. The reader may observe an attractive member of the opposite sex in an advertisement and not attend to the sales message or copy. This occurred with the ad for RCA Colortrack described in this chapter's opening example.

The second risk associated with using stimulus characteristics or unrelated consumer interests to attract attention is that the *interpretation* of the message will be negatively

Courtesy Mt. Bachelor.

ILLUSTRATION 8-7

What is this an ad for? It will attract attention. The critical questions are: Will it draw the reader into the message itself? and Will it convey the type of image the area wants readers of *Outside* magazine to have of Mt. Bachelor?

affected. For example, the use of humor to attract attention to a commercial for insurance may result in the brand being considered inappropriate for serious insurance needs. Thus, caution must be used to ensure that attention-attracting devices do not have a negative impact on attention to, or interpretation of, the main message.

The ad shown in Illustration 8-7 appeared in *Outside* magazine. It uses color, contrast, and size (two full pages) to attract attention. However, the connection between these attention-attracting devices and the brand's features or image is not clear. Ads that rely on stimulus factors not directly related to the product should be thoroughly pretested to determine how the target market interprets them. Does this ad inspire you to want to ski Mt. Bachelor? (Management states that the ad was designed to attract snowboarders who it believes will relate to the ad.)

Developing Warning Labels and Posters

Both ethical and legal considerations require marketers to place warning labels on a wide array of products (cigarettes, alcoholic beverages, many over-the-counter drugs, lawn mowers, power tools, and so forth). These can range from general warnings such as those on cigarette packages to warnings that apply to only a small portion of the population—for example, "Don't take this drug if you have diabetes." The government, consumer groups, and ethical marketers want the warnings to accomplish their primary task—that is, they should effectively alert the potential user to the risk associated with using the product in a manner that allows the consumer to make an informed decision concerning the product. In addition, marketers do not want warnings to detract unduly from the image of the product or cause inappropriately negative assessments of its risk to benefit ratio.

Unfortunately, it appears that some marketers err on the side of protecting their brand's image and sales. For example, in television ads, most warnings or disclosures are presented via only one mode (oral or visual) rather than two and visual disclosures tend to be low contrast (i.e., white lettering on medium or light backgrounds).[93] For these and other reasons, many warning labels are not noticed or are not effectively processed.

Despite the fact that many warnings are ignored, there is substantial evidence that well-designed warnings are attended to and do influence knowledge, beliefs, and, to a lessor extent, behaviors.[94] The challenge, then, is to design warnings with a maximum likelihood of being successful.

Warnings are incorporated into commercials, packages, and point-of-purchase displays, and they are presented in free-standing posters and ads. They should be designed and tested in the same manner as key elements of standard commercials and ads. The first step is to understand the needs and vocabulary of the target audience. As one expert concluded: "Warnings designed with input from consumers about what they wish to know and how and when they wish to know it would not only provide a greater number of options for warning content, it is also likely to increase the probability that a given warning will have its intended effect."[95]

Many of the same issues involving warning labels also arise in design labels to convey nutrition information.[96]

Advertising Evaluation

A successful advertisement (or any other marketing message) must accomplish four tasks:

1. *Exposure.* It must physically reach the consumer.
2. *Attention.* The consumer must attend it to.
3. *Interpretation.* It must be properly interpreted.
4. *Memory.* It must be stored in memory in a manner that will allow retrieval under the proper circumstances.

Advertising research covers all of these tasks. However, most of the effort is focused on attention and, to a lesser extent, memory.

Measures of Exposure Exposure to print media is most frequently measured in terms of circulation. Data on circulation are provided by a variety of commercial firms. The major difficulty with this data is that it frequently is not broken down in a manner consistent with the firm's target market. Thus, a firm may be targeting the lower-middle social class but circulation data may be broken down by income rather than social class. Further, circulation measures are generally based on households and do not provide data on who within a household is exposed to the magazine or newspaper.

Diary reports, in which respondents record their daily listening patterns, and telephone interviews are the two methods used to determine radio listening. Television viewing is measured primarily by **people meters,** which are electronic devices that automatically determine if a television is turned on and, if so, to which channel. They allow each household member to "log on" when viewing by punching an identifying button. The demographics of each potential viewer are stored in the central computer so viewer profiles can be developed.

Measures of Attention The attention-attracting powers of commercials or packages can be partially measured in a direct manner using the techniques described in Table 8-3. Of these techniques, eye tracking appears to offer the greatest potential.

TABLE 8-3

Direct Measures of Attention

1. **Eye pupil dilation.** Changes in the size of the pupil of the eye appear to be related to the amount of attention that a person is giving a message. A pupilometer can measure these changes accurately.
2. **Eye tracking.** An eye camera can track movements of the eyes relative to the ad being read or watched. The paths of the eyes can then be mapped to determine (1) what parts of the message were attended to, (2) what sequence was used in viewing the message, and (3) how much time was spent on each part.
3. **Tachistoscopic test.** A tachistoscope is a slide projector with adjustable projector speeds and levels of illumination. Thus, ads can be shown very rapidly and/or dimly. Ads are tested to determine at what speeds the elements, such as the product, brand, and headline, are recognized. Speed of recognition of various elements in the ads and readership (attention) are highly correlated.
4. **Theater tests.** Theater tests involve showing commercials along with television shows in a theater. Some, such as the one maintained by ASI Market Research, have dials at each seat that viewers use to constantly indicate their interest (attention) in the show or commercial.
5. **Brain wave analysis.** There is some evidence that electroencephalographs can indicate the amount and type of attention given to an advertisement or package.

Indirect measures of attention (which also tap at least some aspects of memory) include theater tests, day-after recall, recognition tests, and Starch scores. *Theater tests* involve showing commercials along with television programs in a theater. Viewers complete questionnaires designed to measure which commercials (and what aspects of those commercials) attracted their attention. **Day-after recall (DAR)** is the most popular method of measuring the attention-getting power of television commercials. Individuals are interviewed the day after a commercial is aired on a program they watched. Recall of the commercial and recall of specific aspects of the commercial are interpreted as a reflection of the amount of attention.

Day-after recall measures of television commercials have been criticized as favoring rational, factual, "hard sell" type ads and high-involvement products while discriminating against feeling, emotional, "soft sell" ads. However, for many product/target market combinations, the latter approach may be superior. In response, substantial work has been done to develop recognition measures for television commercials. **Recognition tests** are tests in which the commercial of interest, or key parts of it, along with other commercials are shown to target-market members. Recognition of the commercial, or key parts of the commercial, is the measure. This technique appears to work better than standard recall measures.[97]

Starch scores are the most popular technique for evaluating the attention-attracting power of print ads. The respondents are shown advertisements from magazine issues they have recently read. For each advertisement, they indicate which parts (headlines, illustrations, copy blocks) they recall reading. Three main "scores" are computed:

1. *Noted.* The percent who recall seeing the ad in that issue.
2. *Seen-associated.* The percent that recall reading a part of the ad that clearly identifies the brand or advertiser.
3. *Read most.* The percent who recall reading 50 percent or more of the copy.

Starch scores allow an indirect measure of attention to the overall ad and to key components of the ad.

Consumer Insight 8-2

Ambush Marketing

Commercial sponsorship of events, particularly sporting events, has become a major marketing activity and a major source of revenue for the events. Sponsor derive a variety of benefits from sponsorship, ranging from exposure of their brand name to image enhancement by association with the event. In the United States, firms spent over $5 billion in sponsorship fees in 1996, with over 16 billion being spent worldwide. Sponsorship is perhaps most obvious and expensive at the Olympics.

Ambush marketing involves "any communication or activity that implies, or from which one could reasonably infer, that an organization is associated with an event, when in fact it is not." Such communications seek to achieve some or all of the benefits of being associated with the event without incurring the cost of sponsorship fees or to overcome exclusive sponsorship rights awarded to a rival.

Ambush marketing can take many forms. One is to sponsor media coverage of the event rather than the event itself. Another is to sponsor a small part of the larger event and then to promote that sponsorship heavily. For example, rather than sponsoring the Olympics, sponsor the U.S. swim team and advertise that sponsorship heavily throughout the Olympics.

A common form of ambush marketing is to advertise heavily during the event. Such advertising can be either one's regular advertisements or it can use ads related to the event. A firm such as Coca-Cola or Pepsi Cola could purchase extensive advertising time during the Olympics on the network carrying the games. Viewers watching the games would then see numerous Coke or Pepsi ads and might conclude that that firm is a sponsor of the Olympics. This conclusion would be more likely if the ads contained Olympic athletes as spokespersons, offered a "salute" to the Olympic athletes, or otherwise used symbols that related directly or indirectly to the Olympics. For example, Wendy's ran ads featuring Olympic gold medalist Kristi Yamaguchi as a spokesperson during the 1992 Olympics while McDonald's was the official sponsor of the U.S. skating team.

Critical Thinking Questions

1. How does ambush marketing work?
2. Ambush marketing does what harm, if any?
3. What ethical issues, if any, arise in ambush marketing?

Source: Special issue, "Ambush Marketing," T. Meenaghan, ed., *Psychology & Marketing,* July 1998.

Measures of Interpretation Marketers investigate *interpretation* primarily through the use of focus groups, theater tests, and day-after recall. *Focus groups* involve a group of 5 to 15 members of the target audience who have a relatively free-form discussion of the meaning conveyed by the advertisement.

Marketers are just beginning to measure the emotional or feeling reactions or meanings that consumers assign to ads. While standard methods do not yet exist, this is clearly an important area for development (more details are provided in Chapter 11).

Ethical Concerns

A host of ethical concerns arise as marketers apply their understanding of the perceptual process. We addressed a number of these issues such as subliminal messages and incorrect consumer inferences earlier in this chapter. In Chapter 20, we will examine some of the regulations that have been created to protect consumers from misuse of perceptual cues.

Most of the ethical concerns in this area relate to the conflict between presenting one's brand in a favorable light and presenting it completely accurately. Consider the following situations:

- An ad shows a plate with a large helping (9 ounces or so) of a food product such as pork. While the helping shown is no larger than that commonly consumed, the calorie count supplied in the ad is for 3 ounces (a recommended serving size).

- Television ads consistently show a particular sport-utility vehicle in extremely rugged terrain. While it is possible that the vehicle could be driven in such terrain, it is designed primarily for on-road operation. Extensive off-road use would likely damage the vehicle.
- A car is advertised as having better acceleration than brand X, better fuel economy than brand Y, and a larger interior than brand Z. These are all true claims, but the advertised brand is worse than each competitor on the two dimensions that are not mentioned for that competitor (i.e., it has worse fuel economy and a smaller interior than brand X.)

Are these practices ethical? Part of the answer resides with consumer expectations and knowledge. That is, to some extent it depends on how consumers interpret the ads.

Many cereal packages show the cereal in a bowl with fruits or berries such as blueberries or banana slices. Some cereals contain these items while others do not. Are those firms that show cereals in a bowl with fruits when they are not included with the cereal unethically trying to mislead the consumer, or are they merely showing their product in a common, appetizing consumption situation?

Consumer Insight 8-2 describes "**ambush marketing,**" in which firms attempt to associate their companies with an event such as the Olympics without becoming an official sponsor. Is this ethical?

SUMMARY

Perception consists of those activities by which an individual acquires and assigns meaning to stimuli. Perception begins with *exposure*. This occurs when a stimulus comes within range of one of our primary sensory receptors. We are exposed to only a small fraction of the available stimuli, and this is usually the result of "self-selection."

Attention occurs when the stimulus activates one or more of the sensory receptors and the resulting sensations go into the brain for processing. Because of the amount of stimuli we are exposed to, we selectively attend to those stimuli that physically attract us (stimulus factors) or personally interest us (individual factors). *Stimulus factors* are physical characteristics of the stimulus itself, such as contrast, size, intensity, color, movement, position, isolation, format, and information quantity. *Individual factors* are characteristics of the individual, such as interests and needs. Both these factors are moderated by the *situation* in which they occur. *Program involvement,* the degree of interest the consumer has in the program or magazine in which the advertisement is embedded, is a situational factor of particular interest to marketers.

Nonfocused attention occurs when we take in information without deliberate effort. *Hemispheric lateralization* is a term applied to activities that take place on each side of the brain. The left side of the brain is concerned primarily with those activities we typically call rational thought and the ability to be conscious and report what is happening. The right side of the brain deals with pictorial, geometric, timeless, and nonverbal information without the individual being able to verbally report it.

A message presented so fast or so softly or so masked by other messages that one is not aware of seeing or hearing it is called a *subliminal message*. Subliminal messages have generated a great deal of interest but do not affect brand choice or other aspects of consumer behavior in a meaningful way.

Interpretation is the assignment of meaning to stimuli that have been attended to. Interpretation is a function of individual as well as stimulus and situation characteristics. *Cognitive interpretation* appears to involve a process whereby new stimuli are placed into existing categories of meaning. *Affective interpretation* is the emotional or feeling response triggered by the stimulus. Interpretation is largely a function of individual learning and expectations that are triggered by the stimulus and moderated by the situation.

Marketers are particularly interested in how consumers *differentiate between brands,* how they *interpret images,* and how they *form inferences* about missing information. Both marketing managers and regulators are concerned with the amount of information that is misinterpreted.

Marketing managers use their knowledge of information processing in a variety of ways. The fact that media exposure is selective is the basis for *media strategy*. *Retailers* can enhance their operations by viewing their outlets as information environments. Both stimulus and personal interest factors are used to attract attention to *advertisements* and *packages*. Characteristics of the target market and the message are studied to ensure that accurate interpretation occurs. The meaning that consumers assign to words and parts of words is the basis for selecting *brand names*. Information processing theory guides a wide range of *advertising evaluation techniques*. Likewise, information processing theory is a basis for *developing warning labels and posters*. Finally, marketers need to be sensitive to the host of ethical issues that arise when developing marketing messages.

KEY TERMS

Adaptation level theory 290
Affective interpretation 296
Ambush marketing 313
Attention 287
Co-branding 306
Cognitive interpretation 296
Consumer inference 303
Contextual priming effects 299
Day-after recall (DAR) 311
Exposure 285
Hemispheric lateralization 294
Individual factors 291
Infomercials 286
Information overload 290
Information processing 284
Interpretation 296
Just noticeable difference (j.n.d.) 300
Muting 286
People meter 310
Perception 284
Perceptual defenses 285
Recognition tests 311
Rhetoric 302
Semiotics 299
Sensory discrimination 300
Sign 299
Situational factors 292
Starch scores 311
Stimulus factors 287
Subliminal stimulus 295
Weber's law 302
Zapping 286
Zipping 286

INTERNET EXERCISES

1. Examine several magazines. Copy two ads that do a very good job of encouraging the reader to visit a Web site. Justify your selection using the principles of perception described in this chapter.
2. Visit one of the following Web sites. Evaluate the site based on the principles of perception covered in this chapter.
   a. http://www.hollywood.com
   b. http://www.absolutvodka.com
   c. http://www.nj.com/yucky
   d. http://www.elle.com
   e. http://www.purina.com
3. Visit several company Web sites until you find one that you feel makes effective use of the principles of perception that we have covered and one that violates these principles. Provide the URL of each and justify your selections.
4. Use the Internet to determine the following. What do you conclude from this?
   a. Who is advertising on the Internet?
   b. Who is using the Internet?
   c. Who is reading the ads on the Internet?

DDB NEEDHAM LIFESTYLE DATA ANALYSES

1. Examine the DDB Needham data in Tables 1a, 2a, 3a, 4a, 5a, 6a, and 7a. What characterizes a person who is unlikely to buy products whose advertising he or she dislikes? Why is this the case? What are the marketing implications of this?

REVIEW QUESTIONS

1. What is *information processing?* How does it differ from *perception?*
2. What is meant by *exposure?* What determines which stimuli an individual will be exposed to? How do marketers utilize this knowledge?
3. What are *zipping, zapping,* and *muting?* Why are they a concern to marketers?
4. What is an *infomercial?* How effective are they?
5. Do consumers seek or avoid commercial information on the Internet?
6. What is meant by *attention?* What determines which stimuli an individual will attend to? How do marketers utilize this?
7. What stimulus factors can be used to attract attention? What problems can arise when stimulus factors are used to attract attention?
8. What is *adaptation level theory?*
9. What is *information overload?* How should marketers deal with information overload?
10. What impact does *program involvement* have on the attention paid to commercials embedded in the program?
11. What is *contextual priming?* Why is it of interest to marketers?
12. What are the six major reasons people watch television?
13. What is meant by *nonfocused attention?*
14. What is meant by *hemispheric lateralization?*
15. What is meant by *subliminal perception?* Is it a real phenomenon? Is it effective?
16. What is meant by *interpretation?*
17. What determines how an individual will interpret a given stimulus?
18. What is the difference between *cognitive* and *affective* interpretation?
19. What is the difference between *semantic* and *psychological* meaning?
20. What is *semiotics?* What is a *sign?*
21. What is *rhetoric?*
22. What is *sensory discrimination?* What is a *just noticeable difference* (j.n.d.)?
23. What is *Weber's law?* Why is it of interest to marketers?
24. What is a *consumer inference?* Why is this of interest to marketers?
25. What is meant by *misinterpretation of a marketing message?* Is it common?
26. How does a knowledge of information processing assist the manager in the following?
    a. Formulating retail strategy.
    b. Developing brand names and logos.
    c. Formulating media strategy.
    d. Designing advertisements and packages.
    e. Developing warning labels and posters.
    f. Evaluating advertising.
27. What is *co-branding?* Is it effective?
28. How is exposure measured? What problems are encountered in this process?
29. Explain the differences between an eye camera, a tachistoscope, and a pupilometer.
30. What is a *Starch score*?
31. What is meant by *day-after recall?*
32. What is meant by *recognition tests?*
33. What is a *people meter?*
34. What ethical concerns arise in applying knowledge of the perceptual process? 
35. What is *ambush marketing?*

DISCUSSION QUESTIONS

36. How could a marketing manager for (*a*) the Mothers Against Drunk Driving, (*b*) Bose stereo equipment, (*c*) a restaurant chain, (*d*) furniture polish, or (*e*) deodorant use the material in this chapter to guide the development of a national advertising campaign? To assist local retailers or organizations in developing their promotional activities? Would the usefulness of this material be limited to advertising decisions? Explain your answer.
37. Anheuser-Busch test-marketed a new soft drink for adults called Chelsea. The product was

advertised as a "not-so-soft drink" that Anheuser-Busch hoped would become socially acceptable for adults. The advertisements featured no one under 25 years of age, and the product contained .5 percent alcohol (not enough to classify the product as an alcoholic beverage). The reaction in the test market was not what the firm expected or hoped for. The Virginia Nurses Association decided to boycott Chelsea, claiming that it "is packaged like a beer and looks, pours, and foams like beer, and the children are pretending the soft drink is beer." The Nurses Association claimed the product was an attempt to encourage children to become beer drinkers later on. The secretary of Health, Education, and Welfare urged the firm to "rethink their marketing strategy." Others made similar protests. Although Anheuser-Busch reformulated the product and altered the marketing mix substantially, the product could not regain momentum and was withdrawn. Assuming Anheuser-Busch was in fact attempting to position Chelsea as an adult soft drink (which appears to have been its objective), why do you think it failed?

38. Develop a brand name for (*a*) a new cold remedy, (*b*) a national car repair chain, (*c*) an Internet grocery shopping service, (*d*) a national magazine for college students, or (*e*) a national travel agency for college students. Justify your name.
39. Develop a logo for (*a*) a new cold remedy, (*b*) a national car repair chain, (*c*) an Internet grocery shopping service, (*d*) a national magazine for college students, or (*e*) a national travel agency for college students. Justify your design.
40. Evaluate the ads in this chapter. Analyze the attention-attracting characteristics and the meaning they convey. Are they good ads? What risks are associated with each?
41. How should television commercials differ depending on the reason people are watching TV (see Consumer Insight 8-1).
42. Develop three co-branded products: one that would be beneficial to both individual brands, one that would benefit one brand but not the other, and one that would benefit neither brand. Explain your logic.
43. What ethical issues arise in ambush marketing? 
44. What problems do you see with people meters?

APPLICATION ACTIVITIES

45. Find and copy or describe examples of marketing promotions that specifically use stimulus factors to attract attention. Look for examples of each of the various factors discussed earlier in the chapter and try to find their use in a variety of promotions (e.g., point-of-purchase, billboards, print advertisements). For each example, evaluate the effectiveness of the stimulus factors used.
46. Repeat Question 45, but this time look for promotions using individual factors.
47. Complete Question 38 and test your names on a sample of students. Justify your testing procedure and report your results.
48. Find two brand names that you feel are particularly appropriate and two that you feel are not very appropriate. Explain your reasoning for each name.
49. Find and describe a logo that you feel is particularly appropriate and one that you feel is not very appropriate. Explain your reasoning.
50. Interview 10 students about their behavior during television and radio commercial breaks. What do you conclude?
51. Interview 10 students about the reason they watch TV. Compare your results with those in Consumer Insight 8-1.
52. Interview 10 students who use the Internet. Determine how they respond to banner ads and the extent to which they attend to various commercial messages on the Internet.
53. Find and copy or describe an ad or other marketing message that you think makes unethical use of the perceptual process. Justify your selection. 

54. Develop an ad but omit information about some key product attributes. Show the ad to five students. After they have looked at the ad, give them a questionnaire that asks about the attributes featured in the ad and about the missing attributes. If they provide answers concerning the missing attributes, ask them how they arrived at these answers. What do you conclude?

REFERENCES

1. *What the Eye Does Not See, the Mind Does Not Remember,* Telecom Research, Inc., undated. See also S. M. Smith, C. P. Haugtvedt, J. M. Jadrich, and M. R. Anton, "Understanding Responses to Sex Appeals in Advertising," in *Advances in Consumer Research XXII,* ed. F. R. Kardes and M. Sujan (Provo, UT: Association for Consumer Research, 1995), pp. 735–39; and P. M. Simpson, S. Horton, and G. Brown, "Male Nudity in Advertisements," *Journal of the Academy of Marketing Science,* Summer 1996, pp. 257–62.
2. J. J. Cronin and N. E. Menelly, "Discrimination vs. Avoidance," *Journal of Advertising,* June 1992, pp. 1–7.
3. T. J. Olney, M. B. Holbrook, and R. Batra, "Consumer Responses to Advertising," *Journal of Consumer Research,* March 1991, pp. 440–50.
4. Ibid.; F. S. Zufryden, J. H. Pedrick, and A. Sankaralingam, "Zapping and Its Impact on Brand Purchase Behavior," *Journal of Advertising Research,* January–February 1993, pp. 58–66; L. van Meurs, "Zapp!" *Journal of Advertising Research,* February 1998, pp. 43–53; and S. Siddarth and A. Chattopadhyay, "To Zap or Not to Zap," *Marketing Science,* no. 2, (1998), pp. 124–38.
5. J. C. Cronin, "In-Home Observations of Commercial Zapping Behavior," *Journal of Current Issues and Research in Advertising,* Fall 1995, pp. 69–75.
6. M. R. Stafford and T. F. Stafford, "Mechanical Commercial Avoidance," *Journal of Current Issues and Research in Advertising,* Fall 1996, pp. 27–38.
7. P. J. Danaher, "What Happens to Television Ratings during Commercial Breaks?" *Journal of Advertising Research,* January 1995, pp. 37–47.
8. van Meurs, footnote 4.
9. A. M. Abernethy, "Differences between Advertising and Program Exposure for Car Radio Listening," *Journal of Advertising Research,* April–May 1991, pp. 33–42.
10. C. Fisher, "Newspaper Readers Get Choosier," *Advertising Age,* July 26, 1993, p. 22.
11. P. S. Speck and M. T. Elliot, "Predictors of Advertising Avoidance in Print and Broadcast Media," *Journal of Advertising,* Fall 1997, pp. 61–76.
12. *TeleNation* (New York: Market Facts, Inc., October 2, 1998), p. 43.
13. K. Haley, "The Infomercial Begins a New Era," *Advertising Age,* January 25, 1993, p. M-3.
14. M. T. Elliot and P. S. Speck, "Antecedents and Consequences of Infomercials," *Journal of Direct Marketing,* Spring 1995, pp. 39–51.
15. K. Maddox, "Survey Shows Increase in Online Usage, Shopping," *Advertising Age,* October 26, 1998, p. S6.
16. See E. T. Popper and K. B. Murray, "Format Effects on an In-Ad Disclosure," in *Advances in Consumer Research XVI,* ed. T. K. Srull (Provo, UT: Association for Consumer Research, 1989), pp. 221–30; and D. M. Krugman et al., "Do Adolescents Attend to Warnings in Cigarette Advertising?" *Journal of Advertising Research,* November 1994, pp. 39–52.
17. J. L. Rogers, "Consumer Response to Advertising Mail," *Journal of Advertising Research,* January 1990, p. 22.
18. "Farm Ads Win Golden Fleece," *The Stars and Stripes,* July 10, 1984, p. 6.
19. G. L. Lohse, "Consumer Eye Movement Patterns on Yellow Pages Advertising," *Journal of Advertising,* Spring 1997, pp. 61–73.
20. *CARR Report No. 250.1A* (Boston: Cahners Publishing Co., undated). See also K. Grønhaug, O. Kvitastein, and S. Gronmo, "Factors Moderating Advertising Effectiveness," *Journal of Advertising Research,* October–November 1991, pp. 42–50.
21. *CARR Report No. 120.3* (Boston: Cahners Publishing Co., undated); and P. H. Chook, "A Continuing Study of Magazine Environment, Frequency, and Advertising Performance," *Journal of Advertising Research,* August–September 1985, pp. 23–33.
22. Footnote 20.
23. J. Meyers-Levy and L. A. Peracchio, "Understanding the Effects of Color," *Journal of Consumer Research,* September 1995, pp. 121–38.
24. See footnote 5.
25. See G. D. Olsen, "Creating the Contrast," *Journal of Advertising,* Winter 1995, pp. 29–44.
26. C. Janiszewski, "The Influence of Display Characteristics on Visual Exploratory Search Behavior," *Journal of Consumer Research,* December 1998, pp. 290–301.
27. D. Walker and M. F. von Gonten, "Explaining Related Recall Outcomes," *Journal of Advertising Research,* July 1989, pp. 11–21.
28. R. C. Goodstein, "Category-Based Applications and Extensions in Advertising," *Journal of Consumer Research,* June 1993, pp. 87–99.
29. R. Pieters, E. Rosbergen, and M. Hartog, "Visual Attention to Advertising," in *Advances in Consumer Research XXIII,* ed. K. P. Corfman and J. G. Lynch (Provo, UT: Association for Consumer Research, 1996), pp. 242–48.
30. M. A. Eastlick, R. Feinberg, and C. Trappey, "Information Overload in Mail Catalog Shopping," *Journal of Direct Marketing,*

Autumn 1993, pp. 14–19. For a different explanation, see Y. Ganzach and P. Ben-Or, "Information Overload, Decreasing Marginal Responsiveness, and the Estimation of Nonmonotonic Relationships in Direct Marketing," *Journal of Direct Marketing,* Spring 1996, pp. 7–12.

31. See D. Maheswaran and B. Sternthal, "The Effects of Knowledge, Motivation, and Type of Message on Ad Processing and Product Judgments," *Journal of Consumer Research,* June 1990, pp. 66–73; and D. J. MacInnis, C. Moorman, and B. J. Jaworski, "Enhancing and Measuring Consumers' Motivation, Opportunity, and Ability to Process Brand Information from Ads," *Journal of Marketing,* October 1991, pp. 32–53.
32. E. Rosbergen, R. Pieters, and M. Wedel, "Visual Attention to Advertising," *Journal of Consumer Research,* December 1997, pp. 305–15.
33. R. G. M. Pieters and T. H. A. Bijmolt, "Consumer Memory for Television Advertising," *Journal of Consumer Research,* March 1997, pp. 362–72
34. See D. L. Hoffman and R. Batra, "Viewer Response to Programs," *Journal of Advertising Research,* August–September 1991, pp. 46–56; K. G. Celuch and M. Slama, "Program Content and Advertising Effectiveness," *Psychology & Marketing,* July–August 1993, pp. 285–99; and K. R. Lord and R. E. Burnkrant, "Attention versus Distraction," *Journal of Advertising,* March 1993, pp. 47–60.
35. K. J. Clancy, "CPMs Must Bow to Involvement Measurement," *Advertising Age,* January 20, 1992, p. 7.
36. G. W. McClung and K. R. France, "The Impact of Program Involvement on Commercial Effectiveness," in *Enhancing Knowledge Development in Marketing,* ed. B. B. Stern and G. M. Zinkhan, (Chicago: American Marketing Association, 1995), pp. 279–87.
37. See V. C. Broach, Jr., T. J. Page, Jr., and R. D. Wilson, "Television Programming and Its Influence on Viewers' Perceptions of Commercials," *Journal of Advertising,* Winter 1995, pp. 45–54; N. T. Tavassoli, C. J. Shultz II, and G. J. Fitzsimons, "Program Involvement," *Journal of Advertising Research,* September 1995, pp. 61–72; K. S. Coulter, and M. A. Sewall, "The Effects of Editorial Context and Cognitive and Affective Moderators on Responses to Embedded Ads"; and V. Starr and C. A. Lowe, "The Influence of Program Context and Order of Presentation on Immediate and Delayed Responses to Television Advertisements"; both in *Advances in Consumer Research XXII,* ed. F. R. Kardes and M. Sujan (Provo, UT: Association for Consumer Research, 1995), pp. 177–83 and 184–89.
38. M. Clancy, "The Television Audience Examined," *Journal of Advertising Research,* July 1994, Special insert; and B. Lee and R. S. Lee, "How and Why People Watch TV," *Journal of Advertising Research,* November 1995, pp. 9–18.
39. For another view of the meaning of mass media, see E. C. Hirschman and C. J. Thompson, "Why Media Matter," *Journal of Advertising,* Spring 1997, pp. 43–60.
40. See D. D. Muehling, R. N. Laczniak, and J. C. Andrews, "Defining, Operationalizing, and Using Involvement in Advertising Research," *Journal of Current Issues and Research in Advertising,* Spring 1993, pp. 21–57.
41. S. Shapiro, D. J. MacInnis, S. E. Heckler, "The Effects of Incidental Ad Exposure on the Formation of Consideration Sets," *Journal of Consumer Research,* June 1997, pp. 94–104.
42. H. E. Krugman, "Sustained Viewing of Television," *Journal of Advertising Research,* June 1980, p. 65; and H. E. Krugman, "Low Recall and High Recognition of Advertising," *Journal of Advertising Research,* February–March 1986, pp. 79–86.
43. See C. Janiszewski, "The Influence of Print Advertisement Organization on Affect toward a Brand Name," *Journal of Consumer Research,* June 1990, pp. 53–65; M. L. Rothschild and Y. J. Hyun, "Predicting Memory for Components of TV Commercials from EEG," *Journal of Consumer Research,* March 1990, pp. 472–78; and C. Janiszewski, "Preattentive Mere Exposure Effects," *Journal of Consumer Research,* December 1993, pp. 376–92.
44. W. B. Key, *Subliminal Seduction* (Englewood Cliffs, NJ: Prentice Hall, 1973); and W. B. Key, *Media Sexploitation* (Englewood Cliffs, NJ: Prentice Hall, 1976).
45. D. L. Rosen and S. N. Singh, "An Investigation of Subliminal Embed Effect on Multiple Measures of Advertising Effectiveness," *Psychology & Marketing,* March–April 1992, pp. 157–73; and K. T. Theus, "Subliminal Advertising and the Psychology of Processing Unconscious Stimuli," *Psychology & Marketing,* May 1994, pp. 271–90.
46. M. Rogers and K. H. Smith, "Public Perceptions of Subliminal Advertising," *Journal of Advertising Research,* March–April 1993, pp. 10–18.
47. C. L. Witte, M. Parthasarathy, and J. W. Gentry, "Subliminal Perception versus Subliminal Persuasion," in *Enhancing Knowledge Development in Marketing,* ed. B. B. Stern and G. M. Zinkhan (Chicago: American Marketing Association, 1995), pp. 133–38; and C. Trappey, "A Meta-Analysis of Consumer Choice and Subliminal Advertising," *Psychology & Marketing,* August 1996, pp. 517–30.
48. M. Rogers and C. A. Seiler, "The Answer Is No," *Journal of Advertising Research,* March 1994, pp. 36–45.
49. T. J. Brown and P. A. Dacin, "The Company and the Product," *Journal of Marketing,* January 1997, pp. 68–84. See also L. A. Manrai, A. K. Manrai, D. Lascu, and, J. K. Ryans, Jr., "How Green-Claim Strength and Country Disposition Affect Product Evaluation and Company Image," *Psychology & Marketing,* August 1997, pp. 511–37.
50. A. Kirmani, "Advertising Repetition as a Signal of Quality, *Journal of Advertising,* Fall 1997, pp. 77–86. See also H. R. Moser and H. E. Johns, "An Empirical Analysis of Consumers' Attitudes toward Attorney Advertising," *Journal of Professional Services Marketing,* no. 1 (1996), pp. 85–104.
51. See L. M. Scott, "The Bridge from Text to Mind," *Journal of Consumer Research,* December 1994, pp. 461–80.
52. See D. Grewal, K. B. Monroe, and R. Krishnan, "The Effects of Price-Comparison Advertising," *Journal of Marketing,* April 1998, pp. 46–59; and D. Grewal, R. Krishnan, J. Baker, and N. Borin, "The Effects of Store Name, Brand Name, and Price Discounts," *Journal of Retailing,* no. 3 (1998), pp. 331–52.
53. R. Friedman, "Psychological Meaning of Products," *Psychology & Marketing,* Spring 1986, pp. 1–15; R. Friedman and M. R. Zimmer, "The Role of Psychological Meaning in Advertising,"

Journal of Advertising, no. 1 (1988), pp. 31–40; and L. L. Golden, M. I. Alpert, and J. F. Betak, "Psychological Meaning," *Psychology & Marketing,* Spring 1989, pp. 33–50.

54. J. Z. Sojka and J. L. Giese, "Thinking and/or Feeling," in *Advances in Consumer Research XXIV,* ed. M. Bruck and D. J. MacInnis (Provo, UT: Association for Consumer Research, 1997), pp. 438–42.

55. See D. G. Mick and C. Buhl, "A Meaning-Based Model of Advertising Experiences," *Journal of Consumer Research,* December 1992, pp. 317–38.

56. M. S. LaTour, "Female Nudity in Print Advertising," *Psychology & Marketing,* Spring 1990, pp. 65–81. See also J. J. Kellaris and R. C. Rice, "The Influence of Tempo, Loudness, and Gender of Listener on Responses to Music," *Psychology & Marketing,* January–February 1993, pp. 15–29; R. W. Pollay and S. Lysonski, "In the Eye of the Beholder," *Journal of International Consumer Marketing* 6, no. 2 (1993), pp. 25–43; W. R. Darley and R. E. Smith, "Gender Differences in Information Processing Strategies," *Journal of Advertising,* Spring 1995, pp. 41–56; and M. Y. Jones, A. J. S. Stanaland, and B. D. Gelb, "*Journal of Advertising,*" Summer 1998, pp. 33–51.

57. B. H. Schmitt, Y. Pan, and N. T. Tavassoli, "Language and Consumer Memory," *Journal of Consumer Research,* December 1994, pp. 419–31; and B. H. Schmitt and S. Zhang, "Language Structure and Categorization," *Journal of Consumer Research,* September 1998, pp. 108–22.

58. B. J. Parker, "Exploring Life Themes and Myths in Alcohol Advertisements through a Meaning-Based Model," *Journal of Advertising,* Spring 1998, pp. 97–111.

59. G. Tom et al., "Cueing the Consumer," *Journal of Consumer Marketing,* Spring 1987, pp. 23–27. See also D. A. Aaker and D. M. Stayman, "Implementing the Concept of Transformational Advertising," *Psychology & Marketing,* May–June 1992, pp. 237–53.

60. J. J. Inman, L. McAlister, and W. D. Hoyer, "Promotion Signal," *Journal of Consumer Research,* June 1990, pp. 74–81.

61. C. K. Hsee and F. Leclerc, "Will Products Look More Attractive When Presented Separately or Together?" *Journal of Consumer Research,* September 1998, pp. 175–86.

62. D. Grewal, H. Marmorstein, and A. Sharma, "Communicating Price Information through Semantic Cues," *Journal of Consumer Research,* September 1996, pp. 148–55.

63. "GF, Coke Tell Why They Shun TV News," *Advertising Age,* January 28, 1980, p. 39.

64. Y. Yi, "Contextual Priming Effects in Print Advertisements," *Journal of Advertising,* March 1993, pp. 1–10; V. K. Prasad and L. J. Smith, "Television Commercials in Violent Programming," *Journal of the Academy of Marketing Science,* Fall 1994, pp. 340–51; B. H. Schmitt, "Context Priming of Visual Information in Advertisements," *Psychology & Marketing,* January 1994, pp. 1–14; K. R. France and C. W. Park, "The Impact of Program Affective Valence and Level of Cognitive Appraisal on Advertisement Processing and Effectiveness," *Journal of Current Issues and Research in Advertising,* Fall 1997, pp. 1–21; J. H. Watt et al., "The Effects of Program Involvement and Commercial Position on Reactions to Embedded Commercials," in *Advances in Consumer Research XXV,* ed. J. W. Alba and J. W. Hutchinson (Provo, UT: Association for Consumer Research, 1998), pp. 492–98; and A. B. Aylesworth and S. B. MacKenzie, "Context Is Key," *Journal of Advertising,* Summer 1998, pp. 17–31.

65. See D. E. Sprott, D. M. Hardesty, and A. D. Miyazaki, "Disclosure of Odds Information," *Journal of Public Policy & Marketing,* Spring 1998, pp. 11–23.

66. D. G. Mick, "Consumer Research and Semiotics," *Journal of Consumer Research,* September 1986, pp. 196–213; R. D. Zakia and M. Nadin, "Semiotics, Advertising and Marketing," *Journal of Consumer Marketing,* Spring 1987, pp. 5–12; and *International Journal of Research in Marketing* 4, nos. 3 and 4 (1988), which are devoted to this topic. See also L. M. Scott, "Understanding Jingles and Needledrop," *Journal of Consumer Research,* September 1990, pp. 223–36.

67. E. C. Hirschman, L. Scott, and W. B. Wells, "A Model of Product Discourse," *Journal of Advertising,* Spring 1998, p. 33–50.

68. F. W. Langrehr and C. L. Caywood, "A Semiotic Approach to Determining the Sins and Virtues Portrayed in Advertising," *Journal of Current Issues and Research in Advertising,* Spring 1995, p. 42.

69. R. Alsop, "Color Grows More Important in Catching Consumers' Eyes," *The Wall Street Journal,* November 29, 1989, p. B.1.

70. M. S. Lans, "Supreme Court OKs Color as Trademark," *Marketing News,* May 5, 1995, p. 13.

71. N. Dawar and P. Parker, "Marketing Universals," *Journal of Marketing,* April 1994, pp. 81–95. See also P. S. Richardson, A. S. Dick, and A. K. Jain, "Extrinsic and Intrinsic Cue Effects on Perceptions of Store Brand Quality," *Journal of Marketing,* October 1994, pp. 28–36; T. Z. Chang and A. R. Wildt, "Impact of Product Information on the Use of Price as a Quality Cue," *Psychology & Marketing,* January 1996, pp. 55–74; and J. Srivastava and A. Mitra, "Warranty as a Signal of Quality," *Marketing Letters,* no. 4 (1998), pp. 327–36.

72. T. A. Shimp, S. Samiee, and T. J. Madden, "Countries and Their Products," *Journal of the Academy of Marketing Science,* Fall 1993, pp. 323–30; C. M. Kochunny, E. Babakus, R. Berl, and W. Marks, "Schematic Representation of Country Image," *Journal of International Consumer Marketing* 5, no. 1 (1993), pp. 5–24; V. Cordell, "Interaction Effects of Country of Origin with Branding, Price, and Perceived Performance Risk"; and I. P. Akaah and A. Yaprak, "Assessing the Influence of Country of Origin on Product Evaluations"; both in *Journal of International Consumer Marketing* 5, no. 2 (1993), pp. 5–20 and 39–53; D. Strutton and L. E. Pelton, "Southeast Asian Consumer Perceptions of American and Japanese Imports," *Journal of International Consumer Marketing* 6, no. 1 (1993), pp. 67–86; T. M. Rogers, P. F. Kaminski, D. D. Schoenbachler, and G. L. Gordan, "The Effect of Country-of-Origin Information on Consumer Purchase Decision Process," *Journal of International Consumer Marketing* 7, no. 3 (1994), pp. 73–109; W. K. Li, K. B. Monroe, and D. K. Chan, "The Effects of Country of Origin, Brand, and Price Information," in *Advances in Consumer Research XXI,* ed. C. T. Allen and D. R. John (Provo, UT: Association for Consumer Research, 1994), pp. 449–57; R. Parameswaran and R. M. Pisharodi,

"Facets of Country of Origin Image," *Journal of Advertising,* March 1994, pp. 43–56; and S. S. Andaleeb, "Country-of-Origin Effects," *Journal of International Consumer Marketing* 7, no. 3 (1995), pp. 29–52.

73. J. J. Kellaris, A. D. Cox, and D. Cox, "The Effect of Background Music on Ad Processing," *Journal of Marketing,* October 1993, pp. 100–14; and G. Brooker and J. J. Wheatley, "Music and Radio Advertising," in *Advances in Consumer Research XXI,* ed. C. T. Allen and D. R. John (Provo, UT: Association for Consumer Research, 1994), pp. 286–91.

74. Y. Pan and D. R. Lehmann, "The Influence of New Brand Entry on Subjective Brand Judgments," *Journal of Consumer Research,* June 1993, pp. 76–86.

75. J. Harris, "The Effects of Promotional Bundling," in *Advances in Consumer Research XXIV,* ed. M. Bruck and D. J. MacInnis (Provo, UT: Association for Consumer Research, 1997), pp. 168–72.

76. R. L. Miller, "Dr. Weber and the Consumer," *Journal of Marketing,* January 1962, pp. 57–61; and J. J. Wheatley, J. S. Y. Chiu, and A. Goldman, "Physical Quality, Price, and Perceptions of Product Quality," *Journal of Retailing,* Summer 1981, pp. 100–16.

77. L. M. Scott, "Images in Advertising," *Journal of Consumer Research,* September 1994, p. 254. See also K. Bremer and M. Lee, "Metaphors in Marketing," in *Advances in Consumer Research XXIV,* ed. M. Bruck and D. J. MacInnis (Provo, UT: Association for Consumer Research, 1997), pp. 419–24.

78. Ibid.; B. J. Phillips, "Thinking Into It," *Journal of Advertising,* Summer 1997, pp. 77–87; and M. Friestad and P. Wright, "Everyday Persuasion Knowledge," *Psychology & Marketing,* March 1999, pp. 185–94.

79. L. A. Peracchio and J. Meyers-Levy, "How Ambiguous Cropped Objects in Ad Photos Can Affect Product Evaluations," *Journal of Consumer Research,* June 1994, pp. 190–204; S. M. Broniarczyk and J. W. Alba, "The Role of Consumers' Intuitions in Inference Making," *Journal of Consumer Research,* December 1994, pp. 393–407.

80. G. V. Johar, "Consumer Involvement and Deception from Implied Advertising Claims," *Journal of Marketing Research,* August 1995, pp. 267–79; and C. Pechmann, "Do Consumers Overgeneralize One-Sided Comparative Price Claims," *Journal of Marketing Research,* May 1996, pp. 150–62.

81. J. C. Andrews, R. G. Netemeyer, and S. Burton, "Consumer Generalization of Nutrient Content Claims in Advertising," *Journal of Marketing,* October 1998, pp. 62–75.

82. J. Jacoby and W. D. Hoyer, "Viewer Miscomprehension of Televised Communications," *Journal of Marketing,* Fall 1982, pp. 12–31.

83. *The Comprehension and Miscomprehension of Print Communications* (New York: The Advertising Educational Foundation, Inc., 1987). See also J. Jacoby and W. D. Hoyer, "The Comprehension/Miscomprehension of Print Communication," *Journal of Consumer Research,* March 1989, pp. 434–43; and R. F. Beltramini and S. P. Brown, "Miscomprehension and Believability of Information Presented in Print Advertising," in *Advances in Consumer Research XXI,* ed. C. T. Allen and D. R. John (Provo, UT: Association for Consumer Research, 1994), pp. 218–23.

84. S. M. Broniarcyzk, W. D. Hoyer, and L. McAlister, "Consumers' Perceptions of the Assortment Offered in a Grocery Category," *Journal of Marketing Research,* May 1998, pp. 166–76.

85. F. Leclerc, B. H. Schmitt, and L. Dube, "Foreign Branding and its Effects on Product Perceptions and Attitudes," *Journal of Marketing Research,* May 1994, pp. 263–70.

86. T. Pavia and J. A. Costa, "The Winning Number," *Journal of Marketing,* July 1993, pp. 85–98; T. Pavia, "Brand Names and Consumer Inference," in *Advances in Consumer Research XXI,* ed. C. T. Allen and D. R. John (Provo, UT: Association for Consumer Research, 1994), pp. 195–200; and K. L. Keller, S. E. Heckler, and M. J. Houston, "The Effects of Brand Name Suggestiveness on Advertising Recall," *Journal of Marketing,* January 1998, pp. 48–57.

87. J. N. Axelrod and H. Wybenga, "Perceptions that Motivate Purchase," *Journal of Advertising Research,* June–July 1985, pp. 19–21.

88. A. M. Levin, J. C. Davis, and I. Levin, "Theoretical and Empirical Linkages between Consumers' Responses to Different Branding Strategies," in *Advances in Consumer Research XXIII,* ed. K. P. Corfman and J. G. Lynch (Provo, UT: Association for Consumer Research, 1996), pp. 296–330; and B. L. Simonin and J. A. Ruth, "Is a Brand Known by the Company It Keeps," *Journal of Marketing Research,* February 1998, pp. 30–42.

89. G. Levin, "Some Logos Hurt Image," *Advertising Age,* September 13, 1993, p. 40.

90. J. Tantillo, J. D. Lorenzo-Aiss, and R. E. Mathisen, "Quantifying Perceived Differences in Type Styles," *Psychology & Marketing,* August 1995, pp. 447–57.

91. A. H. Schechter, "Measuring the Value of Corporate and Brand Logos," *Design Management Journal,* Winter 1993, pp. 33–39.

92. "Ford Boss Outlines Shift to 'Rifle' Media," *Advertising Age,* October 26, 1981, p. 89. See also P. J. Danaher, "Wearout Effects in Target Marketing," *Marketing Letters,* no. 3 (1996), pp. 275–87.

93. M. G. Hoy and M. J. Stankey, "Structural Characteristics of Televised Advertising Disclosures," *Journal of Advertising,* June 1993, pp. 47–58.

94. See E. P. Cox et al., "Do Product Warnings Increase Safe Behavior?" *Journal of Public Policy & Marketing,* Fall 1997, pp. 195–204; J. A. Garretson and S. Burton, "Alcoholic Beverage Sales Promotion"; M. D. Slater et al., "Developing and Assessing Alcohol Warning Content"; J. R. Hankin, J. J. Sloan, and R. J. Sokol, "The Modest Impact of the Alcohol Beverage Warning Label"; and P. S. Ellen, P. F. Bone, and E. W. Stuart, "How Well Do Young People Follow the Label?" all in *Journal of Public Policy & Marketing,* Spring 1998, pp. 35–47, 48–60, 61–69, and 70–85; P. Raghubar and G. Menon, "AIDS and Me," *Journal of Consumer Research,* June 1998, pp. 52–63; A. Zuckerman and S. Chaiken, "A Heuristic-Systematic Processing Analysis of the Effectiveness of Product Warning Labels"; G. K. Rousseau, N. Lamson, and W. A. Rogers, "Designing Warnings to Compensate for Age-Related Changes"; B. Fischoff et al., "What Information Belongs in a Warning?" and D. P. Mackinnon and A. Lapin, "Effects of Alcohol Warnings and Advertisements," all in *Psychology & Marketing,* October 1998, pp. 621–42, 643–62, 663–86, and 707–26; and L. Nohre, et. al., "The Association

between Adolescents' Receiver Characteristics and Exposure to the Alcohol Warning Label" and T. K. Greenfield, K. L. Graves, and L. A. Kaskutas, "Long-Term Effects of Alcohol Warning Labels"; both in *Psychology & Marketing,* May 1999, pp. 245–59 and 261–82.

95. See D. W. Stewart and I. M. Martin, *Journal of Public Policy & Marketing,* Spring 1994, pp. 1–19.

96. See P. M. Ippolito and A. D. Mathios, "New Food Labeling Regulations and the Flow of Nutrition Information to Consumers," *Journal of Public Policy & Marketing,* Fall 1993, pp. 188–205; S. Burton, A. Biswas, and R. Netemeyer, "Effects of Alternative Nutrition Label Formats"; and M. Viswanathan, "The Influence of Summary Information on the Usage of Nutrition Information"; both in *Journal of Public Policy & Marketing,* Spring 1994, pp. 36–47 and 48–60; A. L. Levy, S. B. Fein, and R. E. Shucker, "Performance Characteristics of Seven Nutrition Label Formats"; G. T. Ford, M. Hastak, A. Mitra, and D. J. Ringold, "Can Consumers Interpret Nutrition Information in the Presence of a Health Claim?" C. Moorman, "A Quasi Experiment to Assess the Consumer and Informational Determinants of Nutrition Information Processing Activities"; and M. J. Barone, R. L. Rose, K. C. Manning, and P. W. Miniard, "Another Look at the Impact of Reference Information on Consumer Impressions of Nutrition Information"; all in *Journal of Public Policy & Marketing,* Spring 1996, pp. 1–62.

97. C. R. Duke and L. Carlson, "A Conceptual Approach to Alternative Memory Measures for Advertising Effectiveness," *Journal of Current Issues and Research in Advertising,* Fall 1993, pp. 1–14; E. duPlessis, "Recognition versus Recall"; J. S. Dubow, "Recall Revisited"; L. D. Gibson, "Recall Revisited"; and H. J. Ross, Jr., "Recall Revisited"; all in *Journal of Advertising Research,* May 1994, pp. 75–91, 92–106, 107–108, and 109–11; J. S. Dubow, "Rejoinder to Larry Gibson's Response to 'Recall' "; and J. S. Dubow, "'Revisited' Rejoinder to Hal Ross' Response to 'Recall Revisited' "; both in *Journal of Advertising Research,* July 1994, pp. 70–73 and 74–76; and J. Stapel, "Recall and Recognition," *Journal of Advertising Research,* July 1998, pp. 41–45.

Vito Palmisano/Tony Stone Images.

Learning, Memory, and Product Positioning

chapter nine

■ John Robbins founded EarthSave International in 1998 as a response to the success of his 1987 book, *Diet for a New America.* EarthSave is dedicated to "educating people about the powerful connections between our food, our health and the environment, with the mission of creating a better world by promoting the benefits of healthy and life-sustaining food choices." The animal foods industry spends billions of dollars per year trying to convince people that meat and dairy foods are essential to a well-balanced diet, as well as extremely pleasurable consumption choices. The "milk mustache" campaign alone spent almost $200 million in 1998. Against this, EarthSave believes that "factual food information is more powerful than advertisement fallacies." Therefore, it seeks to help people learn about the consequences of their food choices on their health and on the environment. They believe that if people know the facts, they will alter their eating patterns.

Some of the many food facts that they want people learn include the following.

- Over half of U.S. farm fields are devoted to raising grain for animals. One result is that the production of a single pound of feedlot beef requires 600 gallons of water.
- Every year, livestock farms generate an estimated five tons of manure for every person in the United States. One large chicken complex produces 125 tons of manure per day. These quantities are posing increasingly serious pollution problems.
- A person eating no meat or dairy consumes around 2,500 calories of crop production each day, but people who eat just 30 percent of their food as animal products require crop production of 9,000 calories.
- Each year in the United States, contaminated chicken kills at least 1,000 people and sickens millions more.

- It takes 660 gallons of water per pound of chicken. This would produce 16 pounds of broccoli or enough soybeans for three pounds of tofu.
- A high-protein diet is a major cause of calcium loss.
- An adequate supply of calcium can be obtained in a plant-based diet.
- Dairy products are not essential for human health.

EarthSave operates by encouraging individuals to become members. Members receive a quarterly newsletter. EarthSave provides educational materials including books, brochures, videos, and audio tapes as well as T-shirts and posters. Its Web site (www.earthsave.org) has recent news, articles of interest, a catalog of available material, and relevant links. Local EarthSave chapters provide support for individuals seeking to change their diets. They also sponsor special events, potlucks, and video showings.[1]

As the opening example illustrates, nonprofit organizations are interested in teaching consumers and others about the consequences of their consumption choices. Likewise, firms and business associations such as the Milk Producers Council want consumers to learn about the positive features of their products and services. In this chapter, we discuss the nature of learning and memory, conditioning and cognitive theories of learning, and general characteristics of learning. Implications for marketing managers are also examined within each section. The outcome of consumer learning about a brand and product category—product position—is discussed in the final section.

NATURE OF LEARNING

In the previous chapter, we described information processing as *a series of activities by which stimuli are perceived, transformed into information, and stored.* The four activities in the series are exposure, attention, interpretation, and memory. *Learning* is the term used to describe the processes by which memory and behavior are changed as a result of conscious and nonconscious information processing.

Learning is essential to the consumption process. In fact, consumer behavior is largely *learned* behavior. As illustrated in Figure 9-1, we acquire most of our attitudes, values, tastes, behaviors, preferences, symbolic meanings, and feelings through learning. Our culture and social class, through such institutions as schools and religious organizations, as well as our family, friends, mass media, and advertising, provide learning experiences that greatly influence the type of lifestyle we seek and the products we consume.

A wide array of social organizations attempt to help consumers learn "appropriate" attitudes and behaviors about issues such as racial discrimination, environmental protection, proper nutrition, drinking and driving, and date rape. Marketers expend considerable effort to ensure that consumers learn of the existence and nature of their products. Firms that help consumers learn about their products in an efficient manner often obtain a long-term competitive advantage.[2]

Learning is *any change in the content or organization of long-term memory and/or behavior.*[3] Thus, learning is the result of information processing, as described in the last chapter. Recall from Chapter 8 that information processing may be conscious and deliberate in high-involvement situations. Or, it may be nonfocused and even nonconscious in low-involvement situations.

Learning Is a Key to Consumer Behavior **FIGURE 9-1**

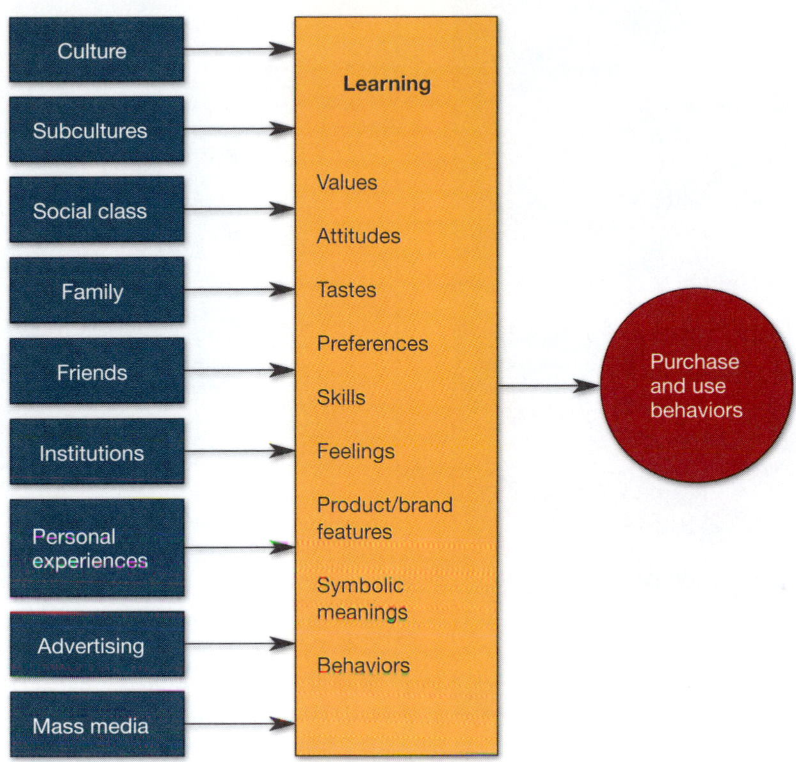

LEARNING UNDER CONDITIONS OF HIGH AND LOW INVOLVEMENT

A moment's reflection will reveal that we learn things in different ways. Preparing for an exam generally involves intense, focused attention. The outcome of these efforts is rewarded with a grade. However, most of our learning is of a much different nature. Most of us know who is playing in the World Series each year even if we don't care for baseball because we hear about it frequently. We can identify clothes that are stylish even though we never really think much about clothing styles. In this section, we are going to describe the various ways consumers learn.

Learning may occur in either a high-involvement or a low-involvement situation. A **high-involvement learning** situation is one in which the consumer is motivated to process or learn the material. For example, an individual reading *Laptop Buyer's Guide* prior to purchasing a computer is probably highly motivated to learn relevant material dealing with the various computer brands. A **low-involvement learning** situation is one in which the consumer has little or no motivation to process or learn the material.[4] A consumer whose television program is interrupted by a commercial for a product he or she doesn't currently use generally has little motivation to learn the material presented in the commercial. Much, if not most, consumer learning occurs in relatively low-involvement contexts.[5]

Consider a person reading a newspaper. Often the reader is focused on the articles in the paper and does not consciously or deliberately read the ads near the articles. However,

®Milky Way. © M&M Mars.

ONCE WOMEN WAITED TO HEAR THREE LITTLE WORDS. NOW IT'S JUST TWO.

Oh, how times have changed. That's not to say romance is out of style, but ignorance certainly is. Because as much as things have changed, it still holds true that knowledge is power. Nowhere is this more evident than when it comes to HIV.

SOME THINGS ARE BEST DONE IN THE PRIVACY OF YOUR OWN HOME. If you decide to get tested for HIV, we invite you to consider the Home Access Express™ HIV test. It's the same laboratory test used by doctors and hospitals— with the decidedly big advantage that you have access to it in the safe, private environment of your own home. You'll also find it interesting to know that it's greater than 99.9% accurate.

Here's how it works: when you call 1.800.HIV.TEST, we send you a kit complete with everything you need for testing*. You then call a separate toll-free number to activate a personal identification code. This anonymous code gives you exclusive access to your test result as well as pre and post-test counseling. Next, you follow the easy sample collection instructions, return your sample to us and call three business days later for your test result.

I'm negative

CALL US IF YOU NEED TO TALK. As part of the testing process, we provide counseling 24 hours a day, seven days a week. We also offer helpful information about HIV, advice on treatment and referrals to health services in your area. Of course, everything is done anonymously because this entire system has been created with the protection of your privacy in mind.

MAKE LOVE WITH YOUR EYES OPEN. This test gives you the knowledge you need to make informed choices about sex in a day and age when even meaningless flings can have meaningful results. $49.95 plus shipping and handling is a small price to pay for the peace of mind it provides. Since all the answers you need are available when you call 1.800.HIV.TEST, the only question is, what are you waiting for?

1.800.HIV.TEST
THE HOME ACCESS HIV I TEST SYSTEM

*For the detection of antibodies to HIV-1. Use as directed. Call 1.800.HIV.TEST for directions and details. ©1996 Home Access Health Corporation, Hoffman Estates, Illinois 60195-5200

© 1996 Home Access Health Corporation.

ILLUSTRATION 9-1

An important judgment in designing an ad is the level of involvement the audience will have with the ad. Involvement is generally based on the interaction of characteristics of the target market, the situation, and the ad or other marketing stimulus.

the reader is exposed to these ads (termed **incidental exposure**). This *incidental exposure has been shown to increase the reader's liking of the brands in these ads despite not being able to recall having seen the ads themselves!* Incidental exposure has also been shown to increase the likelihood that a brand will be included in a consumer's consideration set (the set of brands a consumer would consider purchasing to achieve a purchase goal) across a variety of conditions and product classes.[6] Clearly the low-involvement learning that occurs with incidental exposure is important for marketers and consumers alike.

Involvement is a function of the interaction between the individual, the stimulus, and the situation.[7] For example, an individual not interested in clothing may merely glance at most ads for clothes. However, a clothing ad featuring a celebrity that the consumer greatly admires may cause the individual to examine that ad in some detail (high involvement) and to pay significant attention to the celebrity's clothing. Likewise, consumers who ignore most clothing ads may become much more involved with this type of information if they face a need to buy new clothes soon.

As we will see in the following sections, the way one structures a communication differs based on the level of involvement the audience is expected to have.[8] Illustration 9-1 shows one ad that assumes high-involvement learning and another based on low-involvement learning. Why does one ad assume a highly involved audience and the other a low-involvement audience? What differences do you notice between these two ads? Do those differences make sense?

Learning Theories in High- and Low-Involvement Situations **FIGURE 9-2**

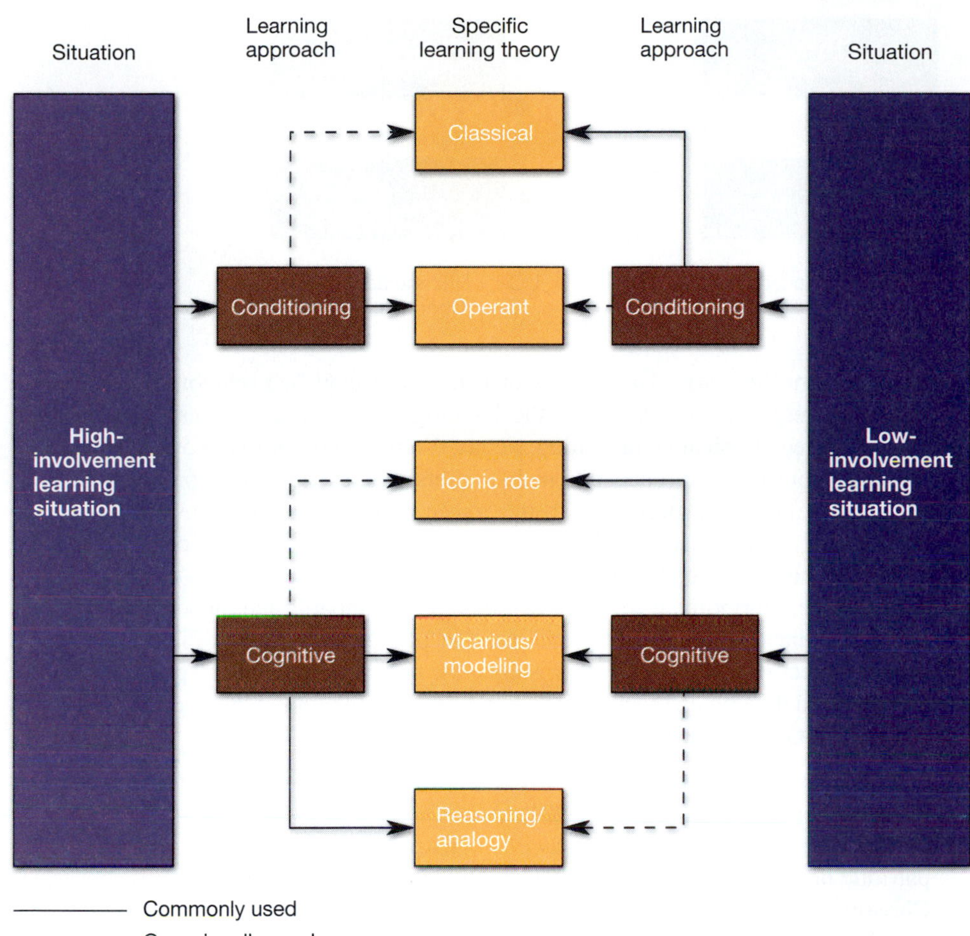

Figure 9-2 shows the two general situations and the five specific learning theories that we are going to consider. The level of involvement is the primary determinant of how material is learned. The solid lines in the figure indicate that operant conditioning, vicarious learning/modeling, and reasoning/analogy are commonly used learning processes in high-involvement situations. Classical conditioning, iconic rote learning, and vicarious learning/modeling tend to occur in low-involvement situations. Each of these specific theories is described in the following pages.

Conditioning

Conditioning refers to learning based on *association of a stimulus (information) and response (behavior or feeling)*. The word *conditioning* has a negative connotation to many of us and brings forth images of robotlike humans. However, conditioned learning simply means that through exposure to some stimulus and a corresponding response, one learns that they go together (or do not go together). There are two basic forms of conditioned learning—classical and operant.[9]

FIGURE 9-3 Consumer Learning through Classical Conditioning

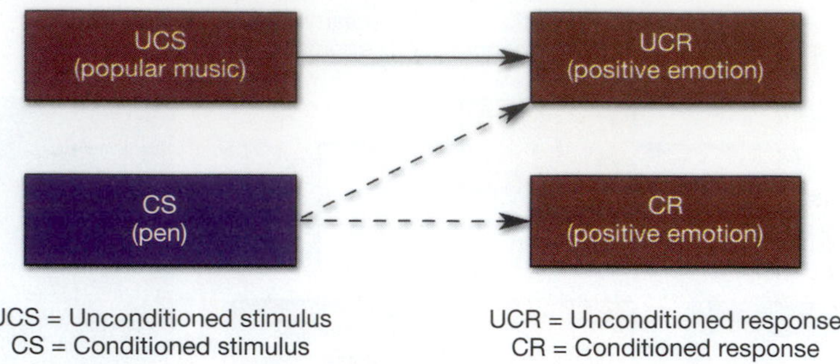

Classical Conditioning The process of using an established relationship between a stimulus and response to bring about the learning of the same response to a different stimulus is called **classical conditioning.** Figure 9-3 illustrates this type of learning.

Hearing popular music (unconditioned stimulus) elicits a positive emotion (unconditioned response) in many individuals. If this music is consistently paired with a particular brand of pen or other product (conditioned stimulus), the brand itself may come to elicit the same positive emotion (conditioned response).[10]

For example, Marlboro cigarettes are presented in billboards and, in countries where it is legal, in media ads showing the brand name or package and a beautiful outdoor scene. Part of the objective of such ads is to associate the positive emotional response to the outdoor scene with the brand. This in turn will increase the likelihood that the individual will like the brand. Other marketing applications include:

- Consistently advertising a product on exciting sports programs may result in the product itself generating an "excitement" response.
- An unknown political candidate may elicit "patriotic feelings" by consistently playing patriotic background music in his or her commercials and appearances.
- Christmas music played in stores may elicit emotional responses associated with giving and sharing, which in turn may increase the propensity to purchase.

Classical conditioning is most common in low-involvement situations. In the Marlboro example described above, it is likely that many consumers devote little or no focused attention to the advertisement, since cigarette ads are low-involvement messages even for most smokers. However, after a sufficient number of low-involvement "scannings" or "glances at" the advertisement, the association may be formed. It is important to note that what is learned is generally not information but emotion or an affective response. If this affective response leads to learning about the product or leads to a product trial, we have this situation:

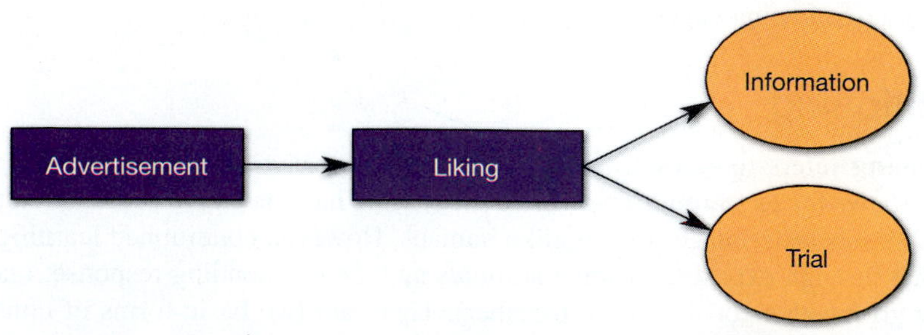

Consumer Learning by Operant Conditioning **FIGURE 9-4**

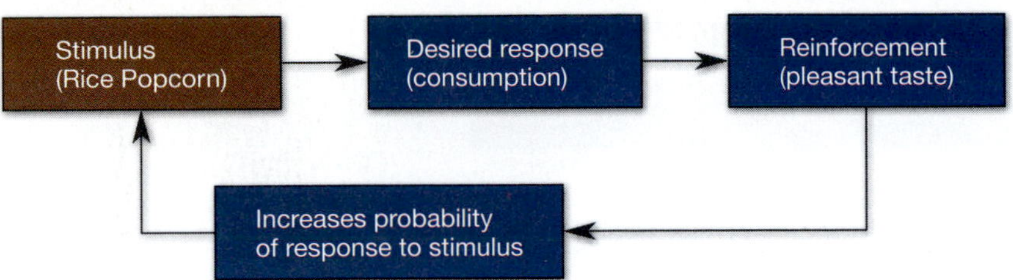

Operant Conditioning *Instrumental learning,* or **operant conditioning,** differs from classical conditioning primarily in the role and timing of reinforcement.[11] Suppose you are the product manager for Pacific Snax's *Rice Popcorn* snack. You believe your product has a light, crisp taste that consumers will like. How can you influence them to learn to consume your brand? One approach would be to distribute a large number of free samples through the mail, at shopping malls, or in stores.[12]

Many consumers would try the free sample (desired response).[13] To the extent that the taste of *Rice Popcorn* is indeed pleasant (reinforcement), the probability of continued consumption is increased. This is shown graphically in Figure 9-4.

Notice that reinforcement plays a much larger role in operant conditioning than it does in classical conditioning. Since no automatic stimulus–response relationship is involved; the subject must first be induced to engage in the desired behavior. Then, this behavior must be reinforced.

Operant conditioning often involves the actual usage of the product. Thus, a great deal of marketing strategy is aimed at securing an initial trial. Free samples (at home or in the store), special price discounts on new products, and contests all represent rewards offered to consumers to try a particular product or brand. If they try the brand under these conditions and like it (reinforcement), they are likely to take the next step and purchase it in the future. This process of encouraging partial responses leading to the final desired response (consume a free sample, buy at a discount, buy at full price) is known as **shaping.** This process is illustrated in Figure 9-5.

In one study, 84 percent of those given a free sample of a chocolate while in a candy store made a purchase, whereas only 59 percent of those not provided a sample made a purchase. Thus, shaping can be very effective. Illustration 9-2 shows an ad designed to induce trial, the first step in shaping. Note that this ad promises a free gift just to try the product and a 20 percent price reduction if the first product is purchased.

While reinforcement increases the likelihood of behavior such as a purchase being repeated, a negative consequence (punishment) has exactly the opposite effect. Thus, the purchase of a brand that does not function properly greatly reduces the chances of future purchases of that brand. This underscores the critical importance of consistent product quality.

Operant conditioning is widely used by marketers. The most common application is to have consistent quality products so that the use of the product to meet a consumer need is reinforcing. Other applications include:

- Direct mail or personal contacts after a sale that congratulates the purchaser for making a wise purchase.

FIGURE 9-5 The Process of Shaping in Purchase Behavior

- Giving "extra" reinforcement for shopping at a store, such as trading stamps, rebates, or prizes.
- Giving "extra" reinforcement for purchasing a particular brand, such as rebates, toys in cereal boxes, or discount coupons.
- Giving free product samples or introductory coupons to encourage product trial (shaping).
- Making store interiors, shopping malls, or downtown areas pleasant places to shop (reinforcing) by providing entertainment, controlled temperature, exciting displays, and so forth.

The power of operant conditioning is demonstrated by an experiment conducted by an insurance company. Over 2,000 consumers who purchased life insurance over a one-month period were randomly divided into three groups. Two of the groups received reinforcement after each monthly payment in the form of a nice "thank-you" letter or telephone call. The third group received no such reinforcement. Six months later, 10 percent of the members of the two groups receiving reinforcement had terminated their policies while 23 percent of those not receiving reinforcement had done so! Reinforcement (being thanked) led to continued behavior (sending in the monthly premium).[14]

Cognitive Learning

Cognitive learning encompasses all the mental activities of humans as they work to solve problems or cope with situations. It involves learning ideas, concepts, attitudes, and facts that contribute to our ability to reason, solve problems, and learn relationships without direct experience or reinforcement. Cognitive learning can range from very simple information acquisition to complex, creative problem solving. Three types of cognitive learning are important to marketers.

Iconic Rote Learning Learning the *association between two or more concepts in the absence of conditioning* is known as **iconic rote learning.** For example, one may see an ad that states, "Ketoprofen is a headache remedy," and associate the new concept "ketopro-

Courtesy Oxmoor House.

ILLUSTRATION 9-2

Marketers design products that they hope will meet consumer needs. When a need is met by a product, the probability of the product being purchased in the future increases. A critical step in this process is the initial purchase or trial of the product. This ad encourages such a trial.

fen" with the existing concept "headache remedy." There is neither an unconditioned stimulus nor a direct reward involved.

A substantial amount of low-involvement learning involves iconic rote learning. Numerous repetitions of a simple message may result in the essence of the message being learned as a result of the consumer scanning the environment. Through iconic rote learning, consumers may form beliefs about the characteristics or attributes of products without being aware of the source of the information. When the need arises, a purchase may be made based on those beliefs.[15]

Vicarious Learning/Modeling It is not necessary for consumers to directly experience a reward or punishment to learn. Instead, we can observe the outcomes of others' behaviors and adjust our own accordingly. Likewise, we can use imagery to anticipate the outcome of various courses of action. This is known as **vicarious learning** or **modeling.**[16]

This type of learning is common in both low- and high-involvement situations. In a high-involvement situation such as purchasing a new suit shortly after taking a job, a consumer may deliberately observe the styles worn by others at work or by role models from other environments, including advertisements. Many ads encourage consumers to image the feelings and experience of using a product.[17] Such images not only enhance learning about the product, they may even influence how the product is evaluated after an actual trial.

A substantial amount of modeling also occurs in low-involvement situations. Throughout the course of our lives we observe people using products and behaving in a great variety of

ILLUSTRATION 9-3

Ads not only convey information and elicit feelings, they can challenge existing assumptions and cause readers to think and reexamine their beliefs.

Reprinted with permission of NIKE, Inc.

situations. Most of the time we pay limited attention to these behaviors. However, over time, we learn that certain behaviors (and products) are appropriate in some situations while others are not.

Reasoning/Analogy The most complex forms of cognitive learning are **reasoning,** including **analogical reasoning.** In reasoning, individuals engage in creative thinking to restructure and recombine existing information as well as new information to form new associations and concepts. The ad in Illustration 9-3 encourages the reader to think about the relationship between mental and physical health and sports participation by girls.

Analogical learning occurs when a consumer uses an existing knowledge base to understand a new situation or object. Suppose your hear about new software programs called off-line Web readers that are designed to download Web pages to PCs. You might learn about this new software by analogical reasoning such as by:

> relating it to something you understand better such as VCRs. You notice that the Web readers and VCRs are designed to retrieve media content. Given this similarity of purpose, you may logically expect them to share other characteristics. Since VCRs record TV programs onto a disk that allows them to be replayed on other VCR players at any desired time, you may conclude that the Web readers will record Web pages onto a disk that can then be accessed from other computers as desired. You may also believe that VCR players are difficult to program and assume that the new Web readers will also be difficult to use properly. At the end of this process, you may have a fairly complete set of beliefs about the new Web reader without having seen or used the product or read or viewed any information about its characteristics.[18]

Summary of Learning Theories with Examples of Involvement Level **TABLE 9-1**

Theory	*Description*	*High-Involvement Example*	*Low-Involvement Example*
Classical Conditioning	A response elicited by one object will be elicited by the second object if both objects frequently occur together.	The favorable emotional response elicited by the word *America* comes to be elicited by the brand Chrysler after a consumer reads that Chrysler plans to use only American-made parts.	The favorable emotional response elicited by a song comes to be elicited by a brand name that is consistently paired with that song even though the consumer does not "pay attention" to the advertising.
Operant Conditioning	A response that is given reinforcement is more likely to be repeated when the same situation arises in the future.	A suit is purchased and the purchaser finds that it does not wrinkle and generates several compliments. A sport coat made by the same firm is then purchased.	A familiar brand of peas is purchased without much thought. They taste "all right." The consumer continues to purchase this brand.
Iconic Rote Learning	Two or more concepts become associated without conditioning.	A jogger learns about various brands of running shoes as a result of closely reading many shoe advertisements that he or she finds enjoyable.	A consumer learns that Apple makes home computers, without ever really "thinking" about Apple advertisements or products.
Vicarious Learning or Modeling	Behaviors are learned by watching the outcomes of others' behaviors or by imagining the outcome of a potential behavior.	A consumer watches the reactions people have to her friend's new short skirt before deciding to buy one.	A child learns that men don't wear dresses without ever really "thinking" about it.
Reasoning/ Analogy	Individuals use thinking to restructure and recombine existing information to form new associations and concepts.	A consumer believes that baking soda removes odors from the refrigerator. Noticing an unpleasant aroma in the carpet, the consumer decides to sweep some baking soda into the carpet.	Finding that the store is out of black pepper, a consumer decides to substitute white pepper.

Summary of Learning Theories

Theories of learning help us understand how consumers learn across a variety of situations. We have examined five specific learning theories: operant conditioning, classical conditioning, iconic rote learning, vicarious learning/modeling, and reasoning/analogy. Each of these learning theories can operate in a high- or a low-involvement situation. Table 9-1 summarizes these theories and provides examples from both high- and low-involvement contexts.

GENERAL CHARACTERISTICS OF LEARNING

Regardless of which approach to learning is applicable in a given situation, several general characteristics of learning are relevant and of interest to marketing managers. Five of the most important are strength of learning, extinction (or forgetting), stimulus generalization, stimulus discrimination, and the response environment.

Strength of Learning

What is required to bring about a strong and long-lasting learned response? How can the HIV Alliance teach you how to eliminate or minimize your risk of AIDS such that you will not forget? How can Revlon teach you about its new line of vitamins and how they differ from other vitamins? The *strength of learning* is heavily influenced by four factors: *importance, reinforcement, repetition,* and *imagery.* Generally, learning comes about more rapidly and lasts longer (1) the more important the material to be learned, (2) the more reinforcement (or punishment) received during the process, (3) the greater the number of stimulus repetitions (or practice) that occurs, and (4) the more imagery contained in the material.

Importance Importance refers to the value that the consumer places on the information to be learned. The more important it is for you to learn a particular behavior or piece of information, the more effective and efficient you become in the learning process.

Importance is the dimension that separates high-involvement learning situations from low-involvement situations. Therefore, high-involvement learning tends to be more complete than low-involvement learning.[19] As we will see, high involvement with the learning situation reduces the need for reinforcement, repetition, and imagery. Unfortunately, marketers are most often confronted with consumers in low-involvement learning situations.

Reinforcement Anything that increases the likelihood that a given response will be repeated in the future is considered **reinforcement.** While learning frequently occurs in the absence of reinforcement (or punishment), reinforcement has a significant impact on the speed at which learning occurs and the duration of its effect.

A *positive reinforcement* is a pleasant or desired consequence. A couple who likes Italian food and dining out sees an ad for a new Olive Garden restaurant in their area and decides to try it. They enjoy the food, service, and ambience. The Olive Garden is now more likely to be selected the next time they dine out.

A *negative reinforcement* involves the removal or the avoidance of an unpleasant consequence. In Illustration 9-4, Head promises to provide high performance while avoiding painful feet. If the ad convinces a consumer to try Head boots and they perform well while feeling comfortable, this consumer is likely to purchase and use the boots and, based on stimulus generalization (discussed shortly), to try other Head products as well.

Punishment is the opposite of reinforcement. It is any consequence that decreases the likelihood that a given response will be repeated in the future. If the couple who tried the Olive Garden restaurant described earlier thought that the service was bad or that the food was poorly prepared, they would be unlikely to patronize this restaurant in the future.

From the above discussion, we can see that there are two very important reasons for marketers to determine precisely what reinforces specific consumer purchases: (1) *to obtain repeat purchases, the product must satisfy the goals sought by the consumer;* and (2) *to induce the consumer to make the first purchase, the promotional messages must promise the appropriate type of reinforcement*—that is, satisfaction of the consumer's goals.

Courtesy Head USA.

ILLUSTRATION 9-4

Reinforcement is anything that increases the probability that a given response will be repeated in the future. It can involve a positive outcome such as providing pleasure or the removal or avoidance of a negative outcome such as sore feet.

Repetition Repetition (or practice) increases the strength and speed of learning. Quite simply, the more times we are exposed to information or practice a behavior, the more likely we are to learn it. The effects of repetition are, of course, directly related to the importance of the information and the reinforcement given. Less repetition of an advertising message is necessary for us to learn the message if the subject matter is very important or if there is a great deal of relevant reinforcement. Since many advertisements do not contain information of current importance to consumers or direct rewards for learning, repetition plays a critical role in the promotion process for many products.

Figure 9-6, based on a study of 16,500 respondents, shows the impact of various levels of advertising repetition over a 48-week period on brands that had either high or low levels of initial awareness. Several features stand out. First, the initial exposure has the largest impact.[20] Second, frequent repetition (once a week) outperforms limited repetition (once every other week or every four weeks). This advantage grows the longer the campaign lasts. Finally, relative gains are much greater for unknown brands.

Both the number of times a message is repeated and the timing of those repetitions affect the extent and duration of learning.[21] Figure 9-7 illustrates the relationship between repetition timing and product recall for a food product. One group of homemakers, represented by the curved line in the figure, was exposed to a food product advertisement once a week for 13 consecutive weeks. For this group, product recall (learning) increased rapidly and reached its highest level during the 13th week, forgetting occurred rapidly, and recall was virtually zero by the end of the year.

A second group of homemakers was exposed to the same 13 direct-mail advertisements. However, they received one ad every four weeks. The zigzag line in the figure shows the recall pattern for this group. Here learning increased throughout the year, but with substantial forgetting between message exposures.

Placing multiple insertions of the same ad in a single issue of a magazine enhances learning. Three insertions generate more than twice the impact of one insertion.[22]

FIGURE 9-6 Impact of Repetition on Brand Awareness for High- and Low-Awareness Brands

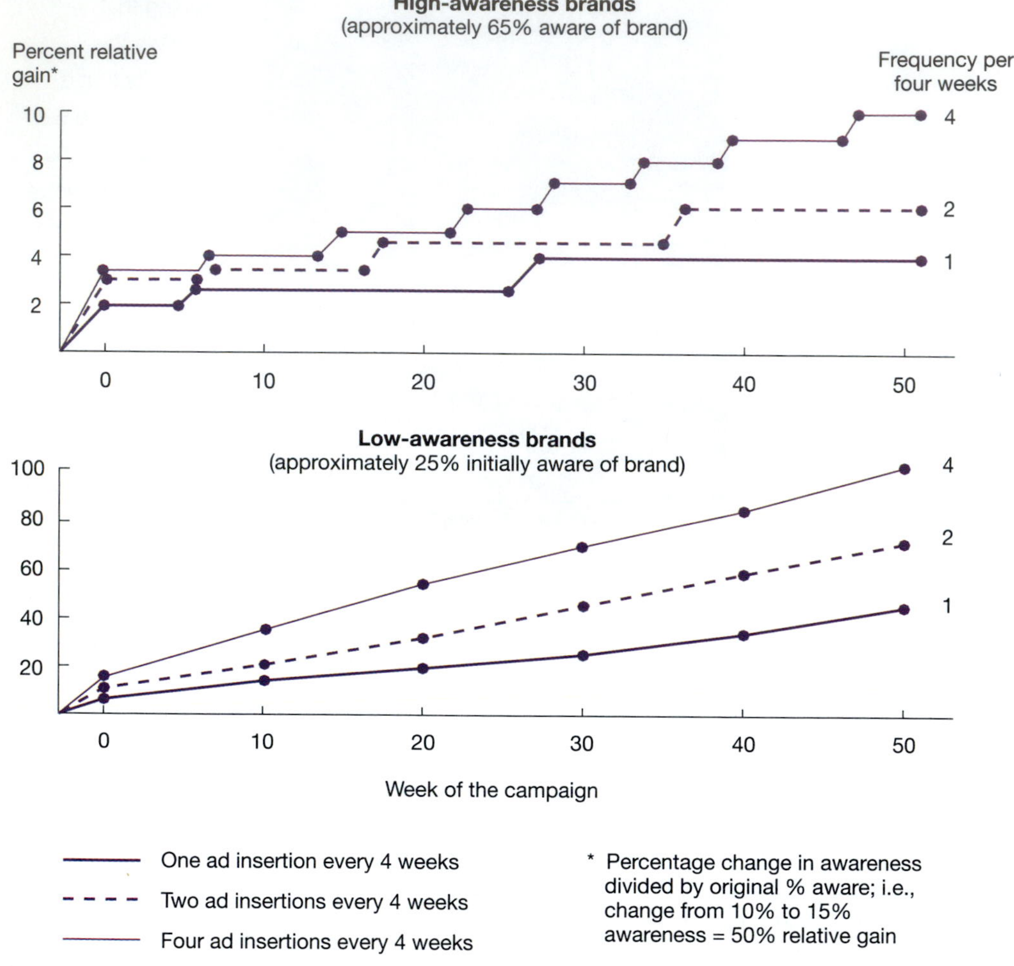

Source: *A Study of the Effectiveness of Advertising Frequency in Magazines,* © 1993 Time Inc. Reprinted by permission.

Concentrating one's messages during a single television broadcast has a similar effect. Compared to one showing of a commercial, three showings during a championship baseball game produced two and one-third times the recall, with 20 percent more positive attitudes and 50 percent fewer negative attitudes.[23] The results below are based on the number of times another commercial appeared during an NFC championship game:

Number of Times Commercial Shown	*Average Recall (percent)*
1	28%
2	32
3	41
4	45

Repetition Timing and Advertising Recall **FIGURE 9-7**

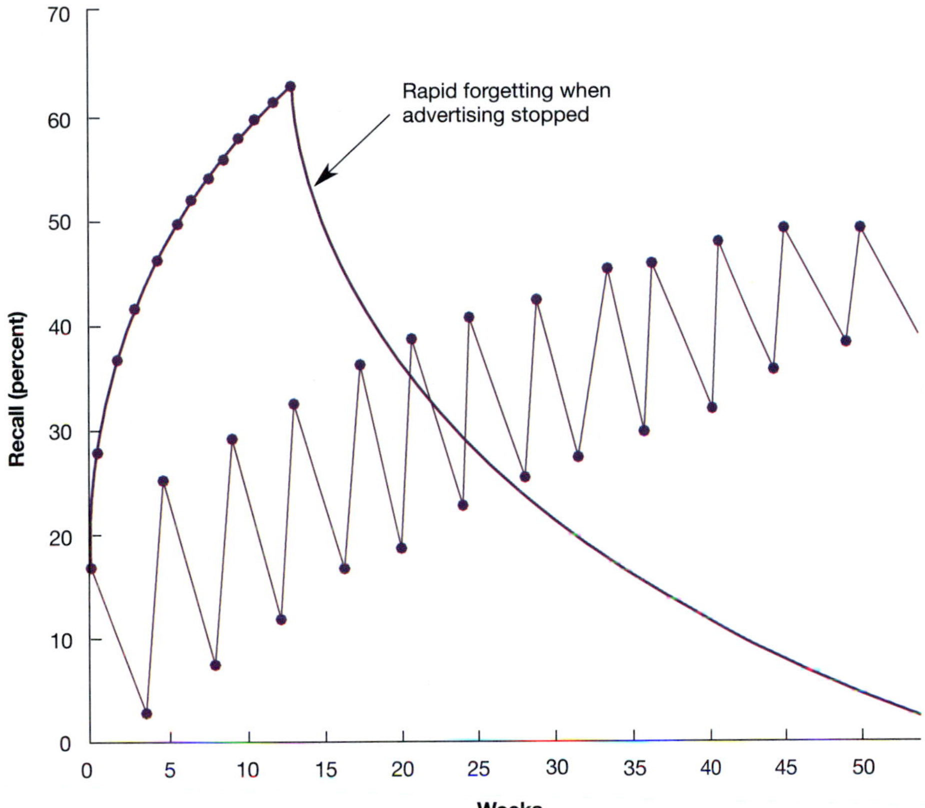

Source: Reprinted from H. J. Zielski, "The Remembering and Forgetting of Advertising," *Journal of Marketing*, January 1959, p. 240, with permission from The American Marketing Association. The actual data and a refined analysis were presented in J. L. Simon, "What Do Zielski's Data Really Show about Pulsing?" *Journal of Marketing Research*, August 1979, pp. 415–20.

Given a finite budget, how should a firm allocate its advertising across a budget cycle? The answer depends on the task. Any time it is important to produce widespread knowledge of the product rapidly such as during a new-product introduction, frequent (close together) repetitions should be used. This is referred to as **pulsing.** Thus, political candidates frequently hold back a significant proportion of their media budgets until shortly before the election and then use a "media blitz" to ensure widespread knowledge of their desirable attributes. More long-range programs, such as store or brand image development, should use more widely spaced repetitions. Likewise, reminder advertising that seeks to reinforce or reaffirm prior learning for an established brand should generally be distributed throughout the year or purchasing season. In either case, learning is likely to be enhanced if different variations of the same basic message are used.[24]

Consumers frequently complain about repetition in advertising, and some even declare that because of excess repetition, "I will never buy that brand!" Thus, there is a fine line for the marketer to balance in terms of repetition. Too much repetition can cause people to actively shut out the message, evaluate it negatively, or pay no attention to it.[25]

Imagery Words, whether a brand name or a corporate slogan, create certain images.[26] For example, brand names such as Camel and Mustang evoke sensory images or well-defined mental pictures. This aids learning, as words high in imagery are substantially easier to learn and remember than low-imagery words. The theory behind the imagery effect is that high-imagery words leave a dual code since they can be stored in memory on the basis of both verbal and pictorial dimensions, while low-imagery words can only be coded verbally.[27]

High-imagery brand names are learned more quickly than are low-imagery names. Likewise, advertising claims consistent with the image evoked by the brand name are easy to recall. Thus, a television brand with a name such as PicturePerfect would be learned more quickly than one named Emporium. Likewise, advertising claims related to picture quality would be associated with the PicturePerfect brand more readily than with the Emporium brand. However, marketers need to be careful when selecting brand names that reflect a single attribute of a product. While claims associated with the attribute in the name are easily associated with the brand, advertised benefits unrelated to the brand (such as sound quality in our PicturePerfect example) are more difficult for consumers to recall compared to the same benefits claimed for a neutral or nonsuggestive brand name.[28]

Pictures *are* images and thus, by definition, have a high level of imagery. Pictures enhance the consumer's visual imagery, which is a particularly effective learning device.[29] They also appear to assist consumers in encoding the information into relevant chunks. Thus, the key communication points of an ad should be in the images elicited by its pictorial component, as this is what will be learned most quickly and firmly.[30]

There is also evidence that echoic memory—memory of sounds, including words—has characteristics distinct from visual memory.[31] Background music that conveys meanings congruent with the meaning being conveyed by the verbal message has been found to increase learning.[32]

Extinction Liggett & Myers' share of the cigarette market slid from 20 percent to less than 4 percent. Much of this decline appears to have resulted from sharply reduced advertising. As one executive stated:

> Some time after the company moved away from advertising and marketing, it became clear that people would quickly forget about our products if we didn't support them in the marketplace.[33]

The above quote emphasizes that marketers want consumers to learn *and* remember positive features, feelings, and behaviors associated with their brands. However, **extinction,** or forgetting as it is more commonly termed, occurs when the reinforcement for the learned response is withdrawn, the learned response is no longer used, or the individual is no longer reminded of the response.

Figure 9-8 illustrates a commonly found rate of forgetting **(decay curve)** for advertising. In this study, aided and unaided recall of four advertisements from *American Machinist* magazine were measured. As can be seen, recall dropped rapidly after five days, then stabilized.

The rate at which extinction occurs is inversely related to the strength of the original learning. That is, the more important the material, the more reinforcement, the more repetition, and the greater the imagery, the more resistant the learning is to extinction.

At times, marketers or regulatory groups desire to accelerate extinction. For example, the American Cancer Society and other organizations offer programs designed to help individuals "unlearn" smoking behavior. Manufacturers want consumers to forget unfavorable publicity or outdated product images.

Corrective advertising, a government requirement that firms remove inaccurate learning caused by past advertising, is described in Chapter 20.

Forgetting over Time: Magazine Advertisement **FIGURE 9-8**

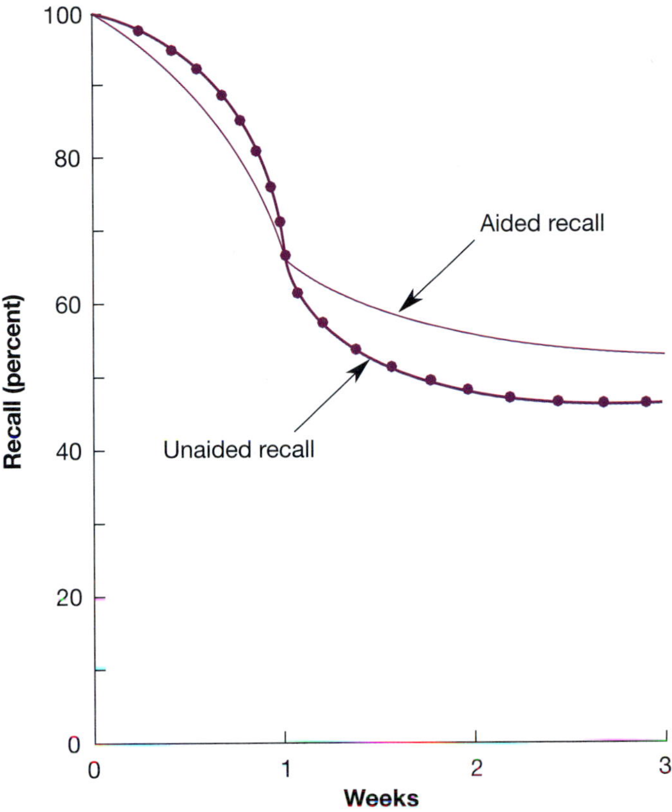

Source: LAP Report #5260.1 (New York: Weeks McGraw-Hill, undated.) Reprinted with permission from McGraw-Hill Companies, Inc.

Stimulus Generalization

Stimulus generalization (often referred to as the *rub-off effect*) *occurs when a response to one stimulus is elicited by a similar but distinct stimulus.* Thus, a consumer who learns that Nabisco's *Oreo Cookies* taste good and therefore assumes that their new *Oreo Chocolate Cones* will also taste good has engaged in stimulus generalization. The fact that stimulus generalization is common provides a major source of brand equity and brand extensions based on brand equity. This area is so important that we devote the last major section of this chapter to it.

Stimulus Discrimination

Stimulus discrimination refers to the process of *learning to respond differently to similar but distinct stimuli.*[34] At some point, stimulus generalization becomes dysfunctional because less and less similar stimuli are still being grouped together. At this point, consumers must begin to be able to differentiate among the stimuli. For example, the management of Bayer aspirin feels that consumers should not see their aspirin as being the same as other brands. In order to obtain a premium price or a large market share, Bayer must teach consumers that its aspirin is distinct from other brands.

Marketers have a number of ways to do this, the most obvious of which is advertising that specifically points out brand differences, real or symbolic. The product itself is frequently altered in shape or design to help increase product differentiation.[35]

For example, Nuprin did not gain market share with ads showing research indicating that two Nuprins gave more headache relief than Extra Strength Tylenol. The campaign was changed to focus on the color of Nuprin *("Little—Yellow—Different—Better")* with a picture of the yellow Nuprin capsules. The campaign made Nuprin the segment's fastest-growing brand. According to the advertising director:

> That Nuprin is yellow is superficial to the superiority, yet it opens people's minds that this product is different.[36]

Response Environment

Consumers generally learn more information than they can readily retrieve. That is, we frequently have relevant information stored in memory that we cannot access when needed. One factor that influences our ability to retrieve stored information is the strength of the original learning.

A second factor affecting retrieval is the similarity of the retrieval environment to the original learning environment.[37] Thus, the more the retrieval situation offers cues similar to the cues present during learning, the more likely effective retrieval is to occur. (This suggests that studying at a desk in a quiet environment rather than on a sofa with music playing might enhance exam performance.) To the extent practical, marketers should do one of two things: (1) configure the learning environment to resemble the most likely retrieval environment, or (2) configure the retrieval environment to resemble the original learning environment.

Matching the retrieval and learning environments requires an understanding of when and where consumers make brand or store decisions. Decisions on brand or store made at home do not have the same set of cues that are available at a retail outlet.

Suppose a firm teaches consumers to have a positive feeling toward its brand of gum by consistently pairing the pronouncement of its brand name with a very pleasant, fun scene in a television ad (classical conditioning). However, it does not show the package, and the name is presented visually only briefly. In the purchase situation, the consumer faces a shelf with many packages but no auditory presentation of brand name. Thus, the retrieval environment is not conducive to triggering the learned response. A better strategy would have been to associate the response with the package, which is what the consumer will encounter in the purchase situation.

Quaker Oats applied this concept in a very direct manner. It developed and ran an extremely popular advertising campaign for Life cereal. As the popularity of the campaign became evident, Quaker placed a photo of a scene from the commercial on the front of the Life cereal package. This enhanced the ability of consumers to recall both affect and information from the commercial and was very successful.[38]

Conclusions on Consumer Learning Thus far, we have examined specific theories and approaches to learning. Knowledge of learning theories can be used to structure communications that will assist consumers in learning relevant facts, behaviors, and feelings about products. We will now turn our attention to an outcome of learning—memory.

MEMORY

Memory is the total accumulation of prior learning experiences. It consists of two interrelated components: short-term and long-term memory.[39] These are *not* distinct physiological entities. Instead, *short-term memory* is that portion of total memory that is currently activated or in use. In fact, it is often referred to as *working memory.*

Short-Term Memory

Short-term memory has a limited capacity to store information and sensations. In fact, it is not used for storage in the usual sense of that term. It is more like a file in a computer system that is currently in use. Active files are used to hold information while it is being analyzed, augmented, and/or altered. After the processing is complete, the reconfigured information is transferred to another system (printed, for example) or returned to a more permanent storage facility such as the hard drive. A similar process occurs with short-term memory. Individuals use short-term memory to hold information while they analyze and interpret it. They may then transfer it to another system (write or type it), place it in long-term memory, or both.

Thus, short-term memory is closely analogous to what we normally call thinking. *It is an active, dynamic process, not a static structure.*

Two basic types of information processing activities occur in short-term memory—elaborative activities and maintenance rehearsal. **Elaborative activities** are *the use of previously stored experiences, values, attitudes, beliefs, and feelings to interpret and evaluate information in working memory as well as to add relevant previously stored information.* Elaborative activities serve to redefine or add new elements to memory. Thus, the interpretation stage of perception as described in Chapter 8 is based on elaborative activities.

Suppose your firm has developed a new product targeted initially at bike riders. The product is a water bottle that one wears strapped to the back with a tube from which the rider can drink without using hands. How will this product be categorized or assigned meaning by the market? The answer depends in large part on *how* it is presented. How it is presented will influence the nature of the elaborative activities that will occur, which in turn will determine how the product is remembered.

Illustration 9-5 shows how *CamelBak*® introduced such a product. First, it used an image-rich name that conveys much of the product's function. Camels are known for their ability to store water and this system is worn on one's back. The visual in the ad clearly, if symbolically, shows the product's primary benefit. The text expands on this theme. Thus, this ad should help trigger elaborative activities that will allow consumers to define this as a new and useful product for providing fluids on bike trips. The high-imagery name should help retention and recall of the key benefits of the product.

Maintenance rehearsal is *the continual repetition of a piece of information in order to hold it in current memory for use in problem solving or transferal to long-term memory.* Repeating the same formula or definition several times before taking an exam is an example. Marketers frequently simulate this by repeating the brand name and/or a key benefit in a prominent manner several times in an ad.

Short-term memory activities involve both concept and imagery manipulation. **Concepts** are abstractions of reality that capture the meaning of an item in terms of other concepts. They are similar to a dictionary definition of a word. Thus, a consumer might bring forth concepts such as water bottle and backpack when first processing the new concept *CamelBak.*

ILLUSTRATION 9-5

Successful new products and brands must enter into memory in a favorable manner, and they must be recalled when required. In this case, the brand name, the visual in the ad, and the ad text will enhance the elaborative activities appropriate for the product.

© Fasttrack Systems, Inc. 1996. Created by Mizuno & Associates, Westlake Village, CA.

Imagery involves concrete sensory representations of ideas, feelings, and objects. It permits a direct recovery of aspects of past experiences. Thus, imagery processing involves the recall and mental manipulation of sensory images, including sight, smell, taste, and tactile sensations. The CamelBak ad might induce some consumers to experience the thirst they felt on their last ride and to feel cool water quenching that thirst. The two tasks below will help clarify the distinctions between concepts and imagery in working memory:

- Write down the first 10 *words* that come to mind when I say "romantic evening."
- Imagine a "romantic evening."

Obviously, marketers often want to elicit imagery responses rather than or in addition to verbal ones. While we are just beginning to study imagery responses, they are a significant part of consumers' mental activities.[40]

Long-Term Memory

Long-term memory is viewed as an unlimited, permanent storage. It can store numerous types of information such as concepts, decision rules, processes, affective (emotional) states, and so forth. Marketers are particularly interested in **semantic memory,** which is the basic knowledge and feelings we have about a concept. It represents our understanding of an object or event at its simplest level. At this level, a brand such as Acura might be categorized as "a luxury car."

A Partial Schematic Memory for Mountain Dew **FIGURE 9-9**

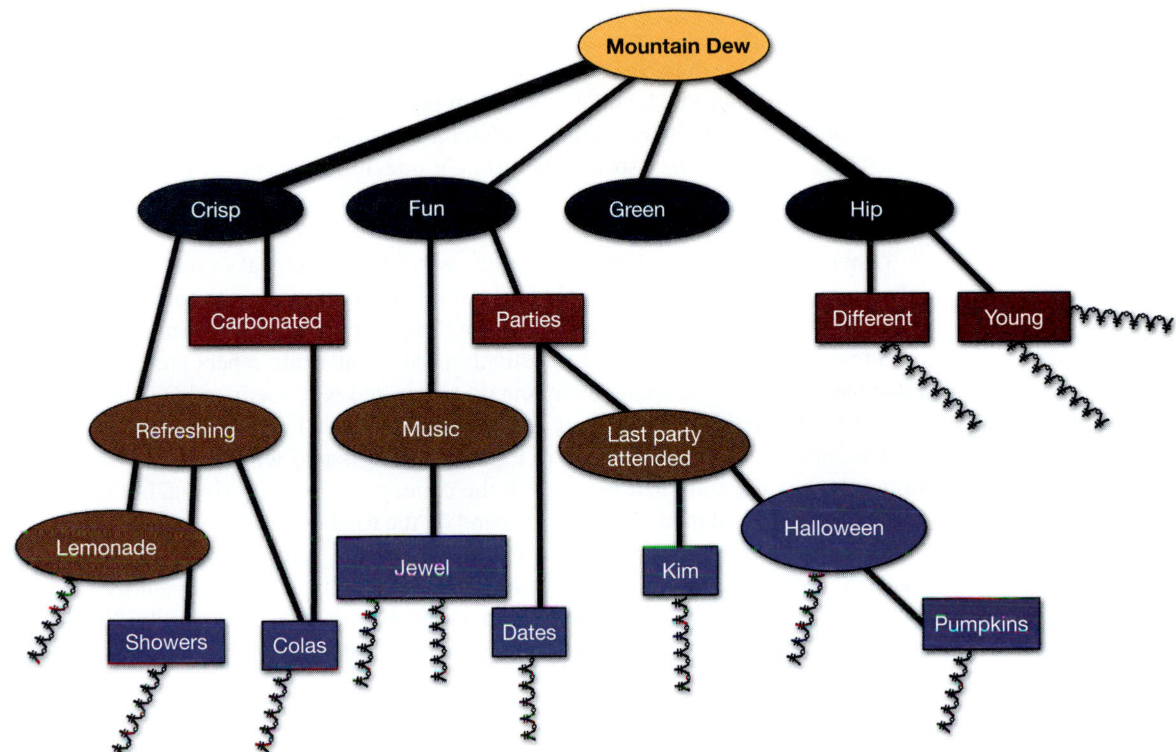

Another type of memory of interest to marketers is **episodic memory.** This is the memory of a sequence of events in which a person participated. These personal memories of events such as a first date, graduation, or learning to drive can be quite strong. They often elicit imagery and feelings. Marketers frequently attempt to evoke episodic memories either because their brand was involved in them or to associate the positive feelings they generate with the brand.

Schema Both concepts and episodes acquire a depth of meaning by becoming associated with other concepts and episodes. A pattern of such associations around a particular concept is termed a **schema** or *schematic memory* (sometimes called a *knowledge structure*). Schematic memory is a complex web of associations. It is this form of memory that is concerned with the association and combinations of various "chunks" of information. Figure 9-9 provides a very simplified example of a schema by showing how one might associate various concepts with *Mountain Dew* to form a network of meaning for that brand. Notice that our hypothetical schema contains *product characteristics, usage situations, episodes,* and *affective reactions.* The source of some of the schema is personal experience, while other aspects may be completely or partially based on marketing activities.[41] The schematic memory of a brand is the same as the brand image (discussed in the next section). It is what the consumer thinks of *and* feels when the brand name is mentioned.

In the partial schema shown in Figure 9-9, concepts, events, and feelings are stored in *nodes* within memory. Thus, the concept "hip" is stored in a node, as are "music," "fun," and "parties." Each of these is associated either directly or somewhat indirectly with Mountain

Dew. *Associative links* connect various concepts to form the complete meaning assigned to an item.

Associative links vary in terms of how strongly and how directly they are associated with a node. In our example, crisp, fun, green, and hip are directly associated with Mountain Dew. However, one or two of these may be very strongly associated with the brand, as crisp and hip are shown to be by the bold lines in our example. Other nodes may have weaker links, such as fun and green. Without reinforcement, the weaker links may disappear over time (over the longer run, so will the stronger ones). Marketers spent enormous effort attempting to develop strong, easily activated links between their brands and desirable product benefits.[42]

Other associations are less direct. Thus, when the individual in our example thinks of Mountain Dew, crisp "comes to mind." After thinking of crisp in the context of a beverage, the concept carbonated is triggered. This, in turn, gives rise to cola drinks.

Some aspects of a schema are relatively permanent while others are transitory. In our example, crisp and fun are likely to remain associated with the brand for quite some time. However, the Halloween party linkage will probably fade fairly quickly.

The memory activation shown in Figure 9-9 originated with the name of a particular brand. If the activation had begun with the concept *hip,* would Mountain Dew arise as a node directly linked to hip? It would depend on the total context in which the memory was being activated. In general, multiple memory nodes are activated simultaneously. Thus, a question like "What is a 'hip' soft drink?" might quickly activate a memory schema that links Mountain Dew directly to hip. However, a more abstract question like "What is hip?" might not. And a request for the name of a hip band would be unlikely to trigger a memory of hip soft drinks.[43]

Schemas exist for all the concepts we hold. Some are very well developed and complex, while others contain few linkages. Marketers expend substantial effort to influence the schema consumers have for their brands. We will discuss this process in detail in the next section of this chapter. Marketers also strive to influence the schema consumers have for consumption situations.

What do you think of when you see the word *thirst?* The various things, including brands, that come to mind constitute the schema for thirst. PepsiCo exerts substantial marketing efforts in an attempt to have its brands, including Mountain Dew, become part of the schema associated with thirst. Brands in the schematic memory for a consumer problem such as thirst are known as the *evoked set.* We will discuss the way consumers and marketers use the evoked set in Chapter 15.

Scripts Memory of how an action sequence should occur, such as purchasing and drinking a soft drink in order to relieve thirst, is a special type of schema known as a **script.** Scripts are necessary for consumers to shop effectively. One of the difficulties new forms of retailing have is teaching consumers the appropriate script for acquiring items in a new manner. This is the problem facing firms wanting to sell products via the Internet. Before these firms can succeed, their target markets must learn appropriate scripts for Internet shopping.

Marketers and public policy officials want consumers to develop scripts for appropriate product acquisition, use, and disposal behavior. For example, using a product or service requires one to learn a process. This process often includes the disposition of the package or some part of the product.[44] Unfortunately, many consumers have learned consumption scripts that do not include appropriate disposition activities such as recycling. Thus, both government agencies and environment groups spend substantial effort attempting to teach consumers consumption scripts that include recycling.

Perhaps the most controversial and complex attempt to teach consumers a script involves HIV prevention among teenagers and young adults. The controversy largely centers on the appropriateness of teaching a script that involves the use of condoms in any sexual encounter versus encouraging a norm against premarital sex. And, as we saw in Chapter 1, even if this controversy did not exist, there is considerable doubt as to the best way to teach the "safe sex script." (Also see Case 4–1.) Other socially desirable scripts involve wearing a seat belt when driving, arranging a "designated driver" or other means of transportation when drinking alcoholic beverages, or watering one's lawn early in the morning for maximum efficiency.

Remembering versus Knowing

Suppose you were asked the price you last paid for a product you purchase periodically, such as a six-pack of Coke. Could you remember? Do you remember the price you usually pay for such a product? Many consumers will not be able to remember this information. Yet many of these same consumers will judge the advertised or actual price of a six-pack of Coke to be "too expensive," "a great deal," or "about average." When asked how they reached such a conclusion, some would reply that they "know a bargain when they see one." We all "know" things for which we cannot recall the source or even the exact nature of our knowledge.

Traditionally, we have thought of remembering, and thus memory, as the ability to recall specific items and events. If you read this chapter and then try to answer the review questions at the end without referring back to the chapter, you are engaging in traditional memory recall. This is referred to as explicit memory. **Explicit memory** is characterized by *the conscious recollection of an exposure event.* In the schema in Figure 9-9, the memory of the Halloween party is likely to be an explicit memory that can be consciously recalled in some detail.

In contrast to remembering, knowing utilizes implicit memory. **Implicit memory** involves *the nonconscious retrieval of previously encountered stimuli.* It is a sense of familiarity, a feeling, or a set of beliefs about an item without conscious awareness of when and how they were acquired. In Figure 9-9, the association of Mountain Dew and hip is most likely an implicit memory.[45]

The distinction between remembering or explicit memory and knowing or implicit memory is important for marketing research, pricing, and advertising strategy. For example, it suggests that measuring advertising effectiveness in terms of advertising recall may not be appropriate for ads aimed establishing a brand image. Much of a brand image will take the form of an implicit memory. A consumer will "know" Mountain Dew is hip, that Levi's are old-fashioned, and that Volkswagen is fun without being able to explain how he or she acquired this knowledge. Thus, recall of the ad or of any of the features of the ad is not as relevant as is its long-term impact on what consumers know (rather than remembers) about the brand.

BRAND IMAGE AND PRODUCT POSITIONING

Brand image refers to the schematic memory of a brand.[46] It contains the target market's interpretation of the product's attributes, benefits, usage situations, users, and manufacturer/marketer characteristics. It is what we think of and feel when we hear or see a brand name.[47] *Company image* and *store image* are similar except they apply to companies and stores rather than brands.

Plymouth's sales are only 40 percent of what they were at Plymouth's peak. Research shows that Plymouth "has little identity" among the first-time buyers that it sees as vital to its future. Steven Bruyn, the car's marketing manager, recently stated: "There is clearly

ILLUSTRATION 9-6

The image of a product or product line is of vital importance to a firm. The Plymouth Prowler will not only meet the needs of a market segment but Chrysler also hopes it will have a positive impact on the image of the Plymouth line.

© Bill Delaney.

no real passion associated with the brand."[48] What should Plymouth's management do? One approach is to attempt to enhance the brand's image through advertising. While doing this, Chrysler took an additional step to add excitement to the image of the entire Plymouth line. It launched the Plymouth Prowler, a $35,000, two-seat, retro-styled roadster (see Illustration 9-6). While the market for the Prowler is estimated to be small, it is hoped that adding it to the Plymouth line will sharpen and enhance the image of the entire line.

Consider the following headlines from recent marketing publications:

- ABC Sets Out in Search of Sharper Brand Image.
- Hardee's Debuts $100 million in Ads to Rebuild Brand.
- Ford Switches Directions to Push Primary Brands
- Brands Still Rule Supreme.

After a number of years of focusing on special promotions and price discounts through coupons, rebates, and sales, major consumer marketers have realized that a focus on establishing and maintaining a strong brand image is critical to long-term success. As the above headlines indicate, this concern cuts across all types of services and products.

How powerful are brand images? Think of *McDonald's, Delia's, Calvin Klein, Coke, Oil of Olay, Amazon.com,* and *Midas*. For many consumers, each of these names conjures up a rich pattern of meanings and feelings. Brand images can be important in any product category.

In high-tech markets, Intel gained a huge advantage by branding its computer chip (see Illustration 16-7). It originally used the expression—"Intel, the Computer Inside"—in advertising. In Japan, this expression had been shortened to "Intel In It." When Intel's attempt to trademark the *386* name for its computer chip failed, it decided to use "Intel Inside." In addition, it decided to provide a cooperative advertising allowance to PC makers who used the logo. Awareness of the chip rose from 22 to 80 percent of home-PC buyers in just two years, and many buyers will only consider computers with the Intel logo.[49]

Hewlett-Packard (H-P) acquired a company image over time that it is now exploiting. Its corporate marketing communications manager described its historic marketing approach as follows: "If we were trying to sell sushi, we would market it as cold, dead fish." However, its technological innovations and trouble-free products such as its *Laser-Jet* and *DeskJet* printers gave it a valuable image among retail buyers. This enabled H-P to enter the home computer market, as described below:

> "So basically, H-P, without having the computers themselves on the shelves, already was viewed as a leader in computer products sold at retail," says Webb McKinney, general manager of the home products division. The new line was marketed as "Not just a PC but an H-P." To the industry's surprise, it gained the number five spot in the home market in three months. "I think it's a great product; I don't want to denigrate it. But it really was the brand," says McKinney.[50]

Product Positioning

Product positioning is *a decision by a marketer to try to achieve a defined brand image relative to competition within a market segment.* That is, marketers decide that they want the members of a market segment to think and feel in a certain way about a brand. This is generally expressed in relation to a competitive brand or a usage situation. The term *product positioning* is most commonly applied to decisions concerning brands, but it is also used to describe the same decisions for stores, companies, and product categories.

Product positioning decisions are strategic decisions. Deciding how a brand should be thought of by a target market relative to competition or usage situations has a major impact on the long-term success of the brand (presuming the firm can create the desired position). Consider Saturn's positioning strategy. Saturn stresses value, made in America by caring workers, and dealers who care about and respect customers and who do not "haggle" over price. Saturn wants to be viewed as superior to its competitors on each of these attributes. If it achieves this desired positioning, it will succeed *to the extent that this position is desired by the target market.*[51] If the target market does not value this image or values the image portrayed by competitors more, Saturn will not succeed.

An important component of brand image is the appropriate usage situations for the product and/or brand. Often marketers have the opportunity to influence the usage situations for which a product or brand is seen as appropriate. What do you think of when you think of cranberry sauce? Odds are that Thanksgiving and perhaps Christmas are part of your image of cranberry sauce. In fact, these are probably the only usage situations that came to mind. However, in one study, sales for cranberry sauce increased almost 150 percent over a three-month period after consumers saw advertisements promoting nontraditional uses. Thus, expanding the usage situation component of cranberry sauce's image could dramatically increase its sales.[52]

The terms *product position* and *brand image* are often used interchangeably. In general, however, product position involves an explicit reference to a brand's image relative to another brand or the overall industry. It is characterized by statements such as "H-P printers are the most reliable printers available." Brand image generally considers the firm's image without a direct comparison to a competitor. It is characterized by statements such as "H-P printers are extremely reliable."

Once a marketer decides on an appropriate product position, the marketing mix is manipulated in a manner designed to achieve that image in the target market. The stimuli that marketing managers employ to influence a product's interpretation and thus its position can be quite subtle.[53] Sunkist Growers has a pectin-based candy available in various fruit flavors (pectin is a carbohydrate obtained from orange and lemon peels). The candy contains no preservatives and less sugar than most fruit jelly candies. Originally, the candy was available in restaurants, hospitals, and, to a limited extent, supermarket candy sections.

FIGURE 9-10 Perceptual Map for Automobiles

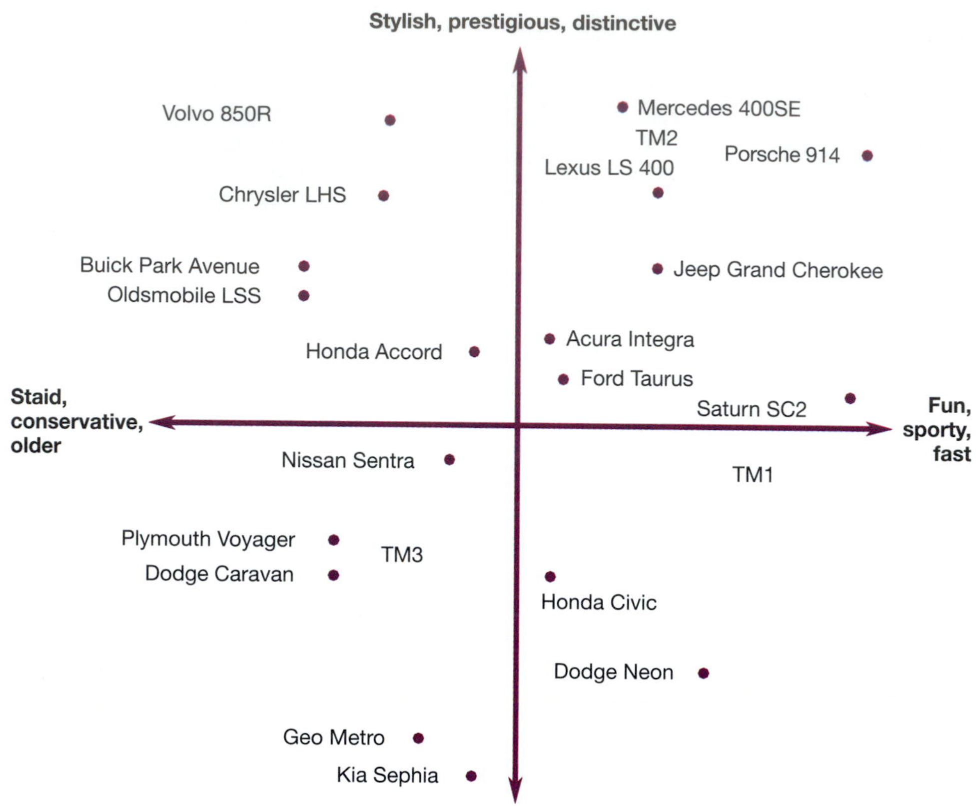

Now, Sunkist Growers is actively promoting the candy, called Sunkist Fruit Gems, as a "healthful, natural" snack. The company hopes to attract adults as well as children. As part of the overall marketing strategy, Sunkist is attempting to distribute the candy through the produce departments of supermarkets. Notice how the distribution plan supports the desired product position or image. A consumer receiving a message that this is a healthful, natural product may agree when the product is found near other healthful, natural products such as apples and oranges.

Marketing managers frequently fail to achieve the type of product image or position they desire because they fail to anticipate or test for consumer reactions. Toro's initial lightweight snow thrower was not successful. Why? It was named the Snowpup, and consumers interpreted this to mean that it was a toy or lacked sufficient power. Sales success came only after a more macho, power-based name was utilized—first Snowmaster and later Toro.

Perceptual mapping offers marketing managers a useful technique for measuring and developing a product's position. Perceptual mapping takes consumers' perceptions of how similar various brands or products are to each other and relates these perceptions to product attributes. Figure 9-10 is a perceptual map for several automobile models. The marketing implications of the positions held by the Buick Park Avenue and the Oldsmobile LSS are serious. Not only are they viewed as being rather unexciting, they also appear to

ILLUSTRATION 9-7

Repositioning a product involves making all aspects of the product consistent with the new position. This includes product features, price, communications, distribution channels, and, as shown here, package or container design.

compete primarily with each other (both are made by GM) rather than with the products of other manufacturers.

This perceptual map also provides the ideal point for three market segments—TM1, TM2, and TM3. These ideal points represent the image/characteristics each segment desires in an automobile. If the models in this map were all that existed, it would indicate that TM1 consumers are not being offered the product they want. At present, they have to spend more than they want and buy a Saturn SC2 or buy a less sporty car than they desire such as the Honda Civic or the Dodge Neon. If this segment is large enough, one or more firms should consider developing a fun, sporty, but fairly low cost, economical car and targeting this group.

Product Repositioning The images consumers have of brands change over time. Thus, H-P may maintain a reputation for having very reliable printers while losing its position as having the most reliable printers in the industry if a superior competitor evolves. Likewise, H-P's image and position could evolve over time based on marketing mix changes initiated by H-P.

The evolution of images and product positions over time is natural and to an extent inevitable. **Product repositioning,** on the other hand, *refers to a deliberate decision to significantly alter the way the market views a product.* This could involve its level of performance, the feelings it evokes, the situations in which it should be used, or even who uses it.

Mug Root Beer is being repositioned to be more appropriate to Generation X and to older teens (its primary target market is 15 to 29 years old). This is noticeably younger than its prior target. To accomplish this repositioning, it is being advertised on television for the first time in five years. It is appearing on shows that appeal to young adults as well as on MTV. In one ad, a young man drinks Mug while flipping the city's master light switch on and off to the beat of the 1970's tune "Love Train."[54] In another ad, a young man drinks Mug while talking to a prairie dog in a pet store about freeing him from his "jail." In addition to advertising and promotion changes, the package was redesigned to a brighter red from its original brown in order to appeal more to this market segment (see Illustration 9-7).

PepsiCo is attempting to reposition Mug primarily in terms of its user group. What do you think of when you hear Midas? If you still think only of mufflers, Midas will not have succeeded in its attempt to expand it image. It wants to be seen as an expert in auto systems

Consumer Insight 9-1

Repositioning the Acura

Honda introduced the Acura into the U.S. market in 1986 as premium car at a relatively low price compared to European imports such as Mercedes and BMW. The car was positioned as a high-performance, precision-crafted automobile priced well below other cars with comparable performance. It was a major success and quickly became the best-selling premium import brand.

In 1995, Acura had its worst sales since its launch. What happened? A number of events eroded the strength of its initial product position. In 1989, Toyota and Nissan launched the Lexus and Infiniti at luxury levels and prices somewhat above the Acura. In early 1990s, Mercedes, BMW, and Audi sharply reduced their prices. Thus, Acura's position as "high performance at a bargain price" was eroded to "high performance at a price a little lower than the competition."

In addition, Honda learned that price and performance were not an adequate foundation. A Honda executive states: "We came to find out that, in the luxury car market, performance isn't enough. The buyers want status, prestige, comfort, and luxury." An executive from Honda's ad agency reflects these concerns: "Acura gets extremely high marks for quality, dependability, and value, but it doesn't perform well in categories like luxurious, expensive-looking, and prestigious. We have to change the image."

Ads for the 1995 and 1996 models dropped the performance theme and focused on luxury. Both the Legend and the Integra are being redesigned and will be replaced by versions with new names. Honda is also expanding the width of the line to include a luxury sport-utility vehicle as well as a lower-priced coupe.

However, just changing the product and the advertising is unlikely to be enough to reposition Acura as a luxury car. The dealership network will also have to change. As one dealer says: "If we're going to be a luxury car franchise, we've got to look like a luxury car franchise. We've got to deliver the image they are projecting." To this end, Honda starting awarding dealers significant prizes based on customer satisfaction scores rather than pure sales volume. It also hired Sandy Corp., the firm that trained Saturn and Infiniti dealers, to teach its dealers how to better serve customers. However, progress on remodeling the aging showrooms is likely to be slow, with sales at an all-time low and 25 percent of the dealers losing money. Likewise, many dealers do not support the image shift and use their share of the brand's advertising dollars in hard sell rather than image ads.

Critical Thinking Questions

1. The Acura did not change yet its product position did. Why? What lesson does this convey?
2. Is Honda likely to succeed in its repositioning strategy?

Source: L. Armstrong, "Acura: Stuck between Gears?" pp. 136–38. Reprinted from the October 2, 1995 issue of *Business Week* by special permission.

and plans to spend $23 million in advertising to reposition itself (it feels it already has the service capabilities to support the image). One ad compares auto repairs to math:

> "Repairing a car is like math. Once you master the basics, then you can build on them. Same as Midas. They excelled in mufflers, and expanded into other systems on your car." The tagline: "Midas Auto Systems Experts. What can we do for you today?"[55]

Consumer Insight 9-1 illustrates the importance of a proper positioning strategy and the difficulty that repositioning can involve.

BRAND EQUITY AND BRAND LEVERAGE

Brand equity is *the value consumers assign to a brand above and beyond the functional characteristics of the product* (though it is generally derived from such features).[56] For example, many people pay a significant premium for Bayer aspirin relative to store brands of aspirin despite the fact that they are chemically identical.

Brand equity is nearly synonymous with the reputation of the brand.[57] However, the term *equity* implies economic value. Thus, brands with "good" reputations have the potential for high levels of brand equity, while unknown brands or brands with weak reputations do not.

Brand equity is based on the image consumers have of the brand. A consumer who believes that a brand delivers superior performance, is exciting to use, and is produced by a company with appropriate social values is likely to be willing to pay a premium for the brand, to go to extra trouble to locate and buy it, to recommend it to others, or to otherwise engage in behaviors that benefit the firm that markets the brand. Thus, one source of economic value from a preferred brand image results from consumers' behaviors toward existing items with that brand name.[58]

Another source of value for a brand image is that consumers may assume that the favorable aspects of the image associated with an existing product will apply to a new product with the same brand name. This is based on the principle of stimulus generalization described earlier in this chapter.

Brand leverage (often termed *family branding, brand extensions,* or *umbrella branding*) refers to marketers capitalizing on brand equity by using the existing brand name for new products.[59] If done correctly, consumers will assign some of the characteristics of the existing brand to the new brand. Recent brand extensions include Bounty paper napkins (previously only paper towels), Tartar Control Listerine, and Toyota ski boats.

However, stimulus generalization does not occur just because two products have the same brand name. There must be a connection between the products. Bacardi is particularly conservative in using its name for fear of adversely affecting sales of Bacardi rum, the world's largest-selling distilled spirit. However, they successfully launched Bacardi Tropical Fruit Mixers (frozen nonalcoholic drinks) based on the following rationale:

> Our research found that tropical drinks—piña coladas and frozen daiquiris—are highly associated with Bacardi rum. We already have credibility in that area, which made this new venture right. Bacardi has a lot of equity in its name; it means quality in areas related to rum . . . But we feel the name wouldn't have that equity in another area. Bacardi wine, for example, wouldn't mean a lot because rum has nothing to do with wine.[60]

In contrast, Campbell's was not able to introduce a spaghetti sauce under the Campbell's name (it used *Prego* instead). Consumer research found that:

> Campbell's, to consumers, says it isn't authentic Italian. Consumers figured it would be orangy and runny like our tomato soup.[61]

Successful brand leverage requires that the original brand have a strong positive image and that the new product fit with the original product on at least one of four dimensions:[62]

1. *Complement.* The two products are used together.
2. *Substitute.* The new product can be used instead of the original.
3. *Transfer.* Consumers see the new product as requiring the same manufacturing skills as the original.
4. *Image.* The new product shares a key image component with the original.

Porsche has a high-quality, sporty image among many consumers. It could logically extend its name to tires (complement), motorcycles (substitute), ski boats (transfer), or sunglasses (image). In fact, it recently introduced a Porsche mountain bike—for $4,500!

What do cosmetics and vitamins have in common? On the surface, very little. However, think about Revlon's image. It is known for skin care and beauty enhancement products. It recently launched Revlon Vitamins with the expression: "Now, Revlon beauty begins from the inside-out." The vitamins are positioned in terms of the specific health benefits associated with each that relate directly to beauty such as nail strength. Will consumers accept this new line because of Revlon's image in beauty and skin care? If they do, Revlon will have successfully used brand leverage to take advantage of its brand equity.

Other examples of successful and unsuccessful brand extensions include the following:

- Gillette was unsuccessful with a facial moisturizer line under the *Silkience* brand name. Silkience's excellent reputation in hair care simply did not translate to face creams.
- Harley-Davidson has applied its name successfully to a wide variety of products, but its Harley-Davidson wine coolers were not successful.
- Levi Strauss failed in its attempt to market Levi's tailored suits for men.
- Country Time could not expand from lemonade to apple cider.
- Life Savers gum did not succeed.
- Coleman successfully expanded from camping stoves and lanterns into a complete line of camping equipment.
- Oil of Olay bar soap is successful in large part due to the equity of the Oil of Olay lotion.

When marketers want to offer a version of a popular brand to distinct market segments with a distinct image from the original brand, they generally need to create a new brand rather than extend the existing one. AT&T did this by creating the Lucky Dog Phone Co. to offer low cost dial-around phone service to cost-focused customers. Likewise, The Gap created Old Navy to target value-oriented students and young families. Miller Brewing uses the Plank Road Brewery to market specialty beers such as Red Dog, Southpaw, and Icehouse. These new brands have images that are distinct from the original brand. Using unique brand names for this purpose avoids diluting or confusing the original brand image.

Brand extensions are sometimes done to bolster the image of the brand rather than to capitalize on its current equity. As described earlier, this was part of the reason the Plymouth Prowler was developed. Mercedes, like Porsche and BMW, has launched a mountain bike with its name attached. However, much of the reason is because mountain bikes have a "hip, active image." A marketer for Mercedes says the firm wants to "appeal to a larger, wider, younger audience."[63] In these cases, the new product is designed to enhance the base brand image and increase its equity.

Brand extensions involve several risks for marketers. One is that a failure of any product with a brand name can hurt all the products with the same brand name (consumers generalize bad outcomes as well as good ones).

Another risk is diluting or unfavorably altering the original brand image.[64] A strong image is generally focused on a fairly narrow set of characteristics. Each additional product added to that product name alters the image somewhat. If too many or too dissimilar products are added to the brand name, the brand image may become diffuse or confused. For example, if Porsche launched skis, backpacks, tennis equipment, fashion clothes for both genders, stereos, and so forth, it would eventually lose its unique meaning. Many feel that Nike is in danger of such a brand dilution as it attaches its name to an ever-wider array of products.

Federal law has recently recognized the danger of brand equity dilution by other firms. Until 1996, a firm in a noncompeting industry could use a famous brand name such as *Apple* if there were no danger of consumer confusion. However, the Federal Trademark Dilution Act of 1995 allows a firm to take action if another uses its brand name or trademark in a way that lessens:

> The capacity of a famous mark to identify and distinguish goods and services, regardless of the presence or absence of (1) competition between the owner of the famous mark and other parties, or (2) likelihood of confusion, mistake, or deception.[65]

This law, which we discuss in more detail in Chapter 20, provides significantly more protection to existing brands but also increases the difficulty of selecting and developing new brand names.

SUMMARY

Consumers must learn almost everything related to being a consumer—product existence, performance, availability, values, preference, and so forth. Marketing managers, therefore, are very interested in the nature of consumer learning.

High-involvement learning occurs when an individual is motivated to acquire the information. *Low-involvement learning* occurs when an individual is paying only limited or indirect attention to an advertisement or other message. Low-involvement learning tends to be limited due to a lack of elaborative activities.

Learning is defined as any change in the content or organization of long-term memory and/or behavior. Two basic types of learning, *conditioning* and *cognition,* are used by consumers.

There are two forms of conditioned learning—classical and operant. *Classical conditioning* refers to the process of using an existing relationship between a stimulus and response to bring about the learning of the same response to a different stimulus.

In *operant conditioning, reinforcement* plays a much larger role than it does in classical conditioning. No automatic stimulus-response relationship is involved, so the subject must first be induced to engage in the desired behavior and then this behavior must be reinforced.

The *cognitive* approach to learning encompasses the mental activities of humans as they work to solve problems, cope with complex situations, or function effectively in their environment. It includes *iconic rote learning* (forming associations between unconditioned stimuli without rewards), *vicarious learning/modeling* (learning by imagining outcomes or observing others), and *reasoning/analogy.*

The strength of learning depends on four basic factors: importance, reinforcement, repetition, and imagery. *Importance* refers to the value that the consumer places on the information to be learned—the greater the importance, the greater the learning. *Reinforcement* is anything that increases the likelihood that a response will be repeated in the future—the greater the reinforcement, the greater the learning. *Repetition* or practice refers to the number of times that we are exposed to the information or that we practice a behavior. Repetition increases the strength and speed of learning. *Imagery* is the degree to which concepts evoke well-defined mental images. High-image concepts are easier to learn.

Remembering a fact or specific event is known as *explicit memory.* Knowing something without awareness of the source or exact nature of the knowledge is referred to as *implicit memory.* Both forms of memory are important to marketers, but implicit memory is particularly important for understanding how consumers form and use brand images.

Stimulus generalization is one way of transferring learning by generalizing from one stimulus situation to other, similar ones. *Stimulus discrimination* refers to the opposite process of learning—responding differently to somewhat similar stimuli.

Extinction, or forgetting, is also of interest to marketing managers. Extinction is directly related to the strength of original learning, modified by continued repetition.

Memory is the result of learning. Most commonly, information goes directly into *short-term memory* for problem solving or elaboration where two basic activities occur—elaborative activities and maintenance rehearsal. *Elaborative activities* are the use of stored experiences, values, attitudes, and feelings to interpret and evaluate information in current memory. *Maintenance rehearsal* is the continual repetition of a piece of information in order to hold it in current memory.

Long-term memory is information from previous information processing that has been stored for future use. It undergoes continual restructuring as new information is acquired. Information is retrieved from retention for problem solving, and the success of the retrieval process depends on how well the material was learned and the match between the retrieval and learning environment.

Brand image, a market segment or individual consumer's schematic memory of a brand, is a major focus of marketing activity. *Product positioning* is a decision by a marketer to attempt to attain a defined brand image, generally in relation to specific competitors. A brand image that matches a target market's needs and desires will be valued by that market segment. Such a brand is said to have *brand equity* because consumers respond favorably toward it in the market. In addition, these consumers may be willing to assume that other products with the same brand name will have some of the same features. Introducing new products with the same name as an existing product is referred to as *brand leverage* or *brand extension.*

KEY TERMS

Analogical reasoning 332
Brand equity 350
Brand image 345
Brand leverage 351
Classical conditioning 328
Cognitive learning 330
Concept 341
Conditioning 327
Decay curve 338
Elaborative activities 341
Episodic memory 343
Explicit memory 345
Extinction 338
High-involvement learning 325
Iconic rote learning 330
Imagery 342
Implicit memory 345
Incidental exposure 326
Learning 324
Long-term memory 342
Low-involvement learning 325
Maintenance rehearsal 341
Modeling 331
Operant conditioning 329
Perceptual mapping 348
Product positioning 347
Product repositioning 349
Pulsing 337
Punishment 334
Reasoning 332
Reinforcement 334
Schema 343
Scripts 344
Semantic memory 342
Shaping 329
Short-term memory 341
Stimulus discrimination 339
Stimulus generalization 339
Vicarious learning 331

INTERNET EXERCISES

1. Visit one of the following Web sites. Evaluate the site in terms of its application of learning principles.
   a. http://www.kraftfoods.com
   b. http://www.pepsi.com
   c. http://www.pg.com
   d. http://www.nike.com
2. Visit several company Web sites until you find one that you feel makes particularly effective use of one or more of the learning theories we have covered and one that makes very little use of these principles. Provide the URL of each and justify your selections.
3. Evaluate the following three Web sites in terms of their ability to create/support a good brand image and product position.
   a. http://www.4adodge.com
   b. http://www.ford.com
   c. http://www.mitsucars.com

REVIEW QUESTIONS

1. What is *learning?*
2. Describe *low-involvement learning*. How does it differ from *high-involvement learning?*
3. What is *incidental exposure?*
4. What do we mean by *cognitive learning,* and how does it differ from the *conditioning theory* approach to learning?

5. Distinguish between learning via classical conditioning and that which occurs via operant conditioning.
6. What is *iconic rote learning?* How does it differ from classical conditioning? Operant conditioning?
7. Define *modeling.*
8. What is meant by *learning by reasoning?*
9. Describe *analogical reasoning.*
10. What factors affect the strength of learning?
11. What is *imagery?*
12. What is meant by *stimulus generalization?* When do marketers use it?
13. Define *stimulus discrimination.* Why is it important?
14. Explain *extinction* and tell why marketing managers are interested in it.
15. Why is it useful to match the retrieval and learning environments?
16. What is *memory?*
17. Define *short-term memory* and *long-term memory.*
18. What is *maintenance rehearsal?*
19. What is meant by *elaborative activities?*
20. What is meant by *imagery in working memory?*
21. What is *semantic memory?*
22. How does a *schema* differ from a *script?*
23. What is *episodic memory?*
24. What is the difference between *knowing* and *remembering?*
25. What is the difference between *implicit memory* and *explicit memory?*
26. What is a *brand image?* Why is it important?
27. What is *product positioning?*
28. What is *perceptual mapping?*
29. What is *brand equity?*
30. What does *leveraging brand equity* mean?

DISCUSSION QUESTIONS

31. How would you select a product position for:
    a. A candidate for governor of your state.
    b. A soft drink targeting children.
    c. A nonprofit organization focused on saving endangered insect species.
    d. A line of clothing targeting Hispanic males.
    e. A brand of yogurt.
32. Is low-involvement learning really widespread? Which products are most affected by low-involvement learning?
33. Almex and Company introduced a new coffee-flavored liqueur in direct competition with Hiram Walker's tremendously successful Kahlua brand. Almex named its new entry Kamora and packaged it in a bottle similar to that of Kahlua, using a pre-Columbian label design. The ad copy for Kamora reads: "If you like coffee—you'll love Kamora." Explain Almex's marketing strategy in terms of learning theory.
34. Describe the brand images the following "brands" have among students on your campus.
    a. Jewel
    b. Your state government
    c. Snapple
    d. Volkswagen
    e. The Catholic Church
    f. The basketball team
35. In what ways, if any, would the brand images you described in response to the previous question differ with different groups, such as (*a*) middle-aged professionals, (*b*) young blue-collar workers, (*c*) high school students, and (*d*) retired couples?
36. What is the relationship between imagery and schema?
37. What is the relationship between remembering and knowing?
38. Evaluate the following illustrations in light of their apparent objectives and target market.
    a. 9-1
    b. 9-2
    c. 9-3
    d. 9-4
    e. 9-5
    f. 9-6
39. How would you teach teenagers a driving script that involved the consistent use of seat belts?

APPLICATION ACTIVITIES

40. Fulfill the requirements of Question 34 by interviewing five male and five female students.
41. Answer Question 35 based on interviews with five individuals from each group.
42. Pick a consumer convenience product, perhaps a personal care product such as deodorant or mouthwash, and create advertising copy stressing (*a*) a positive reinforcement, (*b*) a negative reinforcement, and (*c*) a punishment.
43. Find and describe three advertisements, one based on cognitive learning, another based on operant conditioning, and the third based on classical conditioning. Discuss the nature of each advertisement and how it utilizes that type of learning.
44. Find and describe three advertisements that you believe are based on low-involvement learning and three that are based on high-involvement learning. Justify your selection.
45. Select a product and develop an advertisement based on low-involvement learning and one based on high-involvement learning. When should each be used (be specific)?
46. Select a product that you feel has a good product position and one that has a weak position. Justify your selection. Describe an ad or package for each product and indicate how it affects the product's position.
47. Select a product, store, or service of relevance to students on your campus. Using a sample of students, measure its brand image. Develop a marketing strategy to improve its image.
48. Develop a campaign to reduce the risk of AIDS for students on your campus by teaching them the value of :
    a. Abstinence from sex outside of marriage
    b. "Safe" sex

49. Find a recent brand extension that you feel will be successful and one that you feel will fail. Explain each of your choices.

REFERENCES

1. Based on various documents at EarthSave's home page, www.earthsave.org.
2. B. Wernerfelt, "Efficient Marketing Communication," *Journal of Marketing Research,* May 1996, pp. 239–46.
3. A. A. Mitchell, "Cognitive Processes Initiated by Exposure to Advertising," in *Information Processing Research in Advertising,* ed. R. Harris (New York: Lawrence Erlbaum Associates, 1983), pp. 13–42.
4. See C. Huffman and M. J. Houston, "Goal-Oriented Experiences and the Development of Knowledge," *Journal of Consumer Research,* September 1993, pp. 190–207.
5. See S. A. Hawkins and S. J. Hoch, "Low-Involvement Learning," *Journal of Consumer Research,* September 1992, pp. 212–25; and N. M. Alperstein, "The Verbal Content of TV Advertising and Its Circulation in Everyday Life," *Journal of Advertising,* no. 2 (1990), pp. 15–22.
6. S. Shapiro, S. J. MacInnis, and S. E. Heckler, "The Effects of Incidental Ad Exposure on the Formation of Consideration Sets," *Journal of Consumer Research,* June 1997, pp. 94–104. See also S.-W. Chung and K. Szymanski, "Effects of Brand Name Exposure on Brand Choice," in *Advances in Consumer Research XXIV,* ed. M. Bruck and D. J. MacInnis (Provo, UT: Association for Consumer Research, 1997), pp. 288–94.
7. D. D. Muehling, R. N. Laczniak, and J. C. Andrews, "Defining, Operationalizing, and Using Involvement in Advertising Research," *Journal of Current Issues and Research in Advertising,* Spring 1993, pp. 22–57; and T. B. C. Poiesz and C. J. P. M. deBont, "Do We Need Involvement to Understand Consumer Behavior?" in *Advances in Consumer Research XXII,* ed. F. R. Kardes and M. Sujan (Provo, UT: Association for Consumer Research, 1995), pp. 448–52.
8. See G. D. Olsen, "The Impact of Interstimulus Interval and Background Silence on Recall"; and J. Sengupta, R. C. Goodstein, and D. S. Boninger, "All Cues Are Not Created Equal"; both in *Journal of Consumer Research,* March 1997, pp. 295–303 and 351–61.
9. W. R. Nord and J. P. Peter, "A Behavior Modification Perspective on Marketing," *Journal of Marketing,* Spring 1980, pp. 36–47.
10. See C. Janiszewski and L. Warlop, "The Influence of Classical Conditioning Procedures on Subsequent Attention to the Conditioned Brand," *Journal of Consumer Research,* September 1993, pp. 171–89; T. A. G. Groenland and J. P. L. Schoormans, "Comparing Mood-Induction and Affective Conditioning as Mechanisms Influencing Product Evaluation and Product Choice," *Psychology & Marketing,* March 1994, pp. 183–97; G. Tom, "Classical Conditioning of Unattended Stimuli," *Psychology & Marketing,* January 1995, pp. 79–87; J. Kin, C. T. Allen, and F. R. Kardes, "An Investigation into the Mediational Mechanisms Underlying Attitudinal Conditioning," *Journal of Marketing Research,* August 1996, pp. 318–28; R. P. Grossman and B. D. Till,

"The Persistence of Classically Conditioned Brand Attitudes," *Journal of Advertising,* Spring 1998; and J. Kim, J.-S. Lim, and M. Bhargava, "The Role of Affect in Attitude Formation," *Journal of the Academy of Marketing Science,* Spring 1998, pp. 143–52.

11. For details, see M. L. Rothschild and W. C. Gaidis, "Behavioral Learning Theory: Its Relevance to Marketing and Promotions," *Journal of Marketing,* Spring 1981, pp. 70–78; and J. P. Peter and W. R. Nord, "A Clarification and Extension of Operant Conditioning Principles in Marketing," *Journal of Marketing,* Summer 1982, pp. 102–7.
12. S. Hume, "Sampling Wins Over More Marketers," *Advertising Age,* July 27, 1992, p. 12.
13. H. B. Lammers, "The Effect of Free Samples on Immediate Consumer Purchase," *Journal of Consumer Marketing,* Spring 1991, pp. 31–37.
14. B. J. Bergiel and C. Trosclair, "Instrumental Learning," *Journal of Consumer Marketing,* Fall 1985, pp. 23–28. See also W. Gaidis and J. Cross, "Behavior Modification as a Framework for Sales Promotion Management," *Journal of Consumer Marketing,* Spring 1987, pp. 65–74.
15. See J. R. Rossiter and L. Percy, "Visual Communication in Advertising," in Harris, ed., footnote 3, pp. 83–126. Also see footnote 7; and J. W. Pracejus, "Is More Always Better," in *Advances in Consumer Research XXII,* ed. F. R. Kardes and M. Sujan (Provo, UT: Association for Consumer Research, 1995), pp. 319–22.
16. See footnote 9.
17. For a way to measure such images, see L. A. Babin and A.C. Burns, *Psychology & Marketing,* no. 3 (1998), pp. 261–78.
18. J. Gregan-Paxton and D. R. John, "Consumer Learning by Analogy," *Journal of Consumer Research,* December 1997, pp. 266–85.
19. See R. G. M. Pieters, E. Rosbergen, and M. Hartog, "Visual Attention to Advertising," in *Advances in Consumer Research XXIII,* ed. K. P. Corfman and J. G. Lynch (Provo, UT: Association for Consumer Research, 1996), pp. 242–48; and S. M. Leong, S. H. Ang, and L. L. Tham, "Increasing Brand Name Recall in Print Advertising among Asian Consumers," *Journal of Advertising,* Summer 1996, pp. 65–81.
20. See also J. P. Jones, "Single-Source Research Begins to Fulfill Its Promise," *Journal of Advertising Research,* May 1995, pp. 9–16.
21. See S. N. Singh and C. A. Cole, "The Effects of Length, Content, and Repetition on Television Commercial Effectiveness," *Journal of Marketing Research,* February 1993, pp. 91–104; C. P. Haugtveld, D. W. Schumann, W. L. Schneier, and W. L. Warren, "Advertising Repetition and Variation Strategies," *Journal of Consumer Research,* June 1994, pp. 176–89; S. N. Singh, S. Mishra, N. Bendapudi, and D. Linville, "Enhancing Memory of Television Commercials through Message Spacing," *Journal of Marketing Research,* August 1994, pp. 384–92; E. Ephron, "More Weeks, Less Weight," *Journal of Advertising Research,* May 1995, pp. 18–23; and footnote 19.
22. P. H. Chook, "A Continuing Study of Magazine Environment, Frequency, and Advertising Performance," *Journal of Advertising Research,* August–September 1985, pp. 23–33.
23. J. O. Eastlack, Jr., "How to Get More Bang from Your Television Bucks," *Journal of Consumer Marketing,* Third Quarter 1984, pp. 25–34. Conflicting results are in G. F. Belch, "The Effects of Television Commercial Repetition on Cognitive Response and Message Acceptance," *Journal of Consumer Research,* June 1982, pp. 56–65.
24. H. R. Unnava and R. E. Burnkrant, "Effects of Repeating Varied Ad Executions on Brand Name Memory," *Journal of Marketing Research,* November 1991, pp. 406–16.
25. See M. H. Blair, "An Empirical Investigation of Advertising Wearin and Wearout," *Journal of Advertising Research,* January 1988, pp. 45–50; and G. D. Hughes, "Real-Time Response Measures Redefine Advertising Wearout," *Journal of Advertising Research,* May–June 1992, pp. 61–77.
26. G. M. Zinkhan and C. R. Martin, Jr., "New Brand Names and Inferential Beliefs," *Journal of Business Research,* April 1987, pp. 157–72. See also B. B. Reece, B. G. VandenBergh, and H. Li, "What Makes a Slogan Memorable and Who Remembers It," *Journal of Current Issues and Research in Advertising,* Fall 1994, pp. 42–57.
27. K. R. Robertson, "Recall and Recognition Effects on Brand Name Imagery," *Psychology & Marketing,* Spring 1987, pp. 3–15. See also J. Meyers-Levy, "The Influence of a Brand Name's Association, Set Size, and Word Frequency on Brand Memory," *Journal of Consumer Research,* September 1989, pp. 197–207.
28. K. L. Keller, S. E. Heckler, and M. J. Houston, "The Effects of Brand Name Suggestiveness on Advertising Recall," *Journal of Marketing,* January 1998, pp. 48–57. See also Sengupta, Goodstein, and Boninger, footnote 8.
29. See Leong, Ang, and Tham, footnote 19; M. C. Macklin, "Preschoolers' Learning of Brand Names from Visual Cues," *Journal of Consumer Research,* December 1996, pp. 251–61; and J. C. McCracken and M. C. Macklin, "The Role of Brand Names and Visual Cues in Enhancing Memory for Consumer packaged Goods," *Marketing Letters,* no. 2 (1998), pp. 209–26.
30. D. J. MacInnis and L. L. Price, "The Role of Imagery in Information Processing," *Journal of Consumer Research,* March 1987, pp. 473–91; M. J. Houston, T. L. Childers, and S. E. Heckler, "Picture-Word Consistency and the Elaborative Processing of Advertisements," *Journal of Marketing Research,* November 1987, pp. 359–69; W. J. Bryce and R. F. Yalch, "Hearing versus Seeing," *Journal of Current Issues and Research in Advertising,* Spring 1993, pp. 1–20; and A. C. Burns, A. Biswas, and L. A. Babin, "The Operation of Visual Imagery as a Mediator of Advertising Effects," *Journal of Advertising,* June 1993, pp. 71–85.
31. T. Clark, "Echoic Memory Explored and Applied," *Journal of Consumer Marketing,* Winter 1987, pp. 39–46. See also C. E. Young and M. Robinson, "Video Rhythms and Recall," *Journal of Advertising Research,* July 1989, pp. 22–25.
32. J. J. Kellaris, A. D. Cox, and D. Cox, "The Effect of Background Music on Ad Processing," *Journal of Marketing,* October 1993, pp. 114–25. See also D. W. Stewart, K. M. Farmer, and C. I. Stannard, "Music as a Recognition Cue in Advertising Tracking Studies," *Journal of Advertising Research,* August–September 1990, pp. 39–48.
33. "L&M Lights Up Again," *Marketing & Media Decisions,* February 1984, p. 69.

34. See M. Sujan and J. R. Bettman, "The Effects of Brand Positioning Strategies on Consumers' Brand and Category Perceptions," *Journal of Marketing Research,* November 1989, pp. 454–67.

35. G. S. Carpenter, R. Glazer, and K. Nakamoto, "Meaningful Brands from Meaningless Differences," *Journal of Marketing Research,* August 1994, pp. 339–50.

36. P. Winters, "Color Nuprin's Success Yellow," *Advertising Age,* October 31, 1988, p. 28.

37. See M. C. Macklin, "The Effects of an Advertising Retrieval Cue on Young Children's Memory and Brand Evaluations," *Psychology & Marketing,* May 1994, pp. 291–311; J. W. Park, "Memory-Based Product Judgments"; and E. J. Cowley, "Altering Retrieval Sets"; both in *Advances in Consumer Research XXII,* ed. F. R. Kardes and M. Sujan (Provo, UT: Association for Consumer Research, 1995), pp. 159–64 and 323–27.

38. K. L. Keller, "Memory Factors in Advertising," *Journal of Consumer Research,* December 1987, pp. 316–33. See also C. J. Cobb and W. D. Hoyer, "The Influence of Advertising at the Moment of Brand Choice," *Journal of Advertising,* no. 4 (1985), pp. 5–12; and G. Tom, "Marketing with Music," *Journal of Consumer Marketing,* Spring 1990, pp. 49–53.

39. For differing views, see A. J. Malter, "An Introduction to Embodied Cognition," in *Advances in Consumer Research XXIII,* ed. K. P. Corfman and J. G. Lynch (Provo, UT: Association for Consumer Research, 1996), pp. 272–76; and M. E. Hill, R. Radtke, and M. King, "A Transfer Appropriate Processing View of Consumer Memory," *Journal of Current Issues and Research in Advertising,* Spring 1997, pp. 1–21.

40. See L. M. Scott, "Images in Advertising," *Journal of Consumer Research,* September 1994, p. 254.

41. K. A. Braun, "Postexperience Advertising Effects on Consumer Memory," *Journal of Consumer Research,* March 1999, pp. 319–34.

42. See M. T. Pham and G. V. Johar, "Contingent Processes of Source Identification," *Journal of Consumer Research,* December 1997, pp. 249–66.

43. See E. J. Cowley, "Recovering Forgotten Information," in *Advances in Consumer Research XXI,* ed. C. T. Allen and D. R. John (Provo, UT: Association for Consumer Research, 1994), pp. 58–63.

44. See S. E. Heckler, "The Role of Memory in Understanding and Encouraging Recycling Behavior," *Psychology & Marketing,* July 1994, pp. 375–92.

45. This discussion is based on K. B. Monroe and A. Y. Lee, "Remembering versus Knowing," *Journal of the Academy of Marketing Science,* Spring 1999, pp. 207–225.

46. See E. W. Anderson and S. M. Shogan, "Repositioning for Changing Preferences," *Journal of Consumer Research,* September 1991, pp. 219–32; A. L. Biel, "Converting Image into Equity"; and P. H. Farquhar and P. M. Herr, "The Dual Structure of Brand Associations"; both in *Brand Equity and Advertising,* ed. D. A. Aaker and A. L. Biel (Hillsdale, NJ: Lawrence Erlbaum Associates, 1993), pp. 67–82 and 263–77.

47. See R. H. Coulter and G. Zaltman, "Using the Zaltman Metaphor Technique to Understand Brand Images," in *Advances in Consumer Research XXI,* ed. C. T. Allen and D. R. John (Provo, UT: Association for Consumer Research, 1994), pp. 501–07; and D. Padgett and D. Allen, "Communicating Experiences," *Journal of Advertising,* Winter 1997, pp. 49–62.

48. B. Vlasic, "That Daring Old Company and Its Jaunty Jalopy," *Business Week,* January 15, 1996, p. 31.

49. See D. G. Norris, "Intel Inside," *Journal of Business and Industrial Marketing* 8, no. 1 (1993), pp. 14–24; and N. Arnott, "Inside Intel's Marketing Coup," *Sales & Marketing Management,* February 1994, pp. 78–81.

50. B. Morris, "The Brand's the Thing," *Fortune,* March 4, 1996, p. 84.

51. For a differing view, see G. S. Carpenter, R. Glazer, and K. Nakamoto, "Meaningful Brands from Meaningless Differences," *Journal of Marketing Research,* August 1995, pp. 339–50.

52. B. Wansink, "Making Old Brands New," *American Demographics,* December 1998, pp. 53–58.

53. D. Mazursky and J. Jacoby, "Exploring the Development of Store Images," *Journal of Retailing,* Summer 1986, pp. 145–65.

54. C. Rubel, "Soft Drink Makers Place Future in Youth's Hands," *Marketing News,* May 20, 1996, p. 18.

55. L. Haran, "Midas Wants Motorists to Look Beyond Mufflers," *Advertising Age,* March 11, 1996, p. 3.

56. See K. L. Keller, "Conceptualizing, Measuring, and Managing Customer-Based Brand Equity," *Journal of Marketing,* January 1993, pp. 1–22; The special issue on brand equity, *International Journal of Research in Marketing,* March 1993; P. Feldwick, "What Is Brand Equity Anyway, and How Do You Measure It?" *Journal of the Market Research Society,* April 1996, pp. 85–104; and P. K. Teas and T. H. Grapentine, "Demystifying Brand Equity," *Marketing Research,* Summer 1996, pp. 25–29.

57. See P. Herbig, J. Milewicz, and J. Golden, "A Model of Reputation Building and Destruction," *Journal of Business Research,* September 1994, pp. 23–31.

58. C. J. Cobb-Walgren, C. A. Ruble, and N. Donthu, "Brand Equity, Brand Preference, and Purchase Intent," *Journal of Advertising,* Fall 1995, pp. 25–40; J. A. Quelch and D. Harding, "Brands versus Private Labels," *Harvard Business Review,* January 1996, pp. 99–109; S. J. Agres and T. M. Dubitsky, "Changing Needs for Brands," *Journal of Advertising Research,* January 1996, p. 30; M. K. Agarwal and V. R. Rao, "An Empirical Comparison of Consumer-Based Measures of Brand Equity," *Marketing Letters,* no. 3 (1996), pp. 237–47; E. Crowly and J. Zajas, "Evidence Supporting the Importance of Brands in Marketing Computer Products," *Journal of Professional Services Marketing,* no. 2 (1996), pp. 121–37; and M. S. Sullivan, "How Brand Names Affect the Demand of Twin Automobiles," *Journal of Marketing Research,* May 1998, pp. 154–65.

59. See T. Erdem, "An Empirical Analysis of Umbrella Branding," *Journal of Marketing Research,* August 1998, pp. 339–51.

60. L. Freeman and P. Winters, "Franchise Players," *Advertising Age,* August 18, 1986, pp. 3 and 61.

61. H. Schlossberg, "Slashing through Market Clutter," *Marketing News,* March 5, 1990, p. 6.

62. S. M. Bromiarcyzk and J. W. Alba, "The Importance of the Brand in Brand Extension"; P. A. Dacin and D. C. Smith, "The Effect of

Brand Portfolio Characteristics on Consumer Evaluations of Brand Extensions"; and S. K. Reddy, S. L. Holak, and S. Bhat, "To Extend or Not to Extend"; all in *Journal of Marketing Research,* May 1994, pp. 214–28, 229–42, and 143–62; D. A. Shein and B. H. Schmitt, "Extending Brands with New Product Concepts," *Journal of Business Research,* September 1994, pp. 1–10; B. Sharp, "Brand Equity and Market-Based Assets of Professional Service Firms," *Journal of Professional Services Marketing,*" no. 1 (1995), pp. 3–13; T. Bristol, "Consumers' Beliefs Resulting from Conceptual Combinations," *Psychology & Marketing,* September 1996, pp. 571–89; P. Dyson, A. Farr, and N. S. Hollis, "Understanding, Measuring, and Using Brand Equity," *Journal of Advertising Research,* November 1996, pp. 9–21; M. Lee, J. Lee, and W. A. Kamakura, "Consumer Evaluations of Line Extensions," in *Advances in Consumer Research XXIII,* ed. K. P. Corfman and J. G. Lynch (Provo, UT: Association for Consumer Research, 1996), pp. 289–95; D. M. Boush, "Brand Name Effects on Interproduct Similarity Judgments," *Marketing Letters,* no. 4 (1997), pp. 419–27; A. M. Levin, I. P. Levin, and C. E. Heath, "Movie Stars and Authors as Brand Names," in *Advances in Consumer Research XXIV,* ed. M. Bruck and D. J. MacInnis (Provo, UT: Association for Consumer Research, 1997), pp. 175–81; and B.-D. Kim and M. S. Sullivan, "The Effect of Parent Brand Experience on Line Extension Trial and Repeat Purchase," *Marketing Letters,* no. 2 (1998), pp. 181–93.

63. B. Forrest, "Two-Wheel Drives," *Men's Journal,* November 1996, p. 34.

64. B. Loken and D. R. John, "Diluting Brand Beliefs," *Journal of Marketing,* July 1993, pp. 71–85; V. Lane and R. Jacobson, "The Reciprocal Impact of Brand Leveraging," *Marketing Letters,* no. 3 (1997), pp. 261–71; D. R. John, B. Loken, and C. Joiner, "The Negative Impact of Extensions," *Journal of Marketing,* January 1998, pp. 19–32; and Z. Gurhan-Canli and D. Maheswaran, "The Effects of Extensions on Brand Name Dilution and Enhancement," *Journal Marketing Research,* November 1998, pp. 464–73.

65. R. A. Peterson, K. H. Smith, and P. C. Zerrillo, "Trademark Dilution and the Practice of Marketing," *Journal of the Academy of Marketing Science,* Spring 1999, pp. 255–68; and M. L. Retsky, "Famous Marks Have Legal Protection against Poachers," *Marketing News,* November 9, 1998, pp. 5–6.

Courtesy Swatch/SMH (USA).

Motivation, Personality, and Emotion

Nicolas Hayek performed what some consider to be a business miracle by changing SMH, the Swiss firm best known for its Swatch watch, from a $1.1 billion firm losing $124 million a year to a $2.1 billion firm making $286 million a year. His success was surprising because he ignored the conventional wisdom that firms must seek the lowest labor cost countries to produce products subject to global price competition. SMH is committed to its Swiss home base. The bulk of its technology, people, and production is centered in the Jura Mountains of Switzerland. As Hayek says: "We are all global companies competing in global markets. But that does not mean we owe no allegiance to our own societies and cultures." Part of an interview with Hayek follows. The comments focus on the success of the Swatch watch line he created.

What did you see that others didn't?

I understood that we were not just selling a consumer product, or even a branded product. We were selling an emotional product. You wear a watch on your wrist, right against your skin. You have it there for 12 hours a day, maybe 24 hours a day. It can be an important part of your self-image. It doesn't have to be a commodity. It shouldn't be a commodity. I knew that if we could add genuine emotion to the product, and attack the low end with a strong message, we could succeed.

How do you "emotionalize" a watch? Do you mean to say that Swatch turned something that was mundane and functional into a fashion statement?

That is how most people describe what we did. But it's not quite right.

Fashion is important . . . But take a trip to Hong Kong and look at the styles, the designs, the colors. They make pretty watches over there too.

We are not offering people a style. We are offering them a message. This is an absolutely critical point. Fashion is about image. Emotional products are about message—a strong, exciting, distinct, authentic message that tells people who you are and why you do what you do. There are many elements that make up the Swatch message. High quality. Low cost. Provocative. Joy of life. But the most important element of the Swatch message is the hardest for others to copy. Ultimately, we are not just offering watches. We are offering our personal culture.[1]

As Swatch illustrates, emotion can play an important role in consumer decisions and marketing strategies. This chapter focuses on emotion and two closely related concepts: motivation and personality. *Motivation* is the energizing force that activates behavior and provides purpose and direction to that behavior. *Personality* reflects the common responses (behaviors) that individuals make to a variety of recurring situations. *Emotions* are strong, relatively uncontrollable feelings that affect our behavior. The three concepts are closely interrelated and are frequently difficult to separate.

THE NATURE OF MOTIVATION

Water is virtually cost-free from municipal agencies, yet millions of consumers now pay 1,000 times the price of municipal water to purchase bottled water. While heavily advertised brands such as Perrier are well known, bulk water delivered to homes and offices in 5-gallon containers makes up half the market.

Why do consumers pay to purchase a virtually free item? There appear to be four major purchase motives. Health concerns focusing on nutrition and fitness motivate some users. These individuals want natural, untreated, "pure" water. Safety motivates other purchases. Many consumers are concerned with ground water contamination and reports of deteriorating water quality levels. The third motivating factor is "snob appeal" or status. Ordering or serving Perrier is more chic and higher status than plain water. The final motivation is taste. Some areas have water that many find unpleasant to drink due to its natural taste or taste caused by treatment. The marketing strategy implications of these differing motivations are:

- Safety: Show danger of municipal water. Stress filtration, safe source, low price, and home/office delivery.
- Health: Stress purity, no additives or treatments, moderate price, home/office delivery.
- Status: Stress quality, usage situations, high price; retail, restaurant, and bar outlets.
- Taste: Stress taste, low price, and home/office delivery.

Motivation is *the reason for behavior.* A **motive** is *a construct representing an unobservable inner force that stimulates and compels a behavioral response and provides specific direction to that response.* A motive is why an individual does something. As the example above illustrates, the motivations underlying the consumption of even a "simple" product like water can be quite complex.

There are numerous theories of motivation, and many of them offer useful insights for the marketing manager.[2] This section describes two particularly useful approaches to understanding consumer motivation. The first approach, Maslow's motive hierarchy, is a macro theory designed to account for most human behavior in general terms. The second approach, based on McGuire's psychological motives, uses a fairly detailed set of motives to account for a limited range of consumer behavior.

Maslow's Hierarchy of Needs

Maslow's hierarchy of needs approach is based on four premises:[3]

1. All humans acquire a similar set of motives through genetic endowment and social interaction.
2. Some motives are more basic or critical than others.
3. The more basic motives must be satisfied to a minimum level before other motives are activated.
4. As the basic motives become satisfied, more advanced motives come into play.

Thus, Maslow proposes a motive hierarchy shared by all. Table 10-1 illustrates this hierarchy, briefly describes each level, and provides marketing examples.

Maslow's theory is a good guide to general behavior. It is not an ironclad rule, however. Numerous examples exist of individuals who sacrificed their lives for friends or ideas, or who gave up food and shelter to seek self-actualization. However, we do tend to regard such behavior as exceptional, which indicates the general validity of Maslow's overall approach.[4] It is important to remember that any given consumption behavior can satisfy more than one need. Likewise, the same consumption behavior can satisfy different needs at different times. For example, clothing can satisfy physiological, safety, and/or esteem needs. Illustration 10-1 shows an ad for *patagonia* in which its clothing is associated with self-actualization.

McGuire's Psychological Motives

McGuire has developed a motive classification system that is more specific than Maslow's.[5] McGuire's motives that are of most use to marketing are briefly described in the following sections.

Need for Consistency A basic desire is to have all facets or parts of oneself consistent with each other. These facets include attitudes, behaviors, opinions, self-images, views of others, and so forth. Marketers use this in several ways. First, it makes clear the need for a consistent marketing mix. A product positioned as a luxury product with an elegant design, expensive packaging, limited distribution, and ads that stress exclusiveness should not be priced at or below an average product. This inconsistency would be likely to cause consumers to reject the product. This is basically what happened to Omega watches in the 1980s. As a result, the firm was pushed to the edge of bankruptcy before new management restored a consistent image to the brand.[6]

The second area of marketing interest with consistency is called *cognitive dissonance.* This refers to a tendency of consumers to worry about the wisdom of major purchases after they have been made. Often making a major purchase is not consistent with the need to save money or to make other purchases. We cover this issue in depth in Chapter 18.

Need to Attribute Causation This set of motives deals with our need to determine who or what causes the things that happen to us. Do we attribute the cause of a favorable or unfavorable outcome to ourselves or to some outside force?

Attributing cause is part of the foundation for the use of *rhetorical theory* to understand consumers' responses to persuasive messages, as described in Chapter 8 (page 302). It also underlies an area of research known as **attribution theory.**[7] This approach to understanding the reasons consumers assign particular meanings to the behaviors of others has been used primarily for analyzing consumer reactions to promotional messages (in terms of

TABLE 10-1 Marketing Strategies and Maslow's Motive Hierarchy

I. PHYSIOLOGICAL: Food, water, sleep, and, to an extent, sex, are physiological motives.

Products Health foods, medicines, sports drinks, low-cholesterol foods, and exercise equipment.

Themes Band-Aid—"Blister-proof your feet."
Quaker Oats—"Eating oatmeal is good for your heart."
NordicTrack—"Only NordicTrack gives you a total-body workout."

II. SAFETY: Seeking physical safety and security, stability, familiar surroundings, and so forth are manifestations of safety needs.

Products Smoke detectors, preventive medicines, insurance, retirement investments, seat belts, burglar alarms, sunscreen.

Themes Sleep Safe—"We've designed a travel alarm that just might wake you in the middle of the night—because a fire is sending smoke into your room. You see, ours is a smoke alarm as well as an alarm clock."
Partnership for a Drug-Free America—"Heroin: Dying's the Easy Part."
Revo cycling glasses—"Should've worn Revo" under a picture of a wrecked bike.

III. BELONGINGNESS: Belongingness motives are reflected in a desire for love, friendship, affliation, and group acceptance.

Products Personal grooming, foods, entertainment, clothing, and many others.

Themes Olive Garden Restaurants—"Italians didn't invent sharing. They just made it impossible to resist.
Tums—"You are important. You are loved. You should take your calcium."
J.C. Penney—"Wherever teens gather, you'll hear it. It's the language of terrific fit and fashion."

IV. ESTEEM: Desires for status, superiority, self-respect, and prestige are examples of esteem needs. These needs relate to the individual's feelings of usefulness and accomplishment.

Products Clothing, furniture, liquors, hobbies, stores, cars, and many others.

Themes Sheaffer—"Your hand should look as contemporary as the rest of you."
New Balance—"One more woman chasing a sunset. One more woman going a little farther. One more woman simply feeling alive. One less woman relying on someone else."
Cadillac—"Those long hours have paid off. In recognition, financial success, and in the way you reward yourself. Isn't it time you owned a Cadillac?"

V. SELF-ACTUALIZATION: This involves the desire for self-fulfillment, to become all that one is capable of becoming.

Products Education, hobbies, sports, some vacations, gourmet foods, museums.

Themes U.S. Army—"Be all you can be."
Avia—"She wasn't just training her body, she was training her mind."
Outward Bound School—"Challenges, adventure, growth."

credibility). When consumers attribute a sales motive to advice given by a salesperson or advertising message, they tend to discount the advice. In contrast, similar advice given by a friend would likely be attributed to a desire to be helpful and might therefore be accepted.

The fact that consumers do not passively receive messages but rather attribute sales motives and tactics to ads and the advice of sales personnel means that many of these messages are not believed or are "discounted."[8] Marketers use a variety of means to overcome this. One approach is to use a credible spokesperson such as in Illustration 10-2. This technique is discussed in depth in Chapter 11.

© 1998, 1999 Patagonia, Inc. used with permission. All rights reserved.

ILLUSTRATION 10-1

Appeals to self-actualization focus on individuals challenging themselves and reaching their full potential.

Need to Categorize We have a need to categorize and organize information and experiences in some meaningful yet manageable way.[9] So we establish categories or mental partitions that allow us to process large quantities of information. Prices are often categorized such that different prices connote different categories of goods. Automobiles over $20,000 and automobiles under $20,000 may elicit two different meanings because of information categorized on the basis of price level. Many firms price items at $9.95, $19.95, $49.95, and so forth. A reason is to avoid being categorized in the over $10.00, $20.00, or $50.00 group.

Need for Cues These motives reflect needs for observable cues or symbols that enable us to infer what we feel and know. Impressions, feelings, and attitudes are subtly established by viewing our own behavior and that of others and drawing inferences as to what we feel and think. In many instances, clothing plays an important role in presenting the subtle meaning of a desired image and consumer lifestyle. This is so critical at companies such as Anheuser-Busch that it uses a special clothing consulting firm to tailor clothes for its executives that are consistent with the firm's desired image.

Need for Independence The need for independence and individuality is a characteristic of the American culture, as described in Chapter 3. It is likely that all individuals in all cultures have this need at some level. Americans are taught that it is proper and even essential to express and fulfill this need. In contrast, in countries such as Japan, fulfillment of this need is discouraged, while fulfillment of the need for affiliation is more socially acceptable.

ILLUSTRATION 10-2

Consumers generally attribute selling motives to ads and disbelieve or discount the message. One approach to gain message acceptance is to use a credible source.

Courtesy Bozell Worldwide Inc., Advertising.

Owning or using products and services that are unique is one way consumers express their independence.[10] The increasing popularity of handmade craft goods, original art, antiques, and other unique products reflects this need. Marketers in America have responded to this motive by developing limited editions of products and providing wide variety and customization options. In addition, many products are advertised and positioned with independence, uniqueness, or individuality themes. Dodge is positioning itself as a different, unique, independent car company (see Illustration 10-3).

Need for Self-Expression This motive deals with the need to express one's identity to others. We feel the need to let others know by our actions (which include the purchase and display of goods) who we are and what we are. The purchase of many products such as clothing and automobiles allows consumers to express an identity to others, since these products have symbolic or expressive meanings. Thus, the purchase of the latest in skiwear may reflect much more than a desire to remain warm while skiing. The Swatch example in the chapter-opening vignette relates directly to this need.

Need for Ego-Defense The need to defend our identities or egos is another important motive. When our identity is threatened, we are motivated to protect our self-concept and utilize defensive behaviors and attitudes. Many products can provide ego-defense. A consumer who feels insecure may rely on well-known brands for socially visible products to avoid any chance of making a socially incorrect purchase.

Need for Reinforcement We are often motivated to act in certain ways because we are rewarded for doing so. Products designed to be used in public situations (clothing, furniture, and artwork) are frequently sold on the basis of the amount and type of reinforcement that will be received. Keepsake diamonds uses this motive with an advertisement that states: "Enter a room and you are immediately surrounded by friends sharing your excitement."

This should be familiar to you, as it is the basis for operant learning as described in the previous chapter.

Courtesy BBDO Detroit.

ILLUSTRATION 10-3

Americans tend to respond positively to ads and products that encourage self-expression and "doing your own thing."

Need for Affiliation Affiliation is the need to develop mutually helpful and satisfying relationships with others. As we saw in Chapter 7, group membership is a critical part of most consumers' lives, and many consumer decisions are based on the need to maintain satisfying relationships with others. Marketers frequently use such affiliation-based themes as "Your kids will love you for it" in advertisements.[12]

Need for Modeling The need for modeling reflects a tendency to base behavior on that of others. Modeling is a major means by which children learn to become consumers. The tendency to model explains some of the conformity that occurs within reference groups. Marketers utilize this motive by showing desirable types of individuals using their brands. For example, some Rolex ads devote most of their copy to a description of very successful people such as Picabo Street or Monica Kristensen. They then state that this person owns a Rolex.

Need for Novelty We often seek variety and difference simply out of a need for novelty. Marketers refer to the outcome of this motive as *variety-seeking behavior.* This may be a prime reason for brand switching and some so-called impulse purchasing.[11] The need for novelty is curvilinear and changes over time. That is, individuals experiencing rapid change generally become satiated and desire stability, while individuals in stable environments become "bored" and desire change. The travel industry segments the vacation market in part by promoting "adventure" vacations or "relaxing" vacations to groups, depending on their likely need for novelty. For example, ads for Guatemala placed in magazines such as *Outside* ask: "When was the last time you did something for the first time?" They describe the

ILLUSTRATION 10-4

Most consumers respond positively to ads that appeal to the need for affiliation.

Courtesy Gillette Co.

various outdoor adventures available in that country (see Illustration 12-8). In contrast, ads of the British Virgin Islands in *Travel Holiday* ask: "What less could you want?" and stress the peaceful, tranquil nature of the area (see Illustration 12-3).

Need for Assertion The need for assertion reflects a consumer's need for engaging in those types of activities that will bring about an increase in self-esteem as well as esteem in the eyes of others. Individuals with a strong need for assertion are more likely to complain when dissatisfied with a purchase. The ad in Illustration 10-4 would appeal to the desire for esteem.

MOTIVATION THEORY AND MARKETING STRATEGY

Beck's and Heineken are imported beers that are consumed primarily by confident, upscale, professional men. However, BBDO (a major advertising agency) found through its motivation research that Heineken consumption is driven by a desire for status, whereas Beck's is associated with a desire for individuality. Likewise, both Classico and Newman's Own spaghetti sauces are consumed by upscale, sophisticated adults. However, Classico buyers are motivated by indulgence and romance while Newman's Own buyers are showing ambition and individuality. Since the purchase of each of these brands is caused by a different motive, each requires a distinct marketing and advertising program.[13]

Consumers do not buy products. Instead, they buy motive satisfaction or problem solutions. Thus, consumers do not buy perfume or aftershave lotion (or a chemical compound with certain odoriferous characteristics): Instead, they buy romance, sex appeal, sensual pleasure, sophistication, and/or a host of other emotional and psychological benefits. Managers must discover the motives that their products and brands can satisfy and develop marketing mixes around these motives.

As an example, consumers often buy products and services as a gift for themselves, though they may feel some guilt at being self-indulgent. Motivation research has found that people make such purchases for a variety of motives, including rewarding themselves for an accomplishment.[14] Consistent with this research, Keepsake has run advertising campaigns stressing the appropriateness of self-gifts of diamond jewelry as a reward.

The preceding section provided a number of examples of firms appealing to specific consumer motives. We often find that multiple motives are involved in consumption behavior. In the following sections, we examine (1) how to discover which motives are likely to affect the purchase of a product category or brand by a particular target market, (2) how to develop strategy based on the total array of motives that are operating, and (3) how to reduce conflict between motives.

Discovering Purchase Motives

Suppose a marketing researcher interviewed you and asked why you wear Gap clothes (or own a mountain bike, or use cologne, or whatever). Odds are you would offer several reasons such as "They're in style," "My friends wear them," "I like the way they fit," or "They look good on me." However, there may be other reasons that you are reluctant to admit or perhaps are not even aware of: "They show that I have money," "They make me sexually desirable," or "They show I'm still young." All or any combination of the above motives could influence the purchase of clothes or many other items.

The first group of motives mentioned above were known to the consumer and admitted to the researcher. Motives that are known and freely admitted are called **manifest motives.** Any of the motives we have discussed can be manifest. However, motives that conform to a society's prevailing value system are more likely to be manifest than are those that are in conflict with such values.

The second group of motives described above were either unknown to the consumer or were such that the consumer was very reluctant to admit them. Such motives are **latent motives.** Figure 10-1 illustrates how the two types of motives might influence a purchase.

Given that a variety of manifest and latent motives may be operative in a particular purchase such as that shown in Figure 10-1, the first task of the marketing manager is to determine the combination of motives influencing the target market. Manifest motives are relatively easy to determine. Direct questions (Why did you buy a Cadillac?) will generally produce reasonably accurate assessments of manifest motives.[15]

Determining latent motives is substantially more complex. Sophisticated analytical techniques such as multidimensional scaling can sometimes provide insights into latent motives. "Motivation research" or **projective techniques** are designed to provide information on latent motives. Table 10-2 describes some of the more common projective techniques.

Projective techniques were popular in the 1950s and early 1960s but virtually disappeared from use as marketers began to rely heavily on quantitative measures throughout the 1970s and 1980s. However, these techniques are gaining use again as a way to enhance and enrich the insights that can be gained from more empirical sources. For example, Oreo

FIGURE 10-1 Latent and Manifest Motives in a Purchase Situation

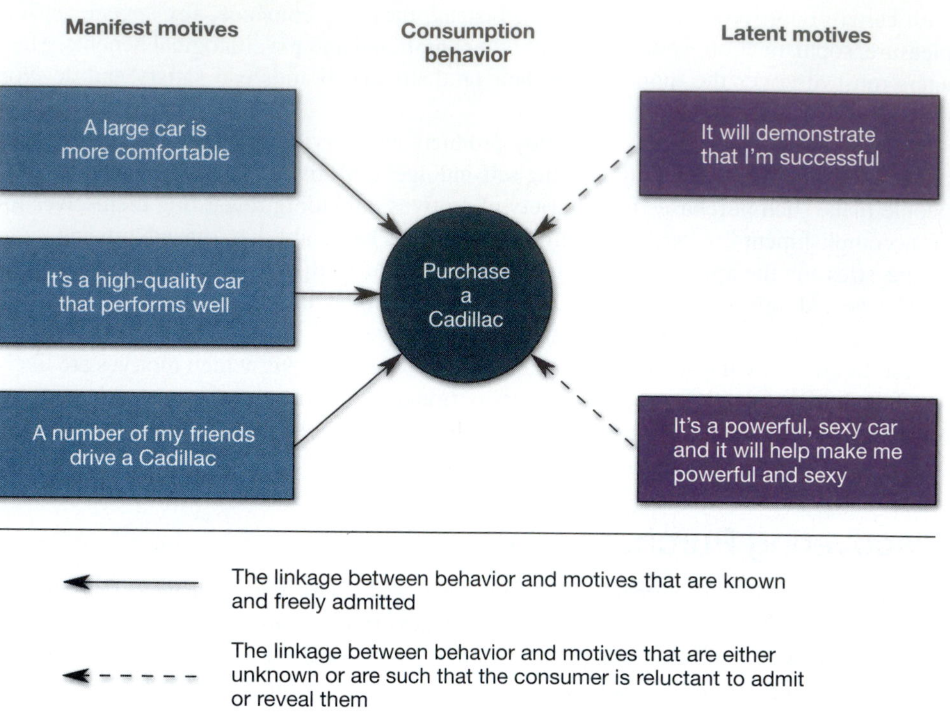

used projective techniques in a focus group setting to gain a fuller understanding of the brand: "We had always known that Oreo evoked strong emotions but what surprised us in these focus groups was that many regarded Oreo as almost 'magical.'" As a result, "Unlocking the Magic of Oreo" became a campaign theme.[16]

Not only are the traditional projective techniques being used at an increasing rate, but also new approaches are being developed.[17] One popular approach is **laddering** or constructing a **means-end** or **benefit chain.**[18] A product or brand is shown to a consumer who names all the benefits that possession or use of that product might provide. Then, for each benefit mentioned, the respondent is asked to identify the benefits that the benefit provides. This is repeated for each round of benefits until the consumer can no longer identify additional benefits.

For example, a respondent might mention "fewer colds" as a benefit of taking a daily vitamin. When asked the benefit of fewer colds, one respondent might identify "more efficient at work" and "more energy." Another might name "more skiing" and "looking better." Both use the vitamin to reduce colds but as a means to different ultimate benefits. How should vitamin ads aimed at each of these two consumers differ?

A similar approach is to use the terms generated in a word association task as the stimulus words in a second round of associations. For example, the term *soap* generates relatively few associations. Among these are clean and fresh. Clean and fresh, however, generate additional responses such as free, relaxed, unhindered, nature, country, and sensual.[19] This type of information is invaluable for developing advertising and positioning strategies.

Motivation Research Techniques **TABLE 10-2**

I. ASSOCIATION TECHNIQUES	
Word association	Consumers respond to a list of words with the first word that comes to mind.
Successive word association	Consumers give the series of words that come to mind after hearing each word on the list.
Analysis and use	Responses are analyzed to see if negative associations exist. When the time to respond (response latency) is also measured, the emotionality of the word can be estimated. These techniques tap semantic memory more than motives and are used for brand name and advertising copy tests.
II. COMPLETION TECHNIQUES	
Sentence completion	Consumers complete a sentence such as "People who buy a Cadillac______________________."
Story completion	Consumers complete a partial story.
Analysis and use	Responses are analyzed to determine what themes are expressed. Content analysis—examining responses for themes and key concepts—is used.
III. CONSTRUCTION TECHNIQUES	
Cartoon techniques	Consumers fill in the words and/or thoughts of one of the characters in a cartoon drawing.
Third-person techniques	Consumers tell why "an average woman," "most doctors," or "people in general" purchase or use a certain product. Shopping lists (describe a person who would go shopping with this list) and lost wallets (describe a person with these items in his wallet) are also third-person techniques.
Picture response	Consumers tell a story about a person shown buying or using a product in a picture or line drawing.
Analysis and use	Same as for completion techniques.

Marketing Strategies Based on Multiple Motives

Once a manager has isolated the combination(s) of motives influencing the target market, the next task is to design the marketing strategy around the appropriate set of motives. This task involves everything from product design to marketing communications. The nature of these decisions is most apparent in the communications area. Suppose that the motives shown in Figure 10-1 are an accurate reflection of a desired target market. What communications strategy should the manager use?

First, to the extent that more than one motive is important, the product must provide more than one benefit and the advertising for the product must communicate these multiple benefits. Communicating manifest benefits is relatively easy. For example, an advertisement for Cadillac states, "From the triple-sanded finish (once with water and twice with oil) to that superbly refined Cadillac ride, the quality comes standard on Cadillac." This is a direct appeal to a manifest motive for product quality. Direct appeals are generally effective for manifest motives, since these are motives that consumers are aware of and will discuss.

However, since latent motives often are less than completely socially desirable, indirect appeals frequently are used. The bulk of the copy of the Cadillac ad referred to above

ILLUSTRATION 10-5

Most ads appeal to multiple motives and desires. Both the pictures and the text can trigger motives.

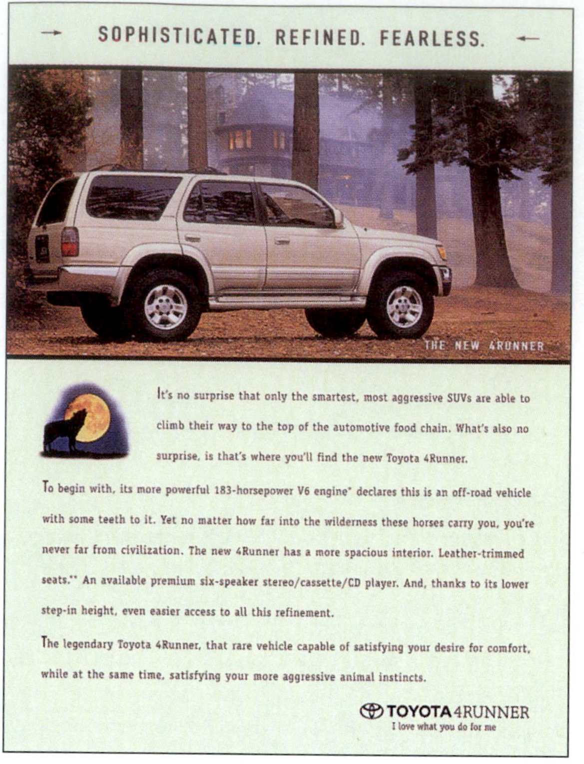

Courtesy Toyota Motor Sales U.S.A., Inc.

focused on the quality of the product. However, the artwork (about 60 percent of the ad) showed the car being driven by an apparently wealthy individual in front of a luxurious club. Thus, a dual appeal was used. The direct appeal in the copy focused on quality, while the indirect appeal in the artwork focused on status.

While any given advertisement for a product may focus on only one or a few purchasing motives, the campaign needs to cover all the important purchase motives of the target market. In essence, the overall campaign attempts to position the product in the schematic memory of the target market in a manner that corresponds with the target market's manifest and latent motives for purchasing the product. To what motives does the ad shown in Illustration 10-5 appeal?

Marketing Strategies Based on Motivation Conflict

With the many motives we have and the many situations in which these motives are activated, there are frequent conflicts between motives. The resolution of a motivational conflict often affects consumption patterns. In many instances, the marketer can analyze situations that are likely to result in a motivational conflict, provide a solution to the motivational conflict, and attract the patronage of those consumers facing the motivational conflict. There are three types of motivational conflict of importance to marketing managers: approach–approach conflict, approach–avoidance conflict, and avoidance–avoidance conflict.

Approach–Approach Motivational Conflict A consumer who must choose between two attractive alternatives faces **approach–approach conflict.** The more equal this attraction, the greater the conflict. A consumer who recently received a large income tax refund (situational variable) may be torn between a vacation (perhaps powered by the novelty motive) and a new mountain bike (perhaps powered by the need for self-expression). This conflict could be resolved by a timely advertisement designed to encourage one or the other action. Or, a price modification, such as "fly now, pay later," could result in a resolution whereby both alternatives are selected.

Approach–Avoidance Motivational Conflict A consumer facing a purchase choice with both positive and negative consequences confronts **approach–avoidance conflict.** A consumer who is concerned about gaining weight yet likes snack foods faces this type of problem. The consumer wants the taste and emotional satisfaction associated with the snacks (approach) but does not want to gain weight (avoidance). The development of lower-calorie snack foods reduces this conflict and allows the weight-sensitive consumer to enjoy snacks and also control calorie intake.

Avoidance–Avoidance Motivational Conflict A choice involving only undesirable outcomes produces **avoidance–avoidance conflict.** When a consumer's old washing machine fails, this conflict may occur. The person may not want to spend money on a new washing machine, or pay to have the old one repaired, or go without one. The availability of credit is one way of reducing this motivational conflict. Advertisements stressing the importance of regular maintenance for cars, such as oil filter changes, also use this type of motive conflict: "Pay me now, or pay me (more) later."

Do Marketers Create Needs?

Marketers are often accused of creating a need for a product that would not exist except for marketing activities, particularly advertising. Mouthwash, deodorant, and jet skis are used as examples of products for which there would be no need had not advertising created one.

Do marketers create needs? The answer depends in part on what is meant by the term *need.* If need is used to refer to a basic motive such as those described earlier in this chapter, it is clear that marketers seldom if ever create a need. Human genetics and the general experiences all humans encounter as they mature basically determine human motives. An analysis of literature and myths across cultures and centuries reveals a remarkably consistent set of human motives.

These common motives involve much more than the first two levels of Maslow's need hierarchy. Long before marketing or advertising appeared, individuals used perfumes, clothing, and other items to gain acceptance, display status, and so forth. Marketing and advertising are not the cause of these basic human motives.

However, marketers do create **demand.** Demand is the willingness to buy a particular product or service. It is caused by a need or motive, but it is not the motive. For example, advertising has helped create a demand for mouthwash. One way some firms did this was to indicate that without mouthwash, one would have bad breathe, and if you had bad breath, people would not like you. This message ties mouthwash to the need for affiliation or belongingness. It does not create the need for affiliation but suggests that using a certain brand of mouthwash is essential for satisfying this need. In so doing, the marketer hopes to create demand for the brand.

Given the definitions above, marketers do not create needs. This does not mean that there are not ethical issues involved in how marketers create demand as well as in the consequences of the demand that is created. Critics feel that creating demand by stressing threats to consumers' esteem or affiliation needs is unethical. For example, the headline in an ad for Retin-A states: "My mom thought I was beautiful (pimples and all) but you can't date your mom." Critics would argue that such ads unduly play on the insecurities of young women in order to generate demand for the brand.

PERSONALITY

While motivations are the energizing and directing force that makes consumer behavior purposeful and goal directed, the personality of the consumer guides and directs the behavior chosen to accomplish goals in different situations. **Personality** is *an individual's characteristic response tendencies across similar situations.*

We can easily (though perhaps not always accurately) describe our own personality or the personality of a friend. For example, you might say that one of your friends is "fairly aggressive, very opinionated, competitive, outgoing, and witty." What you have described are the behaviors your friend has exhibited over time across a variety of situations. These characteristic ways of responding to a wide range of situations should, of course, also include responses to marketing strategies.

There is controversy as to the exact nature of personality, the value of studying such a broad area, and the appropriate way to measure it.[20] However, the concept is a very real and meaningful one to all of us on a daily basis. People do have personalities! Personality characteristics exist in those we know and help us to describe and differentiate between individuals.

Personality theories can be categorized as being either individual theories or social learning theories. All **individual personality theories** have two common assumptions: (1) that all individuals have internal characteristics or traits and (2) that there are consistent and measurable differences between individuals on those characteristics. Most of these theories state that the traits or characteristics are formed at a very early age and are relatively unchanging over the years. Differences between individual theories center on the definition of which traits or characteristics are the most important.

Cattell's theory is a representative example of the individual approach. Cattell believes that traits are acquired at an early age through learning or are inherited. A unique aspect of his approach is the delineation of surface traits or observable behaviors that are similar and cluster together, and source traits that represent the causes of those behaviors. Cattell felt that if one could observe the surface traits that correlate highly with one another, they would identify an underlying source trait. For example, a source trait of assertiveness may account for the surface traits of aggressiveness, competitiveness, and stubbornness. Table 10-3 gives examples of some of Cattell's major source traits and corresponding surface traits.

While Cattell's theory is representative of multitrait individual personality theories (more than one trait influences behavior), there are a number of single-trait theories. Single-trait theories stress one trait as being particularly relevant. Some examples of single-trait theories that have been shown to be relevant to marketing are those that deal with dogmatism, extroversion, neuroticism,[21] cynicism, consumer conformity,[22] vanity,[23] affect intensity,[24] and the need for cognition.[25]

Romanticism/classicism is an individual personality variable that offers useful potential to marketers. Romantics are characterized by being "inspirational, imaginative, creative, intuitive. Feelings rather than facts predominate." Classics tend to be "straightforward, unadorned, unemotional, economical, and carefully proportional." A scale has been developed to measure each component. One study using MBA students as respondents found those classified as romantics preferred vacations that involved warm weather destinations and risky activities such as hang gliding compared to those categorized as classics.[26] For what other product categories do you think these two groups would have differing preferences?

Social learning theories emphasize the environment as the important determinant of behavior.[27] Hence, there is a focus on external versus internal factors. Also, there is little concern with variation between individuals in terms of individual traits. Systematic differences in situations, in stimuli, or in social settings are the major interest of social theorists—not differences in traits, needs, or other properties of individuals. Rather than classifying individuals, social theorists classify situations, an approach not widely used in marketing.

Cattell's Personality Traits* **TABLE 10-3**

Reserved: detached, critical, aloof, stiff	versus	*Outgoing:* warmhearted, easygoing, participating
Affected by feeling: emotionally less stable	versus	*Emotionally stable:* mature, faces reality, calm
Humble: stable, mild, easily led, docile, accommodating,	versus	*Assertive:* aggressive, competitive, stubborn.
Sober: taciturn, serious	versus	*Happy-go-lucky:* enthusiastic
Expedient: disregards rules	versus	*Conscientious:* persistent, moralistic, staid
Shy: timid, threat-sensitive	versus	*Venturesome:* uninhibited, socially bold
Tough-minded: self-reliant, realistic	versus	*Tender-minded:* sensitive, clinging, overprotected.
Practical: down-to-earth	versus	*Imaginative:* bohemian, absentminded
Forthright: unpretentious, genuine, but socially clumsy	versus	*Astute:* polished, socially aware
Self-assured: placid, secure, complacent, serene	versus	*Apprehensive:* self-reproaching, insecure, worrying, troubled
Conservative: respecting traditional ideas, conservatism of temperament	versus	*Experimenting:* liberal, freethinking, radicalism
Group dependent: a joiner and follower	versus	Self-sufficient: resourceful, prefers own decisions
Undisciplined: lax, follows own urges, careless of social rules	versus	*Controlled:* exacting will-power, socially precise, compulsive,
Relaxed: tranquil, torpid, unfrustrated, composed	versus	*Tense:* frustrated, driven, overwrought

*The source trait is in italics.

Source: Adapted from R. B. Cattell, H. W. Eber, and M. M. Tasuoka, *Handbook for the Sixteen Personality Factor Questionnaire* (Champaign, IL: Institute for Personality and Ability Testing, 1970), pp. 16–17. Reprinted by permission of the copyright owner.

THE USE OF PERSONALITY IN MARKETING PRACTICE

While we each have a variety of personality traits and become involved in many situations that activate different aspects of our personality, some of these traits or characteristics are more desirable than others and some may even be undesirable. That is, in some situations we may be shy when we wish we were bold, or timid when we would like to be assertive. Thus, most of us encounter times when we wish some areas of our personality were different.

Many consumer products acquire a **brand personality.**[28] One brand of perfume may project youth, sensuality, and adventure, while another perfume may be viewed as modest, conservative, and aristocratic. In this example, each perfume has a distinct personality and is likely to be purchased by a different type of consumer or for a different situation. Consumers will tend to purchase the product with the personality that most closely matches their own or that strengthens an area in which the consumer feels weak. As one consumer (Ella) stated when explaining why she varied from purchasing the conservative clothing she felt was most suitable for her work:

ELLA: You still have your personality when you're shopping. And I think a part of my personality is something like, "Wow, get the Carole Little (a colorful line of clothing).

INTERVIEWER: So you think your clothes are an expression of yourself?

ELLA: Oh sure, yeah. It tells a lot about your personality.[29]

Marketers are paying increasing attention to brand personalities. For example, Chrysler began trying to establish unique personalities for each of its car brands with the 1997 models and Ford began enhancing the personalities of its products in 1999.[30]

Researchers at Whirlpool Corp. reached the following conclusions concerning brand personalities:[31]

- Consumers readily assign human characteristics to brands even if the brands are not managed or the characteristics are not wanted by the marketers.
- Brand personalities create expectations about key characteristics, performance and benefits, and related services.
- Brand personalities are often the basis for a long-term relationship with the brand.

This research found the following brand personality profiles, including a description of what type of person the brand would be if it were human and what it would do and like, for a Whirlpool and a KitchenAid appliance (the larger the score, the more that trait is associated with the brand):

Whirlpool	*KitchenAid*
Gentle (146)	Sophisticated (206)
Sensitive (128)	Glamorous (186)
Quiet (117)	Wealthy (180)
Good natured (114)	Elegant (178)
30 years old (125)	30 years old (135)
1970s (140)	1990s (167)
Cosmo (132)	Cosmo (136)
Sailing (125)	Theater (124)
Jazz (118)	Classical (126)

The difference in the personality consumers assign to these brands is obvious. What type of target market will each appeal to?

A recent major study found that consumers perceive brand personalities in terms of five basic dimensions, each with several facets (see Figure 10-2). For example, consumers think about the "sincerity" of a brand with respect to its being *down-to-earth, honest, wholesome,* and *cheerful* while its "excitement" dimension consists of its level of being *daring, spirited, imaginative,* and *up-to-date.* A 42-item, Likert scale has been developed to measure brand personality on these dimensions.[32]

An important point from this research is that brands acquire personalities whether marketers want them to or not. These personalities influence purchases. Therefore, marketers need to manage the personalities of their brands. Here is how the head of SMH (maker of Swatch, Omega, and numerous other brands) views it:

My job is to sit in the bunker with a machine gun defending the distinct messages of all my brands. I am the custodian of our messages. I review every new communications campaign for every single brand.[33]

What brand personality is communicated by the ad in Illustration 10-6?

Dimensions of Brand Personality **FIGURE 10-2**

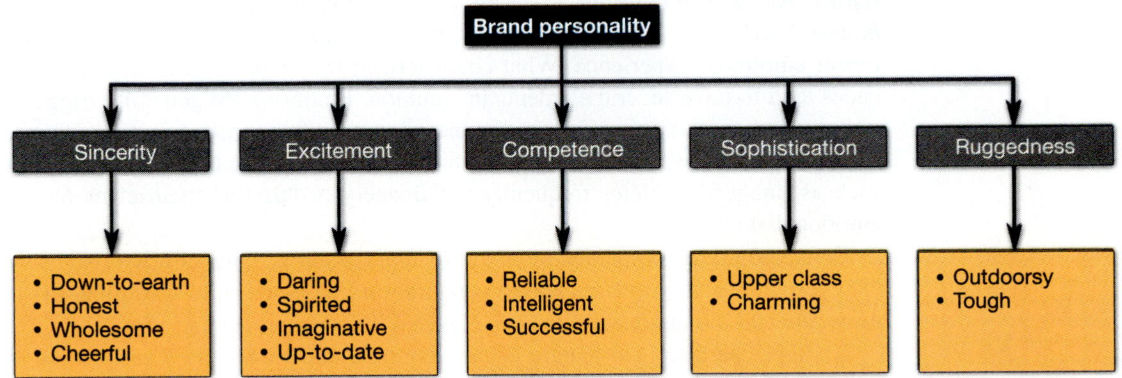

Source: Reprinted with permission from the *Journal of Marketing Research,* published by the American Marketing Association. J. L. Aaker, "Dimensions of Brand Personality," August 1997, p. 352.

Courtesy Bonne Bell, Inc.

ILLUSTRATION 10-6

People assign personalities to brands based on, among other things, the characteristics of the product category, the brand's features, its packaging, and its advertising. What type personality is this brand developing?

EMOTION

Earlier, we defined **emotion** as *strong, relatively uncontrolled feelings that affect our behavior.*[34] All of us experience a wide array of emotions. Think for a moment about a recent emotional experience. What characterized this experience? All emotional experiences tend to have several elements in common. Emotions are generally triggered by *environmental events.* Anger, joy, and sadness are most frequently a response to a set of external events. However, we can also initiate emotional reactions by *internal processes* such as imagery. Athletes frequently use imagery to "psych" themselves into a desired emotional state.

Emotions are accompanied by *physiological changes.* Some characteristic changes are (1) eye pupil dilation, (2) increased perspiration, (3) more rapid breathing, (4) increased heart rate and blood pressure, and (5) elevated blood sugar level.

Another characteristic feature of an emotional experience is *cognitive thought.* Emotions generally, though not necessarily, are accompanied by thinking.[35] The types of thoughts and our ability to think "rationally" vary with the type and degree of emotion.[36] Extreme emotional responses are frequently used as an explanation for inappropriate thoughts or actions: "I was so mad I couldn't think straight."

Emotions also have associated *behaviors.* While the behaviors vary across individuals and within individuals across time and situations, there are unique behaviors characteristically associated with different emotions: fear triggers fleeing responses, anger triggers striking out, grief triggers crying, and so forth.

Finally, emotions involve *subjective feelings.* In fact, it is the feeling component we generally refer to when we think of emotions. Grief, joy, anger, jealousy, and fear feel very different to us. These subjectively determined feelings are the essence of emotion.

These feelings have a specific component that we label as the emotion, such as sad or happy. In addition, emotions carry an evaluative or a like/dislike component. While the terms are used inconsistently in the literature, we use the term *emotion* to refer to the identifiable, specific feeling, and the term *affect* to refer to the liking/disliking aspect of the specific feeling.[37] While emotions are generally evaluated (liked and disliked) in a consistent

FIGURE 10-3 Nature of Emotions

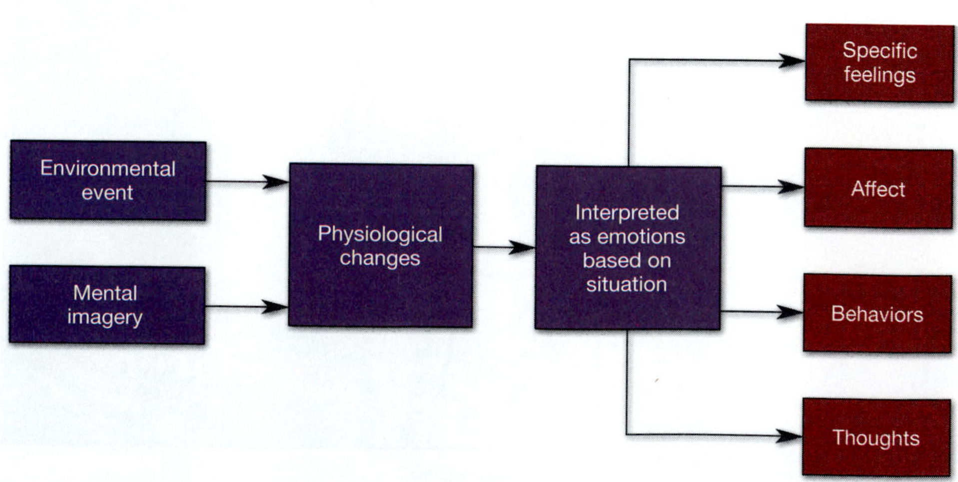

manner across individuals and within individuals over time, there are cultural, individual and situational variations.[38] For example, few of us generally want to be sad or afraid, yet we occasionally enjoy a movie or book that scares or saddens us.

Figure 10-3 reflects current thinking on the nature of emotions.

Types of Emotions

If asked, you could doubtless name numerous emotions and your friends could name many others that did not appear on your list. Thus, it is not surprising that researchers have attempted to categorize or "type" emotions into manageable clusters. Some researchers have suggested that three basic dimensions—pleasure, arousal, and dominance (PAD)—underlie all emotions. Specific emotions reflect various combinations and levels of these three dimensions.[39] Table 10-4 lists the three primary PAD dimensions, a variety of emotions or emotional categories associated with each dimension, and indicators or items that

TABLE 10-4

PAD Emotional Dimensions, Emotions, and Emotional Indicators

Dimension	*Emotion*	*Indicator/Feeling*
Pleasure	Duty	Moral, virtuous, dutiful
	Faith	Reverent, worshipful, spiritual
	Pride	Proud, superior, worthy
	Affection	Loving, affectionate, friendly
	Innocence	Innocent, pure, blameless
	Gratitude	Grateful, thankful, appreciative
	Serenity	Restful, serene, comfortable, soothed
	Desire	Desirous, wishful, craving, hopeful
	Joy	Joyful, happy, delighted, pleased
	Competence	Confident, in control, competent
Arousal	Interest	Attentive, curious
	Hypoactivation	Bored, drowsy, sluggish
	Activation	Aroused, active, excited
	Surprise	Surprised, annoyed, astonished
	Déjà vu	Unimpressed, uninformed, unexcited
	Involvement	Involved, informed, enlightened, benefited
	Distraction	Distracted, preoccupied, inattentive
	Surgency	Playful, entertained, lighthearted
	Contempt	Scornful, contemptuous, disdainful
Dominance	Conflict	Tense, frustrated, conflictful
	Guilt	Guilty, remorseful, regretful
	Helplessness	Powerless, helpless, dominated
	Sadness	Sad, distressed, sorrowful, dejected
	Fear	Fearful, afraid, anxious
	Shame	Ashamed, embarrassed, humiliated
	Anger	Angry, agitated, enraged, mad
	Hyperactivation	Panicked, confused, overstimulated
	Disgust	Disgusted, revolted, annoyed, full of loathing
	Skepticism	Skeptical, suspicious, distrustful

Source: Adapted with permission from M. B. Holbrook and R. Batra, "Assessing the Role of Emotions on Consumer Responses to Advertising," *Journal of Consumer Research,* December 1987, pp. 404–20.

TABLE 10-5

Batra and Holbrook's Emotions and Indicators (Adjectives)*

Emotion	Indicator
Activation	Arousal, active, excited
Skepticism	Skeptical, suspicious
Anger	Angry, enraged, mad
Restful	Restful, serene
Bored	Bored, uninvolved, unimpressed, unexcited
Fear	Fearful, afraid
Desire	Desirous, wishful, full of craving
Social affection	Loving, affectionate, pure
Gratitude	Grateful, thankful, benefited
Sadness	Sad, remorseful, sorrowful
Irritation	Disgusted, irritated, annoyed
Surgency	Playful, entertained, lighthearted

*Administered as "I felt not at all (adjective)/very (adjective)" (seven-point scale).

Source: "Developing a Typology of Affective Responses to Advertising," R. Batra and M. B. Holbrook, *Psychology & Marketing,* Spring 1990, p. 22. Copyright © 1990 by John Wiley & Sons, Inc. Reprinted by permission of John Wiley & Sons, Inc.

can be used to measure each emotion. Table 10-5 provides the same information for a 12-emotion typology developed by Batra and Holbrook.

EMOTIONS AND MARKETING STRATEGY

The opening vignette for this chapter illustrates how Swatch achieved substantial success in part by positioning the brand in emotional terms. While marketers have always used emotions to guide product positioning, sales presentations, and advertising on an intuitive level, the deliberate, systematic study of the relevance of emotions in marketing strategy is relatively new. In this section, we will briefly describe strategies focused on emotion arousal as a product benefit, emotion reduction as a product benefit, and emotion arousal in the context of advertising.

Emotion Arousal as a Product Benefit

Emotions are characterized by positive or negative evaluations. Consumers actively seek products whose primary or secondary benefit is emotion arousal.[40] While positive emotions are sought the majority of the time, this is not always the case ("The movie was so sad, I cried and cried. I loved it. You should see it.").[41]

Many products feature emotion arousal as a primary benefit. Movies, books, and music are the most obvious examples.[42] Las Vegas, Atlantic City, and Disney World are positioned as emotion-arousing destinations, as are various types of adventure travel programs. Long-distance telephone calls have been positioned as emotion-arousing products ("Reach out and touch someone"). Several brands of soft drinks stress excitement and fun as primary benefits. Even automobiles are sometimes positioned as emotion-arousing products:

Toyota—"Oh What a Feeling"; and Pontiac—"We Build Excitement." Stores feature events and environments that arouse emotions such as excitement.[43]

Products often arouse emotions in ways unintended by marketers. Most of us have experienced emotions such as frustration and anger as we have tried to assemble toys and other products or program VCRs and similar devices. In fact, technological products of all types produce paradoxes for many people. A **paradox** occurs when *something is both X and not-X at the same time.* These paradoxes trigger a variety of emotional and behavior responses that have major implications for marketing strategy. Consumer Insight 10-1 provides more detail about paradoxes caused by technological products.

Emotion Reduction as a Product Benefit

As a glance at Table 10-4 or 10-5 indicates, many emotional states are unpleasant to most individuals most of the time. Few of us like to feel sad, powerless, humiliated, or disgusted. Responding to this, marketers design and/or position many products to prevent or reduce the arousal of unpleasant emotions.

The most obvious of these products are the various over-the-counter medications designed to deal with anxiety or depression. Shopping malls, department stores, and other retail outlets are often visited to alleviate boredom or to experience activation, desire, or surgency.[44] Flowers are heavily promoted as an antidote to sadness. Weight-loss products and other self-improvement products are frequently positioned primarily in terms of guilt-, helplessness-, shame-, or disgust-reduction benefits. Personal grooming products often stress anxiety reduction as a major benefit. Charities frequently stress guilt reduction or avoidance as a reason for contributing.[45]

Emotion in Advertising

Emotion arousal is often used in advertising even when emotion arousal or reduction is not a product benefit. Consider the following recent headlines from *Advertising Age:*

- Lee takes emotional path to reach women for Riders.
- Discover's new ads bank on emotion.
- Marketers play heartstrings for ordinary products.
- Emotional appeal of laundry to replace performance claims in ads.

Illustration 10-7 provides an example of the effective use of emotion to attract attention to an ad and to position a line of products. In this ad, the young girl is being introduced to her new foster mother. After a shy start, the girl tries some soup. As the girl tastes the soup she says, "My mother used to make me that soup." "So did mine," says the foster mother. "Why don't I tell you about my mom and then you can tell me about yours." The tag line for the campaign is "Good for the body. Good for the soul."

We are just beginning to develop a sound understanding of how emotional responses to advertising influence consumer behavior,[46] as well as what causes an ad to elicit particular emotions.[47] Therefore, the general conclusions discussed below must be regarded as tentative.[48]

Emotional content in advertisements *enhances their attention attraction and maintenance capabilities.* Advertising messages that trigger the emotional reactions of joy, warmth, or even disgust are more likely to be attended to than are more neutral ads. As we saw in Chapter 8, attention is a critical step in the perception process.

Consumer Insight 10-1

Emotions and the Paradoxes of Technology

The common perception that the Internet can serve as a great time saver while simultaneously consuming large amounts of time is a paradox. A paradox occurs when an object is both X and not-X at the same time. When this is the case, a fixed equilibrium or balance between the opposing conditions is seldom achievable. Therefore, the salience or relevance of the positive or negative features are likely to shift frequently, often due to situational factors, producing a see-saw sensation from positive to negative feelings. Paradoxes produce conflict and ambience, which lead to emotional responses such as anxiety and stress and behavior responses such as avoidance, abandonment, and mastery.

Technology ranging from dishwashers to computers often produces paradoxes for consumers. A recent study uncovered eight central paradoxes associated with the consumption of technological products.

Control/chaos: It can facilitate regulation and order as well as lead to upheaval and disorder. An answering machine allows one to screen messages and answer at one's own choice of time. It can also overflow, provide a large number of messages at one time, and annoy some of those who are trying to reach you.

Freedom/enslavement: It can reduce restrictions and increase benefits or it can increase dependence and add restrictions. A computer allows one to do many things better and faster. However, one quickly becomes dependent on it and is unable to function effectively when a computer is not accessible.

New/obsolete: It provides the newest benefits of scientific knowledge but is soon outdated. Computers, software, cameras, stereo systems, and many other products are changing so rapidly that it is difficult and extremely expensive to be "up-to-date."

Competence/incompetence: It may increase feelings of intelligence and efficacy as well as feelings of ignorance and ineptitude. While one may experience pleasure in mastering many aspects of a technological product such as Excel, most also experience frustration at being unable to fully utilize the capabilities of many such technologies.

Fulfills/creates desires: It fulfills desires while developing or increasing awareness of other desires. The acquisition of a computer meets needs for faster and better word processing but generates desires for printers, zip drives, and additional software.

Assimilation/isolation: It can facilitate human interaction and isolation. Television can be used for interactive activities such as Super Bowl parties and shared experiences such as watching "Dawson's Creek." It also leads to solitary viewing and a lack of family discussion and interaction. The Internet both facilitates communication and restricts it.

Emotions are characterized by a state of heightened physiological arousal. Individuals become more alert and active when aroused. Given this enhanced level of arousal, *emotional messages may be processed more thoroughly* than neutral messages. More effort and increased elaboration activities may occur in response to the emotional state.[49]

Emotional advertisements that *trigger a positively evaluated emotion enhance liking of the ad itself.*[50] For example, "warmth" is a positively valued emotion that is triggered by experiencing directly or vicariously a love, family, or friendship relationship. Ads high in warmth, such as the Campbell's ad in Illustration 10-7, trigger the psychological changes described earlier in this chapter. In addition, warm ads such as these are liked more than neutral ads. Liking an ad has a positive impact on liking the product.

Emotional ads *may be remembered better than neutral ads.*[51] As discussed in Chapter 8, recognition measures, rather than recall measures, may be required to measure this enhanced memory.

Engaging/disengaging: It encourages involvement, flow, and activity while discouraging these same things. Many technologies such as television and computers remove people from direct experience and involvement while simultaneously involving them in a more passive or abstract experience.

Individuals differ in the extent to which they experience these paradoxes and in the degree to which such paradoxes produce anxiety and frustration. However, everyone experiences them to some extent and they arouse both positive and negative emotions in all of us.

Those individuals who find such paradoxes stressful adopt four categories of strategies for avoiding or minimizing them:

Preacquisition avoidance strategies: These include ignoring information about new technologies and refusing or delaying the acquisition of new technological products.

Preacquisition confrontative strategies: Using someone else's technology product temporarily; using buying heuristics such as buying a familiar, widely known brand or a basic, less sophisticated model; engaging in extensive prepurchase learning and extended decision making; and buying extended warranties or maintenance contracts are examples.

Consumption avoidance strategies: After acquiring the new technology (often as a gift or in response to peer pressure) one may still ignore it, abandon it, not repair or maintain it, or use it only under restricted circumstances (the VCR is used for showing rental movies but not for recording movies).

Consumption confrontative strategies: Accommodation (changing one's behaviors to meet the requirements of the new technology); partnering (developing an attachment to the technology), and mastering (thoroughly learning the technology) are common strategies.

Consumers are aware of technology paradoxes and pursue a variety of strategies to cope with them. They are not passive recipients of technology and do not automatically assume that new technologies are net positive benefits.

Critical Thinking Questions

1. What implications does this research have for understanding the diffusion of technological innovations (see Chapter 7 for a discussion of innovation diffusion)?
2. What is your assessment of the benefits and harm that advanced technologies have had for your society?

Source: D. G. Mick and S. Fournier, "Paradoxes of Technology: Consumer Cognizance, Emotions, and Coping Strategies," *Journal of Consumer Research*, September 1998, pp. 123–43.

Repeated exposure to positive-emotion-eliciting ads *may increase brand preference through classical conditioning.*[52] Repeated pairings of the unconditioned response (positive emotion) with the conditioned stimulus (brand name) may result in the positive affect occurring when the brand name is presented.

Brand liking may also occur in a direct, high-involvement manner. A person having a single or few exposures to an emotional ad may simply "decide" that the product is a good, or likable, product. Or that since they like the ad, they will probably like the product. This is a much more conscious process than implied by classical conditioning. For example, The "lizard" ads for Budweiser beer are enjoyed by many. Some of those who enjoy the ads may simply decide that they would enjoy a beer made by a firm with that type of humor.

Advertising using emotion-based appeals is gaining popularity. For example, Warner-Lambert dropped its fact-based comparative ad campaign for its e.p.t. Stick Test home

ILLUSTRATION 10-7

Emotional appeals can play a powerful role in developing a brand image.

© Campbell Soup Company.

pregnancy test in favor of a strong emotional campaign. Its 30-second TV spots capture the moment when a husband learns his wife is pregnant. The wife playfully hints at the news of her pregnancy by chanting the lines from familiar songs that use the word "baby," such as "Baby Face," until her husband catches on.

Measuring Emotional Responses to Ads A variety of approaches for measuring the emotional response to advertisements exist.[53] BBDO, a major ad agency, has a list of 26 emotions it believes can be triggered by advertising. To measure the emotions triggered by an ad, it developed the Emotional Measurement System. Starting with 1,800 pictures of six actors portraying various emotions, the firm used extensive research to narrow the list to 53 that reflect the 26 emotions of interest.

To test a commercial, respondents quickly sort through the 53 pictures and set aside all that reflect how they felt while watching the commercial. The percent of respondents selecting particular pictures provides a profile of the emotional response to the commercial. The system has been used for such companies as Gillette, Pepsi-Cola, Polaroid, and Wrigley.

The **galvanic skin response (GSR)** has been used to measure emotional arousal. GSR involves fitting the respondent with small electrodes that monitor the electrical resistance of the skin. This resistance changes with the very slight changes in perspiration that accompany emotional arousal. The most famous application of GSR is the "lie detector test."

While the validity of the GSR for marketing applications is controversial, evidence is beginning to suggest that it can be a useful measure.[54] Consider the results shown in Table 10-6. This study was conducted for *Better Homes and Gardens* and shows that, in this

TABLE 10-6

Emotional Arousal and Mail Response Rates*

Promotional Claim/Offer	*GSR Score**	*GSR Ranking*†	*Verbal Ranking*†	*Market Results*
1-cent sale	.300	1	4	1
Special saving	.284	2	3	2
Sampler	.248	3	1	3
Macramé	.231	4	2	4

*The higher the score, the higher the arousal.

†Predicted market response.

Source: P. L. LaBarbera and J. D. Tucciarone, "GSR Reconsidered," *Journal of Advertising Research,* September 1995, p. 45.

case, the GSR results were a better predictor of market response than were verbal evaluations of the ads. Blue Cross of Northern California obtained similar results testing a series of television commercials designed to produce calls to an 800 number.

SUMMARY

Consumer motivations are energizing forces that activate behavior and provide purpose and direction to that behavior. There are numerous motivation theories. Maslow's need hierarchy states that basic motives must be minimally satisfied before more advanced motives are activated. It proposes five levels of motivation: physiological, safety, belongingness, esteem, and self-actualization.

McGuire has developed a more detailed set of motives—the needs for consistency, causation, categorization, cues, independence, novelty, self-expression, ego-defense, assertion, reinforcement, affiliation, and modeling.

Consumers are often aware of and will admit to the motives causing their behavior. These are manifest motives. They can be discovered by standard marketing research techniques such as direct questioning. Direct advertising appeals can be made to these motives. At other times, consumers are unable or are unwilling to admit to the motives that are influencing them. These are latent motives. They can be determined by motivation research techniques such as word association, sentence completion, and picture response. While direct advertising appeals can be used, indirect appeals are often necessary. Both manifest and latent motives are operative in many purchase situations.

Because of the large number of motives and the many different situations that consumers face, motivational conflict can occur. In an approach–approach conflict, the consumer faces a choice between two attractive alternatives. In an approach–avoidance conflict, the consumer faces both positive and negative consequences in the purchase of a particular product. And finally, in the avoidance–avoidance conflict, the consumer faces two undesirable alternatives.

The personality of a consumer guides and directs the behavior chosen to accomplish goals in different situations. There are two basic approaches to understanding personality. Individual theories have two common assumptions: (1) all individuals have internal characteristics or traits, and (2) there are consistent differences between individuals on these characteristics or traits that can be measured. Most of the individual theories state that traits are formed at an early age and are relatively unchanging over the years. Social learning theories emphasize the environment as the important determinant of behavior. Therefore, the focus is on external (situational) versus internal factors.

Brands, like individuals, have personalities, and consumers tend to prefer products with brand personalities that are pleasing to them. It is also apparent that consumers prefer advertising messages that portray their own or a desired personality.

Emotions are strong, relatively uncontrollable feelings that affect our behavior. Emotions occur when environmental events or our mental processes trigger physiological changes, including increased perspiration, eye pupil dilation, increased heart and breath rate, and elevated blood pressure and sugar level. These changes are interpreted as specific emotions based on the situation. They affect consumers' thoughts and behaviors. Marketers design and position products to both arouse and reduce emotions. Advertisements include emotion-arousing material to increase attention, degree of processing, remembering, and brand preference through classical conditioning or direct evaluation.

KEY TERMS

Approach–approach conflict 372
Approach–avoidance conflict 373
Avoidance–avoidance conflict 373
Attribution theory 363
Benefit chain 370
Brand personality 375
Demand 373
Emotion 378
Galvanic skin response (GSR) 384
Individual personality theories 374
Laddering 370
Latent motive 369
Manifest motive 369
Maslow's hierarchy of needs 363
Means-end chain 370
Motivation 362
Motive 362
Paradox 381
Personality 374
Projective techniques 369
Social learning theories 374

INTERNET EXERCISES

1. Visit several company Web sites. Find and describe one that makes effective use of an appeal or theme based on the following:
   a. One of Maslow's need hierarchy levels
   b. One of McGuire's motives
   c. An emotional appeal
2. Visit several general interest or entertainment sites on the Internet that contain ads. Find and describe an ad that uses the following:
   a. One of Maslow's need hierarchy levels
   b. One of McGuire's motives
   c. An emotional appeal
3. Monitor a hobby- or product-based interest group for a week. What types of motives and emotions are involved with the activity or product? What are the marketing implications of this?

DDB NEEDHAM LIFESTYLE DATA ANALYSES

1. The DDB Needham questionnaire measures personality by asking people to list characteristics that describe themselves: Use Table 7a to answer the following:
   a. Do any of these personality characteristics seem to be associated with heavy consumption of any of the products or activities? Why do you think this is?
   b. Is product ownership associated with any of these personality characteristics? How would you explain this?
   c. Do any of these personality characteristics appear to influence television show preferences? Why do you think this is?
   d. Do any of these personality characteristics seem to be associated with any of the attitude, interest, or opinion items? Why do you think this is?

REVIEW QUESTIONS

1. What is a motive?
2. What is meant by a motive hierarchy? How does Maslow's hierarchy of needs function?
3. Describe each level of Maslow's hierarchy of needs.
4. Describe each of McGuire's motives.
5. What is meant by motivational conflict, and what relevance does it have for marketing managers?
6. What is a manifest motive? A latent motive?
7. How do you measure manifest motives? Latent motives?
8. How do you appeal to manifest motives? Latent motives?
9. Describe the following motivation research techniques:
   a. Association
   b. Completion
   c. Construction
10. What is personality?
11. Describe the individual and the social learning approaches to personality.
12. How can knowledge of personality be used to develop marketing strategy?
13. What is an emotion?
14. What physiological changes accompany emotional arousal?
15. What factors characterize emotions?
16. How can we type or categorize emotions?
17. How do marketers use emotions in product design and positioning?
18. What is a *paradox?*
19. What types of paradoxes does technology produce? How do consumers cope with technology paradoxes?
20. What is the role of emotional content in advertising?
21. Describe BBDO's Emotional Measurement System.
22. What is the GSR? How do marketers use it?

DISCUSSION QUESTIONS

23. How could Maslow's motive hierarchy be used to develop marketing strategy for the following?
   a. Mothers Against Drunk Driving
   b. Revlon's new vitamin line
   c. EarthSave
   d. A restaurant chain
   e. A candidate for mayor
   f. Toothpaste
24. Which of McGuire's motives would be useful in developing a promotional campaign for the following? Why?
   a. EarthSave
   b. Hair salon
   c. Palm computer
   d. Aftershave lotion
   e. Internet provider service
   f. Mountain bike
25. Describe how motivational conflict might arise in purchasing (or giving to) the following:
   a. EarthSave
   b. Sport-utility vehicle
   c. Discount store
   d. Evian bottled water
   e. Olive Garden restaurant
   f. Health insurance
26. Describe the manifest and latent motives that might arise in purchasing, shopping at, or giving to the following:
   a. United Way
   b. Swimsuit
   c. Stereo system
   d. Toothpaste
   e. Palm computer
   f. A salt water aquarium
27. Do marketers create needs? Do they create demand? What ethical issues are relevant? 
28. How might knowledge of personality be used to develop an advertising campaign for the following?
   a. EarthSave
   b. A candidate for governor
   c. In-line skates

d. A tax service
e. Weber barbecue grills
f. A sport-utility vehicle

29. Using Table 10-3, discuss how you would use one of the personality source traits in developing a package design for an herbal tea.
30. How would you use emotion to develop marketing strategy for the products listed in Question 28?
31. List all the emotions you can think of. Which ones are not explicitly mentioned in Table 10-4? Where would you place them in this table?
32. Does the list of technology paradoxes in Consumer Insight 10-1 make sense to you? Why? Which of these have you experienced? Provide an additional example of each type of paradox.
33. Does the list of consumer responses to technology paradoxes in Consumer Insight 10-1 make sense to you? Why? Which of these have you utilized?

APPLICATION ACTIVITIES

34. Develop an advertisement for two of the items in Question 24 based on relevant motives from McGuire's set.
35. Repeat Question 34 using Maslow's need hierarchy.
36. Repeat Question 34 using emotions.
37. Find and copy or describe two advertisements that appeal to each level of Maslow's hierarchy. Explain why the ads appeal to the particular levels and speculate on why the firm decided to appeal to these levels.
38. Find and copy or describe an ad that contains direct appeals to manifest motives and indirect appeals to latent motives. Explain how and why the ad is using each approach.
39. Select a product of interest and use motivation research techniques to determine the latent purchase motives for five consumers.
40. Have five students describe the personality of the following. To what extent are the descriptions similar? Why are there differences?
    a. Harvard University
    b. Bud Light beer
    c. Porsche
    d. Macintosh computer
    e. A local restaurant
    f. The university bookstore
41. Find and copy two ads with strong emotional appeal and two ads from the same product categories with limited emotional appeal. Why do the companies use different appeals?
    a. Have 10 students rank or rate the ads in terms of their preferences and then explain their rankings or ratings.
    b. Have 10 different students talk about their reactions to each ad as they view it. What do you conclude?
42. Read the article that Consumer Insight 10-1 is based on. Interview five students using the same methodology. Compare your results to those obtained in the article.

REFERENCES

1. W. Taylor, "Message and Muscle," *Harvard Business Review,* March 1993, pp. 99–110.
2. For an example, see C. Moorman and E. Matulich, "A Model of Consumers' Preventive Health Behaviors," *Journal of Consumer Research,* September 1993, pp. 208–28.
3. A. H. Maslow, *Motivation and Personality,* 2nd ed. (New York: Harper & Row, 1970).
4. See R. Yalch and F. Brunel, "Need Hierarchies in Consumer Judgments of Product Designs," in *Advances in Consumer Research XXIII,* ed. K. P. Corfman and J. G. Lynch (Provo, UT: Association for Consumer Research, 1996), pp. 405–10.
5. W. J. McGuire, "Psychological Motives and Communication Gratification," in *The Uses of Mass Communications,* ed. J. G. Blumler and C. Katz (Newbury Park, CA.: Sage Publications,

1974), pp. 167–96; and W. J. McGuire, "Some Internal Psychological Factors Influencing Consumer Choice," *Journal of Consumer Research,* March 1976, pp. 302–19.

6. Footnote 1, pp. 105–6.
7. S. Burton, D. R. Lichtenstein, A. Biswas, and K. Fraccastoro, "The Role of Attributions in Consumer Perceptions of Retail Advertisements Promoting Price Discounts," *Marketing Letters* 5, no. 2 (1994), pp. 131–40.
8. See D. M. Boush, M. Friestad, and G. M. Rose, "Adolescent Skepticism toward TV Advertising and Knowledge of Advertiser Tactics"; and M. Friestad and P. Wright, "The Persuasion Knowledge Model"; both in *Journal of Consumer Research,* June 1994; pp. 1–31 and 165–75; and M. Friestad and P. Wright, "Persuasion Knowledge," *Journal of Consumer Research,* June 1995, pp. 62–74.
9. See B. H. Schmit and S. Zhang, "Language Structure and Categorization," *Journal of Consumer Research,* September 1998, pp. 108–22.
10. M. Lynn and J. Harris, "The Desire for Unique Consumer Products," *Psychology & Marketing,* September 1997, pp. 601–16.
11. S. Menon and B. E. Kahn, "The Impact of Context on Variety Seeking in Product Choice," *Journal of Consumer Research,* December 1995, pp. 285–95; T. H. Dodd, B. E. Pinkleton, and Q. W. Gustafson, "External Information Sources of Product Enthusiasts," *Psychology & Marketing,* May 1996, pp. 291–304; H. C. M. Van Trijp, W. D. Hoyer, and J. J. Inman, "Why Switch?" *Journal of Marketing Research,* August 1996, pp. 281–92; K. L. Wakefield and J. H. Barnes, "Retailing Hedonic Consumption," *Journal of Retailing,* no. 4, (1996), pp. 409–27; B. E. Kahn, R. K. Ratner, and D. Kahneman, "Patterns of Hedonic Consumption Over Time," *Marketing Letters,* no. 1 (1997), pp. 85–96; P. Leszczyc and H. Timmermans, "Store-Switching Behavior," *Marketing Letters,* no. 2 (1997), pp. 193–204; and M. Trivedi, "Using Variety-Seeking-Based Segmentation to Study Promotional Response," *Journal of the Academy of Marketing Science,* Winter 1999, pp. 37–49.
12. See G. M. Zinkhan, J. W. Hong, and R. Lawson, "Achievement and Affiliation Motivation," *Journal of Business Research,* March 1990, pp. 135–43.
13. C. Miller, "Spaghetti Sauce Preference," *Marketing News,* August 31, 1992, p. 5.
14. G. D. Mick, M. DeMoss, and R. J. Faber, "A Projective Study of Motivations and Meanings of Self-Gifts," *Journal of Retailing,* Summer 1992, pp. 122–44.
15. For an excellent approach, see G. Berstell and D. Nitterhouse, "Looking 'Outside the Box,'" *Marketing Research,* Summer 1997, pp. 5–13.
16. C. Rubel, "Three Firms Show that Good Research Makes Good Ads," *Marketing News,* March 13, 1995, p. 18.
17. See T. Collier, "Dynamic Reenactment," *Marketing Research,* Spring 1993, pp. 35–37; G. Zaltman, "Metaphorically Speaking," *Marketing Research,* Summer 1996, pp. 13–20; and C. B. Raffel, "Vague Notions," *Marketing Research,* Summer 1996, pp. 21–23.
18. See J. F. Durgee, G. C. O'Connor, and R. W. Veryzer, "Translating Values into Product Wants," *Journal of Advertising Research,* November 1996, pp. 90–99; J. Gutman, "Means-End Chains as Goal Hierarchies," *Psychology & Marketing,* September 1997, pp. 545–60; and B. Wansink, "Making Old Brands New," *American Demographics,* December 1997, pp. 53–58.
19. J. Langer, "Story Time Is Alternative Research Technique," *Marketing News,* September 1985, p. 19. See also L. L. Golden, M. I. Alpert, and J. F. Betak, "Psychological Meaning," *Psychology & Marketing,* Spring 1989, pp. 33–50; and M. D. Reilly, "Free Elicitation of Descriptive Adjectives for Tourism Research," *Journal of Tourism Research,* Spring 1990, pp. 21–26.
20. J. L. Lastovicka and E. A. Joachimsthaler, "Improving the Detection of Personality-Behavior Relationships in Consumer Research," *Journal of Consumer Research,* March 1988, pp. 583–87; G. R. Foxall and R. E. Goldsmith, "Personality and Consumer Research," *Journal of the Market Research Society,* no. 2 (1988), pp. 111–25; and H. H. Kassarjain and M. J. Sheffet, "Personality and Consumer Behavior," in *Perspectives in Consumer Behavior,* ed. H. H. Kassarjain and T. S. Robertson, (Englewood Cliffs, NJ: Prentice Hall, 1991), pp. 281–303.
21. See T. A. Mooradian, "Personality and Ad-Evoked Feelings," *Journal of the Academy of Marketing Science,* Spring 1996, pp. 99–109; and "I Can't Get No Satisfaction," *Psychology & Marketing,* July 1997, pp. 379–93.
22. D. M. Boush, C. H. Kim, L. R. Kahle, and R. Batra, "Cynicism and Conformity as Correlates of Trust in Product Information Sources," *Journal of Current Issues and Research in Advertising,* Fall 1993, pp. 71–79.
23. R. G. Netemeyer, S. Burton, and D. R. Lichtenstein, "Trait Aspects of Vanity," *Journal of Consumer Research,* March 1995, pp. 612–26.
24. M. Geuens and P. D. Pelsmacker, "Affect Intensity Revisited," *Psychology & Marketing,* May 1999, pp. 195–209.
25. See Y. Zhang, "Responses to Humorous Advertising," *Journal of Advertising,* Spring 1996, pp. 15–32; Y. Zhang, "The Effect of Humor in Advertising," *Psychology & Marketing,* September 1996, pp. 531–45; and S. P. Mantel and F. R. Kardes, "The Role of Direction of Comparison, Attribute-Based Processing, and Attitude-Based Processing in Consumer Preference," *Journal of Consumer Research,* March 1999, pp. 335–51.
26. M. B. Holbrook and T. J. Olney, "Romanticism and Wanderlust," *Psychology & Marketing,* May 1995, pp. 207–22.
27. See F. Buttle, "The Social Construction of Needs," *Psychology & Marketing,* Fall 1989, pp. 196–210.
28. J. J. Plummer, "How Personality Makes a Difference," *Journal of Advertising Research,* January 1985, pp. 27–31; and J. F. Durgee, "Understanding Brand Personality," *The Journal of Consumer Marketing,* Summer 1988, pp. 21–23.
29. V. Larsen and N. D. Wright, "The Mirror and the Lamp, the Mask and the Elephant," in *Advances in Consumer Research XXV,* ed. J. W. Alba and J. W. Hutchinson (Provo, UT: Association for Consumer Research, 1998), p. 101.
30. J. Halliday, "Chrysler Brings Out Brand Personalities with '97 Ads," *Advertising Age,* September 30, 1996, p. 3; and J. Halliday, "Ford Extends Story-Telling Ads," *Advertising Age,* August 24, 1998, p. 3.

31. B. F. Roberson, "Brand Personality and the Brand-Consumer Relationship," Whirlpool Corporation, April 5, 1994. See T. Triplett, "Brand Personality Must Be Managed or It Will Assume a Life of Its Own," *Marketing News,* May 9, 1994, p. 9.

32. J. L. Aaker, "Dimensions of Brand Personality," *Journal of Marketing Research,* August 1997, pp. 347–56.

33. Footnote 1, p. 105.

34. For a thorough discussion, see R. P. Bagozzi, M. Gopinath, and P. U. Nyer, "The Role of Emotions in Marketing," *Journal of the Academy of Marketing Science,* Spring 1999, pp. 184–207.

35. See P. U. Nyer, "A Study of the Relationships between Cognitive Appraisals and Consumption Emotions," *Journal of the Academy of Marketing Science,* Fall 1997, pp. 296–305.

36. See B. J. Babin, J. S. Boles, and W. R. Darden, "Salesperson Stereotypes, Consumer Emotions, and Their Impact on Information Processing," *Journal of the Academy of Marketing Science,* Spring 1995, pp. 94–105.

37. See M. B. Holbrook and J. O'Shaughnessy, "The Role of Emotion in Advertising," *Psychology & Marketing,* Summer 1984, pp. 45–63; and R. Batra and M. L. Ray, "Affective Responses Mediating Acceptance of Advertising," *Journal of Consumer Research,* September 1986, pp. 234–49.

38. See D. J. Moore and W. D. Harris, "Affect Intensity and the Consumer's Attitude toward High Impact Emotional Advertising Appeals," *Journal of Advertising,* Summer 1996, pp. 37–50; L. Dube and M. S. Morgan, "Trend Effects and Gender Differences in Retrospective Judgments of Consumption Emotions," *Journal of Consumer Research,* September 1996, pp. 156–62; M.-H. Huang, "Exploring a New Typology of Emotional Appeals," *Journal of Current Issues and Research in Advertising,* Fall 1997, pp. 24–37, J. L. Aaker and P. Williams, "Empathy versus Pride," *Journal of Consumer Research,* December 1998, pp. 241–61; and M. Geuens and P. D. Pelsmacker, "Affect Intensity Revisited," *Psychology & Marketing,* May 1999, pp. 195–209.

39. M. B. Holbrook and R. Batra, "Assessing the Role of Emotions on Consumer Responses to Advertising," *Journal of Consumer Research,* December 1987, pp. 404–20; and W. J. Havlena, M. B. Holbrook, and D. R. Lehmann, "Assessing the Validity of Emotional Typologies," *Psychology & Marketing,* Summer 1989, pp. 97–112. See also T. J. Page et al., "Measuring Emotional Response to Advertising"; P. A. Stout and J. D. Leckenby, "The Nature of Emotional Response to Advertising"; both in *Journal of Advertising,* no. 4 (1988), pp. 49–52 and 53–57; M. B. Holbrook and R. Batra, "Toward a Standardized Emotional Profile (SEP) Useful in Measuring Responses to the Nonverbal Components of Advertising," in *Nonverbal Communication in Advertising,* ed. S. Hecker and D. W. Stewart (Lexington, MA: D. C. Heath, 1988); and E. Day, "Share of Heart," *Journal of Consumer Marketing,* Winter 1989, pp. 5–12.

40. See N. V. Raman, P. Chattopadhyay, and W. D. Hoyer, "Do Consumers Seek Emotional Situations?" in *Advances in Consumer Research XXII,* ed. F. R. Kardes and M. Sujan (Provo, UT: Association for Consumer Research, 1995), pp. 537–42.

41. See C. Campbell, *The Romantic Ethic and the Spirit of Modern Consumerism* (Oxford: Blackwell, 1987).

42. See K. T. Lacher and R. Mizerski, "An Exploratory Study of the Responses and Relationships Involved in the Evaluation of, and in the Intention to Purchase, New Rock Music," *Journal of Consumer Research,* September 1994, pp. 366–80.

43. See E. Sherman, A. Mathur, and R. B. Smith, "Store Environment and Consumer Purchase Behavior," *Psychology & Marketing,* July 1997, pp. 361–78.

44. See R. A. Westbrook and W. C. Black, "A Motivation-Based Shopper Typology," *Journal of Retailing,* Spring 1985, pp. 78–103; T. C. O'Guinn and R. W. Belk, "Heaven on Earth," *Journal of Consumer Research,* September 1989, pp. 227–38; and footnote 16.

45. B. A. Huhmann and T. P. Brotherton, "A Content Analysis of Guilt Appeals in Popular Magazine Advertisements," *Journal of Advertising,* Summer 1997, pp. 35–45.

46. T. J. Olney, M. B. Holbrook, and R. Batra, "Consumer Responses to Advertising," *Journal of Consumer Research,* March 1991, pp. 440–53; S. P. Brown and D. M. Stayman, "Antecedents and Consequences of Attitude toward the Ad," *Journal of Consumer Research,* June 1992, pp. 34–51; G. Biehal, D. Stephens, and E. Curlo, "Attitude toward the Ad and Brand Choice," *Journal of Advertising,* September 1992, pp. 19–36; P. A. Stout and R. T. Rust, "Emotional Feelings and Evaluative Dimensions of Advertising," *Journal of Advertising,* March 1993, pp. 61–71; and M. H. Huang, "Is Negative Affect in Advertising General or Specific?" *Psychology & Marketing,* May 1997, pp. 223–40.

47. E. Kamp and D. J. MacInnis, "Characteristics of Portrayed Emotions in Commercials," *Journal of Advertising Research,* November 1995, pp. 19–28; H. Baumgartner, M. Sujan, and D. Padgett, "Patterns of Affective Reactions to Advertisements," *Journal of Marketing Research,* May 1997, pp. 219–32; D. W. Miller and L. J. Marks, "The Effects of Imagery-Evoking Radio Advertising Strategies on Affective Responses," *Psychology & Marketing,* July 1997, pp. 337–60; and J. D. Morris and M. A. Boone, "The Effects of Music on Emotional Response," in *Advances in Consumer Research XXV,* ed. J. W. Alba and J. W. Hutchinson (Provo, UT: Association for Consumer Research, 1998), pp. 518–26.

48. See S. P. Brown, P. M. Homer, and J. J. Inman, "A Meta-Analysis of Relationships between Ad-Evoked Feelings and Advertising Responses," *Journal of Marketing Research,* February 1998, pp. 114–26.

49. For a thorough discussion, see H. Mano, "Affect and Persuasion," *Psychology & Marketing,* July 1997, pp. 315–35.

50. See K. R. France, R. H. Shah, and W. W. Park, "The Impact of Valence and Intensity on Ad Evaluation and Memory," in *Advances in Consumer Research XXI,* ed. C. T. Allen and D. R. John (Provo, UT: Association for Consumer Research, 1994), pp. 583–88; and J. P. Murry, Jr., and P. A. Dacin, "Cognitive Moderators of Negative-Emotion Effects," *Journal of Consumer Research,* March 1996, pp. 439–47.

51. M. Friestad and E. Thorson, "Emotion-Eliciting Advertising," in *Advances in Consumer Research XIII,* ed. R. J. Lutz (Provo, UT: Association for Consumer Research, 1986), pp. 111–16.

52. See E. A. Groenland and J. P. L. Schoormans, "Comparing Mood-Induction and Affective Conditioning as Mechanisms Influencing Product Evaluation and Product Choice," *Psychology & Marketing,* March 1994, pp. 183–97.

53. See J. D. Morris and J. S. McMullen, "Measuring Multiple Emotional Responses to a Single Television Commercial," in *Advances in Consumer Research XXI,* ed. C. T. Allen and D. R. John (Provo, UT: Association for Consumer Research, 1994), pp. 175–80.

54. P. L. LaBarbera and J. D. Tucciarone, "GSR Reconsidered," *Journal of Advertising Research,* September 1995, pp. 33–53. See also P. V. Abeele and D. L. MacLachlan, "Process Tracing of Emotional Responses to TV Ads," *Journal of Consumer Research,* March 1994, pp. 586–600; and P. V. Abeele and D. L. MacLachlan, "Process Tracing of Physiological Responses to Dynamic Commercial Stimuli," in *Advances in Consumer Research XXI,* ed. C. T. Allen and D. R. John (Provo, UT: Association for Consumer Research, 1994), pp. 226–32.

Nawrocki Stock Photo Inc.

chapter eleven

Attitudes and Influencing Attitudes

Close your eyes and think of Marlboro cigarettes. What comes to mind? Is it an effeminate, sissy cigarette with an ivory tip or a red beauty tip? Certainly not when one thinks of the Marlboro man!

Philip Morris began marketing Marlboro in 1924 as an extremely mild filter cigarette. In fact, "Mild as May" was its slogan. Early campaigns featured decidedly unmasculine historical characters using the product. By the 1940s, it was promoted as an elegant cigarette primarily for women, though some ads showed men in tuxedos with Marlboros. At this time it came with either an ivory tip or a red beauty tip! It was advertised in a very plush atmosphere and was widely used by women. By the 1950s, the image described above was firmly established. In addition, at that time all filter cigarettes were viewed as somewhat effeminate.

By the mid-1950s, it was becoming increasingly apparent that filter cigarettes would eventually take over the market. Philip Morris decided to make Marlboro acceptable to the heavy user market segment—males. To accomplish this, everything but the name was changed. A more flavorful blend of tobaccos was selected along with a new filter. The package design was changed to red and white with an angular design (more masculine than a curved or circular design). One version of the package was the crushproof box—again, a very rugged, masculine option.

The advertising used "regular guys," not professional models, who typified masculine confidence. The Marlboro cowboy (a real cowboy) was introduced as "the most generally accepted symbol of masculinity in America." To lend credence to the new brand, it was tied to the well-known Philip Morris name with "new from Philip Morris" in the introductory advertising.

How successful was it? What did you think of a few minutes ago when asked to think about Marlboro? This image shift resulted in Marlboro becoming the largest selling brand of cigarettes in the world.

By the 1960s, most adult American males smoked cigarettes and an increasing number of women were beginning to smoke. However, the health hazards of smoking were becoming increasingly well documented. Various groups, particularly the American Cancer Society, began promotional campaigns to reduce smoking. These campaigns used a variety of techniques, including rational arguments, fact sheets, celebrity spokespersons, fear appeals, and humorous appeals.

The results of these attempts to change attitudes and behaviors about smoking have been as impressive as Marlboro's image change. Smoking among adult males in America is lower than it has been in decades. The growth in adult female smoking has stopped. While there has been a recent increase in teenage smoking, there is strong evidence that antismoking advertisements targeting teenagers can change the attitudes of many and noticeably reduce smoking among this group.[1]

As the opening example indicates, businesses and social agencies alike frequently succeed in altering behavior by changing attitudes toward a product, service, or activity. And, as these examples also indicate, these changes can result in injurious or beneficial consumption decisions.

An **attitude** is *an enduring organization of motivational, emotional, perceptual, and cognitive processes with respect to some aspect of our environment.* It is a learned predisposition to respond in a consistently favorable or unfavorable manner with respect to a given object. Thus, an attitude is the way we think, feel, and act toward some aspect of our environment such as a retail store, television program, or product.[2]

Attitudes serve four key functions for individuals:[3]

- *Knowledge function.* Some attitudes serve primarily as a means of organizing beliefs about objects or activities such as brands and shopping. These attitudes may be accurate or inaccurate with respect to "objective" reality, but the attitude will often determine subsequent behaviors rather than "reality." For example, a consumer's attitude toward cola drinks may be "they all taste the same." This consumer would be likely to purchase the least expensive or most convenient brand. This would be true even if, in a taste test, the consumer could tell the brands apart and would prefer one over the others. Firms like Pepsi spend considerable effort to influence consumers' beliefs about colas.
- *Value-expressive function.* Other attitudes are formed and serve to express an individual's central values and self-concept. Thus, consumers who value nature and the environment are likely to develop attitudes about products and activities that are consistent with that value. These consumers are likely to express support for environment protection initiatives, to recycle, and to purchase and use "green" products. We examined this issue in some detail in Chapter 3.
- *Utilitarian function.* This function is based on operant conditioning, as described in Chapter 9. We tend to form favorable attitudes toward objects and activities that are rewarding and negative attitudes toward those that are not. Marketers frequently promise rewards in advertising and conduct extensive product testing to be sure the products are indeed rewarding.
- *Ego-defensive function.* Attitudes are often formed and used to defend our egos and images against threats and shortcomings. Products promoted as very macho may be viewed favorably by men who are insecure in their masculinity. Or, individuals who feel threatened in social situations may form favorable attitudes toward products and brands that promise success or at least safety in such situations. These individuals

would be likely to have favorable attitudes toward popular brands and styles of clothes and to use personal care products such as deodorants, dandruff shampoo, and mouthwash.

Any given attitude can perform multiple functions, though one may predominate. Marketers need to be aware of the function that attitudes relevant to the purchase and use of their brands fulfill or could fulfill for their target markets.

Attitudes are formed as the result of all the influences we have been describing in the previous chapters, and they represent an important influence on an individual's lifestyle. In this chapter, we will examine attitude components, the general strategies that can be used to change attitudes, and the effect of marketing communications on attitudes.

ATTITUDE COMPONENTS

As Figure 11-1 illustrates, it is useful to consider attitudes as having three components: cognitive (beliefs), affective (feelings), and behavioral (response tendencies). Each of these attitude components is discussed in more detail below.

Cognitive Component

The **cognitive component** consists of *a consumer's beliefs about an object. For most attitude objects, we have a number of beliefs*. For example, we may believe that Mountain Dew:

- Is popular with younger consumers.
- Contains a lot of caffeine.
- Is competitively priced.
- Is made by a large company.

Attitude Components and Manifestations FIGURE 11-1

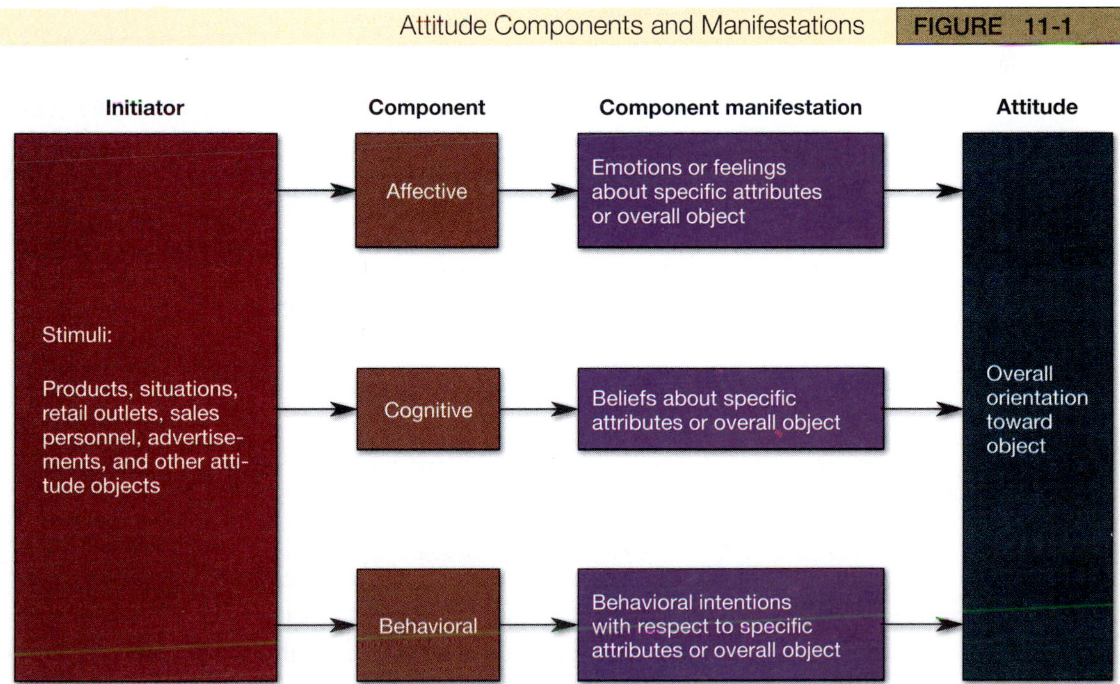

The total configuration of beliefs about this brand of soda represents the cognitive component of an attitude toward Mountain Dew. It is important to keep in mind that beliefs need not be correct or true; they only need to exist.

Many beliefs about attributes are evaluative in nature. That is, high gas mileage, attractive styling, and reliable performance are generally viewed as positive beliefs. The more positive beliefs that are associated with a brand, the more positive each belief is; and the easier it is for the individual to retrieve or recall the beliefs, the more favorable the overall cognitive component is presumed to be.[4] And, since all of the components of an attitude are generally consistent, the more favorable the overall attitude is. This logic underlies what is known as the **multiattribute attitude model.**

There are several versions of this model. The simplest is:

$$A_b = \sum_{i=1}^{n} X_{ib}$$

where

A_b = Consumer's attitude toward a particular brand b
X_{ib} = Consumer's belief about brand b's performance on attribute i
n = Number of attributes considered

This version assumes that all attributes are equally important in determining our overall evaluation. However, a moment's reflection suggests that for some products and individuals, a few attributes such as price, quality, or style are more important than others. Thus, it is often desirable to add an importance weight for each attribute:

$$A_b = \sum_{i=1}^{n} W_i X_{ib}$$

where

W_i = The importance the consumer attaches to attribute i

This version of the model is useful in a variety of situations. However, it assumes that more (or less) is always better. This is frequently the case. More miles to the gallon is always better than fewer miles to the gallon, all other things being equal. This version is completely adequate for such situations.

For some attributes, more (or less) is good up to a point, but then further increases (decreases) become bad. For example, adding salt to a saltless pretzel will generally improve our attitude toward the pretzel up to a point. After that point, additional amounts of salt will decrease our attitude. In such situations, we need to introduce an "ideal point" into the multiattribute attitude model:

$$A_b = \sum_{i=1}^{n} W_i |I_i - X_{ib}|$$

where

I_i = Consumer's ideal level of performance on attribute i

Since multiattribute attitude models are widely used by marketing researchers and managers, we will work through an example using the weighted, ideal point model. The simpler models would work in a similar manner.

Assume that a segment of consumers perceive Diet Coke to have the following levels of performance (the *X*s) and desired performance (the *I*s) on four attributes:

Low price			*I*	*X*				High price
Sweet taste		*I*				*X*		Bitter taste
High status			*I*		*X*			Low status
Low calories	*IX*							High calories
	(1)	(2)	(3)	(4)	(5)	(6)	(7)	

This segment of consumers believes (the *X*s) that Diet Coke is average priced, very bitter in taste, somewhat low in status, and extremely low in calories. Their ideal soda (the *I*s) would be slightly low priced, very sweet in taste, somewhat high in status, and extremely low in calories. Since these attributes are not equally important to consumers, they are assigned weights based on the relative importance a segment of consumers attaches to each.

A popular way of measuring importance weights is with a 100-point **constant-sum scale.** For example, the importance weights shown below express the relative importance of the four soft-drink attributes such that the total adds up to 100 points.

Attribute	*Importance*
Price	10
Taste	30
Status	20
Calories	40
	100 points

In this case, calories are considered the most important attribute, with taste slightly less important. Price is given little importance.

From this information, we can index this segment's attitude toward Diet Coke as follows:

$$
\begin{aligned}
A_{Diet\ Coke} &= (10)(|3-4|)1(30)(|2-6|)1(20)(|3-5|)1(40)(|1-1|) \\
&= (10)(1)1(30)(4)1(20)(2)1(40)(0) \\
&= 170
\end{aligned}
$$

This involves taking the absolute difference between the consumer's ideal soft-drink attributes and beliefs about Diet Coke's attributes and multiplying these differences times the importance attached to each attribute. In this case, the attitude index is computed as 170. Is this good or bad?

An attitude index is a relative measure, so in order to fully evaluate it, we must compare it to the segment's attitudes toward competing products or brands. However, if Diet Coke were perceived as their ideal soft drink, then all their beliefs and ideals would be equal and an attitude index of zero would be computed. Thus, the closer an attitude index calculated in this manner is to zero, the better.

We have been discussing the multiattribute view of the cognitive component as though consumers explicitly and consciously went through a series of deliberate evaluations and summed them to form an overall impression. However, this level of effort would occur only in very high-involvement purchase situations. In general, the multiattribute attitude model merely *represents* a nonconscious process that is much less precise and structured than implied by the model.

ILLUSTRATION 11-1

Individuals differ in their affective reactions to product characteristics. Likewise, the same individual will react differently to the same attributes or outcomes in different situations.

Courtesy Cycle-Ops Products.

Affective Component

Our feelings or emotional reactions to an object represent the **affective component** of an attitude. A consumer who states, "I like Diet Coke," or "Diet Coke is a terrible soda," is expressing the results of an emotional or affective evaluation of the product. This overall evaluation may be simply a vague, general feeling developed without cognitive information or beliefs about the product. Or, it may be the result of several evaluations of the product's performance on each of several attributes. Thus, the statements, "Diet Coke tastes bad," and "Diet Coke is not good for your health," imply a negative affective reaction to specific aspects of the product that, in combination with feelings about other attributes, will determine the overall reaction to the brand.

Since products, like other objects we react to, are evaluated in the context of a specific situation, a consumer's affective reaction to a product may change as the situation changes. For example, a consumer may believe that (1) Diet Coke has caffeine and (2) caffeine will keep you awake. These beliefs may cause a positive affective response when a consumer needs to stay awake to study for an exam and a negative response when he wants to drink something late in the evening that won't keep him awake later.

Due to unique motivations and personalities, past experiences, reference groups, and physical conditions, individuals may evaluate the same belief differently. Some individuals may have a positive feeling toward the belief that "Diet Coke is made by a large multinational firm," while others could respond with a negative reaction. Would you enjoy this situation: "Muscles screaming. Heart pounding. Lungs feeling as if they could burst"? This is the "benefit" the ad shown in Illustration 11-1 promises. Some individuals in some situations do evaluate these outcomes positively!

Despite individual variations, most individuals within a given culture react in a similar manner to beliefs that are closely associated with cultural values. For example, beliefs and feelings about a restaurant with respect to cleanliness are likely to be very similar among individuals in the United States, since cleanliness is highly valued in this culture. Thus, there often is a strong association between how a belief is evaluated and a related value that is of importance within a culture.

While feelings are often the result of evaluating specific attributes of a product, they can precede and influence cognitions. In fact, one may come to like a product without acquiring any cognitive beliefs about the product. Indeed, our initial reaction to a product may be one of like or dislike without any cognitive basis for the feeling. This initial affect can then influence how we react to the product itself.[5]

Behavioral Component

The **behavioral component** of an attitude *is one's tendency to respond in a certain manner toward an object or activity.* A series of decisions to purchase or not purchase Diet Coke or to recommend it or other brands to friends would reflect the behavioral component of an attitude. As we will see in the next section, the behavioral component provides response tendencies or behavioral intentions. *Our actual behaviors reflect these intentions as they are modified by the situation in which the behavior will occur.*

Since behavior is generally directed toward an entire object, it is less likely to be attribute specific than are either beliefs or affect. However, this is not always the case, particularly with respect to retail outlets. For example, many consumers buy canned goods at discount or warehouse-type grocery outlets but purchase meats and fresh vegetables at regular supermarkets. Thus, for retail outlets, it is possible and common to react behaviorally to specific beliefs about the outlet. This is generally difficult to do with products because we have to either buy or not buy the complete product.

Component Consistency

Figure 11-2 illustrates a critical aspect of attitudes: *All three attitude components tend to be consistent.* This means that a change in one attitude component tends to produce related changes in the other components. This tendency is the basis for a substantial amount of marketing strategy.[6]

Attitude Component Consistency **FIGURE 11-2**

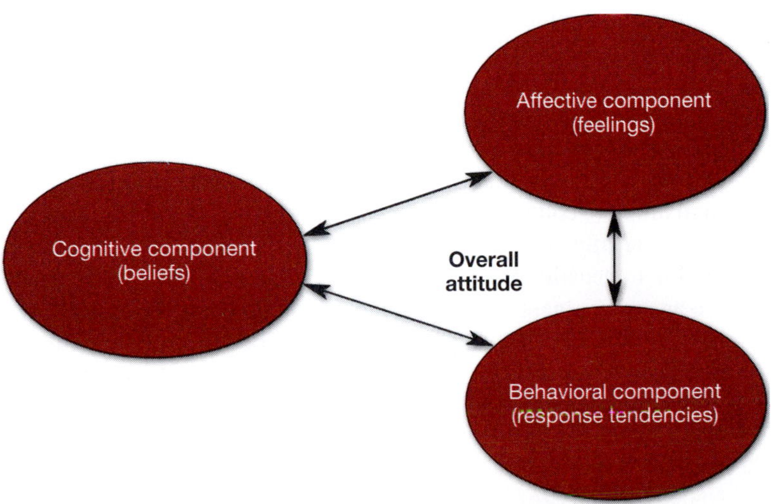

As marketing managers, we are ultimately concerned with influencing behavior. However, it is often difficult to influence behavior directly. That is, we generally are unable to directly cause consumers to buy, use, or recommend our products. However, consumers will often listen to our sales personnel, attend to our advertisements, or examine our packages. We can, therefore, indirectly influence behavior by providing information, music, or other stimuli that influence a belief or feeling about the product if the three components are indeed consistent with each other.

A number of research studies have found only a limited relationship among the three components.[7] Let's examine the sources of this inconsistency by considering an example. Suppose an individual has a set of positive beliefs toward the Palm VII™ organizer and also has a positive affective response to this brand and model. Further, suppose that these beliefs and affect are more favorable toward the Palm VII™ than any other product of this nature. Our customer responds to a questionnaire and indicates these positive beliefs and feelings. However, the consumer does not own a Palm VII™, or purchases another brand or model. Thus, a researcher might conclude that the three components are not consistent.

At least seven factors can operate to reduce the consistency between *measures* of beliefs and feelings and *observations* of behavior.

1. A favorable attitude requires a need or motive before it can be translated into action. Thus, our consumer may not feel a need for a portable organizer or might already own an acceptable, though less preferred, brand.
2. Translating favorable beliefs and feelings into ownership requires ability.[8] One might not own a Palm VII™ or might purchase a less expensive model due to insufficient funds to purchase a Palm VII™.
3. We measured attitudes only toward organizers. Purchases often involve trade-offs not only within but also between product categories. Thus, our consumer might purchase a less expensive organizer in order to save resources to buy skis, a computer, or a vacation.
4. If the cognitive and affective components are weakly held, and if the consumer obtains additional information while shopping, then the initial attitudes may give way to new ones.
5. We measured an individual's attitudes. However, as we saw in Chapter 6, many purchase decisions involve other household members either directly or indirectly. Thus, our shopper may purchase something other than a Palm VII™ in order to better meet the needs of the entire family.
6. We generally measure brand attitudes independent of the purchase situation. However, many items are purchased for, or in, specific situations.[9] A very inexpensive organizer might be purchased if the consumer anticipates access to more sophisticated equipment in the near future.

   The **theory of reasoned action** is based in part on this concept.[10] It holds that behavioral intentions are based on a combination of the attitude toward a specific behavior, the social or normative beliefs about the appropriateness of the behavior, and the motivation to comply with the normative beliefs. Thus, a consumer might have a very favorable attitude toward having a drink before dinner at a restaurant. However, the intention to actually order the drink will be influenced by the consumer's beliefs about the appropriateness of ordering a drink in the current situation (with friends for a fun meal or on a job interview) and her motivation to comply with those normative beliefs.
7. It is difficult to measure all of the relevant aspects of an attitude. Consumers may be unwilling or unable to articulate all of their feelings and beliefs about various products or brands. Therefore, attitude components are sometimes more consistent than our measures suggest them to be.

In summary, attitude components—cognitive, affective, and behavioral—tend to be consistent. However, the degree of apparent consistency between measures of cognitions and affect and observations of behavior may be reduced by a variety of factors, as mentioned above. Further, it is critical to remember that the behavioral component is a response tendency, not an actual behavior. Response tendencies are manifest in many ways short of purchase, such as being receptive to new information about the brand, complimenting others who purchase it, and so forth.

Measurement of Attitude Components

Purchase and use behavior at the brand level are predicted most accurately by overall measures of brand liking or affect. However, since components of attitudes are often an integral part of a marketing strategy, it is important that we be able to measure each component. Common approaches to measuring the components are shown in Table 11-1 and discussed briefly below. Additional details are provided in Appendix A.

Measuring Beliefs In Table 11-1, the beliefs about Diet Coke are measured using a **semantic differential scale.** This scale lists the various attributes and characteristics of a

TABLE 11-1

Measuring Attitude Components

Cognitive Component (Measuring Beliefs about Specific Attributes Using the Semantic Differential Scale)

Diet Coke

Strong taste	—	—	—	—	—	—	—	Mild taste
Low priced	—	—	—	—	—	—	—	High priced
Caffeine free	—	—	—	—	—	—	—	High in caffeine
Distinctive in taste	—	—	—	—	—	—	—	Similar in taste to most

Affective Component (Measuring Feelings about Specific Attributes or the Overall Brand Using Likert Scales)

	Strongly Agree	*Agree*	*Neither Agree nor Disagree*	*Disagree*	*Strongly Disagree*
I like the taste of Diet Coke.	____	____	____	____	____
Diet Coke is overpriced.	____	____	____	____	____
Caffeine is bad for your health.	____	____	____	____	____
I like Diet Coke.	____	____	____	____	____

Behavioral Component (Measuring Actions or Intended Actions)

The last soft drink I consumed was a __________.

I usually drink __________ soft drinks.

What is the likelihood you will buy Diet Coke the next time you purchase a soft drink?

____ Definitely will buy
____ Probably will buy
____ Might buy
____ Probably will not buy
____ Definitely will not buy

brand that might be part of the target market's attitude toward the brand. These characteristics can be discovered through focus group interviews (in-depth discussions with 6 to 12 consumers at a time—see Appendix A), projective techniques, and logical analysis. Each characteristic is presented in terms of the opposite extremes that it might have, such as large/small, light/dark, or fast/slow.

These extremes are separated by five to seven spaces. Consumers are asked to indicate how closely one or the other extreme describes the item being evaluated by placing an X in the appropriate space where the end positions indicate "extremely," the next pair in from either end represent "very," the next pair in indicate "somewhat," and the middle position means "neither-nor."

Consumers' beliefs about the ideal brand are also frequently measured using semantic differential scales. The process is the same as described above except the ideal brand is generally indicated by placing an *I* in the appropriate space rather than an *X*.

The Likert scale described below can also be used to measure beliefs about existing brands and the ideal brand.

Measuring Feelings The Likert scale shown in Table 11-1 also requires a list of the various attributes and characteristics of a brand that might be part of the target market's attitude toward the brand. The list can be generated in the same manner described above for the semantic differential scale.

In a **Likert scale,** the various characteristics the brand might have are placed in statements claiming the brand has a certain characteristic or that the consumer has a specific affective response to the overall brand or an aspect of it. An example is "Going to McDonald's makes me feel happy." Consumers are then asked to state a degree of agreement or disagreement with the statement. As shown in Table 11-1, five levels of agreement are usually used.

In Chapter 10, several sophisticated approaches to measuring affective reactions to advertisements were described. These approaches can also be used to measure the feeling or emotional reactions to a brand or activity.

Measuring Response Tendencies Response tendencies are most often measured by fairly direct questioning, as shown in Table 11-1. For many products, this works quite well. However, for products for which there are strong social norms, such as alcohol or pornography consumption, eating patterns, and media usage, it works less well. People tend to understate the consumption or the intention to consume negative products such as alcohol and to overstate their consumption of positive products such as educational television.

In such cases, carefully worded questions and indirect questions can sometimes help. For example, rather than asking a person about his or her consumption of such products, some researchers ask them to estimate the consumption of other people similar to themselves such as their neighbors or people with similar jobs.

ATTITUDE CHANGE STRATEGIES

The attitude change induced by manipulating the marketing mix for Marlboro, as described in the opening vignette, is a classic in marketing history. As this example illustrates, managers can form and change attitudes toward products and brands. It also raises ethical questions concerning how firms use this knowledge. In addition to ethical issues, it poses difficult challenges to regulators who want to limit the ability of firms to develop favorable attitudes toward products whose consumption may prove harmful to some portion of the population.

Changing Consumer Attitudes

What do you think of when you see the word *plastic?* Would you be pleased to know that the body of a car you are considering purchasing is primarily plastic, or would you prefer metal? Do you feel more comfortable using and recycling a paper cup or a Styrofoam cup? Many consumers think of plastic as cheap, artificial, weak, breakable, nondegradable, environmentally harmful, and otherwise undesirable. These negative attitudes affect consumers' willingness to purchase products containing plastic and their willingness to support legislation restricting the ways plastic is used.

The American Plastics Council recently spent $18 million on a six-month advertising campaign to improve consumers' and legislators' attitudes toward plastic. About $12 million was spent on television advertising, with the rest split between print and radio.

One of the four spots began at a grocery checkout where the clerk sees a shopper with numerous plastic containers and says: "When you look at plastic, you know how it helps things stay fresh and safe and unbreakable and easy to carry. But take another look." (The checkout stand is passed by a moving car and then the stand itself seems to pass in front of a suburban home.) "Plastic also saves energy because it helps make cars lighter and saves gas. And plastic insulation helps save energy at home." (Now the clerk grabs two plastic bags full of groceries.) "Even these strong plastic bags, because they take less energy to make than other grocery bags." The ad closes with the slogan: "Take another look at plastic." (See Illustration 11-3 for an additional ad from the Plastics Council.

Will this campaign succeed? Jackie Prince, a scientist with the Environmental Defense Fund, does not think so:

> People don't dislike plastics; they just don't know what to do with them when they're done. An advertising campaign that focuses on perceptions, on plastics' advantages, is not going to work. You've got to change the underlying reality.

While Prince feels that no advertising campaign can make plastics acceptable to environmentally concerned consumers, advertising expert Bob Garfield is critical of this specific approach to changing attitudes:

> For a campaign such as this to have impact, it must confront consumer mistrust and then convert it, saying, in effect "We know you think we're scum. Here's why you're wrong." Then it could enumerate various plastics myths and one by one explode them, or exhaust viewers with an endless litany of products, from plastic replacement heart valves to Vibram soles, that they cannot live without. A great plastics campaign would first shame us for obsessing about liter bottles to the exclusion of the myriad ways plastic has improved the lives of billions, and then impress us about how the industry, in its own self-interest, is spending millions to make bottle recycling work.

Critical Thinking Questions

1. Will this campaign work? How could it be improved?
2. What dangers does the possibility that advertising can change attitudes significantly present? 
3. Should public schools educate students about commonly used attitude change tactics?

Source: J. Gardner, "Plastics Seek $18M Image Boost," *Advertising Age,* November 9, 1992, p. 12; and B. Garfield, "Plastics Industry Molds Wrong Approach in Ads," *Advertising Age,* November 23, 1992, p. 38.

Consumer Insight 11-1

Consider Consumer Insight 11-1. Can attitudes toward plastic be improved? Is the approach described the best approach? The balance of this chapter is designed to help you develop the knowledge to answer questions such as these.

Change the Affective Component

It is increasingly common for a firm to attempt to influence consumers' liking of their brand without directly influencing either beliefs or behavior. If the firm is successful, increased liking will tend to lead to increased positive beliefs, which could lead to purchase behavior

ILLUSTRATION 11-2

Ads can change the affective component of an attitude toward a brand without altering the belief structure if the ad itself elicits a positive response (is liked). Ads that are primarily pictorial are often used for this purpose, though the pictures themselves convey cognitive as well as emotional meanings.

should a need for the product category arise. Or, perhaps more commonly, increased liking will lead to a tendency to purchase the brand should a need arise, with purchase and use leading to increased positive beliefs. Marketers use three basic approaches to directly increase affect: classical conditioning, affect toward the ad itself, and "mere exposure."

Classical Conditioning One way of directly influencing the affective component is through classical conditioning (see Chapter 9). In this approach, a stimulus the audience likes, such as music, is consistently paired with the brand name. Over time, some of the positive affect associated with the music will transfer to the brand.[11] Other "liked" stimuli, such as pictures, are frequently used for this reason.

Affect toward the Ad As we saw in Chapter 10, liking the advertisement generally increases the tendency to like the product.[12] Positive affect toward the ad may increase liking of the brand through classical conditioning, or it may be a more high-involvement, conscious process. Using humor, celebrities, or emotional appeals increases affect toward the ad. Each is discussed in the last section of this chapter. Illustration 11-2 contains an ad that relies on positive affect.

Ads that arouse negative affect or emotions such as fear, guilt, or sorrow can also enhance attitude change. For example, an ad for a charity assisting refuges could show pictures that would elicit a variety of unpleasant emotions such as disgust or anger and still be effective.[13]

Recent research has also found that affect aroused by the programming surrounding the ad influences how the ad is processed and its impact on attitudes.[14]

Mere Exposure While controversial, there is evidence that affect may also be increased by **mere exposure.**[15] That is, simply presenting a brand to an individual on a large number of occasions might make the individual's attitude toward the brand more positive. Thus, the repetition of advertisements for low-involvement products may well increase liking and subsequent purchase of the advertised brands without altering the initial belief structure.

Classical conditioning, affect toward the ad itself, and mere exposure can alter affect directly and, by altering affect, indirectly alter purchase behavior without first changing beliefs. This has a number of important implications:

- Ads designed to alter affect need not contain any cognitive (factual or attribute) information.
- Classical conditioning principles should guide such campaigns.
- Attitudes (liking) toward the ad itself are critical for this type of campaign (unless mere exposure is being used).
- Repetition is critical for affect-based campaigns.
- Traditional measures of advertising effectiveness focus on the cognitive component and are inappropriate for affect-based campaigns.

Change the Behavioral Component

Behavior, specifically purchase or use behavior, may precede the development of cognition and affect. Or, it may occur in contrast to the cognitive and affective components. For example, a consumer may dislike the taste of diet soft drinks and believe that artificial sweeteners are unhealthy. However, rather than appear rude, the same consumer may accept a diet drink when offered one by a friend (see the discussion of reasoned action above, p. 400). Drinking the beverage may alter her perceptions of its taste and lead to liking; this in turn may lead to increased learning, which changes the cognitive component. Evidence suggests that attitudes formed as a consequence of product trial are strongly held.[16]

Behavior can lead directly to affect, to cognitions, or to both simultaneously.[17] Consumers frequently try new brands or types of low-cost items in the absence of prior knowledge or affect. Such purchases are as much for information ("Will I like this brand?") as for satisfaction of some underlying need such as hunger.

Changing behavior prior to changing affect or cognition is based primarily on operant conditioning (see Chapter 9). Thus, the key marketing task is to induce people to purchase or consume the product while ensuring that the purchase and/or consumption will indeed be rewarding.[18] Coupons, free samples, point-of-purchase displays, tie-in purchases, and price reductions are common techniques for inducing trial behavior (see Illustration 9-2, p. 331). Since behavior often leads to strong positive attitudes toward the consumed brand, a sound distribution system (limited stockouts) is important to prevent current customers from trying competing brands.

Change the Cognitive Component

A common and effective approach to changing attitudes is to focus on the cognitive component.[19] Thus, to change attitudes toward cigarette smoking, the American Cancer Society has presented information on the negative health consequences of smoking. The theory is that by influencing this belief, affect and behavior will then change.

Four basic marketing strategies are used for altering the cognitive structure of a consumer's attitude.

ILLUSTRATION 11-3

The cognitive component of an attitude can be altered by changing current beliefs, adding new beliefs, shifting the importance of beliefs, or changing the beliefs about the ideal product. This ad focuses primarily on changing beliefs.

Courtesy American Plastics Council.

Change Beliefs This strategy involves shifting beliefs about the performance of the brand on one or more attributes. For example, many consumers believe that American cars are not as well made as Japanese cars. A substantial amount of advertising for American automobiles is designed to change this belief. Attempts to change beliefs generally provide "facts" or statements about performance. Illustration 11-3 shows an ad for plastics that is designed to change the belief held by many consumers that plastics are harmful for the environment. Does the attitude change any of your beliefs about plastic?

Shift Importance Most consumers consider some product attributes to be more important than others. Marketers often try to convince consumers that those attributes on which their brands are relatively strong are the most important. For example, Quaker Oatmeal currently stresses the fact that consumption of its ingredients has been shown to reduce the risks of heart disease. It now uses themes such as "Thinking about a heart-healthy breakfast?" to make this attribute more important to consumers.

Add Beliefs Another approach to changing the cognitive component of an attitude is to add new beliefs to the consumer's belief structure. Budweiser recently began promoting freshness in the form of its "born on date" as an important attribute for a beer. Before this campaign, few considered the age of a beer to be a relevant attribute.

Change Ideal The final strategy for changing the cognitive component is to change the perceptions of the ideal brand or situation. Thus, many conservation organizations strive to influence our beliefs about the ideal product in terms of minimal packaging, nonpolluting manufacturing, extensive use of recycled materials, and nonpolluting disposition after its useful life.

INDIVIDUAL AND SITUATIONAL CHARACTERISTICS THAT INFLUENCE ATTITUDE CHANGE

Attitude change is determined by the individual and the situation as well as the activities of the firm or social agency. There are individual differences in how easily individuals will shift attitudes. Some people are more "stubborn" or "closed-minded" or less subject to social influence than are others.[20]

Attitudes that are strongly held are more difficult to change than are attitudes that are weakly held. Think of something you feel strongly about—perhaps your school, your favorite sports team or band, or a disliked behavior such as chewing tobacco. What would be required to change your attitude about this item or activity? Clearly, it would be difficult. First, you would tend to avoid messages that were counter to your attitude. Few committed smokers read articles on the harmful effects of smoking. And, if you do encounter such messages, you tend to discount them. Thus, most marketers do not try to capture sales from consumers who are committed to competing brands. Rather, they focus on those who are less committed, as these consumers are more willing to attend and respond to their messages.

Consumers are not passive when marketers attempt to change their attitudes.[21] Instead, they frequently infer the advertiser's intent and respond to the communications in light of a presumed selling intent. For example, a consumer could respond to the American Plastics Council ad in Illustration 11-3 as follows: "They only want to avoid regulation, so they are trying to fool people. They don't really care about the environment." To avoid such an interpretation, The Council put factual evidence about plastics in the ad. Another approach would have been to use a highly credible source such as a well-known environmentalist or scientist.

The consumer reaction described above presumed a highly involved consumer. Indeed, the ad itself attempts to generate involvement by the use of the question in the headline and the picture of the two apparently identical jugs. If the headline does not generate a fairly high level of involvement and processing, it will fail. An alternative would be to presume limited involvement. Such an ad might feature a pleasant aspect of the environment, a simple headline such as "Plastics make a difference," and limited text. A consumer might glance at this ad and make a connection, perhaps without even "thinking about it," between a healthy environment and plastics.

The **elaboration likelihood model (ELM)** is a theory about how attitudes are formed and changed under varying conditions of involvement as described above.[22] The ELM suggests that brand involvement (the degree of personal relevance of the brand, which may change with the situation) and decision motivation are key determinants of how information is processed and attitudes are changed. High involvement results in a "central route" to attitude change by which consumers deliberately and largely consciously examine and process those message elements that they believe are relevant to a meaningful and logical evaluation of the brand (see Figure 11-3). These elements are elaborated on (combined with other bits of information, related to past experiences and potential outcomes, and so forth), compared to existing knowledge, and combined into an overall evaluation. The multiattribute attitude model represents a high-involvement view of attitude change.

In contrast, low involvement results in a "peripheral" route to attitude change, in which consumers form impressions of the brand based on exposure to the readily available cues in the message regardless of the relevance of those cues to the brand itself. Thus, such aspects as the consumption environment portrayed, the characteristics of the people in the ad, the package, and similar cues may be all that is attended to.

FIGURE 11-3 The Elaboration Likelihood Model

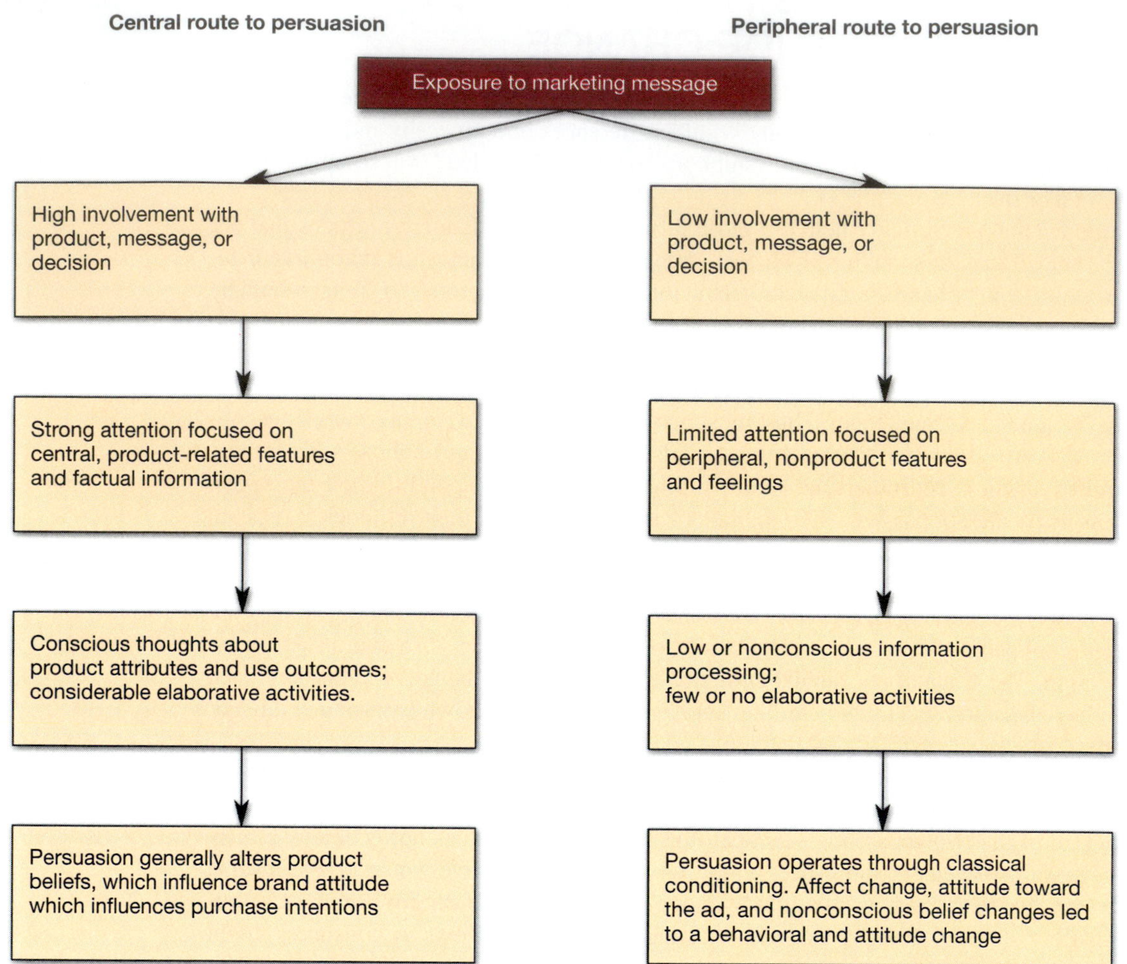

The ELM suggests that vastly different communications strategies are required to communicate effectively with consumers highly involved with the product compared to consumers with little product involvement. In general, more detailed, factual, and logical information can be used in high-involvement, central processing situations. Low-involvement, peripheral route situations generally require limited information, such as pictorial ads that allow quick association of the key attribute with the brand. Or, techniques such as the question headline shown in Illustration 11-3 can be used to increase involvement and processing level.

COMMUNICATION CHARACTERISTICS THAT INFLUENCE ATTITUDE FORMATION AND CHANGE

Attitudes are influenced most strongly when the brand has something unique to offer and the unique benefits of the brand are the focus of the commercial.[23] In this section, we describe communication techniques that enhance attitude change when unique brand features are present as well as when a brand does not have unique benefits. It must be emphasized that, as with all aspects of consumer behavior, individual and situational characteristics interact with the communication features to determine effectiveness.[24]

Source Characteristics

The source of a communication can be an identifiable person, an unidentifiable person (a "typical" homemaker), a company or organization, or an inanimate figure such as a cartoon character. The source of a message is important because consumers respond differently to the same message delivered by different sources.

Source Credibility Influencing attitudes is easier when the target market views the source of the message as highly credible. This is referred to as **source credibility.** Both firms and advocacy groups frequently serve as sources of messages promoting attitude and behavioral changes with respect to products and activities.

Source credibility appears to be composed of two basic dimensions: *trustworthiness* and *expertise.*[25] A source that has no apparent reason other than to provide complete, objective, and accurate information would generally be considered trustworthy. Most of us would consider our good friends trustworthy on most matters. However, our friends might not have the knowledge necessary to be credible in a certain area. While sales personnel and advertisers often have ample knowledge, many consumers doubt the trustworthiness of sales personnel and advertisers because it might be to their advantage to mislead the consumer.

Individuals who are recognized experts and who have no apparent motive to mislead can be influential sources. However, when consumers believe that the firm is paying the source for his or her endorsement, this effectiveness is diminished.[26] Likewise, a relatively unknown individual who is similar to the target market can be an effective spokesperson. In a **testimonial ad,** *a person, generally a typical member of the target market, recounts his or her successful use of the product, service, or idea.* Such ads can be quite effective.[27]

Organizations that are widely viewed as both trustworthy and expert, such as the American Dental Association (ADA), can have a tremendous influence on attitudes. The remarkable success of Crest toothpaste is largely attributable to the ADA endorsement. Underwriters' Laboratories, *Good Housekeeping,* and other trustworthy and expert sources are widely sought for their endorsements. However, such endorsements do not always enhance the believability of the message.[28] Like other sources, they are most likely to be effective when consumers lack the ability to form direct judgments of the product's performance or the value of engaging in the promoted behavior and have faith in the endorsing organization.[29] The following quotes illustrate these points as actual consumers see them.

> I don't like insurance companies. Insurance is such a pain; it's confusing on purpose. You pay all this money in premiums, then when you have to use it; they raise your premiums like you haven't already paid for the service. So if an insurance company was trying to tell me something about AIDS or drinking and driving, I wouldn't believe one word.
>
> "Just say no?" Those people saying that don't live in the projects like I do. They're sitting up in their big offices saying, "all those people got to do is say no." How do they know what my kid's life is like? I've got drug dealers on my corner everyday telling my kids they can get rich and have things if they sell. I have to tell my kids that they have to wait, be patient, go to school, make good grades then they might get a job. So don't try to talk to me if you don't know what my life is like.
>
> If Ronald McDonald or McDonald's speaks, kids and parents will stop and listen because the kids know all the characters and kids like the food. And they have a good history of service in children's charities. It seems like they genuinely care about more than just selling junk food to kids.[30]

Celebrity Sources Celebrities are widely used in advertising in the United States, and evidence indicates that their use may increase a firm's value.[31] The most visible use of celebrity endorsers in recent years has been the mustache campaign for milk (see Illustration 10-2,

ILLUSTRATION 11-4

Celebrity sources and humor can attract attention and help shift attitudes when properly employed. This ad uses both, as well as an element of shock.

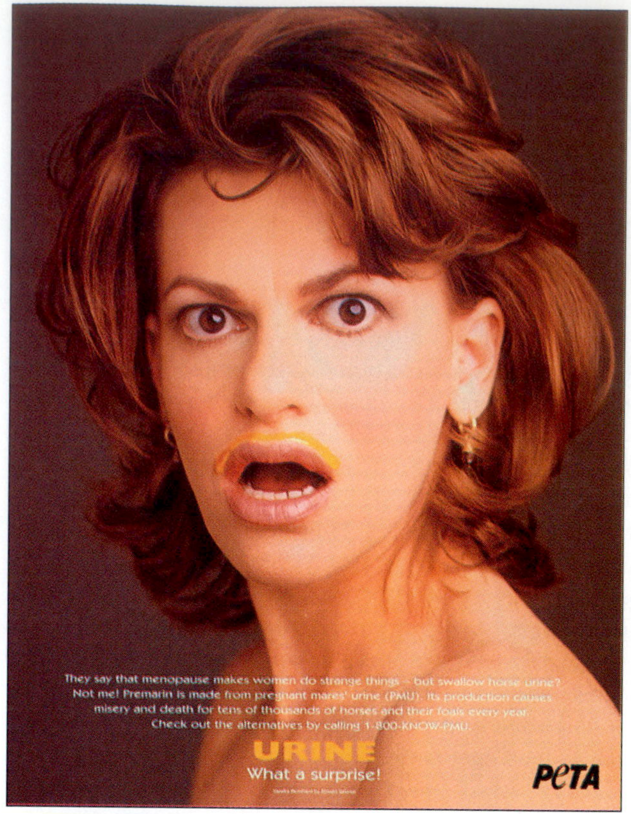

Courtesy PETA; photographer: Robert Serbee; model: Sandra Bernhard.

page 366). People for the Ethical Treatment of Animals (PETA) used comedian Sandra Bernhard in a take-off on the mustache campaign to increase consumer concern about the way horses are used in the preparation of Premarin (see Illustration 11-4).

Celebrity sources may enhance attitude change for a variety of reasons.[32] They may attract more attention to the advertisement than would noncelebrities. Or, in many cases, they may be viewed as more credible than noncelebrities. Third, consumers may identify with or desire to emulate the celebrity. Finally, consumers may associate known characteristics of the celebrity with attributes of the product that coincide with their own needs or desires.

The effectiveness of using a celebrity to endorse a firm's product can generally be improved by matching the image of the celebrity with the personality of the product and the actual or desired self-concept of the target market. For example, skier Picabo Street is leading Nike's attempt to enhance its image and sales among young girls. Her image of reckless enthusiasm and a disregard for the status quo fits with both Nike's image and the desired image of many young women. According to a Nike executive; "Her energy and personality appeal strongly to young girls and we will be using her to support our girls' sports initiatives."[33]

When the three components shown in Figure 11-4 are well matched, effective attitude formation or change can result.[34] For example, celebrity endorsements by Jimmy Connors and Joe Montana are credited with increasing Nuprin's sales almost 25 percent. Their images as maturing athletes now subject to aches and pains matched well with the target market and the product.

Matching Endorser with Product and Target Audience **FIGURE 11-4**

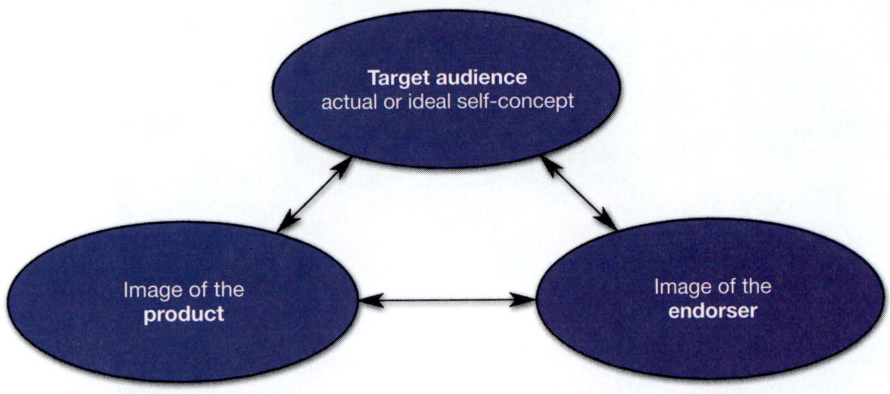

There is evidence that **sponsorship advertising,** a company being the identified sponsor of an event such as the Olympics or a rock concert, works in much the same manner as using a celebrity endorser. That is, the characteristics of the sponsored event may become associated with the sponsoring organization. Such an association is most likely and most effective when the match-up described in Figure 11-4 occurs, with the event taking the place of the endorser.[35]

Using a celebrity as a company spokesperson creates special risks for the sponsoring organization. Few well-known personalities are admired by everyone. Thus, it is important to be certain that most of the members of the relevant target markets will respond favorably to the spokesperson. As the same celebrity endorses additional products, consumers' reactions to the celebrity and the ads containing the celebrity become less positive. Thus, marketers need to limit the number of products "their" celebrities endorse.[36]

An additional risk is that some behavior involving the spokesperson will affect the individual's credibility after he or she is associated with the firm.[37] For example, while serving as spokespersons for the Beef Industry Council, Cybill Shepherd admitted in a magazine interview that she avoided red meat and James Garner had heart surgery. PepsiCo has had problems with commercials featuring Madonna (after a controversial video), Mike Tyson (after his conviction for rape), Magic Johnson (after acquiring AIDS through an admittedly extensive series of affairs), and Michael Jackson (after child molestation charges). Campbell Soup distanced itself from Reggie White after he made controversial remarks concerning homosexuality.

Rather than use celebrity spokespersons, many firms are creating **spokes-characters.**[38] Tony the Tiger and the Green Giant are perhaps the most famous such characters. Spokes-characters can be animated animals, people, products, or other objects. Betty Crocker is an example of a realistic, fictitious human spokesperson, while Count Chocula is a caricature of a fictitious person.

A major advantage of spokes-characters is the ability to have complete control over the character. This eliminates or reduces many of the problems associated with real celebrities. Such characters can come to symbolize the brand and give it an identity that competitors cannot easily duplicate. Illustration 11-5 shows Boxman, who serves as a spokes-character for Arm & Hammer's baking soda.

ILLUSTRATION 11-5

Spokes-characters are gaining popularity. They can add credibility to a message as well as attract attention. Some come to serve as a symbol of the product.

Courtesy Church & Dwight Co., Inc.

Appeal Characteristics

Fear Appeals

The picture at the top of an ad is a snapshot of a young couple sitting together on their back deck. The headline reads: "I woke up in the hospital. Patti never woke up." The copy describes how carbon monoxide poisoning caused the tragedy. The ad, one of a series of similar ads, is for First Alert carbon monoxide detector.

Fear appeals make use of *the threat of negative (unpleasant) consequences if attitudes or behaviors are not altered.* While fear appeals have been studied primarily in terms of physical fear (physical harm from smoking, unsafe driving, and so forth), social fears (disapproval of one's peers for incorrect clothing, bad breath, or inadequate coffee) are also used in advertising.[39]

There is some evidence that individuals avoid or distort extremely threatening messages. At the same time, fear appeals tend to be more effective as higher levels of fear are aroused. Thus, those using fear appeals want to maximize the level of fear aroused while not presenting a threat so intense as to cause the consumer to distort, reject, or avoid the message. This task is made difficult by the fact that individuals respond differently to threats. Thus, the same "threatening" advertisement may arouse no fear in one individual and a high level of fear in another.[40]

Partnership for a Drug-Free America

"TEETH/NATIONAL" :30 DEBB-3237

(MUSIC THROUGHOUT)

It's hard to face what heroin can do to you

Partnership for a Drug Free America

Courtesy Partnership for a Drug-Free America.

ILLUSTRATION 11-6

Fear appeals can be effective at forming, reinforcing, and/or changing attitudes. The ethics of such appeals should be examined carefully before they are used.

Using a fear appeal as a way to gain attention and stress the dangers of heroin use, the Partnership for a Drug-Free America sponsors the ad shown in Illustration 11-6. Is this an effective use of a fear appeal?

Fear appeals are frequently criticized as unethical. The most frequent target of such criticisms are fear appeals based on social anxieties about bad breathe, body odor, dandruff, or soiled clothes. The thrust of these complaints is that these appeals raise anxieties unnecessarily. That is, the injury or harm that they suggest will occur is unlikely to occur or is not really harmful. Fear appeals used to produce socially desirable behaviors such as avoiding drug use or avoiding acknowledged physical risks such a carbon monoxide poisoning are subject to much less criticism even though they often use more intense fear-arousing stimuli.[41]

It has been suggested that the ethics of any given fear appeal be evaluated in terms of its probable effects on three stakeholder groups—society, the consumer, and the firm or organization. These effects are then assessed based on four ethical reasoning approaches—the

ILLUSTRATION 11-7

Humor is used in many countries to attract attention and change attitudes.

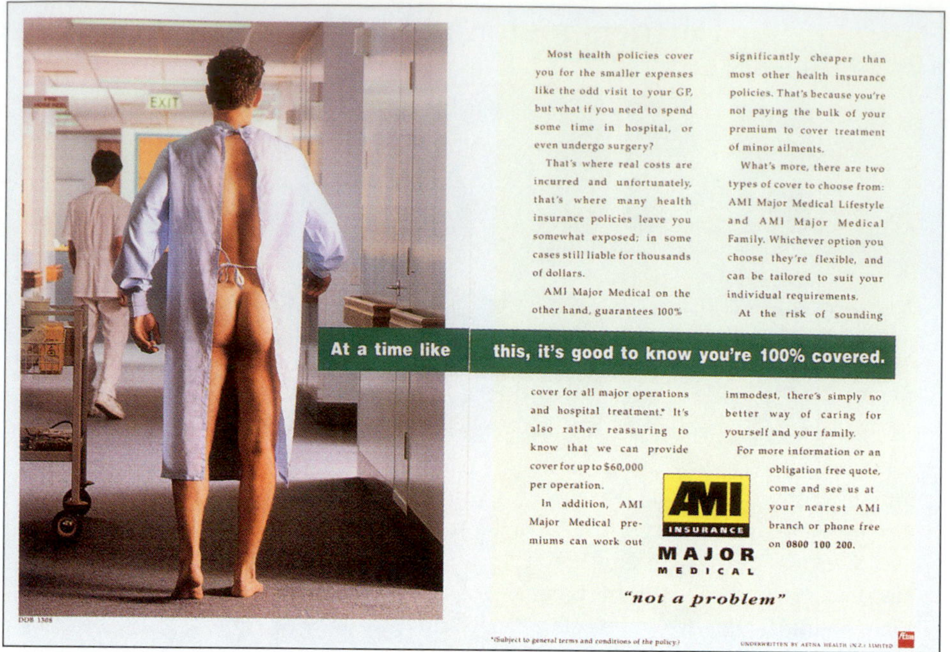

utilitarian (the greatest good for the greatest number), the golden rule (treat others as you want to be treated), Kantian (basic individual rights), or enlightened self-interest (benefits for self with minimum harm to others). This approach is referred to as the ethical effects-reasoning matrix (ERM). It does not produce a decision as to whether a particular fear appeal is ethical. It does ensure that the consequences of the appeal to the key stakeholders are considered from a variety of ethical perspectives.[42]

Humorous Appeals At almost the opposite end of the spectrum from fear appeals are **humorous appeals.**[43] Ads built around humor appear to increase attention to and liking of the ad. Their overall effectiveness is generally increased when the humor relates to the product or brand in a meaningful way and is viewed as appropriate for the product by the target audience.

Illustration 11-7 contains an ad from New Zealand that makes effective use of humor. Note that the humor ties very directly to the product. Other firms that are currently using humorous advertising closely tied to their product include the following:

- A Sunsweet Growers' commercial shows an attractive young woman in a swimsuit with the heading "This is an ad for prunes." As the camera zooms in on her attractive face, the message changes to "You expected something old and wrinkled?"
- Mitsubishi's *Montero Sport* television commercial shows the faces of several men applying mascara, eye shadow, and lipstick as another man drives on a country road. The point is made that the drive is smooth enough to allow the make-up to be applied accurately. At the end of the commercial, the men leave the vehicle as rodeo clowns.
- Air New Zealand's print ads show a smiling flight attendant and a puzzled business traveler. The business traveler says things such as "The flight attendant couldn't stop smiling. What was she on?"

While it is generally recommended that the humor tie directly to the product or brand, Budweiser has had success with its "lizard" campaign despite the fact that the commercial is only loosely tied to the product or brand.

Comparative Ads **Comparative ads** *directly compare the features or benefits of two or more brands.* Comparative ads are more effective than noncomparative ads in generating attention, message and brand awareness, levels of message processing, favorable sponsor brand attitudes, and increased purchase intentions and behaviors. They also evoke a lower level of source believability and a less favorable attitude toward the ad.[44] In addition, they do not always produce the positive benefits described above. At times, the results of such ads are negative for the sponsoring brand and/or positive for the comparator brand. Available evidence suggests that comparative ads should follow these guidelines:[45]

- Comparative advertising may be particularly effective for promoting new or little-known brands with strong product attributes.
- Comparative advertising is likely to be more effective if its claims are substantiated by credible sources.
- Comparative advertising may be used effectively to establish a brand's position or to upgrade its image by association.
- Audience characteristics, especially the extent of brand loyalty associated with the sponsoring brand, are important. Users or owners of the named competitor brands appear to be resistant to comparative claims.
- Since people consider comparative advertisements to be more interesting than noncomparative advertisements (as well as being more "offensive"), these commercials may be effective if the product category is relatively static and noncomparative advertising has ceased to be effective.
- Appropriate theme construction can significantly increase the overall effectiveness of comparative advertising.
- It is important to ascertain how many product attributes to mention in a comparative advertisement.
- Print media appear to be better vehicles for comparative advertisements, since print lends itself to more thorough comparisons.

Emotional Appeals Emotional or feeling ads are being used with increasing frequency. **Emotional ads** *are designed primarily to elicit a positive affective response rather than provide information or arguments.* As we saw in Chapter 10, emotional ads such as those that arouse feelings of warmth trigger a physiological reaction. They are also liked more than neutral ads and produce more positive attitudes toward the product. Emotional advertisements may enhance attitude formation or change by increasing:[46]

- The ad's ability to attract and maintain attention.
- The level of mental processing given the ad.
- Ad memorability.
- Liking of the ad.
- Product liking through classical conditioning.
- Product liking through high-involvement processes.

Illustrations 11-8 and 10-7 (page 384) are designed to elicit emotional responses.

Value-Expressive versus Utilitarian Appeals **Value-expressive appeals** *attempt to build a personality for the product or create an image of the product user.* **Utilitarian appeals** *involve informing the consumer of the functional benefits that are important to the target market.* Which is best under what conditions?

Both theory and some empirical evidence indicate that utilitarian appeals are most effective for utilitarian products and value-expressive appeals are most effective for value-expressive products.[47] That is, one generally should not do image advertising for lawn

ILLUSTRATION 11-8

Ads such as this one evoke powerful emotional responses in some individuals. These emotional responses often facilitate attitude change.

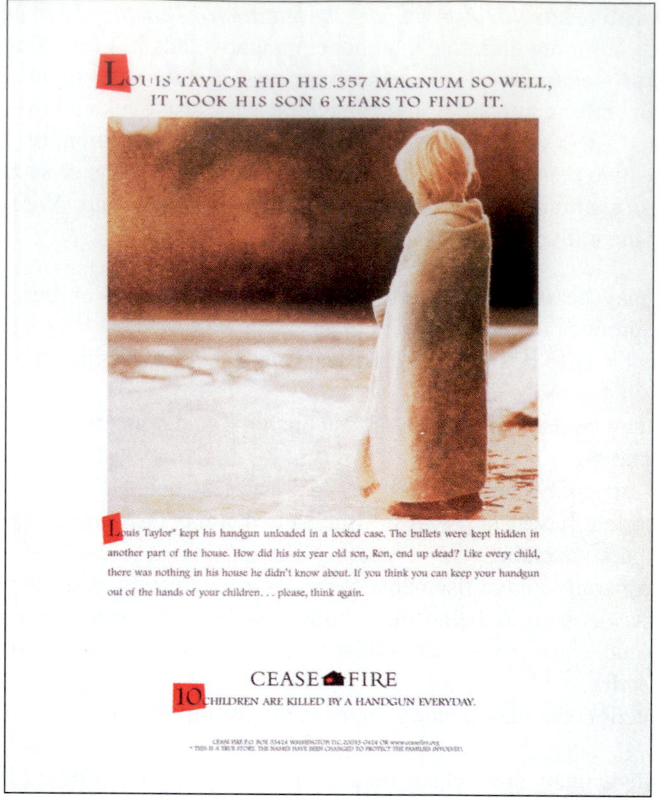

Courtesy Cease Fire, Inc.

fertilizers or factual advertising for perfumes. However, many products such as automobiles, some cosmetics, and clothes serve both utilitarian and functional purposes. Which approach is best for these products? There is no simple answer. Some marketers opt to present both types of appeals, others focus on one or the other, and still others vary their approach across market segments. Illustration 11-9 contains an example of each approach.

Message Structure Characteristics

One-Sided versus Two-Sided Messages In advertisements and sales presentations, marketers generally present only the benefits of their product without mentioning any negative characteristics it might possess or any advantages a competitor might have. These are **one-sided messages,** since only one point of view is expressed. The idea of a **two-sided message,** presenting both good and bad points, is counterintuitive, and most marketers are reluctant to try such an approach. However, two-sided messages are generally more effective than one-sided messages in terms of changing a strongly held attitude. In addition, they are particularly effective with highly educated consumers. One-sided messages are most effective at reinforcing existing attitudes. However, product type, situational variables, and advertisement format influence the relative effectiveness of the two approaches.[48]

Nonverbal Components In Chapter 9, we discussed how pictures enhance imagery and facilitate learning. Pictures, music, surrealism, and other nonverbal cues are also effective in attitude change.[49] Emotional ads, described earlier, often rely primarily or exclu-

Courtesy Palm Computing, Inc.

Courtesy Coty, Inc.

ILLUSTRATION 11-9

Utilitarian appeals generally work best with functional products, while value-expressive appeals work best with products designed to enhance one's image or provide other intangible benefits.

sively on nonverbal content to arouse an emotional response. Nonverbal ad content can also affect cognitions about a product. For example, an ad showing a person drinking a new beverage after exercise provides information about appropriate usage situations without stating "good to use after exercise."

While the impact of nonverbal ad elements is not yet completely understood, it is clear that they can have significant influence.[50] Therefore, the nonverbal portion of advertising messages should be designed and tested with as much care as the verbal portion.

MARKET SEGMENTATION AND PRODUCT DEVELOPMENT STRATEGIES BASED ON ATTITUDES

Market Segmentation

The identification of market segments is a key aspect of marketing. Properly designed marketing programs should be built around the unique needs of each market segment. The importance of various attributes is one way of defining customer needs for a given product. Segmenting consumers on the basis of their most important attribute or attributes is called **benefit segmentation.**[51]

TABLE 11-2

Using the Multiattribute Attitude Model in the Product Development Process

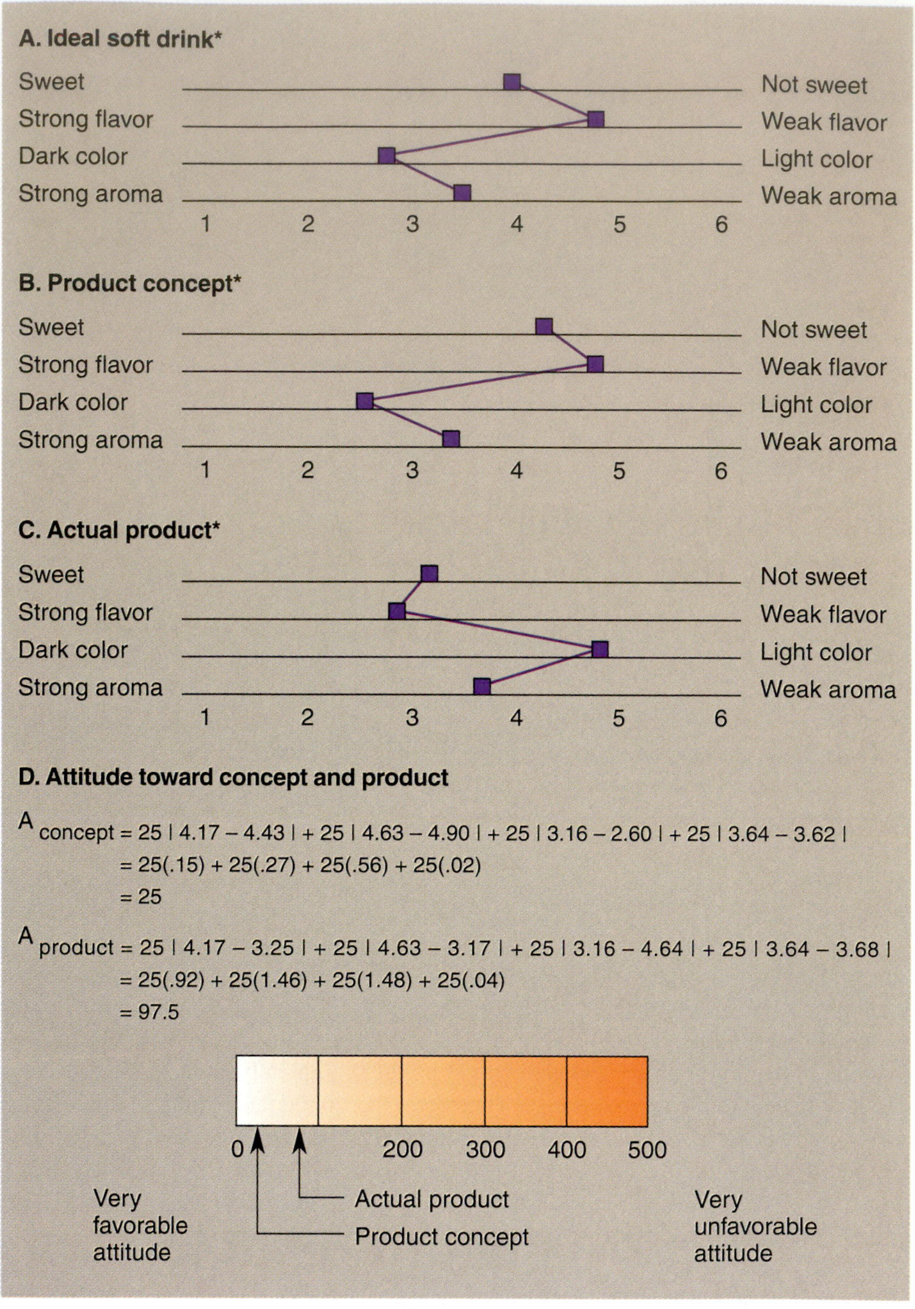

* Measured on a six-point schematic differential scale.

To define benefit segments, a marketer needs to know the importance attached to the respective features of a particular product or service. Then benefit segments can be formed by grouping consumers with similar attribute importance ratings into segments such that within a segment consumers are seeking the same benefit(s).

Additional information about consumers within each segment is obtained to develop a more complete picture of each segment. Then, knowing the primary benefit sought by each segment and the descriptive characteristics of each segment, separate marketing programs can be developed for each of the segments to be served by a particular organization.

Product Development

While the importance consumers attach to key attributes provides a meaningful way to understand needs and form benefit segments, the ideal levels of performance indicate the consumers' desired level of performance in satisfying those needs. Thus, these ideal levels of performance can provide valuable guidelines in developing a new product or reformulating an existing one.

To illustrate how ideal levels can be used in product development, Table 11-2 describes how Coca-Cola used this approach in developing a new soft drink.[52] The first step is to construct a profile of a segment of consumers' ideal level of performance with respect to key attributes of a soft drink. For a particular type of soft drink, four attributes were identified and the average ideal level of performance was obtained from consumer ratings. If there is a wide range of ideal ratings for a particular attribute, further segmentation may be required.

A second step involves creation of a product concept that closely matches the ideal profile. The concept could be a written description, picture, or actual prototype of the product to be developed. As section B shows in Table 11-2, consumers evaluated the product concept developed by Coca-Cola as being fairly close to their ideal level of performance on each of the four attributes. It appears that only their concept of color was off target by being a little too dark.

The next step is to translate the concept into an actual product. When Coca-Cola did this and presented the product to the consumers, they did not perceive it to be similar to either the product concept or their ideal levels of performance (see section C of Table 11-2). While the actual product achieved a reasonable attitude rating, the product concept scored higher (section D, Table 11-2). Thus, the product could benefit from further improvement.

Based on this information, management would attempt to further improve the actual product to better align it with ideal levels of performance prior to market introduction. This same type of procedure can be used to help design ads, packages, or retail outlets.

SUMMARY

Attitudes can be defined as the way we think, feel, and act toward some aspect of our environment. A result of all the factors discussed so far in the text, attitudes influence, as well as reflect, the lifestyle individuals pursue.

Attitudes have three component parts: cognitive, affective, and behavioral. The cognitive component consists of the individual's beliefs or knowledge about the object. The cognitive component is generally assessed by using a version of the multiattribute attitude model. Feelings or emotional reactions to an object represent the affective component of the attitude. The behavioral component reflects overt actions and statements of behavioral intentions with respect to specific attributes of the object or the overall object. In general, all three components of an attitude tend to be consistent with each other.

Attitude change strategies can focus on affect, behavior, cognition, or some combination. Attempts to change affect generally rely on classical conditioning. Change strategies focusing on behavior rely more on operant conditioning. Changing cognitions usually involves information processing and cognitive learning.

Source credibility is composed of two basic dimensions: trustworthiness and expertise. Influencing attitudes is much easier when the source of the message is viewed as highly credible by the target market. Celebrities are widely used as product or company spokespersons. They are most effective when their image matches the personality of the product and the actual or desired self-concept of the target market.

The appeals used to change attitudes are important and are varied. Fear appeals make use of the threat of negative consequences if attitudes or behaviors are not altered. Humorous appeals can also be effective in influencing attitudes. However, the humorous message must remain focused on the brand or main selling point to be effective.

Comparative ads produce mixed results. They are most effective for unknown brands having a strong functional advantage. The decision to use a value-expressive or utilitarian appeal depends on whether the brand fills value-expressive or utilitarian needs. However, this is complicated when the brand fills both types of needs. Emotional appeals have been found to have a strong effect on attitudes toward both the ad and the product.

Two aspects of the structure of the message affect its effectiveness. The effectiveness of one- versus two-sided messages depends largely on the situation and characteristics of the target audience. Nonverbal aspects of the ad, such as pictures, surrealism, and music, also affect attitudes.

Attitudes, particularly the cognitive component, are the basis for market segmentation strategies, such as benefit segmentation, and for new-product development strategies.

KEY TERMS

Affective component 398
Attitude 394
Behavioral component 399
Benefit segmentation 417
Cognitive component 395
Comparative ads 415
Constant-sum scale 397
Elaboration likelihood model (ELM) 407
Emotional ads 415
Fear appeals 412
Humorous appeals 414
Likert scale 402
Mere exposure 405
Multiattribute attitude model 396
One-sided message 416
Semantic differential scale 401
Source credibility 409
Spokes-character 411
Sponsorship advertising 411
Testimonial ads 409
Theory of reasoned action 400
Two-sided message 416
Utilitarian appeals 415
Value-expressive appeals 415

INTERNET EXERCISES

1. Visit several general interest or entertainment sites on the Web that contain ads. Find and describe an ad that attempts to change the following to help form or change attitudes:
   a. Affective component
   b. Cognitive component
   c. Behavioral component
2. Visit several company sites on the web. Find and describe one that attempts to change the following to help form or change attitudes:
   a. Affective component
   b. Cognitive component
   c. Behavioral component
3. Visit several general interest or entertainment sites on the web that contain ads. Find and describe an ad that uses one of the following to help form or change attitudes:
   a. Credible source
   b. Celebrity source
   c. Humorous appeal
   d. Fear appeal
   e. Comparative appeal
   f. Emotional appeal
4. Visit several company sites on the Web. Find and describe one that uses one of the following to help form or change attitudes:
   a. Credible source
   b. Celebrity source
   c. Humorous appeal
   d. Fear appeal
   e. Comparative appeal
   f. Emotional appeal
5. Visit the American Plastics Council Web site (www.plasticsresource.com). What attitude change techniques does it use. Are they effective?

REVIEW QUESTIONS

1. What is an *attitude?*
2. What are the functions of attitudes?
3. What are the components of an attitude?
4. Are the components of an attitude consistent? What factors reduce the apparent consistency between attitude components?
5. What is a *multiattribute attitude model?*
6. What strategies can be used to change the following components of an attitude?
   a. Affective
   b. Behavioral
   c. Cognitive
7. What is meant by *mere exposure?*
8. What is the *elaboration likelihood model (ELM)?*
9. Describe the *theory of reasoned action.*
10. What are the two characteristics of the source of a message that influence its ability to change attitudes? Describe each.
11. What is *source credibility?* What causes it?
12. Why are celebrity sources sometimes effective? What risks are associated with using a celebrity source?
13. Name five possible characteristics of an appeal that would influence or change attitudes. Describe each.
14. Are *fear appeals* always effective in changing attitudes? Why?
15. What characteristics should *humorous ads* have?
16. Are *emotional appeals* effective? Why?
17. Are *comparative appeals* effective? Why?
18. What is a *value-expressive appeal?* A *utilitarian appeal?* When should each be used?
19. What are the two characteristics of the message structure that influence its ability to change attitudes? Describe each.
20. What are the nonverbal components of an ad? What impact do they have on attitudes?
21. When is a *two-sided message* likely to be more effective than a *one-sided message?*
22. How can attitudes guide new-product development?
23. What is a *benefit segment?*

DISCUSSION QUESTIONS

24. Which version of the multiattribute attitude model and which attributes would you use to assess student attitudes toward the following? Justify your answer.
   a. Your university
   b. Crest toothpaste
   c. Plastic grocery bags
   d. Snakes as pets
   e. Mountain Dew
   f. Prunes
25. Assume you wanted to improve or create favorable attitudes among college students toward the following. Would you focus primarily on the affective, cognitive, or behavioral component? Why?
   a. Sierra Club
   b. Prunes
   c. Vegetarianism
   d. Apple computers
   e. Not driving after drinking
   f. Diet Pepsi
   g. Beef
   h. Sugar
26. Suppose you used the multiattribute attitude model and developed a fruit-based carbonated drink that was successful in the United States. Could you use the same model in the following countries? If not, how would it have to change?
   a. India
   b. China
   c. France
   d. Mexico
27. Suppose you wanted to form highly negative attitudes toward drug consumption among college students.
   a. Which attitude component would you focus on? Why?
   b. Which message characteristic would you use? Why?
   c. What type of appeal would you use? Why?
28. What communications characteristics would you use in an attempt to improve college students' attitudes toward the following?
   a. Burger King
   b. Kia automobiles

c. Church attendance
d. Prunes
e. Greenpeace
f. Mountain Dew

29. Is it ethical to use fear appeals to increase demand for the following?
    a. Deodorant among teenagers
    b. Antidandruff shampoo among adults
    c. Smoke alarms among elderly consumers
    d. Handguns among women
30. Name two appropriate and two inappropriate celebrity spokespersons for each of the products or causes in Question 28. Justify your selection.
31. What benefit segments do you think exist for stadium attendance at the following?
    a. College basketball games
    b. Local theater presentations
    c. Major art museums
    d. Professional wrestling matches

APPLICATION EXERCISES

32. Find and copy two magazine or newspaper advertisements, one based on the affective component and the other on the cognitive component. Discuss the approach of each ad in terms of its copy and illustration and what effect it creates in terms of attitude. Also, discuss why the marketer might have taken that approach in each advertisement.
33. Repeat Question 32 for utilitarian and value-expressive appeals.
34. Identify a television commercial that uses a humorous appeal. Then interview five individuals not enrolled in your class and measure their:
    a. Awareness of this commercial
    b. Recall of the brand advertised
    c. Recall of relevant information
    d. Liking of the commercial
    e. Preference for the brand advertised

    Then evaluate your results and assess the level of communication that has taken place in terms of these five consumers' exposure, attention, interpretation, and preferences for this product and commercial.
35. Describe a magazine or television advertisement that uses the following. Evaluate the effectiveness of the ad.
    a. Source credibility
    b. Celebrity source
    c. Testimonial
    d. Fear appeal
    e. Humorous appeal
    f. Emotional appeal
    g. Comparative approach
    h. Extensive nonverbal elements
    i. A two-sided appeal
36. Measure another student's ideal beliefs and belief importance for the following. Examine these ideal beliefs and importance weights and then develop a verbal description (i.e., concept) of a new brand of these items that would satisfy this student's needs. Next, measure that student's attitude toward the concept you have developed in your verbal description.
    a. Soft drink
    b. Restaurant
    c. Bicycle
    d. Toothpaste
    e. Perfume
    f. Senator
37. Use the multiattribute attitude model to assess 10 students' attitudes toward several brands in the following product categories. Measure the students' behavior with respect to these brands. Are they consistent? Explain any inconsistencies.
    a. Magazines
    b. Soft drinks
    c. Toothpaste
    d. Cars
    e. Computers
    f. Local pizza restaurants
38. Develop two advertisements for the following. One ad should focus on the cognitive component and the other on the affective component.
    a. Scope mouthwash
    b. Greenpeace
    c. Mountain Dew
    d. Reducing drinking and driving
    e. Increasing church attendance
    f. Palm organizers
39. Repeat Question 38 using utilitarian and value-expressive appeals.

REFERENCES

1. B. S. Flynn, "Mass Media and School Interventions," *American Journal of Public Health,* July 1994, pp. 1148–50; "Slick TV Ads Divert Child Smoking," *Marketing News,* August 29, 1994, p. 30. See also C. Pechmann and S. Ratneshwar, "The Effects of Antismoking and Cigarette Advertising on Young Adolescents' Perceptions of Peers Who Smoke," *Journal of Consumer Research,* September 1994, pp. 236–51.
2. See R. E. Petty, D. T. Wegener, and L. R. Fabriger, "Attitudes and Attitude Change," *Annual Review of Psychology* 48 (1997), pp. 609–38.
3. D. Katz, "The Functional Approach to the Study of Attitudes," *Public Opinion Quarterly,* Summer 1960, pp. 163–204.
4. See M. Wanke, G. Bohner, and A. Jurkowitsch, "There Are Many Reasons to Drive a BMW," *Journal of Consumer Research,* September 1997, pp. 170–77.
5. R. B. Zajonc, "Feeling and Thinking: Preferences Need No Inferences," *American Psychologist,* February 1980, pp. 151–75. See also Y. Tsal, "On the Relationship between Cognitive and Affective Processes"; and R. B. Zajonc and H. Markus, "Must All Affect Be Mediated by Cognition?" both in *Journal of Consumer Research,* December 1985, pp. 358–62 and 363–64; and J. A. Muncy, "Affect and Cognition," in *Advances in Consumer Research XIII,* ed. R. J. Lutz (Provo, UT: Association for Consumer Research, 1986), pp. 226–30.
6. For an excellent review, see P. A. Dabholkar, "Incorporating Choice into an Attitudinal Framework," *Journal of Consumer Research,* June 1994, pp. 100–18. See also A. Ehrenberg, "In search of Holy Grails"; and A. L. Baldinger and J. Rubinson, "In Search of the Holy Grail"; both in *Journal of Advertising Research,* January 1997, pp. 9–12 and 18–20.
7. I. E. Berger and A. A. Mitchell, "The Effect of Advertising on Attitude Accessibility, Attitude Confidence, and Attitude-Behavior Relationship"; and R. H. Fazio, M. C. Powell, and C. J. Williams, "The Role of Attitude Accessibility in the Attitude-to-Behavior Process"; both in *Journal of Consumer Research,* December 1989, pp. 269–79 and 280–88; M. G. Millar and A. Tesser, "Attitudes and Behavior," in *Advances in Consumer Research XVII,* ed. M. E. Goldberg, G. Gorn, and R. W. Pollay (Provo, UT: Association for Consumer Research, 1990), pp. 86–90; R. E. Petty and J. A. Krosnick, *Attitude Strength* (Mahwah, NJ: Erlbaum, 1995); and S. J. Kraus, "Attitudes and the Prediction of Behavior," *Personality and Social Psychology Bulletin* 21 (1995), pp. 58–75.
8. See A. Sahni, "Incorporating Perceptions of Financial Control in Purchase Prediction," in *Advances in Consumer Research XXI,* ed. C. T. Allen and D. R. John (Provo, UT: Association for Consumer Research, 1994), pp. 442–48.
9. J. A. Cote, J. McCullough, and M. Reilly, "Effects of Unexpected Situations on Behavior-Intention Differences," *Journal of Consumer Research,* September 1985, pp. 188–94.
10. See B. H. Sheppard, J. Hartwick, and P. R. Warshaw, "The Theory of Reasoned Action," *Journal of Consumer Research,* December 1988, pp. 325–43.
11. R. P. Grossman and B. D. Till, "The Persistence of Classically Conditioned Brand Attitudes," *Journal of Advertising,* Spring 1998, pp. 23–31; and J. Kim, J.-S. Lim, and M. Bhargava, "The Role of Affect in Attitude Formation," *Journal of the Academy of Marketing Science,* Spring 1998, pp. 143–52.
12. See K. G. Celuch and M. Slama, "Cognitive and Affective Components of A_{ab} in a Low Motivation Processing Set," *Psychology & Marketing,* March 1995, pp. 123–33; N. S. Hollis, "Like It Or Not, Liking Is Not Enough," *Journal of Advertising Research,* September 1995, pp. 7–16; C. M. Derbaix, "The Impact of Affective Reactions on Attitudes toward the Advertisement and the Brand," *Journal of Marketing Research,* November 1995, pp. 47–79; J. E. Phelps and M. G. Hoy, "The A_{ab}-A_b-PI Relationship in Children," *Psychology & Marketing,* January 1996, pp. 77–105; D. J. Moore and W. D. Harris, "Affect Intensity and the Consumer's Attitude toward High Impact Emotional Advertising Appeals," *Journal of Advertising,* Summer 1996, pp. 37–50; H. Mano, "Affect and Persuasion," *Psychology & Marketing,* July 1997, pp. 315–35; E. Curlo and R. Chamblee, "Ad Processing and Persuasion," *Psychology & Marketing,* May 1998, pp. 279–99; E. Curlo and R. Ducoffe, "Product Use Goals and Attitudinal Response to Ads," *Journal of Current Issues and Research in Advertising,* Spring 1998, pp. 19–32; and M. Geuens and P. D. Pelsmacker, "Affect Intensity Revisited," *Psychology & Marketing,* May 1999, pp. 195–209.
13. See M.-H. Huang, "Is Negative Affect in Advertising General or Specific?" *Psychology & Marketing,* May 1997, pp. 223–40.
14. K. R. France and C. W. Park, "The Impact of Program Affective Valence and Level of Cognitive Appraisal on Advertisement Processing and Effectiveness," *Journal of Current Issues and Research in Advertising,* Fall 1997, pp. 1–21; and A. B. Aylesworth and S. B. MacKenzie, "Context Is Key," *Journal of Advertising,* Summer 1998, pp. 17–31.
15. S. A. Hawkins and S. J. Hoch, "Low-Involvement Learning," *Journal of Consumer Research,* September 1992, pp. 212–25; C. Janiszewski, "Preattentive Mere Exposure Effects," *Journal of Consumer Research,* December 1993, pp. 376–92; M. Vanhuele, "Mere Exposure and the Cognitive-Affective Debate Revisited"; A. Y. Lee, "The Mere Exposure Effect"; both in *Advances in Consumer Research XXI,* ed. C. T. Allen and D. R. John (Provo, UT: Association for Consumer Research, 1994), pp. 264–75; S.-W. Chang, "Effects of Brand Name Exposure on Brand Choice," in *Advances in Consumer Research XXIV,* ed. M. Bruck and D. J. MacInnis (Provo, UT: Association for Consumer Research, 1997), pp. 288–94; and A. Rindfleisch and J. J. Inman, "Explaining the Familiarity-Liking Relationship," *Marketing Letters,* no. 1 (1998), pp. 5–19.
16. L. J. Marks and M. A. Kamins, "The Use of Product Sampling and Advertising," *Journal of Marketing Research,* August 1988, pp. 266–81.
17. See D. S. Kempf, "Attitude Formation from Product Trial," *Psychology & Marketing,* January 1999, pp. 35–50.
18. See G. J. Gaeth et al., "Consumers' Attitude Change Across Sequences of Successful and Unsuccessful Product Usage," *Marketing Letters,* no. 1 (1997), pp. 41–53.
19. R. E. Smith and W. R. Swinyard, "Cognitive Response to Advertising and Trial," *Journal of Advertising,* no. 3 (1988), pp. 3–14;

M. J. Manfredo, "A Test of Assumptions Inherent in Attribute-Specific Advertising," *Journal of Travel Research,* Winter 1989, pp. 8–13; and Y. Yi, "The Indirect Effects of Advertisements Designed to Change Product Attribute Beliefs," *Psychology & Marketing,* Spring 1990, pp. 47–63.

20. See D. M. Boush, C. H. Kim, L. R. Kahle, and R. Batra, "Cynicism and Conformity as Correlates of Trust in Product Information Sources," *Journal of Current Issues and Research in Advertising,* Fall 1993, pp. 71–79; and J. L. Aaker and D. Maheswaran, "The Effect of Cultural Orientation on Persuasion," *Journal of Consumer Research,* December 1997, pp. 315–28.
21. See D. M. Boush, M. Friestad, and G. M. Rose, "Adolescent Skepticism toward TV Advertising and Knowledge of Advertiser Tactics"; and M. Friestad and P. Wright, "The Persuasion Knowledge Model"; both in *Journal of Consumer Research,* June 1994; pp. 1–31 and 165–75; M. Friestad and P. Wright, "Persuasion Knowledge," *Journal of Consumer Research,* June 1995, pp. 62–74; and M. Friestad and P. Wright, "Everyday Persuasion Knowledge," *Psychology & Marketing,* March 1999, pp. 185–94.
22. See R. E. Petty, J. T. Cacioppo, and D. Schumann, "Central and Peripheral Routes to Advertising Effectiveness," *Journal of Consumer Research,* September 1993, pp. 135–46; R. E. Petty and J. T. Cacioppo, "The Elaboration Likelihood Model of Persuasion," in *Advances in Experimental Social Psychology,* ed. L. Berkowitz (Orlando: Academic Press, 1986), pp. 123–205; R. Petty, R. Unnava, and A. J. Strathman, in *Handbook of Consumer Behavior,* ed. T. S. Robertson and J. J. Kassarjain (Englewood Cliffs, NJ: Prentice Hall, 1991), pp. 1–49; K. R. Lord, M.-S. Lee, and P. L. Sauer, "The Combined Influence Hypothesis," *Journal of Advertising,* Spring 1995, pp. 73–85; K. Yoon, R. N. Laczniak, D. D. Muehling, and B. B. Reece, "A Revised Model of Advertising Processing," *Journal of Current Issues and Research in Advertising,* Fall 1995, pp. 53–67; J.-W. Park and M. Hastak, "Effects of Involvement on On-line Brand Evaluations," in *Advances in Consumer Research XXII,* ed. F. R. Kardes and M. Sujan (Provo, UT: Association for Consumer Research, 1995), pp. 435–39; and M. T. Pham, "Cue Representation and Selection Effects of Arousal on Persuasion," *Journal of Consumer Research,* March 1996, pp. 373–87.
23. D. W. Stewart and D. H. Furse, *Effective Television Advertising* (Lexington, MA: Lexington Books, 1986); and D. W. Stewart and S. Koslow, "Executional Factors and Advertising Effectiveness," *Journal of Advertising,* no. 3 (1989), pp. 21–32.
24. See P. M. West and S. M. Broniarczyk, "Integrating Multiple Opinions," *Journal of Consumer Research,* June 1998, pp. 38–51.
25. P. M. Homer and L. R. Kahle, "Source Expertise, Time of Source Identification, and Involvement in Persuasion," *Journal of Advertising,* no. 1 (1990), pp. 30–39; M. E. Goldberg and J. Hartwick, "The Effects of Advertiser Reputation and Extremity of Advertising Claim on Advertising Effectiveness," *Journal of Consumer Research,* September 1990, pp. 172–79; and K. Braunsberger and J. M. Munch, "Source Expertise versus Experience in Hospital Advertising," *Journal of Services Marketing,* no. 1 (1998), pp. 23–38.
26. D. J. Moore, J. C. Mowen, and R. Reardon, "Multiple Sources in Advertising Appeals," *Journal of the Academy of Marketing Science,* Summer 1994, pp. 234–43.
27. R. D. Reinartz, "Testimonial Ads," *Bank Marketing,* March 1996, pp. 25–30.
28. R. F. Beltramini and E. R. Stafford, "Comprehension and Perceived Believability of Seals of Approval Information in Advertising," *Journal of Advertising,* September 1993, pp. 3–13.
29. E. Haley, "Exploring the Construct of Organization as Source," *Journal of Advertising,* Summer 1996, pp. 19–35.
30. Ibid., p. 28.
31. J. Agrawal and W. A. Kamakura, "The Economic Worth of Celebrity Endorsers," *Journal of Marketing,* July 1995, pp. 56–62.
32. R. Ohanian, "Construction and Validation to Measure Celebrity Endorsers' Perceived Expertise, Trustworthiness, and Attractiveness," *Journal of Advertising,* no. 3 (1990), pp. 39–52; R. Ohanian, "The Impact of Celebrity Spokespersons' Perceived Image," *Journal of Advertising Research,* February–March 1991, pp. 46–54; J. Sengupta, R. C. Goodstein, and D. S. Boninger, "All Cues Are not Created Equal," *Journal of Consumer Research,* March 1997, pp. 351–61; and R. Nataraajan and S. K. Chawla, "'Fitness' Marketing," *Journal of Professional Services Marketing,* no. 2 (1997), pp. 119–29. For a different perspective, see G. McCracken, "Who Is the Celebrity Endorser?" *Journal of Consumer Research,* December 1989, pp. 310–21.
33. J. Jenson, "Picabo Street Wins Starring Role in Nike Game Plan," *Advertising Age,* November 11, 1996, p. 3.
34. M. A. Kamins, "An Investigation into the 'Match-up' Hypothesis in Celebrity Advertising," *Journal of Advertising,* no. 1 (1990), pp. 4–13; S. Misra and S. E. Beatty, "Celebrity Spokesperson and Brand Congruence," *Journal of Business Research,* September 1990, pp. 159–73; J. Lynch and D. Schuler, "The Matchup Effect of Spokesperson and Product Congruency," *Psychology & Marketing,* September 1993, pp. 417–45; and M. A. Kamins and K. Gupta, "Congruence between Spokesperson and Product Type," *Psychology & Marketing,* November 1994, pp. 569–86.
35. S. R. McDaniel, "An Investigation of Match-Up Effects in Sport Sponsorship Advertising," *Psychology & Marketing,* March 1999, pp. 163–84.
36. C. Tripp, T. D. Jensen, and L. Carlson, "The Effects of Multiple Product Endorsements by Celebrities on Consumers' Attitudes and Intentions," *Journal of Consumer Research,* March 1994, pp. 535–47.
37. B. D. Till and T. A. Shimp, "Endorsers in Advertising," *Journal of Advertising,* Spring 1998, pp. 67–82.
38. M. F. Callcott and W.-N. Lee, "Establishing the Spokes-Character in Academic Inquiry," in *Advances in Consumer Research XXII,* ed. F. R. Kardes and M. Sujan (Provo, UT: Association for Consumer Research, 1995), pp. 144–51; and M. F. Callcott and B. J. Phillips, "Elves Make Good Cookies," *Journal of Advertising Research,* September 1996, pp. 73–79.
39. D. D. Schoenbachler and T. E. Whittler, "Adolescent Processing of Social and Physical Threat Communications," *Journal of Advertising,* Winter 1996, pp. 37–54.
40. M. S. LaTour and H. J. Rotfeld, "There Are Threats and (Maybe) Fear-Caused Arousal," *Journal of Advertising,* Fall 1997, pp. 45–59. See also T. L. Henthorne, M. S. LaTour, and R. Nataraajan, "Fear Appeals in Print Advertising," *Journal of Advertising,* June 1993, pp. 60–69; J. T. Strong and K. M. Dubas,

"The Optimal Level of Fear-Arousal in Advertising," *Journal of Current Issues and Research in Advertising,* Fall 1993, pp. 93–99; K. R. Lord, "Motivating Recycling Behavior," *Psychology & Marketing,* July 1994, pp. 341–58; and P. A. Keller and L. G. Block, "Increasing the Persuasiveness of Fear Appeals," *Journal of Consumer Research,* March 1996, pp. 448–60.

41. See M. S. LaTour, R. L. Snipes, and S. J. Bliss, "Don't Be Afraid to Use Fear Appeals," *Journal of Advertising Research,* March 1996, pp. 59–66.

42. C. R. Duke, G. M. Pickett, L. Carlson, and S. J. Grove, "A Method for Evaluating the Ethics of Fear Appeals," *Journal of Public Policy & Marketing,* Spring 1993, pp. 120–29.

43. M. C. Weinberger, H. Spotts, L. Campbell, and A. L. Parsons, "The Use and Effect of Humor in Different Advertising Media," *Journal of Advertising Research,* May 1995, pp. 44–56; H. Cho, "Humor Mechanisms, Perceived Humor and Their Relationships to Various Executional Types in Advertising," in *Advances in Consumer Research XXII,* ed. F. R. Kardes and M. Sujan (Provo, UT: Association for Consumer Research, 1995), pp. 191–97; Y. Zhang, "Responses to Humorous Advertising," *Journal of Advertising,* Spring 1996, pp. 15–32; Y. Zhang, "The Effect of Humor in Advertising," *Psychology & Marketing,* September 1996, pp. 531–45; H. E. Sparks, M. G. Weinberger, and A. L. Parsons, "Assessing the Use and Impact of Humor on Advertising Effectiveness," *Journal of Advertising,* Fall 1997, pp. 17–32; and T. W. Cline and J. J. Kellaris, "The Joint Impact of Humor and Argument Strength in a Print Advertising Context," *Psychology & Marketing,* January 1999, pp. 69–86.

44. D. Grewal et al., "Comparative versus Noncomparative Advertising," *Journal of Marketing,* October 1998, pp. 1–15.

45. S. Putrevu and K. R. Lord, "Comparative and Noncomparative Advertising," *Journal of Advertising,* June 1995, pp. 77–91; T. H. Stevenson and L. E. Swayne, "The Use of Comparative Advertising in Business-to-Business Direct Marketing," *Industrial Marketing Management,* January 1995, pp. 53–59; A. Kara, E. Kaynak, and D. Lee, "Upgrading by Association," in *Advances in Consumer Research XXIV,* ed. M. Bruck and D. J. MacInnis (Provo, UT: Association for Consumer Research, 1997), pp. 425–30; J. Halliday, "Survey," *Advertising Age,* May 4, 1998, p. 26; H. Yi, J. E. Phelps, and D. R. Roskos-Ewoldsen, "Examining the Effectiveness of Comparative Advertising," *Journal of Current Issues and Research in Advertising,* Spring 1998, pp. 61–74; N. Donthu, "A Cross-Country Investigation of Recall of and Attitude toward Comparative Advertising," *Journal of Advertising,* Summer 1998, p. 22; and A. Chattopadhyay, "When Does Comparative Advertising Influence Brand Attitude?" *Psychology & Marketing,* August 1998, 461–75.

46. See footnote 12.

47. J. S. Johar and M. J. Sirgy, "Value-Expressive versus Utilitarian Advertising Appeals," *Journal of Advertising,* September 1991, pp. 23–33; S. Sharitt, "Evidence for Predicting the Effectiveness of Value-Expressive versus Utilitarian Appeals," *Journal of Advertising,* June 1992, pp. 47–51; M. R. Stafford and E. Day, "Retail Services Advertising," *Journal of Advertising,* Spring 1995, pp. 57–71; M. E. Slama and R. B. Singley, "Self-Monitoring and Value-Expressive vs. Utilitarian Ad Effectiveness," *Journal of Current Issues and Research in Advertising,* Fall 1996, pp. 39–49; and L. Dube, A. Chattopadhyay, and A. Letarte, "Should Advertising Appeals Match the Basis of Consumers' Attitudes?" *Journal of Advertising Research,* November 1996, pp. 82–89.

48. C. Pechmann, "Predicting When Two-Sided Ads Will be More Effective than One-Sided Ads," *Journal of Marketing Research,* November 1992, pp. 441–53; and A. E. Crowley and W. D. Hoyer, "An Integrative Framework for Understanding Two-Sided Persuasion," *Journal of Consumer Research,* March 1994, pp. 561–74.

49. A. C. Burns, A. Biswas, and L. A. Babin, "The Operation of Visual Imagery as a Mediator of Advertising Effects," *Journal of Advertising,* June 1993, pp. 71–85.

50. See P. W. Miniard, D. Sirdeshmukh, and D. E. Innis, "Peripheral Persuasion and Brand Choice," *Journal of Consumer Research,* September 1992, pp. 226–39.

51. J. W. Harvey, "Benefit Segmentation for Fund Raisers," *Journal of the Academy of Marketing Science,* Winter 1990, pp. 77–86. D. S. P. Cermak, K. M. File, and R. A. Prince, "A Benefit Segmentation of the Major Donor Market," *Journal of Business Research,* February 1994, pp. 121–30; P. J. O'Connor and G. L. Sullivan, "Market Segmentation," *Psychology & Marketing,* October 1995, pp. 613–35; T.-Z. Chang and S.-J. Chen, "Benefit Segmentation," *Journal of Professional Services Marketing,* no. 2 (1995), pp. 69–80; and J. W. Peltier and J. A. Schribrowsky, "The Use of Need-Based Segmentation for Developing Segment-Specific Direct Marketing Strategies," *Journal of Direct Marketing,* Fall 1997, pp. 53–62.

52. H. E. Bloom, "Match the Concept and the Product," *Journal of Advertising Research,* October 1977, pp. 25–27.

CATCH THE ADVENTURE

With surprises around every bend, kayakers and canoers can explore thousands of miles along Belize's rivers, lagoons, marshes and reefs. At dawn or dusk, it's a great way to observe wildlife.

An adventurer's paradise, Belize is your peaceful, English-speaking neighbor only 2 hours from the US. With a diversity of adventure opportunities unmatched by any other country, the people of Belize have protected 40% of the country as parks and reserves. Belize is on the Caribbean coast nestled between Mexico and Guatemala and offers an intriguing mix of tropical forests rich with wildlife, majestic 3,675 foot mountains, mysterious Maya temples, and diving and fishing experiences beyond compare. In a single day you can go from tropical forest to the longest barrier reef in the Western Hemisphere. And the people are as warm and friendly as the climate. Discover Belize. And let the adventures begin.

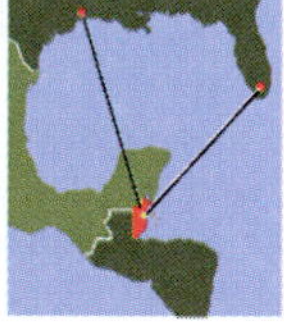

Kayaking in the exotic Upper Sibun River. Photo by Tony Rath.

Contact the Belize Tourism Board at **1-800-624-0686**
or visit us at our website: www.travelbelize.org/kayaking

BELIZE℠ *Mother Nature's best kept secret*

Courtesy Belize Tourism Board.

chapter twelve

Self-Concept and Lifestyle

A marketing study identified five consumer lifestyles in relation to outdoor activities.[1] Each of these lifestyles is described briefly below.

- *Excitement-seeking competitives (16 percent).* Like risk, some danger, and competition, though they also like social and fitness benefits. Participate in team and individual competitive sports. Half belong to a sports club or team. Median age of 32, two-thirds are male. Upper-middle class, and about half are single.
- *Getaway actives (33 percent).* Like the opportunity to be alone or experience nature. Active in camping, fishing, and birdwatching. Not loners; focus on families or close friends. Half use outdoor recreation to reduce stress. Median age of 35, equally divided between men and women.
- *Fitness-driven (10 percent).* Engage in outdoor activities strictly for fitness benefits. Walking, bicycling, and jogging are popular activities. Upscale economically. Median age of 46, over half are women.
- *Health-conscious sociables (33 percent).* Relatively inactive despite stated health concerns. Most involved with spectator activities such as sightseeing, driving for pleasure, visiting zoos, and so forth. Median age 49, two-thirds are female.
- *Unstressed and unmotivated (8 percent).* Not interested in outdoor recreation except as an opportunity for the family to be together. Median age of 49, equally divided between males and females.

What are the marketing implications of this study for Prince tennis equipment, Schwinn bicycles, Jazzercise Inc., and Old Town canoes?

In this chapter, we will discuss the meaning of lifestyle and the role it plays in developing marketing strategies. Lifestyle is, in many ways, an outward expression of one's self-concept. That is, the way an individual chooses to live, given the constraints of income and ability, is heavily influenced by that person's current and desired self-concept. Therefore, we begin the chapter with an analysis of the self-concept. We then describe lifestyles, the ways in which lifestyle is measured, and examples of how lifestyle is being used to develop marketing programs.

SELF-CONCEPT

Self-concept is defined as *the totality of the individual's thoughts and feelings having reference to him- or herself as an object*. It is our perception of ourselves and our feelings toward ourselves. In other words, your self-concept is composed of the attitudes you hold toward yourself.

The self-concept can be divided into four basic parts, as shown in Table 12-1: actual versus ideal, and private versus social. The actual/ideal distinction refers to your perception of *who I am now* **(actual self-concept)** and *who I would like to be* **(ideal self-concept).** The private self refers to *how I am or would like to be to myself* **(private self-concept),** while the social self is *how I am seen by others or how I would like to be seen by others* **(social self-concept).**

All four types of self-concept influence consumer behavior and offer insights for developing marketing strategy. For example, products can be promoted as a means to enhance or maintain a person's private or social self. We will describe marketing applications of self-concept theory after we develop a more complete understanding of its nature and role in the consumption process.

Interdependent/Independent Self-Concepts

The self-concept is important in all cultures. However, those aspects of the self that are most valued and most influence consumption and other behaviors vary across cultures. Researchers have found it useful to categorize self-concepts into two types—independent and interdependent (also referred to as separateness and connectedness).[2]

An independent construal of the self is based on the predominant Western cultural belief that individuals are inherently separate. The **independent self-concept** is *characterized by an emphasis on personal goals, characteristics, achievements, and desires*. Individuals with an independent self-concept tend to be individualistic, egocentric, autonomous, self-reliant, and self-contained. They define themselves in terms of what they have done, what they have, and their personal characteristics that make them distinct from others.

An interdependent construal of the self is based more on the common Asian cultural belief in the fundamental connectedness of human beings. The **interdependent self-concept** is *characterized by an emphasis on family, cultural, professional, and social relationships*.

TABLE 12-1

Dimensions of a Consumer's Self-Concept

Dimensions of Self-Concept	*Actual Self-Concept*	*Ideal Self-Concept*
Private Self	How I actually see myself	How I would like to see myself
Social Self	How others actually see me	How I would like others to see me

Courtesy Woolrich, Inc.

ILLUSTRATION 12-1

Ads work best when their appeal matches the dominant type of self-concept held by the target market. This ad will be effective with the independent self-concept common in Western cultures.

Individuals with an interdependent self-concept tend to be obedient, sociocentric, holistic, connected, and relation oriented. They define themselves in terms of social roles, family relationships, and commonalities with other members of their groups, including ethnic and nationality groups.

Independent and interdependent self-concepts are not discreet categories. Rather they are constructs used to describe the opposite ends of a continuum along which most cultures lie. However, as we stressed in Chapter 2, most cultures are heterogeneous. Therefore, within a given culture, subcultures and other groups will vary on this dimension, as will individuals.[3]

Variation in the degree to which an individual or culture is characterized by an independent versus an interdependent self-concept has been found to influence message preferences, consumption of luxury goods, and the types of products preferred. For example, ads stressing acting alone and autonomy tend to be effective with consumers with independent self-concepts, while ads emphasizing group membership work better with consumers with interdependent self-concepts.[4] The ad in Illustration 12-1 should be very effective with individuals whose independent self-concept is dominant.

Possessions and the Extended Self

Some products acquire substantial meaning to us or are used to signal particularly important aspects of ourselves to others. Belk developed a theory called the *extended self* to explain this.[5] The **extended self** consists of *the self plus possessions*. That is, we tend to define ourselves in part by our possessions. Thus, some possessions are not just a manifestation of our self-concept; they are an integral part of our self-identity. We are, to some extent, what we possess. If we lost key possessions, we would be somewhat different individuals.[6]

While these key possessions might be major items—for example, one's home or automobile—they are equally likely to be smaller items with unique meaning such as a

Consumer Insight 12-1

Tattoos and the Extended Self

Most products and services associated with the extended self are physically separated from the physical self. Until recently, exceptions were limited primarily to hairstyles and coloring, and cosmetics. One could also alter the physical self through exercise, diet, weight training, and plastic surgery. In recent years, body piercing and tattooing have become additional ways to alter both the extended self and the physical self. Tattooing is unique (except for plastic surgery) in that it is a relatively unalterable change to the physical self. It can be done primarily for adornment or beauty enhancement reasons. Or, it can serve primarily as a public or private symbol.

For most of this century, tattooing was not socially acceptable among most social groups in the United States. The most noticeable exception was enlisted men in the Navy, and even then alcohol consumption was frequently involved in the decision to secure a tattoo. This has changed sharply in recent years. Why has this become socially acceptable and what does it mean to the self-concept of those who secure tattoos?

Research on tattoos focuses on four themes—the renaissance of tattooing, the impact of the tattoo on the extended self, the risks associated with acquiring a tattoo, and the satisfaction/dissatisfaction that can result.

A *tattoo renaissance* began in the 1960s with the hippie movement and the evolution of skilled tattoo artists in the San Francisco area. Interest also began to grow in the historical and ethnographic aspects of the tattoo medium. The commercial art world and academic art historians began to pay attention to tattooing as an art form. This, in turn, attracted better tattoo artists. By the early 1990s, public figures, particularly athletes, began to wear visible tattoos, which increased their acceptability among the more venturesome members of "mainstream" society.

Tattoos have meanings on at least three levels. First, there is the meaning associated with *having a*

souvenir, a photograph, a pet, or a favorite cooking pan. These objects have meaning to us beyond their "market value." Consider these quotes from consumers who lost their possessions in natural disasters and who had ample insurance to replace them:

> Yeah, we got better stuff, but it doesn't mean anything to us. It's just stuff.
>
> I had so much love tied up in my things. I can't go through that kind of loss again. What I'm buying now won't be as important to me.
>
> You can't put back or replace what you had. It was too personal—it was customized.
>
> I wanted a different house so that the missing items wouldn't seem gone. I couldn't look in a room and see something was not there anymore.[7]

Products become part of one's extended self for a variety of reasons. Souvenirs often become part of the extended self as representations of memories and feelings:

> You can't really tell what Paris is like . . . you know, a lot of it is just feelings; feelings you can't put into words, or (that) pictures cannot capture . . . They (a hat and blouse) are just reminders.
>
> I had a really wonderful trip and really sort of discovered myself, you know, I learned to be independent on my own. I really didn't have the money to buy this (necklace and boomerang charm), but I decided I wanted something really permanent . . . The boomerang is a symbol of going back there sometime.[8]

Gifts often take on important meanings as representations of relationships (see Chapter 13).

> That gift was my grandfather's ring . . . Even now when I look at it, I think about its past with him and the journeys it took around the world in the Navy back in World War II.

tattoo. While increasingly common, having a tattoo is still far from the norm. Thus, having a tattoo in and of itself makes a statement about the person. A person with a tattoo is still viewed as somewhat of a risk taker or nonconformist. The location of the tattoo also contains meaning. The more visible the tattoo, the more rebellious or nonconforming the individual appears to be. The tattoo itself is a major source of meaning, both private and symbolic. Tattoos may symbolize group membership, interests, activities, relationships, life transitions, accomplishments, or values. Tattoos may be unique and filled primarily with personal meaning or their meaning may be rooted in cultural practice and myths.

Acquiring a tattoo is risky. It is very expensive to remove or alter a tattoo. Thus, if you don't like your tattoo or your tastes change over time, you are at financial risk. There is also the social risk that one's current or future friends, colleagues, or employers will have a negative reaction to the tattoo. Finally, there is still physiological risk associated with acquiring a tattoo.

Finally, there is evaluation and satisfaction or dissatisfaction. As mentioned earlier, dissatisfaction is difficult and expensive to correct. Satisfaction, often at a high level, is a frequent outcome. Some research indicates that this may even produce addiction.

Critical Thinking Questions

1. How does a tattoo affect one's self-concept and become part of one's extended self?
2. Will one or multiple visible tattoos become the norm for younger consumers over the next 10 years?
3. How is the renaissance in tattooing similar to the revival of cigar smoking? How is it different?

Source: Based on J. Watson, "Why Did You Put That There?"; and A. M. Velliquette, J. B. Murray, and E. H. Creyer, "The Tattoo Renaissance"; both in *Advances in Consumer Research XXV*, ed. J. W. Alba and J. W. Hutchinson (Provo, UT: Association for Consumer Research, 1998), pp. 453–60 and 461–67.

The key chain is special because every so often, when I think about who gave it to me, it brings back old thoughts and feelings. It is a symbol of friendship between us, and it keeps us in touch.

[T]here stood Daddy . . . holding a beautiful old violin . . . as proud as I was of the gift at the time, it means more to me today as I raise my first child. My violin is old and dusty now, but I will always treasure it and keep its meaning alive.[9]

Some products become imbued with meaning and value as they are used over time. Use over time allows a product to become associated with an array of memories. A product in one author's extended self is the old, cheap briefcase he purchased to take to his first academic conference many years ago. To his surprise, the briefcase has lasted 30 years and has been on trips through much of the world. Although well worn, it is now "part of" the author and he plans to continue to use it as long as possible.

At other times, a single "peak experience" with a product such as a mountain bike can propel the product into the extended self. A **peak experience** is *an experience that surpasses the usual level of intensity, meaningfulness, and richness and produces feelings of joy and self-fulfillment*.[10] Products that are acquired or used to help consumers with major life transitions (leaving home, first job, marriage, children, and so forth) are also likely to be or become part of the extended self.[11]

Other products quickly or immediately become part of the extended self because they are central to one's private self-concept or serve as an important symbol of one's social self-concept. Skis and computers are examples of products that may quickly become part of the extended self. Consumer Insight 12-1 describes a product that is likely to become part on one's extended self as well as one's physical self.

A scale has been developed to measure the extent to which an item has been incorporated into the extended self.[12] It is a Likert scale (see Appendix A) in which consumers express agreement (from strongly agree to strongly disagree on a seven-point scale) to the following statements:

1. My ______________________ helps me achieve the identity I want to have.
2. My ______________________ helps me narrow the gap between what I am and what I try to be.
3. My ______________________ is central to my identity.
4. My ______________________ is part of who I am.
5. If my ______________________ is stolen from me I will feel as if my identity has been snatched from me.
6. I derive some of my identity from my ______________________ .

Owning a product makes it a part of a person even if it does not become an important part of the person's extended self. The **mere ownership effect** (or the endowment effect) is *the tendency of an owner to evaluate an object more favorably than a nonowner*. This occurs almost immediately upon acquiring an object and increases with time of ownership. Thus, we tend to value an object more after acquiring it than before. We also tend to value objects we own more highly than we value similar objects owned by others.[13]

The concept of the extended self and the mere ownership effect have numerous implications for marketing strategy. One is that communications that cause potential consumers to visualize product ownership might result in enhanced product evaluations. Product sampling or other trial programs may have similar results.

Measuring Self-Concept

Utilizing the self-concept in marketing requires that we be able to measure it. The most common measurement approach is the semantic differential (see Appendix A). Malhotra has developed a set of 15 pairs of adjectives that offer promise of being applicable across a variety of settings. These terms, shown in Table 12-2, were found effective in describing the ideal, actual, and social self-concepts of individuals, as well as the images of automobiles and celebrities.

Using the scales requires consumers to mark each set of adjectives to indicate how well one or the other describes the consumer (now and/or as the consumer would like to be) as well as the product, brand, or celebrity of interest. The end positions indicate "extremely," the next pair in from either end represent "very," the next pair in indicate "somewhat," and the middle position means "neither-nor." Based on this scale, what are your actual and desired private and social self-concepts?

This instrument can be used to ensure a match between the self-concept (actual or ideal) of a target market, the image of a brand, and the characteristics of an advertising spokesperson. For example, Nike undoubtedly studied the desired self-concept of young girls and the image of Picabo Street before selecting her as a primary company spokesperson to this segment.[14]

Another effective method for measuring the congruence between a consumer's self-image and a product image involves the following instructions:

Take a moment to think about (product *x*). Think about the kind of person who typically uses (product *x*). Imagine this person using one or more personal adjectives such as stylish, classy, masculine, sexy, old, athletic, or whatever personal adjectives you can use to describe the typical user of (product *x*). Once you've done this, indicate your agreement or disagreement to the following statement: This (product *x*) is consistent with how I see myself (in situation *y*).[15]

Measurement Scales for Self-Concepts, Person Concepts, and Product Concepts **TABLE 12-2**

1. Rugged	____	____	____	____	____	____	____	Delicate
2. Excitable	____	____	____	____	____	____	____	Calm
3. Uncomfortable	____	____	____	____	____	____	____	Comfortable
4. Dominating	____	____	____	____	____	____	____	Submissive
5. Thrifty	____	____	____	____	____	____	____	Indulgent
6. Pleasant	____	____	____	____	____	____	____	Unpleasant
7. Contemporary	____	____	____	____	____	____	____	Noncontemporary
8. Organized	____	____	____	____	____	____	____	Unorganized
9. Rational	____	____	____	____	____	____	____	Emotional
10. Youthful	____	____	____	____	____	____	____	Mature
11. Formal	____	____	____	____	____	____	____	Informal
12. Orthodox	____	____	____	____	____	____	____	Liberal
13. Complex	____	____	____	____	____	____	____	Simple
14. Colorless	____	____	____	____	____	____	____	Colorful
15. Modest	____	____	____	____	____	____	____	Vain

Reprinted with permission from the *Journal of Marketing Research,* published by the American Marketing Association. Source: N. K. Malhotra, "A Scale to Measure Self-Concepts, Person Concepts, and Product Concepts," November 1981, p. 462.

Using Self-Concept to Position Products

Attempts to obtain our ideal self-concept (or maintain our actual self-concept) often involve the purchase and consumption of products, services, and media.[16] The role of the self-concept is explained by the following logical sequence:

1. An individual has a self-concept. The self-concept is formed through interaction with parents, peers, teachers, and significant others.
2. The self-concept is of value to the individual.
3. Because the self-concept is valued, individuals strive to maintain or enhance their self-concept.
4. Certain products serve as social symbols and communicate social meaning about those who own or use such products.
5. The use of products as symbols communicates meaning to oneself and to others, causing an impact on the individual's private and social self-concepts.
6. As a result, individuals often purchase or consume products, services, and media to maintain or enhance a desired self-concept.

This sequence is reflected in Figure 12-1. This figure and the related discussion imply a rather conscious, deliberate process by which consumers determine their actual and desired self-concept and proceed to purchase products consistent with these concepts. While something like this may occasionally occur, most of the time the process is not deliberate, at least at the conscious level. That is, we may drink diet colas because our desired self-concept includes a slim figure, but we are unlikely to think about the purchase in these terms. However, as the following consumer quote illustrates, on occasion we do.

> And I feel if you present yourself in the right way, people will start to notice. But this leads back to image and self-worth, which can be achieved through having the right clothes and a good haircut . . . having a good portrait of yourself on the outside can eventually lead to an emotionally stable inside.[17]

This suggests that marketers should strive to develop product images that are consistent with the self-concepts of their target markets.[18] While everyone's self-concept is unique,

FIGURE 12-1 The Relationship between Self-Concept and Brand Image Influence

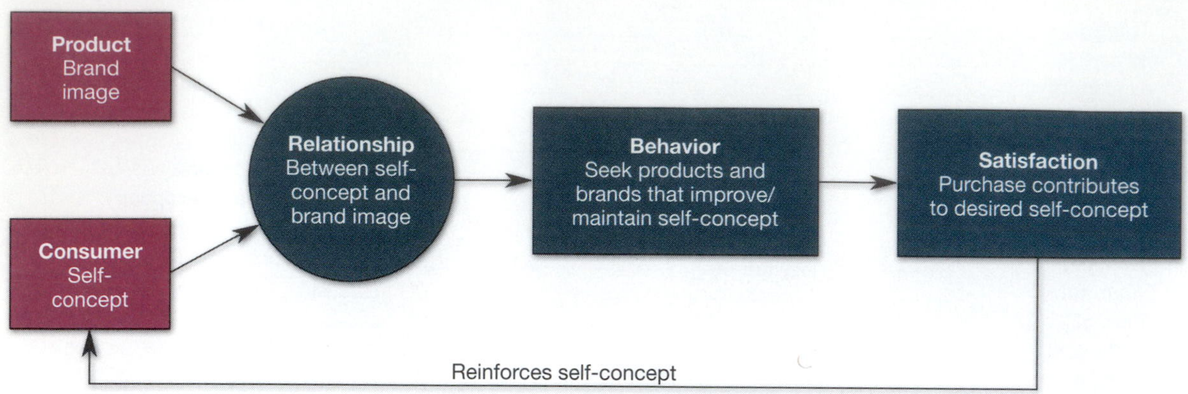

there is also significant overlap across individuals. For example, many consumers see themselves as environmentalists. Companies and products that create an image as being concerned about or good for the environment are likely to be supported by these consumers.

While it has been shown that consumers prefer brands that are similar to their self-concepts, the degree to which they would be attracted to such a brand varies with the *symbolism* and *conspicuousness* of that product class. Furthermore, the interaction between self-concept and product image is situation specific. That is, the situation may heighten or lessen the degree to which a product or store would enhance an individual's self-concept. Further, the ideal image that a consumer wishes to project (ideal social self-concept) varies with the situation. This suggests the need to measure ideal self-concepts in a situational context.[19]

Look at Illustration 12-2. What type of self-concept does this ad appeal to?

Marketing Ethics and the Self-Concept

The self-concept contains many dimensions. Marketers have been criticized for focusing too much attention on the importance of being beautiful, with beautiful being defined as young and slim with a fairly narrow range of facial features. While virtually all societies appear to define and desire beauty, the intense exposure to products and advertisements focused on beauty in America today is unique. Critics argue that this concern leads individuals to develop self-concepts that are heavily dependent on their physical appearance rather than other equally or more important attributes.

Consider the following quotes from two young women:

- I never felt that I looked right. The styles that I always want to wear, I always feel like I look fat. I always have to wear like a long skirt or sweater or at least baggy pants and a tight shirt. Like I can see outfits that I'd love to wear, but I know that I could never wear them. I probably could wear them and get away with it, but I'd be so self-conscious walking around that I'd be like, "oh, my God." Like I always try to look thinner and I guess everybody does.
- I am pretty content with my hair because I have good hair. I have good eyesight (laughs) so I don't have to wear glasses or anything that would make my face look different from what it is. In terms of bad points, well there is a lot. I got a lot of my father's features. I wish I had more of my mother's. My hands are pretty square. I have a kind of a big butt. Then, I don't have that great of a stomach. I like my arms. They're not

Courtesy Ford Motor Company.

ILLUSTRATION 12-2

Ads that position products to match the self-concept of the target market are generally successful. Such ads can appeal to the consumer's actual or ideal, private or social self.

> flabby arms. I like my ankles. It sounds really stupid, but a lot of people have like these trunks and it's very unattractive. So, I don't have huge, fat ankles. One thing I really hate is that I have large calves, which I don't like.[20]

These young women have self-concepts that are partly negative due to their perceptions of their beauty relative to the standard portrayed in the media. Critics of advertising claim that most individuals, but particularly young women, acquire negative components to their self-concepts because very few can achieve the standards of beauty presented in advertising.

The ethical question is complex. No one ad or company has this type of impact. It is the cumulative impact of many ads across many companies reinforced by the content of the mass media that presumably causes some to be overly focused on their physical beauty. And, as stated earlier, concern with beauty existed long before advertising.

THE NATURE OF LIFESTYLE

As Figure 12-2 indicates, our **lifestyle** is basically *how we live*. It is how we enact our self-concept. It is determined by our past experiences, innate characteristics, and current situation. It influences all aspects of our consumption behavior. One's lifestyle is a function of inherent individual characteristics that have been shaped and formed through social interaction as one evolves through the life cycle. Thus, lifestyle is influenced by the factors discussed in the previous chapters—culture, values, demographics, subculture, social class, reference groups, family, motives, emotions, and personality.

FIGURE 12-2 Lifestyle and the Consumption Process

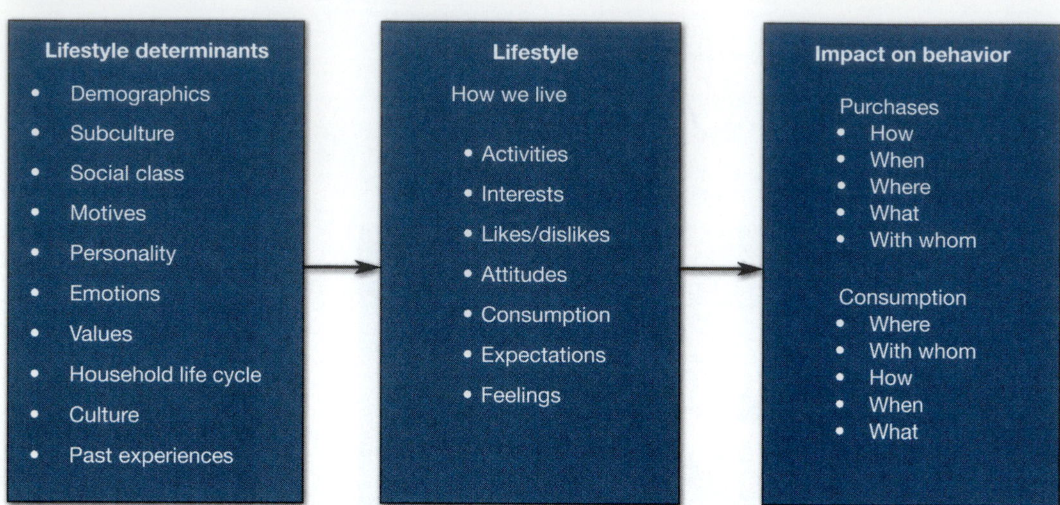

Individuals and households both have lifestyles. While household lifestyles are in part determined by the individual lifestyles of the household members, the reverse is also true.

Our desired lifestyle influences our needs and desires and thus our purchase and use behavior. It determines many of our consumption decisions that, in turn, reinforce or alter our lifestyle.

Lifestyle analysis can be used by marketers with respect to specific areas of consumers' lives, such as outdoor recreation. Many firms have conducted lifestyle studies focused on those aspects of individual or household lifestyles of most relevance to their product or service. For example, the lifestyle study described at the beginning of this chapter focused on outdoor activities. The British Virgin Islands ad shown in Illustration 12-3 would appeal to individuals classified as "getaway actives" and "health-conscious sociables" in this study. A second approach is to study the general lifestyle patterns of a population. This approach is also widely used in practice. Both approaches are described in detail in the next section.

Consumers are seldom explicitly aware of the role lifestyle plays in their purchase decisions. For example, few consumers would think, "I'll have a Starbucks coffee at a Starbucks outlet to maintain my lifestyle." However, individuals pursuing an active, social lifestyle might purchase Starbucks in part because of its convenience, "in" status, and the presence of others at Starbucks' outlets. Thus, lifestyle frequently provides the basic motivation and guidelines for purchases, although it generally does so in an indirect, subtle manner.

In this chapter, we will first discuss the measurement of lifestyles, starting with an activity-specific lifestyle segmentation study. In the next sections, we will describe the primary commercial lifestyles system, VALS2, and a geo-lifestyle system, PRIZM. The final section will describe the emerging work in developing international lifestyle systems.

Measurement of Lifestyle

Attempts to develop quantitative measures of lifestyle were initially referred to as **psychographics.**[21] In fact, the terms *psychographics* and *lifestyle* are frequently used interchangeably. Psychographic research attempts to place consumers on psychological—as opposed to purely demographic—dimensions. Psychographics originally focused on individuals'

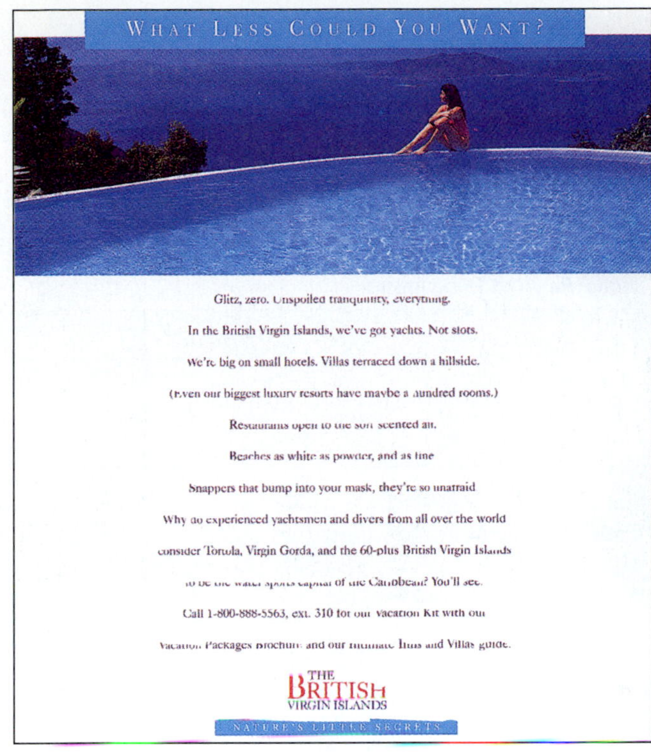

Courtesy FCB/New York.

ILLUSTRATION 12-3

One use of activity-specific lifestyle studies is to understand the market segments that exist in relation to that activity and to develop marketing mixes for the targeted segments. This ad would appeal to individuals classified as "getaway actives" and "health-conscious sociables" in the outdoor activity lifestyle study described at the beginning of this chapter.

activities (behaviors), interests, and opinions. The initial measurement instrument was an AIO inventory (activities, interests, and opinions). **AIO inventories** consist of *a large number of statements (often as many as 300) with which large numbers of respondents express degrees of agreement or disagreement.*

While it is a useful addition to demographic data, marketers found the original AIO inventories too narrow. Now, psychographics or lifestyle studies typically include the following:

- *Attitudes:* evaluative statements about other people, places, ideas, products, and so forth.
- *Values:* widely held beliefs about what is acceptable and/or desirable.
- *Activities and interests:* nonoccupational behaviors to which consumers devote time and effort, such as hobbies, sports, public service, and church.
- *Demographics:* age, education, income, occupation, family structure, ethnic background, gender, and geographic location.
- *Media patterns:* which specific media the consumers utilize.
- *Usage rates:* measurements of consumption within a specified product category. Often consumers are categorized as heavy, medium, light, or nonusers.

A large number of individuals, often 500 or more, provide the above information. Statistical techniques are used to place them into groups whose members have similar response patterns.[22] Most studies use the first two or three dimensions described above to group individuals. The other dimensions are used to provide fuller descriptions of each group. Other studies include demographics as part of the grouping process.[23]

Lifestyle measurements can be constructed with varying degrees of specificity. At one extreme are very general measurements dealing with general ways of living. Examples of

TABLE 12-3

Lifestyle Analysis of the British Cosmetics Market

Cosmetic Lifestyle Segments

1. *Self-aware:* concerned about appearance, fashion, and exercise.
2. *Fashion-directed:* concerned about fashion and appearance, not about exercise and sport.
3. *Green goddesses:* concerned about sport and fitness, less about appearance.
4. *Unconcerned:* neutral attitudes to health and appearance.
5. *Conscience-stricken:* no time for self-realization, busy with family responsibilities.
6. *Dowdies:* indifferent to fashion, cool on exercise, and dress for comfort.

Behaviors and Descriptors

			Retail Outlets*					
	*Cosmetic Use Index**	*Blush Use Index**	*Wallis*	*Miss Selfridge*	*Etam*	*C&A*	*Age† (15–44)*	*Social Class‡*
Self-aware	162	188	228	189	151	102	51%	60%
Fashion-directed	147	166	153	165	118	112	43	56
Green goddesses	95	76	74	86	119	103	32	52
Unconcerned	82	81	70	89	74	95	44	64
Conscience-stricken	68	59	53	40	82	99	24	59
Dowdies	37	19	17	22	52	85	20	62

*100 = Average usage.
†Read as "______ percent of this group is between 15 and 44."
‡Read as "______ percent of this group is in the working and lower middle class."

Source: T. Bowles, "Does Classifying People by Lifestyle Really Help the Advertiser?" *European Research,* February 1988, pp. 17–24.

these are provided in the next sections. More commonly, measurements are product or activity specific, such as the study of outdoor activities described earlier. For example, a study of lifestyles related to fashion clothing included 40 statements such as the following (respondents stated their degree of agreement with each):[24]

I like parties with music and chatting.

I like clothes with a touch of sensuality.

I choose clothes that match my age.

No matter where I go, I dress the way I want to.

I think I spend more time than I should on fashion.

This study also included measures of relevant activities and demographics. The value of such lifestyle information on a particular target market is easy to understand. General or "product free" lifestyles can be used to discover new product opportunities, while product-specific lifestyle analysis may help reposition existing brands.

Table 12-3 presents a small portion of a lifestyle analysis of British women between the ages of 15 and 44. This was an activity/product–specific analysis focused on appearance, fashions, exercise, and health. Six groups were formed based solely on attitudes and values with respect to the four areas mentioned. *After* the groups were formed, very significant differences were found in terms of product usage, shopping behaviors, media patterns, and demographics. Attempts to segment the market using demographics alone produced much less useful results.

Courtesy Wilson McHenry.

ILLUSTRATION 12-4

The Arbitron Company has identified eight lifestyle segments relating to media and computer usage. To which segment will this ad most appeal?

The value of this type of data is obvious. For example, how would you develop a marketing strategy to reach the conscience-stricken segment shown in Table 12-3?

The Arbitron Company discovered eight lifestyles of relevance to media usage. Three are briefly described below. How would you advertise Internet services or direct digital television to each?

- *Fast laners* (14% of population): Younger, overrepresenting Generation X and teenagers. Social and busy, they are impulse shoppers despite slightly below average income. They are heavy users of late-night television, MTV, HBO, contemporary comedies, premium cable services, and pay-per-view. They are open to technology and innovation and are optimistic about the future.
- *Savvy sophisticates* (11% of population): Overrepresents high-income and highly educated baby boomers. They describe themselves as confident, innovative, and curious. They are optimistic about the future but somewhat skeptical about new media possibilities. They own and use more computer, telephone, and communications equipment than any other segment. They read *Newsweek* magazine and watch "60 Minutes" and PBS.
- *The settled set* (17% of population): Older than the general population, with a thrifty, conservative, family values orientation. They watch "Wheel of Fortune" and read *Reader's Digest.* They are not very comfortable with technology and change.[25]

To which of these three groups will the ad in Illustration 12-4 appeal? How should ads for the other two groups differ from this one?

A number of other applications of lifestyle analyses have been reported recently. It was used to develop a successful lottery in Britain,[26] to predict sales at a new department store location,[27] to understand service expectations with respect to health care,[28] to study subcultures in Canada,[29] to compare Hong Kong and Singapore consumers,[30] and to analyze complaint behavior by elderly patients dissatisfied with their health care.[31]

While product- or activity-specific lifestyle studies are very useful, many firms have found general lifestyle studies to be of great value also. Two popular general systems are described next.[32]

THE VALS LIFESTYLES

By far the most popular application of lifestyle and psychographic research by marketing managers is SRI's **VALS2** program. Introduced in 1978 and significantly revised in 1989, VALS2 provides a systematic classification of American adults into eight distinct value and lifestyle patterns.[33] VALS2 has more of a psychological base than the original, which was more activity and interest based. The psychological base attempts to tap relatively enduring attitudes and values. It is measured by 42 statements with which respondents state a degree of agreement or disagreement. The following are some examples:

- I am often interested in theories.
- I often crave excitement.
- I liked most of the subjects I studied in school.
- I like working with carpentry and mechanical tools.
- I must admit that I like to show off.
- I have little desire to see the world.
- I like being in charge of a group.
- I hate getting grease and oil on my hands.

The questions are designed to classify respondents according to their *self-orientation* (similar in many ways to the self-concept), which serves as one of VALS2's two dimensions. SRI has identified three primary self-orientations:

- *Principle oriented.* These individuals are guided in their choices by their beliefs and principles rather than by feelings, events, or desire for approval.
- *Status-oriented.* The actions, approval, and opinions of others heavily influence these individuals.
- *Action-oriented.* These individuals desire social or physical activity, variety, and risk taking.

These three orientations determine the types of goals and behaviors that individuals will pursue.

The second dimension, termed *resources,* reflects the ability of individuals to pursue their dominant self-orientation. It refers to the full range of psychological, physical, demographic, and material means on which consumers can draw. Resources generally increase from adolescence through middle age and then remain relatively stable until they begin to decline with older age.

Based on these two concepts, SRI has identified eight general psychographic segments, as shown in Figure 12-3. Table 12-4 provides a demographic description of each segment. Table 12-5 provides information on product ownership and activities for each segment. Each of these segments is described briefly below.

The VALS2 Segments

Actualizers *Actualizers* are successful, sophisticated, active, "take-charge" people with high self-esteem and abundant resources. They are interested in growth and seek to develop, explore, and express themselves in a variety of ways—sometimes guided by principle and

VALS2 Lifestyle System **FIGURE 12-3**

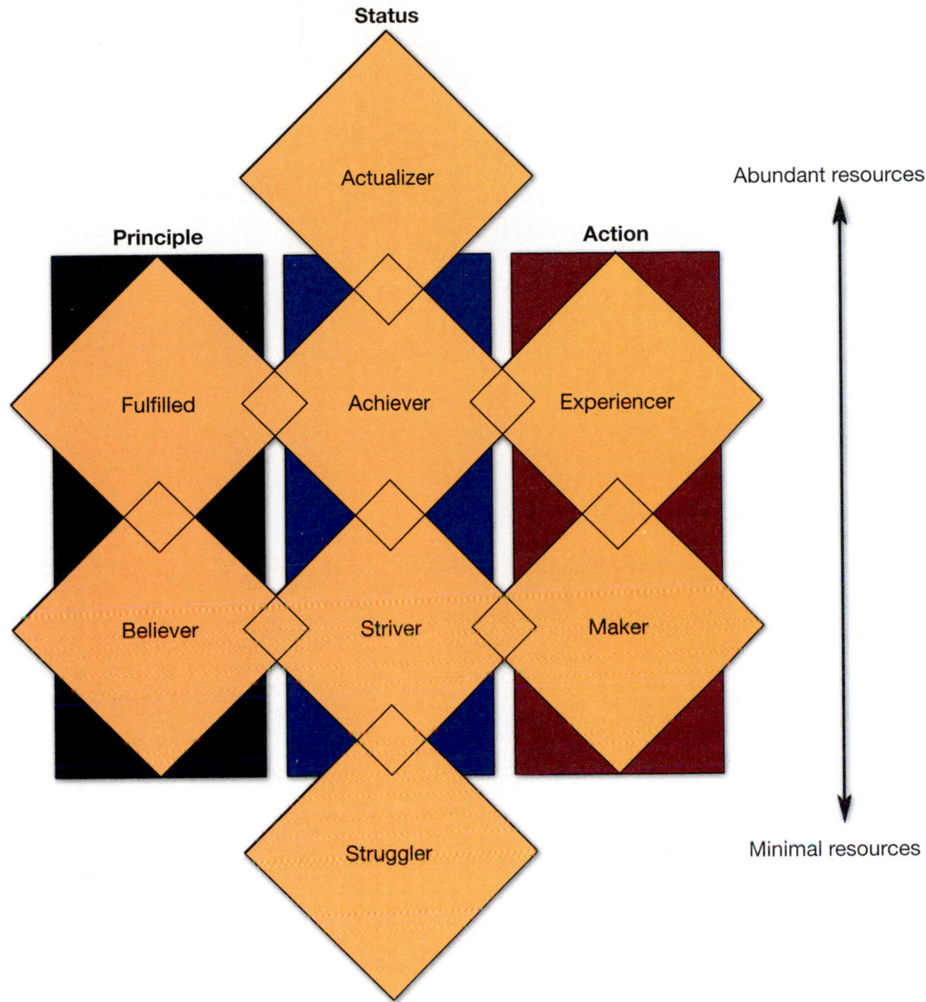

Source: SRI International.

sometimes by a desire to have an effect, to make a change. Image is important to Actualizers, not as evidence of status or power but as an expression of their taste, independence, and character.

Actualizers are among the established and emerging leaders in business and government, yet they continue to seek challenges. They have a wide range of interests, are concerned with social issues, and are open to change. Their possessions and recreation reflect a cultivated taste for the finer things in life. This is borne out in Table 12-5. The ad in Illustration 12-5 would appeal to actualizers.

Fulfilleds and Believers: Principle Oriented Principle-oriented consumers seek to make their behavior consistent with their views of how the world is or should be.

Fulfilleds are mature, satisfied, comfortable, reflective people who value order, knowledge, and responsibility. Most are well educated, and in (or recently retired from) professional occupations. They are well-informed about world and national events and are alert to opportunities to broaden their knowledge. Content with their careers, families, and station in life, their leisure activities tend to center around the home.

TABLE 12-4 VALS2 Segment Demographics

Segment	Percent of Population	Sex (M)	Median Age	Median Income	Education (College)	Occupation (White Collar)	Married
Actualizer	8%	59%	43	$58,000	95%	68%	72%
Fulfilled	11	47	48	38,000	81	50	73
Believer	16	46	58	21,000	6	11	70
Achiever	13	39	36	50,000	77	43	73
Striver	13	41	34	25,000	23	19	60
Experiencer	12	53	26	19,000	41	21	34
Maker	13	61	30	23,000	24	19	65
Struggler	14	37	61	9,000	3	2	47

Source: SRI International.

TABLE 12-5 VALS2 Segment Product Ownership and Activities

	Actualizer	Fulfilled	Believer	Achiever	Striver	Experiencer	Maker	Struggler
Own SLR Camera	163	124	80	138	83	88	115	29
Own bicycle >$150	154	116	90	33	83	120	88	43
Own fishing equipment	87	91	114	87	84	113	142	67
Own backpacking equipment	196	112	64	100	56	129	148	29
Own home computer	229	150	59	136	63	82	109	20
Own pickup truck	72	96	115	104	103	91	147	52
Own sports car	330	116	43	88	102	112	90	5
Barbecue outdoors	125	93	82	118	111	109	123	50
Do gardening	155	129	118	109	68	54	104	80
Do gourmet cooking	217	117	96	103	53	133	86	47
Drink herbal tea	171	125	89	117	71	115	81	68
Drink domestic beer	141	88	73	101	87	157	123	50
Drink imported beer	238	93	41	130	58	216	88	12
Play team sports	114	73	69	104	110	172	135	34
Do cultural activities	293	63	67	96	45	154	63	14
Do risky sports	190	48	36	52	59	283	171	7
Socialize weekly	109	64	73	90	96	231	94	62
Automotive magazines	92	105	50	79	50	254	157	22
Business magazines	255	227	74	179	37	71	33	8
Commentary magazines	274	173	106	87	66	109	49	15
Reader's Digest	58	143	150	90	63	57	87	130
Fish and game magazines	56	83	119	46	37	130	209	79
Literary magazines	533	120	29	77	44	105	45	31

*Figures under each segment are the index for each segment (100 = Average ownership or activity level).
Source: SRI International.

Courtesy Ford Plantation.

ILLUSTRATION 12-5

This ad would appeal to Actualizers' desire for growth and their taste for the finer things in life.

Fulfilleds have a moderate respect for the status quo institutions of authority and social decorum but are open-minded about new ideas and social change. Fulfilleds tend to base their decisions on strongly held principles and consequently appear calm and self-assured. Fulfilleds are conservative, practical consumers; they look for functionality, value, and durability in the products they buy.

Table 12-5 indicates that this group does not socialize much, does not consume beer as much as the average consumer, and is not into cultural activities. However, they drink herbal tea, do gourmet cooking, and own SLR cameras and computers more than the average consumer.

Believers are conservative, conventional people with concrete beliefs based on traditional, established codes: family, church, community, and the nation. Many Believers express moral codes that are deeply rooted and literally interpreted. They follow established routines, organized in large part around their homes, families, and the social or religious organizations to which they belong. As consumers, they are conservative and predictable, favoring American products and established brands.

Table 12-5 indicates the conservative nature of their purchases and activities. Other than the poverty ridden Strugglers, this group is least likely to own a sports car, to consume beer, do risky sports, or to read literary magazines. However, they do exceed the average in owning fishing equipment and pickups, in gardening, and in reading *Reader's Digest*.

The ad in Illustration 12-6 would appeal to both the Fulfilleds and the Believers.

Achievers and Strivers: Status Oriented Status-oriented consumers have or seek a secure place in a valued social setting. They make choices to enhance their position or to facilitate their move to another, more desirable group. Strivers look to others to indicate

ILLUSTRATION 12-6

Both Believers and Fulfilleds have a strong family orientation. This ad would appeal to both groups.

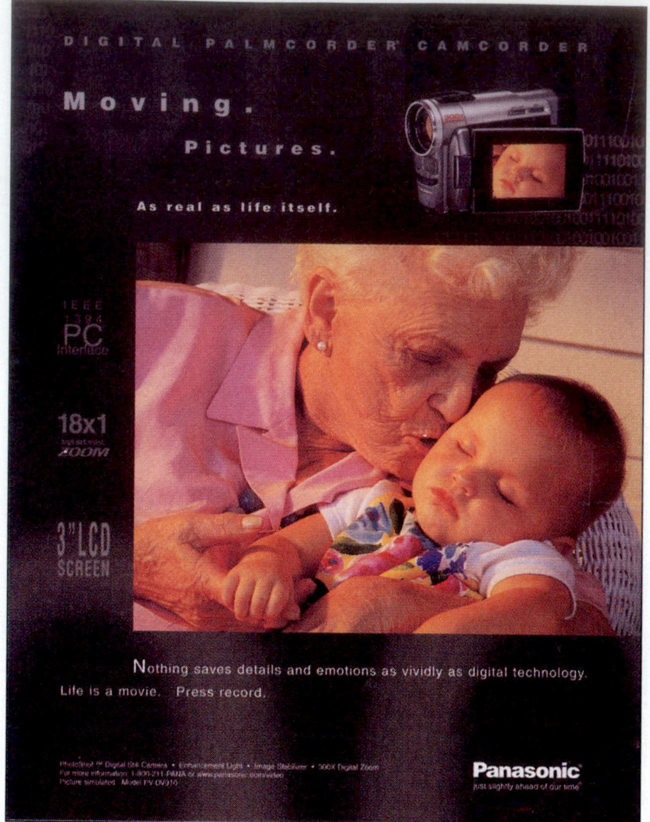

Courtesy Panasonic Video Products.

what they should be and do, whereas Achievers, more resourceful and active, seek recognition and self-definition through achievements at work and in their families.

Achievers are successful career- and work-oriented people who like to, and generally do, feel in control of their lives. They value consensus, predictability, and stability over risk, intimacy, and self-discovery. They are deeply committed to work and family. Work provides them with a sense of duty, material rewards, and prestige. Their social lives reflect this focus and are structured around family, church, and career. Achievers live conventional lives, are politically conservative, and respect authority and the status quo. Image is important to them; they favor established, prestige products and services that demonstrate success to their peers.

Achievers own cameras and computers (Table 12-5) more than average. They also barbecue outdoors, read business magazines, and drink imported beer more than average. The ad in Illustration 12-7 would appeal to Achievers.

Strivers seek motivation, self-definition, and approval from the world around them. They are striving to find a secure place in life. Unsure of themselves and low on economic, social, and psychological resources, Strivers are concerned about the opinions and approval of others. Money defines success for Strivers, who don't have enough of it and often feel that life has given them a raw deal. Strivers are easily bored and impulsive. Many of them seek to be stylish. They emulate those who own more impressive possessions, but what they wish to obtain is generally beyond their reach.

Table 12-5 indicates that Strivers are below average owners of many products, read less than average, but engage in barbecues and team sports more often than the norm.

Courtesy Pagenet.

ILLUSTRATION 12-7

This ad would appeal to the Achievers' family focus, appreciation of prestige products, and comfort with technology.

Experiencers and Makers: Action Oriented Action-oriented consumers like to affect their environment in tangible ways. Makers do so primarily at home and with constructive activity, Experiencers in the wider world through adventure and vivid experiences.

Experiencers are young, vital, enthusiastic, impulsive, and rebellious. They seek variety and excitement, savoring the new, the offbeat, and the risky. Still in the process of formulating life values and patterns of behavior, they quickly become enthusiastic about new possibilities but are equally quick to cool. At this stage of their lives, they are politically uncommitted, uninformed, and highly ambivalent about what they believe.

Courtesy Guatemalan Tourism.

ILLUSTRATION 12-8

Both Actualizers and Experiencers like to try new things and both like risky sports. This ad would be effective with both groups.

Experiencers combine an abstract disdain for conformity with an outsider's awe of others' wealth, prestige, and power. Their energy finds an outlet in exercise, sports, outdoor recreation, and social activities. Experiencers are avid consumers and spend much of their income on clothing, fast food, music, movies, and video. These patterns are reflected in Table 12-5. The ad in Illustration 12-8 would be particularly appealing to this segment. Actualizers would also be attracted by it.

Makers are practical people who have constructive skills and value self-sufficiency. They live within a traditional context of family, practical work, and physical recreation and have little interest in what lies outside that context. Makers experience the world by working on it—building a house, raising children, fixing a car, or canning vegetables—and have sufficient skill, income, and energy to carry out their projects successfully. Makers are politically conservative, suspicious of new ideas, respectful of government authority and organized labor, but resentful of government intrusion on individual rights. They are unimpressed by material possessions other than those with a practical or functional purpose (e.g., tools, pickup trucks, washing machines, or fishing equipment).

Strugglers *Strugglers'* lives are constricted. Chronically poor, with limited educations and skills, without strong social bonds, frequently elderly and concerned about their health, they are often resigned and passive. Because they must struggle to meet the urgent needs of the present moment, they do not show a strong self-orientation. Their chief concerns are for security and safety. Strugglers are cautious consumers. They represent a modest market for most products and services, and they are loyal to favorite brands. As described in Chapter 4, meeting the needs of these consumers is a challenge for both marketers and public policy makers.

Issues and Uses of VALS2

VALS2 is linked with numerous major databases. Both Simmons Market Research Bureau and Mediamark Research classify their respondents into VALS2 categories, which allows additional product and media use analyses. National Family Opinion and the NPD Group also classify members of their national consumer panels using VALS2. Finally, the VALS2 system is linked to all the major geo-demographic systems such as PRIZM (described in the next section of this chapter).

Concerns about VALS2 include the following:

- VALS2 are *individual* measures, but most consumption decisions are *household* decisions or are heavily influenced by other household members.
- Few individuals are "pure" in terms of self-orientation. While one of the three themes SRI has identified may be dominant for most individuals, the degree of dominance will vary, as will the orientation that is second in importance.
- The types of values and demographics measured by VALS2 may be inappropriate for particular products or situations. Product- or activity-specific lifestyles may provide more useful information. For example, VALS2 seems most useful for important or ego-involving purchases. Will it work well for laundry detergent?

Despite these problems, VALS2 is the most complete general segmentation system available. It is widely used by marketing managers. A recent study examined Internet usage by the VALS2 groups. Which groups would you guess to be heavy users? Actualizers are 10 percent of the population but represent 50 percent of the Internet users. Experiencers are also above average users, while Achievers, Believers, Makers, and Strugglers are far below average in usage.[34]

GEO-LIFESTYLE ANALYSIS (PRIZM)

Claritas, a leading firm in this industry, describes the logic of **geo-demographic analysis:**

> People with similar cultural backgrounds, means, and perspectives naturally gravitate toward one another. They choose to live amongst their peers in neighborhoods offering affordable advantages and compatible lifestyles.
>
> Once settled in, people naturally emulate their neighbors. They adopt similar social values, tastes, and expectations. They exhibit shared patterns of consumer behavior toward products, services, media and promotions.[35]

Analyses of this type are known as geo-demographic analyses.[36] They focus on the demographics of geographic areas based on the belief that lifestyle, and thus consumption, is largely driven by demographic factors, as described above. The geographic regions analyzed can be quite small, ranging from standard metropolitan statistical areas, through five-digit ZIP codes, census tracts, and down to census blocks (averaging only 340 households). Such data are used for target market selection, promotional emphasis, and so forth by numerous consumer goods marketers.

Claritas has taken geo-demographic analysis one step further and incorporated extensive data on consumption patterns. The output is a set of 62 lifestyle clusters organized into 12 broad social groups. This is called the **PRIZM** system. Every neighborhood in the United States can be profiled in terms of these lifestyle groups. Eight of the 62 lifestyle clusters are described as follows:

- *Furs and Station Wagons* is typified by "new money," living in expensive neighborhoods in the suburbs. They are well-educated, mobile professionals and managers. They are "winners"—big producers and big spenders.

- *Pools and Patios* once resembled Furs and Station Wagons. Today, their children are grown, leaving aging couples in homes too expensive for younger homemakers. Good educations, high white-collar employment levels, and double incomes assure the "good life."
- *Young Suburbia* is one of the largest clusters, found coast to coast in most major markets. It runs to large, young families and ranks second in incidence of married couples with children. Their relative affluence and high white-collar employment levels distinguish these neighborhoods. As a result, they are strong consumers of most family products.
- *Blue Chip Blues* is similar to Young Suburbia on most dimensions except social rank. Its predominant high school educations and blue-collar occupations are reflected in fewer high-end incomes and lower home values. However, high employment and double incomes yield similar discretionary spending patterns.
- *Blue-Collar Nursery* leads the nation in craftsmen, the elite of the blue-collar world. It is also no. 1 in married couples with children and households of three or more. These are low-density satellite towns and suburbs of smaller industrial cities. They are well paid and very stable.
- *Middle America* is at the center of the socioeconomic scale and is close to the U.S. average on most measures such as age, ethnicity, household composition, and life cycle. It is concentrated in the geographic center of the United States.
- *Emergent Minorities* is almost 80 percent black, the remainder largely Hispanics and other minorities. Emergent Minorities has above-average concentrations for children, almost half of them with single parents. It also shows below-average levels of education and white-collar employment.
- *Shotguns and Pickups* are common in outlying areas and rural communities. It is characterized by large families, headed by blue-collar craftsmen with high school educations. Many are dedicated outdoorsmen.

Unlike the VALS2 typology, PRIZM does not measure values or attitudes (though the distribution of VALS2 types within each geographic area covered by PRIZM is available). It is primarily driven by demographics, with substantial support from consumption and media usage data. Claritas and its competitors are widely used by consumer marketing firms such as General Motors and Hertz.[37]

An illustration of PRIZM lifestyle clusters can be seen in their use to redesign two bowling alleys.

Charlie Boyd operated two similar bowling alleys in the Kansas City suburb of Olathe—Olathe Lanes East (OL East) and Olathe Lanes West (OL West). The two facilities were less than three miles apart and drew most of their patronage from a six square mile area split by a major highway.

When the owner decided to redesign the facilities (due to a fire at one), the firm that was called in to rebuild noticed that the cars of the patrons of OL East were BMWs, sports vans, and other upscale vehicles. In contrast, the cars in the lot at OL West were Fords, Chevrolets, and pickups. This led to questioning, which revealed that the patrons of the two very similar bowling alleys differed in income, education, and food and beverage preferences. Additional research based on the PRIZM clusters revealed that customers at OL East were primarily Young Suburbia (38%), Pools and Patios (30%), and Furs and Station Wagons (23%). In contrast, OL West's bowlers were Middle America (39%), Blue-Collar Nursery (17%), Blue Chip Blues (13%), and Shotguns and Pickups (9%).

Not surprisingly, the reasons the two groups bowled and their desires and expectations differed sharply. The upscale clusters that patronized OL East came for relaxation and exercise. Women in particular came for exercise. Socialization was also important, but these women belonged to other groups and their socialization needs were met elsewhere. Men came to escape the tensions of their professional careers and to relax. They were not interested in bowling as a competitive activity. In fact, they weren't very interested in bowling at all. It was a means to the end of unwinding.

The blue-collar clusters that patronized OL West were much more focused on socializing and bowling. Many of the women's groups bowled several times per week and it served as a major source of socializing. For the men, it was both a place to socialize and to compete with their peers and excel.

These results and the wealth of data on the lifestyles and preferences led to a complete redesign of both facilities. The designers identified 82 surfaces in the facilities and created each one to be consistent with the tastes and needs of the key lifestyle groups. For example, the upscale groups preferred a quite environment, so all aspect of the new facility was designed to dampen noise. Floor-to-ceiling windows were used, and the ultimate overall effect was a modern, stylish, open environment. The OL West facility was done in a folksy, outdoors style. The predominant scheme is peach stucco with blue-green accents.

The goals of the redesigns were to maintain or increase patronage and to increase the food and beverage sales at each facility (the primary source of profit). Within a year, food and beverage sales had increased by 2.5 times the prior level and the profits of both facilities were up sharply. The president of the design firm describes the impact of the project on his business as follows:

> The development of the Olathe lanes facilities changed our business from one driven by traditional interior design into one driven by marketing. Today, we begin every project by looking at customers' lifestyles rather than design trends.[38]

INTERNATIONAL LIFESTYLES: GLOBAL SCAN

Both VALS2 and PRIZM are oriented to the United States. In addition, VALS2 is now available for Japan. As we saw in Chapter 2, marketing is increasingly a global activity. If there are discernible lifestyle segments that cut across cultures, marketers can develop

TABLE 12-6

Global Lifestyle Segments Identified by GLOBAL SCAN

Strivers (26%): young people on the run. Their median age is 31, and their average day is hectic. They push hard to achieve success, but they're hard-pressed to meet all their goals. They're materialistic, they look for pleasure, and they insist on instant gratification. Short of time, energy, and money, they seek out convenience in every corner of their lives.

Achievers (22%): slightly older and several giant steps ahead of the Strivers—affluent, assertive, and on the way up. Opinion leaders and style setters, Achievers shape our mainstream values. They led the way to the fitness craze and still set the standard for what we eat, drink, and wear today. Achievers are hooked on status and fixated on quality, and together with Strivers, create the youth-oriented values that drive our societies today.

Pressured (13%): downtrodden people with more than their share of problems. Largely women from every age group, the Pressured face economic and family concerns that drain their resources and rob much of the joy from their lives.

Adapters (18%): maybe an older crowd, but these folks are hardly shocked by the new. Content with themselves and their lives, they respect new ideas without rejecting their own standards. And they are all ready to take up whatever activities will enrich their golden years.

Traditionals (16%): embody the oldest values of their countries and cultures. Conservative, rooted in the heartland, and tied to the past. Traditionals prefer the tried and true, the good old ways of thinking, eating, and living their lives.

cross-cultural strategies around these segments. Although language and other differences would exist, individuals pursuing similar lifestyles in different cultures should be responsive to similar product features and communication themes.

Not surprisingly, a number of attempts have been made to develop such systems.[39] Large, international advertising agencies have provided much of the impetus behind these efforts. We will describe a system developed by Backer Spielvogel Bates Worldwide (BSBW).

BSBW's **GLOBAL SCAN** is based on surveys of 15,000 consumers in 14 countries (Australia, Canada, Colombia, Finland, France, Germany, Hong Kong, Indonesia, Japan, Mexico, Spain, the United Kingdom, the United States, and Venezuela). It measures over 250 value and attitude components, in addition to demographics, media usage, and buying preferences.

Based on the combination of lifestyle and purchasing data, BSBW found five global lifestyle segments, as described in Table 12-6. While these segments exist in all 14 countries studied thus far, the percentage of the population in each group varies by country, as shown in Figure 12-4.

Suppose you were developing an international strategy for Whirlpool Appliances. You would notice that Strivers are the largest global segment, although this is not true in all countries. A product line targeted at this group would need to be relatively inexpensive and readily available, would require access to credit, and should have a maximum number of convenience features (perhaps at the expense of durability, if this is necessary to keep costs low). The communications theme would stress convenience, gratification, and value. Promotional efforts would be allocated disproportionately to those countries with large concentrations of Strivers. Illustration 12-9 shows an international ad that would appeal to Strivers.

FIGURE 12-4 GLOBAL SCAN Segment Sizes across Countries

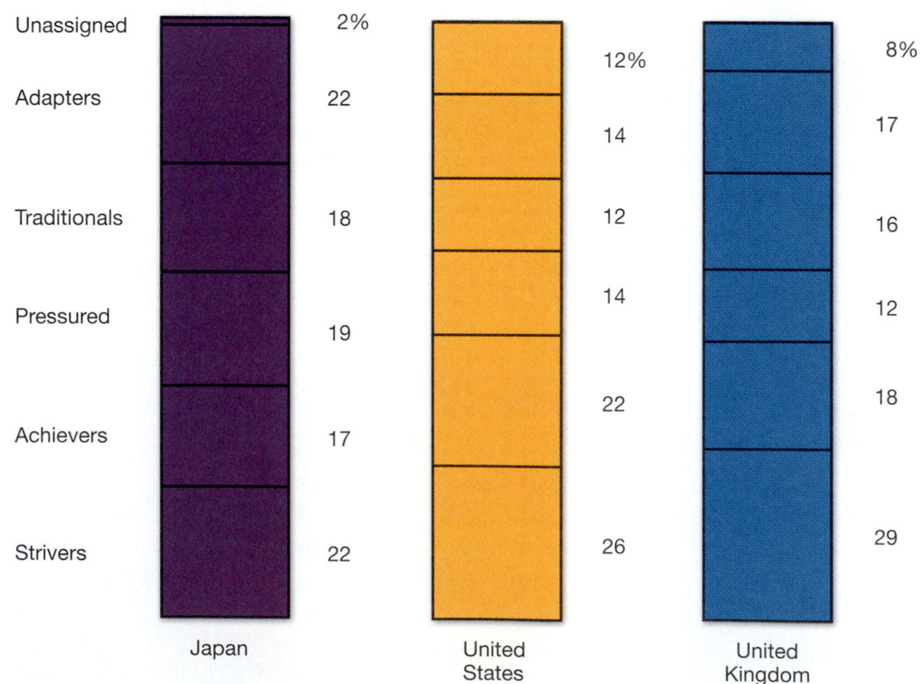

ILLUSTRATION 12-9

The GLOBAL SCAN Striver segment is interested in pleasure and gratification. This ad would appeal to this international group.

SUMMARY

The *self-concept* is one's beliefs and feelings about oneself. There are four types of self-concept: *actual self-concept, social self-concept, private self-concept,* and *ideal self-concept*. The self-concept is important to marketers because consumers purchase and use products to express, maintain, and enhance their self-concepts. Marketers, particularly those working in international marketing, have found it useful to characterize individuals and cultures by whether they have a predominately *independent self-concept* (the individual is the critical component) or an *interdependent self-concept* (relationships are of primary importance).

Our self-concept, the way we define ourselves, typically includes at least some of our possessions. The self-concept, including the possessions one uses to define oneself, is termed the *extended self*.

Lifestyle can be defined simply as how one lives. Lifestyle is a function of one's inherent individual characteristics that have been shaped through social interaction as one moves through one's life cycle. It is how one expresses one's self-concept in actions.

Psychographics is the primary way that lifestyle is made operationally useful to marketing managers. This is a way of describing the psychological makeup or lifestyle of consumers by assessing such lifestyle dimensions as activities, interests, opinions, values, and demographics. Lifestyle measures can be macro and reflect how individuals live in general, or micro and describe their attitudes and behaviors with respect to a specific product category or activity.

The VALS2 system, developed by SRI, divides the United States into eight groups—Actualizers, Fulfilleds, Believers, Achievers, Strivers, Experiencers, Makers, and Strugglers. These groups were derived based on two dimensions. The first dimension is self-orientation, with three categories: *principle oriented* (those guided by their basic beliefs and values); *status oriented* (those influenced by the actions, approval, and opinions of others); and *action oriented* (those who seek social or physical activity, variety, and risks). The second dimension is the physical, mental, and material resources to pursue one's dominant self-orientation.

Geo-lifestyle analysis is based on the premise that individuals with similar lifestyles tend to live near each other. PRIZM is one system that has analyzed demographic and consumption data down to the census block. It has developed profiles of each block in terms of 62 lifestyle clusters.

In response to the rapid expansion of international marketing, a number of attempts have been made to develop lifestyle measures applicable across cultures. GLOBAL SCAN is the largest of these. It has found five segments that exist across the 14 countries it has analyzed to date.

KEY TERMS

Actual self-concept 428
AIO inventory 437
Extended self 429
Geo-demographic analysis 447
GLOBAL SCAN 450
Ideal self-concept 428
Independent self-concept 428
Interdependent self-concept 428
Lifestyle 435
Mere ownership effect 432
Peak experience 431
Private self-concept 428
PRIZM 447
Psychographics 436
Self-concept 428
Social self-concept 428
VALS2 440

INTERNET EXERCISES

1. Visit SRI's VALS2 site (http://future.sri.com/vals/survey.html). Complete the survey for yourself and your parents. Are you and your parents' classifications and the behaviors associated with them accurate?
2. Visit Claritas's Web site (http://www.claritas.com). Report on its approach to lifestyle segmentation.
3. Visit USAData's Web site (http://www.usadata.com). Describe the types of lifestyle data there.

DDB NEEDHAM LIFESTYLE DATA ANALYSES

1. The DDB Needham questionnaire measures personality by asking people to list characteristics that describe themselves. These measures could also be interpreted as measures of self-concept.
   a. Based on Table 7a, do any of these self-concept characteristics seem to be associated with heavy consumption of any of the products or activities? Why do you think this is?
   b. Based on Table 7a, do any of these self-concept characteristics seem to be associated with product ownership? Why do you think this is?
   c. Based on Table 7a, do any of these self-concept characteristics seem to be associated with television show preferences? Why do you think this is?
   d. Based on Table 7a, do any of these self-concept characteristics seem to be associated with any of the attitude, interest, or opinion items? Why do you think this is?
2. Identify attitude, interest, or opinion statements that match those that the text says are associated with one of the VALS2 lifestyle groups. Do the demographics of those who agree with those statements match the demographics associated with the VALS2 groups?
3. Examine the DDB Needham data in Tables 1a, 2a, 3a, 4a, 5a, 6a, and 7a. What characterizes one who is likely to have his or her (*a*) car or (*b*) clothing become part of his or her extended self?

REVIEW QUESTIONS

1. What is a *self-concept?* What are the four types of self-concept?
2. How do marketers use insights about the self-concept?
3. How can we measure the self-concept?
4. How does an *interdependent self-concept* differ from an *independent self-concept?*
5. What is the *extended self?*

6. What is a *peak experience?*

7. What ethical issues arise in using the self-concept in marketing?
8. What do we mean by *lifestyle?* What factors determine and influence that lifestyle?
9. What is *psychographics?*
10. What is an *AIO inventory?*
11. When is a product- or activity-specific psychographic instrument superior to a general one?
12. What are the dimensions on which VALS2 is based? Describe each.
13. Describe the VALS2 system and each segment in it.
14. What is *geo-demographic analysis?*
15. Describe the PRIZM system.
16. Describe the GLOBAL SCAN system.

DISCUSSION QUESTIONS

17. Use Table 12-2 to measure your four self-concepts. To what extent are they similar? What causes the differences? To what extent do you think they influence your purchase behavior?
18. Use Table 12-2 to measure your self-concept (you choose which self-concept and justify your choice). Also measure the image of three celebrities you admire. What do you conclude?
19. What possessions are part of your extended self? Why?
20. Is your self-concept predominantly independent or interdependent? Why?
21. For each of the following products, develop one ad that would appeal to a target market characterized by predominantly independent self-concepts and another for a target market characterized by predominantly interdependent self-concepts.
    a. Dr Pepper
    b. Saturn SC2 (sports car)
    c. Tide laundry detergent
    d. McDonald's
22. Use the self-concept theory to develop marketing strategies for the following products.
    a. United Way contributions
    b. Sears
    c. Marine recruitment
    d. Mountain Dew
    e. Head snowboards
    f. Bonne Bell lipstick
23. Does VALS2 make sense to you? What do you like or dislike about it?
24. How would one use VALS2 to develop a marketing strategy?
25. Develop a marketing strategy based on VALS2 for:
    a. Greenpeace
    b. Ski resort
    c. Bose stereo equipment
    d. Prunes
    e. A new TV series
    f. WNBA
26. Develop a marketing strategy for *each* of the eight VALS2 segments for:
    a. Electric razor (for men)
    b. Vacation package
    c. Mouthwash
    d. TV series
    e. Pepsi
    f. A new magazine
27. Does PRIZM make sense to you? What do you like or dislike about it? Is it really a measure of lifestyle?
28. How would one use PRIZM to develop a marketing strategy?
29. Does GLOBAL SCAN make sense to you?
30. How would you use GLOBAL SCAN to develop marketing strategy?
31. Develop a marketing strategy for each of the GLOBAL SCAN segments for the products in Question 25.
32. The following quote is from Paul Casi, president of Glenmore distilleries: "Selling cordials is a lot different from selling liquor. Cordials are like the perfume of our industry. You're really talking high fashion and you're talking generally to a different audience—I don't mean male versus female—I'm talking about lifestyle."
    a. In what ways do you think the lifestyle of cordial drinkers would differ from those who drink liquor but not cordials?
    b. How would you determine the nature of any such differences?
    c. Of what use would knowledge of such lifestyle differences be to a marketing manager introducing a new cordial?

33. How is one likely to change one's lifestyle at different stages of one's household life cycle? Over one's life, is one likely to assume more than one of the VALS2 lifestyle profiles described? GLOBAL SCAN's?
34. To which VALS2 category do you belong? To which do your parents belong? Which will you belong to when you are your parents' age?
35. Based on the outdoor activity lifestyles described in the chapter opening example, develop a marketing strategy for:
    a. A resort
    b. A fitness club
    c. In-line skates
    d. Schwinn bicycles
    e. Jazzercize Inc.
    f. Old Town canoes
36. Using Table 12-3, develop a cosmetics line and marketing program targeting the following segments.
    a. Self-aware
    b. Fashion-directed
    c. Green goddesses
    d. Unconcerned
    e. Conscience-stricken
    f. Dowdies

APPLICATION ACTIVITIES

37. Develop an instrument to measure the interdependent versus independent self-concept.
38. Use the instrument you developed in Question 37 to measure the self-concepts of 10 male and 10 female students (all of the same nationality). What do you conclude?
39. Develop your own psychographic instrument (set of relevant questions) that measures the lifestyles of college students.
40. Using the psychographic instrument developed in Question 39, interview 10 students (using the questionnaire instrument). Based on their responses, categorize them into lifestyle segments.
41. Find and copy or describe ads that would appeal to each of the eight VALS2 segments.
42. Repeat Question 41 for the five GLOBAL SCAN segments.
43. Identify and describe a male and a female TV personality or role played on television that fits each of the eight VALS2 profiles outlined.
44. Repeat Question 43 for the five GLOBAL SCAN segments.

REFERENCES

1. B. E. Bryant, "Built for Excitement," *American Demographics,* March 1987, pp. 39–42.
2. H. R. Markus and S. Kitayama, "Culture and Self," Psychological Review, no. 2 (1991), pp. 224–53; S. Abe, R. P. Bagozzi, and P. Sadarangani, "An Investigation of Construct Validity and Generalizability of the Self-Concept," *Journal of International Consumer Marketing,* no. 3/4 (1996), pp. 97–123; and N. Y. Wong and A. C. Ahuvia, "Personal Taste and Family Face," *Psychology & Marketing,* August 1998, pp. 423–41.
3. C. L. Wang and J. C. Mowen, "The Separateness-Connectedness Self-Schema," *Psychology & Marketing,* March 1997, pp. 185–207.
4. See footnotes 2 and 3; and C. Webster and R. C. Beatty, "Nationality, Materialism, and Possession Importance," in *Advances in Consumer Research XXIV,* ed. M. Bruck and D. J. MacInnis (Provo, UT: Association for Consumer Research, 1997), pp. 204–10.
5. R. W. Belk, "Possessions and the Extended Self," *Journal of Consumer Research,* September 1988, pp. 139–68; R. Belk, "Extended Self and Extending Paradigmatic Perspective," *Journal of Consumer Research,* June 1989, pp. 129–32. See also M. L. Richins, "Valuing Things"; and M. L. Richins, "Special Possessions and the Expression of Material Values"; both in *Journal of Consumer Research,* December 1994, pp. 504–33; E. Sivadas and R. Venkatesh, "An Examination of Individual and Object-Specific Influences on the Extended Self and Its Relation to Attachment and Satisfaction"; and J. Gentry, S. M. Baker, and F. B. Kraft, "The Role of Possessions in Creating, Maintaining, and Preserving One's Identity"; both in *Advances in Consumer Research XXII,* ed. F. R. Kardes and M. Sujan (Provo, UT: Association for Consumer Research, 1995), pp. 406–18.
6. See S. S. Kleine, R. E. Kleine, Jr., and C. T. Allen, "How Is a Possession 'Me' or 'Not Me'?" *Journal of Consumer Research,* December 1995, pp. 327–43.
7. S. Sayre and D. Horne, "I Shop, Therefore I Am," in *Advances in Consumer Research XXIII,* ed. K. P. Corfman and J. G. Lynch (Provo, UT: Association for Consumer Research, 1996), pp. 323–28.
8. See L. L. Love and P. S. Sheldon, "Souvenirs," in *Advances in Consumer Research XXV,* ed. J. W. Alba and J. W. Hutchinson (Provo, UT: Association for Consumer Research, 1998), pp. 170–74.

9. C. S. Areni, P. Kiecker, and K. M. Palan, "Is It Better to Give than to Receive?" *Psychology & Marketing,* January 1998, pp. 81–109.
10. K. J. Dodson, "Peak Experiences and Mountain Biking," in *Advances in Consumer Research XXIII,* ed. K. P. Corfman and J. G. Lynch (Provo, UT: Association for Consumer Research, 1996), pp. 317–22.
11. C. H. Noble and B. A. Walker, "Exploring the Relationships among Liminal Transitions, Symbolic Consumption, and the Extended Self," *Psychology & Marketing,* January 1997, pp. 29–47.
12. E. Sivadas and K. A. Machleit, "A Scale to Determine the Extent of Object Incorporation in the Extended Self," in *Marketing Theory and Applications* 5, ed. C. W. Park and D. C. Smith (Chicago: American Marketing Association, 1994).
13. S. Sen and E. J. Johnson, "Mere-Possession Effects without Possession in Consumer Choice," *Journal of Consumer Research,* June 1997, pp. 105–17; M. A. Strahilevitz and G. Loewenstein, "The Effect of Ownership History of the Valuation of Objects," *Journal of Consumer Research,* December 1998, pp. 276–89; and K. P. Nesselroade, Jr., J. K. Beggan, and S. T. Allison, "Possession Enhancement in an Interpersonal Context," *Psychology & Marketing,* January 1999, pp. 21–34.
14. J. Jenson, "Picabo Street Wins Starring Role in Nike Game Plan," *Advertising Age,* November 11, 1996, p. 3.
15. M. J. Sirgy et al., "Assessing the Predictive Validity of Two Methods of Measuring Self-Image Congruence," *Journal of the Academy of Marketing Science,* Spring 1997, pp. 229–42.
16. T. R. Graeff, "Image Congruence Effects on Product Evaluations," *Psychology & Marketing,* August 1996, pp. 481–99; J. E. Burroughs, "Product Symbolism, Self Meaning, and Holistic Matching," in *Advances in Consumer Research XXIII,* ed. K. P. Corfman and J. G. Lynch (Provo, UT: Association for Consumer Research, 1996), pp. 463–69; N. Y. C. Wong, "Suppose You Own the World and No One Knows?" in *Advances in Consumer Research XXIV,* ed. M. Bruck and D. J. MacInnis (Provo, UT: Association for Consumer Research, 1997), pp. 197–203; and G. Lantz and S. Loeb, "An Examination of the Community Identity and Purchase Preferences Using the Social Identity Approach," in *Advances in Consumer Research XXV,* ed. J. W. Alba and J. W. Hutchinson (Provo, UT: Association for Consumer Research, 1998), pp. 486–91.
17. S. J. Gould, "An Interpretive Study or Purposeful, Mood Self-Regulating Consumption," *Psychology & Marketing,* July 1997, pp. 395–426.
18. See J. W. Hong and G. M. Zinkham, "Self-Concept and Advertising Effectiveness," *Psychology & Marketing,* January 1995, pp. 53–77.
19. T. R. Graeff, "Consumption Situations and the Effects of Brand Image on Consumers' Brand Evaluations," *Psychology & Marketing,* January 1999, pp. 49–70.
20. J. Meyers-Levy and L. A. Peracchio, "Understanding the Socialized Body," *Journal of Consumer Research,* September 1995, p. 147.
21. See E. H. Demby, "Psychographics Revisited," *Marketing Research,* Spring 1994, pp. 26–30.
22. See J. L. Lastovicka, J. P. Murry, and E. A. Joachimsthaler, "Evaluating the Measurement Validity of Lifestyle Typologies with Qualitative Measures and Multiplicative Factoring," *Journal of Marketing Research,* February 1990, pp. 11–23.
23. See F. W. Gilbert and W. E. Warren, "Psychographic Constructs and Demographic Segments," *Psychology & Marketing,* May 1995, pp. 223–37.
24. W. A. Kamakura and M. Wedel, "Life-Style Segmentation with Tailored Interviewing," *Journal of Marketing Research,* August 1995, pp. 308–17.
25. Publicity release from The Arbitron Company (New York), March 5, 1995. See also K. Shermach, "Study Identifies Types of Interactive Shoppers," *Marketing News,* September 1995, p. 22.
26. E. Kent-Smith and S. Thomas, "Luck Had Nothing to Do with It," *Journal of the Market Research Society,* April 1995, pp. 127–41.
27. P. Leblang, "A Theoretical Approach for Predicting Sales at a New Department Store Location via Lifestyles," *Journal of Direct Marketing,* Autumn 1993, pp. 70–74.
28. A. M. Thompson and P. F. Kaminski, "Psychographic and Lifestyle Antecedents of Service Quality Expectations," *Journal of Services Marketing* 7, no. 4 (1993), pp. 53–61.
29. M. Hui, A. Joy, C. Kim, and M. Laroche, "Equivalence of Lifestyle Dimensions across Four Major Subcultures in Canada," *Journal of International Consumer Marketing,* no. 3 (1993), pp. 15–35.
30. S. H. C. Tai and J. L. M. Tam, "A comparative Study of Chinese Consumers in Asian Markets," *Journal of International Consumer Marketing,* no. 1 (1996), pp. 25–42.
31. A. L. Dolinsky et al., "The role of Psychographic Characteristics as Determinants of Complaint Behavior by Elderly Consumers," *Journal of Hospital Marketing,* no. 2 (1998), pp. 27–51.
32. For a critical review and alternative approach, see D. B. Holt, "Poststructuralist Lifestyle Analysis," *Journal of Consumer Research,* March 1997, pp. 326–50. Alternative lifestyle systems are also described in C. Walker and E. Moses, "The Age of Self-Navigation," *American Demographics,* September 1996, pp. 36–42; and P. H. Ray, "The Emerging Culture," *American Demographics,* February 1997, pp. 29–56.
33. Values and Lifestyles Program. *Descriptive Materials for the VALS2 Segmentation System* (Menlo Park, CA.: SRI International, 1989). See also T. P. Novak and B. MacEvoy, "On Comparing Alternative Segmentation Schemes," *Journal of Consumer Research,* June 1990, pp. 105–9; and Lastovicka, Murry, and Joachimsthaler, footnote 22.
34. R. P. Heath, "The Frontier of Psychographics," *American Demographics,* July 1996, pp. 38–43.
35. *How to Use PRIZM* (Alexandria, VA.: Claritas, 1986), p. 1.
36. See S. Mitchell, "Birds of a Feather," *American Demographics,* February 1995, pp. 40–48.
37. C. Del Vale, "They Know Where You Live," *Business Week,* February 7, 1994, p. 89.
38. B. J. Eichhorn, "Selling by Design," *American Demographics,* October 1996, pp. 45–48.
39. For example, see K. Brunso and K. G. Grunet, "Development and Testing of a Cross-Culturally Valid Instrument," in *Advances in Consumer Research XXII,* ed. F. R. Kardes and M. Sujan (Provo, UT: Association for Consumer Research, 1995), pp. 475–80.

part three

Cases

3-1 Repositioning Las Vegas

After years of being famous for gambling and showgirls, Las Vegas is embarking on a five-year marketing plan to reposition itself from "Sin City" to a family vacation destination. The Las Vegas Convention and Visitors Authority (LVCVA) spent over $27 million on the campaign in 1999. The tagline is "Its anything and everything." However, it does not ignore gambling. The ads use a neon gaming-chip logo and the "Open 24 hours" line continues in all ads. The objective is to increase visitors from 30 million in 1997 to over 38 million in 2002.

A number of developments are making such a repositioning possible. The recent addition of numerous theme-oriented casino hotels provides a wealth of nongambling activities ranging from roller-coaster rides atop skyscrapers to first-class theater to state-of-the art virtual reality experiences to water sports. Top-end retailers such as Neiman Marcus, Versace, and Armani have major outlets in the city. Luxury hotels such as the Four Seasons are providing accommodations that are not tied to gaming.

Nevada's governor is helping the push. He recently visited Latin America and Asia in part to urge airline carriers to open more direct and charter flights to Las Vegas. According to the governor, "Each and every one (of the 20,000 new hotel rooms) is connected to a resort or an attraction worthy of a visit by themselves. In foreign markets, they don't understand the theme park–type attractions we now have." International tourists represent 19 percent of the visitors to Las Vegas now. The city wants to increase that percent to 25 in five years.

While the city hopes to increasingly become a family vacation destination, currently 87 percent of the visitors gamble during their stay.

Discussion Questions

1. What attitudes do you think Americans currently have about Las Vegas? Are these attitudes consistent with it being a family vacation destination? What attitude change strategies should the LVCVA use to change any inappropriate attitudes?
2. How would you describe Las Vegas' current product position? Can this position be altered to include "great family vacation site"? How?
3. What learning theories can the LVCVA use to teach people about the nongaming reasons to visit Las Vegas?
4. What product position would you try to achieve for Las Vegas in each of these countries?
   a. Germany
   b. France
   c. Japan
   d. Taiwan
   e. Mexico
   f. Saudi Arabia
5. Develop an ad to attract a family to Las Vegas using one of the following.
   a. An emotional appeal
   b. The self-concept
   c. One of McGuire's motives
   d. A utilitarian appeal
6. Does Las Vegas have brand equity? If so, how can it use it?
7. Visit the Las Vegas Web site (lasvegas.com). Is it consistent with the desired image? If not, how could it be improved?

Source: Lasvegas.com, M. G. Briones, "Las Vegas Throws the Dice," *Marketing News,* September 1998, p.1; and A. Salomon, "Family Fun in the Desert," *Advertising Age,* August 24, 1998, p. 7.

3-2 Marketing the California Avocado

In 1999, Integrated Marketing Works and the California Avocado Commission conducted another set of minifocus groups (five to seven participants) in an ongoing research program designed to increase their understanding of the consumption of avocados in general and California avocados in particular. This set of interviews focused on light to moderate users in geographic regions with heavy consumption (three in California and three in Colorado) and on nonusers in the light use areas (three with nonusers and one with light/moderate users in Atlanta). All of the groups were composed of 35- to 49-year-old females who were the primary grocery shoppers for their households.

Based on these and previous research studies, users and nonusers were described as follows: Users derive pleasure from both the taste of avocados and from the emotional and usage situations associated with avocado consumption. The following represents the agency's view of how avocados trigger emotional or sensual responses in consumers.

Physical avocado	*Emotional*
Flavor/texture	Delicious, creamy, pizzazz, special
Green	Natural, good for me, friendly
Implied Occasions	Festive, feeling good, fun, upbeat, carefree, happy
Implied Usage	Pizzazz, healthy, satisfying, delicious
Unique	Special, different, fun
California "Aspirational"	Healthy, natural, fun, outdoors, active, feeling good

Barriers to the consumption of avocados by users are price, the fat content, and the view that they are only for special occasions.

Nonusers are actually nonretail purchasers. Many of them have had avocados in restaurants and many are attached to avocados. Thus, they have some of the same "emotional" responses to avocados as do users. They also feel the same barriers. However, in addition, they are unsure of how to purchase one (how do you select a ripe one for use today or one that will ripen for use in three or four days) and how to peel and use them in recipes.

Until recently, California avocados have had virtually no direct competition except in the northeast, where avocados from Mexico have been imported, and the south, where Florida avocados are available. However, with the ongoing removal of trade barriers, it is likely that this competition will spread throughout the country and will involve additional countries. Therefore, the California Avocado Commission wants to develop strong brand image and brand equity for its product. In addition, avocados compete for "share of stomach" with 240 other items in a typical produce department.

In light of the research and the changing competitive situation, two campaigns were prepared—one targeting light/moderate users in core market areas and one targeting nonusers in light usage areas. A description of each campaign and wording for one of the commercials for each follows. Table A contains demographic data relevant to avocado consumption.

Core Market Campaign

Objective Convince current users to buy California avocados more often.

Target Market The target market is moderate to light users, women, 25–54, middle and upper income, families and single households. These individuals are always on the go. They are rushed in shopping and have little time for elaborate food preparation. They like the produce department and feel good about incorporating fresh and natural foods into their diets. They have very rich feelings about avocados. Beyond the physical experience of eating the avocado, there is a rich experiential association that stems from usage—happy, fun, festive, outdoors, natural, upbeat, satisfying, delicious, creamy, special, feeling good, carefree.

The Campaign It will leverage attachment to the product through the physical and emotional attributes to inspire cravings for California avocados that will cause consumers to eat them more often. It will stress the California origin where the best produce comes from. This will also provide an image of natural, fresh, healthy, and tasty. The unique taste will be emphasized. The tone will be evocative, natural, fun. After seeing the ad, consumers should think, "I love California avocados and I need to satisfy my cravings for them more often."

Radio Ad Copy

SOUND EFFECTS: Music under, throughout

ANNOUNCER: In a world where love and good taste are misunderstood . . .

MAN: To hide your love is . . . not . . . good

ANNOUNCER: In a house where love is hard to find . . .

ANNOUNCER: In a kitchen where one woman can love despite looks . . .

WOMAN: Oh avocado, dark and slightly soft when ripe. You may have bumpy skin . . . but I . . . I love you!

TABLE A

Demographics and Avocado Consumption*

Variable	Avocados	Bananas	Apples	Kiwis
Percent of Adults†	41.5%	71.4%	68.8%	14.7%
Age				
18–24 years	82	87	85	80
25–34	106	98	101	108
35–44	109	102	105	108
45–54	114	103	102	107
55–64	108	105	108	114
>64	73	100	93	76
Education				
College graduate	145	108	108	142
Some college	123	104	106	116
High school graduate	73	97	97	89
No degree	72	90	89	55
Occupation				
Professional	121	105	110	143
Managerial/Administrative	148	109	106	111
Technical/Clerical/Sales	94	101	103	101
Precision/Craft	131	102	104	41
Other employed	96	95	95	101
Race/Ethnic Group				
White	104	102	102	104
Black	41	84	85	51
Spanish speaking	184	87	91	81
Region				
Northeast	78	104	109	125
North central	54	110	108	124
South	67	91	90	61
West	239	101	100	119
Household Income				
<$10,000	72	89	84	65
$10,000–19,999	69	94	92	68
$20,000–29,999	87	99	97	83
$30,000–39,999	84	99	102	98
$40,000–49,999	125	103	106	126
$50,000–59,999	101	106	105	112
$60,000–74,999	120	107	109	137
$75,000+	153	106	110	133
Household Structure				
1 person	90	95	88	86
2 people	103	100	99	87
3 or more	102	102	104	112
Any child in HH	101	103	105	107

*100 = Average use or consumption unless a percent is indicated. Base = Female homemakers.
†Purchased in the past 12 months.

Source: *Mediamark Spring 1997* (New York: Mediamark Research Inc., 1997).

ANNOUNCER: In a mouth that craves great taste, there is, the Genuine California Avocado.

WOMAN: Did you ever think a burger could be like this?

MAN: (Mouth full) Hang on . . . (chewing swallows) . . . there . . . what was your question, Love?

ANNOUNCER: The Genuine California Avocado (Fast, like legal disclosure) Opening in markets everywhere today. This fruit is not yet rated.

Underdeveloped Market Campaign

Objective Convince nonpurchasers of California Avocados to buy them at retail supermarkets.

Target Market Basically the same as for the core market. The difference is that avocados are not part of their consideration set when shopping. Since displays for avocados in these regions tend to be small, these consumers may remain unaware of them at retail. While many of these consumers may have had and enjoyed avocados as part of a dish or salad at a restaurant, they may not be aware of its physical appearance and may not recognize it at retail.

The Campaign It is important to differentiate the California avocado from the Florida one (there are noticeable physical differences) in order to avoid building sales for the competition. The campaign will focus on "I know I like California Avocados (guacamole) and now it's easy to enjoy them at home." Why? They aren't hard to pick, purchase, or use and they have a taste unlike anything else. The tone will be fun, sophisticated, and natural. After seeing the ad, people should think: "I've never considered buying a California Avocado before. I know I like them and they're much easier to use than I previously thought. I should buy one next time I'm at the supermarket."

Radio Ad Copy

NARRATOR: It has come to my attention that, due to not knowing exactly what they are, some people out there are using Genuine California Avocados for things other than what they are intended. I have been instructed to tell you that California Avocados are *not* for use as fishing line weights;

SOUND EFFECTS: Buzzer

NARRATOR: A drain plug;

SOUND EFFECTS: Buzzer

NARRATOR: a doggie chew-toy;

SOUND EFFECTS: Buzzer

NARRATOR: A dish scrubber;

SOUND EFFECTS: Buzzer

NARRATOR: A go-kart wheel;

SOUND EFFECTS: Buzzer

NARRATOR: or a videotape machine head-cleaner.

SOUND EFFECTS: Buzzer

NARRATOR: California Avocados *are* intended for use in guacamole;

SOUND EFFECTS: Ding

NARRATOR: sliced on a sandwich;

SOUND EFFECTS: Ding

NARRATOR: or chopped up in salad, and other delicious uses.

SOUND EFFECTS: Ding

NARRATOR: So whatever you do, when you see a California Avocado, think, "Man, I'm really in the mood for a Turkey Avocado Sandwich";

SOUND EFFECTS: Ding

NARRATOR: not, "Say, that thing is just about the same size as the hole in my heating duct."

SOUND EFFECTS: Ding

ANNOUNCER: This has been a word from Genuine California Avocados.

Discussion Questions

1. Evaluate these ads in terms of their ability to capture attention. How will they be interpreted?
2. How can nonusers be taught the proper way to select avocados at retail?
3. In light of increasing competition, what product position should California Avocados strive for?
4. What role does emotion play in the consumption of avocados?
5. Is there any motivational conflict in avocado consumption? If so, what should the California Avocado Commission do about it?
6. Evaluate the attitude change strategy being used.
7. Evaluate the use of humor in these ads. Propose and defend two other approaches.
8. Develop a lifestyle-based television ad to increase avocado consumption.

9. What insights, if any are provided by the demographic data?
10. Develop a marketing campaign to increase avocado use among nonusers.
11. Visit the California Avocado Commission Web site (http://www.avoinfo.com). Evaluate its effectiveness in promoting the consumption of avocados. What behavioral principles and assumptions does it rely on?

Source: Based on materials supplied by the California Avocado Commission. Used with permission.

3-3 Marketing Food Irradiation

Food irradiation was developed in the 1950s. It involves exposing food to ionizing energy such as gamma rays from cobalt-60 or cesium-137. The gamma radiation kills all bacteria, parasites, mold, and fungus in or on agricultural products, including red meat, poultry, fresh fruits, vegetables, herbs, and spices. The U.S. Food and Drug Administration (FDA) began approving irradiation applications in 1963. Now most foods can be treated with irradiation (except red meat, for which approval is expected in 2000, and processed foods such as hot dogs), but they must carry a prominent "Radura" symbol (a stylized flower) along with the phrase "treated with irradiation."

While it sounds exotic, irradiation is similar to X-rays. As the dean of the Yale University of School of Medicine and former FDA commissioner states, "The process of irradiating food does not make food radioactive. Food that is being irradiated never comes in direct contact with radioactive material and the gamma rays or X-rays or electrons used do not have the potential to make the food radioactive."

Forbes magazine ran an article in 1999 entitled, "These People Didn't Have to Die." The article described how nine adult deaths and three stillborn births were caused by tainted hot dogs sold by Sara Lee Corp. In addition to the unmeasurable grief caused by the deaths, Sara Lee faced a $60 million product recall. According to the article, people have been eating irradiated fruit, vegetables, and spices for years (although other sources indicate that irradiated foods rarely appear in American supermarkets), but the pork and chicken industry still make virtually no use of it and it is not allowed on red meats. The article quotes a university scientist as saying: "It (irradiation) could have prevented this outbreak. These people didn't need to die."

Irradiation has been widely used as a food safety measure in Europe for years. Groups such as the World Health Organization and the American Medical Association endorse its use. However, it has yet to "catch on" in the United States. As the CEO of ConAgra states, "ConAgra stands ready to use irradiation technology once public acceptance of irradiation becomes stronger." The primary reason that is advanced for the lack of public acceptance is a phobia about radiation and the absence of a coordinated industry effort to address this concern.

Others suggest that the public is largely indifferent but that a vocal, if small, opposition has prevented widespread acceptance. According to the *Forbes* article:

> A group called Food & Water, Inc., has instilled in a fair number of consumers a visceral fear of the process, as if eating irradiated meat were the equivalent of swallowing radium capsules. Hoping to stop technology in the supermarket if they can't stop it in Washington, D.C., the irradiation opponents have run fear-mongering ad campaigns. Irradiation-bashers also say the meat should carry warning labels suggestive of what you see on hazardous materials cargo.

In addition to concerns about negative health consequences of consuming irradiated foods, some environmentalists object to irradiation on the grounds that the production and use of radioactive materials for this purpose causes further nuclear contamination of the environment.

Despite the efforts of opponents and the lack of aggressive industry activities, a recent survey shows fairly high level of public acceptance of irradiated foods. Among the findings:

- 48 percent favor the use of irradiation to increase the safety of foods such as meat, poultry, and fish, while 26 percent oppose it and 26 percent are undecided.
- 54 percent of those who recall hearing about irradiation in the news favor it compared to 44 percent who do not recall hearing about it.
- Shoppers who have confidence in the safety of nationally branded products are much more favor-

ably inclined toward irradiation than are those who doubt the safety of these brands.

- Males and frequent users of microwaves are particularly supportive of irradiation.

One thing the food industry does agree on: Greater acceptance will require changing the name from *irradiation*. As one industry spokesperson states, "This is a word that has 'radiation' in it, and for many people, that raises (concerns)." In late 1999, at industry's urging, the FDA began consideration of changing the required use of the Radura symbol and the "treated with irradiation" label to alternatives such as "cold pasteurized" and "electronic pasteurization." This issue is not yet resolved, but public opinion appears to be against the new labels.

Several observers have speculated on the apparent reluctance of both the food industry and the firms that provide irradiation services to aggressively promote irradiation. One reason is the large financial cost that some feel will be necessary. Others speculate that the food industry is not pushing the process because it will add to the cost of food—as much as three to seven cents per pound of hamburger meat, for example. Finally, there are some reports that both the appearance and odor of irradiated meats may be altered in unfavorable ways.

One expert summarized the issue as follows:

> To convince people that it's OK to try something new, there has to be an immediate, definitive benefit, enough so that it will alleviate fears about the product. Once there's a clearly stated, overwhelming benefit or advantage to a product, consumers do show they will put aside any reluctance to use the product.

Discussion Questions

1. What type of innovation is irradiated meat? Conduct a diffusion analysis on irradiated meat, using Table 7-4 as a guide.
2. What meaning would the proposed labels "cold pasteurized" and "electronic pasteurization" convey to the average consumer? How would you determine if this would be misleading?
3. What product position should the industry try to obtain for irradiated foods?
4. How could the industry teach consumers about the benefits of irradiated foods?
5. How could the industry change the attitudes of those consumers who are opposed to irradiated foods?
6. How could the Food & Water organization change the attitudes of those in favor of irradiated foods?
7. Visit the Web sites of the Grocery Manufactures of America (www.gmabrands.com) and the Food Marketing Institute (www.fmi.org). Evaluate each in terms of its effectiveness in promoting the use or avoidance of irradiation. What behavior principles does each appear to use?

Source: L. Rothstein, "An Idea Whose Time Has Come—And Gone," *Bulletin of the Atomic Scientists,* July 1998, pp. 7–11; L. Freeman, "'Irradiation' Designation May Finally Become a Sales Pitch," *Marketing News,* September 14, 1998, p. 1; M. Conlin, "These People Didn't Have to Die," *Forbes,* February 8, 1999, p. 54; A. Allen, "Ready for Irradiation," *Food Processing,* August 1999, p. 68; and "Radiation Scandal," *The Ecologist,* August 1999, p. 304.

3-4 Kraft's Umbrella Campaign

Following is part of an interview that *Advertising Age* conducted with Robert Eckert, president and CEO of $16 billion Kraft Foods.

AA: Last year Kraft assigned a major corporate branding effort to J. Walter Thompson USA. When is that coming?

ECKERT: It will be later this year (1998). We are working on the next evolution of using our scale and competing at a higher level. And that is to tie some of these great brand names together.

AA: How specifically?

ECKERT: First, let me tell you where we're trying to go as a company . . . Part of the reason (for success) is that we've started to act less like a holding company and more like an operating company.

AA: How has that worked?

ECKERT: It's been particularly effective for us in sales. When we go to call on a retail customer, there is one person who represents all Kraft and that person has several experts working for him or her who are specialists in a category. We speak with one voice.

We go in and talk about meal solutions broadly, and the fact that consumers are spending 21 minutes in a supermarket, down 25 percent in the last five years—the no. one question in America is "what's for dinner?"

Another advantage we have is that we're the only company that covers breakfast, lunch, and dinner, as well as snacks.

AA: So how does the new corporate campaign fit in?

ECKERT: We have four $1 billion brands—Kraft (cheeses), Maxwell House, Post, and Oscar Mayer. We have 26 other brands with sales between $100 million and $1 billion—household names: Miracle Whip, Philadelphia, Cool Whip, Country Time, DiGiorno. We've been very effective in going into the supermarket and talking about the collection of brands—how you can put these things together to satisfy what busy moms are going through in trying to put together meal solutions.

The next logical step is to do this with consumers as well. So we are working on a marketing program that does recognize what's going on in households today and does bring together our brands to address it. Yes we are working on a campaign. It's more than advertising but advertising is an important component.

AA: This isn't like the ill-fated 1980's "We're Beatrice" branding effort, is it?

ECKERT: My recollection of "We're Beatrice" is that of a brand name on top of things—Stiffel lamps, Samsonite luggage, Fisher nuts, County Line cheese—and it was billed as "a company that makes all these." This, you'll see when we finalize it, it's about what's going on with consumers today and how our products happen to fit into that. It's not about us. That's the absolutely wrong way to do this.

As the $50 million corporate campaign began, Eckert states that its goal wasn't "to hawk our products," but "to show consumers how Kraft understands their food needs and the connections that brings to them whether it's lunch, dinner or snacks." The campaign is to involve all corporate communications—TV and print ads, direct mail and co-marketing, consumer promotion, and the Internet.

The ad agency filmed hours of real families interacting around food to be edited into commercials. According to Eckert, "There's no acting, no scripts. It's very human. It captures how they live . . . how these people work through obstacles." Busy families have essentially changed the way people related to eating: "There are no more fancy meals like we grew up with. Today, your son could be eating a Lunchable, you could be eating something else . . . (but even) if you're only together for 5 or 10 minutes there is a food-based connection."

The first three spots were described by a reviewer as "understated, yet extraordinarily powerful iterations of the family ethic." One portrays a single mom shopping with her teenage sons, another a nuclear family of seven, and the third an extended family get-together. There is no narration, just interview bites and New Age Irish fiddle music in the background. The only "sales" message follows a brief sequence of stylized logo cards of familiar Kraft Labels. The message is "Kraft Foods. We make it taste good, but you make it feel good. Food brings us together. Let's make something good."

Discussion Questions

1. Evaluate Kraft's decision to use this umbrella campaign. What are the benefits and risks?
2. What product position is Kraft striving for? Is this the optimal position for Kraft?
3. Evaluate Kraft's use of emotional appeals in its strategy.
4. How can Kraft effectively teach consumers about the range of products it makes and how these products fit into consumers' lives?
5. Visit Kraft's Web site (http://www.kraftfoods.com). Does it advance the "one image" theme? How? How would you improve it?
6. Assume you are a representative of VALS2. Prepare a proposal for Kraft indicating how your database can help Kraft achieve its goals.

Source: J. Pollack, "Eckert Positions Kraft as Microsoft of Food Industry," *Advertising Age,* March 23, 1998, p. 1.

3-5 Marketing Men's Cosmetics

American males are now spending over $10 billion annually on facelifts, hairpieces, cosmetics, and other "beauty" enhancement products. Men account for 25 percent of cosmetic surgeries. Fighting baldness has become a major business, with hair transplants and toupees accounting for well over $1 billion in annual sales. Rogaine for men was one of the most successful new products of the late 1990s. It now faces competition from pills that fight baldness.

Sales of men's hair colorings quadrupled from the mid 1980s to the mid 90s and are now well over $100 million in annual sales. As baby boomers age and gray, coloring sales are forecast to grow even more. Coloring one's hair was not generally accepted male behavior until in the late 1980s. In the late 1960s, Combe launched *Grecian Formula* hair coloring for men with heavy advertising. While it became somewhat of a joke, it did begin to slowly legitimize the product category. Some feel its ads featuring baseball player Pete Rose were particularly influential. In 1995, a much improved *Grecian Formula* 16 had a 15 percent share of the men's hair coloring market.

In the 1970s, Clairol introduced a line of men's hair dyes called *Great Day,* but significant sales never developed. Combe created the current market surge with its *Just for Men* line, which it introduced in 1987. This line washes out the gray in minutes (*Grecian Formula* used a gradual process that took days to remove all the gray). Along with this major product improvement, Combe managed to move retail placement of the product from the women or general hair care aisle into the men's products aisle. *Just for Men* had 59 percent of the market in 1995. Combe spent $50 million in marketing, mostly on television advertising for *Just for Men* from 1987 through 1995.

In 1993, Clairol launched *Men's Choice,* which captured 13 percent of the market. It spent $4.5 million on advertising in 1995, mostly on radio and magazines, along with regional support for local sports teams and live endorsements from nationally syndicated radio personality Don Imus. Both Clairol and Combe place their advertising on prime-time newscasts, TV sports, and men's and sports magazines.

Clairol's 1996 ads juxtapose images of *Men's Choice* against *Just for Men* and provide reasons why *Men's Choice* is a better product. A spokesperson stated: "It's a bold move but we felt it worked best for men, who are information seekers." This philosophy is reflected in its use of copy-intensive magazine ads, packages, and point-of-purchase materials with a strictly informational format.

Males have three reasons for trying to look good (which, in American society, also implies looking young). First, one's career may be enhanced by looking good, which includes being attractive, fit appearing, and energetic (young). One businesswoman stated:

> Any guy who goes into consulting has to be attractive. It struck me one day: Every time I met a good-looking guy and asked him "So, little boy, what do you do?" he was a consultant. The ugly ones are all accountants.

A second reason for men's concern about looks is to be attractive to women. Many middle-aged men who go through divorce engage in a wide variety of "beauty" enhancement activities. Most women no longer need to rely on men for financial support, which allows them to focus more on the physical and personal characteristics of potential partners.

A final reason is a combination of ego and competitiveness. If looks matter, then competitive men will compete to look good. Knowing that one looks good and/or receiving compliments or "admiring glances" is also gratifying to a person's ego.

In 1995, the men's grooming market was approximately $3.3 billion (figures below in millions of dollars):

Fragrances	$1,600
Shaving	632
Deodorant	537
Hair care	362
Hair color	100
Skin care	100

Recent Developments

While growing, the "explosion" that many expected in the mid-90s still has not occurred as the new century begins. Sales data are not available except for an estimate that skin care sales had grown to $122 million in the four years following the survey shown above. This represents a sound but not overwhelming growth rate of 5 percent a year.

Other evidence of growth is in the accelerating rate of new brands and products targeting men's needs. While this is occurring across all parts of the market, it is particularly true for hair coloring. In 1997, Combe spent $17 million on media advertising to introduce Just 5, a coloring product that works in 5 minutes rather than the usual 25. Revlon spent $40 million in marketing to introduce its ColorStay line, which is the first cream gel on the market. It promises longer lasting color. In late 1998, Revlon launched a new version of this line, called ColorStay naturals.

Research and observation has led those in the industry to reach several conclusions. One is that men are willing to buy and experiment with all kinds and types of new fragrances and colognes, but they almost uniformly do not want anything that smells too strong

TABLE A

Demographics and Male Cosmetic Use*

Variable	Hair Coloring Products	Complexion Care Products	Aftershave/ Cologne[†]	Hand/Body Lotion and Creams[†]
Percent of Males	6.6%	5.3%	10.2%	11.2%
Age				
18–24 years	116	127	112	95
25–34	86	102	108	101
35–44	88	94	100	85
45–54	139	112	104	106
55–64	97	84	83	112
>64	85	78	84	111
Education				
College graduate	90	98	91	90
Some college	102	92	100	96
High school graduate	104	104	104	103
No degree	103	106	105	113
Occupation				
Professional	98	102	97	92
Managerial/ Administrative	96	107	100	72
Technical/Clerical/Sales	95	113	117	112
Precision/Craft	117	108	102	99
Other employed	102	108	111	111
Race/Ethnic Group				
White	92	97	97	84
Black	150	133	133	213
Spanish speaking	72	125	125	114
Region				
Northeast	108	96	96	102
North central	106	112	112	98
South	90	104	104	112
West	102	84	84	81
Household Income				
<$10,000	120	73	90	65
$10,000–19,999	91	85	100	101
$20,000–29,999	80	92	101	116
$30,000–39,999	102	118	85	112
$40,000–49,999	87	86	111	107
$50,000–59,999	92	117	110	102
$60,000–74,999	128	95	95	99
$75,000+	110	114	104	84
Household Structure				
1 person	69	82	98	77
2 people	84	93	100	101
3 or more	115	108	101	104
Any child in HH	110	114	101	112

*100 = Average use or consumption unless a percent is indicated.
[†]Heavy users.

Source: *Mediamark Spring 1997* (New York: Mediamark Research Inc., 1997).

or in any way draws attention to themselves. Another is expressed clearly by Wanda McDaniel of Giorgio Armani: "Men want to look and smell good too!" The challenge according to one expert is:

> How to entice more men to smell good, put gooey things in their hair, and oily lotions on their faces without feeling somehow unmanly?

Table A contains material related to the use of "beauty" items by men.

Discussion Questions

1. Visit the Web sites listed below. Are they effective at promoting their products to men? What behavior principles and assumptions do they rely on?
   a. Combe (http://www.combe.com)
   b. Revlon (http://www.revlon.com)
2. Develop a marketing strategy for Revlon to use to enter the men's skin care/makeup market.
3. Develop a marketing strategy for Combe to use to enter the men's skin care/makeup market.
4. Should Combe use a brand leverage strategy and use the *Just for Men* name for a skin care line? If not, how should it select a name?
5. How, if at all, could Combe use the following as the basis for its appeal for the product line?
   a. Personality
   b. Emotion
   c. Self-concept
6. What motives should Combe appeal to?
7. Persuading many men to use skin care products will require a significant attitude change. Which attitude change techniques would be most appropriate? Which would be least appropriate?
8. What type of brand image and product position would you want this line of skin care products to have?
9. Design an ad for the new line. Explain how it will work at each stage of the perception process.
10. What learning theories would you use to "teach" members of your target market to take proper care of their skin?
11. What demographic groups would be the best target markets?
12. Develop a strategy for Revlon to use to introduce a complete line of men's cosmetics to the following countries.
    a. Japan
    b. Germany
    c. France
    d. Mexico

Source: A. Wallenstein, "Boomers Put New Life in Hair Dye for Men," *Advertising Age,* September 1995, p. 1; A. Farnham, "You're So Vain," *Fortune,* September 9, 1996, pp. 66–82; and G. Boulard, "Men's Personal Care Market," January 1999, pp. 50–54.

3-6 Made in Mexico*

The passage of NAFTA greatly lowered the trade barriers between Canada, the United States, and Mexico. Many manufacturers in each country are actively evaluating opportunities to export to the other two countries, as well as facing increased competition from imports from those countries.

Productos Superiores, Inc., is a leading manufacturer of appliances in Mexico. The firm is considering a major effort to market its brand in the United States. Product testing indicates that its appliances are slightly above average in terms of quality, design, and reliability compared to the brands currently sold in America. Productos Superiores' cost structure is such that its products will cost 10 to 20 percent less than products with similar quality currently selling in the United States.

Productos Superiores' management is very concerned about the image that products made in Mexico have in America. Since Productos Superiores is virtually unknown in the United States, management is concerned that consumers will generalize any image they have of products made in Mexico onto Productos Superiores' products. While it has yet to conduct research on the image that appliances made in Mexico have in the United States, it did find a study on the general image U.S. consumers had of products made in other countries.

Table A contains the results of this study. Respondents were asked to rate "the typical product made in ________________________" on a 1 to 10 scale, with 1 being "very poor" and 10 being "excellent."

Discussion Questions

1. Should Productos Superiores' management be concerned that the relatively weak image of products made in Mexico will be attached to their line of products? Why?

*The company name and data in this case are fictitious.

TABLE A

U.S. Consumer Perceptions of Products Made in Other Countries

Attribute	*United States*	*Japan*	*Germany*	*Taiwan*	*Mexico*
Quality	7.3	8.7	9.1	6.9	5.2
Style	8.2	8.5	8.7	7.1	6.7
Reliability	7.8	8.2	8.9	7.4	5.4
Price	8.3	7.9	6.2	9.1	9.0
Design	8.5	8.2	9.3	7.6	6.2
Prestige	7.4	7.3	8.2	6.9	4.3

2. How can Productos Superiores introduce its appliances and avoid consumers attaching the negative aspects of Made in Mexico to their brand?
3. Develop a marketing strategy, including specific ads, to introduce Productos Superiores appliances into the U.S. market.
4. What product position would you try to establish for Productos Superiores appliances? Why?
5. What learning approach and principles would you use to "teach" consumers about Productos Superiores appliances?
6. How would you establish a favorable attitude for Productos Superiores appliances?
7. What name and logo or tag line would you use for Productos Superiores' appliance line in the United States? Why?
8. Develop an ad or marketing approach to create a positive attitude toward Productos Superiores appliances, focusing on the following components:
   a. Cognitive
   b. Affective
   c. Behavioral
9. Develop an ad or marketing approach to create a positive attitude toward Productos Superiores appliances, using the following:
   a. Humor
   b. Emotion
   c. Utilitarian appeal
   d. Value-expressive appeal
   e. Celebrity endorser
   f. Self-concept
10. What VALS2 lifestyle segment(s) would be the best target market(s) for Productos Superiores appliances? Why?
11. To what motive(s) would you appeal to induce consumers to purchase Productos Superiores appliances?
12. Develop an ad for Productos Superiores appliances that would attract the attention of consumers who are not interested in appliances. Explain how your ad will attract attention and why it will also convey the desired message or image.

3-7 ThirstyDog! and ThirstyCat!

The Original Pet Drink Co., Inc., is a new firm located in Ft. Lauderdale. It recently launched its first product—a line of purified bottled beverages for cats and dogs. The beverages are slightly carbonated, flavored ("crispy beef" for dogs or "tangy fish" for cats), and contain a number of nutritional supplements (see Table A). They are intended to replace tap water for pets and to supplement, but not replace, normal pet food.

Relevant facts about the product include the following: All ingredients have FDA approval for human consumption and the product is approved for human consumption as bottled, no refrigeration is required, the product is Kosher, and its shelf life is six to eight months. Patent protection is not practical. There have been over 15,000 palatability tests conducted on dogs and cats. Most animals (about 70 percent) like the current versions more than tap water. Some need to acquire a taste (it is recommended that the product be the pet's only source of water until it prefers the taste). Others never develop a preference for the product.

Reaction from veterinarians has been mixed. Some praise the product while others refer to it as

TABLE A

Product Ingredients

Ingredient	*Benefit*
Purified carbonated water	No impurities or harmful substances; carbonation acts as a preservative
D-glucose	Energy source
Potassium	Supplies electrolytes for optimal cardiac and other organ functions
Vitamin C	Strong teeth, gums, and bones
Niacin	Maintains stomach and gastrointestinal tract
Pantothenic acid	Prevents dry skin and enhances coat
Leucine	Optimizes carbohydrate utilization
Vitamin B-6	Enhances sense of smell, vision, hearing
Zinc	Strengthens immune system, promotes skin health
Biotin	Maintains healthy skin, paws, and hair
Taurine (cats only)	Optimizes vision and cardiac function
Fructose (dogs only)	Naturally occurring sweetener
Benzoate	Naturally occurring preservative
Sorbate	Naturally occurring preservative
Natural/artificial flavors	Encourages consumption without adding calories
Thirsty Cat! = 20 calories per liter; Thirsty Dog! = 40 calories per liter. No fat or cholesterol.	

"frivolous. It does no harm but don't rely on it to do any good." Research has shown that 42 percent of homeowners with a pet are concerned about giving their pet tap water, 32 percent stated they would try this product after hearing a description of it, and 14 percent are currently giving their cat or dog an alternative to tap water (generally plain bottled water that retails from $.89 per gallon to $2.98 per gallon).

The firm is excited about the product because it has the potential to create an entirely new product category. Furthermore, the potential market appears huge. An average cat consumes a liter of water a week and a relatively small dog consumes 2 to 3 liters a week.

The firm has named the product *ThirstyDog!* and *ThirstyCat!* It is expected to retail at $1.79 to $1.99 per liter bottle. Point-of-purchase displays, brochures, and the package itself will stress the nutritional and health benefits associated with using the product.

Another start-up firm, Dr. George Hill Pet Drinks, is launching a similar product. It also comes in different flavors for cats and dogs. It can be used as a fluid replacement or added to dry dog food. In addition to 12 vitamins and minerals, it contains brewer's yeast, which is commonly used to control fleas. It comes in 32- and 64-ounce milk-jug style bottles. The smaller bottle will retail for around $1.39.

Table B contains demographic data relevant to the ownership of dogs and cats and the purchase of products for them.

Discussion Questions

1. Conduct an innovation analysis (see Table 7-4) and recommend specific diffusion enhancement strategies for ThirstyDog!/ThirstyCat!
2. What product position would you try to establish for ThirstyDog!/ThirstyCat!? Why?
3. What learning approach and principles would you use to "teach" consumers about ThirstyDog!/ThirstyCat!?
4. How would you establish a favorable attitude for ThirstyDog!/ThirstyCat!?
5. What name and logo or tag line would you use for the product? Why?
6. Develop an ad or marketing approach to create a positive attitude toward ThirstyDog!/ThirstyCat!, focusing on the following components:
   a. Cognitive
   b. Affective
   c. Behavioral
7. Develop an ad or marketing approach to create a positive attitude toward ThirstyDog!/ThirstyCat!, using the following:
   a. Humor
   b. Emotion
   c. Utilitarian appeal
   d. Value-expressive appeal
   e. Celebrity endorser
   f. Self-concept
   g. Fear

TABLE B

Demographics and Pet Ownership*

Variable	Cat Owners	Cat Treats	Dog Owners	Dog Treats
Percent of Adults	20.9%	8.0%	27.6%	19.5%
Age				
18–24 years	73	103	73	67
25–34	104	109	106	97
35–44	129	108	137	133
45–54	127	138	112	122
55–64	87	76	88	96
>64	58	62	60	64
Education				
College graduate	129	110	108	109
Some college	113	118	116	120
High school graduate	101	104	100	100
No degree	50	57	69	61
Occupation				
Professional	140	118	122	122
Managerial/Administrative	139	112	121	121
Technical/Clerical/Sales	116	131	124	124
Precision/Craft	147	234	85	85
Other employed	91	79	114	114
Race/Ethnic Group				
White	112	109	109	109
Black	21	39	40	39
Spanish speaking	67	72	77	67
Region				
Northeast	103	122	84	101
North central	106	129	120	137
South	86	66	92	71
West	115	106	108	108
Household Income				
<$10,000	57	65	54	50
$10,000–19,999	73	68	75	63
$20,000–29,999	98	109	96	94
$30,000–39,999	94	106	92	95
$40,000–49,999	122	121	116	119
$50,000–59,999	113	109	137	142
$60,000–74,999	133	122	130	136
$75,000+	130	116	126	133
Household Structure				
1 person	75	83	56	65
2 people	94	102	89	103
3 or more	112	104	120	109
Child <2	76	61	88	62
Child 2–5	75	66	101	73
Child 6–11	114	102	128	109
Child 12–17	128	124	137	133

*100 = Average use or consumption unless a percent is indicated. Base = Female homemakers.

Source: *Mediamark Spring 1997* (New York: Mediamark Research Inc., 1997).

8. Evaluate the ThirstyDog!/ThirstyCat! brand name.
9. What VALS2 lifestyle segment(s) would be the best target market(s) for ThirstyDog!/ThirstyCat!? Why?
10. Based on the demographic data in Table B, what would be the best target(s) market for ThirstyDog!/ThirstyCat!?

3-8 Sugar versus Artificial Sweeteners

Answer the following true/false questions:

1. A teaspoon of sugar contains less than 20 calories.
2. The Academy of General Dentistry recommends a low-sugar diet to minimize risks of tooth decay.
3. The American Dietetic Association does not recommend a reduced-sugar diet for Americans.
4. The Food and Drug Administration (FDA) places sugar on its list of foods that are Generally Recognized as Safe (GRAS).
5. No artificial sweetener is on the FDA's GRAS list.

The answers are true (16 calories), false, true, true, and true. Despite these facts, sugar has steadily lost business to artificial sweeteners. To correct any misperceptions concerning sugar, as well as to counter aggressive marketing activities for artificial sweeteners, the Sugar Association decided to launch a major advertising campaign.

Prior to designing the campaign, the association conducted a major consumer survey to determine demographics, attitudes, and values associated with sugar consumption. Some of the key findings are:

- Eighty-six percent "like" or "love" sweets.
- Sugar and sugar-sweetened foods are associated with the happy, pleasurable moments in life.
- Users of artificial sweeteners like sugar and sugar-sweetened foods to the same extent as nonusers, and they use about as much sugar.
- Heavy-user households (40+ pounds per year) constitute 30 percent of sugar users but represent 77 percent of household sugar consumption. They bake more often and are more likely to eat sugar-sweetened snacks, desserts, and breakfasts. Seventy-five percent have children at home compared to 48 percent of light users (10 pounds or less per year). Heavy users say they "love" sweets, while light and moderate users "like" sweets.
- Over two-thirds of the respondents agreed with these statements: "I feel I can enjoy snacks/desserts because my eating habits are generally healthy." "Enjoying sweets is a natural and normal part of a child's life."
- Over half the respondents felt they should limit their families' consumption of both sugar and artificial sweeteners.

While the results of the survey are generally very positive, officials of the Sugar Association are worried about the continued existence of consumer concern over the quantity of sugar consumed. They are also concerned that the continued extensive promotion of sugar-free products will cause consumers to presume that sugar is somehow bad.

Table A contains demographic data on sugar and artificial sweetener consumption.

Discussion Questions

1. Explain how consumers might "learn" that sugar is bad, based on frequently seen promotions for sugar-free products.
2. Visit the Sugar Association's Web site (http://www.sugar.org). Evaluate its effectiveness in encouraging sugar use. What behavior principles and assumptions does it rely on?
3. What values are involved in the consumption of sugar versus artificial sweeteners?
4. The attitude survey produced strong positive attitudes toward sugar, and yet over half the respondents felt they should limit their families' intake of sugar. How do you account for this?
5. How would you establish a favorable product position for sugar relative to artificial sweeteners?
6. What ethical issues would concern you in developing a product position for sugar?
7. What learning approach and principles would you use to "teach" consumers about sugar?
8. Develop an ad or marketing approach to create a positive attitude toward sugar, focusing on the following components:
   a. Cognitive
   b. Affective
   c. Behavioral
9. Develop an ad or marketing approach to create a positive attitude toward sugar, using the following:
   a. Humor

TABLE A

Demographics and Sugar Consumption*

Variable	*Heavy Users*†	*Light Users*†	*Artificial Sweetener*‡
Percent of Respondents	19.0%	47.2%	23.5%
Age			
18–24 years	62	120	57
25–34	96	102	76
35–44	112	96	95
45–54	117	96	125
55–64	102	97	137
>64	92	99	123
Education			
College graduate	76	109	116
Some college	95	103	101
High school graduate	114	94	98
No degree	105	99	85
Occupation			
Professional	86	107	120
Managerial/Administrative	79	106	112
Technical/Clerical/Sales	02	103	105
Precision/Craft	103	100	71
Other employed	117	96	85
Race/Ethnic Group			
White	102	101	105
Black	98	86	67
Spanish speaking	111	102	92
Region			
Northeast	75	106	97
North central	120	102	102
South	107	90	104
West	89	110	94
Household Income			
<$10,000	83	96	80
$10,000–19,999	114	99	79
$20,000–29,999	116	91	101
$30,000–39,999	102	102	94
$40,000–49,999	99	98	95
$50,000–59,999	117	101	112
$60,000–74,999	85	109	120
$75,000+	82	105	115
Household Structure			
1 person	58	107	99
2 people	89	107	112
3 or more	120	94	93
Child <2	105	96	84
Child 2–5	118	92	79
Child 6–11	131	92	82
Child 12–17	145	87	93

*100 = Average use or consumption unless a percent is indicated.
†Base = Female homemakers.
‡Base = All adults.

Source: *Mediamark Spring 1997* (New York: Mediamark Research Inc., 1997).

b. Emotion
c. Utilitarian appeal
d. Value-expressive appeal
e. Celebrity endorser
f. Self-concept
g. Fear

10. What VALS2 lifestyle segment(s) would be the best target market(s) for sugar? Why?
11. To what motive(s) would you appeal to induce consumers to use sugar?
12. Develop an ad for sugar that would attract the attention of consumers who are not interested in sugar or cooking. Explain how your ad will attract attention and why it will also convey the desired message or image.
13. What, if anything, in Table A should cause the Sugar Association concern?
14. Based on the material in Table A, what demographic groups should the Sugar Association target? Why? How should they approach these groups?

3-9 Antismoking Campaigns Targeting Teens

One expert on teenagers and antismoking messages stated:

> They're struggling desperately to form their own identities, to fit in, relate to other people their own age, particularly to members of the opposite sex. Anything they perceive can help them succeed socially is something they want to do. Any message about dying when you're middle-aged is removed from their intense need of making it through the day socially.

Most antismoking messages in the past have focused on the health hazards of smoking and have had limited impact on teenagers. A 1992 study found slightly over a quarter of both males and females between age 12 and 21 smoked cigarettes. From 1986 through 1994, the percent of high school seniors who smoke a half-pack or more a day (11 percent), the percent who smoke daily (19 percent), and the percent who have smoked in the past month (30 percent) remained constant after declining steadily for the preceding 10 years. A 1993 survey of why teenagers continue to smoke produced the following results:

Percent Responding (multiple responses allowed)

Cigarettes Smoked per Day	*It Relaxes or Calms Me*	*It's Really Hard to Quit*
1–5	57.3%	61.5%
6–15	69.7	74.4
>15	75.4	71.1

Table A provides additional information about teenage smoking.

Antismoking groups are beginning to use new, aggressive social appeals to reduce smoking among teenagers. These ads attempt to be revolting yet humorous. They use the MTV style of different camera angles and fast cuts. The actors are all teenagers, and preaching about health is out. The following are some of the new style ads:

- A girl accidentally drinks from a soda cup that her tobacco chewing boyfriend had used as a spittoon. The voiceover says: "Tobacco: tumor causing, teeth staining, smelly, puking habit."
- A cow is shown breaking wind while the voiceover states: "So what does cigarette smoke and a cow have in common? Harmful methane gas. Yuck? No wonder smoking kills 400,000 people a year, more than AIDS, murder, and suicide combined."
- A young girl smoking a cigarette gushes about the charming boy she has fallen for. As she talks her face turns into a collection of old banana peels, sardines, and dirty socks as she says: "We looked right into each other's eyes—he has THE MOST beautiful eyes—and I say 'Hi, Jason' and he sort of stops and says 'Two words: breath mints.' I mean—what does that mean anyways."

Discussion Questions

1. Why are health appeals generally ineffective with teenagers?
2. Will the new type of appeal succeed? Is there any danger that these new ads could make smoking "cool" rather than disgusting?
3. Design an ad to discourage teenagers from beginning to smoke. Justify your design.
4. Design an ad to cause teenage smokers to quit smoking. Justify your design.
5. Is "teenager" too large a category to reach with one approach or type of ad?

TABLE A

Nicotine Withdrawal Symptoms Reported by Teenagers When Attempting to Quit Smoking

	Days Smoked per Month			
Symptom	*<1*	*1–14*	*15–29*	*30*
Find it hard to concentrate	11.8%	22.8%	39.2%	46.1%
Feel hungry more often	24.4	35.4	43.0	49.0
Feel more irritable	21.4	36.5	55.8	77.0
Strong urge to smoke	21.9	36.3	71.2	81.6
Feel restless	17.0	30.3	49.9	62.6
Feel sad, blue, depressed	9.3	17.9	24.4	28.6

Note: Multiple responses allowed.
Source: Gale Research, 1996.

6. Pick three key concepts from the text and describe how you would use them to design a program to reduce teenage smoking.
7. Evaluate the following Web sites in terms of the material they provide relative to teenage smoking.
   a. http://www.tobacco.org
   b. http://www.nobutz.com

3-10 Bayer Ibuprofen?

For many years, aspirin dominated the market for nonprescription pain relief, and Bayer aspirin dominated the aspirin market. However, in recent years, acetaminophen- and ibuprofen-based pain relievers have taken over much of the market. By 1989, aspirin-based products held only 40 percent of the total analgesics market. This dropped to 35 percent by 1992. At that time, Bayer had a 6.6 percent share of the total analgesics market and 19 percent of the aspirin market. By 1995, Bayer had less than 5 percent of the analgesics market.

Competition in the analgesics market is intense. There are three main types of analgesics—aspirin, acetaminophen, and ibuprofen. There are several advertised brands within each type of analgesic as well as private label and store brands. Product differences within analgesic categories are limited.

The intense competition has given rise to product proliferation and niche strategies. Advil is the leader in the ibuprofen category with a 50 percent share. Motrin, with a 15 percent share, has used three different commercials to target backache, arthritis, and headache pain. It attempts to "maintain the brand's appeal as a general analgesic while reaching out to specific groups of pain sufferers through advertising." The strategy appears to be working, as its share is growing. Nuprin (13 percent share) has attempted to compete with a focus on muscle aches, using celebrities such as Jimmy Connors, Michael Chang, and Joe Montana.

Similar niche strategies are appearing in the acetaminophen and aspirin categories. Acetaminophen-based Midol is attempting to position itself as "the menstrual relief specialist." It further focuses with such line extensions as Midol PM Nighttime Formula and Midol IB Cramp Relief Formula. Tylenol is increasingly positioned in terms of arthritis pain relief, though it is also widely used for headache relief.

The private label and store brands compete on price. They may sell for a third of the price of the national brands.

Recent medical findings indicate that the regular use of aspirin helps certain heart and colon conditions. Bayer introduced Therapy Bayer for this application, but aspirin sales in general and Bayer aspirin sales both continue their relative decline.

In 1995, Bayer launched a $40 million campaign to increase its overall market share. Television ads target the aging baby boomers. One features an older father painlessly horsing around with his younger son after taking Extra Strength Bayer. These ads stress effectiveness. A print campaign for the new Aspirin Regimen Bayer focuses on aspirin's ability to prevent heart attacks and strokes.

Excedrin was historically behind Bayer in the aspirin category. However, it now has a greater total market share in the overall analgesics market. It has managed to grow its market share by aggressively adding line extensions: ibuprofen-based Excedrin IB and acetaminophen-based Excedrin AF and Excedrin PM.

Bayer management is considering introducing nonaspirin-based analgesics using the Bayer name.

Discussion Questions

1. What is Bayer aspirin's current product position?
2. What are the benefits and risks of introducing an acetaminophen- and/or ibuprofen-based analgesic with the Bayer name? Should Bayer do this?
3. If it proceeds, what would it want consumers to learn about the new brands? What learning principles should it use?
4. Develop an ad or series of ads to introduce a Bayer acetaminophen- and/or ibuprofen-based analgesic.
   a. Explain the perception principles that you used to design the ad(s).
   b. Explain the learning principles you used to design the ad(s).
   c. Explain the attitude influence principles you used to design the ad(s).
5. Develop an ad or series of ads to introduce a Bayer acetaminophen- and/or ibuprofen-based analgesic using the following:
   a. Lifestyle-based theme.
   b. Self-concept-based theme.
   c. Personality-based theme.
6. Develop an ad or series of ads to introduce a Bayer acetaminophen- and/or ibuprofen-based analgesic focusing on the following:
   a. Cognitive component of an attitude.
   b. Affective component of an attitude.
   c. Behavioral component of an attitude.

Source: Adapted from P. Sloan, "Bayer to Offer Non-Aspirin Pain Reliever," *Advertising Age,* July 13, 1992, p. 12; and M. Kuntz, "Extra-Strength Aspiration," *Business Week,* May 1, 1995, p. 46.

part four

Consumer Decision Process

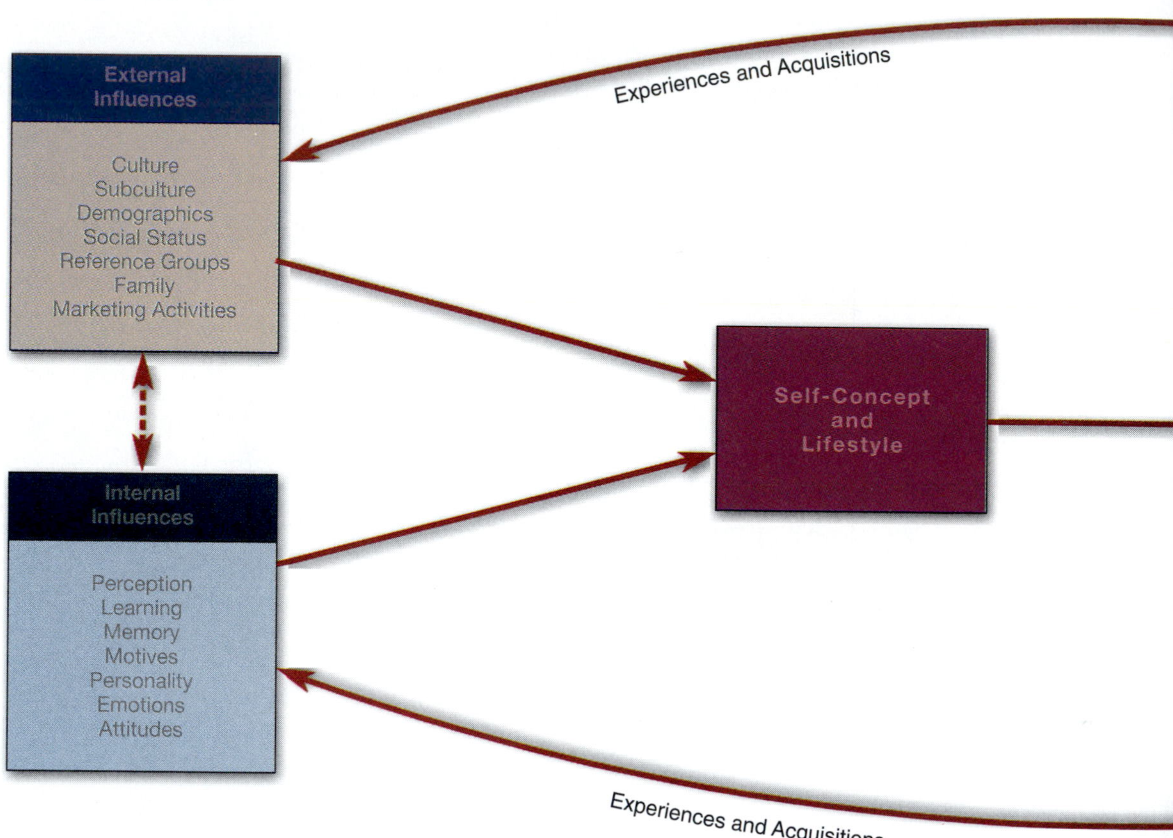

■ Up to now, we have focused on various sociological and psychological factors that contribute to different patterns of consumer behavior. Though these various influences play a significant role in behavior, all behavior takes place within the context of a situation. Chapter 13 provides a discussion of the impact situational variables have on consumer behavior.

Of particular importance to marketers is how situations and internal and external sources of influence affect the purchase decision process. The extended consumer decision process, shown on this page, is composed of a sequence of activities: problem recognition, information search, brand evaluation and selection, store choice and purchase, and postpurchase processes. However, extended decision making occurs only in those relatively rare situations when the consumer is highly involved in the purchase. Lower levels of purchase involvement produce limited or nominal decision making. Chapter 14 describes those various types of decisions and their relationship to involvement. It also analyzes the first stage of the process—problem recognition.

Information search constitutes the second stage of the consumer decision process and is discussed in Chapter 15. Chapter 16 examines the alternative evaluation and selection process. Chapter 17 deals with outlet selection and the in-store influences that often determine final brand selection. The final stage of the consumer decision process, presented in Chapter 18, involves behavior after the purchase. This includes postpurchase dissonance, product or service use, satisfaction, disposition, and repurchase motivation. Both cognitive (thinking) and emotional (feeling) processes are important at each stage of the decision process.

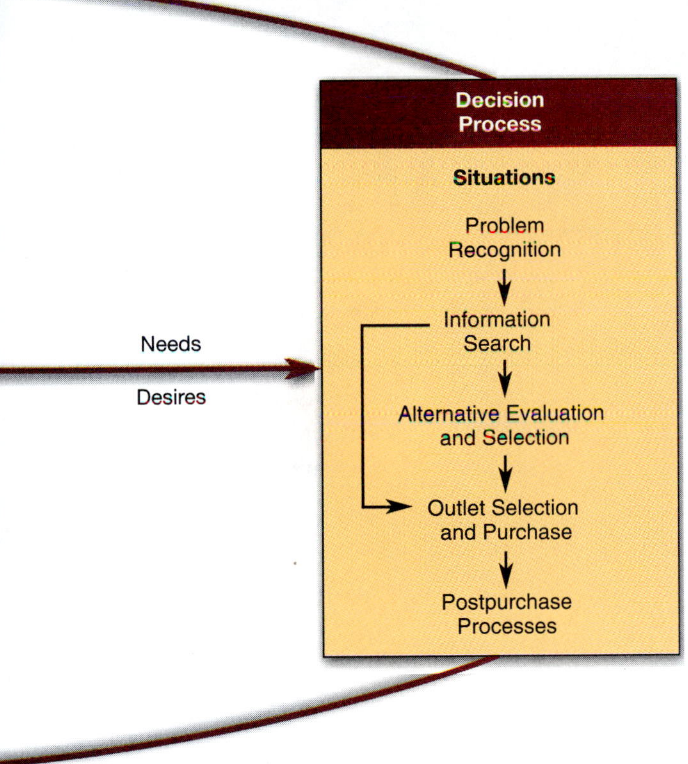

Situational Influences

■ Weddings are a joyous moment in the lives of those involved. The 2.4 million weddings each year in the United States are also big business ($35 billion). Weddings are not only social, legal, and religious rituals, they are also *consumption rituals*. Bridal gowns, tuxedo rentals, bridal showers, wedding gifts, dinners and receptions, rings, honeymoons, and other consumption activities are now an integral part of a wedding. While details differ, ritualized consumption patterns surround this event in most cultures.

■ Freixenet, marketers of Cordon Negro sparkling wine, advertise heavily to this market, "not only for the cases bought, but for exposure of the product" to the many guests. Freixenet offers a free Wedding Beverage Guide, which includes toasts, graces, and paper tuxedos to wrap around the wine bottles. It also provides a coupon good for a $1 refund per bottle.

■ Bridal registries, once limited to department stores, now appear at retailers ranging from Ace Hardware to the Metropolitan Museum of Art. Marshall Field's stresses customer service in its approach to gaining bridal registries. After the wedding, Field's sends a coupon offering discounts on merchandise the couple may not have received from their list. It also hosts an annual "Marriage of Style" show featuring a fashion show, a vendor exhibit area, and a speaker's panel covering topics such as etiquette and finance. Almost 900 people attended a recent show.

■ The Internet is quickly becoming a major part of the "marriage market." The WeddingChannel.com currently makes it easy for couples to create personal wedding pages on the Web where they can post directions and pictures, notify guests of last-minute changes, recount how they met, and so forth. The goal is to have a constantly updated gift registry available. This would allow guests to both learn what gifts the couple desires that they have not yet received and to order those gifts on-line from participating retailers.

■ Walt Disney World capitalizes on this consumption ritual by serving as a wedding site through its Fairytale Weddings department. In the Cinderella wedding, the bride arrives in a glass coach drawn by six white horses complete with a costumed driver and footman. A fairy godmother and stepsisters mix with the guests at the reception, where dessert is served in a white chocolate slipper. Almost two thousand couples are married at Walt Disney World each year.[1]

A wedding is a type of situation known as a ritual situation. As the model we have used to organize this text stresses, the purchase decision and consumption process always occur in the context of a specific situation. Therefore, before examining the decision process, we must first develop an understanding of situations. In this chapter, we will examine the situations in which consumption occurs, the way situations influence consumption behaviors, key characteristics of situations, the nature of ritual situations, and situation-based marketing strategies.

THE NATURE OF SITUATIONAL INFLUENCE

We define **situational influence** as *all those factors particular to a time and place that do not follow from a knowledge of personal (intraindividual) and stimulus (choice alternative) attributes and that have a demonstrable and systematic effect on current behavior.*[2] That is, a situation is a set of factors outside of and removed from the relatively stable or permanent attributes of the individual consumer as well as removed from the characteristics of the primary stimulus object (e.g., a product, a television advertisement) to which the consumer is reacting (e.g., purchasing a product, viewing a commercial).

Consumers do not respond to stimuli such as advertisements and products presented by marketers in isolation. Instead, they respond to marketing influences and the situation simultaneously. To understand a consumer's behavior, we must know about the consumer, about the object such as a product that the consumer is responding to, and the situation in which the response is occurring. This is shown in Figure 13-1.

To integrate the influence of situation into marketing strategy, we must first give careful attention to the degree that the situation *interacts* with a given product and a given set of target consumers.[3] Then we must evaluate the situation more systematically in terms of *when it occurs,* the *strength of its influence,* and the *nature of its influence on behavior*. For example, time spent doing leisure activities is influenced by physical surroundings (e.g., temperature and weather), social influences, and a person's mood. To be effective in marketing a particular leisure activity such as a sports event or movie, a marketer must understand how and when these situational influences will impact a consumer's decision to spend time on that activity.

The consumption process occurs within four broad categories or types of situations: the communications situation, the purchase situation, the usage situation, and the disposition situation.

The Communications Situation

The situation in which consumers receive information has an impact on their behavior. Whether we are alone or in a group, in a good mood or bad, in a hurry or not influences the degree to which we see and listen to marketing communications. Is it better to advertise on a happy or sad television program? A calm or exciting program? These are some of the questions managers must answer with respect to the **communications situation.**[4]

If we are interested in the product and are in a receptive communications situation, a marketer is able to deliver an effective message to us. However, finding high-interest

The Situation Interacts with the Marketing Activity and the Individual to Determine Behavior **FIGURE 13-1**

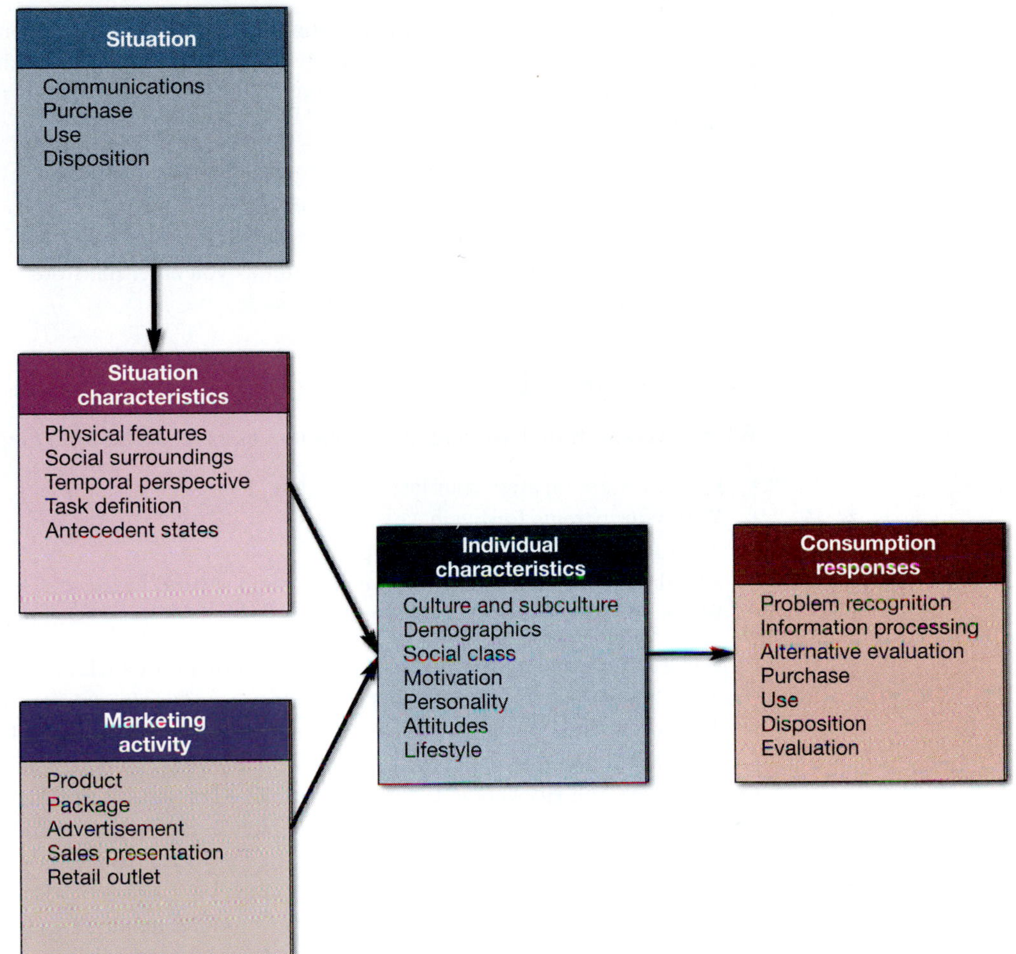

potential buyers in receptive communications situations is a difficult challenge. For example, consider the difficulty a marketer would have in communicating to you in the following communications situations:

- Your favorite team just lost the most important game of the year.
- Final exams begin tomorrow.
- Your roommates only watch comedy programs.
- You have the flu.
- You are driving home on a cold night, and your car heater doesn't work.

The Purchase Situation

Situations affect product selection in a purchase situation. Mothers shopping with children are more apt to be influenced by the product preferences of their children than when shopping without them. A shortage of time, such as trying to make a purchase between classes, can affect the store chosen, the number of brands considered, and the price you are willing to pay.

Marketers must understand how **purchase situations** influence consumers in order to develop marketing strategies that enhance the purchase of their products. For example, how would you alter your decision to purchase a beverage in the following purchase situations?

- You are in a very bad mood.
- A good friend says "That stuff is bad for you!"
- You have an upset stomach.
- There is a long line at the checkout counter as you enter the store.
- You are with someone you want to impress.

The Usage Situation

What beverage would you prefer to consume in each of the following usage situations?

- Friday afternoon after your last final exam.
- With your parents for lunch.
- After dinner on a cold, stormy evening.
- At a dinner with a friend you have not seen in several years.
- When you are feeling sad or homesick.

Marketers need to understand the **usage situations** for which their products are, or may become, appropriate. Based on this knowledge, marketers can communicate how their products can create consumer satisfaction in each relevant usage situation. For example, a recent study found that consuming two 1.5-cup servings of oat-based cereal a day could lower cholesterol. How could General Mills take advantage of this fact to increase sales of its oat-based cereal, Cheerios? A recent ad depicts a dad coming home late from work and having Cheerios for dinner. When asked why by his young daughter, he says "Because they taste just as good at night." (See also Illustration 7-4, page 237.) Research indicates that such expanded usage situation strategies can produce major sales gains for established products.[5]

Marketers also develop products and services based on the situations consumers encounter. As Illustration 13-1 illustrates, Bonne Bell has created a line of fragrances for use with the differing moods consumers experience (or would like to experience).

The Disposition Situation

Consumers must frequently dispose of products and/or product packages after or before product use. As we will examine in detail in Chapter 18, decisions made by consumers regarding the **disposition situation** can create significant social problems as well as opportunities for marketers.

Some consumers consider ease of disposition an important product attribute. These consumers may only purchase items that can be easily recycled. Often disposition of an existing product must occur before or simultaneously with the acquisition of the new product. For example, most consumers must remove their existing bed before using a new one. Marketers need to understand how situational influences affect disposition decisions in order to develop more effective and ethical products and marketing programs. Government and environmental organizations need the same knowledge in order to encourage socially responsible disposition decisions.

Courtesy Bonne Bell, Inc.

ILLUSTRATION 13-1

Consumers' moods vary over the course of time. Astute firms develop products and services relevant to the various moods consumers experience.

How would your disposition decision differ in these situations?

- You have finished a soft drink in a can at a mall. There is a trash can nearby, but there is no sign of a recycling container.
- You have finished reading the newspaper after class, and you note that you are running late for a basketball game.
- You and two friends have finished soft drinks. Both your friends toss the recyclable cans into a nearby garbage container.
- A local charity will accept old refrigerators if they are delivered to the charity. Your garbage service will haul one to the dump for $15. You just bought a new refrigerator. You don't (do) know anyone with a pickup or van.

SITUATIONAL CHARACTERISTICS AND CONSUMPTION BEHAVIOR

A number of features or characteristics of situations influence behaviors across the various types of situations described above. We will describe five key characteristics of situations that help determine the situation's impact on behavior—physical features, social surroundings, time perspectives, task objectives, and antecedent states.[6] These factors have been studied primarily in the United States. While the same characteristics of situation will exist across cultures, one should not assume that the response to those characteristics would be the same. For example, a very crowded store might cause a different emotional reaction among American consumers and Indian consumers.[7]

ILLUSTRATION 13-2

Retail store interiors should provide a physical environment consistent with the nature of the target market, the product line, and the desired image of the outlet.

Courtesy J. T. Nakaoka Associates Architects.

Physical Features

Information Professionals, Inc., offers a service called "advertiming." The service relies on an extensive computer database that compares consumption patterns with the current weather. Based on observed relationships between weather and product category sales, the firm uses weather forecasts to advise its clients on spot advertising buys, sales, point-of-purchase displays, and related issues.

A number of firms have used simpler versions of this approach for some time. For example, Blistex, Inc., and Campbell Soup have based spot radio advertising on weather forecasts for several years. However, Information Professionals provides data on less obvious relationships and products. For example, does hot cocoa sell better on a warm but dark winter day or on a frigid but bright day? The answer is dark and warm. Therefore, cocoa advertisers would be better off timing spot buys and special promotions to coincide with dark, cloudy days as opposed to average days or cold, clear days.[8]

Physical surroundings include decor, sounds, aromas, lighting, weather, and visible configurations of merchandise or other material surrounding the stimulus object. Physical surroundings are a widely recognized type of situational influence, particularly for retail applications.

For example, store interiors are often designed to create specific feelings in shoppers that can have an important cueing or reinforcing effect on purchase. All physical aspects of the store, including lighting, layout, presentation of merchandise, fixtures, floor coverings, colors, sounds, odors, and dress and behavior of sales personnel, combine to produce these feelings, which in turn influence purchase tendencies.[9] A retail clothing store specializing in extremely stylish, modern clothing would want to reflect this to customers in the physical characteristics of the purchase situation. The fixtures, furnishings, and colors should all reflect an overall mood of style, flair, and newness. In addition, the store personnel should appear to carry this theme in terms of their own appearance and apparel. Illustration 13-2 shows the interior of the Bergdorf Goodman men's store in New York City. Its target

Typology of Service Environments **FIGURE 13-2**

Time Spent in Facility	Consumption Purpose: *Utilitarian*		*Hedonic*
Short [minutes]	Dry cleaner Bank	Fast food Hair salon	Facial Coffee at Starbucks
Moderate [hour(s)]	Medical appointment Legal consultation	Business dinner Exercise class	**Theater** **Sporting event**
Extended [day(s)]	Hospital Trade show	**Conference hotel** **Training center**	**Cruise** **Resort**

Note: The darker the shading, the more important the physical features of the servicescape are.

Source: "Customer Response to Intangible and Tangible Service Factors," adapted from K. L. Wakefield and J. G. Blodgett, *Psychology & Marketing,* January 1999, p. 54. Copyright © 1999 John Wiley & Sons. Reprinted by permission of John Wiley & Sons, Inc.

market is males with upscale incomes and taste levels. Its fixtures, design, and layout present an environment appropriate for this group.

The sum of all the physical features of a retail environment is referred to as the **store atmosphere** or environment. A store's atmosphere has been shown to influence shoppers' moods and their willingness to visit and linger. It also influences the consumer's judgments of the quality of the store and the store's image.[10] Perhaps more importantly, a positive mood induced while in the store increases satisfaction with the store, which can produce repeat visits and store loyalty.[11] **Atmospherics** is the process managers use to manipulate the physical retail environment to create specific mood responses in shoppers.

Atmosphere is referred to as **servicescape** when describing a service business such as a hospital, bank, or restaurant.[12] Figure 13-2 classifies services based on the reason the customer is using the service and the length of time the service will be used. The reason for using a service is broadly categorized along a continuum from strictly utilitarian such as dry cleaning to primarily hedonic such as a massage. The time can range from a few minutes to days or weeks. It appears that the physical characteristics and the feelings and image they create become increasingly important as hedonic motives and the time involved with the service increase. Thus, the physical characteristics of a vacation resort may be as or more important than the intangible services provided.

It is important that Figure 13-2 be interpreted correctly. It indicates that the physical environment at Starbucks is more important to the service experience than the physical features of dry cleaners are. *This does not mean that the physical aspects of dry cleaners are not important*. Indeed, an organized, professional-appearing dry cleaning establishment is likely to produce more satisfied customers than one with the opposite characteristics.[13] What the figure does indicate is that the relative importance of tangible physical features increases as one moves to extended, hedonic consumption experiences.

Having established the importance of the physical environment in various contexts, we will now examine some of its components.

Colors The color *red* is effective at attracting consumers' attention and interest. However, while physically arousing, red is also perceived as tense and negative. Softer colors such as *blue* are less attention-attracting and arousing. They are perceived as calm, cool, and positive. Which color would be best for store interiors? Research indicates that blue is superior to red in terms of generating positive outcomes for both the retailer (sales) and the consumer (satisfaction).[14]

As we saw in Chapter 2, the meaning of colors varies across cultures. Therefore, this and all other aspects of the physical environment should be designed specifically for the cultures involved.

Aromas While research is just beginning, there is increasing evidence that odors can have positive effects on consumer shopping behaviors.[15] One study found that a scented environment produced a greater intent to revisit the store, higher purchase intention for some items, and a reduced sense of time spent shopping.[16] Another study found that one aroma, but not another, increased slot machine usage in a Las Vegas casino.[17] A third study reported that a floral-scented environment increased sales of Nike shoes.[18]

Despite these results, it is far from clear if, when, and how scents can be used effectively in a retail environment. In addition, scent preferences are highly individualized such that a pleasant scent to one individual may be repulsive to another. In addition, some shoppers object to anything being deliberately added to the air they breathe, and others worry about allergic reactions.[19]

Music Music influences consumers' moods, which influence a variety of consumption behaviors.[20] Is slow-tempo or fast-tempo background music better for a restaurant? Table 13-1 indicates that slow music increased gross margin for one restaurant by almost 15 percent per customer group compared to fast music! However, before concluding that all restaurants should play slow music, examine the table carefully. Slow music appears to have relaxed and slowed down the customers, resulting in more time in the restaurant and substantially more purchases from the bar. Restaurants that rely on rapid customer turnover may be better off with fast-tempo music.

A study of the impact of music in a supermarket environment found that the tempo of the music (fast or slow) did not affect purchasing behavior. However, the match between the music being played and the customer's music preference did.[21] Another study found that music, particularly music that the audience liked, increased their perception of how

TABLE 13-1

The Impact of Background Music on Restaurant Patrons

Variables	*Slow Music*	*Fast Music*
Service time	29 min.	27 min.
Customer time at table	56 min.	45 min.
Customer groups leaving before seated	10.5%	12.0%
Amount of food purchased	\$55.81	\$55.12
Amount of bar purchases	\$30.47	\$21.62
Estimated gross margin	\$55.82	\$48.62

Source: R. E. Milliman, "The Influence of Background Music on the Behavior of Restaurant Patrons," in the *Journal of Consumer Research,* September 1986, p. 289.

long a wait for a service was. However, it also increased their positive emotional response to the service environment and to the wait itself. And, it increased the consumers' positive behavioral intentions (continue using and recommending the service provider).[22]

Because of the impact that music can have on shopping behavior, firms now exist to develop music programs to meet the unique needs of specific retailers. This music is not like the stereotype of "elevator" or background music such as that generally supplied by Muzak. Background music is designed to mask general noises and to go unnoticed. The new approach is to have foreground music that shoppers will hear and respond to. The music becomes part of the shopping experience.

AEI, a major supplier of foreground music, does intense research on the demographics and psychographics of each client store's customers. The age mix, buying patterns, and traffic flows of each part of the day are analyzed. An AEI spokesperson characterizes its approach as follows:

> Our retailers are passionate about their environment. We call our clients "passion retailers" because their success is tied directly to how you and I view them. Fashion apparel companies like The Limited or The Gap are passionate about their image. They control the factors within their stores that shape the behavior of their buyers. From store fixtures to color schemes, everything is planned to communicate that image, including the music. Besides heat and light, music is the only thing that impacts you 100 percent of the time you are in the store.[23]

Firms such as the Banana Republic, Bath & Body Works, Eddie Bauer, and County Seat use services such as those offered by AEI to help create an appropriate and consistent shopping environment throughout their chains.

Crowding Crowding generally produces negative outcomes for both the retail outlet and the consumer.[24] As more people enter a store and/or as more of the space of the store is filled with merchandise, an increasing percentage of the shoppers will experience a feeling of being crowded, confined, or claustrophobic. Most consumers find these feelings to be unpleasant and will take steps to change them. The primary means of doing this is to spend less time in the store by buying less, making faster decisions, and using less of the available information. This in turn tends to produce less satisfactory purchases, an unpleasant shopping trip, and a reduced likelihood of returning to the store.

Marketers need to design their outlets in a manner that will reduce consumers' perceptions of crowding. This is made difficult by the fact that retail shopping tends to occur at specific times, such as holiday weekends. Retailers must balance the expense of having a larger store than required most of the time against the cost of dissatisfied customers during key shopping periods. Using extra personnel, adding additional checkout lines, and similar measures can enhance the flow of consumers through a store during peak periods and reduce the crowding sensation.

Marketing Strategy and Physical Surroundings Remember that there are many possible behaviors that a marketer could be interested in: actual purchase, shopping (looking), receiving information (such as watching TV advertisements), using a product or service, and so forth. An analysis of nonpurchase motivations for shopping found physical activity and sensory stimulation to be two important motives.[25] Enclosed shopping malls offer clear advantages in providing a safe, comfortable area for leisurely strolls. The sights and sounds of a variety of stores and individuals also provide a high degree of sensory stimulation. Both these factors play an important role in the overall success of shopping centers and other shopping areas. If there are physical aspects of the situation that you can influence and/or control, then you should do so in a manner that will make the physical situation compatible with the lifestyle of your target market.

ILLUSTRATION 13-3

This product is designed to help consumers cope with a potential unpleasant physical situation—allergy symptoms created when engaging in outdoor sports.

Courtesy Quantum Group.

Often you can neither control nor influence the physical situation the consumer will encounter, such as winter versus summer for beverage consumption. In these cases, it is appropriate to alter the various elements of the marketing mix to match the needs and expectations of the target market. Both Dr Pepper and Lipton tea have varied their advertising between summer and winter based on physical changes in the environment and consumers' reactions to these changes.

Products are also designed to help consumers deal with the physical situations they will encounter. Illustration 13-3 is an ad for a product designed to enhance consumers' enjoyment of outdoor activities.

Social Surroundings

Social surroundings are the other individuals present during the consumption process. Our actions are frequently influenced by those around us. For example, Chinese-, Mexican-, and Anglo-Americans prefer different types of food in situations where business associates are present versus those where parents are present.[26]

What would you wear in each of the following situations?

- Studying alone for a final.
- Meeting at the library with a date to study for a final.
- Going to a nice restaurant with a date.
- Meeting a prospective employer for lunch.

Courtesy Allen Edmonds.

ILLUSTRATION 13-4

Even a product such as men's shoes varies depending on the social situation in which it will be used.

Most of us would change our apparel across at least some of these situations. Illustration 13-4 shows how Allen Edmonds designs shoes for different types of social situations.

Social influence is a significant force acting on our behavior, since individuals tend to comply with group expectations, particularly when the behavior is visible. Thus, shopping, a highly visible activity, and the use of many publicly consumed brands are subject to social influences.[27]

Shopping can provide a social experience outside the home for making new acquaintances, meeting existing friends, or just being near other people. Some people seek status and authority in shopping since the salesperson's job is to wait on the customer. This allows these individuals a measure of respect or prestige that may otherwise be lacking in their lives. Thus, consumers, on occasion, shop *for* social situations rather than, or in addition to, products.

Frequently, as a marketing manager, you will not have any control over social characteristics of a situation. For example, when a television advertisement is sent into the home, the advertising manager cannot control whom the viewer is with at the time of the reception. However, the manager can utilize the knowledge that some programs are generally viewed alone (weekday, daytime programs), some are viewed by the entire family (prime-time family comedies), and others by groups of friends (Super Bowl). The message presented can be structured to these viewing situations.

There are a number of occasions where marketing managers can influence the social aspects of a situation. For instance, the advertiser can encourage you to "ask a friend" or, better yet, "bring a friend along." Some firms, such as Tupperware, have been ingenious in structuring social situations that encourage sales.[28] Salespersons know that frequently they can use the shopper's companion as an effective sales aid by soliciting his or her opinion and advice.[29]

Temporal Perspectives

Temporal perspectives are situational characteristics that deal with the effect of time on consumer behavior. Time as a situational factor can manifest itself in a number of ways.[30] The amount of time available for the purchase has a substantial impact on the consumer decision process. In general, the less time there is available (i.e., increased time pressure), the shorter will be the information search, the less available information will be used, and the more suboptimal purchases will be made.[31]

Limited purchase time can also result in a smaller number of product alternatives being considered. The increased time pressure experienced by many dual-career couples and single parents tends to increase the incidence of brand loyalty, particularly for nationally branded products. The obvious implication is that these consumers feel safer with nationally branded or "known" products, particularly when they do not have the time to engage in extensive comparison shopping.

Time as a situational influence affects our choice of stores. A number of retail firms have taken advantage of the temporal perspective factor. Perhaps the most successful of these is the 7-Eleven chain, which caters almost exclusively to individuals who either are in a hurry or who want to make a purchase after regular shopping hours.

Internet shopping is growing rapidly in part due to the time pressures felt by many dual-career and single-parent households. Shopping on the Internet has two important time-related dimensions. First, it has the potential to reduce the amount of time required to make a specific purchase. Second, it provides the consumer with almost total control over *when* the purchase is made (see Chapter 17).

Time pressures have increased demand for high-quality, easy-to-prepare foods, as well as other time-saving products. Illustration 13-5 shows an ad positioning the Palm III connected organizer as a means of gaining control over time. As with other aspects of situational influence, the way time is viewed and responded to varies across cultures (see Chapter 2, page 57).

Task Definition

Task definition is the reason the consumption activity is occurring. The major task dichotomy used by marketers is between purchases for self-use versus gift giving.

Gift Giving Consumers use different shopping strategies and purchase criteria when shopping for gifts versus shopping for the same item for self-use.[32] Consumers give gifts for many reasons.[33] Social expectations and ritualized consumption situations such as birthdays often "require" gift giving independent of the giver's actual desires. Gifts are also given to elicit return favors either in the form of gifts or actions. And, of course, gifts are given as an expression of love and caring.[34]

The type of gift given and desired varies by occasion and gender.[35] One study found that wedding gifts tend to be *utilitarian* (the top four attributes are durability, usefulness, receiver's need, and high performance), while birthday gifts tend to be *fun* (the top four attributes are enjoyability, uniqueness, durability, and high performance). Thus, both the general task definition (gift giving) and the specific task definition (gift-giving occasion) influence purchase behavior, as does the relationship between the giver and the recipient.

Gift giving produces anxieties on the part of both givers and receivers. Gifts communicate symbolic meaning on several levels.[36] The gift item itself generally has a known (or knowable) price that can be interpreted as a measure of the esteem the giver has

3Com and the 3Com logo are registered trademarks. Palm III™ and the Palm III™ logo are trademarks of Palm Computing, Inc., 3Com Corporation or its subsidiaries.

ILLUSTRATION 13-5

In the United States, dual-career and single-parent families as well as increased performance expectations in many jobs have caused consumers to feel "time starved." Products such as the Palm III that are positioned as a means of saving or gaining control of time are generally viewed favorably.

for the receiver. The image and functionality of the gift implies the giver's impression of the image and personality of the receiver. It also reflects on the image and thoughtfulness of the giver.

The nature of a gift can signify the type of relationship the giver has or desires with the receiver.[37] A gift of stationery implies a very different desired relationship between two individuals than does a gift of cologne. Consider these quotes from two different women:

- He actually gave Ann an electric frying pan for Christmas. That's not a gift, it's a chore . . . I tried to control my dismay when I asked Ann how the frying pan made her feel. She said, "I got the feeling he had visions of me barefoot and pregnant." She quit dating him shortly after.
- The biggest moment of revelation, the moment I knew he was "serious" about me was when he showed up with a gift for my daughter. Other men had shown the typical false affection for her in order to get on my good side, but he was only civil and polite to her, never gushy. One day, however, he showed up with a very nice skateboard for my daughter . . . The gift marked a turning point in our relationship. I think for him it marked the time that he decided it would be OK to get serious about a woman with a child.[38]

As the quotes above indicate, the act of giving/receiving a gift can alter the relationship between the giver and receiver. Consumer Insight 13-1 describes this process.

Consumer Insight 13-1

The Impact of Gifts on Relationships

Recent research indicates that receiving a gift has one of six impacts on the existing relationship between the gift giver and the recipient.

Strengthening The gift moves the relationship to a higher level. Feelings of connection, bonding, commitment, and/or shared meaning are enhanced. This often signals a change in the nature of a relationship, such as moving from friendship to a romance.

> It was the first time I knew this guy was serious . . . He must really love me to . . . go outside of these bounds that we had already established . . . Backpacking equipment was really a symbol of who he was. And to sort of share that was to share who he was . . . So, this was one of the first signs that this was a long-term meaningful relationship.

Affirmation Receiving the gift confirms the positive quality of the existing relationship. Existing feelings of affection are validated. These gifts often occur within the context of a ritualized situation such as birthdays or Christmas.

> So bright yellow and orange slices of dried apricots and peaches, sent by my dad, were packages of love I could share with my friends in the dorm . . . My dad and I were so close—it became a hug across the miles.

Negligible The gift receipt has no noticeable effect on the recipient's view of the relationship. These gifts may produce mild positive or negative emotions but do not strengthen or weaken the ties between the giver and receiver.

> My sister sends me this dried fruit every year for Christmas . . . I don't like dried fruit . . . This is minor because it's not like I'm mad at my sister because she sent dried fruit. It's like. "Oh, it's dried fruit again."

Negative Confirmation The receipt of the gift confirms the negative quality of the current relationship. The lack of feelings of connection, bonding, and/or shared meaning is validated. These gifts are almost always associated with ritual situations that virtually require gifting. "Inappropriate" gifts are interpreted not as mistakes but as signals of a lack of interest or an attempt to change the recipient.

> My husband always gets great stuff (from his parents)—things that are tasteful, that he likes and are suited to him. I get this "country" sweatshirt. It is something I would never wear . . . Generally, we are not close, don't talk except when visiting once or twice a year. This same pattern happened several times.

Weakening The gift harms the quality of the relationship between the giver and the receiver. It evokes negative emotions such as anger, embarrassment, or uneasiness. Gifts that impose burdens (reciprocation or care of the gift) or that insult the recipient tend to weaken relationships.

> we opened the one gift from all the employees. Well, when we opened it, we could tell right then and there that it (a frying pan) was used, because there was no packing material or instruction book or warranty . . . it was never the same around the office again.

Severing The gift harms the relationship so severely as to terminate it. Extreme instances of gifts that weaken relationships might terminate them. Gifts that are threatening or that clearly signal that the relationship is over also have this effect.

> And she gave me a shirt. Wrapped. And she recalled the precedent: "I just remembered that your relationship with Tracie ended with a shirt-giving." . . . The immediate impact was that it definitely, you know, was the signal that this was the end.

Critical Thinking Questions

1. What implications do these findings have for manufacturers and/or retailers who market gift items?
2. According to this study, the recipient's response to the gift is the key determinant of its impact on the relationship. What implications does this have for the giver?

Source: C. C. Otnes, and F. F. Brunel, "Gift Receipt and the Reformulation of Interpersonal Relationships," *Journal of Consumer Research*, March 1999, pp. 385–402.

Items received as gifts often take on meaning associated with the relationship or the giver:

- To me, the roses and vase mark the time we became more than friends. I will always keep the vase to symbolize my friendship with him before the relationship, because, like the vase, I will always have his friendship.
- I was given a diamond ring from an old lady that was a very special friend of the family. We were friends, although there was an age difference of 60 years. It reminds me of her—a very nice and very strong personality.[39]

Of course, the meaning and nature of gift giving is culture specific (see Chapter 2, page 62).[40]

Antecedent States

Features of the individual person that are not lasting characteristics—such as momentary moods or conditions—are called **antecedent states.** For example, we all experience states of depression or high excitement from time to time that are not normally part of our individual makeup.

Moods **Moods** are *transient feeling states that are generally not tied to a specific event or object.*[41] They tend to be less intense than emotions and may operate without the individual's awareness. While moods may affect all aspects of a person's behavior, they generally do not completely interrupt ongoing behavior as an emotion might. Individuals use such terms as happy, cheerful, peaceful, and blue to describe their moods.

Moods both affect and are affected by the consumption process.[42] For example, television, radio, and magazine program content can influence our mood and arousal level, which, in turn, influences our information-processing activities.[43]

Moods also influence our decision processes and the purchase and consumption of various products.[44] Positive mood states appear to be associated with increased browsing and "impulse" purchasing. Negative moods also increase impulse and compulsive purchasing in some consumers.[45] Moods also influence perceptions of service and waiting time.[46]

Consumers actively manage their mood states. That is, we often seek situations, activities, or objects that will alleviate negative moods or enhance positive ones. Products and services are one means consumers use to manage their mood states. Thus, a person feeling sad or "down" might view a situation comedy on television, go to a cheerful movie, eat at an upbeat restaurant, or purchase a new compact disc, shirt, or other fun product. Consumers engage in such mood-regulating behavior at a nonconscious level and also at a very deliberate, conscious level:

- [T]here are certain products that I purchase specifically to make me feel better. For instance, occasionally, I enjoy smoking a cigar. Certainly the cigar serves no other purpose than to make me feel good.
- While other cosmetics, perfumes and nice clothes can make me feel good, they seldom have the same power to transform my temperament like a manicure and pedicure can.
- What do freshness, softness, and sensuality have in common? Me, and that's why I use these products that enhance my spirit because using the products is much more than just physical, it's a spiritual voyage as well. One goes from feeling bored, dull, and tired to feeling sexy, beautiful and confident.[47]

Marketers attempt to influence moods and to time marketing activities with positive mood-inducing events. Many companies prefer to advertise during "light" television programs because viewers tend to be in a good mood while watching these shows. Restaurants, bars, shopping malls, and many other retail outlets are designed to induce positive moods in patrons. As discussed earlier, music is often played for this reason.

Since consumers actively manage their moods, marketers can position products and services with "mood enhancement" as one of the benefits. Such positioning can involve direct statement claims such "Give yourself a treat," or "You deserve a break today." It can also be done more subtly through the usage situations shown in advertisements for the product or service.

Momentary Conditions Whereas moods reflect states of mind, *momentary conditions reflect temporary states of being* such as being tired, being ill, having "extra" money, being broke, and so forth. However, for conditions, as for moods, to fit under the definition of antecedent states, they must be momentary and not constantly with the individual. Hence, an individual who is short of cash only momentarily will act differently than someone who is always short of cash.[48]

As with moods, individuals attempt to manage their momentary conditions, often through the purchase or consumption of products and services. For example, individuals feeling tired or sleepy during the day may drink a cup of coffee or a soft drink or eat a candy bar. A variety of medications are sold to relieve physical discomfort associated with overexertion, colds, allergies, and so forth. Pawnshops provide cash for individuals temporarily needing funds, as do banks and other financial institutions. Thus, a great deal of marketing activity is directed toward momentary conditions.

RITUAL SITUATIONS

Rituals are receiving increasing attention by marketing scholars and practitioners. A **ritual situation** can be described as *a set of interrelated behaviors that occur in a structured format, that have symbolic meaning, and that occur in response to socially defined occasions*.[49] Ritual situations can range from completely private to completely public. A completely private ritual situation would be an individual's decision to drink a private toast or say a private prayer on the anniversary of an event with special meaning to the individual. A couple that celebrates their first date by returning to the same restaurant every year is involved in a more public ritual. Weddings, as described in the opening vignette, tend to be even more public. Finally, national and global holidays present very public ritual situations.

Ritual situations are of major importance to marketers because they often involve prescribed consumption behaviors. Every major American holiday (ritual situation) has *consumption rituals* associated with it. For example, more than 60 percent of the toy industry's sales occur at Christmas. Illustration 13-6 shows how M&M's ties into the common American consumption ritual of baking Christmas cookies.

While there is significant variation across individuals and households, there is enough shared behavior that marketers can develop products and promotions around the common ritual situations that arise each year. For example, candy marketers produce and promote a wide array of candies for Valentine's Day.

Marketers also attempt to change or create consumption patterns associated with ritual situations.[50] For example, Halloween cards are being promoted, as are Halloween lights. As we saw in the opening example, a wide array of firms seek to make their products and services part of the consumption pattern associated with weddings. The same is true for most other rites of passage in America such as graduation.

ILLUSTRATION 13-6

Ritual situations often have associated consumption patterns.

M&M's® Chocolate Mini Baking Bits.

SITUATIONAL INFLUENCES AND MARKETING STRATEGY

In previous sections, we described a variety of marketing strategies based on situational influences. Here, we will focus more specifically on the process by which such strategies can be developed.

It is important to note that individuals do not encounter situations randomly. Instead, most people "create" many of the situations they face. Thus, individuals who choose to engage in physically demanding sports such as jogging, tennis, or racquetball are indirectly choosing to expose themselves to the situation of "being tired" or "being thirsty." This allows marketers to develop products, advertising, and segmentation strategies based on the situations that individuals selecting various lifestyles are likely to encounter.

After determining the different situations that might impact the consumption of a product, marketers must determine which products or brands are most likely to be purchased or consumed across those situations. One method of dealing with this question is to jointly scale situations and products. An example is shown in Figure 13-3. Here, *use situations* that ranged from "private consumption at home" to "consumption away from home where there is a concern for other people's reaction to you" were scaled in terms of their similarity and relationship to products appropriate for that situation.

For a use situation described as "to clean my mouth upon rising in the morning," toothpaste and mouthwash are viewed as most appropriate. However, a use situation described as "before an important business meeting late in the afternoon" involves both consumption

FIGURE 13-3 Use Situations and Product Positioning

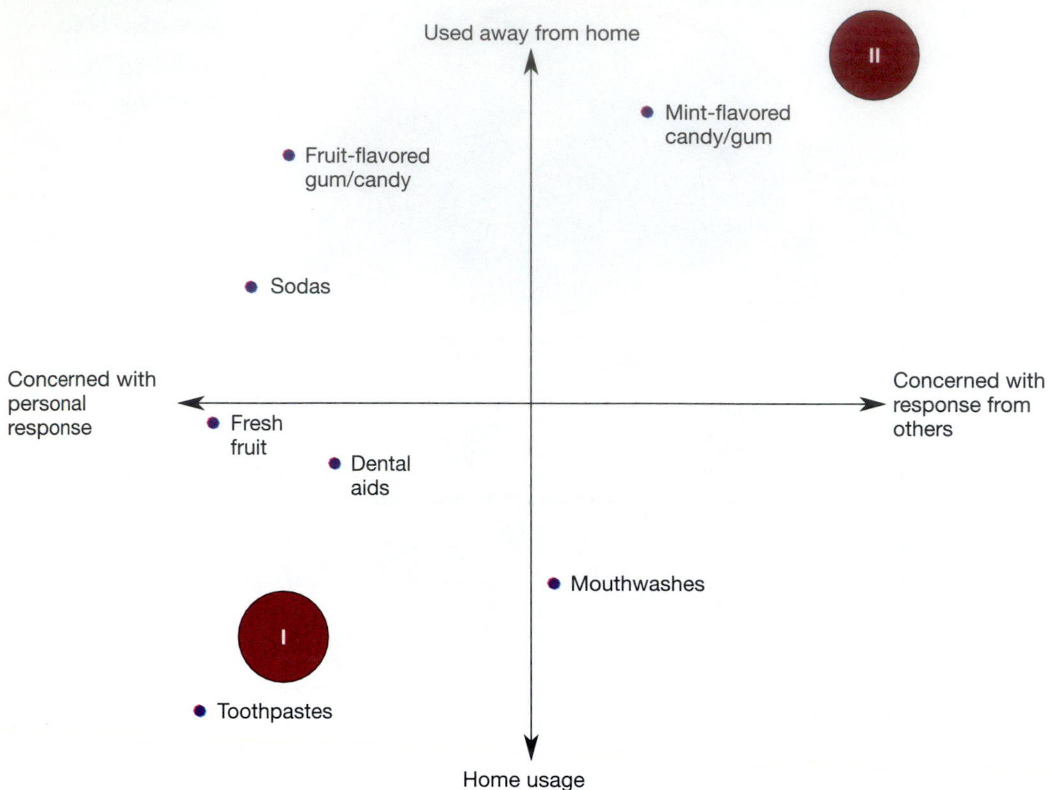

I = Use situation: "To clean my mouth upon rising in the morning."
II = Use situation: "Before an important business meeting late in the afternoon."

away from home and a concern for the response others have to you. As a result, mint-flavored gums or candies are preferred.

Having determined how products are *currently used* across situations can help the marketer develop appropriate advertising and positioning strategies. In our example, a product such as Wrigley's Spearmint gum might advertise its breath freshening capabilities for use in away from home social situations. Or, a marketer may try to change the situations for which a product is used. In Figure 13-3 mouthwash is not seen as appropriate for consumption away from home. What if a version of Scope was developed that one swallowed after use? Could it successfully be promoted for use away from home? Illustration 13-7 shows one of series of ads designed to convince consumers that French wine is appropriate for casual social situations, not just very special celebrations (the primary current use situation).

Another approach for developing situation-based marketing strategies is to follow these five steps:[51]

1. Use observational studies, focus group discussions, depth interviews, and secondary data to discover the various usage situations that influence the consumption of the product.
2. Survey a larger sample of consumers to better understand and quantify how the product is used and the benefits sought in the usage situation by market segment.

Courtesy Food and Wines from France/Sopexa U.S.A.

ILLUSTRATION 13-7

This ad attempts to position French wine as appropriate for casual, fun social situations.

TABLE 13-2 Person–Situation Segments for Suntan Lotions

Suntan Lotion Use Situation	Potential Users of Suntan Lotion				
	Young Children	*Teenagers*	*Adult Women*	*Adult Men*	*Situation Benefits*
Beach/Boat Activities	Prevent sunburn/skin damage	Prevent sunburn while tanning	Prevent sunburn/skin change/dry skin	Prevent sunburn	Container floats
Home/Pools Sunbathing	Prevent sunburn/skin damage	Tanning without sunburn	Tanning without skin damage or dry skin	Tanning without sunburn/skin damage	Lotion won't stain clothes or furniture
Tanning Booth		Tanning	Tanning with moisturizer	Tanning	Designed for sunlamps
Snow Skiing		Prevent sunburn	Prevent sunburn/ skin damage/ dry skin	Prevent sunburn	Antifreeze formula
Person Benefits	Protection	Tanning	Protection and tanning with soft skin	Protection and tanning	

Reprinted with permission from *Journal of Marketing,* published by the American Marketing Association. Adapted from P. Dickson, "Person–Situation: Segmentation's Missing Link," Fall 1982, pp. 56–64.

3. Construct a person–situation segmentation matrix. The rows are the major usage situations and the columns are groups of users with unique needs or desires. Each cell contains the key benefits sought. Table 13-2 illustrates this for suntan lotion.
4. Evaluate each cell in terms of potential (sales volume, price level, cost to serve, competitor strength, etc.).
5. Develop and implement a marketing strategy for those cells that offer sufficient profit potential given your capabilities.

SUMMARY

Marketing managers should view the consumer and marketing activities designed to affect and influence that consumer in light of the situations that the consumer faces. A *consumer situation* is a set of factors outside of and removed from the individual consumer, as well as removed from the characteristics or attributes of the product.

Situations have been classified into a scheme of five objectively measured variables. *Physical surroundings* include geographical and institutional location, decor, sound, aromas, lighting, weather, and displays of merchandise or other material surrounding the product. Retailers are particularly concerned with the effects of physical surroundings. The sum of all the physical features of a retail environment is referred to as the *store atmosphere* or environment. *Atmospherics* is the process managers use to manipulate the physical retail environment to create specific mood responses in shoppers. Atmosphere is referred to as *servicescape* when describing a service business such as a hospital, bank, or restaurant.

Social surroundings deal with other persons present who could have an impact on the individual consumer's behavior. The characteristics of the other persons present, their roles, and their interpersonal interactions are potentially important social situational influences.

Temporal perspectives deal with the effect of time on consumer behavior. It includes such concepts as time of day, time since last purchase, time since or until meals or payday, and time constraints imposed by commitments. Convenience stores have evolved and been successful by taking advantage of the temporal perspective factor.

Task definition reflects the purpose or reason for engaging in the consumption behavior. The task may reflect different buyer and user roles anticipated by the individual. For example, a person shopping for dishes to be given as a wedding present is in a different situation than if the dishes were for personal use.

Antecedent states are features of the individual person that are not lasting or relatively enduring characteristics. *Moods* are such things as temporary states of depression or high excitement, which all people experience. *Momentary conditions* are such things as being tired, ill, having a great deal of money (or none at all), and so forth.

A *ritual situation* can be described as a set of interrelated behaviors that occur in a structured format, that have symbolic meaning, and that occur in response to socially defined occasions. Ritual situations can range from completely private to completely public. Ritual situations are of major importance to marketers because they often involve prescribed consumption behaviors.

Situational influences may have very direct influences, but they also interact with product and individual characteristics to influence behavior. In some cases, the situation will have no influence whatsoever, because the individual's characteristics or choices are so intense that they override everything else. But the situation is always potentially important and therefore is of concern to marketing managers.

KEY TERMS

Antecedent states 491
Atmospherics 483
Communications situations 478
Disposition situations 480
Moods 491
Physical surroundings 482
Purchase situation 480
Ritual situation 492
Servicescape 483
Situational influence 478
Social surroundings 486
Store atmosphere 483
Task definition 488
Temporal perspective 488
Usage situation 480

INTERNET EXERCISES

1. Visit several on-line malls. How would you characterize this shopping situation relative to shopping at an actual mall?
2. What type of store environment does Amazon.com have?
3. Prepare a report listing and describing several useful sites for gathering current information about ritual situations such as marriages or job interviews.
4. Evaluate the WeddingChannel.com.

REVIEW QUESTIONS

1. What is meant by the term *situation?* Why is it important for a marketing manager to understand situation influences on purchasing behavior?
2. What are *physical surroundings* (as a situational variable)? Give an example of how they can influence the consumption process.
3. How does crowding affect shopping behavior?
4. What is *store atmosphere?*
5. What is *atmospherics?*
6. What is a *servicescape?*
7. What are *social surroundings* (as a situational variable)? Give an example of how they can influence the consumption process.
8. What is *temporal perspective* (as a situational variable)? Give an example of how it can influence the consumption process.
9. What is *task definition* (as a situational variable)? Give an example of how it can influence the consumption process.
10. Why do people give gifts?
11. How might the receipt of a gift affect the relationship between the giver and the receiver?
12. What are *antecedent conditions* (as a situational variable)? Give an example of how they can influence the consumption process.
13. What is a *mood?* How does it differ from an *emotion?* How do moods influence consumption behavior?
14. How do people manage their moods?
15. How do *moods* differ from *momentary conditions?*
16. What is meant by the statement, "Situational variables may interact with object or personal characteristics"?
17. Are individuals randomly exposed to situational influences? Why?
18. What is a *ritual situation?* Why are they important?
19. Describe a process for developing a situation-based marketing strategy.

DISCUSSION QUESTIONS

20. Discuss the potential importance of each type of situational influence in developing a marketing strategy to promote the purchase of (gifts to/shopping at):
    a. Christian Children's Fund
    b. McDonald's
    c. T.G.I. Friday's
    d. Mountain Dew
    e. Life insurance
    f. Sears
21. What product categories seem most susceptible to situational influences? Why?
22. Flowers are "appropriate" gifts for women for many situations but seem to be appropriate for men only when they are ill. Why is this so? How might FTD change this?
23. How could the store atmosphere at the following be improved?
    a. The main bookstore near campus
    b. A bank near campus
24. Speculate on what a matrix like the one shown in Table 13-2 would look like for the following:
    a. Pain relievers
    b. Mouthwash

c. Milk
d. Fast-food restaurants
e. Bicycles
f. Coffee

25. Does Table 13-1 have implications for outlets other than restaurants? If yes, which ones and why?
26. Does your shopping behavior and purchase criteria differ between purchases made for yourself and purchases made as gifts? How?
27. Describe a situation in which a mood (good or bad) caused you to make an unusual purchase.
28. Describe a relatively private ritual that you or someone you know has. What, if any, consumption pattern is associated with it.
29. Describe the consumption rituals your family has associated with the following:
    a. Fourth of July
    b. Christmas
    c. Memorial Day
    d. Valentine's Day
    e. Mother's Day
    f. Father's Day
    g. Your birthday

APPLICATION ACTIVITIES

30. Interview five people who have recently purchased the following. Determine the role, if any, played by situational factors.
    a. A paperback book
    b. A dress, suit, or sports coat
    c. Flowers
    d. A nice restaurant meal
    e. A soft drink
    f. Sports equipment
31. Interview a salesperson for the following. Determine the role, if any, this individual feels situational variables play in his or her sales.
    a. Clothing
    b. Automobile
    c. Pets
    d. Jewelry
32. Conduct a study using a small (10 or so) sample of your friends in which you attempt to isolate the situational factors that influence the type, brand, or amount of the following purchased or used.
    a. Fast food
    b. Perfume
    c. Movie rentals
    d. Charity donations
    e. Church attendance
    f. Popcorn or similar snacks
33. Create a list of 10 to 20 use situations relevant to campus area restaurants. Then interview 10 students and have them indicate which of these situations they have encountered and ask them to rank order these situations in terms of how likely they are to occur. Discuss how a restaurant could use this information in trying to appeal to the student market.
34. Visit three stores selling the same product line. Describe how the atmosphere differs across the stores. Why do you think these differences exist?
35. Visit three hair salons. Describe how the servicescape differs across the salons. Why do you think these differences exist?
36. Copy or describe three advertisements that are clearly based on a situational appeal. For each advertisement, indicate:
    a. Which situational variable is involved
    b. Why the company would use this variable
    c. Your evaluation of the effectiveness of this approach
37. Create a wedding gift, birthday gift, and self-use ad for the following. Explain the differences across the ads.
    a. Barbecue grill
    b. Dish set
    c. Power drill
    d. Set of kitchen knives
    e. Food processor
    f. Clock/radio/alarms
38. Interview 10 students and determine instances where their mood affected their purchases. What do you conclude?
39. Interview 10 students and determine the consumption patterns they have with respect to the following. What do you conclude?
    a. Fourth of July
    b. Christmas
    c. Memorial Day
    d. Valentine's Day
    e. Mother's Day
    f. Father's Day

REFERENCES

1. C. Miller, "Til Death Do They Part," *Marketing News,* May 27, 1995, pp. 1–2.
2. R. W. Belk, "Situational Variables and Consumer Behavior," *Journal of Consumer Research,* December 1975, p. 158.
3. See K. S. Lim and M. A. Razzaque, "Brand Loyalty and Situational Effects," *Journal of International Consumer Marketing,* no. 4 (1997), pp. 95–115.
4. See K. R. France and C. W. Park, "The Impact of Program Affective Valence and Level of Cognitive Appraisal on Advertising Processing and Effectiveness," *Journal of Current Issues and Research in Advertising,* Fall 1997, pp. 1–21; and A. B. Aylesworth and S. B. MacKenzie, "Context Is Key," *Journal of Advertising,* Summer 1998, pp. 17–31.
5. B. Wansink, "Making Old Brands New," *American Demographics,* December 1997, pp. 53–58.
6. Ibid.; and I. Sinha, "A Conceptual Model of Situation Type on Consumer Choice Behavior and Consideration Sets," in *Advances in Consumer Research XXI,* ed. C. T. Allen and D. R. John (Provo, UT: Association for Consumer Research, 1994), pp. 477–82. For a different approach, see G. R. Foxall, "Situated Consumer Behavior," *Research in Consumer Behavior* 6 (1993), pp. 113–52.
7. See J. A. F. Nicholls et al., "Situational Influences on Shoppers," *Journal of International Consumer Marketing,* no. 2, pp. 21–39.
8. D. A. Michals, "Pitching Products by the Barometer," *Business Week,* July 8, 1985, p. 45.
9. See S. Grossbart, R. Hampton, B. Rammohan, and R. S. Lapidus, "Environmental Dispositions and Customer Response to Store Atmospheres," *Journal of Business Research,* November 1990, pp. 225–41; and E. Sherman, A. Mathur, and R. B. Smith, "Store Environment and Consumer Purchase Behavior," *Psychology & Marketing,* July 1997, pp. 361–78.
10. See W. R. Swinyard, "The Effects of Mood, Involvement, and Quality of Store Experience on Shopping Intentions," *Journal of Consumer Research,* September 1993, pp. 271–80; J. Baker, D. Grewal, and A. Parasuraman, "The Influence of Store Environment on Quality Inferences and Store Image," *Journal of the Academy of Marketing Science,* Fall 1994, pp. 328–39; W. R. Darden and B. J. Badin, "Exploring the Concept of Affective Quality," *Journal of Business Research* 29 (1994), pp. 101–9; and C. S. Areni, J. R. Sparks, and P. Dunne, "Assessing Consumers' Affective Responses to Retail Environments," in *Advances in Consumer Research XXIII,* ed. K. P. Corfman and J. G. Lynch (Provo, UT: Association for Consumer Research, 1996), pp. 504–09.
11. B. Babin and W. R. Darden, "Good and Bad Shopping Vibes," *Journal of Business Research,* March 1996, pp. 210–60.
12. M. J. Bitner, "Servicescapes," *Journal of Marketing,* April 1992, pp. 57–71. See also J. C. Ward, M. J. Bitner, and J. Barnes, "Measuring the Prototypicality and Meaning of Retail Environments," *Journal of Retailing,* Summer 1992, pp. 194–220; J. Baker, D. Grewal, and M. Levy, "An Experimental Approach to Making Retail Store Environmental Decisions," *Journal of Retailing,* Winter 1992, pp. 445–60; J. Podel, "Bank Design," *Bank Marketing,* May 1994, pp. 10–14; K. L. Wakefield and J. G. Blodgett, "The Importance of Servicescapes in Leisure Service Settings," *Journal of Services Marketing* 8, no. 3 (1994), pp. 66–76; and K. L. Wakefield and J. G. Blodgett, "The Effect of the Servicescape on Customers' Behavioral Intentions in Leisure Service Settings," *Journal of Services Marketing,* no. 6 (1996), pp. 45–61.
13. M. J. Bitner, "Evaluating Service Encounters," *Journal of Marketing,* April 1990, pp. 69–82.
14. See J. A. Bellizzi and R. E. Hite, "Environmental Color, Consumer Feelings, and Purchase Likelihood," *Psychology & Marketing,* September 1992, pp. 347–63.
15. D. J. Mitchell, B. E. Kahn, and S. C. Knasko, "There's Something in the Air," *Journal of Consumer Research,* September 1995, pp. 229–38.
16. E. R. Spangenberg, A. E. Crowley, and P. W. Henderson, "Improving the Store Environment," *Journal of Marketing,* April 1996, pp. 67–80.
17. A. R. Hirsch, "Effects of Ambient Odors on Slot-Machine Usage in a Las Vegas Casino," *Psychology & Marketing,* October 1995, pp. 585–94.
18. M. Wilkie, "Scent of a Market," *American Demographics,* August 1995, pp. 40–49.
19. P. Sloan, "Smelling Trouble," *Advertising Age,* September 11, 1995, p. 1.
20. G. C. Bruner II, "Music, Mood, and Marketing," *Journal of Marketing,* October 1990, pp. 94–104; J. D. Herrington and L. M. Capella, "Practical Applications of Music in Service Settings," *Journal of Services Marketing* 8, no. 3 (1994), pp. 50–65; L. Dube, J.-C. Chebat, and S. Morin, "The Effects of Background Music on Consumers' Desire to Affiliate in Buyer-Seller Interactions," *Psychology & Marketing,* July 1995, pp. 305–19; and C. S. Gulas and C. D. Schewe, "Atmospheric Segmentation," in *Enhancing Knowledge Development in Marketing,* ed. R. Achrol and A. Mitchell (Chicago: American Marketing Association, 1994), pp. 325–30.
21. J. D. Herrington and L. M. Capella, "Effect of Music in Service Environments," *Journal of Services Marketing* 10, no. 2 (1996), pp. 26–41.
22. M. K. Hui, L. Dube, and J.-C. Chebat, "The Impact of Music on Consumers' Reactions to Waiting for Services," *Journal of Retailing,* Spring 1997, pp. 87–104.
23. C. Rudel, "Marketing with Music," *Marketing News,* August 12, 1996, p. 21.
24. See M. K. M. Hui and J. E. G. Bateson, "Testing a Theory of Crowding in the Service Environment," in *Advances in Consumer Research XVII,* ed. M. E. Goldberg, G. Gorn, and R. W. Pollay (Provo, UT: Association for Consumer Research, 1990), pp. 866–73; and S. A. Eroglu and K. A. Machleit, "An Empirical Study of Retail Crowding," *Journal of Retailing,* Summer 1990, pp. 201–21.
25. See R. A. Westbrook and W. C. Black, "A Motivation-Based Shopper Typology," *Journal of Retailing,* Spring 1985, pp. 78–103.
26. D. M. Stayman and R. Deshpande, "Situational Ethnicity and Consumer Behavior," *Journal of Consumer Research,* December 1989, pp. 361–71.

27. See B. Dubois and G. Laurent, "The Functions of Luxury," in *Advances in Consumer Research XXIII,* ed. K. P. Corfman and J. G. Lynch (Provo, UT: Association for Consumer Research, 1996), pp. 470–77; Y. Zhang and B. Gelb, "Matching Advertising Appeals to Culture," *Journal of Advertising,* Fall 1996, pp. 29–46; and T. R. Graeth, "Consumption Situations and the Effects of Brand Image on Consumers' Brand Evaluations," *Psychology & Marketing,* January 1997, pp. 49–70.

28. See J. K. Frenzen and H. L. Davis, "Purchasing Behavior in Embedded Markets," *Journal of Consumer Research,* June 1990, pp. 1–12.

29. See L. L. Price, L. F. Feick, and A. Guskey, "Everyday Market Helping Behavior," *Journal of Public Policy & Marketing,* Fall 1995, pp. 255–66; C. L. Hartman and P. Kiecker, "Buyers and Their Purchase Pals," in *Enhancing Knowledge Development in Marketing,* ed. R. Achrol and A. Mitchell (Chicago: American Marketing Association, 1994), pp. 138–44; and P. Kiecker and C. L. Hartman, "Predicting Buyers' Selection of Interpersonal Sources," in *Advances in Consumer Research XXI,* ed. C. T. Allen and D. R. John (Provo, UT: Association for Consumer Research, 1994), pp. 464–69.

30. See B. L. Gross, "Consumer Response to Time Pressure"; L. K. Anglin, J. K. Stuenkel, and L. R. Lepisto, "The Effect of Stress on Price Sensitivity and Comparison Shopping"; and F. Denton, "The Dynamism of Personal Timestyle"; all in *Advances in Consumer Research XXI,* ed. C. T. Allen and D. R. John (Provo, UT: Association for Consumer Research, 1994), pp. 120–36.

31. M. Hahn, R. Lawson, and Y. G. Lee, "The Effects of Time Pressure and Information Load on Decision Quality," *Psychology & Marketing,* September 1992, pp. 365–78. See also S. M. Nowlis, "The Effect of Time Pressure on the Choice of Brands that Differ in Quality, Price, and Product Features," *Marketing Letters,* October 1995, pp. 287–96; R. Pieters, L. Warlop, and M. Hartog, "The Effect of Time Pressure and Task Motivation on Visual Attention to Brands," in *Advances in Consumer Research XXIV,* ed. M. Bruck and D. J. MacInnis (Provo, UT: Association for Consumer Research, 1997), pp. 281–87; and R. Dhar and S. M. Nowlis, "The Effect of Time Pressure on Consumer Choice Deferral," *Journal of Consumer Research,* March 1999, pp. 369–84.

32. See E. Fisher and S. J. Arnold, "More than a Labor of Love"; and M. DeMoss and D. Mick, "Self-Gifts"; both in *Journal of Consumer Research,* December 1990, pp. 322–32; T. I. Garner and J. Wagner, "Economic Dimensions of Household Gift-Giving," *Journal of Consumer Research,* December 1991, pp. 368–79; and B. H. Schmitt and C. J. Shultz II, "Situational Effects on Brand Preferences for Image Products," *Psychology & Marketing,* August 1995, pp. 433–46.

33. Ibid., pp. 393–417; and M. A. McGrath, "Gender Differences in Gift Exchanges," *Psychology & Marketing,* August 1995, pp. 371–93.

34. R. W. Belk, "The Perfect Gift," in *Gift-Giving,* ed., C. Otnes and R. F. Beltramini (Bowling Green, OH: Bowling Green University Press, 1996), pp. 59–84; and D. R. Horne, S. Sayre, and D. A. Horne, "Gifts," in *Advances in Consumer Research XXIII,* ed. K. P. Corfman and J. G. Lynch (Provo, UT: Association for Consumer Research, 1996), pp. 30–34.

35. S. Athay, "Giving and Getting," *American Demographics,* December 1993, pp. 46–54; C. Otnes, J. A. Ruth, and C. C. Milbourne, "The Pleasure and Pain of Being Close"; and M. Rucker, A. Freitas, and J. Dolstra, "A Toast for the Host"; both in *Advances in Consumer Research XXI,* ed. C. T. Allen and D. R. John (Provo, UT: Association for Consumer Research, 1994), pp. 159–68.

36. See J. F. Sherry, Jr., M. A. McGrath, and S. L. Levy, "The Dark Side of the Gift," *Journal of Business Research,* November 1993, pp. 225–44; C. Otnes, T. M. Lowrey, and Y. C. Kim, "Gift Selection for Easy and Difficult Recipients," *Journal of Consumer Research,* September 1993, pp. 229–44; and C. Otnes, K. Zolner, and T. M. Lowrey, "Inlaws and Outlaws," in *Advances in Consumer Research XXI,* ed. C. T. Allen and D. R. John (Provo, UT: Association for Consumer Research, 1994), pp. 25–29.

37. See M. F. Wolfinbarger and M. C. Gilly, "An Experimental Investigation of Self-Symbolism in Gifts," in *Advances in Consumer Research XXIII,* ed. K. P. Corfman and J. G. Lynch (Provo, UT: Association for Consumer Research, 1996), pp. 458–62; and R. G. M. Pieters and H. S. J. Robben, "Beyond the Horses Mouth," in *Advances in Consumer Research XXV,* ed. J. W. Alba and J. W. Hutchinson (Provo, UT: Association for Consumer Research, 1998), pp. 163–69.

38. R. W. Belk and G. S. Coon, "Gift Giving as Agapic Love," *Journal of Consumer Research,* December 1993, pp. 404–05.

39. C. S. Areni, P. Kiecker, and K. M. Palan, "Is It Better to Give than to Receive?" *Psychology & Marketing,* January 1998, pp. 81–109.

40. S.-Y. Park, "A Comparison of Korean and American Gift-Giving Behaviors," *Psychology & Marketing,* September 1998, pp. 577–93.

41. See R. P. Bagozzi, M. Gopinath, and P. U. Nyer, "The Role of Emotion in Marketing," *Journal of the Academy of Marketing Science,* Spring 1999, pp. 184–206.

42. D. Kuykendall, "Mood and Persuasion," *Psychology & Marketing,* Spring 1990, pp. 1–9; P. A. Knowles, S. J. Grove, and W. J. Burroughs, "An Experimental Examination of Mood Effects," *Journal of the Academy of Marketing Science,* Spring 1993, pp. 135–42; J. Hornik, "The Role of Affect in Consumers' Temporal Judgments," *Psychology & Marketing,* May 1993, pp. 239–55; and J. Hadjimarcou and L. J. Marks, "An Examination of the Effects of Context-Induced Mood States on the Evaluation of a 'Feel-Good' Product," in *Advances in Consumer Research XXI,* ed. C. T. Allen and D. R. John (Provo, UT: Association for Consumer Research, 1994), pp. 509–13.

43. R. Batra and D. M. Stayman, "The Role of Mood in Advertising Effectiveness," *Journal of Consumer Research,* September 1990, pp. 203–14; D. Kuykendall and J. P. Keating, "Mood and Persuasion," *Psychology & Marketing,* Spring 1990, pp. 1–9; M. A. Kamins, L. J. Marks, and D. Skinner "Television Commercial Evaluation in the Context of Program Induced Mood," *Journal of Advertising,* June 1991, pp. 1–14; E. A. G. Groenland and J. P. I. Schoormans, "Comparing Mood-Induction and Affective Conditioning as Mechanisms Influencing Product Evaluation and Product Choice," *Psychology & Marketing,* March 1994, pp. 183–97; K. R. France and C. W. Park, "The Impact of Program Affective Valence and Level of Cognitive Appraisal on Advertisement Processing and Effectiveness, *Journal of Current Issues and Research in Advertising,* Fall 1997, pp. 1–21; and A. B. Aylesworth and C. B. MacKenzie, "Context Is Key," *Journal of Advertising,* Summer 1998, pp. 17–31.

44. See M. T. Curren and K. R. Harich, "Consumers' Mood States," *Psychology & Marketing,* March 1994, pp. 91–107; and J. Hadjimarcou, J. W. Barnes, and R. S. Jacobs, "The Effects of Contest-Induced Mood States on Initial and Repeat Product Evaluations," in *Advances in Consumer Research XXIII,* ed. K. P. Corfman and J. G. Lynch (Provo, UT: Association for Consumer Research, 1996), pp. 337–41.

45. D. W. Rook and M. P. Gardner, "In the Mood," *Research in Consumer Behavior* 6 (1993), pp. 1–28; W. R. Swinyard, "The Effects of Mood, Involvement, and Quality of Store Experience on Shopping Intentions," *Journal of Consumer Research,* September 1993, pp. 271–80; and R. J. Faber and G. A. Christenson, "In the Mood to Buy," *Psychology & Marketing,* December 1996, pp. 803–19.

46. P. A. Knowles, S. J. Grove, and G. M. Pickett, "Mood and the Service Customer," *Journal of Services Marketing* 7, no. 4 (1993), pp. 41–52; and J.-C. Chebat et al., "Impact of Waiting Attribution and Consumer's Mood on Perceived Quality," *Journal of Business Research,* November 1995, pp. 191–96.

47. S. J. Gould, "An Interpretive Study of Purposeful, Mood Self-Regulating Consumption," *Psychology & Marketing,* July 1997, pp. 395–426.

48. See P. A. Walsh and S. Spiggle, "Consumer Spending Patterns," in *Advances in Consumer Research XXI,* ed. C. T. Allen and D. R. John (Provo, UT: Association for Consumer Research, 1994), pp. 35–40.

49. For discussions of rituals and consumer behavior, see D. W. Rook, "The Ritual Dimension of Consumer Behavior," *Journal of Consumer Research,* December 1985, pp. 251–64; B. Gainer, "Ritual and Relationships," *Journal of Business Research,* March 1995, pp. 253–60.

50. See C. Otnes and L. M. Scott, "Something Old, Something New," *Journal of Advertising,* Spring 1996, pp. 33–50.

51. For similar approaches, see P. Dickson, "Person-Situation," *Journal of Marketing,* Fall 1982, pp. 55–64; and D. Ball, C. Lamb, and R. Brodie, "Segmentation and Market Structure When Both Consumer and Situational Characteristics Are Explanatory," *Psychology & Marketing,* September 1992, pp. 395–408.

Michael J. Hruby.

chapter fourteen

Consumer Decision Process and Problem Recognition

In 1995, Schering-Plough Corp. began a major effort to popularize the Ultraviolet (UV) Index. In a joint effort with the National Weather Service, the Environmental Protection Agency, the Centers for Disease Control, and other health groups, the firm wants to make the UV Index part of the local weather forecast. This would indicate the ultraviolet risk level in the local area, including how quickly people will sunburn if unprotected. Initial results revealed that 70 percent of the consumers in the test cities were aware of the index and most increased use of sunscreens because of it.

Why is Schering-Plough spending substantial sums to increase consumer awareness of the risks of unprotected exposure to the sun? It is the dominant firm in the sun care market, where its Coppertone brand has a 27 percent market share. Helping people recognize the danger of sun exposure not only helps these individuals, it may produce increased sales for Schering-Plough.

Coppertone is even covering up Little Miss Coppertone to promote sun protection. As a company spokesperson states:

> After 42 years, Little Miss Coppertone has an important new role. Not only is she a national symbol of fun in the sun, but she is now helping make people aware of the need for UV protection.

Firms such as Schering-Plough not only attempt to cause consumers to recognize the problems associated with ultraviolet exposure, they also develop products to alleviate the problems. For example, Schering-Plough knows that many consumers want to be in the sun and want a tan but don't want to risk the harm associated with ultraviolet radiation. In response, they developed Protect & Tan, a combination water-resistant sun protection lotion and self-tanner.[1]

Problem recognition is the first stage of the consumer decision process. In the opening example, Schering-Plough and various government and private health organizations hope to cause problem recognition among consumers concerning the risk of sun exposure. It is their hope that problem recognition will lead to decisions to protect oneself from inappropriate levels of exposure.

This chapter examines the nature of the consumer decision process and analyzes the first step in that process, problem recognition. Within problem recognition, we focus on (1) the process of problem recognition, (2) the uncontrollable determinants of problem recognition, and (3) marketing strategies based on the problem recognition process.

TYPES OF CONSUMER DECISIONS

The term *consumer decision* produces an image of an individual carefully evaluating the attributes of a set of products, brands, or services and rationally selecting the one that solves a clearly recognized need for the least cost. It has a rational, functional connotation. While consumers do make many decisions in this manner, many others involve little conscious effort. Further, many consumer decisions focus not on brand attributes but rather on the feelings or emotions associated with acquiring or using the brand or with the environment in which the product is purchased or used.[2] Thus, a brand may be selected not because of an attribute (price, style, functional characteristics) but because "It makes me feel good" or "My friends will like it."

While purchases and related consumption behavior driven by emotional or environmental needs have characteristics distinct from the traditional attribute-based model, we believe the decision process model provides useful insights into all types of consumer purchases. As we describe consumer decision making in this and the next four chapters, we will indicate how it helps us understand emotion-, environment-, and attribute-based decisions.

Consumer decisions are frequently the result of a single problem such as running low on gasoline. At other times, they result from the convergence of several problems such as an aging automobile and a growing feeling of inadequacy or low self-esteem. Furthermore, once the decision process begins, it may evolve and become more complex with multiple goals. A consumer noticing a simple need for gas may want to minimize the price paid, avoid one or more brands due to their environmental record, and decide to find a station with food service attached. This consumer may wind up choosing between a station with a lower price and its own food service versus another station with a higher price but with a preferred food outlet such as Taco Bell attached, versus spending the extra time to buy gas at one and food at the other.[3]

As Figure 14-1 indicates, there are various types of consumer decision processes.[4] As the consumer moves from a very low level of involvement *with the purchase situation* to a high level of involvement, decision making becomes increasingly complex. While purchase involvement is a continuum, it is useful to consider nominal, limited, and extended decision making as general descriptions of the types of processes that occur along various points on the continuum. You should keep in mind that the types of decision processes are not distinct but rather blend into each other.

Before describing each type of decision process, the concept of purchase involvement must be clarified. We define **purchase involvement** as *the level of concern for, or interest in, the purchase process triggered by the need to consider a particular purchase.*[5] Thus, purchase involvement is a *temporary state* of an individual, family, or household unit. It is influenced by the interaction of individual, product, and situational characteristics.[6]

Involvement and Types of Decision Making FIGURE 14-1

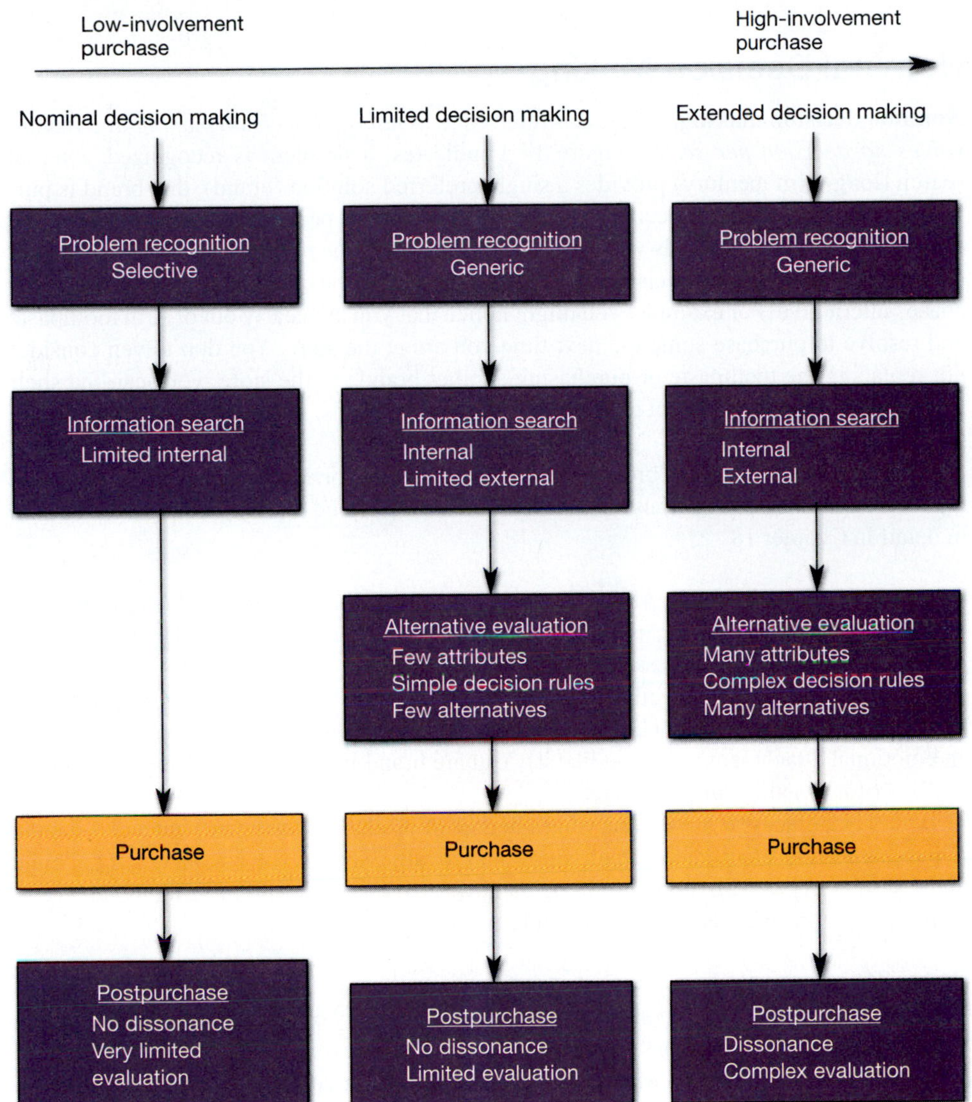

Note that purchase involvement is *not* the same as **product involvement** or enduring involvement.[7] You may be very involved with a brand (Starbucks or Saturn) or a product category (coffee or cars) and yet have a very low level of involvement with a particular purchase of that product because of brand loyalty, time pressures, or other reasons. For example, think of your favorite brand of soft drink or other beverage. You may be quite loyal to that brand, think it is superior to other brands, and have strong, favorable feelings about it. However, when you want a soft drink, you probably just buy your preferred brand without much thought.

Or, you may have a rather low level of involvement with a product (school supplies or automobile tires) but have a high level of purchase involvement because you desire to set an example for a child, impress a friend who is on the shopping trip, or save money.

The following sections provide a brief description of how the purchasing process changes as purchase involvement increases.

Nominal Decision Making

Nominal decision making, sometimes referred to as *habitual decision making* in effect *involves no decision per se.* As Figure 14-1 indicates, a problem is recognized, internal search (long-term memory) provides a single preferred solution (brand), that brand is purchased, and an evaluation occurs only if the brand fails to perform as expected. Nominal decisions occur when there is very low involvement *with the purchase.*

A completely nominal decision does not even include consideration of the "do not purchase" alternative. For example, you might notice that you are nearly out of Aim toothpaste and resolve to purchase some the next time you are at the store. You don't even consider not replacing the toothpaste or purchasing another brand. At the store, you scan the shelf for Aim and pick it up without considering alternative brands, its price, or other potentially relevant factors.

Nominal decisions can be broken into two distinct categories: brand loyal decisions and repeat purchase decisions. These two categories are described briefly below and examined in detail in Chapter 18.

Brand Loyal Purchases At one time, you may have been highly involved in selecting a toothpaste and, in response, used an extensive decision-making process. Having selected Aim as a result of this process, you may now purchase it without further consideration, even though using the best available toothpaste is still important to you. Thus, you are committed to Aim because you believe it best meets your overall needs and you have formed an emotional attachment to it (you like it). You are brand loyal. It will be very difficult for a competitor to gain your patronage.

In this example, you have a fairly high degree of product involvement but a low degree of purchase involvement because of your brand loyalty. Should you encounter a challenge to the superiority of Aim, perhaps through a news article, you would most likely engage in a high-involvement decision process before changing brands.

Repeat Purchases In contrast, you may believe that all catsup is about the same and you may not attach much importance to the product category or purchase. Having tried Del Monte and found it satisfactory, you now purchase it whenever you need catsup. Thus, you are a repeat purchaser of Del Monte catsup, but you are not committed to it.

Should you encounter a challenge to the wisdom of buying Del Monte the next time you need catsup, perhaps because of a point-of-sale price discount, you would probably engage in only a limited decision process before deciding on which brand to purchase.

Limited Decision Making

Limited decision making involves *internal and limited external search, few alternatives, simple decision rules on a few attributes, and little postpurchase evaluation.* It covers the middle ground between nominal decision making and extended decision making. In its simplest form (lowest level of purchase involvement), limited decision making is similar to nominal decision making.[8] For example, while in a store you may notice a point-of-purchase display for Jell-O and pick up two boxes without seeking information beyond your memory that "Jell-O tastes good," or "Gee, I haven't had Jell-O in a long time." In addition, you may have considered no other alternative except possibly a very limited examination of a "do not buy" option. Or, you may have a decision rule that you buy the cheapest brand of instant coffee available. When you run low on coffee (problem recognition), you simply examine coffee prices the next time you are in the store and select the cheapest brand.

Limited decision making also occurs in response to some emotional or environmental needs. For example, you may decide to purchase a new brand or product because you are "bored" with the current, otherwise satisfactory, brand. This decision might involve evaluating only the newness or novelty of the available alternatives.[9] Or, you might evaluate a purchase in terms of the actual or anticipated behavior of others. For example, you might order or refrain from ordering wine with a meal depending on the observed or expected orders of your dinner companions.

In general, limited decision making involves recognizing a problem for which there are several possible solutions. There is internal and a limited amount of external search. A few alternatives are evaluated on a few dimensions using simple selection rules. The purchase and use of the product are given very little evaluation afterwards unless there is a service problem or product failure.

Extended Decision Making

As Figure 14-1 indicates, **extended decision making** involves *an extensive internal and external information search followed by a complex evaluation of multiple alternatives.* It is the response to a high level of purchase involvement. After the purchase, doubt about its correctness is likely and a thorough evaluation of the purchase takes place. Relatively few consumer decisions reach this level of complexity. However, products such as homes, personal computers, and complex recreational items such as backpacks and stereo systems are frequently purchased via extended decision making.

Even decisions that are heavily emotional may involve substantial cognitive efforts. For example, we may agonize over a decision to take a cruise or purchase a new outfit even though the needs being met and the criteria being evaluated are largely emotions or feelings rather than attributes per se, and are therefore typically fewer in number with less external information available.

Marketing Strategy and Types of Consumer Decisions

The brief descriptions of the various types of consumer decisions provided above should be ample to indicate that marketing strategies appropriate for extended decision making would be less than optimal for nominal or limited decisions. As Figure 14-1 illustrates, each stage of the consumption process is affected by purchase involvement. We will describe the first stage, problem recognition, and discuss the marketing applications associated with it in the balance of this chapter. We devote the next four chapters to the remaining four stages of the consumption process and discuss the relevant marketing applications in those chapters.

Our discussion of the decision process is based primarily on studies conducted in America. Although the evidence is very limited, it appears that consumers in other cultures use similar processes.[10]

THE PROCESS OF PROBLEM RECOGNITION

A day rarely passes in which we do not face multiple problems, which we resolve by consuming products and services. Routine problems of depletion, such as the need to get gasoline as the gauge approaches empty, or the need to replace a frequently used food item, are readily recognized, defined, and resolved. The unexpected breakdown of a major appliance such as a refrigerator creates an unplanned problem that is also easily recognized but is often more difficult to resolve. Recognition of other problems, such as the need for a palm-sized electronic organizer, may take longer, as they may be subtle and evolve slowly over time.

Feelings such as boredom, anxiety, or the "blues" may arise quickly or slowly over time. Such feelings are often recognized as problems subject to solution by purchasing behavior (I'm sad, I think I'll go shopping/to a movie/to a restaurant). At other times, such feelings may trigger consumption behaviors without deliberate decision making. A person feeling "restless" may eat snack food without really thinking about it. In this case, the "problem" remains unrecognized (at the conscious level) and the solutions tried are often inappropriate (eating may not reduce restlessness).[11]

Marketers develop products to help consumers solve problems. They also attempt to help consumers recognize problems, sometimes well in advance of their occurrence (see Illustration 14-1).

The Nature of Problem Recognition

Problem recognition is the first stage in the consumer decision process. An **actual state** is *the way an individual perceives his or her feelings and situation to be at the present time.* A **desired state** is *the way an individual wants to feel or be at the present time.* **Problem recognition** is *the result of a discrepancy between a desired state and an actual state that is sufficient to arouse and activate the decision process.* For example, you probably don't want to be bored on Friday night. If you find yourself alone and becoming bored, you would treat this as a problem because your actual state (being bored) and your desired state (being pleasantly occupied) were different. You could then choose to consume a television program, rent a video, call a friend, go out, or take a wide array of other actions.

The kind of action taken by consumers in response to recognized problems relates directly to its importance to the consumer, the situation, and the dissatisfaction or inconvenience created by the problem.

Without recognition of a problem, there is no need for a decision. This condition is shown in Figure 14-2 when there is no discrepancy between the consumer's desired state (what the consumer would like) and the actual state (what the consumer perceives as already existing). Thus, if Friday night arrives and you find yourself engrossed in a novel, your desire to be pleasantly occupied (desired state) and your condition of enjoying a novel would be consistent and you would have no reason to search for other activities.

On the other hand, when there is a discrepancy between a consumer desire and the perceived actual state, recognition of a problem occurs.[12] Figure 14-2 indicates that any time the desired state is perceived as being greater than or less than the actual state, a problem exists. For example, being pleasantly occupied (desired state) would generally exceed being bored (actual state) and result in problem recognition. However, if your roommate

Reprinted with permission of Kemper Distributors Inc.

ILLUSTRATION 14-1

Marketers often attempt to cause consumers to recognize potential problems for which the marketer has a solution. As the ad illustrates, this sometimes involves making consumers aware of problems well before they arise.

suddenly showed up with a rowdy party, you might find yourself with more stimulation (actual state) than the medium level you actually desire. This too would result in problem recognition.

In Figure 14-2, consumer desires are shown to be the result of the desired lifestyle of the consumer (as described in Chapter 12) and the current situation (time pressures, physical surroundings, and so forth as described in Chapter 13). Thus, consumers whose self-concept and desired lifestyle focus on outdoor activities will desire frequent participation in such activities. A current situation of new snow in the mountains or warm weather at the beach would tend to increase their desire to be engaged in outdoor sports.

Perceptions of the actual state are also determined by a consumer's lifestyle and current situation. Consumers' lifestyles are a major determinant of their actual state because that is how they choose to live given the constraints imposed by their resources. Thus, a consumer who has chosen to raise a family, have significant material possessions, and pursue a demanding career is likely to have little free time for outdoor activities (actual state). The current situation—a day off work, a big project due, or a sick child—also has a major impact on how consumers perceive the actual situation.

It is important to note that it is the consumer's perception of the actual state that drives problem recognition, not some "objective" reality. Consumers who smoke cigars may

FIGURE 14-2 The Process of Problem Recognition

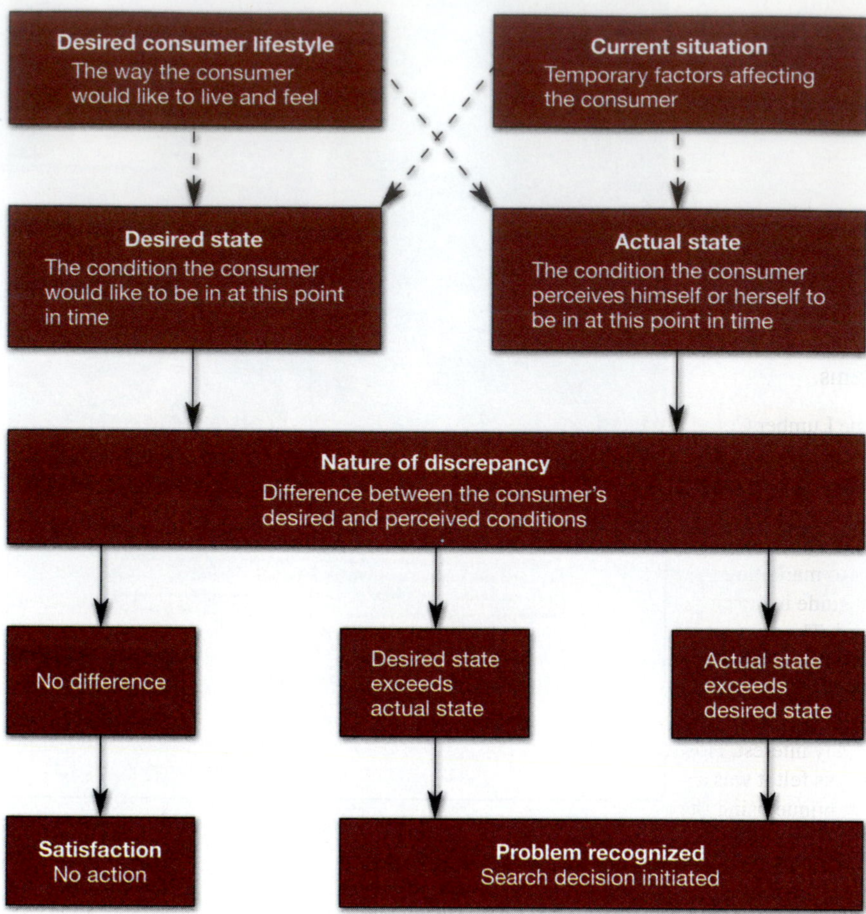

believe that this activity is not harming their health because they do not inhale. These consumers do not recognize a problem with this behavior despite the "reality" that it is harmful.

The Desire to Resolve Recognized Problems

The level of one's desire to resolve a particular problem depends on two factors: (1) *the magnitude of the discrepancy between the desired and actual states,* and (2) *the relative importance of the problem.* An individual could desire to have a car that averages at least 25 miles per gallon while still meeting certain size and power desires. If the current car obtains an average of 22 miles per gallon, a discrepancy exists, but it may not be large enough to motivate the consumer to proceed to the next step in the decision process.

On the other hand, a large discrepancy may exist and the consumer may not proceed to information search because the *relative importance* of the problem is small. A consumer may desire a new Volkswagen and own a 10-year-old Toyota. The discrepancy is large. However, the relative importance of this particular discrepancy may be small compared to other consumption problems such as those related to housing, utilities, and food. Relative importance is a critical concept because all consumers have budget constraints, time constraints, or both. Only the relatively more important problems are likely to be solved. In general, importance is determined by how critical the problem is to the maintenance of the consumer's desired lifestyle.

Types of Consumer Problems

Consumer problems may be either active or inactive. An **active problem** is *one the consumer is aware of or will become aware of in the normal course of events.* An **inactive problem** is *one of which the consumer is not yet aware.* This concept is very similar to the concept of felt need discussed in the Diffusion of Innovations section of Chapter 7 (page 247). The following example should clarify the distinction between active and inactive problems.

Timberlane Lumber Co. acquired a source of supply of Honduran pitch pine. This natural product lights at the touch of a match even when damp, and burns for 15 to 20 minutes. It will not flare up and is therefore relatively safe. It can be procured in sticks 15 to 18 inches long and 1 inch in diameter. These sticks can be used to ignite fireplace fires, or they can be shredded and used to ignite charcoal grills.

Prior to marketing the product, Timberlane commissioned a marketing study to estimate demand and guide in developing marketing strategy. Two large samples of potential consumers were interviewed. The first sample was asked how they lit their fireplace fires and what problems they had with this procedure. Almost all of the respondents used newspaper, kindling, or both, and very few experienced any problems. The new product was then described, and the respondents were asked to express the likelihood that they would purchase such a product. Only a small percentage expressed any interest. However, a sample of consumers that were paid to use the new product for several weeks felt it was a substantial improvement over existing methods and expressed a strong desire to continue using the product. Thus, the problem was there (because the new product was strongly preferred over the old by those who tried it), but most consumers were not aware of it. This is an *inactive problem.* Before the product can be successfully sold, the firm must activate problem recognition.

In contrast, a substantial percentage of those interviewed about lighting charcoal fires expressed a strong concern about the safety of liquid charcoal lighter. These individuals expressed great interest in purchasing a safer product. This is an *active problem.* Timberlane need not worry about problem recognition in this case. Instead, it can concentrate on illustrating how its product solves the problem that the consumers already know exists.

As this example indicates, active and inactive problems require different marketing strategies. Active problems only require the marketer to convince consumers that their brand is the superior solution. Consumers are already aware of the problem. In contrast, inactive problems require the marketer to convince consumers that they have the problem and that the marketer's brand is a superior solution to the problem. This is a much more difficult task.

Illustration 14-2 is an ad that is designed to activate a problem that is inactive for many women. Note that it does not directly compare Skintimate® with other products designed for women. Rather, it focuses on that part of the market that uses soap and water. Many of these consumers do not think about the discomfort associated with this approach (actual state) or are not aware that a superior solution (desired state) exists. Thus, this ad attempts to trigger the recognition of an inactive problem. Skintimate® uses a similar ad targeting women who shave with men's shaving foam.

ILLUSTRATION 14-2

Consumers are often unaware of the fact that they could be more comfortable or satisfied if they changed the way they perform various activities such as shaving. This ad attempts to make consumers aware of an inactive problem.

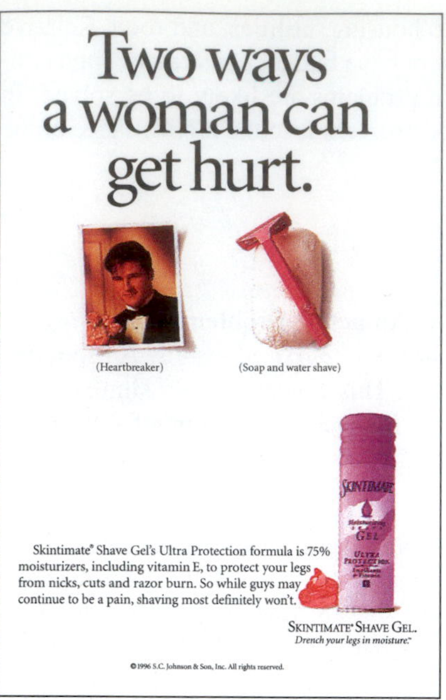

UNCONTROLLABLE DETERMINANTS OF PROBLEM RECOGNITION

A discrepancy between what is desired by a consumer and what the consumer has is the necessary condition for problem recognition. A discrepancy can be the result of a variety of factors that influence consumer desires, perceptions of the existing state, or both. These factors are often beyond the direct influence of the marketing manager, such as a change in family composition. Figure 14-3 summarizes the major nonmarketing factors

FIGURE 14-3 Nonmarketing Factors Affecting Problem Recognition

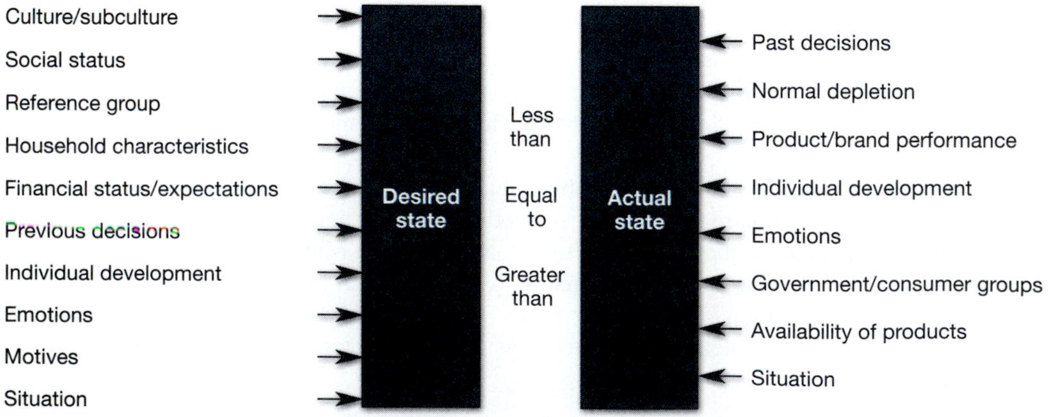

Problem Recognition and Alcohol Consumption

Consumer groups and government officials have been concerned that many consumers do not recognize the danger to health and other problems associated with alcohol use. As a result of these concerns, all alcoholic beverage containers must carry the following warning:

GOVERNMENT WARNING: (1) ACCORDING TO THE SURGEON GENERAL, WOMEN SHOULD NOT DRINK ALCOHOLIC BEVERAGES DURING PREGNANCY BECAUSE OF THE RISK OF BIRTH DEFECTS, (2) CONSUMPTION OF ALCOHOLIC BEVERAGES IMPAIRS YOUR ABILITY TO DRIVE A CAR OR OPERATE MACHINERY, AND MAY CAUSE HEALTH PROBLEMS.

In addition to the label warnings, some groups want all advertising of alcoholic beverages to carry warnings. Additional legislation has been introduced but not passed that would require every print and broadcast ad to carry one of five rotated health warnings.

Two of the five warnings are:

SURGEON GENERAL'S WARNING: DRINKING DURING PREGNANCY MAY CAUSE MENTAL RETARDATION AND OTHER BIRTH DEFECTS. AVOID ALCOHOL DURING PREGNANCY.

WARNING: ALCOHOL MAY BE HAZARDOUS IF YOU ARE USING ANY OTHER DRUGS, SUCH AS OVER-THE-COUNTER, PRESCRIPTION, OR ILLICIT DRUGS.

Research has shown that the current warning is not as effective as other warnings. However, marketers of alcoholic beverages do not want warnings that would unnecessarily alarm consumers or tarnish the overall image of the product. Thus, the task is to develop warnings that clearly communicate the risks and trigger problem recognition in the appropriate audiences without unduly raising concerns among other consumers.

Critical Thinking Questions

1. What responsibilities do marketers have in terms of warning consumers of potential harmful effects of using their products?
2. Is it possible to effectively warn consumers of the health dangers of alcohol consumption without tarnishing the image of the product category?

Consumer Insight 14-1

that influence problem recognition. The marketing factors influencing problem recognition are discussed in the next section of this chapter.

An examination of Figure 14-3 will reveal that most of the nonmarketing factors that impact problem recognition are fairly obvious and logical. Most were described in some detail in prior chapters. As we discussed in Chapter 2, one's culture impacts almost all aspects of one's desired state. For example, the desire to be recognized as an independent, unique person with distinctive behaviors and possessions differs sharply between American and Japanese consumers due to cultural influences.

Previous decisions and individual development were not discussed in earlier chapters. A previous decision to buy a bike or skis could lead to a current desire to have a car rack to carry them. A decision to become a home owner may trigger desires for numerous home and garden items.

Individual development causes many changes in the desired state. As we age, our needs and desires evolve noticeably. An ad for Scotch appearing in men's magazines recognizes this with a headline of "When you were young, you didn't like girls either," appearing over a picture of an attractive woman and a bottle of Scotch. As individuals gain skills, their desires related to those skills change. Beginning skiers, musicians, and gardeners typically desire products that may no longer be appropriate as their skills increase.

Government agencies and various consumer groups actively attempt to trigger problem recognition, often in relation to the consumption of various products. Consumer Insight 14-1 is an example of the government attempting to trigger problem recognition

ILLUSTRATION 14-3

Government agencies and nonprofit groups often attempt to generate problem recognition in consumers. This is often done in an attempt to change behaviors that are harmful to the individual or society.

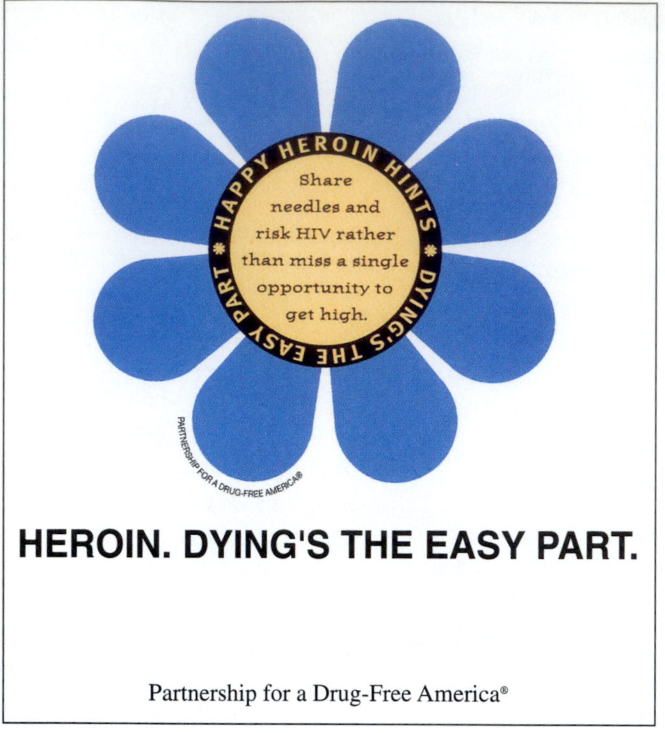

Courtesy Partnership for a Drug-Free America.

among some consumers who drink alcoholic beverages.[13] Illustration 14-3 is an ad used by the Partnership for a Drug-Free America to increase problem recognition related to the dangers of sharing drug needles.

MARKETING STRATEGY AND PROBLEM RECOGNITION

Marketing managers have four concerns related to problem recognition. First, they need to know the problems consumers are facing. Second, managers must know how to develop the marketing mix to solve consumer problems. Third, they occasionally want to cause consumers to recognize problems. Finally, there are times when managers desire to suppress problem recognition among consumers. The remainder of this chapter discusses these issues.

Discovering Consumer Problems

A wide variety of approaches are used to determine the problems consumers face. The most common approach undoubtedly is *intuition.* That is, a manager can analyze a given product category and logically determine where improvements could be made. Thus, soundless vacuum cleaners or lawn mowers are logical solutions to potential consumer problems. The difficulty with this approach is that the problem identified may be of low importance to most consumers. Therefore, several research techniques are also employed.

A common research technique is the *survey,* which asks relatively large numbers of individuals about the problems they are facing. This was the technique used by Timberlane about Honduran pitch pine, as described earlier. A second common technique is *focus groups.* Focus groups are composed of 8 to 12 similar individuals—such as male college students, lawyers, or teenage girls—brought together to discuss a particular topic. A moderator is present to keep the discussion moving and focused on the topic, but otherwise the sessions are free flowing.

Both surveys and focus groups tend to take one of three approaches to problem identification: *activity analysis, product analysis,* or *problem analysis.* A third technique, *human factors research,* does not rely on surveys or focus groups. *Emotion research,* a fourth effort, attempts to discover the role emotions play in problem recognition.

Activity Analysis Activity analysis focuses on a particular activity—for example, preparing dinner, maintaining the lawn, or eating out. The survey or focus group attempts to determine what problems consumers encounter during the performance of the activity. For example, Johnson Wax had a national panel of women report on how they cared for their hair and the problems they encountered. Their responses revealed a perceived problem with oiliness that existing brands could not resolve. As a result, Johnson Wax developed Agree Shampoo and Agree Creme Rinse, both of which became very successful.

A survey of "kitchen problems" among homemakers showed a "lack of organization" to be the most commonly expressed problem. Food storage was not seen as a problem by very many, and dealing with leftovers was a very minor concern.[14]

Product Analysis Product analysis is similar to activity analysis but examines the purchase and/or use of a particular product or brand. Thus, consumers may be asked about problems associated with using their mountain bike or their laptop computer. Curlee Clothing used focus groups to analyze the purchase and use of men's clothing. The results indicated a high level of insecurity in purchasing men's clothing. This insecurity was combined with a distrust of both the motivations and competence of retail sales personnel. As a result, Curlee initiated a major effort to train retail sales personnel through specially prepared films and training sessions.

Problem Analysis Problem analysis takes the opposite approach from the previous techniques. It starts with a list of problems and asks the respondent to indicate which activities, products, or brands are associated with those problems. Such a study dealing with packaging could include questions such as:

- ________________________ packages are hard to open.
- Packages of ________________________ are hard to reseal.
- ________________________ doesn't pour well.
- Packages of ________________________ don't fit on the shelf.
- Packages of ________________________ waste too many resources.

Human Factors Research Human factors research attempts to determine human capabilities in areas such as vision, strength, response time, flexibility, and fatigue and the effect on these capabilities of lighting, temperature, sound and product design. While many methods can be employed in human factors research, observational techniques such as slow-motion and time-lapse photography, video recording, and event recorders are particularly useful to marketers.

This type of research can be particularly useful in identifying functional problems that consumers are unaware of. For example, it can be used in the design of such products as vacuum cleaners, lawn mowers, kitchen utensils, and computers to minimize user fatigue. Recent publicity about carpal tunnel syndrome (injury resulting from repeating the same movements over time, such as inputting data into a computer) has resulted in substantial interest in this area.

ILLUSTRATION 14-4

A key task of marketers is to identify consumer problems and to develop solutions for them. This product is designed to meet the unique needs of some individuals who engage in scuba diving and snorkeling.

Courtesy Pioneer Research.

Emotion Research Marketers are just beginning to conduct research on the role of emotions in the decision process. Common approaches are focus group research and one-on-one personal interviews that focus on either (1) the emotions associated with a certain product or (2) the products associated with reducing or arousing certain emotions. For more subtle or sensitive emotions or products, projective techniques (see Table 10-2, page 371) can provide useful insights.[15] Likewise, the various techniques used to measure emotions and emotional responses to advertising (see Chapter 10) can also be used to measure emotional responses to decision situations.[16]

Responding to Consumer Problems

Once a consumer problem is identified, the manager may structure the marketing mix to solve the problem. This can involve product development or alteration, modifying channels of distribution, changing pricing policy, or revising advertising strategy. For example, many divers and snorkelers want to take pictures of their vacation both on the surface and in the water but don't want the expense and hassle of two cameras. Pioneer developed the *SeaLife ReefMaster* camera in response to this consumer problem (see Illustration 14-4).

As you approach graduation, you will be presented with opportunities to purchase insurance, acquire credit cards, and solve other problems associated with the onset of financial independence and a major change in lifestyle. These opportunities, which will be presented through both personal sales contacts and advertising media, reflect various firms' knowledge that many individuals in your situation face problems that their products will help solve.

Weekend and night store hours are a response of retailers to the consumer problem of limited weekday shopping opportunities. Solving this problem has become particularly important to families with both spouses employed.

The examples described above represent only a small sample of the ways in which marketers react to consumer problem recognition. Basically, each firm must be aware of the consumer problems it can solve, which consumers have these problems, and the situations in which the problems arise.

Helping Consumers Recognize Problems

There are occasions when the manager will want to cause problem recognition rather than react to it. In the earlier example involving the fire starters, Timberlane faced having to activate problem recognition in order to sell its product as a fireplace starter. Toy marketers are attempting to reduce their dependence on the Christmas season by activating problem recognition at other times of the year. For example, Fisher-Price has had "rainy day" and "sunny day" promotions in the spring and summer months. Illustrations 14-1 and 14-2, presented earlier, show attempts to activate problem recognition.

Generic versus Selective Problem Recognition Two basic approaches to causing problem recognition are *generic problem recognition* and *selective problem recognition.* These are analogous to the economic concepts of generic and selective demand.

Generic problem recognition involves a *discrepancy that a variety of brands within a product category can reduce.* Generally, a firm will attempt to influence generic problem recognition when the problem is latent or of low importance and one of the following conditions exists.

- It is early in the product life cycle.
- The firm has a very high percentage of the market.
- External search after problem recognition is apt to be limited.
- It is an industrywide cooperative effort.

Telephone sales programs often attempt to arouse problem recognition, in part because the salesperson can then limit external search to one brand. Cooperative advertising frequently focuses on generic problem recognition. Illustration 14-5 is an example of one of the most notable ongoing campaigns of this type (also see Illustration 10-2, page 366). Note that the copy attempts to make individuals aware of the need for the calcium that milk provides but does not promote any particular brand of milk.

Firms with very large market shares in a product category often can focus on generic problem recognition, since any sales increase will probably come to their brands. However, a smaller firm that generates generic problem recognition for its product category may be generating more sales for its competitors than for itself. Even larger market share firms can lose share if generic problem recognition campaigns are not done carefully. Borden's Creamette is the largest brand of pasta in the United States. It increased its marketing efforts substantially and promoted recipes using pasta. Its sales increased only 1.6 percent compared to the industry's growth of 5.5 percent.[17] Its efforts apparently helped the sales of its competitors more than its own sales.

Selective problem recognition involves *a discrepancy that only one brand can solve.* The ad shown in Illustration 14-6 is focused on creating selective problem recognition. Firms attempt to cause selective problem recognition to gain or maintain market share, while increasing generic problem recognition generally results in an expansion of the total market.

ILLUSTRATION 14-5

This ad will generate problem recognition that any brand of milk could resolve. This is known as generic problem recognition.

Courtesy Bozell Worldwide.

Approaches to Activating Problem Recognition How can a firm influence problem recognition? Recall that problem recognition is a function of the (1) *importance* and (2) *magnitude* of a discrepancy between the desired state and an existing state. Thus, the firm can attempt to influence the size of the discrepancy by altering the desired state or the perceptions of the existing state. Or, the firm can attempt to influence the perception of the importance of an existing discrepancy.

There is evidence that individuals and product categories both differ in their responsiveness to attempts to change desired or perceived existing states.[18] Thus, marketers must be sure that the selected approach is appropriate for their product category and target market.

Many marketing efforts attempt to *influence the desired state.* That is, marketers often advertise the benefits their products will provide, hoping that these benefits will become desired by consumers. The ad in Illustration 14-7 attempts to influence the desired state by showing the need for sports shoes designed for the unique needs of women.

It is also possible to *influence perceptions of the existing state* through advertisements. Many personal care and social products take this approach. "Even your best friend won't tell you . . ." or "Kim is a great worker but this coffee . . ." are examples of messages designed to generate concern about an existing state. The desired state is assumed to be fresh breath and good coffee. These messages are designed to cause individuals to question if their existing state coincides with this desired state.

The Honda ad in Illustration 14-8 attempts to make parents and other adults aware that the common practice (actual state) of two children riding one ATV is not as safe as it may appear. This would trigger problem recognition that would hopefully result in parents restricting such behaviors.

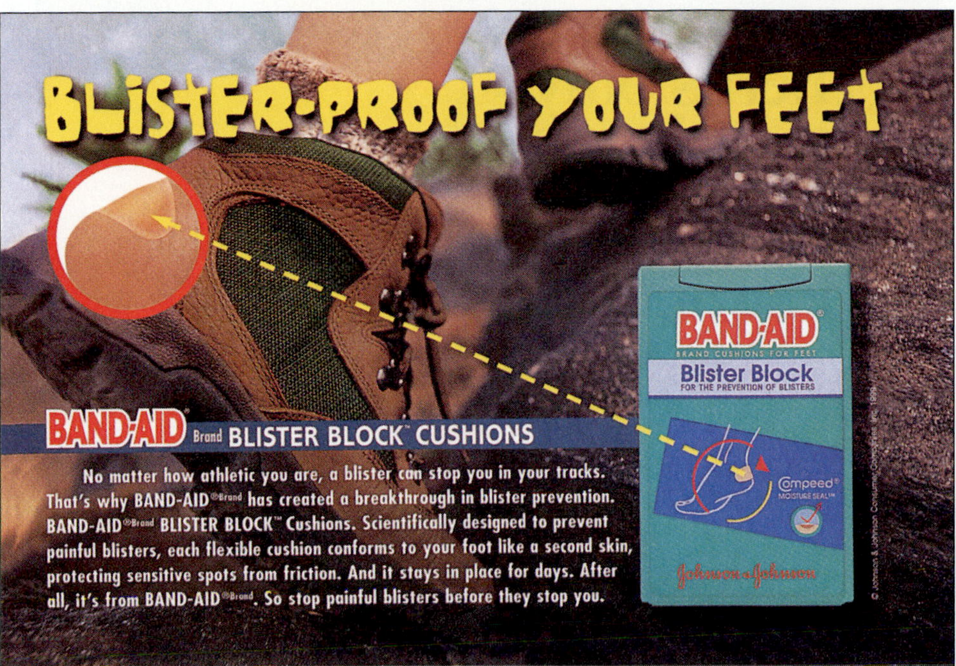

ILLUSTRATION 14-6

This ad will generate problem recognition that is best solved by one brand. This is selective problem recognition.

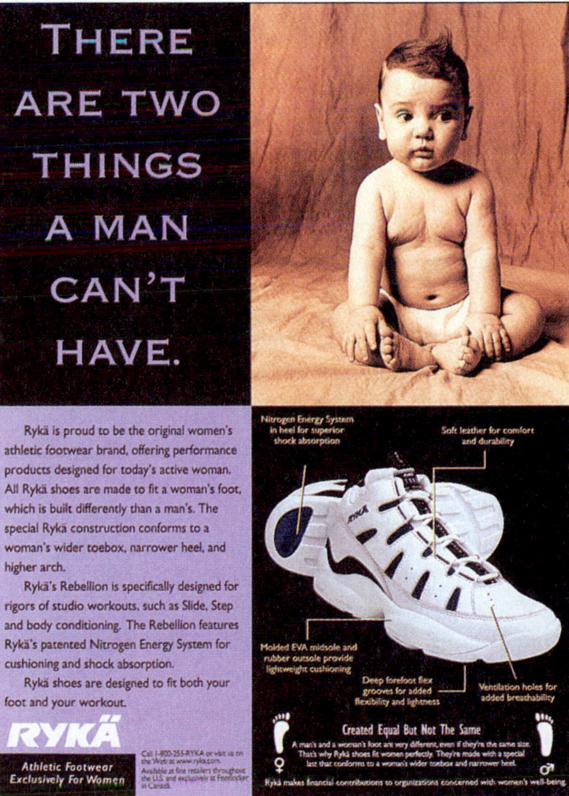

Courtesy Ryka, Inc.

ILLUSTRATION 14-7

This ad attempts to influence the desired state by showing the unique needs of female athletes.

ILLUSTRATION 14-8

Many adults may not be aware that two kids riding on one ATV is unsafe. This ad triggers problem recognition by altering perceptions of the existing state.

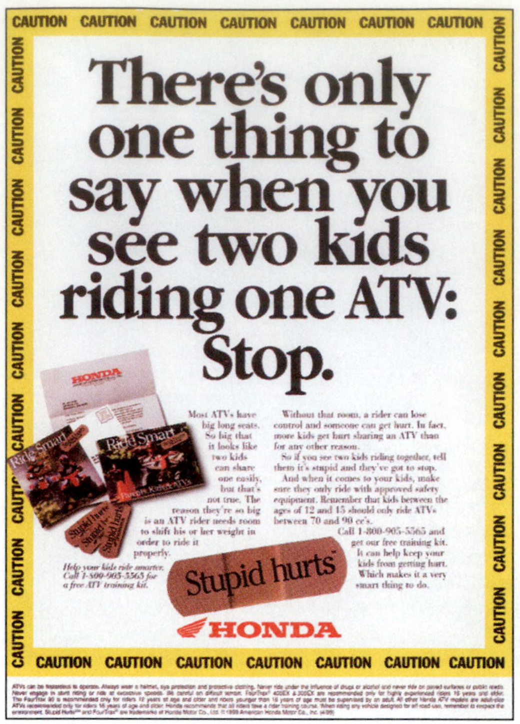

Courtesy American Honda Co.

Critics frequently question the ethics of activating problem recognition. This is (particularly) true for problems related to status or social acceptance. This debate is generally discussed in terms of "creating needs." We discussed this in some depth in Chapter 10 (page 373).

The Timing of Problem Recognition Consumers often recognize problems at times when purchasing a solution is difficult or impossible:

- We decide we need snow chains when caught in a blizzard.
- We become aware of a need for insurance *after* an accident.
- We desire a flower bed full of tulips in the spring but forgot to plant bulbs in the fall.
- We want cold medicine when we are sick but don't feel like driving to the store.

In some instances, marketers attempt to help consumers solve such problems after they arise. For example, some pharmacies will make home deliveries. However, the more common strategy is to trigger problem recognition in advance of the actual problem (see Illustration 14-1). That is, it is often to the consumer's and marketer's advantage for the consumer to recognize and solve potential problems *before* they become actual problems.

While some companies, particularly insurance companies, attempt to initiate problem recognition through mass media advertising, others rely more on point-of-purchase displays and other in-store influences (see Chapter 17). Retailers as well as manufacturers are involved in this activity. For example, prior to snow season, the following sign was placed on a large rack of snow shovels in the main aisle of a large hardware store:

REMEMBER LAST WINTER

WHEN YOU *NEEDED*

A SNOW SHOVEL?
THIS YEAR
BE PREPARED!

Suppressing Problem Recognition

As we have seen, competition, consumer organizations, and governmental agencies occasionally introduce information in the marketplace that triggers problem recognition that particular marketers would prefer to avoid. The American tobacco industry has made strenuous attempts to minimize consumer recognition of the health problems associated with cigarette smoking. For example, a Newport cigarette advertisement showed a happy, laughing couple under the headline, "Alive with pleasure." This could easily be interpreted as an attempt to minimize any problem recognition caused by the mandatory warning at the bottom of the advertisement, "Warning: The Surgeon General has determined that cigarette smoking is dangerous to your health."

Makers of brands with substantial nominal or limited decision purchases do not want their current customers to recognize problems with their brands. Effective quality control and distribution (limited out-of-stock situations) are important in these circumstances. Packages and package inserts that assure the consumer of the wisdom of their purchase are also common.

SUMMARY

Consumer decision making becomes more extensive and complex as *purchase involvement* increases. The lowest level of purchase involvement is represented by *nominal decisions:* a problem is recognized, long-term memory provides a single preferred brand, that brand is purchased, and only limited postpurchase evaluation occurs. As one moves from *limited decision making* toward *extended decision making,* information search increases, alternative evaluation becomes more extensive and complex, and postpurchase evaluation becomes more thorough.

Problem recognition involves the existence of a discrepancy between the consumer's desired state (what the consumer would like) and the actual state (what the consumer perceives as already existing). Both the desired state and the actual state are influenced by the consumer's lifestyle and current situation. If the discrepancy between these two states is sufficiently large and important, the consumer will begin to search for a solution to the problem.

A number of factors beyond the control of the marketing manager can affect problem recognition. The desired state is commonly influenced by (1) culture/subculture, (2) social status, (3) reference groups, (4) household characteristics, (5) financial status/expectations, (6) previous decisions, (7) individual development, (8) motives, (9) emotions, and the (10) current situation.

The actual state is influenced by (1) past decisions, (2) normal depletion, (3) product/brand performance, (4) individual development, (5) emotions, (6) government/consumer groups, (7) availability of products, and the (8) current situation.

Before marketing managers can respond to problem recognition generated by outside factors, they must be able to *measure* consumer problems. Surveys and focus groups using *activity, product,* or *problem analysis* are commonly used to measure problem recognition. *Human factors research* approaches the same task from an observational perspective. *Emotion research* focuses on the emotional causes of and responses to product purchase and use.

Once managers are aware of problem recognition patterns among their target market, they can react by designing the marketing mix to solve the recognized problem. This may involve product development or repositioning, a change in store hours, a different price, or a host of other marketing strategies.

Marketing managers often want to influence problem recognition rather than react to it. They may desire to generate *generic problem recognition,* a discrepancy that a variety of brands within a product category can reduce; or to induce *selective problem recognition,* a discrepancy that only one brand in the product category can solve.

Attempts to *activate problem recognition* generally do so by focusing on the desired state. However, attempts to make consumers aware of negative aspects of the existing state are also common. In addition, marketers attempt to influence the timing of problem recognition by making consumers aware of potential problems before they arise.

Finally, managers attempt to minimize or suppress problem recognition by current users of their brands.

KEY TERMS

Active problem 511
Actual state 508
Desired state 508
Extended decision making 507
Generic problem recognition 517
Inactive problem 511
Limited decision making 506
Nominal decision making 506
Problem recognition 508
Product involvement 505
Purchase involvement 504
Selective problem recognition 517

INTERNET EXERCISES

1. Visit several general interest or entertainment sites on the Web that contain ads. Find and describe an ad that attempts to trigger problem recognition. How does it do this?
2. Visit several company sites on the Web. Find and describe one that attempts to trigger problem recognition. How does it do this?
3. Monitor several chat sites or interest groups for a week. Prepare a report on how a marketer could learn about the consumption problems of consumers by doing this.

REVIEW QUESTIONS

1. What is meant by *purchase involvement?* How does it differ from product involvement?
2. How does consumer decision making change as purchase involvement increases?
3. What is the role of *emotion* in the consumer decision process?
4. How do *nominal, limited,* and *extended decision making* differ? How do the two types of nominal decision making differ?
5. What is *problem recognition?*
6. What influences the motivation to resolve a recognized problem?
7. What is the difference between an *active* and an *inactive problem?* Why is this distinction important?
8. How does lifestyle relate to problem recognition?
9. What are the main uncontrollable factors that influence the *desired* state?
10. What are the main uncontrollable factors that influence the *existing* state?
11. How can you measure problem recognition?
12. In what ways can marketers react to problem recognition? Give several examples.
13. How does *generic problem recognition* differ from *selective problem recognition?* Under what conditions would a firm attempt to influence generic problem recognition? Why?
14. How can a firm cause problem recognition? Give examples.
15. How can a firm suppress problem recognition?

DISCUSSION QUESTIONS

16. What products do you think *generally* are associated with nominal, limited, and extended decision making? Under what conditions, if any, would these products be associated with a different form of decision making?
17. What products do you think *generally* are purchased or used for emotional reasons? How would the decision process differ for an emotion-driven purchase compared to a more functional purchase?
18. What products do you think *generally* are associated with brand loyal decision making and which with repeat purchase decision making? Justify your response.
19. Describe two purchases you have made using nominal decision making, two using limited decision making, and two using extended decision making. What caused you to use each type of decision process?
20. Describe two recent purchases you have made. What uncontrollable factors, if any, triggered problem recognition? Did they affect the desired state, the actual state, or both?
21. How would you measure consumer problems among the following:
    a. High school students
    b. Preteens
    c. Snowboarders
    d. New students on campus
    e. Vegans
    f. Recently retired couples
22. How would you determine the existence of consumer problems of relevance to a marketer of the following:
    a. Stereo equipment
    b. Internet services
    c. Cosmetics
    d. Baby toys
    e. Pet products
    f. Fast foods
23. Discuss the types of products that resolve specific problems that occur for most consumers at different stages of their household life cycle.
24. How would you activate problem recognition for:
    a. United Way donations
    b. Life insurance
    c. A meat-free diet
    d. A gourmet hamburger restaurant
    e. Using a designated driver if drinking
    f. An exercise club for teenagers
25. How would you influence the time of problem recognition for:
    a. Health insurance
    b. Candy as a gift
    c. Health checkups
    d. Flashlight batteries
    e. Swimsuits
    f. Aspirin

APPLICATION ACTIVITIES

26. Interview five other students and identify three consumer problems they have recognized recently. For each problem, determine:
    a. The relative importance of the problem.
    b. How the problem occurred.
    c. What caused the problem (i.e., change in desired or actual states).
    d. What action they have taken.
    e. What action is planned to resolve each problem.
27. Find and describe an advertisement that is attempting to activate problem recognition. Analyze the advertisement in terms of the type of problem and the action the ad is suggesting. Also, discuss any changes you would recommend to improve the effectiveness of the ad in terms of activating problem recognition.
28. Interview five other students and identify three recent instances when they engaged in nominal, limited, and extended decision making (a total of nine decisions). What specific factors appear to be associated with each type of decision?
29. Interview five other students and identify five products that each buys using a nominal decision process. Also, identify those that are based on brand loyalty and those that are merely repeat

purchases. What characteristics, if any, distinguish the brand loyal products from the repeat products?

30. Find and describe two advertisements or point-of-purchase displays that attempt to influence the timing of problem recognition. Evaluate their likely effectiveness.
31. Using a sample from a relevant market segment, conduct an activity analysis for an activity that interests you. Prepare a report on the marketing opportunities suggested by your analysis.
32. Using a sample from a relevant market segment, conduct a product analysis for a product that interests you. Prepare a report on the marketing opportunities suggested by your analysis.
33. Conduct a problem analysis, using a sample of college freshmen. Prepare a report on the marketing opportunities suggested by your analysis.
34. Interview five smokers and ascertain what problems they see associated with smoking.
35. Interview someone from the local office of the American Cancer Society concerning their attempts to generate problem recognition among smokers.

REFERENCES

1. P. Sloan, "UV Index Backs Sunscreen Surge," *Advertising Age,* January 30, 1995, p. 11.
2. J. C. Mowen, "Beyond Consumer Decision Making," *Journal of Consumer Marketing,* Winter 1988, pp. 15–25.
3. See J. R. Bettman, M. F. Luce, and J. W. Payne, "Constructive Consumer Choice," *Journal of Consumer Research,* December 1998, pp. 187–217.
4. For more complex but valuable approaches, see footnote 3 and R. Lawson, "Consumer Decision Making within a Goal-Driven Framework," *Psychology & Marketing,* August 1997, pp. 427–49.
5. Based on A. A. Mitchell, "Involvement: A Potentially Important Mediator of Consumer Behavior," in *Advances in Consumer Research VI,* ed. W. L. Wilkie (Chicago: Association for Consumer Research, 1979), pp. 191–96. See also T. Otker, "The Highly Involved Consumer"; and B. von Keitz, "Consumer Involvement"; both in *Marketing and Research Today,* February 1990, pp. 30–36 and 37–45.
6. Based on H. H. Kassarjian, "Low Involvement: A Second Look," in *Advances in Consumer Research VIII,* ed. K. B. Monroe (Chicago: Association for Consumer Research, 1981), pp. 31–33. See also S. A. Hawkins and S. J. Hoch, "Low-Involvement Learning," *Journal of Consumer Research,* September 1992, pp. 212–25; D. D. Muehling, R. N. Laczniak, and J. C. Andrews, "Defining, Operationalizing, and Using Involvement in Advertising Research," *Journal of Current Issues and Research in Advertising,* Spring 1993, pp. 22–57; and T. B. C. Poiesz and C. J. P. M. deBont, "Do We Need Involvement to Understand Consumer Behavior," in *Advances in Consumer Research XXII,* ed. F. R. Kardes and M. Sujan (Provo, UT: Association for Consumer Research, 1995), pp. 448–52.
7. See M. P. Venkatraman, "Opinion Leadership, Enduring Involvement and Characteristics of Opinion Leaders," in *Advances in Consumer Research XVII,* ed. M. E. Goldberg, G. Gorn, and R. W. Pollay (Provo, UT: Association for Consumer Research, 1990), pp. 60–67; and G. M. Rose, L. R. Kahle, and A. Shoham, "The Influence of Employment-Status and Personal Values on Time Related Food Consumption Behavior and Opinion Leadership," in *Advances in Consumer Research XXII,* ed. F. R. Kardes and M. Sujan (Provo, UT: Association for Consumer Research, 1995), pp. 367–72.
8. W. D. Hoyer, "An Examination of Consumer Decision Making for a Common Repeat Purchase Product," *Journal of Consumer Research,* December 1984, pp. 822–29; and A. d'Astous, I. Bensouda, and J. Guindon, "A Re-Examination of Consumer Decision Making for a Repeat Purchase Product," in *Advances in Consumer Research XVI,* ed. T. K. Srull (Provo, UT: Association for Consumer Research, 1989), pp. 433–38.
9. B. E. Kahn and A. M. Isen, "The Influence of Positive Affect on Variety Seeking among Safe, Enjoyable Products," *Journal of Consumer Research,* September 1993, pp. 257–70; M. Trivedi, F. M. Bass, and R. C. Rao, "A Model of Stochastic Variety-Seeking," *Marketing Science,* Summer 1994, pp. 274–97; S. Menon and B. E. Kahn, "The Impact of Context on Variety Seeking in Product Choice," *Journal of Consumer Research,* December 1995, pp. 285–95; T. H. Dodd, B. E. Pinkleton, and Q. W. Gustafson, "External Information Sources of Product Enthusiasts," *Psychology & Marketing,* May 1996, pp. 291–304; and H. C. M. Van Trijp, W. D. Hoyer, and J. J. Inman, "Why Switch? Product Category-Level Explanations for True Variety-Seeking Behavior," *Journal of Marketing Research,* August 1996, pp. 281–92.
10. See W. J. McDonald, "Developing International Direct Marketing Strategies with a Consumer Decision-Making Content Analysis," *Journal of Direct Marketing,* Autumn 1994, pp. 18–27; and W. J. McDonald, "American versus Japanese Consumer Decision Making," *Journal of International Consumer Marketing* 7, no. 3 (1995), pp. 81–93.
11. See M. DeMoss and D. G. Mick, "Self-Gifts," *Journal of Consumer Research,* December 1990, pp. 322–32.
12. For a more thorough treatment, see G. C. Bruner II and R. J. Pomazal, "Problem Recognition: The Crucial First Stage of the Consumer Decision Process," *Journal of Consumer Marketing,* Winter 1988, pp. 53–63.
13. See M. E. Hilton, "Overview of Recent Findings on Alcoholic Beverage Warning Labels"; J. R. Hankin et al. "The Impact of

Alcohol Warning Label on Drinking during Pregnancy"; K. L. Graves, "An Evaluation of the Alcohol Warning Label"; L. A. Kaskutas, "Changes in Public Attitudes toward Alcohol Control Policies Since the Warning Label Mandate of 1988"; K. R. Laughery et al. "The Role of Cognitive Responses as Mediators of Alcohol Warning Label Effects"; A. M. Fenaughty and D. P. MacKinnon, "Immediate Effects of the Arizona Alcohol Warning Poster"; and M. J. Kalsher, S. W. Clarke, and M. S. Wogalter, "Communication of Alcohol Facts and Hazards by a Warning Poster"; all in *Journal of Public Policy & Marketing,* Spring 1993, pp. 1–90; and T. Barlow and M. W. Wogalter, "Alcoholic Beverage Warnings in Magazine and Television Advertisements," *Journal of Consumer Research,* June 1993, pp. 147–56.

14. J. Parks, "Weary of Kitchen Clutter," *Advertising Age,* September 12, 1994, p. 12.
15. See T. Collier, "Dynamic Reenactment," *Marketing Research,* Spring 1993, pp. 35–37; G. Zaltman, "Metaphorically Speaking," *Marketing Research,* Summer 1996, pp. 13–20; and C. B. Raffel, "Vague Notions," *Marketing Research,* Summer 1996, pp. 21–23.
16. J. D. Morris and J. S. McMullen, "Measuring Multiple Emotional Responses to a Single Television Commercial," in *Advances in Consumer Research XXI,* ed. C. T. Allen and D. R. John (Provo, UT: Association for Consumer Research, 1994), pp. 175–80; G. Levin, "Emotion Guides BBDO's Ad Tests," *Advertising Age,* January 29, 1990, p. 12; and P. L. LaBarbera and J. D. Tucciarone, "GSR Reconsidered," *Journal of Advertising Research,* September 1995, pp. 33–53. See also P. V. Abeele and D. L. MacLachlan, "Process Tracing of Emotional Responses to TV Ads," *Journal of Consumer Research,* March 1994, pp. 586–600; and P. V. Abeele and D. L. MacLachlan, "Process Tracing of Physiological Responses to Dynamic Commercial Stimuli," in *Advances in Consumer Research XXI,* ed. C. T. Allen and D. R. John (Provo, UT: Association for Consumer Research, 1994), pp. 226–32.
17. E. Lesly, "Why Things Are So Sour at Borden," *Business Week,* November 22, 1993, p. 84.
18. See G. C. Bruner II, "Problem Recognition Style," *Journal of Consumer Studies and Home Economics,* no. 14 (1990), pp. 29–40.

Courtesy The Pepsi Cola Company.

chapter fifteen

Information Search

The ability of consumers to search for information has increased radically since the advent of the Internet. The Internet allows easy access to manufacturers' Web sites, to other consumers, and to third parties such as consumer groups and government agencies. It also greatly expands the ability of marketers to provide information to consumers. Marketers can provide information to consumers who are directly seeking information about the firm's products, typically through the company or brand's home page or Web site. Marketers can also provide consumers with information that they are not explicitly seeking by placing ads in other sites on the Web.

Company Web sites can do more than merely provide company and product information to consumers:

- Avon's Web site includes extensive corporate, product, and beauty information. It also has a sweepstakes and topical bulletin boards. Its interactive Avon Beauty Advisor makes recommendations based on individual beauty needs.
- Kraft Foods' site, the "Kraft Interactive Kitchen," provides quick and easy help with food planning, shopping, and preparation chores. It has a searchable cookbook, a recipe box, a shopping list customized to generate a list of ingredients by grocery aisle for selected recipes, a party planner, a meal planner, and recipes by e-mail (recipes delivered to the consumer's e-mail address on a regular schedule).
- Pepsi's Pepsi World/Pepsi Pop Culture site provides updates of new movies, games, and music. It provides free downloads of screensavers and wallpaper and contains contests. A unique feature is the Pepsi Live Webcast Concert series. Pepsi explains its approach as follows: "Simply put, the goal was to reach our core young consumers where they're hanging out (on-line), and give them an innovative, interactive experience."
- Eastman Kodak's site has more than 35,000 pages of information, images, and digital imaging applications. Among the noteworthy features are *PictureThis* postcards that enable site users to

create and send photo-realistic multimedia postcards; rotating feature articles on the individual and emotional aspects of photography; *PhotoNet* on-line, which allows members to store and upload photos on-line; and *PhotoQuilt,* an application that weaves personal stories and pictures into a huge collection arranged into a virtual patchwork quilt.[1]

Note that each of these Web sites provides basic product information similar to that which a consumer could get from a brochure or catalog. However, each site goes much further than this, providing application and usage suggestions often personalized for each consumer. The sites add value for the consumer both in terms of providing easily accessible product information and by adding other information, activities, and applications of relevance to the consumer. These firms want consumers to use their sites not only when explicitly seeking product specific information but on a regular basis for a variety of purposes. This is one way in which the firm can build a relationship with the consumer.

Reaching today's consumer is an extremely challenging task. While many consumers are active searchers and want to be able to interact with the company, other purchasers of the same product are willing to expend little or no effort to obtain product or brand information before making a purchase.

Consumers continually recognize problems and opportunities, so internal and external searches for information to solve these problems are ongoing processes. Searching for information is not free. Information search involves mental as well as physical activities that consumers must perform. It takes time, energy, money, and can often require giving up more desirable activities.

The benefits of information search, however, often outweigh the cost of search. For example, search may produce a lower price, a preferred style of merchandise, a higher quality product, or greater confidence in the choice. In addition, the physical and mental processes involved in information search are, on occasion, rewarding in themselves. Finally, we must keep in mind that consumers acquire a substantial amount of relevant information without deliberate search—through low-involvement learning (see Chapter 9).

NATURE OF INFORMATION SEARCH

Suppose your television quit working, or you noticed that you were low on gas, or you felt particularly restless, or you decided you needed a new suit. What would you do in response to each of these recognized problems? The odds are you would first think or remember how you usually solve this type of problem. This might produce a satisfactory solution (I'd better stop at the next Texaco and fill up), which you proceed to implement. Or, you might decide that you need to get additional information (I'll check the Yellow Pages to see who repairs my brand of television).

Once a problem is recognized, relevant information from long-term memory is used to determine if a satisfactory solution is known, what the characteristics of potential solutions are, what are appropriate ways to compare solutions, and so forth. This is **internal search.** If a resolution is not reached through internal search, then the search process is focused on external information relevant to solving the problem. This is **external search.**

Many problems are resolved by the consumer using only previously stored information. If, in response to a problem, a consumer recalls a single, satisfactory solution (brand or store), no further information search or evaluation may occur. The consumer purchases the recalled brand and *nominal decision making* has occurred. For example, a consumer who catches a cold may recall that Dristan nasal spray provided relief in the past. Dristan then is purchased at the nearest store without further information search or evaluation.

Likewise, a consumer may notice a new product in a store because of the attention-attracting power of a point-of-purchase display. He or she reads about the attributes of the product and recalls an unresolved problem that these attributes would resolve. The purchase is made without seeking additional information. This represents *limited decision making,* involving mainly internal information.

Had the consumer in the example above looked for other brands that would perform the same task or looked at another store for a lower price, we would have an example of limited decision making using both internal and external information. As we move into *extended decision making,* the relative importance of external information search tends to increase. However, even in extended decision making, internal information often provides some or all of the appropriate alternatives, evaluative criteria, and characteristics of various alternatives.[2]

External information can include:

- The opinions, attitudes, behaviors, and feelings of friends, neighbors, relatives, and, increasingly, strangers contacted on the Internet.
- Professional information that is provided in pamphlets, articles, books, the Internet, and personal contacts.
- Direct experiences with the product through inspection, trial, or observation.
- Marketer-generated information presented in advertisements, Web sites, displays, and by sales personnel.

Deliberate external search also occurs in the absence of problem recognition.[3] **Ongoing search** is done both *to acquire information for possible later use and because the process itself is pleasurable*. For example, individuals highly involved with an activity such as backpacking are apt to seek information about backpacking-related products on an ongoing basis without a recognized problem with their existing backpacking equipment. This search could involve reading ads in backpacking magazines, visiting outdoor shops and Web sites, and/or talking with and observing fellow backpackers. These activities would provide the individual with both pleasure and information for future use.

As described in Chapter 7 (page 242), market mavens are actively involved in ongoing search. They engage in ongoing search to stay informed about the market because they enjoy this activity and the social rewards derived from sharing the results of their searches with others.

TYPES OF INFORMATION SOUGHT

A consumer decision requires information on the following:[4]

- The appropriate evaluative criteria for the solution of a problem.
- The existence of various alternative solutions.
- The performance level or characteristic of each alternative solution on each evaluative criterion.

Information search, then, seeks each of these three types of information, as shown in Figure 15-1.

FIGURE 15-1 Information Search in Consumer Decisions

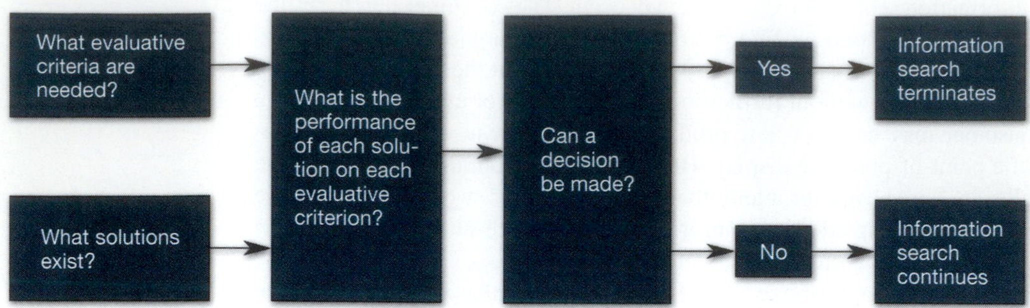

Evaluative Criteria

Suppose you are provided with money to purchase a laptop computer, perhaps as a graduation present. Assuming you have not been in the market for a computer recently, your first thought would probably be: "What features do I want in a computer?" You would then engage in internal search to determine the features or characteristics required to meet your needs. These desired characteristics are your *evaluative criteria.* If you have had limited experience with computers, you might also engage in external search to learn which characteristics a good computer should have. You could check with friends, read reviews in *PC Magazine,* talk with sales personnel, visit computer company Web sites, or personally inspect several computers.

Thus, one potential objective of both internal and external search is *the determination of appropriate evaluative criteria.* Government agencies and consumer organizations want consumers to use "sound" evaluative criteria such as the nutrition content of foods. Marketers want consumers to use evaluative criteria that match their brand's strengths. Thus, both marketers and government agencies provide information designed to influence the evaluative criteria used by consumers. The ad in Illustration 15-1, encourages consumers to use five primary evaluative criteria when choosing a portable computer. Implied in the ad is that using too many evaluative criteria produces unneeded capabilities and unnecessarily high price.

A detailed discussion of evaluative criteria appears in Chapter 16.

Appropriate Alternatives

After (and while) searching for appropriate evaluative criteria, you would probably seek *appropriate alternatives*—in this case brands or, possibly, stores. Again, you would start with an internal search. You might say to yourself:

> IBM, Compaq, Toshiba, Apple, NEC, Niko, Motorola, and HP all make personal computers. After my brother's experience, I'd never buy Niko, I've heard good things about IBM, Apple, and Compaq. I think I'll check them out.

The eight brands that you thought of as potential solutions are known as the **awareness set** or the **consideration set.** The awareness set is composed of three subcategories of

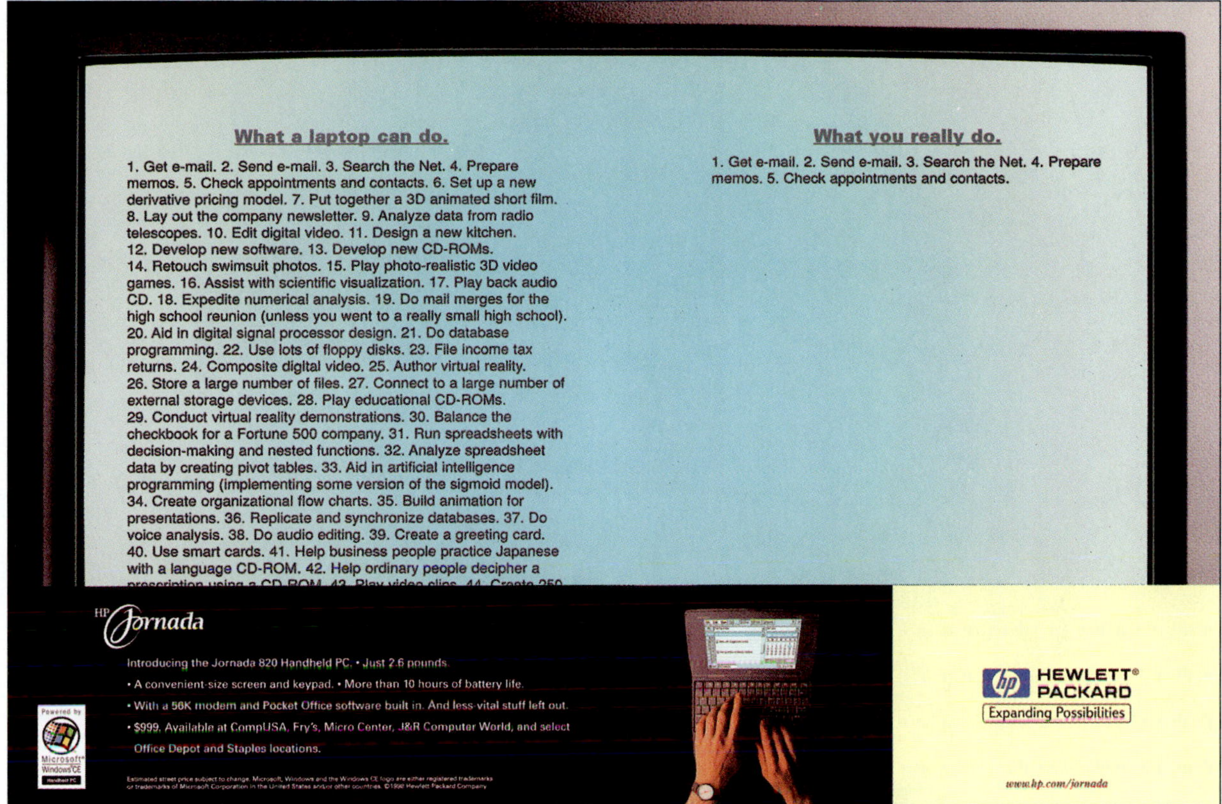

Courtesy Hewlett-Packard Company.

ILLUSTRATION 15-1

Consumers often search for information on the appropriate evaluative criteria to use. This ad seeks to influence the criteria used as well as position HP on those criteria.

considerable importance to marketers.[5] The three brands that you have decided to investigate are known as the **evoked set.** An evoked set *is those brands one will evaluate for the solution of a particular consumer problem.* If you do not have an evoked set for laptop computers, or lack confidence that your evoked set is adequate, you would probably engage in external search to learn about additional alternatives. You may also learn about additional acceptable brands as an incidental aspect of moving through the decision process. Thus, an important outcome of information search is the development of a complete evoked set.

If you are initially satisfied with the evoked set, information search will be focused on the performance of the brands in the evoked set on the evaluative criteria. Thus, the evoked set is of particular importance in structuring subsequent information search and purchase.

The brand you found completely unworthy of further consideration is a member of what is called the **inept set.** Brands in *the inept set are actively disliked or avoided by the consumer.* Positive information about these brands is not likely to be processed even if it is readily available.

In our example, Motorola, Toshiba, NEC, and HP were brands of which you were aware but were basically indifferent toward. They compose what is known as an **inert set.** Consumers will generally accept favorable information about brands in the inert set, although they do not seek out such information. Brands in this set are generally acceptable when preferred brands are not available. Thus, the eight brands in the initial awareness set can be subdivided as follows:

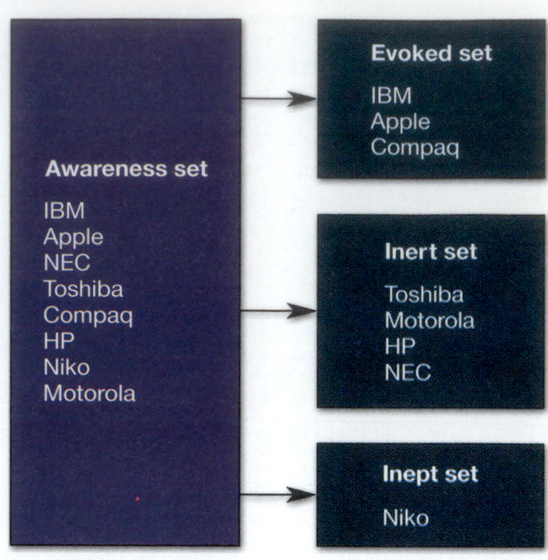

Figure 15-2 illustrates the general relationships among these classes of alternatives.

FIGURE 15-2 Categories of Decision Alternatives

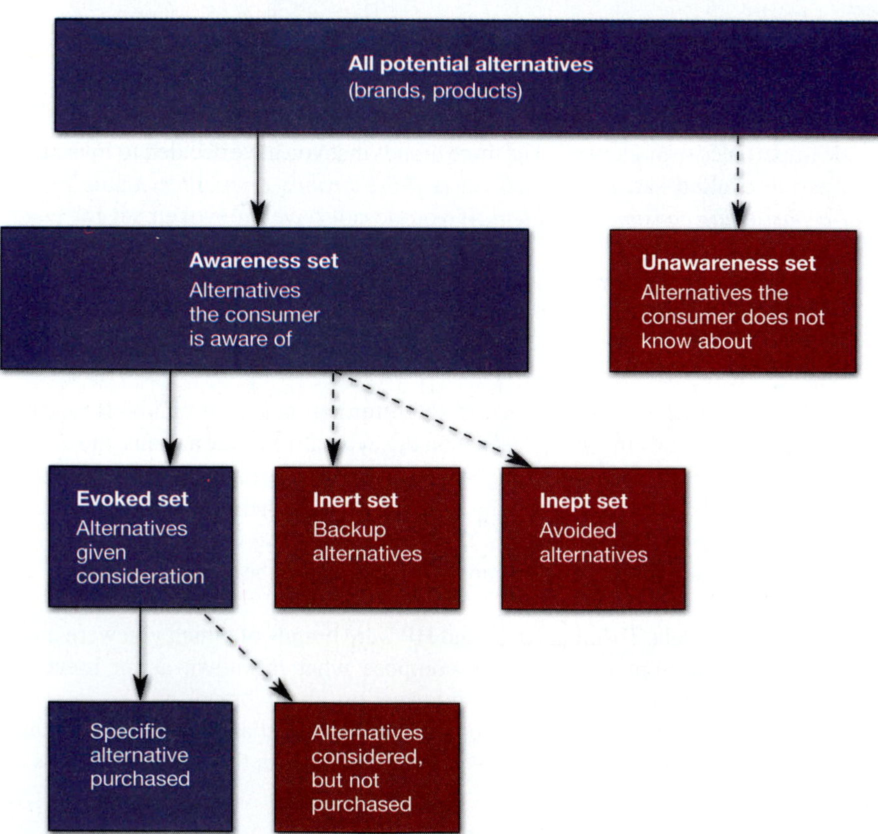

Figure 15-3 illustrates the results of several studies comparing the size of the awareness and evoked sets for a variety of products. Notice that in all cases, the evoked set is substantially smaller than the awareness set. Since the evoked set generally is the one from which consumers make final evaluations and decisions, *marketing strategy that focuses only on creating awareness may be inadequate*. Thus, marketers must strive to have consumers recall their brand in response to a recognized problem *and* consider the brand a worthy potential solution. As we discuss in the next chapter, retail outlets face similar issues.[6]

Alternative Characteristics

To choose among the brands in the evoked set, the consumer compares them on the relevant evaluative criteria. This process requires the consumer to gather information about *each brand on each pertinent evaluative criterion.*[7] In our example of a computer purchase,

Awareness and Evoked Sets for Various Products **FIGURE 15-3**

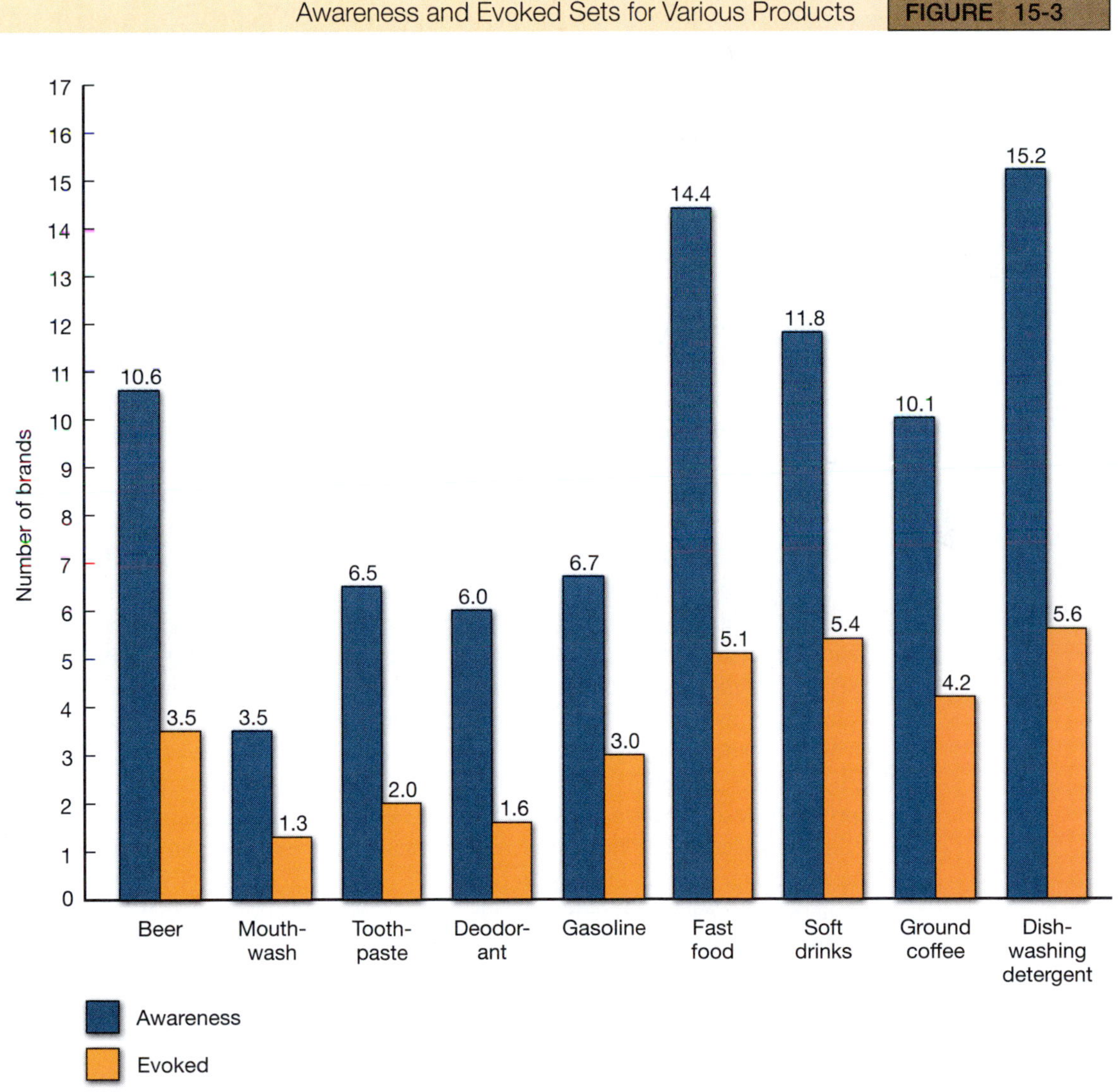

Source: J. Roberts, "A Grounded Model of Consideration Set Size and Composition," in *Advances in Consumer Research XVI,* ed. T. K. Skrull (Provo, UT: Association for Consumer Research, 1989), p. 750.

you might collect information on the price, memory, processor, weight, screen clarity, and accompanying software for each brand you are considering.

In summary, consumers engage in internal and external search for (1) appropriate evaluative criteria, (2) the existence of potential solutions, and (3) the characteristics of potential solutions. However, extensive search generally occurs for only a few consumption decisions. Nominal and limited decisions that involve little or no active external search are the rule. In addition, consumers acquire substantial information without deliberate search through low-involvement learning. Finally, while our discussion has focused on searching for functional information, emotions and feelings are important in many purchases.

SOURCES OF INFORMATION

Refer again to our rather pleasant example of receiving cash with which to purchase a computer. We suggested that you might recall what you know about computers, check with friends and an on-line users group, consult *Consumer Reports* and read reviews in *PC Magazine,* talk with sales personnel, or personally inspect several computers to collect relevant information. These represent the five primary sources of information available to consumers:

- *Memory* of past searches, personal experiences, and low-involvement learning.
- *Personal sources,* such as friends, family, and others.
- *Independent sources,* such as magazines, consumer groups, and government agencies.
- *Marketing sources,* such as sales personnel and advertising.
- *Experiential sources,* such as inspection or product trial.[8]

These sources are shown in Figure 15-4. Consumers decide how many and which sources of information to use at both the macro (personal sources) and micro (my mother) levels. Thus, a purchase decision requires a subset of decisions concerning information seeking.[9]

Internal information is the primary source used by most consumers most of the time (nominal and limited decision making). However, note that information in long-term memory was *initially* obtained from external sources. That is, you may resolve a consumption problem using only or mainly stored information. At some point, however, you acquired that information from an external source, such as direct product experience, friends, or low-involvement learning.

Marketing-originated messages are only one of five potential information sources, and they are frequently found to be of limited *direct* value in consumer decisions.[10] Figure 15-5 shows the important role of personal sources for new residents seeking a professional service. As the figure illustrates, personal sources, particularly friends, dominated the search process for medical and legal services. Personal sources, marketing sources (particularly the Yellow Pages), and physical search were equally important in selecting a veterinarian.

However, marketing activities influence all five sources. Thus, the characteristics of the product, the distribution of the product, and the promotional messages about the product provide the underlying or basic information available in the market. An independent source such as *Consumer Reports* bases its report on the functional characteristics of the product. Personal sources such as friends also must base their information on experience with the product or its promotion (or on other sources that have had contact with the product or its promotion).

A substantial amount of marketing activity is designed to influence the information that consumers will receive from nonmarketing sources. For example, when Johnson & Johnson introduced a new-formula baby bath:

> Product information, demonstrations, monographs, journal ads, and direct-mail programs were targeted at pediatricians and nurses to capitalize on health care professionals' direct contact with

Information Sources for a Purchase Decision **FIGURE 15-4**

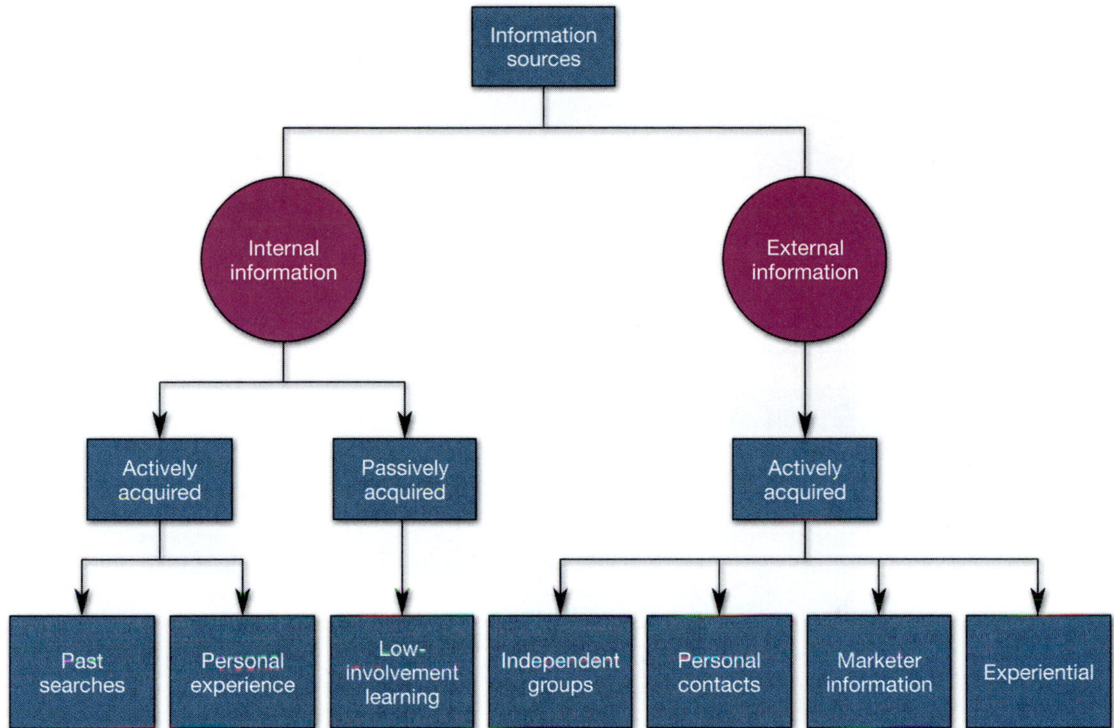

new mothers. Print ads and coupons appeared in baby care publications, and a film exploring the parent–infant bonding process was distributed to teaching centers, hospitals, and medical schools.

In addition, while consumers may not use advertising or other marketer provided data as an immediate input into many purchase decisions, there is no doubt that the continual exposure to advertising frequently influences the perceived need for the product, the composition of the consideration and evoked sets, the evaluative criteria used, and the beliefs about the performance levels of each brand.[11] There is also substantial evidence that advertising for consumer nondurables can have a significant impact on sales even in the short run.[12] Thus, while consumers report only limited direct influence by marketing sources, other types of evidence indicate that the effect may be stronger.

Information Search on the Internet

The **Internet** or **World Wide Web** is a network of computers that any computer with access to a phone connection can join. In addition to the computers and connecting systems, the Internet consists of **Web sites,** specific addresses or files in the network, and **search engines,** programs designed to search the various Web sites and provide the address of and/or access to those with the requested characteristics.

The presence of the Internet is altering consumer information search in ways that are not yet fully understood.[13] Estimates of the number of current users of the Internet range widely, with 40 million U.S. and 5 million Canadian households using the Internet in 2000 a reasonable estimate.[14] A survey conducted late in 1998 found that 45 percent of the adults

FIGURE 15-5 Prepurchase Information Search for Services after a Move

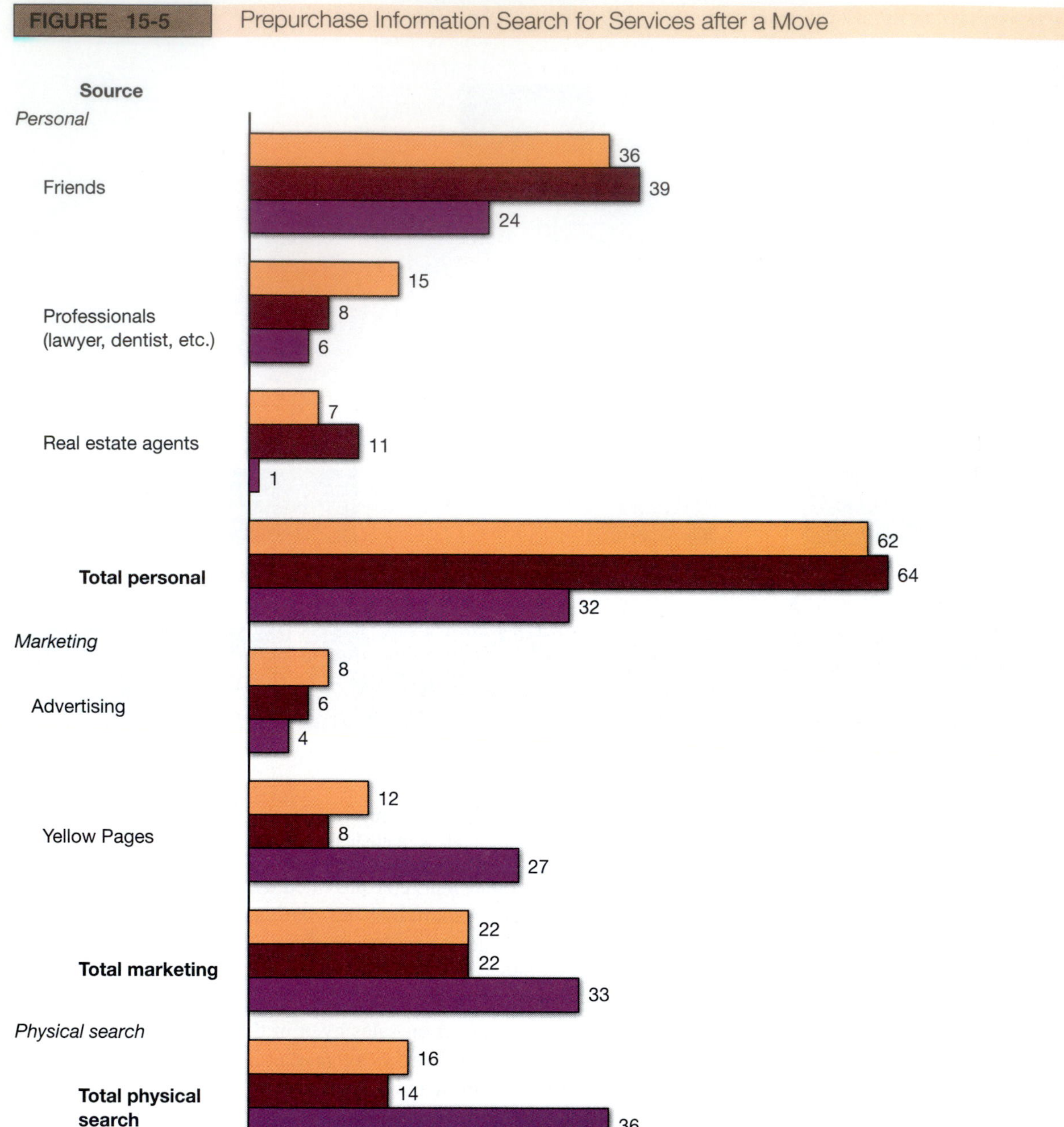

Source: J. B. Freiden and R. E. Goldsmith, "Prepurchase Information Seeking for Professional Services," *Journal of Services Marketing,* Winter 1989, p. 49.

who responded had used the Internet compared to 30 percent in 1997 (and 87 percent of these had used it within the last six months). Clearly, use of the Internet is growing rapidly.

However, as Figure 15-6 shows, the Internet is not used equally by all segments of the population. It should be noted that Internet usage among lower income groups is increasing rapidly as the cost of both hardware and connection services declines.

Household users of the Internet use it in the following ways:[15]

	Activities	*Primary Activity*
Gather news or information	91%	26%
Send e-mail	88	31
Conduct research	79	23
Surf various sites	69	09
Shop	27	01
Post to bulletin boards	23	01
Play games	22	03
Participate in chats	18	04

Users rated "conducting research before making a purchase" as their primary interest for using the Internet in the future. Younger users are more likely to use the Internet for communications purposes, while middle-aged users are more focused on seeking information.[16]

Note that the Internet contains marketer-supplied data in the form of ads associated with search, entertainment, and general information sites, and home pages or Internet Presence Sites. A **home page** or **Internet Presence Site (IPS)** is a Web site developed and maintained by a firm (or another organization or individual) that provides detailed product and company data (or independent data from government and private sources): The Internet also contains personal sources of information on bulletin boards and chat sessions. Among those consumers who had used the Internet in the past six months, over 75 percent had visited a company Web site. Reasons for these visited included:

Seeking product information	90%
Seeking company information	88
Getting coupons, discounts	30
Buying products	23
Entering contests	15

Consumers frequently visit a company Web site because they see it mentioned in traditional media:

Percent visiting a Web site because they saw it mentioned in:	
Magazine/newspaper ad	71%
TV ad	57
Product packaging	49
Radio ad	36
Direct mail	32
Billboard	22

FIGURE 15-6 Characteristics of Internet Users

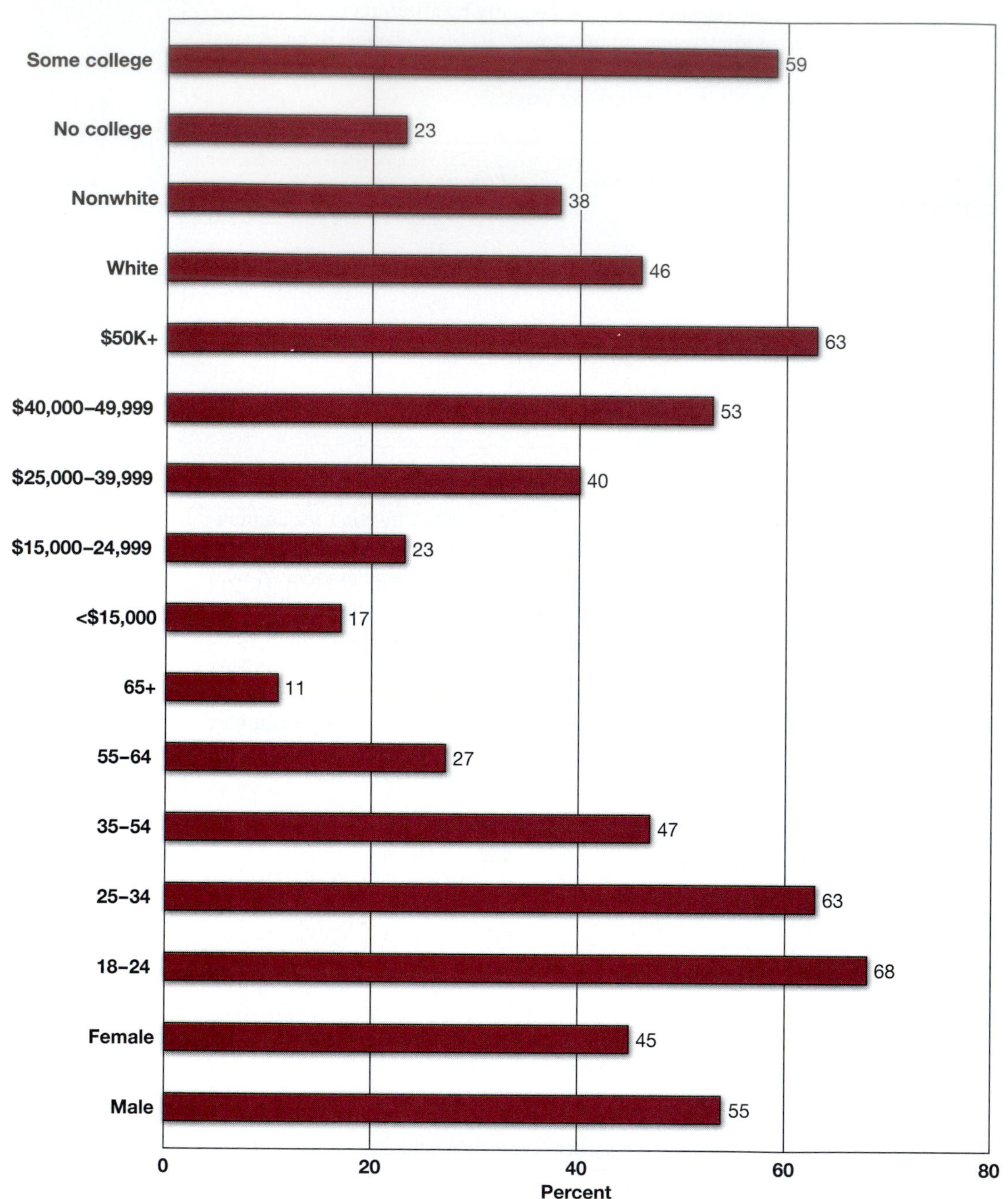

Source: Derived from *Interactive Media Study* (Arlington Heights, IL: Market Facts', Inc. TeleNation, October 1998).

The above data indicate that ads such as the one shown in Illustration 15-2 can be effective in guiding consumers' information search activities to company Web sites. In addition, the presence of a Web address in an advertisement appears to enhance a variety of aspects of the firm's image, including being customer-oriented, responsive, sophisticated, and successful.[17] As Web addresses become the norm, it is possible that their presence will

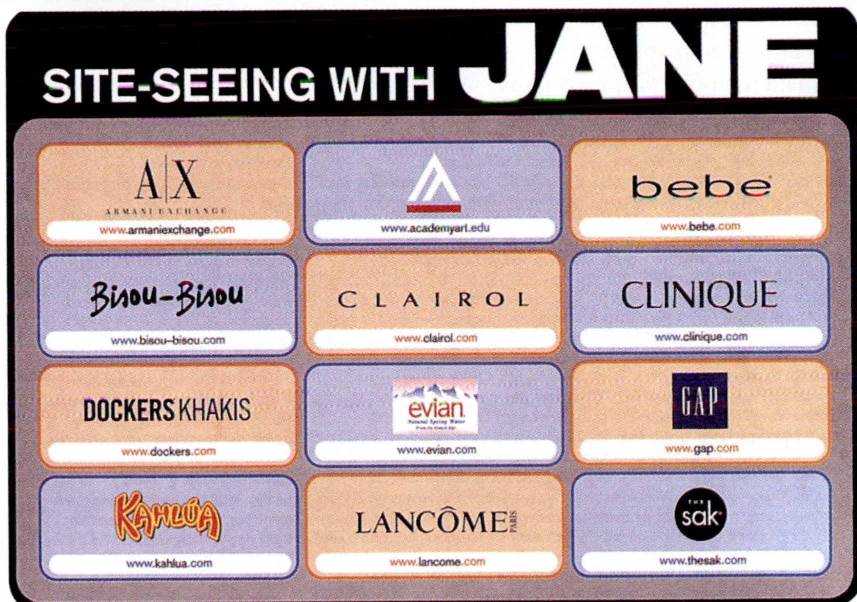

Courtesy Jane Magazine; courtesy Cybergrrl, Inc. (www.cybergrrl.com).

ILLUSTRATION 15-2

The Internet is becoming an important source of information for many consumers and an important marketing tool for many firms. Marketers often use mass media ads and links with other Internet sites to encourage consumers to visit their Web sites.

no longer generate positive image benefits, but their absence might produce negative reactions.

Consumers also encounter ads on the Internet while visiting general information, search, and entertainment sites. These are generally **banner ads** that, when clicked, will take the consumer to the company or products home page or to a special advertisement. About 60 percent of the Internet users surveyed sometimes looked at these ads, but only 10 percent indicated that they did so often or very often. About half click on these ads at least occasionally (only 3 percent do so often).

The Internet is undergoing rapid expansion in terms of usage, capabilities, and characteristics.[18] For example, there are a number of shopping services on the Internet that can search all or most of the retail sites and identify the site with the lowest price for a particular product. The services use **bots,** which are software "robots" that do your searching for you. Some of the services also provide product data and reviews. For example, consumers using the Excite shopping service type in the name of a specific product. Excite's bot then goes to 500 on-line merchants' sites and reports back current data and prices. These services, which are rapidly evolving, are likely to substantially alter the way many consumers search for information.[19]

Marketing Strategy and Information Search on the Internet Marketers have four major decisions with respect to marketing on the Internet:

1. Should we have a company/brand Web site?
2. If we have a Web site, should it be active or passive?
3. Should we advertise on the Web in addition to our Web site?
4. Should we sell our products directly to consumers via the Web?

We will discuss the first three of these issues now. The fourth issue is covered in Chapter 17 on outlet selection.

A Web site is increasingly essential for consumer product companies. As we saw earlier, most Web users visit these sites and Web users tend to be younger, upscale consumers. A firm without a Web site is likely to be viewed as unresponsive and out-of-date. Therefore, the real decision is whether the site itself should focus strictly on providing product and company information (a passive site) or should it contain additional features and activities designed to draw consumers to the site (an active site). The sites described in the chapter-opening example were all active sites.

An active site allows the firm to develop a relationship with consumers over time and provide them with product information as well as other relevant information and entertainment. However, it is also expensive and often appeals to a relatively small percent of the market. Active sites should generally have a natural tie to the activities they are providing. In the opening example, Avon's activities focused on beauty while Kraft's focused on food preparation and shopping. Firms such as Disney would be naturals for active sites, while LifeSavers would be less so.[20] The Pepsi World site shown at the beginning of the chapter is an active site, while the 3Com site in Illustration 15-3 is passive. Note that the 3Com site has many useful features for those who have or are considering acquiring a 3Com product. It is considered a passive site because it does not provide nonproduct-related inducements to visit the site.

Whether a site is active or passive, it needs to be easy to access and negotiate, up-to-date, logical, and focused on customers' needs.[21] The more complex the purchase and/or use of the product, the more complete and interactive the Web site should be. A Web site for a backpack manufacturer should have a series of questions concerning the consumers intended product uses, physical characteristics, and other desires. Based on the responses to these questions, the program would then recommend one or more products from the firm's line, giving the advantages of each. Such an approach would make little sense for simpler products such as breath mints.

As consumers increasingly visit company Web sites, it is likely that consumer expectations for easily accessed, useful information presented in an entertaining format will become the norm. Firms that do not live up to these expectations will see their image and sales decline.

While the use of home pages by marketers is now common, advertising is still quite limited though growing rapidly. Approximately four billion dollars was spent on Internet advertising in 1999, a tiny percentage of total advertising expenditures.[22] However, as marketers learn more about Internet marketing in general and advertising in particular, both

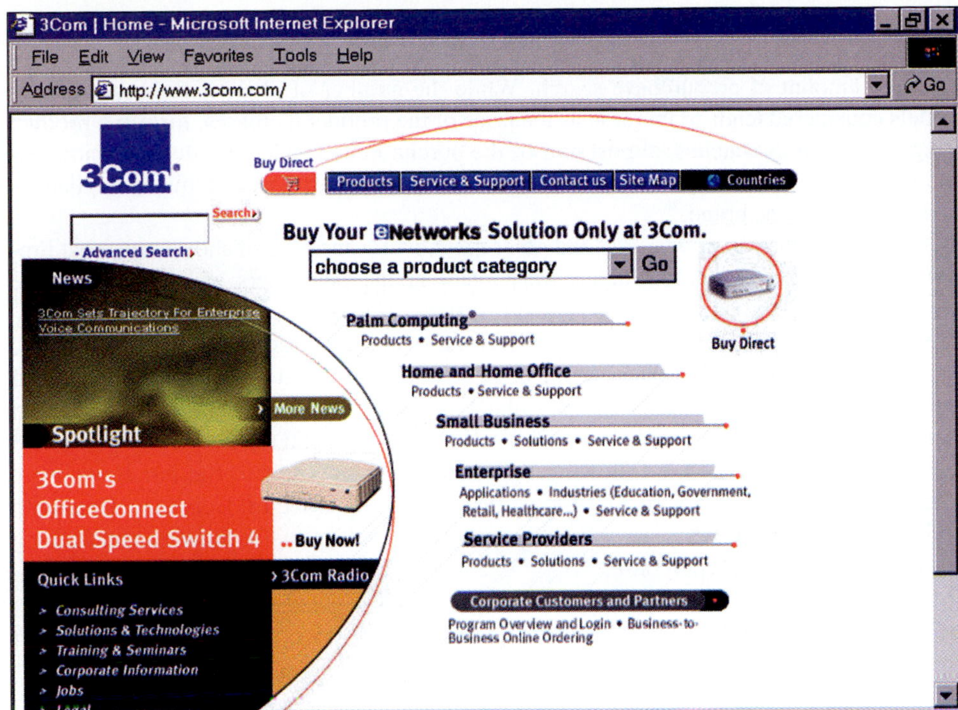

ILLUSTRATION 15-3

Web sites differ in the extent to which they offer nonproduct-related inducements to visit the site. This site is heavily product focused.

the total and relative amounts of advertising done on the Internet are increasing exponentially.[23] In the meantime, marketers are "learning by doing" on the Web. As the CEO of Unilever, a firm with over 40 brand Web sites, states:

> I don't know what's going to happen, but I'm convinced we've got to play and we've got to engage our consumers. This is truly experimental. For me, it's the same as investing in having scientists play with molecules in order to come up with a new product.[24]

AMOUNT OF EXTERNAL INFORMATION SEARCH

Marketing managers are particularly interested in external information search, as this provides them with direct access to the consumer. How much external information search do consumers actually undertake? Most purchases are a result of nominal or limited decision making and therefore involve limited external search immediately prior to purchase. This is particularly true for relatively low-priced convenience goods such as soft drinks, canned foods, and detergents. Therefore, the discussion in this section focuses on major purchases such as appliances, professional services, and automobiles. Intuitively, we would expect substantial amounts of direct external search prior to such purchases.

Different measures of external information search have been used: (1) number of stores visited, (2) number of alternatives considered, (3) number of personal sources used, and (4) overall or combination measures. Each of these measures of search effort assesses a different aspect of behavior, yet each measure supports one observation: *External information search is skewed toward limited search, with the greatest proportion of consumers performing little external search immediately prior to purchase.*

Surveys of *shopping behavior* have shown a significant percent of all durable purchases are made after visiting only one store.[25] The *number of alternatives* considered also shows a limited amount of prepurchase search. While the number of alternative brands and/or models considered tends to increase as the price of the product increases, for some product categories, such as watches, almost half of the purchasers considered only one brand *and* one model. Another study found that 27 percent of the purchasers of major appliances considered only one brand.[26]

Measures of the use of *personal* and other *nonmarket* sources also show somewhat limited levels of search. Approximately 40 percent of the purchasers of a new appliance consulted others, and one-fourth consulted *Consumer Reports*.[27]

Seven separate studies that span 40 years, two product categories, four services, and two countries found remarkable consistency in terms of the total external information search undertaken. These studies classified consumers in terms of their total external information search as (1) nonsearchers, (2) limited information searchers, and (3) extended information searchers.[28] As shown in the following table, approximately half of the purchases were preceded by virtually no external information search, about one-third were associated with limited information search, and only 12 percent involved extensive information seeking immediately prior to the purchase.

Country/Product/Year	*Nonsearchers*	*Limited Searchers*	*Extended Searchers*
America/appliances/1955	65%	25%	10%
America/appliances/1972	49	38	13
America/appliances/1974	65	27	08
Australia/automobiles/1981	24	58	18
America/appliances/1989	24	45	11
America/professional services/1989	55	38	07
Australia/professional services/1995	53	35	12

A given individual might exhibit extended search for one purchase, limited for one, and be a nonsearcher for yet another. However, extended information seeking has been found to be characteristic of some individuals such as market mavens, as described earlier.

Most consumers engage in minimal external information search *immediately* prior to the purchase of consumer durables. The level of search for less important items is even lower. As you will see in the next section, limited information search does not necessarily mean that the consumer is not following a sound purchasing strategy. Nor does it mean that substantial amounts of internal information are not being used.[29]

COSTS VERSUS BENEFITS OF EXTERNAL SEARCH

Why do 50 percent of the buyers of major appliances described above do little or no external search, while 12 percent engage in extensive external search? Part of the answer lies in the differences between the buyers in terms of their perceptions of the benefits and costs of search associated with a particular purchase situation.[30] The ability to make such cost–benefit trade-offs appears to be limited in preschool children but to develop rapidly at about the time they enter school.[31] Thus, most active consumers appear to be able to make search decisions based on their estimates of the costs and benefits involved.

The benefits of external information search can be tangible, such as a lower price, a preferred style, or higher quality product. Or the benefits can be intangible in terms of reduced risk, greater confidence in the purchase, or even providing enjoyment. Perceptions of these benefits are likely to vary with the consumer's experience in the market, media habits, and the extent to which the consumer interacts with others or belongs to differing reference groups. Therefore, one reason 50 percent of major appliance buyers do little or no external search is that they do not perceive significant benefits resulting from such an effort.

Furthermore, acquisition of external information is not free, and consumers may engage in limited search because the costs of search exceed the perceived benefits. The costs of search can be both monetary and nonmonetary. Monetary costs include out-of-pocket expenses related to the search effort, such as the cost of transportation, parking, and time-related costs, including lost wages, lost opportunities, charges for child care, and so forth. Nonmonetary costs of search are less obvious but may have an even greater impact than monetary costs. Almost every external search effort involves some physical and psychological strain. Frustration and conflict between the search task and other more desirable activities, as well as fatigue, may shorten the search effort.

In this section, we are going to examine four basic types of factors that influence the expected benefits and perceived costs of search: *market characteristics, product characteristics, consumer characteristics,* and *situation characteristics*.[32] These four factors and their components are shown in Table 15-1.

Market Characteristics

Market characteristics include the number of alternatives, price range, store distribution, and information availability. It is important to keep in mind that it is the consumer's perception of, or beliefs about, the market characteristics that influence shopping behavior, *not* the actual characteristics.[33] While beliefs and reality are usually related, often they are not identical.

Obviously, the greater the *number of alternatives* (products, stores, brands) available to resolve a particular problem, the more external search there is likely to be. At the extreme, there is no need to search for information in the face of a complete monopoly such as utilities or driver's licenses.

However, if too many models and brands are available, information overload (see Chapter 8) may cause consumers to shop less. In particular, a wide range of models and/or brands may make the search process virtually impossible if the models vary across stores. That is, if one store has two brands with five models each and a second store has the same two brands but with five different models each, the consumer must compare 20 distinct brands/models. In response, many consumers will limit their shopping to a single retail outlet. This leads some marketers to develop a large number of models so that key accounts can have exclusive models and avoid direct price competition with other retailers on those exact models.[34]

The *perceived range of prices* among equivalent brands in a product class is a major factor in stimulating external search. For example, shopping 36 retail stores in Tucson for five popular branded toys produced a total low cost of $51.27 and a total high cost of $105.95. Clearly, efficient shopping for these products in this market would provide a significant financial gain.

However, it appears that something similar to Weber's law may operate in terms of consumers' response to price variations. That is, the percentage savings available from shopping may be as important as the dollar amount. Consumers who perceive the chance

TABLE 15-1

Factors Affecting External Search Immediately Prior to Purchase

Influencing Factor	Increasing the Influencing Factor Causes the Search to:
I. Market Characteristics	
A. Number of alternatives	Increase
B. Price range	Increase
C. Store concentration	Increase
D. Information availability	Increase
1. Advertising	
2. Point-of-purchase	
3. Sales personnel	
4. Packaging	
5. Experienced consumers	
6. Independent sources	
II. Product Characteristics	
A. Price	Increase
B. Differentiation	Increase
C. Positive products	Increase
III. Consumer Characteristics	
A. Learning and experience	Decrease
B. Shopping orientation	Mixed
C. Social status	Increase
D. Age and household life cycle	Mixed
E. Product involvement	Mixed
F. Perceived risk	Increase
IV. Situation Characteristics	
A. Time availability	Increase
B. Purchase for self	Decrease
C. Pleasant surroundings	Increase
D. Social surroundings	Mixed
E. Physical/mental energy	Increase

to save $50 when purchasing a $200 item may be motivated to engage in search but not if the same savings were available for a $5,000 item.[35]

Store distribution—the number, location, and distances between retail stores in the market—affects the number of store visits a consumer will make before purchase. Because store visits take time, energy, and in many cases money, a close proximity of stores will often increase this aspect of external search.[36]

In general, *information availability* is directly related to information use.[37] However, too much information can cause information overload and the use of less information. In addition, readily available information tends to produce learning over time, which may reduce the need for additional external information immediately prior to a purchase.[38] *Advertising, point-of-purchase displays, sales personnel, packages, other consumers,* and *independent sources* such as *Consumer Reports* are major sources of consumer information.

Product Characteristics

Product characteristics such as *price level* and *differentiation* tend to influence external search with higher prices and greater differentiation associated with increased external search.

Consumers appear to enjoy shopping for *positive products*—those whose acquisition results in positive reinforcement. Thus, shopping for flowers and plants, dress clothing, sports equipment, and cameras is viewed as a positive experience by most consumers. In contrast, shopping for *negative products*—those whose primary benefit is negative reinforcement (removal of an unpleasant condition)—is viewed as less pleasant. Shopping for groceries, extermination services, and auto repairs is not enjoyed by most individuals. Other things being equal, consumers are more likely to engage in external search for positive products.[39]

Consumer Characteristics

A variety of consumer characteristics affect perceptions of expected benefits, search costs, and the need to carry out a particular level of external information search. A satisfying *experience* with a particular brand is a positively reinforcing process. It increases the probability of a repeat purchase of that brand and decreases the likelihood of external search. As a result, external search is generally greater for consumers having a limited purchase experience with brands in a particular product category.

However, there is evidence that at least some familiarity with a product class is necessary for external search to occur.[40] For example, external search prior to purchasing a new automobile is high for consumers who have a high level of *general knowledge about cars* and low for consumers who have a substantial level of *knowledge* about existing brands.[41] Thus, consumers facing a completely unfamiliar product category may feel threatened by the amount of new information or may simply lack sufficient knowledge to conduct an external search.

External search tends to increase with various measures of *social status* (education, occupation, and income), though middle-income individuals search more than those at higher or lower levels. *Age* of the shopper is inversely related to information search. That is, external search appears to decrease as the age of the shopper increases. This may be explained in part by increased learning and product familiarity gained with age. New households and individuals moving into new stages of the *household life cycle* have a greater need for external information than established households.

Consumers tend to form general approaches or patterns of external search. These general approaches are termed *shopping orientations*.[42] While individuals will exhibit substantial variation from the general pattern across situations and product categories, many do take a stable shopping approach to most products across a wide range of situations (see Table 17-3, page 608). Other individuals engage in extensive ongoing information search because they are market mavens, as described earlier. A new generation of consumers is emerging that is developing radically different search patterns from prior generations. The **N-Generation** is described in Consumer Insight 15-1.

Consumers who are *highly involved with a product category* generally seek information relevant to the product category on an ongoing basis.[43] This ongoing search and the knowledge base it produces may reduce their need for external search immediately before a purchase. However, this may vary with the nature of their involvement with the product category. One study found that wine enthusiasts who desired variety engaged in significantly more external search than those who were less interested in variety.[44]

Perceived Risk The **perceived risk** associated with unsatisfactory product performance, either instrumental or symbolic, increases information search prior to purchase.[45] Higher perceived risk is associated with increased search and greater reliance on personal sources of information and personal experiences.

Consumer Insight 15-1

The Net-Generation

Some are referring to those aged 2 through their early 20s as the Net-Generation or the N-Generation. Net in this instance refers to the Internet, or more broadly computers and computer communications. This generation is the first in history to grow up with home computers. It is being profoundly affected by the experience and will, in turn, alter the way business, and particularly marketing, is conducted.

The computer, which many older consumers either avoid or struggle to cope with, seems natural to younger consumers. One study found that a four-year-old could be taught to use a mouse in less than five minutes, a fraction of the time it takes to teach an adult. Most children entering kindergarten have used a computer.

It is estimated that there are more than 7 million children in the United States under 18 that are active users of the Internet. Over 90 percent of the students at public universities and community colleges currently have access to the Internet either from their dorms or apartments or from the school library. Worldwide, the number of Internet users doubles every six months.

These children often have more knowledge about computers and related products than their parents. Consider this quote from a 12-year-old who was computer shopping with his father:

> My dad asked about prices, but I kind of hinted around about what kind of capability it has. Most companies will also try to rip you off by telling you Windows is preloaded and stuff like that, but they won't actually give you the disks. I wanted to make sure about that in case it ever crashes.

Not only are these youngsters knowledgeable about computers but they are learning how to use computers to quickly become knowledgeable about virtually anything. They know how to access company literature, consumer reports, government studies, and the opinions of others who have purchased the product by using the Internet. They are increasingly being asked to serve as researchers for major household purchases.

N-Generation members are moving away from television viewing. Children currently watch less TV than their parents and they watch less each year. The time freed is spent on the computer and often on the Internet. The flexibility and interactive nature of the Internet is shaping their views on shopping, gathering information, brands, and virtually all other aspects of marketing.

One writer describes the N-Generation and the challenge it poses to marketers as follows:

> N-Geners are not viewers or listeners or readers. They are users. They reject the notion of expertise as they sift through information at the speed of light by themselves for themselves. It is difficult to convince them that they must have anything.

Critical Thinking Questions

1. How will the N-Generation change marketing practice over the next 10 years?
2. How will the growth of computer communications change the U.S. society over the next 10 years?

Source: D. Tapscott, "The Rise of the Net-Generation," *Advertising Age,* October 14, 1996, p. 31; and B. Layne, "Meet Your Future," *Advertising Age,* November 20, 1995, p. S-12.

Perceived risk is a function of the individual, the product, and the situation. It varies from one consumer to another and for the same consumer from one product to another and from one situation to another. For example, the purchase of a bottle of wine may not involve much perceived risk when buying for one's own consumption. However, the choice of wine may involve considerable perceived risk when buying wine for a dinner party for one's boss. Likewise, it might be perceived as risky if the individual has little knowledge and is buying an expensive bottle for personal consumption.

While perceived risk varies across consumers and situations, some products are generally seen as riskier than others (see Table 17-2, page 606). For example, services are generally perceived as riskier than physical products.[46] Likewise, perceived risk is high for products whose failure to perform as expected would result in a high:

- *Social cost* (e.g., a new suit that is not appreciated by one's peers).
- *Financial cost* (e.g., an expensive vacation during which it rained all the time).
- *Time cost* (e.g., an automobile repair that required the car to be taken to the garage, left, and then picked up later).
- *Effort cost* (e.g., a computer whose hard drive crashes after being loaded with important software).
- *Physical cost* (e.g., a new medicine produces a harmful side effect).

Situation Characteristics

As was indicated in Chapter 13, situational variables can have a major impact on search behavior. For example, recall that one of the primary reactions of consumers to crowded store conditions is to minimize external information search. *Temporal perspective* is probably the most important situational variable with respect to search behavior. As the time available to solve a particular consumer problem decreases, so does the amount of external information search.[47]

Gift-giving situations (*task definition*) tend to increase perceived risk, which, as we have seen, increases external search. Shoppers with limited physical or emotional energy (*antecedent state*) will search for less information than others. Pleasant *physical surroundings* increase the tendency to search for information (at least *within* that outlet). *Social surroundings* can increase or decrease search, depending on the nature of the social setting (see Chapter 13 for a more complete discussion of these issues).

MARKETING STRATEGIES BASED ON INFORMATION SEARCH PATTERNS

Sound marketing strategies take into account the nature of information search engaged in by the target market prior to purchase. Two dimensions of search are particularly appropriate: the type of decision influences the level of search, and the nature of the evoked set influences the direction of the search. Table 15-2 illustrates a strategy matrix based on these two dimensions. This matrix suggests the six marketing strategies discussed in the following sections. As you will see, while there is considerable overlap between the strategies, each has a unique thrust.

TABLE 15-2 Marketing Strategies Based on Information Search Patterns

	Target Market Decision-Making Pattern		
Position	*Nominal Decision Making (no search)*	*Limited Decision Making (limited search)*	*Extended Decision Making (extensive search)*
Brand in Evoked Set	Maintenance strategy	Capture strategy	Preference strategy
Brand Not in Evoked Set	Disrupt strategy	Intercept strategy	Acceptance strategy

ILLUSTRATION 15-4

Firms with a significant group of loyal or repeat purchasers must continually improve their products and communicate their advantages to their customers.

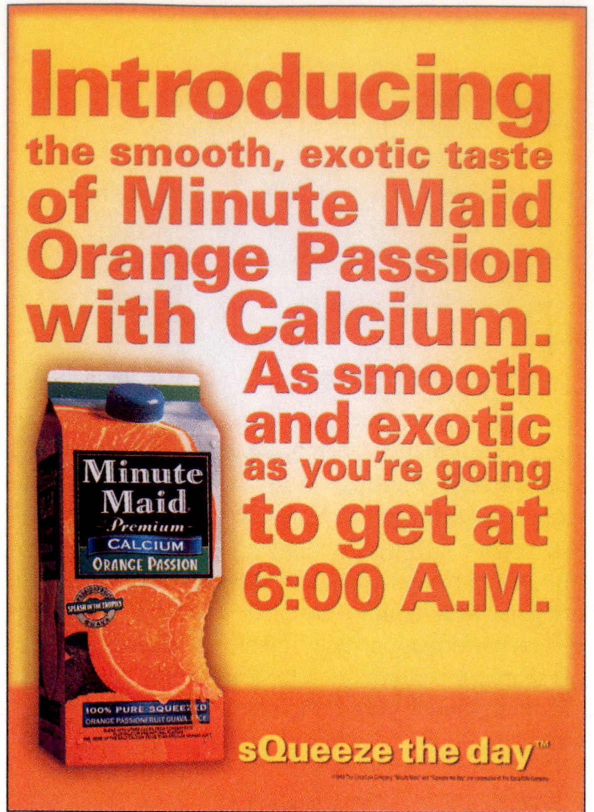

Courtesy The Coca-Cola Company.

Maintenance Strategy

If our brand is purchased habitually by the target market, our strategy is to maintain that behavior. This requires consistent attention to product quality, distribution (avoiding out-of-stock situations), and a reinforcement advertising strategy. In addition, we must defend against the disruptive tactics of competitors. Thus, we need to maintain product development and improvements and to counter short-term competitive strategies such as coupons, point-of-purchase displays, or rebates.

Morton salt and Del Monte canned vegetables have large repeat purchaser segments that they have successfully maintained. Budweiser, Marlboro, and Crest have large brand-loyal purchaser segments. They have successfully defended their market positions against assaults by major competitors in recent years. In contrast, Liggett & Myers lost 80 percent of its market share when it failed to engage in maintenance advertising.[48] Quality control problems caused Schlitz to lose substantial market share.

Illustration 15-4 shows part of Minute Maid's maintenance strategy against the challenge of multiple competitors. Note that the ad stresses the newest improvements that Minute Maid has incorporated.

Disrupt Strategy

If our brand is not part of the evoked set and our target market engages in nominal decision making, our first task is to *disrupt* the existing decision pattern. This is a difficult task since

Courtesy Sprint.

ILLUSTRATION 15-5

Firms trying to disrupt the habitual purchase patterns of consumers who do not consider their brand need attention-attracting advertising and a strong benefit to offer.

the consumer does not seek external information or even consider alternative brands before a purchase. Low-involvement learning over time could generate a positive product position for our brand, but this alone would be unlikely to shift behavior.

In the long run, a major product improvement accompanied by attention-attracting advertising could shift the target market into a more extensive form of decision making. In the short run, attention-attracting advertising aimed specifically at breaking habitual decision making can be successful. Free samples, coupons, rebates, and tie-in sales are common approaches to disrupting nominal decision making. Likewise, striking package designs and point-of-purchase displays may disrupt a habitual purchase sequence.[49] Comparative advertising is also often used for this purpose.

Illustration 15-5 is an example of a disrupt-based strategy. Notice that the ad targets a specific group with a very strong benefit. Strong benefit claims such as this are necessary to disrupt the nominal decision making common in this product category. Phone companies are now making use of extensive telephone sales calls as another approach to disrupting nominal purchase patterns.

Capture Strategy

Limited decision making generally involves a few brands that are evaluated on only a few criteria such as price or availability. Much of the information search occurs at the point-of-purchase or in readily available media prior to purchase. If our brand is one of the brands given this type of consideration by our target market, our objective is to capture as large a share of their purchases as practical.

Since these consumers engage in limited search, we need to know where they search and what information they are looking for. In general, we will want to supply information, often on price and availability, in local media through cooperative advertising and at the point-of-purchase through displays and adequate shelf space. If appropriate for the product category, an active Web site might be beneficial. We will also be concerned with maintaining consistent product quality and adequate distribution.

ILLUSTRATION 15-6

This ad, distributed in newspapers, would be effective as part of a capture or intercept strategy as it gives consumers an immediate incentive to purchase this brand.

Courtesy Pietro's Pizza.

Intercept Strategy

If our target market engages in limited decision making and our brand is not part of their evoked set, our objective will be to intercept the consumer during the search for information on the brands in the evoked set. Again, our emphasis will be on local media with cooperative advertising and at the point of purchase with displays, shelf space, package design, and so forth. Coupons can also be effective. We will have to place considerable emphasis on attracting the consumers' attention, as they will not be seeking information on our brand. If appropriate for the product category, an active Web site could be particularly useful. The promotion shown in Illustration 15-6 was distributed in the newspaper. It would be effective as part of a capture and/or intercept strategy.

In addition to the strategies mentioned above, low-involvement learning, product improvements, and free samples can be used to move the brand into the target market's evoked set.

Preference Strategy

Extended decision making with our brand in the evoked set requires a preference strategy. Since extended decision making generally involves several brands, many attributes, and a number of information sources, a simple capture strategy may not be adequate. Instead, we need to structure an information campaign that will result in our brand being preferred by members of the target market.

The first step is a strong position on those attributes important to the target market. This is discussed in considerable detail in Chapter 16. Next, information must be provided in all the appropriate sources. This may require extensive advertising to groups that do not purchase the item but recommend it to others (e.g., druggists for over-the-counter drugs,

Courtesy Tiger Direct, Inc.

ILLUSTRATION 15-7

This ad assumes an involved search process. It provides substantial data on numerous product features.

veterinarians and county agents for agricultural products). Independent groups should be encouraged to test the brand, and sales personnel should be provided detailed information on the brand's attributes. In addition, it may be wise to provide the sales personnel with extra motivation (e.g., extra commissions paid by the manufacturer) to recommend the product. Point-of-purchase displays and pamphlets should also be available. A well-designed Web site is essential.

The TigerDirect ad shown in Illustration 15-7 is part of an effective preference strategy. It assumes an involved search and provides detailed information relative to multiple product attributes.

Acceptance Strategy

Acceptance strategy is very similar to preference strategy. However, it is complicated by the fact that the target market is not seeking information about our brand. Therefore, in addition to the activities involved in the preference strategy described above, we must attract their attention or otherwise motivate them to learn about our brand. Consider the following quote made by Lee Iaccoca while he was head of Chrysler:

> Our biggest long-term job is to get people in [the showroom] to see how great these cars are—to get some traffic—and let them compare, so we're going head to head on price and value.[50]

Because of this situation, Chrysler implemented an acceptance strategy. In addition to product improvements and heavy advertising, Chrysler literally paid consumers to seek information about their cars! They did this by offering cash to individuals who would test drive a Chrysler product prior to purchasing a new car.

Long-term advertising designed to enhance low-involvement learning is another useful technique for gaining acceptance. Extensive advertising with strong emphasis on attracting attention can also be effective. The primary objective of these two approaches is not to "sell" the brand; rather, they seek to move the brand into the evoked set. Then, when a purchase situation arises, the consumer will seek additional information on this brand.

SUMMARY

Following problem recognition, consumers may engage in extensive internal and external search, limited internal and external search, or only internal search. Information may be sought on (1) the appropriate *evaluative criteria* for the solution of the problem, (2) the existence of various *alternative solutions,* and (3) the *performance* of each alternative solution on each evaluative criterion.

Most consumers, when faced with a problem, can recall a limited number of brands that they feel are probably acceptable solutions. These acceptable brands, the *evoked set,* are the initial ones that the consumer seeks additional information on during the remaining internal and external search process. Therefore, marketers are very concerned that their brands fall within the evoked set of most members of their target market.

Consumer internal information (information stored in memory) may have been actively acquired in previous searches and personal experiences or it may have been passively acquired through low-involvement learning. In addition to their own *memory,* consumers can seek information from four major types of external sources: (1) *personal sources,* such as friends and family; (2) *independent sources,* such as consumer groups, paid professionals, and government agencies; (3) *marketing sources,* such as sales personnel and advertising; and (4) *experiential sources,* such as direct product inspection or trial.

The Internet is changing consumer information search in ways that are not yet fully understood. However, millions of households use the Internet to seek information about companies and products. Marketers must maintain well designed Web sites, referred to as home pages or Internet Presence Sites. In addition, firms are increasingly using the Internet as an advertising medium.

Explicit external information search *after* problem recognition is limited. This emphasizes the need to communicate effectively with consumers prior to problem recognition. Characteristics of the market, the product, the consumer, and the situation interact to influence the level of search.

It is often suggested that consumers generally should engage in relatively extensive external search prior to purchasing an item. However, this view ignores the fact that information search is not free. It takes time, energy, money, and can often require giving up more desirable activities. Therefore, consumers should engage in external search only to the extent that the expected benefits such as a lower price or a more satisfactory purchase outweigh the expected costs.

Sound marketing strategy takes into account the nature of information search engaged in by the target market. The level of search and the brand's position in or out of the evoked set are two key dimensions. Based on these two dimensions, six potential information strategies are suggested: (1) *maintenance,* (2) *disrupt,* (3) *capture,* (4) *intercept,* (5) *preference,* and (6) *acceptance*.

KEY TERMS

INTERNET EXERCISES

1. Find and describe a magazine ad that is particularly effective at causing readers to consult a Web site. Why is it effective?
2. Use the Internet to find information on (*i*) the appropriate evaluative criteria, (*ii*) the available alternatives, and (*iii*) the performance characteristics of the following:
   a. Skis
   b. Sports cars
   c. Diets
   d. Vacation resorts
3. Visit the Web sites of three firms in each of the following product categories. Report on the quality of the information provided at each site
   a. Backpacks
   b. Hotels
   c. Rental cars
   d. Skis
   e. Hot sauces
   f. Fruits
4. Describe three Internet shopping services.
5. Click on three banner ads for similar products. Describe where you encountered the banner ads and evaluate each ad.
6. Visit an Internet store. Compare the information available at that store with the information available at a similar outlet in a mall.

DDB NEEDHAM LIFESTYLE DATA ANALYSES

1. Based on the DDB Needham data, what characterizes one who is likely to read ingredient labels carefully? What are the marketing implications of this? What are the regulatory implications?
2. Examine the DDB Needham data in Tables 1 through 7. What characterizes one who is likely to be confused by nutrition labeling? What are the marketing implications of this?

REVIEW QUESTIONS

1. When does *information search* occur? What is the difference between internal and external information search?
2. What kind of information is sought in an external search for information?
3. What are *evaluative criteria* and how do they relate to information search?
4. How does a consumer's *awareness set* influence information search?
5. What roles do the *evoked set, inert set,* and *inept set* play in a consumer's information search?
6. What are the primary sources of information available to consumers?
7. What is the *Internet?*
8. What is an *Internet Presence Site?*
9. What is the difference between an active and a passive Web site?
10. When should company or brand Web sites be extensive and, if applicable, interactive?
11. What is a *bot?*
12. How do *nonsearchers, information searchers,* and *extended information searchers* differ in their search for information?
13. What factors might influence the search effort of consumers who are essentially one-stop shoppers? How do these factors differ in terms of how they influence information searchers and extended information searchers?
14. What factors have to be considered in the total cost of the information search? How might these factors be different for different consumers?
15. Explain how different *market characteristics* affect information search.
16. How do different *consumer characteristics* influence a consumer's information search effort?
17. How do *product characteristics* influence a consumer's information search effort?
18. How do *situational characteristics* influence a consumer's information search effort?

19. Describe the information search characteristics that should lead to each of the following strategies:
    a. Maintenance
    b. Disrupt
    c. Capture
    d. Intercept
    e. Preference
    f. Acceptance
20. Describe each of the strategies listed in Question 19.

DISCUSSION QUESTIONS

21. Pick a product/brand that you believe would require each strategy in Table 15-2 (six products in total). Justify your selection. Develop a specific marketing strategy for each (six strategies in total).
22. How would you utilize Figure 15-5 to develop a marketing communications strategy for a provider of the services listed?
23. Of the products shown in Figure 15-3, which product class is most likely to exhibit the most brand switching? Explain your answer in terms of the information provided in Figure 15-3.
24. Describe a product and brand that you believe should have an extensive Web site (not necessarily active). Justify your choice and indicate in detail what the site should contain.
25. How should a firm determine if it should have an active Web site?
26. What information sources do students on your campus use when purchasing the following? Consider the various sources listed in Figure 15-4 in developing your answer. Do you think there will be individual differences? Why?
    a. Cosmetics
    b. Car repairs
    c. Upper-division electives
    d. Cold remedies
    e. Weekend entertainment
    f. A pet
    g. Jewelry
    h. Father's Day gifts
27. What factors contribute to the size of the awareness set, evoked set, inert set, and inept set?
28. Discuss factors that may contribute to external information search and factors that act to reduce external search for information before purchase of the following:
    a. Automobile repairs
    b. Life insurance
    c. Restaurant for a special meal
    d. Cold medicine
    e. Sports drinks
    f. Counseling services
29. Is it ever in the best interest of a marketer to encourage potential customers to carry out an extended prepurchase search? Why or why not?
30. What implications for marketing strategy does Figure 15-2 suggest?
31. What role, if any, should the government play in ensuring that consumers have easy access to relevant product information? How should it accomplish this?
32. Describe a recent purchase in which you engaged in extensive search and one in which you did little prepurchase search. What factors caused the difference?
33. What is your awareness set, evoked set, inert set, and inept set for the following? In what ways, if any, do you think your sets will differ from the average member of your class? Why?
    a. Laptop computers
    b. Mouthwash
    c. Mountain bikes
    d. Shoe stores
    e. Perfume
    f. Hair stylists
    g. Restaurants
    h. Detergents

APPLICATION ACTIVITIES

34. Develop an appropriate questionnaire and complete Question 26 using information from 10 students not in your class. Prepare a report discussing the marketing implications of your findings.
35. For the same products listed in Question 33, ask 10 students to list all the brands they are aware of in each product category. Then have them indicate which ones they might buy (evoked set), which

ones they are indifferent toward (inert set), and which brands of those they listed they strongly dislike and would not purchase (inept set). What are the marketing implications of your results?

36. Develop a short questionnaire designed to measure the information search consumers engage in prior to purchasing an expensive recreational or entertainment item or service. Your questionnaire should include measures of types of information sought, as well as sources that provide this information. Also include measures of the relevant consumer characteristics that might influence information search, as well as some measure of past experience with the products. Then interview two recent purchasers of each product, using the questionnaire you have developed. Analyze each consumer's response and classify each consumer in terms of information search. What are the marketing implications of your results?

37. For each strategy in Table 15-2, find one brand that appears to be following that strategy. Describe in detail how it is implementing the strategy.

38. Develop a questionnaire to determine which college students view as positive and which they view as negative. Measure the shopping effort associated with each type. Explain your overall results and any individual differences you find.

REFERENCES

1. "The 1998 CASIE Awards Finalists," *Advertising Age,* October 12, 1998, special section.
2. An outstanding discussion of the trade-off consumers make between memory-based decisions (internal search) and external search is in J. R. Bettman, M. F. Luce, and J. W. Payne, "Constructive Consumer Choice Processes," *Journal of Consumer Research,* December 1998, pp. 187–217.
3. P. H. Bloch, D. L. Sherrell, and N. M. Ridgway, "Consumer Search," *Journal of Consumer Research,* June 1986, pp. 119–26; and P. H. Bloch, N. M. Ridgway, and D. L. Sherrell, "Extending the Concept of Shopping," *Journal of the Academy of Marketing Science,* Winter 1989, pp. 13–22.
4. For a more comprehensive view, see R. Lawson, "Consumer Decision Making within a Goal-Driven Framework," *Psychology & Marketing,* August 1997, pp. 427–49.
5. See D. R. Lehmann and Y. Pan, "Context Effects, New Brand Entry, and Consideration Sets," *Journal of Marketing Research,* August 1994, pp. 364–74; I. Sinha, "A Conceptual Model of Situation Type on Consumer Choice Behavior and Consideration Sets," in *Advances in Consumer Research XXI,* ed. C. T. Allen and D. R. John (Provo, UT: Association for Consumer Research, 1994), pp. 477–82; K. Jedidi, R. Kohli, and W. S. DeSarbo, "Consideration Sets in Conjoint Analysis," *Journal of Marketing Research,* August 1996, pp. 364–72; M. D. Johnson and D. R. Lehmann, "Consumer Experience and Consideration Sets for Brands and Product Categories," in *Advances in Consumer Research XXIV,* ed. M. Bruck and D. J. MacInnis (Provo, UT: Association for Consumer Research, 1997), pp. 295–300; and S. Shapiro, D. J. MacInnis, and S. E. Heckler, "The Effects of Incidental Ad Exposure on the Formation of Consideration Sets," *Journal of Consumer Research,* June 1997, pp. 94–104.
6. R. R. Brand and J. J. Cronin, "Consumer-Specific Determinants of the Size of Retail Choice Sets," *Journal of Services Marketing,* no. 1 (1997), pp. 19–38.
7. D. Butler and A. M. Abernethy, "Information Consumers Seek from Advertisements," *Journal of Professional Services Marketing* 10, no. 2 (1994), pp. 75–92.
8. See S. C. Mooy and H. S. J. Robben, "How Consumers Learn From and About Products," in *Advances in Consumer Research XXV,* ed. J. W. Alba and J. W. Hutchinson (Provo, UT: Association for Consumer Research, 1998), pp. 318–23.
9. C. B. Jarvis, "An Exploratory Investigation of Consumers' Evaluations of External Information Sources in Prepurchase Search," in *Advances in Consumer Research XXV,* ed. J. W. Alba and J. W. Hutchinson (Provo, UT: Association for Consumer Research, 1998), pp. 446–51.
10. For a review and conflicting evidence, see A. A. Wright and J. G. Lynch, Jr., "Communications Effects of Advertising versus Direct Experience When Both Search and Experience Attributes Are Present," *Journal of Consumer Research,* March 1995, pp. 108–18.
11. See C. F. Mela, S. Gupta, and D. R. Lehmann, "The Long-Term Impact of Promotion and Advertising on Consumer Brand Choice," *Journal of Marketing Research,* May 1997, pp. 248–61; and M. J. Sirgy et al., "Does Television Viewership Play a Role in the Perception of Quality of Life?" *Journal of Advertising,* Spring 1998, pp. 125–42.
12. See L. M. Lodish et al., "How T.V. Advertising Works," *Journal of Marketing Research,* May 1995, pp. 125–39; L. D. Gibson, "What Can One TV Exposure Do?" *Journal of Advertising Research,* March 1996, pp. 9–18; and D. R. Riskey, "How T.V. Advertising Works," *Journal of Marketing Research,* May 1997, pp. 292–93.
13. See D. L. Hoffman and T. P. Novak, "Marketing in Hypermedia Computer-Mediated Environments," *Journal of Marketing,* July 1996, pp. 50–68; J. Alba et al., "Interactive Home Shopping," *Journal of Marketing,* July 1997, pp. 38–53; A. Peterson, S. Balasubramanian, and B. J. Bronnenberg, "Exploring the Implications of the Internet for Consumer Marketing"; J. Deighton, "Commentary"; and R. A. Burke, "Do You See What I See?" all in *Journal of the Academy of Marketing Science,* Fall 1997, pp. 329–46, 347–51, and 352–60.
14. J. L. McQuivey, "On-Line Retail Strategies," *The Forrester Report,* November 1998, p. 5.

15. Unless otherwise referenced, this section is based on *Interactive Media Study* (Arlington Heights, IL: Market Facts' TeleNation, October 1998).
16. T. E. Miller, "Segmenting the Internet," *American Demographics,* July 1996, pp. 48–51.
17. L. M. Maddox and D. Mehta, "The Role and Effect of Web Addresses in Advertising," *Journal of Advertising Research,* March 1997, pp. 47–59.
18. See S. C. McDonald, "The Once and Future Web," *Journal of Advertising Research,* March 1997, pp. 21–28.
19. H. Green, "A Cybershopper's Best Friend," *Business Week,* May 4, 1998, p. 84.
20. K. Maddox, "Jupiter Unveils Brand Action Marketing Plan," *Advertising Age,* January 1998, p. 24.
21. J. Eighmey, "Profiling User Responses to Commercial Web Sites," *Journal of Advertising Research,* May 1997, pp. 59–66; R. A. Oliva, "Help Them Find It—Fast," *Marketing Management,* Winter 1998, pp. 36–39; and S. Ghose and W. Dou, "Interactive Functions and Their Impacts on the Appeal of Internet Presence Sites," *Journal of Advertising Research,* March 1998, pp. 29–43.
22. Internet Advertising Bureau Website, www.iab.net, February 3, 2000.
23. See K. Maddox, "P&G's Plan," *Advertising Age*, August 17, 1998, p. 1.
24. B. Synder, "Unilever Speaks UP about Internet Strategy," *Advertising Age,* August 17, 1998, p. 30.
25. R. A. Westbrook and C. Farnell, "Patterns of Information Source Usage among Durable Goods Buyers," *Journal of Marketing Research,* August 1979, pp. 303–12; and J. E. Urbany, P. R. Dickson, and W. L. Wilkie, "Buyer Uncertainty and Information Search," *Journal of Consumer Research,* September 1989, pp. 208–215.
26. Urbany, Dickson, and Wilkie, footnote 25; and *Warranties Rule Consumer Follow-Up* (Washington D.C.: Federal Trade Commission, 1984), p. 26.
27. Ibid.
28. G. Katona and E. Mueller, "A Study of Purchase Decisions," in *Consumer Behavior: The Dynamics of Consumer Reaction,* ed. L. Clark (New York University Press, 1955), pp. 30–87; J. Newman and R. Staelin, "Prepurchase Information Seeking for New Cars and Major Household Appliances," *Journal of Marketing Research,* August 1972, pp. 249–57; J. Claxton, J. Fry, and B. Portis, "A Taxonomy of Prepurchase Information Gathering Patterns," *Journal of Consumer Research,* December 1974, pp. 35–42; G. C. Kiel and R. A. Layton, "Dimensions of Consumer Information Seeking Behavior," *Journal of Marketing Research,* May 1981, pp. 233–39; J. B. Freiden and R. E. Goldsmith, "Prepurchase Information-Seeking for Professional Services," *Journal of Services Marketing,* Winter 1989, pp. 45–55; G. N. Souter and M. M. McNeil, *Journal of Professional Services Marketing* 11, no. 2 (1995), pp. 45–60; and Urbany, Dickson, and Wilkie, footnote 25. See also B. L. Bagus, "The Consumer Durable Replacement Buyer," *Journal of Marketing,* January 1991, pp. 42–51.
29. G. Punj, "Presearch Decision Making in Consumer Durable Purchases," *Journal of Consumer Marketing,* Winter 1987, pp. 71–82.
30. For more elaborate models, see P. A. Titus and P. B. Everett, "The Consumer Retail Search Process," *Journal of the Academy of Marketing Science,* Spring 1995, pp. 106–19; S. Moorthy, B. T. Ratchford, and D. Talukdar, "Consumer Information Search Revisited," *Journal of Consumer Research,* March 1997, pp. 263–277; and S. Putrevu and B. T. Ratchford, "A Model of Search Behavior with an Application to Grocery Shopping," *Journal of Retailing,* no. 4 (1997), pp. 463–86. See also H. Marmorstein, D. Grewal, and R. P. H. Fishe, "The Value of Time Spent in Price-Comparison Shopping," *Journal of Consumer Research,* June 1992, pp. 52–61; and B. T. Ratchford and N. Srinivasan, "An Empirical Investigation of Returns to Search," *Marketing Science,* Winter 1993, pp. 73–87.
31. J. Gregan-Paxton and D. R. John, "Are Young Children Adaptive Decision Makers?" *Journal of Consumer Research,* March 1995, pp. 567–80.
32. For a different model, see J. G. Blodgett, D. J. Hill, and G. Stone, "A Model of the Determinants of Retail Search," in *Advances in Consumer Research XXII,* ed. F. R. Kardes and M. Sujan (Provo, UT: Association for Consumer Research, 1995), pp. 518–23.
33. D. R. Lichtenstein, N. M. Ridgway, and R. G. Netemeyer, "Price Perceptions and Consumer Shopping Behavior," *Journal of Marketing Research,* May 1993, pp. 234–45.
34. M. N. Bergen, S. Dutta, and S. M. Shugan, "Branded Variants," *Journal of Marketing Research,* February 1996, pp. 9–19.
35. D. Grewal and H. Marmorstein, "Market Price Variation, Perceived Price Variation, and Consumers' Price Search Decisions for Durable Goods," *Journal of Consumer Research,* December 1994, pp. 453–60.
36. See B. G. C. Dellaert, "Investigating Consumers' Tendency to Combine Multiple Shopping Purposes and Destinations," *Journal of Marketing Research,* May 1998, pp. 177–89.
37. See C. Moorman, "Market-Level Effects of Information," *Journal of Marketing Research,* February 1998, pp. 82–98.
38. See C. M. Fisher and C. J. Anderson, "The Relationship between Consumer Attitudes and Frequency of Advertising in Newspapers for Hospitals," *Journal of Hospital Marketing* 7, no. 2 (1993), pp. 139–56.
39. S. Widrick and E. Fram, "Identifying Negative Products," *Journal of Consumer Marketing,* no. 2 (1983), pp. 59–66.
40. S. E. Beatty and S. M. Smith, "External Search Effort," *Journal of Consumer Research,* June 1987, pp. 83–95.
41. C. A. Fiske et al., "The Relationship between Knowledge and Search," in *Advances in Consumer Research XXI,* ed. C. T. Allen and D. R. John (Provo, UT: Association for Consumer Research, 1994), pp. 43–50. See also L.-T. Bei and R. Heslin, "The *Consumer Reports* Mindset," in *Advances in Consumer Research XXIV,* ed. M. Bruck and D. J. MacInnis (Provo, UT: Association for Consumer Research, 1997), pp. 151–58.
42. See J. R. Lumpkin; "Shopping Orientation Segmentation of the Elderly Consumer," *Journal of the Academy of Marketing Science,* Spring 1985, pp. 271–89; T. Williams, M. Slama, and J. Rogers, "Behavioral Characteristics of the Recreational Shopper," *Journal of Academy of Marketing Science,* Summer 1985, pp. 307–16; and J. R. Lumpkin, J. M. Hawes, and W. R. Darden, "Shopping Patterns of the Rural Consumer," *Journal of Business Research,* February 1986, pp. 63–81.

43. See G. Wang, S. M. Fletcher, and D. H. Carley, "Consumer Factors Influencing the Use of Nutrition Information Sources," in *Advances in Consumer Research XXII,* ed. F. R. Kardes and M. Sujan (Provo, UT: Association for Consumer Research, 1995), pp. 573–81; and U. M. Dholakia, "Involvement-Response Models of Joint Effects," in *Advances in Consumer Research XXV,* ed. J. W. Alba and J. W. Hutchinson (Provo, UT: Association for Consumer Research, 1998), pp. 499–506.
44. T. H. Dodd, B. E. Pinkleton, and A. W. Gustafson, *Psychology & Marketing,* May 1996, pp. 291–304.
45. G. R. Dowling and R. Staelin, "A Model of Perceived Risk and Intended Risk-Handling Activity," *Journal of Consumer Research,* June 1994, pp. 119–34. See also Turley and LeBlanc, footnote 5; and J. B. Smith and J. M. Bristor, "Uncertainty Orientation," *Psychology & Marketing,* November 1994, pp. 587–607.
46. K. B. Murray, "A Test of Services Marketing Theory," *Journal of Marketing,* January 1991, pp. 10–25.
47. See D. S. Sundaram and R. D. Taylor, "An Investigation of External Search Effort," in *Advances in Consumer Research XXV,* ed. J. W. Alba and J. W. Hutchinson (Provo, UT: Association for Consumer Research, 1998), pp. 440–45.
48. "L&M Lights Up Again," *Marketing and Media Decisions,* February 1984, p. 69.
49. L. L. Garber, "The Package Appearance in Choice," in *Advances in Consumer Research XXII,* ed. F. R. Kardes and M. Sujan (Provo, UT: Association for Consumer Research, 1995), pp. 653–60.
50. R. Gray, "Chrysler Hinges Price on Popularity," *Advertising Age,* October 5, 1981, p. 7.

558

Courtesy Sunbeam Corporation.

Alternative Evaluation and Selection

Sunbeam Appliance Company successfully redesigned its many lines of small kitchen appliances. The redesign of its food processor line illustrates the four-stage process used:

1. A *consumer usage and attitude survey* was used to determine how and for what purpose products in the product category are used, frequency of use, brand ownership, brand awareness, and attitudes toward the product.
2. A *consumer attribute and benefit survey* was used to provide importance ratings of product attributes and benefits desired from the product category, along with perceptions of the degree to which each brand provides the various attributes and benefits.
3. A *conjoint analysis study* (a technique described in this chapter) was used to provide data on the structure of consumers' preferences for product features and their willingness to trade one feature for more of another feature. Conjoint analysis provides the relative importance *each* consumer attaches to various levels of each potential product feature. This allows individuals with similar preference structures to be grouped into market segments.
4. *Product line sales and market share simulations* were used to determine the best set of food processors to bring to the market. Based on the preference structures and sizes of the market segments discovered in step 3 and the perceived characteristics of competing brands, the market share of various Sunbeam product sets was estimated using computer simulations.

The above process involved interviewing hundreds of product category users. Twelve different product attributes were tested and four distinct market segments were uncovered. The existing product line was replaced with four new models (down from six) targeted at three of the four segments. The results were increased market share, reduced costs, and increased profitability.[1]

FIGURE 16-1 Alternative Evaluation and Selection Process

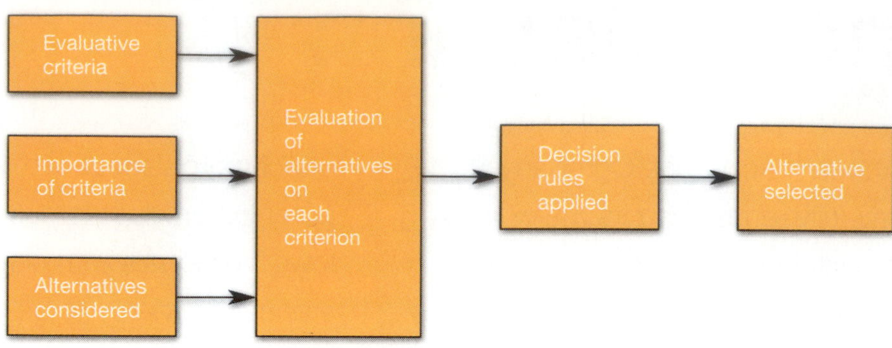

The opening example describes Sunbeam's successful analysis of consumers' desired product benefits (evaluative criteria) and the manner in which they choose between products with differing combinations of benefits. The process by which consumers evaluate and choose among alternatives is illustrated in Figure 16-1.

We will organize our discussion around four basic areas. First, we will provide an overview of the process consumers use to select among alternatives. Then, the nature and characteristics of evaluative criteria (the benefits the product should provide) will be described. After examining evaluative criteria, we focus on the ability of consumers to judge the performance of products on the evaluative criteria. Finally, we examine the decision rules that consumers use in selecting one alternative from those considered.

It is important to remember that many purchases involve little or no evaluation of alternatives. Nominal decisions do not require the evaluation of any alternatives. The last purchase is repeated without considering other information. Limited decisions may involve comparing a few brands (small evoked set) on one or two dimensions (I'll buy Heinz or Del Monte catsup, depending on which is cheaper at Safeway).

HOW CONSUMERS MAKE CHOICES

Any attempt to describe a complex, nonlinear process such as consumer choice necessarily simplifies it and removes much of its richness. Thus, our discussion will make consumer choice seem more logical, structured, rational, and deliberate than it often is. Fortunately, we have all made numerous consumer choices and we know that they are frequently circular, emotional, incomplete, and based on expediency rather than optimality. We also know that the situation plays an important role in the processes we use to make consumer choices. For example, when we are tired or hurried, we are very likely to use different choice processes than we would if we had more energy or time. Consumer Insight 16-1 illustrates how prior purchases in a product category affect the decisions to make current purchases in that category.

In this section, we will examine three aspects of consumer choice: attribute-based versus attitude-based processes, affective choice, and the processes consumers use to construct choices.

Consumer Insight 16-1

Mental Budgeting and Consumer Decisions

Research indicates that consumers allocate their discretionary funds into mental accounts such as entertainment and household expenses. They then track expenditures against these accounts and adjust current purchases based on the balances left in the accounts. Since it is not possible to predict consumption opportunities and needs, this process leads to the overconsumption of some and the underconsumption of others. Consider the following examples.

> Consumer A has mentally allocated some funds for clothing and anticipates buying slacks. During a shopping trip, this consumer decides that her current slacks are still quite stylish. Instead of buying slacks, she uses the money mentally allocated to this purpose to buy a sweater she would not have purchased under normal circumstances.
>
> Consumer B splurges and uses most of her monthly entertainment budget on an evening at the theater. The next week friends ask her to join them for a night on the town. She declines because she had "spent too much money" on the theater evening. However, she could easily afford the night on the town with her friends and would have enjoyed it.

In both cases described above, the consumers made suboptimal decisions because they segregated their financial resources into mental accounts and were reluctant to reallocate to or from other accounts. Thus, Consumer A purchased an unneeded sweater because her "clothing" account had unexpected excess funds while Consumer B missed a fun evening because her "entertainment" account was depleted.

Since consumers have limited time, energy, and capacity for mental (or written) budgets, purchases that are easy to place into an existing budget category are more likely to be tracked and categorized than are less clearcut purchases. For example, attending the theater is easy to classify as entertainment while attending a charity dinner and auction is less clearcut. Easily tracked, representative events are more likely to produce over- or underconsumption.

Critical Thinking Questions

Given that mental budgeting is a common practice and that consumers are reluctant to reallocate resources across "accounts":

1. What are the marketing implications for existing consumer products/services such as clothing, household items, restaurants, and so forth?
2. What are the marketing implications for new-product categories such as Internet provider services?

Source: C. Heath and J. B. Soll, "Mental Budgeting and Consumer Decisions," *Journal of Consumer Research,* June 1996, pp. 40–52.

Attribute-Based versus Attitude-Based Choice Processes

Consider the following two processes a consumer might use to purchase an answering machine:

> *Process 1:* The consumer remembers that the Casio his last roommate had seemed to work well and looked "good," his parents had a Toshiba that also worked well but was rather large and bulky, and his old Samsung had not performed as well as he had expected. He goes to a store and gathers price, recording time, and ease of remote access information on each of these brands. He mentally ranks each brand on these three attributes and his general impression of their quality. Based on these evaluations, he makes a choice.
>
> *Process 2:* The consumer remembers that the Casio his last roommate had seemed to work well and looked "good," his parents had a Toshiba that also worked well but was rather large and bulky, and his old Samsung had not performed as well as he had expected. At the store, he sees that the Casio and Toshiba are about the same price and decides to buy the Casio.

The first example above is attribute-based choice. **Attribute-based choice** *requires the knowledge of specific attributes at the time the choice is made and involves attribute-by-attribute comparisons across brands.* The second example above is attitude-based choice. **Attitude-based choice** *involves the use of general attitudes, summary impressions, intuitions, or heuristics; no attribute-by-attribute comparisons are made at the time of choice.*[2] There can also be combinations of these forms. A common combination would be for overall preferences to be formed based on attitude-based processing, with the final choice adding a brand-by-brand comparison on the price attribute.

Attribute-based choices require the comparison of each specific attribute across all the brands considered. This is a much more effortful and time-consuming process than the global comparisons made when attitude-based choice is involved. It also tends to produce a more nearly optimal decision.

Motivation, information availability, and individual and situational factors interact to determine which choice process will be used. As one would suspect, the greater the motivation to make an optimal decision, the more likely an attribute-based choice will be made. In general, the importance of making an optimal decision increases with the value of the item being considered and consequences of a nonoptimal decision. Thus, attribute-based processing is more likely for a laptop computer or an athletic shoe for a marathoner than it is for an inexpensive calculator or an athletic shoe to wear around campus.

The more specific attribute information a consumer has in memory and the easier it is to access complete attribute-by-brand information, the more likely that attribute-based processing will be used. This can be used by brands that have important attribute-based advantages but that lack strong reputations or images in the target market. The approach would be to make attribute-based comparisons easy by providing the information in an easy to process format such as a brand-by-attribute matrix. Such a matrix could be presented in ads, on packages, in point-of-purchase displays, in brochures, and/or on the firm or brand's Web site. A firm using such a strategy should structure the information so that its brand will be the focal point of comparison. This could be done by listing it first, perhaps in bold or colored type.

A variety of situations influence which choice approach is most likely. As we saw in Chapter 13, task definition influences the importance assigned to many purchases, with gift purchases often being assigned more importance than similar purchases for oneself. Time pressure is a major determinant of the choice process used, with increasing time pressures producing more use of attitude-based decisions. Individuals also differ in their tendency to use each type of choice process. Individuals with a high need for cognition (see Chapter 10) are more likely to make attribute-based choices.

It is important to note that many decisions, even for important products, appear to be attitude-based. Recall from the previous chapter that most individuals collect very little product information from external sources immediately before a purchase. However, many others do. Thus, marketers for most products and services, even expensive, important ones, have a dual task. They must provide information and experiences that produce a strong attitude-based position (for those consumers making an attitude-based choice) *and* they must provide performance levels and supporting information that will result in preference among those consumers making attribute-based choices. Illustration 16-1 contains an ad that encourages attitude-based choice.

Affective Choice

Consider a consumer buying an alarm clock. She inspects several models, noticing many differences among them. Some models have a snooze-alarm feature, some don't. Some have a battery

Courtesy Kohler Company.

ILLUSTRATION 16-1

This ad encourages attitude-based choice by encouraging the consumer to form a general attitude or summary impression that Kohler faucets are bold, stylish, and modern.

backup, others don't. The models also vary on the wake-to-music or wake-to-alarm feature, top-mounted versus side controls, push-button versus rotary or sliding switches, lighted alarm-set indicator, automatic FM frequency control, the type of finish, and the price. She reviews her relative preference for these diverse features, and chooses the model that gives her the best combination of the desired features.

Now consider her buying a dress for an upcoming big social event. Scanning a rack full of dresses in a store, she pulls out a few that seemed nice. One of them particularly caught her eye: she tries it on, and thinks she looks great in it. She tries another one which she thought made her look too conservative. A third one made her look too sexy. Somehow, the first one looked so right for her: a few more minutes of contemplation about what a great impression she would make donning that dress in the party, and she has made up her mind about that dress.[3]

The purchase of the dress is primarily an **affective choice.** Such choices do not lend themselves well to either the attribute-based or the attitude-based choice approaches described in the previous section. Affective choices tend to be more holistic in nature. The brand is not decomposed into distinct components each of which is evaluated separately from the whole. The evaluation of such products is generally focused on the way they will make the user *feel* as they are used. The evaluation itself is often based exclusively or primarily on the immediate emotional response to the product or service:

I'm getting married, and we were looking for a place to have the wedding and we had been to about five or six places . . . this (place) was not quite right . . . and this other place was not quite right . . . but then we went to a place called The Highlander in Glens Falls. I went in the lobby and I knew immediately that this was right. It was immaculately clean, the floor was not just marble but inlaid different types of patterns on the floor . . . its restaurant, the doors were lead and glass and you just knew that this was right . . . You go in there and sure enough they had a wedding coordinator.[4]

Decisions based on affect are said to use the "How do I feel about it" heuristic or decision rule. Consumers imagine or picture using the product or service and evaluate the feeling that this use will produce.[5] For example, a consumer choosing between a weekend at a bed-and-breakfast on the beach and a weekend in a nice hotel in a nearby city might imagine each episode and "see how they feel." The decision would then be made largely or completely on these expected feelings.

Affective choice is most likely when the underlying motive is consummatory rather than instrumental. **Consummatory motives** *underlie behaviors that are intrinsically rewarding to the individual involved.* **Instrumental motives** *activate behaviors designed to achieve a second goal.* For example, one person might read a best-seller for the pleasure of reading the book (consummatory motive) while another might read the same book to be able to appear "with it" to his or her friends (instrumental motive).

Marketers are just beginning to study affect-based decisions.[6] However, it is clear that such decisions require different strategies than the more cognitive decisions generally considered in marketing. For those decisions that are likely to be affective in nature (largely triggered by consumptive motives), marketers should design products and services that will provide positive experiences. They also should help consumers visualize how they will feel during and after the consumption experience. This is particularly important for new brands or products and services. Consumers who have experience with a product or brand have a basis for imagining the affective response it will produce. Those who do not may incorrectly predict the feelings the experience will produce. For example, individuals imagining a whitewater rafting trip may conclude that it would produce feelings of terror rather than exhilaration. Illustration 16-2 contains an ad that helps consumers envision the positive experiences and accompanying feelings they would have at a Beaches resort.

Constructing Consumer Choices[7]

A substantial amount of research on consumer choice has assumed a rational decision maker with well-defined preferences that do not depend on how the options are presented. Each option or alternative in a choice set is assumed to have a value to the consumer that depends only on the characteristics of that option (Option A's absolute value will be the same when compared to Options B and C as when it is compared to any other set of alternatives). The consumer is also assumed to have sufficient skill to calculate which option will maximize his or her value and will choose on this basis. This approach is referred to as *rational choice theory*. The task in rational choice theory is to *identify* or discover the one optimal choice for the decision confronting the decision maker. The decision maker simply collects information on the levels of the attributes of the alternatives, applies preexisting values to those levels, applies the appropriate choice rule, and the superior option is revealed.

While rational choice theory helps us understand many aspects of consumer behavior, it is clearly incomplete. An emerging view is that *many choices are constructed by the consumer as the decision is made.* All consumers have **bounded rationality**—*a limited capacity for processing information.* In addition, consumers often have goals that are different from, or in addition to, selecting the optimal alternative. Therefore, for many decisions consumers do not engage in a strictly rational choice. Instead, they construct a decision

Courtesy Sandals Resorts.

ILLUSTRATION 16-2

In affective choice, consumers mentally anticipate the feelings a consumption experience will produce and base their choice on these anticipated feelings. This ad helps consumers visualize the experiences and thus feelings they will have at this resort.

process that is appropriate for the situation at hand. Rather than simply discovering the best existing alternative, the superior alternative is constructed as the consumer moves through the choice process. This is called **constructive choice.**

Constructive choice is a complex process that we are just beginning to understand. While there are many aspects to this process, we will focus on the currently most useful feature—metagoals.

Consumer Choice Metagoals Consumer choice goals are usually described in terms such as getting "the least expensive calculator with the functions I need," "getting a haircut before class that looks good and costs no more than average," "selecting the best running shoes for my training program," and so forth. These are the specific purchase goals or outcomes the consumer wants to obtain. A **metagoal** refers to *the general nature of the outcome being sought*. The purchase goals just described are examples of a metagoal of *maximizing the accuracy of the decision*. This is the only metagoal assumed in rational choice theory. However, other metagoals exist. Consumers often seek to *minimize the cognitive effort required for the decision*. This is often the goal in nominal and limited decision making. However, it can also play an important role in extended decision making as well. Consumers seeking to minimize effort tend to use simple choice rules, consider fewer alternatives, place more importance on the dominant attribute, and evaluate fewer attributes of each alternative.[8] Consumers may also delay or avoid the decision.[9]

Choices that involve conflicts between valued goals such as safety versus performance in purchasing an automobile or an attractive, low-effort lawn versus the use of pesticides and herbicides can generate significant negative emotions.[10] Thus, another consumer metagoal is to *minimize the experience of negative emotion while making the decision*. One strategy consumers use for this purpose is to avoid or delay the decision and stay with the status quo.

A fourth metagoal is to *maximize the ease with which a decision can be justified*. Consumers are social beings and often feel compelled to justify a decision to others or to themselves. This is particularly true for luxury items and items that are different or more extravagant than those used by one's reference groups. However, one may often feel a need to justify the purchase of common, functional products: "I see you have a new lawn mower. Why did you choose a Honda?" Anticipating the need for such justifications can affect how a consumer makes the initial decision.

These metagoals are not mutually exclusive. In fact, decisions are characterized by multiple goals with differing levels of importance. Further, the relative importance of the goals may change as the consumer constructs the decision process. For example, a consumer deciding to purchase a lawn mower may begin with maximizing the accuracy of the decision as the primary goal. However, as the consumer learns of the vast number of brands, models, and features, minimizing effort may become increasingly important. This importance may increase even more as the consumer spends more time on the choice. As the consumer learns of incompatible features (the model that pollutes the least costs the most and does not perform as well as others) minimizing negative emotion may become more salient. As the consumer moves to the final choice, ease of justification may dominate.

Marketers must understand the metagoals that are likely to be used by consumers purchasing their products and develop product features and marketing communications consistent with those metagoals. It is particularly important for marketers to utilize strategies that assist the consumer with the effort, emotion, and justification of metagoals, as these are the ones most firms have ignored while focusing on rational choice theory.

EVALUATIVE CRITERIA

As the prior discussion described, consumers often make decisions based on affect, on overall attitude toward the brand, or to minimize effort or negative emotion. Many of these types of decisions involve very little consideration of specific product features. However, most decisions involve an evaluation of the likely performance of the product or service on one or more dimensions. **Evaluative criteria** are *the various dimensions, features or benefits a consumer looks for in response to a specific problem*. Before purchasing a computer, you might be concerned with cost, speed, memory, operating system, display, and warranty. These would be your evaluative criteria. Someone else could approach the same purchase with an entirely different set of evaluative criteria.

Nature of Evaluative Criteria

Evaluative criteria are typically product features or attributes associated either with benefits desired by customers or the costs they must incur. Thus, many consumers who want to avoid cavities use toothpaste that contains fluoride. For these consumers, fluoride is an evaluative criterion associated with the benefit cavity prevention. In this case, the evaluative criterion and the desired benefit are not identical and fluoride is important as a feature only to the extent that it helps prevent cavities. In such cases, marketers should

Courtesy Tamron.

ILLUSTRATION 16-3

Consumers are interested in product features only in relation to the benefits those features provide. This ad stresses the ability of the lens to capture memories, rather than its technical characteristics.

stress the benefit the feature will provide the consumer, not just the feature itself. The ad in Illustration 16-3 focuses on the ability of the Tamron zoom lens to capture memories, not on its technical specifications.

In other situations, the product feature and the benefit or cost are the same. For example, price is often an evaluative criterion that is identical to one aspect of cost (as we will see, price can have many meanings).

As we saw earlier, products and services purchased primarily for emotional reasons may involve anticipating the effect of purchase or use on feelings rather than an analysis of product attributes per se. Likewise, a product purchased for use in a social situation often involves anticipation of the reaction of others to the product instead of an analysis of its attributes. In these cases, the anticipated feelings or reactions would be the evaluative criteria.

Evaluative criteria can differ in type, number, and importance. The *type of evaluative criteria* a consumer uses in a decision varies from *tangible* cost and performance features to *intangible* factors such as style, taste, prestige, feelings generated, and brand image.[11] Illustration 16-4 shows how two similar products stress very different types of evaluative criteria. The *Jergens* ad stresses tangible attributes and technical performance. The *Nivea* ad focuses on intangible attributes and feelings.

Evaluative criteria may exist in terms of extremes (lower price or more miles per gallon is better), limits (it must not cost more than $100; it must get more than 25 miles per gallon), or ranges (any price between $85 and $99 is acceptable).[12]

The number of evaluative criteria used depends on the product, the consumer, and the situation. For fairly simple products such as toothpaste, soap, or facial tissue, consumers

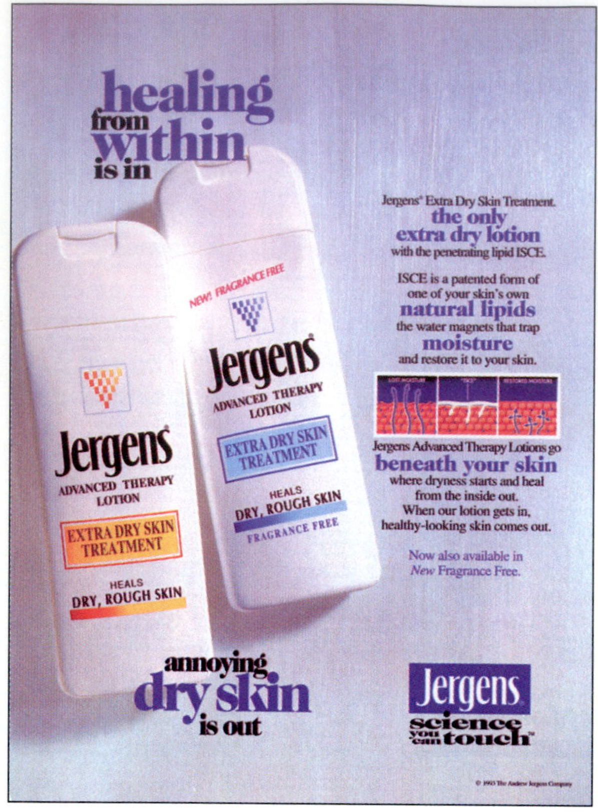

Reprinted by permission of the Andrew Jergen Company.

Courtesy Beiersdorf, Inc.

ILLUSTRATION 16-4

These ads are for the same product category but assume differing evaluative processes by consumers.

use relatively few evaluative criteria. On the other hand, the purchase of an automobile, stereo system, or house may involve numerous criteria. As we will see later, consumers often use a few criteria (price, size, and location of an apartment, for example) to reduce a large set of alternatives to a smaller number. Then, they may use a larger number of criteria to make a final choice. Characteristics of the individual (such as product familiarity and age) and characteristics of the purchase situation (such as time pressure) also influence the number of evaluative criteria considered.[13]

The importance that consumers assign to each evaluative criterion is of great interest to marketers. Three consumers could use the same six evaluative criteria shown in the following table when considering a notebook computer. However, if the importance rank they assigned each criterion varied as shown, they would likely purchase different brands.

	Importance Rank for		
Criterion	*Consumer A*	*Consumer B*	*Consumer C*
Price	**1**	6	3
Processor	5	**1**	4
Display quality	3	3	**1**
Memory	6	**2**	5
Weight	4	4	**2**
After-sale support	**2**	5	6

Consumer A is concerned primarily with cost and support services. Consumer B wants computing speed and power. Consumer C is concerned primarily with ease of use. If each of these three consumers represented a larger group of consumers, we would have three distinct market segments based on the importance assigned the same criteria. Of course, we could have other segments that consider other or additional criteria, such as a built-in modem or battery life.

The importance of evaluative criteria varies among individuals and also within the same individual across situations. For example, a consumer might consider the price of food items to be the most important attribute most of the time. However, when "in a hurry," speed of service and convenient location may be more important.[14]

The evaluative criteria, and the importance that individuals assign them, influence not only the brands selected but if and when a problem will be recognized. This, in turn, influences if and when a purchase of any type will be made. For example, consumers who attach more importance to automobile styling and product image relative to comfort and cost buy new cars more frequently than do those with the opposite importance rankings.[15]

Marketers must understand the criteria consumers use and might use to evaluate their brands for two reasons. First, as we saw in the opening example, understanding these criteria is essential for developing and/or communicating appropriate brand features to the target market. In addition, marketers frequently want to influence the evaluative criteria used by consumers.[16]

Measurement of Evaluative Criteria

Before a marketing manager or a public policy decision maker can develop a sound strategy to affect consumer decisions, he or she must determine:

- Which evaluative criteria are used by the consumer.
- How the consumer perceives the various alternatives on each criterion.
- The relative importance of each criterion.

Consumers sometimes will not or cannot verbalize their evaluative criteria for a product. Therefore, it is often difficult to determine which criteria they are using in a particular brand-choice decision, particularly if emotions or feelings are involved. This is even more of a problem when trying to determine the relative importance they attach to each evaluative criterion.

Determination of Which Evaluative Criteria Are Used To determine which criteria are used by consumers in a specific product decision, the marketing researcher can utilize either *direct* or *indirect* methods of measurement. *Direct* methods include asking consumers what information they use in a particular purchase or, in a focus group setting, observing what consumers say about products and their attributes. Of course, direct measurement techniques assume that consumers can and will provide data on the desired attributes.

In the research that led to the development of Sunbeam's new food processor line, consumers readily described their desired product features and benefits. However, direct questioning is not always as successful. For example, Hanes Corporation suffered substantial losses ($30 million) on its *L'erin* cosmetics line when, *in response to consumer interviews,* it positioned it as a functional rather than a romantic or emotional product. Eventually, the brand was successfully repositioned as glamorous and exotic, although consumers did not *express* these as desired attributes.[17]

Indirect measurement techniques differ from direct in that they assume consumers will not or cannot state their evaluative criteria. Hence, frequent use is made of indirect methods such as **projective techniques** (see Table 10-2, page 371), which allow the person to indicate the criteria someone else might use. The "someone else" is very probably the person being asked, of course, and we have indirectly determined the evaluative criteria used. This approach is particularly useful for discovering emotional-type criteria.

Perceptual mapping is another useful indirect technique for determining evaluative criteria. Consumers judge the similarity of alternative brands, then these judgments are processed via a computer to derive a perceptual map of the brands. No evaluative criteria are specified. The consumer simply ranks the similarity between all pairs of alternatives, and a perceptual configuration is derived in which the consumer's evaluative criteria are the dimensions of the configuration.

For example, consider the perceptual map of beers shown in Figure 16-2. This configuration was derived from a consumer's evaluation of the relative similarity of these brands of beer. Examining this perceptual map, we can identify the horizontal axis on the basis of physical characteristics such as taste, calories, and fullness. The vertical axis is characterized by price, quality, and status. This procedure allows us to understand consumers' perceptions and the evaluative criteria they use to differentiate brands.

There may be attributes that consumers consider important but that they do not use in choosing among brands.[18] Such attributes will generally not be discovered in the techniques we have described. This situation would occur when consumers consider all brands to either be equivalent on the attribute or to be above their desired level. Thus, a consumer might consider all brands of bottled water to be safe to drink (not contaminated). Therefore they do not use this as a criterion when comparing brands. However, ignoring an important but nonsalient feature such as this could have very negative results for the brand. Such features may become salient due to marketer advertising or other publicity such as news reports about contaminated bottled water. Volvo has spent considerable effort over the years to make safety a salient feature for evaluating automobiles.

Determination of Consumers' Judgments of Brand Performance on Specific Evaluative Criteria A variety of methods are available for measuring consumers' judgments of brand performance on specific attributes. These include *rank ordering scales, semantic differential scales,* and *Likert scales* (see Appendix A). The semantic differential scale is probably the most widely used technique.

The **semantic differential scale** lists each evaluative criterion in terms of opposite levels of performance, such as fast–slow, expensive–inexpensive, and so forth. These opposites are separated by five to seven intervals and placed below the brand being considered, as shown below.

Apple PowerBook G3

Expensive	___	X	___	___	___	___	___	Inexpensive
High quality	X	___	___	___	___	___	___	Low quality
Heavy	___	___	___	___	X	___	___	Light
Easy to read display	___	___	___	X	___	___	___	Hard to read display

Perceptual Mapping of Beer Brand Perceptions **FIGURE 16-2**

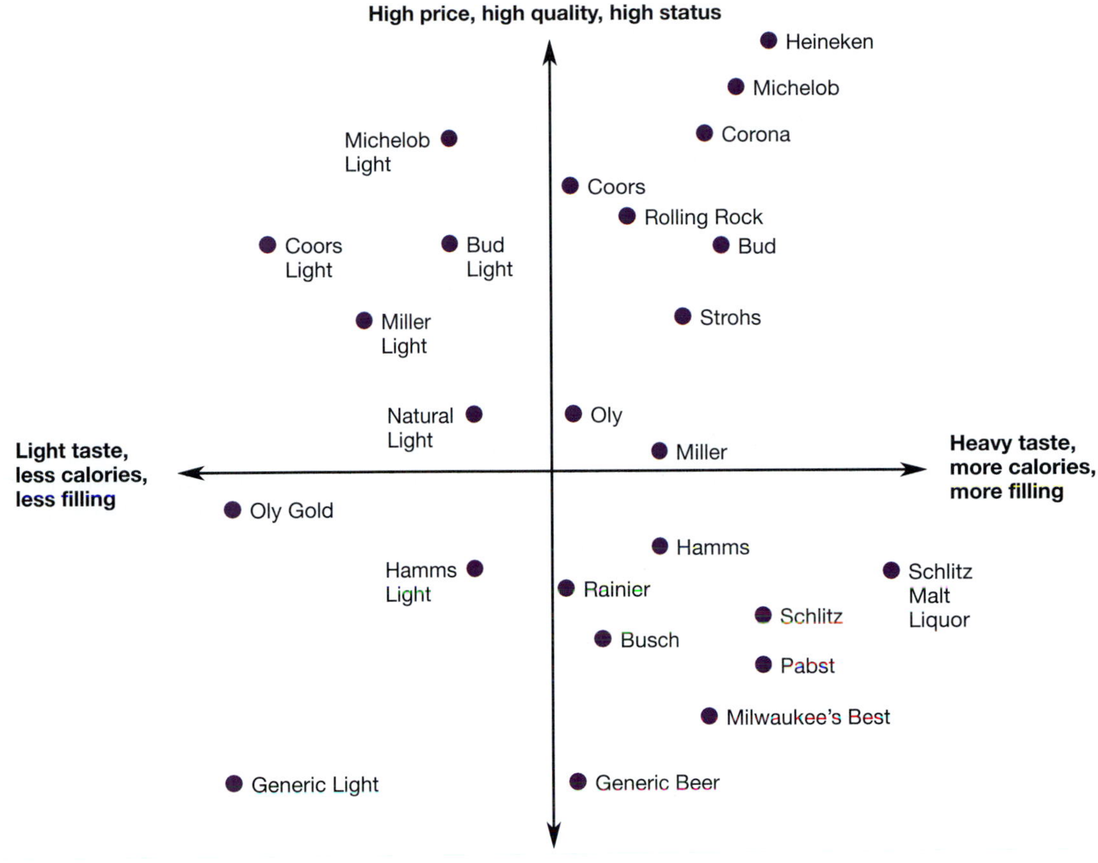

Consumers are asked to indicate their judgments of the performance of the brand by marking the blank that best indicates how accurately one or the other term describes or fits the brand. The end positions indicate *extremely,* the next pair in from the ends means *very,* the next pair in, *somewhat,* and the middle position, *neither-nor*. Thus, the respondent in the example above evaluated the Apple PowerBook G3 as very expensive, extremely high quality, somewhat light, with a display that is neither easy nor hard to read.

None of these techniques are very effective at measuring emotional responses to products or brands. Projective techniques can provide some insights. However, BBDO's Emotional Measurement System and the other approaches designed to measure emotional responses to ads (see Chapter 10) can be adapted to measure responses to products as well.

Determination of the Relative Importance of Evaluative Criteria The importance assigned to evaluative criteria can be measured either by direct or by indirect methods. The **constant sum scale** is the most common method of direct measurement. This method requires the consumer to allocate 100 points to his or her evaluative criteria, depending on the importance of each criterion. For example, in evaluating the importance of notebook computer criteria, a 100-point constant sum scale might produce the following results:

Evaluative Criteria	*Importance (in points)*
Price	5
Processor	35
Display quality	20
Battery life	25
After-sale support	5
Weight	10
Total	100

This consumer rated the processor as much more important than other attributes, with battery life and display quality also important. Weight, after-sale support, and price were not as important. Other evaluative criteria that could have been considered, such as size dimensions and installed RAM capacity, presumably are not important to this consumer or do not differ significantly across brands and therefore have implicit importance weights of zero. If an important attribute is omitted, the results of this approach are not valid. Thus, marketers need to be certain that all salient attributes are considered.

The most popular indirect measurement approach is **conjoint analysis.** In conjoint analysis, the consumer is presented with a set of products or product descriptions in which the potential evaluative criteria vary. For example, in Figure 16-3, a consumer was asked to rank in terms of overall preference 24 different computer designs featuring different levels of four key evaluative criteria. The preferences were then analyzed in light of the variations in the attributes. The result is a preference curve for each evaluative criterion that reflects the importance of that attribute. For example, processor is a particularly important evaluative criterion for this consumer.

Conjoint analysis was used in the Sunbeam example that opened this chapter. Sunbeam tested 12 different attributes, such as price, motor power, number of blades, bowl shape, and so forth. As stated earlier, four segments emerged *based on the relative importance of these attributes*. In order of importance, the key attributes for two segments were:

Cheap/Large Segment	*Multispeed/Multiuse Segment*
$49.99 price	$99.99 price
4-quart bowl	2-quart bowl
Two speeds	Seven speeds
Seven blades	Functions as blender and mixer
Heavy-duty motor	Cylindrical bowl
Cylindrical bowl	Pouring spout

Conjoint analysis is limited to the attributes listed by the researcher. Thus, a conjoint analysis of soft-drink attributes would not indicate anything about calorie content unless

Using Conjoint Analysis to Determine the Importance of Evaluative Criteria for a Computer **FIGURE 16-3**

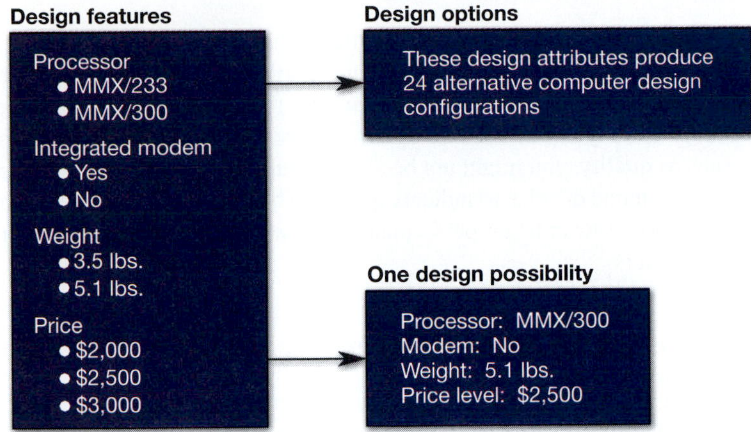

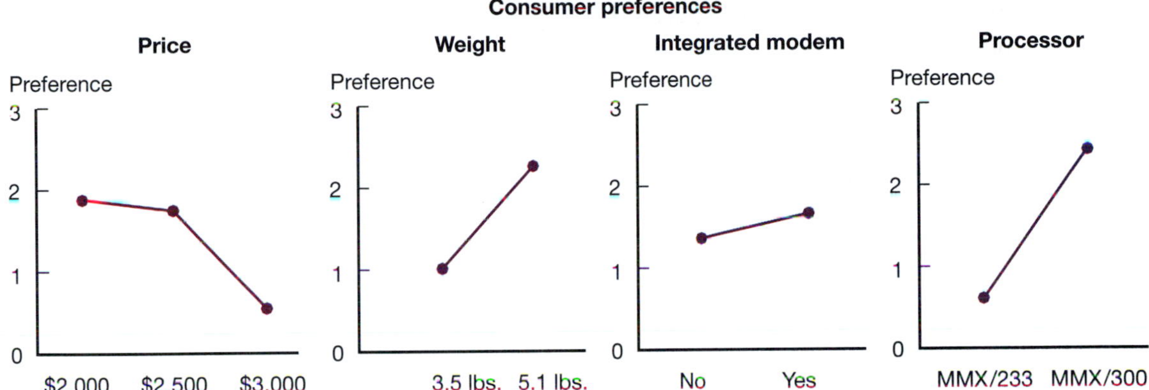

Relative importance

Evaluative criteria	Importance
Processor	45%
Modem	5
Weight	25
Price	25

- Processor is the most important feature in this example, and MMX/300 is the preferred option.
- While price and weight are also important, price becomes important only between $2,500 and $3,000.

the researcher listed it as a feature. The Sunbeam study did not test such attributes as brand name, color, weight, or safety features. If an important attribute is omitted, incorrect market share predictions are likely to result.[19] In addition, conjoint analysis is not well suited for measuring the importance of emotional or feeling-based product choices. For example, what types of attributes would you use to perform a conjoint analysis of perfumes?

INDIVIDUAL JUDGMENT AND EVALUATIVE CRITERIA

If you were buying a notebook computer, you would probably make direct comparisons across brands on features such as price, weight, and display clarity. These comparative judgments may not be completely accurate. For example, the display that is the easiest to read in a five-minute trial may not be the easiest to read over a two-hour work session. For other attributes, such as quality, you might not be able to make direct comparisons. Instead, you might rely on brand name or price to indicate quality. The accuracy of direct judgments and the use of one attribute to indicate performance on another (surrogate indicator) are critical issues for marketers.

Accuracy of Individual Judgments

The average consumer is not adequately trained to judge the performance of competing brands on complex evaluative criteria such as quality or durability. For more straightforward criteria, however, most consumers can and do make such judgments. Prices generally can be judged and compared directly. However, even this can be complex. Is a six-pack of 12-ounce cans of Coca-Cola selling for $2.49 a better buy than two liters priced at 99 cents each? Consumer groups have pushed for unit pricing (pricing by common measurements such as cost per ounce) to make such comparisons simpler. The federal truth-in-lending law was passed to facilitate direct price comparisons among alternative lenders.

The ability of an individual to distinguish between similar stimuli is called **sensory discrimination.** This involves such variables as the sound of stereo systems, the taste of food products, or the clarity of display screens. The minimum amount that one brand can differ from another with the difference still being noticed is referred to as the *just noticeable difference (j.n.d.)*. As we saw in Chapter 8, this ability is not well developed in most consumers. In general, research indicates that *individuals typically do not notice relatively small differences between brands or changes in brand attributes*. In addition, the complexity of many products and services, as well as the fact that some aspects of performance can only be judged after extensive use, make accurate brand comparisons difficult.[20]

The inability of consumers to accurately evaluate many modern products can result in inappropriate purchases (buying a lower quality product at a higher price than necessary).[21] This is a major concern of regulatory agencies and consumer groups, as well as for marketers of high-value brands.

Use of Surrogate Indicators

Consumers frequently use an observable attribute of a product to indicate the performance of the product on a less observable attribute. For example, most of us use price as a guide to the quality of at least some products. An attribute used to stand for or indicate another attribute is known as a **surrogate indicator.**

Consumers' reliance on an attribute as a surrogate indicator of another attribute is a function of its predictive value and confidence value.[22] *Predictive value* refers to the consumer's perception that one attribute is an accurate predictor of the other. *Confidence value* refers to the consumer's ability to distinguish between brands on the surrogate indicator. Thus, a consumer might believe that ingredients accurately indicate (high predictive value) the nutritional value of foods but not use them as indicators due to an inability to make the complex between-brand comparisons (low confidence value).

Perhaps the most widely used surrogate indicator, due in part to its high confidence value, is *price*. Price has been found to influence the perceived quality of shirts, radios, and aftershave lotion, appliances, carpeting, automobiles, and numerous other product categories.[23] These influences have been large, but, as might be expected, they decline with increases in visible product differences, prior product use, and additional product information. Unfortunately, for many products the relationship between price and functional measures of quality is low.[24] Thus, consumers using price as a surrogate for quality frequently make suboptimal purchases.

Brand name often is used as a surrogate indicator of quality. It has been found to be very important when it is the only information the consumer has available and to interact with or, on occasion, replace the impact of price.[25]

Country of manufacture is another widely used indicator of quality.[26] Would you prefer a stereo made in Japan or in Russia? Most consumers would assume the stereo from Japan to be superior. Since many consumers cannot directly judge the quality of products such as stereos, country of manufacture can be an important quality cue.

Warranties are another cue that consumers use to indicate quality. The longer and more inclusive the warranty, the better the quality of the product is assumed to be.[27] *Advertised brands and services* are often assumed to be superior to unadvertised brands.[28] Likewise, *national brands* are frequently considered to be superior to store brands.[29] Packaging, color, and style have also been found to affect perceptions of quality.

Surrogate indicators are based on consumers' beliefs that two features such as price level and quality level generally "go together." Consumers also form beliefs that certain variables do not go together—such as *lightweight* and *strong, rich taste* and *low calories,* and *high fiber* and *high protein.*[30] Marketers attempting to promote the presence of two or more variables that many consumers believe to be mutually exclusive have a high risk of failure unless very convincing messages are used. Thus, it is important for marketers to fully understand consumers' beliefs about the feasible relationships of attributes related to their products.

Evaluative Criteria, Individual Judgments, and Marketing Strategy

Obviously, marketers must understand the evaluative criteria consumers use relative to their products and develop products that excel on these features. All aspects of the marketing communications mix must then communicate this excellence.

Marketers must also recognize and react to the ability of individuals to judge evaluative criteria, as well as to their tendency to use surrogate indicators. For example, most new consumer products are initially tested against competitors in **blind tests.** A blind test is one in which the consumer is not aware of the product's brand name. Such tests enable the marketer to evaluate the functional characteristics of the product and to determine if a j.n.d. over a particular competitor has been obtained without the contaminating or "halo" effects of the brand name or the firm's reputation.

Marketers also make direct use of surrogate indicators. Andecker is advertised as "the most expensive taste in beer." This is an obvious attempt to utilize the price–quality relationship that many consumers believe exists for beer. On occasion, prices are raised to increase sales because of the presumed price–quality relationship. For example, a new mustard packaged in a crockery jar did not achieve significant sales priced at 49 cents but it did at $1.[31]

ILLUSTRATION 16-5

Consumers are often unable to accurately judge the quality or other features of a brand. In such situations, marketers may associate their brands with symbols or processes that consumers do associate with high quality (or other desired characteristics).

Courtesy Solgar Vitamin and Herb Company, Inc.

Marketers frequently use brand names as an indicator of quality.[32] *Elmer's* glue stressed the well-established reputation of its brand in promoting a new super glue (ads for Elmer's Wonder Bond said *Stick with a name you can trust*). Other firms stress *Made in America, Italian Styling,* or *German Engineering.*

Other types of surrogate indicators are also used. A marketer stressing the rich taste of a milk product, for example, would want to make it cream colored rather than white, and a hot, spicy sauce would be colored red. GE guarantees absolute satisfaction with its major appliances for 90 days. This strategy not only greatly reduces any perceived risk associated with purchasing a GE major appliance, it serves as a strong surrogate indicator of product quality. Illustration 16-5 shows how Parve uses its kosher designation as an indicator of quality.

DECISION RULES FOR ATTRIBUTE-BASED CHOICES

As we saw earlier, attribute-based choices involve the comparison of brands on the relevant evaluative criteria. Such comparisons can be structured by brand, in which all the criteria are evaluated and an overall evaluation for one brand is "computed" before another brand is considered. Or, the evaluation can be structured by criteria, in which the value of each alternative on a criterion is assessed and then the next criterion is examined.

As we describe some of the choice rules consumers use to select among alternatives, remember that these rules are representations of imprecise and often nonconscious or

TABLE 16-1

Performance Levels on the Evaluative Criteria for Six Notebook Computers

Evaluative Criteria	Consumer Perceptions*					
	Gateway	*HP*	*Compaq*	*Dell*	*IBM*	*Toshiba*
Price	5	3	3	4	2	1
Weight	3	4	5	4	3	4
Processor	5	5	5	2	5	5
Battery life	1	3	1	3	1	5
After-sale support	3	3	4	3	5	3
Display quality	3	3	3	5	3	3

*1 = Very poor; 5 = Very good.

low-effort mental processes. The following quote is a good representation of a consumer using a complex choice rule (compensatory with one attribute weighted heavily):

> I really liked the Ford (minivan) a lot, but it had the back tailgate that lifted up instead of the doors that opened. I suspect that if that had been available we might have gone with the Ford instead because it was real close between the Ford and the GM. The lift gate in the back was the main difference and we went with the General Motors because we liked the doors opening the way they did. I loved the way the Ford was designed on the inside. I loved the way it drove. I loved the way it felt and everything, but you are there manipulating all these kids and groceries and things and you have got to lift this thing, and it was very awkward. It was hard to lift, and if you are holding something you have got to steer all the kids back, or whack them in the head. So that was a big thing. You know it was a lot cheaper than the GM. It was between $1,000 and $2,000 less than General Motors and because money was a factor, we did go ahead and actually at one point talk money with a (Ford) dealer. But we couldn't get the price difference down to where I was willing to deal with that tailgate is what it comes down to.[33]

Despite the fact that the choice rules we describe are not precise representations of consumer decisions, they do enhance our understanding of how consumers make decisions and provide guidance for marketing strategy.

Suppose you have evaluated a particular model of each of the six notebook computer brands in your evoked set on six evaluative criteria: price, weight, processor, battery life, after-sale support and display quality. Further, suppose that each brand excels on one attribute but falls short on one or more of the remaining attributes, as shown in Table 16-1.

Which brand would you select? The answer would depend on the decision rule you utilize. Consumers use five decision rules: conjunctive, disjunctive, elimination-by-aspects, lexicographic, and compensatory. Consumers frequently use more than one rule to make a single decision. The most common instance of this is using a relatively simple rule to reduce the number of alternatives considered and then to apply a more complex rule to choose among the remaining options. An example would be eliminating from consideration all those apartments that are too far from campus or that rent for more than $700 per month (conjunctive decision rule). The choice from among the remaining apartments might involve carefully trading-off among features such as convenience of location, price, presence of a pool, size of rooms, and so forth (compensatory rule).

The first four rules we will describe are *noncompensatory* rules. This means that a high level of one attribute cannot offset a low level of another. In the apartment example, the consumer described would not consider an apartment that was right next to campus if it cost more than $700 per month. An excellent location cannot compensate for an inappropriate price. In contrast, the last rule is a *compensatory* rule, in which consumers average across attribute levels. This allows a high level of one value to offset a low value of another.

Finally, note that the conjunctive and disjunctive decision rules may produce a set of acceptable alternatives, while the remaining rules generally produce a single "best" alternative.

Conjunctive Decision Rule

The **conjunctive decision rule** establishes minimum required performance standards for each evaluative criterion and selects the first or all brands that surpass these minimum standards. In essence, you would say: "I'll consider all (or I'll buy the first) brands that are all right on the attributes I think are important." For example, assume that the following represent your minimum standards for a notebook computer:

Price	3
Weight	4
Processor	3
Battery life	1
After-sale support	2
Display quality	3

Any brand of computer falling below any of these minimum standards (cutoff points) would be eliminated from further consideration. Referring to Table 16-1, we can see that four computers are eliminated—IBM, Gateway, Dell, and Toshiba. These are the computers that failed to meet *all* the minimum standards. Under these circumstances, the two remaining brands may be equally satisfying. Or, the consumer may use another decision rule to select a single brand from these two alternatives.

Because individuals have limited ability to process information, the conjunctive rule is frequently used to reduce the size of the information processing task to some manageable level. It first eliminates those alternatives that do not meet minimum standards. This is often done in the purchase of such products as homes, computers, and bicycles; in the rental of apartments; or the selection of vacation options. A conjunctive rule is used to eliminate alternatives that are out of a consumer's price range, outside the location preferred, or that do not offer other desired features. Once alternatives not providing these features are eliminated, another decision rule may be used to make a brand choice among those alternatives that satisfy these minimum standards.

The conjunctive decision rule is commonly used in many low-involvement purchases as well. In such a purchase, the consumer evaluates a set of brands one at a time and selects the first brand that meets all the minimum requirements.

If the conjunctive decision rule is used by a target market, it is critical to surpass the consumers' minimum requirement on each criteria. Since the first brand the consumer evaluates that does so is often purchased, extensive distribution and dominant shelf space are important. It is also necessary to understand how consumers "break ties" if the first satisfactory option is not chosen.

Disjunctive Decision Rule

The **disjunctive decision rule** establishes a minimum level of performance for each important attribute (often a fairly high level). All brands that surpass the performance level for *any* key attribute are considered acceptable. Using this rule, you would say: "I'll consider all (or buy the first) brands that perform really well on any attribute I consider to be important." Assume that you are using a disjunctive decision rule and the attribute cutoff points shown below:

Price	5
Weight	5
Processor	Not critical
Battery life	Not critical
After-sale support	Not critical
Display quality	5

You would find Gateway (price), Compaq (weight), and Dell (display quality) to warrant further consideration (see Table 16-1). As with the conjunctive decision rule, you might purchase the first brand you find acceptable, use another decision rule to choose among the three, or add additional criteria to your list.

When the disjunctive decision rule is used by a target market, it is critical to surpass the consumers' requirements on at least one of the key criteria. This should be stressed in advertising messages and on the product package. Since the first brand the consumer evaluates that exceeds one of the requirements is often purchased, again extensive distribution and dominant shelf space are important, as is understanding how consumers "break ties" if the first satisfactory option is not chosen.

Elimination-by-Aspects Decision Rule

The **elimination-by-aspects rule** requires the consumer to rank the evaluative criteria in terms of their importance and to establish a cutoff point for each criterion. All brands are first considered on the most important criterion. Those that do not surpass the cutoff point are dropped from consideration. If more than one brand passes the cutoff point, the process is repeated on those brands for the second most important criterion. This continues until only one brand remains. Thus, the consumer's logic is: "I want to buy the brand that has a high level of an important attribute that other brands do not have."

Consider the rank order and cutoff points shown below. What would you choose using the elimination-by-aspects rule?

	Rank	*Cutoff Point*
Price	1	3
Weight	2	4
Display quality	3	4
Processor	4	3
After-sale support	5	3
Battery life	6	3

Price would eliminate IBM and Toshiba (see Table 16-1). Of those remaining, Compaq, HP, and Dell surpass the weight hurdle (Gateway is eliminated). Notice that Toshiba also exceeded the minimum weight requirement but was not considered because it had been eliminated in the initial consideration of price. Only Dell exceeds the third requirement, display quality.

Using the elimination-by-aspects rule, we end up with a choice that has all the desired features of all the other alternatives, plus one more. In this case, Dell would be selected.

For a target market using the elimination-by-aspects rule, it is critical to surpass the consumers' requirements on one more (in order) of the criteria used than the competition. This competitive superiority should be stressed in advertising messages and on the product package. Firms can also attempt to alter the relative importance that consumers assign to the evaluative criteria.

Lexicographic Decision Rule

The **lexicographic decision rule** requires the consumer to rank the criteria in order of importance. The consumer then selects the brand that performs *best* on the most important attribute. If two or more brands tie on this attribute, they are evaluated on the second most important attribute. This continues through the attributes until one brand outperforms the others. The consumer's thinking is something like this: "I want to get the brand that does best on the attribute of most importance to me. If there is a tie, I'll break it by choosing the one that does best on my second most important criterion."

The lexicographic decision rule is very similar to the elimination-by-aspects rule. The difference is that the lexicographic rule seeks maximum performance at each stage while the elimination-by-aspects seeks satisfactory performance at each stage. Thus, using the lexicographic rule and the data from the elimination-by-aspects example above would result in the selection of Gateway, because it has the best performance on the most important attribute. Had Gateway been rated a 4 on price, it would be tied with Dell. Then, Dell would be chosen based on its superior weight rating.

When this rule is being used by a target market, the firm should try to be superior to the competition on the key attribute. This competitive superiority should be emphasized in advertising. It is essential that the product at least equal the performance of all other competitors on the most important criteria. Outstanding performance on lesser criteria will not matter if a competitor is superior on the most important attribute. If a competitive advantage is not possible on the most important feature, attention should be shifted to the second most important (assuming equal performance on the most important one). If it is not possible to meet or beat the competition on the key attribute, the firm must attempt to make another attribute more important.

The ad shown in Illustration 16-6 emphasizes the ability of this Columbia parka to protect the wearer from bad weather. No other attributes are mentioned. This ad is appropriate for those consumers whose decision rules place primary importance on this attribute.

Compensatory Decision Rule

The four previous rules are *noncompensatory* decision rules, since very good performance on one evaluative criterion cannot compensate for poor performance on another evaluative criterion. On occasion, consumers may wish to average out some very good features with some less attractive features of a product in determining overall brand preference. Therefore, the **compensatory decision rule** states that the brand that rates highest on the sum of the consumer's judgments of the relevant evaluative criteria will be chosen. This can be illustrated as:

$$R_b = \sum_{i=1}^{n} W_i B_{ib}$$

where

R_b = Overall rating of brand b
W_i = Importance or weight attached to evaluative criterion i
B_{ib} = Evaluation of brand b on evaluative criterion i
n = Number of evaluative criteria considered relevant

Courtesy Columbia Sportswear.

ILLUSTRATION 16-6

This ad is ideal for consumers whose decision rules place primary emphasis on this single benefit. Lexicographic and compensatory rules with this attribute as the most important would be examples.

This is the same as the multiattribute attitude model described in Chapter 12. If you used the relative importance scores shown below, which brand would you choose using the compensatory rule?

	Importance Score
Price	30
Weight	25
Processor	10
Battery life	05
After-sale support	10
Display quality	20
Total	100

Using this rule, Dell has the highest preference (see Table 16-1). The calculations for Dell are as follows:

$$
\begin{aligned}
R_{\text{Dell}} &= 30(4) + 25(4) + 10(2) + 5(3) + 10(3) + 20(5) \\
&= 120 + 100 + 20 + 15 + 30 + 100 \\
&= 385
\end{aligned}
$$

Courtesy WinBook Corporation.

Courtesy Transmonde Technologies, Inc.

ILLUSTRATION 16-7

While both ads assume a complex decision process, one emphasizes price as the dominant evaluative criterion while the other focuses on speed.

Products and services targeting consumers likely to use a compensatory rule can offset relatively low performance on some features with relatively high performance on others. However, it is important to have a performance level at or near the competition on the more important features since they receive more weight in the decision than do other attributes. Recall the description of the minivan purchase from the beginning of this section. This customer preferred most of the features of the Ford but bought the GM because Ford was very weak on one key attribute. However, the consumer did express a willingness to change the decision had the price differential been greater. Thus, for compensatory decisions, the total mix of the relevant attributes must be considered to be superior to those of the competition.

Marketing Applications of Decision Rules

As shown below, each decision rule yields a somewhat different choice. Therefore, marketers must understand which decision rules are being used by target buyers in order to position a product within this decision framework.

Decision Rule	*Brand Choice*
Conjunctive	HP, Compaq
Disjunctive	Dell, Compaq, Gateway
Elimination-by-aspects	Dell
Lexicographic	Gateway
Compensatory	Dell

We cannot specify with precision which rules are used by consumers in which situations. However, research clearly indicates that people do *use* the rules.[34] Low-involvement purchases generally involve relatively simple decision rules (conjunctive, disjunctive, elimination-by-aspects, or lexicographic), since consumers will attempt to minimize the mental "cost" of such decisions.[35] High-involvement decisions and purchases involving considerable perceived risk tend to increase evaluation efforts and often may involve not only more complex rules (compensatory) but stages of decision making, with different attributes being evaluated using different rules at each stage.[36] Of course, individual, product, and situational characteristics also influence the type of decision rule used.[37]

A marketing manager must determine, for the market segment under consideration, which is the most likely rule or combination of rules and then develop appropriate marketing strategy. In Illustration 16-7, the Transmonde ad assumes that consumers assign price a critical role in their decision process for this product. In contrast, the WinBook ad from the same magazine assumes that speed is most critical. Both ads assume that a complex decision process is used, as both provide information on numerous other attributes.

SUMMARY

During and after the time that consumers gather information about various alternative solutions to a recognized problem, they evaluate the alternatives and select the course of action that seems most likely to solve the problem. Consumer choices are sometimes based on extremely simple decision rules such as "buy the cheapest brand available." At other times, they are extremely complex, involving multiple stages and processes.

There are a number of ways consumers make choices. *Attribute-based choice* requires the knowledge of the specific attributes of the alternatives at the time the choice is made and involves attribute-by-attribute comparisons across brands. *Attitude-based choice* involves the use of general attitudes, summary impressions, intuitions, or heuristics; no attribute-by-attribute comparisons are made at the time of choice. There can also be combinations of these forms. A common combination would be for overall preferences to be formed based on attitude-based processing, with the final choice adding a brand-by-brand comparison on the price attribute.

Affective choice is another distinct approach consumers use to make selections. Affective choices tend to be holistic in nature. The brand is not decomposed into distinct components, each of which is evaluated separately from the whole. The evaluation of such products is generally focused on the way they will make the user *feel* as they are used. Decisions based on affect are said to use the "How do I feel about it" heuristic or decision rule. Consumers imagine or picture using the product or service and evaluate the feeling that this use will produce.

Affective choice is most likely when the underlying motive is consummatory rather than instrumental. *Consummatory motives* underlie behaviors that are intrinsically rewarding to the individual involved. *Instrumental motives* activate behaviors designed to achieve a second goal.

Rational choice theory assumes a rational decision maker with well-defined preferences that do not depend on how the options are presented. Each option or alternative in a choice set is assumed to have a value to the consumer that depends only on the characteristics of that option. The consumer is also assumed to have sufficient skill to calculate which option will maximize his or her value and will choose on this basis.

While useful, rational choice theory is incomplete. An emerging view is that many choices are constructed by the consumer as the decision is made. All consumers have *bounded rationality*—a limited capacity for processing information. In addition, consumers often have goals that are different from, or in addition to, selecting the optimal alternative. Therefore, for many decisions consumers construct a decision process that is appropriate for the situation at hand. This is called *constructive choice*.

An important part of the theory of constructive choice is the concept of metagoals. A *metagoal* refers to the general nature of the outcome being sought. Four metagoals characterize many consumer choices—maximizing the accuracy of the decision, minimizing the cognitive effort required for the decision, minimizing the experience of negative emotion while making the decision, and maximizing the ease with which a decision can be justified. These goals may shift in importance as the consumer constructs a decision.

Evaluative criteria are the various features or benefits a consumer looks for in response to a specific problem. They are the performance levels or characteristics consumers use to compare different brands in light of their particular consumption problem. The number, type, and importance of evaluative criteria used differ from consumer to consumer and across product categories.

The measurement of (1) which evaluative criteria are used by the consumer, (2) how the consumer perceives the various alternatives on each criterion, and (3) the relative importance of each criterion is a critical first step in utilizing evaluative criteria to develop marketing strategy. While the measurement task is not easy, a number of techniques ranging from direct questioning to projective techniques and multidimensional scaling are available.

Evaluative criteria such as price, size, and color can be judged easily and accurately by consumers. Other criteria, such as quality, durability, and health benefits, are much more difficult to judge. In such cases, consumers often use price, brand name, or some other variable as a *surrogate indicator* of quality.

When consumers judge alternative brands on several evaluative criteria, they must have some method to select one brand from the various choices. Decision rules serve this function. A decision rule specifies how a consumer compares two or more brands. Five commonly used decision rules are *disjunctive, conjunctive, lexicographic, elimination-by-aspects,* and *compensatory*. The decision rules work best with functional products and cognitive decisions. Marketing managers must be aware of the decision rule(s) used by the target market, since different decision rules require different marketing strategies.

KEY TERMS

Affective choice 563
Attitude-based choice 562
Attribute-based choice 562
Blind test 575
Bounded rationality 564
Compensatory decision rule 580
Conjoint analysis 572
Conjunctive decision rule 578
Constant sum scale 571
Constructive choice 565
Consummatory motives 564
Disjunctive decision rule 578
Elimination-by-aspects decision rule 579
Evaluative criteria 566
Instrumental motives 564
Lexicographic decision rule 580
Metagoal 565
Perceptual mapping 570
Projective techniques 570
Semantic differential scale 570
Sensory discrimination 574
Surrogate indicator 574

INTERNET EXERCISES

1. Monitor several chat sites or interest groups for a week. Prepare a report on how a marketer could learn about the following used by consumers by doing this.
   a. Evaluative criteria
   b. Decision rules
2. Visit Conde Nast's site (http://www.concierge.com). Use the Concierge feature in its beach and island finder in the Travel section. What decision rule is this based on?
3. Visit four Web sites for brands in the same product category. Based on the brand information provided and the manner in which it is provided, what decision rule does each brand appear to assume its market uses? If there are differences, how would you explain them?

DDB NEEDHAM LIFESTYLE DATA ANALYSES

1. Based on DDB Needham Tables 1a, 2a, 3a, 4a, 5a, 6a, and 7a, what characterizes individuals who place considerable emphasis on store service as an evaluative criterion? What are the marketing implications of this?

REVIEW QUESTIONS

1. What is *mental budgeting* and how does it affect consumption?
2. How does *attribute-based choice* differ from *attitude-based choice?* When is each most likely?
3. What is *affective choice* and when is it most likely to occur?
4. What is the difference between *consummatory motives* and *instrumental motives?*
5. What is *rational choice* theory?
6. What is meant by *bounded rationality?*
7. What is meant by *constructive choice?*
8. What is a *metagoal?*
9. What are four common metagoals for consumer decisions?
10. What are *evaluative criteria* and on what characteristics can they vary?
11. How can you determine which evaluative criteria consumers use?
12. What methods are available for measuring consumers' judgments of brand performance on specific attributes?
13. How can the importance assigned to evaluative criteria be assessed?
14. What is *sensory discrimination,* and what role does it play in the evaluation of products? What is meant by a *just noticeable difference?*
15. What are *surrogate indicators?* How are they used in the consumer evaluation process?
16. What is the *conjunctive decision rule?*
17. What is the *disjunctive decision rule?*
18. What is the *elimination-by-aspects decision rule?*
19. What is the *lexicographic decision rule?*
20. What is the *compensatory decision rule?*
21. How can knowledge of consumers' evaluative criteria and criteria importance be used in developing marketing strategy?
22. How can knowledge of the decision rules consumers might use in a certain purchase assist a firm in developing marketing strategy?

DISCUSSION QUESTIONS

23. Do you use mental budgeting as described in Consumer Insight 16-1? If so, how has it affected your consumption decisions?
24. Would you use an attribute-based or an attitude-based decision approach to purchasing (or renting or giving to) the following? Would situational factors change your approach?
    a. A special dinner with a friend
    b. A charity
    c. An apartment
    d. A pet
    e. A primary care physician
    f. A Mother's Day present
    g. A mouthwash
    h. A vacation
    i. A notebook computer
25. Repeat Question 24, but speculate on how your instructor would answer. In what ways might his or her answer differ from yours? Why?
26. For which, if any, of the options in Question 24 would you make an affective decision? What role would situational factors play?
27. What metagoals would you use, and what would be their relative importance to you, in purchasing (or renting or giving to) the options in Questions 24?

28. List the evaluative criteria and the importance of each that you would use in purchasing (or renting or giving to) the options in Question 24. Would situational factors change the criteria? The importance weights? Why?
29. Repeat Question 28, but speculate on how your instructor would answer. In what ways might his or her answer differ from yours? Why?
30. Describe two purchase decisions in which you used affective choice, two in which you used attitude-based choice, and two for which you used attribute-based choice. Why did the type of decision process you used vary?
31. Identify five products for which surrogate indicators may be used as evaluative criteria in a brand choice decision. Why are the indictors used, and how might a firm enhance their use (i.e., strengthen their importance)?
32. The table that follows represents a particular consumer's evaluative criteria, criteria importance, acceptable level of performance, and judgments of performance with respect to several brands of mopeds. Discuss the brand choice this consumer would make when using the lexicographic, compensatory, and conjunctive decision rules.

Evaluative Criteria	*Criteria Importance*	*Minimum Acceptable Performance*	**Alternative Brands**					
			Motron	*Vespa*	*Cimatti*	*Garelli*	*Puch*	*Motobecane*
Price	30	4	2	4	2	4	2	4
Horsepower	15	3	4	2	5	5	4	5
Weight	5	2	3	3	3	3	3	3
Gas economy	35	3	4	4	3	2	4	5
Color selection	10	3	4	4	3	2	5	2
Frame	5	2	4	2	3	3	3	3

Note: 1 = Very poor; 2 = Poor; 3 = Fair; 4 = Good; and 5 = Very good.

33. Describe the decision rule(s) you used or would use in buying, renting, or giving to the options listed for Question 24. Would you use different rules in different situations? Which ones? Why? Would any of these involve an affective choice?
34. Describe your last two "major" and your last two "minor" purchases. What role did emotions or feelings play? How did they differ? What evaluative criteria and decision rules did you use for each? Why?
35. Discuss surrogate indicators that could be used to evaluate the perceived quality of the following:
    a. University
    b. Headache remedy
    c. Recreation equipment
    d. Cologne
    e. Canned vegetable line
    f. Automobile
    g. Restaurant
    h. Law office

APPLICATION ACTIVITIES

36. Interview five students to determine if they use mental budgeting and how it affects their purchase decisions. Do your results support Consumer Insight 16-1? How would you explain any differences?
37. Conduct an extensive interview with two students who recently made a major purchase. Have them describe the process they went through. Probe to determine how they constructed this decision.
38. Develop a list of evaluative criteria that students might use in evaluating alternative apartments they might rent. After listing these criteria, go to the local newspaper or student newspaper, select several apartments, and list them in a table similar to the one in Question 32. Then have five other students evaluate this information and have each indicate the apartment they would rent if given only those alternatives. Next, ask them to express

the importance they attach to each evaluative criterion, using a 100-point constant sum scale. Finally, provide them with a series of statements that describe different decision rules and ask them to indicate the one that best describes the way they made their choice. Calculate the choice they should have made given their importance ratings and stated decision rules. Have them explain any inconsistent choices. Report your results.

39. Develop a short questionnaire to elicit the evaluative criteria consumers might use in selecting the following. Also, have each respondent indicate the relative importance he or she attaches to each of the evaluative criteria. Then, working with several other students, combine your information and develop a segmentation strategy based on consumer evaluative criteria and criteria importance. Finally, develop an advertisement for the members of each market segment to indicate that their needs would be served by your brand.
    a. Toothpaste
    b. Lipstick
    c. Sunscreen
    d. Pizza restaurant
    e. Notebook computer
    f. Charity
    g. Pet
    h. Health club
40. Set up a taste test experiment to determine if volunteer taste testers can perceive a just noticeable difference between three different brands of the following. To set up the experiment, store each test brand in a separate but identical container and label the containers *L, M,* and *N*. Provide volunteer taste testers with an adequate opportunity to evaluate each brand before asking them to state their identification of the actual brands represented as *L, M,* and *N*. Evaluate the results and discuss the marketing implications of these results.
    a. Colas
    b. Diet colas
    c. Lemon-lime drinks
    d. Carbonated waters
    e. Chips
    f. Orange juices
41. For a product considered high in social status, develop a questionnaire that measures the evaluative criteria of that product, using both a *direct* and an *indirect* method of measurement. Compare the results and discuss their similarities and differences and which evaluative criteria are most likely to be utilized in brand choice.
42. Find and copy or describe two ads that encourage consumers to use a surrogate indicator. Are they effective? Why? Why do you think the firm uses this approach?
43. Find and copy or describe two ads that attempt to change the importance consumers assign to product class evaluative criteria. Are they effective? Why? Why do you think the firm uses this approach?
44. Find and copy or describe two ads that are based on affective choice. Why do you think the firm uses this approach? Are the ads effective? Why?
45. Interview two salespeople for one of the following products. Ascertain the evaluative criteria, importance weights, decision rules, and surrogate indicators that they believe consumers use when purchasing their product. What marketing implications are suggested if their beliefs are accurate for large segments?
    a. Motorcycles
    b. Beds
    c. Pets
    d. Diamond rings
    e. Dress shoes
    f. Home insurance

REFERENCES

1. A. L. Page and H. F. Rosenbaum, "Redesigning Product Lines with Conjoint Analysis," *Journal of Product Innovation Management,* no. 4 (1987), pp. 120–37.
2. This section is based on S. P. Mantell and F. R. Kardes, "The Role of Direction of Comparison, Attribute-Based Processing, and Attitude-Based Processing in Consumer Preference," *Journal of Consumer Research,* March 1999, pp. 335–52.
3. B. Mittal, "A Study of the Concept of Affective Choice Mode for Consumer Decisions," in *Advances in Consumer Research XXI,* ed. C. T. Allen and D. R. John (Provo, UT: Association for Consumer Research, 1994), p. 256.
4. J. F. Durgee and G. C. O'Connor, "Why Some Products 'Just Feel Right,'" in *Advances in Consumer Research XXII,* ed. F. R. Kardes and M. Sujan (Provo, UT: Association for Consumer Research, 1995), p. 652.
5. M. T. Pham, "Representativeness, Relevance, and the Use of Feelings in Decision Making," *Journal of Consumer Research,* September 1998, pp. 144–59.

6. See K. T. Lacher and R. Mizerski, "An Exploratory Study of the Responses and Relationships Involved in the Evaluation of, and in the Intent to Purchase New Rock Music," *Journal of Consumer Research,* September 1994, pp. 366–80.
7. This section is based on J. R. Bettman, M. F. Luce, and J. W. Payne, "Constructive Consumer Choice Processes," *Journal of Consumer Research,* December 1998, pp. 187–217.
8. See C. A. Mandrik, "Consumer Heuristics," in *Advances in Consumer Research XXIII,* ed. K. P. Corfman and J. G. Lynch (Provo, UT: Association for Consumer Research, 1996), pp. 301–7.
9. See R. Dhar and S. M. Nowlis, "The Effects of Time Pressure on Consumer Choice Deferral," *Journal of Consumer Research,* March 1999, pp. 369–84.
10. See E. C. Garbarino and J. A. Edell, "Cognitive Effort, Affect, and Choice," *Journal of Consumer Research,* September 1997, pp. 147–58; and M. F. Luce, "Choosing to Avoid," *Journal of Consumer Research,* March 1998, pp. 409–33.
11. P. H. Bloch, "Seeking the Ideal Form," *Journal of Marketing,* July 1995, pp. 16–29.
12. G. Kalyanaram and J. D. C. Little, "An Empirical Analysis of Latitude of Price Acceptance in Consumer Package Goods," *Journal of Consumer Research,* December 1994, pp. 408–18.
13. D. J. Mitchell, B. E. Kahn, and S. C. Knasko, "There's Something in the Air," *Journal of Consumer Research,* September 1995, pp. 229–38; D. R. Lichtenstein, R. G. Netemeyer, and S. Burton, "Assessing the Domain Specificity of Deal Proneness," *Journal of Consumer Research,* December 1995, pp. 314–26; D. R. Lichtenstein, S. Burton, and R. G. Netemeyer, "An Examination of Deal Proneness Across Sales Promotion Types," *Journal of Retailing,* no. 2, pp. 283–97; and V. Ramaswamy and S. S. Srinivasan, "Coupon Characteristics and Redemption Intentions," *Psychology & Marketing,* January 1998, pp. 50–80.
14. See A. Ostrom and D. Iacobucci, "Consumer Trade-Offs and the Evaluation of Services," *Journal of Marketing,* January 1995, pp. 17–28.
15. B. L. Bagus, "The Consumer Durable Replacement Buyer," *Journal of Marketing,* January 1991, pp. 42–51.
16. A. Kirmani and P. Wright, "Procedural Learning, Consumer Decision Making, and Marketing Choice," *Marketing Letters* 4, no. 1 (1993), pp. 39–48; G. S. Carpenter, R. Glazer, and K. Nakamoto, "Meaningful Brands from Meaningless Differentiation," *Journal of Marketing Research,* August 1994, pp. 339–50; and S. M. Broniarczyk and A. D. Gershoff, "Meaningless Differentiation Revisited," in *Advances in Consumer Research XXIV,* ed. M. Bruck and D. J. MacInnis (Provo, UT: Association for Consumer Research, 1997), pp. 223–28.
17. B. Abrams, "Hanes Finds L'eggs Methods Don't Work with Cosmetics," *The Wall Street Journal,* February 3, 1983, p. 33.
18. See R. Dhar and S. J. Sherman, "The Effect of Common and Unique Features in Consumer Choice," *Journal of Consumer Research,* December 1996, pp. 193–203; and A. Chernev, "The Effect of Common Features on Brand Choice," *Journal of Consumer Research,* March 1997, pp. 304–11.
19. See K. Jedidi, R. Kohli, and W. S. DeSarbo, "Consideration Sets in Conjoint Analysis," *Journal of Marketing Research,* August 1996, pp. 364–72.
20. See S. H. Ang, G. J. Gorn, and C. B. Weinberg, "The Evaluation of Time-Dependent Attributes," *Psychology & Marketing,* January 1996, pp. 19–35.
21. P. M. Parker, "Sweet Lemons," *Journal of Marketing Research,* August 1995, pp. 291–307.
22. G. L. Sullivan and K. J. Burger, "An Investigation of the Determinants of Cue Utilization," *Psychology & Marketing,* Spring 1987, pp. 63–74. See also N. Dawar and P. Parker, "Marketing Universals," *Journal of Marketing,* April 1994, pp. 81–95.
23. G. J. Tellis and G. J. Gaeth, "Best Value, Price-Seeking, and Prize Aversion," *Journal of Marketing,* April 1990, pp. 35–45; J. Gotlieb and D. Sarel, "The Influence of Type of Advertisement, Price, and Source Credibility on Perceived Quality," *Journal of the Academy of Marketing Science,* Summer 1992, pp. 253–60; J. B. Gotlieb and D. Sarel, "Effects of Price Advertisements," *Journal of Business Research,* May 1991, pp. 195–210; D. R. Lichtenstein, N. M. Ridgway, and R. G. Netemeyer, "Price Perceptions and Consumer Shopping Behavior," *Journal of Marketing Research,* May 1993, pp. 234–45; T.-Z. Chang and A. R. Wildt, "Impact of Product Information on the Use of Price as a Quality Cue," *Psychology & Marketing,* January 1996, pp. 55–75; and G. S. Bobinski, Jr., D. Cox, and A. Cox, "Retail 'Sale' Advertising, Perceived Retailer Credibility, and Price Rationale," *Journal of Retailing,* no. 3 (1996), pp. 291–306.
24. S. Burton and D. R. Lichtenstein, "Assessing the Relationship between Perceived and Objective Price-Quality," in *Advances in Consumer Research XVII,* ed. M. E. Goldberg, G. Gorn, and R. W. Pollay (Provo, UT: Association for Consumer Research, 1990), pp. 715–22; and D. J. Faulds, O. Grunewald, and D. Johnson, "A Cross-National Investigation of the Relationship between the Price and Quality of Consumer Products," *Journal of Global Marketing* 8, no. 1 (1994), pp. 7–25.
25. See P. S. Richardson, A. S. Dick, and A. K. Jain, "Extrinsic and Intrinsic Cue Effects on Perceptions of Store Brand Quality," *Journal of Marketing,* October 1994, pp. 28–36.
26. T. M. Rogers, P. F. Kaminski, D. D. Schoenbachler, and G. L. Gordan, "The Effect of Country-of-Origin Information on Consumer Purchase Decision Process," *Journal of International Consumer Marketing* 7, no. 3 (1994), pp. 73–109; W. K. Li, K. B. Monroe, and D. K. Chan, "The Effects of Country of Origin, Brand, and Price Information," in *Advances in Consumer Research XXI,* ed. C. T. Allen and D. R. John (Provo, UT: Association for Consumer Research, 1994), pp. 449–57; R. Parameswaran and R. M. Pisharodi, "Facets of Country of Origin Image," *Journal of Advertising,* March 1994, pp. 43–56; S. S. Andaleeb, "Country-of-Origin Effects," *Journal of International Consumer Marketing* 7, no. 3 (1995), pp. 29–52; S. I. Lampert and E. D. Jaffe, "Country of Origin Effects on International Market Entry," *Journal of Global Marketing,* no. 2 (1996), pp. 27–52; G. Lantz and S. Loeb, "Country of Origin and Ethnocentrism"; and G. Chakraborty, A. T. Allred, and T. Bristol, "Exploring Consumers' Evaluations of Counterfeits"; both in *Advances in Consumer Research XXIII,* ed. K. P. Corfman and J. G. Lynch (Provo, UT: Association for Consumer Research, 1996), pp. 374–78 and 379–83; G. R. Iyer and J. K. Kalita, "The Impact of Country-of-Origin and Country-of-Manufacture Cues on Consumer Perceptions of Quality and Value," *Journal of*

Global Marketing, no. 1 (1997), pp. 7–28; L. A. Manrai et al., "How Green-Claim Strength and Country Disposition Affect Product Evaluation and Company Image," *Psychology & Marketing,* August 1997, pp. 511–37; S. Janda and C. P. Rao, "The Effect of Country-of-Origin Related Stereotypes and Personal Beliefs on Product Evaluation," *Psychology & Marketing,* October 1997, pp. 689–702; and F. M. Ulgado and M. Lee, "The Korean versus American Marketplace," *Psychology & Marketing,* September 1998, pp. 595–614.

27. See W. Boulding and A. Kirmani, "A Consumer-Side Experimental Examination of Signaling Theory," *Journal of Consumer Research,* June 1993, pp. 11–23.
28. J. E. Urbany et al., "Do Buyers Believe that Advertised Brands Are Better Buys?" in *Enhancing Knowledge Development in Marketing,* ed. D. W. Cravens and P. R. Dickson (Chicago: American Marketing Association, 1993), pp. 434–41.
29. J. Scattone, "Factors Influencing Consumer Perceptions, Attitudes, and Consideration of Store Brands," in *Enhancing Knowledge Development in Marketing,* ed. B. B. Stern and G. M. Zinkhan, (Chicago: American Marketing Association, 1995), pp. 27–33; and footnote 25.
30. K. M. Elliott and D. W. Roach, "Are Consumers Evaluating Your Products the Way You Think and Hope They Are?" *Journal of Consumer Marketing,* Spring 1991, pp. 5–14; and J. Baumgartner, "On the Utility of Consumers' Theories in Judgments of Covariation," *Journal of Consumer Research,* March 1995, pp. 634–43.
31. K. B. Monroe, *Pricing* (New York: McGraw-Hill, 1979), p. 38.
32. C. F. Hite, R. E. Hite, and T. Minor, "Quality Uncertainty, Brand Reliance, and Dissipative Advertising," *Journal of the Academy of Marketing Science,* Spring 1991, pp. 115–22; and P. Sellers, "Brands," *Fortune,* August 23, 1993, pp. 52–56.
33. C. J. Thompson, "Interpreting Consumers," *Journal of Marketing Research,* November 1997, p. 443.
34. M. L. Ursic and J. G. Helgeson "The Impact of Choice and Task Complexity on Consumer Decision Making," *Journal of Business Research,* August 1990, pp. 69–86; and P. L. A. Dabholkar, "Incorporating Choice into an Attitudinal Framework," *Journal of Consumer Research,* June 1994, pp. 100–18.
35. See E. Coupey, "Restructuring," *Journal of Consumer Research,* June 1994, pp. 83–99.
36. See D. L. Alden, D. M. Stayman, and W. D. Hoyer, "Evaluation Strategies of American and Thai Consumers," *Psychology & Marketing,* March 1994, pp. 145–61; and J. E. Russo and F. Lecleric, "An Eye-Fixation Analysis of Choice Processes for Consumer Nondurables," *Journal of Consumer Research,* September 1994, pp. 274–90.
37. See J. G. Helgeson and M. L. Ursic, "Information Load, Cost/Benefit Assessment and Decision Strategy Variability," *Journal of the Academy of Marketing Science,* Winter 1993, pp. 13–20; W. J. McDonald, "The Roles of Demographics, Purchase Histories, and Shopper Decision-Making Styles in Predicting Consumer Catalog Loyalty," *Journal of Direct Marketing,* Summer 1993, pp. 55–65; M. S. Yadav, "How Buyers Evaluate Product Bundles," *Journal of Consumer Research,* September 1994, pp. 342–53; and A. V. Muthukrishnan, "Decision Ambiguity and Incumbent Brand Advantage," *Journal of Consumer Research,* June 1995, pp. 98–109.

Chicks dig us.

Cheap. Cheap.

(www.chicksdigus.com)

BUY.COM

The Internet Superstore

BUYCOMP.COM BUYSOFT.COM BUYBOOKS.COM BUYVIDEOS.COM BUYGAMES.COM

Courtesy Buy.Dot.Com

chapter seventeen

Outlet Selection and Purchase

Can a retailer make money selling many if not most of its items at or below the price it pays for them? Scot Blum, the founder of Buy.com, is betting that you can. The secret—sell on-line, minimize your operating costs, generate very large volumes, and make your profits selling advertising space on your site. Will it work? At this time it is not yet clear. However, sales volumes are $2 million per day and growing rapidly, as are advertising revenues.

Buy.com opened its Internet business in November 1997 as Buycomp.com. It sold computers and related items with a commitment to have the lowest price on the Web for every one of the 30,000 or so items it sells. To do so it uses a unique technology that allows it to search through other on-line sellers' sites and determine their prices. Prices are searched daily. Once the lowest price is determined, Buy.com undercuts it and sends it off to price-comparison search engines, which make it available to comparison shoppers.

To keep costs low, Buy.com does not provide amenities. It does not score well on customer service, ease of use, or overall customer experience. This does not appear to have been a problem for computer-related products. However, Buy.com has recently gone into the book, movie, and video game businesses using the same formula. This puts it in direct competition with Amazon.com and Reel.com. Will the lowest price–limited service concept work here?

Blum plans to stick with the strategy:

> We're going for someone who knows what they want and wants it for the best price. We're trying to keep our site simple, effective, and easy to use—not cluttered with a lot of links and long reviews and stuff.

Since Amazon.com and others offer these features, some customers may use those sites to determine what they want and then buy it from Buy.com (this is known as free-riding). However, the CEO of Amazon.com isn't worried. According to him:

> But with books and music, there's a different dynamic. Customers want selection, ease of use, and a low price—in that order.

Buy.com plans to continue expanding. It has locked up 3,000 Web addresses that start with "Buy," including BuyCars.com, BuyInsurance.com, and even BuyCheesburgers.com.[1]

Selecting a retail outlet involves the same process as selecting a brand, as described in the previous chapters.[2] That is, the consumer recognizes a problem that requires an outlet to be selected, engages in internal and possibly external search, evaluates the relevant alternatives, and applies a decision rule to make a selection. We are not going to repeat our discussion of these steps. However, we will describe the evaluative criteria that consumers frequently use in choosing retail outlets, consumer characteristics that influence the criteria used, and in-store characteristics that affect the amounts and brands purchased.

Before turning to the above topics, we need to clarify the meaning of the term *retail outlet*. It refers to any source of products or services for consumers. In early editions of this text, we used the term *store*. However, increasingly consumers see or hear descriptions of products in catalogs, direct-mail pieces, various print media, on television or radio, or on the Internet and acquire them through mail, telephone, or computer orders. Generally referred to as **in-home shopping,** these sources represent a small but rapidly growing percent of total retail sales. In the next section, we will examine the most dynamic component of in-home shopping, Internet retailing, as well as recent developments in store retailing.

THE RETAIL SCENE

> You're watching "Seinfeld" on TV, and you like the jacket he's wearing. You click on it with your remote control. The show pauses and a Windows-style dropdown menu appears at the top of the screen, asking if you want to buy it. You click "yes." The next menu offers you a choice of colors; you click on black. Another menu lists your credit cards asking which one you'll use for this purchase. Click on MasterCard or whatever. Which address should the jacket go to, your office or your home or your cabin? Click on one address and you're done—the menus disappear and "Seinfeld" picks up where it left off.
>
> Just as you'll already have taught the computer about your credit cards and addresses, you will have had your body measured by a 3-D version of supermarket scanners, so the system will know your exact size. And it will send the data electronically to a factory, where robots will custom tailor the jacket to your measurements. An overnight courier service will deliver it to your door the next morning.[3]

Farfetched? The quote is from Bill Gates, founder of Microsoft. Already, parts of this scenario are possible. Skiers can have their feet scanned into a computer along with data on their skiing style and the computer will provide a list of the brands and sizes of ski boots that will fit best and meet their performance needs. You can also have a "mass-produced" bicycle designed for your body size and produced in an automated factory in a matter of days. So, while Gates' vision may be a bit futuristic, at least some aspects of it will be commonplace in a few years. As is obvious, retailing is one of the most exciting areas in most developed economies.

Internet Retailing

As the Buy.com example at the beginning of the chapter indicates, Internet retailing is a booming and increasingly competitive business (see Chapter 15 for a discussion of the use of the Internet as a source of information for purchases):[4]

	Year	
	2000	*2003*
U.S. households on-line (millions)	38.3	52.8
U.S. households shopping on-line (millions)	17.7	40.3
Average annual household on-line expenditures	$1,864	$2,678
Total U.S. retail expenditures on-line (billions)	$33	$108

Currently, high-income households dominate on-line shopping, with those earning over $50,000 accounting for 74 percent of all Internet sales (compared to 47 percent of all retail sales). However, this is forecast to drop to 66 percent by 2003, as more lower income families begin to use this channel.

Forrester Research categorizes products and services into three categories based on their purchase characteristics relative to Internet shopping:

- *Convenience items:* low-risk discretionary items. Internet sales will be most successful where huge selections and deep discounts are important and easy shipping is available. Examples are books, CDs, flowers, and event tickets.
- *Researched items:* high-information, big ticket planned purchases. Internet sales will be led by items with low style content and those for which "touch" is not important. Examples are leisure travel, computer hardware, consumer electronics, and appliances.
- *Replenishment goods:* moderate cost, high-frequency purchases. Items that are relatively expensive and easy to ship will be most successful. Examples include health care items such as vitamins, beauty aids, and gourmet foods.

Figure 17-1 is Forrester's estimate of the percent of total retail sales that will take place on the Internet in 2003 for several products in each category.

As the opening example discussed, shoppers derive a number of advantages from shopping on the Internet. In Illustration 17-1, eToys.com promotes convenience as a primary advantage of its outlet, with selection and price also mentioned.

For at least some product categories and people, the Internet offers greater selection, convenience, and lower prices than other distribution channels. However, in 1998, less than a third of those using the Internet shopped on it. Why? One study produced the following reasons:[5]

Reasons for Not Shopping on the Internet	*Male*	*Female*
Security concerns	70%	73%
Lack of "touch"	45	54
Unfamiliar merchants	41	37
Too difficult	21	26

As these percentages suggest, females are less likely to shop on-line than are males (19 percent versus 32 percent, according to one survey), a problem that Internet retailers

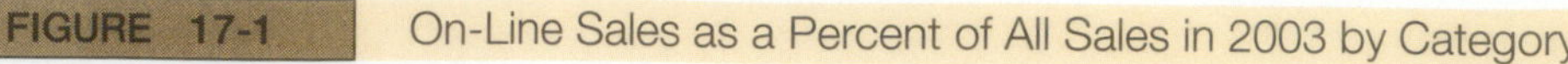

FIGURE 17-1 On-Line Sales as a Percent of All Sales in 2003 by Category

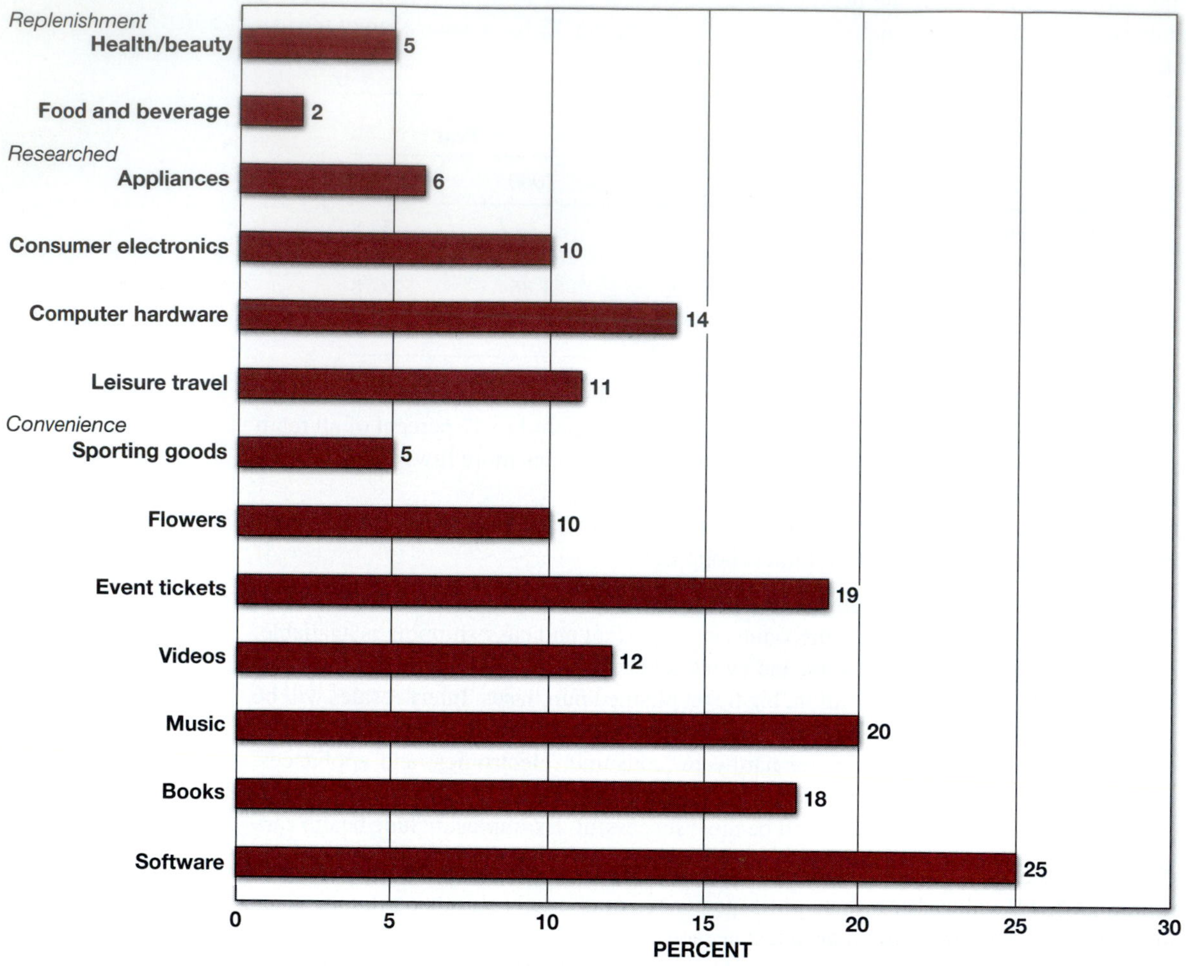

Source: Based on J. L. McQuivey et al., "On-Line Retail Strategies," *The Forrester Report,* November 1998 , p. 8.

are working hard to overcome.[6] One approach is to link on-line retailers such as Lands' End, J. Crew, Godiva Chocolatier, and Gymboree, who cater to women, with popular women's content sites such as iVillage.

Sending a credit card number via the Internet remains a major concern despite programs designed to provide secure transmissions. In addition, Internet shopping, like other forms of in-home shopping, is not viewed as being as satisfying as store shopping by many consumers. This is caused by the inability to physically examine the products, the lack of social interaction involved in the process, and the lack of activity, stimulation, and "getting out of the house or office" provided by store visits.

Consider the following quotes concerning substantial purchases such as cars:

> Part of the enjoyment of it (bargaining) is winning the game. Part of the enjoyment is the pleasure it gives . . . There is the thrill of victory.
>
> My attitude toward buying a car is more like a fight . . . A one-price policy would mean that I automatically lose the fight.

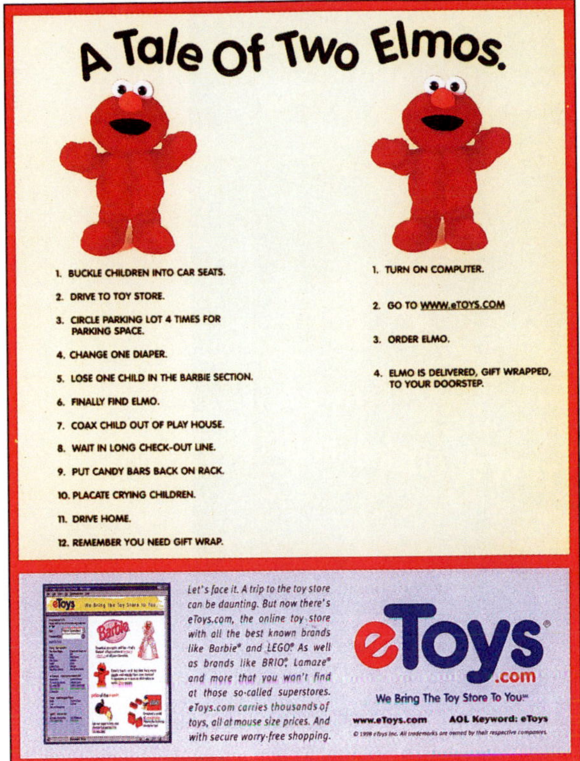

Courtesy eToys, Inc.

ILLUSTRATION 17-1

While some Internet stores such as Buy.com focus almost exclusively on price, others stress selection, information, or, in this example, convenience coupled with selection and price.

I was able to play "Big Man Daddy" in front of my daughters. And they were impressed. In a way I was putting on a show.[7]

These quotes indicate some of the noneconomic value that some consumers obtain from bargaining. Others value different types of interactions that are common in store-based shopping but are not easily duplicated on the Internet.

As we saw in Chapter 15, there are a number of demographic characteristics that vary between those who use the Internet and those who do not. There are also demographic distinctions among those who shop on the Internet and those who use it but do not shop on it. Compared to users who do not shop on it, Internet shoppers tend to have higher education levels, somewhat higher incomes, and to be white, male, and live in the northeast or west. Internet shopping does not appear to vary with age, except that those under 24 and those over 64 shop on-line less than the other age groups.[8]

At present there are very few data on factors other than demographics associated with Internet shopping.[9] Further, the growth of shopping on the Internet and the changes in the nature of Internet shopping are so rapid that many differences between shoppers and nonshoppers are likely to be very transitory.[10]

There is a tendency to think of Internet retailers as distinct from store-based retailers and other forms of in-home shopping such as catalogs. Internet retailers bring to mind startup firms such as Amazon.com, Priceline, and Buy.com. However, most large store-based retailers and catalog firms also have Internet sales sites. Thus, firms such as Eddie Bauer actively market through retail outlets, catalogs, and the Internet. The Internet allows regional retailers such as Eastern Mountain Sports to instantly become national and international in scope (see Illustration 17-2). It also allows traditional retailers such as

ILLUSTRATION 17-2

An Internet sales site instantly converts a regional firm into a national and even international one.

Courtesy Eastern Mountain Sports.

Toys "R" Us and Macy's to reach smaller communities where they could not economically operate before.

Consumer goods manufacturers such as Nike and Avon are increasingly offering their products directly to consumers via the Internet. A deterrent to manufacturers is concern about alienating their traditional distribution channels.

Store-Based Retailing

As we have seen, technology promises exciting changes in the future of nonstore retailing. However, the vast majority of retail sales take place in stores, and this will remain true for the foreseeable future. And today there is an explosion in store-based retailing activities. Brand stores are emerging as major sales volume outlets as well as promotional devices for brands such as Levi's, Nike, Reebok, and OshKosh B'Gosh.[11] The Sharper Image and similar outlets function as adult toy stores where one can play with the latest fun items for adults. Category killers or superstores provide a huge range of brands and variety of items within one product category at low prices. Toys "R" Us and Home Depot are the best known examples.

Giant outlets are not the only way to succeed. McDonald's has found that 75 percent of its customers decide where to eat just five minutes before they make the purchase. Thus, it and its fast-food competitors are building thousands of small outlets inside other outlets such as Wal-Mart, Home Depot, and gas stations. McDonald's is also increasing the value customers receive by providing play areas at outlets catering to families with younger children.

Courtesy Mall of America.

ILLUSTRATION 17-3

One way store-based retailers add value for their customers is by providing a fun shopping environment. This provides an advantage against similar retailers who do not have such an environment, as well as against alternative forms of retailing such as the Internet.

Other firms are pursuing excellence in narrow niches. Sunglass Hut operates small kiosks in malls, airports, and other high-traffic areas. The kiosks carry 1,000 different kinds of sunglasses at very low prices. Byerly's is an upscale supermarket chain that offers a large selection of prepared foods, carpeting to deaden the noise and add to the ambience, and candy that is kept well out of the reach of children.[12] Giant superstores such as Staples, Home Depot, Costco, and Blockbuster are opening ministores in small towns, tiny shopping centers, and downtown areas.[13]

Traditional department stores such as Sears are fighting back with renovations and new product lines. Malls are becoming giant entertainment centers. For example, the Mall of America near Minneapolis is built around an amusement park. It also has a miniature golf course, 9 nightclubs, 45 restaurants, a 14-screen movie complex, and a wedding chapel (see Illustration 17-3).[14] Retailing is clearly an exciting, competitive area. Those retailers who best understand their consumers will be the ones to prosper in the future.

In addition to commercial outlets, a substantial volume of retail trade occurs in noncommercial settings, such as garage sales, flea markets, farmer's markets, swap meets, and consumer-to-consumer (through classified ads and computer bulletin boards).[15]

OUTLET CHOICE VERSUS PRODUCT CHOICE

Outlet selection is obviously important to managers of retail firms such as Amazon.com, Sears, and L. L. Bean. However, it is equally important to consumer goods marketers. There are three basic sequences a consumer can follow when making a purchase decision:

TABLE 17-1

Marketing Strategy Based on the Consumer Decision Sequence

Decision Sequence	Level in the Channel: *Retailer*	*Manufacturer*
1. Outlet First, Brand Second	Image advertising Margin management on shelf space, displays Location analysis Appropriate pricing	Distribution in key outlets Point-of-purchase, shelf space, and position Programs to strengthen existing outlets
2. Brand First, Outlet Second	Many brands and/or key brands Co-op ads featuring brands Price special on brands Yellow Pages listings under brands	More exclusive distribution Brand availability advertising (Yellow Pages) Brand image management
3. Simultaneous	Margin training for sales personnel Multiple brands/key brands High-service or low-price structure	Programs targeted at retail sales personnel Distribution in key outlets Co-op advertising

(1) brand (or item) first, outlet second; (2) outlet first, brand second; or (3) brand and outlet simultaneously.[16]

Our model and discussion in the previous two chapters suggest that brands are selected first and outlets second. This situation may arise frequently. For example, a consumer considering buying a notebook computer may look in relevant consumer publications and talk with knowledgeable individuals. Based on this information, the consumer may select a brand and purchase it from the outlet with the lowest price (or easiest access, best image, service, or other relevant attributes). This has been the process assumed in the discussion thus far in this text.

However, for many individuals and product categories, stores rather than brands form the evoked set.[17] In our notebook computer example, the consumer might be familiar with one store—Campus Computers—that sells personal computers. He or she may decide to visit that store and select a computer from the brands available there.

A third strategy is to compare the brands in one's evoked set at the stores in the evoked set. The decision would involve a simultaneous evaluation of both store and product attributes. Thus, a consumer might choose between a second preferred computer at a store with friendly personnel and excellent service facilities versus a favorite computer at an impersonal outlet with no service facilities.

The appropriate marketing strategies for both retailers and manufacturers differ depending on the decision sequence generally used by the target market. How would a manufacturer's strategy differ depending on whether the brand or store was selected first? A brand-first decision sequence would suggest brand image and feature advertising, Yellow Pages listings by brand, and possibly a limited distribution strategy. An outlet-first choice would tend to produce a focus on point-of-purchase materials, distribution through key outlets, and programs to encourage good shelf space and support from store personnel. Table 17-1 highlights additional strategic implications.

Courtesy Wal-Mart Stores, Inc.

ILLUSTRATION 17-4

Manufacturers often use advertising to create brand demand and to direct consumers to appropriate outlets.

An example of a firm attempting to both create product demand and direct consumers to the appropriate retail outlet is Ponds, which provides advertising dollars for retailers to produce product specific ads such as the one shown in Illustration 17-4. Retailers often share in the cost of such ads. In other cases, firms use retailers' names in the ads as an inducement for the retailer to carry or display the brand.

ATTRIBUTES AFFECTING RETAIL OUTLET SELECTION

The selection of a specific retail outlet, whether before or after a brand decision, involves a comparison of the alternative outlets on the consumer's evaluative criteria. This can involve selecting an outlet type such as the Internet, a catalog, or a store and/or a specific outlet within an outlet type such as Buybooks.com versus Amazon.com. This section considers a number of evaluative criteria commonly used by consumers to select retail outlets. Unfortunately, virtually all of this material is related most directly to choosing from among stores, as little research is available on the other types of choices consumers make.

Outlet Image

A given consumer's or target market's perception of all of the attributes associated with a retail outlet is generally referred to as the **store image.**[18] This is the same as the concept of brand image discussed in Chapter 9. One study found the following nine dimensions and 23 components of these nine dimensions of store image.[19] Notice that the store atmosphere component is primarily affective or feeling in nature.

Dimension	*Component(s)*
Merchandise	Quality, selection, style, and price
Service	Layaway plan, sales personnel, easy return, credit, and delivery
Clientele	Customers
Physical facilities	Cleanliness, store layout, shopping ease, and attractiveness
Convenience	Location and parking
Promotion	Advertising
Store atmosphere	Congeniality, fun, excitement, comfort
Institutional	Store reputation
Post-transaction	Satisfaction

This study focused on stores; the components and probably the dimensions will require adjusting for use with other types of retail outlets. For example, 800 numbers, 24-hour operations, and ample in-bound phone lines (no busy signals) are relevant to the convenience of a catalog merchant such as L. L. Bean, not location and parking as listed in the table. What determines convenience for an Internet site?

A study that focused on the affective component of store image or personality found the following differences across stores (the higher the number, the more the component fits the outlet):[20]

	Affective Component			
Store	*Pleasant*	*Unpleasant*	*Active*	*Sleepy*
JCPenney's	18.5	12.8	13.7	14.3
Kmart	15.2	12.6	14.8	12.9
Macy's	25.2	7.2	19.0	6.7
The Sharper Image	23.5	7.8	22.4	6.9
Victoria's Secret	25.5	9.5	16.0	12.7

Notice that JCPenney's and Kmart are about as strong on the unpleasant component as on the pleasant component, and they are viewed as being neither active nor sleepy. This suggests that shopping motives will have to come from price, selection, or other functional features. In contrast, Macy's is a pleasant, active place to shop. Consumers will shop at stores such as Macy's because they are pleasant and active rather than, or in addition to, their functional characteristics. Victoria's Secret and The Sharper Image are both pleasant places to shop, but the former is a less active experience than the latter. What do these affective results suggest for each firm's marketing strategy?

Marketers make extensive use of image data in formulating retail strategies.[21] First, marketers control many of the elements that determine an outlet's image. Second, differing groups of consumers desire different things from various types of retail outlets.[22] Thus, a focused, managed image that matches the target market's desires is essential for most retailers.[23]

Department stores traditionally attempted to "be all things to all people." As a result, they suffered serious losses to more specialized competitors as markets became increasingly segmented during the 1980s. Their images were too diffuse to attract customers. In response, many have sought to evolve into collections of distinctive specialty stores or stores-within-stores, each with a sharply focused image keyed to a well-defined target market. Sears attempted to capitalize on its reputation for hard-goods while simultaneously

Courtesy Sears & Roebuck.

ILLUSTRATION 17-5

Sears attempted to create an image as a good source for stylish clothes.

developing an image for cosmetics and stylish clothes (see Illustration 17-5). However, this positioning strategy did not work, and Sears recently switched to a price/convenience approach (see Case 4–4).

Other outlets concentrate on one or more attributes that are important to a segment of consumers or that are important to most consumers in certain situations. As we saw earlier, Buy.com emphasizes price as its main competitive advantage. 7-Eleven Food Stores have followed the second approach, which is to provide customers "what they want, when they want it, where they want it." Thus, they focus on providing convenience (easy access, extended hours, quick service) for consumers in those situations where convenience is the key attribute.

Not only individual stores but also store types (discount, department, secondhand), shopping areas (downtown, malls, neighborhoods) and shopping methods (television, phone, catalog, Internet) have images.[24] Thus, retailers should be concerned not only with their own image but also with the image of their shopping type, area, and method. The ability to aggressively portray a consistent, integrated image is a significant advantage for shopping malls. As we saw earlier, many consumers will not shop the Internet due to security concerns associated with using a credit card on the Web. It would benefit all Internet marketers to jointly attack this problem.

Retailer Brands

Closely related to store image are **store brands.** At the extreme, the store or outlet is the brand. The Gap, Victoria's Secret, and Body Shop International are examples. All the items carried in the store are the store's own brand. Traditionally, retailers carried only manufacturers' brands and only a few such as Sears and Wards developed their own house or store brands. In the 1970s, many stores began to develop store brands as low-price alternatives to national brands, and many continue with this approach.[25]

However, increasingly retailers such as Wal-Mart are developing and promoting high-quality brands with either the store's name or an independent name. Sears has been very active and effective in this area. Such brands not only provide attractive margins for these outlets; if they are developed appropriately, they become an important attribute of the outlet; that is, they are another reason for the consumer to shop that store. And importantly, no other outlet can carry this brand. Thus, the Kenmore and Craftsman brands are important features of a Sears store.

Virtually all shoppers now purchase store brands at least some of the time. Store brands represent 15 percent of supermarket sales and 30 percent of apparel sales.[26] Store brands have a large share in the home appliance market as well.

The key to success of store brands seems clear—high quality.[27] The traditional pattern of providing reasonable quality at a low price is no longer necessarily optimal.[28] In fact, stressing quality over price may be particularly beneficial if the brand carries the store's name or will become associated with the store.

Retail Advertising

Retailers use advertising to communicate their attributes, particularly sale prices, to consumers. It is clear that price advertising can attract people to stores. Revealing results were obtained in a major study involving newspaper ads in seven cities for a range of product categories (motor oil, sheets, digital watches, pants, suits, coffee makers, dresses, and mattresses). The impact of the retail advertisements varied widely by product category. For example, 88 percent of those who came to the store in response to the advertisement for motor oil purchased the advertised item, compared to only 16 percent of those responding to the dress ad. Approximately 50 percent of the shoppers overall purchased the advertised item that attracted them to the store.

As Figure 17-2 illustrates, purchases of the advertised item understate the total impact of the ad. Sales of additional items to customers who came to purchase an advertised item are referred to as **spillover sales.** Spillover sales in this study equaled sales of the advertised items. That is, for every $1 spent on the sale item by people who came to the store in response to the advertising, another $1 was spent on some other item(s) in the store.[29]

FIGURE 17-2 Expenditures of Individuals Drawn to a Store by an Advertised Item

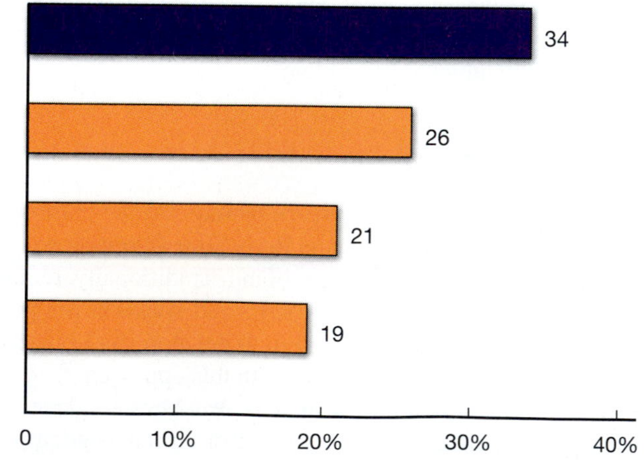

Another study produced the results shown below:[30]

Action	Reason for Visiting Store: *Purchase Promoted Item*	*Other Reason*
Dollars spent on promoted items	$11.30	$ 3.27
Dollars spent on regular items	18.48	21.90
Total	$29.78	$25.17
Store profit	$ 5.64	$ 5.77

Retailers evaluating the benefits of price or other promotions must consider the impact on overall store sales and profits, not just those of the advertised item.

Although a large percentage of retail advertising stresses price, particularly sales price, studies continue to show that price is frequently not the prime reason consumers select a retail outlet. This suggests that many retailers could benefit by stressing service, selection, and/or the affective benefits of their outlets.[31]

As the ad for Buy.com at the beginning of this chapter and the ad in Illustration 17-2 show, Internet retailers advertise in mass media both to attract consumers to their sites and to build an image. Catalog merchants use both mass media and mail to persuade consumers to use their catalogs.

Price Advertising Decisions Retailers face three decisions when they consider using price advertising:

1. How large a price discount should be used?
2. Should comparison or reference prices be used?
3. What verbal statements should accompany the price information?

Consumers tend to assume that any advertised price represents a price reduction or sale price. Showing a comparison price increases the perceived savings significantly. However, the strength of the perception varies with the manner in which the comparison or reference price is presented. A **reference price** is a price in relation to which other prices are compared. In the claim, "Regularly $9.95, now only $6.95," $9.95 is the reference price. An **external reference price** is a price presented by a marketer for the consumer to use to compare with the current price. An **internal reference price** is a price or price range[32] that a consumer retrieves from memory to compare to a price in the market.[33]

Although there are situational influences and individual differences,[34] most consumers understand external reference prices and are influenced by them but do not completely believe them.[35] The reason for the lack of belief is the practice of some retailers of using inflated reference prices. These inflated prices could be "suggested list prices" in markets where virtually all sales are at a lower level. Or, they may reflect prices that the store set for the merchandise originally that were too high and produced few sales. The price reduction being shown then merely corrects an earlier pricing error but does not provide meaningful benefit to the consumer. Since price and sale advertising have a strong impact on consumer purchases, the FTC and many states have special guidelines and regulations controlling their use.

The best approach for retailers seems to be to present the sale price and (1) the dollar amount saved if it is large, (2) the percentage saved when it is large, and (3) both if both are large. Thus, $10 savings on a $200 item should show the dollar savings but not the percent savings. A $10 saving on a $20 item could stress both the dollar and the percent savings.

ILLUSTRATION 17-6

The sale ad presents the sales price and the reference price but not the dollar or percent savings. Is this wise?

A $1.00 saving on a $3.00 item should focus on the percent savings.[36] The regular price could be shown in any of these conditions.[37] The regular price (the price on which the savings are calculated) should be the price at which the store normally sells a reasonable volume of the brand being discounted.

Such words or phrases as "now only," "compare at," or "special" appear to enhance the perceived value of a sale. However, this varies by situation, initial price level and discount size, consumer group, and retail outlet.[38] Thus, a retail manager must confirm these generalizations for his or her store and product line.

Retailers need to use caution in how they use price advertising. Such advertising signals not only the price of the advertised items but also the price level of the store.[39] And, since price level, quality, service, and other important attributes are often linked in the consumer's mind, inappropriate price advertising can have a negative effect on the store's image. Providing a rationale for a sale price such as "a special buy from the manufacturer" may enhance consumers' perceptions of the sale.[40]

The ad in Illustration 17-6 places primary emphasis on the sale price but also shows the reference price. Since both the dollar and the percent savings are relatively large, the research we have reviewed would suggest that both these figures should be presented.

Outlet Location and Size

The location of a retail outlet plays an important role in consumer store choice. If all other things are approximately equal, the consumer generally will select the closest store. Likewise, the size of an outlet is an important factor in store choice. Unless a customer is particularly interested in fast service or convenience, larger outlets tend to be preferred over smaller outlets.

Several methods for calculating the level of store attraction based on store size and distance have been developed. One such model is called the **retail attraction model** (also called the **retail gravitation model**). A popular version of this model is:

$$MS_i = \frac{\frac{S_i}{T_i^{\lambda}}}{\sum_{i=1}^{n} \frac{S_i}{T_i^{\lambda}}}$$

where

MS_i = Market share of store i
S_i = Size of store i
T_i = Travel time to store i
λ = Attraction factor for a particular product category

In the retail gravitation model, store size generally is measured in square footage and assumed to be a measure of breadth of merchandise. Likewise, the distance or travel time to a store is assumed to be a measure of the effort, both physical and psychological, to reach a given retail area. Because willingness to travel to an outlet varies by product class, the travel time is raised to the λ power. This allows the effect of distance or travel time to vary by product.[41]

For a convenience item or minor shopping good, the attraction coefficient is quite large, since shoppers are unwilling to travel very far for such items. However, major high-involvement purchases such as automobiles or specialty items such as wedding dresses generate greater willingness to travel to distant trading areas. When this is the case, the attraction coefficient is small and the effect of travel time as a deterrent is reduced.

There is also evidence that the attraction coefficient should vary depending on the size of the shopping list for that trip.[42] Thus, while the attraction coefficient might be quite large for the purchase of one or two convenience items, it may become much smaller if 30 or 40 such items are to be purchased on the same trip.

Consumers often combine shopping trips and purposes.[43] Thus, a consumer may visit a health club, have lunch with a friend, pick up the laundry, shop for food for the next few days, and pick up a prescription on one trip. Thus, retail patronage is in part a function of an outlet's location in relation to other outlets and consumers' travel patterns. Combining outlets and/or adding departments based on such shopping patterns can produce value for customers and increased revenue for the firm.[44] An example is supermarkets such as Safeway and Albertson's adding pharmacies to their outlets.

Gravitation models have yet to be developed for Internet stores. Current industry wisdom is that size in terms of number of items carried per product category is critically important in attracting customers. Thus, one of Amazon.com's advantages is the vast selection it offers. Distance is not relevant for Internet outlets but ease of searching the site is. Thus, it is likely that some form of gravitation model will be developed for Internet outlets.

CONSUMER CHARACTERISTICS AND OUTLET CHOICE

The preceding discussion by and large has focused on store attributes independent of the specific characteristics of the consumers in the target market. However, different consumers have vastly differing desires and reasons for shopping. This section of the chapter examines two consumer characteristics that are particularly relevant to store choice: perceived risk and shopper orientation.

TABLE 17-2

The Economic and Social Risk of Various Types of Products

Social Risk	Economic Risk: *Low*	Economic Risk: *High*
Low	Wine (personal use)	Personal computer
	Stocks	Auto repairs
	Kitchen supplies	Clothes washer
	Pens/pencils	Insurance
	Gasoline	Doctor/lawyer
High	Fashion accessories	Business suits
	Hairstyles	Living room furniture
	Gifts (inexpensive)	Automobile
	Wine (entertaining)	Snowboard
	Deodorant	Ski suit

Perceived Risk

The purchase of products involves the risk that they may not perform as expected. As described in Chapter 15, such a failure may result in a high:

- *Social cost* (e.g., a hairstyle that is not appreciated by one's peers).
- *Financial cost* (e.g., an expensive pair of shoes that become too uncomfortable to wear).
- *Time cost* (e.g., a television repair that required the set to be taken to the shop, left, and then picked up later).
- *Effort cost* (e.g., a computer disk that fails after being loaded with several hours of work).
- *Physical cost* (e.g., a new medicine that produced a harmful side effect).

The first of these is generally termed *social risk,* while the next three are often considered to be *economic risk.* Table 17-2 shows that socks and gasoline are low in economic and social risk, while hairstyles and small gifts are low in economic risk but high in social risk. Other products, such as personal computers and auto repairs, are low in social risk but high in economic risk. Finally, automobiles and living room furniture are high in both economic and social risk.[45] Table 17-2 also indicates the role of the situation in perceived risk. Wine is shown as low in both social and economic risk when used for personal consumption but high in social risk when served while entertaining.

The perception of these risks *differs* among consumers, based in part on their past experiences and lifestyles. For this reason, **perceived risk** is considered a consumer characteristic as well as a product characteristic.[46] For example, while many individuals would feel no social risk associated with the brand of car owned, others would.

Like product categories, retail outlets are perceived as having varying degrees of risk. Traditional outlets are perceived as low in risk, while more innovative outlets such as the Internet are viewed as higher risk.[47]

The above findings lead to a number of insights into retailing strategy, including the following:

- Nontraditional outlets need to minimize the perceived risk of shopping if they sell items with either high economic or social risk. Lands' End attempts to reduce perceived risk by stressing toll-free ordering, 24-hour toll-free customer service telephones with trained assistants, and a 100 percent satisfaction guarantee. Word of mouth from satisfied customers reinforces these advertised policies.

- Nontraditional outlets need brand-name merchandise in those product categories with high perceived risk. Most Internet retailers feature such items.
- Traditional outlets have a major advantage with high-perceived-risk product lines. These lines should generally be their primary strategy focus. Low-risk items can be used to round out the overall assortment. They can be promoted through point-of-purchase materials and price discounts.
- Economic risks can be reduced through warranties and similar policies. Social risk is harder to reduce. A skilled sales force, known brands, and satisfaction guarantees can help reduce this type of risk.

Shopping Orientation

Individuals go shopping for more complex reasons than simply acquiring a product or set of products. Diversion from routine activities, exercise, sensory stimulation, social interactions, learning about new trends, and even acquiring interpersonal power ("bossing" clerks) are nonpurchase reasons for shopping.[48] Of course, the relative importance of these motives varies both across individuals and within individuals over time as the situation changes.[49] Illustration 17-3 (page 597) shows how malls can provide an inviting environment for activities in addition to shopping.

A shopping style that puts particular emphasis on certain activities or shopping motivations is called a **shopping orientation.** Shopping orientations are closely related to general lifestyle and are subject to similar influences. For example, one study found that retail work experience, stage in the household life cycle, and income help to predict shopping orientation.[50] The results of two distinct approaches to classifying consumers by shopping orientation follow.

Psychographic-Based Shopping Orientations Table 17-3 provides the demographic profiles of seven commonly held shopping orientations. The shopping patterns of each are described below. The percents associated with the groups add to only 78, as 22 percent of the respondents did not fit into any of these seven categories.

Inactive Shoppers (15 percent) have extremely restricted lifestyles and shopping interests. Best characterized by their inactivity, Inactive Shoppers do not engage in outdoor or do-it-yourself activities except for working in the yard or garden. They do not express strong enjoyment or interest in shopping, nor are they particularly concerned about such shopping attributes as price, employee service, or product selection.

Active Shoppers (12.8 percent) have demanding lifestyles and are "tough" shoppers. They engage in all forms of outdoor activities and are usually do-it-yourselfers. Actives enjoy "shopping around," and price is a major consideration in their search. Actives appear to shop more as an expression of their intense lifestyles rather than an interest in finding bargains. Therefore, these shoppers balance price with quality, fashion, and selection in their search for value.

Service Shoppers (10 percent) demand a high level of in-store service when shopping. They usually seek convenient stores with friendly, helpful employees, and they quickly become impatient if they have to wait for a clerk to help them.

Traditional Shoppers (14.1 percent) share Active Shoppers' preoccupation with outdoor activities, but not their enthusiasm for shopping. They actively hike, camp, hunt, and fish, and are do-it-yourselfers who often work on their cars. In general, though, Traditional Shoppers are not price sensitive nor do they have other strong shopper requirements.

Dedicated Fringe Shoppers (8.8 percent) are heavy catalog shoppers. They are do-it-yourselfers and are more likely than average to try new products. They have almost a compulsion for being different. Dedicated Fringe Shoppers are not interested in extensive

TABLE 17-3 Selected Demographic Characteristics of Shopper Types

Characteristics	Shopper Types						
	Inactive	*Active*	*Service*	*Traditional*	*Dedicated Fringe*	*Price*	*Transitional*
Age							
18–34	35.5%	54.6%	40.9%	52.3%	46.3%	36.9%	63.8%
35–44	20.4	21.3	23.7	21.3	21.7	22.4	12.6
45–64	31.5	19.7	28.3	22.9	25.2	29.0	19.1
65 or older	12.6	4.4	7.1	3.5	6.7	11.7	4.5
Sex							
Male	36.1	46.6	48.6	62.3	50.0	25.6	45.0
Female	63.9	53.4	51.4	37.7	50.0	74.4	55.0
Social Class							
Lower	49.9	51.5	43.4	43.7	48.8	45.4	55.9
Middle	46.3	46.0	52.6	53.2	47.5	50.0	40.5
Upper	3.8	2.5	4.0	3.1	3.7	4.6	3.6
Stage of Family Life Cycle (condensed)							
Young singles not living at home	7.7	5.0	6.8	8.0	5.9	2.5	8.5
Young married couples	21.4	38.6	26.4	34.7	33.9	26.5	46.9
Older married couples with dependent children	32.5	34.8	38.8	37.2	29.6	33.5	23.8
Older married couples without dependent children	27.9	20.0	23.1	18.8	27.2	29.3	17.8
Solitary survivors	10.6	1.6	4.9	1.3	3.4	8.2	3.0

socializing. They have little interest in television and radio advertisements and exhibit limited brand and store loyalty.

Price Shoppers (10.4 percent), as the name implies, are most identifiable by their extreme price consciousness. Price Shoppers are willing to undertake an extended search to meet their price requirements, and they rely heavily on all forms of advertising to find the lowest prices.

Transitional Shoppers (6.9 percent) seem to be consumers in earlier stages of the family life cycle who have not yet formalized their lifestyle patterns and shopping values. They take an active interest in repairing and personalizing cars. Most participate in a variety of outdoor activities. They are more likely than average to try new products. Transitional Shoppers exhibit little interest in shopping around for low prices. They are probably "eclectic shoppers" because they appear to make up their minds quickly to buy products once they become interested.

The opportunities for developing segment-specific marketing strategies are clearly evident. For example, Inactive Shoppers might respond to home delivery. Active Shoppers would respond well to entertainment-focused malls, as would transitional shoppers. However, as a single store attempts to target more of the segments, the risk of failure with all groups increases, as many of their desires are, if not mutually exclusive, difficult to meet within the same outlet. Which of these groups would shop at Wal-Mart? Banana Republic? Sears? Which are the best targets for various types of Internet outlets?

Motivation-Based Shopping Orientations of College Students A recent study used projective techniques to ascertain the ways college students approach shopping.[51] It had consumers "Think about an animal that best describes you as a shopper . . . (and) explain what it is about your behavior that makes this animal an appropriate metaphor." One response was, in part:

> The reason I chose a hawk is basically the speed and grace in which my shopping is done. I glide through the mall and when I see what I want I dive in and "attack" it. To extend this metaphor the trip to the mall is short and to the point. Just as a hawk swoops down and kills its prey, I see the item and grab it.

Based on this projective research, six shopping orientations were uncovered.

Chameleons indicated that their shopping styles are situation-specific or constantly changing. Their shopping approach is based on product type, shopping impetus, and purchase task.

Collectors/Gatherers are characterized by their propensity to stockpile items and to purchase large quantities to either save money or alleviate the need for shopping. They attempt to get the best price and take advantage of retailer guarantees.

Foragers are particular and are motivated to purchase only the desired items. They are willing to search extensively and have little store loyalty. They like to shop alone.

Hibernants are indifferent toward shopping. Their shopping patterns are opportunistic rather than need driven and they will often postpone even required purchases.

Predators are purposive and speed oriented in their shopping. They plan before shopping and like to shop alone. They don't enjoy shopping and tend to shop outlets where they are assured of getting the items they need quickly.

Scavengers enjoy shopping both to make purchases and as an activity. They like to go to sales and consider shopping to be entertainment. They make numerous unplanned purchases.

Clearly, differing marketing strategies would be required for each of these orientations.

IN-STORE INFLUENCES THAT AFFECT BRAND CHOICES

As Figure 17-3 indicates, it is not uncommon to enter a retail outlet with the intention of purchasing a particular brand but to leave with a different brand or additional items. Influences operating within the store induce additional information processing and subsequently affect the final purchase decision. This portion of the chapter examines five variables that singularly and in combination influence brand decisions inside a retail store: *point-of-purchase displays, price reductions, store layout, stockout situations,* and *sales personnel.*

The Nature of Unplanned Purchases

The fact that consumers often purchase brands different from or in addition to those planned has led to an interest in *impulse purchases.* **Impulse purchases** are defined as

FIGURE 17-3 Supermarket Decisions: Two-Thirds Are Made In-Store

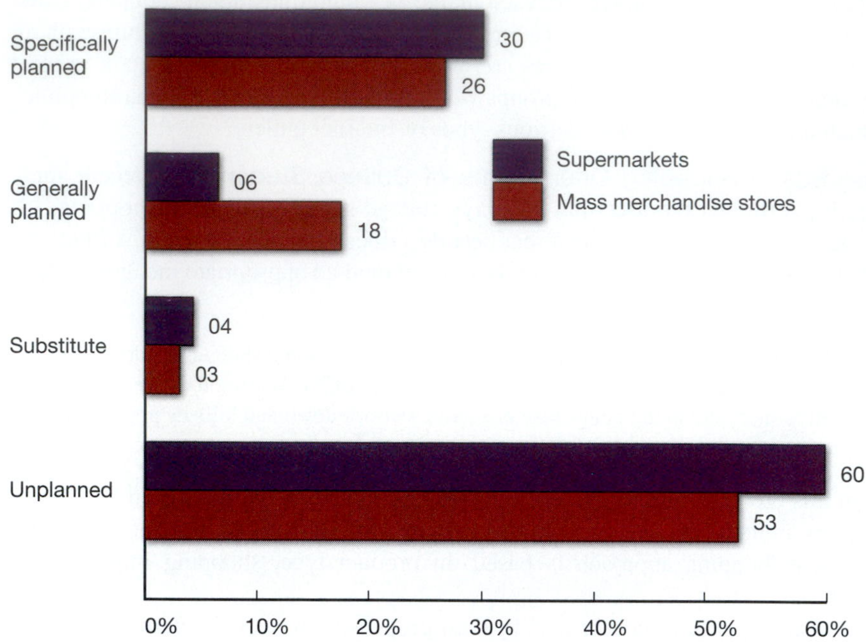

Source: *The 1995 POPAI Consumer Buying Habits Study* (Washington, DC, Point-of-Purchase Institute, www.popai.com, 1995 ©), p. 18.

purchases made in a store that are different from those the consumer planned to make prior to entering the store. Unfortunately, the term *impulse purchase,* and even its more accurate substitute, **unplanned purchase,** implies a lack of rationality or alternative evaluation. However, this is not necessarily true.[52] The decision to purchase Del Monte rather than Green Giant peas because Del Monte is on sale is certainly not illogical. Nor is an unplanned decision to take advantage of the unexpected availability of fresh strawberries.

Considering in-store purchase decisions as the result of additional information processing within the store leads to more useful marketing strategies than considering these purchases to be random or illogical.[53] This approach allows the marketer to utilize knowledge of the target market, its motives, and the perception process to increase sales of specific items. The Point-of-Purchase Advertising Institute uses the following definitions:

- *Specifically planned.* A specific brand or item decided on before visiting the store and purchased as planned.
- *Generally planned.* A prestore decision to purchase a product category such as vegetables but not the specific item.
- *Substitute.* A change from a specifically or generally planned item to a functional substitute.
- *Unplanned.* An item bought that the shopper did not have in mind on entering the store.
- *In-store decisions.* The sum of generally planned, substitute, and unplanned purchases.

Table 17-4 illustrates the extent of purchasing (in the United States and Canada) that is not specifically planned. It reveals that consumers make most item or brand decisions *after* entering the store. Thus, marketing managers not only must strive to position their brand in the target market's evoked set, they also must attempt to influence the in-store decisions of

In-Store Purchase Behavior **TABLE 17-4**

Product	*Specifically Planned*	*Generally Planned*	+ *Substituted*	+ *Unplanned*	= *In-Store Decisions*
Total study average*	30%	61%	4%	60%	70%
Hair care*	23	4	5	68	77
Magazines/Newspapers*	11	3	1	84	89
Oral hygiene products*	30	5	5	61	71
Automotive oil*	21	—	—	79	79
Tobacco products*	32	6	—	61	68
Coffee*	42	5	6	47	58
First aid products*	7	10	—	83	93
Cereal*	33	9	6	52	67
Soft drinks*	40	3	5	51	60
Mixers	23	6	4	68	77
Fresh fruits, vegetables*	67	7	1	25	33
Cold remedies†	28	35	19	18	72
Toothpaste/toothbrushes†	38	31	16	15	62
Antacids/laxatives†	39	37	12	12	61
Facial cosmetics†	40	34	11	15	60

Sources: *The 1995 POPAI Consumer Buying Habits Study* (Washington, DC, Point-of-Purchase Institute, www.popai.com, 1995 ©) and *The 1992 POPAI/Horner Canadian Drug Store Study* (Washington, DC, Point-of-Purchase Institute, www.popai.com, 1992 ©).

their potential consumers. Retailers must not only attract consumers to their outlets; they should structure the purchasing environment in a manner that provides maximum encouragement for unplanned purchases.[54]

In-store marketing strategies are particularly important for product categories characterized by very high rates of in-store purchase decisions. For example, first aid products (93 percent in-store decisions) and oral hygiene products such as toothpaste and mouthwash (89 percent in-store decisions) represent major opportunities. In contrast, fresh fruits, soft drinks, and baby food represent less opportunity for in-store marketing strategies.

We now turn our attention to some of the strategies that manufacturers and retailers can use to influence in-store decisions.

Point-of-Purchase Displays

Point-of-purchase (P-O-P) displays are common in the retailing of many products, and the impact these displays have on brand sales is often tremendous. Figure 17-4 provides a visual representation of this impact for six product categories. Notice the impact that product type has on the effectiveness of P-O-P material. The impact of P-O-P materials also varies with the location of the material, as shown below:

Location	*Percent Sales Increase*
On the shelf	11%
Rear endcap	141
Front endcap	162

FIGURE 17-4 The Sales Impact of Point-of-Purchase Displays

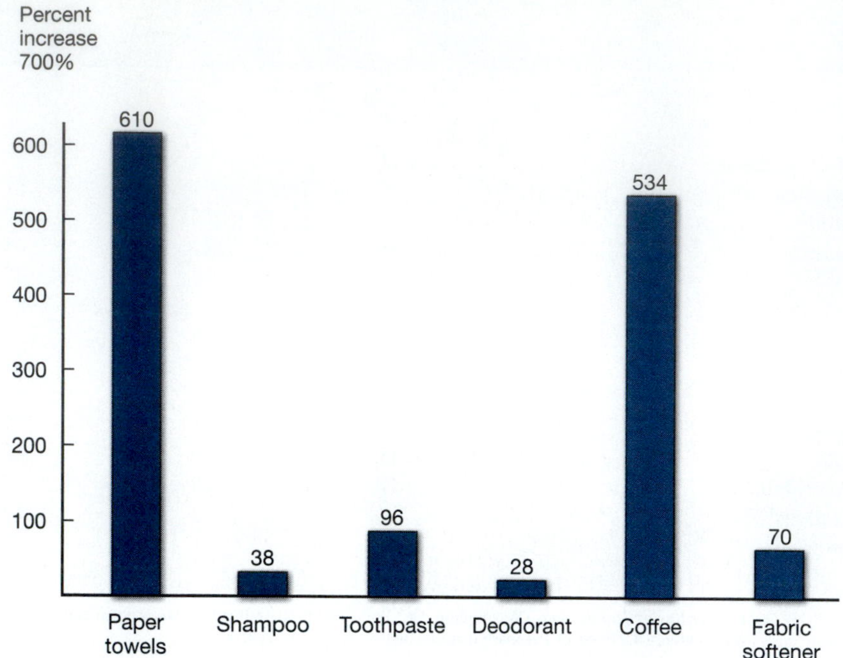

Source: *The POPAI/Kmart/Procter & Gamble Study of P-O-P Effectiveness in Mass Merchandizing Stores Study* (Washington, DC, Point-of-Purchase Institute, www.popai.com, 1993 ©).

Although the sales impact of displays varies widely by product type and location and between brands within a product category, there is generally a strong increase in sales.[55]

Illustration 17-7 shows two successful point-of-purchase displays from different cultures.

Price Reductions and Promotional Deals

Price reductions and promotional deals (coupons, multiple-item discounts, and gifts) are generally accompanied by the use of some point-of-purchase materials. Therefore, the relative impact of each is sometimes not clear.[56] Nonetheless, there is ample evidence that in-store price reductions affect brand decisions. The general pattern, observed in the United States, the United Kingdom, Japan, and Germany, is a sharp increase in sales when the price is first reduced, followed by a return to near-normal sales over time or after the price reduction ends.[57]

Sales increases in response to price reductions come from four sources.[58]

1. Current brand users may buy ahead of their anticipated needs (stockpiling). Stockpiling often leads to increased consumption of the brand, since it is readily available.
2. Users of competing brands may switch to the reduced price brand. These new brand buyers may or may not become repeat buyers of the brand.
3. Nonproduct category buyers may buy the brand because it is now a superior value to the substitute product or to "doing without."
4. Consumers who do not normally shop at the store may come to the store to buy the brand.

Courtesy Matsushita Electric Works, Ltd.

ILLUSTRATION 17-7

Point-of-purchase displays are effective across cultures.

High-quality brands tend to benefit more than brands from lower quality tiers when prices are reduced (and to suffer less when prices are raised).[59] Like brands, households respond to price reductions and deals differently. Younger and less educated consumers tend to be somewhat more responsive to deals.[60] Consumers also differ in their psychological proneness to respond to deals across product categories.[61]

As discussed earlier under price advertising, consumers judge store quality and image in part based on the number and nature of reduced price items in the store.[62] Therefore, retailers need to carefully consider their sale price policies in light of both the sales of the discounted items and the impact these discounts will have on the store image. In addition, "large basket" shoppers (those who purchase a large number of items at one time) prefer "everyday low prices" in which all items in the store have relatively low prices but few are reduced beyond that level ("on sale") to stores with somewhat higher standard prices with many sale items.[63]

Is a shirt from an Internet retailer priced at \$24.95 plus \$5.00 shipping and handling a better or worse deal than the same shirt priced at \$29.95 with shipping and handling free? Consumers tend to perceive the former to be a better deal than the latter. Research has shown that *partitioned prices* (the first scenario above) produced greater demand and a lower recalled total cost than the combined price (the second scenario).[64] This varies with the size of the secondary charge and the reason for it. In many cases this discounting of the secondary charge might be quite logical. In our example, a consumer might reason that the \$5.00 for shipping is no more than it would cost to visit a store to buy a similar shirt and therefore is not comparatively relevant. The implications are clearly that retailers should partition prices whenever there is a sound logical reason to do so *unless* the outlet is striving for a very high-quality (and thus high-price) image.

Consumer Insight 17-1

Why Do So Many Retail Prices End in 99?

Retail prices typically end just below a round number (a number ending in one or more zeros) such as $24.95 rather than $25.00 or $2.49 rather than $2.50. Having the last two digits (the rightmost digits) be 99 is particularly popular for lower priced goods with 95 being more common for higher priced items. Why? Even numbers are probably easier to remember and compare, and adding the cost of several items together is certainly simpler with round numbers.

Two theoretical explanations have been advanced and both have received some support in empirical studies. Both are probably valid but for different consumers and/or situations. The first and most supported explanation is the "left-to-right" theory. Multidigit numbers are processed left to right. As we saw in Chapters 9, 15, and 16, consumers frequently seek to minimize or at least reduce their information processing efforts. Therefore, they may ignore or pay little attention to the rightmost digits in a price. The number of digits receiving limited attention probably depends on the total number present. Thus, a price of $.99 may be interpreted as $.90 while one of $119.99 may be viewed as $110. To the extent that such a mechanism operates, marketers using 99 or 95 rightmost digits are receiving the highest possible price relative to the price consumers will perceive.

Another explanation is the sale-association theory. While many prices end in 99 normally, this is even more common for reduced price items. Therefore, consumers may associate (low-involvement learning) a 99 ending price as a sale or bargain price.

Critical Thinking Questions

1. Is it ethical for retailers to set prices with 99 rightmost digits knowing that consumers will interpret the price to be lower than it is?
2. Why don't consumers simply round up to the next larger number? Wouldn't it be easier to think of $9.99 as $10.00 rather than as $9.90 or even $9.00?

Source: R. M. Schindler and T. M. Kibarian, "Increased Consumer Sales Response through Use of 99-ending Prices," *Journal of Retailing,* no. 2 (1996), pp. 187–99; M. Stiving and R. S. Winer, "An Empirical Analysis of Price Endings with Scanner Data," *Journal of Consumer Research,* June 1997, pp. 57-67; and R. M. Schindler and P. N. Kiby, "Patterns of Rightmost Digits Used in Advertised Prices," *Journal of Consumer Research,* September 1997, pp. 192–201.

Consumer Insight 17-1 explores an additional retailing pricing phenomenon, the tendency to end prices in 99.

Outlet Atmosphere

Store atmosphere is influenced by such controllable attributes as lighting, layout, presentation of merchandise, fixtures, floor coverings, colors, sounds, odors, and the dress and behavior of sales and service personnel. A major uncontrollable component of atmosphere is the number, characteristics, and behavior of customers. Entertainment parks spend substantial time, effort, and resources training their staff. However, as the following quotes indicate, they cannot train their customers, who sometimes have a negative and sometimes a positive impact on the overall atmosphere.

- While standing in line at the Magic Kingdom at Disney some man in front of me continually blew cigar smoke in our faces.
- While standing in line at Universal Studios, these people . . . were using foul language and yelling to get the line moving. It made Universal less enjoyable than it could have been.
- At Busch Gardens we always seemed to be in the same place as this elderly couple and they made sure our two kids could see the animals or dancers.
- I met these really nice people from Canada who talked to me in line waiting for the ET ride.[65]

Atmosphere is referred to as **servicescape** when describing a service business such as a hospital, bank, or restaurant.[66] **Atmospherics** is the process managers use to manipulate the physical retail or service environment to create specific mood responses in shoppers. Internet retailers also have atmospheres that are determined by graphics, colors, layout,

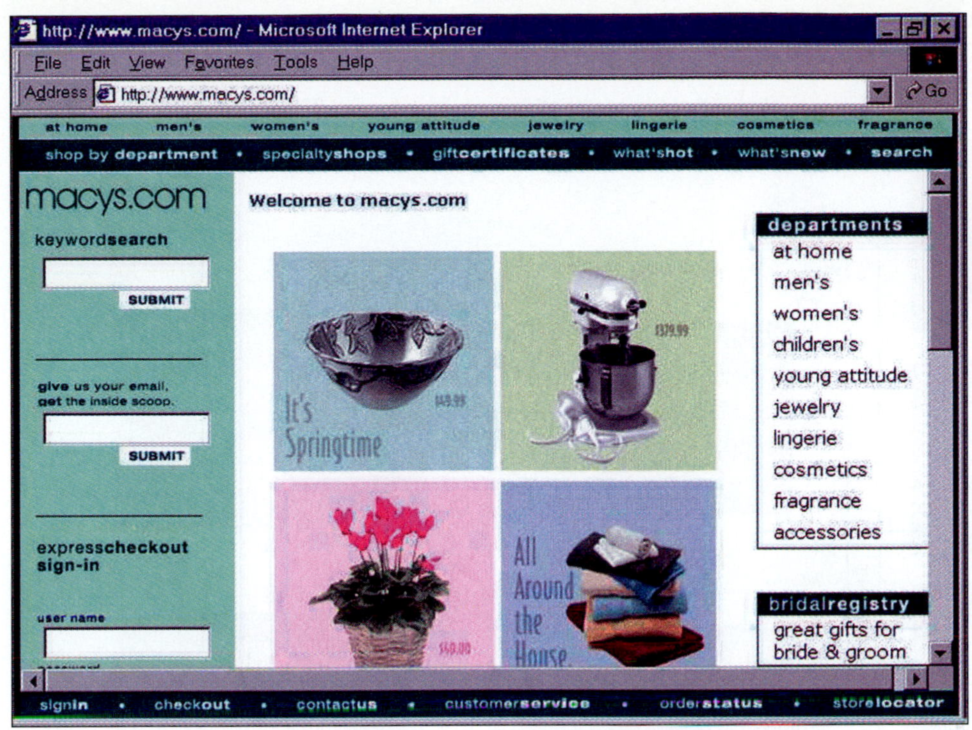

Courtesy Federated Department Stores.

ILLUSTRATION 17-8

Retail Web site designs should take into consideration the atmosphere or feelings they will generate as well as the content and items they will present.

content, interactivity, tone, and so forth. What type of atmosphere is portrayed in Macy's site (Illustration 17-8)? To date, there are no published studies on exactly how Internet retailer atmospheres are developed or how they affect consumption.

A store's atmosphere affects the shopper's mood and willingness to visit and linger. It also influences the consumer's judgments of the quality of the store and the store's image.[67] Perhaps more importantly, a positive mood induced while in the store increases satisfaction with the store, which can produce repeat visits and store loyalty.[68]

Music can have a major impact on the store environment (see page 484). It has been shown to influence the time spent in the store or restaurant, the mood of the consumer, and the overall impression of the outlet.[69] It also enhances perceptions of waiting time for services.[70] However, it is important to match the music to the target audience. As shown below, baby boomers responded positively to classic rock music in a supermarket setting, while older adults did not:[71]

	Baby Boomers			**Older Adults**		
	Classic Rock	*Big Band*	*Top 40*	*Classic Rock*	*Big Band*	*Top 40*
Items purchased	31	11	15	4	12	14
Dollars spent	34	21	21	16	17	24
Shopping minutes	27	16	29	21	30	28

Findings such as these suggest the possibility of using differing music styles during differing times of the day, week, or month if customers with differing music preferences shop at distinct times.

FIGURE 17-5 Store Atmosphere and Shopper Behavior

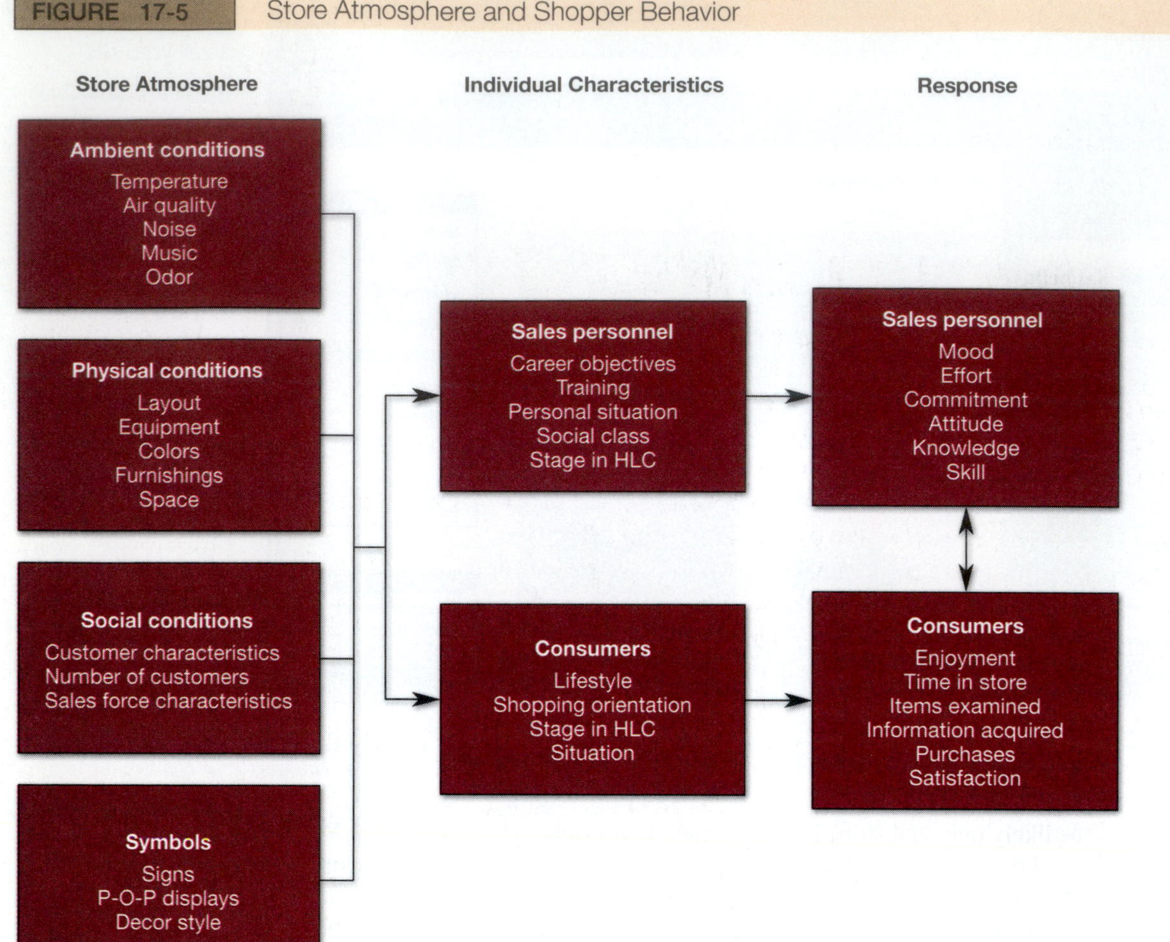

Reprinted with permission from the *Journal of Marketing,* published by the American Marketing Association. Adapted from M. J. Bitner, "Servicescapes," April 1, 1992, pp. 57–71.

Marketers are also beginning to investigate the impact of *odors* on shopping behaviors (see page 484).[72] Early studies suggest that odors can have a positive effect on the shopping experience. However, like music, odor preference varies across customers, so caution must be used to ensure that the aroma is not offensive to target customers. In addition, many consumers don't want anything artificial or unnecessary added to the air they breathe. A firm "spiking" the air with artificial aromas could irritate some consumers as well as risk adverse publicity.

The appearance and behaviors of the employees and the other shoppers in the outlet have a major impact on store atmosphere. The actual design of the store, the colors used,[73] the types of fixtures, the lighting, and similar physical features are also important.

Figure 17-5 illustrates the way store atmosphere influences shopper behavior. Several things in this figure are noteworthy. First, the physical environment interacts with the characteristics of individuals to determine response. Thus, an atmosphere that would produce a favorable response in teenagers might produce a negative response in older shoppers. Second, the store atmosphere influences *both* the sales personnel and the customers, whose interactions then influence each other.

TABLE 17-5

Impact of a Stockout Situation

I. Purchase behavior

A. Purchase a substitute brand or product at the original store. The substitute brand/product may or may not replace the regular brand in future purchases.

B. Delay the purchase until the brand is available at the original store.

C. Forgo the purchase entirely.

D. Purchase the desired brand at a second store. All of the items initially desired may be purchased at the second store or only the stockout items. The second store may or may not replace the original store on future shopping trips.

II. Verbal behavior

A. The consumer may make negative comments to peers about the original store.

B. The consumer may make positive comments to peers about the substitute store.

C. The consumer may make positive comments to peers about the substitute brand/product.

III. Attitude shifts

A. The consumer may develop a less favorable attitude toward the original store.

B. The consumer may develop a more favorable attitude toward the substitute store.

C. The consumer may develop a more favorable attitude toward the substitute brand/product.

Stockouts

Stockouts, the store being temporarily out of a particular brand, obviously affect a consumer's purchase decision. The customer then must decide whether to buy the same brand but at another store, switch brands, delay the purchase and buy the desired brand later at the same store, or forgo the purchase altogether. In addition, the consumer's verbal behaviors and attitudes may change. Table 17-5 summarizes the impacts that a stockout situation may have.[74]

None of the likely outcomes is particularly favorable for the original store or brand. For example, three of the four purchase behaviors involve buying a different brand from the desired brand or delaying the purchase. If a different brand is purchased, it is more likely to be repurchased in the future than it would be had the original brand been available. The manufacturer stands to lose both current and future sales. Thus, effective distribution and inventory management are critical for both manufacturers and retailers.

Sales Personnel

For most low-involvement decisions in the United States, self-service is predominant. As purchase involvement increases, the likelihood of interaction with a salesperson also increases. Thus, most studies of effectiveness in sales interactions have focused on high-involvement purchases such as insurance, automobiles, or industrial products. There is no simple explanation for effective sales interactions. Instead, the effectiveness of sales efforts is influenced by the interactions of:[75]

- The salesperson's knowledge, skill, and authority.
- The nature of the customer's buying task.
- The customer–salesperson relationship.

Thus, specific research is required for each target market and product category to determine the optimal personnel selling strategy.

Consider the following shopping experience:

> I also had lousy service in the store. The salesguy seemed to be trying to sell me the cheaper shoe to get me out the door . . . The thing that irritated me was that I thought I was a fairly knowledgeable

shopper and I thought that they should understand some of these things . . . They weren't very knowledgeable . . . I got the impression they didn't like their jobs.[76]

Is this consumer likely to return to this outlet? Will he recommend it to his friends? It is clear that knowledgeable, helpful salespeople enhance the shopping experience, while those who are not have the opposite effect.

PURCHASE

Once the brand and store have been selected, the consumer must complete the transaction. This involves what is normally called purchasing or renting the product. Traditionally, this involved giving cash to acquire the rights to the product. However, credit plays a major role in consumer purchases in the United States and increasingly in other developed nations as well.

The use of bank credit cards such as Visa, MasterCard, Diners Club, and American Express, and store charge cards such as Sears, Ward's, and JCPenney's, are the main way consumers finance all but major items such as cars or homes.

Of course, credit not only is a means to purchase a product; it is a product itself. Thus, the decision to purchase a relatively expensive item may trigger problem recognition for credit. Since a variety of forms of credit are available, the decision process then may be repeated for this problem.

Businesses need to simplify the actual purchase as much as possible. This involves strategies as simple as managing the time spent in line at the checkout register to more complex operations such as computerized credit checks to minimize credit authorization time. Many businesses appear to overlook the fact that the actual purchase act is generally the last contact the consumer will have with the store on that trip. While first impressions are important, so are final ones. Store personnel need to be not only efficient at this activity but also helpful and personable. Their behaviors and attitudes should reflect the image the store wants the customer to leave with.

SUMMARY

Consumers generally must select outlets as well as products. There are three general ways these decisions can be made: (1) *simultaneously;* (2) *item first, outlet second;* or (3) *outlet first, item second*. Both the manufacturer and the retailer must be aware of the decision sequence used by their target market, as it will have a major impact on their marketing strategy.

The decision process used by consumers to select a retail outlet is the same as the process described for selecting a brand. The only difference is in the nature of the evaluative criteria used. The store's *image* is an important evaluative criterion. The major dimensions of store image are merchandise, service, clientele, physical facilities, convenience, promotion, store atmosphere, institutional, and post-transaction factors. *Store brands* can both capitalize on a store's image and enhance (or detract from) it. Outlet location is an important attribute for many consumers, with closer outlets being preferred over more distant ones. Larger outlets generally are preferred over smaller outlets. These variables have been used to develop *retail gravitation models*. These models can predict the market share of competing shopping areas with reasonable accuracy.

Consumers visit retail shops and shopper areas for a variety of reasons. *Shopping orientation* refers to the general approach one takes to acquiring both brands and nonpurchase satisfactions from various types of retail outlets. Knowledge of a target market's shopping orientations for a product category is extremely useful in structuring retailing strategy.

While in a store, consumers often purchase a brand or product that differs from their plans before entering the store. Such purchases are referred to as *impulse* or *unplanned purchases*. Unfortunately, both of these terms imply a lack of rationality of the decision processes. It is more useful to consider such decisions as being the result of additional information processing induced by in-store stimuli. Such variables as *point-of-purchase displays, price reductions, store layout, store atmosphere, sales personnel,* and brand or product *stockouts* can have a major impact on sales patterns.

Once the outlet and brand have been selected, the consumer must acquire the rights to the item. Increasingly, this involves the use of credit—particularly the use of credit cards. However, major purchases often require the consumer to make a second purchase decision: "What type of credit shall I buy to finance this purchase?" Financial institutions increasingly recognize the opportunities in the consumer credit field and are beginning to utilize standard consumer goods marketing techniques.

KEY TERMS

Atmospherics 614
External reference price 603
Impulse purchase 609
In-home shopping 592
Internal reference price 603
Perceived risk 606
Reference price 603
Retail attraction (gravitational) model 605
Servicescape 614
Shopping orientation 607
Spillover sales 602
Stockouts 617
Store atmosphere 614
Store brand 601
Store image 599
Unplanned purchase 610

INTERNET EXERCISES

1. Visit five Internet retail outlets. Which is the best? Why? Which is the worst? Why?
2. Visit several Internet malls. Describe one that you think is effectively designed and one that you feel is poorly designed. Explain why.
3. Visit two Internet retailers for the same product category. Evaluate the "outlet atmosphere" of each. What, if anything, in the atmosphere provides the following:
   a. Encouragement for impulse purchases
   b. Nonpurchase reasons for visiting
   c. Risk reduction
   d. Service
   e. Fun

DDB NEEDHAM LIFESTYLE DATA ANALYSES

1. Examine the DDB Needham data in Tables 1a, 2a, 3a, 4a, 5a, 6a, and 7a. What characterizes individuals who place considerable emphasis on price as an evaluative criterion? What are the marketing implications of this for store-based retailers? For Internet retailers?

REVIEW QUESTIONS

1. How is the retail environment changing?
2. Describe Internet retailing.
3. The consumer faces both the problem of what to buy and where to buy it. How do these two types of decisions differ?
4. How does the sequence in which the brand/outlet decision is made affect the brand strategy? The retailer strategy?
5. What is a *store image* and what are its dimensions and components?
6. What is a *store brand?* How do retailers use store brands?
7. What key decisions do retailers make with respect to retail price advertising?
8. What is meant by the term *spillover sales?* Why is it important?

9. How does the size and distance to a retail outlet affect store selection and purchase behavior?
10. Describe the model of *retail gravitation* presented in the chapter.
11. How is store choice affected by the *perceived risk* of a purchase?
12. What is meant by *social risk?* How does it differ from *economic risk?*
13. What is a *shopping orientation?*
14. Describe seven psychographic-based shopping orientations.
15. Describe six motivation-based shopping orientations of college students.
16. What is meant by an *in-store purchase decision?* Why is it important?
17. Once in a particular store, what in-store characteristics can influence brand and product choice? Give an example of each.
18. Describe the impact of point-of-purchase displays on retail sales.
19. Describe the impact of price reductions and deals on retail sales.
20. What is meant by *store atmosphere?* How does it affect consumer behavior?
21. What is a *servicescape?*
22. What can happen in response to a *stockout?*

DISCUSSION QUESTIONS

23. Describe Internet retailing in 2005.
24. Name two product categories for which the brand is generally selected first and the outlet second, two for which the reverse is true, and two for which these decisions are generally made simultaneously. Justify your selections. How should marketing strategy differ across these products?
25. How would you measure the image of a retail outlet?
26. Does the image of a retail outlet affect the image of the brands it carries? Do the brands carried affect the image of the retail outlet?
27. The discussion of outlet image lists nine dimensions and 23 components of these nine dimensions of more images. How would this change for the following types of outlets?
    a. Internet stores
    b. Catalog merchants
28. What would you estimate the market share of the following three furniture stores to be if the attraction coefficient for furniture is .5? What if it were 2?
    a. Store A = 10,000 square feet, 15 minutes from the target market
    b. Store B = 20,000 square feet, 30 minutes from the target market
    c. Store C = 40,000 square feet, 75 minutes from the target market
29. Would a form of retail gravitation model work for Internet retailers? What would it look like?
30. How are social and economic risks likely to affect the store choice behavior of consumers shopping for the following?
    a. Dress shirts
    b. Men's socks
    c. Flowers (as a gift)
    d. Therapist
    e. Skis
    f. Soft drinks (self-use)
    g. Vacuum cleaner
    h. Garbage service
31. Describe an appropriate retailing strategy for a department store targeting each of the:
    a. Psychographic-based shopping orientations described in the text.
    b. Motivation-based shopping orientations described in the text.
32. The motivation-based shopping orientations described in the text were developed using a small sample of Canadian students. Do you think these are accurate descriptions of the shopping orientations of students on your campus?
33. What in-store characteristics could retailers use to enhance the probability of purchase among individuals who visit a store? Describe each factor in terms of how it should be used, and describe its intended effect on the consumer for the following products:
    a. Soft drinks
    b. Snowboards
    c. Dessert after a meal
    d. Flowers from a supermarket

e. Cold remedies
f. Lawn fertilizer

34. What site characteristics could Internet retailers use to enhance the probability of purchase among individuals who visit their sites? Describe each factor in terms of how it should be used, and describe its intended effect on the consumer for the following products:
    a. Snowboards
    b. Books from Amazon.com while visiting another site
    c. Flowers while visiting a book site
    d. Books from a book site
    e. Cosmetics from Macy's
    f. Tools from Sears
35. What type of store atmosphere is most appropriate for each of the following store types? Why?
    a. Bicycle shop
    b. Garden supplies
    c. Massage therapist
    d. Personal computers
    e. Luxury automobiles
    f. Casual clothes for teenagers
    g. Expensive furniture
    h. Chinese food restaurant
36. Repeat Question 35 (except for *c*, and *h*) for Internet retailers.
37. Retailers often engage in "loss leader" advertising, in which a popular item is advertised at or below cost. Does this make sense? Why?
38. How would you respond to a stockout of your preferred brand of the following? What factors other than product category would influence your response?
    a. Toothpaste
    b. Frozen pizza
    c. Deodorant
    d. Laptop computer
    e. Mouthwash
    f. Soft drink

APPLICATION ACTIVITIES

39. Pick a residential area in your town and develop a gravitational model for (*a*) nearby supermarkets and (*b*) shopping malls. Conduct telephone surveys to test the accuracy of your model.
40. Develop a questionnaire to measure the image of the following. Have other students complete these questionnaires for three or four competing outlets. Discuss the marketing implications of your results.
    a. Discount stores
    b. Internet bookstores
    c. Pizza restaurants
    d. Internet malls
    e. Convenience stores
    f. Outdoor recreation equipment stores
    g. Nice restaurants
    h. Sears, Wards, Kmart
41. Have 10 students on your campus describe their shopping orientations in terms of animals, as discussed in the section of the text on motivation-based shopping orientations. Combine your descriptions with those of two other students. Do any patterns emerge? Do they match those described in the text? How would you explain the differences?
42. For several of the products listed in Table 17-4, interview several students not enrolled in your class and ask them to classify their last purchase as specially planned, generally planned, substitute, or unplanned. Then combine your results with those of your classmates to obtain an estimate of student behavior. Compare student behavior with the behavior shown in Table 17-4 and discuss any similarities or differences.
43. Arrange with a local retailer (convenience store, drugstore, and so on) to temporarily install a point-of-purchase display. Then set up a procedure to unobtrusively observe the frequency of evaluation and selection of the brand before and while the display is up. Describe your finding.
44. Visit two retail stores selling the same type of merchandise and prepare a report on their use of P-O-P displays. Explain any differences.
45. Interview the manager of a drug, department, or grocery store on their views of P-O-P displays and price advertising.
46. Answer Question 38 using a sample of 20 students. What are the marketing implications of your results?
47. Develop an appropriate questionnaire and construct a new version of Table 17-2, using products

relevant to college students. What are the marketing implications of this table?

48. Determine, through interviews, the general shopping orientations of students on your campus. What are the marketing implications of your findings?

49. Interview 20 students on your campus and determine their Internet shopping behaviors. Divide them into appropriate groups such as heavy-, light-, and nonshoppers and explain why each group behaves as it does.

REFERENCES

1. L. Armstrong, "Anything You Sell, I Can Sell Cheaper," *Business Week,* December 14, 1998, pp. 130–31; and J. W. Gurley, "Buy.com May Fail," *Fortune,* January 11, 1999, pp. 150–51.
2. For differing views, see W. R. Darden and M.-J. Dorsch, "An Action Strategy Approach to Examining Shopping Behavior," *Journal of Business Research,* November 1990, pp. 289–308; and J. A. Lesser and P. Kamal, "An Inductively Derived Model of the Motivation to Shop," *Psychology & Marketing,* Fall 1991, pp. 177–96. The most thorough coverage of this topic is M. Laaksonen, *Journal of Business Research,* September 1993, pp. 3–174.
3. S. Sherman, "Will the Information Superhighway Be the Death of Retailing?" *Fortune,* April 18, 1994, p. 17. For a successful approach, see A. Taylor III, "How to Buy a Car on the Internet," *Fortune,* March 4, 1996, pp. 164–68.
4. J. L. McQuivey et al., "On-Line Retail Strategies," *The Forrester Report,* November 1998, p. 5.
5. *Interactive Media Study* (Arlington Heights, IL: Market Facts' TeleNation, October 1998), p. 9.
6. See M. G. Briones, "On-Line Retailers Seek Ways to Close Shopping Gender Gap," *Marketing News,* September 1998, p. 2.
7. M. A. Jones, P. J. Trocchia, and D. L. Mothersbaugh, "Noneconomic Motivations for Price Haggling," in *Advances in Consumer Research XXIV,* ed. M. Bruck and D. J. MacInnis (Provo, UT: Association for Consumer Research, 1997), pp. 388–91.
8. See footnote 5.
9. See M. A. Eastlick and M. Liu, "The Influence of Store Attitudes and Other Nonstore Shopping Patterns on Patronage of Television Shopping Programs," *Journal of Direct Marketing,* Summer 1997, pp. 14–24.
10. See D. L. Hoffman and T. P. Novak, "Marketing in Hypermedia Computer-Mediated Environments," *Journal of Marketing,* July 1996, pp. 50–68; J. Alba et al., "Interactive Home Shopping," *Journal of Marketing,* July 1997, pp. 38–53; and R. A. Peterson, S. Balasubramanian, and B. J. Bronnenberg, "Exploring the Implications of the Internet for Consumer Marketing"; J. Deighton, "Commentary"; and R. A. Burke, "Do You See What I See?" all in *Journal of the Academy of Marketing Science,* Fall 1997, pp. 329–46, 347–51, and 352–60.
11. M. Kuntz, "These Ads Have Windows and Walls," *Business Week,* February 27, 1995, p. 74.
12. See C. Talmadge, "Retailers Injecting More Fun into Stores," *Advertising Age,* October 30, 1996, p. 38; S. Chandler, "Reinventing the Store," *Business Week,* November 27, 1995, pp. 84–96; and K. Naughton, "Revolution in Retailing," *Business Week,* February 19, 1996, pp. 7–76.
13. S. A. Forest, "Look Who's Thinking Small," *Business Week,* May 17, 1999, pp. 67–70.
14. K. Labich, "What It Will Take to Keep People Hanging Out at the Mall," *Fortune,* May 1995, pp. 102–6.
15. See J. K. Frenzen and H. L. Davis, "Purchasing Behavior in Embedded Markets," *Journal of Consumer Research,* June 1990, pp. 1–12; J. F. Sherry, Jr., "A Sociocultural Analysis of a Midwestern American Flea Market," *Journal of Consumer Research,* June 1990, pp. 13–30; J. F. Sherry, Jr., "Dealers and Dealing in a Periodic Market," *Journal of Retailing,* Summer 1990, pp. 174–200; and R. W. Belk, J. F. Sherry, Jr., and M. Wallendorf, "A Naturalistic Inquiry into Buyer and Seller Behavior at a Swap Meet," *Journal of Consumer Research,* March 1988, pp. 449–70.
16. See J. J. Stoltman, J. W. Gentry, K. A. Anglin, and A. C. Burns, "Situational Influences on the Consumer Decision Sequence," *Journal of Business Research,* November 1990, pp. 195–207.
17. S. A. Finn and J. Louviere, "Shopping-Center Patronage Models," *Journal of Business Research,* November 1990, pp. 259–75; E. J. Wilson and A. G. Woodside, "A Comment on Patterns of Store Choice and Customer Gain/Loss Analysis," *Journal of the Academy of Marketing Science,* Fall 1991, pp. 377–82; A. G. Woodside and R. J. Trappey III, "Finding Out Why Customers Shop Your Store and Buy Your Brand," *Journal of Advertising Research,* November 1992, pp. 59–78; and R. R. Brand and J. J. Cronin, "Consumer-Specific Determinants of the Size of Retail Choice Sets," *Journal of Services Marketing,* no. 1 (1997), pp. 19–38.
18. S. M. Keaveney and K. A. Hunt, "Conceptualization and Operationalization of Retail Store Image," *Journal of the Academy of Marketing Science,* Spring 1992, pp. 165–176. See also D.-N. Lascu and T. Giese, "Exploring Country Bias in a Retailing Environment," *Journal of Global Marketing* 9, no. 1/2 (1995), pp. 41–58.
19. J. D. Lindquist, "Meaning of Image," *Journal of Retailing,* Winter 1974, pp. 29–38; See also R. Hansen and T. Deutscher, "An Empirical Investigation of Attribute Importance in Retail Store Selection," *Journal of Retailing,* Winter 1977–1978, pp. 59–73; and M. R. Zimmer and L. L. Golden, "Impressions of Retail Stores," *Journal of Retailing,* Fall 1988, pp. 265–93.
20. W. R. Darden and B. J. Badin, "Exploring the Concept of Affective Quality," *Journal of Business Research,* February 1994, p. 106.
21. See J. E. M. Steenkamp and M. Wedel, "Segmenting Retail Markets on Store Image," *Journal of Retailing,* Fall 1991, pp. 300–320; and N. Sirohi, E. W. McLaughlin, and D. R. Witink,

"A Model of Consumer Perceptions and Store Loyalty Intentions for a Supermarket Retailer," *Journal of Retailing,* no. 2 (1998), pp. 223–45.

22. See S. W. McDaniel and J. J. Burnett, "Consumer Religiosity and Retail Store Evaluative Criteria," *Journal of the Academy of Marketing Science,* Spring 1990, pp. 101–12; and W. K. Darley and J.-S. Linn, "Store-Choice Behavior for Pre-Owned Merchandise," *Journal of Business Research,* May 1993, pp. 17–31.
23. See W. J. McDonald, "Consumer Preference Structure Analysis," *Journal of Direct Marketing,* Winter 1993, pp. 20–30.
24. W. K. Darley and J.-S. Lim, "Store-Choice for Pre-Owned Merchandise," *Journal of Business Research,* May 1993, pp. 17–31; A. Finn and J. J. Louviere, "Shopping Center Image," *Journal of Business Research,* March 1996, pp. 241–51; and R. B. Settle, P. L. Alreck, and D. E. McCorkle, "Consumer Perceptions of Mail/Phone Order Shopping Media," *Journal of Direct Marketing,* Summer 1994, pp. 30–45.
25. See S. Burton, D. R. Lichtenstein, R. G. Netemeyer, and J. A. Garretson, "A Scale for Measuring Attitude toward Private Label Products," *Journal of the Academy of Marketing Science,* Fall 1998, pp. 293–306.
26. See J. A. Quelch and D. Harding, "Brands versus Private Labels," *Harvard Business Review,* January 1996, pp. 99–109; and A. Z. Cuneo, "Private-Label Lessons," *Advertising Age,* July 27, 1998, p. 1.
27. See P. S. Richardson, A. S. Dick, and A. K. Jain, "Extrinsic and Intrinsic Cue Effects on Perceptions of Store Brand Quality," *Journal of Marketing,* October 1994, pp. 28–36; *The Swing Shopper* (Philadelphia: The Consumer Network, Inc., December 1994); and J. Scattone, "Factors Influencing Consumer Perceptions, Attitudes and Consideration of Store Brands," in *Enhancing Knowledge Development in Marketing,* ed. B. B. Stern and G. M. Zinkhan (Chicago: American Marketing Association, 1995), pp. 27–33.
28. P. S. Richardson, A. K. Jain, and A. Dick, "Household Store Brand Proneness," *Journal of Retailing,* no. 2 (1996), pp. 159–85.
29. *The Double Dividend* (New York: Newspaper Advertising Bureau Inc., February 1977).
30. F. J. Mulhern and D. T. Padgett, "The Relationship between Retail Price Promotions and Regular Price Purchases," *Journal of Marketing,* October 1995, pp. 83–90.
31. See M. R. Stafford and E. Day, "Retail Services Advertising," *Journal of Advertising,* Spring 1995, pp. 57–71.
32. See C. Janiszewski and D. R. Lichtenstein, "A Range Theory of Price Perception," *Journal of Consumer Research,* March 1999, pp. 353–68.
33. See R. A. Briesch, L. Krishnamurthi, and T. Mazumdar, "A Comparative Analysis of Reference Price Models," *Journal of Consumer Research,* September 1997, pp. 202–14. For a different approach, see K. B. Monroe and A. Y. Lee, "Remembering versus Knowing," *Journal of the Academy of Marketing Science,* Spring 1999, pp. 207–25.
34. See V. Kumar, K. Karande, and W. J. Reinartz, "The Impact of Internal and External Reference Prices on Brand Choice," *Journal of Retailing,* no. 3 (1998), pp. 401–26.
35. A. Biswas and S. Bunton, "Consumer Perceptions of Tensile Price Claims," *Journal of the Academy of Marketing Science,* Summer 1993, pp. 219–30; A. Biswas, E. J. Wilson, and J. W. Licata, "Reference Pricing Studies in Marketing," *Journal of Business Research,* July 1993, pp. 239–56; K. D. Frankenberger and R. Liu, "Does Consumer Knowledge Affect Consumer Responses to Advertised Reference Price Claims?" *Psychology & Marketing,* May 1994, pp. 235–51; T. Mazumdar and P. Papatla, "Loyalty Differences in the Use of Internal and External Reference Prices," *Marketing Letters* 6, no. 2 (1995), pp. 111–22; T. A. Suter and S. Burton, "Reliability and Consumer Perceptions of Implausible Reference Prices in Retail Prices," *Psychology & Marketing,* January 1996, pp. 37–54; and M. S. Yadav and K. Seiders, "Is the Price Right?" *Journal of Retailing,* no. 3 (1998), pp. 311–29.
36. T. B. Geath, S. Chatterjee, and K. R. France, "Mental Accounting and Changes in Price," *Journal of Consumer Research,* June 1995, pp. 90–97.
37. See S.-F. S. Chen, K. B. Monroe, and Y.-C. Lou, "The Effects of Framing Price Promotion Messages on Consumers' Perceptions and Purchase Intentions," *Journal of Retailing,* no. 3 (1998), pp. 353–72.
38. See A. Biswas and E. A. Blair, "Contextual Effects of Reference Prices," *Journal of Marketing,* July 1991, pp. 1–12; D. R. Lichtenstein, S. Burton, and E.-J. Karson, "The Effect of Semantic Cues on Consumer Perceptions of Reference Price Ads," *Journal of Consumer Research,* December 1991, pp. 380–91; G. E. Mayhew and R. S. Winer, "An Empirical Analysis of Internal and External Reference Prices," *Journal of Consumer Research,* June 1992, pp. 62–70; A. Biswas, "The Moderating Role of Brand Familiarity in Reference Price Perceptions," *Journal of Business Research,* November 1992, pp. 251–62; A. Biswas and S. Burton, "Consumer Perceptions of Tensile Price Claims in Advertisements," *Journal of the Academy of Marketing Science,* Summer 1993, pp. 217–30; K. N. Rajendran and G.-J. Tellis, "Contextual and Temporal Components of Reference Price," *Journal of Marketing,* January 1994, pp. 22–39; and D. Grewal, H. Marmorstein, and A. Sharma, "Communicating Price Information through Semantic Cues," *Journal of Consumer Research,* September 1996, pp. 148–55.
39. See D. Simester, "Signaling Price Image Using Advertised Prices," *Marketing Science* 14, no. 2 (1995), pp. 166–88.
40. G. S. Bobinski, Jr., D. Cox, and A. Cox, "Retail 'Sale' Advertising, Perceived Retailer Credibility, and Price Rationale," *Journal of Retailing,* no. 3 (1996), pp. 291–306.
41. C. S. Craig, A. Ghosh, and S. McLafferty, "Models of the Retail Location Process: A Review," *Journal of Retailing,* Spring 1984, pp. 5–33.
42. See D. R. Bell, T.-H. Ho, and C. S. Tang, "Determining Where to Shop," *Journal of Marketing Research,* August 1998, pp. 352–69.
43. See B. G. C. Dellaert et al., "Investigating Consumers' Tendency to Combine Multiple Shopping Purposes and Destinations," *Journal of Marketing Research,* May 1998, pp. 177–88.
44. See P. R. Messinger and C. Narasimhan, "A Model of Retail Formats Based on Consumers' Economizing on Shopping Time," *Marketing Science* no. 1 (1997), pp. 1–23.
45. Based on V. Prasad, "Socioeconomic Product Risk and Patronage Preferences of Retail Shoppers," *Journal of Marketing,* July 1975, p. 44.
46. G. R. Dowling and R. Staelin, "A Model of Perceived Risk and Intended Risk-Handling Activity," *Journal of Consumer*

Research, June 1994, pp. 119–34; L. W. Turley and R. P. LeBlanc, "An Exploratory Investigation of Consumer Decision Making in the Service Sector," *Journal of Services Marketing* 7, no. 4 (1993), pp. 11–18; and J. B. Smith and J. M. Bristor, "Uncertainty Orientation," *Psychology & Marketing,* November 1994, pp. 587–607.

47. Settle, Alreck, and McCorkle, footnote 24; and C. R. Jasper and S. J. Ouellette, "Consumers' Perception of Risk and the Purchase of Apparel from Catalogs," *Journal of Direct Marketing,* Spring 1994, pp. 23–36.

48. See R. A. Westbrook and W. C. Black, "A Motivation-Based Shopper Typology," *Journal of Retailing,* Spring 1985, pp. 78–103.

49. See M. A. Eastlick and R. A. Feinberg, "Gender Differences in Mail-Catalog Patronage Motives," *Journal of Direct Marketing,* Spring 1994, pp. 37–44; "The Call of the Mall," *EDK Forecast,* October 1994, pp. 1–3; and "Black, Hip, and Primed to Shop," *American Demographics,* September 1996, pp. 52–58.

50. W. R. Darden and R. D. Howell, "Socialization Effects of Retail Work Experience on Shopping Orientations," *Journal of the Academy of Marketing Science,* Fall 1987, pp. 52–63. See also W. J. McDonald, "Psychological Associations with Shopping," *Psychology & Marketing,* November 1994, pp. 549–68.

51. D. N. Hassay and M. C. Smith, "Fauna, Foraging and Shopping Motives," in *Advances in Consumer Research XXIII,* ed. K. P. Corfman and J. G. Lynch (Provo, UT: Association for Consumer Research, 1996), pp. 510–15.

52. See S. Spiggle, "Grocery Shopping Lists," in *Advances in Consumer Research XIV,* ed. M. Wallendorf and P. Anderson (Provo, UT: Association for Consumer Research, 1987), pp. 241–45; E. S. Iyer, "Unplanned Purchasing," *Journal of Retailing,* Spring 1989, pp. 40–57; and C. W. Park, E. S. Iyer, and D. C. Smith, "The Effects of Situational Factors on In-Store Grocery Shopping Behavior," *Journal of Consumer Research,* March 1989, pp. 422–33.

53. See J. E. Russo and F. Lecleric, "An Eye Fixation Analysis of Choice Processes for Consumer Nondurables," *Journal of Consumer Research,* September 1994, pp. 274–90.

54. See S. E. Beatty and M. E. Ferrell, "Impulse Buying," *Journal of Retailing,* no. 2 (1998), pp. 169–91.

55. See *POPAI/Horner Drug Store Study* (Englewood, NJ: Point-of-Purchase Advertising Institute, 1992); A. J. Greco and L. E. Swayne, "Sales Response of Elderly Consumers to P-O-P Advertising," *Journal of Advertising Research,* September 1992, pp. 43–53; and *POPAI/Kmart/Procter & Gamble Study of P-O-P Effectiveness* (Englewood, NJ: Point-of-Purchase Advertising Institute, 1993). See also D. W. Schumann et al., "The Effectiveness of Shopping Cart Signage," *Journal of Advertising Research,* February 1991, pp. 17–22.

56. See E. T. Anderson and D. I. Simester, "The Role of Sale Signs," *Marketing Science,* no. 2 (1998), pp. 139–55.

57. A. S. C. Ehrenberg, K. Hammond, and G. J. Goodhardt, "The After-Effects of Price-Related Consumer Promotions," *Journal of Advertising Research,* July 1994, pp. 11–21; and P. Papatla and L. Krishnamurthi, "*Journal of Marketing Research,* February 1996, pp. 20–36.

58. See B. E. Kahn and D. C. Schmittlein, "The Relationship between Purchase Made on Promotion and Shopping Trip Behavior," *Journal of Retailing,* Fall 1992, pp. 294–315; K. Helsen and D. C. Schmittlein, "How Does a Product Market's Typical Price-Promotion Pattern Affect the Timing of Households' Purchases?" *Journal of Retailing,* Fall 1992, pp. 316–38; and C. F. Mela, K. Jedidi, and D. Bowman, "The Long-Term Impact of Promotions on Consumer Stockpiling Behavior," *Journal of Marketing Research,* May 1998, pp. 250–62.

59. K. Sivakumar and S. P. Raj, "Quality Tier Competition," *Journal of Marketing,* July 1997, pp. 71–84.

60. See also D. R. Lichtenstein, S. Burton, and R. G. Netemeyer, "An Examination of Deal Proneness Across Sales Promotion Types," *Journal of Retailing,* no. 2 (1997), pp. 283–97.

61. P. K. Tat, "Rebate Usage," *Psychology & Marketing,* January 1994, pp. 15–26; D. R. Lichtenstein, R. G. Netemeyer, and S. Burton, "Assessing the Domain Specificity of Deal Proneness," *Journal of Consumer Research,* December 1995, pp. 314–26; and V. Ramaswamy and S. S. Srinivasan, "Coupon Characteristics and Redemption Intentions," *Psychology & Marketing,* January 1998, pp. 59–80.

62. D. Grewal, R. Krishnan, J. Baker, and N. Borin, "The Effect of Store Name, Brand Name, and Price Discounts on Consumers' Evaluations and Purchase Intentions," *Journal of Retailing,* no. 3 (1998), pp. 331–52.

63. D. R. Bell and J. M. Lattin, "Shopping Behavior and Consumer Preference for Store Price Format," *Marketing Science,* no. 1 (1998), pp. 66–88. See also R. Lal and R. Rao, "Supermarket Competition," *Marketing Science,* no. 1 (1997), pp. 60–80.

64. V. G. Morwitz, E. A. Greenleaf, and E. J. Johnson, "Divide and Prosper," *Journal of Consumer Research,* November 1998, pp. 453–63.

65. S. J. Grove and R. P. Fisk, "The Impact of Other Customers on Service Experiences," *Journal of Retailing,* no. 1 (1997), pp. 63–85.

66. M. J. Bitner, "Servicescapes," *Journal of Marketing,* April 1992, pp. 57–71. See also J. C. Ward, M. J. Bitner, and J. Barnes, "Measuring the Prototypicality and Meaning of Retail Environments," *Journal of Retailing,* Summer 1992, pp. 194–220; R. A. Kerin, A. Jain, and P. J. Howard, "Store Shopping Experience and Consumer Price-Quality-Value Perceptions," *Journal of Retailing,* Winter 1992, pp. 376–98; J. Baker, D. Grewal, and M. Levy, "An Experimental Approach to Making Retail Store Environmental Decisions," *Journal of Retailing,* Winter 1992, pp. 445–60; J. Podel, "Bank Design," *Bank Marketing,* May 1994, pp. 10–14; K. L. Wakefield and J. G. Blodgett, "The Importance of Servicescapes in Leisure Service Settings," *Journal of Services Marketing* 8, no. 3 (1994), pp. 66–76; and K. L. Wakefield and J. G. Blodgett, "Customer Response to Intangible and Tangible Service Factors," *Psychology & Marketing,* January 1999, pp. 51–68.

67. J. Baker, D. Grewal, and A. Parasuraman, "The Influence of Store Environment on Quality Inferences and Store Image," *Journal of the Academy of Marketing Science,* Fall 1994, pp. 328–39; W. R. Swinyard, "The Effects of Mood, Involvement, and Quality of Store Experience on Shopping Intentions," *Journal of Consumer Research,* September 1993, pp. 271–80; and E. Sherman, A. Mathur, and R. B. Smith, "Store Environment and Consumer Purchase Behavior," *Psychology & Marketing,* July 1997, pp. 361–78.

68. B. Babin and W. R. Darden, "Good and Bad Shopping Vibes," *Journal of Business Research,* March 1996, pp. 210–60.

69. J. D. Herrington and L. M. Capella, "Practical Applications of Music in Service Settings," *Journal of Services Marketing* 8, no. 3 (1994), pp. 50–65; L. Dube, J.-C. Chebat, and S. Morin, "The Effects of Background Music on Consumers' Desire to Affiliate in Buyer–Seller Interactions," *Psychology & Marketing,* July 1995, pp. 305–19; J. D. Herrington and L. M. Capella, "Effect of Music in Service Environments," *Journal of Services Marketing* 10, no. 2 (1996), pp. 26–41; C. Rudel, "Marketing with Music," *Marketing News,* August 12, 1996, p. 21; and C. S. Areni, J. R. Sparks, and P. Dunne, "Assessing Consumers' Affective Responses to Retail Environments," in *Advances in Consumer Research XXIII,* ed. K. P. Corfman and J. G. Lynch (Provo, UT: Association for Consumer Research, 1996), pp. 504–9.
70. M. K. Hui, L. Dube, and J.-C. Chebat, "The Impact of Music on Consumers' Reactions to Waiting for Services," *Journal of Retailing,* no. 1 (1997), pp. 87–104.
71. C. S. Gulas and C. D. Schewe, "Atmospheric Segmentation," in *Enhancing Knowledge Development in Marketing,* ed. R. Achrol and A. Mitchell (Chicago: American Marketing Association, 1994), pp. 325–30. Similar results are in J. D. Herrington and L. M. Capella, "Effects of Music in Service Environments," *Journal of Services Marketing,* no. 2 (1996), pp. 26–41.
72. D. J. Mitchell, B. E. Kahn, and S. C. Knasko, "There's Something in the Air," *Journal of Consumer Research,* September 1995, pp. 229–38; E. R. Spangenberg, A. E. Crowley, and P. W. Henderson, "Improving the Store Environment," *Journal of Marketing,* April 1996, pp. 67–80; A. R. Hirsch, "Effects of Ambient Odors on Slot-Machine Usage in a Las Vegas Casino," *Psychology & Marketing,* October 1995, pp. 585–94; M. Wilkie, "Scent of a Market," *American Demographics,* August 1995, pp. 40–49; and P. Sloan, "Smelling Trouble," *Advertising Age,* September 11, 1995, p. 1.
73. See A. E. Crowley, "The Two-Dimensional Impact of Color on Shopping," *Marketing Letters* 4, no. 1, pp. 59–69.
74. W. H. Motes and S. B. Castleberry, "A Longitudinal Field Test of Stockout Effects on Multi-Brand Inventories," *Journal of the Academy of Marketing Science,* Fall 1985, pp. 54–68; and M. A. Emmelhainz, J. R. Stock, and L. W. Emmelhainz, "Consumer Responses to Retail Stock-Outs," *Journal of Retailing,* Summer 1991, pp. 138–47.
75. See D. M. Szymanski, "Determinants of Selling Effectiveness," *Journal of Marketing,* January 1988, pp. 64–77; D. A. McBane, "Empathy and the Salesperson," *Psychology & Marketing,* July 1995, pp. 349–70; D. Strutton, L. E. Pelton, and J. R. Lumpkin, "Sex Differences in Ingratiatory Behavior," *Journal of Business Research,* September 1995, pp. 35–45; and O. W. DeShields, Jr., A. Kari, and E. Kaynak, "Source Effects in Purchase Decisions," *International Journal of Research in Marketing* 13 (1996), pp. 89–101.
76. B. B. Stern, G. J. Thompson, and E. J. Arnould, "Narrative Analysis of a Marketing Relationship," *Psychology & Marketing,* no. 3 (1998), pp. 195–214.

Courtesy The Ritz-Carlton, L.L.C.

Postpurchase Processes, Customer Satisfaction, and Customer Commitment

■ From the first time a guest registers at a Ritz-Carlton hotel, every preference and special order is entered into a database accessible from all the chain's hotels. Employees carry special note cards on which guest comments and concerns are noted for subsequent entry into the database. Thus, the next time a customer checks into a Ritz-Carlton, the hotel will know if an iron should be in the room, if bed turn-down is desired, or if a particular type of room is preferred. The guest's needs can then be met without the guest having to make requests.

The Ritz-Carlton loyalty program is also customized. Most hotel programs provide points per stay that can be redeemed for upgrades, free nights, or other predetermined and limited prizes. "When we recognize guests for their long stays or repeat business, we recognize them with something that's appropriate for them." Recognition awards are often chosen at a staff meeting held at the start of each shift, where a list of guests and their preferences is reviewed. For example, if a guest who prefers a room with an ocean view is visiting for the fifth time and the staff sees that a deluxe room with that view is available, they will upgrade the guest. When the guest checks in, the registration clerk will give the upgrade with a thank you. However, "you should always tell the guest why he or she is being rewarded. That way a customer won't expect rewards every visit."[1]

FIGURE 18-1 Postpurchase Consumer Behavior

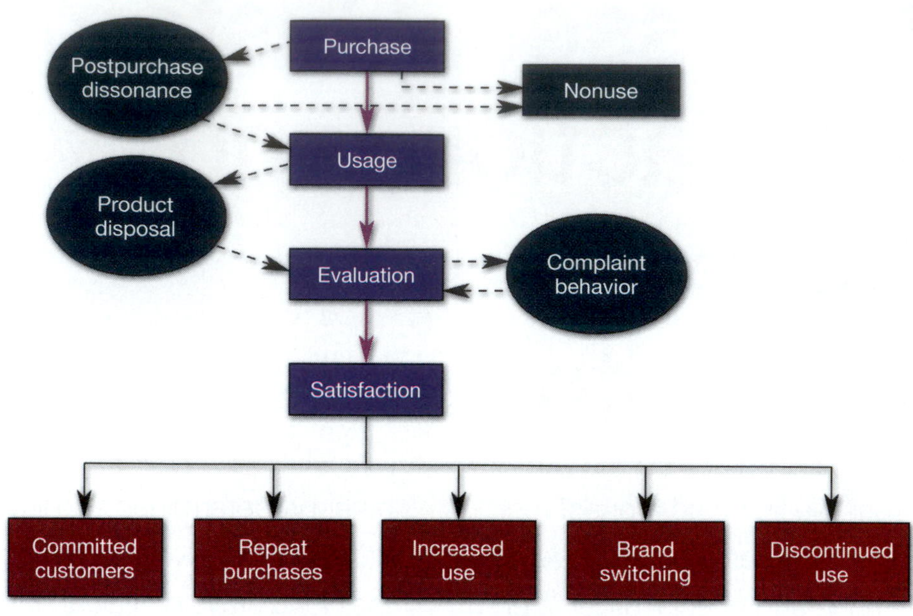

Rare only a few years ago, customer loyalty programs are now common in American firms. The objective of such programs is to increase the satisfaction, commitment, and retention of key customers. In this chapter, we will examine the postpurchase processes that produce customer satisfaction and commitment and the marketing strategies these processes suggest.

Figure 18-1 illustrates the relationships among the postpurchase processes. As the figure indicates, some purchases are followed by a phenomenon called *postpurchase dissonance*. This occurs when a consumer doubts the wisdom of a purchase he or she has made. Other purchases are followed by nonuse. The consumer keeps or returns the product without using it. Most purchases are followed by product use, even if postpurchase dissonance is present. Product use often requires the disposition of the product package and/or the product itself. During and after use, the purchase process and the product are evaluated by the consumer. Unsatisfactory evaluations may produce complaints by those consumers. Appropriate responses by the firm may reverse the initial dissatisfaction among those who complained. The result of all these processes is a final level of satisfaction, which in turn can result in a loyal, committed customer, one who is willing to repurchase, or a customer who switches brands or discontinues using the product category.

POSTPURCHASE DISSONANCE

> I still like it (the dining room set) a whole lot better than what we used to have. But I think if we had taken longer we would have gotten more precisely what we wanted. I mean we got a great deal. You couldn't get that for that price, so I am happy with the money part of it, but some days I wish we had spent more and gotten something a bit different.[2]

This is a very common reaction after making a difficult, relatively permanent decision. Doubt or anxiety of this type is referred to as **postpurchase dissonance.**[3] Figure 18-1 indicates that some, but not all, consumer purchase decisions are followed by postpurchase dissonance. The probability of a consumer experiencing postpurchase dissonance, as well as the magnitude of such dissonance, is a function of:

- *The degree of commitment or irrevocability of the decision.* The easier it is to alter the decision, the less likely the consumer is to experience dissonance.
- *The importance of the decision to the consumer.* The more important the decision, the more likely dissonance will result.
- *The difficulty of choosing among the alternatives.* The more difficult it is to select from among the alternatives, the more likely the experience and magnitude of dissonance. Decision difficulty is a function of the number of alternatives considered, the number of relevant attributes associated with each alternative, and the extent to which each alternative offers attributes not available with the other alternatives.
- *The individual's tendency to experience anxiety.* Some individuals have a higher tendency to experience anxiety than do others. The higher the tendency to experience anxiety, the more likely the individual will experience postpurchase dissonance.

Dissonance occurs because making a relatively permanent commitment to a chosen alternative requires one to give up the attractive features of the unchosen alternatives. This is inconsistent with the desire for those features. Thus, nominal and most limited decision making will not produce postpurchase dissonance, since these decisions do not consider attractive features in an unchosen brand that do not also exist in the chosen brand. For example, a consumer who has an evoked set of three brands of detergent could consider them to be equivalent on all relevant attributes except price and, therefore, always purchases the least expensive brand. Such a purchase would not produce postpurchase dissonance.

Because most high-involvement purchase decisions involve one or more of the factors that lead to postpurchase dissonance, these decisions often are accompanied by dissonance. And, since dissonance is unpleasant, consumers generally attempt to avoid or reduce it. Avoiding dissonance involves actions taken before the purchase is made by either avoiding/delaying the decision or using a purchase decision rule that will minimize regret.

Decisions that involve giving up some or all of a desirable feature to obtain (more of) a slightly more desirable feature often generate negative emotions while the decision is being made. These negative emotions may be sufficient to cause the consumer to avoid or delay the decision (I'll just keep this car a while longer.).[4] This suggests that firms marketing products such as automobiles, vacation homes, expensive vacation packages, and similar products train their salespeople to help minimize these negative emotions. Advertising that stresses the fun and positive emotions of the decision outcome and incentive programs that encourage consumers to continue with the purchase process could also be effective.

Consumers may also use decision rules designed to minimize the experience of postpurchase doubt. Such a rule would focus on minimizing the regret or doubt that a decision might produce rather than maximizing the value or benefits of the decisions. The following choice exemplifies this rule:

> And I think that fear was one reason that we bought the General Motors van because we were afraid that if we bought the Ford . . . Well, there is a feeling that if something is too much less, then you start asking yourself why is it that much less . . . We had read how Ford uses more automatization in their manufacturing and we knew that it cost them less to make a car than GM. So we knew that there was a real reason for why theirs is so much cheaper, but you keep asking yourself, "Am I going to kick myself for this? Am I going to wish that I spent more and gotten the other one?"[5]

After the purchase is made, the consumer may utilize one or more of the following approaches to reduce dissonance:

- Increase the desirability of the brand purchased.
- Decrease the desirability of rejected alternatives.

ILLUSTRATION 18-1

Advertisements for high-involvement purchase items can serve to confirm the wisdom of a purchase as well as to influence new purchasers.

Courtesy DaimlerChrysler Corporation.

- Decrease the importance of the purchase decision.
- Reverse the purchase decision (return the product before use).

While postpurchase dissonance may be reduced by internal reevaluations, searching for additional external information that serves to confirm the wisdom of a particular choice is also a common strategy. Naturally, information that supports the consumer's choice acts to bolster confidence in the correctness of the purchase decision.

The consumer's search for, or heightened receptiveness to, information *after* the purchase greatly enhances the role that advertising and follow-up sales efforts can have. To build customer confidence in choosing their brand, many marketers of consumer durables such as major appliances and automobiles send recent purchasers direct-mail materials designed in large part to confirm the wisdom of their purchase. Local retailers can place follow-up calls to make sure the customer is not experiencing any problems with the car or appliance and to reduce any dissonance. Even a simple message such as "Thanks for buying a new Saturn from us. We know you'll be happy with your decision. Is there anything we can do to help you enjoy your new car more?" can reduce dissonance and increase satisfaction.

Many advertisements help recent purchasers confirm the wisdom of their purchase as well as attract new purchasers. Imagine that you have just purchased a new Plymouth Neon after agonizing between it and several other options. Now you are wondering if you made the best choice. At this point, you are likely to be very receptive to positive information about the Neon. So, if you encounter the ad shown in Illustration 18-1, you are apt to read it.

A concept very similar to postpurchase dissonance can be termed **consumption guilt.** Consumption guilt occurs when some negative emotions or guilt feelings are aroused by the use of a product or service. A person driving a large car may experience some negative feelings due to concern over resource utilization and pollution. This quote illustrates consumption guilt quite clearly.

> I have to count calories much more than I did before. I still buy a sundae once in a while but the joy of eating ice cream will probably forever be connected with a guilt over eating something so unhealthy. When I think about it, I realize that most products make me feel good and bad at the same time.[6]

Marketers of products whose target markets might experience consumption guilt need to focus on validating the consumption of the product. They need to find ways to give the consumer permission or a rationale for indulging in that consumption act.

PRODUCT USE AND NONUSE

Product Use

Most consumer purchases involve nominal or limited decision making and therefore arouse little or no postpurchase dissonance. Instead, the purchaser or some other member of the household uses the product without first worrying about the wisdom of the purchase. And, as Figure 18-1 shows, even when postpurchase dissonance occurs, it is still generally followed by product use.

Marketers need to understand how consumers use their products for a variety of reasons. Understanding both the functional and symbolic ways in which a product is used can lead to more effective product designs. For example, Nike uses observation of basketball players at inner-city courts to gain insights into desired functional and style features. One insight gained through these observations is that the process of putting on and tying/buckling basketball shoes before a match is full of meaning and symbolism. In many ways, it is the equivalent of a knight putting on armor before a jousting match or combat. Nike has used this insight in several aspects of its shoe designs.

Use innovativeness refers to a consumer using a product in a new way.[7] Marketers who discover new uses for their products can greatly expand sales. Two products that are famous for this are Arm & Hammer's baking soda and WD-40. Arm & Hammer discovered that consumers were using its baking soda for a variety of noncooking uses such as deodorizing refrigerators. It now advertises such uses. WD-40, a lubricant, is renowned for the wide array of applications that consumers suggest for it—including as an additive to fish bait and for removing gum from a carpet.

Many firms attempt to obtain relevant information on product usage via surveys using standard questionnaires. Such surveys can lead to new-product development, indicate new uses or markets for existing products, or indicate appropriate communications themes. For example, what product positioning and advertising themes are suggested by Figure 18-2? However, observation, depth interviews, and case studies often produce deeper insights:

- During the summers, several Chicago organizations offer "architectural boat cruises" on the Chicago River. They compete on the architectural credentials of their guides, the sites shown, and the boats used. One company did a standard survey and virtually all the respondents checked "interest in architecture" as a "very important" or "extremely important" reason for taking the cruise. However, depth research with 50 passengers showed that architecture was a relatively minor reason for their being there. Most of the Chicago residents were there as a means to entertain out-of-town guest on a nice day. This finding resulted in very different positioning and advertising themes for the sponsoring firm.

FIGURE 18-2 Product Usage Index for VCRs and Microwaves

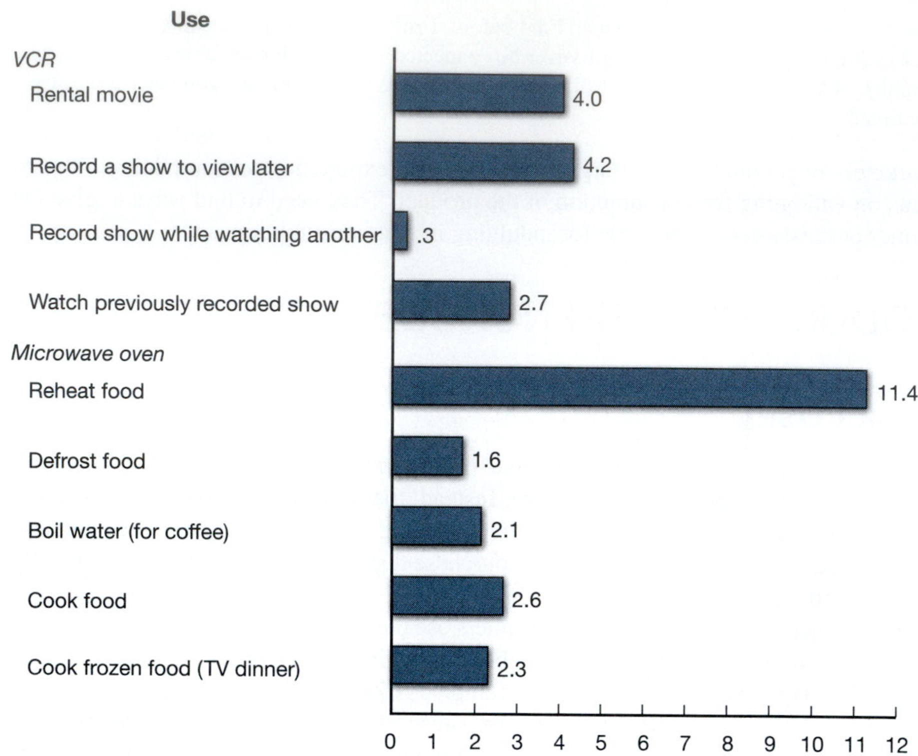

Note: Figures refer to the average number of days per month a product is used for that specific purpose.

Source: Adapted from S. Ram and H. J. Jung, "The Conceptualization and Measurement of Product Usage," *Journal of the Academy of Marketing Science,* Academy of Marketing Science, Winter 1990, pp. 67–76.

- A few years back, a number of upscale frozen gourmet dinner entrees were introduced with great expectations—which none achieved. Researchers observed the frozen food cases that still sold the product and found that, while most consumers ignored it, a few bought substantial quantities. Interviews with these consumers revealed that they were not using them for home meals but rather were preparing them in the office microwave for lunch. They stated that good restaurants were too slow, inconvenient, and expensive for lunch and fast-food places lacked quality and nutrition. This led to opportunities to reposition a line for office-based lunch consumption and to develop a line of high-quality, nonfrozen entrees suitable for office preparation and consumption.[8]

Use behavior can vary regionally. For example, there are major regional variations in how coffee is consumed—with or without cream, with or without sugar, in a mug or a cup, and so forth. Thus, a coffee marketer may find it worthwhile to prepare regional versions of the major advertising theme to reflect regional usage patterns.

Retailers can frequently take advantage of the fact that the use of one product may require or suggest the use of other products. Consider the following product "sets": houseplants and fertilizer, bikes and helmets, cameras and carrying cases, sport coats and ties, and dresses and shoes. In each case, the use of the first product is made easier, more enjoyable, or safer by the use of the related product. Retailers can promote such items jointly,

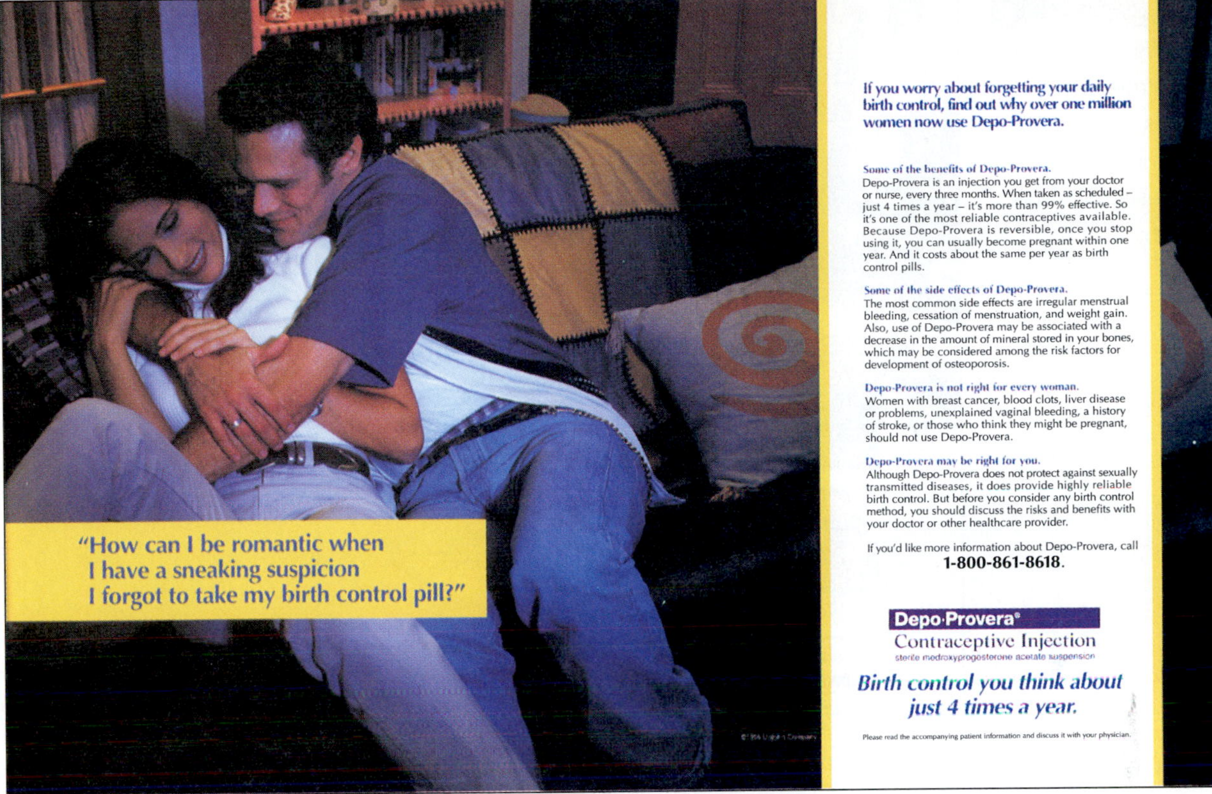

Courtesy Pharm & Upjohn, Inc.

ILLUSTRATION 18-2

Consumers frequently discontinue using, or use improperly, products that require consistent daily behaviors over long periods of time or that are otherwise difficult to use correctly. Firms that are able to redesign such products in a manner that makes them easier to use can gain a competitive advantage.

display them together, or train their sales personnel to make relevant complementary sales. However, to do so requires a sound knowledge of how the products actually are utilized.

Stringent product liability laws and aggressive civil suits also are forcing marketing managers to examine how consumers use their products. These laws have made firms responsible for harm caused by products *not only when the product is used as specified by the manufacturer but in any reasonably foreseeable use of the product.* Thus, the manufacturer must design products with both the primary purpose *and* other potential uses in mind. This requires substantial research into how consumers actually use products.

When marketers discover confusion about the proper way to use a product, it is often to their advantage to teach consumers how to use it. At other times, a firm can gain a competitive advantage by redesigning the product so that it is easier to use properly (see Illustration 18-2).

Product Nonuse

As Figure 18-1 indicates, not all purchases are followed by product use. **Product nonuse** occurs *when a consumer actively acquires a product that is not used at all or used only sparingly relative to its potential use.*[9]

For many products and most services, the decisions to purchase and to consume are made simultaneously. When one orders a meal in a restaurant, one is also deciding to eat the meal at that time. However, a decision to purchase food at a supermarket requires a second decision to prepare and consume the food. The second decision occurs at a different

ILLUSTRATION 18-3

Advertisements can encourage purchases, consumption of previously purchased products, or both.

Courtesy Campbell Soup Company.

point in time and in a different environment from the first. Thus, nonuse can occur because the situation or the purchaser changes between the purchase and the potential usage occasion. For example, a point-of-purchase display featuring a new food item shown as part of an appealing entree might cause a consumer to imagine an appropriate usage situation and to purchase the product. However, without the stimulus of the display, the consumer may not remember the intended use or may just "never get around to it." Nonuse situations such as the following are common:[10]

- *Wok*—"I wanted to try and cook stirfry but I didn't take time out to use it."
- *Skirt*—"My ingenious idea was that I'd lose a few pounds and fit into the size 4 rather than gain a few and fit into the size 6. Obviously, I never lost the weight, so the skirt was snug."
- *Gym membership*—"Couldn't get in the groove to lift."

In such cases, the consumer has wasted money and the marketer is unlikely to get repeat sales or positive referrals. Many such purchases are difficult for the marketer to correct after the purchase. In other cases, consumers would have used the product if reminded or motivated at the proper time. In the last example, good records would indicate that this member was not using the gym. A personal mail or telephone invitation to come in might be enough to get this person started.

Campbell Soup has conducted research that shows that most homes have several cans of Campbell's soup on hand. Therefore, a major goal of its ads is to encourage people to consume soup at the next appropriate meal, through such tactics as radio commercials aired prior to mealtime. Since consumers have the product available, the task is not to encourage purchase but to motivate near-term consumption. The ad in Illustration 18-3 would serve to encourage both the purchase of Campbell's soup and the near-term consumption of soup already on-hand.

DISPOSITION

Disposition of the product or the product's container may occur before, during, or after product use. Or, for products that are completely consumed such as an ice-cream cone, no disposition may be involved.

The United States produces several hundred million tons of household and commercial refuse a year, over 1,500 pounds per person, not including industrial waste. Many landfills are rapidly being filled. Collection and dumping costs for most urban and suburban areas continue to climb. Environmental concerns involving dioxins, lead, and mercury are growing. Clearly, disposition is a major concern for marketers.

Millions of pounds of product packages are disposed of every day. These containers are thrown away as garbage or litter, used in some capacity by the consumer, or recycled. Creating packages that utilize a minimal amount of resources is important for economic reasons as well as being a matter of social responsibility. Producing containers that are easily recyclable or that can be reused also has important consequences beyond social responsibility. As we saw in Chapter 3, some market segments consider the recyclable nature of the product container to be an important product attribute. These consumers anticipate disposition of the package as an attribute of the brand during the alternative evaluation stage. Thus, ease of package disposition (including the absence of a package) can be used as a marketing mix variable in an attempt to capture these market segments.

Marketers are responding to consumers' concerns with recyclable packaging, as the following examples illustrate:

- Rubbermaid is repositioning its trash barrel line to a Recycling Container line. The new line has four models designed to store newspapers, cans, bottles, and yard waste.
- Procter & Gamble uses recycled paper in 80 percent of its product packaging and is packaging liquid Spic and Span, Tide, Cheer, and Downy in containers made from recycled packages.
- Mobil Chemical Co. recently introduced Hefty degradable trash bags. Poly-Tech Inc. sells Ruggies and Sure-Sac degradable bags (however, the bags require exposure to sunlight to degrade).
- The plastics industry has introduced a coding system that identifies a container's plastic resin composition and indicates whether it can be recycled.

For many product categories, a physical product continues to exist even though it may no longer meet a consumer's needs. A product may no longer function physically (instrumental function) in a manner desired by a consumer. Or, it may no longer provide the symbolic meaning desired by the consumer. An automobile that no longer runs is an example of a product ceasing to function instrumentally. An automobile whose owner decides it is out of style no longer functions symbolically (for that particular consumer). In either case, once a replacement purchase is made (or even before the purchase), a disposition decision must be made.

Figure 18-3 illustrates the various alternatives for disposing of a product or package. Unfortunately, while "throw it away" is only one of many disposition alternatives, it is by far the most widely used by consumers. Governmental and environmental agencies work hard to change these behaviors, as do some firms. Other firms, however, continue to use unnecessary or hard to recycle packaging and product components. Some of these same

FIGURE 18-3 Disposition Alternatives

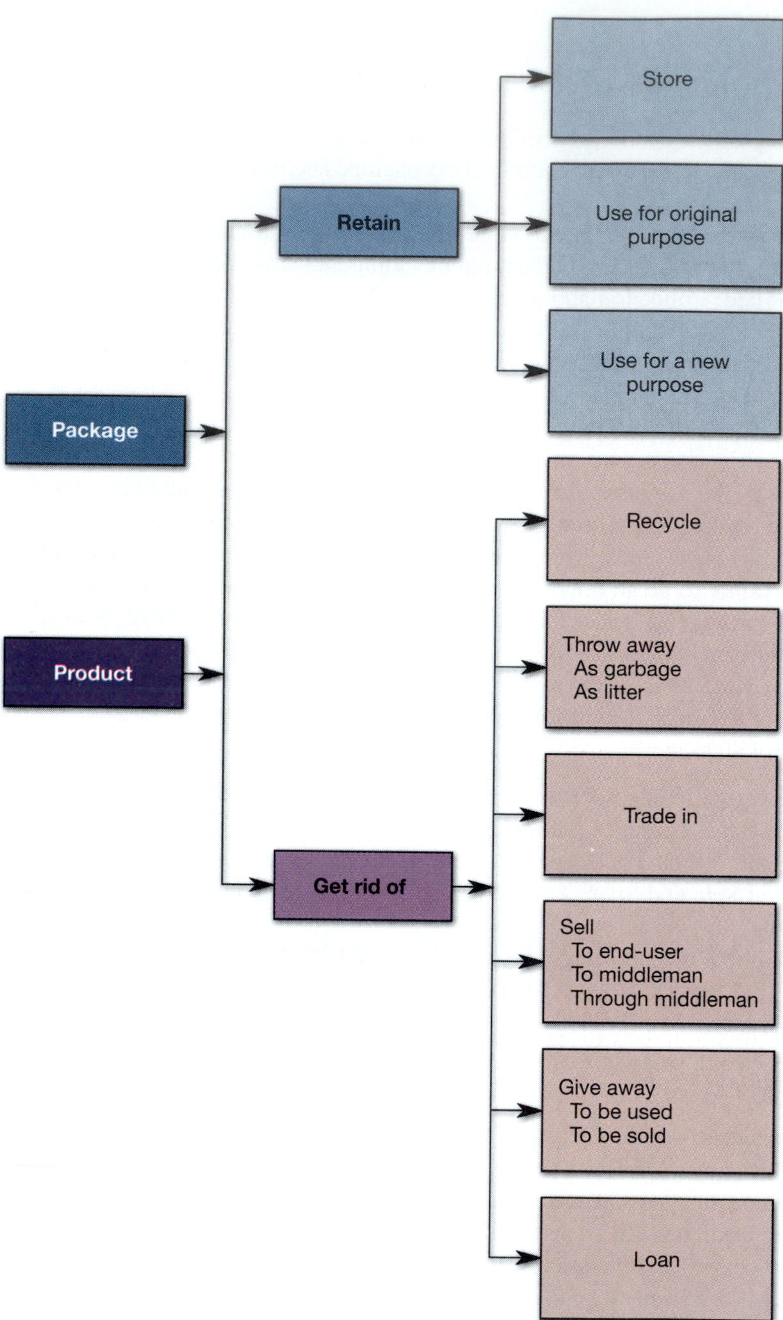

firms also spend millions of dollars campaigning against stricter laws on recycling and product/package disposition.

Relatively little is known about the demographic or psychological characteristics of individuals who tend to select particular disposal methods, though "green" consumption values in general are associated positively with most measures of social status such as education and income. It appears that situational variables such as the availability of storage space, the current needs of friends, the availability of recycling or charitable organizations, and so forth are also important determinants of disposition behavior.

Product Disposition and Marketing Strategy

Why should a marketing manager be concerned about the disposition of a used product? Perhaps the best reason is that the cumulative impact of these decisions has a major impact on the quality of the environment and the lives of current and future generations. However, there are also short-term economic reasons for concern. Disposition decisions affect the purchase decisions of both the individual making the disposition and other individuals in the market for that product category.

There are four major ways in which disposition decisions can affect a firm's marketing strategy. First, disposition sometimes must occur before acquisition of a replacement because of physical space or financial limitations. For example, because of a lack of storage space, a family living in an apartment may find it necessary to dispose of an existing bedroom set before acquiring a new one. Or, someone may need to sell his current bicycle to raise supplemental funds to pay for a new bicycle. If consumers experience difficulty in disposing of the existing product, they may become discouraged and withdraw from the purchasing process. Thus, it is to the manufacturer's and retailer's advantage to assist the consumer in the disposition process.

Second, frequent decisions by consumers to sell, trade, or give away used products may result in a large used product market that can reduce the market for new products. **Consumer-to-consumer sales** occur *when one consumer sells a product directly to another without a commercial intermediary*. Garage sales, swap meets, flea markets, classified ads, and postings on electronic bulletin boards are growing rapidly. Thrift stores, featuring used clothing, appliances, and furniture, run by both commercial and nonprofit groups, are also growing. While there are no precise estimates of the total amount of such sales, they are an important part of the economy. Low-income consumers are the primary shoppers at thrift stores, while most economic groups engage in consumer-to-consumer sales.

A manufacturer may want to enter such a market by buying used products or taking trade-ins and repairing them for the rebuilt market. This is common for automobile parts such as generators and, to a lesser extent, for vacuum cleaners and other appliances.

A third reason for concern with product disposition is that the United States is not completely a throwaway society. Many Americans continue to be very concerned with waste and how their purchase decisions affect waste. Such individuals might be willing to purchase, for example, a new vacuum cleaner if they were confident that the old one would be rebuilt and resold. However, they might be reluctant to throw their old vacuums away or to go to the effort of reselling the machines themselves. Thus, manufacturers and retailers could take steps to ensure that products are reused. The same consumers prefer to buy from companies that provide recyclable products and that practice recycling themselves. Illustration 18-4 shows Canon's attempt to inform consumers of its recycling activities and concerns.

The fourth reason is that environmentally sound disposition decisions benefit society as a whole and thus the firms that are part of that society. Firms' owners and employees live and work in the same society and environment as many of their consumers. Their environment and lives are affected by the disposition decisions of consumers. Therefore, it is in their best interest to develop products, packages, and programs that encourage proper disposition decisions.

ILLUSTRATION 18-4

Proper product disposition is important to many consumers. Canon describes recycling programs for its products as well as for materials it uses.

Our name is known around the world as a pioneer in technology. And our commitment to developing innovative and reliable products in this country has been clear for over 40 years. But concern for the environment is also a big part of our nature.

Our Clean Earth Campaign, for example, started as a program to recycle used toner cartridges from Canon products. Today, it has grown to include partnerships with such leading environmental organizations as the National Park Foundation, the Nature Conservancy and the National Wildlife Federation. Within each organization, we're sponsoring programs to preserve the health and well being of our great wilderness.

Of course, Canon is also hard at work in the corporate environment. From our National Office Paper Recycling Project, to our ozone-free and ENERGY STAR℠ compliant copiers, we're helping to conserve and protect our natural resources for generations to come.

Imagine. A world where technology and nature exist in harmony. Clearly, it's the vision you'd expect from a leader like Canon.

Canon

Courtesy Canon U.S.A., Inc.

PURCHASE EVALUATION AND CUSTOMER SATISFACTION

As we saw in Figure 18-1, a consumer's evaluation of a purchase is influenced by the purchase process itself, postpurchase dissonance, product use, and product/package disposition. Not all purchase evaluations are influenced by each of these four components. Rather, they are potential influencing factors that may affect the evaluation of a particular purchase. You should also note that the outlet or the product or both may be involved in the

TABLE 18-1

Expectations, Performance, and Satisfaction

Perceived Performance Relative to Expectation	Expectation Level: *Below Minimum Desired Performance*	Expectation Level: *Above Minimum Desired Performance*
Better	Satisfaction*	Satisfaction/Commitment
Same	Nonsatisfaction	Satisfaction
Worse	Dissatisfaction	Dissatisfaction

*Assuming the perceived performance surpasses the minimum desired level.

evaluation.[11] Consumers may evaluate each aspect of the purchase ranging from information availability to price to retail service to product performance.[12] Overall satisfaction with a purchase could include satisfaction with the purchase process, including the information available for the decision and the experience of actually making the purchase, as well as satisfaction with the service or product purchased.[13] In addition, satisfaction with one component such as the product may be influenced by the level of satisfaction with other components such as the salesperson.[14] However, keep in mind that nominal decisions and many limited decisions are actively evaluated only if some factor, such as an obvious product malfunction, directs attention to the purchase.

The Evaluation Process

A particular alternative such as a product, brand, or retail outlet is selected because it is thought to be a better overall choice than other alternatives that were considered in the purchase process. Whether that particular item was selected because of its presumed superior functional performance or because of some other reason, such as a generalized liking of the item or outlet, consumers have a level of expected performance for it. The expected level of performance can range from quite low (this item or outlet isn't very good but it's the only one available and I'm in a hurry) to quite high.[15] As you might suspect, expectations and perceived performance are not independent. Up to a point, we tend to perceive performance to be in line with our expectations.[16]

After (or while) using the product, service, or outlet, the consumer will perceive some level of performance. This perceived performance level could be noticeably above the expected level, noticeably below the expected level, or at the expected level. As Table 18-1 indicates, satisfaction with the purchase is primarily a function of the initial performance expectations and perceived performance relative to those expectations.[17]

In Table 18-1, you can see that an outlet or brand whose performance confirms a low-performance expectation generally will result in neither satisfaction nor dissatisfaction but rather with what can be termed *nonsatisfaction.* That is, you are not likely to feel disappointment or engage in complaint behavior. However, this purchase will not reduce the likelihood of a search for a better alternative the next time the problem arises.

A brand whose perceived performance fails to confirm expectations generally produces dissatisfaction. If the discrepancy between performance and expectation is sufficiently large, or if initial expectations were low, the consumer may restart the entire decision process. The item performing below expectations most likely will be placed in the inept set (see Chapter 15) and no longer be considered. In addition, complaint behavior and negative word-of-mouth communications may be initiated.

When perceptions of product performance match expectations that are at or above the minimum desired performance level, satisfaction generally results. Likewise, performance above the minimum desired level that exceeds a lower expectation tends to produce satisfaction. Satisfaction reduces the level of decision making the next time the problem is recognized. That is, a satisfactory purchase is rewarding and encourages one to repeat the same behavior in the future (nominal decision making). Satisfied customers are also likely to engage in positive word-of-mouth communications about the brand.

Product performance that exceeds expected performance will generally result in satisfaction and sometimes in commitment. Commitment, discussed in depth in the next section, means that the consumer is enthusiastic about a particular brand and is somewhat immune to actions by competitors.

Table 18-1 focuses only on the chosen alternative. However, the evaluation of the chosen alternative is somewhat dependent on the quality of the set of alternatives from which it was selected. A clearly superior choice may be held to lower standards than one that was nearly equal to one or more unchosen alternatives.[18] Other situational factors such as mood also impact how individuals evaluate products and services,[19] as do individual characteristics.[20]

The need to produce satisfied consumers has important implications both for product performance and the positioning of promotional claims. Since dissatisfaction is, in part, a function of the disparity between expectations and perceived performance, unrealistic consumer expectations created by promotional exaggeration can contribute to consumer dissatisfaction.

The need to develop realistic consumer expectations poses a difficult problem for the marketing manager.[21] For a brand or outlet to be selected by a consumer, it must be viewed as superior on the relevant combination of attributes. Therefore, the marketing manager naturally wants to emphasize its positive aspects. If such an emphasis creates expectations in the consumer that the item cannot fulfill, a negative evaluation may occur. Negative evaluations can produce brand switching, unfavorable word-of-mouth communications, and complaint behavior. Thus, the marketing manager must balance enthusiasm for the product with a realistic view of the product's attributes.

Determinants of Satisfaction Since performance expectations and actual performance are major factors in the evaluation process, we need to understand the dimensions of product and service performance. A major study of the reasons customers switch service providers found competitor actions to be a relatively minor cause. Most customers did not switch from a satisfactory provider to a better provider. Instead, they switched because of perceived problems with their current service provider. The nature of these problems and the percent listing each as a reason they changed providers follow (the percents sum to more than 100, as many customers listed several reasons that caused them to switch service providers):[22]

- *Core service failure* (44 percent)—mistakes (booking an aisle rather than the requested window seat), billing errors, and service catastrophes that harm the customer (the dry cleaners ruined my suit).
- *Service encounter failures* (34 percent)—service employees were uncaring, impolite, unresponsive, or unknowledgable.
- *Pricing* (30 percent)—high prices, price increases, unfair pricing practices, and deceptive pricing.
- *Inconvenience* (21 percent)—inconvenient location, hours of operation, waiting time for service or appointments.
- *Responses to service failures* (17 percent)—reluctant responses, failure to respond, and negative responses (it's your fault).
- *Attraction by competitors* (10 percent)—more personable, more reliable, higher quality, better value.

- *Ethical problems* (7 percent)—dishonest behavior, intimidating behavior, unsafe or unhealthy practices, or conflicts of interest.
- *Involuntary switching* (6 percent)—service provider or customer moves, or a third-party payer such as an insurance company requires a change.

Other studies have found that waiting time has a major impact on evaluations of service.[23] Consumers have particularly negative reactions to delays over which they believe the service provider has control and during which they have little to occupy their time.[24] Obviously, firms should attempt to minimize the delays encountered by their customers. If delays are unavoidable, the cause should be clearly indicated, as well as accurate estimates of the duration.[25] To the extent possible, consumers should be provided with activities or entertainment during the delay.[26]

Not surprisingly, the nature and extent of personal contact with customers in service encounters is of critical importance in determining customer satisfaction. While extended, personalized customer contact is expensive, it is also very effective at increasing satisfaction and repeat purchase intentions.[27]

Many firms now "guarantee" their services. These guarantees can range from inclusive and general—"Satisfaction guaranteed"—to specific in terms of coverage and pay out—"Delivery in 30 minutes or it's free." Such service guarantees can increase expected performance levels and patronage (and costs).[28]

For many products, there are two dimensions to performance: instrumental, and expressive or symbolic. **Instrumental performance** relates to *the physical functioning of the product*. That the product operates properly is vital to the evaluation of a dishwasher, sewing machine, or other major appliance. **Symbolic performance** relates to *aesthetic or image-enhancement performance*. For example, the durability of a sport coat is an aspect of instrumental performance, while styling represents symbolic performance.

Is symbolic or instrumental performance more important to consumers as they evaluate product performance? The answer to this question undoubtedly varies by product category and across consumer groups. However, a number of studies focusing on clothing provide some insights into how these two types of performance are related.

Clothing appears to perform five major functions: protection from the environment, enhancement of sexual attraction, aesthetic and sensuous satisfaction, an indicator of status, and an extension of self-image. Except for protection from the environment, these functions are all dimensions of symbolic performance. Yet studies of clothing returns, complaints about clothing purchases, and discarded clothing indicate that physical product failures are the primary cause of dissatisfaction. One study on the relationship between performance expectations, actual performance, and satisfaction with clothing purchases reached the following general conclusion:

> Dissatisfaction is caused by a failure of instrumental performance, while complete satisfaction also requires the symbolic functions to perform at or above the expected levels.[29]

Other research has found that negative performance on a feature such as waiting time or ease of use has a stronger effect on satisfaction than does positive performance on that same feature.[30] This suggests that both products and services focus on meeting expectations across all relevant features before maximizing performance on a few.

In addition to symbolic and instrumental performance, products also provide affective performance. **Affective performance** is *the emotional response that owning or using the product provides*.[31] It may arise from the instrumental and/or symbolic performance or from the product itself. That is, a suit that produces admiring glances or compliments may produce a positive affective response. Or, the affective performance may be the primary product benefit, such as for an emotional movie or novel.

DISSATISFACTION RESPONSES

Figure 18-4 illustrates the major options available to a dissatisfied consumer.[32] The first decision is whether or not to take any external action. By taking no action, the consumer decides to "live with" the unsatisfactory situation. This decision is a function of the importance of the purchase to the consumer, the ease of taking action, and the characteristics of the consumer involved.[33] It is very important to note that even when no external action is taken, the consumer is likely to have a less favorable attitude toward the store or brand.

Consumers who take action in response to dissatisfaction generally pursue one or more of five alternatives. As Figure 18-4 indicates, most of these alternatives are damaging to the firm involved both directly in terms of lost sales and indirectly in terms of a customer with a less favorable attitude. Therefore, marketers should strive to minimize dissatisfaction *and* to effectively resolve dissatisfaction when it occurs.

Consumers are satisfied with the vast majority of their purchases. Still, because of the large number of purchases that individuals make each year, most individuals experience dissatisfaction with some of their purchases. For example, one study asked 540 consumers if they could recall a case in which one or more of the grocery products they normally purchase was defective. They recalled 1,307 separate unsatisfactory purchases.

These purchases produced the following actions (the study did not measure negative word-of-mouth actions such as warning friends):

- 25 percent of these unsatisfactory purchases resulted in brand switching.
- 19 percent caused the shopper to stop buying the products.
- 13 percent led to an in-store inspection of future purchases.
- 3 percent produced complaints to the manufacturer.
- 5 percent produced complaints to the retailer.
- 35 percent resulted in the item being returned.

FIGURE 18-4 Dissatisfaction Responses

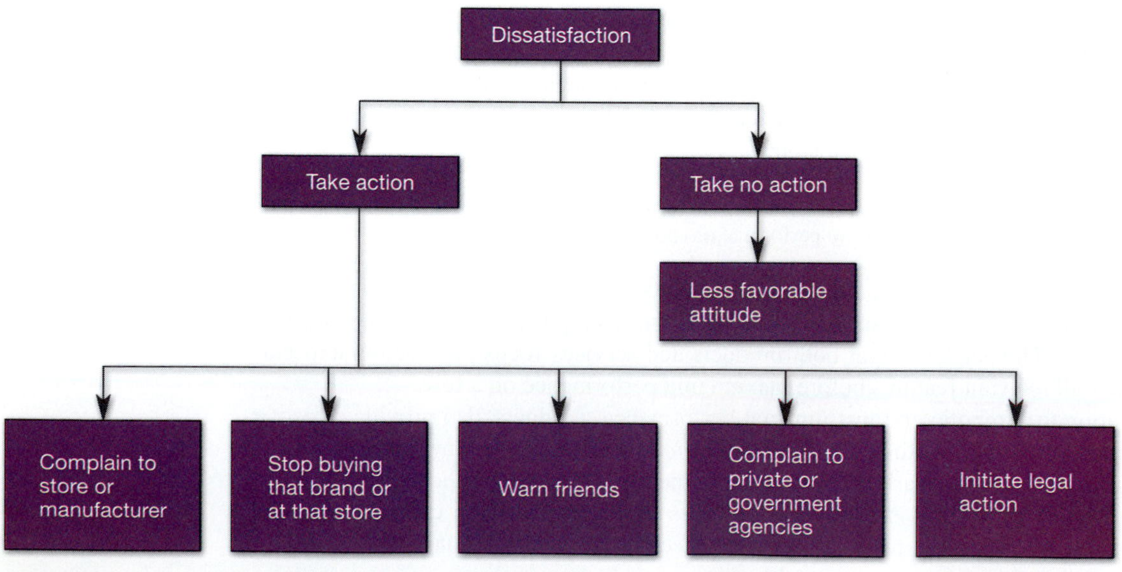

In a similar study of durable goods, 54 percent of the dissatisfied customers said they would not purchase the brand again, and 45 percent warned their friends about the product.[34]

Marketing Strategy and Dissatisfied Consumers

> I feel mad. I put it in my Christmas letter to 62 people across the country. I mean, I told everybody don't buy one of these things because the transmission is bad.[35]

The above quote is a marketer's nightmare. Firms need to satisfy consumer expectations by (1) creating reasonable expectations through promotional efforts and (2) maintaining consistent quality so the reasonable expectations are fulfilled. Since dissatisfied consumers tend to express their dissatisfaction to their friends, dissatisfaction may cause the firm to lose future sales to the unhappy consumer's friends as well as to the unhappy consumer.[36]

When a consumer is dissatisfied, the most favorable consequence is for the consumer to communicate this dissatisfaction to the firm but to no one else. This alerts the firm to problems, enables it to make amends where necessary, and minimizes negative word-of-mouth communications. Many firms have discovered that customers whose complaints are resolved to their satisfaction are even more satisfied than are customers who did not experience a problem in the first place.[37] In addition, complaints generally work to the consumer's advantage as firms attempt to redress the problem.

Unfortunately, many individuals do not communicate their dissatisfaction to the firm involved. Those who do complain tend to have more education, income, self-confidence, and independence, and are more confident in the business system than those who do not complain.[38] In our society, and more so in many others, we are taught not to complain. Therefore, complaining takes emotional energy:

> I find it hard to say anything when I'm unhappy (with a purchase). It takes talking to myself all the way to the store. I say, "how do I say that?" I practice it. If I can get my husband to do it, I will. I'm very uncomfortable, even afterwards. I don't want people to think that I'm such a crab or not be liked or not think, "That's not such a nice lady."[39]

Complaints about products frequently go to retailers and are not passed on to manufacturers. Many firms attempt to overcome this by establishing and promoting "consumer hot lines"—toll-free numbers that consumers can use to contact a representative of the firm when they have a complaint. General Electric spends $10 million a year on its 800-number "Answer Center," which handles 3 million calls annually. GE feels that the payback is "multiple times" that.[40] Procter & Gamble provides the following examples of benefits received from its hot line:

- Duncan Hines brownie mix: "We learned that people in high-altitude areas need special instructions for baking, and these soon were added to the packages. We also found that one of the recipes on a box label was confusing, so we changed it."
- Toothpaste: "We spotted a pattern of people complaining that they couldn't get the last bit of toothpaste out of the tube without it breaking, so the tubes were strengthened."
- A sudden group of calls indicated that the plastic tops on Downy fabric softener bottles were splintering when twisted on and off, creating the danger of cut fingers. P&G identified the supplier of the fragile caps and learned that it had recently changed its formula. The new-formula caps were becoming brittle as they aged. Most of the bad caps had not left the factory, and P&G simply replaced them. Thus, a costly (financially and imagewise) product recall was avoided.

- P&G also receives calls with positive testimonials. These are forwarded to the appropriate advertising agency, where they are analyzed for insights into why people like the product. Several P&G campaigns have been based on these unsolicited consumer comments.[41]

While hot lines and other procedures increase the ease with which consumers can express a complaint, they are not sufficient. Most consumers who complain want a tangible result. Failure to deal effectively with this expectation can produce increased dissatisfaction. Therefore, firms need to resolve the cause of consumer complaints, not just give the consumers the opportunity to complain.[42] For example, Burger King, which receives up to 4,000 calls a day on its 24-hour hot line (65 percent are complaints), resolves 95 percent of the problems on the initial call. To be certain the customers are truly satisfied, 25 percent are called back within a month.

Unfortunately, many corporations are not organized to effectively resolve and learn from consumer complaints. This area represents a major opportunity for many businesses.[43] In fact, for many firms, retaining once-dissatisfied customers by encouraging and responding effectively to complaints is more economical than attracting new customers through advertising or other promotional activities.[44] It has been estimated that it costs only one-fifth as much to retain an old customer as to obtain a new one.[45] Training those employees who deal directly with customers to use appropriate communication styles and empowering them to resolve problems as they arise is one way firms can increase customer satisfaction and retention.[46]

Anticipating dissatisfaction and removing the potential cause before it occurs can pay substantial benefits to a firm. A few years ago, a problem was discovered with the Intel Pentium chip. The problem was rare and would affect very few users under only limited applications. Intel was slow to acknowledge and respond to the problem. This in turn generated a significant amount of negative publicity, which harmed the company's image and sales.[47] Contrast Intel's response and results to those of LifeScan:

LifeScan, a Johnson & Johnson company, makes meters that diabetics use to monitor their blood sugar levels. Several years ago, a single meter was found to be defective. In response, the company notified 600,000 customers virtually overnight and recalled the entire product line. Customers responded positively to this show of concern by LifeScan. Its market share has increased by 7 percent since the recall.

To create and retain highly satisfied customers, LifeScan has a full-time manager of customer loyalty who works closely with the marketing and customer service departments to measure and improve customer satisfaction and retention. Customer service representatives field 1.3 million calls per year and are trained and empowered to make decisions to satisfy each caller. These service reps also play a key role in new-product development activities.

LifeScan offers its customers a 24-hour toll-free hot line, telecommunications capability for the deaf (diabetes contributes to hearing impairment), 24-hour meter replacement (meters are stored at Federal Express in Memphis to make this possible), educational information, a newsletter, and a five-year product warranty. Additional services are provided to distributors and health care professionals.

To ensure that these activities are effective, LifeScan maintains daily phone statistics, conducts quarterly satisfaction surveys to supplement the annual satisfaction survey, and stays in touch with its customers in other ways as well.[48]

LifeScan reacted before all but one of its customers had a chance to experience dissatisfaction. This quick action resulted in increased customer loyalty and sales. Consumer Insight 18-1 indicates how Whirlpool and Otis Elevator use their customer service databases to solve customer problems and complaints before they occur.

Responding to Customer Problems before They Occur

Consumer Insight 18-1

Whirlpool

At Whirlpool, a computer system recently raised a warning. A few customers had reported a serious water leak in their washing machines after only a few loads had been washed. Engineers quickly located the problem—a faulty hose clamp. Production was halted and the clamp was replaced on all in-process machines, those in inventory, and those at dealers. More importantly, the few hundred consumers who had purchased the new model were identified by Whirlpool's customer database. These consumers were quickly notified and mechanics were sent to their homes to replace the clamp.

Not only were customers kept from experiencing an annoying and possibly damaging problem, Whirlpool avoided potential negative publicity as well as claims for property damage. As the director of consumer assistance stated: "Imagine the property-damage liability if there had been a leak in a fifth-floor apartment."

Whirlpool maintains records on 15 million customers and more than 20 million installed appliances, some dating back to the 1960s. It uses specialized database computers to scan volumes of records in parallel and seek out faint but significant patterns.

Otis Elevator

Otis Elevator's centralized service center, OtisLine, handles 1.2 million calls a year. Half are for unscheduled repairs. When answering such a call, the service rep punches in a code that identifies the customer's building. Immediately, a record of the equipment and its repair history appears. A series of canned questions elicits the essential new information. Within minutes, a radio message dispatches the appropriate Otis technician to the building.

This fast, efficient postproblem service is only a minor part of the picture. The technician completes a report on the problem and the needed repairs. A full-time 20-member engineering team reviews each case and has the computer scan for similar cases. The results may involve a design change in an elevator model or a change in the recommended maintenance schedule.

These two cases illustrate the power of bringing technology to focus on customer service issues. A recent study of large U.S. and European firms found that 70 percent had customer service as the main focus for their investments in technology.

Critical Thinking Questions

1. What ethical concerns are associated with maintaining and using a database like Whirlpool's?
2. What type of database should your university maintain on its students?

Source: Reprinted from the March, 21, 1994 issue of *Business Week* by special permission.

CUSTOMER SATISFACTION, REPEAT PURCHASES, AND CUSTOMER COMMITMENT

Pizza Hut's customer satisfaction department conducts an aggressive customer satisfaction campaign at all of its company-owned outlets. A key part of the campaign is a major, ongoing survey of about 50,000 customers per week.

A percentage of all customers who have pizza delivered or who take it out are telephoned within 24 hours. The interview is limited to four minutes. A system is in place to ensure that at least 60 days elapse before a customer is interviewed again. In addition, one out of every 20 to 30 dine-in customer is given a coupon at the bottom of their receipt and a toll-free number to call to participate in a six-minute interview. Two-thirds of those who respond to this offer do so within 24 hours, so the dining experience is still fresh in their memory.

Half of the store manager's quarterly bonus is linked to the survey results. Thus, it serves as a motivational and control device for the managers. In addition, it identifies problems quickly and allows managers to solve them before the image of the outlet or of Pizza Hut is harmed.

The survey focuses only on customer satisfaction issues that the manager can control. Thus, questions concerning value, price, and brand image are not used. Instead, the survey's focus is on service, food quality, and the purchase experience.

The surveys have identified systemwide problems as well as issues at individual stores. When Pizza Hut launched its Stuffed Crust Pizza, initial sales were strong, but repeat sales did not materialize. The surveys revealed the nature of the service problems associated with the new product and enabled the firm to take corrective action. It also provided insights that Pizza Hut can use in future new-product introductions.[49]

Pizza Hut is typical of the many American firms that have responded to increased competition by focusing their efforts on producing satisfied customers rather than on producing short-term sales. As we just saw, customers who are not satisfied are unlikely to continue using a brand and they are likely to communicate to friends and associates the causes of their dissatisfaction. In contrast, satisfied customers are likely to repurchase the brand the next time a need arises. Increasing customer satisfaction can thus lead directly to an increase in firm profitability.[50]

However, given increasingly sophisticated and value-conscious consumers and multiple brands that perform at satisfactory levels, producing satisfied customers is necessary but not sufficient for many marketers. Instead, the objective is to produce committed or brand-loyal customers.

Figure 18-5 illustrates the composition of the buyers of a particular brand at any point in time. Of the total buyers, some percent will be satisfied with the purchase. As we have seen, marketers are spending considerable effort to make this percent as high as possible. The reason is that, while many satisfied customers will switch brands,[51] satisfied customers are more likely to become or remain repeat purchasers than are dissatisfied customers. **Repeat purchasers** continue to buy the same brand though they do not have an emotional attachment to it.

FIGURE 18-5 Creating Committed Customers Is Increasingly the Focus of Marketing Strategy

As we saw earlier, some dissatisfied customers may also become or remain repeat purchasers. These individuals will not perceive any available satisfactory alternatives or will believe that the expected benefits of renewed search are not worth the expected costs. However, they may engage in negative word-of-mouth and are very vulnerable to competitors' actions.

While repeat purchasers are desirable, *mere* repeat purchasers are very vulnerable to competitor actions. That is, they are buying the brand due to habit or because it is readily available where they shop, or because it has the lowest price, or for similar superficial reasons. These customers have no commitment to the brand. That is, they are not brand loyal. **Brand loyalty** is defined as *consistently purchasing a brand over time due to an emotional attachment to the brand.*[52]

Service and store loyalty are generally defined in the same or a similar manner.[53] Thus, a brand (store or service) loyal, or **committed customer,** has an emotional attachment to the brand or firm. The customer likes the brand in a manner somewhat similar to friendship. Consumers use expressions such as *I trust this brand, I like this outlet,* and *I believe in this firm* to describe their commitment:

> I tried it myself one time and eventually adopted a taste for it. Now I drink it all the time. I have it every morning after I come in from my run. I drink it after I clean the house. I always have a glass of it in my hand. That's me. I am very loyal to Gatorade. I would say that I am very loyal to that. I know they have other brands of that now, I see coupons all the time, but I have never even picked up a bottle of them. Never even tried them. Because I like Gatorade a lot. I really do.[54]

Brand loyalty can arise through identification, where a consumer believes the brand reflects and reinforces some aspect of the consumer's self-concept. This type of commitment is most common for symbolic products such as automobiles. Brand loyalty may also arise through performance so far above expected that it delights the customer.[55] Such superior performance can be related to the product or the firm itself or, as mentioned earlier, to the manner in which the firm responds to a complaint or a customer problem.

Committed customers are unlikely to consider additional information when making a purchase. They are also resistant to competitors' marketing efforts—for example, coupons. Even when loyal customers do buy a different brand to take advantage of a promotional deal, they generally return to their original brand for their next purchase.[56] Committed customers are more receptive to line extensions and other new products offered by the same firm. They are also more likely to forgive an occasional product or service failure.[57]

Finally, committed customers are likely to be a source of positive word-of-mouth communications. This is extremely valuable to a firm. Positive word-of-mouth communications from a committed customer increases both the probability of the recipient becoming a customer and of the recipient sharing the positive comments with a third person[58]—"I haven't eaten at Aron's yet but Kim raves about the food and service."

For all of these reasons, committed customers are much more profitable to the firm than mere repeat purchasers who, in turn, are more profitable than occasional buyers. However, since the cost of creating committed customers varies by industry and competitive setting, so does their relative profitability.[59]

Repeat Purchasers, Committed Customers, and Profits

Churn is a term used to refer to *turnover in a firm's customer base*. If a firm has a base of 100 customers and 20 leave each year and 20 new ones become customers, it has a churn rate of 20 percent. Reducing churn is a major objective of many firms today. Why? It typically costs more to obtain a new customer than to retain an existing one, and new customers generally are not as profitable as longer term customers. Consider the profits generated by one credit card firm's customers over time:[60]

Year	*Profits*
Acquisition cost	($51)
Year 1	30
Year 2	42
Year 3	44
Year 4	49
Year 5	55

Acquisition costs include such expenses as advertising, establishing the account, mailing the card, and so forth. First-year profits are low because many new customers are acquired due to a promotional deal of some type. In addition, their initial usage rate tends to be low and they don't use all the features. This is a common pattern for both consumer and industrial products. Auto service profits per customer increased from $25 the first year to $88 in the fifth year, while an industrial laundry found they went from $144 to $258.

Figure 18-6 shows the sources of the growth of profit per customer over time. Price premium refers to the fact that repeat and particularly committed customers tend to buy the brand consistently rather than waiting for a sale or continually negotiating price. Referrals

FIGURE 18-6 Sources of Increased Customer Profitability Over Time

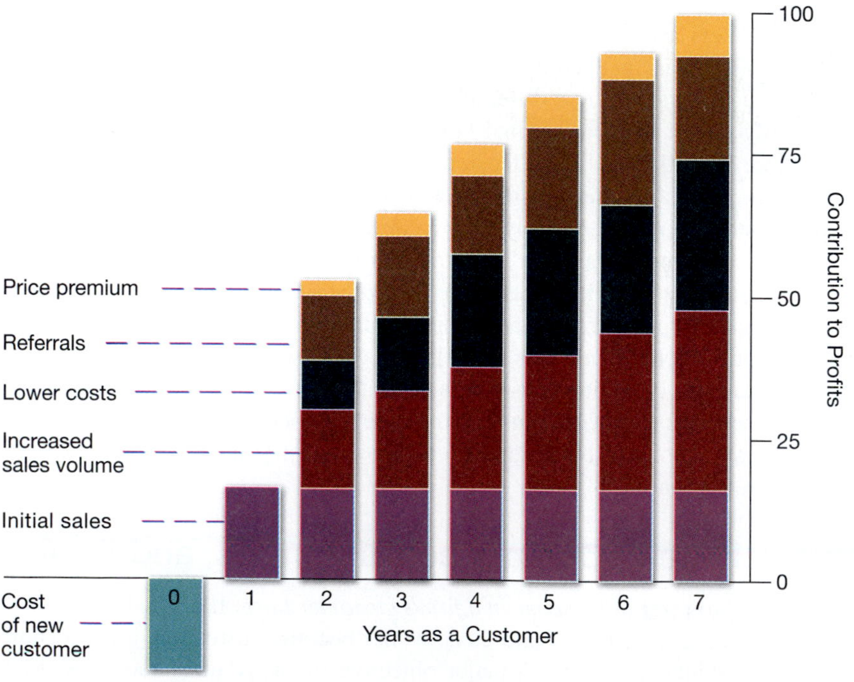

are profits generated by new customers acquired due to recommendations from existing customers. Lower costs occur because both the firm and the customer learn how to interact more efficiently over time. Finally, customers tend to use a wider array of a firm's products and services over time.

While many of these profit sources will come from mere repeat purchasers, to fully capture a customer's profit potential, a firm needs to produce committed customers. For example, willingness to pay the full price and actively providing referrals are primarily characteristics of committed customers. More importantly, it is difficult to maintain mere repeat purchasers over long time periods.

While committed customers are most valuable to a firm, reducing churn can have a major impact on profit even if the retained customers are primarily repeat purchasers. Reducing the number of customers who leave a firm in a year increases the average "life" of the firm's customer base.[61] As we saw earlier, the longer a customer is with a firm, the more profits the firm derives from that customer. Thus, a stable customer base tends to be highly profitable per customer. Reducing the number of customers who leave various types of firms each year by 5 percent has been found to increase the average profits per customer as follows:[62]

Firm Type	*Percent Increase in Average Profits per Customer*
Auto service	30%
Branch banks	85
Credit card	75
Credit insurance	25
Insurance brokerage	50
Industrial laundry	45

The motivation for marketers to retain customers is obvious. Phil Bressler, the co-owner of five Domino's Pizza outlets in Maryland, found that a regular customer was worth more than $5,000 over the 10-year life of the franchise agreement. He makes sure that every employee in every store is constantly aware of that number. Poor service or a bad attitude may cost the outlet several thousands of dollars, not just the $10 or $15 that might be lost on the single transaction![63]

Repeat Purchasers, Committed Customers, and Marketing Strategy

An important step in developing a marketing strategy for a particular segment is to specify the objectives being pursued. Several distinct possibilities exist:

1. Attract new users to the product category.
2. Capture competitors' current customers.
3. Encourage current customers to use more.
4. Encourage current customers to become repeat purchasers.
5. Encourage current customers to become committed customers.

Each of the objectives listed above will require different strategies and marketing mixes. The first two objectives require the marketer to convince potential customers that the

FIGURE 18-7 Customer Satisfaction Outcomes

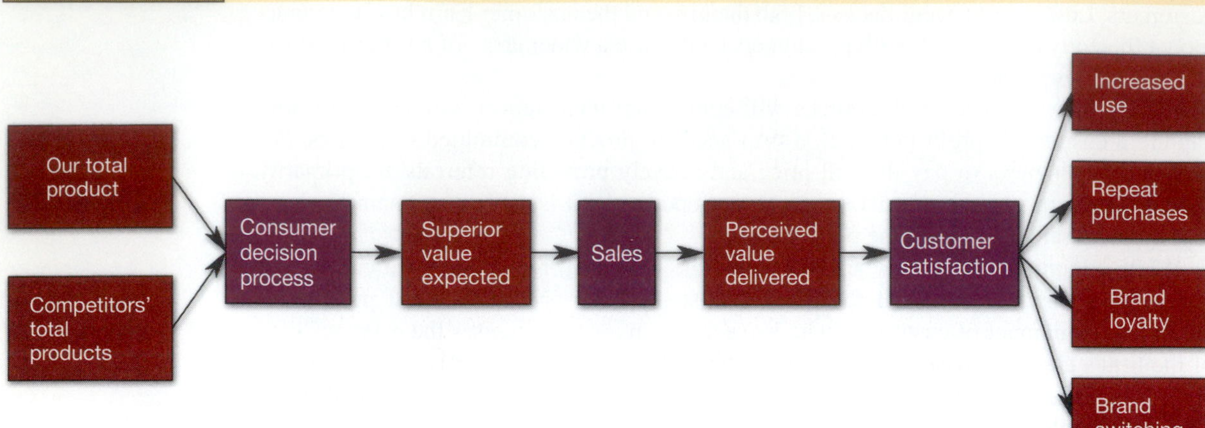

marketer's brand will provide superior value to not using the product or to using another brand. This is shown in the first four stages of Figure 18-7. Advertisements promising superior benefits, coupons, free trials, and similar strategies are common approaches. While some firms are content to consider the sale the last step, smart firms now realize the critical importance of retaining customers after the initial sale. This is true even for infrequently purchased items (rather than repeat sales, the marketer wants positive, or at least neutral, word-of-mouth communications).

The next three objectives focus on marketing to the firm's current customers. All require customer satisfaction as a necessary precondition. As Figure 18-7 indicates, this requires that the firm deliver the value expected by the customer. Techniques for creating satisfied customers were described earlier. Marketing efforts focused on a firm's current customers are generally termed *relationship marketing.*

Relationship Marketing An attempt to develop an ongoing, expanding exchange relationship with a firm's customers is called **relationship marketing.** In many ways, it seeks to mimic the relationships that existed between neighborhood stores and their customers many years ago. In these relationships, the store owner knew the customers not only as customers but also as friends and neighbors. The owner could anticipate their needs and provide help and advice when needed. Relationship marketing attempts to accomplish the same results but, because of the large scale of most operations, must use databases, "customized mass communications," and advanced employee training and motivation.[64] Consider the following example:

Lees Supermarkets, a family-owned and operated company, started a Shoppers Club that records the purchases of members. Frequent or heavy shoppers are offered special incentives and deals. These offers can be customized based on past purchasing patterns. In addition, last Thanksgiving, 600 regular, high-volume members were rewarded with free turkeys. Such an unexpected reward can produce delight and loyalty among key customers.[65]

Relationship marketing has five key elements:[66]

1. Developing a core service or product around which to build a customer relationship.
2. Customizing the relationship to the individual customer.

3. Augmenting the core service or product with extra benefits.
4. Pricing in a manner to encourage loyalty.
5. Marketing to employees so that they will perform well for customers.

This list of elements makes it clear that relationship marketing is centered on understanding consumer needs at the individual consumer level.[67]

As stated earlier, relationship marketing can be used to encourage increased usage, repeat purchases, and/or customer commitment.

Given satisfied customers, a marketer may encourage those customers to use more of the brand or related products and services offered by the firm.[68] This may involve convincing those customers who use more than one brand to use the marketer's brand a higher percentage of the time. This is a key objective of frequent-flier programs that award higher "points" per mile the more miles flown on the airline in a year. Another approach to increasing consumption is to show new ways to use the brand or new situations for which it is appropriate.

A substantial amount of effort is currently being focused on the fourth objective—encouraging repeat purchases.[69] While these programs are generally called **customer loyalty programs,** many are designed to generate repeat purchases rather than committed customers.[70] In addition to frequent-flier programs offered by most major airlines, programs designed to generate repeat purchases include the following:

- Saks-Fifth Avenue (Saks First) and Sears (Best Customer) identify frequent shoppers and make them members of their store "clubs." As members, they receive extra services, preshopping at sales, fashion newsletters, and so forth.
- Arby's Restaurants has Club Arby's, which electronically tracks purchases and offers food prizes to repeat customers.
- Waldenbooks' Preferred Customer Program offers discounts and rebates to repeat purchasers. It also segments its membership based on the types of books each customer buys. This allows it to deliver customized direct-mail ads to its frequent shoppers.

While programs such as those described above are often very effective at generating repeat purchases, they do not necessarily create committed customers.[71] Committed customers have a reasonably strong emotional attachment to the product or firm. Generating committed customers requires that the firm consistently meet or exceed customer expectations. Further, customers must believe that the firm is treating them fairly and is, to some extent at least, concerned about their well-being. Thus, *generating committed customers requires a customer-focused attitude in the firm.* It also requires that this attitude be translated into actions that meet customers' needs.[72]

United Airline Mileage Plus attempts to create committed customers through the services it provides its passengers and through an extensive frequent-flier program that gives increasing rewards the more one flies. For example, members of its Premier members get to board early—a privilege greatly appreciated by frequent fliers. The program has numerous affiliates, which allows members to earn miles through credit card purchases, hotel stays, car rentals, phone calls, and a host of other activities (see Illustration 18-5). Miles can be redeemed for up-grades, tickets, cruises, vacations, and so forth.

Developing committed customers for a retailer requires the retailer to understand customer desires at every stage of the shopping process, from retail advertisements through disposition of the products. At every stage, the retailer needs to move beyond customer satisfaction through customer delight and to customer affection. At the buying stage, the following types of retail actions at an appliance store are examples of the requirements for

ILLUSTRATION 18-5

Successful customer loyalty programs are based on understanding the needs of key customers and providing benefits of value to them.

"© 1999 Hertz System, Inc. Hertz is a registered service mark and trademark of Hertz System, Inc."

each level of customer response:[73]

Satisfaction	Courteous, knowledgeable salespeople, speed and efficiency in completing transactions, credit.
Delight	Sales associates with electronic notepad to scan UPCs disclosing complete product information, chocolate-covered silver dollar thank-you candies, recycled paper package in the right color, special order gladly taken.
Affection	Individual birthday sales, database on individual buying patterns and requirements, discounts and awards instantly given based on past purchases, thank-you cards and gift certificate in the mail.

SUMMARY

Following some purchases, consumers experience doubts or anxiety about the wisdom of the purchase. This is known as *postpurchase dissonance.* It is most likely to occur (1) among individuals with a tendency to experience anxiety, (2) after an irrevocable purchase, (3) when the purchase was important to the consumer, and (4) when it involved a difficult choice between two or more alternatives.

Whether or not the consumer experiences dissonance, most purchases are followed by product use. This use may be by the purchaser or by some other member of the purchasing unit. Monitoring product usage can indicate new uses for existing products, needed product modifications, appropriate advertising themes, and opportunities for new products. Product liability laws have made it increasingly important for marketing managers to be aware of all potential uses of their products.

Product nonuse is also a concern. Both marketers and consumers suffer when consumers buy products that they do not use or use less than they intended. Thus, marketers frequently attempt to influence the decision to use the product as well as the decision to purchase the product.

Disposition of the product or its package may occur before, during, or after product use. Understanding disposition behavior has become increasingly important to marketing managers because of the ecological concerns of many consumers, the costs and scarcity of raw materials, and the activities of federal and state legislatures and regulatory agencies.

Postpurchase dissonance, product usage, and disposition are potential influences on the purchase evaluation process. Consumers develop certain expectations about the ability of the product to fulfill instrumental and symbolic needs. To the extent that the product meets these needs, satisfaction is likely to result. When expectations are not met, dissatisfaction is the likely result.

Taking no action; switching brands, products, or stores; and warning friends are all common reactions to a negative purchase evaluation. A marketing manager generally should encourage dissatisfied consumers to complain directly to the firm and to no one else. Unfortunately, only a fairly small, unique set of consumers tends to complain to the firm. Developing such strategies as consumer hot lines can increase the percentage of dissatisfied consumers who complain to the firm.

After the evaluation process and, where applicable, the complaint process, consumers have some degree of repurchase motivation. There may be a strong motive to avoid the brand, a willingness to repurchase it some of the time, a willingness to repurchase it all of the time, or some level of brand loyalty or customer commitment, which is a willingness to repurchase coupled with a psychological commitment to the brand.

Marketing strategy does not always have the creation of brand loyalty as its objective. Rather, the manager must examine the makeup of the brand's current and potential consumers and select the specific objectives most likely to maximize the overall organizational goals.

Relationship marketing attempts to develop an ongoing, expanding exchange relationship with a firm's customers. It is used to increase brand usage, repeat sales, or customer commitment.

KEY TERMS

Affective performance 641
Brand loyalty 647
Churn 647
Committed customer 647
Consumer-to-consumer sales 637
Consumption guilt 630
Customer loyalty programs 651
Instrumental performance 641
Postpurchase dissonance 628
Product nonuse 633
Relationship marketing 650
Repeat purchasers 646
Symbolic performance 641
Use innovativeness 631

INTERNET EXERCISES

1. Monitor several product- or activity-related chat sites or interest groups for a week. Prepare a report on how a marketer could learn about the following by doing this:
   a. Customer satisfaction levels and customer commitment
   b. Product use
   c. Customer evaluation processes
2. Find a company site that helps the company in terms of relationship marketing. Describe and evaluate this effort.
3. Find a product, company, or brand site that helps the consumer use a product properly or effectively. Describe and evaluate this effort.

DDB NEEDHAM LIFESTYLE DATA ANALYSES

1. What characterizes individuals who feel they have acquired too much debt? What are the marketing implications of this? What are the regulatory implications of this?
2. What characterizes people who become committed enough to favorite brands to resist other brands when they are on sale? What are the marketing implications of this?

REVIEW QUESTIONS

1. What are the major postpurchase processes engaged in by consumers?
2. How does the type of decision process affect the postpurchase processes?
3. What is postpurchase dissonance? What characteristics of a purchase situation are likely to contribute to postpurchase dissonance?
4. What actions do consumers take to avoid postpurchase dissonance before the purchase?
5. In what ways can a consumer reduce postpurchase dissonance?
6. What is meant by product nonuse and why is it a concern of marketers?
7. What is meant by the disposition of products and product packaging, and why does it interest governmental regulatory agencies and marketers?
8. What factors influence consumer satisfaction? In what way do they influence consumer satisfaction?
9. What is the difference between instrumental and symbolic performance, and how does each contribute to consumer satisfaction?
10. What is affective performance?
11. What courses of action can a consumer take in response to dissatisfaction? Which are used most often?
12. What would marketers like consumers to do when dissatisfied? How can marketers encourage this?
13. What is churn? How does it affect profits?
14. What are the sources of increased profits from longer term customers?
15. What is the relationship between customer satisfaction, repeat purchases, and committed customers?
16. What is the difference between repeat purchasers and committed customers?
17. Why are marketers interested in having committed customers?
18. What are five objectives that a marketing strategy for a particular segment might have? How will marketing strategies differ across the five objectives that a firm might have for a particular segment?
19. What is relationship marketing? What strategies are involved?

DISCUSSION QUESTIONS

20. How should retailers deal with consumers immediately after purchase to reduce postpurchase dissonance? What specific action would you recommend, and what effect would you intend it to have on the recent purchaser of (gift to):
    a. Automobile repair
    b. Cable TV
    c. Mouthwash
    d. Mountain bike
    e. United Way
    f. A dog
21. How should manufacturers deal with consumers immediately after purchase to reduce postpurchase dissonance? What specific action would you recommend, and what effect would you intend it to have on the recent purchaser of:
    a. Mountain bike
    b. Toothbrush
    c. Stereo system
    d. Life insurance
22. Discuss how you could determine how consumers actually use the following. How could this information be used to develop marketing strategy?
    a. Microwave
    b. Mountain bike
    c. Laptop computer
    d. Athletic shoes
    e. Bleach
    f. Bottled water
23. How would you go about measuring consumer satisfaction among purchasers of the following? What questions would you ask, what additional information would you collect, and why? How could this information be used for evaluating and planning marketing programs?
    a. Internet access
    b. Snowboards
    c. Mexican food restaurant
    d. Auto repairs

e. Sweaters
f. Athletic shoes

24. Based on those characteristics that contribute to postpurchase dissonance, discuss several product purchases that are most likely to result in dissonance and several that will not create this effect.
25. What level of product dissatisfaction should a marketer be content with in attempting to serve a particular target market? What characteristics contribute to dissatisfaction, regardless of the marketer's efforts?
26. Describe the last time you were dissatisfied with a purchase. What action did you take? Why?
27. Are you a "mere" repeat purchaser of any brand, service, or outlet? Why are you not a committed customer? What, if anything, would make you a committed customer?
28. Are you a committed customer to any brand, service, or outlet? Why?
29. Design a customer loyalty program for a local Mexican food restaurant.

APPLICATION ACTIVITIES

30. Develop a brief questionnaire to determine product nonuse among college students and the reasons for it. With several classmates, interview 50 students. What do you conclude?
31. Develop a questionnaire designed to measure consumer satisfaction of a clothing purchase of $50 or more. Include in your questionnaire items that measure the product's instrumental, symbolic, and affective dimensions of performance, as well as what the consumer wanted on these dimensions. Then, interview several consumers to obtain information on actual performance, expected performance, and satisfaction. Using this information, determine if consumers received what they expected (i.e., evaluation of performance) and relate any difference to consumer expressions of satisfaction. What are the marketing implications of your results?
32. Develop a survey to measure student dissatisfaction with service purchases. For purchases they were dissatisfied with, determine what action they took to resolve this dissatisfaction and what was the end result of their efforts. What are the marketing implications of your findings?
33. Develop a questionnaire to measure repeat purchase behavior and brand loyalty. Measure the repeat purchase behavior and brand loyalty of 10 students with respect to the following. Determine why the brand loyal students are brand loyal.
    a. Pizza restaurants
    b. Toothpaste
    c. Deodorant
    d. Soft drinks
    e. Grocery stores
    f. Bookstores
34. With the cooperation of a major durables retailer, assist the retailer in sending a postpurchase letter of thanks to every other customer immediately after purchase. Then, approximately two weeks after purchase, contact the same customers (both those who received the letter and those who did not) and measure their purchase satisfaction. Evaluate the results.
35. Interview a grocery store manager, a department store manager, and a restaurant manager. Determine the types of products their customers are most likely to complain about and the nature of those complaints.
36. Measure 10 students' disposition behaviors with respect to the following. Determine why they use the alternatives they do.
    a. Soft-drink containers
    b. Magazines
    c. Food cans
    d. Newspapers
    e. Plastic items
    f. Large items
37. Implement Question 22 with a sample of students.
38. Implement Question 23 with a sample of students.
39. Interview 20 students to determine which, if any, customer loyalty programs they belong to, what they like and dislike about them, and the impact they have on their attitudes and behaviors. What opportunities do your results suggest?

REFERENCES

1. G. Conlon, "True Romance," *Sales & Marketing Management,* May 1996, pp. 88–89; permission conveyed through the Copyright Clearance Center.
2. G. J. Thompson, "Interpreting Consumers," *Journal of Marketing Research,* November 1997, p. 444.
3. The basic theory of cognitive dissonance, of which postpurchase dissonance is a subset, is presented in L. Festinger, *A Theory of Cognitive Dissonance* (Stanford, CA.: Stanford University Press, 1957).
4. M. F. Luce, "Choosing to Avoid," *Journal of Consumer Research,* March 1998, pp. 409–33.
5. See footnote 2.
6. S. J. Gould, "An Interpretative Study of Purposeful, Mood Self-Regulating Consumption," *Psychology & Marketing,* July 1997, pp. 395–426.
7. See S. Ram and H.-S. Jung, "Innovativeness in Product Usage"; and N. M. Ridgway and L. L. Price, "Exploration in Product Usage"; both in *Psychology & Marketing,* January 1994, pp. 57–84; and K. Park and C. L. Dyer, "Consumer Use Innovative Behavior," in *Advances in Consumer Research XXII,* ed. F. R. Kardes and M. Sujan (Provo, UT: Association for Consumer Research, 1995), pp. 566–72.
8. G. Berstell and D. Nitterhouse, "Looking 'Outside the Box,'" *Marketing Research,* Summer 1997, pp. 5–11.
9. A. B. Bower and D. E. Sprott, "The Case of the Dusty Stair-Climber," in *Advances in Consumer Research XXII,* ed. F. R. Kardes and M. Sujan (Provo, UT: Association for Consumer Research, 1995), pp. 582-87. See also B. Wansink and R. Deshpande, "*Marketing Letters* 5, no.1 (1994), pp. 91–100.
10. Bower and Sprott, footnote 9, p. 585.
11. See D. Halstead, D. Hartman, and S. L. Schmidt, "Multisource Effects on the Satisfaction Process," *Journal of the Academy of Marketing Science,* Spring 1994, pp. 114–29.
12. See K. A. Hunt and S. M. Keaveney, "A Process Model of the Effects of Price Promotions on Brand Image," *Psychology & Marketing,* November 1994, pp. 511–32.
13. R. A. Spreng, S. B. MacKenzie, and R. W. Olshavsky, "A Reexamination of the Determinants of Consumer Satisfaction," *Journal of Marketing,* July 1996, pp. 15–32.
14. See B. G. Goff, J. S. Boles, D. N. Bellenger, and C. Stojack, "The Influence of Salesperson Selling Behaviors on Customer Satisfaction with Products," *Journal of Retailing,* no. 2 (1997), pp. 171–83.
15. See V. A. Zeithaml, L. L. Berry, and A. Parasuraman, "The Nature and Determination of Customer Expectations of Service," *Journal of the Academy of Marketing Science,* Winter 1993, pp. 1–12; K. E. Clow, D. L. Kurtz, J. Ozment, and B. S. Ong, "The Antecedents of Consumer Expectations of Services," *Journal of Services Marketing,* no. 4 (1997), pp. 230–48.
16. See J. Ozment and E. A. Morash, "The Augmented Service Offering for Perceived and Actual Service Quality," *Journal of the Academy of Marketing Science,* Fall 1994, pp. 352–63; and G. B. Voss, A. Parasuraman, and D. Grewal, "The Roles of Price, Performance, and Expectations in Determining Satisfaction in Service Exchanges," *Journal of Marketing,* October 1998, pp. 48–61.
17. For discussions of both conceptual and measurement issues, see J. J. Cronin, Jr., and S. A. Taylor, "Measuring Service Quality"; and T. A. Oliva, R. L. Oliver, and I. C. MacMillan, "A Catastrophe Model for Developing Service Strategies"; both in *Journal of Marketing,* July 1992, pp. 55–69 and 83–96; R. A. Peterson and W. R. Wilson, "Measuring Customer Satisfaction," *Journal of the Academy of Marketing Science,* Winter 1992, pp. 61–72; E. W. Anderson and M. W. Sullivan, "The Antecedents and Consequences of Customer Satisfaction for Firms," *Marketing Science,* Spring 1993, pp. 125–43; R. K. Teas, "Expectations, Performance Evaluation, and Customers' Perceptions of Quality," *Journal of Marketing,* October 1993, pp. 18–34; A. Parasuraman, V. A. Zeithaml, L. L. Berry, "Reassessment of Expectations as a Comparison Standard"; J. J. Cronin, Jr., and S. A. Taylor, "SERVPERF versus SERVQUAL"; and R. K. Teas, "Expectations as a Comparison Standard"; all in *Journal of Marketing,* January 1994, pp. 111–39; S. F. Gardial, "Comparing Consumers' Recall of Prepurchase and Postpurchase Product Evaluation Experiences," *Journal of Consumer Research,* March 1994, pp. 548–60; R. L. Oliver, "Attribute Need Fulfillment in Product Usage Satisfaction," *Psychology & Marketing,* January 1995, pp. 1–17; M. D. Johnson, E. W. Anderson, and C. Fornell, "Rational and Adaptive Performance Expectations in a Customer Satisfaction Framework," *Journal of Consumer Research,* March 1995, pp. 695–707; P. J. Danaher, "Using Conjoint Analysis to Determine the Relative Importance of Service Attributes," *Journal of Retailing*, no. 2 (1997), pp. 235–60; and K. Gupta and D. Stewart, "Customer Satisfaction and Customer Behavior," *Marketing Letters,* no. 3 (1996), pp. 249–63.
18. See C. Droge, D. Halstead, and R. D. Mackoy, "The Role of Competitive Alternatives in the Postchoice Satisfaction Formation Process," *Journal of the Academy of Marketing Science,* Winter 1997, pp. 18–30; and K. A. Taylor, "A Regret Theory Approach to Assessing Consumer Satisfaction," *Marketing Letters,* no. 2 (1997), pp. 229–38.
19. A. Mattila, "An Examination of Consumers' Use of Heuristic Cues in Making Satisfaction Judgments," *Psychology & Marketing,* August 1998, pp. 477–500.
20. L. Dube and M. S. Morgan, "Trend Effects and Gender Differences in Retrospective Judgments of Consumption Emotions," *Journal of Consumer Research,* September 1996, pp. 156–62; T. R. Shaffer and D. L. Sherrell, "Consumer Satisfaction with Health-Care Services," *Psychology & Marketing,* May 1997, pp. 261–285; and T. A. Mooradian and J. M. Oliver, "'I Can't Get No Satisfaction,'" *Psychology & Marketing,* July 1997, pp. 379–92.
21. See K. E. Clow and J. L. Beisel, "Managing Consumer Expectations of Low-Margin, High-Volume Services," *Journal of Services Marketing* 9, no. 1 (1995), pp. 33–46.
22. S. M. Keaveney, *Journal of Marketing,* April 1995, pp. 71–82.
23. S. Taylor, "Waiting for Service," *Journal of Marketing,* April 1994, pp. 56–69; S. Taylor and J. D. Claxton, "Delays and the Dynamics of Service Encounters," *Journal of the Academy of Marketing Science,* Summer 1994, pp. 254–64; and S. Taylor, "The Effects of Filled Waiting Time and Service Provider Control Over the Delay on Evaluations of Service," *Journal of the Academy of Marketing Science,* Winter 1995, pp. 38–48.

24. For related issues, see P. Kumar, M. U. Kalwani, and M. Dada, "The Impact of Waiting Time Guarantees on Customers' Waiting Experiences," *Marketing Science,* no. 4 (1997), pp. 295–314; and M. K. Hui, M. V. Thakor, and R. Gill, "The Effect of Delay Type and Service Stage on Consumers' Reactions to Waiting," *Journal of Consumer Research,* March 1998, pp. 469–79.

25. See M. K. Hui and D. K. Tse, "What to Tell Consumers in Waits of Different Lengths," *Journal of Marketing,* April 1996, 81–90.

26. M. K. Hui, L. Dube, and J.-C. Chebat, "The Impact of Music on Consumers' Reactions to Waiting for Services," *Journal of Retailing,* no. 1 (1997), pp. 87–104; and G. Tom, M. Burns, and Y. Zeng, "Your Life on Hold," *Journal of Direct Marketing,* Summer 1997, pp. 25–31.

27. See B. Mittal and W. M. Lassar, "The Role of Personalization in Service Encounters," *Journal of Retailing,* no. 1 (1996), pp. 95–109; R. A. Spreng and R. D. Mackoy, "An Empirical Examination of a Model of Perceived Service Quality and Satisfaction," *Journal of Retailing*, no. 2 (1996), pp. 210–14; N. Sirohi, E. W. McClaughlin, and D. R. Wittink, "A Model of Consumer Perceptions and Store Loyalty Intentions for a Supermarket Retailer," *Journal of Retailing,* no. 2 (1998), pp. 223–45; and W. O. Bearden, M. K. Malhotra, and K. H. Uscategui, "Customer Contact and the Evaluation of Service Experiences," *Psychology & Marketing,* December 1998, pp. 793–809.

28. See G. H. G. McDougall, T. Levesque, and P. VanderPlaat, "Designing the Service Guarantee," *Journal of Services Marketing,* no. 4 (1998), pp. 278–93; and A. M. Ostrom and D. Iacobucci, "The Effect of Guarantees on Consumers' Evaluation of Services," *Journal of Services Marketing,* no. 5 (1998), pp. 362–78.

29. I. E. Swan and L. J. Combs, "Product Performance and Consumer Satisfaction: A New Concept," *Journal of Marketing,* April 1976, pp. 25–33.

30. V. Mittal, W. T. Ross, Jr., and P. M. Baldsare, "The Asymmetric Impact of Negative and Positive Attribute-Level Performance on Overall Satisfaction and Repurchase Levels," *Journal of Marketing,* January 1998, pp. 33–47. See also G. J. Gaeth et al., "Consumers' Attitude Change Across Sequences of Successful and Unsuccessful Product Usage," *Marketing Letters,* no. 1 (1997), pp. 41–53.

31. See H. Mano and R. L. Oliver, "Assessing the Dimensionality and Structure of the Consumption Experience," *Journal of Consumer Research,* December 1993, pp. 451–66.

32. See J. Singh, "A Typology of Consumer Dissatisfaction Response Styles," *Journal of Retailing,* Spring 1990, pp. 57–97; J. Singh, "Voice, Exit, and Negative Word-of-Mouth Behaviors," *Journal of the Academy of Marketing Science,* Winter 1990, pp. 1–15; K. Grønhaug and O. Kvitastein, "Purchases and Complaints," *Psychology & Marketing,* Spring 1991, pp. 21–35; S. W. Kelley and M. A. Davis, "Antecedents to Customer Expectations for Service Recovery," *Journal of the Academy of Marketing Science,* Winter 1994, pp. 52–61; and M. Davidow and P. A. Dacin, "Understanding and Influencing Consumer Complaint Behavior," in *Advances in Consumer Research XXIV,* ed. M. Bruck and D. J. MacInnis, (Provo, UT: Association for Consumer Research, 1997), pp. 450–56.

33. J. Singh and R. E. Wilkes, "When Consumers Complain," *Journal of the Academy of Marketing Science,* Fall 1996, pp. 350–65; and K. P. N. Morel, T. B. C. Poiesz, and H. A. M. Wilkie, "Motivation, Capacity and Opportunity to Complain," in *Advances in Consumer Research XXIV,* ed. M. Bruck and D. J. MacInnis, (Provo, UT: Association for Consumer Research, 1997), pp. 464–69.

34. See also S. P. Brown and R. F. Beltramini, "Consumer Complaining and Word-of-Mouth Activities," in *Advances in Consumer Research XVI,* ed. T. K. Srull (Provo, UT: Association for Consumer Research, 1989), pp. 9-11; and J. E. Swan and R. L. Oliver, "Postpurchase Communications by Consumers," *Journal of Retailing,* Winter 1989, pp. 516–33.

35. Footnote 2.

36. M. L. Richins, "Negative Word-of-Mouth by Dissatisfied Consumers," *Journal of Marketing,* Winter 1983, pp. 68–78; M. L. Richins, "Word-of-Mouth as Negative Information," in *Advances in Consumer Research XI,* ed. T. C. Kinnear (Provo, UT: Association for Consumer Research, 1984), pp. 687–702; and M. T. Curren and V. S. Folkes, "Attributional Influences on Consumers' Desires to Communicate about Products," *Psychology & Marketing,* Spring 1987, pp. 31–45.

37. See R. A. Spreng, G. D. Harrell, and R. D. Mackoy, "Service Recovery," *Journal of Services Marketing* 9, no. 1 (1995), pp. 15–23; M. A. Hocutt, G. Chakraborty, and J. C. Mowen, "The Impact of Perceived Justice on Customer Satisfaction," in *Advances in Consumer Research XXIV,* ed. M. Bruck and D. J. MacInnis (Provo, UT: Association for Consumer Research, 1997), pp. 457–63; and L. Dube and M. F. Maute, "Defensive Strategies for Managing Satisfaction and Loyalty in the Service Industry," *Psychology & Marketing,* December 1998, pp. 775–91.

38. A literature review and model is in N. Stephens and K. P. Gwinner, "Why Don't Some People Complain?" *Journal of the Academy of Marketing Science,* Summer 1998, pp. 172–89. See also A. L. Dolinsky et al. "The Role of Psychographic Characteristics as Determinants of Complaint Behavior," *Journal of Hospital Marketing,* no. 2 (1998), pp. 27–51.

39. Ibid.

40. B. Bowers, "For Firms, 800 Is a Hot Number," *The Wall Street Journal,* November 9, 1989, p. B-1.

41. J. A. Prestbo, "At Procter & Gamble, Success Is Largely Due to Heeding Consumer," *The Wall Street Journal,* April 29, 1980, p. 23.

42. See C. Goodwin and I. Ross, "Consumer Evaluations of Response to Complaints," *Journal of Consumer Marketing,* Spring 1990, pp. 39–47; and J. G. Blodgett, D. J. Hill, and S. S. Tax, "The Effects of Distributive, Procedural, and Interactional Justice on Postcomplaint Behavior," *Journal of Retailing,* no. 2 (1997), pp. 185–210.

43. See F. F. Reichheld, "Learning from Customer Defections," *Harvard Business Review,* March 1996, pp. 56–69.

44. C. Fornell and B. Wernerfelt, "Defensive Marketing Strategy by Customer Complaint Management," *Journal of Marketing Research,* November 1987, pp. 337–46.

45. P. Sellers, "What Customers Really Want," *Fortune,* June 4, 1990, pp. 58–62.

46. B. A. Sparks, G. L. Bradley, and V. J. Callan, "The Impact of Staff Empowerment and Communication Style on Customer Evaluations," *Psychology & Marketing,* August 1997, pp. 475–93.

47. See N. C. Smith, R. J. Thomas, and J. A. Quelch, "A Strategic Approach to Managing Product Recalls," *Harvard Business Review,* September 1996, pp. 102–12.

48. T. Tripett, "Product Recall Spurs Company to Improve Customer Satisfaction," *Marketing News,* April 11, 1994, p. 6.

49. C. Rubel, "Pizza Hut Explores Customer Satisfaction," *Marketing News,* March 25, 1996, p. 15.

50. E. W. Anderson, C. Fornell, and D. R. Lehmann, "Customer Satisfaction, Market Share, and Profitability," *Journal of Marketing,* July 1994, pp. 53–66.

51. T. O. Jones and W. E. Sasser, Jr., "Why Satisfied Customers Defect," *Harvard Business Review,* November 1995, pp. 88–95; P. P. Leszczyc and H. J. P. Timmermans, "Store-Switching Behavior," *Marketing Letters,* no. 2 (1997), pp. 193–204; and B. Mittal and W. M. Lassar, "Why Do Customer Switch?" *Journal of Services Marketing,* no. 3 (1998), pp. 177–94.

52. See A. S. Dick and K. Basu, "Customer Loyalty," *Journal of the Academy of Marketing Science,* Spring 1994, pp. 99–113; A. L. Baldinger and J. Rubinson, "Brand Loyalty," *Journal of Advertising Research,* November 1996, pp. 22–34; A. Ehrenberg, "Description and Prescription," *Journal of Advertising Research,* December 1997, pp. 17–22; K. S. Lim, "Brand Loyalty and Situational Effects," *Journal of International Consumer Marketing,* no. 4 (1997), pp. 95–115; and U. M. Dholakia, "An Investigation of Some Determinants of Brand Commitment," in *Advances in Consumer Research XXIV,* ed. M. Bruck and D. J. MacInnis (Provo, UT: Association for Consumer Research, 1997), pp. 381–87.

53. R. G. Javalgi and C. R. Moberg, "Service Loyalty," *Journal of Services Marketing,* no. 3 (1997), pp. 165–79; R. East et al., "Customer Defection from Supermarkets," in *Advances in Consumer Research XXV,* ed. J. W. Alba and J. W. Hutchinson (Provo, UT: Association for Consumer Research, 1998), pp. 507–12.

54. S. Fournier, "Consumers and Their Brands," *Journal of Consumer Research,* March 1998, p. 355.

55. R. L. Olvier, R. T. Rust, and S. Varki, "Customer Delight," *Journal of Retailing,* no. 3 (1997), pp. 311–36.

56. See J. Deighton, C. M. Henderson, and S. A. Neslin, "The Effects of Advertising on Brand Switching and Repeat Purchasing," *Journal of Marketing Research,* February 1994, pp. 28–43.

57. See D. Bejou and A. Palmer, "Service Failure and Loyalty," *Journal of Services Marketing,* no. 1 (1998), pp. 7–22.

58. M. Johnson, G. M. Zinkham, and G. S. Ayala, "The Impact of Outcome, Competency, and Affect on Service Referral," *Journal of Services Marketing,* no. 5 (1998), pp. 397–415.

59. E. W. Anderson, C. Fornell, R. T. Rust, "Customer Satisfaction, Productivity, and Profitability," *Marketing Science,* no. 2 (1997), pp. 129–45.

60. F. F. Reichheld and W. E. Sasser, Jr., "Zero Defections," *Harvard Business Review,* September 1990, pp. 105–11; and R. Jacob, "Why Some Customers Are More Equal than Others," *Fortune,* September 19, 1994, pp. 215–24.

61. See S. Li, "Survival Analysis," *Marketing Research,* Fall 1995, pp. 17–23.

62. Reichheld and Sasser, footnote 60, p. 110.

63. See also S. Lingle, "How Much Is a Customer Worth?" *Bank Marketing,* August 1995, pp. 13–16.

64. See the special issue on relationship marketing, *Journal of the Academy of Marketing Science,* Fall 1995; and G. E. Gengler and P. P. Leszczyc, "Using Customer Satisfaction Research for Relationship Marketing," *Journal of Direct Marketing,* Winter 1997, pp. 23–29.

65. L. Freeman, "Marketing the Market," *Marketing News,* March 2, 1998, p. 1. Other examples are in G. B. Voss and Z. G. Voss, "Implementing a Relationship Marketing Program," *Journal of Services Marketing,* no. 11 (1997), pp. 278–98; B. G. Yovovich, "Scanners Reshape the Grocery Business," *Marketing News,* February 16, 1998, p. 1; and G. Brewer, "The Customer Stops Here," *Sales & Marketing Management,* March 1998, pp. 31–36.

66. L. L. Berry, "Relationship Marketing of Services," *Journal of the Academy of Marketing Science,* Fall 1995, pp. 236–45.

67. See N. Bendapudi and L. L. Berry, "Customers' Motivations for Maintaining Relationships with Service Providers," *Journal of Retailing,* Spring 1997, pp. 15–37.

68. B. Wansink and M. L. Ray, "Estimating an Advertisement's Impact on One's Consumption of a Brand," *Journal of Advertising Research,* May 1992, pp. 9–16.

69. See T. G. Vavra, "Rethinking the Marketing Mix to Maximize Customer Retention," in *Enhancing Knowledge Development in Marketing,* ed. D. W. Cravens and P. R. Dickson (Chicago: American Marketing Association, 1993), pp. 262–68.

70. See G. Levin, "Marketers Flock to Loyalty Offers," *Advertising Age,* May 24, 1993, p. 13; C. Miller, "Rewards for the Best Customers," *Marketing News,* July 5, 1993, p. 1; J. Fulkerson, "It's in the Cards," *American Demographics,* July 1996, pp. 38–43; and J. Passingham, "Grocery Retailing and the Loyalty Card," *Journal of the Market Research Society,* January 1998, pp. 55–63.

71. See G. T. Gundlach, R. S. Achrol, and J. T. Mentzer, "The Structure of Commitment in Exchange," *Journal of Marketing,* January 1995, pp. 78–92; and L. O'Brien and C. Jones, "Do Rewards Really Create Loyalty?" *Harvard Business Review,* May 1995, pp. 75–82.

72. See F. Rice, "The New Rules of Superlative Services"; and P. Sellers, "Keeping the Buyers"; both in *Fortune,* Autumn–Winter 1993, pp. 50–53 and 56–58; and G. A. Conrad, G. Brown, and H. A. Harmon, "Customer Satisfaction and Corporate Culture," *Psychology & Marketing,* October 1997, pp. 663–74.

73. A. Taher, T. W. Leigh, and W. A. French, "Augmented Retail Services," *Journal of Business Research,* March 1996, pp. 217–28.

Cases

4-1 Will Sex Sell?

Sexually transmitted diseases (STDs) such as AIDS remain a major health threat to many groups, particularly younger people. The U.S. government recently launched an AIDS prevention campaign that included TV spots promoting condom use. A variety of firms have also been promoting condom use, though their efforts have been handicapped by the refusal of the three major television networks to air condom ads. Despite record levels of promotion by the federal government and private firms, condom sales were flat or declined during the mid-1990s and have grown only slowly in the late 1990s.

Condom sales grew at a double-digit rate in the late 1980s. This growth was spurred by former Surgeon General C. Everett Koop's report strongly advocating the use of condoms to stem the spread of AIDS. The CDC (Centers for Disease Control and Prevention) followed up by mailing to every U.S. household a pamphlet explicitly discussing condoms. This effort, coupled with Rock Hudson's highly publicized death from AIDS, caused the product category sales to increase by 40 to 50 percent. However, when sales growth stalled, even the announcement that Magic Johnson was HIV-positive caused only a small increase in condom use.

Surveys conducted for the CDC indicate that slightly less than half of sexually active teenagers use condoms. Many experts believe this figure to be overstated. According to an expert on marketing to youth:

> It's very P.C. [politically correct] to say you use them, but I think it's less than that. It's such a hard sell. There's a lot of cultural baggage to overcome. Guys feel there's less enjoyment and it's not macho, and I just don't know how many girls would force the issue. They have to be taught how to do this with grace and panache. Marketers really have to take a bottoms-up approach, going in depth over all the issues relative to sex and how condom usage fits in, and that's going to take a lot of insight into the consumer.

Other experts believe that the tendency for young adults to believe that nothing really bad can happen to them is a major factor in the limited use of condoms among one of the most at-risk groups.

In the mid-1990s, the U.S. government began to encourage the use of condoms through a series of public service announcements (PSAs) on television. One ad shows a frisky little condom in its package as it springs from a dresser drawer and skitters across the bedroom floor awaking a sleeping cat as it passes. Then it jumps onto a bed and dives under the sheets where a couple appears to be in passionate embrace. A voice-over says: *It would be nice if latex condoms were automatic, but since they're not, using them should be.*

Another PSA, prepared in both English and Spanish, shows a Hispanic couple. She unbuttons his shirt. He pulls off her earring. She kicks off a shoe. Then she asks: *Did you bring it?* He replies: *I forgot it.* She concludes the evening by turning on the light and saying: *Then forget it.* There are also two PSAs promoting abstinence. ABC has provided significant airtime for both the condom and the abstinence PSAs.

These ads have been criticized for a variety of reasons, including not targeting specific at-risk communities such as young gay men, targeting too old an audience (over 25), not indicating that lubricants such as petroleum jelly can eliminate a condom's ability to protect against disease, and for promoting sexual activity rather than abstinence outside of a marriage relationship.

While all three major networks have agreed to run the federal government–provided PSAs, none of them will show company commercials for condoms. Fox began accepting such commercials in 1992 but is stringent in what it will allow for content. For example, it turned down a commercial for Lifestyles condoms that featured a close-up of a woman saying: *I'll do a lot for love, but I'm not ready to die for it.* In contrast, many cable program channels such as MTV accept condom advertising.

According to one expert, condom marketers face three serious limitations: (1) they are limited in what they can say and what media they can use, (2) they are pressured by activists who want to see generic appeals (safe sex/disease prevention) that do not serve company goals, and (3) constant criticism from powerful critics who believe that any marketing of condoms to young people inappropriately promotes sexual promiscuity.

Ansell, which markets Lifestyles condoms (the number two selling brand), has used several approaches over the past 10 years. The first featured ads in college newspapers with headlines that state *More thoughtful than a box of chocolates* and an offer of a $1 sample kit and coupons. A television ad (limited to a few cable channels) showed a group of women stating that they *never would with a guy that calls you Oooo baby, never would with guys who high-five,* and finally, *never with a guy who thinks he can get away with not wearing a condom.* The ad closes with a picture of a Lifestyles box and a voice-over saying: *Not with me. Not in this day and age.*

Based on extensive consumer research, in the mid-1990s Ansell launched three separate marketing programs targeting women, Xers (18- to 30-year-olds), and Hispanics. The research revealed that the younger consumers were suffering from "safe-sex fatigue."

"Everyone out there was selling the same way: fear of STDs and AIDS and HIV. And while those are still very real fears, it's gotten to the level of 'tune out and turn off'," according to Carol Carrozza, Ansell's marketing director. "People in this group don't like to be preached to . . . they're sick of that." Ansell's promotion to this group includes a contest with a $10,000 first prize asking these consumers to send in a 30-second video telling how they would sell condoms and safer sex. The contest is being promoted with spots on college radio stations. There is also a print ad that shows a pay phone on a wall covered with graffiti. Standing out from the other graffiti is the headline:

> Looking for people with sex on their mind! Must be willing to perform, creativity a plus! Call 1-800-551-5454

The text at the bottom of the ad tells how to enter the video contest.

Ansell's research revealed that many women were mortified at the idea of having to actually purchase condoms. Ansell decided to confront this issue directly. First, the LifeStyles name is gender neutral in contrast to names such as Trojan, which have a more masculine connotation. Packaging is also designed to be gender neutral. It is also color coded so that buyers can quickly select the style they want.

A print ad targeting women showed a young woman wearing a fake nose and glasses. The headline is: "You'd be amazed at what I used to go through to buy condoms." The copy describes the pain of "facing a sea of condom boxes, when someone walks by. You quickly pick up toothpaste, mouthwash, anything to avoid people knowing what you really came in for. Well, thanks to LifeStyles, I've finally put my disguises in the drawer." The ad has an 800 number readers can call for literature on safer sex, coupons, and LifeStyles samples.

Ansell targets Hispanics with bilingual packages and limited Spanish-language advertising.

In 1998, Ansell made a major change in its advertising approach. The ads, which debuted on the Howard Stern show in New York and Los Angeles and appeared on CBS stations in Chicago and Boston as well as MTV and Comedy Central, eschew the normal focus on protection and responsibility. Instead they imply pleasure and show couples on a motorcycle, dancing, and in bed. The television campaign was accompanied by a racy print campaign showing a nearly nude couple. It appeared in *Glamour* magazine and as a poster in 425,000 college newspapers. Copy in the ad describes the six unique styles of the Lifestyles line.

The new advertising theme was followed by new "Easy-Open, Easy-On" packaging (and advertising promoting it) in 1999. The new packages resemble individual butter packs, with a tabbed, peel-off top that unveils a condom inside a plastic circular container. Ads for the new package continue a sexually explicit approach. Part of one print ad is:

> "GETTING IT ON" JUST GOT A LOT EASIER
>
> Nothing throws cold water on the heat of passion like fumbling with a hard to open condom. With LifeStyles new Condom discs, those days are over.

Discussion Questions

1. What type of decision process is typically used in the decision to purchase and use condoms?
2. Why is condom use limited among sexually active young people?
3. What are the ethical issues involved in promoting condom use? 
4. What actions should the government take to promote either abstinence or the use of condoms, given the dangers of AIDS? 
5. Should the networks accept condom advertising? Why? 
6. Assume you are the marketing manager for one of the major condom marketers. Develop a marketing program to increase the percentage of condom use among sexually active young people. Describe how each stage of the decision process is considered in your strategy.

7. Assume you are the national manager for a regional or national chain of the following. How would you attempt to increase sales of condoms in your outlets? What risks, if any, would your program have?
   a. Grocery stores
   b. Convenience stores
   c. Pharmacies (selling primarily prescription drugs and over-the-counter medicines and beauty aids)
   d. Drugstores
8. Evaluate Ansell's new advertising approach.
9. Does Ansell's new advertising approach raise any ethical questions?

Source: C. Miller, "Condom Sales Cool Off," *Marketing News,* February 28, 1994, p. 14; A. Z. Cuneo, "Anti-AIDS Effort Draws Criticism," *Advertising Age,* May 2, 1994, p. 40; C. Miller, "Condom Maker Asks Consumers to Come Up with Their Own Ads," *Marketing News,* April 24, 1995, p. 2; H. Rotfeld, "Condom Companies Face Unfair Marketing Limitations," *Marketing News,* May 11, 1998, p. 14; M. Wilkie, "Condom Ads Will Debut," *Advertising Age,* August 10, 1998, p. 8; and C. Bittar, "Lifestyles Adds Sex "Peel" to Condoms," *Brandweek,* February 1, 1999, p. 73.

4-2 South Hills Mall Kids' Club

South Hills Mall is an enclosed shopping center located in the hub of a concentrated retail area along U.S. Route 9 in Poughkeepsie, New York. The mall has 90 stores and is anchored by Sears, Hess's, and Kmart. South Hills attracts all demographic groups, but older shoppers (over 45 years of age) are responsible for nearly half of the center's sales. The mall is positioned to appeal to Middle America's desire for value and service.

A two-level, superregional, upscale center with 5 anchors and 167 stores recently opened on the parcel adjacent to South Hills. The competing center has strong appeal for young and middle-aged shoppers (under 45 years of age) and also attracts a large percentage of shoppers with incomes exceeding $50,000.

With the opening of the new center, South Hills Mall began to lose its share of the young family shoppers (ages 20 to 45). The erosion of this key shopper group negatively impacted traffic and sales.

To counter the increased competition, Jill Hofstra, marketing director for South Hills Mall, developed the South Hills Mall Kids' Club with these objectives in mind:

- Reinforce the South Hills Mall's position as a provider of genuine value and extra services to shoppers.
- Develop a program that will give South Hills Mall the competitive edge in building loyalty and frequency of visits from the young-family shopper group.
- Strengthen sales and traffic from this key shopper group.

The Kids' Club

To attract the young-family shopper group, Hofstra decided to target children with a consistent message, using a monthly direct-mail program. The message was to deliver an incentive or promise of value to stimulate shopping visits to the mall. Thus, the Kids' Club was born.

The club was launched in January with a day of festivities, including clowns, jugglers, music, marionette shows, and face painters. In addition, the local police department conducted child-fingerprinting sessions, the traffic safety commission provided children's safety sessions, and the mall merchants sponsored in-store activities and giveaways.

To recruit members, invitations were sent to 550 prospective Kids' Club members, and the event was also promoted in print and radio advertising. Over 1,600 children turned out and received their free membership kit, free button, balloon, and T-shirt.

Kids' Club is geared for children 12 and under. Membership is free and very easy. Kids or their parents fill out an application at the Customer Service Center. Then, every month, members receive a postcard outlining special surprises and promotions geared toward them and their families. In addition to the excitement of receiving their own personal mail, kids enjoy the fun of solving a different riddle each month and discovering what their surprise gift will be.

In February, the Kids' Club sponsored a local circus performance and gave away tickets to the show. Redeeming the Kids' Club postcards for free Valentine's Day stickers created a 20.6 percent response rate. In March, 27.6 percent of Kids' Club members took advantage of a free photo with the Easter Bunny.

April's special promotion included free inflatable kites and a chance to win a pair of tickets to a play (29 percent response). In May, kids created a mug for Mother's Day, and in June, they picked up a free gift for Dad. The July beachball giveaway attracted hundreds of children.

New babies are invited to join the club. New parents receive a packet that includes Kids' Club registration, a bib, and shoelaces with the Kids' Club logo. They also are informed of the mall's free stroller policy and receive coupons from the mall merchants. Recruitment of new members is done through mall signage, periodic print and radio advertising, and customer service personnel. Mall merchants also have the chance to get involved by signing up new members, sponsoring a particular month's giveaway, or coordinating merchandising activities.

Kids' Club is designed so that everyone wins. Kids love the free surprises. Parents enjoy receiving special messages about mall events. The mall hopes to gain increased traffic and shopper loyalty when Kids' Club members and their families visit the Customer Service Center to redeem their postcards each month.

Discussion Questions

1. What view of the household decision process is reflected in this program?
2. This program will have the most appeal to children of what age?
3. In what ways could this program be improved?
4. What ethical issues are associated with this program?

5. Will this program increase repeat shopping at the center? Will it increase center loyalty? Justify your answers.
6. How does this program utilize situational influences?
7. What view of the consumer decision process is reflected in this program?

Source: This case was prepared by, and is used with permission of, Jill A. Hofstra, Certified Marketing Director, South Hills Mall.

4-3 Evaluating Retail Advertising

A large department store wanted to better understand the effectiveness of its retail promotions. The store, which had above-average quality and competitive prices, typically ran newspaper and radio advertisements during a retail promotion. Its television advertising was primarily institutional and did not address specific retail promotions. While the management team knew that they had to advertise their retail promotions, they never felt comfortable with the effectiveness of these efforts.

Advertising Study

Prepromotion Survey To better understand its advertising effectiveness, a study of advertising exposure, interpretation, and purchases was conducted. Fifty in-depth interviews were conducted with members of the store's target market to determine the appropriate merchandise, price, ad copy, and media for the test. In addition, the store's image and that of three competing stores were measured.

Based on this information, a line of merchandise that would appeal to target consumers was selected. The retail promotion was run for one week. Full-page newspaper ads promoting the retail merchandise were run each day in the two local newspapers. Radio advertisements also ran on radio stations whose listener demographics matched the target market. Eight radio advertisements were aired each day of the promotion, two in each of four time slots: early morning, midday, early evening (7–10 PM), and late evening (after 10 PM).

In-Promotion Survey Each evening, a sample of 100 target market consumers was interviewed by telephone as follows:

1. Target consumers were asked if they had read the newspaper or listened to the radio that day. If so, how extensively? This would determine their exposure to the advertisement.
2. After a general description of the merchandise, they were asked to recall any related retail advertisements they had seen or heard.
3. If they recalled the ad, they were asked to describe the ad, the merchandise promoted, sale prices, and the sponsoring store.
4. If they were accurate in their ad interpretation, they were asked to express their intentions to purchase.
5. Additional questions that could be useful in future promotions targeted at this consumer segment were also asked.

Postpromotion Survey Immediately following the retail promotion, 500 target market consumers were surveyed to determine what percentage of the target market actually purchased the promoted merchandise. It also determined which sources of information influenced them in their decision to purchase and the amount of their purchase.

Results of Study Figure A shows that, while ad exposure (75 percent) and ad awareness (68 percent) were high, correct interpretation of the ad was low. Only 43 percent of those exposed to and aware of the

Overall Ad Effectiveness and Market Penetration **FIGURE A**

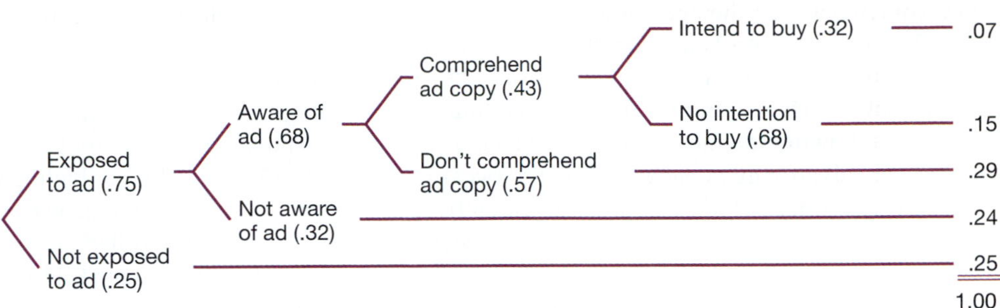

ad copy could accurately recall important details, such as which store was promoting the retail sale. Of those who did comprehend the ad copy, 33 percent intended to respond by purchasing the advertised merchandise. This yields an overall intention to buy, based on the ad, of 7 percent. As shown in Figure A, the biggest area of lost opportunity was due to those who did not accurately interpret the ad copy.

The postpromotion survey estimated that only 4.2 percent of the target market consumers made purchases of the promotional merchandise during the promotion period. However, the average total amount of purchase was $45, roughly double the average price of the promotion merchandise. In terms of how these buyers learned of the promotion, 46 percent mentioned newspaper A, 23 percent mentioned newspaper B, 15 percent learned of the sale through word-of-mouth communication, and 10 percent mentioned the radio.

Overall, the retail promotion yielded almost $100,000 in sales and was judged a success in many ways. However, management was concerned over the results presented in Figure A, since a significant sales opportunity was missed by not achieving a higher level of ad comprehension. Management believes that a more effective ad would have at least 75 percent correct interpretation among those aware of the ad. This in turn would almost double sales with no additional cost.

Discussion Questions

1. Discuss the learning and retention of information in this case within the context of high- and low-involvement learning. Why might some target consumers have higher levels of involvement in learning of this retail promotion than others?
2. Discuss Figure A and why the overall estimated market penetration (7 percent) was higher than actual market penetration (4.2 percent). How might this model be improved to achieve a more accurate estimate of market penetration?
3. With respect to future retail advertising promotions, what recommendations would you make to improve the overall profitability of the advertising effort? Recall that management's ultimate concern was to achieve a "bigger response per dollar spent."
4. Is management realistic in desiring 75 percent correct interpretation among those aware of the ad? What could be done to improve interpretation?

4-4 Can Sears Survive?

A 1992 story on Sears in *Advertising Age* explained:

> The task facing Sears is very, very difficult. Sears has to set completely new strategies that are responsive to the new realities. For one thing, it has to make its stores attractive. Consumers have a myriad of retailing choices, and they are also conservative and frugal. Retailers first must make them want to spend and second induce them to spend at their store. Sears is not good at that; it doesn't stand out, and *it doesn't stand for anything* [italics added]. Do you know any woman who wants a Sears' cocktail dress? Its hard goods get in the way of its soft goods and vice versa.

Sears decided to tackle this challenge head-on. It closed 113 outdated stores, replaced its phone book–thick all-inclusive catalog with 23 specialty catalogs, started carrying popular brands, accepted credit cards other than its own, moved its clothing lines to more fashionable items, and started a $4 billion renovation project for its remaining stores.

In 1993, it launched its "Softer Side of Sears" campaign to draw middle-income women shoppers to Sears' soft goods and fashion items. The campaign cleverly juxtaposed things such as hammers, batteries, and tires versus items such as satiny robes, stylish black dresses, and sexy shoes. The idea was to get women between the ages of 25 to 54 into the stores. That group controls at least 70 percent of all dollars spent at Sears. In one ad a woman said, "I came in for a DieHard—and I left with something drop dead," showing the model in a sexy black dress. Sears' advertising agency was able to tweak the idea to cover dozens of categories. Eventually, it evolved the tag line into "Come See the Many Sides of Sears."

One reason for the strategy was research revealing that while women were the primary purchasers of Sears major hard-goods, Kenmore appliances, and Craftsman tools, they went elsewhere for fashion and personal items. Sears had few major brands of apparel to offer, and its store brands were not widely popular.

Sears' Chairman Arthur Martinez described the goal of the campaign as follows:

> We've listened carefully to the women who shop at Sears for their families and homes and we know that they want affordable, fashionable apparel for themselves. We want the campaign to disarm the skeptics and pleasantly surprise our customers and feature the kind of merchandise that's on our sales floor right now.

Initial results were encouraging. Sales and profit increases were above the industry average for the next three years. Revenue per square foot of selling space increased from $289 at year-end 1992 to $353 at the end of 1995. However, by late 1999, Sears was announcing depressed earnings, a managerial shake-up, a 1,400 employee layoff at its headquarters, and a new marketing campaign.

The new campaign will be more value focused, with the theme: "The Good Life at a Great Price. Guaranteed. Sears." Sears is expected to spend over $600 million on advertising in the first year of the new campaign. Mark A. Cohen, Sears' executive vice president of marketing, says:

> Whether we like it or not, we're in a price game war, a value shootout with all our competition. With the "softer side" campaign, the customer feedback has been "We love the commercials, imagery and models, but we don't find those goods at Sears."

The campaign is the final piece in a series of changes the retailer announced early this year (1999), including offering more trendy brand-name clothing, reaching out to younger consumers with concert tours and teenage advisory panels, remodeling its stores and selling merchandise on the Internet.

Cohen said the new campaign, which continues to target women, is intended to emphasize Sears' entire product line, positioning the chain as a one-stop-shopping destination for so-called lifestyle goods. One new TV ad, highlighting Sears' Fieldmaster private-label brand, depicts a man in a flannel-style shirt, sleeves rolled up, as he rock-climbs. The ad notes that the "rugged shirt" is $22.50, then adds, "For the man who fears nothing . . . except shopping." After one last view of the man, now looking puzzled, the scene cuts to the Fieldmaster logo and the new slogan.

The Future?

Some experts say the rescue of the company from the brink of bankruptcy in 1992 only delayed the inevitable. Middle-priced stores such as Sears, JCPenney, and Montgomery Ward are being squeezed from both ends, by higher-priced competitors such as Macy's and Bloomingdale's and discount and specialty shops such as Wal-Mart, Gap, and Abercrombie & Fitch.

One analyst said Sears has suffered in recent years as one of the last of a dying breed—the department store. Retailers that are now called department stores are really large apparel stores that sometimes have housewares, he said. The other retailers to move into the void are discounters, such as Wal-Mart, which beat Sears on price.

"There's much more competition, and Sears, at its core, still has a cost structure that is quite a bit higher than their competition," one Chicago analyst said. "What happened was that companies like Wal-Mart came along . . . They were able to build a different model and grew up with a better cost structure from the get-go."

One analyst is concerned that Sears' new tag line could apply to any of a dozen different retailers. "A very good measure of how well your campaign is connected to your brand is if you put a competitor's logo at the end of it and it works. If it does, then you haven't done your job."

Discussion Questions

1. What is Sears' store image and position? What should it be?

2. Evaluate the new ad campaign compared to the old.
3. What criteria do the groups listed below use to select an outlet to purchase (*i*) dress clothes, (*ii*) casual clothes, (*iii*) power tools, and (*iv*) appliances?
   a. Teenagers
   b. Retired men
   c. Middle-aged professional men
   d. Young professional women
   e. Older working-class women
4. How should Sears determine the type of atmospherics it should have?
5. How would you encourage women who come to Sears for hard-goods to purchase clothing items?
6. Develop a marketing strategy for Sears targeting the following groups.
   a. Hispanics
   b. African-Americans
   c. Teenagers
   d. Middle-class women 25 to 50
   e. Middle-class men over 50

Source: S. Hume, "Sears' Next Struggle," *Advertising Age,* October 5, 1992, p. 4; "Sears Trades its 'Softer Side' for Fresher Image," *Los Angeles Times,* August 18, 1999, p. C-5; and J. Mann, "Sears Unable to Deliver on Ad Campaign's Promises," *Kansas City Star,* August 24, 1999.

4-5 The Most Recognized and Respected Brand in the World?

What is the most recognized and respected brand in the world? Old, established brands such as Coca-Cola, McDonald's, and IBM could certainly make a case for this title. However, an upstart firm aims to topple these giants and claim this title for itself. Starbucks' stated company objective is "to establish Starbucks as the most recognized and respected brand in the world."

Starbucks was founded in 1971 by three academics. In Berkeley, California, the three friends met a Dutchman, Alfred Peet, who ran a coffee shop that was the focal point for the emerging food scene in the area. The three academics moved to Seattle and opened a coffee shop in Pike's Market featuring the fresh, high-quality beans used by Peet. They named the shop Starbucks after the coffee-loving first mate in Herman Melville's Moby Dick.

In 1982, Howard Schultz joined Starbucks as director of marketing and retail sales. In 1983, while visiting in Italy, he was struck by the enormous number of coffee shops where Italians started the day and later gathered to chat. "As soon as I saw it, I knew we should be doing this."

This revelation started the transformation of Starbucks. Sales of gourmet coffee in the United States have risen approximately 25 percent a year in the 1990s, and Starbucks sales have grown even more rapidly.

Schultz bought Starbucks from the three original owners in 1987. The firm lost money for three straight years while Schultz attempted to encourage consumption of darker, richer coffees. With a very limited budget, the firm began with billboards and transit ads with the headline "Familiarity breeds contempt" to encourage consumers to try the new product.

Schultz targeted 35- to 45-year-olds with higher-than-average incomes and educations. Women received slightly more emphasis than men. A manager described the basic strategy as follows: "We were trying to appeal to the top and have the market move to us."

Positive word-of-mouth communications, limited but effective advertising, a decision to provide brewing equipment and beans to restaurants, and consistent product quality led to eventual success in Seattle. By distributing the beans through mail order with ads in magazines such as *The New Yorker,* Starbucks began to develop national awareness.

Soon Washington state was saturated with Starbucks coffee shops (which sell coffee for on-premise consumption as well as to go, and also the coffee beans). California was targeted next, and outlets were opened in Washington, D.C., Denver, and Chicago. By late 1999, there were approximately 2,500 Starbucks outlets with around 500 of these located outside the United States. The firm plans to open 500 new stores in Europe and another 500 in Asia in the next three years. It also plans to continue opening around a store a day in the United States.

Starbucks is considering launching a major television campaign but is concerned that its educational message doesn't translate well into a 30-second commercial. Therefore, it is considering an infomercial. Management is also concerned that standard advertising might destroy the unique mystique that surrounds Starbucks coffee.

Starbucks is facing challenges from numerous coffee bars that have appeared everywhere. Many of these are in portable stands and are set up in mall parking lots, gas station driveways, and virtually anywhere there is a high traffic flow. Also, machines now produce higher quality coffee than in the past. Virtually all grocery stores now sell "gourmet" coffee beans (including Starbucks), which can be ground in the store or taken home whole.

Schultz plans to continue Starbucks torrid growth through the continued opening of new outlets as described earlier and new products cobranded and/or distributed with strategic partners.

In 1996, Starbucks and Dreyer's Grand Ice Cream Inc. formed a partnership. Dreyer's now distributes various flavors of Starbucks coffee ice cream such as Expresso Swirl and Javachip throughout the United States. Starbucks is also the flavor in Redhook Brewery's Double Black Stout beer.

Starbucks also worked with Capitol Records to produce several Starbucks' jazz CDs that are sold through Starbucks outlets. Its most recent activity in this area was to sponsor (along with Beyond Music and the Sundance Channel) "Where Music Meets Film: Live from the Sundance Film Festival," a CD compilation of songs performed at the 1999 Sundance Music Studio. Starbucks will have exclusive distribution rights through its retail outlets and Web site for the first eight weeks after the recording is released.

Starbucks' largest partnership is now with PepsiCo. This venture produces the cold, bottled coffee drink, Frappuccino. The product carries the Starbucks label and is distributed by Pepsi. A similar joint effort between Pepsi and Lipton produced the number one seller in ready-made iced tea.

Starbucks also has a wholly owned subsidiary, Tazo Tea company, which markets a line of innovative, premium teas.

Discussion Questions

1. What caused the major growth in the sales of gourmet coffee in the United States?
2. What caused Starbucks' success?
3. Should Starbucks conduct a major television advertising campaign? Justify your answer.
4. Should Starbucks prepare and use an infomercial? Justify your answer.
5. What types of situational factors could Starbucks use in its marketing strategy?
6. What risks are associated with using the Starbucks name on other products? What are the gains? Do you think it is a wise strategy?
7. Can Starbucks become one of the worlds most recognized and respected brand names by 2010? What will it have to do to accomplish this goal?
8. Develop a strategy for Starbucks to use to expand into Mexico and South America.
9. Visit Starbucks' Web site (www.starbucks.com).
   a. Evaluate the site in terms of its communications effectiveness.
   b. Evaluate the site as a retail outlet.
   c. Evaluate Starbucks' program for social responsibility. Does it receive proper recognition for its actions? If not, what, if anything, should it do about it?

4-6 Managing a Product Failure at Saturn

Saturn, a division of General Motors, advertises around the theme:

> A different kind of company.
>
> A different kind of car.

Though Saturn cars generally cost less than $20,000, the firm attempts to provide its customers with the same level of service and consideration typically associated with expensive luxury cars. Its stated objective is to be "the friendliest, best-liked car company in America." The manager of two dealerships in Maryland states:

> We're going to do more than what the customer expects, and in the long run, I think it will enhance our image.

Saturn's attempt to build an image of a high-quality car built by skilled, caring workers and sold in helpful, nonpressure dealerships received two small tests in its first two years. In one, it had to recall 1,836 cars that had received improper coolant. In another, it had to repair 1,480 cars with faulty seat-back recliners. In the second case, the firm made a TV commercial showing a Saturn representative flying to Alaska to fix the car of a resident who had purchased it in the lower 48.

However, in 1993, Saturn began receiving reports of a wire short-circuiting and causing a fire. Thirty-four fires (no injuries) were reported. Saturn faced a dilemma. A recall would involve 350,000 cars and a direct expense of as much as $35 million. Any negative publicity associated with the recall could seriously depress sales. Saturn had yet to break even, and General Motors was under serious financial pressure.

Saturn managers decided to deal with the problem in a manner consistent with its company objective described earlier. It quickly notified all purchasers of the affected cars and asked them to contact their dealers to have the defective wire replaced at no charge. The dealerships extended their operating hours, hired extra personnel, arranged door-to-door pickup and delivery, provided free car washes, and often provided barbecues or other festivities. All the repaired cars had a courtesy card placed inside that said:

> We'd like to thank you for allowing us to make this correction today. We know an event like this will test our relationship, so we want to repeat to you our basic promise—that everyone at Saturn is fully committed to making you as happy a Saturn owner as we can.

According to Steve Shannon, Saturn's director of consumer marketing, the decision to handle the recall in this manner was simple:

> The measure of whether we are a different kind of company is how we handle the bad times as well as the good. We're trying to minimize the inconvenience and show that we stand behind the cars, so that our owners don't lose faith in us or the cars.

How have consumers responded to the recall? Kim Timbers learned of the recall from friends who had heard of it on news reports before she received her letter from Saturn. She took her car to the dealer, who served her coffee and doughnuts during the 25-minute repair. Her response:

> I expected this would be my first bad experience with Saturn. But it was so positive, I trust them even more than when I purchased the car.

Discussion Questions

1. Describe the evaluative process and outcome that Timbers went through.
2. Saturn is attempting to create committed customers. Do you think it is succeeding? Why?
3. Evaluate the manner by which Saturn handled the recall. What options did it have?
4. How do you think publicity about the recall affected Saturn's image among nonowners?
5. How can Saturn determine if the direct cost of the recall is justified in terms of consumer response?
6. What should Saturn do after the recall is over?

4-7 Closing the Gender Gap in Internet Retail Shopping

According to a recent survey, males (55 percent) are more likely to use the Internet than are females (45 percent). This difference is even larger for shopping on-line. In this survey, 23 percent of on-line women had made a purchase on-line compared to 35 percent of on-line men. Another study had figures of 19 percent for women and 32 percent for men. This is the opposite of the situation in most other distribution channels and represents both a huge challenge and opportunity for Internet retailers.

As indicated in Chapter 17, both men and women who use the Internet site security concerns as the primary reason for not shopping on it. However, more women (54 percent) than men (45 percent) mention "lack of touch" as a nonshopping reason. This may relate somewhat to the different types of items typically purchased by men and women.

Many women use the Internet to explore issues and access information on issues of specific concern to women. Traffic at the four leading sites for women's content—iVillage, Wire Networks, HomeArts, and AOL Studio's Electra—has been growing at 200 to 300 percent a year. These sites provide content and bulletin boards and chat rooms on issues such as health, career management, and relationships.

Kathryn Creech, general manager of HomeArts, which brings together content from Hearst publications such as *Cosmopolitan* and *Good Housekeeping,* describes its operation as follows: "We aggregate the audience by putting together great content that attracts a number of people, then sell advertisers and direct marketers a chance to reach those women."

Firms such as L.L. Bean, Lands' End, J. Crew, and Gymboree pay to link to HomeArts. Content sites are still trying to determine the best way to market to encourage women to shop on-line. According to Creech:

> Integrating shopping opportunities with the content is really important. That's how the mainstream audience will become familiar with and comfortable with shopping online. It could be as simple as planning a recipe. If a woman

is learning about cooking Chinese cooking through the Web site, the idea is to provide the chance for her to buy what she needs to make dinner.

Sports Superstore Online is linked to iVillage and AOL's Electra. The iVillage link is to the firm's home page, which is not designed for women, while the Electra link is to a storefront created specifically for women. The firm is using this experiment to determine the best approach. However, even within the main store, each section such as golf or footwear has a "women only" section featuring products designed specifically for females.

The following quotes from senior executives at HomeArts and iVillage summarize the current status of on-line retailing to women.

For most sites like HomeArts, I think it's fair to say that we're all still learning how to make commerce work.

No one has cracked the code yet for the way women want to shop on-line.

Discussion Questions

1. Why do a smaller percentage of female Internet users shop on-line than male Internet users?
2. What types of products are women most likely to buy on-line? Would these categories differ for men? What implications does this have for Internet marketing?
3. What decision process do consumers go through when deciding to buy on-line? Do males and females use different processes or use the same process but reach different decisions?
4. What image does Internet shopping have for males? Females?
5. How should the following firms increase their Internet sales to women?
   a. Sears
   b. Victoria's Secret
   c. Revlon cosmetics
   d. Reebok
   e. The Gap
   f. Dell computers
6. Visit one of the four sites mentioned in the case. Report on the types of companies linked to each and the manner by which they are linked.
7. Visit one of the four sites mentioned in the case. Visit five of the sites linked to it. To what extent is each linked site uniquely designed to reflect the source of the link (the content site)? Select and evaluate the best and the worst of the five links.

Source: M. G. Briones, "On-Line Retailers Seek Ways to Close Shopping Gender Gap," *Marketing News,* September 14, 1998, p. 2; J. L. McQuivey, "On-Line Retail Strategies," *The Forrester Report,* November 1998; *Interactive Media Study* (Arlington Heights, IL: Market Facts' TeleNation, October 1998); and H. Stapinski, "You Go, Girls!" *American Demographics,* January 1999, pp. 47–51.

4-8 The American Egg Board

In 1945, per capita egg consumption was 402. By 1997, that figure had dropped to 236. Consumption has rebounded somewhat to an estimated 254 in 1999. Shell egg (eggs purchased in the shell for consumption rather than as an existing ingredient in a product such as a cookie) had a similar decline, hitting an all-time low of 170 in 1996. In 1999, per capita shell egg consumption was up to 176.

The sharp decline in per capita egg consumption has a number of causes. General changes in lifestyles and eating patterns have favored the use of cereals and other prepared foods over eggs. The massive advertising of cereal companies has caused consumers to shift their breakfast preferences away from eggs (the leading cereal brand often has an ad budget five times larger than the budget of the American Egg Board).

While the two factors described above hampered egg sales, the 1960's association of high cholesterol levels with heart disease had a devastating impact. Many mass media reports from 1960s through the 1990s stressed the importance of cholesterol reduction as a means of reducing heart disease. Eggs have perhaps the highest concentration of cholesterol of any food product. The early reports recommended sharply reducing dietary cholesterol (cholesterol that one eats such as that found in eggs). This caused many consumers to recognize a problem with their current eating patterns (particularly egg consumption) and to seek and consume alternatives.

As research continued, it became increasingly clear that dietary cholesterol was not nearly the culprit it was initially thought to be. Instead, cholesterol produced by one's own body is the major problem. The consumption of fats, particularly saturated fats, tends to increase cholesterol (particularly the most harmful type of cholesterol) in many people. However, eggs and other cholesterol containing foods continued to be shunned by consumers.

Starting in 1996, several fairly widely reported studies have shown that moderate amounts of dietary cholesterol (egg) consumption do not pose a risk of increased body cholesterol for most consumers. However, even these studies have produced only a modest resurgence in egg consumption (per capita consumption of shell eggs has increased less than an egg a month since 1996).

The American Egg Board (AEB)

The AEB is the industry association that promotes eggs. To provide information about consumers' attitudes and knowledge about eggs and to assess the effectiveness of its "I Love Eggs" campaign (its previous marketing effort), AEB completed a three-part consumer research study in early 1998. Over one-third of consumers reported feeling better about eggs than they did just two years earlier, and most consumers in 1998 admit that they are no longer as concerned about cholesterol as they were before.

Research also showed that convenience is still a growing problem for eggs, particularly on weekdays when the time spent at breakfast is growing shorter. Although they are no longer afraid of eggs, many consumers are not aware of the nutritional positives that eggs have to offer, particularly the quality of protein in an egg. Surprisingly, AEB research showed that one barrier to increased egg consumption is that consumers don't even think of eggs at breakfast.

In 1998, AEB spent $20 million promoting eggs, with $11 million devoted to advertising. This was a sharp increase from prior years and was associated with a new theme: *"If It Ain't Eggs, It Ain't Breakfast."* The president of AEB states: "When consumers think about breakfast, we want them to think about eggs." The campaign will try to reach consumers when they are thinking about breakfast by sponsoring NBC's "Today Show" concert series.

Launched in the spring, the new campaign shifted the American Egg Board's focus from combating negative publicity about eggs and cholesterol to celebrating the nutritional positives of eggs and protein. The ads will state that one large egg a day makes good nutritional sense as part of a balanced diet. The ads will continue to use the "Incredible egg" slogan that was launched in 1976, as well as the "I love eggs" slogan.

The 1998 AEB Annual Report describes the campaign as follows:

> The "If It Ain't Eggs" campaign grew out of the idea that although a cold bowl of cereal or a bagel on the run might be fast, and they might fill you up, they just aren't breakfast. The television and radio campaign uses music to remind people about their favorite family meal in a fun, folksy way. It is a shift from changing attitudes about cholesterol to changing behavior and encouraging consumers to eat eggs more often.
>
> The television commercial features three generations coming together to prepare a family breakfast with eggs as the centerpiece. It includes mouthwatering footage of a variety of egg dishes in order to "trigger the crave" for eggs. As permission to eat the eggs they love, the spot includes a protein message to educate consumers about the nutritional benefits of eggs.
>
> The overall campaign goal to "Capture the Weekend Breakfast" remained intact. More breakfasts continue to be eaten on weekends, and most weekend breakfasts still don't include eggs. Thus, weekend breakfast remains AEB's greatest opportunity to increase consumption. Television and radio advertising was emphasized during three-day holiday weekends throughout the year to encourage consumers to include eggs in the additional breakfast occasion.

In addition to advertising, the AEB engages in "consumer education" and generates significant publicity. It describes some of its educational activities as follows.

> For hard-to-reach young parents and their children, a new booklet, *We Are Eggstra Special,* was developed and distributed to over 163,000 chain and individually owned day care centers, Head Start facilities, and elementary schools with prekindergarten and kindergarten classes as well as to early childhood education district supervisors.
>
> The booklet features hands-on activities for children not yet old enough to read—elementary math measurements, simple science and art projects, songs, poems, raps, and other language arts activities and, of course, cooking—all within a multicultural theme. Included in the mailing was a reproducible letter to parents announcing the program and providing both nutrition and food safety tips. With the completion of the preschool program, AEB has now provided accurate, up-to-date information to teachers at all levels of childhood education.
>
> Seven years after its original release, *The Incredible Journey from Hen to Home* was given a facelift and an update. With jazzed-up colors and a new pocket folder, the material for 4th- through 6th-grade use was particularly revised in the areas of nutrition and food safety to include

the Food Guide Pyramid and Fight BAC!™ campaign. More than 104,000 copies of the new *Journey* kit edition were sent to schools nationwide at the end of the year.

Following up on the previously released kit for active older adult programs, three new issues of a coordinating *Rediscover Eggs!* newsletter were sent to 4,000 retirement living communities, neighborhood senior centers, and nutrition sites. Each issue—bearing the seal of the American Academy of Family Physicians Foundation for credibility—contained articles on nutrition and food safety, recipes, egg craft instructions, and answers to common questions.

A video was produced to coordinate with *The Incredible Classroom Eggsperience* middle/high school print kit produced last year. The film was mailed to 25,000 family and consumer science department heads, media specialists, and classroom educators.

According to AEB, in 1998 eggs were prominently featured 87 times in 25 magazines with a combined circulation of 204,439,472. Some of the articles included:

- "Eggs for Supper," a five-page feature in *Good Housekeeping.*
- "The Case for Eggs," a six-page feature in *Cooking Light.*
- "Eggs Over Easy," three pages in *Parenting.*
- "The Good Egg," a four-page spread in *House Beautiful.*
- "The Truth about Eggs" in *Bon Appetit.*
- "Perfect Omelet" features in *Ladies Home Journal, Parents,* and *Woman's World.*

AEB attempts to influence opinion leaders in a variety of ways. In 1998, a recipe contest was conducted among members of the International Association of Culinary Professionals (IACP) in conjunction with their Kids in the Kitchen Network section. IACP members in all sections—cookbook authors and food writers, cooking school owners, members of the food press, food media personalities, consultants, and entrepreneurs—were invited to submit recipes children could cook with or without help. Rather than prizes being awarded to the recipe developers, each selected a child/family charity or elementary, middle, or high school to receive a cash donation. The recipes are being compiled into a cook booklet to be publicized and distributed nationally.

In terms of general publicity, AEB focused on generating widespread attention for a study published in the *Journal of the American College of Nutrition,* which showed that even people with moderately high cholesterol can eat two eggs a day. A multidimensional publicity campaign resulted in positive news stories in leading national magazines such as *Good Housekeeping* and *First for Women;* a syndicated story by the Gannett News Service reaching over 500 newspapers across the country; and feature television segments on "Dr. Dean," a syndicated health program, and FOX's "Good Day New York."

In the winter, AEB teamed up with The Pennsylvania State University's Center for Sports Medicine to launch a national nutrition/fitness campaign to showcase eggs as an ideal food for active people. Educational materials, including a consumer brochure, *"Foods That Fuel: A Guide to Eating Your Way to Fitness,"* emphasized the importance of consuming "fuel foods" such as eggs for optimal energy and maximum performance.

Table A provides demographic data relevant to egg consumption.

Discussion Questions

1. Consumers appear to have recognized a problem with egg consumption. Why is it so difficult to get them to "unrecognize" this problem?
2. Why don't consumers eat more eggs?
3. According to the research, eggs are not in the evoked set for breakfast for many consumers. What can the AEB do to change this?
4. What decision process do consumers use to decide what to have for breakfast during the week? During the weekend?
5. What evaluative criteria do consumers use in selecting a food for breakfast? Do these change from weekdays to weekends?
6. What insights do the demographic data offer AEB?
7. How can AEB use situations to increase egg consumption?
8. Evaluate AEB's new campaign.

Sources: J. Pollack, "Egg Board Budgets $11 mil," *Advertising Age,* May 25, 1998, p. 10; J. Neff, "The Great Egg Breakthrough," *Food Processing,* January 1998, p. 25; and the American Egg Board Web site (www.aeb.com).

TABLE A

Demographics and Egg Consumption*

Variable	Used in Last Six Months	Heavy User†	Light User‡	Egg Alternatives (last 30 days)
Percent of Respondents	84.0%	33.2%	24.2%	12.7%
Age				
18–24 years	103	108	100	66
25–34	105	104	112	68
35–44	103	119	84	78
45–54	101	114	86	112
55–64	94	82	99	156
>64	93	68	108	160
Education				
College graduate	104	86	124	94
Some college	102	99	110	86
High school graduate	100	105	90	99
No degree	93	106	79	129
Occupation				
Professional	103	97	114	95
Managerial/Administrative	103	83	126	83
Technical/Clerical/Sales	104	98	109	72
Precision/Craft	108	133	90	113
Other employed	98	116	78	85
Race/Ethnic Group				
White	101	99	104	101
Black	93	105	78	98
Spanish speaking	99	117	70	130
Region				
Northeast	98	96	100	108
North central	104	99	106	101
South	100	111	91	95
West	97	85	110	101
Household Income				
<$10,000	89	79	102	134
$10,000–19,999	100	106	94	94
$20,000–29,999	99	113	92	114
$30,000–39,999	101	99	96	102
$40,000–49,999	106	99	106	67
$50,000–59,999	105	102	105	101
$60,000–74,999	102	95	112	95
$75,000+	102	102	102	89
Household Structure				
1 person	90	47	154	100
2 people	100	86	112	119
3 or more	103	125	76	89
Child <2	106	123	91	92
Child 2–5	106	129	75	78
Child 6–11	105	136	68	74
Child 12–17	102	141	65	90

*100 = Average use or consumption unless a percent is indicated. Base = Female homemakers.
†More than two dozen in last 30 days.
‡Less than two dozen in last 30 days.

Source: *Mediamark Spring 1997* (New York: Mediamark Research Inc., 1997).

part five

Organizations as Consumers

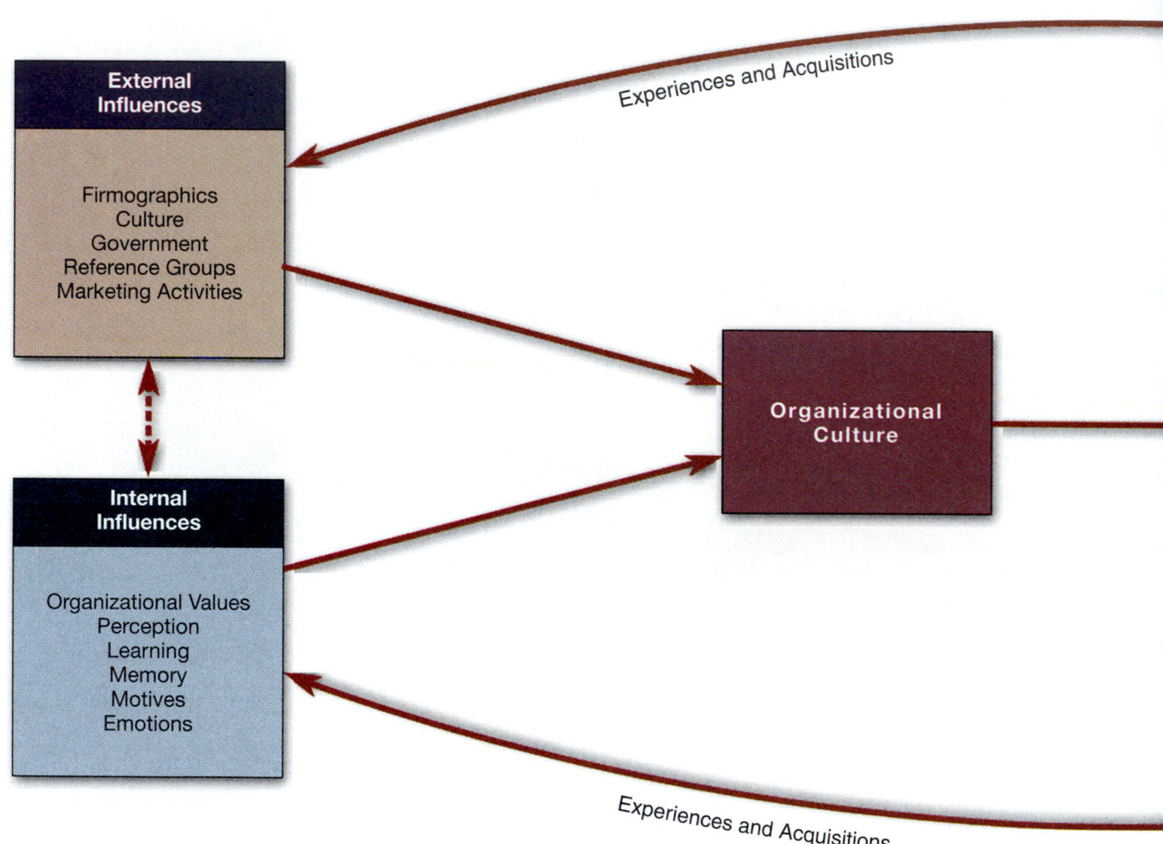

■ The stereotype of organizational buying behavior is one of a cold, efficient, economically rational process. Computers rather than humans could easily, and perhaps preferably, fulfill this function. In reality, nothing could be further from the truth. In fact, organizational consumer behavior is as "human" as individual and household consumer behavior.

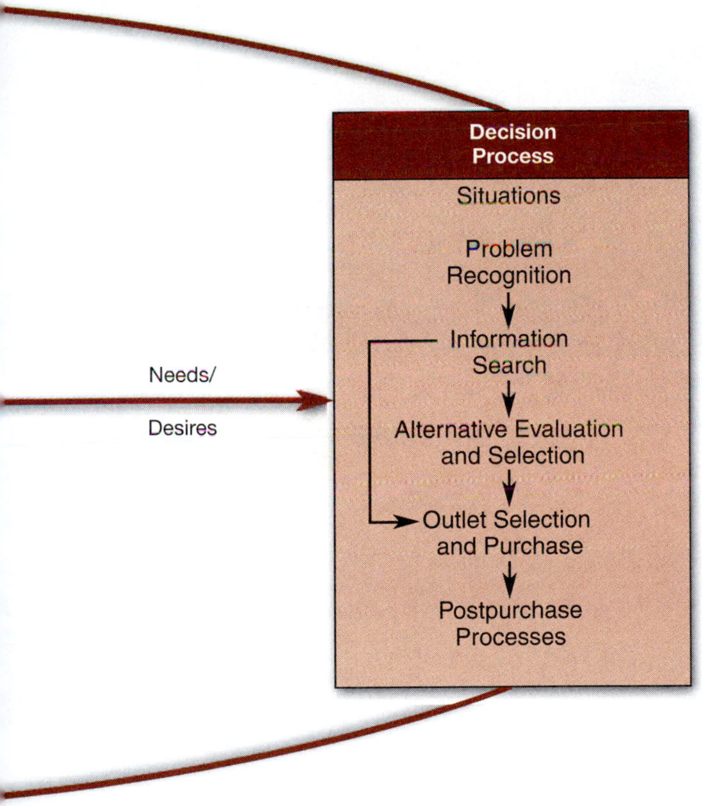

Decision Process

Situations

Problem Recognition → Information Search → Alternative Evaluation and Selection → Outlet Selection and Purchase → Postpurchase Processes

Needs/ Desires

Organizations pay price premiums for well-known brands and for prestige brands. They avoid risk and fail to properly evaluate products and brands both before and after purchase. Individual members of organizations use the purchasing and consumption process as a political arena and attempt to increase their personal, departmental, or functional power through purchasing. Marketing communications are perceived and misperceived by organization members. Likewise, organizations learn correct and incorrect information about the world in which they operate.

Organizational purchase decisions take place in situations with varying degrees of time pressure, importance, and newness. They typically involve more people and criteria than do individual or household decisions. Thus, the study of organizational buying behavior is a rich and fun-filled activity.

On this and the facing page is a version of our model of consumer behavior modified for organizational buying. Chapter 19 explains these modifications.

"PATIENCE IS A VIRTUE."

–CHAUCER

"ENOUGH IS ENOUGH."

–WESTERN UNION

Haven't you spent enough time waiting to collect from your customers? Maybe that's why when they finally decide to pay, you should tell them to send their money by Western Union Quick Collect.® The Quick Collect service delivers guaranteed good funds in minutes. In fact, we're the fastest way to send good funds.

And the most convenient, with over 20,000 Western Union agent locations in the U.S.

For more information, ask your manager to call 1-800-525-6313. The sooner the better, because while patience may be a virtue, too much can ruin your business.

WESTERN UNION | QUICK COLLECT

The fastest way to collect good funds.℠

Courtesy First Data Corporation.

Organizational Buyer Behavior

One of Western Union's important organizational market segments is collection agents. There are about 100,000 collection agents in 1,300 collection offices in the United States. Collection offices include collection agencies, credit card–issuing banks, mortgage companies, and finance companies.

Collectors request payment from debtors in a variety of ways—hand delivery, regular mail, or overnight mail of a check or money order are the most common. Western Union markets Quick Collect as an alternative means. With Quick Collect, the debtor pays at one of Western Union's 18,000 locations. The payment is then transferred to the collection agent within 15 minutes, eliminating the "check-is-in-the-mail" story as well as eliminating earnings lost while payment is in transit.

According to Quick Collect's product manager:

> We want the collectors to tell debtors to use Quick Collect every time. We needed to build awareness but more important, to establish relationships with individual collectors, which we felt we could do by rewarding them for being good at their job.

Western Union developed a revolving reward program that targets individual agents with a new one-month promotion every six months. The constant flow of new programs keeps the agents interested and participating.

A recent program used a scratch-and-win game. Collection managers received posters, game boards, and a one-month supply of scratch-off tickets. Every time a debtor paid using Quick Collect, the agent involved received a ticket. The agents had a 1-in-86 chance to win a prize such as a cellular phone or CD player. Another box on the ticket had a letter that agents could accumulate to try to spell "Quick Collect." Those who succeeded (about one per month) received a grand prize of air travel for two anywhere in the United States. The program is credited with increasing the use of Quick Collect by 30 percent.

To further develop its relationship with agents, Western Union publishes a quarterly magazine, the *Professional Collector,* which now has a circulation of 100,000. It contains lifestyle features and industry-specific articles on topics such as legal developments. It is designed to help the collectors see their jobs as a professional career. The reward program is incorporated into the magazine through a feature called the Champion Collector. Managers nominate their top agents. Winners' names are listed in this part of the magazine and they receive a plaque.

Western Union credits these programs as a major reason Quick Collect has experienced double-digit annual growth for the past seven years.[1]

Purchase decisions by businesses are often described as "rational" or "economic." However, businesses and other organizations are made up of individuals. These individuals, not "the organization," make the purchase decisions. Thus, as we saw in the opening example, they respond to contests and loyalty programs just as individual consumers do. Illustration 19-1 reflects the fact that communicating with organizational buyers involves many of the same principles of perception used to reach household buyers—for example, color, contrast, and humor.

However, organizations are not just a collection of individuals. Organizations do develop unique rules and cultures that influence the behavior of their members. Thus, it is important that we understand the unique characteristics of organizations that relate to their purchasing behavior.

Firms spend over $50 billion a year on **business-to-business marketing.**[2] Spending this money wisely requires a thorough understanding of organizational buyer behavior. Under-

ILLUSTRATION 19-1

Ads targeting organizational buyers need to be interesting and attention attracting as well as informative.

Courtesy Compaq Computer Corporation.

standing organizational purchasing requires many of the same skills and concepts used to understand individual consumer or household needs. While larger and often more complex, organizations—like individual consumers—develop preferences, memories, and behaviors through perceptions, information processing, and experience. Likewise, organizations develop cultures that create relatively stable patterns of behaviors over time and across situations.

Like households, organizations make many buying decisions. In some instances, these buying decisions are routine replacement decisions for a frequently purchased commodity product or service such as paper or pens. At the other end of the continuum, organizations face new, complex purchase decisions that require careful problem definition, extensive information search, a long and often very technical evaluation process, perhaps a negotiated purchase, and a long period of use and postpurchase evaluation.

Because there are many similarities between analyzing consumer behavior and analyzing organizational buyer behavior, our basic conceptual model of buyer behavior still holds. Of course, some aspects of the model, such as social status, do not apply, but most others apply with some modification. The purpose of this chapter is to discuss how this model of consumer behavior should be modified for application to organizational buying behavior and how the concepts of this model operate when marketing to organizations rather than to individual consumers or households.

ORGANIZATIONAL CULTURE

At the hub of our consumer model of buyer behavior is self-concept and lifestyle. Organizations also have a type of self-concept in the beliefs and attitudes the organization members have about the organization and how it operates. Likewise, organizations have a type of lifestyle in that they have distinct ways of operating. We characterize these two aspects of an organization as its **organizational culture** (see Figure 19-1). Organizational culture is much like lifestyle in that organizations vary dramatically in how they make decisions and how they approach problems involving risk, innovation, and change.[3] The term **corporate culture** is often used to refer to the organizational culture of a business firm.

Organizational culture reflects and shapes organizational needs and desires, which in turn influence how organizations make decisions. For example, the Environmental Protection Agency, the Red Cross, and IBM are three large organizations. Each has a different organizational culture that influences how it gathers information, processes information, and makes decisions.

Organizations occasionally seek to change their organizational culture. Jack Welch, the CEO of General Electric Company, has sought to make GE more aggressive and entrepreneurial. To accomplish this, he has changed many values and organizational behaviors with respect to taking risks and challenging conventional thinking. It is his hope that this change in organizational culture will create a more responsive, faster growing company.

Another example is Nike. Imagine how it has changed from a tiny startup operation to a small, innovative company to a worldwide marketer of sports shoes and clothing. At each stage of organizational evolution, Nike's culture changed, which, in turn, altered how it purchased products and services. Xerox markets to both General Electric and Nike. These are two very different kinds of organizations, and both are undergoing change. As a result, Xerox and others must analyze and understand the buyer behavior of each organization in order to develop marketing strategies that best serve the needs of each organizational customer or customer segment.

FIGURE 19-1 Overall Model of Organizational Buyer Behavior

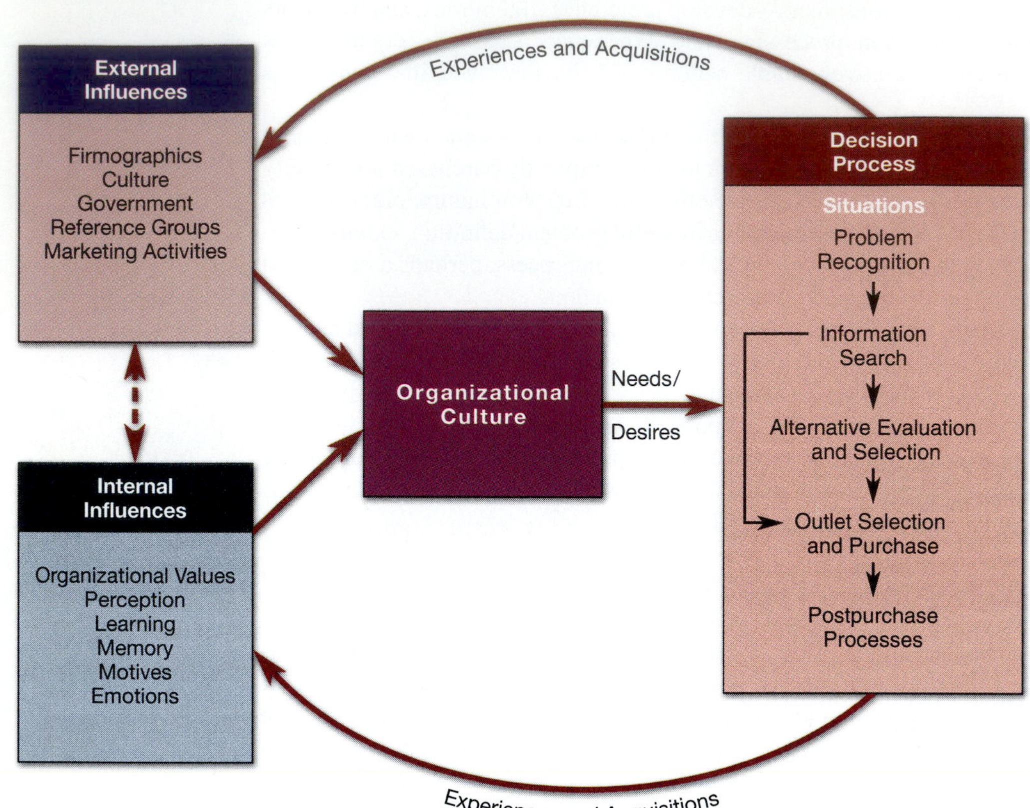

EXTERNAL FACTORS INFLUENCING ORGANIZATIONAL CULTURE

Firmographics

We discussed earlier the important role of consumer demographics in understanding consumer behavior. Firmographics are equally important. **Firmographics** involve both organization characteristics—for example, size, activities, objectives, location, and industry category—and characteristics of the composition of the organization—for example, gender, age, education, and income distribution of employees.[4]

Size Large organizations are more likely to have a variety of specialists who attend to purchasing, finance, marketing, and general management, while in smaller organizations one or two individuals may have these same responsibilities. Larger organizations are generally more complex, since more individuals participate in managing the organization's operations. The fact that there are often multiple individuals involved in the purchase decision in a large organization means that advertising and sales force efforts must be targeted at various functions in the firm. Each message might need to stress issues of concern only to that function. The same purchase decision in a smaller firm might involve only the owner

TABLE 19-1

Organizational Activities Based on Organizational Objective and Nature of Activity

General Organizational Objective	Nature of Organizational Activity		
	Routine	*Complex*	*Technical*
Commercial	Office management	Human resource management	New-product development
Governmental	Highway maintenance	Tax collection	Space exploration
Nonprofit	Fund raising	Increase number of national parks	Organ donor program
Cooperative	Compile industry statistics	Establish industry standards	Applied research

or manager. Different media would be required to reach this person, and one message would need to address all the key purchase issues.

Activities and Objectives The activities and objectives of organizations influence their style and behavior. For example, the Navy, in procuring an avionics system for a new fighter plane, operates differently than Boeing does in purchasing a very similar system for a commercial aircraft. The Navy is a government organization carrying out a public objective, while Boeing seeks a commercial objective at a profit.

Table 19-1 is a matrix that provides examples of the interface between broad organizational objectives and activities. Organizational objectives can be categorized as commercial, governmental, nonprofit, and cooperative. The general nature of organizational activity is described as routine, complex, or technical. For example, a government organization purchasing highway maintenance services would operate differently from a government organization procuring missiles. Likewise, a cooperative wholesale organization set up as a buying cooperative for several retailers would have a different organizational culture from a cooperative research institute set up by firms in the semiconductor industry. And a nonprofit organization involved in organ donations is likely to differ from one organized to gather industry statistics.

Commercial firms can be usefully divided into public firms (stock is widely traded) and private firms (one or a few individuals own a controlling share of the firm). In public firms, management is generally expected to operate the firm in a manner that will maximize the economic gains of the shareholders. These organizations face consistent pressures to make economically sound, if not optimal, decisions.

However, about half of all business purchases involve privately held firms whose CEO is often the controlling shareholder. In this situation, the firm can and frequently does pursue objectives other than profit maximization. One study found motives such as the following to be driving the management of such firms:[5]

- Building a place for the entire family to work and be involved.
- Having complete, autocratic control over an environment.
- Build a lasting "empire."
- Becoming wealthy.
- Doing what the family expects.
- Avoiding corporations or working for others.
- Obtaining status.
- Improving the world or the environment.

Segmenting these firms based on the motives of the owners is a useful approach for developing sales messages. For example, Micron Electronics is targeting the owners and

ILLUSTRATION 19-2

Industrial ads appeal to the values and personal concerns of managers, not just economic or product issues.

Courtesy Micron Electronics Inc.

managers of smaller, entrepreneurial firms. Its ads position it as understanding and caring about the needs and concerns of these individuals more than the larger PC firms do. One ad states: "They wouldn't give you the time of day. They said you weren't a player . . . They're holding on line three." The ad in Illustration 19-2 recognizes that the long hours these entrepreneurs work is not just for selfish reasons.

Location As we saw in Chapter 5, there are a number of regional subcultures in the United States. These subcultures influence organizational cultures as well as individual lifestyles. For example, firms on the west coast tend to be more informal in their operations than those on the east coast. Dress is more casual, relationships are less formalized, and business is on more of a personal level in the west than elsewhere in the country. The midwest and south also have unique business styles. Marketing communications and sales force training need to reflect these differences.

These location-based cultural differences are magnified as one enters foreign cultures. Firms that open branches outside their home countries frequently experience some difficulties managing the workforce and operating within the local community. Selling to organizations outside a firm's home culture poses even more challenges than selling to households in that culture (see Chapter 2). For example:

> To get a bank in China's Sichuan province last year to buy more than 100 ATMs, Diebold had to offer the bank 23 units for free. Diebold's distributor was coerced into buying a floor in a building the bank had invested in. And the distributor, as well as Thorpe McConville, Diebold's general manager and CEO, and Kevin Wu, a deputy GM, had to get approval from 10 people in a variety of the bank's departments. "You've always got to meet with 8 to 12 people, all of whom have a different agenda," Ku says. "And you've got to be prepared for political chaos."
>
> The sales cycle took six months. McConville paid four visits to Sichuan, each time taking the prospects out for lunch, dinner, or karaoke.[6]

Industry Category Two firms can be similar in terms of size (large), location (Illinois), activity (manufacturing), objective (profit), and ownership (public), and still have sharply differing cultures due in part to being in differing industries. If one of the two firms described above manufactured heavy equipment and the other computers, we would expect differing cultures to exist.

Organization Composition Organization cultures influence the behaviors and values of those who work in the organizations. However, the types of individuals who work in the organization also heavily influence organization cultures. An organization composed primarily of young, highly educated, technically oriented people (say, a software engineering firm) will have a different culture from an organization composed primarily of older, highly educated, nontechnical individuals (say, an insurance firm). While the culture of most organizations is influenced more by the characteristics of the founder and top managers, the overall composition of the organizational membership is also important.

Macrosegmentation **Macrosegmentation** groups organizations with distinguishing firmographics into market segments. These segments, based on differences in needs due to firmographics, are called *macrosegments*.[7] Micron Electronics' decision to focus on smaller firms described earlier is an example. First Chicago, one of America's largest banks, states:

> We've tried too long to be everything to everyone. We're in the process of rolling out a strategy in all our branches where we segment customers and tailor our marketing campaigns to those segments.

Two of the macrosegments being targeted are midsized and small businesses. Each segment will have a marketing team that focuses on that segment.[8]

As we discuss later, this is quite different from microsegmentation based on the decision-making unit's needs and preferences. Thus, organizational markets can have a two-tiered segmentation scheme referred to as macro- and microsegmentation.[9]

In Table 19-2, electricity-producing utilities were first grouped into 12 macrosegments based on size, location, and type of ownership. These 12 segments were found to have differences in their needs with respect to price, product quality, warranty, spare parts availability, and several other purchase criteria. This information was sufficient to allow the development of focused strategies for each segment. However, as we will see shortly, differences in customer loyalty, a microsegmentation variable, were used to further segment each of the 12 groups.

Culture/Government

Variations in values and behaviors across cultures affect organizations as well as individuals. For example, in most American firms shareholder or owner wealth is a dominant decision criteria. Corporate downsizing has resulted in hundreds of thousands of workers and managers losing their jobs at a time when corporate profits are soaring. These actions have been acceptable in the America society. Similar corporate behavior would not be accepted in much of Europe or Japan. In these societies, worker welfare is often on a par with or above concern about corporate profit. Plant closure laws, layoff regulations, and worker benefits tend to be much higher than in America.

In America, Japan, and most of Europe, bribery and similar approaches for making sales are not acceptable, and these governments enforce a wide array of laws prohibiting such behaviors. In America, both the legal and social constraints against bribery are strong enough to make corporate gift giving from a supplier to a buyer difficult or impossible.[10] In

TABLE 19-2

Organizational Segmentation Strategy Based on Firmographics

Served Market Several thousand firms that purchase electrical equipment for conversion and regulation of electricity.

Firmographics These electric utilities differ on the basis of:

Size: Large, medium, and small.
Location: Four geographical regions.
Organizational: Public utilities, rural electric co-ops, investor-owned utilities, and industrial firms.

Customer Needs Based on these organizational demographics, meaningful differences were found for 12 distinct segments on the basis of the following purchase criteria:

1. Price.
2. Quality.
3. Warranty.
4. Availability of spare parts.
5. Reliability.
6. Ease of installation.
7. Maintenance requirements.
8. Energy losses.
9. Appearance of product.

Customer Loyalty Each of the 7,000 potential customers were classified on the basis of customer loyalty as:

Firm loyal: Very loyal and not likely to switch.
Competitive: Preferred vendor, but number two is very close.
Switchable: A competitor is the preferred vendor, but we are a close second.
Competitor loyal: Very loyal to a competitor.

Marketing Strategy

1. For each segment, focus on specific needs important to that segment.
2. Increase customer-need-specific market communications to *each* of the 12 segments.
3. Increase sales coverage to customers classified as "competitive" and "switchable," while decreasing coverage of those classified as "firm loyal" and "competitor loyal."

Results The year the marketing strategy was implemented, total market demand *decreased* by 15 percent. In addition, one of the three sales regions did not implement the strategy. Shown below are the percent changes in sales by sales region and customer loyalty. Which sales region do you think did not participate in the need-based organizational marketing strategy? If you selected region 3, you're right!

	Sales Region		
Customer Loyalty	*1*	*2*	*3*
Loyal	+2%	+3%	+3%
Competitive	+26	+18	−9
Switchable	+16	+8	−18
Competitor loyal	−4	−3	−4
Total	+18%	+12%	−10%

Source: Adapted from Dennis Gensch, "Targeting the Switchable Industrial Customer," *Marketing Science,* Winter 1984, pp. 41–54.

other parts of the world, "bribes" are an expected part of many business transactions. This poses a difficult ethical dilemma for firms doing business in these regions. Ignoring any legal constraints imposed by the American government, should an American firm provide an expensive "gift" to the purchasing agent in a foreign country where it is common knowledge that such gifts are essential to do business with the country's firms?

In many parts of the world, businesses and governments are partners or at least work closely together. In the United States, an arm's-length or even adversarial relationship is more common. Consider the following description of IBM's relationship with the U.S.

Reference Group Infrastructure for Personal Computers and Microprocessors **FIGURE 19-2**

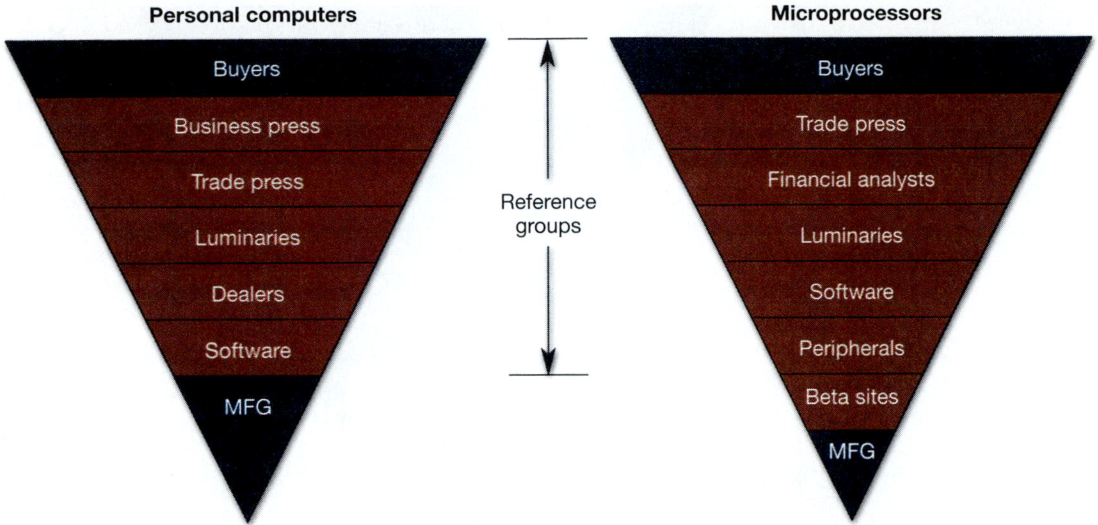

Source: Adapted from Regis McKenna, *The Regis Touch: The New Marketing Strategies for Uncertain Times* (Reading MA: Addison-Wesley Publishing, 1985).

government and its consequences:

> IBM's deal-making culture developed out of one of the greatest legal battles in history, the 13-year attempt by the U.S. Department of Justice to break IBM's monopoly on the market for mainframe computers. In the end, IBM settled the suit by consenting to some minor restrictions—such as not announcing in advance products that might chill competitors' sales—but at a cost as high as $100 million. A legal staff of hundreds was employed for the duration of the dispute. This ordeal left deep scars on the IBM psyche, resulting in a preoccupation with secrecy, an aversion to putting commitments in writing, and an elaborate system of legal reviews for even the most routine business transactions. At IBM, every press release, speech, and product disclosure is subject to legal approval, leading to interminable delays. This culture is unsuited to the fast-moving environment of the personal computer business.[11]

Will Microsoft's battle with the U.S. government have a similar effect on its culture?

Reference Groups

Reference groups influence organizational behavior and purchasing decisions.[12] Perhaps the most powerful type of reference group in industrial markets is that of lead users. **Lead users** are *innovative organizations that derive a great deal of their success from leading change*. As a result, their adoption of a new product, service, technology, or manufacturing process is watched and often emulated by the majority.[13]

Other reference groups such as trade associations, financial analysts, and dealer organizations also influence an organization's decision to buy or not buy a given product, or to buy or not buy from a given supplier. **Reference group infrastructure** refers to the flow of purchase influence within an industry. The success of a new technology product depends on how the firm influences the reference groups located along the continuum separating it from its consumer market. The more the firm gains positive endorsement or use throughout this infrastructure, the greater the chance of customers treating it as a preferred source of supply. Figure 19-2 provides two illustrations of this concept.

FIGURE 19-3 Combining Lead User and Infrastructure Reference Groups

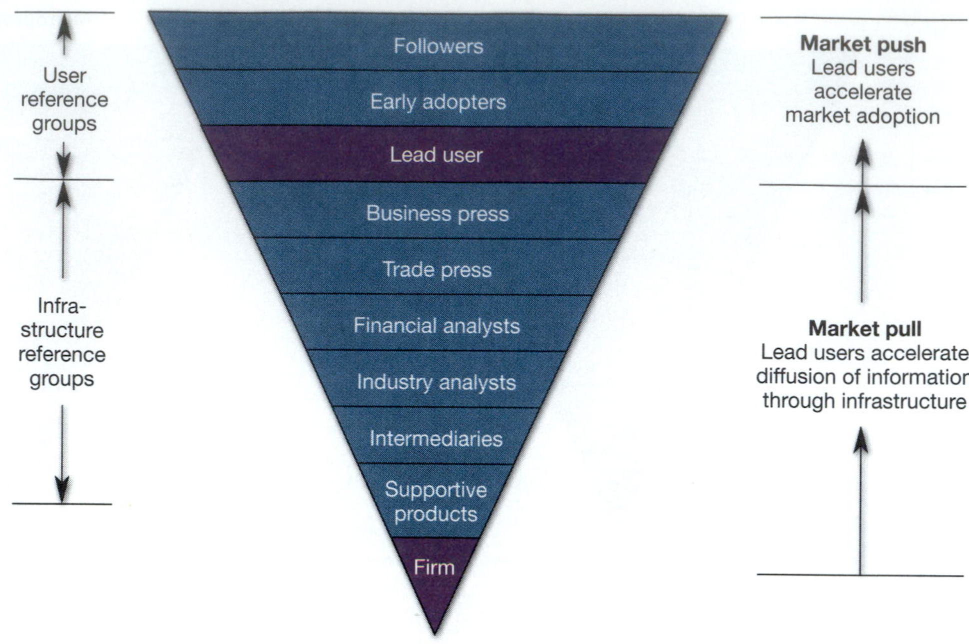

Source: Roger Best and Reinhard Angellhard, "Strategies for Leveraging a Technology Advantage," *Handbook of Business Strategy,* 1988.

If we combine the concept of lead users with the reference group infrastructure, as shown in Figure 19-3, we have a more comprehensive picture of organizational reference group systems. Since the lead users play such a critical role, their adoption of a product, technology, or vendor can influence the overall infrastructure in two powerful ways. First, a lead-user decision to adopt a given supplier's innovative product adds credibility to the product and supplier. This in turn has a strong positive impact on the infrastructure that stands between the firm and its remaining target customers. Second, a lead-user decision to purchase will have a direct impact on firms inclined to follow market trends.

The strategy implication of this is clear. Marketers of new industrial products, particularly technology products, should focus initial efforts on securing sales to visible lead users.

INTERNAL FACTORS INFLUENCING ORGANIZATIONAL CULTURE

Organizational Values

IBM and Apple Computer both manufacture and market computers. However, each organization has a distinct organizational culture. IBM is corporate, formal, and takes itself seriously. Apple is less formal, creative, and promotes a more open organizational culture. Marketing managers must understand these differences in order to best serve the respective organizational needs.

Courtesy BMC Software, Inc.

ILLUSTRATION 19-3

Ads should appeal to the values of the businesses they are targeting. This ad will appeal to businesses and individuals that value competition.

As you examine the eight common business values shown below, think of how IBM might differ from Apple, Nordstrom's from Kmart, Amazon.com from Barnes and Noble, or FedEx from the U.S. Postal Service. Each is a large organization, but each has a unique set of values that underlies its organizational culture. To the degree that organizations differ on these values, a firm marketing to them will have to adapt its marketing approach.

1. Risk taking is admired and rewarded.
2. Competition is more important than cooperation.
3. Hard work comes first, leisure second.
4. Individual efforts take precedence over collective efforts.
5. Any problem can be solved.
6. Active decision making is essential.
7. Change is positive and is actively sought.
8. Performance is more important than rank or status.

The values as stated above are representative of an innovative organization that seeks change, views problems as opportunities, and rewards individual efforts. It is hard to imagine the U.S. Postal Service or many other bureaucratic organizations encouraging such values. On the other hand, these values underlie many high-technology startup organizations.

The ad in Illustration 19-3 would appeal to organizations and individuals with a competitive orientation.

Shared Values and Value Conflicts Individuals and organizations both have values. Unfortunately, these value sets are not always consistent. As a result, two different value

ILLUSTRATION 19-4

Well done industrial advertising campaigns will often work across cultures to enhance the image of the firm.

Courtesy 3M.

systems can be operating within an organization. To the degree that these value systems are consistent, decision making and implementation of decisions will move smoothly.[14]

The distinction between individual values/objectives and organizational values/objectives is critical. Marketers must recognize that individuals may make purchasing decisions on behalf of the organization that are based solely on the values/objectives of the organization, solely on the values/objectives of the individual, or on a compromise between the two. Thus, marketers must recognize situations where conflict between individual and organizational values/objectives exists and how it is likely to be resolved. Then they must design products and communications based on this knowledge.[15]

Perception

To process information, a firm must go through the same sequential stages of exposure, attention, and interpretation as consumers. Of course, given the more complex nature of organizations, the processes involved are also more complex.[16] A business customer develops certain images of seller organizations from their products, people, and organizational activities. Like people, organizations have memories and base their decisions on images or memories they have developed. Once an image is formed by an organization, it is very difficult to change. Therefore, it is important for an organization to develop a sound communications strategy to build and reinforce a desired image or brand position.[17]

Illustration 19-4 shows an ad from 3M's *1, 2, 3M* campaign that was very successful. The challenge was to unify 3M's 60,000 products and provide the organization with a meaningful image. It was important to show that not only are 3M products exciting technologically but that they are useful and make a difference in peoples' lives. The campaign was highly successful in the United States, France, Latin America, and Australia. Research showed that

Impact of Ad Size on Inquiries **FIGURE 19-4**

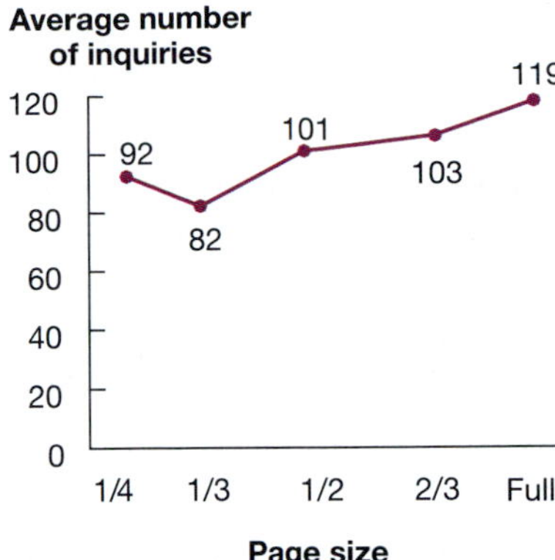

Source: *CARR Report No. 250.1* (Boston: Cahners Publishing Co., undated).

perception of 3M as an innovative company with innovative products went from 10 to 51 percent, overall favorable impression of 3M increased from 65 to 85 percent, and the likelihood of recommending 3M and its products moved from 71 to 91 percent.[18]

Ad size and repetition have a positive effect on awareness and action. One major study found a 20 percent gain in awareness when two or more ads are placed in the same issue of a specialized business magazine compared to only one.[19] The size of the advertisement also affects action in the form of inquiries generated by the advertisement. A study of 500,000 inquiries to ads run in *Plastic World, Electronics Design News,* and *Design News* found that full-page ads were much more effective at generating inquiries than smaller ads (see Figure 19-4).

The potential power of industrial advertising can be seen in its impact on sales of an industrial safety product. Sales in the first year of the ad campaign increased almost fourfold, with advertising in one trade publication using an eight-page advertising schedule: six black and white ads and two color ads. When three color spreads were added to the schedule, sales continued to climb. When ad frequency was again increased, this time to six black and white single-page ads and 11 color spreads, product sales rose to 6.7 times pre-campaign sales.[20]

While advertising plays an important role in communicating to organizations, direct sales calls are the most important element of the communications mix in most industrial markets. This is the case despite the high cost of such calls:[21]

Industry	*Average Cost Per Sales Call*
Manufacturing	$159
Service	$106
Retail	$99
Wholesale distribution	$81
All companies	$113

One reason for the significant role of salespeople is that businesses are not just economic entities. Business buyers prefer to do business with firms they know, like, and trust.

Those relationships are most often formed between members of the firms involved, with sales personnel being the most common representative of the selling organization. As one successful salesperson states:

> You have to have a great product but you also have to make the customer like you as a salesperson.[22]

Firms marketing to organizations increasingly use the Internet to provide information about the firm, its products, its prices, and terms and conditions.[23] They also use it to generate leads for telephone or direct sales calls and to solicit orders either on the Internet or via an 800 number. Internet usage is becoming so common in organizational markets that firms without a strong Internet presence are increasingly at a disadvantage.

Learning

Like individuals, organizations learn through their experiences and perceptions.[24] Positive experiences with vendors are rewarding and tend to be repeated. Purchasing processes and procedures that prove effective tend to be institutionalized in rules and policies. Likewise, negative experiences with vendors produce learning and avoidance behavior, and purchasing procedures that don't work are generally discarded. Developing the capacity to learn efficiently is increasingly a key to organizational success.[25]

Motives and Emotions

Organizational decisions tend to be less emotional than many consumer purchase decisions. However, because humans with psychological needs and emotions influence these decisions, this aspect of marketing to an organizational customer cannot be overlooked or underestimated.

Quite often there is considerable personal or career risk in organizational purchase decisions. The risk of making a bad purchase decision can elicit feelings of self-doubt or psychological discomfort. These are personal emotions that will influence purchase decisions. FedEx appeals to risk avoidance with ads that ask, in essence:

> How do you explain to your boss that the important papers didn't arrive but you saved the company $5 by using a less expensive overnight mail service?

PURCHASE SITUATION

The buying process is influenced by the complexity and difficulty of the decision task. Less complex, low-risk, routine decisions are generally made by an individual or a small group without extensive effort. At the other extreme are organizational decisions that are complex and have major organizational implications. A continuum of purchase situations lies between these two extremes.[26] A useful categorization of organizational purchase situations is provided in Table 19-3 and described in the following paragraphs.[27]

You should note that this is similar to the purchase involvement construct discussed in Chapter 14. For consumers, we divided the purchase involvement continuum into three categories—nominal, limited, and extended. The industrial purchase situation has a larger range of complexity than most individual or household decisions and so has six rather than three categories. However, the two are quite similar.

Casual Purchase This situation occurs when the purchase is of minor importance, there is little uncertainty surrounding the purchase, there are multiple vendors, and the buyer has

TABLE 19-3 Organizational Purchase Situations and Buying Responses

	1 *Casual*	*2* *Routine Low Priority*	*3* *Simple Modified Rebuy*	*4* *Judgmental New Task*	*5* *Complex Modified Rebuy*	*6* *Strategic New Task*
Situational Characteristics						
Purchase importance	Of minor importance	Somewhat important	Quite important	Quite important	Quite important	Extremely important
Task uncertainty	Little uncertainty	Moderately uncertain	Little uncertainty	Great amount of uncertainty	Little uncertainty	Moderately uncertain
Extensiveness of choice set	Much choice	Much choice	Narrow set of choices	Narrow set of choices	Much choice	Narrow set of choices
Buyer power	Little or no power	Moderate power	Moderate power	Moderate power	Strong power position	Strong power position
Buying Activities						
Search for information	No search made	Little effort at searching	Moderate amount of search	Moderate amount of search	High level of search	High level of search
Use of analysis techniques	No analysis performed	Moderate level of analysis	Moderate level of analysis	Moderate level of analysis	Great deal of analysis	Great deal of analysis
Proactive focus	No attention to proactive issues	Superficial consideration of proactive focus	High level of proactive focus	Moderate proactive focus	High level of proactive focus	Proactive issues dominate purchase
Procedural control	Simply transmit the order	Follow standard procedures	Follow standard procedures	Little reliance on established procedures	Follow standard procedures	Little reliance on established procedures

Source: Reprinted with permission from the *Journal of Marketing,* published by the American Marketing Association. M. D. Bunn, "Taxonomy of Buying Decision Approaches," January 1993, p. 47.

limited purchasing power. The typical purchase response involves no effort to search for information, no analysis is performed, no consideration is given to proactive issues (strategic and long-term considerations), and substantial procedure control is exercised.

Routine Low-Priority Purchase This process tends to occur for repetitive purchases that are somewhat important, with a moderate level of uncertainty, a substantial number of choices available, and a moderate amount of buyer power. It involves limited search effort, a moderate amount of analysis, superficial consideration of proactive issues, and standard rules and procedures.

Simple Modified Rebuy This strategy is used when the purchase is quite important to the firm, there is little uncertainty, a narrow set of choices, and moderate buyer power. It requires a moderate amount of search and analysis, a high level of proactive focus, and a tendency to follow standard procedures.

Judgmental New Task This approach tends to occur when the buying decision is quite important, there is substantial uncertainty, a narrow set of choices, and the firm has moderate buyer power. The firm engages in moderate search, analysis, and proactive focusing but with little reliance on established procedures (since there is no precedent to follow, the firm must "decide as it goes").

Complex Modified Rebuy This process is used when the decision is quite important, with little uncertainty, many choices, and strong buyer power. Extensive search, sophisticated analysis, a strong proactive focus, and adherence to established procedures characterize it.

Strategic New Task This task occurs when the decision is extremely important to the firm, there is a moderate level of uncertainty, a narrow set of choices, and the firm has strong buyer power. It involves a high level of search, extensive analysis, an intense focus on proactive issues, but little reliance on established procedures.

Clearly, the marketing strategy and tactics for one particular type of purchase situation would be inappropriate for others. Thus, marketers must understand the purchase task confronting their organizational consumers and develop appropriate marketing strategies.

ORGANIZATIONAL PURCHASE PROCESS

Decision-Making Unit

Decision-making units (DMUs) are the individuals (representing functional areas and management) within an organization that participate in making a given purchase decision. These are often referred to as **buying centers.** They are often relatively permanent for recurring decisions and ad hoc for nonroutine ones. Large, highly structured organizations ordinarily involve more individuals in a purchase decision than do smaller, less formal organizations. Important decisions are likely to draw into the decision process individuals from a wider variety of functional areas and organizational levels than are less-important purchase decisions.[28]

The decision-making unit can be partitioned by area of functional responsibility and type of influence. Functional responsibility can include specific functions such as manufacturing, engineering, transportation, research and development, and purchasing, as well as general management. Each function views the needs of the organization differently and as a result uses different importance weights or evaluative criteria.

TABLE 19-4

Service Attribute Importance for Retail and Wholesale Buyers and Operations Personnel

*Attribute**	*Buyer Rating*	*Operations Rating*
Ease of placing orders	**4.01**	3.71
Line-item availability	**4.55**	4.31
Packages clearly identified	4.46	**4.82**
Meets appointments	4.46	**4.73**
Delivers when requested	**4.87**	4.70
Delivered sorted and segregated	4.36	**4.75**
Palletizing/unitizing capability	3.72	**4.37**
Master carton packaging quality	3.81	**4.48**
Shelf unit packaging quality	3.97	**4.29**
Complete/accurate documentation	4.54	**4.81**
Well-documented deal/style codes	4.36	**4.60**
Length of order cycle	**4.14**	3.61
Consistency of order cycle	**4.38**	3.88

*Measured on a 1 to 5 scale, with 5 being very important and 1 being not at all important. All are significantly different at the .05 level.

Adapted from M. B. Cooper, C. Droge, and P. J. Daugherty, "How Buyers and Operations Personnel Evaluate Service," *Industrial Marketing Management,* no. 20 (1991), p. 83.

In Table 19-4, we see that buyers in retail and wholesale firms assign different priorities to the performance of suppliers than do the operations people in those same firms. Firms marketing to these retailers and wholesalers must meet the needs of each group and communicate that to each group. Note that focusing only on the buyers, a common strategy, is not likely to be successful.

How the final purchase decision is made is in part determined by individual power, expertise, the degree of influence each functional area possesses in this type decision, how the organization resolves group decision conflicts, and the nature of the decision.[29]

Members of the decision-making unit play various roles, such as information gatherer, key influencer, decision maker, purchaser, and/or user.[30] A plant manager could play all five roles, while corporate engineers may simply be sources of information. The role a function plays in an organizational decision varies by type of decision and organizational culture.

Decision-making units are likely to vary over the product life cycle. Consider the changes in the decision-making unit that took place in the purchase of microprocessors by an original equipment manufacturer over the stages of the microprocessor's product life cycle. Early stages in the life of a new product presented a judgmental new-task decision that required a large DMU. As the product grew in its utilization, a simple modified rebuy decision evolved, as did a change in the structure of the DMU. Finally, as the microprocessor moved into a mature stage, it became a routine low-priority decision involving primarily the purchasing function. These changes are illustrated below:

Stage of Product Life Cycle	*Type of Purchase Situation*	*Size of DMU*	*Key Functions Influencing the Purchase Decision*
Introduction	Judgmental new task	Large	Engineering and R&D
Growth	Simple modified rebuy	Medium	Production and top management
Maturity	Routine low priority	Small	Purchasing

TABLE 19-5

Decision Process in Purchasing Microcomputers for a Large Insurance Company

Stages of the Purchase Decision Process	*Key Influences within Decision-Making Unit*	*Influences Outside the Decision-Making Unit*
Problem recognition	Office manager Sales manager	Field sales agents Administrative clerks Accounting manager Microcomputer sales representative
Information search	Data processing manager Office manager Purchasing manager	Operations personnel Microcomputer sales representative Other corporate users Office systems consultant
Alternative evaluation	General management Data processing manager Office manager Sales manager Purchasing manager	Office systems consultant Microcomputer sales representative
Purchase decision	General management Office manager Purchasing manager	
Product usage	Office manager Sales manager	Field sales agents Administrative clerks Accounting personnel Microcomputer sales representative
Evaluation	Office manager Sales manager General management	Field sales agents Administrative clerks Accounting personnel

Microsegmentation As described earlier, macrosegmentation allows a marketer to group customers with like needs and firmographics into market segments. **Microsegmentation** is the grouping of organizational customers on the basis of similar decision-making units or styles. For example, customer organizations that are heavily dominated by technical people might be segmented from those dominated by purchasing agents and finance managers. This type of segmentation can be the primary segmentation approach or it can be used to further segment macrosegments that were defined based on firmographics.[31]

Refer back to Table 19-2. This market was first segmented based on firmographics into 12 macrosegments. These segments had a number of distinct product and service needs. However, as shown in the table, each of these 12 segments was further segmented into microsegments based on their level of loyalty to the firm or a competitor. The results of this two-level segmentation approach were increased profits and market share.

Organizational Decisions

Because organizational decisions typically involve more individuals in more complex decision tasks than do individual or household decisions, marketing efforts to affect this process are much more complex.[32] Shown in Table 19-5 are stages in the decision process

Group Involvement in the Decision Process in Hi-Tech Organizations **TABLE 19-6**

	Percent Involved in Each Stage of Decision Process					
Stages of Decision Process	*Board of Directors*	*Top Management*	*Head of Department*	*Lab Technician or Operator*	*Purchasing Manager or Buyer*	*Finance Manager Accountant*
Recognizing the need to purchase	7%	26%	70%	30%	0%	3%
Determining product specifications	0	33	74	33	3	0
Deciding which suppliers to consider	3	33	56	14	19	0
Obtaining quotations and proposals	0	26	52	19	14	3
Evaluating quotations and proposals	7	63	63	3	11	7
Final product or supplier selection	21	48	48	7	11	0

Source: Reprinted from *Industrial Marketing Management,* Vol. 15, R. Abratt, "Industrial Buying in Hi-Tech Markets," p. 295. Copyright 1986, with permission from Elsevier Science.

and sources of influence at each stage in a large insurance company's decision to add microcomputers to its office management function. Altogether, there were 12 separate sources of influence, each with different levels of influence and affecting different stages of the purchase decision process.

To have a chance to win this large contract, a selling firm must provide relevant information to each source of influence. This is not a simple task, given that each source of influence has different motives and different criteria for evaluating alternative products, as well as different media habits.

Problem Recognition In Table 19-5, the sales manager and office manager played the key role in recognizing the need to add microcomputers to their organization. Recognition of this problem, however, could have come about in several ways. In this instance, a continuing problem between field sales agents and internal administrative clerks led the office manager and sales manager to recognize the problem. Aiding their recognition of the problem were accounting personnel and microcomputer sales representatives who called on the office manager. The combination of these sources of influence eventually led to an increased level of importance and the subsequent stage of information search.

Table 19-6 demonstrates that in hi-tech markets, the head of a department is most likely to recognize a problem or need to purchase. Perhaps more important is that purchasing managers are not a source of problem recognition. This points out the danger of salespeople only calling on purchasing people. As shown in Table 19-6, problem recognition and determining specifications often occur without much involvement of purchasing personnel.

ILLUSTRATION 19-5

Internet marketing to organizational buyers is growing exponentially.

Courtesy Value America.

Information Search Information search can be both formal and informal.[33] Site visits to evaluate a potential vendor, laboratory tests of a new product or prototype, and investigation of possible product specifications are part of formal information search. Informal information search can occur during discussions with sales representatives, while attending trade shows, or reading industry-specific journals. Industrial buyers search for information both to help make the best decision and to support their actions and recommendations within the organization.[34]

Increasingly organizational buyers are searching for product and price information on the Internet. Business-to-business Internet sales are exploding and are much larger than household sales (see Illustration 19-5).

Evaluation and Selection The evaluation of possible vendors and selection of a given vendor often follows a **two-stage decision process.**[35] The first stage is making the buyer's approved vendor list. A conjunctive decision process is very common. Using this decision rule, the organization screens out potential vendors that do not meet all its minimum criteria. In a government missile purchase, 41 potential manufacturers of a missile electronics system were first identified. After site visits to inspect manufacturing capability and resources, this list of 41 was pared down to 11 that met the government's minimum criteria.

A second stage of organizational decision making could involve other decision rules such as disjunctive, lexicographic, compensatory, or elimination-by-aspects. For the government purchase discussed above, a lexicographic decision process was next used, with the most important criterion being price. Using this decision rule, two vendors were selected.

The process of evaluation and selection is further complicated by the fact that different members of the decision-making unit have differing evaluative criteria. In Table 19-7, we

TABLE 19-7 Evaluative Criteria and Organizational Role

Evaluative Criteria Used in Purchase Decision	Functional Role in Organization			
	Purchasing	*Management*	*Engineering*	*Operations*
Vendor offers broad line	X	X		
Many product options available	X	X		
Ease of maintenance of equipment			X	X
Competence of service technicians		X	X	X
Overall quality of service		X	X	
Product warranty	X	X	X	X
Delivery (lead time)				X
Time needed to install equipment	X			X
Construction costs	X		X	X
Vendor has the lowest price	X	X	X	
Financial stability of vendor	X		X	X
Vendor willing to negotiate price	X			
Vendor reputation for quality	X	X	X	
Salesperson competence		X	X	X
Compatibility with equipment	X	X		
Available computer interface	X			

Source: Adapted from D. H. McQuiston and R. G. Walters, "The Evaluative Criteria of Industrial Buyers: Implications for Sales Training," *The Journal of Business and Industrial Marketing,* Summer–Fall 1989, p. 74.

see that purchasing, management, engineering, and operations use differing sets of performance criteria. For example, purchasing is more concerned with pricing policies, terms and conditions, and order status; engineers are more concerned with product knowledge, product operations, and applications knowledge. A salesperson calling on these accounts would need to understand and respond to the unique as well as the shared criteria of these purchase influencers.

It is generally assumed that business purchases are strictly economic, with the goal of maximizing the profits of the purchasing organization.[36] We have indicated several times in this chapter that power, prestige, security, and similar noneconomic criteria also play important roles in business purchase decisions. A recent study found that there are organizations that buy "green" similar to the "green consumers" we described in Chapter 3. These organizations have policies and/or individual champions for socially responsible buying behavior by the organization.[37] Firms wishing to do business with these organizations must meet their requirements for products produced in an environmentally sound manner. The ad in Illustration 19-6 would appeal to these firms.

Purchase and Decision Implementation Once the decision to buy from a particular organization has been made, the method of purchase must be determined. From the seller's point of view, this means how and when they will get paid. In many purchases, payment is not made until delivery. Others involve progress payments. For a firm that is working on the construction of a building or a highway, or developing a new military aircraft that will take several years, the method of payment is critical. Many businesses offer a price discount for payment within 10 days. Others may extend credit and encourage extended payment over time.

ILLUSTRATION 19-6

Firms make decisions for more than economic reasons.

Courtesy Georgia Pacific.

On an international basis, purchase implementation and method of payment are even more critical. Some countries prohibit the removal of capital from their country without an offsetting purchase. This led Caterpillar Tractor Company to sell earthmoving equipment in South America in exchange for raw materials, such as copper, which it could sell or use in its manufacturing operations. Another company signed a long-term contract at a very low price when the exchange rate favored the seller. This ensured the seller a good price when the exchange rate fluctuated and provided the buyer with a lower-than-average price.

TABLE 19-8 Customer and Management Perceptions of the Importance of After-Sale Services

After-Sales Service Item	Importance of Service Item			Ratings of Service		
	Customers	*Managers*	*Gap*	*Customers*	*Managers*	*Gap*
Attitude and behavior of technician	11.5	8.4	3.1	7.04	7.56	−.52
Availability of technical service staff	16.1	12.9	3.2	7.64	8.12	−.48
Repair time when service needed	15.4	17.4	−2.0	6.36	7.71	−1.35
Dispatch of breakdown call	15.5	9.8	5.7	6.92	7.57	−.65
Availability of spare parts during call	10.0	10.1	−.1	7.16	7.49	−.33
Service contract options	5.2	6.8	−1.6	6.88	7.48	−.60
Price–performance ratio for services rendered	8.1	14.5	−6.4	6.12	7.30	−1.18
Response time when service needed	18.2	20.1	−1.9	5.92	7.09	−1.17

Source: H. Kasper and J. Lemmink. "After-Sales Service Quality: Views between Industrial Customers and Service Managers," *Industrial Marketing Management* 18 (1989), p. 203.

Consumer Insight 19-1

Organizational Relationship Marketing

W. W. Grainger distributes maintenance, repair, and operating (MRO) supplies to organizational buyers. To enhance its services to its customers, it formed Grainger Consulting Services (GCS), which helps customers understand and minimize the total cost of MRO supplies management.

Pharma Labs (a disguised name) is a pharmaceuticals manufacturer. GCS worked with Pharma on a fee basis to analyze its MRO supplies cost. It applied its models and research methods to four primary areas: processes (from how the need for items is identified to payment of invoices), products (product price, usage factors, brand standardization and application), inventory (on-hand value and carrying costs), and suppliers (performance, consolidation, and value-adding services provided).

Among other outcomes of the study, GCS recommended that Pharma consolidate its MRO supplies purchases. Pharma agreed and initiated a national account agreement with Grainger. Grainger placed a representative on-site with Pharma to manage the purchase and inventory processes. This freed a Pharma maintenance technician who had been purchasing MRO supplies full-time to return to more value-adding activities in his department.

After six months, the various actions taken by Pharma based on the GCS report produced $387,000 in cost savings. Grainger's sales to Pharma increased from $50,000 to $350,000 per year! Thus, both companies benefited from their relationship.

Critical Thinking Questions

1. Is this truly relationship marketing? Why or why not?
2. What opportunities does Grainger's approach suggest for other types of firms marketing to organizations? To households?

Source: Reprinted by permission of *Harvard Business Review.* From "Business Marketing: Understanding What Customers Value," by James C. Anderson and James A. Narus, November 1998.

Terms and conditions—payments, warranties, delivery dates, and so forth—are both complex and critical in business-to-business markets. One U.S. manufacturer of steam turbines lost a large order to a foreign manufacturer because its warranty was written too much to the advantage of the seller.

Usage and Postpurchase Evaluation After-purchase evaluations of products are typically more formal for organizational purchases than are household evaluations of purchases. In mining applications, for example, a product's life is broken down into different components such that total life-cycle cost can be assessed. Many mines will operate different brands of equipment side-by-side to determine the life-cycle costs of each before repurchasing one in larger quantities.

A major component of postpurchase evaluation is the service the seller provides during and after the sale.[38] Table 19-8 indicates the importance that one group of customers and managers assigned to different aspects of after-sales service. Notice that the managers did not have a very good understanding of what was important to their customers. The table indicates that they also viewed their service performance more favorably than their customers did. This firm seems unlikely to produce satisfied customers.

Similarly to households, dissatisfied organizational buyers may switch suppliers and/or engage in negative word-of-mouth communications. Firms marketing to organizations pursue strategies similar to those followed by consumer marketers in dealing with dissatisfied customers. They seek to minimize dissatisfaction and to encourage those who become dissatisfied to complain to them and to no one else.[39]

Relationship marketing is at least as important in industrial marketing as it is in consumer marketing. The basic idea at the organizational level is for the seller to work closely with the buyer over time with the objective of enhancing the buyer's profits or operations while also making a profit.[40] Consumer Insight 19-1 describes a successful example of organizational relationship marketing.

SUMMARY

Like households, organizations make many buying decisions. In some instances, these buying decisions are routine replacement decisions; at other times, they involve new, complex purchase decisions. Six purchase situations are common to organizational buying: *casual, routine low priority, simple modified rebuy, judgmental new task, complex modified rebuy,* and *strategic new task*. Each of these purchase situations will elicit different organizational behaviors.

Organizations have a style or manner of operating that we characterize as organizational culture. *Firmographics* (organization characteristics such as size, activities, objectives, location, and industry category, and characteristics of the composition of the organization such as the gender, age, education, and income distribution of employees) have a major influence on organizational culture. The process of grouping buyer organizations into market segments on the basis of similar firmographics is called *macrosegmentation*.

Reference groups play a key role in business-to-business markets. *Reference group infrastructures* exist in most organizational markets. These reference groups often include third-party suppliers, distributors, industry experts, trade publications, financial analysts, and key customers. *Lead users* have been shown to be a key reference group that influences both the reference group infrastructure and other potential users.

Other external influences on organizational culture include the local culture in which the organization operates and the type of government it confronts. Internal factors affecting organizational culture include organizational values, perception, learning, memory, motives, and emotions.

Organizations hold values that influence the organization's style. Individuals in the organization also hold these values in varying degrees. When there is a high degree of shared values between the individuals and the organization, decision making occurs smoothly.

Organizations also develop images, have motives, and learn. Seller organizations can affect how they are perceived through a variety of communication alternatives. Print advertising, direct mail, and sales calls are the most common. Whereas organizations have "rational" motives, their decisions are influenced and made by people with emotions. A seller organization has to understand and satisfy both to be successful. Organizations learn through their experiences and information-processing activities.

The organizational decision process involves problem recognition, information search, evaluation and selection, purchase implementation, and postpurchase evaluation. Quite often, a seller organization can influence the information search such that it establishes the choice criteria to be used in evaluation and selection. A conjunctive process is typical in establishing an evoked set, and other decision rules are used for selecting a specific vendor.

Purchase implementation is more complex and the terms and conditions more important than in household decisions. How payment is made is of major importance. Finally, use and postpurchase evaluation are often quite formal. Many organizations will conduct detailed in-use tests to determine the life-cycle costs of competing products or spend considerable time evaluating a new product before placing large orders. Satisfaction is dependent on a variety of criteria and on the opinions of many different people. To achieve customer satisfaction, each of these individuals has to be satisfied with the criteria important to him or her.

KEY TERMS

Business-to-business marketing 676
Buying center 690
Corporate culture 677
Decision-making units (DMUs) 690
Firmographics 678
Lead user 683
Macrosegmentation 681
Microsegmentation 692
Organizational culture 677
Reference group infrastructure 683
Terms and conditions 697
Two-stage decision process 694

INTERNET EXERCISES

1. Evaluate the Detroit office of J. Walter Thompson's Web site (http://www.jwtworld.com).
2. Evaluate MCI's Web site (http://www.mci.com).
3. Evaluate Advertising Age's Web site (http://adage.com).
4. Pick an industrial market and compare the Web sites of the top three firms. Which is best? Why?

REVIEW QUESTIONS

1. How can an organization have a culture? What factors contribute to different organizational cultures?
2. How would different organizational activities and objectives affect organizational culture?
3. What are *organizational values?* How do they differ from personal values?
4. What is meant by *shared values?*
5. What are *firmographics,* and how do they influence organizational culture?
6. Define *macrosegmentation,* and describe the variables used to create a macrosegmentation of an organizational market.
7. Define *microsegmentation,* and describe the variables used to create microsegments.
8. What types of reference groups exist in organizational markets?
9. What are *lead users,* and how do they influence word-of-mouth communication and the sales of a new product?
10. What is a *decision-making unit?* How does it vary by purchase situation?
11. How are purchase decisions made when there is disagreement within the DMU?
12. How can a seller organization influence perceptions of a buyer organization?
13. What are *organizational motives?*
14. What is a *two-stage decision process?*
15. Why can purchase implementation be a critical part of the organizational decision process?
16. What are the six purchase situations commonly encountered by organizations? How do organizations typically respond to each situation?

DISCUSSION QUESTIONS

17. Describe three organizations with distinctly different organizational cultures. Explain why they have different organizational cultures and the factors that have helped shape the style of each.
18. Describe how IBM might vary in its organizational culture from the following. Justify your response.
    a. Dell Computer
    b. Compaq
19. Discuss how the following pairs differ from each other in terms of organizational activities and objectives. Discuss how these differences influence organizational cultures.
    a. Your university/a large consulting firm
    b. The Navy/the United Way
    c. Amazon.com/Sears
    d. Kmart/Disney World
20. What determines whether an individual's values or the organization's values will prevail in a purchase decision (given that they conflict)?
21. Discuss how IBM might use a macrosegmentation strategy to sell computers to businesses.
22. Discuss how IBM might use a microsegmentation strategy to sell computers to businesses.
23. Discuss how a small biotechnology firm could influence the reference group infrastructure and the lead users to accelerate adoption of its products in the market.
24. Discuss the marketing implications of the decision-making structure shown in Table 19-5. Then, using the information shown in Table 19-5, discuss how you would develop your marketing strategy for this purchase situation.

25. "Industrial purchases, unlike consumer purchases, do not have an emotional component." Comment.
26. Review Table 19-2. For what other industries would this be a sound approach?
27. For each of the six purchase situations described in the chapter, describe a typical purchase for the following:
    a. A large manufacturer
    b. A small advertising agency
    c. The Marines
    d. Your university
    e. A fast-food chain

APPLICATION ACTIVITIES

28. Interview an appropriate person at a large and at a small organization and ask each to identify purchase situations that could be described as casual, routine low priority, simple modified rebuy, judgmental new task, complex modified rebuy, and strategic new task. For each organization and purchase situation, determine the following:
    a. Size and functional representation of the decision-making unit.
    b. The number of choice criteria considered.
    c. Length of the decision process.
    d. Number of vendors or suppliers considered.
29. For a given industrial organization, arrange to review the trade publications to which it subscribes. Identify three industrial ads in these publications that vary in copy length, one very short (under 100 words), one with approximately 150 words, and one very long (over 250 words). Arrange to have these ads read by three or four people in the organization. Have each reader rank the ads in terms of preference (independent of product or manufacturer preference). Then ask each to describe what they like or dislike about each ad. Discern the role that copy length played in their evaluation.
30. Review two issues of three magazines targeting organization buyers or members. What percent of the ads contain emotional or other noneconomic appeals?
31. Interview a representative from a commercial, governmental, nonprofit, and cooperative organization. For each, determine its firmographics, activities, and objectives. Then relate these differences to differences in the organizational cultures of the organizations.
32. Interview a person responsible for purchasing for a business or government agency. Have that person describe and evaluate any attempts at relationship marketing by its suppliers. What do you conclude?
33. For a given organization, identify its reference groups. Create a hierarchical diagram, as shown in Figure 19-3, and discuss how this organization could influence groups that would in turn create favorable communication concerning this organization.

REFERENCES

1. G. Conlon, "True Romance," *Sales & Marketing Management,* May 1996, pp. 86–87.
2. C. Kosek, "Business-to-Business Grabs $51.7 Billion," *Advertising Age,* June 1996, p. S-4.
3. See R. Deshande and F. E. Webster, Jr., "Organizational Culture and Marketing," *Journal of Marketing,* January 1989, pp. 3–15; and S. Kitchell, "Corporate Culture, Environmental Adaptation, and Innovation Adoption," *Journal of the Academy of Marketing Science,* Summer 1995, pp. 195–205.
4. H. Hlavacek and B. C. Ames, "Segmenting Industrial and Hi-Tech Markets," *Journal of Business Strategy,* Fall 1986, pp. 39–50.
5. K. M. File and R. A. Prince, "A Psychographic Segmentation of Industrial Family Businesses," *Industrial Marketing Management,* May 1996, pp. 223–34.
6. G. Brewer, "An American in Shanghai," *Sales & Marketing Management,* November 1997, p. 42. See also N. D. Albers-Miller and B. Gelb, "Business Advertising Appeals as a Mirror of Cultural Dimensions," *Journal of Advertising,* Winter 1996, pp. 57–70.
7. See R. L. Griffith and L. G. Pol, "Segmenting Industrial Markets," *Industrial Marketing Management,* January 1994, pp. 39–46.
8. G. Brewer, "Selling an Intangible," *Sales & Marketing Management,* January 1998, pp. 52–58.
9. See S. P. Kalafatis and V. Cheston, "Normative Models and Practical Applications of Segmentation in Business Markets," *Industrial Marketing Management,* no. 26 (1997), pp. 519–30.
10. See F. Gibb, "To Give or Not to Give," *Sales & Marketing Management,* September 1994, pp. 136–39.

11. J. Kaplan, *Startup* (New York: Houghton Mifflin, 1995). p. 120.
12. Adapted from J. H. Martin, J. M. Daley, and H. B. Burdg, "Buying Influences and Perceptions of Transportation Services," *Industrial Marketing Management,* no. 17 (1988), pp. 311–12.
13. A. N. Link and J. Neufeld, "Innovation vs. Imitation: Investigating Alternative R&D Strategies," *Applied Economics,* no. 18 (1986), pp. 1359–63.
14. G. Badovick and S. Beatty, "Shared Organizational Values: Measurement and Impact upon Strategic Marketing Implementation," *Journal of the Academy of Marketing Science,* Spring 1987, pp. 19–26.
15. J. F. Tanner, Jr., "Predicting Organizational Buyer Behavior," *Journal of Business and Industrial Marketing,* Fall 1990, pp. 57–64.
16. D. I. Gilliland and W. J. Johnston, "Toward a Model of Business-to-Business Marketing Communications Effects," *Industrial Marketing Management,* no. 26 (1997), pp. 15–29.
17. See S. M. Mudambi, P. Doyle, and V. Wong, "An Exploration of Branding in Industrial Markets," *Industrial Marketing Management,* no. 26 (1997), pp. 433–46; and J. Lapierre, "The Role of Corporate Image in the Evaluation of Business-to-Business Professional Services," *Journal of Professional Services Marketing,*" no. 1 (1998), pp. 21–41.
18. L. Hochwald, "It's the Sizzle that Sells," *Sales & Marketing Management,* April 1997, pp. 51.
19. *CARR Report No. 120.3* (Boston: Cahners Publishing Co., undated).
20. "Study: Increase Business Ads to Increase Sales," *Marketing News,* March 14, 1988, p. 13.
21. M. Marchetti, "Hey Buddy, Can You Spare $113.25?" *Sales & Marketing Management,* August 1997, pp. 69–77.
22. G. Conlon, "A Day in the Life of Sales," *Sales & Marketing Management,* September 1997, pp. 42–63.
23. See E. D. Honeycut, Jr., T. B. Flaherty, and K. Benassi, "Marketing Industrial Products on the Internet," *Industrial Marketing Management,* no. 27 (1998), pp. 63–72.
24. See J. M. Sinkula, "Market Information Processing and Organizational Learning," *Journal of Marketing,* January 1994, pp. 35–45; and G. T. M. Hult and E. L. Nichols, Jr., "The Organizational Buyer Behavior Learning Organization," *Industrial Marketing Management,* May 1996, pp. 197–207.
25. D. A. Garvin, "Building a Learning Organization," *Harvard Business Review,* July 1993, pp. 78–91; and S. F. Slater and J. C. Narver, "Market Orientation and the Learning Organization," *Journal of Marketing,* July 1995, pp. 63–74.
26. See W. J. Johnson and J. E. Lewin, "Organizational Buying Behavior," *Journal of Business Research,* January 1996, pp. 1–15.
27. M. D. Bunn, "Taxonomy of Buying Decision Approaches," *Journal of Marketing,* January 1993, pp. 38–56. See also R. R. Dholakia, J. L. Johnson, A. J. Della Bitta, and N. Dholakia, "Decision-Making Time in Organizational Buying Behavior," *Journal of the Academy of Marketing Science,* Fall 1993, pp. 281–92; and M. D. Bunn, "Key Aspects of Organizational Buying," *Journal of the Academy of Marketing Science,* Spring 1994, pp. 160–69.
28. H. Brown and R. Brucker, "Charting the Industrial Buying Stream," *Industrial Marketing Management,* no. 19 (1990), pp. 55–61.
29. E. J. Wilson, G. L. Lilien, and D. T. Wilson, "Developing and Testing a Contingency Paradigm of Group Choice in Organizational Buying," *Journal of Marketing Research,* November 1991, pp. 452–66; R. Ventakesh, A. K. Kohli, and G. Zaltman, "Influence Strategies in Buying Centers," *Journal of Marketing,* October 1995, pp. 71–82; and M. A. Farrell and B. Schroder, "Influence Strategies in Organizational Buying Decisions," *Industrial Marketing Management,* no. 25 (1996), pp. 293–303.
30. M. Berkowitz, "New Product Adoption by the Buying Organization: Who Are the Real Influencers?" *Industrial Marketing Management,* no. 15 (1986), pp. 33–43.
31. See L. Meredith, "A Customer Evaluation System," *Business & Industrial Marketing* 8, no. 1 (1993), pp. 58–72.
32. S. J. Puri and C. M. Sashi, "Anatomy of a Complex Computer Purchase," *Industrial Marketing Management,* January 1994, pp. 17–27; and E. Day and J. C. Barksdale, Jr., "Organizational Purchasing of Professional Services," *Journal of Business and Industrial Marketing* 9, no. 3 (1994), pp. 44–51.
33. See A. M. Weiss and J. B. Heide, "The Nature of Organizational Search in High-Technology Markets," *Journal of Marketing Research,* May 1993, pp. 220–33.
34. P. M. Doney and G. M. Armstrong, "Effects of Accountability on Symbolic Information Search and Information Analysis by Organizational Buyers," *Journal of the Academy of Marketing Science,* Winter 1996, pp. 57–65.
35. G. Gordon, R. Calantone, and C. A. diBenedetto, "How Electrical Contractors Choose Distributors," *Industrial Marketing Management,* no. 20 (1991), pp. 29–42; E. Day and H. C. Barksdale, Jr., "How Firms Select Professional Services," *Industrial Marketing Management,* no. 21 (1992), pp. 85–91; A. G. Lockett and P. Naude, "Winning a Large Order," *Industrial Marketing Management,* no. 20 (1991), pp. 169–75; and J. B. Heide and W. M. Weiss, "Vendor Consideration and Switching Behavior for Buyers in High-Technology Markets," *Journal of Marketing,* July 1995, pp. 30–43.
36. See K. N. Thompson, B. J. Coe, and J. R. Lewis, "Gauging the Value of Suppliers' Products," *Journal of Business and Industrial Marketing* 9, no. 2, pp. 29–40.
37. M. E. Drumwright, "Socially Responsible Organizational Buying," *Journal of Marketing,* July 1994, pp. 1–19.
38. K. Smith, "Service Aspects of Industrial Products," *Industrial Marketing Management,* no. 27 (1998), pp. 83–93.
39. S. W. Hansen, J. E. Swan, and T. L. Powers, "Encouraging 'Friendly' Complaint Behavior in Industrial Markets," *Industrial Marketing Management,* no. 25 (1996), pp. 271–81.
40. D. J. Flint, R. B. Woodruff, and S. F. Gardial, "Customer Value Change in Industrial Marketing Relationships," *Industrial Marketing Management,* no. 26 (1997), pp. 163–75; and M. H. Morris, J. Brunyee, and M. Page, "Relationship Marketing in Practice," *Industrial Marketing Management,* no. 27 (1998), pp. 359–71.

Cases

5-1 Mack Trucks' Integrated Communications Campaign

Mack Trucks, Inc., was established in 1900. For 90 years it dominated the construction and refuse segments of the Class 8 (large) truck market. In fact, the expression "Built like a Mack truck" came to stand for solid, rugged construction. Unfortunately, 70 percent of the demand for large trucks is in the highway or over-the-road hauling segment, and this is also the segment with the highest growth rate.

Until the late 1980s, Mack did not compete in the over-the-road segments. The products it did supply were not well received. In 1990, Mack was purchased by the French automaker Renault V. I. A plan to become a major competitor in the critical highway market segment was developed and implemented. The first stage involved the development and launch of two new over-the-road truck lines. According to Brian Taylor, Mack's vice president of marketing:

> We developed a product line that had good ergonomics. It was roomy and it had a smooth ride, but we faced a challenge with communicating those changes to our customers.

The firm hired Carmichael Lynch and Carmichael Lynch Spong, two firms specializing in marketing research, advertising, and public relations, to work with Mack to develop an integrated communications campaign. The firm began with a series of primary and secondary research studies.

Research Studies

Four basic sources of information were used to guide the development of the integrated campaign.

1. Perceptual maps were derived that identified how Mack trucks were perceived relative to competing brands. The maps revealed that they were viewed as durable but not very comfortable.
2. Focus group sessions and one-on-one interviews with current and prospective Mack customers isolated additional driver and operator needs and concerns. This research helped identify the criteria the trucks would need to meet to be in the buyer's consideration set.
3. Industry trade publications frequently conduct surveys of fleet operators, truck owners, and truck drivers. These surveys cover a wide range of issues, including desired truck features and shortcomings. These surveys were obtained and analyzed.
4. News clippings and other sources of data describing quality or service problems Mack had experienced in the past were also studied.

These studies indicated that Mack faced a significant communications challenge. According to Taylor, "'Built like a Mack truck' served us well in our core business, but it did not have a good connotation in the over-the-road segment. And that was a perception we had to change." Jack Supple, president of Carmichael Lynch, stated the challenge this way: "We had to create a campaign—an impression—in which customers would be willing to suspend their disbelief that Mack was more than they knew."

Objectives

Three primary objectives were developed for the campaign:

1. Change the perception of Mack trucks from "rugged, tough, and uncomfortable to drive," to "the most comfortable and driveable over-the-road trucks."
2. Change the perception of Mack engines from "heavy, expensive, and low tech," to "ideal for over-the-road applications, very economical and reliable."
3. Increase the number of over-the-road fleet buyers who have Mack in their consideration sets.

Accomplishing these objectives would require a change in Mack's current positioning from:

> Mack is a great old brand. But they can't compete for my business because they don't have a package that meets my needs.

to:

> Mack's turning things around. The CH model with the E7 engine is the right combination for my fleet. Plus, these guys really want my business.

This leads to the following positioning statement:

> The new Mack is the proud result of combining Mack tradition and unequaled driveability.

The Communications Strategy

The communications strategy integrated advertising, sales promotion, direct marketing, and public relations. For the advertising campaign, Mack's traditional bulldog was made hip in six new print ads with racing stripes, sunglasses, a champagne glass, or other symbols of change and uniqueness. The ads were colorful with limited text. Each focused on one key attribute such as fuel economy. The tagline for the campaign was "Drive one and you'll know."

The sales promotion program consisted of the "Bulldog National Test Drive Tour." This tour allowed truckers to test-drive a new Mack truck at truckstops and trade shows throughout the country.

The direct marketing program included an 800 number in all print advertising that readers could use to get information about the nearest dealer, the test drive promotion, or to request specific model information. The "Fleet Focus" part of the campaign mailed materials to nearly 1,200 non-Mack fleet customers urging them to consider Mack in their next purchase and providing material to support that recommendation. Dealers were provided with qualified lead cards generated from the 800 number, the test drives, and the direct-mail program.

Throughout the campaign, numerous news releases and articles were provided to trade publications. There was also an eight-city media tour in which Mack discussed its commitment to the public and the over-the-road segment. Mack redesigned the quarterly, 24-page *Bulldog* magazine to reflect the firm's customer service orientation.

Discussion Questions

1. Is this program likely to succeed? Why or why not? What, if anything, would you change?
2. Is a "hip" bulldog an appropriate symbol for a serious industrial product like a truck?
3. Why are Mack and its agencies so concerned with customer perception when its products are so good?
4. What criteria do you think fleet buyers have for including a brand in their consideration set? How do you think they choose from among the brands in the consideration set?
5. Why did the "built like a Mack truck" theme not work for the over-the-road segment?
6. How would you alter the campaign for use in these countries?
   a. Japan
   b. Germany
   c. China
   d. Brazil

Source: "Mack Ads Propel Sales." Reprinted with permission from *CRA/Advertising Age*, September 18, 1995.

5-2 Kenestic Inc.

Kenestic, Inc., specializes in the manufacture and marketing of molded plastic products with unique durability, resistance to breakage, and long life. These products are used as components of other products such as automobiles, planes, and manufacturing equipment. Over time, Kenestic has developed an expertise in molded plastic that goes far beyond that of most of its competitors. In fact, most of Kenestic's products command a 15 to 25 percent price premium because of their unique performance capabilities.

Products and Customer Needs

Kenestic product development has focused on tough applications in which the wear life (how long the product lasts) and problems with breakage are important factors in buying decisions. These are applications in which the ability to mold plastic into unique shapes and its light weight give it an advantage over metal products but for which strength and impact resistance requirements are higher than normal. In these applications, product failure often results in considerable repair expenses, loss of productivity, inconvenience, and occasionally physical danger. Kenestic's target market consists of firms that Kenestic management feels make products that could use Kenestic's superior performance plastic.

Kenestic recently surveyed its customers' needs. Shown in Table A are customer importance ratings of purchase criteria and customer perceptions of Kenestic relative to competitors. On the top three most important purchase criteria, Kenestic is rated

TABLE A

Kenestic's Current Customers' Needs and Kenestic's Perceived Performance

Purchase Criteria	Importance	Competitive Position
Wear life of product	25%	Very good
Breakage	20	Very good
After-sale support	15	Very good
Price of product	14	Poor
Availability	10	Very poor
Delivery	10	Poor
Design productivity	6	Poor

TABLE B

Kenestic's Noncustomers' Needs and Kenestic's Perceived Performance

Purchase Criteria	Importance	Competitive Position
Availability	30%	Very poor
Design productivity	25	Poor
Price	20	Poor
Delivery	15	Poor
Wear life	5	Very good
After-sale support	3	Very good
Breakage	2	Very good

ahead of its competition. While Kenestic's prices are higher, customers are willing to buy its products because of its superior performance on the top three purchase criteria. For the three least important purchase criteria, Kenestic is rated behind its competitors.

Noncustomer Survey

The customer needs and perceptions shown in Table A are those of existing customers served by Kenestic. Because the noncustomer base within its target market was many times larger than its current customer base, Kenestic also conducted a noncustomer survey to find out more about noncustomer needs and perceptions of Kenestic.

A portion of the noncustomer survey results are shown in Table B. While noncustomer perceptions of Kenestic relative to competition are similar to those of existing customers, their needs are very different. Noncustomers rated availability, price, and design productivity as their three most important purchase criteria. These are among the bottom four purchase criteria for existing customers.

Customer Decision Process

The wide difference in customer and noncustomer needs led to a recognition that the company did not adequately know how purchase decisions were made by either existing customers or noncustomers. While Tables A and B demonstrate differences in purchase criteria, these results do not provide sufficient insight into how these purchase criteria were used in a purchase decision. To find out, a purchase decision study was conducted, using a random sample of both customers and noncustomers.

The results of the purchase decision survey are shown in Figure A.

In making a decision to buy, customers first ask whether wear life or breakage is a serious issue. In 90 percent of user applications, it is not a problem. Thus, Kenestic's key benefits are not relevant for 90 percent of its potential customers' applications.

If the application does warrant concern for wear life and/or breakage, availability is the next key concern. Kenestic products are not available when needed 30 percent of the time. If they are available, decision makers look at price in relationship to the product's economic value—the overall cost of the product including price, savings from increased wear life and potential damage from breakage, and added value derived from after-sale support. In 75 percent of the applications where wear life and/or breakage are a problem, Kenestic wins the business. However, this sequence results in only slightly over a 5 percent share.

In applications where wear life or breakage is not a concern, the decision process focused on design productivity, where Kenestic was weak. Because of

Customer Decision Process **FIGURE A**

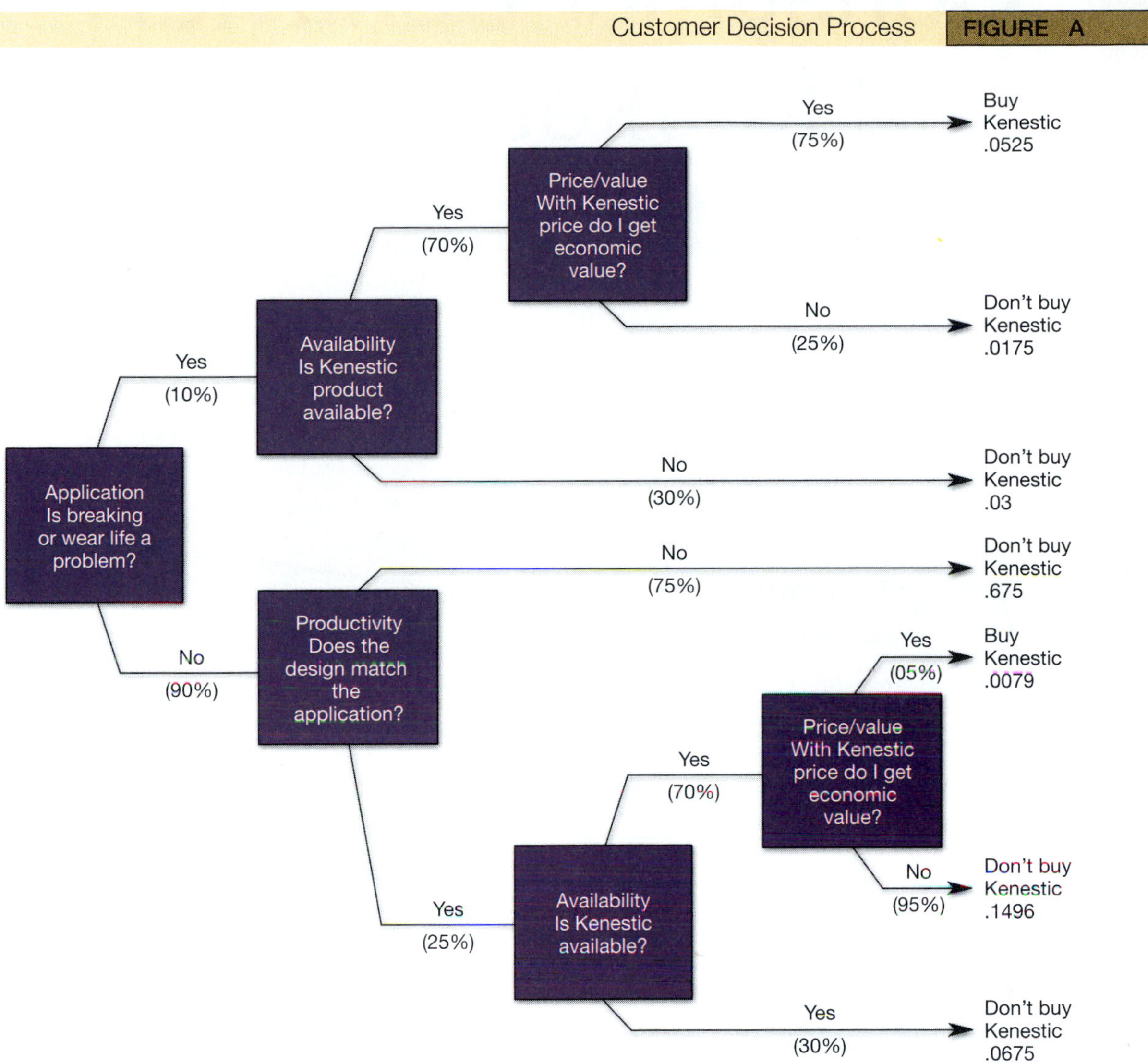

poor performance in this area, the company was not considered in 75 percent of these applications. When the Kenestic product did fit the application, it was available 70 percent of the time. However, because higher price was not offset with savings due to wear life, breakage, or after-sales support, Kenestic only obtained 5 percent of these purchases. The net impact is less than a 1 percent share of these applications.

Figure A demonstrates where and why Kenestic obtains its market share, but more importantly, it reveals where and why it loses market share. While its overall market share is around 6 percent, it has almost a 50 percent market share when wear life and breakage are important. Outside this area of application, the company is unable to obtain a 1 percent market share.

Discussion Questions

1. What are the limitations to looking at just customer or noncustomer ratings of purchase criteria?
2. What additional benefits can be obtained by understanding how purchase decisions are made?
3. Where should Kenestic focus its efforts, and what would be the impact of these efforts?
4. Explain how Kenestic's high price is offset in applications where wear life, breakage, and after-sale support are important. Also, explain why the economic value of the product is less attractive in applications where wear life and breakage are not a concern.

part six

Consumer Behavior and Marketing Regulation

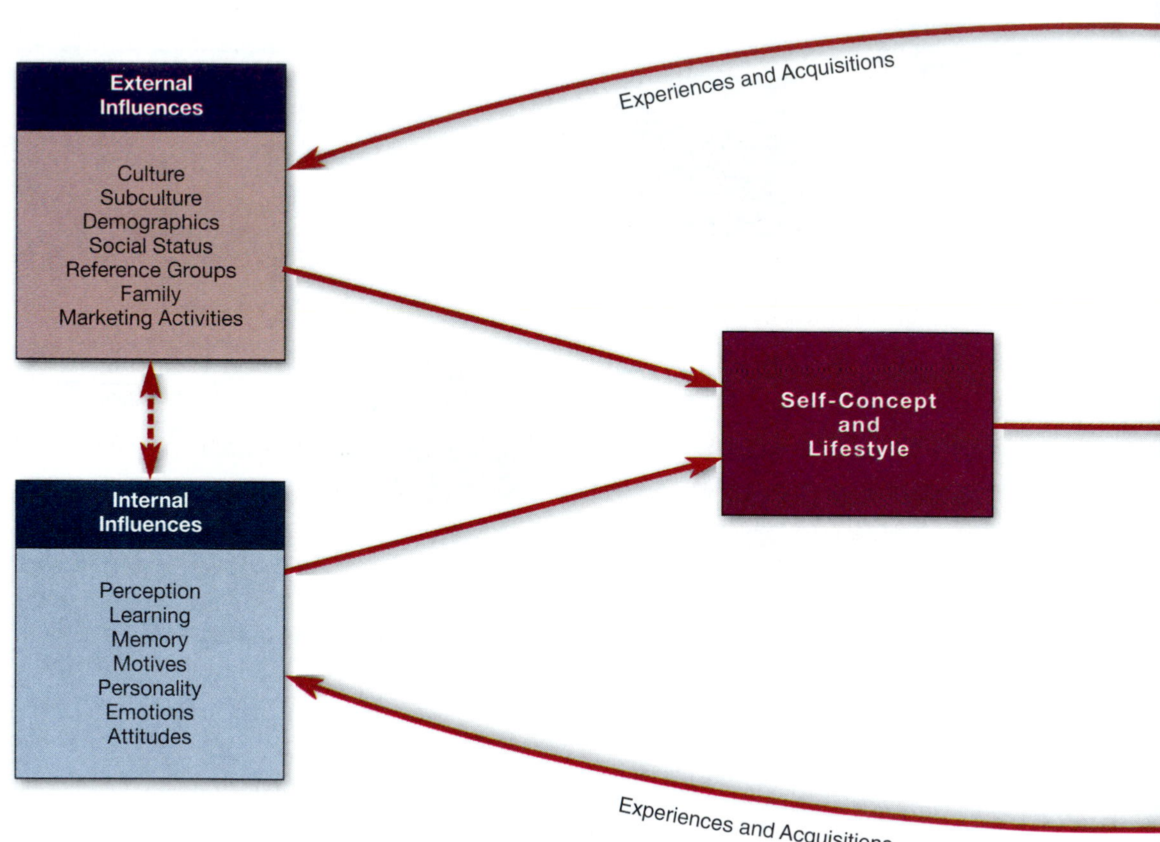

■ Throughout the text, we have emphasized that a knowledge of consumer behavior is as important to those who would regulate consumer behavior as it is to those who engage in marketing activities. Government officials, consumer advocates, and citizens all need to understand consumer behavior to develop, enact, and enforce appropriate rules and regulations for marketing activities. Consumers, in particular, need to understand their own behaviors and how their purchase and consumption behaviors help determine the type of marketplace and society we have.

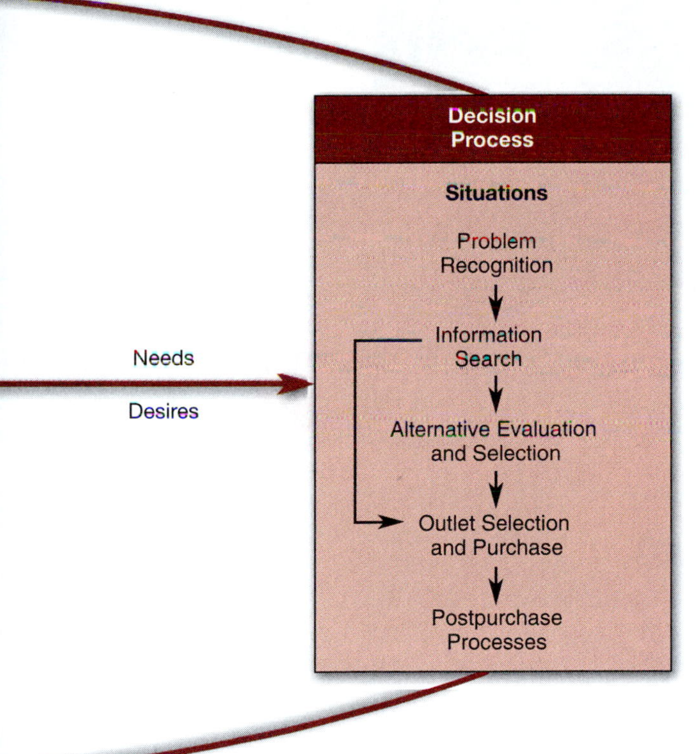

In this section, we will briefly analyze the current consumerism movement. This movement arose in the 1960s as a result of general dissatisfaction with the marketing system and specific marketing practices. For the past 35 years, it has had varying degrees of influence on regulatory policy and the sales of individual firms.

A common objective of the consumerism movement is the regulation of marketing activities. There is particular concern focused on marketing to children. The concern arises because of the large amount of time children spend watching television and using the Internet and the limited ability of children to comprehend commercial messages. Regulations also cover advertising, product, and pricing practices aimed at adults.

In Chapter 20, we cover all of these issues as they relate to a knowledge of consumer behavior.

© Agence France Presse.

Marketing Regulation and Consumer Behavior

Calvin Klein ignited a storm of controversy over "kiddie porn" in advertising. The firm denied any intention to portray children in a sexual or pornographic manner. According to the firm, the intent was to convey the idea that today's teens "have a real strength of character and independence."

The cause of the controversy was an advertising campaign that appeared in magazines, billboards, and on television featuring teenaged models in provocative poses and, in some of the television ads, making suggestive comments. For example, one television commercial featured a slim young man with no shirt on standing next to a step ladder in an empty room:

OFF-CAMERA MALE VOICE: Go ahead, show me what you can do.

MODEL: I'm not sure what to do.

VOICE: What do you do when you just stand around and you hear a good song on the radio or CD?

MODEL: I mosh, I like, run around the room.

VOICE: You march?

MODEL: Yeah, mosh.

VOICE: Go ahead:

The model dances around the ladder.

VOICE: That's a pretty good mosh.

MODEL: Thanks.

Other television ads had similar approaches. One of the print ads featured a young female in a foldout magazine insert in a very suggestive pose. Some reactions to these ads from adults included:

- They gave me the willies! That purple shag carpet and the '70s-style wood paneling make me think of some dirty, sex-crazed old man with kids in the "playroom."
- The kids looked very unsure of themselves, and the man's voice sounded like a scummy animal.

- At first I must admit I was titillated by the centerfold shot, then disgusted when I saw how old she was.

A number of organizations, including The Catholic League, Morality in Media, and Agudah Israel of America, called for boycotts of Calvin Klein products. However, others, like the president of Gryo Advertising, defended the campaign:

> Young consumers see the campaign as twisted in a good way while older ones won't get it. They won't see the humor in it. It's kind of cheesy '80s to show some hot babe with her shirt coming undone. The Calvin Klein ads are cooler because they're kinda scary. There's nothing offensive in the ads. They're just disturbing and people don't know why. People say it's kiddie porn, and all Calvin Klein has to say is, "If you see that then you are seeing something that's not there," and he's right. The most offensive thing in there is the purple shag carpeting.

Another ad agency executive states that:

> It's almost tongue in cheek, but no one's getting the joke. It's way above a lot of kids' heads. This is almost too sophisticated for them to get the sexual element.

Indeed, interviews with some teenagers support this view:

- Amy (16)—It's just another commercial on TV. I've seen worse—have you ever watched NYPD Blue? Commercials matter to a certain extent. It really matters what's in fashion. I buy jeans that look good.
- Karen (15)—I thought they were funny. That guy behind the camera was asking some stupid questions. I didn't get why he was asking those questions. It's definitely a sexual thing, but to say child pornography is stupid.
- Libby (18)—I looked at the ads in the magazines and the models were skinny with long legs, and I figured, I'm skinny and I have pretty long legs. I just figured that was me, so I bought a pair. But I don't think it's in good taste to show young models who are so thin and unhealthy looking. Levi's is catering to the same age group, and the models are skateboarding and playing outside.[1]

As the opening example indicates, marketing practices are sometimes controversial. One ad agency executive concluded that "(in a) mass market, and that's where Calvin Klein is, you can't target one audience and eliminate the rest. Some people decided this campaign was very bad. But from a purely marketing standpoint, that doesn't matter. The real question is, do young people like these ads?"[2]

We believe that the last statement made by this executive is wrong for a variety of reasons. First, individual consumers and/or consumer groups may boycott brands that engage in marketing practices that they find offensive even if the primary target market likes them. In this case, if parents find the ads offensive, they may restrict their children's ability to purchase Calvin Klein products. If enough consumers become sufficiently upset with specific actions, they or consumer groups that represent them will demand regulatory action at the local, state, or federal level. More importantly, *marketing is not, or at least should not be, just about selling products*. It should enhance the lives of those affected by it. Ads that degrade or exploit individuals or groups do not, in the long run, meet the test of enhancing consumer welfare. Unfortunately, as the opening vignette indicates, it is not always easy to determine what constitutes exploitation.

Marketing is a highly visible, important activity. It affects the lives of individuals, the success of nonprofit groups, and the profits of businesses. As we have indicated throughout the text, there are many issues where the appropriate ethical action for marketers is not clear-cut. As a marketing manager, you will face many such situations in your career. However, society has declared that other marketing actions are clearly inappropriate. It has done so by enacting laws and regulations that prohibit or require specific marketing actions. In this chapter, we are going to examine the regulation of marketing practices. Regulating marketing activities requires the same level of understanding of consumer behavior as does managing marketing programs. Our consideration of the regulation of marketing practices will separate regulations designed to protect children from those designed to protect adults.

Before we begin our analysis of marketing regulation, we briefly explore the nature of **consumerism**—*a social movement with the purpose of enhancing the power of buyers relative to that of sellers.* The consumerism movement has been the major source of regulations focused specifically on protecting consumers for the past 35 years.

CONSUMERISM

There have been several consumerism movements in the history of the United States (similar patterns have occurred in most countries). By **consumerism movement** we mean *a sustained period of political activity by consumers who are dissatisfied with various aspects of the marketing system.* Such movements generally produce boycotts of some firms or products and legislation designed to remedy at least some of the problems concerning consumers.

The current consumerism movement began in the early 1960s. Many suggest that it was crystallized in 1962 when President John F. Kennedy presented his famous Consumers' Bill of Rights in a speech to Congress:

1. The right to safety: to be protected against the marketing of goods which are hazardous to health or life.
2. The right to be informed: to be protected against fraudulent, deceitful, or grossly misleading information, advertising, labeling, or other practices, and to be given the facts needed to make an informed choice.
3. The right to choose: to be assured, wherever possible, access to a variety of products and services at competitive prices; and in those industries in which competition is not workable and government regulation is substituted, an assurance of satisfactory quality and service at fair prices.
4. The right to be heard: to be assured that consumer interest will receive full and sympathetic consideration in the formulation of government policy, and fair and expeditious treatment in its administrative tribunals.

The consumerism movement is not a well-organized political group or set of groups with a precise, long-term agenda. Rather, it refers to a state of mind in many consumers that inclines them to support a boycott or regulatory actions suggested by more active consumer groups. While some consumers are concerned about marketing activities aimed at children, others are concerned about environmental or social issues. Many belong to no direct consumerism groups. However, by responding in a proconsumerism manner to polls, by voting for proconsumer candidates and legislation, and by buying certain brands rather than others, they give strength to the movement.

Large numbers of consumers do not become disenchanted with the marketing system without cause. A high level of consumer dissatisfaction or distrust suggests that marketers either do not understand consumer behavior sufficiently to effectively meet consumer needs or they do understand consumer behavior and choose to misuse this understanding to take advantage of consumers. Both of these factors are undoubtedly true to an extent. Many other factors also contribute to general consumer dissatisfaction. Some of these include the following:

- The marketplace is much more impersonal than in the past. With the disappearance of the small local store, consumers must generally deal with strangers in an impersonal environment. (Note that consumers voted for this impersonal environment with their shopping choices.)
- Product complexity has increased dramatically. Until the late 1950s, many consumers understood how most of the products they purchased functioned and could repair them if necessary. However, the advent of the transistor, the computer chip, and sophisticated engine designs left most consumers technologically illiterate. Consumers can no longer directly evaluate a product or many services.
- Advertising has become more intrusive. With global competition increasing the number of firms in each product category and technology increasing the number of product categories and media, the number of advertisements has grown almost exponentially. The increase in two-earner families and single-parent families and, until recently, a decline in real wages has placed time and financial constraints on many individuals. These individuals need to make sound purchases but often lack the information and time to do so.
- The mass media are quick to publicize unethical or questionable practices by marketers. Thus, evening news shows give prime coverage to the actions of a few firms. However, this coverage gives some the impression that fraud and dangerous products are more widespread than they are.
- Many individuals would like the United States to be less materialistic and more concerned with other values. They would like to restrict marketing activities in an attempt to limit Americans' focus on "things."

As the list above suggests, marketing activities are a vital part of our society and they are affected by many of the same forces that affect other parts of our lives. In this chapter, we will focus on those issues raised by the consumerism movement that are under the control of marketing managers and that a knowledge of consumer behavior can influence.

The consumerism movement's interests evolve over time as the legal structure and marketing practices change. However, a concern for marketing activities focused on children has been a central concern of the current movement since its beginning. For example, in response to pressure from consumer groups, in 1990 Congress passed the Children's Television Act in an attempt to improve the quality of the programming presented to children. In 1996, the Federal Communications Commission issued new rules under this act that require stations to air three hours of educational programming targeting children 16-years-old and under per week, tightened the definition of educational programming, and provided rules for the labeling of such programs.

We will first examine the regulation of marketing activities targeting children and then examine some of the important regulatory issues involved in marketing to adults.

REGULATION AND MARKETING TO CHILDREN

The regulation of marketing activities aimed at children focuses primarily on advertising and product safety. The product safety issues are concerned with appropriate product design and materials. We will focus our attention on advertising and other promotional activities targeting children as consumers. The regulation of these activities rests heavily on theories of children's consumer behavior, particularly their information-processing skills.

There are a variety of state, federal, and voluntary guidelines and rules governing marketing to children. Despite these rules, many feel that some marketers continue to take advantage of children and that the overall marketing system, particularly advertising, is socializing children to value things (products) rather than intangibles such as relationships and integrity.

One basis for the concern over marketing to children is based on *Piaget's stages of cognitive development* (Chapter 6, page 212), which indicate that children lack the ability to fully process and understand information (including marketing messages) until around 12 years of age. This theory and the research that supports it is the basis for most regulation of advertising aimed at children and, according to critics, for some marketing programs that deliberately exploit children.

Concerns about the Ability of Children to Comprehend Commercial Messages

Quebec's Consumer Protection Act prohibits commercial advertising to persons under 13 years of age. The U.S. Federal Trade Commission has considered proposals to eliminate all advertisements to young children and advertisements for sugared food products aimed at older children.

The American advertising industry's primary self-regulatory body, the National Advertising Division (NAD) of the Council of Better Business Bureaus, maintains a special unit to review advertising aimed at children—the **Children's Advertising Review Unit (CARU).** Some of the guidelines relating to information processing that guide CARU's policing of children's advertising are shown in Table 20-1.

CARU and others are interested in the impact that the *content* of children's advertising has, as well as the ability of children to process advertising messages. However, our current focus is limited to children's abilities to *comprehend* advertising messages (we discuss content issues in the next section). There are two components to this concern: (1) Can children discern the differences between program and commercial? and (2) Can children understand specific aspects of commercials, such as comparisons?

TABLE 20-1

Information-Processing-Related Guidelines of the Children's Advertising Review Unit

1. Care should be taken not to exploit a child's imagination. Fantasy, including animation, is appropriate for younger as well as older children. However, it should not create unattainable performance expectations nor exploit the younger child's difficulty in distinguishing between the real and the fanciful.
2. The performance and use of a product should be demonstrated in a way that can be duplicated by the child for whom the product is intended.
3. All price representations should be clearly and concisely set forth. Price minimizations such as "only" or "just" should not be used.
4. Program personalities or characters, live or animated, should not promote products, premiums, or services in or adjacent to programs primarily directed to children in which the same personality appears.
5. Children have difficulty distinguishing product from premium. If product advertising contains a premium message, care should be taken that the child's attention is focused primarily on the product. The premium message should be clearly secondary.

Source: *Self-Regulation Guidelines for Children's Advertising,* Children's Advertising Review Unit, Council of Better Business Bureaus, Inc. © 1991, 1996. Reprinted with permission of the Council of Better Business Bureaus, Inc.

Do Children Understand the Selling Intent of Commercials? Research suggests that younger children have at least some difficulty understanding the selling intent of commercials. However, there is some evidence that young children are aware of the selling intent but cannot verbalize this intent.[3] Currently, the advertising industry strives to separate children's commercials from the programs by prohibiting overlapping characters and by using *separators* such as: "We will return after these messages."

This problem is growing in intensity, as children's products are increasingly the "stars" of animated children's television programs or movies.[4] Familiar examples of this approach are *Teenage Mutant Ninja Turtles* and *Pokémon*. Increasingly, product lines and television programs and movies are being designed jointly with a major objective being sales of the toy line. Parents have expressed concerns ranging from the effects that toy-based programming has on their children's behaviors and emotional development to the belief that such programming may replace other more creative and child-oriented programs.[5]

This concern has led to a variety of proposals to restrict or eliminate such programs. These proposals have produced an ongoing debate about who controls the television set. One argument is that it is the parent's responsibility to monitor and regulate their children's viewing behaviors. If a sufficient number of parents find such programs inappropriate and refuse to let their children watch them, advertisers will quit sponsoring them and they will no longer be available. Another argument is that today's time-pressured parents do not have time to screen all the shows their children watch. Furthermore, tremendous peer pressure can develop for children to watch a particular show and/or own the products associated with it. Denying a child the right to watch such a show then causes arguments and resentments. Therefore, society should set appropriate standards within which broadcasters should operate.

Can Children Understand the Words and Phrases in Commercials? The second aspect of comprehension involves specific words or types of commercials that children might misunderstand. For example, research indicates that disclaimers such as "Part of a nutritious breakfast," "Each sold separately," and "Batteries not included," are ineffective with preschool children.[6] Not only do young children have a difficult time understanding these phrases, an analysis of Saturday morning advertising aimed at children revealed that most such disclaimers are presented in a manner that does not meet the Federal Trade Commission's "Clear and Conspicuous" requirements for such disclaimers.[7]

For example, one toy ad contained this disclaimer: "TV Teddy comes with one tape. Other tapes sold separately." However, it appeared near the bottom of the screen in lettering that measured only 3.5 percent of the screen height against a multicolor background. It was not repeated by an announcer and appeared for less than three seconds. A child would have to read at 200 words per minute to read the message! Unfortunately, this treatment of the disclaimer is more the rule than the exception.

The CARU has special rules for comparison advertising and prohibits price minimizations such as "only," and "just." It also suggests specific phrasing for certain situations such as "your mom or dad must say it's OK before you call," rather than "ask your parents' permission." Cases involving CARU and the information-processing skills of children include the following:

- *LJN Toys.* A television commercial for its Photon electronic target game showed the guns appearing to shoot red laser beams. The commercial included a visual disclaimer: "Red beam for illustration only." Because the commercial ran during children's programming, the CARU challenged the adequacy of the disclaimer.
- *Mattel Toys.* A TV commercial showed Monstroid, a figure in its Masters of the Universe line, apparently grabbing other figures automatically. Copy said, "Now, a raging

terror grabs hold of the universe . . . When Monstroid gets wound up, it grabs . . . " CARU challenged the ad on the basis that children would not understand that Monstroid's grip is manually operated.[8]

- *Hasbro.* A TV commercial directed to children promoted a "My Little Pony" movie for "only" $1. CARU challenged the use of price minimizations such as only or just "because children aren't sophisticated enough to comprehend the relative value of money."[9]

Likewise, the Federal Trade Commission (FTC) applied sanctions to Lewis Galoob Toys and its ad agency. The ads cited showed a doll dancing and a toy airplane flying, both of which require human assistance. The ads also failed to disclose that assembly was required for certain toy sets. Finally, the firm failed to "clearly and conspicuously" disclose that the two toys shown together had to be purchased separately. An FTC spokesperson noted that the ads never appeared on network stations and speculated that the networks' internal review processes for children's ads would have precluded their being shown.[10]

Concerns about the Effects of the Content of Commercial Messages on Children

Even if children accurately comprehend television ads, there are concerns about the effects the content of these messages has on children. These concerns stem in part from the substantial amount of time American children spend viewing television. Children between 2 and 11 years of age spend more than 25 hours per week watching television and are thus exposed to almost 25,000 television commercials per year.[11] This viewing is spread throughout the week, though prime time (Monday–Sunday, 7:30–11:00 PM) is most popular except for younger viewers, who watch Saturday morning programs extensively.

The large amount of time children devote to watching television, including commercials, gives rise to two major areas of concern:

- The impact of commercial messages on children's values.
- The impact of commercial messages on children's health and safety.

Four of the six basic "principles" that underline the CARU's guidelines for advertising directed at children focus on these concerns (the other two are concerned with children's information-processing capabilities). They are:

1. Recognizing that advertising may play an important role in educating the child, advertisers should communicate information in a truthful and accurate manner with full recognition that the child may learn practices from advertising that can affect his or her health and well-being.
2. Advertisers are urged to capitalize on the potential of advertising to influence behavior by developing advertising that, wherever possible, addresses itself to positive and beneficial social behavior such as friendship, kindness, honesty, justice, generosity, and respect for others.
3. Care should be taken to incorporate minority and other groups in advertisements in order to present positive and prosocial roles and role models wherever possible. Social stereotyping and appeals to prejudice should be avoided.
4. Although many influences affect a child's personal and social development, it remains the prime responsibility of the parents to provide guidance for children. Advertisers should contribute to this parent–child relationship in a constructive manner.

Several of the specific guidelines derived from these principles are provided in Table 20-2.

TABLE 20-2

Content-Related Guidelines of the Children's Advertising Review Unit

1. Representation of food products should be made so as to encourage sound use of the product with a view toward healthy development of the child and development of good nutritional practices. Advertisements representing mealtime should clearly and adequately depict the role of the product within the framework of a balanced diet. Snack foods should be clearly represented as such, and not as substitutes for meals.
2. Children should not be encouraged to ask parents or others to buy products. Advertisements should not suggest that a parent or adult who purchases a product or service for a child is better, more intelligent, or more generous than one who does not. Advertising directed toward children should not create a sense of urgency or exclusivity—for example, by using words like "now" and "only."
3. Benefits attributed to the product or service should be inherent in its use. Advertisements should not convey the impression that possession of a product will result in more acceptance of a child by his or her peers. Conversely, it should not be implied that lack of a product will cause a child to be less accepted by his or her peers. Advertisements should not imply that purchase and use of a product will confer upon the user the prestige, skills, or other special qualities of characters appearing in advertising.
4. Advertisements for children's products should show them being used by children in the appropriate age range. For instance, young children should not be shown playing with toys safe only for older children.
5. Advertisements should not portray adults or children in unsafe situations, or in acts harmful to themselves or others. For example, when athletic activities (such as bicycle riding or skateboarding) are shown, proper precautions and safety equipment should be depicted.

Source: *Self-Regulatory Guidelines for Children's Advertising,* Council of Better Business Bureaus, Inc. © 1991, 1996. Reprinted with permission of the Council of Better Business Bureaus, Inc.

Health and Safety Consumer groups are concerned that advertising may promote unsafe or dangerous behavior in children. In many instances, children view advertising directed at adults and the consequences are potentially harmful, as described below:

> A television commercial for Calgonite automatic dishwasher detergent showed a woman inside an automatic dishwasher. The commercial was withdrawn voluntarily after CARU received a complaint that a three-year-old child had climbed into a dishwasher shortly after viewing the commercial.[12]

The problem caused by the Calgonite commercial illustrates the difficulty of complying with the safety guideline. This commercial was not aimed at children nor shown during a children's program. The fact that children watch prime-time television extensively places an additional responsibility on marketers.

Ensuring that advertisements portray only safe uses of products is sometimes difficult, but it is not a controversial area. Advertising of health-related products, particularly snack foods and cereals, is much more controversial. The bulk of the controversy focuses on the heavy advertising emphasis placed on sugared products. Advertising sugared products does increase their consumption. However, this same advertising may also increase the consumption of related products, such as milk. What is not known (and probably cannot be determined) are the eating patterns that would exist in the absence of such advertising. That is, if children did not know about cereals such as Cap'n Crunch, would they eat a more nutritious breakfast, a less nutritious breakfast, or perhaps no breakfast at all? However, extensive viewing of child-oriented advertising has been found to correlate with low nutritional awareness.[13]

Unfortunately, some marketers have not been very responsible in this area. For example, children's diets are higher in overall fat and saturated fat than health guidelines call for and obesity among children is increasing. In the early 1990s, the percentage of high-fat foods advertised during Saturday morning children's TV programs increased from 16 percent of all food advertising to 41 percent. Most of the ads are for fast food, particularly hamburgers and pizzas. Such advertising undoubtedly influences children's food choices and subsequent health. It should be noted that other successful marketers of products consumed by children, such as Coca-Cola and PepsiCo, do not advertise on children's shows.[14]

Values Advertising is frequently criticized as fostering overly materialistic, self-focused, and short-term values in children. One reason is the magnitude of advertising focused on kids. For example, in one month Nike ran 90 commercials for its shoes on MTV and only 21 on sports programs.[15] Many persons are concerned that this consistent pressure to buy and own things is producing negative values in children.

Advertising has also been charged with portraying undesirable stereotypes of women and minority groups. Unfortunately, we do not have sound evidence about the impact of advertising on children's values. However, CARU principles and guidelines strongly encourage advertisers to portray positive values in advertisements aimed at children. About 10 percent of all complaints to CARU involve the area of values.

Most ads aimed at children meet all CARU guidelines. However, some would claim that thousands of similar ads, all promoting the acquisition of products, have the cumulative effect of distorting children's values. These individuals want regulations that sharply limit the amount of advertising that can be directed at children.

Summary of Television Advertising and Children CARU recently examined 604 hours of children's programming on ABC, NBC, CBS, USA Network, Nickelodeon, and two independent broadcasters. There were 10,329 commercials aired during the 604 hours. Of these 10,329 commercials, 385 were in violation of one of CARU's guidelines. Fast-food ads accounted for 109 of the violations, with Burger King having 83. The most common offense was to devote most of the commercial to describing a premium rather than the primary product. CARU guidelines require that ads aimed at children emphasize the product.

Advertiser compliance was highest on the three networks (which have their own review processes) with a 2 percent violation rate, independent stations were next at 3.7 percent, while 5 percent of the ads on cable violated the CARU guidelines.[16] Thus, the vast majority of ads meet CARU guidelines. However, given the enormous amount of time children spend watching television, most will see many ads that are in violation of these guidelines. In addition, these guidelines do not address such issues as advertising high-fat foods. Nor do they (nor could they) oppose generating desires for products that many families cannot afford. Nonetheless, CARU has greatly enhanced the level of responsibility in advertising aimed at children. Many consumer advocates would like it to expand the areas it covers and increase the stringency of its rules.

Controversial Marketing Activities Aimed at Children

There are a number of marketing activities targeted at children in addition to television advertising that are controversial and for which various regulatory proposals are being considered. We describe three in this section.

Kids' Clubs One of the fastest growing ways to market to children is **kids' clubs.**[17] Firms such as Fox, Chuck E. Cheese, Toys "R" Us, Burger King, Disney, Hyatt, and Delta

TABLE 20-3

The Nickelodeon Club

The Characteristics of the Club	A one-year membership (which includes a subscription to *Nickelodeon Magazine*) costs $9.95 (but a special $7.95 introductory offer is advertised in the premiere issue). The magazine, with an insert promoting club membership, was launched in May 1990 through Pizza Hut. That insert promised special "kids-only" prices on club merchandise and "special offers or discounts" at Pizza Hut, Universal Studios in Florida, and TCBY yogurt. In addition to eight pages of ads, *Nickelodeon Magazine* devoted nine pages to the "Nick Store," where club merchandise is offered at two prices, a kid's price and a higher adult's price. One-third (17 of 52) of its pages sells things to kids. Other popular kid's magazines with no club affiliation tend to devote a smaller percent of their pages of advertising: One-fourth (22 of 80) pages of *Sports Illustrated for Kids* is ads, as is about one-sixth to one-tenth of *3-2-1 Contact.* Club members will also be sent product samples and coupons from Nick Club advertisers.
What the Nickelodeon Club Promises Advertisers	You (the advertiser) can capture all the excitement of the Nickelodeon name, the on-air attitude, and the off-air environment, by delivering your product message or coupon to the young consumers of today and the brand-loyal customers of tomorrow. With the Nick Nack Pack (product samples and coupons mailed to kids) and the *Nickelodeon Magazine,* Nick offers you home delivery of an entire generation—the Nickelodeon generation. The preceding quote is from the packet Nickelodeon sends to prospective advertisers. It also quotes the Nickelodeon/Yankelovich Youth Monitor: "All kids tend to influence their parents across a number of categories—clothing, food, entertainment, nontraditional and larger ticket items." Among the data given: "60% of kids buy products because they have coupons for them." While the kids are joining a fun club, Nickelodeon is building a large database of names. Along with the Sassy and MTV clubs, Nickelodeon offers to sell its kids' club membership list to direct-mail advertisers.

Source: **Selling America's Kids,** © 1990 by Consumers Union of U.S., Inc., Yonkers, NY 10103-1057, a nonprofit organization. Reprinted with permission from *Consumer Reports,* 1990, for educational purposes only. No commercial use or photocopying permitted. To subscribe, call 1-800-234-1645 or visit us at www.ConsumerReports.org.

Airlines sponsor kids' clubs. The clubs typically provide membership certificates, a magazine, the chance to win prizes, and discounts or coupons for products offered by the sponsor. Kids' clubs vary widely in what they offer the members and how ethically they are run. Here is how Consumers Union characterized the majority of them:

> In a real club, kids are likely to find friends, shared interests and activities, and opportunities for fun and growth. In the promotional clubs common years ago, kids were likely to get membership cards, decoder rings, or other symbols that reinforced loyalty to the sponsoring radio or TV program, comic, or other product. In one of the new kids' clubs, kids are likely to get hard sell from many advertisers, a monthly magazine cum sales catalog, discount coupons, and other powerful incentives to buy.
>
> Clubs disguise commercial messages. Kids are invited to join something that promises to be "theirs," but turns out to be a way of manipulating them to buy things. The ad messages come disguised as "advice from your club," making them more difficult to resist.[18]

Table 20-3 describes the Nickelodeon Club and an advertisement that Nickelodeon used to attract advertisers to its club magazine. The selling intent of this club seems apparent.

Consumers Union has the following recommendation for regulating kids' clubs:

> The Federal Trade Commission should recognize that kids' clubs, whose purpose is to sell products, may mislead children, even if the commercial nature of the clubs is obvious to adults. The FTC should require kids' clubs to provide a substantial nonmerchandising service or activity for kids. Clubs intending to sell members' names in mailing lists should disclose that fact and give kids the opportunity to keep their names off the list.

Would the Burger King Kids' Club described below meet the requirements recommended by Consumers Union?

> Kids (or their parents) can pick up a membership form at any Burger King for free. After it is sent in, they receive a kit containing a membership certificate, stickers, a membership card and iron-on transfers for T-shirts. On their birthdays, they receive a card good for a free meal at their local Burger King. Bimonthly Kids' Club newsletters are distributed through the restaurants. A quarterly 32-page, full-color magazine is sent to the members' homes. There are three different versions of the magazine geared to the age of the member. Each issue has six pages of outside advertising. Burger King does not sell its membership list.[19]

Advertising in the Classroom In 1989, Whittle Communications created a substantial controversy when it launched a closed-circuit television network (Channel One) that would provide 12 minutes of news to participating schools. If the schools' teachers agree to have their students watch the program most days, they receive the TV equipment free. However, the news program contains two minutes of commercials. Unlike home viewing, watching this news program is not voluntary and students cannot skip to other channels when the commercials are aired. It is now in over 12,000 middle and high schools. Research indicates that the commercials are having an impact on the students.[20]

Another major controversy arose when a teenager in Georgia was suspended from school for wearing a Pepsi T-shirt on "Coke day."[21] The school had an exclusive contract with Coca-Cola. While such events generate substantial publicity, numerous corporations place direct and indirect ads in schools everyday:

- American Airlines sponsored a package of materials designed to teach children to read maps and globes. It was distributed to 9,500 teachers in communities served by American. A company spokesperson described their motivation as: We thought it important to be a good corporate citizen and do things in schools that would benefit the learning experience. Today's students are tomorrow's workers. Of course, they're also tomorrow's airline passengers, we wanted them to learn the American name and to be familiar with the brand.
- Cover Concepts distributes book covers to schools for free. Over 60 million were distributed in a recent year. However, the covers contain ads for firms. Firms can target the schools and classes where their message will appear. Firms such as Nike, Nickelodeon, Procter & Gamble, and Quaker Oats are clients.[22]
- Many first-grade teachers use the AT&T Adventure Club, which includes student newsletters, classroom posters, and teaching guides. It is designed to develop an understanding of communications and to build AT&T brand awareness.
- Scholastic Inc., one of the nation's largest publishers of books and magazines for children, developed a program for Minute Maid to encourage 3.7 million elementary school kids to read a book a week over their summer vacation. Kids who sent away for a chart to keep track of their progress also received coupons for Minute Maid products. For each coupon redeemed, Minute Maid donated 10 cents to a nonprofit organization that promotes reading.

TABLE 20-4

"Educational" Materials Supplied to Schools

Corporate Sponsor	Teaching Material	Promotional Content
Polaroid	Polaroid Education Program (lesson book, camera—"A visual approach to teaching basic skills")	*High.* Mentions "Polaroid" in every lesson and assignment, and requires 10 proofs of film purchase for the camera.
Kodak	Corkers (bulletin board ideas) & Teaching Tips from Kodak (tips from teachers on using photography to teach)	*Low.* Encourages taking photos but never mentions "Kodak."
Chef Boyardee	Teach . . . Good Nutrition (sets of reproducible masters)	*High.* Has its name and logo on every master; names its products in all recipes; and just encourages kids to eat pizza (no nutrition education).
McDonald's	Nutrient Pursuit (poster and activity to teach the four basic food groups)	*Low.* Its name isn't on the materials, but its logo is on the masters. Nutrition education is weak.
Tampax	Mysteries of Me (lesson plans and masters for three activities)	*High.* Pushes using Tampax by name, gives girls a coupon to order a $3 starter kit or a free sample, and has its name on the poster.
Procter & Gamble	Perspectives (case studies of P&G's past to teach economics and history)	*Moderate.* Builds P&G's image and talks about its products, but doesn't "sell."
	Food Preparation (booklet and worksheets)	*Moderate.* Uses P&G brand-name products in recipes, and includes coupons for free P&G products "for demonstrations/discussions."
Reynolds Wrap	"Preserve Freshness and Flavor with The Best Wrap Around" poster with teaching guide on back	*High.* Shows more than 30 foods wrapped in aluminum foil; says "Freeze in it! Cook in it! Store in it!" All information pushes using foil.
Almond Board of California	"Everybody's Nuts About Almonds" poster with teaching guide on back	*High.* Shows only almonds and package; "Nutrition" teaching guide shows why almonds are nutritionally superior to other nuts, including peanuts, and why they're so healthy—one-sided and misleading.

Source: **Selling America's Kids,** © 1990 by Consumers Union of U.S., Inc., Yonkers, NY 10103-1057, a nonprofit organization. Reprinted with permission from Consumer Reports, 1990, for educational purposes only. No commercial use or photocopying permitted. To subscribe, call 1-800-234-1645 or visit us at www.ConsumerReports.org.

- Even school lunch menus now contain advertising. The Jefferson County Kentucky school district estimated that it saved $200,000 on menu costs in a test of the program.[23]

Table 20-4 describes a number of other "educational materials" programs offered by marketers for use in schools and Consumers Union's evaluation of the promotional content of these materials. Consumers Union and other groups want schools to be "ad-free" zones. They feel that all material provided to schools by organizations should be:

- Accurate: Be consistent with established facts, appropriately referenced, and current.
- Objective: Present all relevant points of view, and clearly state the sponsor's bias.

- Complete: Not mislead by omission.
- Nondiscriminatory: Avoid ethnic, age, race, and gender stereotypes.
- Noncommercial: Not contain any of the sponsor's brand names, trademarks, related trade names, or corporate identification in the text or illustrations; avoid implied or explicit sales messages.
- Evaluative: Encourage cognitive evaluation of the subject taught.

While many firms would agree with most of the above requirements, complete compliance with the noncommercial standard would greatly reduce the motivation of firms to provide valuable (sometimes) material to the schools.

Internet Marketing and Children Children are becoming major users of the Internet. Not surprisingly, marketers are beginning to use the Internet to communicate with kids. Two major concerns emerge: invading children's privacy and exploitation of children through manipulative sales techniques.[24]

Privacy Issues An example of invading children's privacy is the KidsCom communications playground (targeting kids 4 to 8), which requires children to provide their name, age, sex, and e-mail address in order to enter the site. It also requests their favorite TV show, music groups, and the name of the child who referred them to KidsCom. Once in the playground, they can earn "KidsCash," which can be redeemed for prizes by supplying additional personal information.

An industry study found that almost 90 percent of children's sites on the Internet collect personal information from the children. Slightly over half provide some disclosure about their information practices, but less than a fourth ask children to check with their parents before they provide information and less than 10 percent give parents control over information collected from children.[25] Two studies by the Center for Media Education (CME), one of a random sample of children's Web sites and the second of the 80 most popular sites for children, found:[26]

	Random Sample	*Most Popular Sites*
Collect personal information	95%	88%
Post their privacy policies	27	75
Attempt to get parental consent	6	26
Get verifiable parental consent	3	13

Concern over the invasion of children's privacy motivated Congress to pass the Children's Online Privacy Protection Act (COPPA) in 1998. It authorized the FTC to develop specific rules to implement the provisions of the act (see Table 20-5). The FTC developed a set of rules which it began enforcing in April 2000.

Even before COPPA was passed, the FTC had initiated action against Web sites that it judged were unfairly collecting personal data from children. For example, GeoCities agreed to an FTC ruling requiring it to erase any information collected from the 40,000 kids in its database unless a parent consents to it being kept. It also agreed to ensure that any firms who acquired this data erase it.[27]

Exploitive Activities The Center for Media Education considers exploiting children to involve such techniques as building "playgrounds" that are primarily commercial in intent

TABLE 20-5

Key Provisions of COPPA

The Act requires that commercial Web sites that collect personal information from children under 13 obtain prior parental consent before they collect that information. The Act only applies to Web sites (or portions thereof) directed to children or to Web sites that knowingly collect personal information from children under 13. The Act does not apply to nonprofits.

Notice: Parents have the right to be notified about data collection and use practices. The parent must be informed about what information will be collected, how it will be used, and to whom and in what form the information will be disclosed to others. The notice must be prominently displayed and unavoidable.

Prior Parental Consent: With certain exceptions, information cannot be collected from children, used, or disclosed unless the Web site operator has obtained verifiable parental consent through "reasonable effort."

Prevention of Further Use: Parents have the right to prevent further use of already collected personal identifying information and to prevent future collection of information from the child.

Collection of Personal Information Must Be Limited: The collection of personal identifying information for a child's participation in a game, prize, offer, or other activity on the Web site must be limited to what is reasonably necessary for the activity.

Access to Information: Parents of children under 13 have the right to access and review a description of the specific types of personal identifying information collected from the child, and Web sites operators must provide reasonable means to the parent to obtain the information itself that has been collected from the child.

and blending advertising and content in sophisticated ways. For example the Web site for Kellogg's is described by the Center for Media Education as follows:

> [It] makes full use of Snap, Crackle, & Pop, Tony the Tiger, and Toucan Sam. The three elves are the hosts of the Clubhouse, welcoming children to explore the different rooms and encouraging them to participate in all the various activities. Youngsters can color pictures of the spokescharacters, download Rice Krispies Treats recipes, and do word-find puzzles. The Kellogg General Store sells licensed merchandise: Tony the Tiger watches, Toucan Sam sweatshirts, and Snap, Crackle & Pop T-shirts are just a few of the items that can be ordered on-line.

The ethical and regulatory issues involved in Internet marketing to children are explored in depth in Case 6–1 (pages 737–739). The Center for Media Education recommends the following principles to guide development of on-line commercial services:

1. Personal information should not be collected from children, nor should personal profiles of children be sold to third parties.
2. Advertising and promotions targeted at children should be clearly labeled and separated from content.
3. Children's content areas should not be directly linked to advertising sites.
4. There should be no direct interaction between children and product spokespersons.
5. There should be no on-line microtargeting of children (commercial or promotions developed for individual children), and no direct-response marketing.

REGULATION AND MARKETING TO ADULTS

Regulation of marketing activities aimed at adults focuses on consumer information, product features, and pricing practices. As Consumer Insight 20-1 shows, there is increasing demand for regulation to protect the privacy of adults, particularly on the Internet.

Consumer Insight 20-1

Internet Privacy Issues Concerning Adults

Privacy issues are an increasing area of concern for consumer groups and marketers. Currently, many magazines sell their subscription lists to various firms who use the information for direct marketing campaigns. Some charities sell or otherwise make available their donor lists. American Express recently announced plans to sell extensive information on its cardholders to merchants. These data would be combined with data on 175 million Americans compiled by KnowledgeBase. KnowledgeBase has information on age, marital status, family composition, household ownership, and so forth. By combining this demographic data with American Express purchase records, American Express plans to develop mailing lists of customers most likely to buy certain products, which it will sell to other firms. Cardholders can keep their names off the list by calling or writing American Express, but the company has no plans to explicitly inform its customers of this use of their purchase records.

While the dissemination of subscription and credit card data is a concern, most attention is currently focused on the privacy of data collected on the Internet. The FTC is giving the Internet commerce industry an opportunity to show that self-regulation will work but has promised strict regulation if it does not. Consumer groups are pressuring Congress to pass legislation requiring privacy protection. In response, a number of industry groups, including the Better Business Bureau, the Direct Marketing Foundation, and TrustE, are working on guidelines and technologies to help protect privacy while still allowing marketers to use data to direct messages to targeted audiences.

One of the reasons the concern about Internet privacy is so strong is that data are collected with the consumer explicitly providing it. When a person visits a Web site, that fact can be recorded (his or her Web address at a minimum), as well as what parts of the site are visited, what information is requested, what links are accessed, and so forth, without the consent or even knowledge of that person. Other information may be collected in a more direct manner. Information from various sites and sources can be pooled to develop individual profiles.

Critical Thinking Questions

1. Is American Express's proposed use of its purchase data ethical? Why or why not? If you think it is unethical, do you think it should be illegal? What consequences would outlawing this use of data have?
2. Develop a set of guidelines for Internet privacy.

Source: P. Laamiell, "American Express Plan to Market Customer Information Draws Fire," *Marketing News,* June 8, 1998, p. 7; I. Teinowitz, "Online Privacy Rules Proposed to Ease Threat to E-Commerce," *Advertising Age,* April 27, 1998, p. 3; and K. M. Bayne, "Privacy Still Burning Web Issue," *Advertising Age,* June 29, 1998, p. 37.

Consumer Information

There are three major concerns focused on the information that marketers provide to consumers, generally in the form of advertisements—the accuracy of the information provided, the adequacy of the information provided, and the cumulative impact of marketing information on society's values. We will briefly look at advertising's impact on our values before focusing on the accuracy and adequacy of consumer information.

Marketing and Values We discussed the impact of advertising on values in the previous section on advertising to children. The concern is the same for advertising directed at adults—the long-term effect of a constant flow of messages stressing ownership and/or narcissistic values may be negative both for individuals and society. For example, an ad for Musk by Alyssa Ashley recently appeared in a magazine read by teenage females. It consisted of a picture of a young teenage girl on the back of a motorcycle driven by a scruffy looking man with long hair, a beard, and a tattoo. The girl's dress is pulled up to the top of her thigh. The only other content was a picture of the product package and the headline—"Sometimes even good girls want to be bad." Many would argue that this ad promotes inappropriate values and behaviors.

ILLUSTRATION 20-1

Ads that stress beauty and attractiveness are often effective. Some critics charge that the cumulative effect of thousands of such ads over time results in too much value being placed on these attributes. Others note that beauty was deemed desirable and actively pursued long before the advent of advertising.

Courtesy JCPenney Co.

Most ads for women's cosmetics and clothing, emphasize beauty (see Illustration 20-1), while others stress sex appeal as a major benefit. Each individual ad including Illustration 20-1 is probably harmless. However, some critics charge that when people see such themes repeated thousands of times for hundreds of products, they learn to consider a person's looks to be more important than other attributes.[28] This can lead to injurious consumption patterns such as excessive tanning despite knowledge of the associated health hazard.[29] Further, those who cannot afford such products or who are not "good-looking" suffer. Others would argue that individuals have been concerned with their looks and possessions in virtually all cultures and times. They argue that advertising does not cause a society's values, it merely reflects them.

Portrayals of beauty and casual attitudes toward sex are not the only ways advertisements are argued to influence values. The portrayal of women in the mass media in general and in advertising in particular often has been limited to stereotypical roles or as decoration.[30] This in turn can influence the concepts girls develop of themselves and their role choices. Of course, many firms now portray females in a more positive, realistic fashion. The ad for Jane, shown in Illustration 20-2 stresses positive values while still promoting a beauty enhancement product. The Nike ad in Illustration 9-3 (page 332) has generated a positive response from many woman as well as advertising critics. A television version of the ad combines quick camera takes and slow-motion shots of teenage girls on a playground, with images of girls playing on swing sets and monkey bars. The

Courtesy Sassaby Cosmetics, Inc.

ILLUSTRATION 20-2

This ad has been praised for its positive portrayal of young women.

sound portion is a variety of girls' voices describing the long-term benefits of female participation in sports:

> I will like myself more; I will have more self-confidence if you let me play sports. If you let me play, I will be 60 percent less likely to get breast cancer. I will suffer less depression if you let me play sports.
>
> I will be more likely to leave a man who beats me. If you let me play, I will be less likely to get pregnant before I want to; I will learn what it means to be strong.[31]

The manner in which ethnic groups, the elderly, and other social groups are portrayed in ads and the mass media can impact the way members of these groups view themselves as well as the way others see them.[32] Marketers need to ensure that their ads reflect the diversity of the American society in a manner that is realistic and positive for all the many groups involved. These portrayals should involve both the content of the ads and the shows sponsored by the ads.[33] For example, several Hispanic groups are considering a boycott of the major networks and some of their sponsors due to the virtually complete absence of Hispanic roles and actors on network television.

Consumer Information Accuracy The salesperson tells you "My brand is the best there is." Does he or she need scientific proof to make such a statement? At what point does permissible puffery become misleading and illegal? Does it vary by the situation? The consumer group involved?[34]

An ad shows a pair of very attractive female legs. The headline reads "Her legs are insured for $1,000,000. Her policy came with one minor stipulation. Schick Silk Effects." Schick Silk Effects is a woman's razor. How do you interpret this ad? Many would assume

ILLUSTRATION 20-3

Is imitation "the sincerest form of flattery" or a source of consumer confusion?

© 1994 Paul F. Kilmer.

that the insurance company insisted on her shaving with this device before they would issue the policy. This suggests that the insurance company considers this razor to be very good at protecting women's legs while they shave.

However, in exceedingly fine print at the very bottom of the ad is this disclaimer: "Policy condition included by insurer at the request of Warner-Lambert Co." Warner-Lambert is the firm that markets Silk Effects. In other words, the firm that owns the razor had the requirement that this razor be used placed in the insurance policy. This leads to a very different interpretation of the ad. *Should this ad be illegal? Is it unethical?*

Suppose you saw a snorkel or swim fins with the National Association of Scuba Diving Schools' "Seal of Approval" on the package. What would this mean to you? Many of us would interpret it to mean that the product had been tested by the association or was manufactured to conform to a set of standards established by the association. However, the FTC charged that the seal was *sold* for use on diving products *without tests or standards*.[35]

Research shows that the more baking soda a toothpaste contains, the more effective it is in cleaning away plaque and deep stains. How much baking soda should a toothpaste contain before it can be called a "baking soda" toothpaste? There is no rule. Arm & Hammer's contains 65 percent baking soda, while Crest Baking Soda Toothpaste has 20 percent.[36] *Should there be rules for labels such as this or is the required contents listing enough?*

Illustration 20-3 shows several major national brands and several competing brands with similar packages. Are consumers misled by such packages? Are the firms who build brand equity through their product development and marketing efforts being "ripped off"

TABLE 20-6

Regulation and the Interpretation of Marketing Messages

- The 4th U.S. Circuit Court of Appeals ruled that meat from a turkey thigh can be called a "turkey ham" even if it contains no pork. A lower court had reached the opposite conclusion. The ruling appeared to rely heavily on a technical definition of the term *ham*.
- Maximum Strength Anacin's claim that it is "the maximum strength allowed" was ruled illegal because it "implies that an appropriate authority has authorized the sale of products like Maximum Strength Anacin." No such authorization exists.
- The Association of Petroleum Re-Refiners petitioned the FTC to reconsider its requirement that all re-refined oil products "clearly and conspicuously" label the origin of the product. This has meant that "made from used oil" appears on all labels. The association feels that this disparages the quality of such lubricants, and they want to use the phrase "recycled oil product" instead.
- A court issued an injunction stopping the distribution of a new brand of gloves trademarked Blueberry because of potential confusion with an existing brand trademarked Cranberry. Each trademark contained a picture of the fruit with the name.
- Keebler Company's claim of "Baked not fried" for Wheatables and Munch'ems snack crackers was challenged before the NAD. While the crackers are baked, they are sprayed with vegetable oil after baking and have a fat content similar to fried products.
- Under the Federal Trademark Dilution Act (FTDA), Hasbro was able to stop the use of the Internet name candyland.com for a sexually explicit Web site because the site would injure the value of its registered trademark Candy Land (a line of children's games). Courts have generally held that only the owners of registered trademarks can use them as Web site addresses.

by imitators? Or, are these legitimate attempts to position competing products as being similar to the brand leaders?[37]

Because of such problems, various businesses, consumer groups, and regulatory agencies are deeply concerned with the interpretation of marketing messages. However, determining the exact meaning of a marketing message is not a simple process. Table 20-6 illustrates some of the areas where controversy over the interpretation of various marketing messages has existed.

Obtaining accurate assignments of meaning is made even more difficult by the variation in information-processing skills and motivations among different population groups.[38] For example, this warning was ruled inadequate in a product liability case involving a worker who was injured while inflating a truck tire:

> Always inflate tire in safety cage or use a portable lock ring guard. Use a clip-on type air chuck with remote valve so that operator can stand clear during tire inflation.

The court held that (1) "There is a duty to warn *foreseeable* users of all hidden dangers" and (2) "in view of the unskilled or semiskilled nature of the work and the existence of many in the workforce who do not read English, warnings *in the form of symbols* might have been appropriate since the employee's ability to take care of himself was limited."[39] Thus, marketers must often go to considerable lengths to provide messages that the relevant audience will interpret correctly.

Fortunately, we are developing considerable knowledge on effectively presenting such difficult messages as product risks, nutrition, and affirmative disclosures (see Chapter 8). In addition, consumer research is being used by both marketers and the courts to determine if an ad is misleading.[40]

The examples above indicate the difficulty of regulating the explicit verbal content of ads. Regulating the more subtle meanings implied by the visual content of ads is much more difficult.[41] For example, some are critical of beer advertisements that portray active young adults in groups having fun and consuming beer. These critics contend that the visual message of these ads is that alcohol consumption is the appropriate way for young adults to be popular and have fun. Recently, both government and business self-regulatory groups have begun regulating visual communications.

- The FTC recently challenged ads for Beck's beer that featured young adults drinking on a sailing ship. It charged that the ads promoted unsafe marine conduct.
- The NAD required Balance Bar to drop all claims referring to clinical studies and *visuals of physicians* in its advertising after ruling that its formula was not proved to be "clinically effective for the general population."

Corrective advertising is *advertising run by a firm to cause consumers to "unlearn" inaccurate information they acquired as a result of the firm's earlier advertising*. Three examples of corrective advertising messages follow:

- "Do you recall some of our past messages saying that Domino sugar gives you strength, energy, and stamina? Actually, Domino is not a special or unique source of strength, energy, and stamina. No sugar is, because what you need is a balanced diet and plenty of rest and exercise."
- "If you've wondered what some of our earlier advertising meant when we said Ocean Spray cranberry juice cocktail has more food energy than orange juice or tomato juice, let us make it clear: we didn't mean vitamins and minerals. Food energy means calories. Nothing more.

  "Food energy is important at breakfast since many of us may not get enough calories, or food energy, to get off to a good start. Ocean Spray cranberry juice cocktail helps because it contains more food energy than most other breakfast drinks.

  "And Ocean Spray cranberry juice cocktail gives you and your family vitamin C plus a great wake-up taste. It's . . . the other breakfast drink."
- Sugar Information, Inc.: "Do you recall the messages we brought you in the past about sugar? How something with sugar in it before meals could help you curb your appetite? We hope you didn't get the idea that our little diet tip was any magic formula for losing weight. Because there are no tricks or shortcuts; the whole diet subject is very complicated. Research hasn't established that consuming sugar before meals will contribute to weight reduction or even keep you from gaining weight."

While the effectiveness of corrective advertising has been debated, the FTC considers it a useful tool in protecting the public. Likewise, firms injured by the false claims of competitors often request it as a remedy (Power Bar has requested the FTC to require Balance Bar to run corrective ads concerning the clinical claims described earlier). However, a recent court ruling has challenged the conditions under which the FTC can require corrective advertising. Significantly, the challenge centers on how strongly the false impression must be learned before corrective advertising is necessary to erase it.[42]

Adequacy of Consumer Information It is important that consumers have not only accurate information but adequate information as well. To ensure information adequacy, a number of laws have been passed, such as the federal truth-in-lending legislation. This law requires full disclosure of finance charges and other aspects of credit transactions.

Nutritional labeling has been required for years and was significantly revised in 1990. While research findings on the impact of such labels are mixed, the labels do provide valuable information to many consumers. A consistent stream of consumer behavior

ILLUSTRATION 20-4

Do consumers benefit from this level of required information, or does information overload set in?

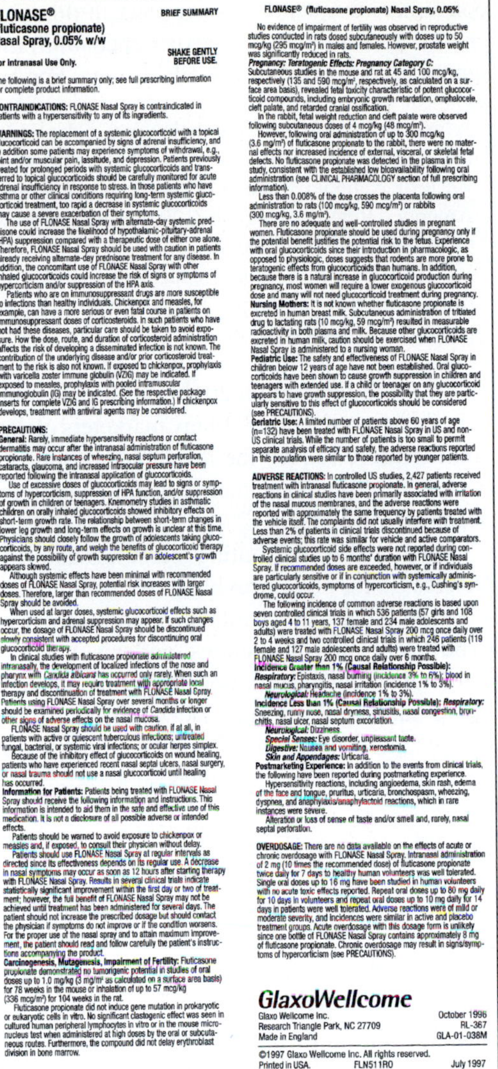

FLONASE®
(fluticasone propionate)
Nasal Spray, 0.05% w/w

BRIEF SUMMARY

SHAKE GENTLY BEFORE USE.

For Intranasal Use Only.

The following is a brief summary only; see full prescribing information for complete product information.

CONTRAINDICATIONS: FLONASE Nasal Spray is contraindicated in patients with a hypersensitivity to any of its ingredients.

WARNINGS: The replacement of a systemic glucocorticoid with a topical glucocorticoid can be accompanied by signs of adrenal insufficiency, and in addition some patients may experience symptoms of withdrawal, e.g., joint and/or muscular pain, lassitude, and depression. Patients previously treated for prolonged periods with systemic glucocorticoids and transferred to topical glucocorticoids should be carefully monitored for acute adrenal insufficiency in response to stress. In those patients who have asthma or other clinical conditions requiring long-term systemic glucocorticoid treatment, too rapid a decrease in systemic glucocorticoids may cause a severe exacerbation of their symptoms.

The use of FLONASE Nasal Spray with alternate-day systemic prednisone could increase the likelihood of hypothalamic-pituitary-adrenal (HPA) suppression compared with a therapeutic dose of either one alone. Therefore, FLONASE Nasal Spray should be used with caution in patients already receiving alternate-day prednisone treatment for any disease. In addition, the concomitant use of FLONASE Nasal Spray with other inhaled glucocorticoids could increase the risk of signs or symptoms of hypercorticism and/or suppression of the HPA axis.

Patients who are on immunosuppressant drugs are more susceptible to infections than healthy individuals. Chickenpox and measles, for example, can have a more serious or even fatal course in patients on immunosuppressant doses of corticosteroids. In such patients who have not had these diseases, particular care should be taken to avoid exposure. How the dose, route, and duration of corticosteroid administration affects the risk of developing a disseminated infection is not known. The contribution of the underlying disease and/or prior corticosteroid treatment to the risk is also not known. If exposed to chickenpox, prophylaxis with varicella zoster immune globulin (VZIG) may be indicated. If exposed to measles, prophylaxis with pooled intramuscular immunoglobulin (IG) may be indicated. (See the respective package inserts for complete VZIG and IG prescribing information.) If chickenpox develops, treatment with antiviral agents may be considered.

PRECAUTIONS:
General: Rarely, immediate hypersensitivity reactions or contact dermatitis may occur after the intranasal administration of fluticasone propionate. Rare instances of wheezing, nasal septum perforation, cataracts, glaucoma, and increased intraocular pressure have been reported following the intranasal application of glucocorticoids.

Use of excessive doses of glucocorticoids may lead to signs or symptoms of hypercorticism, suppression of HPA function, and/or suppression of growth in children or teenagers. Knemometry studies in asthmatic children on orally inhaled glucocorticoids showed inhibitory effects on short-term growth rate. The relationship between short-term changes in lower leg growth and long-term effects on growth is unclear at this time. Physicians should closely follow the growth of adolescents taking glucocorticoids, by any route, and weigh the benefits of glucocorticoid therapy against the possibility of growth suppression if an adolescent's growth appears slowed.

Although systemic effects have been minimal with recommended doses of FLONASE Nasal Spray, potential risk increases with larger doses. Therefore, larger than recommended doses of FLONASE Nasal Spray should be avoided.

When used at larger doses, systemic glucocorticoid effects such as hypercorticism and adrenal suppression may appear. If such changes occur, the dosage of FLONASE Nasal Spray should be discontinued slowly consistent with accepted procedures for discontinuing oral glucocorticoid therapy.

In clinical studies with fluticasone propionate administered intranasally, the development of localized infections of the nose and pharynx with *Candida albicans* has occurred only rarely. When such an infection develops, it may require treatment with appropriate local therapy and discontinuation of treatment with FLONASE Nasal Spray. Patients using FLONASE Nasal Spray over several months or longer should be examined periodically for evidence of *Candida* infection or other signs of adverse effects on the nasal mucosa.

FLONASE Nasal Spray should be used with caution, if at all, in patients with active or quiescent tuberculous infections; untreated fungal, bacterial, or systemic viral infections; or ocular herpes simplex.

Because of the inhibitory effect of glucocorticoids on wound healing, patients who have experienced recent nasal septal ulcers, nasal surgery, or nasal trauma should not use a nasal glucocorticoid until healing has occurred.

Information for Patients: Patients being treated with FLONASE Nasal Spray should receive the following information and instructions. This information is intended to aid them in the safe and effective use of this medication. It is not a disclosure of all possible adverse or intended effects.

Patients should be warned to avoid exposure to chickenpox or measles and, if exposed, to consult their physician without delay.

Patients should use FLONASE Nasal Spray at regular intervals as directed since its effectiveness depends on its regular use. A decrease in nasal symptoms may occur as soon as 12 hours after starting therapy with FLONASE Nasal Spray. Results in several clinical trials indicate statistically significant improvement within the first day or two of treatment; however, the full benefit of FLONASE Nasal Spray may not be achieved until treatment has been administered for several days. The patient should not increase the prescribed dosage but should contact the physician if symptoms do not improve or if the condition worsens. For the proper use of the nasal spray and to attain maximum improvement, the patient should read and follow carefully the patient's instructions accompanying the product.

Carcinogenesis, Mutagenesis, Impairment of Fertility: Fluticasone propionate demonstrated no tumorigenic potential in studies of oral doses up to 1.0 mg/kg (3 mg/m² as calculated on a surface area basis) for 78 weeks in the mouse or inhalation of up to 57 mcg/kg (336 mcg/m²) for 104 weeks in the rat.

Fluticasone propionate did not induce gene mutation in prokaryotic or eukaryotic cells in vitro. No significant clastogenic effect was seen in cultured human peripheral lymphocytes in vitro or in the mouse micronucleus test when administered at high doses by the oral or subcutaneous routes. Furthermore, the compound did not delay erythroblast division in bone marrow.

FLONASE® (fluticasone propionate) Nasal Spray, 0.05%

No evidence of impairment of fertility was observed in reproductive studies conducted in rats dosed subcutaneously with doses up to 50 mcg/kg (295 mcg/m²) in males and females. However, prostate weight was significantly reduced in rats.

Pregnancy: Teratogenic Effects: Pregnancy Category C: Subcutaneous studies in the mouse and rat at 45 and 100 mcg/kg, respectively (135 and 590 mcg/m², respectively, as calculated on a surface area basis), revealed fetal toxicity characteristic of potent glucocorticoid compounds, including embryonic growth retardation, omphalocele, cleft palate, and retarded cranial ossification.

In the rabbit, fetal weight reduction and cleft palate were observed following subcutaneous doses of 4 mcg/kg (48 mcg/m²).

However, following oral administration of up to 300 mcg/kg (3.6 mg/m²) of fluticasone propionate to the rabbit, there were no maternal effects nor increased incidence of external, visceral, or skeletal fetal defects. No fluticasone propionate was detected in the plasma in this study, consistent with the established low bioavailability following oral administration (see CLINICAL PHARMACOLOGY section of full prescribing information).

Less than 0.008% of the dose crosses the placenta following oral administration to rats (100 mcg/kg, 590 mcg/m²) or rabbits (300 mcg/kg, 3.6 mg/m²).

There are no adequate and well-controlled studies in pregnant women. Fluticasone propionate should be used during pregnancy only if the potential benefit justifies the potential risk to the fetus. Experience with oral glucocorticoids since their introduction in pharmacologic, as opposed to physiologic, doses suggests that rodents are more prone to teratogenic effects from glucocorticoids than humans. In addition, because there is a natural increase in glucocorticoid production during pregnancy, most women will require a lower exogenous glucocorticoid dose and many will not need glucocorticoid treatment during pregnancy.

Nursing Mothers: It is not known whether fluticasone propionate is excreted in human breast milk. Subcutaneous administration of tritiated drug to lactating rats (10 mcg/kg, 59 mcg/m²) resulted in measurable radioactivity in both plasma and milk. Because other glucocorticoids are excreted in human milk, caution should be exercised when FLONASE Nasal Spray is administered to a nursing woman.

Pediatric Use: The safety and effectiveness of FLONASE Nasal Spray in children below 12 years of age have not been established. Oral glucocorticoids have been shown to cause growth suppression in children and teenagers with extended use. If a child or teenager on any glucocorticoid appears to have growth suppression, the possibility that they are particularly sensitive to this effect of glucocorticoids should be considered (see PRECAUTIONS).

Geriatric Use: A limited number of patients above 60 years of age (n=132) have been treated with FLONASE Nasal Spray in US and non-US clinical trials. While the number of patients is too small to permit separate analysis of efficacy and safety, the adverse reactions reported in this population were similar to those reported by younger patients.

ADVERSE REACTIONS: In controlled US studies, 2,427 patients received treatment with intranasal fluticasone propionate. In general, adverse reactions in clinical studies have been primarily associated with irritation of the nasal mucous membranes, and the adverse reactions were reported with approximately the same frequency by patients treated with the vehicle itself. The complaints did not usually interfere with treatment. Less than 2% of patients in clinical trials discontinued because of adverse events; this rate was similar for vehicle and active comparators.

Systemic glucocorticoid side effects were not reported during controlled clinical studies up to 6 months' duration with FLONASE Nasal Spray. If recommended doses are exceeded, however, or if individuals are particularly sensitive or if in conjunction with systemically administered glucocorticoids, symptoms of hypercorticism, e.g., Cushing's syndrome, could occur.

The following incidence of common adverse reactions is based upon seven controlled clinical trials in which 536 patients (57 girls and 108 boys aged 4 to 11 years, 137 female and 234 male adolescents and adults) were treated with FLONASE Nasal Spray 200 mcg once daily over 2 to 4 weeks and two controlled clinical trials in which 246 patients (119 female and 127 male adolescents and adults) were treated with FLONASE Nasal Spray 200 mcg once daily over 6 months.

Incidence Greater than 1% (Causal Relationship Possible):
Respiratory: Epistaxis, nasal burning (incidence 3% to 6%); blood in nasal mucus, pharyngitis, nasal irritation (incidence 1% to 3%).
Neurological: Headache (incidence 1% to 3%).

Incidence Less than 1% (Causal Relationship Possible): ***Respiratory:*** Sneezing, runny nose, nasal dryness, sinusitis, nasal congestion, bronchitis, nasal ulcer, nasal septum excoriation.
Neurological: Dizziness.
Special Senses: Eye disorder, unpleasant taste.
Digestive: Nausea and vomiting, xerostomia.
Skin and Appendages: Urticaria.

Postmarketing Experience: In addition to the events from clinical trials, the following have been reported during postmarketing experience.

Hypersensitivity reactions, including angioedema, skin rash, edema of the face and tongue, pruritus, urticaria, bronchospasm, wheezing, dyspnea, and anaphylaxis/anaphylactoid reactions, which in rare instances were severe.

Alteration or loss of sense of taste and/or smell and, rarely, nasal septal perforation.

OVERDOSAGE: There are no data available on the effects of acute or chronic overdosage with FLONASE Nasal Spray. Intranasal administration of 2 mg (10 times the recommended dose) of fluticasone propionate twice daily for 7 days to healthy human volunteers was well tolerated. Single oral doses up to 16 mg have been studied in human volunteers with no acute toxic effects reported. Repeat oral doses up to 80 mg daily for 10 days in volunteers and repeat oral doses up to 10 mg daily for 14 days in patients were well tolerated. Adverse reactions were of mild or moderate severity, and incidences were similar in active and placebo treatment groups. Acute overdosage with this dosage form is unlikely since one bottle of FLONASE Nasal Spray contains approximately 8 mg of fluticasone propionate. Chronic overdosage may result in signs/symptoms of hypercorticism (see PRECAUTIONS).

GlaxoWellcome
Glaxo Wellcome Inc.
Research Triangle Park, NC 27709
Made in England

October 1996
RL-367
GLA-01-038M

Printed in USA. FLN511R0 July 1997

Courtesy Glaxo Wellcome, Inc.

research since these rules were enacted has uncovered a number of potential improvements in the manner in which the information is presented (see Chapter 8). Unfortunately, as with many such programs, those who are relatively disadvantaged in terms of education and income are least able to use this type of information.[43]

Marketers, consumer groups, and public officials would like consumers to have all the information they need to make sound choices. One approach is to provide all potentially relevant information. This approach is frequently recommended by regulatory agencies and is required for some product categories such as drugs. Problems with this approach can arise, however. For example, a relatively simple, one-page advertisement for Flonase nasal spray required the second full page of small type shown in Illustration 20-4 telling of dosage, precautions, and warnings in order to comply with federal full-disclosure regulations.

The assumption behind the full-disclosure approach is that each consumer will utilize those specific information items required for the particular decision. Unfortunately, consumers frequently do not react in this manner, particularly for low-involvement purchases. Instead, they may experience *information overload* (see Chapter 8, page 290) and ignore all or most of the available data. For example:

> A federal act required banks belonging to the Federal Reserve to explain to their customers the detailed protections built into money transfer systems available in electronic banking. Thus, Northwestern National Bank of Minneapolis was forced to create and mail a pamphlet explaining Amended Regulation E to its 120,000 customers. At a cost of $69,000 the bank created and mailed the 4,500-word pamphlet.
>
> In 100 of the pamphlets, the bank placed a special paragraph that offered the reader $10 just for finding that paragraph. The pamphlets were mailed in May and June. As of August, not one person had claimed the money![44]

Examine Illustration 20-4 carefully. Would you read this ad (the ad was slightly larger than this reproduction)? Many marketers claim that such ads add to the costs of advertising and therefore reduce the available consumer information without an offset in consumer benefit.[45] Many consumer advocates agree that the current approach is not meeting the needs of consumers.

A new issue confronting marketers and regulators is disclosure in Internet advertising. Disclosure involves providing relevant qualifiers to advertising claims such as "limited to stock on hand," or "available at participating outlets only." The FTC requires disclosures to be "clear and conspicuous" and this standard has been translated into clear guidelines for print, television, and radio ads. What constitutes "clear and conspicuous" on the Internet? Is it a banner? A pop-up? Does it need a frame around it? This is yet another area where knowledge of consumer information processing and consumer research can help produce effective regulatory guidelines.

Product Issues

Consumer groups have two major concerns with products—*Are they safe?* and *Are they environmentally sound?* A variety of federal and state agencies are involved in ensuring that products are safe to use. The most important are the Food and Drug Administration and the Consumer Product Safety Commission. Product safety is generally not a controversial issue. However, it is impossible to remove all risk from products.

Should tricycles be banned? Accidents involving tricycles are a major cause of injury to young children. Manufacturers, consumer groups, and individuals differ on where the line should be drawn and who should draw it. Some feel that tricycles should indeed be banned. Others feel that parents should decide if their children should ride tricycles. However, both would agree that information on both the risks of tricycle riding and ways of reducing the risk should be made available to purchasers (though there is disagreement on who should make the data available and how it should be made available). Of course, tricycles represent only one of many products subject to such a debate.

We examined consumers' desires for environmentally sound products in some detail in Chapter 3. As indicated there, many consumers want products whose production, use, and disposition produce minimal environmental harm. Many marketers are striving to produce such products. Nonetheless, many consumer groups want regulations requiring faster movement in this area and required, rather than voluntary, compliance with environmental standards.

Potentially injurious products such as guns, tobacco products, and alcoholic beverages are subject to a wide variety of regulations at the federal, state, and even city level. A recent controversy in this area is the introduction of "alcoholic lemonades." These beverages are

ILLUSTRATION 20-5

What regulations, if any, are appropriate for this controversial product category?

bottled like beer or soft drinks, often have cartoon character labels, contain about the same amount of alcohol as beer, but are flavored like lemonade, which almost completely masks the alcohol taste (see Illustration 20-5).

Critics contend that the drinks are designed to hook teenagers on alcohol. According to one 16-year-old girl:

> They taste just like lemonade. That's why we drink them. You can drink them so fast. They just go right down.[46]

Should such products be banned? Attempts are being made to restrict the types of labels they can have as well as the way they can be advertised. *How would you deal with this issue?*

Pricing Issues

Consumer groups want prices that are fair (generally defined as competitively determined) and accurately stated (contain no hidden charges). The Federal Trade Commission is the primary federal agency involved in regulating pricing activities.

Unit pricing is *the presentation of price information on a common basis such as per ounce across brands.* Such information, when properly displayed, can greatly facilitate price comparisons.

Perhaps the most controversial pricing area today is the use of reference prices. An **external reference price** is a price provided by the manufacturer or retailer in addition to the actual current price of the product. Such terms as *Compare at $X, Usually $X, Suggested retail price $Y—Our price only $X* are common ways of presenting reference prices (see Chapter 17, page 603). The concern arises when the reference price is one at which no or few sales actually occur. While most states and the federal government have regulations concerning the use of reference prices, they are difficult to enforce. Given the history of abuse of reference prices, it is not surprising that many consumers are skeptical of them.

SUMMARY

Consumerism is a loose, unstructured social movement with the purpose of enhancing the power of buyers relative to the power of sellers. The current consumerism movement began in the 1960s, as large numbers of consumers became increasingly dissatisfied with marketing practices. However, such nonmarketing forces as the increasing technological sophistication of products, increased time and financial pressures on many families, and consumer choices that produced an impersonal marketplace have also contributed to the consumerism movement.

Consumer groups often attempt to change the marketing practices of individual firms or industries through discussion, publicity, or boycotts. However, the solution preferred by many groups is governmental regulation. Four major areas of continuing concern to consumer groups and regulators are marketing to children, consumer information, pricing issues, and product issues.

Marketing to children is a major concern to the consumerism movement. A major reason for this concern is evidence based on Piaget's theory of cognitive development that children are not able to fully comprehend commercial messages. This had led to rules issued by both the Federal Trade Commission (FTC) and the Children's Advertising Review Unit (CARU) of the National Advertising Division (NAD) of the Council of Better Business Bureaus. These rules focus mainly on being sure that commercials are clearly separated from the program content and that the words and pictures in the commercials do not mislead children having limited cognitive skills.

In addition to concerns about children's comprehension of advertisements, there is concern about the effect of the content of commercials on children. The extensive advertising of high-fat and high-sugar products raises a concern about its effect on the health of children. Since children watch a substantial amount of prime-time television, there is also a danger that ads aimed at adults will inspire children to take inappropriate actions. In addition, there is concern that the enormous amount of advertising that children view will lead to values that are overly materialistic.

There are a number of marketing activities aimed at children other than television advertising that cause concerns. Kids' clubs with a strong emphasis on sales to children have been strongly criticized. Corporate programs that place strong sales messages in "educational" materials supplied to schools have also come under attack. Children's advocates are now particularly concerned about marketing to children on the Internet.

Regulators and business alike are also concerned that adults receive accurate and adequate information about products. The cumulative impact of numerous ads focusing on narcissistic values and product ownership on society's values is a controversial issue.

The consumerism movement, regulators, and responsible marketers want consumers to have sufficient, adequate information to make sound purchase decisions. Attempts to regulate the amount of information provided sometimes overlook information overload and are not effective.

The focus of the consumerism movement on products is twofold: *Are they safe?* and *Are they environmentally sound?*

Concern with pricing is that prices be fair and accurately presented in a manner that allows comparison across brands.

KEY TERMS

Children's Advertising Review Unit (CARU) 713
Consumerism 711
Consumerism movement 711
Corrective advertising 728
External reference price 731
Kids' clubs 717
Unit pricing 731

INTERNET EXERCISES

1. Visit the Federal Trade Commission Web site (http://www.ftc.gov).
   a. What issues involving television advertising to children appear?
   b. What issues involving Internet marketing to children appear?
   c. What other issues involving marketing to children appear?
2. Visit the Better Business Bureau Web site (http://www.bbb.org).
   a. What issues involving television advertising to children appear?
   b. What issues involving Internet marketing to children appear?
   c. What other issues involving marketing to children appear?
3. Visit the Center for Media Education Web site (http://www.cme.org/cme).
   a. What issues involving television advertising to children appear?
   b. What issues involving Internet marketing to children appear?
   c. What other issues involving marketing to children appear?
4. Visit the TrustE Web site (http://www.truste.com).
   a. Evaluate its approach to privacy.
   b. Evaluate the Kids TrustE seal.
5. Visit one of the sites listed below. Evaluate the effectiveness of the site in terms of marketing to children and the degree to which it represents an ethically sound approach to marketing to children.
   a. http://www.kidscom.com
   b. http://www.colgate.com/Kids-world/
   c. http://www.oscar-mayer.com
   d. http://www.disney.com
6. Visit several companies' Web sites. Evaluate the accuracy and completeness of the data provided at those sites.
7. Visit the Federal Trade Commission Web site (http://www.ftc.gov).
   a. What issues involving advertising to adults appear?
   b. What issues involving Internet marketing to adults appear?
   c. What other issues involving pricing to adults appear?
   d. What issues involving product safety appear?
   e. What other marketing issues involving adults appear?
8. Visit the Better Business Bureau Web site (http://www.bbb.org).
   a. What issues involving advertising to adults appear?
   b. What issues involving Internet marketing to adults appear?
   c. What other issues involving pricing to adults appear?
   d. What issues involving product safety appear?
   e. What other marketing issues involving adults appear?

DDB NEEDHAM LIFESTYLE DATA ANALYSES

1. What characterizes individuals who feel there is too much sex in advertising? What are the marketing implications of this? What are the regulatory implications of this?
2. What characterizes individuals who refuse to buy a brand whose advertising they dislike? What are the marketing implications of this? What are the regulatory implications of this?
3. What characterizes individuals who feel that big companies are just out for themselves? What are the marketing implications of this? What are the regulatory implications of this?

REVIEW QUESTIONS

1. What is the *consumerism movement?* What are its objectives?
2. What is the *Consumers' Bill of Rights?*
3. What caused the consumerism movement to come into existence?
4. What are the major concerns in marketing to children?
5. What are the two main issues concerning children's ability to comprehend advertising messages?
6. What is *CARU?* What does it do? What are some of its rules?
7. What are the major concerns about the effect of the *content* of commercial messages on children?
8. What are the issues concerning the impact of advertising on children's health and safety?
9. What are the issues concerning the impact of advertising on children's values?
10. What are the concerns associated with kids' clubs sponsored by commercial firms?
11. How do firms advertise in the classroom? What issues does this raise? What is Consumers Union's recommendation concerning advertising in the classroom?
12. Why are consumer advocates worried about marketing to kids on the Internet?
13. What are the issues concerning the impact of advertising on adults' values?
14. What are the concerns with *consumer information accuracy?*
15. What are the concerns with *consumer information adequacy?*
16. What is *information overload?*
17. What is *corrective advertising?*
18. What are the major consumerism issues with respect to products?
19. What are the major consumerism issues with respect to prices?
20. What is *unit pricing?*
21. What is a *reference price?* What is the concern with reference prices?

DISCUSSION QUESTIONS

22. A television advertisement for General Mills' Total cereal made the following claim: "It would take 16 ounces of the leading natural cereal to equal the vitamins in 1 ounce of fortified Total." The Center for Science in the Public Interest filed a petition against General Mills claiming that the advertisement is deceptive. It was the center's position that the claim overstated Total's nutritional benefits because the cereal is not 16 times higher in other factors important to nutrition.
    a. Is the claim misleading? Justify your answer.
    b. How should the FTC proceed in cases such as this?
    c. What are the implications of cases such as this for marketing management?
23. In recent years, manufacturers of meat products have introduced a product labeled as "turkey ham." The product looks like ham and tastes like ham but it contains no pork; it is all turkey. A nationwide survey of consumers showed that most believed that the meat product contained both turkey and ham. The USDA approved this label based on a dictionary definition for the technical term *ham:* the thigh cut of meat from the hind leg of any animal. Discuss how consumers processed information concerning this product and used this information in purchasing this product. (One court ruled the label to be misleading but was overruled by a higher court.)
    a. Is the label misleading?
    b. How should the FTC proceed in such cases?
24. Do you consider yourself to be a consumerist? Why, or why not?
25. What, if anything, would you add to the Consumers' Bill of Rights?
26. How much, if any, advertising should be allowed on television programs aimed at children?
27. Should there be special rules governing the advertising of food and snack products to children?
28. Does advertising influence children's values? What can the FTC and/or CARU do to ensure that

positive values are promoted? Be precise in your response.

29. What rules, if any, should govern kids' clubs?
30. What rules, if any, should govern marketing to kids on the Internet?
31. What rules, if any, should govern advertising and promotional messages presented in the classroom?
32. Does advertising influence or reflect a society's values?
33. Do you agree that beer advertisements portraying groups of active young adults having fun while consuming beer teach people that the way to be popular and have fun is to consume alcohol?
34. Do you think corrective advertising works? Evaluate the three corrective messages described in the text.
35. "Since riding tricycles is a major cause of accidental injury to young children, the product should be banned." State and defend your position on this issue.
36. How, if at all, would you regulate the new lemonade-flavored alcoholic beverages?
37. To what extent, if at all, do you use nutrition labels? Why?
38. Do you believe reference prices generally reflect prices at which substantial amounts of the product are normally sold?

APPLICATION ACTIVITIES

39. Interview 10 students and determine their degree of concern and activities with respect to consumerism issues. What do you conclude?
40. Watch two hours of Saturday morning children's programming on a commercial channel. Note how many commercials are run. What products are involved? What are the major themes? Would hundreds of hours of viewing these commercials over the course of several years have any impact on children's values?
41. Interview a child 2 to 4 years of age, one between 5 and 7, and one between 8 and 10. Determine their understanding of the selling intent and techniques of television commercials.
42. Interview two children who belong to one or more kids' clubs. Describe the club and the child's reactions to it. Determine the extent to which the club is successful in selling things to the child.
43. Interview two grade school teachers and get their responses to material provided by corporations and Consumers Union's proposed rules for such materials.
44. Repeat Question 40 for prime-time television and adults.
45. Find and copy or describe two ads that you feel are misleading. Justify your selection.
46. Visit a large supermarket. Identify the best and worst breakfast cereal considering both cost and nutrition. What do you conclude?

REFERENCES

1. J. DeCoursey, "Klein's Apology Wearing Thin," *Advertising Age,* September 4, 1995, p. 35; J. Brady, "Fueling the Heat," *Advertising Age,* September 4, 1995, p. 1; P. Sloan and J. DeCoursey, "Gov't Hot on Trail of Calvin Klein Ads," *Advertising Age,* September 11, 1995, p. 1; A. Sachs, "Kiddie Porn or Bad Taste," *Advertising Age,* September 18, 1995, p. 52; and C. Miller, "Sexy Sizzle Backfires," *Marketing News,* September 25, 1996, pp. 1–2.
2. Miller, footnote 1, p. 2.
3. See M. C. Martin, "Children's Understanding of the Intent of Advertising," *Journal of Public Policy & Marketing,* Fall 1997, pp. 205–16.
4. "NAD Slams Spot from Mattel," *Advertising Age,* October 19, 1987, p. 6; and S. Weinstein, "Fight Heats Up against Kids' TV 'Commershows,'" *Marketing News,* October 9, 1989, p. 2.
5. L. Carlson, R. N. Laczniak, and D. D. Muehling, "Understanding Parental Concern about Toy-Based Programming," *Journal of Current Issues and Research in Advertising,* Fall 1994, pp. 59–72.
6. M. A. Stutts and G. G. Hunnicutt, "Can Young Children Understand Disclaimers?" *Journal of Advertising,* no. 1 (1987), pp. 41–46.
7. R. H. Kolbe and D. D. Muehling, "An Investigation of the Fine Print in Children's Television Advertising," *Journal of Current Issues and Research in Advertising,* Fall 1995, pp. 77–95.
8. "VLI Is Challenged," *Advertising Age,* February 16, 1987, p. 12.
9. "NAD Ruling Gives Total Victory," *Advertising Age,* July 17, 1989, p. 41.
10. S. W. Colford, "FTC Hits Galoob, Agency for Ads," *Advertising Age,* December 10, 1990, p. 62.

11. R. Weisskoff, "Current Trends in Children's Advertising," *Journal of Advertising Research,* March 1985, pp. 12–14.

12. "B-M Drops Spots after Query by NAD," *Advertising Age,* April 20, 1981, p. 10.

13. A. R. Wiman and L. M. Newman, "Television Advertising and Children's Nutritional Awareness," *Journal of the Academy of Marketing Science,* Spring 1989, pp. 179–88.

14. E. DeNitto, "Fast-Food Ads Come under Fire," *Advertising Age,* February 14, 1994, p. S-14.

15. See *Selling America's Kids* (Yonkers, NY: Consumers Union Educational Services, 1990), p. 14.

16. S. W. Colford, "Top Kid TV Offender: Premiums," *Advertising Age,* April 29, 1991, p. 52.

17. C. Miller, "Marketers Hoping Kids Will Join Club," *Marketing News,* January 31, 1994, pp. 1–2.

18. See footnote 15, p. 15.

19. See footnote 17, p. 2.

20. See J. E. Brand and B. S. Greenberg, "Commercials in the Classroom," *Journal of Advertising Research,* January 1994, pp. 18–27.

21. J. Schwartz, "Schools for Sale?" *Marketing News,* August 17, 1998, p. 12.

22. C. Miller, "Marketers Find a Seat in the Classroom," *Marketing News,* June 20, 1994, p. 2.

23. B. Bosch, "What's for Lunch? Coupons," *Advertising Age,* November 27, 1995, p. 3.

24. This section is based on K. Montgomery and S. Pasnik, *Web of Deception* (Washington, D.C.: Center for Media Education, 1996).

25. I. Teinowitz, "FTC Chief Asks Congress to Ensure Privacy on Web," *Advertising Age,* June 8, 1998, p. 53.

26. "Many Kids' Web Sites Continuing to Collect Personal Information," Center for Media Education, July 19, 1999.

27. I. Teinowitz, "GeoCities Settles FTC Privacy Case," *Advertising Age,* August 17, 1998, p. 4.

28. See B. G. Englis, M. R. Solomon, and R. D. Ashmore, "Beauty *Before* the Eyes of Beholders," *Journal of Advertising,* June 1994, pp. 49–64; M. C. Martin and P. F. Kennedy, "Social Comparison and the Beauty of Advertising Models," in *Advances in Consumer Research XXI,* ed. C. T. Allen and D. R. John (Provo, UT: Association for Consumer Research, 1994), pp. 365–71; C. R. Wiles, J. A. Wiles, and A. Tjernlund, "The Ideology of Advertising," *Journal of Advertising Research,* May, 1996, pp. 57–66; and M. C. Martin and J. W. Gentry, "Stuck in the Model Trap," *Journal of Advertising,* Summer 1997, pp. 19–33.

29. S. Burton, R. G. Netemeyer, and D. R. Lichtenstein, "Gender Differences for Appearance-Related Attitudes and Behaviors," *Journal of Public Policy & Marketing,* Fall 1994, pp. 60–75.

30. For research in these areas, see R. W. Pollay and S. Lysonski, "In the Eye of the Beholder," *Journal of International Consumer Marketing* 6, no. 2 (1993), pp. 25–43; D. Walsh, "Safe Sex in Advertising," *American Demographics,* April 1994, pp. 24–30; and R. H. Kolbe and D. Muehling, "Gender Roles and Children's Television Advertising," *Journal of Current Issues and Research in Advertising,* Spring 1995, pp. 49–64.

31. C. Rubel, "Marketers Giving Better Treatment to Females," *Marketing News,* April 22, 1996, p. 10.

32. See L. Langmeyer, "Advertising Images of Mature Adults," *Journal of Current Issues and Research in Advertising,* Fall 1993, pp. 81–91; C. R. Taylor and J. Y. Lee, "Not in *Vogue,*" *Journal of Public Policy & Marketing,* Fall 1994, pp. 239–45; T. H. Stevenson and P. E. McIntyre, "A Comparison of the Portrayal and Frequency of Hispanics and Whites in English Language Television Advertising"; and M. T. Elliott, "Differences in the Portrayal of Blacks"; both in *Journal of Current Issues and Research in Advertising,* Spring 1995, pp. 65–86; J. M. Bristor, R. G. Lee, and M. R. Hunt, "Race and Ideology," *Journal of Public Policy & Marketing,* Spring 1995, pp. 48–59; E. J. Wilson and A. Biswas, "The Use of Black Models in Specialty Catalogs," *Journal of Direct Marketing,* Autumn 1995, pp. 47–56; and K. Karande and A. Grbavac, "Acculturation and the Use of Asian Models in Print Advertisements," *Enhancing Knowledge Development in Marketing* (Chicago: American Marketing Association, 1996), pp. 347–52.

33. See L. J. Shrum, "Television and Persuasion," *Psychology & Marketing,* March 1999, pp. 119–40.

34. See A. Simonson and M. B. Holbrook, "Permissible Puffery versus Actionable Warranty in Advertising and Salestalk," *Journal of Public Policy & Marketing,* Fall 1993, pp. 216–33.

35. "Diving Association May Not Use 'Seal of Approval' Unless Based on Tests," *FTC New Summary,* May 21, 1982, p. 1. See R. F. Beltramini and E. R. Stafford, "Comprehension and Perceived Believability of Seals of Approval Information in Advertising," *Journal of Advertising,* September 1993, pp. 4–13.

36. J. Pollack, "Arm & Hammer Brand Fights Toothpaste Rivals," *Advertising Age,* July 27, 1998, p. 2.

37. See J.-N. Kapferer, "Brand Confusion," *Psychology & Marketing,* September 1995, pp. 551–68.

38. C. A. Cole and G. J. Gaeth, "Cognitive and Age-Related Differences in the Ability to Use Nutritional Information in a Complex Environment," *Journal of Marketing Research,* May 1990, pp. 175–84; and W. Mueller, "Who Reads the Label?" *American Demographics,* January 1991, pp. 36–40.

39. B. Reid, "Adequacy of Symbolic Warnings," *Marketing News,* October 25, 1985, p. 3.

40. M. L. Retsky, "Survey Research Is Useful in False Advertising Cases," *Marketing News,* April 27, 1998, p. 8; and M. L. Retsky, "Misleading Ads Could Be as Litigious as Outright Lies," *Marketing News,* August 3, 1998, p. 5.

41. See G. V. Johar, "Consumer Involvement and Deception from Implied Advertising Campaigns," *Journal of Marketing Research,* August 1995, pp. 267–79.

42. I. Teinowitz, "FTC Faces Test of Ad Power," *Advertising Age,* March 30, 1998, p. 26.

43. See R. P. Hill, D. L. Ramp, and L. Silver, "The Rent-to-Own Industry and Pricing Disclosure Tactics," *Journal of Public Policy & Marketing,* Spring 1998, pp. 3–10.

44. "$10 Sure Thing," *Time,* August 4, 1980, p. 51.

45. See M. Wilkie, "Rx Marketers 'Test' FDA Guides on Print DTC Ads," *Advertising Age,* April 6, 1998, p. 18.

46. D. Leonhardt, "A Little Booze for the Kiddies," *Business Week,* September 23, 1996, p. 158.

Cases

6-1 Internet Marketing to Children

In 1996, the Center for Media Education (CME) released a report on the use of the Internet in marketing to children. This report has triggered a wide-ranging debate on the proper use of marketing tactics on the Internet focused on children. The CME has identified two major areas of ethical concern that might require new or revised regulations: invasion of privacy of children and unfair or deceptive advertising.

Children and the Internet

Millions of children now use the Internet regularly. The Internet has many desirable features for children (as well as adults). They can use it to communicate with friends and to make new friends. They can share ideas and seek new information. They can interact with programs and control the timing and content of the communications environment. New developments are announced almost daily that increase the value and pleasure of using the Internet. Sites such as NASA's Jason project and PBS's Electronic Field Trips expose children to places, people, and ideas that challenge and broaden their view of the world.

Marketing managers have observed both children's increasing use of the Internet and the ability of the Internet to provide a unique communications environment. Here is how CME characterizes this process:

> Ad agencies have begun to devote major resources to using on-line media to give their clients unprecedented access to children. A perfect example is Saatchi & Saatchi, which has set up special units to carefully study children on-line and to develop sophisticated marketing strategies to target them. Cultural anthropologists have been hired to examine the nature of "kids culture"; researchers have studied how children process information and respond to advertising; and psychologists have conducted one-on-one sessions with sample groups of children. These experts found that children, whose "learning skills are at their peak," can easily master the new media's learning curve, which is often daunting for adults. They also determined that the on-line world corresponds to the "four themes of childhood . . . attachment/separation, attainment of power, social interaction, and mastery/learning." And, perhaps most important, they found that when children go on-line, they quickly enter the "flow state," that "highly pleasurable experience of total absorption in a challenging activity." All these factors make on-line media a perfect vehicle for advertising to children. Says Greun (director of Saatchi & Saatchi Interactive): "There is nothing else that exists like it for advertisers to build relationships with kids."

Many would argue that there is nothing wrong with advertisers building relationships with kids. Many would also argue that advertisers should feel free to use the most efficient media to build these relationships. However, the Internet is so unique and potentially powerful that it requires a thoughtful analysis before being considered just an efficient media. First, unlike other media that children confront, the Internet is largely immune from adult supervision—once a child masters it, he or she can visit many sites. Parents cannot easily monitor the locations visited nor can they easily keep up with the content of the numerous sites. Second, the Internet is interactive. It can respond to you based on how you respond to it. This is qualitatively different from other media. Third, the Internet can "learn." Internet programs can record and recall past interactions with consumers. This allows fully customized messages.

The unique powers of the Internet lead to the potential for abuse.

Invasion of Children's Privacy and Microtargeting

The CME report identified two questionable means of collecting data from children: incentives and tracking. Using such data to develop individualized offers and appeals (micromarketing) is also an ethical issue.

Incentives for Data A number of firms require children to supply data in order to visit a site. The CME considers many nonmandatory requests for personal data to be inappropriate as well. Here is how CME characterizes two such sites:

- Taking advantage of children's desire to belong to a group, the Splash Kids on the Microsoft Network promises to make children "Splash Kids" if they cooperate and answer questions about themselves . . . a Sony Discman is offered as a prize. A prominently placed icon, which reads "Sign-Up and Win," is linked to the questionnaire.

- At the Batman Forever site, supplying personal information becomes a test of loyalty. "Good citizens of the Web, help Commissioner Gordon with the Gotham Census," children are urged. Although the survey uses the guise of a virtual city's census, much of the information sought by this questionnaire pertains to purchasing habits and video preferences.

These approaches cause concern because younger children are not sophisticated enough to realize how the data may be used and therefore cannot make an informed judgment about providing the data.

Tracking Children Computer technologies allow firms to track all the interactions that users have on-line (contacts, not content). This is referred to as clickstream data or mouse droppings. Thus, it is possible to determine the sites visited by children.

Microtargeting Children Microtargeting is developing and delivering unique ads to each individual. While direct-mail marketers have been doing this for some time, the Internet makes it far easier to microtarget children. Today, many children's sites send new visitors unsolicited e-mail urging them to return, often promising new activities, gifts, or contests. The concern is that these simple approaches will soon incorporate much more personal data to develop sharply focused sales messages. One researcher describes the danger and the allure as follows:

> Instead of doing a commercial that's roughly targeted to boys five to seven, which is a lot of the advertising on Saturday morning TV, now you're targeting a particular boy, who has a particular interest in a particular program, who lives in a house, whose parents have a certain income . . . At that level of targeting, I think the opportunity for manipulation becomes much greater . . . we've never really existed before in an information environment where the TV could reach out to your child and say, "Bob, wouldn't you like to have this new action figure, just like in the movie you saw last week?"

Unfair Advertising to Children On-Line

The Federal Trade Commission has rules regarding advertising on television programs targeting children, including ones that (1) require "separators" between children's programs and commercials, (2) forbid the host of a children's show from directly promoting products to children, and (3) limit the amount of advertising time in children's programs. While these rules are difficult to apply to "action hero" television programs where the product and the show are an integrated whole, they do not yet exist as far as the Internet is concerned. The CME has identified three practices of concern in this area.

Branded Environments What some marketers consider excellent children's advertising, the CME sees as an invasive level of advertising:

> [C]reate an ad that's as much fun as the content (such as) games that kids can play that involve the products . . . then there'll be a reason for kids to click on the ads and interact with them and enjoy them.

This quote is from the head of Kids Site 3000 on America Online. The concern that the CME and others have is the inability of children to critically evaluate this environment and to understand and react to the selling intent.

Disney is one of the children's sites that raises concerns with the CME:

> In the Toy Story section alone, children can download movie clips, sound clips, computer icons, wallpaper patterns, coloring book pages, and a "Toy Story" concentration game. The bottom of each page of the website includes a "Sign-in" button that invites visitors to share personal information and to receive regular Disney on-line updates. The site also hypes its new on-line shopping area, The Disney Store, which is overflowing with children's merchandise.

Blended Advertising and Content Children often have difficulty separating commercials from program content. On the Internet, it is common to merge entertainment activities and commerical content:

> One of the sites easily reached from Nickelodeon's area on AOL is Mootown's website UdderNet, where there are a variety of activities tied to Mootown Snackers (snack foods). Children are invited to play the Cow Chip Toss Game and Mootown Hide and Seek. The Global Lunch Box is used to gather personal information from visitors.

Relationships through Spokescharacters Consider this quote from a Saatchi and Saatchi executive:

> Marketers here have an unparalleled opportunity to get kids actively involved with brands. Brand characters, brand logos, brand jingles, brand video, by cutting, pasting and coloring with these elements . . . it's very important that kids can change what they see and manipulate what they see and author new things based on elements

that we give them to put together. Advertisers can give kids public places to post these characters and also provide activities for kids to do together. And all, of course, within the brand environment and using brand spokespersons or other brand icons.

An example of using spokescharacters can be found on the Mighty Morphin Power Rangers Web site:

Click on any of the Power Rangers below to send them a quick note . . . I will get your letter delivered, no matter where in the Universe the Power Rangers and Monsters are, and I will forward their reply to you within 24 hours.

Discussion Questions

1. Do you share CME's concerns as described above? Why or why not?
2. What ethical responsibilities does a marketer have when communicating with kids via the Internet?
3. What, if any, regulations would you suggest for communicating with children via the Internet?
4. Should the following groups be allowed to communicate with children via the Internet? What restrictions, if any, should be applied?
   a. "Mainstream" religious groups
   b. "Mainstream" political groups
   c. "Fringe" religious groups
   d. "Radical" political groups
   e. Foreign governments
5. Visit two Web sites for children and evaluate their good and bad features.
   a. www.pbs.org/insidepbs/learningservices/eft.html
   b. www.batmanforever.com
   c. www.spectracom.com/description.html
   d. www.colgate.com/Kids-world/
   e. www.oscar-mayer.com

6-2 PETA's Anti-Fur Campaign

PETA, People for the Ethical Treatment of Animals, conducts a strong anti-fur campaign as part of its overall mission. Jannette Patterson, PETA's executive director, describes its program as follows:

PETA's mission statement is: Animals are not ours to eat, wear, experiment on, or use for entertainment. This encompasses our international Anti-Fur Campaign, which is directed toward consumers. Our goal is to expose the truth about the cruelty of the fur industry and to stimulate public discussion about fur garments and fur accessories, as most people will choose not to support an industry that exploits and abuses animals for fashion.

Celebrity involvement is a crucial part of this effort. Pamela Anderson Lee, Kim Basinger, Sheryl Lee, Kathy Najimy, and many other actors and models have posed for advertisements and posters bearing the message that "we'd rather go naked than wear fur." [See the opening illustration for Chapter 1 and Illustration A.] Bea Arthur and other celebrities have filmed public service announcements asking fur-owners to clear their consciences by donating their furs to PETA for use in protests.

Famous drag queens, including Lady Bunny, have lent a comic twist to the campaign at "Fur Is a Drag" fashion shows in New York and London, hosted by singer k.d. lang and *Saturday Night Live*'s gender-neutral Julia "Pat" Sweeney.

Public demonstrations in cities throughout the world draw public and media attention to the plight of mink, beavers, foxes, and other animals on fur farms. Clever street theater and striking visual images distinguish these protests: mass "funerals" for animals skinned of their fur; activists painted cadaver-white lying inside coffins underneath a banner reading, "I Wouldn't Be Caught Dead in Fur;" sexy "Leopard Ladies" wearing nothing but spots and a tail behind a banner reading, "Only Animals Should Wear Fur;" a caged human in a fox costume.

The fur industry's cruelty and misrepresentation to the public have been exposed by PETA's undercover investigations. In a fur sting, supermodel Magali wore a hidden video camera into fur salons and documented the salespeople denying the truth—that animals are drowned, electrocuted, and trapped before being made into fur garments. Clothing designer Stella McCartney, daughter of Sir Paul and Linda, narrated a video exposing filthy, inhumane conditions and the cruel slaughter of animals on an Illinois fur farm.

The success of PETA's ongoing campaign can be found in the fur industry's own trade journals. The *Trapper & Predator Caller* reports, "During recent interviews, only one fur buyer reported having a firm order in hand 'for only a few hundred XXL raccoon' for the trim trade. New York brokers have been 'deafeningly quiet this fall,' according to one large Midwest fur buyer."

Table A contains demographic data relevant to fur consumption.

Discussion Questions

1. Evaluate PETA's overall marketing strategy.
2. Evaluate the strategy of using nudes in the billboard.

TABLE A

Demographics and Fur Consumption*

Variable	Fur Coat, Jacket, Stole	Cloth Coat
Percent of Adults[†]	3.4%	7.5
Age		
18–24 years	189	85
25–34	140	102
35–44	111	121
45–54	65	107
55–64	63	104
>64	35	74
Education		
College graduate	93	127
Some college	116	115
High school graduate	102	99
No degree	81	53
Occupation		
Professional	117	142
Managerial/Administrative	99	137
Technical/Clerical/Sales	109	113
Precision/Craft	277	58
Other employed	110	105
Race/Ethnic Group		
White	96	105
Black	115	66
Spanish speaking	127	45
Region		
Northeast	153	148
North central	102	146
South	67	60
West	102	70
Household Income		
<$10,000	77	35
$10,000–19,999	115	57
$20,000–29,999	74	101
$30,000–39,999	109	100
$40,000–49,999	116	96
$50,000–59,999	108	131
$60,000–74,999	130	158
$75,000+	84	139
Household Structure		
1 person	59	77
2 people	90	105
3 or more	117	103
Any child in HH	122	95

*100 = Average use or consumption unless a percent is indicated.
Base = All women.
[†]Purchased in the past 12 months.

Source: *Mediamark Spring 1997* (New York: Mediamark Research Inc., 1997).

ILLUSTRATION A

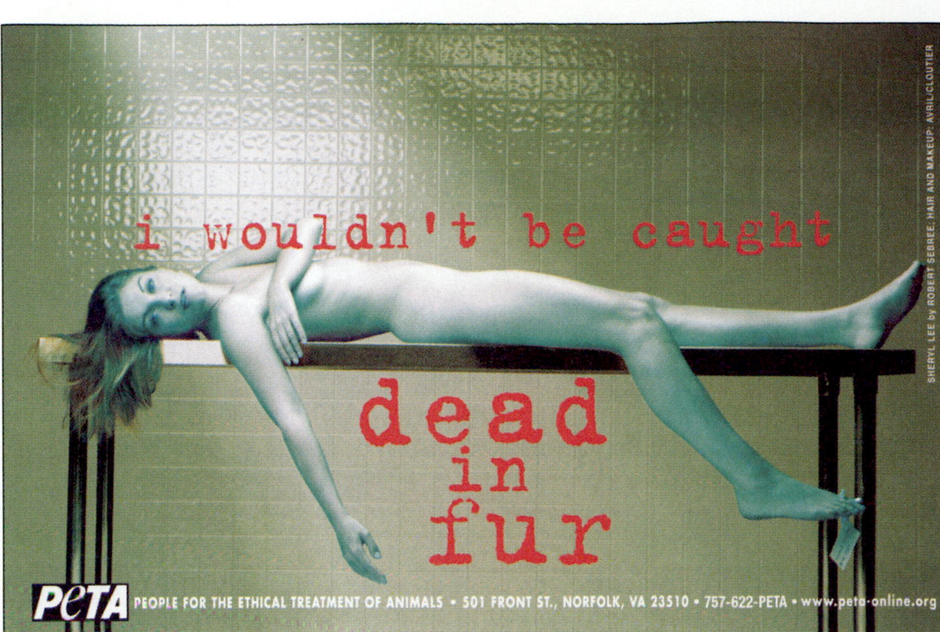

Courtesy PETA.

3. Evaluate the strategy of using Sandra Bernhard in the mustache ad.
4. PETA could use actual photos of animals being kept in appalling conditions or killed in inhumane ways in billboards and ads. Would you recommend this strategy? Justify your response.
5. What insights does the demographic data in Table A provide PETA?
6. Evaluate PETA's Web site (www.peta-online.org).
7. Develop a strategy for PETA to reduce fur use.
8. If you were the fur industry, how would you counter PETA's actions?
9. How should PETA alter its approach for these countries?
   a. Japan
   b. Germany
   c. France
   d. Great Britain

Appendix A

Consumer Research Methods

In this appendix, we want to provide you with some general guidelines for conducting research on consumer behavior. While these guidelines will help you get started, a good marketing research text is indispensable if you need to conduct a consumer research project or evaluate a consumer research proposal.

SECONDARY DATA

Any research project should begin with a thorough search for existing information relevant to the project at hand. Internal data such as past studies, sales reports, and accounting records should be consulted. External data, including reports, magazines, government organizations, trade associations, marketing research firms, advertising agencies, academic journals, trade journals, and books, should be thoroughly researched.

Computer searches are fast, economical means of conducting such searches. Most university and large public libraries have computer search capabilities, as do most large firms. However, computer searches will often miss reports by trade associations and magazines. Therefore, magazines that deal with the product category or that are read by members of the relevant market should be contacted. The same is true for associations (for names and addresses, see *Encyclopedia of Associations,* Gale Research Inc.).

SAMPLING

If the specific information required is not available from secondary sources, we must gather primary data. This generally involves talking to or observing consumers. However, it could involve asking knowledgeable others, such as sales personnel, about the consumers. In either case, time and cost constraints generally preclude us from contacting every single potential consumer. Therefore, most consumer research projects require a sample—a deliberately selected portion of the larger group. This requires a number of critical decisions, as described below. Mistakes made at this point are difficult to correct later in the study. The key decisions are briefly described below.

Define the Population

The first step is to define the consumers in which we are interested. Do we want to talk to current brand users, current product-category users, or potential product-category users? Do we want to talk with the purchasers, the users, or everyone involved in the purchase process? The population as we define it must reflect the behavior on which our marketing decision will be based.

Specify the Sampling Frame

A sampling frame is a "list" or grouping of individuals or households that reflects the population of interest. A phone book and shoppers at a given shopping mall can each serve as a sampling frame. Perfect sampling frames contain every member of the population one time. Phone books do not have households with unlisted numbers; many people do not visit shopping malls, while others visit them frequently. This is an area in which we generally must do the best we can without expecting a perfect frame. However, we must be very alert for biases that may be introduced by imperfections in our sampling frame.

Select a Sampling Method

The major decision at this point is between a random (probability) sample and a nonrandom sample. Nonrandom samples, particularly judgment samples, can provide good results. A judgment sample involves the deliberate selection of knowledgeable consumers or individuals. For example, a firm might decide to interview the social activity officers of fraternities and sororities to estimate campus attitudes toward a carbonated wine drink aimed at the campus market. Such a sample might provide useful insights. However, it might also be biased, since such individuals are likely to have a higher level of income and be more socially active than the average student.

The most common nonrandom sample, the convenience sample, involves selecting sample members in the manner most convenient for the researcher. It is subject to many types of bias and should generally be avoided.

Random or probability samples allow some form of a random process to select members from a sample frame. It may be every third person who passes a point-of-purchase display, house addresses selected by using a table of random numbers, or telephone numbers generated randomly by a computer. If random procedures are used, we can calculate the likelihood that our sample is not representative within specified limits.

Determine Sample Size

Finally, we must determine how large a sample to talk to. If we are using random sampling, there are formulas that can help us make this decision. In general, the more diverse our population is and the more certain we want to be that we have the correct answer, the more people we will need to interview.

SURVEYS

Surveys are systematic ways of gathering information from a large number of people. They generally involve the use of a structured or semistructured questionnaire. Surveys can be administered by mail, telephone, or in person. Personal interviews generally take place in shopping malls and are referred to as mall intercept interviews.

Each approach has advantages and disadvantages. Personal interviews allow the use of complex questionnaires, product demonstrations, and the collection of large amounts of data. They can be completed in a relatively short period of time. However, they are very expensive and are subject to interviewer bias. Telephone surveys can be completed rapidly, provide good sample control (who answers the questions), and are relatively inexpensive. Substantial amounts of data can be collected, but it must be relatively simple. Interviewer bias is possible. Mail surveys take the longest to complete and must generally be rather short. They can be used to collect modestly complex data, and they are very economical. Interviewer bias is not a problem.

A major concern in survey research is nonresponse bias. In most surveys, fewer than 50 percent of those selected to participate in the study actually do participate. In telephone and personal interviews, many people are not at home or refuse to cooperate. In mail surveys, many people refuse or forget to respond.

We can increase the response rate by callbacks in telephone and home personal surveys. The callbacks should be made at different times and on different days. Monetary inducements (enclosing 25 cents or $1) increase the response rate to mail surveys, as do prenotification (a card saying that a questionnaire is coming) and reminder postcards.

If less than a 100 percent response rate is obtained, we must be concerned that those who did not respond differ from those who did. A variety of techniques are available to help us estimate the likelihood and nature of nonresponse error.

EXPERIMENTATION

Experimentation involves changing one or more variables (product features, package color, advertising theme) and observing the effect this change has on another variable (consumer attitude, repeat purchase behavior, learning). The variable(s) that is changed is called an *independent* variable. The variable(s) that may be affected is called a *dependent* variable. The objective in experimental design is to structure the situation so that any change in the dependent variable is very likely to have been caused by a change in the independent variable.

The basic tool in designing experimental studies is the use of control and treatment groups. A *treatment group* is one in which an independent variable is changed (or introduced) and the change (or lack of) in the dependent variable is noted. A *control group* is a group similar to the treatment group except that the independent variable is not altered. There are a variety of ways in which treatment and control groups can be combined to produce differing experimental designs.

In addition to selecting an appropriate experimental design, we must also develop an experimental environment. In a laboratory experiment, we carefully control for all outside influences. This generally means that we will get similar results every time we repeat a study. Thus, if we have people taste several versions of a salad dressing in our laboratory, we will probably get similar preference ratings each time the study is repeated with similar consumers (internal validity). However, this does not necessarily mean that consumers will prefer the same version at home or in a restaurant (external validity).

In a field experiment, we conduct our study in the most relevant environment possible. This often means that unusual outside influences will distort our results. However, if our results are not distorted, they should hold true in the actual market application. Thus, if we have consumers use several versions of our salad dressing in their homes, competitor actions, unusual weather, or product availability might influence their response (internal validity). However, in the absence of such unusual effects, the preferred version should be preferred if actually sold on the market.

QUESTIONNAIRE DESIGN

All surveys and many experiments use questionnaires as data collection devices. A questionnaire is simply a formalized set of questions for eliciting information. It can measure (1) behavior—past, present, or intended; (2) demographic characteristics—age, gender, income, education, occupation; (3) level of knowledge; and (4) attitudes and opinions. The process of questionnaire design is outlined in Table A-1.

TABLE A-1

Questionnaire Design Process

1. *Preliminary decisions*
   Exactly what information is required?
   Exactly who are the target respondents?
   What method of communication will be used to reach these respondents?
2. *Decisions about question content*
   Is this question really needed?
   Is this question sufficient to generate the needed information?
   Can the respondent answer the question correctly?
   Will the respondent answer the question correctly?
   Are there any external events that might bias the response to the question?
3. *Decisions about the response format*
   Can this question best be asked as an open-ended, multiple-choice, or dichotomous question?
4. *Decisions concerning question phrasing*
   Do the words used have but one meaning to all the respondents?
   Are any of the words or phrases loaded or leading in any way?
   Are there any implied alternatives in the question?
   Are there any unstated assumptions related to the question?
   Will the respondents approach the question from the frame of reference desired by the researcher?
5. *Decisions concerning the question sequence*
   Are the questions organized in a logical manner that avoids introducing errors?
6. *Decisions on the layout of the questionnaire*
   Is the questionnaire designed in a manner to avoid confusion and minimize recording errors?
7. *Pretest and revise*
   Has the final questionnaire been subjected to a thorough pretest, using respondents similar to those who will be included in the final survey?

ATTITUDE SCALES

Attitudes are frequently measured on specialized scales.

Noncomparative rating scales require the consumer to evaluate an object or an attribute of the object without directly comparing it to another object. Comparative rating scales provide a direct comparison point (a named competitor, "your favorite brand," "the ideal brand"). An example of each follows:

Noncomparative Rating Scale
How do you like the taste of Diet Pepsi?

Like it very much	Like it	Dislike it	Strongly dislike it
_____	_____	_____	_____

Comparative Rating Scale
How do you like the taste of Tom's of Maine compared to Ultra Bright?

Like it much more	Like it more	Like it about the same	Like it less	Like it much less
_____	_____	_____	_____	_____

Paired comparisons involve presenting the consumer with two objects (brands, packages) at a time and requiring the selection of one of the two according to some criterion such as overall preference, taste, or color. Rank order scales require the consumer to rank a set of brands, advertisements, or features in terms of overall preference, taste, or importance. The constant sum scale is similar except it also requires the respondent to allocate 100 points among the objects. The allocation is to be done in a manner that reflects the relative preference or importance assigned each object. The semantic differential scale requires the consumer to rate an item on a number of scales bounded at each end by one of two bipolar adjectives. For example:

Honda Accord

Fast	*X*	___	___	___	___	___	___	Slow
Fancy	___	___	___	___	___	*X*	___	Plain
Large	___	___	___	*X*	___	___	___	Small
Inexpensive	___	___	___	___	*X*	___	___	Expensive

The instructions indicate that the consumer is to mark the blank that best indicates how accurately one or the other term describes or fits the attitude object. The end positions indicate "extremely," the next pair in from the ends indicates "very," the middlemost pair indicates "somewhat," and the middle position indicates "neither-nor." Thus, the consumer in the example rates the Honda Accord as extremely fast, very plain, somewhat expensive, and neither large nor small.

Likert scales ask consumers to indicate a degree of agreement or disagreement with each of a series of statements related to the attitude object, such as the following:

1. *Macy's is one of the most attractive stores in town.*

Strongly agree	Agree	Neither agree nor disagree	Disagree	Strongly disagree
___	___	___	___	___

2. *The service at Macy's is* not *satisfactory.*

Strongly agree	Agree	Neither agree nor disagree	Disagree	Strongly disagree
___	___	___	___	___

3. *The service at a retail store is very important to me.*

Strongly agree	Agree	Neither agree nor disagree	Disagree	Strongly disagree
___	___	___	___	___

To analyze responses to a Likert scale, each response category is assigned a numerical value. These examples could be assigned values such as Strongly agree = 1 through Strongly disagree = 5, the scoring could be reversed, or a +2 through −2 system could be used.

DEPTH INTERVIEWS

Depth interviews can involve one respondent and one interviewer, or they may involve a small group (8 to 15 respondents) and an interviewer. The latter are called focus group interviews, and the former are termed individual depth interviews or one-on-ones. Groups of four or five are often referred to as minigroup interviews. Depth interviews in general are commonly referred to as qualitative research. Individual depth interviews involve a one-to-one relationship between the interviewer and the respondent. The interviewer does not have a specific set of prespecified questions that must be asked according to the order imposed by a questionnaire. Instead, there is freedom to create questions, to probe those responses that appear relevant, and generally to try to develop the best set of data in any way practical. However, the interviewer must follow one rule: He or she must not consciously try to affect the content of the answers given by the respondent. The respondent must feel free to reply to the various questions, probes, and other, more subtle ways of encouraging responses in the manner deemed most appropriate.

Individual depth interviews are appropriate in six situations:

1. Detailed probing of an individual's behavior, attitudes, or needs is required.
2. The subject matter under discussion is likely to be of a highly confidential nature (e.g., personal investments).
3. The subject matter is of an emotionally charged or embarrassing nature.
4. Certain strong, socially acceptable norms exist (e.g., child-care) and the need to conform in a group discussion may influence responses.
5. A highly detailed (step-by-step) understanding of complicated behavior or decision-making patterns (e.g., planning the family holiday) is required.
6. The interviews are with professional people or with people on the subject of their jobs (e.g., finance directors).

Focus group interviews can be applied to (1) basic need studies for product ideas creation, (2) new-product ideas or concept exploration, (3) product-positioning studies, (4) advertising and communications research, (5) background studies on consumers' frames of reference, (6) establishment of consumer vocabulary as a preliminary step in questionnaire development, and (7) determination of attitudes and behaviors.

The standard focus group interview involves 8 to 12 individuals. Normally, the group is designed to reflect the characteristics of a particular market segment. The respondents are selected according to the relevant sampling plan and meet at a central location that generally has facilities for taping or filming the interviews. The discussion itself is "led" by a moderator. The competent moderator attempts to develop three clear stages in the one- to three-hour interview: (1) establish rapport with the group, structure the rules of group interaction, and set objectives; (2) attempt to provoke intense discussion in the relevant areas; and (3) attempt to summarize the groups' responses to determine the extent of agreement. In general, either the moderator or a second person prepares a summary of each session after analyzing the session's transcript.

PROJECTIVE TECHNIQUES

Projective techniques are designed to measure feelings, attitudes, and motivations that consumers are unable or unwilling to reveal otherwise. They are based on the theory that the description of vague objects requires interpretation, and this interpretation can only be based on the individual's own attitudes, values, and motives.

Table 10-2 provides descriptions and examples of the more common projective techniques.

OBSERVATION

Observation can be used when (1) the behaviors of interest are public, (2) they are repetitive, frequent, or predictable, and (3) they cover a relatively brief time span. An observational study requires five decisions:

1. *Natural versus contrived situation.* Do we wait for a behavior to occur in its natural environment, or do we create an artificial situation in which it will occur?
2. *Open versus disguised observation.* To what extent are the consumers aware that we are observing their behavior?
3. *Structured versus unstructured observation.* Will we limit our observations to predetermined behaviors, or will we note whatever occurs?
4. *Direct or indirect observations.* Will we observe the behaviors themselves or merely the outcomes of the behaviors?
5. *Human or mechanical observations.* Will the observations be made mechanically or by people?

PHYSIOLOGICAL MEASURES

Physiological measures are direct observations of physical responses to a stimulus such as an advertisement. These responses may be controllable, such as eye movements, or uncontrollable, such as the galvanic skin response. Eye-tracking cameras allow researchers to determine how long a consumer looks at each element in a stimulus such as a point-of-purchase display, ad, or package, and the sequence in which they are examined. Galvanic skin response can be measured (via a "lie detector") to detect the intensity of emotional responses to ads or packages.

Appendix B

Consumer Behavior Audit*

In this section, we provide a list of key questions to guide you in developing marketing strategy from a consumer behavior perspective. This audit is no more than a checklist to minimize the chance of overlooking a critical behavioral dimension. It does not guarantee a successful strategy. However, thorough and insightful answers to these questions should greatly enhance the likelihood of a successful marketing program.

Our audit is organized around the key decisions that marketing managers must make. The first key decision is the selection of the target market(s) to be served. This is followed by the determination of a viable product position for each target market. Finally, the marketing mix elements—product, place, price, and promotion—must be structured in a manner consistent with the desired product position. This process is illustrated in Figure B-1.

Consumer Influences Drive Marketing Decisions **FIGURE B-1**

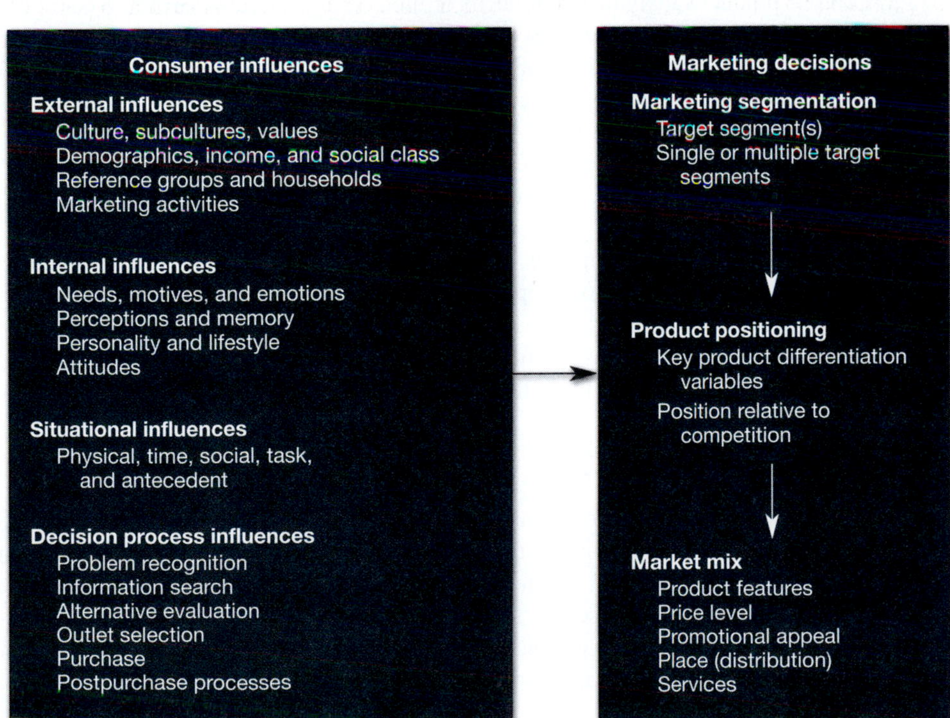

*Revised by Richard Pomazal of Wheeling Jesuit College.

MARKET SEGMENTATION

Market segmentation is the process of dividing all possible users of a product into groups that have similar needs the products might satisfy. Market segmentation should be done prior to the final development of a new product. In addition, a complete market segmentation analysis should be performed periodically for existing products. The reason for continuing segmentation analyses is the dynamic nature of consumer needs.

A. External influences
   1. Are there cultures or subcultures whose value system is particularly consistent (or inconsistent) with the consumption of our product?
   2. Is our product appropriate for male or female consumption? Will ongoing gender-role changes affect who consumes our product or how it is consumed?
   3. Do ethnic, social, regional, or religious subcultures have different consumption patterns relevant to our product?
   4. Do various demographic or social-strata groups (age, gender, urban/suburban/rural, occupation, income, education) differ in their consumption of our product?
   5. Is our product particularly appropriate for consumers with relatively high (or low) incomes compared to others in their occupational group (ROCI)?
   6. Can our product be particularly appropriate for specific roles, such as students or professional women?
   7. Would it be useful to focus on specific adopter categories?
   8. Do groups in different stages of the household life cycle have different consumption patterns for our product? Who in the household is involved in the purchase process?

B. Internal influences
   1. Can our product satisfy different needs or motives in different people? What needs are involved? What characterizes individuals with differing motives?
   2. Is our product uniquely suited for particular personality types? Self-concepts?
   3. What emotions, if any, are affected by the purchase and/or consumption of this product?
   4. Is our product appropriate for one or more distinct lifestyles?
   5. Do different groups have different attitudes about an ideal version of our product?

C. Situational influences
   1. Can our product be appropriate for specific types of situations instead of (or in addition to) specific types of people?

D. Decision process influences
   1. Do different individuals use different evaluative criteria in selecting the product?
   2. Do potential customers differ in their loyalty to existing products/brands?

PRODUCT POSITION

A product position is the way the consumer thinks of a given product/brand relative to competing products/brands. A manager must determine what a desirable product position would be for each market segment of interest. This determination is generally based on the answers to the same questions used to segment a market, with the addition of the consumer's perceptions of competing products/brands. Of course, the capabilities and motivations of existing and potential competitors must also be considered.

A. Internal influences
   1. What is the general semantic memory structure for this product category in each market segment?

2. What is the ideal version of this product in each market segment for the situations the firm wants to serve?

B. Decision process influences

1. Which evaluative criteria are used in the purchase decision? Which decision rules and importance weights are used?

PRICING

The manager must set a pricing policy that is consistent with the desired product position. Price must be broadly conceived as everything a consumer must surrender to obtain a product. This includes time and psychological costs as well as monetary costs.

A. External influences

1. Does the segment hold any values relating to any aspect of pricing, such as the use of credit or "conspicuous consumption"?
2. Does the segment have sufficient income, after covering living expenses, to afford the product?
3. Is it necessary to lower price to obtain a sufficient relative advantage to ensure diffusion? Will temporary price reductions induce product trial?
4. Who in the household evaluates the price of the product?

B. Internal influences

1. Will price be perceived as an indicator of status?
2. Is economy in purchasing this type of product relevant to the lifestyle(s) of the segment?
3. Is price an important aspect of the segment's attitude toward the brands in the product category?
4. What is the segment's perception of a fair or reasonable price for this product?

C. Situational influences

1. Does the role of price vary with the type of situation?

D. Decision process factors

1. Can a low price be used to trigger problem recognition?
2. Is price an important evaluative criterion? What decision rule is applied to the evaluative criteria used? Is price likely to serve as a surrogate indicator of quality?
3. Are consumers likely to respond to in-store price reductions?

DISTRIBUTION STRATEGY

The manager must develop a distribution strategy that is consistent with the selected product position. This involves the selection of outlets if the item is a physical product, or the location of the outlets if the product is a service.

A. External influences

1. What values do the segments have that relate to distribution?
2. Do the male and female members of the segments have differing requirements of the distribution system? Do working couples, single individuals, or single parents within the segment have unique needs relating to product distribution?
3. Can the distribution system capitalize on reference groups by serving as a means for individuals with common interests to get together?
4. Is the product complex such that a high-service channel is required to ensure its diffusion?

B. Internal influences
   1. Will the selected outlets be perceived in a manner that enhances the desired product position?
   2. What type of distribution system is consistent with the lifestyle(s) of each segment?
   3. What attitudes does each segment hold with respect to the various distribution alternatives?

C. Situational influences
   1. Do the desired features of the distribution system vary with the situation?

D. Decision process factors
   1. What outlets are in the segment's evoked set? Will consumers in this segment seek information in this type of outlet?
   2. Which evaluative criteria does this segment use to evaluate outlets? Which decision rule?
   3. Is the outlet selected before, after, or simultaneously with the product/brand? To what extent are product decisions made in the retail outlet?

PROMOTION STRATEGY

The manager must develop a promotion strategy, including advertising, nonfunctional package design features, publicity, promotions, and sales force activities that are consistent with the product position.

A. External factors
   1. What values does the segment hold that can be used in our communications? Which should be avoided?
   2. How can we communicate to our chosen segments in a manner consistent with the emerging gender-role perceptions of each segment?
   3. What is the nonverbal communication system of each segment?
   4. How, if at all, can we use reference groups in our advertisements?
   5. Can our advertisements help make the product part of one or more role-related product clusters?
   6. Can we reach and influence opinion leaders?
   7. If our product is an innovation, are there diffusion inhibitors that can be overcome by promotion?
   8. Who in the household should receive what types of information concerning our product?

B. Internal factors
   1. Have we structured our promotional campaign such that each segment will be exposed to it, attend to it, and interpret it in the manner we desire?
   2. Have we made use of the appropriate learning principles so that our meaning will be remembered?
   3. Do our messages relate to the purchase motives held by the segment? Do they help reduce motivational conflict if necessary?
   4. Are we considering the emotional implications of the ad and/or the use of our product?
   5. Is the lifestyle portrayed in our advertisements consistent with the desired lifestyle of the selected segments?
   6. If we need to change attitudes via our promotion mix, have we selected and properly used the most appropriate attitude-change techniques?

C. Situational influences
   1. Does our campaign illustrate the full range of appropriate usage situations for the product?

D. Decision process influences
   1. Will problem recognition occur naturally, or must it be activated by advertising? Should generic or selective problem recognition be generated?
   2. Will the segment seek out or attend to information on the product prior to problem recognition, or must we reach them when they are not seeking our information? Can we use low-involvement learning processes effectively? What information sources are used?
   3. After problem recognition, will the segment seek out information on the product/brand, or will we need to intervene in the purchase decision process? If they do seek information, what sources do they use?
   4. What types of information are used to make a decision?
   5. How much and what types of information are acquired at the point of purchase?
   6. Is postpurchase dissonance likely? Can we reduce it through our promotional campaign?
   7. Have we given sufficient information to ensure proper product use?
   8. Are the expectations generated by our promotional campaign consistent with the product's performance?
   9. Are our messages designed to encourage repeat purchases, brand loyal purchases, or neither?

PRODUCT

The marketing manager must be certain that the physical product, service, or idea has the characteristics required to achieve the desired product position in each market segment.

A. External influences
   1. Is the product designed appropriately for all members of the segment under consideration, including males, females, and various age groups?
   2. If the product is an innovation, does it have the required relative advantage and lack of complexity to diffuse rapidly?
   3. Is the product designed to meet the varying needs of different household members?

B. Internal influences
   1. Will the product be perceived in a manner consistent with the desired image?
   2. Will the product satisfy the key purchase motives of the segment?
   3. Is the product consistent with the segment's attitude toward an ideal product?

C. Situational influences
   1. Is the product appropriate for the various potential usage situations?

D. Decision process influences
   1. Does the product/brand perform better than the alternatives on the key set of evaluative criteria used by this segment?
   2. Will the product perform effectively in the foreseeable uses to which this segment may subject it?
   3. Will the product perform as well or better than expected by this segment?

CUSTOMER SATISFACTION AND COMMITMENT

Marketers must produce satisfied customers to be successful in the long run. It is often to a firm's advantage to go beyond satisfaction and create committed or loyal customers.

1. What factors lead to satisfaction with our product?
2. What factors could cause customer commitment to our brand or firm?

NAME INDEX

L

M

N

U

V

W

Y

Z

CASE INDEX

SUBJECT INDEX

A

B

N

O

T